Child Psychology

Child Psychology

Pathways to Good Practice

Edited by
Helen Pote
Royal Holloway University of London
Egham Hill, UK

Anna Picciotto
Whittington Health NHS Trust
Magdala Ave, London, UK

Clare Norris
Hertfordshire Parternship NHS Trust
Hatfield, Hertfordshire, UK

WILEY Blackwell

This first edition first published 2024

Registered Offices
John Wiley & Sons, Inc., 111 River Street, Hoboken, NJ 07030, USA
John Wiley & Sons Ltd, The Atrium, Southern Gate, Chichester, West Sussex, PO19 8SQ, UK

For details of our global editorial offices, customer services, and more information about Wiley products visit us at www.wiley.com.

Wiley also publishes its books in a variety of electronic formats and by print-on-demand. Some content that appears in standard print versions of this book may not be available in other formats.

Library of Congress Cataloging-in-Publication Data applied for:

PB ISBN: 9781119861188

Cover Design: Wiley
Cover Image: © South Downs Way crosses Bignor Hill

Set in 9.5/12.5pt STIXTwoText by Straive, Chennai, India

To our fantastic children – Freddie, Alice, Billy, Lily, Bea, Chloe and Louis, who have taught us so much and helped us to remember that things don't always go the way the psychology textbooks suggest.

Contents

Contributors *xi*
Foreword *xix*
Acknowledgements *xxi*

Part I Frameworks for Practice *1*

1 **An Introduction to Child Psychology in Practice** *3*
Helen Pote, Anna Picciotto and Clare Norris

2 **Theory and Evidence in Practice** *13*
Clare Norris, Helen Pote and Anna Picciotto

3 **A Developmental Approach to Assessment and Formulation** *39*
Anna Picciotto, Helen Pote and Clare Norris

4 **Supervision and Self-reflection** *75*
Helen Pote, Anna Picciotto and Clare Norris

5 **Legal and Professional Contexts** *100*
Pinder Kaur and Chris Marshall

6 **Frameworks of Service Delivery** *130*
Duncan Law

7 **Inclusivity, Diversity and Power** *151*
Fatima Bibi

8 **Working with Goals and Monitoring Progress and Outcomes** *176*
Duncan Law

9 **Collaboration and Co-production** *188*
Shaun Liverpool and Paula Bailey

Part II Evidence-informed Practice *209*

10 **Adolescence** *211*
Emma Silver

11 **Sleeping, Feeding and Toileting Difficulties for Young Children** *238*
Pinder Kaur and Lauren Bryan

12 **Behavioural Difficulties and Parenting Interventions** *298*
Emma Karwatzki and Kajal Patel

13 **Emotional Difficulties** *323*
Vicki Curry and Maria Loades

14 **Complex Emotional Difficulties** *357*
Zoë Maiden

15 **Eating Difficulties and Disorders** *407*
Tara Porter

16 **Paediatrics and Long-term Health Conditions** *427*
Sophie Bennett and Kristina Soon

17 **Disrupted Attachments** *451*
Clare Norris and Jade Weston

18 **Young People with Intellectual Disabilities** *492*
Nancy Sheppard and Catherine Day

Part III Growing Areas of Practice *527*

19 **Neurodivergence** *529*
Imogen Newsom-Davis and Anita Marsden

20 **Working in Schools** *579*
Anna Picciotto, Joe Hickey and Sian Barnett

21 **Perinatal and Infant Mental Health** *613*
Jane Iles, Zoe Darwin and Florence Bristow

22 **Mental Health Crisis and Inpatient Care for Children and Young People** *642*
Aspa Paspali

23 **Youth Offending and Forensic Interventions** *690*
Simone Fox and Vicky Thakordas-Desai

24 **Digital Practice** *713*
Helen Pote

25 **Youth Community Practice** *733*
Katerina Alexandraki, Laura Casale, Jessica Davies, Rupert Goodman, Tasir Joseph, Jake Lake, Rachel McKail and Jon Oliver

26 **Working within Children's Social Care** *763*
Clare Norris and Omar Timberlake

27 **Trauma-informed Practice** *800*
Sian Barnett

Index *825*

Contributors

Paula Bailey is a Registered Mental Health Nurse and Systemic Family Psychotherapist and Programme Leader and Senior Lecturer in MSc child and adolescent mental health & wellbeing at Edge Hill University. Paula's research focuses on the impact of mental health on family members in both child and adult mental health services.

Sian Barnett is a Clinical Psychologist and CAMHS Manager. She completed her Doctorate in Clinical Psychology at University College London, in 2003, and has worked in CAMHS for 20 years. She manages the Islington Schools Team, Trauma-informed Practice in Schools Team (iTIPS), Children's Centres and Incredible Years Parenting Groups teams. She has an interest in whole system approaches to trauma, offering supervision, training, consultation and reflective practice to help staff support children and families.

Sophie Bennett is a Clinical Academic Psychologist specialising in child and adolescent mental health. Her work focuses on developing and evaluating methods to ensure that children and young people who have emotional or behavioural difficulties in the context of a chronic physical illness are able to have both their mental and physical healthcare needs met in an integrated way. She has a particular interest in increasing access to psychological treatments through 'low-intensity' interventions, including peer support.

Fatima Bibi is a Consultant Clinical Psychologist working in a North London NHS Mental Health Trust. She has led on innovating mental health services for marginalised children and young people, specifically those who present within the criminal justice system. Fatima specialises in adapting evidence-based psychological approaches to make them more accessible and appropriate for children and young people who typically fall through the net of mainstream mental health services. She is also an associate clinical tutor and provides training, consultation and supervision in relation to diversity and inclusion on clinical psychology doctorate courses.

Florence Bristow is a Highly Specialist Clinical Psychologist in perinatal mental health, working across NHS services and in private practice. She has significant experience of delivering evidence-based psychological therapies for women, infants and their families experiencing mental health difficulties during the transition to parenthood. She has a particular interest in supporting parent–infant relationships and identifying the needs of partners and family members in the perinatal period. She has worked at both local and national levels to inform the development and transformation of perinatal services.

Lauren Bryan is a Lecturer and Academic Tutor on the Professional Doctorate in Clinical Psychology programme at Royal Holloway, University of London. Alongside her academic role, Lauren also continues to practice as a Highly Specialist Clinical Psychologist. Her clinical work is predominantly with children, young people and their families within NHS Child and Adolescent Mental Health Services (CAMHS) and also in independent practice.

Vicki Curry has worked as a Clinical Psychologist in NHS CYP-MH services for over 25 years and has a particular interest in the adaptation of CBT for use in a child and family settings. She has been Programme Director for child CBT and CYP-IAPT-related postgraduate courses for UCL/Anna Freud centre, for many years and has provided CBTCYP-related trainings for professionals and organisations across the United Kingdom and Europe.

Zoe Darwin is a Reader in health research at the University of Huddersfield. Her research field is psychosocial aspects of pregnancy, birth and early parenting. Zoe's particular interest concerns perinatal mental health and wellbeing in all parents and those pursuing parenthood, with an emphasis on experiences and needs of individuals and families.

Catherine Day is Clinical Director of a private practice in the Cayman Islands, an inclusive trauma and attachment service for people with and without disabilities/neurodiversity. She is a consultant clinical psychologist, Certified Theraplay® practitioner, supervisor & trainer-in-training, intensive interaction practitioner/mentor, EMDR trained, DDP Level 2 trained. She trained and worked in the NHS in the United Kingdom and is now involved in many government and NPO initiatives in the Caymen Islands to support people with disabilities at the level of policy, advocacy and service provision.

Simone Fox is a Consultant Clinical and Forensic Psychologist and Multisystemic Therapy (MST) Consultant. She is employed by South London and Maudsley NHS Foundation Trust. Previously she was Deputy Clinical Director and a Senior Lecturer on the doctorate in clinical psychology programme, Royal Holloway, University of London. She has significant experience working with young people and families in the community and custodial settings. She has worked with adult mentally disordered offenders in medium-secure units and prisons. She has experience in undertaking psycho-legal assessments for adults and young people in the criminal justice system.

Joe Hickey is a Senior Clinical Psychologist and Interpersonal Psychotherapist in NHS Tayside's Perth CAMHS and an Associate Clinical Tutor with University College London's doctorate in clinical psychology. He has a special interest in school-based mental health interventions. His previous roles in Islington CAMHS included school-based clinician, Mental Health Support Teams Manager and Joint Manager of the School CAMHS team. He also has experience as a teaching assistant in specialist SEN schools and as a postgraduate tutor at the Anna Freud Centre.

Jane Iles is a Clinical and Research Psychologist, working as a Joint Programme Director on the University of Surrey PsychD clinical psychology training programme. Jane has a background in perinatal mental health research, with specific interests in birth trauma and working to support whole families. Jane has worked on early years parenting programmes and a number of research studies in this field. Clinically, Jane has worked as a clinical psychologist in CAMHS.

Emma Karwatzki is the Programme Director for the Doctorate in Clinical Psychology at University of Hertfordshire. Emma has worked in NHS children and young people's services for the past two decades, latterly as a consultant lead clinical psychologist. Emma's research interests are in the area of family, children and young people's mental health and she has a number of published outputs in the field. In addition to her doctoral training, Emma has postgraduate qualifications in leadership, supervision and systemic practice.

Pinder Kaur is an Indian British-born Lecturer at Royal Holloway, University of London and a practicing Clinical Psychologist. She has predominantly worked with children and families throughout her work in the NHS for over 18 years, in London, community-based settings specialising in family and parenting-based work.

Duncan Law is a Consultant Clinical Psychologist with over 30 years experience working in adult and child mental health settings. He is Visiting Professor in the Department of Clinical, Educational and Health Psychology, University College London and Director of MindMonkey Associates. He was a director and founder member of the Child Outcomes Research Consortium and has broad knowledge of working with goals and feedback and outcome tools. He has extensive experience in service and organisational development, in the United Kingdom and internationally. Above all his focus is on the effective application of complex psychological ideas in ways that make them accessible and acceptable, to enrich and enhance lives.

Shaun Liverpool is a Chartered Psychologist, Researcher and Lecturer in child and adolescent mental health and wellbeing at Edge Hill University. Shaun's research focuses on the design, development, delivery and evaluation of digital interventions to help children/young people and their parents/carers cope with mental health challenges.

Maria Loades is a Reader in clinical psychology at the University of Bath. Her clinical and research interests are on adolescent depression, specifically scalable, timely and effective treatments, including for under-served populations. Maria still practises as a practitioner psychologist and CBT therapist within the Bristol region.

Zoë Maiden is a Senior Clinical Psychologist and Senior Lecturer at Kings College London. She is currently the module lead for the post-graduate diploma in cognitive behaviour therapy for children and young people. Clinically, Zoë works in the National and Specialist CAMHS Trauma, Anxiety and Depression Clinic (N&S CAMHS TAD) at South London and Maudsley NHS Trust. Zoë has significant experience of teaching CBT to professionals of varying experience and working therapeutically with young people with severe and complex difficulties.

Anita Marsden is a Clinical Psychologist working in an NHS community paediatric service in Sussex, England. Anita has worked alongside autistic and neurodivergent individuals for over 20 years in a variety of roles, clinical and academic. Anita is passionate about developing strength-focused neuro-affirmative practice and is on a journey to align her service and clinical practice with the needs of communities of experts by experience (of which she is also a member, as a neurodivergent individual and parent carer).

Chris Marshall is a Senior Lecturer in psychology at Royal Holloway University London. Chris is the Course Lead for the MSc (Apprenticeship) in Clinical Associate Psychology (Child). He qualified as a clinical psychologist from the University of Surrey in 2014 and works clinically in a child and adolescent mental health service (CAMHS) in London.

Imogen Newsom-Davis is a Consultant Clinical Psychologist and Paediatric Neuropsychologist. She has held both clinical and academic psychology roles for over 25 years, including Consultant Lead for Neurodevelopmental Psychology at Great Ormond Street Hospital NHS Foundation Trust. Imogen has a special interest in increasing understanding and support for young people with complex and atypical neurodivergent profiles. She continues to provide honorary NHS and clinical research services alongside independent practice.

Clare Norris has over 20 years' experience as a Clinical Psychologist working with children, their families and caring networks in numerous settings within the NHS, children's social care and in private practice. She specialises in the assessment and intervention with traumatised and attachment-disordered children, their families and caring networks. For 10 years she was Clinical Lecturer at the University of Hertfordshire's doctoral course in clinical psychology, lecturing in the area of child and adolescent mental health and children's social care and publishing related research papers. She is currently Lead Clinical Psychologist for Hertfordshire County Council's award-winning Family Safeguarding Service, (an innovative re-modelling of child protection services which, as a result of the successful evaluation by the Department of Education, is being implemented across the United Kingdom).

Aspa Paspali is a Child and Adolescent Psychiatrist with a decade of experience as an NHS consultant. She completed her medical training in the Aristotle University of Thessaloniki, Greece, and specialised in child and adolescent psychiatry at the South London & Maudsley NHS Foundation Trust. She is currently the CAMHS clinical lead in Whittington Health NHS Trust, overseeing community CAMHS, in-patient and paediatric liaison services. She works with adolescents who present in mental health crisis and/or with severe mental illness, and their families, and has recently led the development of the North Central London CAMHS Dialectical Behavioural Therapy (DBT) Service.

Kajal Patel is a Chartered Clinical Psychologist and has worked clinically with children and young people and their families since 2004. Kajal is currently working in independent practice in London offering therapeutic interventions, clinical supervision and neurodevelopmental assessments. Prior to this Kajal was Lead Psychologist and Professional Lead for

Psychology and Psychotherapy in Kingston CAMHS (NHS). Kajal co-led the implementation of Children's CYP-IAPT in Richmond and Kingston CAMHS and remains passionate about empowering young people and collaborative practice.

Anna Picciotto has worked in child and adolescent mental health for more than two decades as a Clinical Psychologist and has specialised in community service provision for much of her career. Anna now leads CAMH services in an integrated-care organisation. The service comprises an in-patient general adolescent unit, a paediatric MH team and one of the largest and most well-respected NHS community-based MH services for children in the United Kingdom, offering all schools, early years and social care teams easier access to specialist psychological services. For many years her innovative service has offered direct psychological work and consultation to schools and is part of the roll out of mental health support teams for schools. Her clinical practice is integrative, influenced strongly by systemic and developmental psychology. Anna has supervised, taught and written extensively on the evidence base for practice in schools.

Tara Porter is a Clinical Psychologist and Author. She was the Lead Psychologist in an NHS CAMHS eating disorders team for almost two decades. She worked on the NHS England-funded national training programme in CAMHS eating disorders in 2017, 2019 and 2023. She is an Associate Tutor on the doctorate programme for clinical psychologists at UCL. Tara is the author of the *You Don't Understand Me: The Young Woman's Guide to Life*, which was a Sunday Times Bestseller in the United Kingdom and has been published around the world. She regularly writes articles about mental health in journals and the mainstream media, and speaks and teaches about mental health.

Helen Pote is Director of Clinical Programmes for Psychological Practitioners at Royal Holloway with over 25 years' experience training psychologists and working as a Clinical Psychologist with children and families across health, education and research settings. Helen's research focuses on practitioners' digital competences, child mental health and behaviour, family functioning and mental health literacy, with a particular focus on digital interventions. She chairs the South East Research Network for schools (RHUL) and the Committee for Digital Healthcare, Division of Clinical Psychology, British Psychological Society. She is on the editorial board of the *Journal of Family Therapy*.

Nancy Sheppard is a Consultant Clinical Psychologist who manages a specialist CAMHS for children with disabilities. She is employed by the Tavistock and Portman NHS Trust and has worked in the neurodevelopmental field for over 30 years. She has a particular interest in adapting psychodynamic and cognitive analytic therapeutic approaches to support emotional wellbeing and to build confidence in parents and carers parenting a child with additional needs. Over her career she has also played a significant role in training both clinical and educational psychologists and other professionals working in this field.

Emma Silver is a Consultant Clinical Psychologist with over 25 years' experience working with young people and families from different backgrounds in a range of settings. She has led clinical services for young people in the community and education and provides supervision and consultation to organisations in public, charity and private sectors. She has developed and led training for clinical psychologists and other psychological practitioners at University College London, where she has been engaged in research, most recently exploring social media and mental health.

Kristina Soon has worked as a Clinical Psychologist in paediatrics for more than 20 years, implementing and adapting CBT for young people, and their families, affected by procedural fear, stigma, challenges in adhering to complex medical regimes and significant changes to their health/illness status in order to optimise physical and mental health outcomes. Kristina has also led the Children, Young People and Families programme on the UCL doctorate in clinical psychology course for many years and continues to pursue a research interest with young people managing the psychosocial impacts of physical differences.

Vicky Thakordas-Desai is a Consultant Forensic Psychologist working within the West Midlands CAMHS provider collaborative and Clinical Lead for the Family Drug and Alcohol Court (FDAC) service in Birmingham. Vicky has significant experience working with children, young people and adults conducting psychological risk assessments for criminal, civil and quasi court proceedings. She has a specialist interest in the assessment, treatment and management of risk of violent offending particularly in relation to developmental trauma, offending behaviour and mental health difficulties in children and adolescents in the community. Vicky is also a media contributor having appeared on several television crime documentaries.

Omar Timberlake has experience as a Clinical Psychologist working with children, families and adults in numerous settings within the NHS, children's social care and in private practice. He specialises in the assessment of children and adults in the context of trauma and risk for the family courts and working with young people with neurodevelopmental disorders in a school-based setting. He has additionally provided teaching at University of Hertfordshire on attachment and trauma and has a specialist interest in children and young people's experiences within the care system.

Jade Weston is a Clinical Psychologist who has worked with care-experienced and adopted children and their carers, care leavers and families on the edge of care. She has worked within children's social care, NHS, CICs and voluntary adoption agency settings and draws on a range of trauma- and attachment-informed approaches. She has also worked as a senior lecturer and admissions tutor on a doctorate in clinical psychology training programme. She is care-experienced and has set up the Care-Experienced Psychology Network to support aspiring, trainee and qualified psychologists who are care-experienced.

MAC–UK – Katerina Alexandraki, Laura Casale, Jessica Davies, Rupert Goodman, Tasir Joseph, Jake Lake, Rachel McKail and Jon Oliver are staff members at MAC-UK, which is a mental health charity with a vision to see a society where excluded young people inspire and lead the solutions to inequality and the impact of this on mental health, with the resources, capabilities and investment to do so. Central to the work is co-production, which strives to have young people, communities and organisations as equal partners in the design, delivery and evaluation of the work, and promotes shared decision making along the way. MAC-UK seeks to also impact services and systems. Alongside the expertise of young people, communities and services, the work draws on ideas from youth work, psychology and public health to inform practice.

Foreword

Oh how I wish I had had this book when I was starting out on my career in child psychology! It really is the go-to handbook for all things related to child mental health, and I really do mean 'all things'. It somehow manages to be comprehensive in both the topics that it covers and the handling of each topic.

The authors of each chapter are genuine expert practitioners in their fields, and readers can benefit from their expertise, their experience, their knowledge and their wisdom. There is also a certain warmth and compassion in the way that the book has been both written and compiled, which is nourishing and nurturing, and inspires rather than intimidates.

The book starts by helping readers develop their clinical competence and confidence by covering important broad areas of practice. It then focuses on specific areas of practice before considering emerging areas of practice. Helping readers to develop knowledge and competence will in turn increase their clinical decision-making ability as well as help them to feel more confident.

Working in this field can be challenging at times, and as the stress levels increase it can sometimes be difficult to think straight. But this book acts as a guide enabling readers to remain focused on what is important and to make better decisions.

Although relevant in any child mental health context, this book is particularly useful in a UK context, where there has been an expansion of the workforce and the development of many new roles. This book makes evidence-informed approaches accessible to readers regardless of their background training and their particular role.

David Trickey
Consultant Clinical Psychologist
Co-director of the UK Trauma Council

Acknowledgements

A great many people have contributed to this book in different ways. We particularly thank:

The chapter authors, who have given precious time to write their chapters alongside very busy day jobs, responding to tight turnarounds with tolerance.

Graeme Jeffs for merciless proofreading at crucial stages of this process and Marie Ruhle for editorial assistance and indexing.

Our families and friends, who have supported us in making this book a reality, through patience, kind words of encouragement and childcare, and especially Philip Hughes for East Sussex hospitality and the original artwork on the front cover.

All our supervisors, mentors and colleagues, through many years of study and clinical practice, who have taught us so much and encouraged us to take risks with our own learning.

The children, young people and their families and carers, the NHS and public services that have been at the heart of our careers for the past 30 years.

And finally, the inspiring students and practitioners who we have had the privilege to work with at the start of their careers and who always challenge us to think and continue to keep us enthusiastic about our psychological practice.

Part I

Frameworks for Practice

1

An Introduction to Child Psychology in Practice

Helen Pote, Anna Picciotto and Clare Norris

1.1 Overview

> 'Tell me and I forget, teach me and I may remember, involve me and I learn.'
>
> Benjamin Franklin

Starting off as a child psychological practitioner can be daunting. There are so many things to learn: How do young people develop? What are the risk and protective factors for a range of psychological difficulties? How do you talk to young people and their families to assess their needs? What evidence informed approaches might help them resolve any difficulties? The path to gaining this knowledge and developing the necessary skills may seem challenging for the novice practitioner. For young people and their families, the path to addressing their psychological distress is equally challenging and at times very confusing. The young person may be frightened, overwhelmed and often lacking in hope. You offering them support and learning alongside them in a collaborative and curious fashion is a great starting point for helping them and becoming a competent child psychological practitioner as you do so. In your journey to becoming more confident in your skills, be compassionate and encouraging to yourself, just as you would be to the young people you work with. Notice the things you do well alongside the areas of practice you wish to improve, expect to make mistakes and aspire to learn from them.

This book is designed for psychological practitioners and clinicians working in child mental health; apprentices, students, trainees and newly qualified professionals starting out in their careers as well as more experienced practitioners who may be seeking an overview of child mental health practice or of a specific service area. It covers frameworks of practice, the evidence base for working in specific settings and with specific presentations or diagnoses, and emerging areas of practice and service development.

Each chapter is written by an experienced practitioner or practitioners, who are skilled in and passionate about their field. Writing styles differ in each chapter, just as therapeutic styles differ in clinical practice. Whilst each chapter gives an overview of its topic and evaluates the current evidence base, inevitably the lens of the author/s will have shaped

Child Psychology: Pathways to Good Practice, First Edition.
Edited by Helen Pote, Anna Picciotto and Clare Norris.

their interpretation and presentation in a unique way. We think this is a strength for the reader, both those who are developing their own way of working and those who are more established. It reflects the real world, of working in clinical teams with practitioners from multiple disciplines, with different training, backgrounds and experience. Competent and confident practitioners should never stop learning from and questioning their colleagues, embracing and encouraging plurality of thinking and of practice.

1.2 The UK NHS Context

Child mental health services in the United Kingdom and the National Health Service (NHS) are political; they are shaped by governmental policy and funding, and practitioners are working within the intersections of biology, physical health, wealth and poverty, race, culture, society, environment, government policy and contemporary ideology. Practitioners need to be able to consider a range of perspectives when working with children, young people, their caring networks and other agencies. They need to challenge ideas and practice and to listen to difference and dissent, however uncomfortable this may be, seeing them as a sign of strength and an opportunity for growth and development. Crucially, this includes seeking out and giving real weight to the views of experts by experience: children and young people, and the adults that care for them, at all stages of the development and evaluation of treatment and services.

In our view, there has never been a more exciting time to work in child mental health; in the United Kingdom, and in many countries internationally, the emotional health and wellbeing of children and young people is less stigmatised, and viewed as the shared responsibility of the young person, their carers and professional networks. There is a public appetite to provide support and to help tackle what can feel like a tsunami of emotional difficulties young people and their carers are having to navigate. Within the United Kingdom and the NHS, child mental health is a priority service area and there is a commitment to redressing historical funding inequities.

Changes are being implemented in the way public mental health services for children and young people are delivered in the United Kingdom. Acceptance of the age at which children and young people's services should end and adult mental health services begin is shifting, reflecting both our increasing understanding of brain development and maturity and essential differences between the structure of child and adult services and how interventions are delivered.

There is an increasing emphasis on universal settings for young people, such as schools, being 'mentally healthy' and supporting the development of positive emotional health and wellbeing, to prevent more serious mental health difficulties from developing and to identify difficulties as they emerge in order to intervene early. Mental health services are encouraged to be provided as 'in-reach' – embedded into the settings which children, young people, families and carers are already accessing. Services are no longer solely based in mental health clinics or hospitals, although those services that are continue to have an essential place in the range of services available. Choice for service users, whatever their background or resources, in what model or service is accessed, and how and where it is delivered, is being given increasingly high value (NHS Long Term Plan, 2019).

This provides expanding opportunities for practitioners to work not only directly with children, young people, families and carers, but also as trainers and consultants to the networks around them and in leadership roles, advising on policy and service developments.

1.3 A Vision for Confident Child Psychological Practitioners

What might a good child psychological practitioner offer? One of the editors of this book interviewed senior managers of psychological services to see what they wanted from newly qualified clinical psychologists (Pote & Taylor, 2016). The focus was on leadership across a range of specialities, but managers' answers were illuminating; they noted that junior psychological practitioners would need to:

- Have a sound knowledge of clinical presentations, their assessment and treatment.
- Develop strong therapeutic skills in evidence-based models.
- Clearly and confidently communicate psychological ideas and skills with other professionals.
- Take responsibility in teams and lead on risk management.
- Be visible and active members of the multidisciplinary team.
- Be outward-facing, 'big-picture' thinkers, interested in changes in the NHS and be aware of the broader political and legal contexts of practice.
- Demonstrate some business acumen, including a clear ability to take initiative and show an entrepreneurial spirit to develop clinical services effectively (see Figure 1.1).

We have seen that competent child psychological practitioners offer all of this, and their ability to think and act systemically, seeing the needs of the child in context are important building blocks for broader development. In this book we hope to encourage development of all these skills.

In our experience supervising and supporting child psychological practitioners, there are seven elements that make up successful practitioners, which are described in Table 1.1 using the acronym ACHIEVE.

1.4 Developing Clinical Confidence as a Practitioner

Novice practitioners should not expect themselves to be immediately or 'naturally' confident in their clinical practice. As discussed throughout this book, clinical confidence is something that develops over time. Rightly so: clients would not want practitioners to be over-confident in their abilities on their first day of practice before their skills have developed; one would not expect a singer to take the lead role in a big-budget musical after their first singing lesson, no matter how great their talent. Clinical competence and confidence should develop hand in hand, and are reliant on experience over time. Unfortunately, new practitioners sometimes feel they have to present a 'veneer' of competence and confidence to their supervisors when this is far from how they are actually feeling. This is especially true when their work is being evaluated, but it can have a negative impact on learning and make it difficult for supervisors to judge the right amount of support to offer the practitioner.

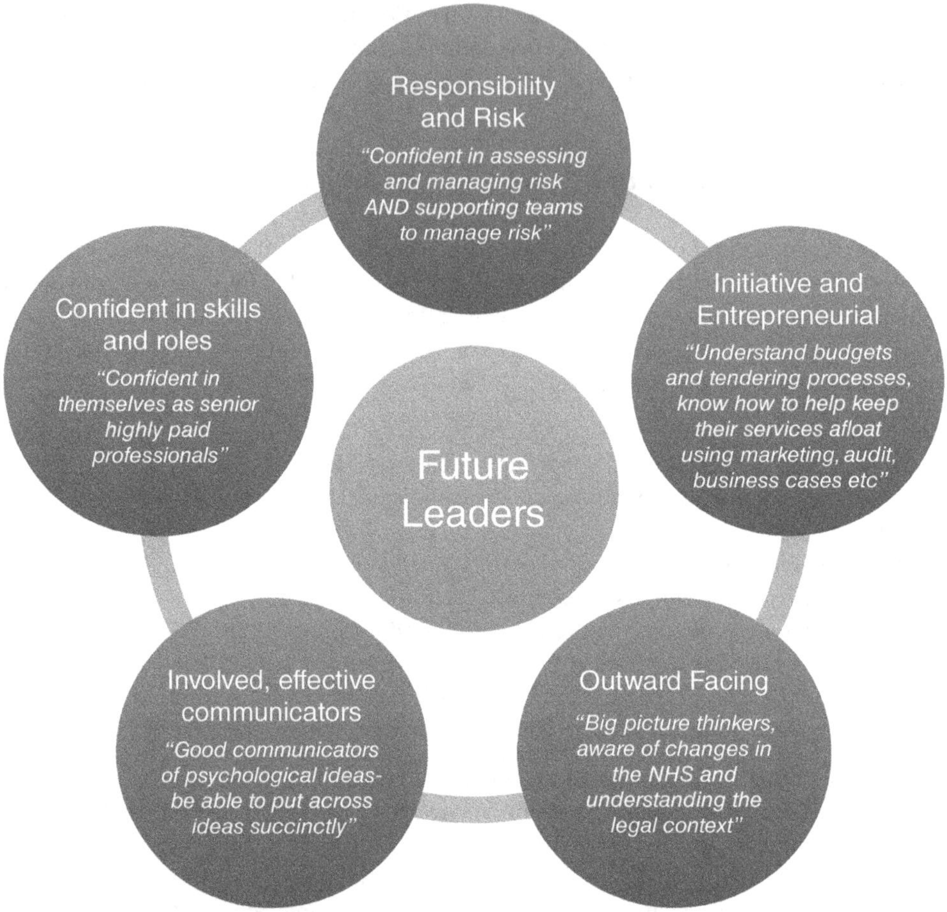

Figure 1.1 What do managers look for in newly qualified psychological practitioners? *Source:* Adapted from Pote and Taylor (2016).

Although being able to contain one's own anxiety in the room with clients is important, so too is being able to ask for help and acknowledge 'not-knowing' with those in a position to support the practitioner's development. This experience of feeling anxious or fraudulent when starting out in clinical practice is common but can be particularly difficult in child service contexts when younger practitioners, often without children themselves, are 'positioned' as experts by families and professionals seeking psychological advice.

Inexperience does not equate to incompetence. Sometimes, novice practitioners are so focussed on the things that they do not know, have not yet experienced or are concerned about trying, that they forget to note the areas of practice where they have good core clinical skills. These core skills are often those originally outlined by Carl Rogers in the 1950s (e.g., Rogers, 1957), which he labelled 'core conditions for therapy': empathy, congruence and unconditional positive regard. Figure 1.2 shows how these might be demonstrated in child psychological practice. Novice practitioners should take some time to notice how they demonstrate these core skills in their everyday interactions with family, friends, colleagues

Table 1.1 The seven elements of confident child psychological practitioners: ACHIEVE.

A	**Aptitude**: having a sound knowledge of child development, clinical presentations, their assessment and treatment and an ability to think creatively to apply theoretical knowledge to build an understanding of the child in context.
C	**Critical thinking**: an ability to think independently, critically and problem solve, to evaluate the clinical evidence base and personalise interventions to meet the individual client's needs.
H	**Holistic approach:** an ability to understand the child in the context of their family, culture and community. Recognising the impact of health, social and financial inequalities on presenting difficulties. Managing complex family difficulties with multiple members experiencing distress.
I	**Interpersonally skilled**: able to work collaboratively with clients across the age span and with members of the multidisciplinary team as well as with professionals from other agencies. Ensuring that different perspectives are communicated clearly and understood.
E	**Evaluative**: able to work reflectively and form a balanced self-evaluation of the work and clinical decision making. Ability to respond to feedback from clients and professionals to develop self and others, in order to improve the quality of the work.
V	**Values driven**: Alignment with NHS values: dignity, respect, equality and compassion. Ensuring that practice is self-reflective, inclusive and anti-discriminatory.
E	**Ethical practice:** Including an ability to work hard, take responsibility and show initiative in offering services that are in children's best interest.

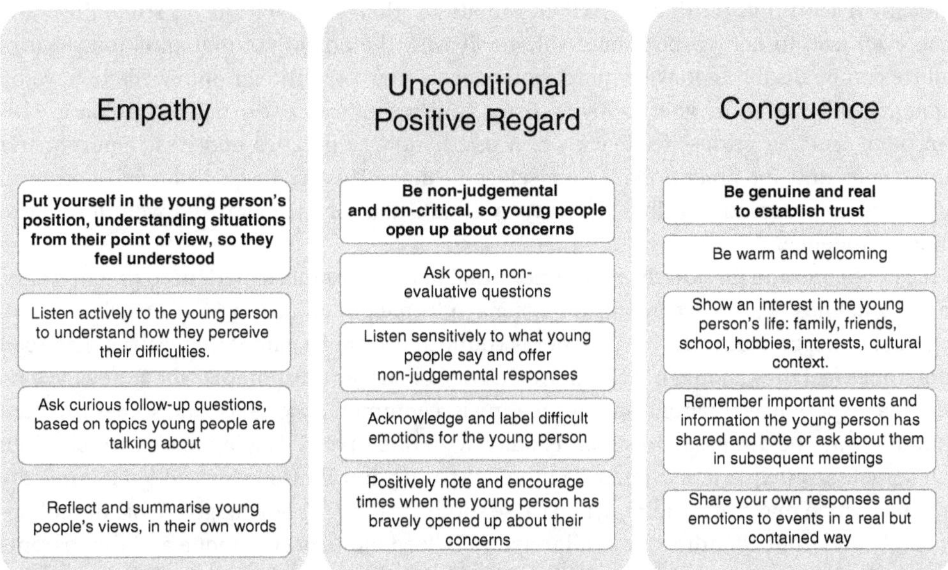

Figure 1.2 Core skills for child psychological practitioners. Clark & Beck, 2011 / Guilford Press.

and clients. They are likely to be more adept at these skills than they imagine and noting when they are demonstrating these core skills well can be an important first step in building clinical confidence. Often displaying these core skills in a first assessment session with young people is a key part of what the practitioner needs to do to start to build a therapeutic alliance and to keep the client engaged; it forms the foundation for the information gathering and psychological work to come. Focussing on these core skills and making an emotional connection with the client is perhaps a more important first step than learning the theoretical and technical skills that can pre-occupy novice practitioners.

The pace of learning and exposure to novel situations are critical in developing clinical confidence. No-one develops their confidence in a new skill by thinking about it, they develop confidence by actually practising the new skill or being in the new situation. It is noticeable that in child psychological practice, where supervisors are concerned about the vulnerability of their young clients and are often keen to be very supportive of their supervisees, the pace of trying out new skills might be slow. Sometimes exposure to new tasks can be too slow and this allows practitioners' anxieties about the work to build up, which can impede confidence. It is important for practitioners to observe others at work and have clinical opportunities quickly enough to allow early opportunities for in vivo practice of skills, with accompanying time for supervisor feedback and self-reflection. See Chapter 4, later in the book for a more detailed consideration of this.

It is important to practice what we preach as psychological practitioners; applying behavioural techniques like graded exposure to novel or fearful clinical situations, repeatedly facing these situations and practicing these skills until anxiety dissipates (Clark & Beck, 2011). It is sometimes helpful to think about this as learning to take risks with one's own learning, putting oneself in situations that are likely to be stretching, and may even lead to failure, but being able to sit with the anxiety of that situation. Fear of failure can be disabling for new practitioners; as a new practitioner one needs to develop enough resilience to be able to invite, listen and respond to constructive feedback. This can often feel like critical feedback when one is new to practice and it is important for supervisors and for practitioners themselves to make this feedback balanced, noting in each clinical observation things that went well and that practitioners did well in order to build confidence.

It can be common for novice practitioners and, in fact, for more experienced practitioners, to feel what has been described as 'imposter syndrome'. In child and family work this feeling can be exaggerated if the practitioner is young and/or not a parent themselves. They can sometimes feel they should not be offering advice or supporting parents when they have no personal experience of parenting. This feeling is a common experience and something that should always be discussed in supervision or with one's peers. Having one's own children can sometimes help a practitioner be more empathic, but it also brings added complexity and bias which may not be helpful, and these should also be acknowledged. Working collaboratively and understanding that children and indeed families are unique and that parents are experts on their own children will reduce the need to feel like an expert on parenting oneself.

Peer support can be really helpful in supporting practitioners to address these common concerns. We, the editors of this book, met as undergraduate psychology students. We have, over the years, been an essential source of professional support and guidance for each other, enabling us to develop confidence in our roles, particularly as we have faced new challenges in our careers. One's own support network is important and novice practitioners need to be proactive in creating it. Use the people around you to develop your thinking and help you to manage the emotional demands of the work.

Taking a developmental perspective is key to developing clinical confidence. This is not only in relation to the young people we see, understanding how they are growing and developing and noticing that many skills or cognitive processes are latent, but also in relation to oneself as a practitioner (see Chapter 3 for further discussion of a developmental approach to practice). Over the course of one's career a practitioner changes considerably, first learning new skills, then developing a personal style and clinical areas of expertise. Personally, they will also change and develop, moving on through their own individual and family life-cycle. Self-reflection on one's own development is essential for understanding how one's own developmental position might link to that of the young people and families the practitioner is working with. Being aware of your own position and the biases it brings is critical in being able to connect and empathise with clients and supports anti-discriminatory practice (See Chapter 7 to think about how to put this into place in practice).

Having this developmental, self-reflective approach is particularly important when circumstances are personally challenging. Such circumstances may mirror some of the themes of one's clinical work with families, for example when they are a result of life events such as bereavement, divorce, domestic abuse or struggling with one's own parenting. These events can impact personal self-confidence and also professional self-efficacy. It is important to attend to personal wellbeing at these times and discuss the impact of these events on the work in supervision as well as through personal therapy, if necessary. Long term, these events may enrich clinical work but in the midst of a crisis practitioners should not be afraid to take the steps that are required to support themselves, to ensure they are offering the best service they can to their clients and maintaining their fitness to practice. Indeed, this is required as part of Health and Care Professions Council (HCPC) standards, the regulatory body through which many psychological practitioners in the United Kingdom are registered to practice (HCPC, 2023).

There are times during a practitioner's career when the clinical environment itself can impact on one's clinical confidence. For example, when the tasks are simply too complex for the level of training, or where staffing levels or resources are inadequate, or when the work does not match the practitioner's interests or values. Practitioners need to recognise when this is the case and not expect themselves to be able to perform 'perfectly' in every setting. One common example for novice practitioners is struggling to work with complex family presentations as a lone practitioner or agency, where there are multiple social, psychological and economic needs that will not all be met through psychological interventions alone. It is important for practitioners to recognise what needs they cannot meet and acknowledge this to themselves and to families. This is critical, as striving to meet all needs, including those beyond one's control as a practitioner can lead to burnout. Being 'good enough' can be tough when faced with vulnerable children, as the practitioner may have strong feelings of responsibility to meet all of the child's needs. Recognising one's limits, and avoiding a 'saviour mentality' in which the practitioner takes sole responsibility for 'curing' others and which is disempowering to one's clients, is important to enable the clinician to continue practice in the long term. Being compassionate to oneself, to families and to other professionals can help, recognising that people are usually doing their best to meet a child's needs in difficult circumstances.

Finally, thinking about the trajectory of one's own career as a child psychological practitioner is important. The range of clinical opportunities are very rich, bringing varied opportunities to work with young people from birth to late adolescence, across community, health, social and forensic settings. Adult and child-focussed competencies will develop in work with young clients, their siblings, peers, parents, professionals and communities. Presenting issues span physical, social and mental health concerns, and practitioners will often be working with complex cases with difficulties that fall across these domains. One thing is for sure, a career as a child psychological practitioner is rarely dull and always presents novel learning opportunities and the possibility of working in different services. Being adaptive and flexible is important over your career to sustain interest and commitment and ensure you are doing work with just the right amount of challenge. Think about how you want your career to develop over time, where your passions lie and what is the right fit for you between work you enjoy and skills you have to offer. Remember, you don't have to learn everything all at once. We hope this book will start you off on an interesting career path.

Top Tips from the Editors

- Keep your clients' needs at the centre of your learning journey.
- Expect your competence and confidence to grow over time, hand in hand.
- Show self-compassion, notice things you do well alongside areas for development to encourage confidence building.
- Listen to others and be open to feedback, reflect on feedback rather than feeling you need to respond immediately.
- Be curious, asking questions and acknowledging what you don't yet know.
- Expect to make mistakes and discuss these with supervisors and peers to maximise learning.
- Expect to feel anxious when facing novel clinical situations and use psychological techniques to contain this.
- Reflect on your own competence limits and be aware of how your personal or work context may affect your competence.
- Developing a support network is important and novice practitioners need to be proactive in drawing on people around them to gain support.

1.5 How to Use this Book

This book does not have to be read sequentially. Each chapter is written to stand independently, however they have been grouped into three sections: Frameworks of Practice; Evidence Informed Practice and Growing Areas of Practice. Section I focuses on the core competencies that any psychological practitioner working in this area needs to develop, alongside the broader contexts, history and frameworks that surround child mental health practice and inform how it is organised and delivered. This section covers the cycle of practice outlined by the British Psychological Society (BPS) (BPS, 2017): assessment, formulation, intervention, evaluation and communication. The limitations of the current evidence base is acknowledged, and a critical, reflective approach is encouraged. The importance of good supervision structures to support the development of self-reflection and inclusive practice is emphasised and it also includes chapters focusing on ethical and inclusive practice, on engagement with children, young people and their caring networks and on the meaningful co-production of services.

Section II focuses on the main presenting issues in child psychological practice across the age range. There are chapters dedicated to specific chronological age groups such as common presentations in the under-fives and the difficulties typically presented during adolescence. Other chapters focus on a particular presenting issue or a range of presenting issues that are grouped together in classifications of mental health difficulties, such as emotional difficulties, eating disorders and behavioural difficulties. Within this section, there are also chapters dedicated to children and young people (CYP) with particular characteristics, acknowledging that those CYP and their families and systems may need dedicated and adapted services, such as those with intellectual difficulties and neurodivergence. Each chapter in Section II includes an introduction to the topic and its relevance to future practice, a review of the evidence-base and National Institute for Health and Care Excellence (NICE) and other policy guidelines, critical reflections on the evidence base and suggestions for future research. Crucially, the view and voices of the CYP, their families and systems in each area of practice are outlined. Guidance on how psychological assessments, formulation and interventions may be carried out and evaluated are included, incorporating empirical examples of clinical practice. There is an acknowledgement of the clinical challenges and ideas about how they may be addressed. Finally, future directions for psychological practice in that area of child psychological practice are discussed.

The final section of the book focuses on specific areas of child psychology in practice that are new, growing or in a period of rapid change: working with adolescents, with CYP in crisis or in perinatal services; the development of community outreach or embedded services such as those based within youth justice services, youth community practice, schools and their families or children's social care; and innovations to practice that will increase access and efficacy: the use of digital technologies and the development of whole systems approaches for services such as trauma informed practice.

1.6 Conclusion

New practitioners bring a wealth of ideas, experiences and innovation to child psychological practice. Crucially, they also bring an energy and enthusiasm without which services would stagnate and their adaptation to a changing world would be impossible.

This is not a book about the development of 'perfect practice', but we hope it will be a starting point, describing some of the challenges and dilemmas we all face as clinicians and the importance of questioning, of taking risks and of learning from mistakes.

References

British Psychological Society. (2017). *BPS practice guidelines.* https://www.bps.org.uk/guideline/bps-practice-guidelines-2017

Health and Care Professions Council. (2023). *Standards.* https://www.hcpc-uk.org/standards/

NHS. (2019). Long term plan. https://www.longtermplan.nhs.uk/

Pote, H., & Taylor, C. (2016). Clinical psychologists as future leaders: Project evaluation: Phase 1. RHUL Grant Report for Health Education England – London.

Rogers, C. R. (1957). The necessary and sufficient conditions of therapeutic personality change. *Journal of Consulting Psychology, 21*(2), 95–103.

2

Theory and Evidence in Practice

Clare Norris, Helen Pote and Anna Picciotto

Children and young people in psychological distress deserve to receive the most effective treatments available, and these should be tailored to meet their individual needs and life circumstances. To achieve this, it is important for child psychological practitioners to take a curious and critical approach towards the theoretical models and research evidence that guides their practice. Practitioners need to think about what the literature currently tells us and what is still unknown about the psychological distress that young people and their families experience. Child-focused psychological theories and models of mental health are not yet sufficiently explanatory, from a developmental and biopsychosocial perspective, to clearly direct clinical practice with young people. The evidence base is limited because many interventions have been developed and evaluated with a proportion of young people, but lack more inclusive or comprehensive research. This chapter seeks to encourage this curious stance and will consider the scientist-practitioner approach used in psychological training and services before reviewing some of the limitations of the evidence base and diagnostic frameworks when working with young people. Finally, the cycle of practice that psychological practitioners follow to assess, formulate, intervene and evaluate their work with young people is introduced and key therapeutic models that are often useful to inform this cycle are briefly outlined.

2.1 Scientist-practitioner and Evidence-based Practice Models

Clinical child psychology is based on a scientist-practitioner model: psychologists are both practitioners, who apply theory and knowledge in practice, and scientists, who base their practice on existing research and evidence as well as generating evidence and research from their own practice. These two aspects require integration if child psychological practitioners are to become competent and confident practitioners who remain helpful to their clients over the course of their careers. By integrating research with practice, it is assumed that the psychological practitioner will deliver effective psychological services and enable research that is of direct relevance to their clients' outcomes (Jones & Mehr, 2007).

Child Psychology: Pathways to Good Practice, First Edition.
Edited by Helen Pote, Anna Picciotto and Clare Norris.

Within services, psychological practitioners are required to use the scientist-practitioner approach to offer evidence-based practice, integrating the best research evidence with clinical expertise whilst attending to client characteristics, preferences and feedback. When applying this approach to children, the development and life stage of the child or young person (CYP) alongside their family context requires careful consideration. Practitioners must understand the developmental norms for a CYP at that particular age, within that particular culture and consider if the research evidence they are drawing upon has relevance to that developmental and cultural context. In practice, child practitioners must keep abreast of the research literature, theoretical advances and clinical guidelines to understand the most effective approaches to psychological assessment and intervention and integrate this with what they have learned about the individual client during the assessment. They must pay close attention to the client's goals and preferences and bring together all of this information into a formulation and treatment plan that guides the psychological intervention and is regularly reviewed with direct feedback from the client. Increasingly, the delivery of evidence-based practice can be compromised by limited resources and service structures so practitioners need to take a flexible, pragmatic and reflective approach when delivering services, especially when evidence for a specific client group or service model is only just emerging.

The scientist-practitioner needs to demonstrate three core competencies in integrating evidence successfully into their practice (Stoltenberg & Pace, 2007), being:

- A consumer of science – reading, understanding, critically appraising and utilising sound relevant research findings in practice.
- An evaluator of science – continuously appraising and modifying their practice based on an ongoing evaluation of the efficacy of their practice.
- A producer of science – carrying out their own research and contributing to the growing evidence base of the profession.

As a consumer of the research evidence base, it is important for the practitioner to note that child-focused research has lagged behind that for adults, for different ethical and practical reasons. However, there is now a strong body of research evidence for the efficacy of child psychological interventions across a range of mental health presentations. This has been important in ensuring that the theories and research driving practice is developmentally appropriate. It has led to the creation of a rich collection of child-focused practice policies and clinical guidelines that have shaped the infrastructure of child health services.

The most influential guidance for child practice and the development of child mental health services comes from the National Institute for Health and Care Excellence (NICE), who produce national guidance for the National Health Service (NHS) on the cost effectiveness and efficacy of physical and mental health treatments across England, Wales and Northern Ireland.[1] The guidance is based on systematic reviews of high-quality research evidence, and includes public consultation on the draft guidance prior to publication. NICE guidelines are usually updated every 3 years and they inform policy and contribute to commissioning decisions and the allocation of resources within the NHS. They also aim to guide practitioners in their everyday practice and choice of

1 In Scotland, services are required to consider Scottish Medicines Consortium (SMC) advice.

effective interventions (see the NICE (2018b, 2018c) 'Into practice guide' for advice on implementing clinical guidelines to improve services and practice).

Similar clinical guidelines exist internationally to guide psychological practitioners, but the delivery of child mental health services is inequitable. This has led to World Health Organization (WHO) initiatives to ensure that the gap between the population in need of mental health intervention and those who can access care is reduced, particularly for those in low- and middle-income countries (LMICs) who often have the most limited access to research and clinical resources (Lancet Global Mental Health Group, 2007).

2.2 Critical Reflections on the Evidence Base

The evidence base in child psychological practice and the practice of evidence-based approaches has been subject to criticism. Each chapter in this book will include a critical examination of the evidence base from a developmental and contextual perspective but themes regarding the limitations of the evidence base are briefly presented in this section. Readers are directed to Fonagy et al. (2015) *What Works for Whom: A Critical Review of Treatments for Children and Adolescents,* for a more detailed discussion.

2.2.1 Types of Evidence and Clinical Trials

In health research, there is often a prescribed or restricted view of what is acceptable evidence. A hierarchy of research evidence exists in medical and psychotherapy research that places those studies that are considered less susceptible to bias at the top of the hierarchy. This 'levels of evidence' approach judges clinical trials, and particularly those using randomisation with some level of blinding for the assignment of treatment groups (randomised controlled trials (RCTs)), as the gold standard of research design. International standards of good practice (e,g. CONSORT guidelines, Moher et al., 2010) and trial registration ensure quality control in the conduct and reporting of these clinical trials. Practitioners are encouraged to choose the highest level of evidence available to support their clinical judgements and this frequently means relying on RCT evidence. Recently, quality appraisal and synthesis of clinical trial data using systematic reviews and meta-analysis has filtered research findings to answer specific questions about the efficacy of different psychological interventions in child practice, this has supported evidence-based clinical decision making. These reviews can be helpful in both determining treatment outcomes and identifying active mechanisms for change, which are important in personalising interventions. For an example, see Baker et al. (2021).

The key aim of RCTs is to compare two or more interventions to determine efficacy over time. There are many strengths inherent in their longitudinal design that allow conclusions to be drawn about the specific impact of the intervention in improving client psychological outcomes. Participants are carefully selected against pre-determined criteria and randomly allocated to different treatment conditions, to control for individual differences such as demographics, symptom severity and level of functioning. Interventions are delivered in a standardised, manualised way to ensure treatment fidelity and reduce differences in the therapists' application of interventions. The design allows active treatments to be compared with a control group with no intervention (such as a waiting list group) or another active comparison condition (such as treatment as usual or another model of therapy). Standardised outcome measures are commonly used to try to achieve reliable and valid assessments of psychological symptoms or clinical levels of psychological distress/disorders.

In practice, there are limitations to an RCT approach (Deaton & Cartwright, 2018):

1. Sample sizes – large trials are needed for randomisation of patients to ensure that individual differences do not have an impact on results and to determine that any change in primary outcome variables, such as mental health symptoms, is due to the intervention alone. Large trials are unusual in psychotherapy research, due to cost and practical considerations, but are essential if statistical analysis is to be sufficiently powered to provide an accurate assessment of the effect of the intervention.
2. Bias towards specific interventions – as RCTs are a major undertaking and are expensive, this limits the amount of time an intervention can be offered for, so briefer interventions (such as Cognitive Behaviour Therapy (CBT)) are more likely to be studied than longer-term therapies. Similarly, interventions that are structured, easily manualised and have a specific symptom or disorder focus lend themselves more easily to an RCT design than unstructured, complex psychological interventions.
3. Practical and ethical issues for suitable control conditions – use of randomised controlled comparisons means that some clients who are in psychological distress are denied an effective intervention or their treatment is delayed. Delaying treatment can be particularly problematic for CYP participants who may be at a critical phase of development or might specifically benefit from early intervention at first onset of a psychological difficulty. Furthermore, clients are not passive recipients of treatment but have preferences for different therapeutic interventions and this may introduce bias in relation to treatment adherence and dropouts. Careful attention to statistical analysis methods, including intention to treat analysis, is therefore important.
4. Treatment fidelity – although manualisation attempts to reduce individual differences between practitioners implementing an intervention, in practice this is difficult to achieve. Therapist adherence to the intervention is often measured by self-report rather than observational data and individual differences between therapists, such as their allegiance to the intervention and levels of skills and experience, can also introduce bias. Therapists' contributions to therapy can be differentiated into three conceptual dimensions: their skills, the techniques they employ and their personal qualities (e.g. warmth, empathy and perceived sincerity). It is difficult to separate the effect of the therapeutic technique or model from the therapist's personal factors, experience and skill (Roth & Fonagy, 2005).

2.2.2 Generalisability of Research Evidence

Evidence generated with adult participants should not be applied to child-focused practice without careful consideration of the developmental and cohort differences between child and adult populations. Yet time and again, adult theoretical models, protocols for psychological intervention and outcome research evidence from clinical adult trials are transposed onto child practice without sufficient consideration.

The evidence base from child-focused clinical trials is also limited in its generalisability in several ways. In clinical research trials, eligible participants are often defined in relation to a single psychiatric diagnosis and young people with mixed or complex presentations are not included in samples to protect internal validity. The *Diagnostic and Statistical Manual of Mental Disorders*, fifth edition (*DSM-5*, American Psychiatric Association, 2013) is commonly used for defining research inclusion and exclusion criteria. This has been criticised for its poor sensitivity to developmental factors in its taxonomy and disorder categorisation, even though the current edition aimed to develop more precise criteria for child presentations. Furthermore, in clinical settings, CYP are often complex and rarely as straightforward in their presentations as in research trials. This is particularly the case for younger children as their difficulties may just be emerging, or may have not differentiated into clear or specific diagnostic categories (Target & Fonagy, 2005; Fonagy et al., 2015).

Another important issue related to generalisability is the social, contextual and demographic make-up of the samples used to form the evidence base. The evidence base for CYP and their families is compromised by an over-reliance on samples from white high-income backgrounds who are English speakers, by using mothers as primary respondents, by gender bias for samples related to specific difficulties and by a lack of specificity in reporting demographic factors related to poverty and levels of education for samples overall. Reasons for under-representation of some participants include language, physical, educational and financial barriers to participation as well as negative experiences and mistrust of health services. An active approach to increase diversity of participation in research is required (National Health Service England, 2023).

It is sometimes difficult to directly translate research findings about psychological interventions into clinical practice. The need for scientific rigour in research trials looking at efficacy inevitably changes the nature of the psychological interventions investigated. The desire for internal validity (finding cause and effect) leads to the use of techniques and conditions that are rarely seen in everyday clinical practice. Thus, external validity (the extent to which findings can be generalised to clinical practice) is compromised. Additional effectiveness trials and implementation research in usual practice settings is required to ensure the psychological interventions being evaluated are going to be helpful to real CYP presenting to services in psychological distress. The recent growth of implementation science to psychotherapy research has been helpful in supporting this research into practice process and ensuring CYP benefit from the research findings in routine psychological services (Bauer & Kirchner, 2020). Implementation science explores the factors that might affect the uptake of clinical innovation in routine settings and seeks to overcome those barriers.

2.2.3 Efficacy and Cost-effectiveness

The efficacy and cost effectiveness of different psychotherapeutic interventions and how this has been established internationally, beyond High Income Countries (HICs) is questionable (Tiley & Kyriakopoulos, 2018). In the United Kingdom (UK), NICE guidance has been controversial, in particular because of the weight given to the cost effectiveness of treatments, which leaves it open to accusations of political influence. With any research evidence, scientist-practitioners should critically evaluate the source; its context and author intentions. When looking at NICE guidance, practitioners should note the combination of resource and clinical effectiveness factors that shape the document.

There are further specific developmental issues in appraising the child psychotherapy evidence base that child psychological practitioners should consider:

1. Measures of symptomatology in CYP are usually derived from several informants: teachers, parents/carers, the CYP themselves and the practitioner. These measures correlate poorly, and measuring overall outcomes and symptom level change reliably for child psychological interventions is therefore complex.
2. Most psychological interventions can only be offered to CYP if they have the life circumstances to support it. For example, to engage in traditional therapeutic interventions in clinic settings CYP may need practical assistance to travel and attend. Each specific intervention model brings its own engagement requirements from caregivers, relying on their competence and motivation to ensure the CYP benefits from the treatment offered; for family therapy there is a need for family members to actively engage in the treatment together; in child psychodynamic psychotherapy, the parents or carers are often required to engage in concurrent therapeutic work; for CBT, caregivers may be required to undertake psychoeducation and support the implementation of new behavioural strategies.
3. Intervention plans are often multifaceted in child services and do not represent the single intervention model preferred in clinical trials. A range of different interventions are more commonly needed with children simultaneously due to the systems they are part of and the combination of difficulties they present with. For example, a single referral for school-based anxiety and reluctance to attend school, may result in an intervention package comprising individual therapy for the child, alongside psychoeducation offered to parents and a school-level consultation with teachers to support mental health literacy. Multiple outcomes for the CYP and their family may be more or less relevant to different people and services involved and determining which are the most meaningful and how best to measure them can be challenging.
4. Understanding and measuring psychological changes seen over the course of a clinical trial needs to attend carefully to developmental factors such as: the chronological and developmental age range of participants; natural maturation during the course of a trial; and normative expected functioning for different psychological mechanisms at different ages (such as cognitive biases, Slavny et al., 2019).

Thus, although RCTs are a powerful tool that help researchers draw some implications from trials, their limitations need to be recognised and the difficulties in the application to child clinical practice understood. They should therefore be integrated with other research designs and other forms of evidence to inform clinical practice guidance and the commissioning of services. Other useful designs include: controlled trials without randomisation, or 'quasi-experiments'; experimental single case designs; cohort studies where groups of patients are allocated to treatments; case control studies, with professional opinion based on clinical experience; descriptive studies; qualitative studies; uncontrolled studies; and reports of expert committees.

2.3 Critical Reflections on Diagnostic Classifications of Child Mental Health Disorders

The most commonly used classification of psychological disorders used in the UK is the *DSM-5* (American Psychiatric Association 2013). Most treatment outcome studies are conducted on samples selected in accordance with *DSM-5* and, less frequently, the International Classification of Diseases (ICD, currently in its 11th edition, World Health Organization, 2022). Such categorisation adheres to a medical model that suggests mental health diagnoses exist and can be identified and classified and that diagnosis can lead to the most appropriate treatment for that disorder.

Despite the widespread acceptance and influence of medicalisation and psychiatric diagnosis, it has been subject to criticism and controversy and there have been calls for a different approach (Bebbington, 2015; Cosgrove & Krimsky, 2012; Critical Psychiatric Network, 2013; Francis, 2013; Johnstone & Boyle, 2018). The reader is directed to texts such as Johnstone and Boyle's *Power, Threat, Meaning Framework* commissioned by the Division of Clinical Psychology (Johnstone & Boyle, 2018) for an in-depth critique of psychiatric diagnostic classifications. It presents an alternative framework for the description of patterns of emotional distress and functional psychological difficulties using a multifactorial and contextual approach. Individual chapters in this book will discuss the advantages and disadvantages of psychiatric diagnosis and the limitations of diagnostic classifications for specific conditions related to CYP mental health.

Within child services the use of psychiatric classification frameworks has both advantages and disadvantages. Some CYP and their families report benefiting from receiving a diagnosis in terms of aiding their understanding and self-management of psychological difficulties and accessing treatment and professional services. Others report experiencing both public stigma and self-stigma following diagnosis and describe it as having a negative and limiting impact on their lives and identities (Kaushik et al., 2016). The reliability and validity of psychiatric classification systems for CYP is often criticised, particularly their poor developmental sensitivity and attention to childhood prevalence figures, to enable age-related diagnostic criteria to be clearly specified. To address these concerns, the *DSM-5* features a new lifespan approach to mental health and has specifically updated some of its criteria to capture more precisely emotional, cognitive and behavioural symptoms presenting in CYP. The issue of CYP presenting with more than one diagnosable condition (co-morbidity) has already been discussed; these are particularly relevant for a range of neurodevelopmental difficulties presenting in childhood. Child psychological practitioners need to ensure that a full psychological understanding of the child is at the centre of their formulation, and that interventions are not simply planned using diagnostic categories.

Given the above limitations, some psychological practitioners and researchers conclude that the current diagnostic systems do not assist them in understanding the aetiology or development of an individual's difficult thoughts, feelings or behaviour (e.g. Bebbington, 2015; Cosgrove & Krimsky, 2012; Critical Psychiatric Network, 2013; Francis, 2013; Johnstone & Boyle, 2018 Thomas & Longden, 2013). It may be that the adoption of this medicalised framework in health services has also marginalised research demonstrating links between social and personal adversity and psychological distress. There is evidence that behaviours, thoughts and feelings can be understood in terms of people's contexts and life experiences (see research on impact of adverse life experiences e.g. Felitti et al., 1998; Koplan & Chard, 2015).

In clinical practice, however, psychological practitioners frequently work alongside medically trained colleagues such as child and adolescent psychiatrists as part of multidisciplinary teams, and biological experiences are considered in the same way that social and psychological experiences are during assessment. Similarly, pharmacological treatments may be offered alongside psychological interventions (Shah & Mountain, 2007).

What alternatives exist for practising psychologists to the main diagnostic frameworks? Child psychological practitioners often prefer to focus on a description of the person's difficulties and the impact on their lives. A psychological formulation is developed with the young person (and, if appropriate, their family) focusing on the development and maintenance of their difficulties in their current context to give an understanding and meaning to their experiences. The next section (and Chapter 3 on assessment and formulation) outlines this individual psychological formulation approach and introduces a popular structure to guide psychological case formulation – the 5Ps model (Padesky, 2020), illustrating how this is used to inform theory-driven, evidence-based practice.

2.4 The Cycle of Practice of Child Psychological Practitioners

The British Psychological Society (BPS) outlines the cycle of clinical/professional practice for psychological practitioners taking a scientist-practitioner model, where the practitioner is continuously appraising and modifying their practice based on an evaluation of its efficacy (BPS, 2017). Psychological practice is underpinned by five core competencies:

1. A detailed **assessment** of the client's difficulties in their context using multiple measures and informants. Importantly, eliciting the CYP's, their carers' and professional network's goals.
2. Developing an agreed **formulation** (understanding) with the CYP and their family of their difficulties and how they may have developed. This formulation integrates psychological theories and research evidence with the individual client's clinical assessment to develop a psychological understanding of the difficulties, which informs the intervention plan.
3. Agreeing and implementing the best **psychological intervention** to address the CYP and their system's difficulties. This should be based on the best available evidence and align with the CYP and their carer's values and choices.
4. **Evaluating** the outcome of that intervention at intervals using multiple measures and informants to review progress and adapting the intervention when necessary.
5. **Communicating** progress through reporting and reflecting on outcomes to the CYP and their systems and caring networks.

Psychological practitioners thus contribute to the evidence base as a producer of science, carrying out their own research and offering practice-based evidence. This may be specific to their own practice and service, such as through audits and service evaluations. Audit and research skills are essential competencies for psychological practitioners working in child settings (Roth et al., 2011). Audit aims to evaluate how closely assessment, formulation, intervention and implementation are delivered against a set of previously given practice standards. Audit also evaluates how protocols and procedures, for example related to consent or recording of activity, have been followed by the practitioner and the service.

Many child psychological practitioners contribute to the knowledge and evidence base for the practice of child psychology within the profession once they are working. Effectiveness or qualitative studies carried out in clinical practice rather than research settings may lack the scientific rigour of RCTs but are recognised as essential contributions to clinical practice. Examples of helpful practice-based evidence include service experience and satisfaction surveys; single-case experimental designs to evaluate psychological interventions; and qualitative research exploring young people's experiences. This evidence can directly feed into clinical and service improvements particularly if quality improvement methodology is carefully applied to focus on a specific area for improvement and test the effect of an applied solution. An example of this might be a series of small-scale research projects investigating if access to a service is inclusive across the range of ethnically diverse communities of CYP and families in the local area where the service is based. This might involve first defining the scale and nature of the problem through data collection, before co-producing possible solutions with CYP, testing these solutions in practice, and using the results to determine the development of more effective service guidelines and care pathways to achieve sustainable organisational change.

2.5 The Importance of Reflexivity and Supervision

Psychological practitioners are constantly having to make important decisions within their clinical practice that can have a significant impact on CYP's lives. Decisions about what to assess, what is included in a formulation, what intervention to implement, with whom and for how long can be guided by the evidence base and good-practice guidelines but they will also be influenced by factors related to the individual practitioner, which the practitioner must reflect upon to support evidence-based decision making and practice.

Reflexivity is the capacity of an individual to examine their own feelings, reactions and motives and how they influence their decisions and actions. Without this reflective capacity, decision making can be subject to bias related to a practitioner's beliefs and assumptions, as factors such as their life experience, cultural background, gender and own experience of being parented all shape their beliefs and assumptions. Without engaging in reflection, the practitioner is less likely to develop awareness of their own beliefs or the factors that have shaped them (unconscious bias) and the impact they are having. In clinical sessions with CYP, for example, the practitioner may make assumptions, lack curiosity, focus on specific areas of concern, limit hypotheses or formulations or simply not attend to whether their language and behaviour is inclusive (see Chapter 7).

Supervision is an essential space to support the development of reflexivity. Through the supervisory relationship, assumptions and biases that the psychological practitioner may not be aware of can be brought to the fore and examined safely. It is helpful for regular feedback from CYP and families to be brought into these supervision conversations, to monitor the impact of clinical decisions and reflect on the practitioner's behaviour in sessions. Continuing professional development and self-care also allow time and space for the practitioner to reflect, develop knowledge and skills and maintain their own wellbeing, all of which are important in supporting the practitioner to maintain an engaged and curious stance in their interactions with clients (see Chapter 4).

2.6 The Main Theoretical Models and Interventions Applied by Child Psychological Practitioners

Child psychological practitioners can develop knowledge and skills in applying different theoretical models that support the understanding of CYP experiencing psychological distress. These theoretical models support the collaborative formulation process between practitioner, CYP and their systems. Each model has associated clinical applications that guide the assessment and intervention process. The different therapeutic models differ across several dimensions, including:

1. The psychological construct to change – focusing on, for example, emotions, behaviours, cognitions or relationship patterns.
2. The client focus – intervening with the child, family or the wider system.
3. The role of the therapist – who might assume an active versus reflective approach, or hold an expert versus a collaborative position.

The theoretical models of child psychological practice most widely applied are outlined briefly. Further discussion of these models and their implementation in specific practice settings will be discussed in later chapters.

2.6.1 Psychodynamic Theory and Therapy

The psychodynamic approach originates from the work of Sigmund Freud and his colleague Josef Breuer in the 1890s (Breuer & Freud, 1956, 1957). It has evolved considerably since its psychoanalytic origins and has been developed further by other leaders in the field (e.g. Anna Freud, 1928, 1936; Carl Jung, 1923; Melanie Klein, 1955). The psychoanalytic and psychodynamic approaches have similarities but are quite distinct in theory and practice.

The focus of psychoanalytic theory is the CYP's unconscious thoughts, feelings and conflicts that are proposed to have contributed to the development of their distress and difficulties in functioning. Psychoanalytic therapy associated with these models can be frequent and extended, with several sessions per week spread over one or more years. The aim is to assist the CYP to develop insight or awareness of these unconscious thoughts and feelings and how they contribute to patterns of behaviour in their lives. This happens through the relationship with the therapist and the therapist's close observations and interpretations of the CYP's utterances, behaviour and play.

Psychodynamic theory and psychodynamic therapy are used as umbrella terms covering a range of therapies that draw upon psychoanalytic principles and integrate these with developmental, attachment and neurological theories (Midgely et al., 2017). The focus is on the internal world of the CYP and how this has developed through their early relational experiences. Interventions are usually briefer with less frequent sessions than in more formal psychoanalytic therapy, occurring once a week for approximately 4 to 6 months.

The focus on the individual therapeutic relationship within psychoanalytic and psychodynamic approaches has meant they have been harder to evaluate in traditional RCTs, which rely on manualised interventions. It has therefore been difficult to evidence their efficacy, but recent syntheses of the evidence base suggests these approaches can be effective for CYP (Midgely & Kennedy, 2011; Midgely et al., 2017).

Shorter-term psychodynamic psychotherapy models have been devised (e.g. Rawson, 2002) and implemented with CYP. This approach contributes to many other more recently developed therapies for CYP and their families such as: Mentalisation Based Therapy (Rossouw & Fonagy, 2012); Dynamic Interpersonal Therapy (Lemma et al., 2011); Short-term Psychodynamic Therapy (Briggs et al., 2015; Gatta et al., 2019; Midgley et al., 2013). Increasingly, child and adolescent psychodynamic psychotherapists may work in an applied way in a broad range of clinical settings, using a psychodynamic theoretical approach to their formulation of the CYP and family's presentation, but offering brief interventions.

Play has been central to the practice of psychodynamic therapy with children in order to access the child's unconscious experiences, desires, thoughts and emotions (e.g. Anna Freud, 1928; Lowenfeld, 1935; Klein, 1955). Psychodynamic psychotherapy has been combined with other therapeutic models such as person-centred approaches (Rogers, 1951) to create play therapy models (Axline, 1947) that have continued to develop into many of today's play therapy approaches (Landreth, 2002; Moustakas, 1953, 1997; Schaefer, 1983) and/or creative therapy models integrating art, drama and music (Cattanach, 2003; Jennings et al., 2005). In these therapies, CYP express themselves through creative media instead of conversation and this has benefits particularly for children who may struggle to verbalise their thoughts and feelings. There is an increasing evidence base for the efficacy of play and creative therapies for a broad range of child and adolescent presentations (see Ray et al., 2001).

2.6.2 Attachment Theory and Therapy

Attachment Theory was developed by John Bowlby in the 1960s (Bowlby, 1969). It has been researched and further developed by developmental psychologist Mary Ainsworth in the 1960s and 1970s (Ainsworth, 1978) and later Crittenden (2008). The theory proposes that, from birth, infants show proximity seeking behaviour towards a primary caregiver (attachment figure), particularly when experiencing a stressful situation. This relationship forms the basis of social and emotional development. The responses of the attachment figure are crucial and lead to the development of patterns of attachment that shape the child's internal working models. These models guide their feelings, thoughts and expectations about relationships and determine how they form and sustain relationships with others.

Ainsworth et al., (1978) developed the concept of the attachment figure as a 'secure base' from which the infant can explore and return. Three attachment styles describing how the child relates to their caregiver and other people were identified: *secure attachment, insecure avoidant attachment* and *insecure anxious attachment*. A fourth attachment style: *insecure disorganised attachment style* was recognised later (see Bretherton, 1992 for further details). In the 1980s, attachment theory was further developed and applied to adults (Hazen & Shaver, 1987). American psychologist, Patricia Crittenden has elaborated further classifications of forms of avoidant and ambivalent attachment behaviour, in her dynamic-maturational model (DMM) of attachment and adaptation (Crittenden, 2008). This model has become popular in assessing and describing an individual's attachment style.

The theory suggests that emotional and behavioural difficulties occur when attachment relationships have been disrupted or are absent, negative or abusive (Bowlby, 1969). The aim in attachment-based therapy is to modify the child's internal working model through reparative experiences in their current relationship with the therapist and with their caregivers. These interventions usually include a combination of sessions with the child and caregivers together and alone, as well as intervention with the child's systems, including their school and professional networks. In many interventions the carers' attachment experiences and styles are also a focus of therapy addressing any difficulties that may interfere with the development of attachment relationships with the child.

There is a growing evidence base for the efficacy of attachment-based parenting interventions (Barlow et al., 2016; Gregory et al., 2020; Rose & O'Reilly, 2017; Woodhouse, 2018). Examples of such therapies are: Dyadic Developmental Psychotherapy (DDP, Hughes, 1997, 2006), Theraplay® (Booth & Jernberg, 2010); Circle of Security (Powell at al., 2014); Video Interactive Guidance (Kennedy & Underdown, 2018) and Mentalisation-based Therapy for Parents (Redfern, 2015). See Chapters 12 and 16 for further details on these.

2.6.3 Behavioural Theory and Therapy

Behavioural interventions are based on theories of classical conditioning (Pavlov, 1927), conditioned behaviourism (Watson, 1930), operant conditioning (Skinner, 1953), Reciprocal Inhibition Theory (Wolpe, 1958, 1990) and Social Learning Theory (Bandura, 1986). All of these focus us on the environmental antecedents and consequences that shape a young person's behaviour. Behavioural therapy considers psychological difficulties as learned behaviours associated with life experiences and the aim is to modify the behaviours so that the CYP has improved functioning.

The focus is therefore on observing and changing what happens before or after the difficult behaviours in the environment (the *antecedents* and *consequences*). Today, behavioural interventions are often combined with cognitive therapy, but pure behaviour therapy continues to be practiced and is an effective evidence-based intervention for certain psychological difficulties, such as phobias and behaviours that challenge (Antony, 2014; Wilson, 2008). Recent evidence-based examples include Positive Behaviour Support, which is often applied with CYP on the autistic spectrum or with a diagnosed learning disability. In addition, many parenting interventions with a strong evidence base for young children have behavioural therapy as a main component, for example the Triple P Parenting Program (Sanders, 1999) and the Incredible Years parenting programmes (Webster-Stratton, 2005). See Chapter 12, Chapter 19 and Chapter 18 for further details of these interventions.

2.6.4 Cognitive Theory and Therapy

Cognitive therapy has its foundations in the theory developed by Beck in the 1960s. Beck developed cognitive models of the main affective disorders (e.g. depression, Beck et al., 1979; anxiety, Beck et al., 1985; and issues managing anger, Beck, 1999). Cognitive theory purports that the CYP has developed unhelpful or dysfunctional cognitions (thoughts) that are beliefs and assumptions developed through their life experiences. These cognitions are linked in a bidirectional way to unhelpful emotions and patterns of behaviour. The aim of the cognitive therapy is to work collaboratively with the young person to identify and modify these cognitions and assumptions and to develop more helpful ways of thinking. This, in turn, will have a positive impact on their emotions and behaviours. Intervention sessions are often weekly, spread over 6 to 20 weeks. Offering self-guided psychoeducation as a precursor to practitioner-led interventions is common.

During the 1980s and 1990s, cognitive and behavioural models and interventions were merged into CBT. A series of disorder-specific cognitive-behavioural theoretical models and detailed practice guidelines were developed, such as those for adult panic disorder (e.g. Barlow, 1988; Clark, 1988) and child anxiety (see Rapee et al., 2009 for a review). CBT's concepts, models of intervention and outcomes have been extensively and rigorously studied and there is significant evidence of its efficacy for many common psychological difficulties experienced by both adults and children (Beck & Dozois, 2014; Oud et al., 2019). In contrast to other approaches, the CBT model fits well with an RCT design; with brief manualised interventions for specific psychological difficulties and focused symptom outcome measurement. CBT has therefore become one of the most popular therapeutic interventions in child services in the UK and has been identified by NICE as the first-choice evidence-based intervention for many psychological disorders for both adults and children (e.g. anxiety, Obsessive Compulsive Disorder, post-traumatic stress disorder (PTSD)). In children's services there has been a focus on CBT delivered directly to young people and on parent facilitated CBT, both with positive outcomes (Cardy et al., 2020; Creswell et al. 2020). More recently, CBT research has developed to consider the active ingredients of interventions, looking at variables that might predict, moderate and mediate psychological outcomes thus enabling practitioners to understand how the therapy is working and thereby offer opportunities to personalise interventions based on the evidence (Bertie & Hudson, 2021). See Chapters and 14 for more detailed discussions of CBT interventions for CYP.

The combination of theories and techniques from behavioural and cognitive therapies sometimes alongside other theories (e.g. Mindfulness from Buddhist-based meditation) has led to what is known as third wave CBT (Hayes & Hoffman, 2017). The most prominent of these is dialectical behaviour therapy (DBT; Dimeff & Linehan, 2001). DBT was initially developed for adults with a diagnosis of emotionally unstable (borderline) personality disorder (EUPD). It is an adaptation of CBT but also uses a mixture of individual and group psychotherapy with the aim of modifying the difficult patterns of cognitions, emotions and behaviours associated with EUPD (e.g. emotion regulation difficulties and interpersonal difficulties). The approach has been adapted and applied to CYP and there have been studies showing its effectiveness (Feigenbaum, 2007; Quinn, 2009) particularly for CYP who self-harm or show suicidal behaviours (e.g. Perepletchikova et al., 2011). DBT is discussed in more detail in Chapter 22.

Mindfulness (meta-cognitive awareness of one's own inner processes such as thoughts, feelings, impulses) originated from Buddhist philosophy and meditation was secularised and simplified in the 1970s by Jon Kabat-Zinn who developed an 8-week mindfulness course for patients with chronic medical conditions (Kabat-Zinn, 1996). Since that time, Mindfulness has become a popular treatment for adults with various disorders and conditions. More recently, it has been adapted for applications with CYP with varying results (See Butterfield et al., 2020 for a critical review of the evidence base).

2.6.5 Systemic Theory and Therapy

Systemic theories are interpersonal, relational models that understand the CYP in context; focusing on the reciprocal influences that are at play between different contextual layers: biological, physical, psychological and sociocultural (Bronfenbrenner, 2000). Ideas from biological and mechanical systems, such as cybernetics (the study of communication and control) were applied to understand the functioning of families and other human systems (Bateson, 1972; Bowen, 1966). Three key aspects of family-systems theory help us understand young people in context (Pote, 2020):

1. The family is an interactive whole, comprised of subsystems that affect each other reciprocally. Hierarchical power structures and alliances may exist within families, which can maintain positive and difficult interactional patterns between young people and their caring networks.
2. Family roles and behaviours form predictable patterns that are reciprocal or circular. These repeat over time and may reappear intergenerationally. As young people develop, the interactional patterns, the roles and rules governing the family interactions have to adapt and family members have to shift roles. Often psychological distress within the family occurs at these points of transition and renegotiation.
3. The broader sociocultural context is critical and mutually influences the interactions in the family system and their rules for living. These rules are often challenged at times of transition, such as adolescence, and affect what the family views as acceptable behaviour.

Three strands of family-therapy models have developed from Family Systems theory and Cybernetics: the Milan method of systemic therapy (Selvini-Palazzoli et al., 1978), the structural (Minuchin, 1981) and strategic therapeutic approaches (Haley, 1976). Through intervening with different behaviours or beliefs these models have a common focus on the interpersonal relationships and the systems that surround the referred CYP, such as their family, school and community. They view psychological distress and dysfunction as occurring not within the individual but in the context of relational and communication difficulties within the system, and modifications of these across the system is the focus of therapy. The systemic approach is most commonly applied to CYP and their family but has also been applied to larger systems, such as schools or residential care homes, with the aim of broader system change.

Postmodern theoretical developments have also influenced systemic therapy; constructivism (Maturana & Varela, 1987), the concept that an individual constructs their own representations of reality and their understanding of the world, and social constructionism

(Gergen, 1985), the theory that reality is socially created through interactional, conversational and relational processes. These have led to a second wave of family therapies. One example of these is the postmodern model (Anderson & Goolishan, 1986) that is commonly practiced today, using techniques such as the reflecting team approach (Andersen, 1987, 1991).

Narrative therapy (developed by White & Epston, 1990) has been influenced by postmodern social constructionism along with Derrida's (1976) concept of deconstruction, Foucault's (1975) ideas about dominant and subjugated discourses and Bruner and Luciarello's research (1989) on the importance of narrative structure in meaning making for humans (see Boston, 2000 for further discussion of these models).

Systemic therapy is a widely applied psychotherapeutic approach with CYP and there is a growing body of research positively evaluating its efficacy in comparison to other therapeutic approaches (see Carr, 2018; Carr et al., 2020 for systematic reviews of research in this field). Similarly there is a growing evidence base for the effectiveness of narrative therapy with CYP in different contexts and for different presentations (see Dulwich Centre (n.d.) for a collection of research literature on the effectiveness of narrative therapy, including some evidence-based studies and randomised controlled trials). Narrative therapy has been combined with cognitive therapy for an effective intervention for children with obsessive compulsive disorder (see Banting & Lloyd, 2017; March and Mulle, 1998; McLuckie 2006).

2.6.6 Other Evidence-based Approaches

There are many well-evaluated intervention models for CYP that combine different therapeutic approaches. Some of these have been adapted from adult therapy models.

An example is interpersonal psychotherapy (IPT), which was developed by Klerman and Weisman in the 1970s for major depression but has been applied successfully to other mental health disorders (Cuijpers at al., 2016). It combines attachment, psychodynamic and CBT models and focuses on interpersonal relationships that may be contributing to the person's depression. It has been adapted for adolescents with depression (IPT-A) and is producing some good outcomes (see Duffy et al., 2019). There is also a family-based version (Family-based Interpersonal Therapy (FB-IPT). The reader should see Dietz (2020) for further information and a review of the evidence.

Multisystemic therapy (MST) is an example of an approach based on an amalgamation of different models including systemic, strategic, structural therapies and cognitive behaviour therapy (Henggeler et al., 1998). It is a multifaceted, intensive, short-term community and home-based intervention applied to the different systems that a CYP is part of. It is usually applied to CYP with challenging and complex social, emotional and behavioural (conduct) disorders but has also evolved and been applied to other challenging issues presented by CYP (see Henggeler & Schaeffer, 2016 for a review of its application and evidence base).

2.6.7 Conclusions and Practical Implications

In everyday practice most child psychological practitioners draw on and integrate different theoretical models in their practice, based on their assessment and formulation of the child or young person's difficulties in the context of their family and systems. They monitor and evaluate the CYP and their systems' responses to these interventions in terms of progress and adapt their approach in accordance with this feedback (the practice cycle).

The intervention the practitioner applies will be informed by the evidence base and guidance (such as those offered by NICE). Many other factors also come into play when planning treatment: their own and their supervisor's skill base; training and preference and allegiance to different theoretical models and interventions; the service offer (what is available within that service including and agreed care and treatment pathways, length of therapy, room availability, training of staff); and the preference and choice of the CYP and their family and their motivation to engage in different types of therapy (the 'fit').

The clinical example (Box 2.1) illustrates an evidence-based practice approach for a young person referred to a child psychological practitioner and demonstrates the implementation of the cycle of practice.

Box 2.1 Clinical example

Context: Lacey, a 13-year-old girl, was referred by her social worker to a psychology service embedded within Children's Social Care. Her mother was White British and her father was from an Irish Traveller background (though she had had no contact with him throughout her life). Lacey was removed from her mother's care aged 11 and had been placed in a permanent foster placement since the age of 12 under a care order, having been living with temporary foster carers for a year. When she lived with her family of origin, Lacey experienced sexual abuse from her mother's partner over several years. She presented with symptoms of PTSD including heightened anxiety, nightmares, sleep disturbance, flashbacks and difficulties regulating her emotions (particularly anger). She had self-harmed in the past as a coping strategy, but this was much improved since she had been living with her foster family. At the time of the referral, she had fallen out with her boyfriend, and the foster family's elderly pet cat had died. These events were seen to have destabilised Lacey and she had started to feel an increase in the urge to self-harm. Lacey and her foster carers sought support to address her difficulties as they were impacting on all aspects of her life, including her ability to attend school regularly, to develop and sustain peer relationships, and to go out in the community.

Assessment

In accordance with NICE and BPS guidance on carrying out assessments with CYP the assessment used multiple methods and informants, including interviews with the foster parents, birth mother, the young person (YP), schoolteacher and social worker as well as reviewing the local authority care records and the medical records. There was a joint assessment appointment with the YP and her foster parents.

Standardised measures were those recommended by CORC (Clinical Outcome Research Consortium, the UK's leading membership organisation that collects and uses evidence to improve CYP's mental health) and the NICE guidelines for children looked after (NICE, 2021).

They included administration of standardised questionnaires using multiple informants: Strength and Difficulties Questionnaire (SDQ, Goodman, 1997); Revised Children's Anxiety and Depression Scale (RCADS, Chorpita et al., 2000); Impact of Life Events Scale-Revised (ILE-R, Weiss & Marmar, 1996); goal-based outcomes (Law & Jacob, 2015); and Parenting Stress Index (PSI, Berry & Jones, 1995).

During the assessment, the practitioner drew out a genogram with the family.

The assessment was carried out over five sessions as it was recognised that it would take time for Lacey to develop trust in the professionals, connected to her past abusive experiences. Consent was always obtained from Lacey for her participation and any information sharing with others. The local authority had parental responsibility (PR) for Lacey, so their consent was also obtained throughout (see Chapter 26 and Chapter 5 for more details on PR).

Formulation

The 5P structure was used for the formulation. A summary of the main factors are:

Presenting issues: anxiety symptoms, depressive symptoms, nightmares, sleep disturbance, flashbacks, difficulties regulating her emotions, urges to self-harm and school avoidance.

Predisposing factors: childhood trauma and abuse, absent father, reconstituted family, loss of main caregiver.

Precipitating factors: difficulties with peers at school and out in the community, falling out with her boyfriend, the death of family pet.

Perpetuating factors: avoidance of going out in the community, interacting with peers and school avoidance, avoidance of painful memories, not asking for support, withdrawing from others.

Protective factors: positive relationship with foster carers and social worker, previous reduction in self-harming, motivation to engage in mental health support.

The assessment concluded that Lacey was presenting with complex trauma due to repeated experiences of trauma throughout her childhood. The 5P formulation integrated psychological theories, primarily attachment theory and cognitive behavioural theory, in order to understand how Lacey's anxious and withdrawn behaviours were connected to her disrupted attachments and experiences of abuse. The formulation mapped how the avoidant anxious behaviours were being reinforced in the current context. This formulation was shared with Lacey, her carers and social worker.

Intervention: The NICE guidelines (2018a) for the treatment of complex PTSD are the same as for a single trauma PTSD but acknowledge that extra time needs to be built in to the length of the intervention to enable the development of trust with the person, to manage any issues that may be a barrier to engaging in the approach (such as self-harming), to take into account the safety and the stability of the person when carrying out the intervention and to work with the person to plan any ongoing support or residual symptoms.

(Continued)

Box 2.1 (Continued)

For CYP of Lacey's age, the recommended treatment is an individual trauma-focused CBT intervention (NICE, 2018a). This information was shared with Lacey and her carers and consent was sought for her to engage in this approach. Lacey was nervous of engaging with the CBT approach as she avoided all memories and triggers associated with her past abuse and it had been explained that the approach would require exposure to these memories. However, she agreed to engage in the initial stages of the intervention (psychoeducation, stabilisation and developing coping strategies and strategies to regulate her emotions).

Lacey attended sessions (sometimes accompanied by her foster carer) and engaged well with the initial stages of the intervention (stabilisation). However, Lacey also encountered many destabilising life events (her birth mother became pregnant again, her older sibling entered a secure unit and she fell out with her best friend) that resulted in her symptoms worsening and she started self-harming again. These events also led to issues with engagement and at times, Lacey would not attend sessions. The psychological practitioner employed various ways of promoting engagement and the continuation of a positive therapeutic relationship (such as visiting Lacey at home, going for walks with her, listening to music with her if she did not want to talk and maintaining a relationship by making phone contact and sending therapeutic letters). Twenty sessions were focused on dealing with engagement, promoting the relationship, discussing the events, assisting Lacey to problem solve, the development of coping strategies and ways to regulate her emotions.

The service was only commissioned to deliver brief psychological interventions (up to 20 sessions). If further interventions were needed, then a referral had to be made to the local child and adolescent mental health service (CAMHS). A referral would therefore need to be made to CAMHS for the next phase of the CBT for trauma intervention (exposure to painful memories).

Evaluation: The same standardised measures (outlined earlier) were repeated following the 20 sessions. It showed that the intervention had led to some positive improvements in Lacey's anxiety and depressive symptoms and her urges to self-harm had been reduced. Her relationships with other had improved as had her attendance at school. There had been some movement towards Lacey's and her carer's goals and her carers reported less stress. However, many of the PTSD symptoms remained (such as sleep disturbance, nightmares and anxiety when out in the community) and a referral to CAMHS was discussed for CBT exposure therapy.

Communication: The psychological practitioner compiled a report describing the intervention and the outcomes and recommendations for further support from CAMHS and shared it with the YP, referrer and foster carers. Consent was obtained from the YP and Children's Social Care (corporate parents) to share the information in the report.

Referral to CAMHS

Lacey was keen to continue therapy aimed at reducing her symptoms of PTSD. However, she was not sure the CBT approach was the best approach for her given her fear and avoidance and she was also afraid of transitioning to another service to carry out this intervention. Her foster carers were concerned that any exposure therapy or change in therapist would increase her self-harming. Alternative approaches for PTSD that also have an evidence base for efficacy were discussed (such as Eye Movement Desensitisation Reprocessing (EMDR), Shapiro, 2018) and Narrative Exposure Therapy (NET, Schauer et al., 2011). However, the local CAMHS did not have any practitioners trained in EMDR so that was not available. Several practitioners in CAMHS had recently attended a NET training course and were receiving NET supervision to become accredited.[2]

Lacey was nervous of the NET approach but liked the idea of developing a visual lifeline of her life and experiences as she had never had the chance to talk through her life experiences. She therefore agreed to sessions with the CAMHS professional to develop her lifeline. To aid transition, her original therapist had some joint sessions with Lacey, the foster carer and the CAMHS therapist. The NET protocol was adapted so that Lacey's professional network (e.g. the school and social workers) were also informed about the approach. Lacey responded well to the approach and the sessions developing her lifeline. She chose to share her lifeline with her social worker, foster carers and designated schoolteacher. Lacey chose to continue with the therapy.

The case was written up in a report and the positive outcome of the NET approach was communicated to the service allowing funds to be made available for others to be trained in this approach as an alternative to trauma focused CBT, giving CYP, families and carers presenting with these difficulties more choice of treatment.

2.7 Conclusion and Key Points

This chapter has outlined the scientist-practitioner model, evidence-based practice and critically discussed some of the limitations of the evidence base for psychotherapeutic interventions for CYP. It has introduced the cycle of practice of assessment, intervention, outcomes, evaluation and communication in clinical practice. The main theoretical approaches to child and adolescent therapy were discussed and along with further reading recommendations on the approaches and their evidence base.

A clinical example was presented to illustrate applying the cycle of practice in a clinical context within a psychological service embedded in children's social care.

The clinical example presented shows how many factors influence the decisions that are made in clinical practice throughout the process of assessment, formulation and treatment, in addition to consulting the evidence base and the outcome of a psychological intervention. These include local mental health service limitations and recourse issues, CYP's personal preferences and goals, the psychological practitioner and their supervisor's model preferences and skill base and life events that impact on the therapeutic relationship and the CYP and their family's ability to engage in a psychological intervention. It also highlights the need for psychological practitioners to be reflective and flexible in terms of their practice to meet the CYP and their family's needs.

2 NET is a strengths-based exposure approach that combines CBT and narrative approaches and has been shown to be efficacious particularly in treating refuges that have multiple and complex trauma. It has been adapted for application to children.

References

Ainsworth M. D. S., Blehar M. C., Waters E., Wall S. N. (1978/2015). *Patterns of attachment: A psychological study of the strange situation*. Taylor & Francis.

American Psychiatric Association. (2013a). *Diagnostic and statistical manual of mental disorders: DSM-5* (5th ed.) American Psychiatric Publishing.

Andersen, T. (1987). The reflecting team: dialogue and meta-dialogue in clinical work. *Family Process, 26*, 415–428.

Andersen, T. (1991). *The reflecting team: dialogues and dialogues about dialogues*. Norton.

Anderson, H., & Goolishan, H. (1986). Problem Determined Systems – towards transformation in family therapy. *Journal of Strategic & Systemic Therapies, 5*, 1–13.

Antony, M. M. (2014). Behaviour therapy. In R. Corsini and D. Wedding (Eds.), *Current psychotherapies* (10th ed, pp. 193–229). Thompson.

Axline, V. M. (1947). *Play therapy; the inner dynamics of childhood*. Houghton Mifflin.

Baker, H. J., Lawrence, P. J., Karalus, J., Creswell, C., & Waite, P. (2021). The effectiveness of psychological therapies for anxiety disorders in adolescents: A meta-analysis. *Clinical Child and Family Psychology Review, 24*(4), 765–782. https://doi.org/10.1007/s10567-021-00364-2.

Bandura, A. (1986). Social foundations of thought and action: A social cognitive theory. *American Psychologist, 44*, 1175–1184.

Banting, R., & Lloyd, S. (2017). A case study integrating CBT with narrative therapy externalizing techniques with a child with OCD: How to flush away the Silly Gremlin. A single-case experimental design. *Journal of Child and adolescent Psychiatric Nursing, 30*(2). 80–89. https://doi.org/10.1111/jcap.12173.

Barlow, D. H. (1988). *Anxiety and its disorders: The nature and treatment of anxiety and panic*. Guilford Press.

Barlow, J., Schradermcmillan, A., Axford, N., Wrigley, Z., Sonthalia, S., Wilkinson, T., Rawsthorn, M., Toft, A., & Coad, J. (2016). Review: Attachment and attachment-related outcomes in preschool children – a review of recent evidence. *Child and Adolescent Mental Health, 21*(1), 11–20.

Bateson, G. (1972). *Steps to an ecology of mind: Collected essays in anthropology, psychiatry, evolution, and epistemology*. Jason Aronson.

Bauer, M. S., & Kirchner, J. (2020). Implementation science: What is it and why should I care?. *Psychiatry research, 283*, 112376. https://doi.org/10.1016/j.psychres.2019.04.025.

Bebbington, P.E. (2015). A commentary on Kendler. *Psychological Medicine, 45*(6), 1119–1120.

Beck, A., (1979). *Cognitive therapy of depression*. Guilford Press.

Beck, A. T. (1999). *Prisoners of hate: The cognitive basis of anger, hostility, and violence*. HarperCollins.

Beck, A. T., & Dozois, D. J. A. (2014). Cognitive theory and therapy: Past, present, and future. In S. Bloch, S. A. Green, & J. Holmes (Eds.), *Psychiatry: Past, present, and prospect* (pp. 366–382). Oxford University Press. https://doi.org/10.1093/med/9780199638963.003.0020.

Beck, A. T., Emery, G., & Greenberg, R. L. (1985). *Anxiety disorders and phobias: A cognitive perspective*. Basic Books/Hachette Book Group.

Beck, A. T., Rush, A., Shaw, B., & Emery, G. (1979). *Cognitive Therapy of Depression*. New York: The Guilford Press.

Berry, J. O., & Jones, W. H. (1995). The Parental Stress Scale: Initial psychometric evidence. *Journal of Social and Personal Relationships, 12*(3), 463–472. https://doi.org/10.1177/0265407595123009.

Bertie, L. A., & Hudson, J. L. (2021). CBT for childhood anxiety: Reviewing the state of personalised intervention research. *Frontiers in Psychology, 12*, 722546. https://doi.org/10.3389/fpsyg.2021.722546.

Booth, P. B., & Jernberg, A. M. (2010). *Theraplay: Helping parents and children build better relationships through attachment-based play*. Jossey-Bass.

Boston, P. (2000). Systemic family therapy and the influence of post-modernism. *Advances in Psychiatric Treatment, 6*, 450–457. https://doi.org/10.1192/apt.6.6.450.

Bowen, M. (1966). The use of family theory in clinical practice. *Comprehensive Psychiatry, 7*(5), 345–374. https://doi.org/10.1016/S0010-440X(66)80065-2.

Bowlby J (1969/1999). Attachment. Attachment and loss (vol. 1, 2nd ed.). Basic Books.

Bretherton, I. (1992). The origins of attachment theory: John Bowlby and Mary Ainsworth. *Developmental Psychology, 28*(5), 759–775. https://doi.org/10.1037/0012-1649.28.5.759.

Breuer, J., & Freud, S. (1956). On the psychical mechanism of hysterical phenomena (1893). *The International Journal of Psychoanalysis, 37*, 8–13.

Breuer, J., & Freud, S. (1957). *Studies on hysteria*. Basic Books.

Briggs, S., Maxwell, M., & Keenan, A. (2015). Working with the complexities of adolescent mental health problems: applying time-limited adolescent psychodynamic psychotherapy (TAPP). *Psychoanalytic Psychotherapy, 29*(3), 314–329. https://doi.org/10.1080/02668734.2015.1086414.

British Psychological Society. (2017). *BPS Practice Guidelines*.

Bronfenbrenner, U. (2000). Ecological systems theory. In A. E. Kazdin (Ed.), *Encyclopedia of Psychology* (Vol. 3, pp. 129–133). Oxford University Press.

Bruner, J., & Lucariello, J. (1989). Monologue as narrative recreation of the world. In K. Nelson (ed.), *Narratives from the Crib* (pp. 73–97). Harvard University Press

Bruner, J. S., & Luciarello, J. (1989). Monologue as narrative recreation of the world. In K. Nelson (ed.), *Narratives from the Crib* (pp.73–97). Harvard University Press.

Butterfield, K. M., Roberts, K. P., Feltis, L. E., & Kocovski, N. L. (2020). What is the evidence in evidence-based mindfulness programs for children? *Advances in Child Development and Behavior, 58*, 189–213. https://doi.org/10.1016/bs.acdb.2020.01.007.

Cardy, J. L., Waite, P., Cocks, F., & Creswell, C. (2020). A systematic review of parental involvement in cognitive behavioural therapy for adolescent anxiety disorders. *Clinical Child and Family Psychology Review, 23*(4), 483–509. https://doi.org/10.1007/s10567-020-00324-2.

Carr, A. (2015). *The Handbook of Child and Adolescent Clinical Psychology* (3rd ed.). Routledge.

Carr, A. (2018). Couple therapy, family therapy and systemic interventions for child-focused problems: the current evidence base. *Journal of Family Therapy, 41*(2), 153–213.

Carr. A., Pinquart, M., & Haun, M.W. (2020). Research-informed practice of systemic therapy. In M. Ochs, M., M. Borcssa, & J. Schweitzer (eds.), *Systemic Research in Individual, Couple and Family Therapy and Counseling* (pp. 319–347). Springer.

Cattanach, A. (2003). *Introduction to Play Therapy*. Routledge.

Chorpita, B. F., Yim, L., Moffitt, C., Umemoto, L. A., & Francis, S. E. (2000). Assessment of symptoms of DSM-IV anxiety and depression in children: a revised child anxiety and depression scale. *Behaviour Research and Therapy, 38*(8), 835–855. https://doi.org/10.1016/s0005-7967(99)00130-8.

Clark, D. M. (1988). A cognitive model of panic attacks. In S. Rachman & J. D. Maser (Eds.), *Panic: Psychological perspectives* (pp. 71–89). Lawrence Erlbaum Associates, Inc.

Cosgrove, L., & Krimsky, S. (2012). A comparison of DSM-IV and DSM-5 panel members' financial associations. *PloS Medicine*, *9*(3), e1001190. https://doi.org/10.1371/journal.pmed.1001190.

Critical Psychiatry Network. (2013, May 23). Statement by the Critical Psychiatry Network on the new DSM-5. https://www.criticalpsychiatry.co.uk/news/statement-by-the-critical-psychiatry-network-on-the-new-dsm-5/.

Creswell, C., Waite, P., & Hudson, J. (2020). Practitioner review: Anxiety disorders in children and young people – assessment and treatment. *Journal of Child Psychology and Psychiatry, and Allied Disciplines, 61*(6), 628–643. https://doi.org/10.1111/jcpp.13186.

Crittenden, P. M. (2008). *Raising parents: Attachment, parenting and child safety*. Willan Publishing.

Cuijpers, P., Donker, T., Weissman, M. M., Ravitz, P., & Cristea, I. A. (2016). Interpersonal psychotherapy for mental health problems: A comprehensive meta-analysis. *American Journal of Psychiatry, 173*(7), 680–687. https://doi.org/10.1176/appi.ajp.2015.15091141.

Deaton, A., & Cartwright, N. (2018). Understanding and misunderstanding randomized controlled trials. *Social Science and Medicine, 210*, 2–21. https://doi.org/10.1016/j.socscimed.2017.12.005.

Derrida, J. (1976). *Of Grammatology*. Johns Hopkins University Press.

Dietz, L. J. (2020). Family-based interpersonal psychotherapy: An Intervention for preadolescent depression. *The American Journal of Psychotherapy, 73*(1), 22–28. https://doi.org/10.1176/appi.psychotherapy.20190028.

Dimeff, L., & Linehan, M.M. (2001). Dialectical behavior therapy in a nutshell. *The California Psychologist, 34*, 10–13.

Duffy, F., Sharpe, H., & Schwannauer, M. (2019). Review: The effectiveness of interpersonal psychotherapy for adolescents with depression – a systematic review and meta-analysis. *Child and Adolescent Mental Health, 24*(4), 307–317. https://doi.org/10.1111/camh.123.

Dulwich Centre. (n.d.). Evidence for the effectiveness of Narrative Therapy https://dulwichcentre.com.au/collection-evidence-for-the-effectiveness-of-narrative-therapy/.

Feigenbaum, J. (2007). Dialectical behaviour therapy: An increasing evidence base, *Journal of Mental Health, 16*(1), 51–68. https://doi.org/10.1080/09638230601182094.

Felitti, V. J., Anda, R. F., Nordenberg, D., Williamson, D. F., Spitz, A. M., Edwards, V., Koss, M. P., & Marks, J. S. (1998). Relationship of childhood abuse and household dysfunction to many of the leading causes of death in adults: The Adverse Childhood Experiences (ACE) study. *American Journal of Preventive Medicine, 14*(4), 245–258. https://doi.org/10.1016/S0749-3797(98)00017-8.

Fonagy, P., Cottrell, D., Phillips, J., Bevington, D., Glaser, D., & Allison, E. (2015). *What works for whom? A critical review of treatments for children and adolescents* (2nd ed.). Guilford Press.

Foucault, M. (1975). *The Archaeology of Knowledge*. Tavistock Press

Francis, R. (2013, February 6). *Report of the Mid Staffordshire NHS Foundation Trust Public Inquiry*. https://www.gov.uk/government/publications/report-of-the-mid-staffordshire-nhs-foundation-trust-public-inquiry.

Freud, A. (1928). *Introduction to the technique of child analysis*. International Psycho-Analytical Press.

Freud, A. (1936). *The ego and the mechanisms of defence*. Karnac.

Gatta, M., Miscioscia, M., Svanellini, L., Spoto, A., Difronzo, M., de Sauma, M., & Ferruzza, E. (2019). Effectiveness of brief psychodynamic therapy with children and adolescents: An outcome study. *Frontiers in Pediatrics, 7*, 501. https://doi.org/10.3389/fped.2019.00501.

Gergen, K. J. (1985). The social constructionist movement in modern psychology. *American Psychologist, 40*(3), 266–275. https://doi.org/10.1037/0003-066X.40.3.266.

Gergen, K.J. (1999). *An invitation to social construction. Sage.*

Goodman, R. (1997). The strengths and difficulties questionnaire: A research note. *Child Psychology & Psychiatry & Allied Disciplines, 38*(5), 581–586. https://doi.org/10.1111/j.1469-7610.1997.tb01545.x.

Gregory, M., Kannis-Dymand, L., & Sharman, R. (2020). A review of attachment-based parenting interventions: Recent advances and future considerations. *Australian Journal of Psychology, 72*, 109–122. https://doi.org/10.1111/ajpy.12270.

Haley, J. (1976). *Problem solving therapy*. Jossey-Bass

Hayes, S. C., & Hofmann, S. G. (2017). The third wave of cognitive behavioral therapy and the rise of process-based care. *World Psychiatry: Official Journal of the World Psychiatric Association (WPA), 16*(3), 245–246. https://doi.org/10.1002/wps.20442.

Hayes, S. C., & Hofmann, S. G. (2018). A psychological model of the use of psychological intervention science: Seven rules for making a difference. *Clinical Psychology: Science and Practice, 25*(3), e12259. https://doi.org/10.1111/cpsp.12259.

Hazan, C., & Shaver, P. (1987). Romantic love conceptualized as an attachment process. *Journal of Personality and Social Psychology, 52*(3), 511–524. https://doi.org/10.1037/0022-3514.52.3.511.

Henggeler, S., Borduin, C.M., Schoenwald, S.K., Pickrel, S.G., Rowland, M.D., & Cunningham, P.B. (1998). *Multi-systemic treatment of antisocial behavior in children and adolescents*. Guilford Press.

Henggeler, S.W. and Schaeffer, C.M. (2016), Multisystemic Therapy®: Clinical overview, outcomes, and implementation research. *Family Process, 55*, 514528. https://doi.org/10.1111/famp.12232.

Hughes D. (1997). *Facilitating developmental attachment*. Jason Aronson.

Hughes D. (2006). *Building the bonds of attachment* (2nd ed.). Jason Aronson.

Jennings, S., Cattanach, A., Mitchell, S., Chesner, A., Meldrum, B., & Nfa, S. M. (2005). *The handbook of dramatherapy*. Routledge.

Johnstone, L., & Boyle, M. with Cromby, J., Dillon, J., Harper, D., Kinderman, P., Longden, E., Pilgrim, D., & Read, J. (2018). *The Power Threat Meaning Framework: Towards the identification of patterns in emotional distress, unusual experiences and troubled or troubling behaviour, as an alternative to functional psychiatric diagnosis*. British Psychological Society.

Jones, J. L., & Mehr, S. L. (2007). Foundations and assumptions of the scientist-practitioner model. *American Behavioral Scientist, 50*(6), 766–771. https://doi.org/10.1177/0002764206296454.

Jung, C.G. (1923). *Psychological types*. Harcourt Brace.

Kabat-Zinn, J. (1996). *Full catastrophe living: Using the wisdom of your body and mind to face stress, pain and illness*. Piatkus.

Kabat-Zinn, J. (2003). Mindfulness-based interventions in context: Past, present, and future. *Clinical Psychology: Science and Practice, 10*(2), 144–156. https://doi.org/10.1093/clipsy.bpg016.

Kaushik, A., Kostaki, E., Kyriakopoulos, M. (2016). The stigma of mental illness in children and adolescents: A systematic review. *Psychiatry Research, 243*, 469–494, https://doi.org/10.1016/j.psychres.2016.04.042.

Kennedy, H., & Underdown, A. (2018). Video interaction guidance: Promoting secure attachment and optimal development for children, parents and professionals. In P. Leach

(Ed.), *Transforming infant wellbeing: Research, policy and practice for the first 1001 critical days* (pp. 224–237). Routledge/Taylor & Francis Group. https://doi.org/10.4324/9781315452890-23.

Klein, M. (1955). The psychoanalytic play technique. *American Journal of Orthopsychiatry, 25*(2), 223-237.

Koplan, C., & Chard, A. (2015). Adverse early life experiences. In M. T. Compton & R. S. Shim (Eds.), *The social determinants of mental health* (pp. 47–75). American Psychiatric Publishing, Inc.

Lancet Global Mental Health Group. (2007). Scale up services for mental disorders: A call for action. *The Lancet, 370*(9594), 1241–1252

Landreth, G. L. (2002). *Play therapy: The art of the relationship* (2nd ed.). Brunner-Routledge.

Law, D., & Jacob, J. (2015). *Goals and Goals Based Outcomes (GBOs): Some useful information* (3rd ed.). CAMHS Press.

Lemma, A., Target, M., & Fonagy, P. (2011). *Brief dynamic interpersonal therapy: A clinician's guide*. Oxford University Press.

Lowenfeld, M. (1935). *Play in childhood*. Mac Keith Press.

March, J. S., & Mulle, K. (1998). *OCD in children and adolescents: A cognitive-behavioral treatment manual*. Guilford Press.

Maturana, H. R., & Varela, F. J. (1987). *The tree of knowledge: The biological roots of human understanding*. New Science Library/Shambhala Publications.

McLuckie, A. (2006). Narrative family therapy for paediatric obsessive compulsive disorder. *Journal of Family Psychotherapy, 16*(4), 83–106.

Midgley, N., Cregeen, S., Hughes, C., & Rustin, M. (2013). Psychodynamic psychotherapy as treatment for depression in adolescence. *Child and Adolescent Psychiatric Clinics of North America, 22*(1), 67-82. https://doi.org/10.1016/j.chc.2012.08.004.

Midgley, N., & Kennedy, E. (2011). Psychodynamic psychotherapy for children and adolescents: a critical review of the evidence base. *Journal of Child Psychotherapy, 37*, 232–260. https://doi.org/10.1080/0075417X.2011.614738.

Midgley, N., O'Keeffe, S., French, L., & Kennedy, E. (2017). Psychodynamic psychotherapy for children and adolescents: an updated narrative review of the evidence base. *Journal of Child Psychotherapy, 40*(1), 1–23. https://doi.org/10.1080/0075417X.2017.1323945.

Minuchin, S. (1981). *Family therapy techniques*. Harvard University Press.

Moher, D., Hopewell, S., Schulz, K. F., Montori, V., Gotzsche, P. C., Deveraux, P. J., … Altman, D. G. (2010). Research methods & reporting CONSORT 2010 Explanation and Elaboration: updated guidelines for reporting parallel group randomised trials. *British Medical Journal, 340*, c869.

Moustakas, C. E. (1953). *Children in play therapy: a key to understanding normal and disturbed emotions*. McGraw-Hill.

Moustakas, C. E. (1997). *Relationship play therapy*. Jason Aronson.

NICE. (n.d.). Into practice guide. https://www.nice.org.uk/about/what-we-do/into-practice/resources-help-put-guidance-into-practice.

NICE. (2018a). Post traumatic stress disorder (NG116).

NICE. (2018b). Principles for putting evidence-based guidance into practice. National Institute for Health and Care Excellence.

NICE. (2018c). Practical steps to improving the quality of care and services using nice guidance. National Institute for Health and Care Excellence.

NICE. (2021). Looked after children and young people (NG205).

National Health Service England. (2023). Increasing diversity in research participation: A good practice guide for engaging with underrepresented groups. https://www.england.nhs.uk/aac/wp-content/uploads/sites/50/2023/02/B1905-increasing-diversity-in-research-participation.pdf.

Oud, M., De Winter, L., Vermeulen-Smit, E., Bodden, D., Nauta, M., Stone, L., ... Stikkelbroek, Y. (2019). Effectiveness of CBT for children and adolescents with depression: A systematic review and meta-regression analysis. *European Psychiatry, 57*, 33–45. doi:10.1016/j.eurpsy.2018.12.008

Padesky, C. A. (2020). *Collaborative case conceptualization: Client knows best*. Guilford Press.

Palazzoli, M.S., Boscolo, L., Cecchin, G., & Prata, G. (1980). Hypothesizing-circularity-neutrality: three guidelines for the conductor of the session. *Family Process, 19*, 3–12.

Pavlov, I. P. (1927). *Conditioned reflexes: an investigation of the physiological activity of the cerebral cortex*. Oxford University Press.

Perepletchikova, F., Axelrod, S. R., Kaufman, J., Rounsaville, B. J., Douglas-Palumberi, H., & Miller, A. L. (2011). Adapting Dialectical Behaviour Therapy for children: Towards a new research agenda for paediatric suicidal and non-suicidal self-injurious behaviours. *Child and Adolescent Mental Health, 16*(2), 116–121. https://doi.org/10.1111/j.1475-3588.2010.00583.x.

Pote, H. (2020). Family context. In *Encyclopedia of Child and Adolescent Development*. S. Hupp and J. Jewell (Eds). John Wiley & Sons, Inc.

Powell, B., Cooper, G., Hoffman, K., & Marvin, R. S. (2014). *The circle of security intervention: Enhancing attachment in early parent–child relationships*. Guilford Press.

Quinn, C. R. (2009). Efficacy of dialectical behaviour therapy for adolescents. *Australian Journal of Psychology, 61*, 156–166. https://doi.org/10.1080/00049530802315084.

Rapee, R. M., Schniering, C. A., & Hudson, J. L. (2009). Anxiety disorders during childhood and adolescence: origins and treatment. *Annual Review of Clinical Psychology, 5*, 311–341. https://doi.org/10.1146/annurev.clinpsy.032408.153628.

Rawson P. (2002). *Short-term psychodynamic psychotherapy: An analysis of the key principles*. Karnac Books.

Ray, D., Bratton, S., Rhine, T., & Jones, L. (2001). The effectiveness of play therapy: Responding to the critics. *International Journal of Play Therapy, 10*(1), 85–108.

Redfern, Sheila. (2015). *Reflective parenting: A guide to understanding what's going on in your child's mind*. Taylor Francis. https://doi.org/10.4324/9781315764108.

Rogers C. R. (1951). *Client-centred therapy*. Mifflin.

Rose, J., & O' Reilly, B. (2017). A systematic review of attachment-based psychotherapeutic interventions for adopted children. *Early Child Development and Care, 187*(12), 1844–1862.

Rossouw, T.I., & Fonagy, P. (2012). Mentalizatised treatment for self-harm in adolescents: a randomized controlled trial. *Journal of the American Academy of Child & Adolescent Psychiatry, 51*(12), 1304–1313. https://doi.org/10.1016/j.jaac.2012.09.018.

Roth, A., Calder, F., & Pilling, S. (2011). A Competence Framework for Child and Adolescent Mental Health Services. https://www.ucl.ac.uk/clinical-psychology//CORE/child-adolescent-competences/CAMHS%20Competences%20Framework_V1%20(2).pdf.

Roth, A., & Fonagy, P. (2005). *What works for whom: A critical review of psychotherapy research* (2nd ed.). Guilford Publications.

Sanders, M. R. (1999). Triple P-Positive Parenting Program: towards an empirically validated multilevel parenting and family support strategy for the prevention of behavior and emotional problems in children. *Clinical Child and Family Psychology Review, 2*(2), 71–90. https://doi.org/10.1023/a:1021843613840.

Schaefer, C. E. (Ed.). (1993). *The therapeutic powers of play*. Jason Aronson.

Schauer, M., Neuner, F., & Elbert, T. (2011). *Narrative exposure therapy: A short-term treatment for traumatic stress disorders* (2nd rev. and expanded ed.). Hogrefe Publishing.

Selvini-Palazzoli, M. (1978*) Self-starvation: From individual to family therapy in the treatment of anorexia nervosa*. Jason Aronson, New York.

Shah, P., & Mountain, D. (2007). The medical model is dead – long live the medical model. *The British Journal of Psychiatry, 191*(5), 375–377.

Shapiro, F. (2018). *Eye Movement Desensitization and Reprocessing (EMDR) therapy: Basic principles, protocols, and procedures* (3rd ed.). Guilford Press.

Skinner, B. F. (1953). *Science and human behavior*. Macmillan.

Slavny, R., Sebastian, C., & Pote, H. (2019). Age-related changes in cognitive biases during adolescence, *Journal of Adolescence, 74*, 63–70. https://doi.org/10.1016/j.adolescence.2019.04.007.

Stoltenberg, C., & Pace, T. (2007). The scientist-practitioner model: now more than ever. *Journal of Contemporary Psychotherapy, 37*, 195–203. https://doi.org/10.1007/s10879-007-9054-0.

Target, M., & Fonagy. P. (2005). The psychological treatment of child and adolescent psychiatric disorders. In A. Roth & P. Fonagy. *What works for whom: A critical review of psychotherapy research* (2nd ed.). Guilford Publications.

Thomas, P., & Longden, E. (2013). Madness, childhood adversity and narrative psychiatry. *Caring. Medical Humanities, 39*(2), 109–114. https://doi.org/10.1136/medhum-2013-010397.

Tiley, C., & Kyriakopoulos, M. (2018). Evidence-based practice in a multicultural world: changing with the times. *British Journal of Psychiatry International, 15*(3), 55–57. https://doi.org/10.1192/bji.2018.14.

Watson, J. B. (1930). *Behaviorism* (Rev, ed.). University of Chicago Press.

Webster-Stratton, C. (2005). The Incredible Years: a training series for the prevention and treatment of conduct problems in young children. In E. D. Hibbs & P. S. Jensen (Eds.), *Psychosocial treatments for child and adolescent disorders: Empirically based strategies for clinical practice* (pp. 507–555). American Psychological Association.

Weiss, D. S., & Marmar, C. R. (1996). The Impact of Event Scale – Revised. In J. Wilson & T. M. Keane (Eds.), *Assessing psychological trauma and PTSD* (pp. 399–411). Guilford.

White, M., & Epston, D. (1990). *Narrative means to therapeutic ends*. W.W. Norton.

Wilson. G. T. (2008). Behaviour therapy. In R. Corsini and D. Wedding (Eds), *Current Psychotherapies* (8th ed). Thompson.

Wolpe, J. (1958). *Psychotherapy by reciprocal inhibition*. Stanford University Press.

Wolpe, J. (1990). *The practice of behaviour therapy* (4th ed.). Pergamon Press.

Woodhouse, S. S. (2018). Attachment-based interventions for families with young children. *Journal of Clinical Psychology, 74*, 1296–1299.

World Health Organization. (2022). ICD-11: International classification of diseases (11th revision). https://icd.who.int/.

3

A Developmental Approach to Assessment and Formulation

Anna Picciotto, Helen Pote and Clare Norris

3.1 Understanding Children and Young People in Context

Children and young people (CYP) do not exist as individuals in isolation but are born into contexts and systems, functioning within their immediate and extended family and carers, their culture of origin, educational settings and the culture and communities in which they live. In order to understand the child and to know how best to effect change, attention needs to be given to these contexts and the history and developmental stage of the family and care network as well as to those of the individual. Developmentally informed psychological assessments that pay attention to context will gather information from a wide range of informants (young person (YP), family, school, referrer and other professionals) and draw on multiple methods for data collection (interviews, observations and standardised assessments). This comprehensive approach enables the psychological practitioner to develop individualised formulations jointly with the CYP and family to guide their intervention plans.

This chapter will take a broad approach to the assessment of psychological difficulties in CYP, considering the context and content of the referral, the multiple factors that will impact on a child's presentation and difficulties, what sources to use to obtain a fuller assessment, what to ask and how to ask it. It will then describe how to develop a psychological formulation of the difficulties in a collaborative way using different theoretical models, how to share the formulation with CYP and their parents/carers and networks and how to revisit the formulation as treatment progresses.

3.2 A Systemic Approach to Assessment and Formulation

Urie Bronfenbrenner (1974) most clearly outlined this approach with his Ecological Systems Theory, describing five inter-related systems that impact on the child and influence its development, and by doing so rejected earlier, unidirectional, staged models of development. Psychological models that were intrapersonal in nature were reconsidered, for example theories of psychosexual development (Freud, e.g. 1905); psychosocial

Child Psychology: Pathways to Good Practice, First Edition.
Edited by Helen Pote, Anna Picciotto and Clare Norris.

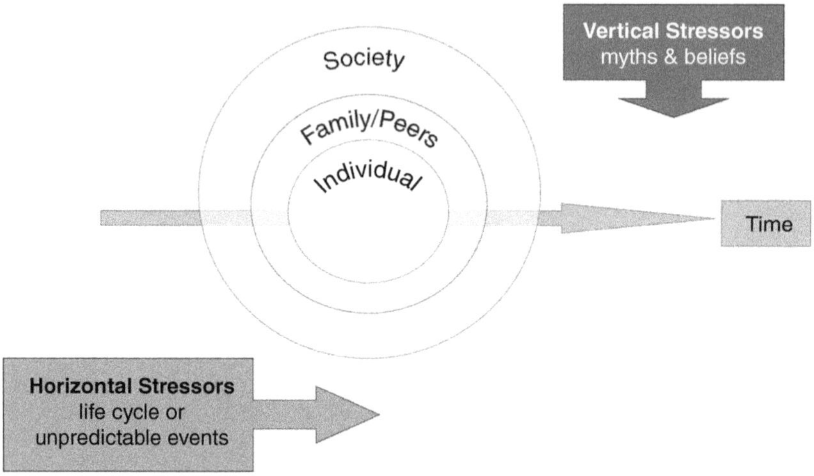

Figure 3.1 Understanding the child in context: Adapted from Bronfenbrenner, Ecological Systems Theory (1974) and Carter & McGoldrick, Family Life Cycle Model (2006).

development (Erikson, 1959); behavioural approaches (Watson, e.g. 1913; Skinner, e.g. 1938); cognitive development (Piaget, e.g. 1952, 1954; Vygotsky, e.g. 1978). In addition, relational models that focused on the quality of parent–child contexts were challenged to consider the broader societal context, for example: Attachment theory (Bowlby, e.g. 1969; Ainsworth, e.g. 1979; Ainsworth et al. 1978); Social learning theory (Bandura, e.g. 1977). For an introduction to psychological models that have been influential on child practice see Chapter 2, and more detailed discussion in relation to specific presenting issues throughout the book.

Since its inception, much of the research into child psychopathology has been based on Bronfenbrenner's model. In clinical practice, it was developed and applied to families by Carter and McGoldrick (1989), who developed the Family Life Cycle Model, to understand how the individual young person functions in the context of their family and community over time (see Figure 3.1). Their model identifies stages of family development, each with its own developmental tasks, transition points and predictable and unpredictable stressors (see Table 3.1). It recognises cultural and societal norms and differences which will impact on how a family will move through the life cycle and sees individual development and developmental tasks as taking place within that broader context and the individual's emotional relationships. Revisions of the model by the authors (Carter & McGoldrick, 2006) have recognised the rapidly evolving concept of 'family' in the late twentieth and twenty-first centuries and critiqued some of its cultural and heteronormative assumptions, such that it has become much less 'normative' in nature when used in current practice.

Assessment of identified 'difficulties' for a child are not therefore considered in isolation but should include an understanding of the development of the wider family network and its history, and should place them within their cultural and societal context. That is not to say that the earlier individual, intrapersonal theories do not form part of an understanding of a CYP's presentation or formulation, but just that none of them on their own will be sufficient to inform the formulation or treatment plan.

Table 3.1 Family life cycle stages (adapted from Carter & McGoldrick, 1989).

Stage	Emotional process	Developmental Tasks
Leaving home – single young adults	Accepting responsibility for self	Differentiation of self from family of origin Development of intimate peer relationships
Joining of families through partnership	Adaptation and commitment to new system	Establishment of identity as couple – with peers and families of origin
Families with young children	Accepting new members into the system	Making space for children Realignment of relationships with wider family
Families with adolescents	Flexing family boundaries	Shift in parent–child relationship Shift in caring for older generation Focus on midlife issues
Launching children and moving on	Accepting changes to family system	Renegotiation of dyadic relationship Development of adult–adult relationships Dealing with disabilities and death
Families in later life	Accepting shift in generational roles	Maintaining functioning in face of decline Making room in the system for the experience of seniors Dealing with and preparing for death

Individual, family and societal factors provide risk and protective influences on child development both in terms of predisposition and maintenance of any difficulties that arise. These will impact differently depending on the stage of the family life cycle that they take place in and the other processes, transitions and stressors that are occurring concurrently for the child and family.

Transitions and making adaptations over time are difficult for young people and their families. As families move between different developmental stages, family members each have to adapt their behaviour, assumptions, expectations, language and roles. Such transitions are often the times when young people and their families struggle to cope and can be a trigger for asking for help and engaging with professional services. Table 3.1 describes the stages within the Family Life Cycle Model, and summarises the emotional processes for the family during those stages, and the family developmental tasks.

3.3 Assessment

A developmental approach to an assessment of a CYP's mental health difficulties will involve seeking information from multiple sources, including the CYP, their family and often the school and their wider professional network (such as children's social care).

It may involve using different methods of data collection, including clinical interviews, measures focused on symptoms and functioning, psychometric testing and naturalistic observation of the CYP, for example in school.

In psychological therapy with CYP, assessment rarely takes place in a finite amount of time, in a prescribed way and only at the start of an episode of care or treatment. How long it takes, what it is focused on and what methods and sources are used will be individual, and determined by the Child Practitioner, service model, client and the reason for the referral.

3.3.1 Consent, Contracting and Setting Up

Before the assessment starts, being curious about the referral that has been received is essential: who made the referral and whose views are presented in it? Even if the CYP and family has consented to the referral, the degree to which they understood what they were being referred for and the service they were being referred into, how much they felt that they had a choice and gave informed consent will vary and will depend on multiple factors. Legal factors about consent (the age and capacity of the young person to consent to their own treatment, Gillick competence and Fraser guidelines, and parental responsibility) must also be considered (see Chapter 5 for a detailed outline of this).

There is a difference between referrals that have been requested or made by a parent, carer or young person and those that have been suggested by a professional. The relationship the family has with the referrer and the power that the referrer holds will also be significant. Systemic models encourage the psychological practitioner to see the referral in context, understanding that referrers are not 'neutral' in the process of seeking help for a client, they will have identified difficulties for which the referral might be a solution (see the work of the Milan systemic therapists detailing 'the problem of the referring person': Palazzoli et al., 1980).

For example, a referral made by a social worker or member of school staff may be harder for a parent/carer to decline or question if they believe their or their child's care might be affected or fear that statutory processes or negative consequences (such as child protection processes, school exclusions) will be put in place if they do not consent. Clients may accept a referral to 'please' a referrer, and referrers may refer out of a sense of despair or 'stuckness' in their own relationship or work with the client.

It is important to remember that the 'problem' the referrer is trying to solve may be broader than the needs of the individual child who is referred for psychological services. For example, a school may consistently refer young people with learning and behavioural problems for psychological help as they find them difficult to manage in the context of expanding class sizes and reduced special educational needs resources or behaviour specialists within the education system. Referrers will have specific goals in mind about what they hope the referral will achieve and these goals are important for the psychological practitioner to understand, alongside the goals that the young person and family are bringing. This will support shared decision making about whether individual assessment and intervention is appropriate or an intervention higher up the system might be more fruitful, for example providing psychological consultation to teachers to enable them to support young people with additional needs. In sum, referrers will have an investment in the process and will influence the client's understanding and take up of the offer of psychological help, so it is important to consider their role.

Before families attend an assessment meeting with a psychological practitioner, they will have often already sought guidance from other people in their community, for example, from relatives, friends, GPs, health visitors and/or other parents. They may have received helpful or sometimes conflicting advice, but a professional psychological practitioner may not be their preferred choice of help giver. Large-scale surveys have found that young people most frequently identify family members as the people they favour most in helping them with mental health problems, with friends the next popular source of help (Yap et al., 2013). When identifying preferred professionals to help with their mental health problems most young people nominated their GP, over psychological professionals as the professional they would seek help from. Surveys have also shown that young people's beliefs about the causes of mental health influence their help seeking behaviour; if young people believed mental health problems were a personal weakness rather than an illness, they preferred informal sources of help such as friends, family and teachers rather than doctors, psychologists and counsellors. They also thought that these professionals would be less helpful in addressing their concerns (Yap et al., 2011). The Thrive Framework for CYP mental health services (Wolpert et al., 2014), outlined in Chapter 6, describes the importance of CYP and families having choice in how they are supported and the option of being directed to psychoeducation and self-help resources when appropriate, rather than a referral necessarily resulting in professional 'treatment'.

Reder and Fredman (1996) describe how the family's relationships with the referrer and other helpers can influence the development of a relationship with the psychological practitioner. They term this the 'relationship to help'. This is an important concept for the psychological practitioner to explore with the family, referrer and others in the system early on in assessments, as these relationships will influence the therapeutic relationship and process, which can impact trust in and engagement with psychological assessments and interventions, sometimes even before the first contact. Box 3.1 outlines some questions to consider when the referral is first received.

Box 3.1 Helpful questions when considering referrals

1. Did the client ask for help and if so, what did they first ask for help with? Is that what they have been referred for?
2. Are the client/s' views included in the referral and are they the same or different to those of the referrer?
3. Was/were the client/s wanting/expecting a referral to a psychological practitioner? Or did they, for example, go to a GP with physical symptoms, which the GP has interpreted as psychological, or were having difficulties with school, which school staff have interpreted as defiance?
4. What have the family been told/ do they understand about the service they have been referred to and why they have been referred?
5. What is the CYP developmental level and what is their view and understanding of the referral?
6. What consent and confidentiality issues does the CYP's age/developmental level raise? Are there any other ethical or consent issues to consider, for example parental responsibility status, or parental consent to treatment in the context of separation or divorce?

(Continued)

Box 3.1 (Continued)

7. What is the cultural background of the child/young person/family? What impact might this have on how they might feel about the referral and the service?
8. What language has the referrer used to describe the presentation? Value-laden descriptions?
9. Have they been referred for psychological support in the past? What for? How did it go?

Depending on the structure and processes of the service the practitioner is working in, it is usually helpful to arrange the first appointment directly with the client to agree a mutually convenient appointment time, within service parameters. This may be done with a young person themselves and/or with their parents/carers and can help the process of engaging them with the service being offered. The psychological practitioner and the family may already have views about whether all the people involved should be seen together initially, whether more than one initial appointment should be offered (for example, to give space for parents/carers/children/YP to talk away from each other or where different family members (such as separated parents) are not able to attend appointments together) and/or whether within the same appointment, family members can be offered time to be seen together and apart.

Referrers and/or other professionals (school staff, social workers, family support workers) may also be invited to join initial appointments with the consent of the client/s.

There will be service practicalities that will also influence who is invited to initial appointments and how the appointments are structured (for example, is more than one practitioner conducting the first appointment, and do they have access to more than one clinical space that will enable separating parents and CYP for part of the appointment?). Giving as much choice as possible to the CYP and parent/carers is an important part of the process of engagement and establishing them from the start as an active agent in their own change process (see Chapter 8 for more detail about this).

Explaining the nature of the service that the client has come to, what will happen in the appointment and clarifying why people in the room think they are there is an important part of setting up and contracting for the work. In some services, this will have been covered in the appointment letter, but nevertheless it is important to go over it again in person, not least because not everyone in the room will necessarily have seen the appointment letter or been involved in the pre-appointment work.

It is helpful for the psychological practitioner to ask how parents/carers may have explained the appointment and the service to the CYP, to use their language where appropriate, and to fill in the gaps in an age and developmentally appropriate way. The psychological practitioner might introduce a CYP mental health service in this way:

> Can you tell me what you explained to X about coming here today, and then I can fill in any gaps? This service is called CAMHS, which stands for Child and Adolescent Mental Health Service – mental health can sound really off-putting, I know, but it really means emotional health and wellbeing – we see children and young people where there may be worries about how they are feeling, sometimes about how things

> are at home, with families, sometimes about school, sometimes about relationships between people in the family. Today we have about an hour to talk together about how things are for you and your family, what things are going well and whether there are things that might be more difficult that we might be able to help with.

3.3.2 Confidentiality

Parameters around and limits to confidentiality and sharing information with other people must be explicit in all first appointments and explained in age and developmentally appropriate language. New practitioners can sometimes feel anxious about having this conversation, worrying that it might jeopardise therapeutic engagement. Building it in as a routine part of contracting at the start of all clinical work can help to normalise this process.

One way of talking about confidentiality is described here:

> The things we talk about today are 'confidential'[1] – that means that I won't talk about them with other people outside my team, unless you tell me something that makes me worried about your/your child's safety, or the safety of another child or young person. Then I would have to talk to other people about that, in order to make sure you/your child or the other child/ren were safe. I would usually tell you if that was the case, before I talked to someone else. Sometimes we might think it would be helpful to share information with other people who work with you or look after you/your child, like school staff, your parents, your social worker – but we would agree what we were going to share and the best way of doing that beforehand.

Putting people at their ease as much as possible is a principal task of the first appointment. If they are not at ease, it will be impossible for the psychological practitioner to gather full and reliable assessment information or set the foundations for intervention work together. Remember that, however familiar you are with the setting and the work, for many CYP and families, coming to see you may be strange, awkward and daunting. If they have been to the service or a similar service before, that will not necessarily mean that they feel comfortable coming again. CYP and families or carers may have a range of emotions including anxiety, shame, hopelessness and anger. They may feel blamed by the referral, and they may be frustrated if they have waited a long time for the appointment. For the new psychological practitioner some of these feelings, particularly anxiety, may mirror their own feelings in approaching the first meeting. They may be concerned about their own competence, for example: *Will I manage all the people in the room? Will I be able to remember all the areas to cover in the assessment? What do I do if child protection issues come up? How can I help people with parenting when I have no experience with children? How can I ask such personal questions without it feeling like I'm prying?* It is important that the novice practitioner uses supervision to prepare well for initial meetings with clients, addressing any anxieties or triggers for their own emotional responses so they can be open to supporting the family to feel at ease.

How the psychological practitioner tries to 'engage' the CYP/family will depend on many things – the theoretical model of the practitioner and their supervisor, who is at the

1 It is important not to use the word 'private' here, which can hold connotations of secrets and shame.

appointment, the age and stage of the CYP, where they are being seen and the presenting issues. Thinking about how to engage younger children is important, and getting the balance right between being a friendly professional and being too informal can be difficult initially. Novice practitioners can sometimes feel the need to hold a 'very professional' or 'expert' position for families that can impede engagement. Usually, engaging with the children directly is a helpful first step, asking them open questions, using their name and discussing things they are interested in or feel proud of. Asking about things they have brought with them to the appointment (toys, soft toys or commenting on school bag or uniform) can be a useful way in. If parents/carers observe practitioners to be engaging with and interested in their child, they will often relax more easily into the assessment meeting.

When engaging children, consideration should be given to how the room is set up. The room should be checked for any hazards, especially if the appointment is taking place outside a traditional clinic setting (for example at a school or GP surgery) and the room is also used for other purposes. Developmentally appropriate toys and activities should be made available to help the child feel more comfortable. Some drawing materials, dolls and puppets are usually helpful as tools to aid and support assessment, by offering the child non-verbal means to express emotions, relationships and life events. Children and young people often find toys and activities can help to relax them and can aid concentration, rather than being distracting.

Assessment appointments can feel 'problem saturated' (White & Epston, 1990) and an important part of the assessment and engagement process should involve getting to know the CYP and family more broadly. Systemic practitioners highlight the importance of 'joining' with the family using strengths-based and narrative approaches, which view clients as experts in their own stories and experiences (Freeman et al., 1997). Therefore, the psychological practitioner's stance as respectful and collaborative, open and enquiring, is very important in achieving successful engagement with families.

Engaging adolescents and older young people requires different skills (see Chapter 10). Service-user feedback frequently reports young people experiencing practitioners as out of touch and patronising. Participatory qualitative research with adolescents has identified five key themes in young people's descriptions of their ideal mental health practitioner (Stubbing & Gibson, 2022): *Someone like me, Someone I connect with, Someone who protects my space, Someone who treats me as an equal,* and *Someone who works in the right way for me.* Asking how the people in the room view the referral and the appointment and what they hope to get out of it, and acknowledging their choice about being there is essential in setting up a collaborative relationship with adolescents right from the start.

It is important to note that, however well prepared the psychological practitioner might try to be, appointments with children and young people can often bring surprises, including unexpected people joining the appointment (siblings, extended family) as well as or instead of the people that were expected. Flexibility and an ability to think on one's feet is helpful, including having the confidence to request that an appointment be rescheduled, if necessary, when the right people can be present. Noticing who comes or is brought to an appointment can inform the assessment and formulation, without judgement but with curiosity: Is a parent able to prioritise the needs of one sibling over others? Do both parents join? Might there be a relationship between who does or does not attend and the reason for the referral?

First appointments can feel, to the client and psychological practitioner, like a barrage of fact-seeking questions, more for the practitioner's benefit than the client's, so pacing of the assessment meetings and ensuring it is focusing on the CYP and family's priorities is an important consideration (see Chapter 8). It is important to remember that for some CYP, and for families and carers, being asked about their feelings and experiences can have a powerfully 'normalising' effect – for the first time they may have the experience that someone understands how they are feeling and that they may not be the only person to have felt that way. The psychological practitioner not being shocked by what they are being told can be similarly powerful. Being able to cover enough ground to be able to start with the client, to make sense of their difficulties and to meaningfully involve them in the process involves skills in balancing structure, content and emotional attunement, which practitioners develop over time.

3.4 Clinical Interviews

3.4.1 What to Cover in the Assessment Interview, and How to Ask

Assessments can take place over one or several appointments and will often include multiple sources or 'informants' – the CYP, family members including parents/carers, professionals involved in their care including school staff, social workers and GPs. This section of the chapter includes examples of questions that can be asked during clinical assessment appointments. They are phrased as if being asked of the CYP/family, but similar questions could be also asked of other professionals involved in the CYP's care. Table 3.2 describes the broad areas to be followed in an assessment interview.

At the start of the first interview, it can be helpful to outline what will be covered. The psychological practitioner might say:

> If it's ok with you, I'd like to ask about you and what has brought you here today – what the concerns are and what life is like at the moment? Then it's really

Table 3.2 The assessment interview.

Area	Content
1. The reason for referral	What prompted the referral and has brought them to the appointment. Why now? Put crudely, what's the problem, for whom and for how long?
2. Current context	The external contexts for the CYP, the family and home/s, race/culture/religion, education, community. Strengths and resources.
3. Family history	The wider family history and context: parents, siblings, extended family. Relationships, moves, traumas, losses, family physical and mental health.
4. Individual developmental history	Pregnancy and birth, developmental milestones, social relationships, education history, physical and mental health.

helpful for me to be able to go right back, to ask about your family background, and what things were like before, right back to when you were a baby. This is so that I can have a wider picture of you and your family that can help to try to make sense of how things are now, and to see what might be helpful.

3.4.2 The Reason for the Referral

When is a Problem a Problem? When and why a presentation, behaviour or pattern of behaviours is considered a symptom or a 'problem' and who it is a problem for is important to be curious about. Psychological practitioners will explore the perception and understanding of the behaviour for all key people: who is worried, about what, for how long and what might it be representing for them? Different and opposing reports of a child's behaviour across contexts can reflect the variety of ways they are being perceived and experienced by adults, and what is being expected of them, rather than necessarily objective differences in behaviour. For example, a child's behaviour may be experienced as 'anger' and trigger particular responses such as anxiety or fear in a parent who is a survivor of domestic abuse, but the same behaviour might be experienced as lively or mischievous by another parent or a teacher. These different perceptions will in turn influence whether the parents/school determine this to be problematic behaviour and will ultimately shape their differing responses to it.

What does and does not constitute 'normal' emotional responses and behaviour in childhood is to a large extent a matter of perception that is subject to familial, cultural and societal influences. However, the predominant approach in services is to use diagnostic frameworks for categorising and describing emotional and behavioural difficulties with the most widely accepted nomenclature being the *Diagnostic and Statistical Manual of Mental Disorders* (5th ed.; *DSM–5*; American Psychiatric Association, 2013). There is significant debate about the appropriateness of using such frameworks for CYP as they may not be sensitive enough to pick up on the complex, and changing developmental presentations seen during childhood or be sufficiently nuanced to account for the developmental differences between children and adults. The *DSM-5* does provide a common language for practitioners and is widely used in research settings, which may be helpful in advancing the understanding and treatment of difficulties.

When first considering a referral and assessing need, the psychological practitioner should try to understand how the behaviour might 'fit', or not, in the family and the wider network, which will be influenced by multiple factors including culture, societal norms, values and current family pressures. The Milan group (Palazzoli et al., 1980) describe 'the problem of the referring person' stressing the importance of considering what the possible role or function of the presenting difficulty might be for the person or people that have identified the 'problem' and what purpose might it be serving for them.

It is also important that the practitioner is aware of their own assumptions and biases that they will bring with them to the referral and assessment process (see Chapter 4 and Chapter 7 for more details).

To what extent these considerations can be explored prior to a first appointment will depend on the service the psychological practitioner is working in. Some services will have a separate intake or triage system that will involve contacting clients and/or referrers to obtain more information that will inform shared decision making about which

Table 3.3 Example questions – the presenting problem.

Questions	Suggested wording
How long has [the difficulty] been going on for?	Can you remember when you first started to feel… Can you remember when it wasn't there? It sounds like you have been feeling like this for a long time. I'm wondering what it is that's changed, that led to this referral now?
Who has noticed? What are the views of the CYP and other key people in the family about it?	What does [grandparent, other parent, family friend] think? If [other parent, teacher, grandparent] was here, what would they say about it?
Are there times when it's better or worse? What or who helps?	Is it the same in school and at home, in different family environments (e.g. grandparents/separated parents)? Are school holiday times different? Is it different when in 1:1 situations, for example, when other siblings are not there?
What have you already tried?	I can see that you attended [a parenting course] a few years ago. Can you tell me what that was like? Did it make any difference? You had some counselling in school last year – what was that like?

practitioner, team or therapy the referral will be allocated to and what the first appointment will look like, including who will be invited. In other services, this is carried out by the practitioner when the referral is made or allocated to them. Questions that the psychological practitioner might ask about the presenting problems are suggested in Table 3.3.

3.4.3 Assessing Risk

The assessment of how safe a child or young person is, both in terms of their own mental health and risk-taking behaviours and in terms of their contextual risk of harm from others (child protection and safeguarding) is central to the initial triage stage when a referral is first received, and to the subsequent assessment. At the triage stage, an assessment of risk will guide how rapidly the referral should be responded to and by whom. CYP presenting in a mental health crisis, risk factors and how to assess and treat it is described in detail in Chapter 22.

Tables 3.4 and 3.5, provide examples of questions that can be used to ask about both mental health and safeguarding risk to a CYP.

Practitioners at all stages of training and clinical practice can find talking about harmful behaviour and risk of harm difficult and anxiety provoking, with common concerns being: *Will I lose the engagement of the CYP/family if I talk about these things? Will I make the situation worse? Will I increase the risk if I ask about self-harm or suicidal thoughts?* The most important factors in assessing risk and safety are:

- paying close attention to what is being said and not said,
- taking it seriously,
- not being afraid to ask uncomfortable questions, and
- knowing where to go for advice and support and drawing on that if at all concerned

Table 3.4 Example questions – self-harm and suicidal thoughts.

Category	Example questions
Self-harm	Have you ever hurt yourself on purpose? When was the last time you hurt yourself? Can you show me [the cut/s]?
	Can I ask whether anyone knew about it? Did you talk to anyone about it? How did they react?
	When you feel like hurting yourself, how do you stop yourself (distraction techniques)?
Suicidal thoughts or ideation	Can I ask whether you have ever felt so sad/down/low/depressed that you have thought about ending your life? Can you tell me about it? Can you remember what stopped you?
	Do you still have thoughts about that now? How often do you have those thoughts? When was the last time?
	When you think about it, do you have ideas about how you might do it?
	How do you manage those thoughts now?

Table 3.5 Example questions: child protection and safeguarding.

Category	Example questions
Domestic violence and abuse	Is there any violence or aggression between you/your parents? Can you tell me about it? Was [CYP] there when it happened?
	How do you [CYP] feel when it happens? Does [parent/carer] know how you feel?
	Have you been asked not to tell anyone? Have you talked to anyone about it? What happened?
Physical abuse and chastisement	How do you react when [CYP] behaves like that? Have you ever responded physically/hit them?
Contextual safeguarding	How safe do you feel in your community/environment? Do you feel that you can say 'no' to your friends/peers? Do you feel that you are made to do things that you feel uncomfortable doing?

This last point is particularly important for practitioners working as a lone mental health professional outside of traditional clinic settings, such as within school or social care environments. Before they start working in such settings, the psychological practitioner should make sure they are aware of who they can go to for advice and what the governance structures are in that setting as well as those of their own service, and local children's social care duty and advice systems. They should also have talked explicitly about confidentiality and the parameters around it at the start of the appointment.

The legal parameters to both mental health risk and safeguarding and the duty of care for all practitioners are described in Chapter 5.

3.4.4 Current Context

Family and Home: Understanding who is in the CYP's family in its broadest sense gives the psychological practitioner information about the context that the CYP is living in. Drawing out a genogram can be a helpful place to start and can lead into the discussion on family history, described later. A genogram is a pictorial representation of the family members, their relationships, their ages and gender identity, presenting issues and life events such as deaths and partnerships/marriages across time, spanning three or more generations of the family. A genogram goes beyond a family tree because it includes information about how family members interact with each other as well as lineage (Burnham, 2002, 2012). The genogram can be completed with the CYP and can draw out strengths and resources available to them and the parent or carer. Of course, the information that is gathered will be the interpretation of the people in the room when drawing out the genogram, including their perceptions, experience and biases. Exploring differences of opinion and perceptions of life events in the assessment with the family can inform the therapy. It can give helpful pointers for areas to cover in the rest of the assessment, identifying strengths and conflicts in relationships, losses and transitions including separations, deaths and relocation. Figure 3.2 shows some of the basic symbols used routinely by psychological practitioners but many online guides exist with detailed guidance (e.g. www.therapistaid.com).

Genograms can be broadened out to include other important figures in the CYP/family's life – friends, pets, teachers, social workers and to depict a wide range of different and more complicated relationships.

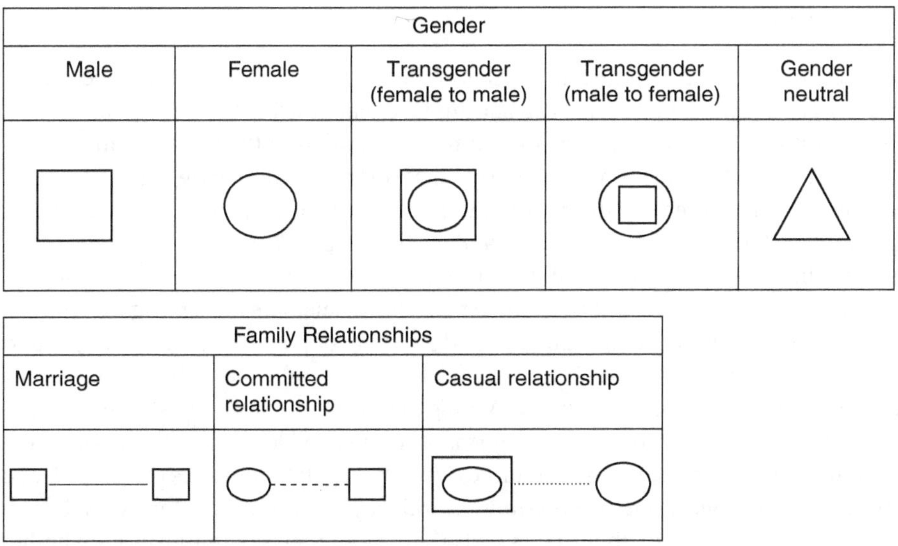

Figure 3.2 Genogram symbols.

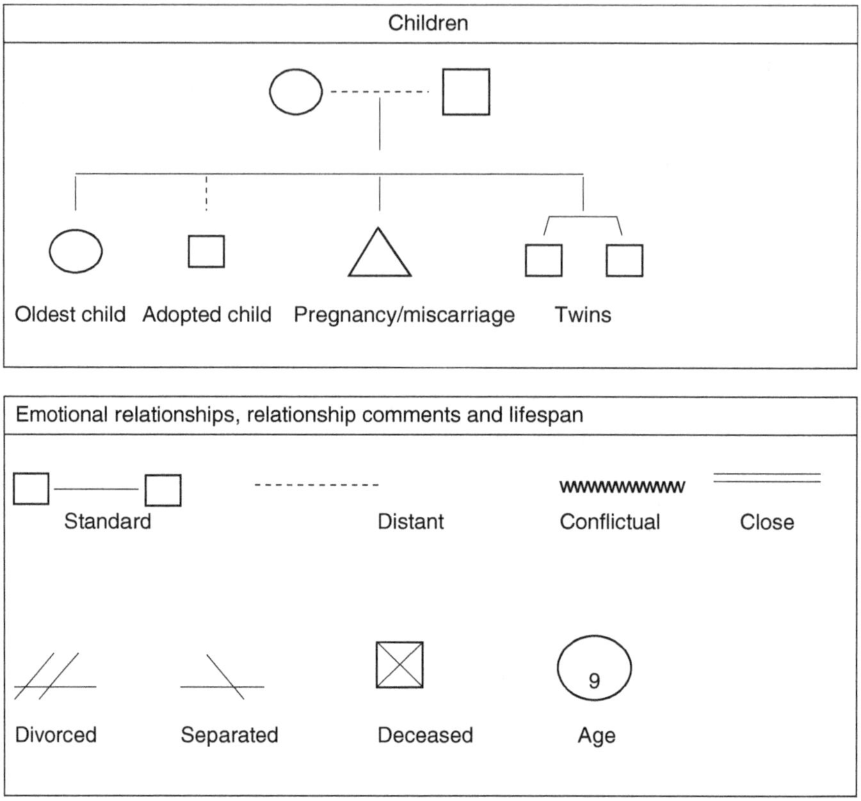

Figure 3.2 (*Continued*)

Community: Exploring the significant aspects of the CYP and family's culture and values, including religion, race and ethnicity, can start to take place during the genogram exercise described and may also be included as part of the exploration of the wider family history (Burnham, 2012). It is helpful for practitioners to have mapped out their own genogram and reflected upon diverse aspects of their own culture before using genograms in assessments with families (see Shellenberger et al., 2007 and Chege et al., 2022).

Questions about housing, work and current schooling will also give the psychological practitioner important broader information to place the immediate presenting difficulty in a wider, social context as well as starting to build a picture of possible resources to support the intervention. It will also give information about how safe the CYP and/or family feels in their home and their community. Asking about the cultural, racial and religious origin of family members can provide information about wider support networks and possible conflicts and clashes. It can also start to identify societal influences on the CYP and family that may be impacting on the presentation and may bring resources for its resolution.

Understanding how a family themselves feels they 'fit' in their community and whether they feel themselves to be marginalised or part of a dominant culture is important and will support conversations about experiences of discrimination including racism.

Practitioners can feel anxious about talking about race, religion and culture and describe feeling worried about using incorrect language and 'getting it wrong', but genuine interest

Table 3.6 Example questions – community.

Area	Questions
Socioeconomic status	What do [people in the household] do? Do you work? Where do you live?
Race/culture	How do you/your family identify in terms of race or ethnicity?
Faith/religion	Are you/family members religious? Tell me about your Faith. Tell me about the sorts of celebrations or rituals your family participates in?
Community	Have you lived here for a long time? Do you have friends/family nearby? Describe your neighbourhood to me. Do you feel safe around your neighbourhood? Can you go out on your own or with friends?
School	What school does the CYP and any siblings attend? How are siblings experiencing school?
Friends	Do you have friends in school/outside school? Can you tell me their names (for younger children)?
	What do you like to do with them? Do you see them outside school?
	What social media apps/platforms do you go on? How do you think they affect you/how you feel?

and curiosity and not assuming knowledge or understanding can help to promote trusting relationships. Not talking about these areas, on the other hand can convey indifference and even ignorance (see Chapter 7).

It is also important to ask here about the CYP's current friendships and peer relationships both in school (if relevant) and outside. This will include social media usage and involvement, as both a positive and potentially negative or harmful influence (see Chapter 10 and Chapter 22 for more discussion on this).

Table 3.6 suggests questions than can be asked in relation to community.

3.4.5 Family History

An exploration of a CYP's family history provides the background to the current presentation. It is helpful to do this chronologically, to understand what life was like for the family before the CYP was born, how the parents met and what their own families of origin were like. These factors may have influenced their experience of becoming parents and of parenting and co-parenting, and their interpretation of the CYP's current presentation. This part of the assessment will include information about any changes, losses or traumas that the wider family has experienced, including migration, domestic violence and abuse and racial trauma. It should cover the parents'/carers' own experience of being parented and can yield important information about possible misalignments between expectations and the experience of parenting both between the parents/carers and also with both sides of the extended family. This discussion can flow naturally whilst creating a genogram with the CYP/family (described earlier).

The psychological practitioner should ask about all pregnancies, not just that of the referred CYP, including any pregnancies lost through miscarriage, termination or still birth.

Table 3.7 Example questions – family history.

Area	Example questions
Parental relationship	Can I ask how you first met? Had you been together for long before [eldest child] was born?
	How do you get on/communicate now?
	Can I ask what your relationship has been like? Has there been any violence or aggression between you, now or in the past?[2]
Pregnancy and birth	Was it an expected pregnancy? How did you feel about being pregnant/becoming parents [first time and this time, if different]?
	How were you during the pregnancy? Any medical complications? Was there any drug or alcohol use whilst you were pregnant? Any stresses during the pregnancy? Any changes to the family?
	Who else was around when you were pregnant/were having the baby? Extended family relationships? Support networks?
	How was the birth? Was it as you expected/wanted it to be?
	Was having a baby how you imagined it would be?
	How did sibling/s react to becoming a big brother/sister?
Family physical, mental health and neurodevelopmental history	Has anyone in the family had any health difficulties (physical or mental health)? Is there any history of neurodiversity in the family?
	Is there any experience of addictions or drug and alcohol misuse in the family now or in the past?
	Does [CYP] remind you of anyone else in the family?
Family trauma history	Has anyone in your family experienced trauma or loss?
	Have you/anyone in your family ever been treated poorly because of your beliefs/ethnicity/race?
Experiences of and beliefs about [CYP] mental health services	Has anyone in the family needed the support of mental health services? What was that like?
	What is your family/culture perspective on therapy, or getting help for mental health?
History of involvement with services	Have you ever had support from other services, such as social workers or family support workers? What was that like?

Asking about siblings, how children in the family adapted to subsequent births, and what life has been like for them also gives important information – both in terms of understanding additional stressors families might be managing, but also possible familial patterns, whether to do with genetic, biological, environmental, cultural or social factors.

Table 3.7 suggests questions that the child practitioner can ask in relation to family history.

2 Questions about parental tensions and conflict including domestic violence and abuse are important but need to be asked sensitively. The child practitioner should be guided by the parent about whether this can be talked about in front of the CYP or whether a separate opportunity should be offered.

3.4.6 Individual Developmental History

This section of the assessment will include information about how the CYP has developed during the pregnancy, through the birth to now and will cover biological factors such as temperament as well as environmental factors that might have influenced their development. It should also include information about the CYP outside the 'problem' or the reason for referral: what are their interests and strengths? It may be interwoven with asking about the current presentation and the family history, as questions will overlap – for example, asking about the current context can include finding out about the CYP more broadly, what they enjoy doing, when the 'problem' is not as difficult; asking about infancy and early milestones across all five domains of early development (gross motor, fine motor, language, cognitive, and social-emotional and behavioural), how the baby fed, slept, what sort of baby they were (smiley, cried a lot, needed to be held). These questions will naturally open up discussion about how the child was experienced by the parent/s, what the family circumstances were at the time and what support was or was not available from the wider network.

The extent to which the parent or carer remembers and how they talk about early weeks and months can also be significant. It can give an indication of the attachment relationship and level of attunement between the parent/carer and the CYP, although it is important that this is not over-interpreted, and that the psychological practitioner considers the role of their own individual assumptions and cultural biases when drawing conclusions or making interpretations.

Table 3.8 provides some examples of questions the psychological practitioner can ask about the individual development of the CYP.

When carrying out an assessment, it is helpful to have in mind a broad overview of 'typical' child development – how an infant/child might be expected to have developed within an age range, across different domains. This is summarised in Table 3.9, but these are bound by cultural norms and standards.

The psychological practitioner should refer to more detailed standardised tools for the evaluation of early child development and developmental milestones for the under-fives, particularly when conducting multidisciplinary developmental assessments; for example, the Bayley Scales of Infant and Toddler Development – fourth version (Bayley4, Bayley & Aylward, 2019) or the World Health Organization (WHO) – Global Scales for Early Development Package (World Health Organization, 2023). Practitioners must ensure standardised assessments are appropriate for the developmental and language abilities of the child, the context and population (Bedford et al., 2013; Boggs et al., 2019; Munoz Chereau et al., 2021).

3.5 Observation and Naturalistic Data Collection

3.5.1 Observation in Clinical Appointments

The psychological practitioner's in-person observations of behaviour and interactions as they occur in the clinical appointment provide important additional information to aid the assessment. That said, they should be interpreted with caution, as they are occurring in an

Table 3.8 Example questions – individual development.

Area	Example questions
Pregnancy and birth	How was the pregnancy? Were there any complications with the baby or mother/person who carried the baby? And the birth? Where was it and who was there? Any medical interventions after the baby was born? What were those first hours after birth like?
Birth order	Does the referred CYP have siblings? How did they react to the birth? How did they get on and how do they get on now?
Temperament	What sort of baby were they? How did they sleep? How did they feed? How did they respond to others?
Milestones	Was [he/she] a healthy baby? Were there any concerns about their development (motor/cognitive/language)? How did they sleep, feed, wean? What was toilet training like?
Socialisation	Can you remember what they liked to play with when they were little, around 2 or 3 years? Did they like to play alone, with others? How did they play with others, what was sharing like? Did they go to play groups/nursery/stay and plays? What was that like? How did they get on with other adults? Extended family, teachers?
Education	When did they first go somewhere where you left them (nursery/school)? How was that? Did it take them long to settle? How do they manage their schoolwork? What's the best thing about school? And any things you don't like so much? Favourite subject? Favourite teacher?

unfamiliar, strange and often anxiety-provoking environment. They nevertheless add an extra layer to the assessment and can tell the practitioner something about the relationship between the people in the room, how they respond to the setting and to talking, how able they are to hear from each other.

Questions to hold in mind during an assessment appointment are given in Table 3.10.

3.5.2 Naturalistic Observations

Observing CYP in other real-life settings outside the clinical appointment can provide additional information to support an assessment. This can be helpful, particularly when there are different descriptions of a CYP's behaviour or functioning, for example from school staff and parents/carers.

Naturalistic observations by practitioners, where the CYP is not aware that they are being observed, allow the psychological practitioner to get an understanding of behaviour, interactions with others and responses and reactions to ordinary situations in a familiar environment, outside an artificial clinic setting. They also allow a more independent observation of behaviour in that setting – carried out by a practitioner rather than an adult involved in their care (parent/carer/teacher), although all observations will be subject to the biases of the observer. They can allow observation of interactions that would not

Table 3.9 Stages of individual child development.

Chronological age of child	Area of development			
	Physical (fine and gross motor skills)	Social-emotional	Cognitive	Language
Infancy Birth to 1 year	Holding up head Weight-bearing Rolling Sitting up Crawling Pulls to stand Grasping objects Weaning from milk (breast or bottle) to solid food Development of sleep, reduction in night waking	Smiling (6 weeks) Selective attention to primary caregiver Comfort-seeking behaviour Development of self-soothing behaviours (sucking thumb) Recognition of familiar faces Development of attachment relationships (preference for primary carer/s)	*Sensorimotor* Exploration of environment through senses Manipulate objects Understand object permanence Development of language	Vocalisations (coos, chuckles) Reacts to voices Responds to name Understands single words Word sounds (ma-ma/da-da) Single word sentences
Toddlerhood 1–2 years	Standing unaided Walking Running Development of fine motor skills (holding crayon) Eat with utensil Throw a ball	Beginnings of shyness – separation anxiety (9–18 months) Beginnings of development of empathy (e.g. responding to crying in others) Showing fear Seeking out attention Shared attention (pointing) Parallel play with peers		Two-three word sentences Understand simple questions and instructions

(*continued*)

Table 3.9 (Continued)

Chronological age of child	Area of development			
	Physical (fine and gross motor skills)	**Social-emotional**	**Cognitive**	**Language**
Early Childhood 2–6 years	Toilet training Use stairs Hop, skip and jump Catch a ball with both hands Brush teeth Ride tricycle/ scooter	Development of independence and autonomy Showing defiance Understand jokes Expresses range of emotions Pretend play Development of cooperation with peers Wanting to please peers Development of understanding of gender and gender identity	*Pre-operational* Symbolic representation Egocentrism	Use of longer sentences Questioning (Why?) Use of past tense
Middle childhood 6–13 years	Ride bike Develop sports skills Tie shoe laces Manage buttons and zips Use tools Onset of puberty	Development of peer relationships Development of self-esteem	*Concrete operational* Logical thinking Concrete problem-solving Increased concentration/listening	Understanding complex words and ideas Development of grammar Learning to read/write
Adolescence 13+ years	Puberty Growth spurt Sexual maturation Become more agile and less clumsy Refine visual–spatial coordination Ongoing frontal lobe brain development	Primacy of peer relationships Separation from carers Development of romantic and sexual relationships Risk taking behaviours Development of self-esteem and resilience	*Formal operational* Development of executive functioning Abstract thinking Hypothetical problem -solving Deductive reasoning	Increasing skill with complex grammar and vocabulary

Table 3.10 Observations during the clinical appointment.

Area	Questions
Parent/CYP relationship	How do the parent/s/carers/CYP interact in the session? Do you sense warmth/hostility between them? How does either react if the other shows emotion (upset/anger)? Is there evidence of role-reversal in their relationship?
	Does the parent/carer allow the CYP appropriate space to be part of the assessment (answering questions, allowing them to be seen alone)?
	Is the parent able to put themselves in the CYP's shoes (to mentalise)? Can they tolerate differences of opinion?
Adult relationships	If more than one adult (parent/carer) attends the appointment, what are your observations of their relationship? Do they agree/disagree? Can they tolerate differences of opinion?
Parenting	How does the parent/carer enforce boundaries (for example, if the CYP doesn't want to go into the session or doesn't want to leave)? How does the parent/care respond if the CYP does not want to engage?
	How does the parent/carer impose boundaries in the face of challenging behaviour from CYP such as climbing/throwing toys/furniture? How do they manage sibling dynamics, if more than one child is present?
CYP	How does the CYP engage with you? Able to maintain eye contact? Able to join in the conversation in a developmentally appropriate way?
	What is their body language like? Are they still/fidgety?
	If other siblings are brought to the appointment, what is the quality of their interaction?

be seen in a clinical appointment: in a school observation, it is possible to observe how the CYP responds to their peers, to requests and demands from figures in authority (teachers), how they respond to different environments and expectations (unstructured play and lunchtimes; structured teaching; independent study; group working) and how they respond to transitions and separations (moving from playtime to class, and at the start and end of the day).

Live observations carried out by practitioners can take different forms: taking notes for the duration of the observation from which they then extract themes or patterns; making a note of every time a behaviour or pattern of behaviours occurs and how long it lasts; noting what the CYP's behaviour is at regular time intervals.

Disadvantages of naturalistic observations by practitioners are that what is being observed cannot be predicted, manipulated or controlled and can only be interpreted as a 'snapshot' of the CYP's style of behaviour and interaction rather than as fully representative.

It is more straightforward for these sorts of observations to most commonly form part of assessments of younger (pre-school or primary age children) in nursery or school settings, partly because naturalist school observations of older young people is practically more difficult as they generally do not remain in one classroom, and the observer is therefore more noticeable as they have to move around the school with the young person.

Table 3.11 Setting up a naturalist observation.

Area	Considerations
Practicalities	Discuss with the teacher/other professional how you will be positioned in the setting. How will they make the CYP known to you if you haven't met them before? How will you be introduced to the group/class? Consider how you will respond if you are asked by children who you are. How will they let you know if, for example, the CYP is not going to be in the setting that day (e.g. is off sick from school)?
What is/are your question/s?	This will inform what you want to observe and therefore when you will need to go to the school. Are you interested in social interaction/peer/adult relationships? Do you want to see how the CYP responds to transitions (e.g. moving from playground to class; home-times)? In a school observation, consider observing different learning and social opportunities. Talk to parents/carers/staff about what they think would be most important for you to observe (e.g. structured learning/independent study).
Talk to adults in the setting	Can you take the opportunity to talk to the teacher about the CYP after the observation? Can they tell you how 'typical' they felt the CYP was during the observation? Was there anything unusual about period of time you observed (e.g. a different teacher to normal)?

Areas to consider when arranging to conduct a naturalistic observation are described in Table 3.11.

3.5.3 Sampling

Naturalistic observations can be carried out over longer periods of time, most commonly by asking an adult who spends time with the CYP (parent/carer/teacher) to observe and record what happens every time specific behaviours occur, or to observe and record what behaviour is being displayed at particular points during a day, at random or specified time points. An example of this would be a parent/carer keeping a record or diary every time a young person displayed anxiety, recording when the event took place, what was happening before and after it and who was present, or a teacher recording what happened every time a child was asked to move from one setting to another. This information can support the psychological practitioner to notice patterns and moderating or mediating variables. Disadvantages of sampling methods of observation are how time-consuming they are for the observer, and how accurate the observer's recording is, which is subject to recording bias and difficult to verify.

3.5.4 Questionnaires and Routine Outcome Measures

Psychological practitioners frequently obtain additional information about areas of behaviour, 'symptoms' and how a CYP is functioning through the use of questionnaires and measures, sometimes called 'routine outcome measures' (ROMs). Chapter 8, describes the use of such measures, the pitfalls and how they can best be used as 'tools' to support

Table 3.12 Points for consideration when using routine outcome measures

Area	Considerations
Who is completing them?	The same measures can be completed by different people: CYP/parent or carer/teacher. Differences in responses should be treated as additional information to inform the assessment and formulation and can be discussed in the appointment.
	Are there barriers to them being completed, such as language or intellectual ability? Some measures are routinely available in different languages, but many are not. Does the person completing the measure need support? An interpreter? Can they read/write?
When are they completed?	Many services send ROMs to CYP/ parents and carers and sometimes schools as well prior to a first appointment. Sometimes this is to inform a decision about which team should provide a service or assessment (to identify a 'threshold') and sometimes it is to provide a 'baseline' to measure progress. Ideally, the timing of any initial measures should be tailored to the CYP to avoid alienating them from the service they have been referred to.
	When they are received prior to the first appointment, it can be helpful to use them as a 'way in' to exploring particular areas that the measures have highlighted. This also gives the message to the CYP and family that they have been taken seriously and completing them is a meaningful part of the process.
How should they be used?	Measures should be used to support and enhance the information that is provided during the clinical appointment/s. They should not be used on their own to provide a diagnosis.

and supplement the assessment and therapeutic process. Table 3.12 details the important points to consider when using such measures.

3.5.5 The Use of Screening Tools and Psychometric Assessments

Specific measures may be used to understand whether a CYP's difficulties might be an indication of an underlying neurodivergence such as Autism Spectrum Disorder (ASD) or Attention Deficit and Hyperactivity Disorder (ADHD). They are used as screening tools, to supplement a clinical assessment in order to support a recommendation for a specialist neurodevelopmental assessment. Chapter 19, describes these measures and their uses in detail.

Understanding the intellectual functioning of a CYP can be an important part of an assessment to aid formulation and treatment planning. There is wide geographical variation in terms of which service or services carry out such assessments and when. In general, Children's and Young People's Mental Health (CYPMH) services will conduct them when there is a question about mental health difficulties and/or when trying to understand whether identified presenting difficulties might be better understood in terms of intellectual functioning. In reality, many CYP presenting with behaviours that challenge will have an underlying intellectual disability, neurodivergence, or both, frequently undiagnosed (see Chapter 18, Chapter 19 and Chapter 23). Screening and being able to identify when to refer on for a specialist assessment is therefore a crucial skill for the psychological practitioner.

Chapter 18, describes the main psychometric assessment tools available for CYP, and what to consider when selecting them.

3.6 Formulation

Formulation is a way of summarising and integrating the different forms of information and knowledge that have been gathered through the assessment and applying psychological theory and sometimes diagnostic classifications to that information to help to make sense, with the client, of the difficulties that they are experiencing. Its purpose is to inform intervention planning and help the psychological practitioner and the client to make shared decisions about where and how to intervene and with whom.

Formulation can be thought of as an evolving story or set of ideas or hypotheses that try to make sense of the presenting difficulties and give direction for future action. It offers a structured explanatory framework, including how difficulties developed, what is maintaining them and how they may relate to each other (Division of Clinical Psychology (DCP), 2011; Johnstone & Dallos, 2014). The hypotheses focus on the contributing, preceding and maintaining factors that affect an individual's psychological, emotional, interpersonal and behavioural problems (Eells, 1997). Formulation can be applied to a specific set of problems or a difficulty that affects a client, their family, or even difficulties that arise within an organisation.

Johnstone and Dallos (2014) highlight that formulation is sometimes portrayed as an *event* in research and psychological texts, but in clinical practice it, instead, reflects an *ongoing* iterative process, something to be built on throughout the assessment and treatment process. Formulation involves suggestion, discussion, reflection, feedback and revision that is intricately part of the process of psychological intervention. As a strong alliance forms, clients will continually feel more able to trust their psychological practitioner and offer additional information, which perhaps felt too personal or shameful to share early on in the assessment. As clients begin to make connections between different aspects of their life through the formulation process, they will come to see other pieces of information as relevant to share with the practitioner. Similarly, the practitioner will feel able to introduce more curious and challenging questions once they have established an empathic and collaborative relationship with the client. All of this information enriches and shapes the evolving formulation.

Formulations differ across therapeutic models and these differences include:

- the factors that each therapeutic approach focuses upon as most relevant (for example intrapersonal vs interpersonal factors);
- theoretical and psychological concepts that are drawn upon to offer explanation;
- the degree of emphasis on reflexivity;
- an expert versus collaborative stance;
- engagement with medical models and diagnostic frameworks;
- the focus on identifying 'truth' versus 'usefulness'; and
- how a formulation is developed and subsequently shared.

Which theoretical models psychological practitioners draw upon to guide formulations will be largely dependent not only upon their own interests but their training, place of work and their supervisor. The quality of formulation will be dependent upon the quality and thoroughness of the assessment, as described earlier. A 'high-quality' formulation should additionally be informed by the evidence base, which can be obtained through research journals and up to date NICE guidelines. This will suggest ways forward regarding intervention and will also highlight if no such specialist psychological support is indicated.

Formulating is, therefore, an integral part of the work that psychological practitioners do. Formulations can be useful in numerous ways: creating them collaboratively and sharing them with clients (discussed later) can support a shared understanding of and give meaning to difficulties they are experiencing, how they may have developed, what might be maintaining them and the impact they are having on their lives. In collaborative formulations, the client has a role in the development of the formulation and so is likely to feel that it includes their own view and is more likely to match their experience. As formulations develop over time, they offer a way to test out hypotheses and facilitate new questions and areas of exploration in the work with clients (DCP, 2011). Clients can feel heard by the practitioner, and this can help the development of a trusting relationship and support engagement.

Within a therapeutic intervention, the formulation can also be shared by the client with others in their lives, both personally and amongst the professionals they may be working with. Similarly, the team that the psychological practitioner is based within can also be informed by formulations. They can be used to highlight risk and safeguarding concerns, deepen understanding around what has contributed to such risk factors and help guide fellow professionals to think about multidisciplinary and multiagency approaches to intervention and support.

Sharing a formulation with others becomes important within the context of children's services. There are multiple layers at which psychological work can have an influence that can bring about positive change for a CYP and/or their family. For example, when thinking about a child, the formulation can have an impact on their parents, wider family members, staff at school that are supporting the child, the key social worker, children's practitioner, other specialist workers and managers who are coordinating and making decisions around the case. Formulations can also support families in accessing specific services to meet their needs particularly when they go alongside a diagnostic assessment.

3.6.1 Approaching Formulation

A common structure for developing a formulation used by child psychological practitioners is referred to as the 5Ps model, which incorporates *Presenting, Predisposing, Precipitating, Perpetuating,* and *Protective* factors to help draw together the assessment information. This model was developed in adult cognitive behavioural therapy (CBT) contexts (Padesky, 2020) and would benefit from additional focus on child development and current functioning across the five areas of development for use in a child context. However, the 5Ps framework is widely used and can be a useful first step for child psychological practitioners developing their formulation skills (see Table 3.13).

A word of caution here: the 5Ps framework is only implicitly a psychological formulation. That is, it encourages the practitioner to note psychological risk and protective factors

Table 3.13 The 5Ps model of formulation

The 'P'	Related questions
Presenting difficulties	What is the 'problem'? What has the CYP been referred for? How long has it been going on?
Predisposing factors	What contributed to the development of the current difficulties? Individual/family/contextual factors?
Precipitating factors	What are the triggers to the current presentation?
Perpetuating factors	What is maintaining the difficulties (keeping them going, stopping them from getting better)?
Protective factors	What are the strengths and resilience in the CYP and family? What resources are available? What makes the problems better?

and psychological processes from the assessment information, but it does not explicitly integrate these with psychological theory to develop a full psychological formulation. To develop a fuller formulation, which has more validity and explanatory power, the psychological practitioner must integrate or overlay psychological theory and research evidence onto the 5Ps framework.

There are many psychological theoretical models that practitioners can call upon to do this, many more than can be covered in this chapter and to the depth they deserve. These typically include psychodynamic, attachment, cognitive behavioural, systemic, narrative, solution-focused, integrative and social constructionist approaches. An integrative formulation allows the psychological practitioner to draw upon more than one theoretical model to inform the formulation (for example, incorporating attachment theory, systemic theory and CBT). The principal theoretical models used in psychological formulations in child practice are described later. These brief descriptions should be read in conjunction with Chapter 2, which describes the models and their evidence base in detail.

Psychodynamic: It is important to note that psychodynamic approaches to formulation can be used alone or alongside other approaches to inform and support a broader understanding of a CYP's difficulties. A psychodynamic formulation's central focus is on the importance of unconscious processes within the individual. Depending upon the approach to psychodynamic work, there is an emphasis on attending to transference/counter transference, identifying associations and patterns within relationships. This approach can target common areas of focus such as how particular symptoms or difficulties can arise and how they are maintained (Johnstone & Dallos, 2014). A psychodynamic formulation involves gaining information regarding the client's background, relationships and experiences of trauma. This will require discerning which information to attend to and particular emphasis is placed on the client's past and present relationships (Summers & Martindale, 2018). There is a more generic approach to structure hypotheses formed around the stress-vulnerability model (Zubin, 1977), that identifies predisposing, precipitating and perpetuating factors, and attends to how these different factors connect. Some approaches focus upon underlying vulnerabilities and defences that individuals may have, and other approaches explore factors that raise or lower one's inner psychological security (Thorgaard, 2009). Malan's (1979) triangles specifically focus upon repeating patterns within an individual's relationships. CYP formulations will usually incorporate Attachment Theory (e.g. Bowlby, 1969; Ainsworth, 1978; Ainsworth et al., 1979), hypothesising about the nature and security of the CYP's relationships with their principal caregivers. It can also be used to inform hypotheses about parents' attachment relationships with their own caregivers, and how these might have impacted on the development and maintenance of the current difficulties.

Cognitive behavioural therapy: CBT consists of interventions and techniques that are underpinned by cognitive and behavioural theories rooted in research evidence (Beck, 1995). In formulation, this includes a focus upon learned behaviours and the role of thoughts on how individuals feel and subsequently act. Distorted or dysfunctional thinking is positioned as influencing a person's mood and behaviour, and from this, psychological distress can arise. The model suggests that early life experiences can help develop beliefs about oneself, others and the world. These are termed 'core global beliefs' that are identified as rigid, often over-generalised and give rise to dysfunctional assumptions that generate rules for living, which serve to help the individual cope and function with their core beliefs. Situations that challenge these assumptions and rules for living can give rise to 'negative thoughts and images', which are conscious and go on to influence mood, anxiety and behaviour (Beck, 1995).

The experience of low mood and anxiety can lead to unhelpful behaviours such as avoidance, which prevents challenging unhelpful beliefs and may lead to further low mood. This may also result in a lack of fulfilling and rewarding behaviours that may be supportive of wellbeing and self-confidence (Martell et al., 2010). The experience of low mood and anxiety can also increase unhelpful thoughts. CBT often focuses on how to help break these 'vicious cycles' by learning to challenge unhelpful beliefs, expectations, and unhelpful behaviours (Hawton et al., 1989). Low self-esteem can arise out of experiencing early life events that have implications for ideas about the self and lead to negative conclusions of an individual's worth or value as a person (Fennell, 2009).

Dudley and Kuyken (2018) highlight that the evidence base for CBT is largely the result of research conducted on single disorders, whereas in clinical practice, co-morbidity is often the norm for presenting clients. To address this, they have proposed a principle-based approach to formulation, which differs from the wide range of manuals for specific disorders. This principled approach highlights the importance of combining both the perspective of the practitioner and the client to help form a shared understanding of the development and maintenance of the client's difficulties. Thus, this is a collaborative approach, improving the engagement of the client and increasing the likelihood that they will find the formulation acceptable and pertaining to their lived experience. This includes emphasising not just the client's difficulties but also their strengths to help build resilience. They recommend using the generic 5Ps model of formulation as a framework for connecting an individual's experiences to the cognitive model. Box 3.2 provides an example of using the 5Ps model of formulation.

Systemic approaches: Dallos and Stedmon (2018) highlight that systemic approaches to formulation identify the therapeutic process as interactional and collaborative and regard the formulation as something that is done with the family, as opposed to coming directly from the therapist to the family. This does not seek to be objective, but an active process of asking questions, thinking about the type of questions and way in which they are asked, provides 'moment to moment feedback', bringing about new information that can shape the relationship with the family. Thus, there has been a move within systemic theory from an expert position to a constructivist position (see Chapter 2), acknowledging the subjective nature of knowledge. This approach highlights that individuals within a family may disagree, holding differing understandings and explanations of what is occurring. Vetere and Dallos (2003) summarise a synthesis of approaches to systemic formulation that include deconstruction of the problem, maintaining patterns and feedback loops, beliefs and explanations, emotions and attachments, and contextual factors.

Other systemic approaches to formulation have included Cronen and Pearce (1982), who take a communication perspective that is rooted in social constructionism. In this approach, the actions of people come together to produce patterns, which involve the events and objects of the social world they live in. These events and objects of that social world are constructed by interweaved activities of multiple persons. Attention here is directed by the stories told, and these stories make lives meaningful.

As described in Section 3.2.1 (Assessment), the expanded family life cycle by Carter and McGoldrick (2005), is a key component of assessment and formulation in clinical practice with CYP and families. This identified that social systems, such as families, experience stressors and distress that occur at points where significant and fundamental changes need to be made by the system. Transitions can be points of distress that create destabilising effects within families.

Incorporating narrative therapy (e.g. White & Epston, 1990) to clinical formulations allows the psychological practitioner to separate the 'problem' from the CYP/family ('externalising') and to elicit strengths and alternative hypotheses when making sense of the difficulties with the client.

Box 3.2 Clinical example: Using the 5Ps model of formulation

What is presented here is an example of assessment and formulation in practice, highlighting the stages and sources of assessment, and how the psychological practitioner uses the 5Ps model collaboratively with the family together to make sense of the difficulties together, and to plan an initial approach to treatment.

Referral

Cynthia was referred to CAMHS by her GP when she was eight. Her mother, Julie, had taken her to the GP because she had never slept through the night. The referral was 'triaged' by the CAMHS Intake team, who spoke to Julie on the phone. Julie explained that although Cynthia had never slept well, the situation at home had become intolerable because Julie had gone back to work and Cynthia's younger siblings (twins, aged four) had started school. The difficulties were now impacting on the whole family.

Setting up

The first assessment appointment was arranged by the psychological practitioner the case had been allocated to, Sisa (Black British), over the phone with Julie. Julie said that she would attend with Cynthia, but that Cynthia's father, Patrick, would not be able to join the appointment because he would be at work. Julie requested that the appointment take place during the school day, so that the younger children would be at school. This could be accommodated by Sisa. Julie explained that she had told Cynthia that they needed to go to see someone to help her to sleep like her brother and sister do. Cynthia had been upset and didn't want to come.

Initial Assessment

The first appointment was in the CAMHS clinic in a room that had some toys, including a doll's house. Sisa brought some A3-sized paper and coloured pens. When she collected Cynthia and Julie from the waiting room, Cynthia had been playing with some cars. Sisa suggested that Cynthia could bring the cars with her to the clinic room if she wanted, which she did.

Once in the room, Sisa introduced herself. She asked Cynthia what her mum had told her about coming to the appointment, but Cynthia said that she couldn't remember, and Julie said that it was to get some help so that she could sleep better. Sisa introduced the service and what form the appointment would take and explained about confidentiality (see Section 3.2.1). She also said that lots of children can feel worried about coming to the clinic, and it can feel strange talking to someone that you don't know, but that she wanted to get to know Cynthia and Julie a bit, and that they could also play with the toys and do some drawings, if she wanted. She commented on the cars, and Cynthia said that she had the same cars at home, which she liked to play with, with her brother and sister. Cynthia played with the cars throughout the session, organising them by size and colour.

Sisa asked about who lived at home with Cynthia, and suggested that they draw out the family together, which Cynthia agreed to do. Cynthia chose the colour pens to use for the different people at home.

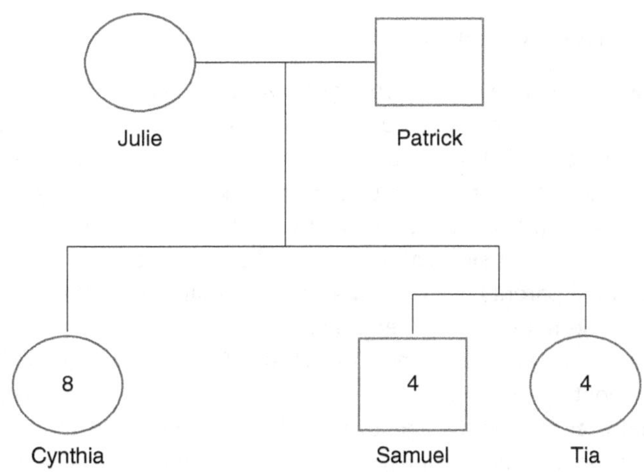

(Continued)

Box 3.2 (Continued)

The reason for the referral

Sisa asked if Cynthia and Julie could explain what had led to Julie going to the GP. Julie said that Cynthia struggles to go off to sleep and one of her parents has to sit in her room for up to an hour whilst she falls asleep, and they then sneak out. If she wakes up during this time the process has to be repeated which can take up to 3 hours a night. She can also wake several times in the night and comes to the parents' bedroom and refuses to go back to her room. Usually, Cynthia's father ends up sleeping in Cynthia's bed and Cynthia sleeps with Julie. Cynthia was quiet whilst Julie was speaking. Julie said quietly to Sisa that it has caused difficulties between the parents, and they have spoken about separating.

Julie said that she has gone back to work recently, and the exhaustion is interfering with her work. Cynthia's siblings sleep well. Cynthia has her own bedroom, and her siblings sleep together in a separate bedroom.

Julie reported that Cynthia has always been a poor and restless sleeper since birth and always struggled to go off to sleep on her own. They have tried many things such as night lights, music, leaving the door open, but nothing has helped. The only time Cynthia sleeps well is when the family go on holiday, and the whole family sleeps in the same room.

Cynthia's difficulties sleeping became more pronounced (she started waking more in the night and refusing to go back to her bed), following the birth of the twins when she was three and a half. Cynthia also started to have nightmares approximately 2 years ago following a house move and after watching the film Toy Story for the first time.

Julie also described Cynthia as having 'meltdowns' that last several hours that can be triggered by her not getting her own way, having her tablet removed from her or can seem to come out of the blue. The tantrums started when she was three but have got more intense and frequent over time.

Current context and family history

Cynthia lives with her parents and younger twin siblings (Samuel and Tia, aged 4). Julie is White British, born in London and Cynthia's father is of Black African (Ghanaian) descent, who came to live in the UK (London) when he was nine to live with an aunt who has since died. Both parents are solicitors, who work full-time. They met at University in London and have remained living in West London in a comfortable three-bedroom house. The family are practising Catholics. They have two cats.

The paternal grandparents live in Ghana, and paternal grandfather suffers with early onset dementia. The family hasn't been back to Ghana to visit the paternal extended family since the twins were born because of the Covid-19 pandemic, and Cynthia's father worries about his parents.

The maternal grandfather died before Cynthia was born and the maternal grandmother has had mobility issues for the past 2 years, since having a heart operation, and is reliant on a wheelchair. Julie has responsibilities helping to support her mother who lives outside London, which takes up a lot of time at weekends.

Cynthia is in Year 3 in the local Catholic primary school, and her siblings have recently started at the same school in the Reception class.

Cynthia's parents had difficulties conceiving and Cynthia and her siblings were born from in vitro fertilisation (IVF). It had been a stressful process for the family with many failed attempts. Her parents were considered older parents as they were both in their 40s when Cynthia was born.

Julie said, although they didn't come from the same backgrounds and their upbringings had been very different, that she and Patrick always used to agree on how to parent the children and they are both very involved in looking after them. She said that things have got more difficult over the past few years, and now they often seem to choose the easiest option to enable them to get as much sleep as possible. Sisa asked if Julie could tell her a bit more about their backgrounds and how they were brought up, and Julie said that her father had been very strict, had smacked her and her sister if they misbehaved and they and their mother had been scared of him. She had always said that she would never be that sort of parent when she had children herself. Going to university had allowed Julie to 'escape' from her father. Julie had always shared a bedroom with her sister, and they had been very close, but her sister has lived in France for 15 years. Patrick had been sent to the UK to get a better education, as he was the only boy in his family. He was very close to the aunt who he lived with when he came to the UK and described her as very gentle. He had had to share a bedroom with his two male cousins, which he hadn't liked because they were unkind to him.

Developmental History

Cynthia was born 7 weeks early and was in a special care baby unit (SCBU) for 2 weeks and was tube fed.

Cynthia met all her developmental milestones with the exception of her speech being slightly delayed. She fed well and there were no concerns, apart from her sleep as an infant – she would fall asleep feeding and was difficult to settle.

Cynthia struggled with separation from her parents when she went to nursery and then to primary school and would cry and refuse to go inside. However once at school she was reported to settle. The teachers report that she struggles with peer relationships and can be dominant over her peers, which some do not like. She also struggles with concentration and is easily distracted. She presents as bright and is considered above average in her academic achievements. At the age of five, Cynthia decided that she did not like her name and has wanted to be known as Ryder. She had an obsession with the TV programme Paw Patrol and her parents felt this was because one of the characters had this name.

Following the first assessment appointment, Sisa discussed the case in supervision, and began to pull together information from the referral and initial appointment into a 5Ps formulation (see Table 3.14).

Following supervision, Sisa contacted Julie and asked if it would be possible to arrange an appointment with both parents without Cynthia, in order to share some

(Continued)

Box 3.2 (Continued)

Table 3.14 Cynthia's 5Ps formulation.

The 'P'	Clinical example	Relevant theoretical models
Presenting difficulties	Sleep difficulties since birth; restless sleep, difficulties falling asleep alone, waking several times in the night and refusing to go back to bed. Temper outbursts that last several hours. Separation anxiety when going to school. Significant impact on parents, family life and child	Attachment theory Behavioural theory
Predisposing factors	Biological: Born via IVF. Premature birth, tube fed, in SCBU. Restless and poor sleep from birth. Delayed speech. Obsessional interests and oddities in wanting to be known as a different name. 'Special' baby as parents struggled to conceive. Parents' experiences of being parented, of how to set boundaries and of sharing a bedroom with siblings. The importance of education in the family. Dominant personality/ emotion regulation difficulties from a young age. Difficulties with attention and easily distracted.	Attachment theory Psychodynamic theory Neuropsychology/ developmental child psychology theories Systemic theory
Precipitating	Birth of siblings. House move. Starting school. Covid-19. Watching film that led to nightmares. Mother returning to work.	Systemic theory Attachment theory
Perpetuating factors	Parents relationship difficulties. Parent's exhaustion, need to work and have caring responsibilities. Responses of parents reinforcing the behaviour (e.g. letting Cynthia sleep in their bed, giving in to Cynthia's demands e.g. over the tablet).	Behaviour theory Systemic theory
Protective/ Positive Factors	Cynthia's intelligence. Good relationships with her siblings. Can be caring towards others and pets. High socioeconomic status. Wanted and loved children. There have been times when she has slept well. Parental shared faith and values Church community support.	Attachment theory/ Resiliency theory Systemic theory Solution-focused/ Narrative theory

of her ideas about the difficulties. They were able to arrange a 5.00 pm appointment, and the parents organised for the children to be at friends' houses.

At that appointment, Sisa started to draw out the start of the 5Ps formulation, highlighting the strengths (Protective factors) in the family and in Cynthia. It seemed to make sense to the parents that things had got harder over the past few years since the birth of the twins, the pandemic and worries about their parents. They wondered how much Cynthia had felt excluded, and that those external pressures had made it more difficult to give her attention on her own, and to agree a coordinated approach to managing Cynthia's sleep difficulties and tantrums. But they also started to think that having the twins had made them notice that Cynthia had always seemed different, and that even when they hadn't had so much else going on, she had been difficult. They talked about the high energy levels that Cynthia had always had (always 'on the go', no 'down time'). They also talked about her not liking noisy environments and finding it very difficult when the twins cried when they were smaller. Sisa added this information to the formulation.

Sisa did some further reading informed by Behavioural theories about the importance of sleep routines in establishing consistent boundaries at bedtime and establishing sleep cues. She discussed these in supervision and her supervisor suggested she also return to some of the neurodevelopmental models that had been introduced to her – so Sisa looked over some common checklists for ADHD and Autism symptoms in order that she was familiar enough to notice any signs of neurodivergence for Cynthia.

Together, the parents and Sisa agreed that it would be helpful to do some work on consistent parenting approaches to try to improve the sleep difficulties and respond to the tantrums, as they felt that these were the most pressing problems. But at the same time, Sisa would arrange for a different practitioner (who hadn't already met Cynthia) to carry out an observation of Cynthia at her school to look at possible features of neurodivergence (Autism and/or Attention Deficit and Hyperactivity Disorder) because of the descriptions of difficult relationships with her peers and possible difficulties with concentration and energy levels (see Chapter 19). Sisa also gave the parents and the school some screening questionnaires that looked specifically at ADHD and social communication difficulties, as well as a sensory processing questionnaire. The parents and Sisa agreed that, even (or maybe especially) if there were an underlying neurodivergence, they wanted to work on how they support and parent Cynthia and to try to get back to working more closely together.

3.7 Conclusion

This chapter has discussed the importance of taking a broad developmental approach to the assessment and formulation of mental health difficulties of children and young people, considering the multiple contexts in which they exist and the developmental stage of the family and its other members, as well as of the individual. In CYPMH services, assessment and formulation should be fluid, dynamic processes that will be modified as the treatment progresses, as more information becomes available to the psychological practitioner and the family. The formulation can be used as an active ingredient of the therapeutic process, increasing collaboration, the sense of clients' voices being actively heard, and ultimately, engagement in therapy.

References

Ainsworth, M. D. S. (1979). Attachment as related to mother-infant interaction. In J. S. Rosenblatt, R. A. Hinde, C. Beer, & M-C. Busnel (Eds.), *Advances in the study of behavior* (Vol. *9*, pp. 1–51). Academic Press.

Ainsworth, M. D. S., Blehar, M. C., Walters, E., & Wall, S. (1978). *Patterns of attachment: A psychological study of the Strange Situation.* Psychology Press.

American Psychiatric Association. (2013). *Diagnostic and statistical manual of mental disorders* (5th ed.). https://doi.org/10.1176/appi.books.9780890425596.

Bandura, A. (1977). *Social learning theory.* Prentice Hall.

Bayley, N., & Aylward, G.P. (2019). *Bayley Scales of Infant and Toddler Development – fourth version (Bayley4).* Pearson.

Bedford, H., Walton, S., & Ahn, J. (2013, June). Measures of child development: A review. Policy Research Unit in the Health of Children, Young People and Families, Centre for Paediatric Epidemiology and Biostatistics, UCL Institute of Child Health. https://discovery.ucl.ac.uk/id/eprint/1521166/1/Bedford_Measures_Child_Development.pdf.

Beck, J. S. (1995). *Cognitive therapy: Basics and beyond.* Guilford Press.

Boggs, D., Milner, K. M., Chandna, J., Black, M., Cavallera, V., Dua, T., Fink, G., Ashish, K. C., Grantham, S., Hamadani, J., Hughes, R., Mani, K., McCoy, D.C., Tann, C., & Lawn, J. E. (2019). Rating early child development outcome measurement tools for routine health programme use. *Archives of Disease in Childhood, 104*, S22–S33.

Bowlby, J. (1969). *Attachment and loss*, Vol. *1. Attachment.* Hogarth Press and the Institute of Psycho-Analysis.

Bronfenbrenner, U. (1974). Developmental research, public policy, and the ecology of childhood. *Child Development*, *45*(1), 1–5. https://doi.org/10.2307/1127743.

Burnham, J. B. (2002). *Family therapy: First steps towards a systemic approach.* Routledge.

Burnham, J. (2012). Developments in the Social GGRRAAACCEEESSS: Visible-invisible and voiced-unvoiced. In I. Krause (Ed.), *Culture and reflexivity in systemic psychotherapy: Mutual perspectives* (pp.139–160). Karnac.

Carter, B., & McGoldrick, M. (1989). *The changing family life cycle: A framework for family therapy* (2nd ed.). Gardner.

Carter, B., & McGoldrick, M. (2005). Overview: The expanded family life cycle. Individual, family and social perspectives. In B. Carter & M.Goldrick, (Eds.), *The expanded family life cycle* (3rd ed., pp. 1–24). Pearson.

Carter, E., & McGoldrick, M. (Eds.). (2006). *The expanded family life cycle: Individual, family, and social perspectives.* Allyn and Bacon.

Chege, C. N., Fu, M., Bustrum, J. M., & Jenks, E. H. (2022). The Worldview Genogram: A process model for enhancing diversity responsiveness and competence in education, training, and clinical supervision. Psychological Services. Advance online publication. https://doi.org/10.1037/ser0000719.

Cronen, V. E., & Pearce, W. B. (1982). The communication of meaning in family systems. *Family Process, 21*(2), 137–148.

Dallos, R., & Stedmon, J. (2018). Formulation in practice. In l. Johnstone, & R. Dallos (Eds.), *Formulation in psychology and psychotherapy: Making sense of people's problems* (2nd ed., pp. 31–48). Routledge.

Division of Clinical Psychology. (2011). *Good practice guidelines on the use of psychological formulation.* British Psychological Society.

Dudley, R., & Kuyken, W. (2018). Formulation in cognitive-behaviour therapy: A relational approach. In J. Johnstone & J. Dallos (Eds.), *Formulation in psychology and psychotherapy: Making sense of people's problems* (2nd ed., pp. 147–160). Routledge.

Eells, T. D. (Ed.). (1997). *Handbook of psychotherapy case formulation.* Guilford Press.

Erikson, E. (1959). Identity and the life cycle: Selected papers. *Psychological Issues, 1*(1), 1–171.

Fennell, M. J. V. (2009). *Depression, anxiety, and cognitive therapy: A practitioner's guide.* John Wiley & Sons.

Freeman, J. C., Epston, D., & Lobovits, D. (1997). *Playful approaches to serious problems: Narrative therapy with children and their families.* W. W. Norton & Co.

Freud, S. (1905). *Three contributions to the theory of sex.* The Standard Edition of the Complete Psychological Works of Sigmund Freud, Vol. VII, 7–63.

Hawton, K., Salkovskis, P. M., Kirk, J., & Clark, D. M. (Eds.). (1989). *Cognitive behaviour therapy for psychiatric problems: A practical guide.* Oxford University Press.

Johnstone, L., & Dallos, R. (2014). *Formulation in psychology and psychotherapy: Making sense of people's problems.* American Psychological Association.

Malan, D. (1979). *Individual psychotherapy and the science of psychodynamics.* Butterworth.

Martell, C. R., Dimidjian, S., & Herman-Dunn, R. (2010). *Behavioural activation for depression: A clinician's guide.* Guilford Press.

Munoz Chereau, B., Ang, L., Outhwaite, L., Dockrell, J., & Heffernan, C. (2021). Measuring early child development across low and middle-income countries: A systematic review. *Journal of Early Childhood Research, 19*(4), 443–470.

Padesky, C. A. (2020). Collaborative case conceptualization: Client knows best. *Cognitive and Behavioral Practice, 27*(4), 392–404. https://doi.org/10.1016/j.cbpra.2020.06.003.

Palazzoli, M.S., Boscolo, L., Cecchin, G., & Prata, G. (1980). The problem of the referring person. *Journal of Marital and Family Therapy, 6*, 3–9. https://doi.org/10.1111/j.1752-0606.1980.tb01699.x.

Piaget, J. (1952). *The origins of intelligence in children.* International Universities Press.

Piaget, J. (1954). *The construction of reality in the child.* Basic Books.

Reder, R., & Fredman, G. (1996). The relationship to help: interacting beliefs about the treatment process. *Clinical Child Psychology and Psychiatry, 1*(3), 457–467.

Shellenberger, S., Dent, M. M., Davis-Smith, M., Seale, J. P., Weintraut, R., & Wright, T. (2007). Cultural genogram: A tool for teaching and practice. *Families, Systems, & Health, 25*(4), 367–381. https://doi.org/10.1037/1091-7527.25.4.367.

Skinner, B. F. (1938). *The behaviour of organisms: An experimental analysis.* Appelton-Century.

Stubbing, J., & Gibson, K. (2022). What young people want from clinicians: Youth-informed clinical practice in mental health care. *Youth, 2*(4), 538–555. https://doi.org/10.3390/youth2040039.

Summers, A., & Martindale, B. (2013). Using psychodynamic principles in formulation in everyday practice. *Advances in Psychiatric Treatment, 19*(3), 203–211.

Thorgaard, M. V. (2009). Understanding psychosis. In P. M. Westen, & J. D. Morrison (Eds.). *A handbook for the assessment of children and adolescents with psychotic and mood disorders* (pp. 1–22). Guilford Press.

Vetere, A., & Dallos, R. (2003). *Working systemically with families: Formulation, intervention and evaluation.* Karnac Books.

Vygotsky, L. S. (1978). *Mind in society: The development of higher psychological processes.* Harvard University Press.

Watson, J. B. (1913). Psychology as the behaviourist views it. *Psychological Review, 20*(2), 158–177.

White, M., & Epston, D. (1990). *Narrative means to therapeutic ends.* Norton.

Wolpert, M., Harris, R., Jones, M., Hodges, S., Fuggle, P., James, R., Wiener, A., Mckenna, C., Law, D., & Fonagy, P. (2014). THRIVE: The AFC-Tavistock model for CAMHS. CAMHS.

World Health Organization. (2023). Global scales for early development (GSED) v1.0 https://www.who.int/publications/i/item/WHO-MSD-GSED-package-v1.0-2023.1

Yap, M., Reavley, N., & Jorm, A. F. (2013). Where would young people seek help for mental disorders and what stops them? Findings from an Australian national survey. *Journal of Affective Disorders, 147*(1–3), 255–261. https://doi.org/10.1016/j.jad.2012.11.014

Yap, M., Wright, A., & Jorm, A. (2011). The influence of stigma on young people's help-seeking intentions and beliefs about the helpfulness of various sources of help. *Social Psychiatry and Psychiatric Epidemiology, 46*(12), 1257–1265.

Zubin, J. (1977). Vulnerability: A new view of schizophrenia. In L. Wynne, R. L. Cromwell, & S. Matthysse (Eds.), *The nature of schizophrenia: New approaches to research and treatment* (pp. 47–53). Wiley-Interscience.

4

Supervision and Self-reflection

Helen Pote, Anna Picciotto and Clare Norris

4.1 Introduction

How do we develop the skills to be an effective psychological practitioner? Early research in a variety of health and business workplaces determined that practice skills development comes through the mutual interaction of three elements – confidence, challenge and support (Eraut et al., 2001). Through training, the psychological practitioner should develop both their clinical competence and clinical confidence. These constructs are related but quite distinct. Clinical competence in applied psychology can be defined as 'the judicious application of communication, knowledge, technical skills, clinical reasoning, emotions, values, and contextual understanding for the benefit of the individual [...] being served' (Barber et al., 2007, p. 494). Distinctly, clinical confidence is the self-perceived ability to deal with clinical scenarios and is a prerequisite for the practitioner to be able to fully participate in clinical activities, take helpful risks with their clinical development and ultimately grow into an experienced and fulfilled practitioner.

In applied psychology practice supervision has been key in bringing these elements together for novice and experienced practitioners – this enables the development of sound clinical judgement, which ensures safe and effective practice. Good-quality initial training and supervision is important in developing psychologists' confidence, but continuing professional development, post-qualification supervision and participating in personal therapy have also been identified by psychologists as important in developing their clinical confidence (McMahon & Hevey, 2015).

Most research on the development of clinical skills and confidence comes from the fields of nursing and medical training. For example, Dornan et al. (2006), interviewed medical students and found that, to reach their ultimate goal of helping patients, they must develop two mutually reinforcing qualities; one is practical competence; the other is a state of mind that includes confidence, motivation and a sense of professional identity. These two qualities were clearly enhanced by practical experience in the health workplace, as long as this experience went beyond passive observations and involved students in active participation in practice, with clear learning objectives, working with supervisors who were both supportive and challenging. The key message from medical settings is that for

Child Psychology: Pathways to Good Practice, First Edition.
Edited by Helen Pote, Anna Picciotto and Clare Norris.

practice skills and confidence to develop, learners must be in a safe, supportive learning relationship but importantly this relationship and the placement learning environment must require action and provide challenge in order for the learner to extend their skills by taking risks with their own learning.

This chapter will explore the development of clinical competences and confidence and how these are supported through the supervision process. It will define supervision and discuss its importance before detailing a range of useful supervision models for working with young people and their families. It will consider self-reflective skills considered necessary for professional practice. Throughout, it will discuss how both supervision and self-reflection might contribute to the development of the psychological practitioner's clinical judgement and confidence over their career.

4.2 Supervision – definition

Many definitions of supervision have been offered in the field of applied psychology, but all contain elements that emphasise the development of personal-professional learning through a supportive relationship, the safety and wellbeing of the client, the evaluative nature of the relationship and the professional gatekeeping role, especially when working with novice practitioners (Hughes & Youngson, 2009; Scaife, 2019).

The British Psychological Society (BPS) uses the definition of supervision developed by Derek Milne. He defines supervision as 'the formal provision, by approved supervisors, of a relationship-based education and training that is case-focused and which manages, supports, develops and evaluates the work of junior colleagues' (Milne, 2007, p. 3). This is incorporated in the supervision policy of the Division of Clinical Psychology (BPS, 2014).

Pilling and Roth have developed a framework for supervision competences for psychological practitioners and offer a detailed definition of its components (Pilling & Roth, 2014). They understand supervision as:

> a formal but collaborative relationship which takes place in an organisational context, which is part of the overall training of practitioners, and which is guided by some form of contract between a supervisor and a supervisee. The expectation is that the supervisee offers an honest and open account of their work, and that the supervisor offers feedback and guidance which has the primary aim of facilitating the development of the supervisee's therapeutic competences, but also ensures that they practice in a manner which conforms to current ethical and professional standards.
>
> (Roth & Pilling, 2008, p. 4)

This overarching framework of supervision is complemented by theory specific supervision models (e.g. CBT, Systemic), which are discussed later in this chapter.

Professional governance is critical in supervision. The supervisor is required to have 'super-vision' – looking out for both the training needs of the supervisee and the clinical needs of their clients and ensuring clients get the best possible service to address their difficulties. This 'super-vision' is not an easy task to achieve and importantly, it is a relational task that relies on the establishment of a safe and trusting professional learning relationship between supervisor and supervisee. When established, a positive supervision relationship enables:

- acquisition of psychological knowledge and ability to apply this to practice;
- development of clinical skills and techniques;
- observation of clinical practice (of supervisor and supervisee);
- self-reflection and personal-professional development;
- growth in supervisee clinical confidence;
- monitoring of safe and ethical practice – meeting the standards for the profession and clinical service; and
- effective evaluation of skills and professional gatekeeping.

The supervision relationship is reciprocal, both supervisor and supervisee should be learning through the process of supervision, remaining open to observations, feedback and reflections on their practice, which aid continuous professional development. Learning through supervision is a lifelong activity and not something reserved for the novice practitioner.

Clinical supervision is one of the common professional activities performed by psychological practitioners but often it comes without a great deal of preparatory training. Registration of psychological supervisors is varied through national professional or registration bodies, often with no official registration requirement. This is surprising give the critical role supervision plays in the training and registration of psychological practitioners.

Supervision supports both practitioners and their clients; ensuring safe and effective psychological assessments and interventions that are delivered in line with professional and service standards and values. These are its primary aims, but supervision is also seen as critical in developing confidence in psychological practice.

Only through supervisory discussion of developing skills can the novice child psychological practitioner begin to make connections between their own questions and actions, joining the theoretical and scientific models they are learning with the empathic insights they are feeling, as they hear the psychological distress of young people and families. In essence, supervision helps practitioners connect theory to their behaviours, thoughts and emotions in order to respond professionally and helpfully to their clients. This supervisory process also enables the novice psychological practitioner to develop self-reflective skills that allow them to practice more independently and confidently, eventually making those connections between theory and practice on their own, in the absence of the supervisor.

4.3 Supervision Standards and Safe Practice

Having regular, protected supervision time, based on clear contracted goals is a usual expectation for child psychological practitioners. For pre-registration training 1–2 hours a week of formal supervision contact time is the norm set out by most psychological professional bodies for a full-time practitioner.

Child psychological practitioners are required to adhere to the professional codes of conduct and ethics from their professional or registration body, including guidelines about supervision. This guidance should be read alongside this chapter and, depending on the specific psychological profession, is likely to be issued by the British Psychological Society,

Health and Care Professions Council, the British Association of Behavioural and Cognitive Psychotherapies or the United Kingdom Council for Psychotherapy. These policies and guidance will outline:

- supervision hours required,
- supervisor and supervisee responsibilities,
- supervision competencies required,
- ethical and conduct standards, and
- conferred professional role titles to use.

Examples of professional standards include the following, but readers should consult their professional body website for additional relevant guidance:

- British Psychological Society (2014) Division of Clinical Psychology, Guidelines on Clinical Supervision, Leicester, BPS.
- British Psychological Society (2017) Professional Practice Guidelines. Leicester, BPS.
- British Psychological Society (2018) Code of Ethics and Conduct. Leicester, BPS.
- Health & Care Professions Council (2016) Guidance on Conduct and Ethics for Students. London: HCPC.
- Health & Care Professions Council (2016) Standards of Conduct, Performance & Ethics. London: HCPC.
- British Association of Behavioural and Cognitive Psychotherapy (n.d.), Supervision Guidance https://babcp.com/Supervision-Guidance
- British Association of Behavioural and Cognitive Psychotherapy (n.d.), Standards of Conduct, Performance and Ethics https://babcp.com/About/Governance-and-Policy/Policies-and-Documents/BABCP-Standards-of-Conduct-Performance-and-Ethics

When involved in supervision, the responsibilities of the supervisee at all stages of training and practice, include:

- *Consent:* Inform clients that practice is supervised. Explain the purpose of this and that the limits of confidentiality will include discussion with the supervisor.
- *Preparation:* Prepare items for an agenda and share in advance of the supervision meeting if possible. Make sure that clinical information to present at supervision is collated so it can be shared efficiently. Setting and sticking to an agenda is important and each supervisor/supervisee will have their own preference for agenda content. Some of the key agenda items are outlined in the sample supervision record in Box 4.1.
- *Open Communication* Share clinical information and information about clinical practice and performance in an open manner. For psychological practitioners in training, clinical responsibility is shared between the supervisor and supervisee, but this is only the case if supervisees have shared clinical information that would enable the supervisor to be able to make a sound clinical judgement. Withholding clinical information is not in the best interests of the client or the supervisee, so being open is important, particularly if the supervisee has faced personal or clinical challenges, is concerned they have not met best practice standards or have made a clinical error. Making mistakes is a normal part of learning.
- *Reflection* Be prepared to engage in reflective conversations and self-reflection. This will include personal conversations to enhance self-awareness of one's attitudes, feelings,

assumptions and biases (conscious and unconscious), which will be influencing the clinical work. In turn, the clinical work will reciprocally influence the practitioner's position and they should monitor how the work is impacting them.

- *Responsiveness* Respond to feedback and guidance from the supervisor, actioning decisions promptly and communicating the outcomes clearly to the supervisor.
- *Recording* Make sure actions arising from supervision are recorded and agreed with the supervisor and entered into the clinical record, in accordance with service protocols and guidance.

Box 4.1 Sample supervision record

Psychology Supervision Record

Date:
Name of Supervisor:
Name of Supervisee:
Clinical Team:
Agreed Agenda:

1. Clinical – e.g. clients to discuss, outcome tracking to note
2. Reflection – e.g. noting relational reflections and sociocultural factors
3. Information sharing – e.g. team and organisational information, life events
4. Theory and evidence – e.g. useful references and upcoming training events
5. Learning goals – e.g. identify any competence areas for development for the supervisee
6. Supervision process – e.g. review of any supervision issues, relational or procedural
7. Summary of agreed actions

Action and discussion recording:

Clinical case /Clinical issue (anonymised)	Discussion themes/ideas	Actions agreed

Signed: **J. Bloggs** (supervisee) **A. Person** (supervisor)

One important feature of well-conducted supervision is clear written recording of goals and actions agreed. This protects both the supervisor and supervisee; ensuring they are sharing clinical responsibilities and executing their supervision duties appropriately. Like clinical notes, supervision notes should clearly distinguish fact and agreed action from opinion and ideas discussed (see Box 4.1). A note in the client's clinical record of any agreed actions in supervision about their clinical care should also be made as soon as possible after supervision.

Risk management and reporting is a crucial responsibility within supervision. All child psychological practitioners (pre-registration and qualified) must discuss risk management in supervision and make sure they are familiar with local risk procedures within their employing organisation. The practitioner should raise any client or staff risk issues with their supervisor as soon as possible and record the discussion and any outcomes in the clinical and supervision notes with speed and accuracy.

Risk management will also include keeping oneself safe as a practitioner. Relevant lone working and safety in the workplace guidelines should be consulted as well as policies on bullying and harassment. Part of keeping oneself safe as a practitioner is attending to self-care. Recently, the levels of stress and burnout within the psychological workforce has been recognised alongside the need for compassionate, supportive supervision and management to aid psychological practitioners in the workplace. Experience of mental health problems within the profession are common, as they are in all communities. Encouraging practitioners to disclose any current difficulties with their own mental health is particularly important within the supervisory relationship. Supervision is a resource for all practitioners, enriching their empathy and clinical skills in many ways but it is important that practitioners with mental health problems receive support within the supervision relationship in order that they can recognise any signs of increasing distress that may compromise their fitness to practice.

Compassionate management is an empathic approach to supervision and management that should: provide opportunities for self-care; ensure regular check-ins with staff; allow flexibility in scheduling and working practices; and offer training and other resources that can prevent burnout (West, 2021). Such an approach encourages supervisees (and supervisors) to raise personal stressors, life events and mental health difficulties in order that they can have reflective conversations about the impact of the work upon them and receive appropriate support. Many psychological practitioners may fear the stigma such disclosure might bring (Tay et al., 2018) so it is important that supervisors support a non-judgemental approach to discussing lived experience of mental health problems for supervisees (Scior et al., 2020).

4.4 Effective Supervision

So, is there evidence that supervision actually helps this process of connecting theory to practice and supports positive client outcomes, practitioner skills, confidence and self-reflection? What is the mechanism of change underpinning supervision that leads to effective outcomes for supervisees and clients? Milne (2009; Milne & Reiser, 2012) has explored these questions within clinical psychology and focused on the important role of the learning alliance in supervision in order for it to be effective. Milne developed evidence-based clinical supervision (EBCS) guidelines through systematic reviews of the supervision evidence and expert consensus. These guidelines outlined four key elements of effective supervision, which align to Kolb's learning cycle (Kolb, 1984) and emphasise experiential learning for the supervisee.

1. Educational needs assessment: defining relevant competencies to establish a learning contract.
2. Goal-setting: problem solving and setting supervision session agendas to address the needs outlined in the learning contract.
3. Supervision methods: Supervisor–supervisee learning alliance and supervisors' judgements about how to address clinical issues and enable the supervisee learning – for example by demonstrating a therapeutic technique.
4. Evaluation: monitoring processes and outcomes for supervisees (clinical competencies) and clients (psychological functioning) using feedback and standardised measures.

4.4.1 Measuring Supervision Process and Outcomes

The effectiveness of supervision has been measured in a variety of ways (e.g. observational ratings and self-report) using multiple informants (e.g. supervisor, supervisee and client). Supervision success has been judged using client variables (did they recover and were they satisfied with the practitioner?), therapist competence (knowledge and skills) as well as the quality of the supervisory alliance. A sample of measures that might be helpful to practitioners in child contexts are discussed later.

In using all of these scales, the practitioner needs to carefully consider issues of consent for the young person (Care Quality Commission (CQC), 2019). Many of the scales require video recordings of practice and this may be considered not to be in the best interests of the child or of direct clinical benefit to them. Young people should be consulted, and consent sought for recordings and use of measures. The practitioner needs to explain in simple terms how these recordings might improve the quality of the work that they are completing together with the young person. See Chapter 5, for further information on capacity and consent seeking with young people.

4.4.2 Observational Tools to Measure Practitioner Competence

These are often used in supervision to guide assessment of and feedback on the supervisee's skill development. Some tools are generic and others dependent on the therapeutic model being used by the practitioner. The University College London website offers a suite of competence frameworks and measurement tools that are helpful for novice practitioners in mapping their skills and setting learning targets within supervision (https://www.ucl.ac.uk/pals/research/clinical-educational-and-health-psychology/research-groups/competence-frameworks).

A common tool used to measure CBT practitioner competence is the Cognitive Therapy Rating Scale-Revised (CTS-R) originally developed by Beck and colleagues in the United States and revised by Blackburn et al. (2001). The scale is very commonly used in adult psychological practice but its reliability and validity were questioned for CBT offered to young people. This led to the development of the Cognitive Behaviour Therapy Scale for Children and Young People (CBTS-CYP) (Stallard et al., 2014). They found high face reliability and internal validity of the CBTS-CYP using a sample of 61 child CBT practitioners and, when compared to the CTS-R, found good convergent validity. However, the CBTS-CYP has not been validated further than this small sample and, as the authors note, requires further validation with younger children. Items on the scale include behavioural experiments, cognitive challenging and reframing.

The Systemic Practice Scale (SPS) is a tool commonly used in children's services to evaluate practitioner systemic competencies. Developed by Butler and colleagues (2018), the scale mimics the CTS-R structure, but focuses on relational skills such as circular questions and use of reflecting teams. Its use has been qualitatively evaluated in practice by supervisors and supervisees and has been found to be a useful measure of systemic competence if used collaboratively (Parker et al., 2021).

4.4.3 Client Feedback

The supervision process can be improved by incorporating feedback from clients. This might include self-ratings of their clinical symptoms and their experience of clinical sessions. Supervisors should use this feedback from young people and families to support improvements in their supervisee's practice. Collaborative partnership working has become an increasing focus of child psychological practice in the past 10 years. Young people are asked for their feedback at all stages of the therapeutic process. Organisations also routinely ask for feedback from young people to inform service planning and quality improvements.

Toolkits to enable practitioners to increase participation from young people and seek their feedback in meaningful ways has been developed (e.g. CAMHS Outcome Research Consortium (CORC) Outcome and Experience Resources https://www.corc.uk.net/outcome-experience-measures). Brief measures included there such as the Session Rating Scale and Session Feedback Questionnaire offer simple visual analogue scales for young people to provide feedback on therapeutic engagement and whether practitioners are demonstrating core listening and engagement skills with young people. Psychological practitioners are encouraged to bring such session-by-session ratings and client-outcome monitoring measures to supervision to add to the clinical discussion (see Chapter 8 and Chapter 9, for further discussion and detail of measures available).

4.4.4 Measuring Supervision Quality and the Supervisory Alliance

Measuring supervision quality and the supervisory alliance and considering its impact in developing the supervisee's clinical skills has become an increasing focus of effective supervision models. Milne and Reiser (2011) developed an observational instrument for describing 23 supervisor and supervisee behaviours that are critical to effective supervision – the Supervision Adherence and Guidance Evaluation (SAGE). This tool has three dimensions and may be useful to supervisees and supervisors in developing and monitoring their relationship:

- The common factors (non-specific factors underlying effective supervision and psychotherapy).
- The supervision cycle (specific supervisors' behaviours that are believed to facilitate optimal learning).
- The supervisee's learning (specific areas of learning that are impacted by the previous two points).

4.4.5 Clinical Simulations

Clinical simulations to support supervision and competence have recently come to the fore, with some emerging evidence that clinical simulation-based education may be helpful in developing clinical psychology competence and confidence. These methods require novice psychological practitioners to interact with actors whilst being observed and measuring their clinical competence. Sessions are often video recorded, and this allows for an abundance of rich performance feedback to be shared with the student. A small mixed-methods study by Sheen et al. (2021) demonstrated that these clinical simulations might be helpful in improving competences measured using standard scales (e.g. CTS-R) but did not demonstrate that they were more effective than traditional case-based discussions. Students preferred the simulation-based approach and were more confident that their skills would transfer to real world settings than when they simply had case-based education. Further research in this area is warranted.

For medical practitioners, digital clinical simulations have been developed using extended reality (virtual and augmented reality (VR/AR)) to enable practitioners to practice their skills repeatedly and receive detailed feedback without the costs of live simulation using actors and with no risk of harm to the client. Emerging evidence suggests that in specific contexts, such as surgical training, virtual methods can be superior to standard training methods in developing surgical competences (Mao et al., 2021). Application of these digital simulations of client and practitioner within psychological practice is just emerging, and includes the integration of artificial intelligence. This is an area for future ethical consideration and outcome research (Fiske et al., 2019).

4.5 Useful Supervision and Learning Models for Child Psychological Practice

As supervision grew within clinical practice so did theoretical approaches to understanding and guiding the supervision process. These models fall into two broad camps: developmental or integrated models and orientation-specific therapy models. Both are considered briefly in this section with references to signpost readers who wish to explore these models further.

4.5.1 Developmental and Integrated Models

These models focus on the learning stages and supervisory support required to move the practitioner from novice to experienced clinical practice. These approaches to supervision underpin development of various types of professional activity not just psychological practice; focusing on cognitive and emotional factors (e.g. self-awareness), motivation and autonomy and how these change over time (see Stoltenberg et al., 1998). For the novice psychological practitioner, each of these factors is proposed to progress through three different levels as clinical expertise is developed and must span a variety of domains such as assessment and client conceptualisation. These models also detail different tasks for supervisors at each development level, progressing from providing didactic learning opportunities, structure and containment of anxiety to later encouragement of autonomy and finally facilitating personal-professional integration across all the domains of practice. These developmental models are rather normative and have received mixed support from research into the process of supervision and skills development, but they are intuitively helpful in emphasising both supervisee and supervisor roles in the learning process over time.

4.5.2 Competence Models

These models describe the competencies common to supervision of psychological therapies across all therapeutic modalities, some are general whilst others pay attention to the specific competences related to therapeutic modalities such as CBT, systemic and psychodynamic supervision. Roth and Pilling (2008) developed a popular general competence model for supervision, which has been influential in supervision training in applied psychology and used across children and young people talking therapies training. The model can be viewed at: https://www.ucl.ac.uk/pals/research/clinical-educational-and-health-psychology/research-groups/core/competence-frameworks-8.

It describes generic competences required for all supervisors, such as the skills in forming and maintaining the supervisory alliance, so is also useful to supervisees in considering what skills will help them to make the most of supervision. Similar general supervision competence models have been produced internationally for example in the United States and Australia (Falender et al., 2004). The focus of these generic models on measuring practitioner competences and integrating review of client goals and measurement of client psychological outcomes into the supervision conversations has been particularly important for enhancing evidenced based practice. For a more detailed discussion see Chapter 8.

4.5.3 The Seven-eyed Supervision Model

The seven-eyed supervision model is a helpful one in child services, it draws on systemic, psychoanalytic, cognitive-behavioural and humanistic models as well as learning theory. Developed initially by Peter Hawkins and adapted by Robin Shohet for use in the helping professions this model is reflective and encourages culturally sensitive practice (Hawkins & Shohet, 2012) and it has been developed further (Hawkins & McMahon, 2020). It draws on two connected systems; the client work system (the client, supervisee interventions and the supervisee–client alliance) and the supervisory system (supervisor, supervisee and supervisory alliance) and sets these within broader layers of context. The seven-eyed model describes seven modes (or foci), which it encourages the supervisor and supervisee to pay attention to: the client; the interventions used; the therapeutic relationship; the supervisee; the supervisory alliance; the supervisor; and the wider context. By reflecting on each mode, the supervisor and supervisee can understand the areas for skills development and the impact of the supervisee/supervisor on the work and the work on each of them. In practice, a study on group supervision showed high levels of attention were paid to client and supervisee actions alongside discussion of the wider context, but less attention was given to the therapeutic alliance, supervisory alliance and the supervisor's role (Lawrence, 2019). Observational research on its use with health practitioners in youth mental health settings (including clinical psychologists) demonstrated the model's value in identifying areas of supervisee practice that required further development (McMahon et al., 2022). Attention to the wider contextual factors is critical in this model and it often makes use of Burnham's social graces model in achieving this. See Chapter 7 for further information.

4.5.4 Cognitive Behavioural Supervision Model

CBT supervision models are also prominent in child psychology practice. Friedberg (2018) notes the importance of supervision as a method of quality control, supporting psychological practitioners delivering CBT to maintain model fidelity. He reports that self-report by practitioners that they are delivering CBT is clearly not supported by observational studies. Friedberg outlines important components of effective CBT supervision:

> core elements embedded in good supervision of CBT with young people, including training in case conceptualisation, ethical and legal alertness, multicultural responsiveness, employing collaborative empiricism and guided discovery, measurement-based care, technical proficiency, as well as addressing trainees' beliefs about the clinical work.
>
> (Friedberg, 2018, p. 2)

The CBT supervision model emphasises the importance of a supportive, authentic supervisory alliance and encourages the use of audio and video recordings as well as didactic instruction, Socratic methods, and practising and modelling therapy behaviour to enhance supervisee cognitive behavioural competence development (Milne, 2017).

4.5.5 Systemic Reflective Supervision Models

Systemic models of supervision that consider relational and reflective aspects of practice and apply these to the supervision relationship are very helpful in child practice contexts. These supervision models have often been delivered in a live way, with observations of the primary therapist by a supervisor and systemic team. The models lend themselves to an interpersonal understanding of the multiple layers of context related to a young person's presenting issue and supervision often privileges the self of the therapist and attends to cultural issues and power in more detail than other models (Daniel & Burck, 2010). For a more detailed discussion of systemic supervision internationally see the special edition of the *Journal of Family Psychotherapy* (Northey & Rivett, 2020). Sherbersky and colleagues (2021) have considered digital practice and noted that the range of systemic supervision contexts delivered in-person are all possible online but there is a need for additional attention to the supervisory alliance to support learner containment in the delivery of digital supervision. Adapting all of the supervision models detailed in this chapter for online delivery is an important area for future debate and research (see Chapter 24 for further discussion).

Reflecting team models have long been used in systemic therapy with clients and these can also be helpfully applied to supervision (Reichelt & Skjerve, 2013). Consider the following exercise, which can be used in group peer supervision (small groups of four to five practitioners) based on the reflecting team format. It aims to introduce new perspectives and circular descriptions of issues that practitioners feel stuck in their clinical work (see Box 4.2).

Box 4.2 Reflecting team supervision exercise
Step One: One person (the supervisee) in the group identifies a clinical case they feel stuck with and writes down their understanding of the problem. **Step Two**: Another person (the supervisor) acts as the interviewer asking the supervisee about the situation. Encourage them to describe situation: What do they feel stuck with and why? What have they done to get unstuck? What contextual factors in their workplace are keeping them stuck? and so forth. It is important for this conversation to focus on the 'stuckness' of the practitioner and not the clients' difficulties per se. Whilst this conversation is happening the other members of the group (the reflectors) just listen and don't engage in the conversation in any way. **Step Three**: The reflectors then have a conversation in front of the supervisor and supervisee offering their understanding/hypotheses about the 'stuckness' for 5 minutes, following the rules for reflecting teams about being respectful, tentative and curious in their observations and comments. Whilst this conversation is happening the supervisor and supervisee just listen and don't engage in the conversation in any way. **Step Four**: The supervisor invites the supervisee to comment on aspects of the reflecting team conversation that have been helpful, thought provoking or have introduced new ideas and difference into their thinking and can support them in moving forward with the clinical work.

4.6 Common Problems with Supervision

Over the years in training and supervising trainee clinical psychologists and when talking to both supervisors and supervises about their supervision experiences, some common concerns that arise within the supervisory alliance have been noticed.

4.6.1 Practitioner Flexibility and the Complexity of Real-life Clinical Work

It is important for supervisees to take the clinical examples they read about in psychology books with a pinch of salt (including the examples in this book). Clients are individuals, they are unpredictable, complex and they don't conform to the psychological models being offered to them. Therapeutic interventions offered might not be a good fit for clients, and this is likely to present challenges if practitioners are not able to remain flexible and think on their feet in clinical sessions. This nuanced flexibility to meet the needs of the individual client is just as important as following the model when you are learning new skills. Clearly, being a scientist-practitioner is important and drawing on the evidence base to design formulations and treatments is essential in order to be offering clients the best treatment – but it is not the only skill. The scientist-practitioner model fails to emphasise the creativity and flexibility that is required to keep clients engaged and trusting of the therapist. Sometimes novice practitioners compare themselves to case examples in books and think if they are not delivering therapy exactly by the book, they're not doing it correctly. At other times novice practitioners compare themselves to their supervisors who have been developing their flexible application to therapeutic interventions and problem-solving issues in sessions for years. This can lead to some insecurities and a sense in new practitioners that they are fraudulent. This contributes to *imposter syndrome*, the sense that if someone were to watch their therapy, they will be found out to not be good enough.

4.6.2 Avoiding Feedback and Observations

Imposter syndrome can inhibit supervisees in engaging in seeking observations and feedback from their supervisors, even though they know that logically this would be helpful in developing their skills. Establishing a good supervisory relationship can really help here, in providing a safe and trusting space to show one's practice and open up to feedback and challenge. In maximising learning it is important to take risks with one's own learning and remain as open as possible to observations and feedback. Setting up observations can be highly anxiety provoking for the novice practitioner, observations can feel like medicine, 'you know it's good for you, but it doesn't make it more palatable to swallow'. Keeping open to feedback from others is a really important part of developing not only skills but also clinical confidence. Don't let anxiety and any catastrophic thoughts about how the observations will go stand in the way. The best intervention for anxiety is exposure to avoided fearful situations. Taking the same approach to facing observations and inviting feedback from supervisors can be helpful. Usually, the feedback isn't anywhere near as negative as novice practitioners imagine. The observations should be set up carefully, with enough opportunity for the supervisor to offer balanced feedback. As discussed, many tools for structured feedback on practice and competencies exist. At a minimum a list of practice strengths and areas for behavioural improvement should be detailed, this gives supervisee direction and encourages specific skills development.

4.6.3 Critical Self-evaluation

In developing one's clinical decision making and confidence it is important for new psychological practitioners not to judge their own practice too negatively. They need to offer a balanced view of their practice strengths and weaknesses both to themselves and to their supervisor. Whenever novice practitioners are asked how they might improve their practice, they can often offer a long list, but when asking what they think they doing really well in sessions or might be proud of, the list is much shorter and sometimes non-existent. Being balanced in self-evaluation is really important, imagine trying to teach a person a new skill, one would not only give feedback about the things that they were doing wrong or needed to improve. In order to shape practitioners' future skills and grow their confidence one might use the process of operant conditioning to reward and remind them of their positive practice, things that they are doing well. This not only increases the positive practice behaviour but also increases confidence and a sense of self-efficacy in their own skills. Practitioners should take the same approach in relation to their own self-evaluation and learning: balance feedback when reflecting on tasks completed, write lists with positives and areas to improve after each session and make sure that the positives are equal in number to the more constructive feedback.

4.6.4 Finding Constructive Criticism Difficult

It can often be hard for supervisors to give more critical feedback and they will be hypervigilant to supervisee's responses. Practitioners should make sure they remain open to critical feedback, delivered constructively, they should try to take the feedback in the spirit of learning rather than becoming defensive. Taking this stance can be particularly hard for new psychological practitioners who are accustomed to academic success. They may not be used to critical feedback and may not have failed anything previously or struggled to acquire new skills. This can lead to catastrophic thoughts about failure that remain at the forefront of practitioner's minds and inhibit learning and experimentation with new skills and clinical opportunities. As earlier, facing these fears and putting oneself in learning situations that raise anxieties is really the only way of developing the skills and becoming the best practitioner possible for clients. Discussion in supervision about how supervisors and supervisees like to approach learning is critical in developing a good supervisor alliance. Perhaps the supervisee prefers a graded approach, with plenty of reading and observation of skills first before trying a new clinical skill. Other learners may prefer to throw themselves into the deep end, after some brief preparatory reading, favouring 'learning from doing' before reflecting and reading further.

4.6.5 Dealing with Uncertainty

Clinical practice brings the unexpected. Every time a practitioner meets with a new client they are faced with novel clinical decisions and uncertainty and this continues throughout clinical practice. Some of these decisions are easy. They follow what has been read in books or has been detailed in psychological theory or evidence. Other clinical decisions need to rely on individual judgement, common sense and the practitioner's ability to think on their feet. As discussed, these skills are just as important but can pose dilemmas for novice practitioners who are under the supervision of others. Some practitioners may be concerned that they need to check out all decisions with their supervisor, they might be nervous of the responsibility of clinical practice and can feel quite deskilled in just making ordinary common-sense judgements. Developing confidence in one's own clinical decision making requires one to experiment and make decisions on one's own. Supervisees are jointly responsible with their supervisor for the clinical decision made so it is important to take the supervisor's advice but also begin to consider one's own individual, independent thoughts on the clinical matters. Checking out these decisions and reflecting on them in supervision after the event helps practitioners evaluate the impact of their clinical decisions (positive and negative) and understand how they might have done things differently. This is not to say the supervisee or supervisors' judgement is superior, sometimes they just have a different clinical approach or style. If supervisors are concerned about a supervisee's clinical judgements it is critical they can be honest about this and take appropriate action, in order to prioritise the best interests of the client but this should be done supportively in the context of encouraging new knowledge and skills.

4.6.6 Poor Supervisory Alliance

Just like any other social relationship supervision can encounter communication difficulties, relational conflicts and breakdowns in trust. When in training, supervisees find it very difficult to address these relational concerns, they feel supervisor are misjudging them, offering harsh or critical feedback and very often they fear a failure of a clinical training placement, a loss of job or a poor reference will result. Taking a step back and examining the relational aspects of the supervision alliance is crucial when supervision relationships are not going well. It is important to understand the communication patterns that are occurring in conversations that are going well and conversations that lead to conflict. Trying to understand the wider context and service pressures that may be impacting on this relationship. Key to addressing difficulties in supervision is clearly recording agreed actions to avoid miscommunications and seeking advice and support from training providers or other managers in the service in resolving conflicts, as they may be able to offer impartial advice and intervene when other problem solving has failed.

4.6.7 Different Approaches to Structured Learning

Looking back at the learning and supervision models presented earlier in this chapter it is notable that supervisor and supervisee may have a different learning style and be at very different stages of their learning journey. If ignored, this will impact strongly on the success of the supervision process. For example, the supervisee may prefer a structured approach to learning with a fixed supervision agenda and explicit examples of theory–practice links and active practising of clinical skills. If paired with a reflective supervisor who is an experienced and integrative practitioner, it may be difficult for the pair to find the right structured agenda for supervision, achieving the right balance between reflection and detailed action planning. If the supervisor is at the stage of unconscious competence such that their own practice has become second nature to them, bringing forth the explicit theory that is underpinning practice may be harder and require the supervisee to ask gentle enquiring questions to support the theory–practice links such as: What ideas were you thinking about that led you to ask about the client's early family history? Why were you asking the client about support in their community? Do you always ask for specific thoughts that the client notices when they are feeling anxious? Why? Would you ever invite a client's partner to join them for a session? Discussing both supervisors and supervisees' approach to learning and their preferences for the organisation of supervision sessions right at the start of the supervision relationship and then reviewing this regularly (at least once a month) is really important so that a shared, productive supervision process can be maintained.

4.7 Self-reflection - Definition

Scaife (2010) defines reflection as the process of thinking analytically about what we are thinking, feeling and doing in order to shape future action. The process of self-reflection is often claimed as a critical part of training as a psychological practitioner and essential for personal and professional development throughout one's career. The co-occurrence of reflection and action in this definition is important; curious self-reflection is used to inform clinical decision making and practice, and thinking about oneself in detail is not done for its own sake but in order to improve the clinical practice for clients. Milne and

Reiser (2020) has emphasised the importance of supervision and reflective discussion in the supervisory alliance as critical in supporting psychological practitioners to reduce work stress and burnout while delivering effective psychological therapies.

Reflection has played a key role in most psychological models of practice. Psychoanalytic traditions consider reflection within the context of the therapeutic relationships, bringing in concepts such as transference and counter-transference (Bateman & Fonagy, 2007). Systemic models focus more on therapist self-reflexivity and relational reflexivity, and the idea of owning one's position when sharing reflections with clients through methods such as Reflecting Teams (Andersen, 1991). Cognitive behavioural models have also started to consider therapists' reflection as a key skill and the work of Bennett-Levy has been important introducing models of self-practice/self-reflection into CBT models (Bennet-Levy et al., 2015).

The systemic models have focused most explicitly on the concept of therapist curiosity and self-reflexivity:

> Self-reflexivity focuses especially on the effect of the therapy process on the therapist and the way that this is a source of (resource for) change in the family. In order to use self-reflexivity it will be necessary for the therapist to be alert to their own constructions, functioning and prejudices so that they can use their self effectively with the family.
>
> (Pote et al., 2001, p. 11).

Cecchin considered the therapist position in relation to the client's difficulties and their experiences. His model of curiosity and self-reflection draws heavily on social constructionism (Cecchin, 1987). He considered how these interactions could never be truly neutral due to the influences of power within our society and in turn the influence of power upon the therapeutic relationship. Rather the therapist should be curious about how their own beliefs, behaviour and language shape the therapeutic encounter. For example, Cecchin would argue that, as therapists, we need to be curious about how these beliefs shape the questions we might choose to ask or choose to avoid in therapeutic conversations. Similarly, the therapist should be curious about the client's beliefs, their interactions and the questions they focus on or ignore during assessment and the course of therapy. What is not said may be just as important as what is said. What we choose to focus on in the therapeutic discussion will be influenced by our own culture, beliefs and experiences as people, and our client's responses but also the system within which we are working. This work context includes the psychological model that informs our work, the team constraints about how long we can meet with people, and the legal and professional structures within the employing organisation and society, such as workload expectations and staff support available.

4.8 Why is Reflection Important to Clinical Practice?

Self-reflection can enhance the therapeutic relationship. Working with children and families is emotive work. We will have all been part of family or caring systems as we grew up and these experiences shape our expectations of the usual patterns of relating in families, what change might be needed and what might be helpful therapist responses to support change in these contexts. In essence, everyone has been a child so when working with children it is important to examine the practitioners' own beliefs and expectations in relation to children and their caregivers. Examining these beliefs is proposed to lead to increased empathy and collaborative practice. Not examining these beliefs and expectations runs the risk of them overshadowing evidenced based clinical decision making. See the supervision example in Box 4.3.

Box 4.3 Supervision example I

Consider an example from clinical practice in a child development service, where regular multidisciplinary assessment of children's cognitive and functional skills take place. The supervisor and supervisee, both from a White British middle-class background, had not discussed any aspects of their own development or educational experiences as children. The supervisee, Alice, a trainee psychological practitioner, had been diagnosed with Dyslexia at around 8 years of age and had found the whole process difficult, feeling criticised at school and at home for not meeting expectations. When Jake, a 10-year-old, white British boy, attends clinic for an ADHD assessment, the family note his diagnosis of Dyslexia. Alice feels immediate empathy and alignment with Jake, in assessment sessions they form a good engagement. Alice reports, in supervision, that she found it harder to engage Jake's parents and was not able to gather a full developmental history as requested by the supervisor. The supervisor could not understand why the task had not been completed as the trainee was usually excellent at engaging parents and was always diligent in completing tasks. The supervisor used gentle reflective questions with Alice to prompt discussion of personal-professional issues: What barriers were getting in the way of you completing the task? Were any personal issues coming up for you in working with this family? How did you understand your good connection with the child compared to the parents in the session? Exploring this with the Alice led them examine some of the beliefs she had developed from her own personal childhood experiences, which were impacting on the approach to engaging the parents in this assessment. This reflection supported Alice to try fresh strategies to engage with the parents in the next meeting.

Novice practitioners are often concerned about their youth, limited life experience or the fact they do not have experience as parents or of interacting with children. They fear this will impede their collaborative relationship with families and impact on engagement and the success of their interventions. All of this can leave practitioners with a strong sense of imposter syndrome when working with families. It is important for psychological practitioners to address this, as imposter syndrome has been associated with compassion fatigue and burnout in mental health professionals (Clark et al., 2022). Key to overcoming this is to develop a high level of curiosity and self-reflection about their own experiences and the experiences of the families they are working with. This supports engagement and establishes empathy and an ability to walk in the shoes of family members despite differences in experience.

Cultural reflexivity is a key aspect of reflection that psychological practitioners need to develop. This enables them to explore aspects of power, whiteness gender, privilege, diversity and equality in their clinical work and support them in addressing discrimination and taking an anti-racist and anti-discriminatory stance in their professional practice (Patel & Keval, 2018). Common tools like Burnham's Social Graces model enable supervisor and supervisee to reflect together about social and cultural aspects of client, supervisee and supervisor identity, which will be constructing the clinical work and supervision process (Burnham, 2012). See the supervision examples presented in Box 4.4. In doing so, they can identify aspects of their unconscious bias that may be having a negative impact on the client experience or outcomes, or defining service structures unhelpfully (See Chapter 7 for further discussion).

Box 4.4 Supervision example II

Jade is a newly qualified child psychological practitioner from a White British working-class background, working in a service close to where she grew up. One of her first allocated cases is Grace a 17-year-old Black-British young woman, of Jamaican heritage, who is experiencing symptoms of depression and low self-esteem following some peer relationship problems at school. The client is from a very similar working-class background to Jade, she has grown up and lives close to where Jade lives, has a similar family make up and goes to a school near to where Jade went to school. Jade feels quite comfortable working with the young woman and her family and thinks they have established a close collaborative therapeutic relationship using CBT models. The supervisory relationship is new, and she and her supervisor haven't talked about Jade's own background or experiences.

Jade's supervisor, who is from a White middle-class background, notices that Jade seems to be making assumptions about Grace and her family, for topics that she has not talked about in sessions with them. Topics include Grace's experience of the school system and her aspirations for job roles in the future. The supervisor decides to explore these assumptions in supervision by completing a cultural genogram and reading and discussing the paper 'Fifty Ways to Leave … your Racism' (Patel & Keval, 2018), which promotes identifying and exploring one's own discourses and considers the broader context of whiteness and racism. Through this, Jade began to be more curious with Grace about her educational and family experiences, and in future sessions, she used open questions to explore Grace's experiences and beliefs about the presenting problems and the role of psychological support. Grace was able to share some painful past experiences of racial bullying at school that were shaping her beliefs and contributing to her current difficulties. Jade was able to reflect, in supervision, about the danger of making assumptions about clients' experiences and the importance of exploring both similarities and differences in establishing positive working alliances.

Ways to support anti-racist and anti-discriminatory practice in supervision has been helpfully addressed in the systemic supervision literature. Pendry (2012) and Patel (2011) have both noted how such practice is underpinned by careful consideration of power in the supervisory relationship and the need for supervisors (whose role puts them in an elevated power position) to take responsibility for initiating conversations about race and racism. Challenging inequalities is an important task for the supervisor in order to practice ethically and attend to any fears the supervisee might have about raising issues of discrimination.

Another area where reflection is important is that of safe practice and risk management. Practitioners need to be able to notice, identify, reflect and respond to emotional reactions they are experiencing in their relationships with clients. These emotional reactions should be a guide to practitioners, helping them notice unspoken distress and areas of concern. This is especially important when working in child-protection contexts or with children who find it hard to express themselves due to environmental or individual factors such as learning disabilities. Often practitioners report feeling uncomfortable or uncertain about a relationship within the family or facts that are being reported before there is any concrete evidence of forms of abuse. Trusting these emotional reactions and being able to disentangle which emotions are specific to this family and which arise from the practitioner themselves is an important area for reflection. Supervision is critical in developing this felt sense of concern as the supervisor can encourage reflection on these emotions through curiosity about the therapeutic relationship (Totsuka, 2014). See Chapter 5 for a more detailed discussion of safeguarding practice.

4.9 Common Problems in Becoming Self-reflective

4.9.1 Sharing Personal Information

The importance of discussing personal values and circumstances can be hard for new practitioners to understand. Practitioners might be unsure about how much personal information to share with supervisors and when the time is right to do this. Like any relationship, it is important to establish trust and share things when it feels comfortable, but the supervisee may want to consider what information it would be helpful for their supervisor to know upfront and prepare some information on this for the first meeting. Completing a genogram together in supervision can be a good way of sharing information and reflecting on personal experiences, context and values. Sharing these personal values is important because they will influence the hypotheses the practitioner develops about clients and the ones that they do not. The supervisor can encourage and support reflective conversations in supervision about alternative perspectives that might be outside the personal experience of the supervisee. This will enrich the work and is likely to make it more culturally, sensitive and clinically helpful. Shellenberger et al. (2007) assert that it is helpful for practitioners to have mapped out their own genogram and reflected upon diverse aspects of their own culture before using genograms in assessments with families and offers the 'cultural genogram' reflective exercises to achieve this in supervision. These have been built on recently to ensure the whole worldview of practitioners, including their values, are considered in detail (Chege et al., 2022).

4.9.2 Reflection vs Action

There is a balance to strike between reflection and action in clinical work and team working. Psychological practitioners sometimes find this a hard balance to strike, preferring to stick at the level of reflection and discussion without translating this into action that may be beneficial to clients. Being a reflective practitioner brings many opportunities for enhanced clinical action. These may include:

- Encourage discussion of difficulties that may be hard to bring out into the open.
- Ask questions that may have been previously neglected or ignored.
- Attend to cultural differences between client and therapist.
- Be curious about beliefs that may underpin difficulties or inform solutions.
- Challenge cultural biases, discriminatory or racist practices.
- Invite contributions from marginalised voices within systems.
- Support clients and colleagues in developing their own self-reflective capacities.

4.9.3 Reflection on Capabilities

Letting people know when you are struggling personally or with clinical work is hard. Sometimes novice practitioners think they have to be able to manage everything that they face. They consider that highlighting areas outside their competence or comfort will reflect badly on their performance evaluations. This is simply not true, clinical practice guidelines focus on the need for practitioners to work within their level of competence and emphasise their responsibility to highlight to others, particularly their supervisors, if they feel they are at risk of going beyond this. The supervisor will then be in a position to develop the supervisee's experience in a graded way in order that these clinical challenges are met. The other stance that practitioners sometimes portray is the illusion that they are coping with everything and that nothing phases them. Presenting such a wholly competent and confident portrait is simply unrealistic. It is important to allow discussion of any personal challenges within supervision and reflect on why these are difficult. This will help the development of reflective skills and in turn enable the practitioner to be more in tune in their clinical relationships. It is particularly important to discuss life events or personal challenges that may be compromising one's clinical fitness to practice. This can be particularly hard for novice therapists, especially when they are being evaluated by their supervisors, but it is nonetheless essential in order to keep themselves and their clients safe and offer them the best service possible. See the supervision examples presented in Box 4.5.

Box 4.5 Supervision example III

Consider Marcus, a 26-year-old British-Filipino trainee clinical psychologist, who has been doing very well on his course (placements and academic assignments) and is about halfway through his training. He has recently had the really difficult news that his dad is dying of cancer. He is working in an older people's service and many of the clients are suffering with chronic health problems though none of his current clients have cancer. Marcus is naturally distressed by some of the clinical work but is concerned now whether he is able to carry on with his work as usual. Marcus fears being evaluated negatively as 'not resilient' and decides not to mention the family circumstances to his supervisor or course tutor. In the past, the supervisor has made comments about the importance of being resilient in this sort of clinical context and Marcus is worried if he talks about his own personal circumstances and stress, and the impact on his work, he might be judged negatively or as unfit to practice. Marcus finds that some mornings he is struggling to go to work, especially when he has to see a particular client with depression and health concerns. In a session with this client, they reveal they are having investigations for cancer and Marcus has tears in his eyes in the session. He finishes the session and is pleased how he managed to contain his emotions and gather the assessment information. However, he is finding it very difficult to develop a systemic formulation of the difficulties the client is experiencing. His supervisor has asked Marcus to present this at the next supervision session and he is worried his competence will be judged as below standard if he is not able to produce it.

In this supervision scenario it is natural for novice (and experienced) practitioners to deliberate the personal and professional boundaries they wish to maintain in supervision. Considering the personal impact of the work on oneself and assessing one's own capabilities and fitness to practice is a reflective and iterative skill that is usually best done in collaboration with other professionals and one's supervisor. It takes some courage to raise personal distress and difficult life circumstances in supervision, especially when one's practice is being evaluated. Novice practitioners often worry about their emotions overwhelming them or being judged as unprofessional in these instances. Remembering that openness in communication is key to maintaining the supervisory alliance is important. The supervisor may have noticed some distress for Marcus and be wondering how to address it sensitively, conversely, they may have seen changes in his behaviour but have no explanation to understand such shifts. Disclosing personal issues and working together in supervision to openly reflect on the impact of personal life circumstances on the work and in turn the impact of the clinical work on personal resilience and coping is usually the most helpful solution. This is the safest and most professional approach and one that puts the supervisees and clients' needs at the forefront of the supervision. Being able to acknowledge when stressful life events are impacting one's work and reflecting on one's own fitness to practice is an important skill to develop and part of psychological practitioners' responsibilities under professional codes of conduct.

4.10 Conclusion

Using supervision to enhance the clinical effectiveness of one's own practice and develop the practice of other professionals is a key skill for psychological practitioners. Yet scant attention is often paid to the competencies, models and process of supervision by novice practitioners. By engaging in self-reflection during supervision about how one learns and by exploring the personal and professional connections that underpin the development of their competencies practitioners can become more effective and in tune with their clients.

References

Andersen, T. (1991). *The reflecting team: Dialogues and dialogues about dialogues.* Norton.

Barber, J. P., Sharpless, B. A., Klostermann, S., & McCarthy, K. S. (2007). Assessing intervention competence and its relation to therapy outcome: A selected review derived from the outcome literature. *Professional Psychology: Research and Practice, 38*(5), 493.

Bateman, A., & Fonagy, P. (2007, April 1). The use of transference in dynamic psychotherapy. *American Journal of Psychiatry, 164*(4). https://doi.org/10.1176/ajp.2007.164.4.680.

Bennett-Levy, J., Thwaites, R., Haarhoff, B., Perry, H., & Padesky, C. A. (2015). *Experiencing CBT from the inside out: A self-practice/self-reflection workbook for therapists (self-practice/self-reflection guides for psychotherapists.* Guilford Press.

Blackburn, I. M., James, I. A., Milne, D. L., Baker, C., Standart, S., Garland, A., & Reichelt, F. K. (2001). The revised cognitive therapy scale (CTS-R): psychometric properties. *Behavioural and Cognitive Psychotherapy, 29*, 431–446.

British Psychological Society, Division of Clinical Psychology. (2014, October 25). *Policy on supervision.* https://doi.org/10.53841/bpsrep.2014.inf224.

Burnham, J. (2012). Developments in Social GRRRAAACCEEESSS: Visible–invisible and voiced–unvoiced. In I. B. Krause (Ed.), *Culture and reflexivity in systemic psychotherapy: mutual perspectives* (pp. 139–161). Routledge. https://doi.org/10.4324/9780429473463.

Butler, C., Sheils, L., Lask, J., Joscelyne, T., Pote, H., & Crossley, J. (2018). Measuring competence in systemic practice: development of the 'Systemic Family Practice – Systemic Competency Scale' (SPS). *Journal of Family Therapy, 42.* https://doi.org/10.1111/1467-6427.12251.

Care Quality Commission. (2019, July). *Brief guide: Capacity and competence in under 18s.* https://www.cqc.org.uk/sites/default/files/Brief_guide_Capacity_and_consent_in_under_18s%20v3.pdf.

Cecchin, G. (1987). Hypothesizing, circularity, and neutrality revisited: an invitation to curiosity. *Family Processing, 4*, 405–413. https://doi.org/10.1111/j.1545-5300.1987.00405.x.

Chege, C. N., Fu, M., Bustrum, J. M., & Jenks, E. H. (2022). *The worldview genogram: A process model for enhancing diversity responsiveness and competence in education, training, and clinical supervision.* Psychological Services. Advance online publication. https://doi.org/10.1037/ser0000719.

Clark, P., Holden, C., Russell, M., & Downs, H. (2022, April 30). The impostor phenomenon in mental health professionals: Relationships among compassion fatigue, burnout, and compassion satisfaction. *Contemporary Family Therapy, 44*, 185–197. https://doi.org/10.1007/s10591-021-09580-y.

Daniel, G., & Burck, C. (2010). *Mirrors and reflections: Processes of systemic supervision* (Systemic Thinking and Practice Series). Karnac Books.

Dornan, T., Bosuizen, H., King, N., & Scherpbier, A. (2006). Experience-based learning: A model linking the processes and outcomes of medical students' learning. *Medical Education, 41*(1), 84–91.

Eraut, M., Alderston, J., Cole, G., & Senker, P. (2001). The impact of the manager on learning in the workplace. In F. Reeve, M. Cartwright, & R. Edwards (Eds.), *Supporting lifelong learning: Volume II: Organising learning* (pp. 91–108). Routledge. https://doi.org/10.4324/9780203996720.

Falender, C. A., Erickson Cornish, J. A., Goodyear, R., Hatcher, R., Kaslow, N. J., Leventhal, G., Shafranske, E., Sigmon, S. T., Stoltenberg, C., & Grus, C. (2004). Defining competencies in psychology supervision: A consensus statement. *Journal of Clinical Psychology, 60*(7), 771–785.

Fiske, A., Henningsen, P., & Buyx, A. (2019, May 9). Your robot therapist will see you now: ethical implications of embodied artificial intelligence in psychiatry, psychology, and psychotherapy. *Journal of Medical Internet Research, 21*(5), e13216.

Friedberg, R. D. (2018). Best practices in supervising cognitive behavioral therapy with youth. *World Journal of Clinical Pediatrics, 7*(1), 1–8. https://doi.org/10.5409/wjcp.v7.i1.1.

Hawkins, P., & McMahon, A. (2020). *Supervision in the helping professions* (5th ed.). McGraw-Hill.

Hawkins, P., & Shohet, R. (2012). *Supervision in the helping professions* (4th ed.). McGraw-Hill/ Open University Press.

Hughes, J., & Youngson, S. (Eds.). (2009). *Personal development and clinical psychology*. British Psychological Society/ Wiley Blackwell.

Kolb, D. A. (1984). *Experiential learning: Experience as the source of learning and development*. Prentice-Hall.

Mao R. Q., Lan, L., Kay, J., Lohre, R., Ayeni, O. R., Goel, D. P., & Sa, D. (2021, July 17). Immersive virtual reality for surgical training: A systematic review. *Journal of Surgery Research, 268*, 40–58. https://doi.org/10.1016/j.jss.2021.06.045.

McMahon, A., & Hevey, D. (2015). 'It has taken me a long time to get to this point of quiet confidence': What contributes to therapeutic confidence for clinical psychologists? *Clinical Psychologist, 21*(3), 195–205. https://doi.org/10.1111/cp.12077.

McMahon, A., Jennings, C., & O'Brien, G. (2022). A naturalistic, observational study of the seven-eyed model of supervision. *The Clinical Supervisor, 41*(1), 47–69. https://doi.org/10.1080/07325223.2021.2022060.

Milne, D. (2007). An empirical definition of clinical supervision. *British Journal of Clinical Psychology, 46*(4), 437–447. doi: 10.1348/014466507X197415. PMID: 17535535.

Milne, D. (2009). *Evidence-based clinical supervision: Principles and practice.* BPS Blackwell.

Milne, D. (2017). *Evidence-based CBT supervision: Principles and practice.* Wiley-Blackwell.

Milne, D., & Reiser, R. (2011). SAGE: A scale for rating competence in CBT supervision. *The Cognitive Behaviour Therapist, 4*, 123–138. doi:10.1017/S1754470X11000079

Milne, D., & Reiser, R. (2012). A rationale for evidence-based clinical supervision. *Journal of Contemporary Psychotherapy, 42*, 1–11. https://doi.org/10.1007/s10879-011-9199-8.

Milne, D., & Reiser, R. (2020). *Supportive clinical supervision: Enhancing well-being and reducing burnout through restorative leadership*. Pavilion.

Northey, W., & Rivett, M. (2020). Editorial to the special issue of the Journal for Family Psychotherapy: International Approaches to Innovative Supervisory Practice. *Journal of Family Psychotherapy, 31*(3), 73–78. https://doi.org/10.1080/08975353.2020.1823144.

Parker, C., Smithson, J., Limond, J., Sherbersky, H., & Butler, C. (2021), Student and supervisor experiences of the Systemic Practice Scale (SPS): A discourse analysis. *Journal of Family Therapy, 43*, 793–818. https://doi.org/10.1111/1467-6427.12318.

Patel, N. (2011). Difference and power in supervision: The case of culture and racism. In I. Fleming & L. Steen (Eds.) *Supervision and clinical psychology: Theory, practice and perspectives* (2nd ed., pp. 96–117). Routledge. https://doi.org/10.4324/9780203805817.

Patel, H., & Keval, H. (2018). Fifty ways to leave … your racism. *Journal of Critical Psychology, Counselling and Psychotherapy, 18*(2), 61–79.

Pendry, N. (2012). Race, racism and systemic supervision. *Journal of Family Therapy, 34*(4), 403–418.

Patel, N. (2011). Difference and power in supervision: The case of culture and racism. In I. Fleming & L. Steen (Eds.) *Supervision and clinical psychology: Theory, practice and perspectives* (2nd ed., pp. 96–117). Routledge. https://doi.org/10.4324/9780203805817.

Pilling, S., & Roth, A. D. (2014). The competent clinical supervisor. In C. E. Watkins, Jr., & D. L. Milne (Eds.), *The Wiley International Handbook of Clinical Supervision* (pp. 20–37). Wiley Blackwell. https://doi.org/10.1002/9781118846360.ch2.

Pote, H., Stratton, P., Cottrell, D., Shapiro, D., & Boston, P. (2001). Systemic family therapy manual. University of Leeds: The Family Therapy Research Centre. https://www.researchgate.net/publication/257311618_Final_LFTRC_Manual.

Reichelt, S., & Skjerve, J. (2013). The reflecting team model used for clinical group supervision without clients present. *Journal of Marital and Family Therapy, 39*, 244–255. https://doi.org/10.1111/j.1752-0606.2012.00298.x.

Roth, A. D., & Pilling, S. (2008). A competence framework for the supervision of psychological therapies. Report for the Care Services Improvement Partnership (CSIP). Skills for Health and NHS Education for Scotland (NESS). https://www.researchgate.net/profile/Stephen-Pilling/publication/265872800_A_competence_framework_for_the_supervision_of_psychological_therapies/links/5727a25e08ae586b21e2963e/A-competence-framework-for-the-supervision-of-psychological-therapies.pdf.

Scaife, J. (2010). *Supervising the reflective practitioner: An essential guide to theory and practice*. Routledge. https://doi.org/10.4324/9781315824192.

Scaife, J. (2019). *Supervision in clinical practice: A practitioner's guide* (3rd ed.). Routledge.

Scior, K., Rüsch, N., White, C., & Corrigan, P. (2020). Supporting mental health disclosure decisions: The honest, open, proud programme. *The British Journal of Psychiatry, 216*(5), 243–245. https://doi.org/10.1192/bjp.2019.256.

Sheen, J., Sutherland-Smith, W., Thompson, E., Youssef, G. J., Dudley, A., King, R., Hall, K., Dowling, N., Gurtman, C., & McGillivray, J. A. (2021). Evaluating the impact of simulation-based education on clinical psychology students' confidence and clinical competence. *Clinical Psychologist, 25*(3), 271–282. https://doi.org/10.1080/13284207.2021.1923125.

Shellenberger, S., Dent, M. M., Davis-Smith, M., Seale, J. P., Weintraut, R., & Wright, T. (2007). Cultural genogram: A tool for teaching and practice. *Families, Systems, & Health, 25*(4), 367–381. https://doi.org/10.1037/1091-7527.25.4.367.

Sherbersky, H., Ziminski, J., & Pote, H. (2021). The journey towards digital systemic competence: Thoughts on training, supervision and competence evaluation. *Journal of Family Therapy, 43*, 351–371. https://doi.org/10.1111/1467-6427.12328.

Stallard, P., Myles, P., & Branson, A. (2014). The cognitive behaviour therapy scale for children and young people (CBTS-CYP): Development and psychometric properties. *Behavioural and Cognitive Psychotherapy, 42*(3), 269–282.

Stoltenberg, C. D., McNeill, B., & Delworth, U. (1998). *IDM Supervision: An integrated developmental model for supervising counsellors and therapists*. Jossey-Bass.

Tay, S., Alcock, K., & Scior, K. (2018). Mental health problems among clinical psychologists: Stigma and its impact on disclosure and help-seeking. *Journal of Clinical Psychology, 74*(9), 1545–1555. https://doi.org/10.1002/jclp.22614.

Totsuka, Y. (2014). Which aspects of social GGRRAAACCEEESSS grab you most?' The social GGRRAAACCEEESSS exercise for a supervision group to promote therapists' self-reflexivity. *Journal of Family Therapy, 36*(1), 86–106. https://doi.org/10.1111/1467-6427.12026.

West, M. (2021). *Compassionate leadership: Sustaining wisdom, humanity and presence in health and social care*. Swirling Leaf Press.

5

Legal and Professional Contexts

Pinder Kaur and Chris Marshall

5.1 Introduction

The legal context and professional issues that are specific to working with children and families can feel like an overwhelming and complex area. Whilst the law and guidelines may be 'black and white' on what is legal or not, what is a child protection issue or not, the reality of navigating these is firmly in the 'grey', requiring the practitioner to apply their clinical skills to the specific relationships and context in these situations. This chapter will aim to balance legislation and professional guidance in this area with plenty of practical guidance.

5.2 Consent

Children and young people (CYP) [1] should be involved as much as possible in decisions about their health care (Department of Health, 2017; Young Minds, Amplified, 2020). As a child psychological practitioner, working collaboratively with CYP is important and supported by evidence demonstrating its positive impact on the experience of care (e.g. Wolpert, 2014) and intervention outcomes (e.g. Cirasola et al., 2021).

However, supporting a CYP's care within child mental health settings can become complex around issues of consent (Paul, 2004; Shaw, 2001). It is often their parent, carer or other concerned adults (e.g. school) who are worried about the CYP and wish for them to get support. The young person may not want help. Additionally, the CYP's understanding of what an assessment and intervention involves may be at a different level from the understanding of their parent's/carers, as well as the developmental and individual differences between CYP's understanding.

Navigating these differences requires some knowledge of the legal framework that underpins consent for CYP and the legalities of parental responsibility (PR). Crucially, this needs to be sensitively applied to the unique circumstances of the CYP. This section of the chapter will summarise key aspects of the legal framework relevant to consent, definitions, guidance

1 'Children' refers to children under the age of 16 and 'Young person' refers to a child aged 16 or 17. When talking about both children and young people this has been abbreviated to 'CYP'.

Child Psychology: Pathways to Good Practice, First Edition.
Edited by Helen Pote, Anna Picciotto and Clare Norris.

Definitions

Child: A person under the age of 16.

Young person: A person aged 16 or 17.

Competence: The individual's ability to understand information about the proposed intervention/treatment and make a decision based on that understanding. Competence is the equivalent term used in place of capacity for children under the age of 16.

Consent: The voluntary and continuing permission of the client to receive a particular treatment based on the knowledge of the purpose, nature, likely effects and risk of that treatment, including the likelihood of success and any alternatives to it.

Children Act (1989): A UK Act of Parliament that centres the welfare of the child as the court's paramount concern. It is underpinned by the idea that children are best cared for within their family but not at the expense of suffering and avoidable significant harm. It assigns legal duties of responsibilities and duties of care to parents and local authorities.

Gillick competent: A term used in England and Wales referring to an assessment in a wider medical context on whether a child (under 16) can consent to their own medical treatment without the need for parental permission and knowledge.

Fraser guidelines: These are a set of guidelines that were developed alongside the Gillick Competency test and is specific to advice around contraception, sexual health, sexual transmitted diseases treatment and termination of pregnancy.

Human Rights Act (1998)*: A UK Law incorporating the rights set out in the European Convention of Human Rights (ECHR) that sets out the fundamental rights and freedoms that everyone in the UK is entitled too, including the right to life, freedom from torture, respect for privacy and family life.

Mental Capacity Act (2005): A UK act of Parliament that provides a legal framework around decision making for people aged 16 and over. Capacity should be assumed unless demonstrated otherwise, people must be helped to make their own decisions, 'unwise' decisions are permitted and do not equate to a lack of capacity, decisions must be made in the best interests of a person who is assessed as lacking capacity, treatment and care should be the least restrictive of their basic rights and freedoms.

Parental responsibility: Refers to the legal duties, powers and responsibilities individual(s) have in respect of their child or young person.

United Nations Convention on the Rights of the Child (UNCRC; 1989): An international Human Rights treaty made of 54 articles detailing the specific rights of children under the age of 18. All countries that sign up to the UNCRC are bound by international law to ensure they implement this (usually referred to as 'ratifying' the treaty within their domestic law and policy): 196 countries, including the UK, have signed up and ratified the treaty.

*Following the UK's exit from the European Union in 2020 the UK Government at the time of writing was seeking to replace the Human Rights Act with the 'Bill of Rights.'
**Legislation and Law can change; this box is correct as of April 2023.

Figure 5.1 Definitions.

on how to assess competence and capacity to consent and the role of parents/carers in relation to this. Figure 5.1 orients the reader to key definitions used in this chapter.

5.2.1 Competence and Consent in Decision Making

As a psychological practitioner, you are required to explicitly seek consent from the appropriate individual to proceed with your involvement (British Psychological Society

(BPS) BPS, 2018). The Law's approach to consent rests on the dichotomy of whether an individual is 'competent' or 'not competent' (Shaw, 2001). Competence refers to the person's ability to think through and understand information and make a decision on the basis of that information. Only a competent person can give valid consent. In England and Wales, the capacity of a young person aged 16 or 17 to consent falls under the Mental Capacity Act (MCA; 2005) whilst capacity to consent for children under 16 is determined by assessing whether they are 'Gillick competent'. In Scotland capacity and consent in CYP is covered by the Adults with the Incapacity Act (2000), Age of Legal Capacity Act (1991) and the Children Act (Scotland; 1995).

5.2.2 Decision Making and Young People Aged 16 and 17

Under the MCA, (2005) 16 and 17 year olds are presumed to have the same capacity as adults to consent to or refuse their care. This presumption of capacity means you can proceed with the young person's consent alone, unless there is a reason to believe the young person lacks capacity. Whilst legally it is acceptable to proceed with the young person's consent alone, in a clinical context, typically, a parent/carer may be involved and have consented initially to the referral on behalf of their child. You can proceed with your initial contact with the family and young person on this basis and then proactively seek consent from the young person to continue with your assessment and intervention. Box 5.1 illustrates one way of doing this in a clinical session.

Box 5.1 Script 1

Gaining consent from a young person aged 16–17. A conversation with Mohammed (he/him) aged 16, about proceeding to an assessment of the referred difficulties when it is their parent who made the referral.

Therapist: It looks like your parent made the referral to our service for low mood difficulties – they mention that you were in support of the referral to our team, and I wanted to check again that you were aware of this…? And if you yourself want to go ahead and meet with me to talk about these low mood difficulties?

Mohammed: Yes, I asked my mum to get me help at the Doctor's surgery – I was just too down to do it as well. I actually wasn't sure at first because I've never been to this place, called CAMHS, but what you said doesn't sound so bad, especially as its online sessions.

Therapist: Would you like to go ahead with the rest of the session exploring what has been going on for you? This will involve me asking questions about how the difficulties have developed, what helps, what doesn't help and completing a questionnaire together. Let me know if there are any questions about what I have just described.

Mohammed: I'm okay to go ahead and have a session with you, sure.

Therapist: Great, thank you. I will check in again on how it's going for you in the session. I am now going to give you a bit more information about how we store your information, what happens to my written notes and then will check again if it's still okay with you to continue.

Parents/carers may not be aware that their 16 or 17 year old child is being treated as an adult with respect to consent for their psychological treatment and the implications this will have on privacy and confidentiality of the work. Therefore, your assessment session should clarify consent and the basis on which you are proceeding (e.g. acknowledge parent's and young person's consent to the referral and that the assessment and intervention will continue to proceed on the basis of the young person's consent and where appropriate with their parents/carers agreement). Box 5.2 illustrates one way of differentiating consent. The parent's role may vary from direct involvement in an intervention (e.g. multisystemic therapy; Henggeler et al., 2009) to minimal involvement (e.g. individual Cognitive Behavioural Therapy (CBT) for social anxiety) therefore, making parents/carers and young people aware of this will be important for engagement with the work and transparency around roles and expectations.

Box 5.2 Script 2

Explaining consent to a Mei-Ling (she/her), mum to 17-year-old Mimi (they/them) and implications of moving forward with Mimi's consent.

Therapist: I wanted to talk about the next steps in this process together. Mei-Ling, you kindly supported Mimi to seek help and gave permission on behalf of Mimi to be referred to us, now that I have met with Mimi we are continuing to meet with their direct permission or consent for the assessment and intervention.

Mei-Ling: okay…so I am not needed anymore then, I guess (nervous laughter)?

Therapist: It's clear from our assessment today that you are important and supported Mimi to seek help for the first time, this is a big step. You may also be able to appreciate that because these sessions are going to primarily involve Mimi only that I need to have Mimi's consent to continue.

Mei-Ling: Okay, that makes sense the sessions are definitely for them.

Therapist: What this also means is that what Mimi and I talk about is private and confidential with a few exceptions around risk and harm that I will discuss in a moment…

Mei-Ling: Oh…

Therapist: …Sometimes when parents/carers hear that sessions are private or confidential they may worry or feel a bit 'in the dark', which can be difficult when they want to be able to help. This is not an uncommon feeling. There may be other feelings about this too and we can talk about this. What Mimi and I will do in our next session is talk about how to involve you in ways that feel may feel helpful to them, and it would be good to hear your thoughts on this too in case you have ideas or expectations about Mimi coming to see me.

Mei-Ling: Okay that sounds like something useful to do, I just want to know how I can help Mimi really.

If a Young Person Aged 16 and 17 Lacks Capacity to Consent: If a young person struggles to understand information about the specific decision relating to their care, struggles to retain information in their mind, is unable to weigh up the information and communicate their decision with adaptations, support, time and minimal pressure, you may suspect the young person lacks capacity to consent. In these instances, it is important to seek the advice of colleagues with additional knowledge in this area and use supervision to discuss and ensure fidelity to the MCA (2005) guidance. These may lead to a few outcomes including delaying the decision to a time when the young person may be able to make the decision or undertaking a Mental Capacity assessment.

5.2.3 Decision Making in Children under 16 Years Old

Legally, a parent with parental responsibility (PR; to be discussed in Section 5.2.4) can consent for their child's treatment under 16 and this is sufficient to proceed with assessment and intervention. Whilst this might be legally acceptable, clinically, there is a duty of care to support the legal and ethical rights of children all ages to determine what happens to them in in their care (BPS, 2018). However, from a developmental perspective there will be a range of decision-making abilities amongst children. Therefore, as part of the assessment the practitioner should also be assessing whether a child under 16 has the competence to understand their intervention and if they can autonomously make a decision to participate on the basis of this. This assessment is referred to as the 'Gillick competence' test.

Use this as a checklist to guide if a child under 16 is Gillick competent

1. Present **information** to the child regarding the specific decision they need to make on:
   - The nature of the difficulties assessed by you/team.
   - The nature of the recommended intervention and any alternatives.
   - Known risks and benefits of interventions, no intervention or known alternatives.
   - Known longer-term consequences of each option.
   - That there is a decision to make.
   - That decisions have consequences.
2. In order to **enhance understanding of the information** presented above:
   - Present adequate information in an age-appropriate way and adapted to their communication needs (verbally in chunks, visually, written service leaflets/website information, recorded, use an interpreter, etc.).
   - Give the child time to think.
   - Give the child time to ask questions.
   - Have regular points in your delivery of the information to check understanding.
3. Decision making can be **supported** by:
   - A supportive parent–child relationship.
   - A positive therapeutic relationship and trust.
   - No pressure (including time pressure) and panic.
   - No judgement.

A child/young person is Gillick competent if they can:

- Retain information.
- See how it applies to them.
- Weigh the issues in balance.
- Arrive at a decision and communicate this to others.

(Kaur, 2022) Reprinted with permission https://medium.com/@drpinderkaur/gillick-competence-c059d4ac6659

Figure 5.2 Guide to assessing Gillick competence.

In 1985, Victoria Gillick, a mother in Norfolk contacted her local Health Authority to seek assurance that children under the age of 16 would not be given contraception and sexual health-based care without parental knowledge and consent. This was in response to a written leaflet from the health authority she had come across. The local authority refused to give this assurance and so Mrs Gillick brought a legal case against them: Gillick v. West Norfolk & Wisbech Area Health Authority (1985).

Initially, Mrs Gillick's case was dismissed in the High Court, but she appealed and the decision was overturned. It was against this decision that the Health Authority appealed to the House of Lords and the case was examined. The Health Authority's appeal eventually overturned the decision, determining that children could be assessed as competent to receive sexual health based care as set out by Lord Fraser's guidelines. Lord Scarman added a further stipulation to the guidelines that a child had to understand what was involved. Gillick competence is applied to decisions in a wider medical context, including psychological and psychiatric care. Lord Fraser's guidelines are applied in a sexual health context.

There is no lower age limit for the guidelines to be applied, however, children under the age of 13 are not legally able to consent to sexual activity (Sexual Offences Act, 2003) and so regardless of their assessed competence using Lord Fraser's guidance the child would need to be referred to the local safeguarding team. Mrs Gillick continued her campaign long after the final decision.

Figure 5.3 Spotlight on the context and development of the Gillick competence test and Fraser guidelines.

Gillick competence defines competence as the child's 'intelligence and ability' to understand the information about the proposed treatment, which includes the treatment's purpose, nature, likely effects and risks, changes of success and availability of any alternatives. There are no set questions for the assessment, but several areas need to be considered and a guide is presented in Figure 5.2.

There is no lower age limit for Gillick competence to be applied. However, Bailey and Harbour (1999) suggest it would be inappropriate for a person under the age of 13 years to consent to treatment without a parent's involvement. Figure 5.3 presents further context of the development of Gillick competence and Fraser guidelines and Script 5.3 demonstrates one way of applying Gillick competence.

Box 5.3 gives an example of applying Gillick competence.

Box 5.3 Applying Gillick Competence

At the end of an assessment the psychological practitioner explains what psychological intervention might be helpful and seeks consent to proceed with this intervention plan. They also discuss the child's (Sam; he/him) parent's role in the sessions.

Therapist: I wanted to check if you want to go ahead with what we have discussed. Even though both your mums have said that it's fine, it's really important for me to get your permission or what we call 'consent' to go ahead too. Is it okay if check this with you? You don't have to decide straight away, just take your time and listen for now.

Sam: Okay.

(Continued)

Box 5.3 (Continued)

Therapist: I now understand that you are worried about people you love dying and that when these thoughts pop into your head you have to do certain repeating actions. These actions and these thoughts are taking up a lot of time and getting in the way of schoolwork, having fun and sometimes make you want to escape life … does that sound about right?

Sam: Yes, I hate it so much.

Therapist: It seems like your experiences fits the description of obsessive-compulsive difficulties, usually called 'OCD' for short, and it's really important for me to understand what this looks like for you specifically because everyone's experience is different. Does that make sense?

Sam: Yes, I think I have OCD too – I saw it on TikTok, you know they're like 30 second online videos on social media, and it makes so much sense. I thought 'that's definitely me…'.

Therapist: I'm glad that was a helpful experience, it would be good to talk a bit more about social media later actually, I'll make a note on our agenda.

Therapist: So fortunately, we are able to try to help you here at CAMHS with these thoughts and experiences. What this involves is a talking therapy called Cognitive Behavioural Therapy, or CBT for short, where we work to understand how you get stuck on these thoughts that pop into your mind, which lead to those physical experiences you described and then those repeating actions you do to try to 'cancel out' the thoughts.

First, we get to know the thoughts and how they show up, using diaries and tracking them. We then put this in to our 'map' or formulation of what's going on for you. Then we gradually work towards challenging some of the ways these thoughts get in the way by doing something called ERP, exposure response prevention, where you 'expose' yourself to the tricky thought and then 'prevent' or stop yourself from doing the thing that seems to help in the short term but in the long term just keeps you feeling 'trapped' as you described. I've described a lot just now, and all this happens step by step, we work together. Does that make sense?

Sam: Do I have to stop my actions? I don't want my mum and nan to die.

Therapist: Not yet. Any changes to what you do at the moment to keep safe will always be done when we have spoken things through, and you feel ready enough.

Sam: Okay, that's good. I'm not ready to be thrown in the deep end.

Therapist: Of course, that's not how it works here. In our service we use a six session and review model. What this means is we will meet for six sessions and then we will have a planned review to make sure we are on track to helping you meet your goal of 'beating down the "family death thoughts" from 9.5/10 stress to 4/10 stress.' We will usually refer to your goal and your experience of the sessions regularly anyway. The review is usually a good point to also invite your parents for some of the session so that they are updated if you would find that helpful at the time as well.

Sam: That would be good.

Therapist: Sometimes parents like to be kept updated after each session, usually just by joining the last 5–10 minutes of the session. What do you think?

Sam: I'd rather keep it for myself – that's important to me.

Therapist: Sure, is there another way we can keep your parents updated? When we met together you might remember your mum, Sylvie, in particular wanted to know how she could help you.

Sam: Maybe you could email me and her me the homework you mentioned? Or she can join the last 5 minutes every few sessions, not every session though…I'm not sure…

Therapist: That's okay – have a think about it and let me know the next time we meet if that's okay? I'll make a note to remind myself to follow up on this when we meet. And it may be there are times it feels helpful to me to involve your parents, we know that having support or a positive team on your side to help reach your therapy goals can be really beneficial when there is a supportive relationship – can I revisit this with you if I feel this way?

Sam: Sure.

Therapist: Okay, the next bit is for me to let you know that whilst this is the recommended therapy for your experiences you do have other options. As you know due to the waiting list your sessions won't start until 4 weeks' time. In the meantime, you could join our waiting list information sessions.

Sam: It's okay to wait. I have that book my nan bought me.

Therapist: Some people find the waiting list information sessions helpful – they have a 'de-stress information session' that people tend to like because of the ideas you get to relax your body. I'll send you the list in case you change your mind and want to attend the group sessions, it's not a problem if you do change your mind. There's information on the list if you want to join one or two of those. It's not a replacement for the work that we are going to start but may help with the wait and to pick up one or two helpful ideas to manage day to day.

Sam: Okay, thank you.

Therapist: And you of course can change your mind about whether you want to go ahead for our sessions, things might change for you. As it stands now based on what you are experiencing and that you are looking to quieten down the thoughts and stop the repeating actions. The therapy I described, called Cognitive Behavioural therapy, has the most evidence shown to help with this and is the recommended treatment. If you choose to not go for this, it may be that things continue as they are or get more difficult without support.

If a Child Under the Age of 16 Lacks Competence: The level of understanding that is sufficient will vary with complexity and gravity of the decision. A child may lack the competence to make a specific decision because they have not developed the maturity, cognitive capacity and understanding to make the decision. Another reason they may lack competence is because other factors are involved that affect their ability to make some types of decisions, for example, a learning disability. In the context of a learning disability further guidance on how to support children to be meaningfully involved in their care should be sought. In either case, legally, the child will be considered to 'lack' Gillick competence and consent should be sought from an adult with parental responsibility. While a child may not be in a position to provide active consent for psychological therapies-based intervention, it is still important to establish they do not actively dissent.

5.2.4 Parental Responsibility

Under Section 3 the Children Act 1989 PR refers to the rights, duties, powers and responsibilities an individual has in respect of their child or young person. PR includes the right to consent to treatment on behalf of a child or young person. Mothers have automatic PR. Not all parents automatically have PR. See Figure 5.4 for differences across the UK. When a child or young person lacks the competence or capacity to give valid consent to their care it is usually sufficient for only one adult with PR to provide consent in order to proceed with a treatment care plan (Children Act, 1989, Section 2). An adult's PR ends when their child turns 18.

A child and family assessment should seek to establish key people who hold PR for the child regardless of whether they are present in the child's life and with their up-to-date contact details where possible. Local Authorities may acquire PR when a child is made subject to care order or interim care order by the court. Looked after children have 'corporate parents' under Section 22(3) of the Children Act (2004), which typically consists of their social worker and team bound by a duty of care to safeguard and promote their welfare.

Despite being able to proceed with one adult's PR, if there is another adult with PR in the child's life it is good practice to seek their views and involvement. However, this will require careful discussion first, as each family's circumstances will vary and potentially change over the course of your input with the child and their family.

For example, it would be inappropriate to seek consent from a second parent with PR who has been abusive to the child. If one parent is absent due to separation involving conflict with the first parent, then it may not be appropriate to broach issues around the estranged parent's consent without weighing up the risk and benefits to the child at that point in time. This does not mean that their role should be excluded completely if therapeutically it may be indicated, for example it may be assessed as helpful to include the second parent if you are working on sleep-related challenges and they have weekly overnight contact with them. This is where clinical judgement underpinned by a good assessment and formulation along with clinical supervision helps approach these dilemmas sensitively with the child at the centre of the work.

If an adult with PR opposes another adult with PR consent, then the responsibility is with the opposing parent to obtain a 'Prohibited Steps Order' under Section 8 of the Children's Act (1989). This may involve potentially navigating difficult feelings expressed about the practitioner by each parent. Supervision will be important to give clarity on boundaries

Who has parental responsibility?
There are variations across the UK and depending on the year the child was born.

- A **mother*** has automatic parental responsibility.
- A **father** usually has parental responsibility if:
  - The father was married to the mother at the time of birth or
  - The father is listed on the birth certificate for births registered from 15 April 2002 in Northern Ireland, 1 December 2003 in England and Wales and 4 May 2006 in Scotland.
- If married parents later divorce both keep parental responsibility.
- **Unmarried parents**
  An unmarried father can gain parental responsibility by:
  - Jointly registering on the birth certificate after the dates specified above.
  - Getting a parental responsibility agreement with the mother.
  - Getting a parental responsibility order from a court.
  - Additionally, if a father marries the mother after the child's birth in Northern Ireland only and continues to live in Northern Ireland, he acquires parental responsibility.
- **Births registered outside the UK**
  - If a child is born outside the UK and comes to live in the UK, parental responsibility depends on the UK country they are now living in.
- **Same sex partners**
  - Both have parental responsibility if they were civil partners or married at the time of treatment (e.g. donor insemination or fertility treatment).
  - If they were not civil partners or married the second parent can get parental responsibility by applying to the courts for parental responsibility if a parental agreement was made.
  - Becoming a civil partner of the other parent and make a parental responsibility agreement or jointly registering the birth.

Source: Adapted from https://www.gov.uk/parental-rights-responsibilities/who-has-parental-responsibility / last accessed June 04 2023.

Looked After Children
There are some children who are under the care of the Local Authority who are sometimes referred to as 'Looked After Children; LAC' or 'children in care'. There are differences between England, Scotland and Wales on the definition of a 'Looked After Child' but parental responsibilities are the same. The local authority typically places a looked after child with a suitable carer and setting and reviews their CYP's care regular as executors of parental responsibilities.

***Mother:** A 'mother' was recently determined in the High Court and Court of Appeals (R (McConnell and YY) v. Registrar General, 2020) to be the label referred to the person who has the biology to birth a baby, regardless of their gender. This arose when Freddy McConnell, a transgender man in England, who birthed his babies sought to be identified as 'father, parent or gestational parent' on his children's birth certificate. The appeal response stated that reform of terminology needed to be take place in a broader parliamentary context. The application of the Law itself, that a 'mother' was not being used in a 'gendered' way was upheld.

Figure 5.4 Parental responsibility.

amongst conflicting parental views and responsibilities to the CYP. Understanding the co-parenting relationship may be helpful to the formulation of the child's referred difficulty.

Both parents and young people need to be informed and involved as much as possible in their care and decisions about their care. Parents may well be directly involved in the care plan proposed, as research shows some types of parental involvement and practice is beneficial to a young person's therapy outcomes. The benefits of involving parents in child and adolescent interventions varies from them being key mechanisms for change for adolescents with conduct problems (e.g. Huey et al., 2000) to their contribution to sustained change in anxiety interventions (e.g. Manassis et al., 2014).

5.2.5 Documenting Assessments of Competence and Capacity

Documenting the initial basis for believing a CYP's consent or competence in their clinical record is important. Any subsequent conversations on consent (whenever they arise throughout the course of contact with the child) should be recorded in their clinical notes.

5.2.6 Withdrawing Consent – CYP

A CYP's refusal or withdrawing consent during treatment in a therapy space may reflect ambivalence, anxiety or other difficult feelings about work or it may be a clear withdrawal of consent from proceeding further. It is helpful to:

- Allow time for discussions around the CYP's feelings about the intervention. What's changed for them and in what way? How much are the practitioner and the therapy contributing to their feelings? How workable might these be?
- Problem solve around the challenges the child or young person is raising (e.g. are there practical things that might make a difference such as shorter sessions, fortnightly, different day and time, do they need a balance between active therapy work and 'problem-free talk?').
- Be additionally sensitive and curious about the experience of CYP from minoritised groups, where there might be challenges around feeling understood by services. Use supervision to make sense of the structural inequalities and social factors that may lead to distress and perceived hesitation in being helped through your sessions.
- Make an interim revised plan around the challenge point with clear review point.
- Discuss in supervision – bring a video recording or video clips of the session to discuss if this is routine in the work.

5.2.7 Parents who Refuse Treatment for their Child

Parents have a duty of care to their child to obtain essential 'medical assistance'. The practitioner, and the team/network around the child will need to think carefully about the basis on which the parents/carers are refusing the intervention for their child. The guidance above will also support conversations around understanding the parent/carer's position.

If it is felt that, after these conversations the parents/carers are refusing an intervention that the practitioner and their team feel would be essential for the child's assessed difficulties, then support should be sought from the service's legal team and named safeguarding contact to discuss whether the parents/carers are holding the 'best interests' of their child in mind when making this decision. It may be that the parent/carers' refusal to treat is part of a wider pattern of neglect or abuse and so it will be important to consult with local safeguarding teams to discuss whether a safeguarding assessment is needed to safeguard and promote the welfare of the child. It is important to seek consent to have these discussions with colleagues outside the service about the parent's decision making. Exceptions to this are where the risk to the CYP would increase in doing so. Initial discussions may be held anonymously and safeguarding teams within the NHS and Local Authority usually have an experienced professional 'on Duty' to discuss these very dilemmas.

5.2.8 The Mental Health Act (1983, 2007) and In-patient Care

In England and Wales, the Mental Health Act (MHA; Department of Healh, 2007) is the main piece of legislation guiding compulsory in-patient admission and treatment. The MHA is usually used when there is a concern that the individual is assessed as needing urgent assessment and treatment, usually by a psychiatric-led multidisciplinary team, due to the risk of harm to themselves or others and they cannot be supported with this in the community. Due to the infringement on a person's life, if detained under the MHA, it is important to follow the detailed legislation on how to proceed. Amendments made to the MHA in 2007 include duties in relation to under 18s being placed in age-appropriate settings, suitable to their needs. The MHA can be used with children of any age but the decision to use this is complex and involves a number of factors. Specific training should be undertaken to understand the Mental Health Act, its applications and your specific role and duties in relation to the Act.

If the CYP has capacity to consent to an in-patient admission, then they should be admitted 'informally'. Additional consent by a person with parental authority is not legally required but it continues to be good practice to involve the CYP's parents/carers in decision making, if the CYP also consents to this information being shared.

If a child under 16 is not competent and therefore lacks capacity to make the decision to be admitted to hospital, then an adult with PR can consent to an admission for their child. However, relying on parental consent alone can become problematic as not all subsequent decisions that need to be made will fall under the scope of their PR.

If a young person aged 16 and 17 lacks capacity to consent to an admission, then they can be admitted in their 'best interests' providing it does not amount to a 'Deprivation of their Liberty'. The Deprivation of Liberty Safeguards is the procedure prescribed in law that protects an individual's rights if they are, or may become, deprived of their liberty in a hospital setting in England and Wales. Psychological practitioners working in crisis and in-patient settings should seek specialised training on the MHA and its applications as providing more depth to the MHA is beyond the scope of this chapter (See Chapter 22).

5.2.9 Key points from this section

- It is good practice to include both parents, children and young people in decisions about their care.
- One parent with PR can consent on behalf of their child for a referral, assessment and intervention if their child is under 16.
- Under 16-year-olds are not assumed to be competent to consent to their treatment and so they should be proactively assessed on whether they can also make decisions about their care and this test of their competence to make decisions is referred to as the 'Gillick competence test'.
- A child should be supported to make decisions about their care with developmentally appropriate information, time and support. Even if a child cannot give valid consent or assent it is still important to gain their co-operation and have an understanding of the child's evolving capacity to make decisions about their care.
- A Gillick competent child can refuse their care.

- It is important to document the basis on which you determine the child's competence to proceed or not proceed with your care.
- Young people's (aged 16 and 17) decision-making powers are similar to adults and fall under the Mental Capacity Act (2005).
- 16 and 17 year olds are assumed to have capacity to consent unless proved otherwise. They do not need a parent with PR to proceed with their care. Although it is good clinical practice to discuss potential benefits.
- Consent to your intervention can be withdrawn by the child, adult with PR and young person 16 and over at any time. Therapeutically, you may wish to balance challenges to the intervention carefully with explicit withdrawal of consent.
- CYP can refuse treatment and intervention and if this decision is considered to be against their best interests or it puts them at risk of harm to themselves or others the Mental Health Act (1983) may be used.
- Parents/carers can refuse treatment and intervention for their child and if it is against the child's best interests then the courts may become involved.

5.3 Safeguarding

5.3.1 Introduction

Children do not choose their parents, caregivers or families. In the early years, children are entirely dependent on carers to attend to their needs to facilitate development. As the child develops, other systems grow in importance including peers, those in education and the wider society. Research has repeatedly shown the devastating effects that abuse and neglect have on child development and mental health (Howe, 2005).

Psychological practitioners often find themselves sitting with a child who they may suspect to be experiencing a form of abuse and/or neglect. They may also be in the position of having concerns about a child's wellbeing.

This section of the chapter will firstly consider what is meant by safeguarding, and a systems-based model published by the BPS (2018) will be outlined. This framework conceptualises safeguarding within multiple systems intersected by a range of themes highlighted by Serious Care Reviews. Secondly, consideration will be given to how safeguarding concerns can be best responded to as they occur in the process of in-person and virtually offered clinical work. In this part of the chapter, 'children' will be used to refer to those aged under 18.

5.3.2 Definitions

What is meant by safeguarding children? Statutory guidance defines it as 'protecting children from maltreatment; preventing impairment of children's health or development; ensuring that children are growing up in circumstances consistent with the provision of safe and effective care and taking action to enable all children to have the best outcomes'. (Working Together to Safeguard Children, DfE, 2022). Figure 5.5 provides information about the Children Act (1989, 2004) and the Children and Social Work Act (2017).

A history of child protection started in 1889 with the passing of the 'Children's Charter'. For the first time in documented history, the Police could arrest anyone causing a child harm. Over the course of 100 years various amendments, new legislation and policies have been devised and implemented. By the late 1980s, it was clear that existing legislation had become complicated and burdensome to the point where professionals in local authority services, tasked with protecting children, were increasingly unclear about how to act.

Children Act (1989)
The Children Act (1989) reformed the law to simplify existing legislation and strengthen the safeguarding protections for children. These included:

Section 17 – enquiries and provision of services for children in need. These include children who, without the intervention of services, will have difficulty of achieving or maintaining a reasonable standard of health or development including children who are diagnosed disabled.
Section 20 – provision of accommodation to children who require it.
Section 47 – enquiries and provision of services for children at risk of or suffering significant harm.

Fundamentally, the Children Act made it clear that safeguarding children was the responsibility of everyone, and those professionals in a position of responsibility for children are duty-bound to report and record as appropriate any concerns they may have for the safety of children.

Children Act (2004)
In January 2003, Lord Laming published his report following an investigation into the reasons for Victoria Climbié's death. Victoria Climbié was an 8-year-old Ivorian girl who was tortured and murdered in by her great-aunt assisted by her great-aunt's partner. She died on 25 February 2000. Lord Laming's report identified several opportunities where professionals, across a range of services including those from social services, police and health, could have intervened to protect Victoria, but did not. The report concluded that the framework of the Children Act (1989) did not require revision – the main concerns related to issues in implementation.
Various measures to improve implementation of the Children Act were published in 2004. These included the creation of Children's Trust Boards and Local Safeguarding Children Boards (LSCBs) tasked with promoting co-operation between agencies and to make safeguarding and welfare of children a key part of professional's everyday practice.

Children and Social Work Act (2017)
In 2017, the Children and Social Work Act amended the Children Act (2004) to further enhance co-operation of local agencies. The LSCBs were replaced with local safeguarding partnerships (LSPs) who determine the processes for safeguarding in their locality.

Figure 5.5 The Children Act (1989, 2004) and Children and Social Work Act (2017).

Safeguarding, in terms of child protection is concerned with addressing incidents of abuse and neglect. Abuse has been categorised as physical (when a child is deliberately hurt, causing physical harm); emotional (when a child is continually emotionally mistreated) and sexual (when a child is forced or enticed to take part in sexual activities). Neglect occurs when a child's basic physical and/or emotional needs are not being consistently met.

There are certain forms of abuse that pervade all categories. Defined as context abuse or extra-familial abuse, these are experiences of significant harm that occur beyond the familial context where parents' and carers' scope of influence is limited. Examples include child sexual exploitation (a child is coerced or groomed into exploitative situations and relationships), bullying and cyberbullying, female genital mutilation and child trafficking.

5.3.3 A Systems Model of Safeguarding

Child psychological practitioners are familiar with the process of conceptualising complex and multifaceted ideas within a theoretical model. *Safeguarding Children and Young People: Every Psychologist's Responsibility* (British Psychological Society, 2018) is a key text for every practitioner. The guidance proposes a systems-based model to aid decision making in safeguarding practice. This involves comprehensively taking account of the multiple systems surrounding a child while recognising there are a range of influencing factors that shape the responses of those within systems. The model can be used to formulate safeguarding concerns, consider risk and resilience within those formulations and use the formulation to inform suitable interventions. A brief overview of the model now follows.

Systems: The model places the child at the centre and then, in ever-widening concentric circles the systems fan out with parents/carers and family in the innermost circle (most influence) followed by education, peers, the community, professionals, organisations and society in decreasing levels of influence over the child. As the child moves through developmental stages, other systems will become more or less important. For example, it is known that peers have an increasing sphere of influence in adolescence compared to early childhood (Wang et al., 2007). It is also known that systems do not operate in isolation, but rather interact to decrease or increase risk. It is useful to keep in mind both the systems as a whole and the individuals/groups within that system.

Influencing factors: The second part of the BPS (2018) model proposes several factors that traverse each of the layers. SCRs take place where abuse and/or neglect are suspected or known to be a significant contributory factor to a child or vulnerable adult suffering a serious injury or death. The findings from SCRs are disseminated and utilised in policy with the aim of preventing similar incidents from occurring in the future. The factors within this model were selected from themes identified across a range of SCRs as being important for everyone in a safeguarding role. Influencing factors include values and ethics, knowledge and learning, power, culture, resources and finances, attitudes and heuristics, relationships and trust, group and stress.

A significant challenge for practitioners is in how to respond to instances when a child discloses a safeguarding concern or there are aspects about their presentation and/or interaction with parents/caregivers that leaves the practitioner feeling concerned. This will be considered more fully in the second part of this safeguarding section. Firstly there follows an exploration of the influencing factors of relationship/trust and knowledge/learning proposed through a series of questions that encourage the practitioner to think carefully about their readiness and the readiness of their service to manage safeguarding concerns when they arise. Consideration of the remaining influencing factors will be interspersed throughout.

5.4 Relationships and Trust

5.4.1 Introduction

The importance of relationship and trust can be considered throughout the systems in which the child resides (i.e. ranging from parents/carers to society). Starting with how the practitioner develops therapeutic relationships with children and their parents followed by how they understand the relationships children have with their friends and the parents of those friends and onto thinking about the various relationships the child and parents have with individuals within wider networks, such as school.

5.4.2 How Would the Practitioner Define the Quality of the Therapeutic Relationship with the Children they Meet?

There is substantial evidence highlighting the importance of the therapeutic relationship on mental health outcomes (Wampold, 2015). Excellent verbal and non-verbal clinical skills, the carefully held balance between validation and change techniques (Dimeff & Linehan, 2001) and how the relationship is attended to, particularly where significant differences exist between therapist and child, are some of the key influences on development of the therapeutic relationship (Hartley et al., 2022). A well-functioning therapeutic relationship is a pre-requisite for children to feel able to discuss concerns of a safeguarding nature with their practitioner. Recent research exploring children's perspectives of an effective safeguarding system highlight their repeated commentary on the importance of feeling that they will be believed when speaking about concerns of a safeguarding nature, that they will have their concerns validated and acted upon. This is more likely to occur if attention is paid to the relationship from the start, ruptures are managed when they occur and the relationship quality is regularly reviewed through observation, conversation and use of questionnaires such as the Session Rating Scale (Duncan et al., 2003).

5.4.3 How are Professional Boundaries Understood?

An important professional issue to consider is how minded the practitioner is to the creation and maintenance of appropriate boundaries, which are vital for the development of therapeutic relationships and how safe children feel in talking about issues of safety in their lives (Ryan et al., 2021). Boundaries can be implicit (unspoken or assumed) such as the child (and parent) expecting the practitioner to be empathic and for them to be the focus. Explicit boundaries, by contrast are discussed, often at the first meeting and include understanding of confidentiality, length of appointments, the therapy being offered and what is expected. Reflecting on clinical practice and discussion in supervision is key to protecting oneself from boundary violations that arise from misconduct and/or poor application of skills.

5.4.4 Do Children and their Carers Understand the Principles of Confidentiality?

Children and their carers need to be informed of confidential criteria at the first point of contact and have this information adapted according to the developmental stage of the child. It is also helpful to provide periodic reminders. The BPS *Practice Guidelines* (2017) provide information for child psychological therapists. In summary, clinical material discussed is privileged between child and psychological practitioner unless information is disclosed that places the child at risk of harm from themselves, from others and/or to others.

In most situations, it would be explained to the child why confidentiality needs to be broken, their consent to share information would be sought and what the next steps are in terms of who the information will be shared with explained. If consent is not provided, the practitioner will need to decide if overriding consent is in the child's best interests. In exceptional circumstances, it may be necessary to breach confidentiality without informing the child. For example, if telling the child what is planned might potentially increase the risk of harm.

5.4.5 How are the Relationships between the Child and their Parents/carers?

Another strand to consider in therapeutic work is the quality of relationships between the child and members of their family at home. High-quality relationships where family members are able to mentalise and communicate sensitively with one another is predictive of good mental health and reduced risk of safeguarding concerns (Rossouw et al., 2021).

A helpful question can be is how often are the child and their caregivers seen together. The developmental age of the child can mean that an indirect intervention with the caregivers is appropriate to achieve the therapeutic goal(s). With a developmentally older child, the clinical work might be direct and only involve caregivers to a degree. Children and caregivers will have their own views about relationships at home and seeing them together can provide opportunities for discussing these relationships.

Mentalising theory is a useful framework for conceptualising how child maltreatment occurs, and this can be particularly helpful when working with parents where abuse/neglect has occurred. Mentalising is concerned with the ability and capacity to accurately imagine the mental states of self and others (Allan & Fonagy, 2006). One hypothesis for why child maltreatment occurs is because the caregiver finds themself in a position where significant difficulty is experienced in their ability to mentalise the child (Byrne et al., 2019). A range of evidence-based interventions are available that support the development and maintenance of mentalising within families with the aim of reducing the incidence and likelihood of child maltreatment. For further details, please see Midgley and Vrouva (2012).

5.4.6 Is the Team Cohesive, with Good Communication between Colleagues?

The BPS model (2018) invites child psychological practitioners to think about and reflect on the teams they work in and the relationships they have with colleagues both within and across services. Much like the children being worked with and the emotional containment being provided, practitioners also need to feel a sense of containment when speaking to colleagues about their concerns, that they will be taken seriously with time given to formulate these concerns.

This can be difficult when working in busy teams where time is a precious commodity due to waiting lists and busy diaries, for example. Teams may give the implicit (and sometimes explicit) message is that as an autonomous practitioner, the practitioner's role is to manage risk themselves. When team dynamics such as these exist, it is vital to raise concerns through the various mechanisms available including clinical supervisors and safeguarding leads as well as formal channels of escalation within services.

5.4.7 How is the Practitioner's Relationship with Colleagues in Other Agencies?

Working as a child psychological practitioner is a busy and demanding role. It can be difficult enough to spend sufficient time developing relationships with one's own colleagues! Findings from SCRs repeatedly highlight the communication failures between agencies as a contributory factor to serious incidents (Firmin, 2020). There are a range of things that can aid relationship development. When starting in a new service, take the time to visit other agencies and attend multiagency meetings. Taking the time to develop relationships with social workers and safeguarding leads in local schools, for example, can facilitate the sharing of information and collaborative approach to safeguarding. Please see Edwards (2011) as a starting point for further thinking and ideas on the subject of building inter-agency relationships.

5.4.8 Is the Practitioner Able to Discuss Safeguarding Concerns in Clinical Supervision Freely?

Under the BPS practice guidelines (2017), child psychological practitioners should have access to regular clinical supervision in which the content and processes of their clinical work can be discussed and reflected upon. A well-functioning supervisory alliance that is looked after by supervisor and supervisee is vital for the supervisee feeling able to explore hypotheses in a supportive, but curiously challenging manner (Corrie & Lane, 2015). In the case of immediate safeguarding concerns, it is not appropriate to wait for scheduled clinical supervision. Clinical supervision is a space for reflecting once a social care referral has been made and for formulating instances where the child psychological practitioner has concerns but needs to consider the various potential issues influencing them. For example, the quality of the therapeutic relationship with the child and their carers, family culture and issues of difference.

5.5 Knowledge and Learning

5.5.1 Introduction

The second influencing factor to be considered is how the practitioner's own knowledge informs them about what abuse/neglect is and how to recognise it, together with the national/local procedures for responding to safeguarding concerns.

Maltreatment of children can be hard to recognise. One of the findings from the SCR following Victoria Climbié's death was the failure of professionals in recognising the extent of abuse and neglect she suffered (Laming, 2003). There are a variety of ways in which knowledge about safeguarding can be developed and maintained. It is vital that child psychological practitioners keep up-to-date with local and national Child Protection guidelines. These are regularly updated following SCRs.

5.5.2 Does the Practitioner have Knowledge of the Vulnerability Factors for Children Suffering Maltreatment?

A challenge faced by child psychological practitioner (and for others working with children) is in recognising the early warning signs of maltreatment. The important of recognising early signs cannot be underestimated. Robust research evidence points to the far reaching and long-term consequences of the adverse child experiences (ACEs) for children's development and wellbeing (for further details see Hays-Grudo & Morris, 2020).

A range of factors exist that increase the vulnerability of a child experiencing abuse and neglect. Holding these in mind when undertaking clinical work is the first step towards considering the level of risk for maltreatment. The National Institute for Health and Care Excellence (NICE) has compiled a list based on research and outcomes of SCRs (NICE, 2017) that are summarised in Figure 5.6. The presence of one or more vulnerability factor does not predict with certainty that maltreatment will occur but they are useful to keep in mind when assessing and formulating risk.

Socioeconomic factors

- Poverty
- Poor housing

Parental factors

- Substance misuse problems, which can reduce the physical, cognitive and emotional capacity for keeping a child's needs in mind.
- History of domestic abuse for a myriad of reasons including the risk of children being injured in the crossfire if they attempt to mediate and reduced parental capacity for childcare. Cultural or religious beliefs in the need for marriage preservation can prevent people from seeking help or leaving their partners.
- Emotional volatility.
- Mental health problems that significantly impact on the tasks of parenting.
- Lack of social support for the family. For example, a young mother who has acrimonious relationships with her wider family or the couple who married outside their own religion, ostracised by their respective families/community and are raising children alone.
- Parents who hold certain beliefs about spirit possession or have other strong religious convictions often interpret children's behaviour as being evidence of the presence of evil for which the remedies are harmful.

Child factors

- Child who is physically and/or learning disabled because they may have an impaired capacity to resist or avoid abuse.
- Temperament for example, those children who are more active and impulsive.
- Age and gender increase vulnerability for certain types of abuse and neglect. For example, boys may be less likely to disclose sexual exploitation.
- Children attempting to develop their self-identity in families where members may have very different religious, cultural or ethnic backgrounds. This may translate into a variety of expectations such as appearance, behaviour, life choices. For example, children in foster families or children raised in Western culture whose parents grew up in a significantly different culture.

Factors that predict recurring or persistent child abuse and neglect

- Parent or carer that does not engage with services.
- There have been one or more previous episodes of child abuse or neglect.
- The parent or carer has a mental health or substance misuse problem that has a significant impact on the tasks of parenting.
- There is chronic parental stress.
- The parent or carer experienced abuse or neglect as a child.
- In efforts to be culturally sensitive, professionals can sometimes inadvertently accept substandard care.

Figure 5.6 Vulnerability factors for child abuse and/or neglect Adapted from NICE, 2017.

In addition to factors found to increase vulnerability of a child to abuse and/or neglect, a range of warnings signifying a child's experience of maltreatment have been documented (e.g. HM Government, 2015; NICE, 2017). The reader is encouraged to develop familiarity with the indicators of harm, which are covered in Tables 5.1–5.3 and 5.4.

5.5.3 What Might be the Factors Influencing Formulation of Risk?

Formulating risk is the process of understanding the issues underpinning risk concerns from a range of sources (e.g. the child, carers, school) within a structure that enables the creation of interventions predicted to manage the risk of harm to self, others and from others.

Table 5.1 Physical abuse.

Definition	Warning signs to look out for
Occurs when someone inside or outside the family unit deliberately physically hurts a child and can take a number of different forms such as hitting, burning and/or shaking. Physical harm may also be caused when a parent or carer deliberately induces illness in a child or fabricates symptoms of an illness.	• Frequent injuries • Unexplained bruises, cuts, burns or bite marks

Table 5.2 Emotional abuse.

Definition	Warning signs to look out for
Emotional abuse is the 'persistent emotional maltreatment of a child' (HM Government, 2015, p. 7). This can take the form of bullying in person or online via social networks, online games or mobile phones, exposure to domestic abuse and parental direct psychological abuse.	• The child worries a great deal about doing something wrong • Unusually withdrawn, often has no friends • In the carer–child interaction you notice verbal and non-verbal behaviours that signal withdrawal of attention • The parent frequently blames their problems on the child • The child is frequently compared in a negative way to other siblings or other children • The carer behaves in a way that has the strong potential to humiliate the child

Table 5.3 Sexual abuse.

Definition	Warning signs to look out for
Physical or non-physical (e.g. forcing a child to watch graphic material) sexual activities with a child that can be inter familial (within families) and extra familial (outside of families).	• Physical sexual health problems • Children who have knowledge of sexual activities, use specific sexual language and/or try to initiate sexual games that is inappropriate for their age and stage of development

Table 5.4 Neglect.

Definition	Warning signs to look out for
A child's basic physical and emotional needs are consistently not met.	• The child is wearing clothes that are dirty, inappropriate (e.g. not wearing a coat in winter) or not fit for wearing • Appointments are frequently missed • Carers who do not seek immediate medical care for their children when they are ill or injured • Children who repeatedly harm themselves or others

Therefore, it is important for child psychological practitioner to ensure the voices within the multiple systems are represented within the formulation. A suggested approach to achieving this aim is to utilise the systems model outlined in this chapter within a model of team formulation (Division of Clinical Psychology, 2011). This approach enables representatives from across systems (e.g. parent, family member, teacher, social worker, youth worker) to actively explore together the various influences that are occurring to create concerns around risk. The opportunity is afforded to consider how each member of the formulation team views the problem, potential solutions and who is responsible for which part. The adolescent mentalisation-based integrative therapy (AMBIT) model espouses an approach to supporting teams and developing avenues of help to vulnerable adolescents (Bevington & Fuggle, 2012; Fuggle et al., 2015), which provides a useful framework for organising team formulation meetings.

Important questions to reflect on during team formulation include:

- Who holds power across and within systems? Are certain voices more privileged and taken more seriously and if so, why might this be and what effect does it have on the risk formulation?
- Are there particular cultural and diversity issues at play? Have these been taken account of in the formulation?
- What thinking biases might be present within individual members and as a group?
- What role do resources and finance play in the understanding of risk and in the available solutions?
- A group identity emerges when individuals are bought together for a specific purpose. How does the group identity and its associated culture and norms impact on the risk formulation? Research has shown the power of groupthink (when group members act in such a way to prevent conflict, for example, by confirming to the majority view) and over-optimism on decision making that is often not in the best interest of the child (Munro, 1999).

Spending time reflecting on the questions posed in this section will aid the process of making decisions when safeguarding concerns are presented by children.

Our attention now turns to what to consider, and actions required when the practitioner is faced with a safeguarding concern.

5.6 Managing Safeguarding Concerns in the Immediacy

> You are in an appointment with a child, in person or virtually. You might be on your own with them or a parent might be present. Perhaps they tell you something directly that leaves you feeling concerned for their safety or they exhibit unusual verbal and/or non-verbal behaviour that worries you. You may have been in this situation on many occasions, or this might be the first time. What you know is that it is your responsibility to explore further and consider your role in preventing or stopping maltreatment.

There exists a range of documents that provide guidance on managing concerns in the moment, processes to follow after a disclosure or if a concern is suspected. These documents include; *What To Do if You're Worried a Child is Being Abused* (HM Government, 2015); *Child Abuse and Neglect* (NICE, 2017); *CAMHS: Learning from Serious Case Reviews* (National Society for the Prevention of Cruelty to Children (NSPCC), 2017); *Principles for Conducting Virtual Consultations with Children and Young People* (Royal College of Paediatrics and Child Health, 2021). Child psychological practitioners will have access to local policies on safeguarding practitioners working with vulnerable children and will undertake mandatory and regular safeguarding training. The material presented next has been drawn from existing safeguarding guidelines referenced earlier in the paragraph, and from clinical practice from within various multidisciplinary teams.

5.6.1 At the Point of Disclosure or Concern is Suspected

- The practitioner may well experience an emotional reaction to what the child is telling them. Developing reflexive practice (i.e. noticing, processing and responding appropriately to cognitive and affective states in the moment) is an integral part of training (Bager-Charleson, 2020). Utilising this ability is key to noticing and managing one's own emotional response so one can remain present for the child. Hearing children's experiences of maltreatment can be very difficult. It is crucial to ensure time is taken to debrief with someone afterwards.
- Take your time, slow down the conversation and avoid interrupting the child. It is important to let them speak at their own pace. Recognise and respond to their verbal and non-verbal language (i.e. reflect, check understanding, use their language) and remember that it may take several conversations for them to share what's happened. Be patient.
- Just as you would with any other child, show compassion as well as concern. This may be the first time a child has opened up about an issue of safety. Validating comments such as 'You've been really brave today' can be helpful.
- Carefully consider the way questions are phrased, particularly avoiding leading questions that is, 'Did he say, he would then…' instead, 'Can you tell me what happened next?'. It is important to ensure you remain as non-biased as possible as formal investigations may be one of the next steps.
- If the child's caregiver(s) are present, make sure there is an opportunity to observe and talk to the child on their own.

- Parents/carers may explain that their cultural or religious beliefs instruct them to parent in certain ways. While it is important to remain culturally sensitive, if a child is at risk of or subject to actual harm, action is required. Information derived from case reviews where issues of culture and religion contributed to child abuse and/neglect have highlighted the importance of professionals balancing the need to remain respectful while remaining alert for signs where attempts are made to conceal child protection issues behind religious and cultural practice (NSPCC, 2014).
- Keep in mind the developmental age of the child when having these conversations. Some children may benefit from writing things down or drawing out what has been happening.
- Children have been clear about what they want from those providing safeguarding. For example, in addition to being listened to, children need to know what action will be taken, how and with whom. It is important for the purposes of maintaining the therapeutic relationship that children are kept informed throughout the process especially if they want their disclosure to be kept confidential and that isn't possible (Department for Education, 2022).

5.6.2 Following the Disclosure

Steps Involving the Child

- Explain to the child what will happen next. If this involves breaking confidentiality, explain why it is necessary. Ensure they understand about being kept informed of the steps along the way. Do they understand the process of referring to Children Social Care (CSC) and the reasons for this? Language should be adapted according to the developmental age of the child.
- Consider whether it is safe for the child to leave the appointment to return home. There are times when it is appropriate to ask another practitioner to sit with the child while a supervisor, safeguarding lead or another member of the team is consulted to consider next steps. For example, the child says they know they will be beaten for returning home late.
- Social media is an important part of children's lives. It is a key medium in which they communicate with their peers and friends, which can be a source of both resilience and risk. Understanding how they understand and use social media is important for monitoring risk.

Steps Involving Children's Social Care and the Practitioner's Own Service

- Make a phone call to the local CSC team explaining the reasons for the call. This needs to be followed up with a written referral. Accurately represent their words, using their actual words unless there is a good reason not to, for example if this would include information about another child or young person. Discuss if there are issues of culture and/or religion contributing to the concerns.
- Discuss with the triaging social worker as to whether it is appropriate to inform the child's caregivers of the referral. If the caregivers are linked directly to the safeguarding concern, there may be reasons for not informing them initially of the referral to CSC (e.g. if informing them increases the risk of harm to the child).

- Always discuss with a supervisor and service safeguarding lead. The timing of this conversation will depend on the urgency of the safeguarding concern (e.g. there may be no time if there is an immediate concern). Following a referral, take some time to reflect on the process and debrief with another practitioner if one is available. Share your concerns and reasons for referral at your team meeting to seek other perspectives and agree next steps with regards to care.
- Children's social care have 24 hours to provide a response to a safeguarding concern. When the referral is received, they will review the information and RAG rate (red = high risk; amber = moderate risk; green = low risk). Their ability to RAG rate is dependent on your ability to provide accurate and comprehensive information from your discussions. If you have not received a reply acknowledging your referral and/or you haven't received a reply within a timeframe that you thought the referral warranted, then it is your duty to contact CSC to follow up on your concerns.
- Following a referral, record the concerns and actions on the service's electronic records system. This will include a risk assessment on the concerns relating to harm from others to self and from others. Many systems have an alert system that requires activation so that any practitioners accessing the child's record will see immediately that a safeguarding concern has been raised.
- Children may disengage from child mental health services following a disclosure, particularly if action to safeguard was taken without their consent. Their disengagement, while understandable, increases risk. There may be a need to transfer care to another practitioner or to find alternative methods for engagement (e.g. changing the venue, moving from face-to-face to virtual appointments).

Steps Involving the Child's Parents/carers

- If you do inform the child's caregivers, it is important to provide clear reasons for the referral and what the next steps are. Parents may ask what the options are following an assessment from CSC. Familiarising yourself of these options beforehand is important (e.g. knowing the difference between sections defining 'Child in Need' and 'Child Protection' in the Children Act (1989, 2004).
- Access to the Internet can be very difficult for parents to manage, but it is important that they and children understand that while the Internet offers a great deal, there are websites that encourage harm. Supporting children to remain curious and 'fact-check' information they read can be undertaken during an assessment and/or intervention.

5.6.3 Post-referral

Steps Involving the Child and/or Parents/carers

- There may be times when the child and/or caregivers disagree or convey strong emotions to the practitioner regarding the decision to refer to CSC. Attempting to repair these ruptures can salvage the therapeutic relationship. However, there may be times when this isn't possible and either they disengage from the service or they require transfer to another practitioner. As compassionate child psychological practitioners, this can be difficult to manage. Having space to reflect and think through with a supervisor and/or team is important.

- When practitioners meet carers of the child who appear to share their values, are concerned and express a desire to be helpful there is a tendency to overestimate their ability to protect the child from harm. On some occasions, practitioners may even find themselves viewing them as equal partners. We have to remain mindful of their desire to be helpful (e.g. some carers will deliberately present in this way in order to dull the practitioner's radar for risk) and ensure they are cognitively and affectively equipped to support any interventions.
- Paying attention to fathers is another important point raised in SCRs. Involving fathers in assessments and risk plans is crucial because of the positive impact they can provide. For example, rectifying under-involvement of a father can reduce the stress on the mother enabling improvements in her cognitive and affective capacities for thinking about the child (Chung, 2021).

Steps Involving Children's Social Care and Your Service

- The local authority has the duty to investigate concerns about any child who is physically present in their area, even if the child is a resident of a different local authority. These will form part of Section 20 or Section 47 enquiries each of which have different timescales for completion.
- They may decide that the child has not been harmed and is not at risk and no further action is necessary (although the case could be referred to other agencies if appropriate).
- If they decide that the child may be at risk, an initial assessment is necessary to gather more information. This initial assessment must be completed within 7 working days of the referral to the child protection team.
- If at any point during the assessment process it becomes apparent that the child is in immediate danger, the team can apply for an emergency court order. An emergency protection order allows a child to be removed from home for up to 8 days.
- A range of options may be available following referral, including early help interventions, parenting programmes and therapeutic interventions, which will vary depending on the child's age and need.
- If the child remains open to CSC, the practitioner should keep in touch with the assigned social worker. They should discuss with them (and their supervisor and team) and agree their part in addressing the presenting problems in the care plan. This will be informed by the collaboratively derived psychological formulation. From a cognitive behavioural perspective, it is useful to ask the question, 'what is maintaining this child's mental health difficulties?'. The answer to this question will determine the extent and nature of the psychological practitioner's continuing involvement. For example, if it was theorised that a child is suffering from depression and this is attributed to their experience of chronic and continuing emotional abuse from their parents, the parental behaviour needs to be addressed within the remit of CSC prior to initiating an evidence-based treatment for childhood depression. This may need to be explained to the parents/carers if they experience confusion as to why their child is not currently receiving psychological treatment (although may remain open to mental health services).
- As the referring practitioner and/or continuing co-ordinator of the child's care, the practitioner may be expected to attend multiagency meetings to consider ongoing risks and management plans. Child psychological practitioners often attend Child in Need

meetings, Core Groups and Child Protection Conferences. These meetings require a report beforehand. It is useful for practitioners to familiarise themselves with the structure of these reports and what information is required. Finding sufficient time to complete reports can often be challenging. It is important to consider the audience reading the report or letter, adjust accordingly, provide explanations in lay terms and avoid using acronyms. It's important to allot time for completion ensuring the child and caregiver's voice is captured in the report. It is best practice to ensure the child (if developmentally appropriate) and/or parents/carers have an opportunity to read and comment on the report before it is submitted.

- Colleagues in other services may have different perceptions of risk and complexity in mental health. Spending time seeking their views to aid development of a truly collaborative formulation can ensure that services are 'on the same page'. This can address paralysis within systems when each sees the problem and its solution in different ways.
- Child mental health services, like all services, have practitioners joining and leaving. When a new practitioner takes over, they will not have the knowledge and experience of the child's abuse history. It is important to take the time to review notes as this is a crucial part of keeping in mind the 'whole picture' rather than just what is happening in the present.

5.7 Virtual Appointments and Safeguarding

Covid-19 changed the landscape in how child psychological practitioners undertake their clinical work. One of these is the provision of virtual appointments. There are numerous benefits to this including improved flexibility of timings and location the appointment can take place in (e.g. appointments at school). One challenge for the child psychological practitioner has been to consider safeguarding practices within the context of virtual appointments.

The Royal College of Paediatrics and Child Health (2021) have provided helpful safeguarding guidelines, which are adapted here for child psychological practitioners based clinical experience:

- It is important to check in the child's medical record as to whether there is a safeguarding alert in the same way as would happen prior to a face-to-face appointment.
- Older children may prefer to keep their cameras off. It is important they can be seen. Arrangements for use of cameras can be discussed in the intervention planning stage.
- Observe the interactions between the child and their parents.
- When the child is on their own, does the verbal and non-verbal body language indicate concern about being overheard? Does it appear that someone else is present in the room, but off-camera? If so, consider exploring the reasons someone else is present. If this doesn't seem appropriate, then consider ending the appointment and arranging a face-to-face session.
- The use of a code phrase that you have agreed with the child in a separate conversation can be helpful. The code phrase is designed to indicate to you that the child is concerned about something, but they can't talk about it virtually. Arrange a face-to-face appointment as soon as you can to discuss further.

- If you have safeguarding concerns at any stage, you should convert a virtual consultation to a face-to-face assessment.

The objective of this section in the chapter was to explore the child psychological practitioner's role in safeguarding children from the perspective of 'readiness to act' and what to consider when faced with a disclosure or when warning signs are observed. The BPS model (2018) provides a comprehensive systems model that includes a range of themes drawn from Serious Case Reviews to help to conceptualise and think broadly about safeguarding concerns so the psychological practitioner is as equipped as they can be to ensure that children remain safe from harm.

5.8 Conclusion

This chapter focused on the legal responsibilities that apply to consent when the referred client is a CYP and the professional and ethical guidance to do with safeguarding CYP. Whilst both legal and professional issues are connected, the area can become complex and there are differences between the two. The law operates in a binary system and professional issues that arise from applying this, including safeguarding issues, require multiple considerations including the parent–child relationship, balancing differing perspectives and mediation skills. This chapter has aimed to support the psychological practitioner with legal concepts and knowledge to do with consent, practical guidance and a comprehensive systems model to formulate decision-making strategies in a safeguarding context.

References

Allen, J. G., & Fonagy, P. (Eds.). (2006). *The handbook of mentalization-based treatment*. John Wiley & Sons, Inc.

Bager-Charleson, S. (2020). *Reflective practice and personal development in counselling and psychotherapy* (3rd ed.). Sage Publications Ltd.

Bailey, P., & Harbour, A. (1999). The law and a child's consent to treatment (England and Wales). *Child Psychology and Psychiatry Review, 4*, 30–34.

Bevington, D., & Fuggle, P. (2012). Supporting and enhancing mentalization in community outreach teams working with hard-to-reach youth: The AMBIT approach. In N. Midgley & I. Vrouva (Eds.), *Minding the child: Mentalization-based interventions with children, young people and their families* (pp. 163–186). Routledge/Taylor & Francis Group.

Bevington, D., Fuggle, P., Fonagy, P., Target, M., & Asen, E. (2012). Innovations in practice: Adolescent mentalization-based integrative therapy (AMBIT) – a new integrated approach to working with the most hard to reach adolescents with severe complex mental health needs. *Child and Adolescent Mental Health, 18*(1), 46–51.

British Psychological Society. (2017, August). *Practice guidelines*. https://www.bps.org.uk/sites/www.bps.org.uk/files/Policy/Policy%20-%20Files/BPS%20Practice%20Guidelines%20%28Third%20Edition%29.pdf

British Psychological Society. (2018, June). *Safeguarding children and young people: Every psychologist's responsibility*. https://www.bps.org.uk/sites/www.bps.org.uk/files/Policy/

Policy%20-%20Files/Safeguarding%20Children%20and%20Young%20People%20%28June %202018%29.pdf

Byrne, G., Sleed, M., Midgley, N., Fearon, P., Mein, C., Bateman, A., & Fonagy, P. (2019). Lighthouse parenting programme: Description and pilot evaluation of mentalization-based treatment to address child maltreatment. *Clinical Child Psychology and Psychiatry, 24*(4), 680-693.

Children Act. (1989). https://www.legislation.gov.uk/ukpga/1989/41/contents

Children Act. (2004). http://www.legislation.gov.uk/ukpga/2004/31/contents

Children and Social Work Act. (2017). http://www.legislation.gov.uk/ukpga/2017/16/contents/enacted

Chung, H. (2021). Shared care, father's involvement in care and family well-being outcomes: A literature review. *Government Equalities Office.* https://assets.publishing.service.gov.uk/government/uploads/system/uploads/attachment_data/file/957538/Shared_care_and_well-being_outcomes-_Literature_review.pdf

Cirasola, A., Midgley, N., Fonagy, P., Impact Consortium, & Martin, P. (2021). The alliance-outcome association in the treatment of adolescent depression. *Psychotherapy (Chic), 58*(1), 95–108.

Corrie, S., & Lane, D. A. (2015). *CBT Supervision.* SAFE Publications Ltd.

Department for Education. (2022). *Working together to safeguard children. Statutory guidance on inter-agency working to safeguard and promote the welfare of children.* https://www.gov.uk/government/publications/working-together-to-safeguard-children--2

Department of Health and Social Care. (2022). *Care and support statutory guidance.* https://www.gov.uk/government/publications/care-act-statutory-guidance/care-and-support-statutory-guidance

Department of Health. (2007). *The Mental Health Act (1983, 2007).* HMSO. https://www.legislation.gov.uk/ukpga/1983/20/contents

Dimeff, L., & Linehan, M. M., (2001). Dialectical behaviour therapy in a nutshell. *The California Psychologist, 34,* 10–13.

Division of Clinical Psychology. (2011, December). *Good practice guidelines on the use of psychological formulation.* http://www.sisdca.it/public/pdf/DCP-Guidelines-for-Formulation-2011.pdf

Duncan B. L., Miller S. D., Sparks J., Claud D., Reynolds L., Brown J., & Johnson L., (2003). The session rating scale: Preliminary psychometric properties of a 'working' alliance measure. *Journal of Brief Therapy, 3*(1), 3–12.

Edwards, A. (2011). Building common knowledge at the boundaries between professional practices: Relational agency and relational expertise in systems of distributed expertise. *International Journal of Educational Research, 50*(1), 33–39.

Firmin, C. (2020). *Contextual safeguarding and child protection: Rewriting the rules.* Taylor & Francis.

Fuggle, P., Bevington, D., Duffy, F., & Cracknell, L. (2015). The AMBIT approach: Working with hard to reach youth. *Mental Health Review Journal, 21*(1), 61–72.

Hartley, S., Redmond, T., & Berry, K. (2022, January 14). Therapeutic relationships within child and adolescent mental health inpatient services: A qualitative exploration of the experiences of young people, family members and nursing staff. *PLoS One.* https://doi.org/10.1371%2Fjournal.pone.0262070

Hays-Grudo, J., & Morris, A. S. (2020). *Adverse and protective childhood experiences: A developmental perspective*. American Psychological Association.

Henggeler, S. W., Schoenwald, S. K., Borduin, C. M., Rowland, M. D., & Cunningham, P. B. (2009). *Multisystemic therapy for antisocial behavior in children and adolescents* (2nd ed.). Guilford Press.

HM Government. (2015, March). *What to do if you're worried a child is being abused. Advice for practitioners*. https://assets.publishing.service.gov.uk/government/uploads/system/uploads/attachment_data/file/419604/What_to_do_if_you_re_worried_a_child_is_being_abused.pdf

Howe, D. (2005). *Child Abuse and Neglect. Attachment, Development and Intervention*. Palgrave Macmillan.

Huey, S. J., Henggeler, S. W., Brondino, M. J., & Pickrel, S. G. (2000). Mechanisms of change in multisystemic therapy: reducing delinquent behavior through therapist adherence and improved family and peer functioning. *Journal of Consulting and Clinical Psychology, 68*(3), 451–467.

Kaur, P. (2022). *Gillick competence, what is it and why is it important?* A checklist guide for therapists. https://medium.com/@drpinderkaur/gillick-competence-c059d4ac6659

Laming, W. H. (2003). *The Victoria Climbie inquiry: Report of an inquiry by Lord Laming* (Cm. 5730). The Stationery Office. https://assets.publishing.service.gov.uk/government/uploads/system/uploads/attachment_data/file/273183/5730.pdf

Manassis, K., Lee, T. C., Bennett, K., Zhao, X. Y., Mendlowitz, S., Duda, S., Saini, M., Wilansky, P., Baer, S., Barrett, P. M., Bodden, D., Cobham, V., Dadds, M. R., Flannery-Schroeder, E., Ginsburg, G., Heyne, D., Hudson, J., Kendall, P. C., Liber, J. M., … Wood, J. J. (2014, May). Types of parental involvement in CBT with anxious youth: A preliminary meta-analysis. *Journal of Consulting and Clinical Psychology, 82*(6). https://doi.org/10.1037/a0036969

Midgley, N., & Vrouva, I. (Eds.). (2012). *Minding the child: Mentalization-based interventions with children, young people and their families*. Routledge.

Munro, E. (1999). Common errors of reasoning in child protection work. *Child Abuse & Neglect, 23*, 745–758.

National Institute for Health and Care Excellence (NICE). (2017, October). *Child abuse and neglect*. https://www.nice.org.uk/guidance/ng76/chapter/Recommendations#factors-that-increase-vulnerability-to-child-abuse-and-neglect

National Society for the Prevention of Cruelty to Children. (2014). *Culture and faith: Learning from case reviews*. https://learning.nspcc.org.uk/media/1332/learning-from-case-reviews_culture-and-faith.pdf

National Society for the Prevention of Cruelty to Children. (2017). *CAMHS: Learning from case reviews. Summary of the risk factors and learning for improved practice for child and adolescent mental health services*. https://learning.nspcc.org.uk/media/1330/learning-from-case-reviews_camhs.pdf

Paul, M. (2004). Decision-making about children's mental health care: Ethical challenges. *Advances in Psychiatric Treatment, 10*(4), 301–311.

R (McConnell and YY) v Registrar General [2020] EWCA Civ 559.

Rossouw, T., Wiwe, M., & Vrouva, I. (Eds.). (2021). *Mentalization-based treatment for adolescents: A practical treatment guide*. Routledge.

Royal College of Paediatrics and Child Health. (2021, January). *Principles for conducting virtual consultations with children and young people.* https://www.rcpch.ac.uk/sites/default/files/generated-pdf/document/Principles-for-conducting-virtual-consultations-with-children-and-young-people.pdf

Ryan, R., Berry, K., Law., & Hartley, S. (2021, March 25). Therapeutic relationships in child and adolescent mental health services: A Delphi study with young people, carers and clinicians. *International Journal of Mental Health Nursing, 30*(4). https://doi.org/10.1111/inm.12857

Shaw, M. (2001). Competence and consent to treatment in children and adolescents. *Advances in Psychiatric Treatment, 7*(2), 150–159.

Wampold, B. E., (2015, September 25). How important are the common factors in psychotherapy? An update. *World Psychiatry, 14*(3). https://doi.org/10.1002%2Fwps.20238

Wang, A., Peterson, G., & Morphey, L. K. (2007). Who is more important for early adolescents' developmental choices? Peers or parents? *Marriage & Family Review, 42*, 95–122.

Wolpert, M. (2014). *Closing the gap through changing relationships.* The Health Foundation.

Young Minds, Amplifed (2020): *Evolving by Involving. Involving young people and their parent/carers in mental health care. Transforming participation across young people's mental health* https://www.youngminds.org.uk/media/0lcbhmqd/evolving-by-involving.pdf

6

Frameworks of Service Delivery

Organising Systems to Deliver Best Psychological Care
Duncan Law

6.1 Overview

This chapter is about service delivery frameworks. At first glance, the idea of a whole chapter on service delivery might seem, well, potentially a little dull and not a high priority for practitioners eager to provide the best care they can to children and young people (CYP). Well, the challenge in this chapter is to demonstrate that service delivery frameworks are all about good clinical care.

Good service frameworks help us provide best clinical care by ensuring that systems are organised to:

- promote good mental health,
- mitigate against psychological harm,
- identify need,
- ensure that a CYP's journey through the system is smooth and effective, and
- provide them with the best, and most appropriate clinical care for their needs

There is little debate about the *need* for service delivery frameworks, but there is much to discuss on *how* the system around CYP's mental health is structured (CAMHS Tier 4 Report Steering Group, 2014; Department of Health, 2015; HM Government, 2011; National CAMHS Review, 2008; NHS Health Advisory Service, 1995). They are much more than just frameworks to delivery therapy services, they are about *the whole* system that exists around CYP mental health. The value placed on service delivery frameworks mirrors how we, as a society, value mental wellbeing and how children are valued. It is deeply political; get it wrong and there is the potential to exacerbate generations of social injustice and flame inequality, get it right and there is an opportunity to not only improve the mental health of a generation, but also to improve their life chances in education, physical health, employment, relationships and as parents to future generations.

This chapter aims to:

- highlight the need for service delivery frameworks,
- address the issues that underlie this need,

Child Psychology: Pathways to Good Practice, First Edition.
Edited by Helen Pote, Anna Picciotto and Clare Norris.

- offer a brief history of service delivery in CYP mental health focusing on recent the frameworks that have the most influence today, and
- end by looking to the future and setting the challenge for the next wave of practitioners.

6.2 Introduction

Given this is a book about children and young people's mental health and this chapter is about service delivery, let me start by sharing something about my own childhood that is pertinent to both.

As an adolescent, back in the early 1980s, I had what I now know to have been an anxiety disorder. I say: 'I now know to have been an anxiety disorder', because at the time I had no idea what was 'wrong' with me. The anxiety significantly impacted my social life, my education and my participation in sport. I was worried, my family were worried about me, the school were worried too, they tried to get help for me and yet I received no professional help for my mental health difficulties. Fortunately, with the help of family and friends I was able to get on with my life and effectively manage the difficulties and deal with them effectively to a point where the anxiety was under control and eventually diminished enough to no longer have an impact on my life.

Looking back, I am now thankful for the experience I had. My limited, lived experience of mental health issues has proved a great asset as a practitioner. It also has driven my interest in service delivery. I got better, but it took a while, and those were some of the most difficult months of my life. I now realise that if my difficulties had been recognised as a mental health issue, I might have received an appropriate mental health intervention and I might have got better, sooner, but after all these years, this aspect of my personal experience is water under the bridge. What still bothers me, and drives my interest is topic, is not the fact that this happened to me: a white, British, cis male, from a stable family that although being far from affluent, was not deprived by any definition, I had not experienced trauma and I was reasonably bright and emotionally literate. Rather, the fact that if someone like me could experience a system not being effective, then how many others, especially those from far less privileged backgrounds, might the system not work for?

You might argue that this experience is of little relevance today, it happened a long time ago when children's mental health services were very different. Of course, much has changed in children's mental health services but sadly, one fact remains true that, as with this experience back in the 1980s, still today, most children who have a mental health difficulty will struggle to get appropriate support from a qualified mental health professional (Green et al., 2005; Sadler et al., 2018).

By implication there are a significant number of CYP (even if this is a significant minority) for whom the system does works, and they get a good experience of service. We know from clinical outcomes and satisfaction data (see also Chapter 8) that many CYP and their families have a very positive and effective experience of Child and Adolescent mental health services (CAMHS) (Sadler et al., 2018; Wolpert et al., 2016). There is no doubt that significant aspects of the CYP mental health system works and work well, improving lives, transforming lives and saving lives. There is equally little doubt that many lose out on such opportunities, and the reasons they lose out is due, in some significant part, to the mental health systems currently in place and how society chooses to organise service delivery.

For a number of young people with mental health difficulties, as will be argued later in this chapter, the most appropriate help will not necessarily need to come from a qualified mental health professional. What needs to be ensured is that there are systems in place, wherever children and young people are, that actively work to keep CYP in good mental health, identify those who have a mental health need, work to understand the story behind the difficulty and find the most appropriate intervention to help. In a nutshell this is what service delivery systems are all about. How to do this is the main subject of this chapter: how to organise the system in the best way possible to provide help, to those who need it in a way that is timely, respectful, and appropriate to the need.

6.3 Levels of Mental Health Need in CYP

Before this chapter continues to look at service delivery, some understanding of the level of need an effective system should be organised around is required. This is not a straightforward question to answer.

6.3.1 Prevalence and Demand

Early approaches to estimating need in CYP mental health focused on estimating the *demand* on services: how many children might ask for help from services (Kurtz, 1996). Later, a much more comprehensive study (certainly in terms of coverage) was reported on at the start of this century, by a psychiatry led team of researchers (Green et al., 2005). Their aim was to try to estimate the numbers of CYP in the community who might show a level of symptomology that was likely to indicate a mental illness.

To do this they used a sophisticated screening tool that had been developed for the task (Goodman et al., 2000). The tool looked at both symptoms and the impact of these symptoms on the child's life. The focus was not just on problem behaviours but also on behaviours that were indicative of positive mental wellbeing, the screening questionnaire focused on both *strengths and difficulties* and became known as the strengths and difficulties questionnaire or SDQ (again, see Chapter 8 for further details). They begin to identify CYP with observable behaviours which, if they were clustered in a particular way and with a certain degree of severity, might indicate a young person who, should they meet a psychiatrist, might be diagnosed with a mental illness.

Outputs from the screening tool were followed up by face-to-face clinical interviews that also explored a range of other issues including help seeking behaviour (Green et al., 2005). This survey, which became the benchmark of future prevalence surveys, estimated that at any one time, in the UK, about 1 in 10 CYP, between the ages of 5 and 16, would meet criteria for a diagnosable mental health disorder. Whereas the numbers who actually received any direct help from a trained mental health practitioner were much, much lower. They estimated that less than a third of CYP with a significant mental health issue received support from CAMHS directly.

The survey helpfully made the distinction between 'prevalence' and 'demand'. The team recognised the real difference between the number of CYP who might have a problem that could be defined as a mental health issue: *prevalence*, and those who came into contact with children's mental health services: *demand*. As was illustrated in the personal example, shared earlier in this chapter, just looking at demand for services hides the real level of need. If services are only organised around demand, then the potentially massive need that prevalence rates highlight may be missed.

The difference in the numbers between prevalence rates and demand on services highlights the gap in the system between those with a mental health need and those coming to the attention of mental health services. This raises important questions about what creates and maintains the gaps between someone having a mental health issue and someone seeking and finding appropriate help for it. The reasons for this gap are complex but some of the themes relate to awareness of mental health issues, stigma, accessibility of services and the provision of services that are provided in a way that are acceptable to CYP and their families (Faulconbridge et al., 2019a).

6.3.2 The Need for Prevention

There is an even bigger hidden need. Even if a sophisticated view of need is taken, which includes prevalence rather than just demand, the focus is still on a very medical view of mental health, which tries to distinguish between its absence or presence that is, 'do you have a mental illness or not?'. As will be described shortly, until recently nearly all mental health delivery frameworks focused on providing services to those who already had a mental health problem, usually one that would meet some predetermined diagnostic criteria. However, this misses an enormous opportunity for applied psychology namely, to understand and develop parts of a mental health system that focuses on positive mental wellbeing and an active focus on interventions that seek to *prevent* mental health issues (Faulconbridge et al., 2019b). Historical approaches to estimating demand that have focused on need, as defined by the presence of a 'problem', become organised around problems and the resolution of problems once they are present. More comprehensive systems are concerned with at how to prevent the problems in the first place.

If we look at parallels in physical health systems, we are into the realms of public health initiatives, protection from disease for example, through vaccination (something that has become all too familiar with over recent years), or road safety initiatives, such as the enforced wearing of seatbelts and speed limits, to prevent road traffic incidents and consequent physical injury. These initiatives acknowledge that the application of physical health theory and research can be actively and effectively applied to prevent problems rather than just dealing with them once they arrive. Services, looked at in this way, become organised around both *prevention* and *treatment*.

We can look at the impact of seatbelts on preventing death in the UK and show the impact of a preventative physical health measure (Webster, 2020). Unfortunately, no such robust data exists around preventative measure in mental health. This is, in part, due to the greater complexity of cause and effect of mental health and preventative measures. It is much harder to measure the numbers of CYP with a *need* to be actively helped to stay mentally well, but this should not stop us from organising mental health systems to focus on preventative interventions, and study their impacts on mental well-being (Troy et al., 2022).

Recent (pre-Covid) updates on prevalence rates in CYP indicate a significant increase in demand on services with a backdrop of an increase, but a much smaller increase, in prevalence of mental health issues in the community; an increase to one in eight CYP having a diagnosable mental health disorder (Sadler et al., 2018), suggesting demand is rising much faster than the community prevalence rate. However, the overall trend, as is so often the case with averaging data, masks a more complex story of bigger increases in mental health difficulties in some parts of the population than in others. In other words, there seem to be some groups of CYP for whom mental health issues are increasing at a much greater rate than others. One of the groups who have shown significantly poorer mental health, are older adolescent females estimated to be one in four (Green et al., 2005). As will be explored in the Section 6.4, the Covid-19 pandemic had a big impact on CYP mental health and, although the data is still being collected and analysed post-pandemic, it is clear that both prevalence and demand have significantly increased in recent years, but the impact has been far from equal across society (Jefferey et al., 2021).

In summary, it is difficult to get a picture of the true level of need of CYP mental health across society, and if the need cannot be estimated accurately, then how can it be ensured that systems are adequately resources to meet the need?

6.4 Resource Issues in the CYP Mental Health System

It is important to name something explicitly at this point, that is often shied away from, certainly in policy and commissioning discussion about CYP mental health: the gap in CYP mental health need and service provision is largely due to a lack of resources. Whatever way need is estimated, there is not, and never has been, enough resource within children's mental health services to meet that need effectively. The lack of resource in the CYP mental health system is largely a result of inadequate funding; successive governments, both national and local, have never made sufficient funds (money) available to truly aim to meet the mental health needs of children and young people. Indeed, in recent years government has acknowledged this with policy aiming to meet the needs of two-thirds of CYP with mental health issues (Department of Health, 2015). This still leave a staggering 33% of CYP with serious mental health issues with no government funded services at all. This is political, if this was the ambition for cancer care or diabetes care there would quite rightly be an outcry, but somehow this is seen as acceptable by government when it comes to CYP mental health.

One final point of clarity before moving on is that, although closely connected to money, the possibility to meet the mental health need in society is not purely a financial one. If services are to be provided that are equitable and effective in meeting need, how practitioners and practitioners work is as important as the resources that are at their disposal to work with. If the premise that there is not enough resource to go round to meet the need equitably and adequately is accepted, there are two options: first, fight, demand, campaign and vote, for more resource (this is political, as stated above), and second, use the precious resources available in the most efficient and effective ways to provide the best service possible.

However, this is where it starts to get really tricky, what does an efficient and effective service look like and what does it look like when commissioners and providers of services are grappling with the inherent lack of resource in the system? If there was one way of answering this there would be one perfect service delivery framework that could be signed up to, and this would be a short chapter. The fact is, the answer to this question is one for debate driven by our judgement on what effective looks like and driven, consciously or otherwise, by values and moral judgements on (in)equality.

6.4.1 Health Inequalities

It is widely known that healthcare systems are inequitable: some people and some groups of people are more likely to get more resource, better treatment and better outcomes than others (Marmot, 2020). This is true even in better-funded healthcare systems (Ramraj et al., 2016). It is also true in the UK healthcare systems some parts have better funding than mental health for example, cardiology and oncology. In all healthcare systems some people get better care than others.

6.4.2 Lessons from the Pandemic

More recently the Covid-19 pandemic shone a spotlight on health inequalities in a way that has highlighted some uncomfortable facts about health, mental health and of particular interest here, CYP's mental health. This section will take a look at some of the lessons from the pandemic and what it has highlighted about health inequality.

One of the really important reminders the pandemic has given (if indeed a reminder was necessary) is that mental health issues are largely the result of environmental factors, or at very least, severely impacted by the environments that CYP inhabit. A huge event such as the Covid-19 pandemic, with its impact on all aspects of everyone's life, has unsurprisingly had a huge impact on people's mental health (World Health Organization, 2022). One of the surprises is that the pandemic has not been detrimental to everyone's mental health: there are some groups of CYP who have appeared to flourish with regard to their mental wellbeing, whilst most others have experienced a large and negative impact (Jeffery et al., 2021). These impacts have not been distributed with any equity across communities. In summary, and at risk of oversimplifying the nuance of the impact, the metal health of those CYP with already good resources: emotional, financial and social, has tended to be less badly impacted than young people in environments with already fewer resources.

6.4.3 Prejudice and Inequality

It is also widely known that environmental issues impact some groups much more than others. Black, Asian and other minority ethnic groups tend, on the whole, to live in parts of society where resources are scarcer (Marmot, 2020). Furthermore, LGBTQ+ young people have fared less well during the Covid pandemic than other young people. The same is true of young women and young people with existing mental health difficulties (Jeffery et al., 2021).

So why are these health inequalities so stark? Well, if there is insufficient resource to go round there will always be unfairness somewhere in the system. This unfairness tends, on the whole, to be placed with minority groups, those who have less of a voice in the system and have been less involved in the development of services (Marmot, 2020). This is partly historical (see Section 6.5). Acknowledging that inequality and racism, sexism and homophobia are part of what has driven the development of services historically and accepting that steps must be taken to address and redress these systemic imbalances is essential for more equitable current and future service delivery frameworks.

How might these inequalities, driven by prejudice, start to be addressed? Well, this is a complex question for which there is no room to give it the justice it deserves in this chapter. What follows here is an admittedly oversimplistic resume of the issues. Prejudice exists where there is lack of knowledge, and it is exacerbated when resources are limited and the better resourced majority fear losing their advantage to the less well-resourced 'other'. This leads to a feeling of being under threat, and when people feel under threat, they tend to hold on more tightly to what they have. At the same time threat impacts on the ability to mentalise the other and with that, empathy is lost, which further exacerbates our lack of understanding which, in turn, exacerbates the threat. The problem perpetuates and is amplified. How do we begin to address this cycle of prejudice, which is inherent in all aspects of society? Caring and well-meaning mental health professionals are not exempt from human fallibilities and therefore are not exempt from prejudice. One way to begin to mitigate against this is to seek knowledge and understanding, to cede power and resource to the less powerful and less well resourced (Marmot, 2020).

What does this look like in mental health service provision? Well, it is what good 'co-production' looks like. Service delivery models that are driven by genuine co-production can begin to mitigate against some aspects of prejudice and ignorance. On a positive note, co-production is starting to be seen as a fundamental principle of good mental health provision (Department of Health, 2015) (see Box 6.1 for an example of co-production in action, and Chapters 9 and 24, for more details).

Box 6.1 Clinical example: MAC-UK – a co-produced service delivery framework

Probably the best example of a service where co-production was genuinely central to its service delivery, is MAC-UK. MAC-UK is a London-based charity that began to experiment with genuine co-production, working with CYP to build mental health provision from the ground up.

In its early days, MAC-UK genuinely lived its philosophy of ceding power to local communities and working with them to build new types of mental health provision, which were young people led. It was an attempt to provide services that were more acceptable and accessible particularly to the disenfranchised youth of inner-city London who tended to be under-represented as recipients of appropriate mental health care, but overly represented in the criminal justice system. MAC-UK and other organizations that recognized the limitations of current mental health provision, particularly for young people in marginalized communities who had experienced multiple trauma discrimination, demonstrated that hearing the voice of young people and supporting them to be heard could have transformative effects on how services were structured and how the whole understanding of mental health need and provision could be challenged and disrupted.

The story of MAC-UK started around 2008 when a recently qualified white female psychologist, Charlie Alcock, recognized that the black young men she saw in her local community, outside of the mental health service she worked in, were not being seen *in* the service. She employed a real co-production philosophy, by going to where the under-represented group were, to join them in their environment, to seek understanding and knowledge about their worlds, and to ask *them* what they wanted. She learnt that NHS mental health services did not work for them for a number of reasons including stigma, their physical location and the systems lack of ability to support some of the very complex needs they had across a range of domains: poverty, racism, trauma, housing issues. What Charlie heard from this disenfranchised group was that they wanted *'Music and Change'* (MAC). Somewhere they could go that was safe and where they could make music. Charlie set up a music studio in a safe house and through the music and safety, the young people began to share their stories. Trauma was often a central theme.

MAC-UK was staffed with clinical psychologists who held a broad view of what a mental health intervention looked like for the young people they worked with. For some it was the opportunity to find meaning though music, to be helped to find housing, or suitable education provision, with others it was to be supported through the criminal justice system. These were mental health interventions in their own right, and through these interactions the young people and the psychologists began to establish trust, which led to further work around trauma.

MAC-UK was an example of how services might look if they were created from the community up, with the young people's voice at the heart of the development. MAC-UK looked very different from traditional mental health service, there were no clinical spaces and no appointments, it was more like a youth club staffed by highly skilled mental health professionals who met the young people where they were at and were led by the young people, guided by the philosophy that *'every interaction counts'*. Every interaction was a mental health intervention.

It would be great to say that MAC-UK got it completely right, and that we should all copy of the MAC-UK approach, but reality is far messier when trying to apply a genuine coproduction philosophy. What MAC-UK did to get right, was that they had a guiding set of principles through which they aimed to address health inequalities for some communities. The application of these principles within society proved a much more complex and difficult thing to achieve. However, what should be held on to is that the MAC-UK experiment demonstrated that it is possible to apply the principles of co-production to create more equitable and accessible services.

Like any word that becomes en vogue, there is a danger that it loses its meaning and loses its power. The term 'co-production' is one such word that is in danger of becoming watered down to be mere tokenistic involvement from service users. Real co-production is where service provision starts with a clean sheet, engaging and joining with local communities to understand where they are at, what their needs and priorities are. It is about working with people to jointly create or 'co-produce' services that are acceptable

(Continued)

Box 6.1 (Continued)

and accessible to that particular community with service providers. Co-production leads to services that are recognized and accepted by those communities as people who can be trusted rather than groups to be suspicious of. Without trust, people are not open to learning and without learning they cannot change. One of the fundamentals of any good therapy is to build trust. The mistake sometimes made by practitioners is the belief that trust only exits between individuals, namely the client and the practitioner, when the reality is that trust exists between communities and systems, within which individual trust might flourish.

This is not an easy thing to do. Labelling groups and individuals who for whom existing services are not accessible or acceptable, as 'hard-to-reach' or 'ambivalent' serves to protect services from accepting the failures of the system. This needs to be turned on its head, accepting that it is services, not individuals, that are hard-to-reach and if systems are to change to address inequalities, the ambivalence of the decision makers and providers must be acknowledged.

6.5 A Brief History of Child Mental Health Provision

This chapter started with a bit of personal ancient history. It will now revisit the past for a while with a brief history lesson of children's mental health services. It can be helpful to have some idea of the past to help understand why current systems are organised as they are and, more helpfully, how this understanding of the past might be used to provide clues as to how systems might be changed and improved. Of course, throughout the history of humanity, families and communities, to a large extent, managed the mental wellbeing of their children without recognition that this is what they were doing, and without formal mental health systems and services to support them. It should not be forgotten that the largest part of the workforce in CYP mental health services are, and always have been, parents and grandparents.

Some of the earliest *formal* children's mental health services can be credited to the work of Anna Freud, youngest child of the father of psychoanalysis, Sigmund Freud. Anna Freud's pioneering work in the 1950s paved the way for what later became child guidance clinics with an emphasis on education attainment as much as mental wellbeing (Midgley, 2012). It was only towards the end of the 1980s that something resembling modern day children and adolescent mental health services began to develop (NHS Health Advisory Service, 1995). The following sections will describe four of the most influential stands of CYP mental, that have shaped the system and are still having impact on how it is organised today.

6.5.1 The Tired, Tiered System

It is the NHS Health Advisory Service (HAS) report in 1995 that is most often credited, or blamed, for the four-tier system that still has a grip on much of children's mental health provision even to this day. It was in the HAS report that a four-level system was first comprehensively described. The four-tier system as described in the slightly later CAMHS review was:

> "**Tier 1:** Services provided by practitioners working in universal services (such as GPs, health visitors, teachers and youth workers), who are not necessarily mental health specialists. They offer general advice and treatment for less severe problems, promote mental health, aid early identification of problems and refer to more specialist services.
>
> **Tier 2:** Services provided by specialists working in community and primary care settings in a unidisciplinary way (such as primary mental health workers, psychologists and paediatric clinics). They offer consultation to families and other practitioners, outreach to identify severe/complex needs, and assessments and training to practitioners at Tier 1 to support service delivery.
>
> **Tier 3:** Services usually provided by a multidisciplinary team or service working in a community mental health clinic, child psychiatry outpatient service or community settings. They offer a specialised service for those with more severe, complex and persistent disorders.
>
> **Tier 4:** Services for children and young people with the most serious problems. These include day units, highly specialised outpatient teams and inpatient units, which usually serve more than one area." (CAMHS Review, 2008, p. 17)

To be fair, the HAS report was merely *describing* a system that already existed rather than making a recommendation for a new four-tier system, organised around problem severity. For the next 20 years children's mental health services were commissioned around this tiered system. There was a brief period in the early 2000s where the four-tier system was described in the, 'Every Child Matters', policy document, as a three-tiered system: universal, targeted and specialist (Department for Education, 2003). However soon, the specialist services were again subdivided into 'specialist' and 'highly specialist' and the four-tiered framework was back.

The tiered system is not fundamentally flawed as an idea, but its execution in real-world settings began to cause increasing difficulties for children and young people trying to access the higher tiers of the pyramid. Many young people and their families found it difficult to access more specialist help finding the service provision at the higher tiers to be inadequately resourced to meet the demand (National CAMHS Review, 2008). There were further anomalies of the different parts of the system not being coterminous, leaving gaps in provision. This resulted in young people being told: 'Your problem isn't bad enough for specialist help at Tier 3 CAMHS' only to find there was even less provision (or sometimes no provision) of lower-level support at Tier 2. In addition, the four-tier framework paid little if any attention to managing flow through the service that is, how to avoid children being stuck at Tier 3 because there was insufficient provision to be '*stepped down*' to Tier 2. Furthermore, it was a system that was organised around mental *ill-health* and gave no weight to long-term strategies of mental health promotion and prevention. People's lived experience, both young people and professionals, in and out of child mental health services, became one of frustration with a lack of provision, long weighting times, and dealing with unreasonable levels of bureaucracy. These experiences left the tiered system looking and feeling rather tired and outdated before new frameworks began to replace it.

The Rise of Participation and Co-production

Driven, in part by growing frustration and often poor experience of trying to get mental health support for children, pressure groups began to organise to give more voice to young people with lived experience of mental health and mental health systems. Organisations such as YoungMinds, the children's mental health charity, were at the forefront of this new movement. They, along with other organisations, began to advocate for young people's participation to influence and improve existing child and adolescent mental health services. This advocacy soon brought together young people with lived experience of mental health challenges and experience of services.

They showed the value of listening to the voice of young people to help create better systems of service delivery, and to disrupt the orthodoxy of professionally led services. Traditionally, professionals in CYP mental health took on the expert, paternalistic role of 'We know what's best for you.' This had led to the development of services with the professional at the centre of the system. The rise of participation and the power of young people's voices were amplified by organisations such as YoungMinds. This started to shift the narrative away from young people being seen as a 'problem to be treated', to one of them being seen as leading the solution. Their influence grew and soon the new participation movement was beginning to influence service delivery and government policy (CAMHS Tier 4 Report Steering Group, 2014). Young people's participation in service design and delivery is now the norm although the quality of participation is extremely variable across systems. This shift has created services that are becoming young person centred – although there is still a long way to go.

Some organisations were to take this idea much further and began to experiment with genuine co-production. Working with CYP to build mental health provision from the ground up. MAC-UK typified this revolutionary approach (see Box 6.1 and Chapter 25).

6.5.2 CAPA: The Choice and Partnership Approach

In parallel to the participation movement, in the early 2000s, professionals in two specialists CAMHS teams: East Hertfordshire and Richmond, began to try to make the existing system work better. The driver for the choice and partnership approach (CAPA) was an attempt to make best use of the available resources within CAMHS at the time. It aimed to organise services to provide the most appropriate and timely support for those who most needed it and could best use the resource on offer. It brought in service improvement and transformation methodology, particularly 'lean theory' combined with the values of participation and collaborative goal setting and partnership work in therapy (York & Kingsbury, 2013). At its heart was the stance of wanting to work with families in a way that acknowledged and harnessed a shared expertise approach. CYP and their families were seen as experts in their lives and mental health professionals brought a different expertise.

Working together and sharing these perspectives and knowledge resulted in more effective (better and faster) therapy (Clark et al., 2018).

Central to CAPA are the '5 Big Ideas', that combine a values driven clinical approach wrapped in an effective and efficient service delivery plan:

1. Choice
2. Selecting core partnership practitioner
3. Core and specific partnership work
4. Job planning
5. Peer-group discussion

Choice: Choice is the first contact point between CYP and CAMHS professionals. It combines elements of traditional assessment in that the aim is to understand the story of the problem the client is bringing. However, it differed from traditional mental health assessments at the time, which tended to be very structured with the purpose of categorising the problem in terms of diagnosis and severity. Choice appointments on the other hand, aimed to be collaborative, putting the CYP's voice at the centre by listening to them and hearing their goals and wishes about what they wanted to change about their own lives, synthesising the joint expertise to develop a joint formulation of the problem. The aim of the choice appointment was to reach a 'choice point' where options of ways forward were honestly set out with the CYP and their family, and the pros and cons discussed (York & Kingsbury, 2013).

The outcome of the Choice appointment again differed from the traditional assessment where the task was to decide if the CYP had a diagnosable mental health problem in which case the treatment was proscribed by the professional and the best treatment was normally one that involved an 'expert' mental health practitioner. In CAPA the outcome acknowledges that there are other ways to help young people improve their mental well-being, one of which might be to work with a mental health practitioner, but alternatives might include life changes: change of school, change of friends or self-help resources, all of which might not necessarily need the ongoing support of a mental health service. Or, the process of working with a practitioner for one session might lead to the realisation that the CYP and family might already be doing everything that is helpful to reach their goal and, again, might not need ongoing mental health support to do it. Using close family bereavement as an example, it almost always tends to lead to a high level of mental distress, but the mental distress is often best be resolved by the family taking, crying, remembering and processing the loss together. CAPA respects the choices of the CYP and family and aims not to over professionalise or pathologise mental distress.

Of course, for many, getting help from a professional might still be the best option. In which case the choice process helps ensure those moving to the help or 'Partnership' stage, are those who might be in a better position to use it and have the appropriate need for it.

Selecting Core Partnership Practitioner: If ongoing professional help is the outcome of the Choice appointment, the person goes into the 'Partnership' phase of the work. The next part of the CAPA process is to 'match' the client to a therapist with the right skills to help them. This is usually not the therapist who offered the Choice appointment. Again, this differed from traditional approaches where CYP were usually assessed and treated by the first practitioner they met in CAMHS at assessment (whether they were the best person to work with them or not). Matching therapist to the needs and goals of the client gave the opportunity to use resources in the most effective way for better outcomes, by providing a therapist with the right skills to work with the CYP (York & Kingsbury, 2013).

The matching process also ensured that the Choice therapist had genuinely understood the goals of the CYP and had reached a 'choice point'. This made sure that the receiving Partnership therapist, and the client, had clarity on the agreed aims of the intervention. Collaboratively agreed goals provide focus to the intervention, which otherwise might drift, taking more resource for one client, which leaves less resource for others. The others are usually those sitting on a waiting list to be seen (see also Chapter 8). The focus on the ending, right at the start of therapy, helped with 'letting go' when the work had been optimally helpful, rather than holding on to CYP because not all problems had been fully resolved.

Core and Specific Partnership Work: In CAPA, Partnership work (the main body of the intervention) is segmented into two pathways: 'Core' and 'Specific'. Core work constitutes the majority of work in the service. In CAPA services most people can be helped by core-level work, to have quick access to something that will help (York & Kingsbury, 2013). This relies on practitioners within services having, or being trained to have, a broad or extended skill set to be able to provide good-quality, evidence-informed interventions to a range of needs.

CAPA calculates the resources (number of sessions) typically needed for a Core Partnership intervention. It requires services to have reliable data on the average length of a Core Partnership. This figure varies depending on the service but tends to hover around the seven to eight session mark. Remember this is an average figure and allows for the fact that some core interventions may take only a few sessions and others may end up taking longer. There is a myth that CAPA dictates people can only be seen for seven to eight sessions and no more. This myth derives from a misunderstanding of how CAPA calculates the average session numbers.

Having Partnership work segmented in this way, creates flexibility in the workforce that reduces internal bottlenecks in the service (which usually manifest as internal waiting lists) and protects the skills and resources needed for more specific interventions.

Specific Partnerships are interventions that are known to need significantly more (or sometimes significantly fewer) sessions than the average core intervention. Activities such as cognitive assessments might been seen as specific partnership work that requires fewer than seven sessions, whereas eating disorders, psychosis, conduct disorders can be predicted to need more resource (sessions) right from the start.

Job Planning: The focus on segmented resource allocation allows services to begin to think in terms of resource and need. This is crucial to the next aspect of CAPA: Job planning. Once predictions of likely need and likely resource are estimated services can work out their *capacity* by calculating how much direct clinical time the practitioners in their service have to deliver direct clinical care: Choice and Partnership work. To do this practitioners' time needs to be job planned (York & Kingsbury, 2013).

Of course, the demand on any practitioner's time is much more than direct clinical work, there are notes to be written, training to be attended, supervision, research, teaching and so forth. Job planning all practitioners' time within a service, allows the capacity in the system to be calculated. In CAPA, capacity is the collective number of hours available for direct clinical work with CYP and their families. With a bit of simple mathematics, how many Choice appointments can be offered and how many Partnership slots would need to be available to match CYP to a partnership therapist without there being any internal waits can be worked out. Remember not all CYP will need or choose to go into Partnership work.

Job planning also enables services to see how time (resources) are consumed outside direct clinical care. This understanding can help spot inefficiencies in the system and see where resources can be 'flexed' if demand temporarily increases. The aim is to try to create a smooth flow through the system, with the capacity matching the demand, and if there is a match, waiting lists are eliminated as long as the numbers of CYP coming into the system equals the numbers leaving the service, in any given period of time.

Peer-group Discussion: The final component or 'big idea' in CAPA is regular peer-group discussions. Cross-discipline discussions share knowledge and broaden core skills. They also help practitioners hone their collaborative goal setting skills. They can help unstick cases that have started to drift and, vitally, they can help practitioners have the confidence to 'let go' of CYP and end treatment.

Peer discussion also has a very necessary human component, it brings people together and strengthens relationships, all of which can facilitate better team functioning, with the aim of providing better clinical work.

CAPA was not unique in the practices and values it drew on, but the whole package combining these practices was what made it work better than previous frameworks. It drew attention to the tricky issue of managing resources to meet demand and gave a process to maximise flow through the system and a method to understand the system in terms of demand and capacity.

Now, the idea of collaborative practice is much more mainstream, but 20 years ago it was a challenge to the orthodoxy. Perhaps because of the very welcome shift across most services to better collaboration, CAPA has sometimes been misunderstood as being only about job planning and session numbers. Where services lose sight of the big picture that combines best clinical practice with service delivery and only contributes on the structural aspects of CAPA, it tends to lose its efficacy as the values at the heart of it get lost, leaving practitioners and clients frustrated. It led to myths about the approach as being as being about, numbers, counting and control, rather than it being about collaborative working and respect. The other strongly held myth about CAPA is that 'it gets rid of waiting lists'. This is true to an extent in that the model keeps a keen focus on efficient and effective interventions that keep flow through the system, unsticking bottlenecks and entry and exit, and flexing capacity to meet increases in demand (Clark et al., 2018). However, it is not magic, no system, however flexible can keep a balance between demand and capacity if demand is too great, or resources are insufficient, even for an efficient service.

Although CAPA still worked within the traditional four-tier system it began to pave the way for a less professionally led approach to mental health and began to shift the narrative from a severity-led system, to one that focused more closely on the needs, goals and wishes of the CYP and their family. It focused on the need to increase capacity by making the best use of the available resource in the system. This need to make best use of resources by providing the best possible clinical interventions was built on by the Children and Young People's Improving Access to Psychological Therapies (CYP IAPT) programme.

6.5.3 CYP IAPT

In around 2013, Children and Young People's IAPT, began to grow from the adult IAPT model. Adult IAPT had begun to transform adult mental health services by providing evidence-based talking therapies, largely cognitive behaviour therapy (CBT), for adults with mild to moderate anxiety and depression. The children's version of the programme, like CAPA, was organised around making best use of existing resources (Shafran et al., 2014). It also acknowledged the power of CYP voice in the system and the value of using feedback and outcome tools (Fonagy & Clark, 2015; Kingsbury et al., 2013). It was similarly organised around improving the quality of mental health provision in children's mental health services, by making evidence-based interventions available across CAMHS (Shafran et al., 2014). However, it was fundamentally different from the adult model in both its ambition and execution. CYP IAPT aimed to transform *all* of children's mental health services.

The drive was to ensure that children's mental health services were organised to provide the best evidence-based interventions in ways that were accessible and acceptable to the children and young people they served (Shafran et al., 2014).

The framework was organised a set of principles of best practice:

- Making the best evidence-based therapies available to CYP who could most benefit from them.
- Improving access to services by opening up CAMHS to self-referral, increasing awareness of mental wellbeing issues within communities and working to reduce stigma.
- Encouraging better participation to improve services development and during interventions to provide better personalised care,
- Amending the use of routine outcome monitoring across all interventions to provide outcomes-focused, goal-oriented interventions and to gather data to demonstrate the cost benefit of investment in CYP mental health (Fonagy et al., 2017; Shafran et al., 2014; Kingsbury et al., 2013.

In order to support the quality improvement initiatives, the CYP IAPT programme was wrapped in an implementation package which included:

- Training for existing CAMHS staff in best evidence-based interventions.
- Training for supervisor and service leads to support and sustain the implementation.
- Implementation packages were delivered through local 'collaboratives' led by regional universities, bringing together local NHS, local authority and third-sector providers to share learning and best practice (Fonagy et al., 2017).

CYP IAPT did not proscribe a service delivery framework as such, it left services to structure themselves in whatever way would best fit local need and existing service delivery, as long as the CYP IAPT principles were embedded across the whole CYP mental health system. In this sense, CYP IAPT was more a quality-improvement programme that impacted on service delivery frameworks, rather than a delivery framework in its own right.

As with CAPA, CYP IAPT worked within the existing tiered framework, with the aim of improving it. Also, like CAPA, it aimed to improve services by providing more effective interventions that, in turn, would increase capacity in services. Its focus on outcomes was where it added value. This drive gave the possibility of working out how many 'Partnership' appointments might be needed to lead to an *effective* clinical outcome and enable services to better calculate capacity. However, CYP IAPT still aimed, primarily, to impact on the part of system that was focused on mental health *problems*. It was the THRIVE framework that provided a genuine whole system framework around CYP mental health, that focused on *prevention* **and** *intervention*.

6.5.4 The THRIVE framework

The first iteration of the THRIVE Framework emerged in 2014 (Wolpert et al., 2014 and it evolved over the next 5 years (Wolpert et al., 2019). It aimed to provide an holistic mental health framework that met the mental health needs of *all* children and young people aged 0–25 years.

The framework is organised around need, rather than diagnosis or severity. It is organised around the idea that, at any point in time, all CYP can be categorised into five groupings based on their primary mental health need at that time. The five needs-based groupings are: Thriving, Getting Advice, Getting Help, Getting More Help and Risk Support. The groupings are fluid and dynamic in that CYP might move between them depending on their changing needs at different times in their childhood (Wolpert et al., 2019).

Thriving

The thriving CYP at the centre of the framework is what makes it a proper, whole system approach, and what makes it different from what came before. This grouping acknowledges the majority of CYP who at any one time have good mental health. The needs of CYP who fall into this group is to receive active effective prevention and promotion strategies to support and maintaining their mental wellbeing (Faulconbridge et al., 2019b).

It also acknowledges that there are groups of CYP who have additional or underlying vulnerabilities to developing mental health issues such as: poverty, trauma or neglect, learning disability or physical health problems; alongside environmental factors including injustice, discrimination and inequalities. It recommends that the system is organised to ensure these groups have access to effective prevention and mental health promotion strategies that meet their needs (Wolpert et al., 2019).

Getting Advice

Some CYP might move from the thriving centre because of worries they have about their own mental wellbeing, or worries someone else has about them. For many, what they will need is good-quality advice. Typical in this group might be CYP who are showing mental distress due to adjusting to life changes or temporary difficulties in their life such as bereavement or changes of school. Their distress may be mild or severe but they do not need (or want) direct professional help other than to be given advice about how best to manage their situation and to be directed to good sources of information such as self-help guides, or good-quality online resources (Wolpert et al., 2019).

This group might also contain CYP with more severe mental health issues, but who for good reasons, choose to receive advice rather than therapy. For example, it might be a young person with bulimia who is not ready to work with professionals and wants to know more about their difficulties and what might help. They might choose to try to work through things with their family without having a mental health professional involved. As long as there were no serious risk issues, the system might direct them to resources such as the 'BEAT' website, which has excellent resources and advice for CYP and their parents about eating disorders. Similarly, it might include CYP who have been receiving therapy but feel things are in a suitably good place to be 'let go of' to manage and maintain their gains within their own community and family. Their need at this point is to receive good advice from professionals about how best to do this.

Getting Help and Getting More Help

These two groupings map directly onto the CAPA Core and Specific partnership. This group comprises of those who need a goal-focused intervention working alongside a professional with the appropriate skills to help. These interventions could be delivered by a mental health practitioner, but not exclusively. In THRIVE, 'An intervention is any form of help related to a mental health need in which a professional takes responsibility for input directly with a specified individual or group. The professional may not necessarily be a trained mental health provider, but may be a range of people who can provide targeted, outcomes-focused help to address the specific mental health issue' (Wolpert et al., 2019, p. 8).

For example, the professional may be a teaching assistant applying a structured graded exposure plan for a child with a classroom-based anxiety. The work may be supervised by a mental health professional but not directly delivered by then.

The distinction between Getting Help and Getting More Help (like in CAPA) is based on the *resources* likely to be needed to lead to a successful outcome, not the severity of the problem. CYP falling into the Getting Help group are likely to be those who need CBT for low mood or anxiety, a parenting intervention, family therapy or focused psychotherapy.

Those who need 'more help' are those CYP who are expected to need a more substantial resource to make improvement. These tend to be CYP with more complex mental health issues for example, an autism spectrum condition with severe obsessive compulsions, developmental trauma. This grouping does not necessarily relate to the severity of the presenting issue; in some instances, CYP with high levels of emotional distress, might readily be helped with relatively low amounts of resource (Wolpert et al., 2019).

Unlike CAPA, the resource allocation in these two needs-based grouping are not specified but left to the local system to decide the right level of allocation.

Getting Risk Support

This grouping is for CYP who have not benefitted from Getting Help but who have the need to be kept safe as they continue to display very high levels of risk.

The THRIVE framework authors suggests: 'The aim of specifying a category of Getting Risk Support is for all partners to be clear that what is being provided is managing risk ONLY. It is important to note that there are likely to be risk management aspects in all groupings. However, in the context of high concerns but lack of therapeutic progress for those in this group, risk management is the sole focus' (Wolpert et al., 2019, p. 10).

It would be hoped that CYP move quickly from this 'risk support' need grouping, back into 'getting more help' when there are more able to make use of therapeutic support on offer.

The THRIVE Framework Principles

The THRIVE Framework purposefully does not dictate how local systems best implement the framework. Like CYP IAPT and CAPA that preceded it, it draws on principles from both frameworks and from CYP participation. The THRIVE principles include a needs-led approach, with shared decision making at its heart, that includes partnership working across the different agencies (health, social care, education) and (like CYP IAPT) the care is evidence based and outcomes focused (Wolpert et al., 2019). However, implementation of the framework does rely on solid multiagency collaboration and protocols which most areas struggle to achieve (Farr et al., 2021). This is partly due to the organisation of the political structures of local and national government but also down to the lack of resources to facilitate and implement change effectively.

So, we are back to the funding issue as a major limiter of change and improvement across CYP mental health services. This should not overwhelm us, but should energise us to continue to innovate and make best use of the resources we have.

6.6 The Future of CYP Mental Health Provision

So where does this leave CYP mental health services? Although there has been definite progress this century, none of the current service delivery frameworks fully meet the definition of a 'good service delivery framework' we set out at the start of this chapter: to promote good mental health, mitigate against psychological harm, identify need, ensure that a child or young person's journey through the system is smooth and effective, and to provide them with the best, and most appropriate clinical care for their needs. THRIVE gets closest in setting out the best principles but falls short of demonstrating how these might be delivered in practice.

This leave a challenge to the next cohort of mental health professionals to build on the good foundations that have been laid and continue to build a system that is properly resourced, accessible and mitigates against prejudice and inequality. This is no easy task but there are opportunities that might help. The challenge for the next generation will be to be creative in where and how the best preventative and curative mental health care to children and young people is delivered.

Not much good came out of the Covid-19 pandemic but one thing that was transformational with regard to CYP mental health services was the rapid move to offering and delivering interventions online (Worsley et al., 2022). This has shown to be an effective and flexible way to deliver psychological interventions and good quality advice and support (Lehtimaki et al., 2021).

The harnessing of information technology will surely be one of the developments in the future, that might truly provide more accessible, effective and flexible mental health services. The surface has only just begun to be scratched when considering the potential value artificial intelligence in mental health settings might be able to offer (Fiske et al., 2019) (see Chapter 24 for more on this). Online working has shown us that good mental health care does not need to be tied to a mental health setting. Work has already begun to move mental health interventions to be more embedded into communities, be that schools (see Chapter 21), sports settings, or whole community approaches. Good-quality psychological theory and research needs to be better and to be applied more effectively. This will necessitate a rethinking of what a mental health intervention looks like: how interventions are delivered and by whom, to be able to deliver comprehensive services to all who can benefit particularly focusing on those at the margins of society who have traditionally been let down by current service models. Initiatives such as the SECURE STAIRS framework (Taylor et al., 2018; Anna Freud National Centre for Children and Families, 2022) for integrated care, are examples of innovations where mental health professionals work closely with the people who already have a relationship with the young person they are wanting to help. These approaches have been rolled out across the criminal justice system in England, in Young Offender institutions and secure children's homes, with promising effects.

And finally, systems need to have sufficient reach to actively engage with *all* children and young people particularly those whose voice society finds it harder to hear, particularly young people with learning disabilities, the very young and those for whom the English language is a challenge. These are not insignificant challenges for an already under-resourced system. The role of mental health professionals must be seen as not just those who deliver services through interventions but also as a driving force to improve and expand them.

References

Anna Freud National Centre for Children and Families. (2022). *Independent evaluation of the Framework for Integrated Care (SECURE STAIRS)*. Anna Freud National Centre for Children and Families. https://www.annafreud.org/media/15923/secure-stairs-independent-evaluation-exec-summary.pdf.

CAMHS Tier 4 Report Steering Group. (2014). *Child and Adolescents Mental Health (CAMHS) tier 4 report*. NHS England. https://www.england.nhs.uk/wp-content/uploads/2014/07/camhs-tier-4-rep.pdf.

Clark, S., Emberly, D., Pajer, K., Delong, E., McWilliam, S., Bagnell, A., Abidi, S., Casey, B., & Gardner, W. (2018). Improving access to child and adolescent mental health care: The choice and partnership approach. *Journal of the Canadian Academy of Child and Adolescent Psychiatry, 27*(1), 5–14.

Department for Education. (2003). *Every Child Matters*. Her Majesty's Stationery Office.

Department of Health. (2015). *Future in mind: Promoting, protecting and improving our children and young people's mental health and wellbeing*. NHS England. https://assets.publishing.service.gov.uk/government/uploads/system/uploads/attachment_data/file/414024/Childrens_Mental_Health.pdf.

Farr, J., Moore, A., Bruffell, H., Hayes, J., Rae, J. P., & Cooper, M. (2021). The impact of a needs-based model of care on accessibility and quality of care within children's mental health services: A qualitative investigation of the UK i-THRIVE Programme. *Child: Care, Health and Development, 47*(4), 442–450.

Faulconbridge, J., Hunt, K, Fatimilehin, Y., Laffan, A., & Law, D. (2019a). Risk factors, protective factors and resilience: How can we nurture psychological wellbeing in children and young people. In J. Faulconbridge, K. Hunt, & A. Laffan. (Eds.), *Improving the psychological wellbeing of children and young people: Effective prevention and early intervention across health, education and social care* (pp. 13–50). Jessica Kingsley.

Faulconbridge, J., Hunt, K., & Laffan, A. (Eds.). (2019b). *Improving the psychological wellbeing of children and young people: Effective prevention and early intervention across health, education and social care*. Jessica Kingsley.

Fiske, A., Henningsen, P., & Buyx, A. (2019). Your robot therapist will see you now: Ethical implications of embodied artificial intelligence in psychiatry, psychology, and psychotherapy. *Journal of Medical Internet Research, 21*(5), e13216. https://doi.org/10.2196/13216.

Fonagy, P., & Clark, D. M. (2015). Update on the improving access to psychological therapies programme in England: commentary on … children and young People's improving access to psychological therapies. *BJPsych Bulletin, 39*(5), 248–251.

Fonagy, P., Pugh, K., & O'Herlihy, A. (2017). *The children and young people's improving access to psychological therapies (CYP IAPT) programme in England*. Wiley.

Goodman, R., Ford, T., Simmons, H., Gatward, R., & Meltzer, H. (2000). Using the Strengths and Difficulties Questionnaire (SDQ) to screen for child psychiatric disorders in a community sample. *The British Journal of Psychiatry, 177*(6), 534–539.

Green, H., McGinnity, A., Meltzer, H., Ford, T., & Goodman, R. (2005). *Mental health of children and young people in Great Britain, 2004*. Palgrave Macmillan. https://sp.ukdataservice.ac.uk/doc/5269/mrdoc/pdf/5269technicalreport.pdf.

HM Government. (2011). *No health without mental health: A cross-government mental health outcomes strategy for people of all ages*. Department of Health. https://assets.publishing.service.gov.uk/government/uploads/system/uploads/attachment_data/file/138253/dh_124058.pdf.

Jeffery, M., Lereya, T., Edbrooke-Childs, J., Deighton, J., Tait, N., & Cortina, M. A. (2021). *Emerging evidence: Coronavirus and children and young people's mental health*. Evidence based Practice Unit London. https://www.annafreud.org/media/13549/emergingevidence7.pdf.

Kingsbury, S., Rayment, B., Fleming I., Thompson, P., & York, A. (2013). CYP IAPT principles in Child & Adolescent Mental Health services. *Values and standards 'Delivering with and delivering well'*. CAMHS Press. https://www.england.nhs.uk/wp-content/uploads/2014/12/delvr-with-delvrng-well.pdf.

Kurtz, Z. (1996). *Treating children well: A guide to using the evidence base in commissioning and managing services for the mental health of children and young people*. Mental Health Foundation.

Lehtimaki, S., Martic, J., Wahl, B., Foster, K. T., & Schwalbe, N. (2021). Evidence on digital mental health interventions for adolescents and young people: Systematic overview. *JMIR Mental Health, 8*(4), e25847.

Marmot, M. (2020). Health equity in England: The Marmot review 10 years on. *The BMJ, 363*, m693. https://doi.org/10.1136/bmj.m693.

Midgley, N. (2012). *Reading Anna Freud*. Routledge.

National CAMHS Review. (2008). *Children and young people in mind: The final report of the National CAMHS Review*. National Child and Adolescents Mental Health Review. https://dera.ioe.ac.uk/10845/1/dh_090398.pdf.

NHS Health Advisory Service. (1995). *Child and adolescent mental health services: Together we stand. The commissioning, role and management of child and adolescent mental health services*. Her Majesty's Stationery Office.

Ramraj, C., Shahidi, F. V., Darity Jr,, W., Kawachi, I., Zuberi, D., & Siddiqi, A. (2016). Equally inequitable? A cross-national comparative study of racial health inequalities in the United States and Canada. *Social Science & Medicine, 161*, 19–26. https://doi.org/10.1016/j.socscimed.2016.05.028.

Sadler, K., Vizard, T., Ford, T., Goodman, A., Goodman, R., & McManus, S. (2018). *Mental health of children and young people in England, 2017: Trends and characteristics*. NHS Digital.

Shafran, R., Fonagy, P., Pugh, K., & Myles, P. (2014). Transformation of mental health services for children and young people in England. In R. S. Beidas and P. C. Kendall (Eds.), *Dissemination and implementation of evidence-based practices in child and adolescent mental health* (pp. 158–178). Oxford University Press.

Taylor, J., Shostak, L., Rogers, A., & Mitchell, P. (2018). Rethinking mental health provision in the secure estate for children and young people: a framework for integrated care (SECURE STAIRS). *Safer Communities, 17*(4), 193–201. http://dx.doi.org/10.1108/SC-07-2018-0019.

Troy, D., Anderson, J., Jessiman, P. E., Albers, P. N., Williams, J. G., Sheard, S., Geijer-Simpson, E., Spencer, L., Kaner, E., Limmer, M., Viner, R., & Kidger, J. (2022). What is the impact of structural and cultural factors and interventions within educational settings on promoting positive mental health and preventing poor mental health: A systematic review. *BMC Public Health, 22*(1), 1–16. https://doi.org/10.1186/s12889-022-12894-7.

Webster, E. (2020). *Seat belts: Time for action*. Parliamentary Advisory Council for Transport Safety. https://www.pacts.org.uk/wp-content/uploads/Report-4.pdf.

Wolpert, M., Harris, R., Hodges, S., Fuggle, P., James, R., Wiener, A., McKenna, C., Law, D., York, A., Jones, M., Fonagy, P., Fleming, I., & Munk, S. (2019). *THRIVE framework for system change*. CAMHS Press. https://www.annafreud.org/media/9254/thrive-framework-for-system-change-2019.pdf.

Wolpert, M., Harris, R., Jones, M., Hodges, S., Fuggle, P., James, R., Wiener, A., Mckenna, C., Law, D., & Fonagy, P. (2014). *THRIVE: The AFC-Tavistock model for CAMHS*. CAMHS Press. https://repository.tavistockandportman.ac.uk/941/1/Thrive%20model%20for%20CAMHS.pdf.

Wolpert, M., Jacob, J., Napoleone, E., Whale, A., Calderon, A., & Edbrooke-Childs, J. (2016) *Child- and parent-reported outcomes and experience from child and young people's mental health services 2011–2015*. CAMHS Press.

World Health Organization. (2022). *Mental health and Covid-19: early evidence of the pandemic's impact*. World Health Organization. https://www.who.int/publications/i/item/WHO-2019-nCoV-Sci_Brief-Mental_health-2022.1.

Worsley, J., Hassan, S., Nolan, L., & Corcoran, R. (2022). 'Space to hide': experiences of remote provision across child and adolescent mental health services (CAMHS). *BMC Health Services Research, 22*(1), 1350.

York, A., & Kingsbury, S. (2013). *The choice and partnership approach: A transformational service model*. CAPA Publications.

7

Inclusivity, Diversity and Power

Fatima Bibi

The purpose of this chapter is to introduce the themes of inclusivity, diversity and power and their relevance to working as a child psychological practitioner. The chapter begins by defining and exploring the concepts of inclusion, diversity and power in relation to clinical practice. Current challenges pertaining to these themes within social, organisational, professional and clinical contexts relating to mental health are then outlined. Key frameworks, ideas and guiding principles are presented to assist practitioners on their journey developing the skills to practice in more inclusive and equitable ways. Whilst each section is separate and presented in an arbitrary way, they are no doubt interrelated and there will be repeated themes that will emerge throughout. Reflective and reflexive practice are a crucial part of the process of exploring inclusivity, diversity and power and exercises have been provided to stimulate thoughts and insights, which may ripen within the reader over time. Some of the content of this chapter may make for uncomfortable reading and may elicit a range of emotions. However, it is through the process of addressing complex, difficult and painful issues and engaging in self-reflection that a meaningful exploration of inclusion, power and diversity can truly take place.

The objective of the chapter is not to provide an exhaustive list or in-depth account of any single approach, but rather an overview to introduce some ideas and frameworks that may be helpful. Importantly, through the use of case studies, the voices and experiences of children, young people, parents and professionals have been incorporated to situate ideas in real-life experiences. All identities have been anonymised and pseudonyms are used to protect the confidentiality of those who have contributed. It is important to identify from the outset that themes around racial, ethnic and cultural diversity dominate much of the discussion in this chapter. This is not to minimise or ignore the importance of discussion around other aspects of difference, but rather to focus on an aspect of diversity that is still riddled with significant challenges. Shedding light on the mechanisms and structures that maintain racial, ethnic and cultural inequality, and exploring the ideas and frameworks that can be applied to try to address them in practice will no doubt have utility in relation to all aspects of diversity.

Child Psychology: Pathways to Good Practice, First Edition.
Edited by Helen Pote, Anna Picciotto and Clare Norris.

7.1 Introduction

Practicing as a child psychological practitioner involves working with and alongside diverse groups of people occupying a range of identities including race, religion, gender, sexuality and socioeconomic status. It also involves practicing in social, political and economic contexts, and within discourses that continue to systematically privilege certain groups and marginalise others in a multitude of ways. Psychological theory and practice do not exist in a vacuum outside the powerful social, political and economic structures that perpetrate and maintain inequality. On the contrary, 'psy' professions (including psychology, psychotherapy and psychiatry) have emerged as a scientific discipline within the historical context of eugenics, imperialism and colonisation, which upheld deeply embedded Eurocentric, patriarchal, racist, homophobic and ableist ideologies. Whilst times have moved on, bringing with it an effort to shift the ethos and value base of therapy professions, the legacy of these ideologies continue and are woven into the fabric of current psychological theories, training, research, therapies and services.

As child psychological practitioners, acknowledging the historical and contextual foundations of the discipline orients practitioners better to the deep-seated origins of the challenges that need to be addressed when trying to practice in more equitable and inclusive ways. In addition to this, it is important to take into consideration the broader context around mental health services, which are couched in a wider social milieu of systemic challenges and structural inequalities including discrimination, and stark wealth disparities. Such disparities materialise within social, organisational, professional and clinical contexts in relation to mental health in a number of ways. It is therefore important to broaden the lens when thinking about mental and emotional distress to accommodate and attend to the impact of contextual factors. Indeed, it is incumbent upon all therapists to examine and engage in issues around inclusion, power and diversity, reflecting on their own values and worldviews and how they may be complicit in maintaining inequality. Such insights can enable practitioners to recognise and amend their practice in the service of providing more inclusive and equitable care for the families, children and young people they seek to support.

An ancient and well-worn adage, more recently revived by Spiderman in the Marvel movies says that 'with great power comes great responsibility'. Child psychological practitioners are in no way super-heroes or all powerful. On the contrary, experiences of powerlessness, especially as a student, trainee and newly qualified practitioners are commonplace. However, in spite of such experiences working as a child psychological practitioner involves occupying a position of relative power with the potential to collude with *or* challenge and resist exclusion, discrimination and marginalisation. Not only is it the legal and professional duty of all practitioners to be aware of diversity and inclusion in accordance with the Equality Act (2010), Health and Care Professions Council (HCPC) and British Psychological Society (BPS) standards, it is possible to argue that it is the moral and ethical responsibility of practitioners to ensure inclusive and non-discriminatory practice.

7.2 Inclusion, Diversity and Power

Inclusivity can be defined as 'the practice or policy of providing equal access to opportunities and resources for people who might otherwise be excluded or marginalised, such as those having physical or mental disabilities or belonging to other minority groups' (Oxford English Dictionary).

Diversity can be defined as 'the practice or quality of including or involving people from a range of different social and ethnic backgrounds and of different genders, sexual orientations, etc' (Oxford English Dictionary). This also includes culture, which can be defined as socially constructed and shared patterns of behaviour that include the language, thoughts, communications, actions, customs, beliefs, values and practices amongst groups of people.

Power refers to a complex set of processes that can operate in abstract and concrete ways (Boyle & Johnstone, 2020). Nelson and Prilleltensky (2005) propose that the defining features of power relate to:

- The capacity and opportunity to fulfil or obstruct personal, relational or collective needs.
- Existing as overt or covert, subtle or blatant, hidden or exposed.
- Structural factors such as social class, gender, ability, race afford differential levels of power.
- Having psychological and political sources, manifestations and consequences.
- The exercise of power can apply to self, others and collectives.

Therapy professions have long struggled with significant challenges around inclusivity and diversity across multiple levels including issues around access to therapies for minoritised groups, the over-representation/under-representation of certain groups within different parts of the mental health system and the lack of diversity amongst therapists to name but a few. The concepts of inclusion, power and diversity in the context of the therapy professions are complex and intimately linked. In trying to understand how they relate to one another, it seems pertinent to centralise the notion of power, since it is those individuals, groups and discourses in positions of relative power and privilege that are ultimately able to oppress, exclude and marginalise.

7.2.1 Foucault on Power

Philosopher and French postmodernist Michel Foucault's ideas on power and knowledge are helpful in illuminating how seemingly innocuous social practices and dominant 'truths' can serve to oppress and marginalise. Foucault (1982) wrote about the subtle and evasive aspects of power that operate in concealed ways to control human experience and behaviour. Foucault's conceptualisation of power leads us away from a focus on power that is wielded by certain groups in explicit acts of domination or coercion ('Traditional Power') into the more dispersed and concealed forms of power characterising modern liberal democratic societies ('Modern Power'). He argues that power in the modern age is everywhere, creating social discipline and conformity to cultural prescriptions of socially accepted ways of being. He proposed that it is through an internalisation of these prescriptions that people regulate or 'police' themselves, and ways of being that do not fit with the narrow range of socially accepted norms and regulations become counterproductive and create distress.

According to Foucault, each society has its 'regime of truth' and 'discourses', which are culturally constructed ideas and practices about reality. He proposed that discourses construct 'knowledge', and that some categories of thinking and lines of argument have come to be generally taken as 'truths' while other ways of thinking/being/doing are marginalised. Discourses therefore produce both knowledge and power simultaneously. Foucault uses the term 'power/knowledge' to signify that power is constituted through accepted forms of knowledge, scientific understanding and 'truth'. The production of power according to Foucault lies with those in positions of privilege, to sustain the interests of a selective few.

Foucault's conception of power as an everyday, socialised and embodied phenomena highlights that we are all implicated in, and impacted by the cultural norms and regulations and can therefore easily become unintentional agents of coercion to certain norm and prescriptions. According to Foucault, professions are integral to the machinery of social control as they create 'knowledge' and 'truths', reinforcing wider social inequalities and the status quo of power relations. As practitioners working within the 'psy' professions, it is therefore essential to critically examine one's own relationship to power, and the 'knowledges' or 'truths' enacted in practice that may serve to further marginalise and oppress certain individuals, groups and ideas whilst privileging others.

7.3 Social Context

The UK has a long-standing problem with child poverty, with recent figures showing that one in every four children lives in poverty (data from the Joseph Rowntree Foundation, 2021). Children living in poverty are four times more likely to have mental health problems compared to children from high-income families (Pople & Rees, 2017). In addition, black and minority ethnic children are more likely to be living in poverty than white British children (Platt, 2014). It is beyond the scope of this chapter to chart the complex and historical factors that have created such troubling circumstances. The combination of government policies, chronic spending cuts to public services, changes in employment markets and the rising cost of living are the most likely and significant contributors. At the time of writing this chapter, the UK (like many parts of the world) is still recovering from the repercussions of the Covid-19 pandemic and is currently living through the worst cost of living crisis for 40 years due to a series of geopolitical and macroeconomic events. Such incidents further compound pre-existing problems around childhood poverty and its impact on mental health.

It is against the backdrop of such challenging of social, political and economic contexts that many families, children and young people are trying to navigate mental and emotional wellbeing. The impact of social inequalities is rarely acknowledged as being as significant (or for some, more significant), than abuse and difficulties within the home. For many individuals, families and communities, the impact of living in overcrowded housing in impoverished neighbourhoods, inadequate access to food and heating, insufficient access to basic resources and severe financial hardship will no doubt have a very real bearing on individual and collective mental health. Challenging experiences of broader social systems (e.g. housing, employment agencies, social support organisations) may serve to diminish an individual's sense of agency in effecting change in their lives, further compounding social and emotional distress. The tendency for mainstream approaches to situate problems within individuals and their relationships obscures the possibilities for a much richer and more holistic understanding of distress, and importantly key areas of intervention.

7.4 Ecological Systems Theory

There are a number of models that seek to accommodate context when thinking about mental and emotional distress. The ecological systems theory was developed by

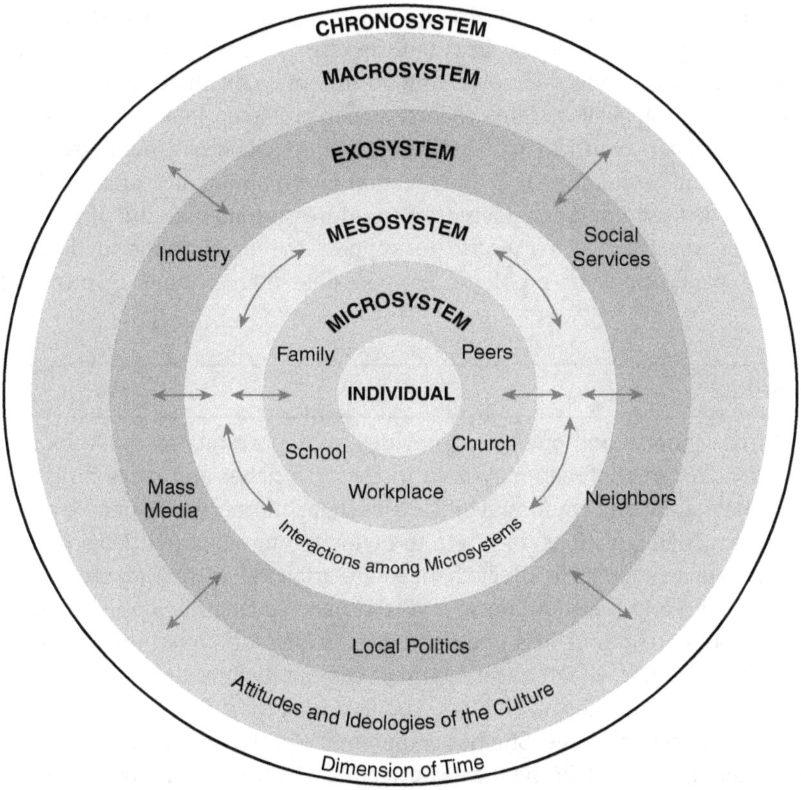

Figure 7.1 Ecological systems that impact on development and distress. Source: Adapted from *Ecological Systems Theory*, Discourses on Learning in Education (learningdiscourses.com).

Russian-American Psychologist Uri Bronfenbrenner in the 1970s to highlight the embeddedness of people in wider social and environmental contexts, and how it can impact on development and distress (Bronfenbrenner 1979, 1992). Bronfenbrenner, identifies five distinct yet interrelated environmental systems that influence on child development (see also Figure 7.1):

- The microsystem: individuals, institutions and groups that most immediately and directly impact the child's development.
- The mesosystem: relationships between the microsystems in which the child is directly involved for example, a child's school and parents
- The exosystem: the link between social settings in which the child does not actively participate but is impacted by for example the child's parents' place of work
- The macrosystem: the outermost layer in the child's environment comprised of cultural values, customs and social norms within which the microsystems and mesosystems are embedded. Includes attitudes and ideologies of the culture based on geographic location, socioeconomic status, poverty and ethnicity.
- The chronosystem: Societal events and transitions over the life course.

The ecological metaphor shifts the focus away from individualistic explanations of distress and attends to the exchanges between the individual, family and importantly their interactions with, and experiences of broader social systems. It is understood that there is a complex and dynamic interplay between the child and the different contexts they are embedded in, each having their own unique influence on the individual, and vice-versa. According to ecological systems theory, social problems including unstable housing, inadequate income, conflicts with criminal justice agencies, unemployment, educational challenges can be functional in the creation and maintenance of difficulties and must therefore be assessed and considered when addressing mental and emotional distress (Hepworth et al., 2010). An exercise to support the practitioner to develop more contextualised conceptions of problems and possible interventions is provided in Box 7.1.

Box 7.1 Exercise

This section with its vignette and questions provides an opportunity to think about how a more contextualised approach may help to create a richer and more holistic understanding of the mental and emotional difficulties that children, young people and families present with. Such questions may help to generate more possibilities around different ways of providing support to effect change in relation the presenting problem.

Ayesha is 15 years old and is struggling with anxiety and self-harm. She lives with her mum and two younger siblings in a one bedroom flat. Ayesha's mum lost her job during the Covid-19 pandemic, which has meant that the family have been struggling financially. Ayesha struggled to keep up with her studies during the pandemic as a result of not having Internet access at home. She has completely withdrawn from her studies and is no longer attending school, or the local youth club, which was shut down due to funding difficulties. She has stopped connecting with her friends and rarely leaves her home as she does not have access to any money. Ayesha has been referred to Social Services by her school due to lack of attendance, which has created difficulties in the relationship between her mother and the school. Ayesha's mum is also struggling with her own mental health difficulties and has not been able to access support.

1. In what ways do the social and economic circumstances of Ayesha's life contribute to and maintain the distress that she is experiencing?
2. What role do the systems around her play (directly and/or indirectly) in contributing to and maintaining the distress?
3. What are the risks of not taking this into consideration when working with Ayesha and her mum?
4. What benefits could there be in creating space in therapeutic conversations to acknowledge the impact of wider contextual factors for Ayesha and her mum?
5. In addition to mental health interventions, what other types of support could Ayesha and her family benefit from to support and sustain their mental and emotional well-being?
6. How could a therapeutic practitioner support this?
7. What challenges may come up in relation to this and how might they be addressed?

7.5 Organisational and Service Context

Service level data shows that just 16% of those who access Child and Adolescent Mental Health Services (CAMHS) are from black and minority ethnic backgrounds (Department of Health, 2015). Children from black and minority ethnic backgrounds are much less likely to be referred to CAMHS services via GPs, compared to referrals from school, social services or the criminal justice system (Edbrooke-Childs et al., 2016). When they do access mental health services, children from black and minority ethnic groups are less likely to complete treatment and demonstrate significantly higher drop-out rates (Chui et al., 2021). Whilst there is little research into the specific reasons for the this, the available data paints a worrying picture in relation to the equity, accessibility and appropriateness of current mental health services for minoritised children and young people. Research on adult populations indicates that a number of factors contribute to the under-utilisation of mental health services for black and minority ethnic communities including language barriers, stigma around mental illness, power imbalances between practitioners and service users, and insensitivity and discrimination towards the needs of minority ethnic service users (Memon et at., 2016). A clinical example of a minority ethnic child's experience of mental health services is described in Box 7.2.

Box 7.2 Clinical example: Tola's experience of mental health services

Tola is a 13-year-old boy of black Nigerian heritage who moved to the UK with his family aged 8. He was referred to CAMHS by Social Services to engage with a psychological intervention for 'behavioural difficulties' at school. Tola had previously been given diagnoses of 'Conduct Disorder', 'Oppositional Defiance Disorder' and 'Attention Deficit Hyperactivity Disorder'. Following months of non-engagement, Tola shared that he was not interested in accessing psychological therapies. He said that he didn't understand what any of the labels he had received meant, and that the assessments he had been required to participate in were intrusive, repetitive and upsetting for him. Tola shared that the labels he received made him feel like there was something wrong with him, and that he didn't want to talk to strangers as that didn't make sense to him. He described struggling to trust professionals in positions of power. He shared that his uncle had recently been 'locked away' and medicated in a 'mental hospital', which made him fearful of what would happen to him. Tola shared that his family had different ideas around what would be helpful for him, and that he felt stuck in between what his family and the services around him thought would be 'best' for him. He was discharged from CAMHS for 'non-engagement'.

Tola's experience epitomizes issues of exclusion, labelling and being 'done to' many young black and minority ethnic people report within mainstream institutions including education, criminal justice and mental health. The cumulative and long-term impact of this can be to engender a deep-seated mistrust of professionals. Fear of mental health services in specific communities is unfortunately founded on the

(Continued)

Box 7.2 (Continued)

prevalence of forceful and more punitive experiences of services for example, black men showing signs of mental distress are far more likely to be perceived as a threat and criminalized (Edbrooke-Childs et al., 2016). Tola's experience also highlights the unhelpful effects of not exploring or accommodating alternative ideas (his families or his own) about what could be helpful for him.

It is perhaps obvious to state that the lack of culturally sensitive and appropriate interventions for children and families from diverse cultural backgrounds will most likely impact engagement, and the efficacy of interventions in a negative way. Tribe (2005) suggests that Western cultural approaches to mental health focus on individual pathology, while in other cultures there may be more of a focus on community or familial processes. However, the set-up of mental health services, guidelines for clinical practice and dominant therapeutic interventions continue to be offered in a decontextualised way, reflecting cultural concepts of personhood, distress and recovery that can be unsuitable for black and minority ethnic children and families. The construct of culture within the therapeutic professions is usually referring to that of the 'other', and very rarely the invisible culture that informs the main psychological models, or that of the therapist or dominant group. Yet it is these deeply embedded cultural values, beliefs and practices that serve to recreate power imbalances within the structures and procedures of organisations resulting in potentially discriminatory processes that have adverse consequences for minoritised groups (Patel, 1992).

7.6 Cultural Competence

The concept of 'cultural competence' was developed in the United States in the 1980s as a framework for addressing diversity and inequality within healthcare systems. It has been defined as a set of congruent behaviours, attitudes and policies that come together in a system or among professionals that enables them to work effectively with people regardless of difference (Cross et al., 1989). Practicing in a culturally competent way includes an awareness of one's own culture, and the curiosity and willingness to learn about the cultural practices and worldview of others. Whaley and Davis (2007) highlight that a culturally competent approach incorporates a variety of practices and strategies to address the challenge of cultural diversity in mental health services which includes:

- acknowledging the importance of culture,
- addressing cross-cultural relations,
- an awareness of the power imbalances that occur as result of cultural differences,
- increasing knowledge of other cultures and traditions, and
- adapting interventions to meet the unique cultural needs of clients.

According to Betancourt et al. (2003) a culturally competent healthcare system is one that acknowledges and incorporates cultural proficiency at every level of the organisation. Indeed, cultural competence can be addressed at multiple levels, including at a wider organisational level (e.g. policies relating to equity, improving representation), at the workforce and practitioner level (e.g. training, drawing on cultural mediators) and at the level of interventions (e.g. cultural adaptations to existing psychological models). Embedding cultural competence in this way increases the likelihood of creating a widespread culture of inclusivity and respect for diversity within organisations to make mental health services more accessible, acceptable and effective for people from diverse cultural backgrounds and communities. It can be helpfully conceptualised as an evolving process over an extended period of time in which individuals, teams and organisations can be at varying levels of awareness, knowledge and skills along the continuum of cultural competence (Ogundare, 2019). Dedicated training, individual supervision and group reflection spaces can facilitate the process of building competence through increasing knowledge, sharing insights and generating ideas around overcoming barriers.

Despite its wide dissemination and implementation across health and education settings in the United States, the idea of cultural competence has been challenged. According to Greene-Moton and Minkler (2020), the term 'competence' implies a top-down approach in which those in a position of relative power and privilege decide on the content and process of measuring competence. Others have argued that the term itself is a misnomer as we cannot ever be truly competent in another's culture (Chavez, 2018), especially since culture is not a fixed, homogeneous, intrinsic characteristic of individuals or groups (Guarnaccia & Rodriguez, 1996). Kirmayer (2012) proposes that the approach to cultural competence must consider culture as being in a constant state of flux and change as a result of interactions between individuals, groups and the multiple networks and institutions they engage with. This view of culture foregrounds issues of power, identity and the sources of structural inequality, enabling practitioners to understand better and redress injustice that can be ignored or perpetuated by culturally blind health systems (Fraser & Honneth, 2003).

7.6.1 Cultural Humility

In more recent years, the concept of 'cultural humility' has gained popularity within the fields of health and mental health to assist practitioners in more effectively addressing the needs of individuals from diverse cultural backgrounds. The term was first coined by paediatricians and public health practitioners Melanie Tervalon and Jann Murray-García in 1998, who define it as 'a lifelong commitment to self-evaluation and critique, to redressing power imbalances … and to developing mutually beneficial and non-paternalistic partnerships with communities on behalf of individuals and defined populations' (p. 123). Tervalon and Murray-García (1998) emphasised the importance of widening the definition of 'culture' beyond just racial or ethnic identity, to incorporate for example, the culture of the health practitioner, which also requires humility when working with individuals, families and communities.

The concept of cultural humility places an emphasis on issues of power and vulnerability, and the complexity of identities (e.g. that even in sameness there is difference). It recognises that practitioners can never be fully competent in another person's culture due to the evolving and dynamic nature of individual identities, thus centralising curiosity and self-reflection with no specified end point. Cultural competence aims to shift both healthcare organisations and practitioners towards actively recognising where they are complicit with power imbalances in order to create better dialogue and accountability. Engaging with cultural humility enables practitioners to develop a deeper understanding of their cultural identities, how this shapes their worldviews, beliefs and biases, and how their cultural identities intersect with power, privilege, and oppression (Mosher et al., 2017). Foronda et al.'s (2016) recent analysis of cultural humility across health and mental health disciplines identified five key attributes that practitioners should strive for in the process of practicing cultural humility:

- *Openness* – the practitioner retains an open mind, is open to engaging in cross-cultural interactions and is open to new ideas and worldviews.
- *Self-awareness* – the practitioner actively gains awareness into their own strengths, limitations, values, beliefs, biases and behaviour.
- *Egoless* – the practitioner displays humbleness and modesty, retaining a respectful stance towards difference that this underpinned by the belief that all people are equal.
- *Supportive interaction* – the practitioner engages in interactions with others that result in positive exchanges.
- *Self-reflection and critique* – the practitioner engages in a continual process of reflecting on aspects of self through deep introspection individually and in supervision.

Table 7.1 highlights the distinction between cultural competence and cultural humility and Box 7.3 includes an exercise to support practitioners to stimulate reflections around cultural competence and cultural humility.

Box 7.3 An exercise to support practitioners to stimulate reflections around cultural competence and cultural humility.

These questions are intended to generate reflections around practitioners' own cultures, and to stimulate ideas around how to engage in cultural competence and cultural humility in the workplace.

1. How would you describe your cultural identity?
2. How much does your cultural identity align with the dominant social culture of the city/country that you live in?
3. Are there aspects that don't align? How do you navigate this?
4. In what ways has your cultural identity shifted (if at all) over time or in specific contexts? If so, what has this been in response to?
5. What advantages and/or disadvantages has your cultural identity afforded you in your personal and professional life?
6. How is easy or difficult have you found these questions so far? What are thoughts around why this is?
7. What's your experience of working with people from different cultures?
8. What might be your blind spot of biases?
9. What would support you to engage in practices of cultural and competence and cultural humility in your place of work?
10. What might get in the way? How would you address them?
11. What steps can you start or continue to take?

Table 7.1 The differences between cultural competence and cultural humility.

	Cultural competence	Cultural humility
Objective	To increase knowledge and understanding of one's own culture and that of others	To engage in an ongoing process of self-reflection, acknowledging one's own biases in relation to cultural difference
Priorities	Gaining knowledge, training to gain competence and expertise	Reflective and reflexive practice, co-learning to develop a flexible and humble approach
Focus	Differences in terms of group identity and group boundaries	Focus on the individual (self and other) and the dynamic nature of culture and identity
Benefits	• Helps practitioners to build knowledge and increase awareness of other cultures • May help to improve engagement with people from diverse cultural backgrounds	• Acknowledges the complexity of identities and that a practitioner will never be fully competent in another's culture or experiences. • Encourages lifelong learning with no end goal • Addresses damaging power dynamics that may impede relationships with service users
Limitations	• Implies an end point, that 'competence' can be acquired in another's culture • Reinforces notion that cultures are static, categorical and monolithic, which can lead to stereotyping • Implies a top-down approach in disseminating and measuring competence	• Addressing the complexity of identity and its relationship to power can be challenging • No end point, which can engender apathy

7.7 Professional Context

A lack of representation amongst practitioners within the 'psy' disciplines has been a long-standing problem within mental health professions. Black and minority ethnic individuals are still significantly under-represented in the UK clinical psychology workforce and in the wider psychological professions (Scior et al., 2016), making up only 9.6% of qualified Clinical Psychologists in England and Wales (Health and Social Care Information Centre, 2013). Data published by the BPS shows that in the UK 88% of psychologists are white and 80% are female (British Psychological Society, 2015), a demographic that has remained unchanged since the 1970s. Unlike medicine and veterinary science, the profession has made very little progress in diversifying its ethnic profile in spite of the numerous inclusion and widening access initiatives that have been put forward since at least 1989 (Tong et al., 2019, Newnes, 2021). Whilst the narrative around diversity, access and inclusion has gained more traction over the years, the systemic barriers that maintain inequality within the profession remain. Deep-seated social inequalities no doubt play a role, often affording individuals from dominant affluent groups advantages in gaining entry onto training courses for example, easier access to opportunities, financial privileges (Wood & Patel, 2017).

Inequity of access appears to be a small part of a much bigger problem in light of the experiences of minoritised people on training courses. For example, the small number of applicants from minoritised groups who are selected onto clinical psychology training, including black and minority ethnic people, those who are disabled and people who identify as being from working-class backgrounds report experiences of marginalisation, being stereotyped and subject to overt and covert discrimination within clinical psychology training (Adetimole et al., 2005). Black and minority ethnic clinical psychology trainees in a 2016 study reported feeling exhausted by the expectation to lead on discussions around racism and cultural experiences, with some needing to request additional support in addressing experiences of racism whilst on training (Paulraj, 2016). Moreover, as Wood and Patel (2017) point out, the presence of a few trainees from minoritised backgrounds does not 'neutralise criticisms of the profession as being predominantly White, Eurocentric and discriminatory' (p. 10).

Eugene Ellis (2021), psychotherapist and founder of the Black, African and Asian Therapy Network (BAATN) highlights that psychotherapy and counselling predominantly represent heterosexual, cis-gendered, middle-class white people. According to McInnis (2020) white therapists stand to gain from white privilege, which refers to the invisible and unearned set of assets that society provides to those with white skin (McIntosh, 2003). White privilege denotes both obvious and less-obvious advantages that white people may be unaware of having, equating to a position of structural advantage. It encompasses pervasive cultural assumptions of white people's worth; presumed greater social status and increased freedom to move, buy, work, play and speak freely. The effects of white privilege manifest within professional, educational and personal contexts as the right to assume the universality of one's own experiences, perceiving oneself as morally neutral and normative and marking others as different or the 'other' (Martin-McDonald & McCarthy, 2008). In the context of therapy, white privilege is reproduced and maintained through the pervasive and unquestioned discourses that frame the work of the therapist as intervening with the 'other' for 'them' to be more like 'us'. It is therefore essential to apply a critical lens in therapeutic practice to reflect on power, inequality and social difference to refrain from entering into oppressive practices. Box 7.4 presents a minority ethnic trainee's experience of clinical psychology training.

Box 7.4 Layla's experience of clinical psychology training

'I was so excited to get onto the training after years of persevering. The excitement quickly gave way to a constant feeling of stress, and at times dread. Not because of the workload but because of feelings of being the odd one out. The funny thing is, everyone was so nice and appeared respectful. But the narrative around difference seemed to be one of deficit and disability. Assumptions around domestic violence, oppression and ignorance in black and minority ethnic communities were rife in the subtext of conversations, implicitly positioning other groups as somehow more primitive or less sophisticated. The more infuriating part was the emphasis on 'celebrating diversity' for example, people loving how exotic and colourful everything was in my culture. Conversations around racism, oppression, colonization, white privilege and structural inequality were at best tricky, and at worst, non-existent. My clumsy attempts to start to articulate my thoughts were met with defensiveness and accusations of inverted racism and prejudice against privileged white people. I couldn't understand how a group of such intelligent, gentle and well-meaning people could be so aggressive in their denial of their relative privilege and unconscious bias.'

Layla's experience captures important themes around the challenges of addressing diversity on training courses including storying difference as somehow problematic or moving too quickly into celebrating diversity. Not participating in the painful work of acknowledging and reflecting on structural and institutional racism and other power relations within therapy trainings creates the risk of producing therapists who are ill equipped to address these themes with service users in helpful or meaningful ways.

7.8 Social Graces

The Social GGRRAAACCEEESSS framework (herein referred to as social graces) developed by Systemic Therapists Burnham (1992) and Roper-Hall (1998) is a helpful scaffold for therapists to critically examine issues of power and social difference. Burnham (1992) initially developed the GGRRAAACCEEESSS acronym as a way of naming and drawing attention to aspects of personal and social identity that afford people different levels of power and privilege. These evolved, initially from nine graces to 15 areas of social difference including gender, geography, race, religion, age, ability, appearance, class, culture, ethnicity, education, employment, sexuality, sexual orientation and spirituality (Burnham, 2012; also see Figure 7.2). The 'social' prefix was subsequently added in order to capture the relational and socially constructed nature of these differences.

The social graces framework encourages practitioners to assess their relationship with aspects of social difference, and promotes curiosity in considering issues of power, oppression and connection (Butler, 2015). Examining the individual graces separately, and with equal importance allows for each aspect of identity to be considered in depth, and for the practitioner to explore how particular aspects of social difference are visible and invisible, and those that go voiced and unvoiced in supervisory and therapeutic settings (see Figure 7.3). It provides a useful lens through which to identify our own implicit biases and blind spots, and reflect on the impact of our identities, positions and assumptions on therapeutic practice. According to Burnham et al. (2008), examining social difference is essential to the co-creation of therapeutic contexts, as therapists are most likely to be pulled towards exploring issues that they privilege or feel most skilled in focusing on. Exploring social graces can facilitate and engender curiosity, enabling the therapist to name power differentials, and ultimately identify and address their own privilege.

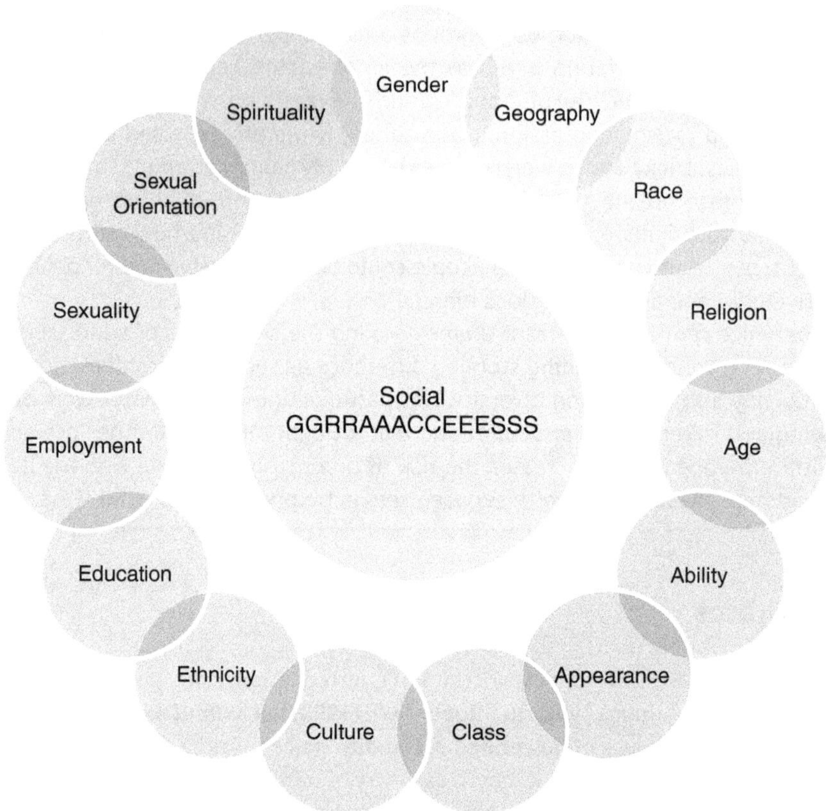

Figure 7.2 Aspects of identity or Social GGRRAAACCEEESSS. Source: Adapted from: https://www.basw.co.uk/sites/default/files/styles/inline_image/public/social-graces.jpg?itok=XOJdLxTp.

Burnham and Harris (2002) encourage practitioners to consider social graces as being in a reflexive relationship with other another, and consider the influence of relational contexts in activating different aspects of identity. Burnham proposes that the social graces should not be thought of as a linear list, but instead more like a kaleidoscope, or 'collide-scope', where aspects of social difference can be foregrounded or backgrounded depending on context and time (Totsuka, 2014). The collide-scope metaphor was intended to increase therapists' awareness of their relative position in terms of social difference and the positionality of the people they work with. According to Partridge and McCarry (2017) the social graces framework enables practitioners to not only reflect on how their social identities influence a situation, but to put these reflections to use through informing future actions in responding to sameness and difference. It also enables practitioners to explicitly identify dominant discourses that privilege dominant social identities (white, middle class, male, heteronormative, able bodied etc.), and to consider alternatives for future actions that are more inclusive. Box 7.5 provides an exercise to guide practitioner exploration of social graces to promote reflexivity.

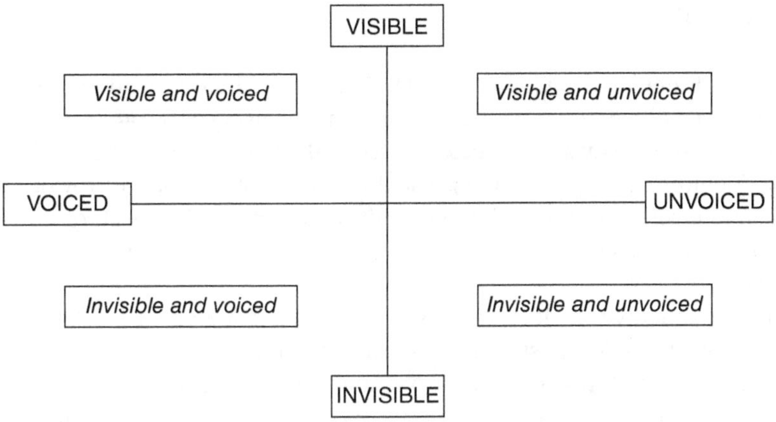

Figure 7.3 Visible and invisible, voiced and unvoiced. Source: Burnham, 2012, p. 146. Reproduced here with the author's kind permission.

Box 7.5 Exercise to guide practitioner exploration to promote reflexivity

Totsuka (2014) developed an exercise to facilitate the exploration of the relationships with different aspects of social graces in supervision as a way of promoting therapist reflexivity. The exercise consists of identifying and mapping out the influences of different aspects of social graces and exploring how and why some of them come to be more privileged than others. It can be used in the context of supervision (individual or group) in which the supervisee/s and supervisor are able to share different aspects of social difference and examine relative power and privilege. The questions here, taken from Totsuka's (2014) exercise can help practitioners to intentionally develop an awareness of, and engage with, the impact of their own identities.

1. Which aspects of the social graces grab you most and why?
2. Which ones did not grab you and why?
3. Can you think of important personal experiences that related to those aspects?
4. How is your view of yourself influenced by the social graces? How have these contributed to any strengths and areas of resilience you have?
5. What is your experience of privileges/lack of privileges in relation to the aspects of the social graces you chose?
6. What are the things you may take for granted?
7. What are the daily effects of your privileges/lack of privileges on your life and on your relationship with others?

It may be helpful to map out on Figure 7.3 the visible/invisible and voiced/unvoiced social graces as they apply to you in relation to your work. Consider the aspects of identity that would be helpful to share with colleagues, and the people you are working with.

7.9 Intersectionality

Whilst the social graces framework is a powerful tool that enables therapists to reflect on aspects of power and social difference, it has been argued that focusing on separate aspects of identity overlooks the complexity and richness created at the 'intersection' where different aspects of social identity meet (Butler, 2015). The theory of intersectionality provides a particularly helpful framework to examine the complexity of how multiple aspects of social identity combine in the contexts of power inequality to create experiences of oppression and systemic injustice.

The theory of intersectionality was developed by US law professor Kimberlé Crenshaw (1989), who defined it as way of 'understanding the ways that multiple forms of inequality or disadvantage sometimes compound themselves and create obstacles that often are not understood among conventional ways of thinking' (p. 149). The key tenets of intersectionality theory hold that people are shaped by their simultaneous membership of multiple interconnected social identities (e.g. race, gender, class), and that the interaction between these combined social identities takes place within a context of connected systems and structures of power (e.g. institutions, laws, policies). It is the interaction or intersection between multiple social identities and power relations in the context of wider systems that creates structural inequalities, which are reflected as relative privilege or disadvantage. This is depicted visually in Figure 7.4.

Intersectionality draws attention to the way different aspects of diversity interconnect to generate qualitatively different and unique experiences of inequality for individuals due to the way that oppressive responses to difference (e.g. racism, homophobia, sexism, ableism) interact and reinforce each other. Examining the multiple and simultaneous ways that an individual can be oppressed at the same time provides a richer and more multidimensional account of experience, avoiding the risk of considering oppression as existing within separate aspects of identity (Chantler, 2005). Patterns of oppression are contextually defined and intersecting, and attending to them in this way allows the

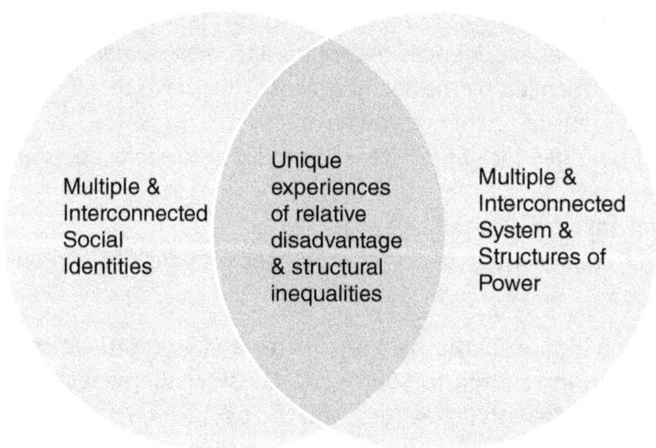

Figure 7.4 The relationship between the central tenets of intersectionality.

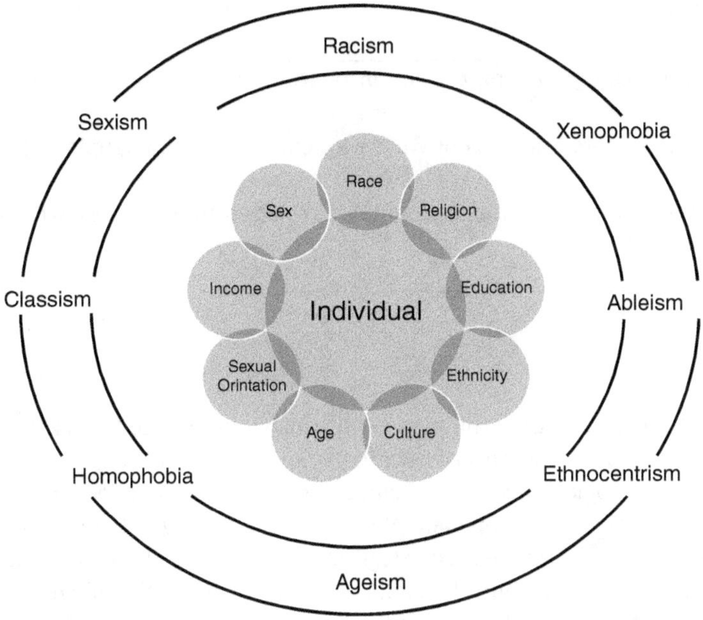

Figure 7.5 Intersectionality wheel illustrating how intersecting categories can shape individual identity (not exhaustive).

therapist to attend to structural differences and power inequalities within the complexity of individual experience. For example, knowing that a woman lives in a racist society is insufficient for fully understanding her experience of racism. Her sexuality, age and socioeconomic status must be taken into account in order to begin to fully understand her unique experience of discrimination (Collins, 2000). Also, the relative importance of each aspect of identity in contributing to the overall experience of oppression will vary between individuals, and therefore it can only be determined through exploring it with those it concerns (Hankivsky, 2014) (see also Box 7.6).

Box 7.6 An exercise for practitioners to explore the intersections of aspects of identity.

This exercise, adapted from knowledge.translation.net, aims to help individuals explore the intersection of aspects of identity in relation to advantages and/or disadvantages or experiences of discrimination in their lives. Use Figure 7.5 to explore areas where you have experienced advantage or disadvantage in your life.

1. What intersecting categories make up your identity?
2. Circle the social identities that bring you advantage or privileges.
3. Underline the social identities in relation to which you have experienced disadvantage or discrimination.
4. Are there intersections between categories of identity that have created more pronounced experiences of advantage/disadvantage for you? In what contexts?

(Continued)

Box 7.6 (Continued)

5. How do your intersecting categories impact you in relation to your work? And on your place in society?
6. How might your place in society impact your work with children, young people and families?
7. How might you apply ideas around intersectionality in relation to your work with children, young people and families?

7.10 Clinical level

Even a cursory review of the academic underpinnings of the main clinical models used in mental health services quickly reveals their overwhelmingly Eurocentric and North American roots. The dominant psychological theories and clinical models were all indeed developed in imperialist countries (Western Europe and North America) using data extracted from Western populations. The evidence base used to legitimise the use of these models and ideas is presented as scientific and value-neutral (Patel, 2003), and disproportionally represents Western, educated, industrialised, rich, democratic nations (Henrich et al., 2010), just 5% of the global population (Arnett, 2016). Yet, as philosopher Thomas Kuhn (1962) points out, scientific discourses do not emerge in a social vacuum and are intricately bound up in specific cultural paradigms that inform how people perceive the world and make sense and meaning of experiences.

By virtue of emerging within Western cultural traditions, modern 'psy' disciplines are deeply aligned with Western philosophies, norms, social values and agendas (Rose, 1998). Notions of body and mind as separate entities (rooted in Cartesian dualism), individualism, reductionism and an ego-centric conceptualisation of the human condition are at the core of dominant Western clinical models (Kirmayer, 2012). Tribe (2005) purports that Western psychological approaches are grounded in a model that is preoccupied with individual intrapsychic processes or individual pathology, whereas other traditions may be embedded in more relational or sociocentric notions of the self with a focus on kinship and collectivism. The deep-rooted historical Eurocentricity of psychological theory and practice thus creates significant challenges in attempting to make it applicable for more diverse groups. Box 7.7 gives a clinical example of a minority ethnic service user's experience of mental health services.

Box 7.7 Clinical example: Salma's experience of therapy

Salma is a 46-year-old Bangladeshi woman who moved to the UK in her 30s. She was referred for Cognitive Behavioural Therapy (CBT) by a social worker due to symptoms of severe anxiety following a racist attack on her son at his school. Salma stopped sending her son to school due to worries about further attacks and often worried about the safety of her family. She was keen to access support as the anxiety symptoms were getting in the way of daily functioning for both her and her family. Salma met with the CBT therapist for three sessions, after which she stopped engaging. She describes her experience of therapy as follows:

'She was a very nice lady. I could tell that she really wanted to help but it didn't really work for me ... I didn't see how thinking about what was going inside my mind and body was going to make everything better. The difficulties were to do with my children, family and how I could keep them safe because if something affects one person it affects us all.'

Salma's experience of therapy demonstrates how certain psychological approaches can fail in their utility for people from diverse backgrounds. Individualizing the distress and locating it within her did not fit with Salma's view of the problem or how to address it. Whilst manualized CBT approaches can be very effective for many people, their inherent assumptions around notions of the self may not fit for people from different cultures who don't construe distress in ways that are congruent with the prevailing psychological paradigm that underpin such approaches. Imposing such ideas on people not only runs the risk of disqualifying their ways of making sense of the human experience but can also serve to maintain deeply embedded inequalities in the system which means that some benefit from services more than others.

For those, like Salma who do not fit into the relatively monocultural norms of Western conceptualisations of health and well-being, mainstream interventions rooted in these ideas may bear little relevance or worse can perpetuate distress. Rimke (2016) highlights that dominant Eurocentric psychological approaches can serve to obscure systemic and structural oppression as explanations for mental distress, promoting individualised formulations of socially based problems. Social unrest, lack of affordable and stable housing, unemployment, the erosion of pensions, rising food and energy prices, toxic work environments, discrimination and community level trauma (historical or current) can all create mental distress, yet the overwhelming message provided by 'psy' experts implies that people's struggles are internally produced and strictly personal. Afuape (2016) points out that the locating of distress within individual psyches places the onus and responsibility for recovery solely on individuals and their coping mechanisms. The blind and uncritical application of individualising approaches not only risks promoting ideas around personal defectiveness and responsibility, but also risks entering into colonising and oppressive practices (Hughes & Bisimwa, 2015).

Whilst they may not be mandatory on UK training courses there are a number of psychological approaches that make space for more contextualised and inclusive ideas of well-being, and in which distress in not solely understood in intrapsychic terms but within the sociopolitical, historical and cultural context of a person's life. These include Liberation Psychology, Community Psychology, Critical Community Psychology, the Power Threat Meaning Framework, Co-ordinated Management of Meaning, and Narrative Therapy. Many of these approaches centralise power imbalances and structural inequality within the conceptualisation of distress, focusing on not just individual level interventions, but also those aimed at collective wellbeing, and wider systems level changes as part of the therapeutic endeavour. It is beyond the scope of this chapter to present all of these approaches and it is urged that the reader explores at least some of them further. Relevant references for further reading are provided at the end of the chapter. In Box 7.8 readers are presented with an exercise to support the consideration of the impact of inequality, power and discourses on service users.

Box 7.8 An exercise to support the consideration of the impact of inequality, power and discourses on service users.

The vignette and questions here provide an opportunity to think about how themes around structural inequalities, power imbalances and problematising discourses can be taken in to consideration when working with children, young people and families.

Daniel is a 15-year-old boy who has been referred for CBT for 'anger management' as part of a Court order. He was known to Youth Offending Services after being caught supplying class B drugs, and for fighting with other boys at school. Daniel has had difficult experiences with school teachers, and is at risk of being excluded from school. He has also experienced regular stop and searches by the police, with whom he has a difficult relationship. Daniel lives in an area with high levels of community-level violence between groups of young people, and very little resources for people his age.

Daniel was born in the UK and his parents are from Jamaica. His mother has multiple jobs to provide for the family and his father is unable to work due to long-standing difficulties with immigration (as his mother was part of the Windrush generation). Daniel has two sisters who are high academic achievers. He has a close relationship with his grandmother. Daniel has previously been offered therapy and was described as 'not psychologically minded' as a result of 'failing' to engage with CBT interventions.

1. How is Daniel being constructed in this context by mainstream services? How is the problem being constructed?
2. What kind of knowledge is being privileged and what ideas do they reinforce? What are the possible effects of this on Daniel, and his family?
3. What is the construction of change in this context?
4. What wider societal discourses might Daniel be up against for example, those relating to masculinity, being a young black person, discourses around education?
5. What kinds of things feed these discourses?
6. How might you embody, and resist these discourses if you were working with Daniel?
7. In what ways could Daniel's behaviour be viewed as a response or an act resistance to these discourses?
8. How might personal and community level injustice (e.g. racism, deprivation) be impacting on Daniel and his family in direct and indirectly?
9. Can you think of ways in which political policy impacts on Daniel and his family?
10. What other kinds of knowledge/theories/approaches could be helpful in working with Daniel?

7.11 Conclusion

This chapter has presented some of the current challenges in relation to themes of inclusivity, diversity and power within the multiple and interconnected contexts that child psychological practitioners will encounter within their training and practice. The chapter highlights that inequality and under-representation permeate all aspects of the 'psy' professions. This points to the pervasive, entrenched and interconnected nature of these issues, reinforcing and reproducing wider social inequalities and power relations. Dismantling the infrastructure that upholds such inequality is thus far beyond any individual practitioner. However, it is through genuine accountability at a practitioner level to the people being served that the profession is more likely to be able to start to make a collective shift towards becoming inclusive and more accommodating of diversity across multiple aspects of identity.

This chapter highlights that addressing issues of inclusivity, power and diversity is a dynamic and lifelong process that requires ongoing curiosity, humility and courage to engage with it in any meaningful way. The frameworks, ideas, case studies, vignettes and exercises presented provide opportunities for practitioners to develop an intentional awareness in relation to inclusion and diversity, and to interrogate themselves, their relationship to power and the dominant ideas that inform mainstream mental health practice. Indeed, it is through the consistent practice of self- and relational reflexivity, and reflexivity with regards to epistemology (the construction of knowledge and culturally bound understanding of reality) that practitioners will gain the skilfulness to practice in inclusive and equitable ways. Whilst this is a complex, emotive and at times challenging topic, it is hoped that this chapter has in some way moved, inspired or enrolled child practitioners to embark on, or continue further along the journey in contributing towards not just a fairer profession, but a fairer world.

Suggested Reading List

Liberation Psychology

Afuape, T., & Hughes, G. (eds.). (2015). *Liberation practices: Towards emotional wellbeing through dialogue.* London: Routledge.

Community Psychology

Orford, J. (2008). *Community psychology: Challenges, controversies and emerging consensus.* John Wiley & Sons.

Critical Community Psychology

Kagan, C., Burton, M., Duckett, P., Lawthom, R., & Siddiquee, A. (2019). *Critical community psychology: Critical action and social change.* Routledge.

The Power Threat Meaning Framework

Boyle, M., & Johnstone, L. (2020). *A straight talking introduction to the Power Threat Meaning Framework: An alternative to psychiatric diagnosis.* PCCS Books.

Co-ordinated Management of Meaning

Pearce, W. B. (2004). The coordinated management of meaning (CMM). In W. B. Gudykunst (Ed.), *Theorizing about intercultural communication* (pp. 35–54). Sage.

Narrative Therapy

Freedman, J., & Combs, G. (1996). *Narrative therapy*. Norton.

References

Adetimole, F., Afuape, T., & Vara, R. (2005). The impact of racism on the experience of training on a clinical psychology course: Reflections from three Black trainees. *Clinical Psychology Forum*, *48*, 11–15.

Afuape, T. (2016). Beyond awareness of 'difference' and towards social action: 'Solidarity practice' alongside young people. *Clinical Child Psychology and Psychiatry*, *21*(3), 402–415.

Arnett, J. J. (2016). The neglected 95%: Why American psychology needs to become less American. In. A. E. Kazdin (Ed.), *Methodological issues and strategies in clinical research* (pp. 115–132). American Psychological Association.

Betancourt, J. R., Green, A. R., & Carrillo, J. E. (2003). Defining cultural competence: A practical framework for addressing racial/ethnic disparities in health and health care. *Public Health Reports*, *118*(4), 293.

Boyle, M., & Johnstone, L. (2020). *A straight talking introduction to the Power Threat Meaning Framework: An alternative to psychiatric diagnosis*. PCCS Books.

British Psychological Society. (2015). *Clinical psychology workforce project*. Division of Clinical Psychology. https://www.bps.org.uk/sites/www.bps.org.uk/files/Page%20-%20Files/Clinical%20Psychology%20Workforce%20Report%20%282015%29.pdf.

Bronfenbrenner, U. (1979). *The ecology of human development: Experiments by nature and design*. Harvard University Press.

Bronfenbrenner, U. (1992). *Ecological systems theory*. Jessica Kingsley.

Burnham, J. (1992). Approach-method-technique: Making distinctions and creating connections. *Human Systems*, *3*(1), 3–26.

Burnham, J. (2012). The importance of being aware of, sensitive to, and competent in. In I. B. Krause *Culture and reflexivity in systemic psychotherapy: Mutual perspectives* (pp. 139–159). Karnak Books, Ltd.

Burnham, J., Alvis Palma, D., & Whitehouse, L. (2008). Learning as a context for differences and differences as a context for learning. *Journal of Family Therapy*, *30*(4), 529–542.

Burnham, J., & Harris, Q. (2002). Emerging ethnicity. In K. N. Dwivedi (Ed.), *Meeting the needs of ethnic minority children: including refugee, Black, and mixed parentage children: A handbook for professionals*. Jessica Kingsley.

Butler, C. (2015). Intersectionality in family therapy training: Inviting students to embrace the complexities of lived experience. *Journal of Family Therapy*, *37*(4), 583-589.

Chantler, K. (2005). From disconnection to connection: 'Race', gender and the politics of therapy. *British Journal of Guidance & Counselling*, *33*(2), 239–256.

Chavez, V. (2018). Cultural humility: Reflections and relevance for CBPR. In N. Wallenstein, B. Duran, J. G. Oetzel, & M. Minkler (Eds.), *Community-based participatory research for health: Advancing social and health equity* (pp. 357–362). John Wiley & Sons.

Chui, Z., Gazard, B., MacCrimmon, S., Harwood, H., Downs, J., Bakolis, I., Polling, C., Rhead, R., & Hatch, S. L. (2021). Inequalities in referral pathways for young people accessing secondary mental health services in south east London. *European Child & Adolescent Psychiatry*, *30*(7), 1113–1128.

Collins, P. H. (2000). Gender, black feminism, and black political economy. *The Annals of the American Academy of Political and Social Science*, *568*(1), 41–53.

Crenshaw, K. (1989). Demarginalizing the intersection of race and sex: A black feminist critique of anti-discrimination doctrine. *The University of Chicago Legal Forum, 1*(8), 139–167.

Cross, T., Bazron, B., Dennis, K., & Isaacs, M. (1989). *Towards a culturally competent system of care: A monograph on effective services for minority children who are severely emotionally disturbed*. CASSP Technical Assistance Center.

Department of Health. (2015). *Future in mind: Promoting, protecting and improving our children and young people's mental health and wellbeing*. NHS England. https://assets.publishing.service.gov.uk/government/uploads/system/uploads/attachment_data/file/414024/Childrens_Mental_Health.pdf

Edbrooke-Childs, J., Newman, R., Fleming, I., Deighton, J., & Wolpert, M. (2016). The association between ethnicity and care pathway for children with emotional problems in routinely collected child and adolescent mental health services data. *European Child & Adolescent Psychiatry*, *25*, 539–546.

Ellis, E. (2021). *The race conversation: An essential guide to creating life-changing dialogue*. Confer Books.

Foronda, C., Baptiste, D. L., Reinholdt, M. M., & Ousman, K. (2016). Cultural humility: A concept analysis. *Journal of Transcultural Nursing*, *27*(3), 210–217.

Foucault, M. (1982). The subject of power. In H. Dreyfus & P. Rainbow (Eds.), *Michael Foucault: Beyond structuralism and hermeneutics*. Harvester Wheatsheaf.

Fraser, N., & Honneth, A. (2003). *Redistribution or recognition? A political-philosophical exchange*. Verso.

Greene-Moton, E., & Minkler, M. (2020). Cultural competence or cultural humility? Moving beyond the debate. *Health Promotion Practice*, *21*(1), 142–145.

Guarnaccia, P. J., & Rodriguez, O. (1996). Concepts of culture and their role in the development of culturally competent mental health services. *Hispanic Journal of Behavioral Sciences*, *18*(4), 419–443.

Hankivsky, O. (2014). Rethinking care ethics: On the promise and potential of an intersectional analysis. *American Political Science Review*, *108*(2), 252–264.

Health and Social Care Information Centre. (2013). NHS workforce, summary of staff in the NHS: Results from September 2012 census. NHS Digital. https://digital.nhs.uk/data-and-information/publications/statistical/nhs-workforce-statistics-overview/nhs-workforce-summary-of-staff-in-the-nhs-results-from-september-2012-census

Henrich, J., Heine, S. J., & Norenzayan, A. (2010). The weirdest people in the world?. *Behavioral and Brain Sciences*, *33*(2–3), 61–83.

Hepworth, D. H., Rooney, R. H., Rooney, G. D., Strom-Gottfried, K., & Larsen, J. A. (Eds.). (2010). Assessment: Understanding and exploring problems and strengths. In *Direct Social Work Practice: Theory and Skills* (pp. 171–194). Brooks-Cole.

Hughes, G., & Bisimwa, N. A. (2015). Hard to reach services? Liberating ourselves from the constraints of our practice. In T. Afuape & G. Hughes (Eds.), *Liberating ourselves from the constraints of our practice* (pp. 171–181). Routledge.

Joseph Rowntree Foundation. (2021). Overall UK poverty rates. Joseph Rowntree Foundation. https://www.jrf.org.uk/data/overall-uk-poverty-rates#:~:text=In%202020%2F21%2C%20around%20one,living%20in%20poverty%20(27%25)

Kirmayer, L. J. (2012). Cultural competence and evidence-based practice in mental health: Epistemic communities and the politics of pluralism. *Social Science & Medicine*, *75*(2), 249–256.

Kuhn, T. S. (1962). *The structure of scientific revolutions* (1st ed.). University of Chicago Press.

Martin-McDonald, K., & McCarthy, A. (2008). 'Marking' the white terrain in indigenous health research: Literature review. *Journal of Advanced Nursing*, *61*(2), 126–133.

McInnis, E. M. (2020). An African psychology perspective on white supremacy within UK clinical psychology. *The Journal of Critical Psychology, 20*(3), 5–15.

McIntosh, P. (2003). White privilege: Unpacking the invisible knapsack. In S. Plous (Ed.), *Understanding prejudice and discrimination* (pp. 191–196). McGraw Hill.

Memon, A., Taylor, K., Mohebati, L. M., Sundin, J., Cooper, M., Scanlon, T., & De Visser, R. (2016). Perceived barriers to accessing mental health services among black and minority ethnic (BME) communities: A qualitative study in Southeast England. *BMJ Open*, *6*(11).

Mosher, D. K., Hook, J. N., Captari, L. E., Davis, D. E., DeBlaere, C., & Owen, J. (2017). Cultural humility: A therapeutic framework for engaging diverse clients. *Practice Innovations*, *2*(4), 221.

Nelson, G., & Prilleltensky, I. (2005). *Community psychology: In pursuit of liberation and well-being*. Palgrave Macmillan.

Newnes, C. (2021). *Racism in psychology: Challenging theory, practice and institutions.* Routledge.

Ogundare, T. (2019). Culture and mental health: Towards cultural competence in mental health delivery. *The Italian Journal for Interdisciplinary Health and Social Development. Journal of Health and Social Sciences, 5*(1), 023–034. https://doi.org/10.19204/2019/cltr6

Partridge, K., & McCarry, N. (2017). Graces that bite: Unleashing the GRR in the graces. *Context*, *151*, 7–10.

Patel, N. (1992). Psychological disturbance, social support and stressors: A community survey of immigrant Asian women and the indigenous population. *Counselling Psychology Quarterly*, *5*(3), 263–276.

Patel, N. (2003). Clinical psychology: Reinforcing inequalities or facilitating empowerment? *The International Journal of Human Rights, 7*(1), 16–39.

Paulraj, P. S. (2016). *How do Black trainees make sense of their 'identities' in the context of clinical psychology training?* (Unpublished doctoral dissertation) University of East London.

Platt, L. (Ed.). (2014). *Millennium Cohort Study: initial findings from the Age 11 survey*. Centre for Longitudinal Studies, Institute of Education.

Pople, L., & Rees, G. (2017). Good childhood report. *The Children's Society.* https://www.childrenssociety.org.uk/what-we-do/resources-andpublications/the-good-childhood-report-2017.

Rimke, H. (2016). Introduction – Mental and emotional distress as a social justice issue: Beyond psychocentrism. *Studies in Social Justice, 10*(1), 4–17.

Roper-Hall, A. (1998). Working systemically with older people and their families who have 'come to grief'. In P. Sutcliffe, G. Tufnell, & U. Cornish (Eds.), *Working with the dying and bereaved: Systemic approaches to therapeutic work* (pp. 177-206). Macmillan.

Rose, N. (1998). *Inventing our selves: Psychology, power, and personhood.* Cambridge University Press.

Scior, K., Wang, M., Roth, A., & Alcock, K. (2016). Underrepresentation in the profession: What's been done and what are the priorities going forward? Commentary on Celia Grace Smith's ethics column. *Clinical Psychology Forum, 280*, 12–13.

Tervalon, M., & Murray-García, J. (1998). Cultural humility versus cultural competence: A critical distinction in defining physician training outcomes in multicultural education. *Journal of Health Care for the Poor and Underserved, 9*(2), 117–125.

Tong, K., Peart, A., & Rennalls, S. J. (2019). Reframing our stories: Addressing barriers faced by Black people trying to access a career in clinical psychology. *Clinical Psychology Forum, 323*, 14–19.

Totsuka, Y. (2014). 'Which aspects of social GGRRAAACCEEESSS grab you most? 'The social GGRRAAACCEEESSS exercise for a supervision group to promote therapists' self-reflexivity. *Journal of Family Therapy, 36*, 86–106.

Tribe, R. (2005). Working with interpreters. In K. H. Barrett & W. H. George (Eds.), *Race, culture, psychology and law* (pp. 163–176). Sage.

Whaley, A. L., & Davis, K. E. (2007). Cultural competence and evidence-based practice in mental health services: A complementary perspective. *American Psychologist, 62*(6), 563.

Wood, N., & Patel, N. (2017). On addressing 'Whiteness' during clinical psychology training. *South African Journal of Psychology, 47*(3), 280–291.

8

Working with Goals and Monitoring Progress and Outcomes

In Collaboration with Young People

Duncan Law

8.1 Can a Question Save a Life?

This is a chapter about working with goals and monitoring outcomes. It could easily be a chapter that jumps into discussing tools, measures, numbers and statistics, which is often the focus of discussions on outcome measures. These important issues will be covered later, but the chapter starts with a story about how a question might save a life …

> There was once an adolescent, who is now a young adult and doing well. When they were a teenager, they were troubled by lots of thoughts and strong feelings about things that happened to them in the past, that they felt overwhelmed by. These feelings had gone on for a long time and they felt hopeless that anything could change. At that time, they felt the only way to stop being overwhelmed by these tremendously difficult and troubling feelings was to end their own life.
>
> Luckily, people around them noticed they were troubled. The school noticed and spoke to the young person who told them that they were planning to take an overdose. The school was rightly worried and decided to speak to the young person's mother who was also very concerned. The young person's mother did not feel she could keep her child safe so, she decided to take her teenage child to hospital. There the young person was triaged by a nurse and later assessed by a medic, who then involved the liaison psychiatry team. The young person remembers speaking to many professionals over the next 24 hours. They remember being asked a whole battery of questions, but the more they were asked the more overwhelmed they felt and the stronger their suicidal feelings became. The professionals decided that they needed to offer risk support to the young person and decided they should be admitted to the in-patient adolescent unit that was located within the same hospital.
>
> The young person remembers the hospital porter coming to take them from the emergency department over to the in-patient unit. The hospital porter had with them a wheelchair. There was nothing unusual about this as hospital porters are used to

Child Psychology: Pathways to Good Practice, First Edition.
Edited by Helen Pote, Anna Picciotto and Clare Norris.

taking people around hospitals, some of whom might struggle with the journey on foot. The young person remembers the porter asking them a question: 'So, do you want to walk or ride?'. The young person, for the first time in a long time, and certainly the first time in the past 24 hours, started to see a glimmer of hope. They experienced that moment, that question, as a turning point in their life, where they felt they might be able to be helped – in a sense, that simple question 'walk or ride?', had saved their life.

Let us pause for a moment here and think what was it about that question that was so transformative for this young person? Well, for the young person what made the difference was that they had been given a choice. They felt that up until then all the questions they had been asked had felt as if they were for the benefit of the professionals and not for the young person, and all decisions about them were made without their involvement. Their experience of being taken to hospital against their will, being assessed and having decisions made about them made the young person feel that their freedoms were being taken away from them, and the more they felt their options shrinking, the more terrified and overwhelmed they felt and the stronger the suicidal thoughts became.

Looking back the young person can see that the professionals and adults around them had been trying to act in then young person's best interest, to keep them safe, although it did not feel like that at the time. On reflection the young person can see that *what* the professionals did was helpful but *how* they did it was experienced as deeply troubling for the adolescent.

So, why start a chapter on goals and outcome monitoring with this story? Well, because it focuses on two fundamental issues in working with young people, namely the vital importance of being thoughtful not only of what is done: the 'task', it's also how it's done; the 'process'.

The young person in the story had experienced the professionals' questions as being for the professionals' benefit, they were asked in a way that made the young person feel that they were seen as nothing more than a problem to be processed. The focus of the professionals was too much on the task: what's the problem? what's the risk? what's the treatment? The porter's question, on the other hand, was seen by the young person as a genuine recognition of them as a person, a human with an intentional mind (Fonagy & Allison, 2014), with hopes and wishes even though, at the time, they felt close to hopeless. The young person felt that if this person could see them as a person rather than a problem, then there was hope that the professionals at the in-patient unit, and others, might do the same.

It also highlights the importance of choice and discussing with young people options that might be available to them, however limited, and helping them consider what they might want. In the case of the story, it was simple and immediate 'walk or ride?'. In therapy and other mental health interventions, practitioners want to understand the longer-term or medium-term wishes of what a young person wants to be different in their life as a result of working with them (Law, 2018).

Most of the time, these considerations might make the difference between whether a young person chooses to engage with the practitioner or not but sometimes, how things are done can have a profound impact on people's lives. These important issues must be kept in mind as feedback and outcome tools are looked at in the rest of this chapter.

8.2 Feedback and Outcome Tools

The feedback and outcome tools that monitor progress and outcomes, are generally based around questions, mostly standardised questionnaires, forms or checklists, either paper-based or digital. They are typically completed by the young person or by someone who knows them such as a parent, caregiver or a teacher. In many Children and Young People's Mental Health (CYPMH) services the questionnaires are referred to as 'routine outcome measures' (ROMs) and their completion is often viewed as a bureaucratic process to 'get data', an inconvenient task to be tolerated and endured by therapist and client alike (Law & Wolpert, 2014). There is real danger in holding and enacting such a narrative around feedback and outcome tools; if practitioners view them in this way then clients are likely to see them in this way too. At best this will lead to clients responding in ways that lead to understandably poor, inaccurate information back from the young people as they will experience the use of these measures as part of a reductionist, dehumanising process reducing them from a person to merely a set of problems. At worst, this use of ROMs could put a young person off from engaging in help, with all the negative consequences that follow. However, if practitioners can see the genuine value in those same questionnaires as tools, primarily to help do a better job with clients, and they are then embedded in the therapeutic process, they become part of the endeavor to be curious about the person as a whole, to enhance the ability to understand and connect with them.

Part of the problem in how the practitioner and the clients see and value these tools is in seeing them as 'routine outcome measures'; 'routine' can mean *something done without thinking,* when actually they are sophisticated clinical tools that should always be used meaningfully and thoughtfully (Law & Wolpert, 2014). The term 'outcome' suggests we might only be interested in whether people are better or worse at the end of an intervention. In therapy, a great opportunity can be missed if only the beginning is compared with the end of an intervention (Lambert, 2007). They can be better understood as ways to get additional feedback along the therapy journey so the way of working can be tweaked and the chances of helping the young person reach a good outcome can be improved (Duncan et al., 2010). Finally, calling them 'measures' instils them with potentially misleading sense of accuracy (Law, 2022).

> "When it comes to 'measuring' minds or mental health. When we speak of these tools as measures (which we will do, and this is an important part of their function) we need to remember that when we attempt to measure minds, they are not fixed and rigid objects like a stick of wood, but they are dynamic and fluid and hard to pin down. So, the 'measurements' we get are likely to have a high degree of inaccuracy."
>
> (Law, 2022, p. 65).

The inaccuracy or 'error' in what the tools measures is not a problem as long as this is kept in mind when attempts are made to track a persons mental health (Deighton et al.,

2014). The numbers obtained from these tools give an indication of someone's state of mind. The ratings (numbers) should always be seen as an invitation to a further conversation, to understand the context in which the young person made the rating. Used meaningfully they are helpful tools, not absolute measures (Law & Wolpert, 2014).

8.3 Working with Goals and the Goal-based Outcome Tool

To ease into this way of thinking about feedback on outcome tools in more detail, this section starts by looking at working with goals (Law, 2018) and the goal-based outcome (GBO) tool (Law, 2019) in mental health interventions.

To understand where working with goals fits, it is helpful to understand the value of shared decision making (SDM) and collaborative practice. Collaborative goal setting is seen as a vital part of SDM (Martin & Feltham, 2020). In children and young people's mental health services, goal setting has been shown to help young people feel more included in their care (Law et al., 2018) and facilitates a better therapeutic alliance (Tyron & Winograd, 2011). Working with goals is a core component across most therapeutic modalities (Grey et al., 2018) and has demonstrated utility across a range of presenting issues (Krause et al., 2022; Rupani et al., 2014).

The GBO tool is a clinical tool with simple and straightforward origins (about 20 years ago) as a way of reminding practitioners to ask young people and families about what they hoped to achieve through a mental health intervention (York & Kingsbury, 2009). Soon it was realised that adding a simple 0 to 10 scale meant that a baseline rating could be obtained at the start of therapy that allowed progress towards therapy goals to be tracked (Law, 2006). From these very simple origins, as a purely clinical tool, a number of studies have shown the GBO to have reasonably robust psychometric properties (Duncan et al., 2023; Edbrooke-Childs et al., 2015; Krause et al., 2022). There is also two randomised control trials currently underway (as yet unpublished) where tentative results seem to show that the use of the GBO may lead to better outcomes.

The GBO is an idiographic tool; what is tracked, using a simple 0 to 10 scale, is defined by the client (Law, 2019). Such client-defined outcome measures or ideographic patient-rated outcome measures (I-PROMs) allow the client to define their own focus for the intervention (Sales et al., 2023). This ensures that what is tracked in therapy has meaning to the client. The tool measures progress on the issues that the person themself most wants to work on (Law, 2019).

The GBO tool is a prompt to ask clients the deceptively simple question: 'What do you want to be different in your life?' as a result of engaging in therapeutic or other mental health intervention. However, before the young person can answer this question, an environment needs to be created where they can explore/discover/dare-to-share, their hopes and wishes for the future (Law, 2022). This process requires a great deal of clinical skill. Goal setting should be integrated into usual clinical conversations, but with a focus on reaching an understanding of what the young person genuinely wants to be different in their lives: their goals. As one young person put it: 'goals should emerge from the stories young people tell about themselves and their lives', this is an excellent piece of clinical advice. When young people are actively engaged in decisions about their care, it can lay the foundations of a good therapeutic relationship (Tryon & Winograd, 2011) and help them feel more motivated to change (Law et al., 2018).

Usually, CYP are invited to set up to three intervention goals (Law & Jacob, 2015). Once goals are set, the GBO provides a simple and intuitive way to track progress. The brevity of the scale makes it easy to integrate into every session so goal progress can be tracked and discussed (Law, 2019).

8.4 Other Monitoring and Outcome Tools

Alongside goal-focused tools, other tools that are useful to monitor progress and outcomes in clinical interventions fall into three broad categories:

- tools that focus on the person's 'symptoms',
- tools that focus on the person's 'functioning', and
- tools that focus on the 'therapeutic alliance'.

There are many different tools that fall under these categories, but some of the most widely used examples are discussed below.

8.4.1 Symptom-focused Tools

Symptom-focused tools are designed to track changes in the problems or 'symptoms' a person may be experiencing. The two most widely used symptom-focused tools in CYPMH services in the UK are the 'Revised Child and Adolescent Anxiety and Depression Scales' (RCADS) (Chorpita et al., 2005) and the Strengths and Difficulties Questionnaire (SDQ) (Goodman, 2011), both of which ask about a wide range of difficulties a child with mental health issues might experience (see Box 8.1).

Both tools invite the young person, or someone who knows them well, to look at a list of symptoms and rate which ones they are currently experiencing. This style of checklist tends to give us lots of information about the types of problems a person is struggling with and can be used to build hypotheses about the nature of their difficulties. If used at the first session, they can provide a 'baseline' measure of a person's problems. If repeated at the end of an intervention, the ratings can be compared to give an indication of progress made, or 'outcome'. Even better is to use the tools repeatedly throughout the course of an intervention. The RCADS (Chorpita et al., 2005), has short subscales, that can be used to track more specific problem areas, for example, low mood, generalised anxiety, or obsessive compulsive disorder (OCD). In this way progress can be monitored at each session and the ratings used to facilitate discussions with the young person about progress: What is helping? What is not? What aspect of the intervention might be helpful to change?

Both the SDQ and RCADS are 'normed', in that they allow comparison of the young person completing the questionnaire with a cohort of young people with whom the tool was developed, to establish the comparative severity of the symptomatology.

It is important to take great care when administering these standardised, symptom-based, nomothetic tools. It was these sorts of tools that the adolescent in our opening story was subjected to in the many assessments they went through when in crisis. They experienced the use of these tools in a way that felt reductive. The young person felt they were being categorised by their symptoms and their level of risk, rather than being seen as a whole person, albeit with some serious difficulties at that time.

This can be the danger with these tools; young people can experience them as merely a piece of paper with no value or meaning to them if they are not properly introduced (Wolpert, 2014). Furthermore, symptom-focused tools, largely developed by white, Western academics and developed and tested in largely white, Western communities, can be experienced as imposing a particular Western psychiatric view of mental health: that mental health issues are an illness made up of symptoms located in an individual (Timimi, 2010). They can create an unhelpful narrative focusing on 'what's wrong with you?', missing the more helpful contextual issues of 'what has happened to you?' (Johnstone & Boyle, 2018). Administered without a careful therapeutic context around them, young people can experience them as dehumanising. Used well, there is real value in using these tools both to us as the practitioner and to the young person (Wolpert, 2014).

Box 8.1 I'm not alone!

Let me share another brief story, at this point in the chapter; this time of symptom-focused tools being used well. Some years ago, I was supervising a recently qualified clinical psychologist who was starting to use the RCADS as a way of gathering information, in an effective and timely way as part of the assessment (or Choice appointment – see Chapter 6) process. My supervisee was a skilled practitioner who understood the value of using symptom-focused tools. They had taken time to explain carefully the value of using the RCADS for themselves, as a practitioner, but most importantly how it could add value for the young person. The young person began filling out the RCADS and soon, became tearful. The practitioner noticed the tears and asked the young person about them. The young person replied that, up until coming to the service she felt that she was 'really going mad' and that she was the 'only person in the world' who felt the way that she did. However, completing the RCADS she began to answer questions that resonated with what she had been experiencing over the previous months. She described the tears as tears of relief. She explained that for someone to have created this questionnaire with questions that were so relevant to her own experience of herself, meant that she could not be the 'only person in the world' who felt like this, in fact there must be many other people who shared her difficult and troubling experiences. Answering the questionnaire made her feel hopeful that she was not alone with these difficulties and that she might be understood by someone who could help.

Throughout the intervention the practitioner and young person agreed to return to the helpful questions in the RCADS, using the subscales of the tool. The practitioner and the young person used the tool to monitor progress in therapy and using the young person's rating of themselves to facilitate further conversations about the therapeutic process, what was helping, and what was not and the wider changes in the young

(Continued)

Box 8.1 (Continued)

person's life that were contributing to her symptom reduction. It was also used to help focus the work on the symptoms that still troubled her and, by looking back at the baseline rating at the first assessment she was able to get a real sense of the progress she has made since then.

I do not want to pretend that every young person's experience will be like the one described here, indeed for some young people questionnaires will feel like a test. However, it is the job of practitioners to explain and discuss the potential value of the tools, creating a context in which the young person is more likely to experience the tool as helpful and valuable.

8.4.2 Functioning-focused Tools

Functioning-focused tools track changes in the impact a person's mental health issues are having on their life: 'functioning'. Such as the Child Outcome Rating Scale (CORS) (Casey et al., 2020) which asks about the CYPs functioning across four domains: 'School', 'Family', 'Me' and 'Everything Else'. The SDQ also has a built-in impact or functioning scale that can be used alongside the full symptom-focused part of the SDQ or can be used on its own and is brief enough to be used at every session: 'The impact/session-by-session scale' (Hall et al., 2015).

Tools that focus more on functioning are less prone to cultural bias and are more culturally sensitive because they focus on the impact of the issues, 'How big a problem is this for you?' and make fewer assumptions about what the underlying causes of the problem might be. Whether symptom, or functioning-focused tools are used depends on the utility of the tool for the young person, for practitioners and for the wider needs of the service.

8.4.3 Therapeutic-alliance-focused Tools

The therapeutic alliance is a complex and evolving construct (Ardito & Rabellino, 2011). Is the therapy working? Is it helping to reach the goals? Is what is happening in therapy important? Does the client feel listened to? Does the young person understand what is being said? All this, and more, goes into creating a feeling of working in collaboration with the therapist. The therapeutic alliance is an indicator of the quality of relationship between the client and the practitioner. The quality of the therapeutic relationship is one of the most important foundations for therapeutic change (Horvath & Luborsky, 1993). So, it is vital that attention is paid to the quality of the therapeutic alliance and the tools in this category aim to help do just that.

Tools that help practitioners focus on and understand the quality of the therapeutic alliance between practitioner and client, work by asking questions to facilitate open communication and generate feedback on how well the young person feels that the practitioner is working with them. One of the most widely used of these tools is the Session Rating Scale (SRS) (Duncan et al., 2003). The SRS invites a child to rate four domains: how much the child felt listened to; how important they felt what happened in the session was;

how much they liked what the therapist did in the session; and how much they wished they could do something different in the session.

As with the GBO, these are deceptively simple questions to ask that require a great deal of clinical skill to engender honest feedback from young people. This is no easy task given the power imbalance between practitioner and client. Giving helpfully critical feedback to a practitioner often feels risky to a young person. This is, in part, due to cultural priming to acquiesce when asked for feedback. If someone is asked by an acquaintance 'How are you?', they are culturally programmed to respond 'fine thank you', whether they are feeling fine or not! If ever one goes out for a meal one is likely to be asked, 'is everything alright with your meal?' and will generally respond 'yes, thank you!' regardless of the quality.

To facilitate honest, helpful, critical feedback attention needs to be paid to the process that communicates a wish to be open to learning and change, in the same way that practitioners want to encourage young people they work with to be open to learning through therapy to facilitate their own change. This is particularly true for CYP who may have experienced trauma (Law, 2022).

In order to encourage helpful feedback, it is important to amplify and praise a young person who 'dares' to be even a little bit critical. If we can encourage children and young people to share what they do not like about therapy, and about their therapists, it may be possible to change what we do to improve the relationship and be more helpful (Duncan et al., 2010).

This kind of feedback also links with ideas of service-user participation (see Chapter 9 for further discussion on this topic). Participation is usually seen as an activity that happens at a service level, but giving feedback to practitioners on an ongoing basis, during the course of therapy, is also a form of participation. What some young people have described as 'everyday participation' (Law et al., 2018).

8.5 Why are Monitoring and Outcome Tools Necessary?

Each of the tools described earlier: goal-focused, symptom-focused, functioning-focused, and those wishing to understand the quality of the therapeutic alliance, all have utility in their own right. Used individually or in conjunction with one another, and integrated into a meaningful clinical exchange, these tools can provide invaluable information that may not be available without using them. Research evidence suggests that monitoring and outcome questionnaires elicit qualitatively different information from young people. Tools help to do things better, and this is just as true of using feedback and outcome, or monitoring tools. This additional information, used well and in conjunction with what is obtained from talking, gives the practitioner more to work with and more chance of being more effective (Lambert, 2007).

Research evidence is clear, from adult mental health settings, that using feedback tools, in conjunction with therapy conversations, reduces drop-out and can lead to quicker and better outcomes for the people seeking help (Lambert, 2007; Shimokawa et al., 2010). There has been less-extensive research in CYP settings to provide the same level of evidence of their efficacy (Bergman et al., 2018) but the body of research points in a similar direction highlighting growing evidence of the utility of these tools in enhancing clinical practice (Bickman et al., 2011; Cooper et al., 2021).

Alongside improving the efficacy of interventions, the data, which is a byproduct of the effective use of these tools, can facilitate better reflective practice, aid supervision and can be used as a service on a system level to help to develop practice-based evidence on the efficacy of interventions in real-world settings.

The utility of these tools is well recognised and mandated across the national health service in England and the rest of the UK. The CYP IAPT programme (see Chapter 6 for further discussion) introduced and embedded a core set of measures to be used across all CYPMH services. The current mandate is for all CYP and their families to complete a GBO alongside a symptom-focused measure such as the RCADS or SDQ, together with information on the client's experience of the service and their satisfaction with it using the CHI ESQ (NHS England, 2015). This data is extracted from electronic patient records and is analysed by the NHS to help better monitor and understand the overall efficacy of the CYPMH system more broadly.

8.6 The Future

The regular use of feedback and outcome tools or monitoring and outcome measures in mental health is a relatively new venture and particularly new in CYPMH settings. Many of the measures used in these settings were developed to have a research function rather than to be used as clinical tools (e.g. RCADS and SDQ). Those tools that were developed specifically to be used in clinical settings for example, the GBO, CORS and SRS, still require further research to robustly test their efficacy. The development and utility of such tools is still in its infancy.

Although reasonably robust tools for use with the majority of CYP who come into contact with mental health services are available, there is still a great deal of work to be done to develop tools, practices and processes that work effectively with more specific populations, such as young people with learning difficulties, with neurodiversity and those young people who experience themselves as being on the fringes of society such as looked after children and those in the criminal justice system. Recent developments and interest in more ideographic and client-defined measures are taking steps in the right direction. However, harnessing the potential that computerised technology, machine learning and artificial intelligence have, will provide the potential to both expand the capacity to improve feedback and hear the voice of young people who, currently, are not heard. Real progress will have been made when effective feedback can be elicited from CYP with severe and profound learning disabilities and those who do not have capacity for verbal communication. It is hard to predict what these feedback tools will look like, but one thing is for certain, they are unlikely to be questionnaire based. A profound wish would be to look back at this chapter in 5 to 10 years' time and see an enormous development in the use of technology to improve what is measured, and how feedback is received in ways that are much more collaborative, much more relevant to the needs and wishes of the young people we work with and are much more sophisticated in analysing and synthesising data that enhances and supports continually improving clinical practice. For now, the fact that we have tools that are currently available, that help us do better work, is a good enough reason for using them, until we have better.

References

Ardito R. B., & Rabellino, D. (2011). Therapeutic alliance and outcome of psychotherapy: historical excursus, measurements, and prospects for research. *Frontiers of Psychology, 2*, 270.

Bergman, H., Kornør, H., Nikolakopoulou, A., Hanssen-Bauer, K., Soares-Weiser, K., Tollefsen, T. K., & Bjørndal, A. (2018). Client feedback in psychological therapy for children and adolescents with mental health problems. *Cochrane Database of Systematic Reviews, 8*, CD011729.

Bickman, L., Kelley, S. D., Breda, C., de Andrade, A. R., & Riemer, M. (2011). Effects of routine feedback to clinicians on mental health outcomes of youths: Results of a randomized trial. *Psychiatric Services, 62*(12), 1423–1429.

Casey, P., Patalay, P., Deighton, J., Miller, S. D., & Wolpert, M. (2020). The Child Outcome Rating Scale: Validating a four-item measure of psychosocial functioning in community and clinic samples of children aged 10–15. *European Child & Adolescent Psychiatry, 29*(8), 1089–1102.

Chorpita, B. F., Moffitt, C. E., & Gray, J. (2005). Psychometric properties of the Revised Child Anxiety and Depression Scale in a clinical sample. *Behaviour Research and Therapy, 43*(3), 309–322.

Cooper, M., Duncan, B., Golden, S., & Toth, K. (2021). Systematic client feedback in therapy for children with psychological difficulties: Pilot cluster randomised controlled trial. *Counselling Psychology Quarterly, 34*(3–4), 21–36.

Deighton, J., Croudace, T., Fonagy, P., Brown, J., Patalay, P., & Wolpert, M. (2014). Measuring mental health and wellbeing outcomes for children and adolescents to inform practice and policy: A review of child self-report measures. *Child and Adolescent Psychiatry and Mental Health, 8*(1), 1–14.

Duncan, C., Cooper, M., & Saxon, D. (2023). Test-retest stability, convergent validity, and sensitivity to change for the Goal-based Outcome tool for adolescents: Analysis of data from a randomized controlled trial. *Journal of Clinical Psychology, 79*(3), 683–696.

Duncan, B. L., Miller, S. D., Sparks, J., Claud, D., Reynolds, L., Brown, J., & Johnson, L. (2003). The Session Rating Scale: Preliminary psychometric properties of a 'working' alliance measure. *Journal of Brief Therapy, 3*(1), 3–12.

Duncan, B. L., Miller, S. D., Wampold, B. E., & Hubble, M. A. (2010). *The heart and soul of change: Delivering what works in therapy*. American Psychological Association.

Edbrooke-Childs, J., Jacob, J., Law, D., Deighton, J., & Wolpert, M. (2015). Interpreting standardized and idiographic outcome measures in CAMHS: What does change mean and how does it relate to functioning and experience? *Child and Adolescent Mental Health, 20*(3), 142–148.

Fonagy, P., & Allison, E. (2014). The role of mentalizing and epistemic trust in the therapeutic relationship. *Psychotherapy, 51*(3), 372.

Goodman, R. (2001). Psychometric properties of the Strengths and Difficulties Questionnaire. *Journal of the American Academy of Child and Adolescent Psychiatry, 40*(11), 1337–1345.

Grey, N., Byrne, S., Taylor, T., Shmueli, A., Troupp, C., Stratton, P., Sefi, A., Law, R., & Cooper, M. (2018). Goal-oriented practice across therapies. In M. Cooper & D. Law (Eds.), *Working with goals in psychotherapy and counselling* (pp. 161–180). Oxford University Press.

Hall, C. L., Moldavsky, M., Taylor, J., Marriot, M., Goodman, R., Sayal, K., Hollis, C. (2015). Piloting electronic session-by-session monitoring in Child and Adolescent Mental Health Services: A preliminary study. *Child and Adolescent Mental Health, 20*(3), 171–174.

Horvath A. O., & Luborsky L. (1993). The role of the therapeutic alliance in psychotherapy. *Journal of Consulting Clinical Psychology, 61,* 561–573.

Johnstone, L., & Boyle, M. (2018). The power threat meaning framework: An alternative nondiagnostic conceptual system. *Journal of Humanistic Psychology.* https://doi.org/10.1177/0022167818793289

Krause, K. R., Edbrooke-Childs, J., Singleton, R., & Wolpert, M. (2022). Are we comparing apples with oranges? Assessing improvement across symptoms, functioning, and goal progress for adolescent anxiety and depression. *Child Psychiatry & Human Development, 53*(4), 737–753.

Lambert, M. (2007). Presidential address: What we have learned from a decade of research aimed at improving psychotherapy outcome in routine care. *Psychotherapy Research, 17*(1), 1–14.

Law, D. (2006). *Goal Based Outcomes (GBOs): Some Useful Information.* CORC publications.

Law, D. (2018). Goal-oriented practice. In M. Cooper & D. Law (Eds.), *Working with goals in psychotherapy and counselling* (pp. 161–180). Oxford University Press.

Law, D. (2019). *The goal-based outcome (GBO) tool: Guidance notes.* MindMonkey Associates.

Law, D. (2022a). Tools to make low intensity interventions with children and youth more effective. In S. Bennett, P. Myles-Hooton, J. Schleider, & R. Shafran (Eds.), *Oxford guide to brief and low intensity interventions for children and young people* (p. 64). Oxford University Press.

Law, D. (2022b). Working with goals and trauma in youth mental health. *International Journal of Environmental Research and Public Health, 19*(17), 11048.

Law, D., & Jacob, J. (2015). *Goals and Goal-based Outcomes (GBOs): Some useful information* (3rd Ed.). CAMHS Press.

Law, D., Martin, K., Jeremy, G., Feltham, A., & Ingram, B. (2018). Everyday participation: Rethinking involvement and participation in children and young people's mental health settings. *The Child & Family Psychology Review, 6*(1), 40–45.

Law, D., & Wolpert, M. (Eds.). (2014). *Guide to using outcomes and feedback tools with children, young people and families.* CAMHS Press.

Martin, K., & Feltham, A. (2020). Shared decision-making with young people in mental health services. In L.-M. Brady (Ed.), *Embedding young people's participation in health services: New approaches* (pp. 31–52). Policy Press.

NHS England (2015). *Local transformation plans for children and young people's mental health and wellbeing: Guidance and support for local areas.* NHS England.

Rupani, P., Cooper, M., McArthur, K., Pybis, J., Cromarty, K., Hill, A., Levesley, R., Murdoch, J., & Turner, N. (2014). The goals of young people in school-based counselling and their achievement of these goals. *Counselling Psychotherapy Research, 14,* 306–314.

Sales, C. M. D., Ashworth, M., Ayis, S., Barkham, M., Edbrooke-Childs, J., Faísca, L., Jacob, J., Xu, D., & Cooper, M. (2023). Idiographic patient reported outcome measures (I-PROMs) for routine outcome monitoring in psychological therapies: Position paper. *Journal of Clinical Psychology, 79*(3), 596–621.

Shimokawa, K., Lambert, M. J., & Smart, D. W. (2010). Enhancing treatment outcome of patients at risk of treatment failure: Meta-analytic and mega-analytic review of a psychotherapy quality assurance system. *Journal of Consulting and Clinical Psychology, 78*(3), 298–311.

Timimi, S. (2010). The McDonaldization of childhood: Children's mental health in neo-liberal market cultures. *Transcultural Psychiatry, 47*(5), 686–706.

Tryon, G. S., & Winograd, G. (2011). Goal consensus and collaboration. *Psychotherapy, 48*, 50–57.

Wolpert, M. (2014). Uses and abuses of Patient Reported Outcome Measures (PROMs): Potential iatrogenic impact of PROMs implementation and how it can be mitigated. *Administrative Policy of Mental Health, 41*, 141–145.

York, A., & Kingsbury, S. (2009). *The Choice and Partnership Approach: A guide to CAPA*. Child and Adolescent Mental Health Services Network.

9

Collaboration and Co-production

Shaun Liverpool and Paula Bailey

This chapter explores the process of engaging young people and their primary carers with services. The chapter provides a descriptive analysis of the emotional experiences of carers when accessing mental health support for their child followed by an exploration of how carers' emotional experiences influence their decision to engage with services. The chapter then explores how carers and practitioners involve young people in care and treatment decisions resulting in a framework to help practitioners develop the kinds of knowledge, approaches, values and personal qualities that could be beneficial when working with families. The chapter also extends previous chapters by focusing on the involvement of young people and carers in assessments, formulations, treatment planning, service development and research. Clinical examples are used throughout to illustrate these aspects of working with young people and their families.

9.1 Considerations to Collaborate on Decisions Around Young People's Mental Health Care

Children and young people's mental health problems have high prevalence, tend to co-occur, potentially predict further health problems, and impact different areas of the child or young person's life (Jensen & Steinhausen, 2015; Kieling et al., 2011; Perou et al., 2013; Polanczyk et al., 2015). Once mental health symptoms are suspected, the families experience many decisions, such as,

- how, when and from where to seek help (Wolpert et al., 2015).
- agreeing on the diagnostic tests or assessments (Berger et al., 2017).
- agreeing on the goals of treatment (Bradley et al., 2013; Law & Jacob, 2015).
- agreeing on treatment options when more than one treatment option is available (Ahmed et al., 2017; Hayes et al., 2018).

Therefore, service providers are usually called upon to provide psychoeducation, assessments, formulations and facilitate treatment planning.

Although carers are recognised in the literature and in law as important members of the decision-making process it is often difficult for them to engage efficiently for reasons

Child Psychology: Pathways to Good Practice, First Edition.
Edited by Helen Pote, Anna Picciotto and Clare Norris.

outlined later (Allan, 2004; Benson & Pinnaro, 2015; Haine-Schlagel & Walsh, 2015; Gondek et al., 2017). As a result, healthcare professionals report low participation from carers (Baker-Ericzén et al., 2013; Boland et al., 2017); carers report feeling isolated and excluded by services (Andershed et al., 2017); and there are treatment disagreements between carers, practitioners and young people (Simmons et al., 2013). In some instances, child and carer maybe in conflict due to Children and young people (CYP) behavioural symptoms of mental health problems (e.g. irritability, avoidance) and both parent and child then experience stress and distress because of the mental health concerns. The parents may also have mental health difficulties leading to issues with participation and engagement (children with mental health problems are more likely to have a parent with mental health problems). Additionally, the need to participate in and collaborate on decision making in child health settings has been associated with added stressors for the carers involved (Adams & Levy, 2017). Nonetheless, researchers, practitioners and policy makers suggest that there are significant benefits when young people and their primary carers are involved in care and treatment decisions through the shared-decision process (Edbrooke-Childs et al., 2015).

CYP sometime access mental health services as involuntary or unwilling participants, meaning they are told they should or must go to services. As such those CYP could be considered as 'involved' with/in services rather than 'engaged' with/in the service as active participants (Srinath et al., 2019). The Care Quality Commission's (2018) review, 'Are we listening?', captured these perspectives from CYP and their carers alongside a wide range of systems involved with children and young people such as schools, health, social care, voluntary and community organisations. The review (Care Quality Commission, 2018) also recognised the need for CAMHS services to encourage active engagement of CYP through individualised partnership approaches and shared decision making within services.

9.2 Shared Decision Making in Young People's Mental Health Settings

Shared decision making has been broadly defined as the involvement of service users in the process of making decisions where there are important reasonable competing treatment options (Charles et al., 1997; Légaré & Thompson-Leduc, 2014). Charles et al. (1999) further described shared decision making as a cognitive, emotional and relational process where service providers and service users collaborate. At its core, the shared-decision-making literature perceives service users as competent and having the capacity to participate in the shared-decision-making process. Another key assumption is that multiple care or treatment options exist with competing outcomes and substantial uncertainty. Together these have important ethical and practical implications, further highlighting a need for a deeper understanding of how shared decision making is implemented in settings like children and young people's mental health services.

Shared decision making experts acknowledge that shared decision making in youth psychotherapy may take many forms. However, at its core, these experts suggest that the shared decision making process must, at a minimum:

- include the youth, the caregiver, or both in a decision-making process with the practitioner, with the possibility of including other stakeholders as well;

- facilitate sharing information bidirectionally, with the practitioner sharing information about psychopathology and treatment options, and receiving information about the youth's symptoms, and the youth and caregiver's preferences, values and goals; and
- determine the course of action collaboratively, through a process of discussion, compromise and agreement (Charles et al., 1997).

Based on these core principles and the essential and ideal elements of shared decision making (Makoul & Clayman, 2006), Langer and Jensen-Doss (2018) developed the following sample shared-decision-making protocol that is specific to young people's mental health settings:

- discuss preferred roles in treatment planning.
- specify decisions to be made.
- present the available options for each decision.
- determine pros and cons of each option.
- design preliminary treatment plan.
- implement progress monitoring.

This process suggests that either the child or parent or both should be involved in the decision-making process in order to achieve shared decision making. The model therefore claims to adapt to the complexities of the triad relationship in treatment planning in young people's mental health settings with young people being involved as much as they are willing and able to. A recent study has also extended this discourse and proposed that shared decision making in young people mental health settings should be viewed as a process involving key decision makers (i.e. carers, healthcare professionals and young people), as developmentally appropriate, sharing information and views, and all parties taking steps (i.e. informed or involved) to build a consensus about the preferred care and treatment option (Liverpool et al., 2021).

9.3 Factors Influencing Involvement and Collaborations with Services

Generally, the evidence on barriers and facilitators to shared decision making are divided into categories of knowledge, attitudes, agreement, lack of expectancy/hope and behaviours among service users and service providers (Adams & Levy, 2017). Reviews commonly highlight specific barriers such as patient/family characteristics (e.g. demographics and child health status), service constraints (e.g. time taken for consultation and trust in service providers), power imbalance, lack of available evidence-based treatment options, and service providers limited knowledge of shared-decision-making skills (Boland et al., 2019; Gondek et al., 2017).

Apart from the main influence of service users' capacity to be involved (e.g. age and health status) in shared decision making, positive attitudes, behaviours and better mental health appear to increase engagement with the shared-decision-making process. For example, common facilitators to shared decision making in general healthcare include: positive provider attitude and behaviours, positive impact on the clinical process, quality information, patients' health outcomes and encouragement of support systems (Covvey et al., 2019; Garvelink et al., 2019; Bee et al., 2015). Additionally, broader paediatric studies suggest family factors (e.g. cultural norms), impact on the family, community standards and policies, previous experience (e.g. help-seeking) as other factors influencing the shared-decision-making process (Boland et al., 2019; Wyatt et al., 2015). The limited literature specific to young people's mental health has reported similar facilitators (Gondek et al., 2017) with recent findings adding that practitioners' skill of containment may be unique to shared decision making in young people's mental health settings (Hayes et al., 2019). Hayes and colleagues also highlighted that carers generally express their capability to be involved in decision making. However, when carers are experiencing feelings of sadness or having low mood, it inhibited their involvement in the shared-decision-making process (Hayes et al., 2020).

Despite these common factors, some researchers suggest that emotions can impact carers' preference to be involved in shared decision making (Légaré et al., 2013) and threaten carers' assumed role in the decision-making process (Jackson et al., 2008). Carers in young people's mental health settings also report lower involvement in care and treatment decisions compared to families of young people with a physical health condition (Butler et al., 2014).

Carers of young people with mental health problems have been described as experiencing an *emotional roller coaster* between hope and hopelessness or emotional stress and strain (Corcoran et al., 2017; Corcoran et al., 2015; Laugesen & Groenkjaer, 2015; Lipstein et al., 2012). More specifically, researchers have identified denial, scepticism, trust and stigma as factors influencing carers' involvement in treatment decisions (Ahmed et al., 2013; Taylor et al., 2006). On reviewing the qualitative evidence, seven themes that best-described carers' experience of having a child with mental health problems that may influence their capacity to engage with services are:

- anxiety and frustration.
- isolation and powerlessness.
- blame, guilt and shame.
- exhausted and overwhelmed.
- distress and sadness.
- empowerment and respect.
- relief and hope.

Based on these emotional states, carers are sometimes less likely to seek help or engage with the shared decision process when experiencing emotions like blame, guilt and shame (Auert et al., 2012; Baker-Ericzén et al., 2013; Barnett et al., 2016; Boden et al., 2016; Bradby et al., 2007; Brinkman et al., 2009; Bull & Whelan, 2006; Chavira et al., 2017; Coletti et al., 2012; Harden, 2005a, 2005b; Hovish et al., 2012; Levy et al., 2016; Mychailyszyn et al., 2008). These low feelings can also impact a carer's ability to keep appointments, to disclose diagnoses or the use of alternative treatments or to adhere to medications and other therapeutic interventions (An, 2017; Attride-Stirling et al., 2004; Arcia et al., 2004; Charach et al., 2006; Jackson & Peters, 2008; Peters & Jackson, 2009; Shyu et al., 2010; Matthews et al., 2011; Bussing et al., 2012; Bone et al., 2015; Gray & Donnelly, 2015; Lundkvist-Houndoumadi et al., 2016; Eaton et al., 2017; Lindly et al., 2017; Pishva, 2017).

However, when carers are able to reappraise the situation (Hodgetts et al., 2013; Nicholas et al., 2016), thus experiencing more positive feelings like empowerment and respect, they are more involved in their child's mental health care and treatment. Similarly once carers stopped viewing service providers as discriminatory or 'medication focused', they began to trust the healthcare professionals and become more available to collaborate in their child's care (Davis et al., 2012). Some carers suggest that the attitude of service providers sometimes creates a feeling of family competence, which can motivate families to participate in early interventions (Coogle & Hanline, 2016). This level of involvement can be key to making carers feel more confident in implementing strategies on their own (Edwards et al., 2018). Additionally, having confidence in the health professionals can allow parents to relinquish some of the responsibility of care as an advocate and be more involved in care as equals thereby forming a partnership. This usually fosters increased willingness from families to cooperate and collaborate with services (Andershed et al., 2017; Coates, 2016).

On a practical level, some families may need additional information to support their involvement in the decision-making process (Davis & Kollins, 2012; Grant et al., 2016). However, once contact with the service provider is established, carers describe feeling more informed, listened to and respected (Andershed et al., 2017). This level of support alongside support from practitioners and other carers of children in similar situations also encourages parents to engage and collaborate more with services (Ahmed et al., 2017; Gerdes et al., 2014). Similarly, once carers notice improvements in their child after the recommended treatment, they are more likely to continue to engage with services. With this acceptance, carers begin to be more hopeful and as a result are more likely to get involved in care and treatment (Markoulakis et al., 2012).

9.4 Clinical Examples

Consider the clinical examples shown in Boxes 9.1, 9.2 and 9.3 that present scenarios of children and young people and their families/caregivers. The clinical examples amplify aspects that could and should be considered when involving children and young people and families/caregivers in care and treatment decisions. Within the clinical examples consideration of the child or young person's age and capacity would be required. It is recommended where possible children and young people should be informed and/or involved as active participants in the shared-decision-making process. It is therefore the responsibility of service providers to provide child-friendly materials and information to help CYP understand choices and decision making in relation to all aspects of their care including the potential outcomes of the treatment decision being made. As for capacity, it is recommended that the CYP's capacity to be actively involved in shared decision making, and similarly that of the carers, is not assumed based on their diagnosis or symptoms. Similarly, capacity to be involved should not be based on language barriers, having learning disabilities or cultural differences. Regular reviews of capacity and desire for active involvement should take place, particularly if there is potential that being involved is causing additional distress to the child/young person and/or their families/caregivers. To summarise, assessment of capacity should be ongoing and iterative with explicit invitations to be involved.

Box 9.1 Clinical example: Morgan

Morgan is a 17-year-old female who currently lives with her mother and stepfather. She has contact with her birth father regularly and has a younger brother and older sister who live with their father. Morgan has been involved with CAMHS since she was 16 years old following episodes of self-harm, suicide attempts, anxiety and depressed mood. This followed a disclosure to a school teacher of historical childhood abuse.

Morgan had been assessed by CAMHS and was offered systemic family psychotherapy and individual CBT sessions within CAMHS. Morgan refused family therapy but did engage in some sessions of CBT before her attendance became sporadic following a change of CBT therapist.

After 6 months in CAMHS Morgan began experiencing what appeared to be auditory hallucinations and as a result was referred to the ARMS (At Risk Mental State) pathway of the early intervention psychosis (EIP) service locally for assessment. The EIP service is a cross-over service working with people from the age of 14 years upwards.

Morgan was offered a screening assessment by the EIP service however a diagnosis of psychosis was inconclusive. Morgan and her family had then been offered an extended assessment, a consultant psychiatrist assessment and a psychological needs assessment. Following assessment, Morgan and her family were offered home-based systemic family therapy and clinical psychology, the focus being an integrated approach to trauma-focused family intervention.

Throughout contact with EIP Morgan remained under the primary care of CAMHS, her allocated care coordinator managed the communication between Morgan, her family and EIP services. She was under the care of the CAMHS consultant psychiatrist who liaised regularly with the consultant psychiatrist in EIP.

Morgan was having monthly contact with her care coordinator in CAMHS and seeing the consultant psychiatrist on a bi-monthly basis for review until her transition to adult services aged 18.

This example amplifies the many services, assessments and interventions that young people experiencing trauma and their families/caregivers face. The importance of understanding factors that influence involvement and collaboration are carefully considered. In doing so they can reduce the emotional and practical burden on those accessing services and increase the likelihood of more successful partnership working to ensure successful intervention outcome.

In Morgan's case trust was a key factor in her engaging with services and more so with interventions. Taking time to actively engage and collaborate with Morgan aimed to reduce issues of trust and amplify feelings of empowerment, respect and partnership. For Morgan's family their feelings of anxiety, frustration, hopelessness and guilt had been overwhelming. This often got in the way of them being able to meaningfully engage with services and particularly family interventions (Royal College of Psychiatrists, 2022). It was important to ensure that the transitions process for the family and Morgan was well communicated and that additional services such as EIP offered a consistent approach to intervention. Communication with Morgan and her family

(Continued)

Box 9.1 (Continued)

about the integrative approach to family interventions was essential, helping them to see the potential challenges and benefits of working together on the early childhood trauma Morgan experienced and its impact on them all over time. Family intervention was implemented for 9 months and was successful in terms of outcome, engagement and collaboration. This process was then mirrored in the move from child to adult services, meaning Morgan and her family had a much more consistent, seamless transition between and through services. They described feeling valued, involved and hopeful about the transition process on evaluation of intervention.

Box 9.2 Clinical example: Jacob

Jacob is a 10-year-old male who currently lives with his mother, father and older brother (aged 13). Jacob has been referred to CAMHS via his GP following several visits alongside his mother. She is concerned that Jacob is becoming increasing anxious and agitated about attending school and is refusing attendance currently. He is frequently experiencing outbursts of anger and has threatened and hit both parents and his brother on numerous occasions. His mother believes this is escalating. She has also noted low mood and expression of suicidal thoughts from Jacob several times over the past few weeks.

CAMHS have offered an assessment appointment and following this assessment and information from Jacob's parents have also referred Jacob to the Autistic Spectrum Disorder Services (ASD) team for further assessment. The CAMHS team have offered Jacob a psychological assessment with the clinical psychologist to identify his needs and potential interventions within these services. Jacob is currently care coordinated by a CAMHS nurse practitioner with whom he has engaged well.

This example focuses on the need to work across boundaries. Jacob is engaging currently with his primary school, primary care services, CAMHS and is referred into specialist services for assessment of ASD.

A number of authors have noted the impact of ASD on individual and family quality of life (Fong et al., 2020; Ono et al., 2019; Posserud et al., 2018). This is something that both CAMHS and ASD services would need to be focused on. Whole-family approaches to engagement, collaboration and decision making in service involvement and intervention is essential for Jacob and his family. Involving other stakeholders such as the school would also play a key role in ensuring a consistent approach to collaboration through effective and responsive communication between key services. 'At least 1 in 10 children with ASD will be referred to CAMHS for intervention' (Roughan et al., 2019, p. 2). With resources limited this also requires flexibility and collaboration between services and alongside Jacob and his family.

Jacob has engaged well with his care coordinator, she has been able to assess his capacity in relation to decision making, Jacob is able to take on information about the challenges and benefits of his plan of care and subsequent interventions. His care coordinator identifies his preferences, values and goals noting he would like to work on a one-to-one basis with the psychologist and would also like to work with his parents. Jacob is reluctant to do any interventions with his older brother and this is something that his parents and the care coordinator are exploring further with Jacob to identify the pros and cons of including or excluding his brother in family-focused sessions. This is a positive example of a shared-decision-making process that is enabling family-focused engagement to address parental issues such as anxiety, distress and feelings of being overwhelmed alongside acknowledging and addressing the needs of Jacob as an individual.

Creative and flexible approaches with Jacob may enhance his experience of individual work focused on his distress, aggression and school refusal. In the current absence of a diagnosis of ASD the CAMHS team should consider collaboration with Jacob's school and the ASD team to identify ways in which interventions may be tailored to support Jacobs mental health difficulties whilst awaiting ASD assessment outcomes.

Working with parents in terms of psychoeducation should be included once diagnosis is reached. Family-focused interventions within CAMHS will offer parents the support they need whilst awaiting ASD assessment outcomes and provide opportunities for Jacob and his parents to work together in developing strategies to manage his experiences safely.

Box 9.3 Clinical example: Tomasz

Tomasz a 14-year-old male who currently lives with his mother father and two younger sisters aged 11 and 9. He and his family are Polish, his father has some understanding of the English language and his mother does not speak English but can understand a little; interpreters would be required for any interventions or assessments that Tomasz and his parents or siblings require. Tomasz's father moved to the UK when Tomasz was 5 years old to find work, his mother and sister followed and the youngest child was then born in in the UK. Tomasz's father presented with Tomasz via the GP as he had concerns about Tomasz related to his anxiety, low mood, isolation and significant loss of weight over the past 8 months. He suggested that his anxiety started when his father left for the UK and he had remained anxious since this time. He noted Tomasz has a great many rituals around cleaning his room and worries about checking the house for danger. His restriction of food started when he was being bullied at high school for being overweight and this has escalated recently when he noticed he was frequently purging and insistent on walking everywhere to 'keep fit'. The GP ordered a range of physical health screens for Tomasz and a referral to CAMHS for assessment. Following CAMHS assessment Tomasz was referred to the eating disorder pathway (EDP) where assessment will commence.

Tomasz has been translating for his parents with health practitioners, his father is concerned that Tomasz is sometimes missing information out particularly when it relates to food and weight loss, as such he has requested an outside interpreter to attend sessions remotely. Both parents are experiencing high levels of distress, they

(Continued)

Box 9.3 (Continued)

talk with EDP team about how long they have had to wait for assessment and feeling that nothing has really changed, if anything they fear Tomasz is getting progressively worse. The suggest if they challenge him in any way he will isolate himself and increase physical activity or purging. They are experiencing high levels of distress and hopelessness. They find the assessment session frustrating due to language barriers and often resort to Google translate. Tomasz himself is fatigued when having to translate and as such is refusing to speak in sessions. Working on collaboration and engagement with Tomasz and his parents has become a focus for the EDP. They have also acknowledged the need to adapt the process of assessment when including translators, often taking on average longer than sessions without interpreters. Language barriers increase difficulties for CYP and their families in relation to accessing services, engagement and collaboration and interventions (van der Boor & White 2020). Ensuring the family have access to interpreters as needed will increase the likelihood of greater collaboration and engagement with services. Utilising an interpreter from the same language and culture to further enhance understanding of specific cultural and social expectation should also be explored. This can enable the EDS team to determine choices and preferences of Tomasz and his parents in terms of decision-making processes, assessment, formulation and treatment planning. This aims to positively enhance the experience of Tomasz and his family as being 'alongside services', whilst also offering services a greater understanding of their individual and collective needs.

9.5 An Affective-appraisal Approach for Involvement in Young People's Mental Health Settings

To further understand how to work with families, interviews and focus groups with carers and healthcare professionals reveal that it is important to acknowledge that carers are 'expected to, but not always able to' engage in shared decision making (Liverpool et al., 2021). Carers and practitioners express that emotions generally influence carers' involvement in care and treatment decisions and in some instances, they describe the reverse may also occur where the involvement also affects carers' emotional state. It was also clear that both negative and positive emotions influenced involvement. More expectedly, negative emotional states resulted in parents not being actively involved in shared decision making and positive emotions encouraged involvement. Carers and practitioners also highlight that in some instances, the negative emotions appear to complicate the shared-decision-making process as it could make it difficult to participate even if they wanted to. However, practitioners also express that negative emotions could make some carers more 'forceful' suggesting a form of over-involvement. Similarly, some positive emotions, like when carers are comfortable or fully trusting of the practitioners, they may decide to be less involved with shared decision making thereby leaving all the decisions to the practitioners.

The affective-appraisal approach to shared decision making recognises that affect and appraisal interact in shaping the shared decision making process, influencing each other in a circular way where the decision may elicit the emotional reaction, that in turn influences the shared decision making process, that again may influence a change in the emotional reaction. It is therefore suggested that adequately supporting carers and young people can activate them to engage in high-quality shared decision making. In this way, emotional support would allow the identification of carers' values and needs associated with shared decision making, thus enriching the shared decision making experience.

9.6 Involving Young People and Carers in Service Development, Service Improvement, Co-production and Research

Adopting a co-design process based on service users and service providers experiences (referred to as experience-based co-design) can be a useful approach for service improvement (Green et al., 2020). In these types of designs, experiences can be gathered from staff, young people and carers via observation and interviews. The critical experiences in relation to the service can then be identified and fed back to participants using innovative strategies like puppet storytelling. This iterative process could allow for young people, carers and staff to then prioritise the areas of service improvement. Once completed a summary of the findings can be presented using creative tools (e.g. drawings, posters, animations) and shared with a wider group of staff and service users. Discussions based on the findings can then allow staff and families, especially young people, to identify and implement activities to improve the service. In this way there is room to explore the unique experiences of various services throughout the service improvement process.

Although experience-based co-design could face particular challenges in young people's mental health settings, the components can be adapted (Boden et al., 2018). For example, see the activities outlined in Box 9.4 and those described in previous chapters. This is especially recommended owing to the nature and context of individual experiences. For example, if personal experiences from young people and their families were collected and shared with other service users this could trigger some incidences of re-traumatising. This is common when working with adverse childhood events where discussion around childhood abuse can arouse anger and pain in CYP who experienced similar traumas. Further to this, issues of confidentiality and anonymity may need to be considered. Despite the potential success of experience-based co-design, time and cost can be major barriers to carrying out this approach to involving carers and young people in service improvement (Locock et al., 2020). Therefore, it can be sometimes beneficial to capture experiences from existing literature and service-user profiles and practitioner notes to support this process.

It is a well-established notion that the involvement of service users in the research process is important to ensure that research is carried out 'with' and not 'about' service users. As a result, patient and public involvement activities are also advocated for across all types of health research (Bagley et al., 2016). Yet, some voices are sometimes missed or under-represented. There is some evidence to suggest that patient and public involvement improves the quality of research (Blackburn et al., 2018). However, researchers agree there are also some challenges such as low levels of engagement and input, when involving the public in research (Staniszewska et al., 2011). Therefore, more efforts are needed to ensure equality, diversity and inclusivity are considered when co-designing service-improvement initiatives (see Box 9.4). Nonetheless, obtaining input from end-users of a service is useful for informing further development and implementation of interventions that can be valuable (Bagley et al., 2016). Based on the Salzburg statement (Salzburg Global Seminar, 2011), the following recommendations have been proposed for service improvement and intervention development around shared decision making. Notably these can be modified to improve different aspects of services.

- Ensure carers and young people are invited to be part of the care and treatment decision making process while considering the following:
  - age and capacity of the young person,
  - how much the young person wishes to have the carer 'involved' or 'informed', and
  - how much or what support the family needs in order to be involved.
- Review practitioners' time schedules so they can provide sufficient time and encourage carers and young people to ask questions and raise concerns during and within sessions.
- Highlight the need for emotional support to be provided to carers especially at the initial stages of accessing services or at crucial decision making time points.
- Propose a need for a key person at the service that can provide answers to more general questions or be a liaison between practitioners and families especially during periods when there is a changeover of service providers.
- Consider the inclusion of the primary carer or key person (i.e. an advocate for the family who is not the primary service provider) at multidisciplinary meetings when care and treatment options are being considered.
- Review the role of carer support groups and explore the potential for further responsibilities.
- Highlight the need for shared decision making support interventions as an adjunct to routine care.
- Suggest that when shared decision making interventions are being developed to be used in young people's mental health settings that the following are considered:
  - patient and public involvement is at the core of design, development, testing and implementation;
  - equal voices are given to service users and services providers; and
  - interventions are accessible, acceptable, suitable and appropriate for the population, easy-to-use, useful and do not incur additional time burden to the service providers and the service users.

Box 9.4 Clinical example: Including service users in the development of interventions to improve services

This example describes a real-world example of the process used to co-design and develop an evidence-based intervention called 'Power Up for Parents'. 'Power Up for Parents' is a novel digital web application to promote shared decision making in young people's mental health settings. The app is expected to be downloaded onto the carers mobile device and during key decision-making periods carers will document preferences and answers to questions and concerns that could help inform value-based judgements. For example, when thinking of medications for depression, carers usually have concerns that could go beyond side effects. By using the app carers could maintain an audit trail that they can then share with their child and the practitioner. The app also offer brief stress-relief interventions like deep breathing exercises to help carers during stressful periods. This example illustrates the multiple layers of collaboration and engagement required to support co-production with young people and their families to enhance the quality of services. First, empirical studies were conducted by professionals to justify the need for the development of a new intervention to improve the experiences of shared decision making in young people's mental health settings. The two key studies associated with the foundation work included a scoping review of already existing interventions to identify gaps and suitability of the currently available interventions and a qualitative study to explore needs among practitioners, CYP and their families. Together the studies revealed that none of the existing interventions supported the shared-decision process in line with all the essential elements required for shared decision making in child mental health settings. In addition, none of the available interventions offered emotional support for carers during key decision making periods. The following steps were then taken to involve relevant stakeholders in the development of 'Power Up for Parents':

Steering Committee
From conception, a steering committee was formed consisting of three primary carers with experience of having a child with a mental health problem. The carers were appointed as part of the steering committee after expressing interest based on various discussions and presentations of the research evidence. The committee was ideal for consensus forming and was mainly responsible for ensuring that the development process was transparent and unbiased. At this stage it was important to consider the diversity among the group so guidance could be offered on any cultural adaptations that became necessary. For example, when considering images to include on the app, the committee were able to point out that the images utilised only captured heterosexual nuclear families. This was an important contribution that led to significant changes in how we considered images for the app.

Service user involvement activities with carers
Carers as secondary service users were also invited to attend consultation meetings to share views and opinions on whether the proposed intervention and changes were fit for purpose. For example, the team wanted to know if the use of phones and other digital devices would be a useful tool to incorporate for new interventions. Therefore, the consultations were useful to obtain lived-experience expert advice on the research and the intervention design. This helped the team gain insight into how primary carers may use digital health interventions. As an initial step, an email consultation was conducted with the Family Research Advisory Group at the National Children's Bureau. This was a useful step as the advisory group already had set meetings and they could share ideas and discussions among themselves before responding to the

(Continued)

Box 9.4 (Continued)

email. The response rate (~nine carers) was fairly good since the coordinator of the advisory group sent frequent reminders to the group. Information about the aims of the intervention with specific questions to generate ideas was shared with the primary carers. Based on the responses, early stages of the development process began and developers were able to start sketching what the intervention could look like. An example of how the intervention might be used was then presented to the group at a scheduled meeting. The pros and cons of digital versus other formats of decision-making tools were discussed along with general thoughts and concerns on the intervention design. The consultations revealed that if a digital intervention is to be useful it should be simple and easy to use, as carers generally did not see themselves as experts in technology. The advisory group provided several suggestions to use as a guide based on apps they frequently used. For example, they recommended mirroring or taking inspiration for formatting from popular online shopping or fitness apps. Based on these discussions, the prototype was then refined and updated before the final meeting. At the final meeting, a presentation of the prototype followed by a group discussion was held, to examine the penultimate version of the intervention. There were further discussions on how carers could use and benefit from the intervention in practice. All attendees were encouraged to share their honest opinions and views as they were seen as critical friends to the project. Activities were also used to further encourage engagement. For example, carers were asked to think about worse and best case scenarios if offered the intervention by a trusted practitioner. Further refinement of the prototype was then carried out based on feedback received. One important upgrade after the sessions was to add a diary or note-taking feature as carers felt they needed to quickly capture details when their child was in distress so they could remember it at the next appointment with the practitioner.

Showcase event with practitioners and researchers
At a planned showcase event, the prototype was presented to practitioners, researchers and intervention developers who were asked to provide feedback and specifically provide input to improve the interactivity of the intervention. The purpose of attending this event was two-fold: 1) to obtain interest from the practitioners and researchers as they would be asked to endorse/promote the use of the intervention; and 2) to provide practitioners with a basic understanding of the purpose and functionality so they would be able to guide carers through the app as well. Three round-table discussions followed, and input was obtained from a total of 12 experts in the area of young people's mental health. Attendees at the event had a specific interest in digital interventions to prevent, treat and promote young people's mental health. This event was part of larger conference and therefore did not require additional effort from the app development team. Notably, it was important to consider including a range of practitioners with varying years of experiences and different types of expertise.

Public engagement

A survey to elicit the public's opinion on the preferred mode of delivery for a shared decision making resource was conducted using social media platforms like Facebook, Twitter and Instagram. These platforms were selected as they were the most commonly used media at the time of the study. This approach was also a useful suggestion from the steering committee. They highlighted the importance of hearing the voices of a wider, more diverse group of people who are or may become service users or service providers. Responses from practitioners, carers and young people were in favour of a web resource. Consequently, three carers and four young people from the Anna Freud National Centre for Children and Families attended two workshops and provided email feedback on two versions of the webpage before agreeing on the final version. The purpose of the workshops and emails was to encourage ongoing discussion about the different features and the usability of the intervention itself. At the first workshop carers and young people explored what shared decision making meant and a consensus was reached for a family friendly definition that could be displayed on the homepage of the app. At the second workshop participants were involved in designing paper prototypes of the webpage. During the workshops CYP and carers enjoyed drawing and using colours to help design sketches of what the intervention could look like. Consequently, the images were professionally designed, and the content updated based on feedback received from the two rounds of email input. The output from this work informed the welcome screen when accessing the 'Power Up for Parents' intervention. One important contribution from the public engagement activity was to reconsider the name of the intervention. Some attendees at the workshops highlighted that not everyone may identify with the label 'parent' as non-biological carers sometimes feel excluded. Based on this the name of the intervention was design to be editable. So anyone using the intervention can change the word 'parent' to a word more appropriate to them. For example, one carer edited the name to reflect 'Power Up for Tom' as Tom was the name of her grandson and she was his primary carer.

Summary

The activities and steps taken to co-design and develop 'Power Up for Parents' are not meant to be prescriptive but can be used as a guide to inform the development of other interventions to be used in CYP mental health settings. The different strands of engagement described in this example were deemed appropriate for developing a complex intervention like 'Power Up for Parents' but variations of this approach may be used for other interventions and in other settings. Since low engagement is possible among this population, we recommend using multiple approaches/activities (e.g. social media, emails and face-to-face (or virtual)) to ensure the voices of key stakeholders and end-users are captured. By adopting this approach, it is anticipated that there will be a better chance of uptake and/or acceptability of the new intervention. This can then be tested in pilot and feasibility studies before proceeding to larger studies and implementation plans.

References

Adams, R. C., & Levy, S. E. (2017). Shared decision-making and children with disabilities: Pathways to consensus. *Pediatrics, 139* (6), 1–11. https://doi.org/10.1542/peds.2017-0956

Ahmed, R., Borst, J., Wei, Y. C., & Aslani, P. (2017). Parents' perspectives about factors influencing adherence to pharmacotherapy for ADHD. *Journal of Attention Disorders, 21*(2), 91–99. https://doi.org/10.1177/1087054713499231

Ahmed, R., McCaffery, K. J., & Aslani, P. (2013). Factors influencing parental decision making about stimulant treatment for attention-deficit/hyperactivity disorder. *Journal of Child & Adolescent Psychopharmacology, 23*(3), 163–178.

Allan, L. Q. C. (2004). The Children Act 1989. In J. Payne-James, I. Wall, & P. Dean (Eds.), *Medicolegal Essentials in Healthcare* (2nd ed., pp. 159–166). https://doi.org/10.1017/CBO9780511545559.018

An, S. L. (2017, March). Parent training occupational therapy program for parents of children with Autism in Korea. *Occupational Therapy International, 4741634.*

Andershed, B., Ewertzon, M., & Johansson, A. (2017). An isolated involvement in mental health care – experiences of parents of young adults. *Journal of Clinical Nursing, 26*(7–8), 1053–1065. https://doi.org/10.1111/jocn.13560

Arcia, E., Fernandez, M. C., & Jaquez, M. (2004). Latina mothers' stances on stimulant medication: Complexity, conflict, and compromise. *Journal of Developmental and Behavioral Pediatrics, 25*(5), 311–317. https://doi.org/10.1097/00004703-200410000-00002

Attride-Stirling, J., Davis, H., Farrell, L., Groark, C., & Day, C. (2004). Factors influencing parental engagement in a community child and adolescent mental health service: A qualitative comparison of completers and non-completers. *Clinical Child Psychology and Psychiatry, 9*(3), 347–361. https://doi.org/10.1177/1359104504043918

Auert, E. J., Trembath, D., Arciuli, J., & Thomas, D. (2012). Parents' expectations, awareness, and experiences of accessing evidence-based speech-language pathology services for their children with autism. *International Journal of Speech-Language Pathology, 14*(2), 109–118.

Bagley, H. J., Short, H., Harman, N. L., Hickey, H. R., Gamble, C. L., Woolfall, K., Young, B., & Williamson, P. R. (2016). A patient and public involvement (PPI) toolkit for meaningful and flexible involvement in clinical trials – a work in progress. *Research Involvement and Engagement, 2*(15). https://doi.org/10.1186/s40900-016-0029-8

Baker-Ericzén, M. J., Jenkins, M. M., & Haine-Schlagel, R. (2013). Therapist, parent, and youth perspectives of treatment barriers to family-focused community outpatient mental health services. *Journal of Child and Family Studies, 22*(6), 854–868. https://doi.org/10.1007/s10826-012-9644-7

Barnett, E. R., Boucher, E. A., Neubacher, K., & Carpenter-Song, E. A. (2016). Decision-making around psychotropic medications for children in foster care: Perspectives from foster parents. *Children and Youth Services Review, 70*, 206–213. https://doi.org/10.1016/j.childyouth.2016.09.012

Bee, P., Price, O., Baker, J., & Lovell, K. (2015). Systematic synthesis of barriers and facilitators to service user-led care planning. *British Journal of Psychiatry, 207*(2), 104–114. https://doi.org/10.1192/bjp.bp.114.152447

Benson, R., & Pinnaro, C. (2015). Autonomy and autism: Who speaks for the adolescent patient? *AMA Journal of Ethics, 17*(4), 305–309.

Berger, Z. D., Brito, J. P., Ospina, N. S., Kannan, S., Hinson, J. S., Hess, E. P., Haskell, H., Montori, V. M., & Newman-Toker, D. E. (2017). Patient-centred diagnosis: Sharing diagnostic decisions with patients in clinical practice. *BMJ Clinical Research, 359*, j4218. https://doi.org/10.1136/bmj.j4218

Blackburn, S., McLachlan, S., Jowett, S., Kinghorn, P., Gill, P., Higginbottom, A., Rhodes, C., Stevenson, F., & Jinks, C. (2018, May). The extent, quality and impact of patient and public involvement in primary care research: A mixed methods study. *Research Involvement and Engagement.* https://doi.org/10.1186/s40900-018-0100-8

Boden, Z. V. R., Larkin, M., Hickman, G., Newton, E., Fenton, K., & Thompson, J. (2016). The experiential impact of hospitalisation: Parents' accounts of caring for young people with early psychosis. *Clinical Child Psychology & Psychiatry, 21*(1), 145–155. https://doi.org/10.1177/1359104515581716

Boden, Z., Larkin, M., & Springham, N. (2018). Using experience-based co-design to improve inpatient mental health spaces. In P. Reavey & L. McGrath (Eds.), *The Handbook of Mental Health and Space: Community and Clinical Applications*. (pp. 1–14). Routledge.

Boland, L., Graham, I. D., Légaré, F., Lewis, K., Jull, J., Shephard, A., Lawson, M. L., Davis, A., Yameogo, A., & Stacey, D. (2019, January). Barriers and facilitators of pediatric shared decision-making: A systematic review. *Implementation Science, 14*(7). https://doi.org/10.1186/s13012-018-0851-5

Boland, L., Kryworuchko, J., Saarimaki, A., & Lawson, M. L. (2017). Parental decision making involvement and decisional conflict: A descriptive study. *BMC Pediatrics, 17*(1), 146. https://doi.org/10.1186/s12887-017-0899-4

Bone, C., O'Reilly, M., Karim, K., & Vostanis, P. (2015). 'They're not witches. ...' Young children and their parents' perceptions and experiences of Child and Adolescent Mental Health Services. *Child: Care, Health & Development, 41*(3), 450–458. https://doi.org/10.1111/cch.12161

Bradby, H., Varyani, M., Oglethorpe, R., Raine, W., White, I., & Helen, M. (2007). British Asian families and the use of child and adolescent mental health services: A qualitative study of a hard to reach group. *Social Science and Medicine, 65*(12), 2413–2424.

Bradley, J., Murphy, S., Fugard, A. J. B., Nolas, S., & Law, D. (2013). What kind of goals do children and young people set for themselves in therapy? Developing a goals framework using CORC data. *Child & Family Clinical Psychology Review, 1*(1), 8–18.

Brinkman, W. B., Sherman, S. N., Zmitrovich, A. R., Visscher, M. O., Crosby, L. E., Phelan, K. J., & Donovan, E. F. (2009). Parental angst making and revisiting decisions about treatment of attention-deficit/hyperactivity disorder. *Pediatrics, 124*(2), 580–589.

Bull, C., & Whelan, T. (2006). Parental schemata in the management of children with attention deficit-hyperactivity disorder. *Qualitative Health Research, 16*(5), 664–678.

Bussing, Regina, Zima, B. T., Mason, D. M., Porter, P. C., & Garvan, C. W. (2012). Receiving treatment for attention-deficit hyperactivity disorder: Do the perspectives of adolescents matter? *Journal of Adolescent Health, 49* (1), 7–14. https://doi.org/10.1016/j.jadohealth.2010.08.014

Butler, A. M., Elkins, S., Kowalkowski, M., & Raphael, J. L. (2014). Shared decision making among parents of children with mental health conditions compared to children with chronic physical conditions. *Maternal and Child Health Journal, 19*(2), 410–418. https://doi.org/10.1007/s10995-014-1523-y

Care Quality Commission (2018). *Are we listening? Review of children and young people's mental health services*. Care Quality Commission. https://www.cqc.org.uk/sites/default/files/20180308b_arewelistening_report.pdf

Charach, A, Skyba, A., Cook, L., & Antle, B. J. (2006). Using stimulant medication for children with ADHD: What do parents say? A brief report. *Journal of the Canadian Academy of Child and Adolescent Psychiatry, 15*(2), 75–83.

Charles, C., Gafni, A., & Whelan, T. (1997). Shared decision-making in the medical encounter: What does it mean? (or it takes at least two to tango). *Social Science & Medicine, 44*(5), 681–692. https://doi.org/10.1016/S0277-9536(96)00221-3

Charles, C., Gafni, A., & Whelan, T. (1999). Decision-making in the physician–patient encounter: Revisiting the shared treatment decision-making model. *Social Science and Medicine, 49*(5), 651–661. https://doi.org/10.1016/S0277-9536(99)00145-8

Chavira, D. A., Bantados, B., Rapp, A., Firpo-Perretti, Y. M., Escovar, E., Dixon, L., Drahota, A., & Palinkas, L. A. (2017). Parent-reported stigma and child anxiety: A mixed methods research study. *Children and Youth Services Review, 76*, 237–242. https://doi.org/https://doi.org/10.1016/j.childyouth.2017.03.013

Coates, D. (2016). Client and parent feedback on a Youth Mental Health Service: The importance of family inclusive practice and working with client preferences. *International Journal of Mental Health Nursing, 25*(6), 526–535. https://doi.org/10.1111/inm.12240

Coletti, D J, Pappadopulos, E., Katsiotas, N. J., Berest, A., Jensen, P. S., & Kafantaris, V. (2012). Parent perspectives on the decision to initiate medication treatment of attention-deficit/hyperactivity disorder. *Journal of Child and Adolescent Psychopharmacology, 22*(3), 226–237. https://doi.org/10.1089/cap.2011.0090

Coogle, C. G., & Hanline, M. F. (2016). An exploratory study of family-centred help-giving practices in early intervention: Families of young children with autism spectrum disorder. *Child & Family Social Work, 21*(2), 249–260.

Corcoran, J., Berry, A., & Hill, S. (2015). The lived experience of US parents of children with autism spectrum disorders: A systematic review and meta-synthesis. *Journal of Intellectual Disabilities, 19*(4), 356–366. https://doi.org/10.1177/1744629515577876

Corcoran, J., Schildt, B., Hochbrueckner, R., & Abell, J. (2017). Parents of children with attention deficit/ hyperactivity disorder: A meta-synthesis, Part I. *Child and Adolescent Social Work Journal, 34*(4), 281–335. https://doi.org/10.1007/s10560-016-0465-1

Covvey, J. R., Kamal, K. M., Gorse, E. E., Mehta, Z., Dhumal, T., Heidari, E., Rao, D., & Zacker, C. (2019). Barriers and facilitators to shared decision-making in oncology: a systematic review of the literature. *Supportive Care in Cancer, 27*(5), 1613–1637. https://doi.org/10.1007/s00520-019-04675-7

Davis, C. C., Claudius, M., Palinkas, L. A., Wong, J. B., & Leslie, L. K. (2012). Putting families in the center: family perspectives on decision making and ADHD and implications for ADHD care. *Journal of Attention Disorders, 16*(8), 675–684.

Davis, N. O., & Kollins, S. H. (2012). Treatment for co-occurring attention deficit/hyperactivity disorder and autism spectrum disorder. *Neurotherapeutics, 9*(3), 518–530. https://doi.org/10.1007/s13311-012-0126-9

Eaton, K., Ohan, J. L., Stritzke, W. G. K., Courtauld, H. M., & Corrigan, P. W. (2017). Mothers' decisions to disclose or conceal their child's mental health disorder. *Qualitative Health Research, 27*(11), 1628–1639. https://doi.org/10.1177/1049732317697096

Edbrooke-Childs, J., Jacob, J., Argent, R., Patalay, P., Deighton, J., & Wolpert, M. (2015). The relationship between child- and parent-reported shared decision making and child-, parent-, and clinician-reported treatment outcome in routinely collected child mental health services data. *Clinical Child Psychology and Psychiatry, 21*(2), 324–338. https://doi.org/10.1177/1359104515591226

Edwards, A. G., Brebner, C. M., McCormack, P. F., & MacDougall, C. J. (2018). From 'parent' to 'expert': How parents of children with autism spectrum disorder make decisions about which intervention approaches to access. *Journal of Autism and Developmental Disorders, 48*(6), 2122–2138. https://doi.org/10.1007/s10803-018-3473-5

Fong, V. C., Gardiner, E., & Iarocci, G. (2020) Can a combination of mental health services and ADL therapies improve quality of life in families of children with autism spectrum disorder? *Quality of Life Research, 29*, 2161–2170. https://doi.org/10.1007/s11136-020-02440-6

Garvelink, M. M., Boland, L., Klein, K., Nguyen, D. V., Menear, M., Bekker, H. L., Eden, K. B., LeBlanc, A., O'Connor, A. M., Stacey, D., & Légaré, F. (2019). Decisional Conflict Scale use over 20 years: The anniversary review. *Medical Decision Making, 39*(4), 301–314. https://doi.org/10.1177/0272989X19851345

Gerdes, A. C., Lawton, K. E., Haack, L. M., & Schneider, B. W. (2014). Latino parental help seeking for childhood ADHD. *Administration and Policy in Mental Health, 41*(4), 503–513.

Gondek, D, Edbrooke-Childs, J., Velikonja, T., Chapman, L., Saunders, F., Hayes, D., & Wolpert, M. (2017). Facilitators and barriers to person-centred care in child and young people mental health services: A systematic review. *Clinical Psychology & Psychotherapy, 24*(4), 870–886. https://doi.org/10.1002/cpp.2052

Grant, N., Rodger, S., & Hoffmann, T. (2016). Intervention decision-making processes and information preferences of parents of children with autism spectrum disorders. *Child: Care, Health and Development, 42*(1), 125–134.

Gray, C., & Donnelly, J. (2015). 'Unheard voices: The views of traveller and non-traveller mothers and children with ASD': Erratum. *International Journal of Early Years Education, 23*(2), 226.

Green, T., Bonner, A., Teleni, L., Bradford, N., Purtell, L., Douglas, C., Yates, P., MacAndrew, M., Dao, H. Y., & Chan, R. J. (2020). Use and reporting of experience-based codesign studies in the healthcare setting: a systematic review. *BMJ Quality & Safety, 29*, 64–76.

Haine-Schlagel, R., & Walsh, N. E. (2015). A review of parent participation engagement in child and family mental health treatment. *Clinical Child and Family Psychology Review, 18*(2), 133–150. https://doi.org/10.1007/s10567-015-0182-x

Harden, J. (2005a). Parenting a young person with mental health problems: Temporal disruption and reconstruction. *Sociology of Health and Illness, 27*(3), 351–371.

Harden, J. (2005b). 'Uncharted waters': The experience of parents of young people with mental health problems. *Qualitative Health Research, 15*(2), 207–223.

Hayes, D., Edbrooke-Childs, J., Town, R., Wolpert, M., & Midgley, N. (2019). Barriers and facilitators to shared decision making in child and youth mental health: clinician perspectives using the Theoretical Domains Framework. *European Child and Adolescent Psychiatry, 25*(8), 655–666. https://doi.org/10.1007/s00787-018-1230-0

Hayes, D., Edbrooke-Childs, J., Town, R., Wolpert, M., & Midgley, N. (2020). Barriers and facilitators to shared decision-making in child and youth mental health: Exploring young person and parent perspectives using the Theoretical Domains Framework. *Counselling and Psychotherapy Research, 20*(1), 57–67. https://doi.org/10.1002/capr.12257

Hayes, D., Town, R., & Lemoniatis, E. (2018). *Developing and piloting i-THRIVE grids*. iThrive.

Hodgetts, S., Savage, A., & McConnell, D. (2013). Experience and outcomes of stepping stones triple P for families of children with autism. *Research in Developmental Disabilities, 34*(9), 2572–2585. https://doi.org/10.1016/j.ridd.2013.05.005

Hovish, K., Weaver, T., Islam, Z., Paul, M., & Singh, S. P. (2012). Transition experiences of mental health service users, parents, and professionals in the United Kingdom: A qualitative study. *Psychiatric Rehabilitation Journal, 35*(3), 251–257. https://doi.org/10.2975/35.3.2012.251.257

Jackson, D., & Peters, K. (2008). Use of drug therapy in children with attention deficit hyperactivity disorder (ADHD): maternal views and experiences. *Journal of Clinical Nursing, 17*(20), 2725–2732. https://doi.org/10.1111/j.1365-2702.2008.02444.x

Jensen, C. M., & Steinhausen, H. (2015). Comorbid mental disorders in children and adolescents with attention-deficit/hyperactivity disorder in a large nationwide study. *Attention Deficit and Hyperactivity Disorders, 7*(1), 27–38. https://doi.org/10.1007/s12402-014-0142-1

Kieling, C., Baker-Henningham, H., Belfer, M., Conti, G., Ertem, I., Omigbodun, O., Rhode, L. A., Srinath, S., Ulkuer, N., & Rahman, A. (2011). Child and adolescent mental health worldwide: Evidence for action. *The Lancet, 378*(9801), 1515–1525. https://doi.org/10.1016/S0140-6736(11)60827-1

Langer, D. A., & Jensen-Doss, A. (2018). Shared decision-making in youth mental health care: Using the evidence to plan treatments collaboratively. *Journal of Clinical Child and Adolescent Psychology, 47*(5), 821–831. https://doi.org/10.1080/15374416.2016.1247358

Laugesen, B., & Groenkjaer, M. (2015). Parenting experiences of living with a child with attention deficit hyperactivity disorder: a systematic review of qualitative evidence. *JBI Database of Systematic Reviews and Implementation Reports, 13*(11), 169–234. http://ovidsp.ovid.com/ovidweb.cgi?T=JS&CSC=Y&NEWS=N&PAGE=fulltext&D=emexb&AN=620287215

Law, D., & Jacob, J. (2015). *Goals and goal based outcomes (GBOs): Some useful information* (3rd ed.). *CAMHS Press*. https://www.corc.uk.net/media/1219/goalsandgbos-thirdedition.pdf

Légaré, F., Moumjid-Ferdjaoui, N., Drolet, R., Stacey, D., Härter, M., Bastian, H., Beaulieu, M. D., Borduas, F., Charles, C., Coulter, A., Desroches, S., Friedrich, G., Gafni, A., Graham, I. D., Labrecque, M., Leblanc, A., Légaré, J., Politi, M., Sargeant, J., & Thomson, R. (2013). Core competencies for shared decision making training programs: Insights from an international, interdisciplinary working group. *Journal of Continuing Education in the Health Professions, 33*(4), 267–273. https://doi.org/10.1002/chp.21197

Légaré, F., & Thompson-Leduc, P. (2014). Twelve myths about shared decision making. *Patient Education and Counseling, 96*(3), 281–286. https://doi.org/10.1016/j.pec.2014.06.014

Levy, S. E., Frasso, R., Colantonio, S., Reed, H., Stein, G., Barg, F. K., Mandell, D. S., & Fiks, A. G. (2016). Shared decision making and treatment decisions for young children with autism spectrum disorder. *Academic Pediatrics, 16*(6), 571–578.

Lindly, O., Thorburn, S., Heisler, K., Reyes, N., & Zuckerman, K. (2017). Parent disclosure of complementary health approaches used for children with autism spectrum disorder: Barriers and facilitators. *Complementary Therapies in Medicine, 35*, 47–52.

Lipstein, E. A., Brinkman, W. B., & Britto, M. T. (2012). What is known about parents' treatment decisions? A narrative review of pediatric decision making. *Medical Decision Making, 32*(2), 246–258. https://doi.org/10.1177/0272989X11421528

Liverpool, S., Hayes, D., & Edbrooke-Childs, J. (2021). An affective-appraisal approach for parental shared decision making in children and young people's mental health settings: A qualitative study. *Frontiers in Psychiatry, 12*, 626848. https://doi.org/10.3389/fpsyt.2021.626848

Locock, L., Graham, C., King, J., Parkin, S., Chisholm, A., Montgomery, C., Gibbons, E., Ainley, E., Bostock, J., Gager, M., Churchill, N., Dopson, S., Greenhalgh, T., Martin, A., Powell, J., Sizmur, S., & Ziebland, S. (2020). Understanding how front-line staff use patient experience data for service improvement: an exploratory case study evaluation. *NIHR Journals Library.*

Lundkvist-Houndoumadi, I., Thastum, M., & Nielsen, K. (2016). Parents' difficulties as co-therapists in CBT among non-responding youths with anxiety disorders: Parent and therapist experiences. *Clinical Child Psychology and Psychiatry, 21*(3), 477–490. https://doi.org/10.1177/1359104515615641

Makoul, G., & Clayman, M. L. (2006). An integrative model of shared decision making in medical encounters. *Patient Education and Counseling, 60*(3), 301–312. https://doi.org/10.1016/j.pec.2005.06.010

Markoulakis, R., Fletcher, P., & Bryden, P. (2012). Seeing the glass half full: benefits to the lived experiences of female primary caregivers of children with autism. *Clinical Nurse Specialist, 26*(1), 48–56. https://doi.org/10.1097/NUR.0b013e31823bfb0f

Matthews, R. A., Booth, S. M., Taylor, C. F., & Martin, T. (2011). A qualitative examination of the work-family interface: Parents of children with autism spectrum disorder. *Journal of Vocational Behavior, 79*(3), 625–639. https://doi.org/10.1016/j.jvb.2011.04.010

Mychailyszyn, M. P., dosReis, S., & Myers, M. (2008). African American caretakers' views of ADHD and use of outpatient mental health care services for children. *Families, Systems, & Health, 26*(4), 447–458.

Nicholas, D. B., Zwaigenbaum, L., Ing, S., MacCulloch, R., Roberts, W., McKeever, P., & McMorris, C. A. (2016). 'Live it to understand it': The experiences of mothers of children with autism spectrum disorder. *Qualitative Health Research, 26*(7), 921–934. https://doi.org/10.1177/1049732315616622

Ono, E., Friedlander, R., & Salih, T. (2019). Falling through the cracks: How service gaps leave children with neurodevelopmental disorders and mental health difficulties without the care they need. *BCMJ, 61*(3), 114–124.

Perou, R., Bitsko, R. H., Blumberg, S. J., Pastor, P., Ghandour, R. M., Gfroerer, J. C., Hedden, S. L., Crosby, A. E., Visser, S. N., Schieve, L. A., Parks, S. E., Hall, J. E., Brody, D., Simile, C.M., Thompson, W. W., Baio, J., Avenevoli, S., Kogan, M. D., Huang, L. N., & Centers for Disease Control and Prevention. (2013). *Mental health surveillance among children–United States, 2005–2011. Morbidity and Mortality Weekly Report*. Surveillance Summaries.

Peters, K., & Jackson, D. (2009). Mothers' experiences of parenting a child with attention deficit hyperactivity disorder. *Journal of Advanced Nursing, 65*(1), 62–71.

Pishva, R. (2017). Becoming therapeutic agents: A grounded theory of mothers' process when implementing cognitive behavioural therapy at home with an anxious child. *Clinical Psychology & Psychotherapy, 24*(3), 766–784. https://doi.org/10.1002/cpp.204

Polanczyk, G. V., Salum, G. A., Sugaya, L. S., Caye, A., & Rohde, L. A. (2015). Annual research review: A meta-analysis of the worldwide prevalence of mental disorders in children and adolescents. *Journal of Child Psychology and Psychiatry, 56*(3), 345–365. https://doi.org/10.1111/jcpp.12381

Posserud, M., Hysing, M., Helland, W., Gillberg, C., & Lundervold, A. J. (2018). Autism traits: The importance of "co-morbid" problems for impairment and contact with services: Data from the Bergen Child Study. *Research in Developmental Disabilities, 72*, 275–283. https://doi.org/10.1016/j.ridd.2016.01.002

Roughan, L. A, Parker, J. R., & Mercer, L. (2019). Improving interventions for parents of children and young people with autism spectrum disorder (ASD) in CAMHS. *BMJ Open Quality, 8*, e000261. https://doi.org/10.1136/bmjoq-2017-000261

Royal College of Psychiatrists. (2022). *National clinical audit of psychosis: England national report for the early intervention in psychosis audit 2021/2022*. Healthcare Quality Improvement Partnership. www.rcpsych.ac.uk/NCAP

Salzburg Global Seminar. (2011). Salzburg statement on shared decision making. *BMJ*. https://doi.org/10.1136/bmj.d1745

Shyu, Y. I. L., Tsai, J. L., & Tsai, W. C. (2010). Explaining and selecting treatments for autism: Parental explanatory models in Taiwan. *Journal of Autism and Developmental Disorders, 40*(11), 1323–1331.

Simmons, M. B., Hetrick, S. E., & Jorm, A. F. (2013). Making decisions about treatment for young people diagnosed with depressive disorders: a qualitative study of clinicians' experiences. *BMC Psychiatry, 13*, 16. https://doi.org/10.1186/1471-244x-13-335

Srinath, S., Jacob, P., Sharma, E., & Gautam, A. (2019). Clinical practice guidelines for assessment of children and adolescents. *Indian Journal of Psychiatry, 61* (2), 158–175. https://doi.org/10.4103/psychiatry.IndianJPsychiatry_580_18

Staniszewska, S., Brett, J., Mockford, C., & Barber, R. (2011). The GRIPP checklist: Strengthening the quality of patient and public involvement reporting in research. *International Journal of Technology Assessment in Health Care, 27*(4), 391–399. https://doi.org/10.1017/S0266462311000481

Taylor, M., O'Donoghue, T., & Houghton, S. (2006). To medicate or not to medicate? The decision-making process of Western Australian parents following their child's diagnosis with an attention deficit hyperactivity disorder. *International Journal of Disability, Development and Education, 53*(1), 111–128. https://doi.org/10.1080/10349120500510115

van der Boor, C.F., & White, R. (2020). Barriers to accessing and negotiating mental health services in asylum seeking and refugee populations: The application of the candidacy framework. *Journal of Immigrant Minority Health, 22*, 156–174. https://doi.org/10.1007/s10903-019-00929-y

Wolpert, M., Harris, R., Hodges, S., Fuggle, P., James, R., Wiener, A., McKenna, C., Law, D., York, A., Jones, M., & Fonagy, P. (2015). THRIVE elaborated. https://www.annafreud.org/media/3214/thrive-elaborated-2nd-edition29042016.pdf

Wyatt, K. D., List, B., Brinkman, W. B., Prutsky Lopez, G., Asi, N., Erwin, P., Wang, Z., Domecq Garces, J. P., Montori, V. M., & LeBlanc, A. (2015). Shared decision making in pediatrics: A systematic review and meta-analysis. *Academic Pediatrics, 15*(6), 573–583. https://doi.org/10.1016/j.acap.2015.03.011

Part II

Evidence-informed Practice

10

Adolescence

Emma Silver

10.1 Introduction

Adolescence has often been portrayed as a problematic period of life that young people, families and society must endure. Around fourth century BC, Aristotle described this period of life as a time when young people are unstable and lacking in self-control, and in the early twentieth century, Stanley Hall (1904) famously described adolescence as a time of 'storm and stress', turbulent, with conflict and mood swings. But most young people do not present in this stereotypical troubled way. In some cultures, the child's entry to adolescence is celebrated, with young people bringing significant advances to society, yet unfortunately this is not yet the dominant narrative.

For some, the idea of working with young people in complex systems is interesting and exciting, while for others it feels uncomfortable and anxiety provoking. Whether or not practitioners are drawn towards or deterred from wanting to work with young people probably relates to a range of factors including their own experiences of adolescence, how young people are portrayed in society, clinical experiences and training, knowledge, sense of competence and confidence with this age group. This chapter aims to offer a greater understanding of adolescence and some ideas to apply to clinical practice. It gives an overview of adolescent development, including the biological, psychological and social changes, and their relationships to each other that are happening as the young person negotiates this phase. It describes how young people are working out who they are and how and where they fit in, negotiating their relationships and online worlds, and considers ways to be interested in and engaged with these important aspects of their lives. Along the way, this chapter will notice how things can become tricky for some young people and their families and consider ways of conceptualising those difficulties. Examples from clinical practice highlight some of the issues and dilemmas intrinsic to working with this age group. It is written from a transtheoretical developmental perspective because, whatever the therapeutic model/approach (e.g. CBT, psychodynamic, systemic), the setting (e.g. clinic, school, inpatient unit), the clinical presentation and who turns up (e.g. young person, family, social worker, teacher), understanding and working within the developmental context is central.

Child Psychology: Pathways to Good Practice, First Edition.
Edited by Helen Pote, Anna Picciotto and Clare Norris.

10.2 What Do We Mean by Adolescence?

> negotiating the relationship between adult and infantile structures; the transition from life in the family to life in the world; the finding and establishing of an identity ...; in short, the capacity to manage separation, loss, choice, independence, and perhaps disillusionment with life on the outside. (Waddell, 1998, p. 126)

Waddell captures the essence of the developmental tasks of adolescence, but adolescence does not have a straightforward definition. It is often described as the years from the onset of puberty to the time when the young person attains a 'stable role' in society. Given the large cultural differences in societal expectations of young people, adolescence could be considered a social construct, however, there are descriptions of typical adolescent behaviours across different human cultures, across species, and documented across history, identifying it as a distinct phase of development (Blakemore 2018b). Adolescence is a window of development bridging childhood and adulthood characterised by profound biological, psychological and social change (Blakemore, 2018b; Johnson et al., 2009). What *is* socially constructed is how the span of the adolescent period is defined – as the age of becoming legally adult differs across cultures (Defoe et al., 2022), and this in turn tends to define the adolescent period in that culture and context.

Although there is a looseness to the edges of this phase of development, and the World Health Organization defines adolescence as 10 to 19 years, for the purposes of this chapter, adolescence is defined as the period between 10 and 24 years of age (Patton et al., 2016). This reflects the ongoing physical maturation, for example, significant brain development that extends at least into mid-20s (see Section 10.5), eruption of the third molars (wisdom teeth), as well as the later age at which many social milestones that previously signified adulthood are now reached (e.g. partnering, parenting and economic independence) that is apparent in all countries to varying degrees (Sawyer et al. 2018). Although many adult legal privileges start at age 18, the adoption of adult roles and responsibilities generally occurs later. Whilst there is great individual variation in trajectories between adolescents during this period, the young person usually negotiates a range of external challenges that tend to include establishing peer friendships, developing intimate and sexual relationships, managing demands in education, learning to be more independent, leaving the family home, gaining employment, while maintaining and changing family relationships (Sawyer et al., 2018). The focus of these challenges and ages at which they happen may differ across cultural contexts, but generally occur in those adolescent years. At the same time, the adolescent also faces a number of internal/biological changes, from the development of secondary sexual characteristics under hormonal control, to a protracted process of brain maturation (Andrews et al., 2020). To understand adolescence, one needs to consider all the levels it expresses – biological, psychological, cultural and social.

10.2.1 A Time of Opportunity, Vulnerability and Challenges

Adolescence is a time of great opportunity and promise, but also vulnerability, with approximately three-quarters of all lifetime psychological disorders emerging by the end of this stage (Kessler et al., 2007). Half of all mental health disorders in adulthood start by age 14, with most going undetected and untreated (WHO, 2022). In terms of overall health, according to the WHO (2022), although adolescents aged 10 to 14 years have the lowest risk of death of all age groups, the leading cause of death amongst adolescents and young adults (older adolescents) are injuries (including road traffic injuries and drowning), violence, self-harm and conditions related to becoming a mother. According to the WHO (2021) one in seven 10 to 19 year olds experiences a mental disorder, and suicide is the fourth leading cause of death in 15 to 29 year olds. In England the most recent government survey reported that 20% of 7 to 16 year olds and 22% of young people aged 17 to 24 years had a probable mental disorder (Newlove-Delgado et al., 2022). Until puberty, the rates of depression in children are low but significantly increase in adolescence, as does the gender disparity, with twice as many girls presenting with symptoms. The mental health presentations seen in adolescence alongside depression are an increase in anxiety disorders (including social anxiety), eating disorders, conduct disorder, gender dysphoria, substance abuse, psychosis, and more general difficulties with emotional dysregulation and self-harm behaviours. Young people who have successfully masked social communication difficulties and other neurodevelopmental presentations as a younger child are likely to struggle more as they go into secondary school when there is an increased need to understand their broadening and less predictable social world (see Chapter 19 for further discussion). Some young people are more at risk of mental health problems due to their living conditions, stigma, discrimination or exclusion, or lack of access to quality support or services (WHO, 2021). This chapter will not discuss specific mental health presentations, which are covered elsewhere in this book, but will instead consider a wider framework to understand and work with adolescents.

For a practitioner working with young people, there are opportunities and challenges. It is a privilege to work with young people when they are open to discovery, learning through experience, have increased capacity for reflection, and at a time when a helpful intervention can have far reaching consequences, potentially to change the trajectory of their lives, and by doing so have an impact on one's own. However, it can also be challenging to engage young people, maintain helpful boundaries, manage the competing wishes of the young person in their family/career/school systems and understand and manage risk behaviours.

The services in which psychological practitioners work (and how they are funded/commissioned) can create other challenges to supporting young people through this period. While the definition here of adolescence goes beyond 18 years old (to reflect societal roles and advances in knowledge of brain development), most children and young people's services (secondary education, children's social care, and child and young people's mental health services in the UK) end at 18, leaving a service transition gap through which vulnerable young people can fall (see Section 10.8).

From a broader perspective, it is young people who tend to challenge society, by questioning the dominant narratives and re-defining boundaries, which can helpfully move society on in ways that previous generations could not have imagined. For the practitioner, cultural identity (meaning culture in its broadest sense; Burnham, 2012) includes the generational culture that they themselves grew up in. This, together with their wider identity will impact how they understand themselves, and with that understanding, will impact their interaction with clients. By the very nature of this phase of development, working with young people necessitates challenging the practitioner's own assumptions and reflecting on values. As expected, this generation of young people are bringing different ideas, values and behaviours to those that have come before. Previous generations have successfully challenged the status quo in different countries, for example, regarding laws pertaining to racial segregation and sexuality. The current generation is taking up issues such as climate change, gender and racism in new and exciting ways that are challenging for society and will inevitably bring about significant changes.

Just as young people are questioning the wider society, their curiosity, creativity and experiences can be invaluable in making changes to how mental health services are developed and run. Involving young people in the development of their services can be rewarding and successful, both at an individual level for those young people involved and at a wider service level to improve access and the experiences for young people. Ideas around collaboration and co-production are discussed in detail in Chapter 9.

10.3 Adolescent Identity Development

Developing a sense of 'who we are' is considered to be a primary task in adolescence. This is a profoundly social process by which the young person begins to individuate from a family unit and establish a coherent identity that is embedded within a network of peer connections and social and cultural contexts (Erikson 1968; Granic et al., 2020). As capabilities and characteristics change over time, adolescents construct their identities, and these are shaped by their relationships, individual and contextual factors. Adolescents try to create continuity and 'self-sameness' by integrating their past, present and future selves into a personal narrative about their lives (McAdams, 2001; Pasupathi et al., 2007).

Self-identity develops throughout one's life, but in adolescent years young people are more focused on how they are seen by others. They become more aware of the gaze of others and how they are judged by others, and this affects how they feel (proud, ashamed, embarrassed, content, etc.). This is complicated, because they appear and are experienced differently in different contexts (home, school class, friends at a party, online social media). Adolescents compare themselves to others and realise that they too are being judged, and value is placed on those judgements, so they become even more aware of the views of others. Elkind's 'imaginary audience' described the way that adolescents believe that everyone is observing and judging them (Elkind, 1967). This is exacerbated with the use of social media where there seems to be no reprieve from the viewing and the views of others.

Adolescents are trying out, evaluating and changing aspects of themselves in their relationships with peers, family and online, and revising their identity over time. As they go through this process there can be increased exploration, information gathering, discussion and reflection, with the young person open to new experiences. They may sit with a way of being for a while and seem more stable, then reconsider, during which there can be a period of emotional instability and they can be more vulnerable to low mood and anxiety, and more sensitive to the gaze (and criticism) of others. This shifting between periods of uncertainty and growth is a normal part of adolescence. Just as for everyone, the part of a young person's identity that is most salient at one time may not be at another time.

For example, a psychological practitioner's identity as a psychologist may be important at a certain time of their life or in particular contexts, whereas at other times or place it would be their ethnic identity, or their identity as a parent or child that is most salient for them. When working clinically with adolescents it is important not to assume that one part of their identity is most important to them at that time or there is a risk of closing down conversations and, in the practitioner's position of power, permission is not given to talk about other aspects of their identity that are more salient.

Parents and young people are confronted with the important task of negotiating their roles and relationships during this phase. Applying ideas from attachment theory (Bowlby, 1969), parents and children are working together to maintain their relationship in a manner consistent with models developed from their own experience of being parented – from cognitive representations derived from their history of interactions with caregivers. Adolescents whose childhood experiences were of caring, responsive parenting tend to be able to maintain these emotional bonds throughout this period of change, whereas adolescents and parents with a history of difficult and unresponsive parental interactions are likely to have more difficult interactions during adolescence (Rosenstein & Horowitz, 1996). Some adolescents may wish to create distance from their parents as soon as possible, while others may be unwilling or struggle to take up demands on them for increased autonomy.

Piaget's (1952) 'formal operational' stage of cognitive development describes the period from about 11 to 15 years when the young person develops abstract thinking, the ability to hypothesise and deduce answers and explore ideas about imagined futures (including perfect worlds and idealised parents). With the emergence of abstract thought, the adolescent begins to see their parent in a different way, less idealised. The change of image is not usually distressing for the adolescent because it supports their emerging sense of individuality and cognitive–emotional separation from the family. However, it can be a difficult time for parents who can feel criticised and hurt. Parents need to manage their emotional responses to allow for their child's inevitable disappointment in them (e.g. De Goede et al., 2009). Some young people, in order to achieve a stable sense of self, keep their perceptions of their parent as idealised, because reappraisal of that model would be experienced as a disappointment and would challenge their established sense of self. This ongoing idealisation could hinder the separation process, and some presenting problems in young people can be considered in this framework as part of the formulation. For example, symptoms of OCD (reassurance seeking) and anorexia (needing to be monitored/fed) maintain a closeness and prevent development of autonomy and separation.

Alongside adolescents' increased awareness of the views of others, they are becoming more aware of their own thoughts and feelings and developing an increased capacity for self-reflection. They tend to be more inward looking as they are focusing on working out who they are, where they fit, and using their increased cognitive development to try things out. It is normal for them to be more 'egocentric' (Elkind, 1967) , which parents and other adults can find frustrating. It seems that the changes in the brain (described later) are preparing the adolescent for the required social understanding and self-reflection to survive in the adult world. The changes in the adolescent brain are thought to be triggered by hormone changes in puberty.

10.4 Puberty

The surge of hormones, marking the onset of adolescence, typically begins at 9 to 10 years of age in girls and at 10 to 12 years of age in boys and triggers physical changes (including breast development, the development of pubic and axillary hair, rapid physical growth and changes in facial structure) prior to the onset of menstruation in girls, which is on average around 12–13 years. The changes in hormones impact the developing brain and behaviour (Peper & Dahl, 2013).

Rates of depression are approximately equal between boys and girls before the onset of puberty, after which, rates for depression in girls are approximately twice that of boys (Bromet et al., 2011; Salk et al., 2017). More advanced 'pubertal status' (i.e. the level of development incorporating visible body changes, e.g. breasts, body shape, skin, hair) has been linked to depressive disorders and is thought to help explain gender differences in rates of depression (Lewis et al., 2018). For girls, starting puberty earlier than one's peers is a risk factor for internalising symptoms (Ullsperger & Nikolas, 2017), and severe levels of depressive symptoms (Hamlat et al., 2019). However, hormonal changes are not singularly associated with increased depression in girls, rather it is a more complex relationship between a range of factors. This time of puberty, or early adolescence, coincides with a period of socioemotional change, and with greater importance on peer relationships, girls are negotiating their friendships, which can be tricky and can increase their fear of rejection. McGuire et al.'s (2019) study indicated that girls with earlier onset of puberty and a more advanced pubertal status, and those who express a high level of concern about social rejection were more likely to report worsening depressive symptoms.

How young people experience puberty relates to their gender, age of onset, family, social and cultural context. The changing body of a young person can affect how they see themselves and how people view and treat them, creating a cycle. Making sense of bodily changes, what meanings are given to them, their relationship to their body, how they see themselves and how others treat them all impact on their experience and can impact on their developing sense of identity. For some young people, the changes in their body can be feel very uncomfortable, and for those who are questioning their gender identity, the onset of puberty can be particularly stressful. Difficulties in gender identity development happen at different times in life, some earlier in childhood, while for others these occur after the start of puberty, sometimes in the context of broader identity questioning and other psychological difficulties (Churcher Clarke & Spiliadis, 2019).

Psychological practitioners need to be curious about a young person's experience of puberty, and how they were experienced by others, as it may be an important factor in the formulation of their sense of identity and their current struggles (see Box 10.1). At the same time as the body is changing, so is the brain, in particular the areas required to negotiate their changing social world.

10.5 The Adolescent Brain

It had been thought that much of the brain's development happened in the very early years of life, but research over the past 25 years has shown that the human brain goes on developing, and that adolescence is a time of enormous neuronal change and growth (Blakemore, 2018b). The brain undergoes substantial structural change in terms of grey and white matter volume, surface area and cortical thickness (Giedd et al., 1999; Tamnes et al., 2017), with MRI studies showing changes during childhood and continuing into the mid-20s. Throughout adolescence the reduction in grey matter is thought to be related to a decrease in synaptic connections driven by a specialisation in the adolescent brain. This 'synaptic pruning' is a process where connections that are used in a particular environment are retained and strengthened while synapses that are not being used are eliminated. This implies that the adolescent's environment (home, education, social life, hobbies etc.) contributes to shaping their brain (Blakemore, 2018b). The increase in white volume is thought to reflect, at least partly, the strengthening of the connections between brain regions, leading to faster and more efficient information processing. The timing and trajectories of brain changes are based on averages, varying across individuals, with one source of variation likely to be puberty. Although there is not a direct, causal relationship between brain functioning and behaviour, some knowledge of the adolescent brain aids our understanding of adolescent experience and behaviours.

10.5.1 Social Brain

Developments in neuroscience suggest that our brains have evolved so that we can negotiate our social worlds (Leiberman, 2015). Some of the last areas of the brain to mature during development are located within the 'social brain', that is, networks related to social cognitive processes such as perspective taking, emotional regulation and the management of relationships (Andrews et al., 2020). These developments are reflected in a period of heightened social sensitivity, during which peer relationships are very important and there is increased vulnerability to the negative effects of social isolation and peer rejection (Orben et al., 2020), with social interactions playing a crucial role in the development of identity (Granic et al., 2020; Rageliené, 2016). Around this time, adolescents are striving to find their place in a larger peer group, with increased time spent with peers relative to family. Carers/teachers sometimes minimise the young person's challenges with their friendship issues, but there is evidence that our brain networks react similarly to social exclusion (in a game) as they do to physical pain, indicating the importance of our social connections (Blakemore, 2018b). Research has linked the quality and nature of peer interactions in adolescence with a range of psychological, educational, physical health and behavioural outcomes (Almquist, 2009; Almquist & Östberg, 2013; Menting et al., 2015; Modin et al., 2011).

10.5.2 Risk

Adolescents across different cultures are more likely than any other age group to take risks, peaking around age 19 (Steinberg et al., 2018). This would seem to be a functional part of development, as we need to take risks – to learn, take new opportunities and have a range of different experiences – in order for the brain to grow. Risk taking is an indication of flexible, trial-and-error learning allowing for creativity and innovation, which can be beneficial for the individual and society. Taking extreme risks can be dangerous, while not taking risks to avoid anxiety can limit learning and development. For an overview of types of risk taking across different age groups see Willoughby et al. (2021). They challenge the idea of younger adolescents in the current generation taking more risks and conclude that it is older adolescents and young adults who are likely to take more risks over what they describe as a range of domains. Risk-taking behaviours in adolescence are not straightforward as not all young people take risks, and there are different sorts or risks. Our understanding is being enhanced by the evolving research on the adolescent brain.

Adolescents are more likely than adults to take risks when in the presence of peers (Gardner & Steinberg, 2005; Shepherd et al., 2011), and this effect is more pronounced when the peers report a preference for risk-taking behaviour (Bingham et al., 2016). One well-replicated study (Steinberg, 2007) involves playing a driving video game while the brain is MRI scanned. The game involves taking risks to stop (avoiding a crash) or go (gaining more rewards) at lights. Comparing adults and adolescents, with or without peers watching, the group that consistently takes most risks are adolescents in the presence of their peers. This is context specific – even if adolescents think peers are watching it produces the same increased risk, whereas this is not the case if it is a young adult or a parent observing (Steinberg, 2014). Translated to everyday life, adolescents are more likely to have a car crash when they are driving with friends than alone or with parents.

Two distinct but interacting psychological processes have been hypothesised as important to adolescent risk taking: impulsivity and sensation seeking. The Life-span Wisdom Model (Romer, 2010; Romer et al., 2017), describes a gradual reduction in risk taking and impulsivity between childhood and adulthood, which is supported by the development of executive function skills and a maturation of the prefrontal cortex. In parallel, there is an increase in sensation seeking that peaks around adolescence and coincides with increased activity in limbic and prefrontal networks associated with reward sensitivity (Chambers et al., 2003; Romer & Hennessy, 2007). The reward regions of the brain are highly sensitive at this time, and we are most influenced by rewards in adolescence than at other times in our lives, which may be adaptive for exploration and learning. As this increase in reward seeking occurs before the full development of the cognitive control system and its connections to areas of the socioemotional system (self-regulation and impulse control), which happens over the course of adolescence, it is thought that the gap between the development of these brain areas relates to a period of heightened vulnerability to risk taking during earlier adolescence (Steinberg, 2008). What this means is that although younger adolescents may generally have good decision-making skills, when they are in emotionally laden situations (e.g. with friends) their emotional brain takes over and in those situations they are more likely to take risks.

Given the importance of social acceptance during adolescence, and some evidence of hypersensitivity to the effects of social rejection (Andrews et al., 2020), it is not surprising that adolescents are more likely to take risks (e.g. health and legal) when with their peers. What an adult/parent would consider to be a 'risky behaviour' (e.g. smoking/drug use) may be considered less risky by the young person than the effects of social rejection, and rather than an irrational choice, their decision could be understood as adaptive, given that social rejection is a risk factor for adolescent onset depression and anxiety (Blakemore, 2018a).

Box 10.1 Clinical example: Puberty, relationships, developing identity

Katy, a white British young person, came into services in her early 20s with very low mood and using drugs and alcohol as a way of managing her feelings. She grew up in a family with an older brother and both parents until her parents separated when she was 14 years old. She lived with her mother and had intermittent contact with her father. Both parents worked in hospitality, involving working late nights. Katy was now working in a bar and had started a modelling career with some initial success. She came across as confident and it seemed important for her to show that she was okay, although this mask was becoming more difficult to maintain. It was hard for Katy to be compassionate to herself; she blamed herself for her experiences, some of which were traumatic, and the 'choices' she made in her early teens.

When I asked about puberty and her early adolescence, Katy explained that she developed large breasts before her peers, and she looked like a curvy young woman by the time she started secondary school (at 11 years old). She was aware of both her parents being taken up by their own struggles and the values that her mother placed on looking (sexually) attractive and being popular. Katy tried to live up to these standards and suppressed her feelings and any other aspects of herself to gain much needed approval from her mother. In identity theory terms, this conditionality of parental interest would be ripe for developing 'false-self behaviour' and prevent the young person's 'true-self' development, which has been related to low self-esteem (Harter, 2012).

In the context of parental neglect (parents taken up with stresses in their own lives, working late nights, relationship conflict and drug use), she was vulnerable to the attention of much older boys which initially made her feel good. She desperately wanted to belong to this group of teenagers, particularly to not be rejected by the girl who had introduced her to the group, whose friendship she valued. She used drugs and alcohol to fit in and she felt obliged to engage in sexual activity with the older boys in the group. She took these risks with others alongside the fear of rejection and being isolated (the bigger risk). She acknowledged that at the time some of it was exciting, particularly the feeling of taking risks and getting away with it (parents not knowing) and feeling more grown up than her peers. However, she was developing her identity and a sense of her self-worth in relation to her sexualised body, and a confusion about connection and intimacy. Later, as an older teenager, she learnt to use substances to manage difficult feelings. She did not imagine that she was a victim of abuse, and she did not want to see herself that way because she believed she was behaving 'like a naughty teenager'.

Influenced by ideas from narrative therapy (see Vetere & Dowling, 2017), it was helpful to think with Katy about the context she was living in at that time, how her bodily changes were experienced by herself and others, parental views, the lack of adult protection and support, her experience of the gaze of older boys/men, and the wider narratives about women and girls that were also part of her online world. We thought about the 'choices' she made in the contexts of power differences and

(Continued)

Box 10.1 (Continued)

her wish as a young adolescent to feel connected and be included by peers, but mostly not to be rejected. Beginning to bring in these contexts allowed Katy to create a different narrative that helped her to be more compassionate to herself, empowered and to start to make sense of patterns in relationships that impacted on her mood.

10.6 Young People's Online Worlds

With the background of heightened risk taking and peer influence, several authors have hypothesised the potentially transformative impact of Social Media (SM) on young people's social interactions, their identity formation (Granic et al., 2020; Subrahmanyam & Šmahel, 2011) and social and emotional wellbeing (Crone & Konijn, 2018; Spies Shapiro & Margolin, 2014). The 2022 Ofcom children and parent media use and attitudes report (Ofcom, 2022) indicated that nearly all children aged 3 to 17 years went online in 2021, with video sharing platforms (e.g. TikTok and YouTube) being the most popular online activity (95%). As SM offers novel opportunities for social experimentation, exploration and connection, that come with new challenges and risks, as much interest needs to be paid in young people's online lives as their offline lives.

The evidence for the relationship between SM use and mental health is mixed, and there is a need for more sophisticated research in this area with adolescents (Valkenburg, 2022). There is some good evidence for sleep disruption amongst heavy SM users (Scott et al., 2019), and heavy digital screen users more generally (Orben & Przybylski, 2020b). This is important because sleep disturbance has been linked to social difficulties, as well as a wide range of mental health problems during adolescence (Tarokh et al., 2016). Systematic reviews and meta-analyses of overall levels of SM use indicate a weak association between higher usage and poorer mental health (Abi-Jaoude, et al., 2020; Orben & Przybylski, 2020a), including symptoms of depression, anxiety and general distress (Abi-Jaoude et al., 2020; Keles, et al., 2019; McCrae et al., 2017; Orben, 2020a). However, it is not possible to attribute causality, and studies that try to explore this (e.g. using longitudinal design) indicate mixed evidence, suggesting possible reciprocal effects : high levels of SM use may impact negatively on mental health and poorer mental health may also drive increased SM use (Aalbers et al., 2019; Frison & Eggermont, 2017; Hunt et al., 2018; Mosquera et al., 2020; Orben, 2020; Orben & Przybylski, 2019). There is emerging evidence that how someone engages with SM is likely to be more important than how much (Blum-Ross & Livingstone, 2018; Nesi et al., 2020; Orben & Przybylski, 2020b), for example, active engagement (e.g. connecting with friends) may be more helpful than passively scrolling, particularly if it involves comparing oneself to others. More specifically, whilst judgemental comparisons for example, comparing one's attractiveness or wealth to others', are typically associated with negative outcomes (Yang et al., 2021), non-judgemental comparisons for example, of opinions and perspectives for informational purposes, may actually lead to mental health benefits (Park and Baek, 2018). While passive use may be problematic specifically in instances where it leads to judgemental social comparisons, it can be considered that some kinds of active use can also be problematic, such as broadcasting (Winstone et al., 2022). The use and impact of SM is likely to be dependent on individual differences, and some studies have supported the 'rich-get-richer' view of online communication, that is, those who already have good offline friendships might benefit most from digital interaction, while those with a liability to mental health issues might be more susceptible to the negative effects (Odgers & Jensen, 2020).

Given that the adolescent brain is generally more sensitive to reward yet has not yet developed all the skills to regulate emotions, it is easy to see how some young people may find it tricky to manage some SM platforms and gaming because of the way they are designed to be implicitly reinforcing. Parents often talk of conflict triggered when wanting their child to come off a screen. Psychoeducation with both parents and young people about the affordances of the platforms they're using as well as strategies to manage their relationship conflict (see Chapter 12) can be helpful.

In terms of the positive effects of SM use, it can provide opportunities including learning (Bruguera et al., 2019), financial revenue and career opportunities (Tang et al., 2012), access to news (Nielsen & Schrøder, 2014) and entertainment, peer support and specialist knowledge (Naslund et al., 2016). SM can provide opportunities for young people to create and explore self-identities (e.g. creating a profile, posting content, testing out ideas) and learn how to manage impressions of others and receiving feedback from others (Nadkarni & Hofmann, 2012). For many young people there is not an option to <u>not</u> engage with SM (e.g. during Covid-19), and it is an implicit part of some careers, (e.g. the music industry), so supporting them to use it in ways that enhance their wellbeing can be an important part of psychological practitioners' work. SM may be supportive for some young people with pre-existing mental health difficulties, for example, through mental health initiatives, online support and provision of specialist information (Luxton et al., 2012; Moorhead et al., 2013; Naslund et al., 2016). For further discussion of risks and benefits of SM use, see Hayes et al. (2022).

Tibber and Silver (2022) present a transdiagnostic cognitive-behavioural conceptualisation of the positive and negative roles of social media and the impact on mental health and wellbeing in adolescents, with a focus on social/interpersonal processes and their interaction with common mental health difficulties, such as anxiety and depression. It uses a 'contextualist approach' to recognise the significance of interactions between the individual, the technology, their patterns of SM use and the nature in which they are engaging (and the broader social context in which it occurs) and consider the importance of the function and consequences of use. Using a cognitive-behavioural framework, they give ideas around how to include young people's online worlds in assessment and intervention. An exploration of a young person's online world needs to be an integral part of the assessment process when completing psychological work, as for some young people their online life may be as rich as their online world. For example, exploring values - what is important to them - and whether their behaviour online (and offline) fits with these (see below for examples). Whilst this will incorporate asking about explicit online risks, particularly where risky behaviour is indicated more generally (See Chapter 22 for further discussion of this), the assessment of their online worlds should go further than this. It can include patterns of use, online relationships and interactions more generally, and thinking together about how these might interact with existing difficulties – in positive and negative ways. The paper (Tibber & Silver, 2022) offers some ideas for questions to open up conversations with young people about their social media use, for example:

> *General questions about SM use to increase awareness*: Do you have a good sense of how much you are using SM at the moment? Are you, or is anyone else, worried that you spend too much time on SM? Is your SM use interfering with other activities? Is it interfering with your sleep? Do you use SM late at night or just before bed? Would you like to reduce your level of use? Would you like to change your pattern of use, for example, when you use it?
> *Questions to activate a critical engagement with social media and increase agency*: What SM platforms do you typically use? Can you tell me more about these? What can you do on them? What materials are you able to share? What additional features and utilities do they have? Can anyone see your posts or is it a closed network?

These questions may lead to psychoeducation or SM-literacy training on platform design and associated affordances, with the aim of increasing the use of SM platforms that support values-consistent behaviour and decrease the use of SM platforms that support values-inconsistent behaviour (see Box 10.2).

> *Questions about their motivations for using SM*: Do you meet people through SM? What sort of things do you find it useful for – sharing homework, seeing what other people are doing, keeping up to date with what's going on?

These questions can help the young person notice when their behaviour is consistent or inconsistent with their values, particularly relating to social values. This assumes that when we behave in line with our values, we tend to feel more comfortable and better in ourselves.

> *Questions about specific online behaviours and modes of engagement:* Do you feel in control of what you are doing? Do you feel able to stop when you want to, or need to? Or do you lose your sense of time and the outside world? To what extent do you interact with others directly? To what extent do you find yourself comparing your life to the lives of others? And how realistic do you think they are?

The questions help to explore sense of control, interaction with others or comparing self with others.

> *Questions about risk behaviour*: Have you ever been exposed to material online, or received messages online, that made you feel uncomfortable or unsafe? Have you ever felt threatened or coerced online? Have you ever experienced online bullying?

This can also include questions about financial risks, and what they are viewing online, particularly if there are concerns around sexual behaviour (e.g. legality of the sorts of pornography being viewed). For further examples and ideas for intervention see Tibber and Silver (2022) and Box 10.2.

Box 10.2 Clinical example: Integrating SM use in clinical understanding and intervention

Leyla was a 16-year-old girl of Pakistani British heritage, living in cramped inner-city housing with her family of three generations. Her mother came to the UK from Pakistan in her late teens to marry Leyla's father, who had grown up in the UK. Leyla was the eldest of five siblings and she recently moved to a new college to study her A levels. Leyla accessed the service because she had been very low in mood and, following a suicide attempt and brief admission to hospital, she was followed up by the local adolescent mental health crisis team. Her parents were worried about her, but Leyla felt disconnected from them in the context of their different generational and cultural experiences. She was highly intelligent and valued her academic ability, which had become an important part of her identity, but her low mood was impacting her performance at college, which fed into negative thoughts and feelings about herself and her future. With her consent, a member of the clinical team talked to the college and to parents to help them understand the impact of her low mood on her learning and find new ways to support Leyla in education and at home.

In our sessions initially we explored issues of intersectionality, including class, gender and ethnicity that helped with engagement, and in developing an understanding of Leyla's life. We co-constructed a CBT formulation that helped make sense of why she was feeling the way she was and how her beliefs about herself, others and the world had developed in context. We understood how her hopelessness increased in relation to her struggles academically, as she placed value (and hope) on changing her life through academic achievement, which was not supported by her family in the context of cultural and family beliefs around gender roles.

Together we considered her behaviour and relationships offline and her SM use and online relationships. She tended to use some SM to passively scroll through and watch videos, not actively engaging with people online or posting. She also accessed information online relating to her academic work and news information. She tended not to connect with friends online – she had become more isolated during the Covid-19 pandemic when college went online, and she didn't have the usual opportunities to establish new friendships in person. Now that college was back to usual teaching, she was struggling to engage with her peers in the context of having had some time away from college, her increased concerns about how she was perceived by others (particularly in relation to her drop in grades) and her low mood. Through exploration of her values, she became more aware of the consequences of her online and offline behaviours and how they fitted with or took her away from her values. For example, she became aware of a tendency to compare herself to a general online world of 'pretty white wealthy girls' who seemed to be living lives that were closed to her, which also perpetuated negative beliefs about herself and impacted on her mood (feelings of disconnection and isolation). Over the course of our sessions, we explored the costs and benefits of alternative

(Continued)

Box 10.2 (Continued)

online spaces that Leyla might access in order to connect with others who she could relate to better (e.g. people who looked more like her and had shared values). By gradually changing her SM use she was exposed to the stories of others, more similar to herself, who had succeeded in different areas of their lives. She started to feel a greater sense of connection and more hopefulness about herself and her future.

10.7 Implications for Clinical Practice

10.7.1 Engaging Adolescents

The therapeutic relationship has long been emphasised as a critical element in psychotherapy. In their research exploring the therapeutic relationship with adolescents whose therapy was successful (CBT for moderate depression), Wilmots et al., (2019), identified an underlying theme whereby adolescents felt that their autonomy and individuality was respected within the relationship, whilst simultaneously being given opportunities to experience emotional closeness with their therapist. This makes sense, given the developmental frame of a struggle between autonomy and inter-dependence. They described a positive therapeutic relationship where the therapist was warm and friendly while simultaneously being a professional, allowing for both autonomy and emotional connection, which reflects previous psychotherapy research (Binder et al., 2011). Feeling known, understood and accepted sets the stage for therapy and this includes an understanding and acceptance of the young person's developing cultural identity (culture in its broadest sense), and in doing so, a requirement for practitioners to reflect on their own cultural identities. For more ideas around exploring cultural identity see the Multicultural Orientation Framework (Davis et al., 2018). The therapist stance of unconditional acceptance and positive regard (Rogers, 1957) allows for trust to develop to enable sharing without feeling judged. This is particularly important in adolescence when the views of others are critical. Clinical experience of ruptures in relationships with young people are often when they felt judged by something said or by the therapists' behaviour. These are important moments to notice because psychological practitioners sometimes will not get it right. Noticing and commenting on these moments of adolescent–adult tension gives an opportunity to repair the relationship, and the experience of rupture and repair can be a helpful part of the therapy process (e.g. Cirasola & Midgeley, 2022).

It can be tricky to get this therapeutic balance right – both friendly and professional. Therapists can fall into being too friendly without the required boundaries to contain the relationship, making it more difficult further on into the work when, for example, there is a disclosure of risk/concerns that need to involve other parts of the young person's system (e.g. school, family, social care). Conversely, therapists can be too rigid in adhering to a therapeutic model that doesn't give enough space to develop a genuine connection.

How psychological practitioners position themselves, or how they are positioned, is important for setting up a safe therapeutic relationship. It can be helpful to consider how the young person may consider the relationship (mentalising), what their expectations may be of the practitioner and what they think the practitioner expects of them. They have, and may have had, lots of different relationships with adults (parents/carers, social worker, teacher, sports coach, music teacher, previous counsellor, etc.), some of which they may have experienced as helpful, but others may have been difficult, conflictual, authoritarian or abusive. Their response to feeling constrained may have been to push the boundaries, leading to conflict and to the adult responding with more constraints on the young person's autonomy. How they see the practitioner and their expectations of this relationship will partly depend on their previous relationship experiences. The practitioner may know very little about these other relationships when they first meet, but there may be clues in the referral and how they present with a parent/carer and with the practitioner at that first meeting. It is important that the practitioner tries to position themselves differently from these other relationships, and this starts by setting the frame for the meeting (see Chapter 3 for more detail on this).

It is not unusual to be faced with the parents/carers and young people feeling upset and angry with each other. In tracking the latest conflict between them (which may have been the decision to come to the clinic that day) it is possible to hear about their interaction in detail. Here it is helpful to give space to each person's experiences of the interaction, running through the event to hear both what they did (behaviour), felt in the moment (emotions) and their thoughts about what the other person was thinking or intending (mentalising). By tracking a recent event in this way the therapist is positioning themselves in a genuinely curious and neutral position, and everyone's experiences and stories are valid. This can be a new experience for a child (or others) in a family, where their views may not have been heard or understood.

Adolescents who don't easily engage with services are often described as 'hard to reach'. Young people might not agree with this attribute, or question if there is something about the service that doesn't fit for them. Is a clinic the best place to meet the young person, or would a more neutral setting work better? Can practitioners be creative in how to connect, perhaps join the young person in an activity? Sometimes walking in the park and talking can be an effective way of working with some young people. How practitioners think about attendance is important, and how a service responds to non-attendance can be helpful or a hinderance to engagement. Clients from chaotic backgrounds often find it difficult to regulate their emotions and can feel overwhelmed at the experience of therapy so at times they do not attend as a way of managing this experience. This is illustrated in the clinical example in Box 10.3, the young person did not attend as a way of managing his relationship with the therapist, yet he used the service in a way that met his goals at that time. He responded well to agreed text reminders, check-in calls, shorter intermittent meetings (rather than a usual 50-minute weekly session). Hearing young people's views about what fits for them and adapting how services work to meet their needs is important and an interesting, challenging part of the role (See Chapter 25 and Chapter 9 for further discussion).

Box 10.3 Clinical example: Engaging the reluctant young person

'I don't want to see another patronising old cow....' He shouted when his mother called to refer with concerns about conflict at home and poor school attendance. Ashley was a 15-year-old dual heritage British boy (white and black Caribbean) from a working-class inner-city home, living with his white mother and 6-year-old white half-sister. He had some contact with his father, but this was inconsistent, and there had been previous domestic violence. He attended a local mixed secondary school where there were conflicts with peers and some difficult relationships with teachers. He had poor attendance, and his mother, who was struggling as a single parent, found it difficult to support him to get to school. There were lots of heated arguments at home, although no physical violence. The more school he missed the harder it had become as he fell behind despite his good academic ability, and this impacted his mood. Fortunately, he had a Head of Year (Black Caribbean) who believed in his ability and was keen to work together with the service to develop strategies to support Ashley.

Ashley came to the first session on his own, sat, arms folded, said very little and looked annoyed. I commented on him seeming to be irritated and wondered whose idea it was to come. Ashley let me know that it was his mother's idea and he only attended to avoid another argument. I said that I appreciated him coming today, which couldn't have been easy, and now he was here maybe we could see what it could be like, and that he could leave at any time. I learnt from Ashley that he had seen lots of people like me, and that no one had been helpful. Understandably, he didn't see the point of doing it again. Alongside his hopelessness about this process, there was a worry that he would fail his GCSEs and not get to college. This last bit was important information as it included a wish for things to be different. Given his experiences with services and other unhelpful adults, I asked if he could help me, especially as a white woman, to know how to do this better. Turning it round to empower a young person with the knowledge to help me do a better job for them and other young people can be a useful tool in engagement. He told me about the list of people he'd seen before and the sorts of things that happened that he didn't like. He referred to this as his 'bullsh*t list'. Ashley was given permission to tell me when what I was doing was going to put me on that list. It became something we returned to in future sessions to elicit his feedback on how we were working together. Coming alongside Ashley maintained his sense of autonomy and helped develop trust with an adult that afforded opportunities to bring in other adults to support his access to education. Ashley did make use of therapy, but not in the traditional way. He made a connection and then withdrew and returned when he felt comfortable enough to reconnect. This was a good enough intervention, and he did enough in his last year in school to get to college, which was his goal of therapy.

10.7.2 Working with Young People

The developmental framework helps practitioners to understand what is within the normal range of adolescent experiences and what may be a problem, and who it is a problem for. For example, we know that adolescents experience 'social anxiety' as part of the developmental process, so for it to be a problem at a clinical level we would expect that their (response to) anxiety would be impacting significantly on their lives. If a young person presents with low mood/emotional lability and self-harm, it is important to take their distress seriously (not see them as a 'moody teenager'), try to make sense of their ways of managing their feelings while assessing risk, and develop strategies with them around safety. This is where a good assessment is important (see Chapters 3 and 22).

Some young people take risks with their peers, (e.g. experimenting with drugs and alcohol). This may present as a problem for their parent/carer but not for the young person. When a parent/carer and young person have different views of the problem there is no easy solution, and practitioners must try to see it from both sides. They can hear the parent's concerns about their child engaging with risky behaviours, and they can also see the young person's view – who may feel that they don't have a problem or don't see that talking to someone (outside their friends) could be helpful for them. By hearing both sides, channels are kept open so that the young person can come if they want to, but they can't be dragged into therapy. Instead, it is important to try to find ways to make it accessible to them, so that they may feel able to come. Many young people, like Ashley, are sent by someone else (usually when under 16 years), and their definition of what the problem is, and their goals may be different from the parent/carer/school's views. However, often there are similar goals that can be elicited in the work together, such as to reduce conflict between them (see Chapter 8).

The good news is that for many adolescents their increased capacity for self-reflection allows for engagement in more exploratory talking therapies that younger children find more difficult. Their level of cognitive development – the ability for abstract thinking and hypothesis testing (Piaget, 1952), and learning through exploration, creativity and taking risks enables them to engage in therapies such as cognitive behavioural therapy (CBT), for example using Socratic questioning, behavioural experiments and problem-solving strategies (Beck, 1976; Fuggle et al., 2012). Young people's increasing mentalising capacity can be enhanced with the use of a range of circular questions (systemic), and they can make good use of relational therapies (e.g. Interpersonal psychotherapy, psychodynamic therapy). Practitioners should be aware that stage models of cognitive development (e.g. Piaget, 1952) are generalised and have their limitations, and some young people remain quite concrete in their thinking into adulthood, while for others they may be able to think more abstractly at different times. For example, while an adolescent may be able to philosophise about the rights and wrongs of a complex political stance, they may not – especially when feeling anxious or very low in mood – be able to apply this high level of cognitive 'rationality' to their own situation, and at those times the practitioner may find it helpful to return to more specific concrete examples to support their ideas in sessions.

When one considers how young people are negotiating separation and autonomy and their developing identity, alongside their internal world, attention needs to be paid to the systems in which they exist (including family, school, peers, social media, culture) and formulations need to be relational, even when the choice of intervention is with the individual. Sometimes working with other parts of the system, rather than working directly with the young person may be a more appropriate intervention.

10.7.3 Parents of Adolescents

This section discusses some of the dilemmas for parents/carers of adolescents. For an overview of interventions with parents see Chapter 12.

Most families the manage the ups and downs of family life with adolescents, but this time of transition can bring about feelings of loss, confusion or being deskilled in their roles. Parents are reminded of their own adolescence in their families, which may bring a helpful parenting roadmap, and/or elicit differences in views and parenting styles between parents/co-parents (that increases conflict) or indicate a need to do things differently to not repeat patterns across generations. It can be tricky to find a new path and may be more difficult where there are generational cultural differences. These can be helpful areas to explore in work with parents (see Byng-Hall, 1995).

Young people often feel that they are experiencing things intensely for the first time, and that it is unique to them, and that others (particularly parents/adults) will not understand. Parents may find this frustrating, or even amusing, as if they themselves were never young. But young people's experiences are genuinely different from their parents because they are growing up in a different generational context (and for some a different country, culture etc.). For example, young people growing up with SM are having a significantly different experience to their parents' teenage years. Parents can be encouraged to acknowledge these differences and be genuinely interested in what it is like for their children.

It could seem that parental influences reduce as a child moves into adolescence, but this is not really the case, and parents need to know that even though their child may want to spend less time with them, they, and their opinions and behaviours, and their relationship with their child still very much matter. Branje et al.'s (2021) review of adolescent identity research over the past 10 years reported that identity development is closely embedded in relationships with family members and friends. At this stage parents are required to understand that their children are thinking individuals who are embracing possible futures and that instead of giving directions in the way that they needed to for their younger child, parents can now suggest ideas and options to explore. Supporting a parent to maintain their position of authority while developing negotiation and problem-solving skills with their child can engender a positive relationship for both. However, this can be difficult for parents around issues where risk is perceived differently and where they may not feel they have the knowledge (e.g. alcohol/drugs, SM). Psychological practitioners can signpost parents to information so they can clarify their views and feel more confident to discuss and negotiate these topics with their child (identifying their 'bottom line') to support appropriate exploration with risk minimisation.

Understandably, many parents fear the sorts of risks their child will take as they go into their teenage years. It can be useful to explore with parents what taking risks means to them. Knowing that risk taking is important for development and learning, parents can support activities where the young person is encouraged to take risks in relatively safe contexts (e.g. climbing/parkour, skateboarding, various sports, music, art – trying out new ideas and pushing limits), and support them to socialise with peers safely by negotiating the boundaries with their adolescent (e.g. managing their safety around how they travel, time they return home). The anxieties that some parents experience are very real due to the environments in which they live, and they have a dilemma about how to protect their children whilst giving them opportunities to explore and develop skills they need. For example, parents of black adolescent boys in a city may be more fearful when their sons go out with friends – an anxiety based within the reality of structural racism within society (see YMCA, 2020). It is important that these experiences are heard and validated and that practitioners come alongside parents in their dilemmas.

Positive parental monitoring is a key protective factor for reduced mental health problems in adolescence (Cadman et al., 2022). This refers to parents' knowledge of their adolescent's whereabouts, their peers, who they tend to spend time with, relationships, and their social and school activities. The parents' knowledge and involvement in their adolescent's life also reflects whether they will come to them for support and share information, and reflects a sense of trust and safety that comes with appropriate levels of involvement. When a young person presents with severe mental health symptoms, parents are often required to be more involved and vigilant, perhaps checking in more with their child, and may be part of their agreed risk management protocol. It is not unusual for parents who have been looking after their teenager through a mental health crisis to feel really worried about them even when their symptoms and risks have reduced. It can be hard for them to know what is 'adolescence' and what are the signs of a mental health problem re-emerging. This can be a delicate time for families, when parents have had to be more vigilant and are now needing to renegotiate their relationship with their child while their anxiety continues to be high. The work towards ending may be to support parents as they negotiate their child's autonomy and dependence, acknowledging their struggles in separation both from their child and perhaps from the service and therapists that have supported them all through difficult and scary times. For other parents and young people the work may be supporting them to access adult services for further support.

10.8 Transition to Adult Services

Most services (e.g. Children and Young People's Mental Health Services – CYPMHS, also known as Child & Adolescent Mental Health Services – CAMHS in the UK) end at 18 years, and while some young people no longer need support, others have ongoing needs and require transfer to Adult Mental Health Services (AMHS). For a number of reasons, this is not an easy transition, and many young people fall between the gap in services at this age (see Singh & Toumainen, 2015). Those who are more likely to access adult services are young people presenting with psychosis, but those with emotional and/or neurodevelopmental presentations are less likely to access a service and have more difficulties in that transition (Singh et al., 2010). Those most vulnerable at this age are looked after children who do not have parents/family to advocate for them and may have also changed key workers in the care system at this time.

The differences in cultures between CAMHS and AMHS can make it more difficult for the professionals and the young people and families to enable a good transition. For example, services for children/young people tend to use fewer diagnostic labels but usually AMHS require a firm mental health diagnosis to access a specific part of the service. If they don't fit that diagnostic system, it can mean that young people can be left without support despite having ongoing needs. For those who do get to adult services, there may be difficulties with access because they tend to be set up for adults and not young people, without the flexibility and support and family involvement that some young people need. Young people have reported that they do not feel prepared or supported during transition, and feel insecure at the loss of the familiar, and anxious about unfamiliar adult services, and that their voices are not heard during this transition process. For some it can feel like 'having to move house due to a flood' rather than a planned process determined by choice, and informed decision making (Wilson et al., 2015).

In response to these issues and the needs of young people, some services, commissioners and young people have come together to generate creative solutions. The National Institute for Health and Care Excellence (NICE, 2016) guidelines for transition from children's to adults' services for young people using health or social care services, aim to help young people and their carers to have a better experience of transition by improving the way it is planned and carried out. Singh and Toumainen (2015) described some new models of care in different countries that try to manage this transition time and consider that rather than trying to fix a bridge between the two service providers, there should be a 'radical redesign with a seamless new pathway within a stigma free, youth friendly specialist model'. The NHS Long-Term Plan (National Health Service, 2019) is committed to moving to 0–25s services for both physical and mental health, with service delivery based on need rather than age.

'Minding the Gap' in Camden, London, is one such initiative that has brought together NHS child and adult mental health services, non-statutory services and young people to co-construct a pathway for young people to access appropriate mental health support beyond age 18. While culture change and redesign of services is a longer-term goal, examples of more simple interventions to aid transition are: to identify all 17 year olds on caseloads so transition can be planned ahead; AMHS employ a transitions champion or a CAMHS practitioner to support referrals of young people; regular transition meetings across services to discuss potential referrals; and provide joint training for AMHS and CAMHS practitioners on working with young people.

The transition boundary spans the maximum risk period for the emergence of serious mental disorders, so it is important for future services to be focusing on this time of transition in young people's mental health care as it has the potential to transform outcomes in young people's mental health.

10.9 Conclusion

Adolescence is a period of development when young people acquire the physical, cognitive, emotional and social resources that are the foundation for their adult lives. It can be a time of great opportunity and a time of fragility. What happens during these years has a significant impact on their later life and wellbeing. For psychological practitioners, it is an opportune time to intervene, with developmental changes facilitating use of a range of talking therapies to work collaboratively with young people at a time in their lives that can change trajectories into the next generation. Considering young people's presentations within the framework of adolescent development – biological, social, emotional, psychological – allows for a broader understanding through which practitioners can make sense of the young person's struggles in their contexts and adapt services and interventions to meet their needs. Although there are inherent challenges to this work, being genuinely interested in young people's lives, being creative in engaging young people, working flexibly and collaboratively allows young people to be empowered to make use of the available resources (e.g. with peers, in education, online, in services, in their families) to support their mental health.

References

Aalbers, G., McNally, R. J., Heeren, A., de Wit, S., & Fried, E. I. (2019). Social media and depression symptoms: A network perspective. *Journal of Experimental Psychology: General, 148,* 1454–1462.

Abi-Jaoude, E., Treurnicht Naylor, K., & Pignatiello, A. (2020). Smartphones, social media use and youth mental health. *Canadian Medical Association Journal, 192,* E136–141.

Almquist, Y. (2009). Peer status in school and adult disease risk: A 30-year follow-up study of disease-specific morbidity in a Stockholm cohort. *Journal of Epidemiology and Community Health, 63,* 1028–1034.

Almquist, Y. B., & Östberg, V. (2013). Social relationships and subsequent health-related behaviours: Linkages between adolescent peer status and levels of adult smoking in a Stockholm cohort. *Addiction 108*(3), 629–637.

Andrews, J. L., Ahmed, S., & Blakemore, S.-J. (2020). Navigating the social environment in adolescence: the role of social brain development. *Biological Psychiatry, 89,* 109–118.

Beck, A. (1976). *Cognitive therapy and the emotional disorders.* International University Press.

Binder, P., Moltu, C., Hummelsund, C., Sagen, S. H., & Holgersen, H. (2011). Meeting an adult ally on the way out into the world: Adolescent patients' experiences of useful psychotherapeutic ways of working at an age when independence really matters. *Psychotherapy Research, 21*(5), 554– 566.

Bingham, C. R., Simons-Morton, B. G., Pradhan, A. K., Li, K., Almani, F., Falk, E. B., Shope, J. T., Buckley, L., Ouimet, M. C., & Albert, P. S. (2016). Peer passenger norms and pressure: Experimental effects on simulated driving among teenage males. *Transportation Research Part F: Traffic Psychology and Behaviour, 41,* 124–137.

Blakemore, S.-J. (2018a). Avoiding social risk in adolescence. *Currents Directions in Psychological Science 27,* 116–122.

Blakemore, S.-J. (2018b). *Inventing ourselves: The secret life of the teenage brain.* Doubleday.

Blum-Ross, A., & Livingstone, S. (2018). The trouble with 'screen time' rules. In G. Mascheroni, G., Ponte, C., & Jorge, A. Borås (Eds.), *Digital parenting – the challenges for families in the digital age* (pp. 179–188). The International Clearinghouse on Children, Youth and Media.

Bowlby, J. (1969). *Attachment and loss, Vol. 1: Attachment.* Basic Books.

Branje, S., de Moor, E. L., Becht, A. I., & Spitzer, J. (2021). Dynamics of identity development in adolescence: A decade in review. *Journal of Research on Adolescence, 31(*4), 908–927.

Bromet E., Andrade L. H., Hwang I., Sampson N. A., Alonso J., De Girolamo, G., de Graaf, R., Demyttenaere, K., Hu, C., Iwata, N., Karam, A. M. Kaur, J., Kostyuchenko, S., Lépine, J.-P., Levinson, D., Matschinger, H., Mora, M. E. M., Oakley Browne, M., … Kesler, R. C. (2011). Cross-national epidemiology of DSM-IV major depressive episode. *BMC Medicine, 9,* 90.

Bruguera, C., Guitert, M., & Romeu, T. (2019). Social media and professional development: A systematic review. *Research in Learning Technology, 27*. https://doi.org/10.25304/rlt.v27.2286

Burnham, J. (2012). Developments in social GRRRAAACCEEESSS: Visible-invisible and voiced-unvoiced. In I-B. Krause (Ed.) *Culture and reflexivity in systemic psychotherapy. Mutual perspectives*. Karnac.

Byng-Hall. J. (1995). *Rewriting family scripts: Improvisation and systems change*. Guilford Press.

Cadman, T., Paul, E., Culpin, I., Sallis, H., Bould, H., & Pearson, R. (2022). Parental monitoring longitudinally associates with reduced risk of adolescent mental health problems. *Journal of Affective Disorders Reports, 10*, 100420.

Chambers, A.R., Taylor J.R., & Potenza, M.N. (2003). Developmental neurocircuitry of motivation in adolescence: A critical period of addiction vulnerability. *American Journal of Psychiatry 160*(6), 1041–1052.

Churcher Clarke, A., & Spiliadis, A. (2019). 'Taking the lid of the box': The value of extended clinical assessment for adolescents presenting with gender identity difficulties. *Clinical Child Psychology and Psychiatry, 24*(2) 338–352.

Cirasola, A., & Midgley, N. (2022). The alliance with young people: Where have we been, where are we going? *Psychotherapy, 60*(1), 110–118. https://doi.org/10.1037/pst0000461

Crone, E. A., & Konijn, E. A. (2018) Media use and brain development during adolescence. *Nature Communications, 9*(588), 1–10.

Davis, D. E, DeBlaere, D., Worthington, C. E., Rivera, D., Van Tongeren, D. R., & Placares, V. (2018). The multicultural orientation framework: A narrative review. *Psychotherapy, 55*(1), 89–100.

De Goede, I. H., Branje, S. J., & Meeus, W. H. (2009). Developmental changes in adolescents' perceptions of relationships with their parents. *Journal of Youth and Adolescence, 38*, 75–88.

Defoe, I. N., Rap, S. E., & Romer, D. (2022). Adolescents' own views on their risk behaviors, and the potential effects of being labeled as risk-takers: A commentary and review. *Frontiers in Psychology, 13*, 945775. doi: 10.3389/fpsyg.2022.945775

Elkind, D. (1967). Egocentrism in adolescence. *Child Development, 38*(4), 1025–1034.

Erikson, E. K. (1968). *Identity, Youth, and Crisis*, Norton.

Frison, E., & Eggermont, S. (2017) Browsing, posting, and liking on Instagram: The reciprocal relationships between different types of Instagram use and adolescents' depressed mood. *Cyberpsychology, Behavior, and Social Networking 20*(10), 603–609.

Fuggle, P., Dunsmuir, S., & Curry, V. (2012). *CBT with Children, Young People and Families*. SAGE.

Gardner, M., & Steinberg, L. (2005). Peer influence on risk taking, risk preference, and risky decision making in adolescence and adulthood: An experimental study. *Developmental Psychology, 41*(4), 625–635.

Giedd, J. N., Blumenthal, J,. Jeffries, N. O., Castellanos, F. X., Liu, H., Zijdenbos, A., Paus, T., Evans, A. C., & Rapoport, J. L. (1999). Brain development during childhood and adolescence: A longitudinal MRI study. *Nature Neuroscience 2*, 861– 863.

Granic, I., Morita, H., & Scholten, H. (2020). Beyond screen time: identity development in the digital age. *Psychological Inquiry, 31*, 195–223.

Hall, G. S. (1904). *Adolescence (Vols. 1 & 2)*. Prentice Hall.

Hamlat E. J., Snyder H. R., Young J. F., & Hankin B. L. (2019). Pubertal timing as a transdiagnostic risk for psychopathology in youth. *Clinical Psychological Science, 7,* 411–449.

Harter, S. (2012). *The construction of the self, developmental and sociocultural foundations* (2nd ed.). Guildford Press.

Hayes, B., James, A., Barn, R., & Watling, D. (2022). Children's risk and benefit behaviours on social networking sites. *Computers in Human Behavior, 130,* 107147.

Hunt, M. G., Marx, R., Lipson, C., & Young, J. (2018). No more FOMO: limiting social media decreases loneliness and depression. *Journal of Social and Clinical Psychology, 37,* 751–768.

Johnson, S. B., Blum, R. W., & Giedd, J. N. (2009). Adolescent maturity and the brain: the promise and pitfalls of neuroscience research in adolescent health policy. *Journal of Adolescent Health, 45,* 216–221.

Keles, B., McCrae, N., & Grealish, A. (2019). A systematic review: the influence of social media on depression, anxiety and psychological distress in adolescents. *International Journal of Adolescence and Youth, 25,* 79–93.

Kessler, R. C., Amminger, G. P., Aguilar-Gaxiola, S., Alonso, J., Lee, S., & Ustün, T. B. (2007). Age of onset of mental disorders: a review of recent literature. *Current Opinion in Psychiatry, 20,* 359–364.

Lieberman, M. (2015). Introduction to social cognitive neuroscience. In A. Toga (Ed.), *Brain mapping: An encyclopedic reference* (pp. 1–2). Elsevier.

Lewis G., Ioannidis K., van Harmelen A.-L., Neufeld S., & Stochl J., (2018). The association between pubertal status and depressive symptoms and diagnoses in adolescent females: A population-based cohort study. *PLoS One, 13,* e0198804.

Luxton, D. D., June, J. D., & Fairall, J. M. (2012). Social media and suicide: A public health perspective. *American Journal of Public Health, 102* (suppl 2), S195.

McAdams, D. P. (2001). The psychology of life stories. *Review of General Psychology, 5,* 100–122. https://doi.org/10.1037/1089-2680.5.2.100

McCrae, N., Gettings, S., & Purssell, E. (2017). Social media and depressive symptoms in childhood and adolescence: A systematic review. *Adolescent Research Review, 2,* 315–330.

McGuire, T. C., McCormick, T., Koch, M. K., & Mendle, J. (2019). Pubertal maturation and trajectories of depression during early adolescence. *Frontiers in Psychology, 10,* 1362. https://doi.org/10.3389/fpsyg.2019.01362

McLaughlin, K. A., Hatzenbuehler, M. L., & Hilt, L. M. (2009). Emotion dysregulation as a mechanism linking peer victimization to internalizing symptoms in adolescents. *Journal of Consulting Clinical Psychology, 77,* 894–904.

Menting, B., Van Lier, P. A. C., Koot, H. M., Pardini, D., & Loeber, R. (2015). Cognitive impulsivity and the development of delinquency from late childhood to early adulthood: moderating effects of parenting behavior and peer relationships. *Development and Psychopathology, 28,* 167–183.

Modin, B., Östberg, V., & Almquist, Y. (2011). Childhood peer status and adult susceptibility to anxiety and depression. A 30-year hospital follow-up. *Journal of Abnormal Child Psychology, 39,* 187–199.

Moorhead, S. A., Hazlett, D. E., Harrison, L., Carroll, J. K., Irwin, A., & Hoving, C. (2013). A new dimension of health care: Systematic review of the uses, benefits, and limitations of social media for health communication. *Journal of Medical Internet Research, 15,* e85.

Mosquera, R., Odunowo, M., McNamara, T., Guo, X., & Petrie, R. (2020). The economic effects of Facebook. *Experimental Economics, 23*, 575–602.

Nadkarni, A., & Hofmann, S. G. (2012). Why do people use Facebook? *Personality and Individual Differences, 52*, 243–249.

Naslund, J. A., Aschbrenner, K. A., Marsch, L. A., & Bartels, S. J. (2016). The future of mental health care: Peer-to-peer support and social media. *Epidemiology and Psychiatric Sciences, 25*, 113–122.

Nesi, J., Telzer, E. H., & Prinstein, M. J.(2020). Adolescent development in the digital media context. *Psychological Inquiry 31*(3), 229–234.

Newlove-Delgado, T., Marcheselli, F., Williams, T., Mandalia, D., Davis, J., McManus, S., Savic, M., Treloar, W., & Ford, T. (2022). *Mental Health of Children and Young People in England, 2022.* NHS Digital.

National Health Service. (2019). The NHS long-term plan. https://www.longtermplan.nhs.uk/

National Institute for Health and Care Excellence. (2016). *Transition from children's to adults' services for young people using health or social care services.* National Institute for Health and Care Excellence. https://www.nice.org.uk/guidance/ng43

Nielsen, R. K., & Schrøder, K. C. (2014). The relative importance of social media for accessing, finding, and engaging with news. *Digital Journalism, 2,* 472–489.

Odgers, C. L. and Jensen, M. R. (2020). Annual research review: Adolescent mental health in the digital age: facts, fears, and future directions. *Journal of Child Psychology and Psychiatry, 61*(3): 336–348. doi:10.1111/jcpp.13190

Ofcom. (2019). *Children and parents: Media use and attitudes report* 2018. https://www.ofcom.org.uk/__data/assets/pdf_file/0024/134907/children-and-parents-media-use-and-attitudes-2018.pdf

Ofcom. (2022). *Children and parents: Media use and attitudes report* 2022. https://www.ofcom.org.uk/__data/assets/pdf_file/0024/234609/childrens-media-use-and-attitudes-report-2022.pdf

Orben, A. (2020). Teenagers, screens and social media: a narrative review of reviews and key studies. *Social Psychiatry and Psychiatric Epidemiology, 55*(4), 407–414.

Orben, A., & Przybylski, A. K. (2019). Screens, teens, and psychological well-being: Evidence from three time-use-diary studies. *Psychological Science 30*(5), 682–696.

Orben, A. and Przybylski, A. K. (2020a). Reply to: Underestimating Digital Media Harm. *Nature Human Behaviour, 4*(4), 349–351.

Orben, A., & Przybylski, A. K. (2020b). Teenage sleep and technology engagement across the week. *PeerJ, 8*, e8427.

Orben, A., Tomova, L., & Blakemore, S. J. (2020). The effects of social deprivation on adolescent development and mental health. *The Lancet Child & Adolescent Health*, *4*(8), 634–640. https://doi.org/10.1016/S2352-4642(20)30186-3

Park, S. Y., & Baek, Y. M. (2018). Two faces of social comparison on Facebook: the interplay between social comparison orientation, emotions, and psychological well-being. *Computers in Human Behavior, 79*: 83–93.

Pasupathi, M., Mansour, E., & Brubaker, J. R. (2007). Developing a life story: Constructing relations between self and experience in autobiographical narratives. Human Development, 50, 85–110. https://doi.org/10. 1159/000100939

Patton G. C., Sawyer, S. M., Santelli, J .S., Ross, D.A., Afi fi ,R., Allen, N.B., Arora, M., Azzopardi, P., Baldwin, W., Bonell, C., Kakuma, R., Kennedy, E., Mahon, J., McGovern, T., Mokdad, A. H., Patel, V., Petroni, S., Reavley, N., Taiwo, K., … Viner, R. M. (2016). Our future: A Lancet commission on adolescent health and wellbeing. *The Lancet Commissions, 387.*

Peper, J. S., & Dahl, R. E. (2013). Surging hormones: Brain-behavior interactions during puberty. *Current Directions in Psychological Science, 22*(2), 134–139.

Piaget, J. (1952). *The Origins of Intelligence.* International United Press.

Rageliené, T. (2016). Links of Adolescents identity development and relationship with peers: A systematic literature review. *Journal of the Canadian Academy of Child and Adolescent Psychiatry 25*(2), 97–105.

Rogers, C. R. (1957). The necessary and sufficient conditions of therapeutic personality change. *Journal of Consulting Psychology, 21*(2), 95–103.

Romer, D. (2010). Adolescent risk taking, impulsivity, and brain development: Implications for prevention. *Developmental Psychobiology, 52,* 263–276.

Romer, D., & Hennessy, M. (2007). A biosocial-affect model of adolescent sensation seeking: the role of affect evaluation and peer-group influence in adolescent drug use. *Prevention Science, 8,* 89–101.

Romer, D., Reyna, V. F., & Satterthwaite, T. D. (2017). Beyond stereotypes of adolescent risk taking: placing the adolescent brain in developmental context. *Developmental Cognitive Neuroscience, 27,* 19–34.

Rosenstein, D. S., & Horowitz, H. A. (1996). Adolescent attachment and psychopathology. *Journal of Consulting and Clinical Psychology, 64*(2), 244–253. https://doi.org/10.1037/0022-006X.64.2.244

Salk R. H., Hyde J. S., & Abramson L. Y. (2017). Gender differences in depression in representative national samples: meta-analyses of diagnoses and symptoms. *Psychological Bulletin, 143,* 783–822.

Sawyer, S. M., Peter S. A. Wickremarathne, D., & Patton, G.C. (2018). The age of adolescence. *The Lancet Child and Adolescent Health, 2*(3), 223–228.

Scott, H., Biello, S. M., & Woods, H. C. (2019). Social media use and adolescent sleep patterns: cross-sectional findings from the UK Millennium Cohort Study. *BMJ Open, 9,* e031161.

Shepherd, J. L., Lane, D. J., Tapscott, R. L., & Gentile, D. A. (2011). Susceptible to social influence: Risky 'driving' in response to peer pressure. *Journal of Applied Social Psychology, 41,* 773–797.

Singh, S. P., Paul, M., Ford, T., Kramer, T., Weaver, T., McLaren, S., Hovish, K., Islam. Z., Belling, R., & White, S. (2010). Process, outcome and experience of transition from child to adult mental healthcare: Multi-perspective study. *British Journal of Psychiatry, 197,* 305–312.

Singh, S. P., & Tuomainen, H. (2015). Transition from child to adult mental health services: needs, barriers, experiences and new models of care. *World Psychiatry, 14*(3), 358–361.

Spies Shapiro, L. A., & Margolin, G. (2014). Growing up wired: social networking sites and adolescent psychosocial development. *Clinical Child and Family Psychology Review, 17*(1), 1–18. https://doi.org/10.1007/s10567-013-0135-1

Steinberg, L. (2007). Risk taking in adolescence: New perspectives from brain and behavioral science. *Current Directions in Psychological Science, 16*(2), 55–59.

Steinberg, L. D. (2008). A social neuroscience perspective on adolescent risk taking. *Developmental Review, 28*, 78–106.

Steinberg, L. D. (2014). *Age of opportunity: lessons from the science of adolescence*. Huffington Mifflin.

Steinberg, L., Icenogle, G., Shulman, E. P., Breiner, K., Chein, J., Bacchini, D., Chang, L., Chaudhary, N., Giunta, L. D., Dodge, K. A., Fanti, K. A., Lansford, J. E., Malone, P. S., Oburu, P., Pastorelli, C., Skinner, A. T., Sorbring, E., Tapanya, S., Tirado, L. M. U., … Takash, H. M. S. (2018). Around the world, adolescence is a time of heightened sensation seeking and immature self-regulation. *Developmental Science, 21*(2), 10.1111/desc.12532. https://doi.org/10.1111/desc.12532

Subrahmanyam, K., & Šmahel, D. (Eds.). (2011). Constructing identity online: Identity exploration and self-presentation. In *Digital Youth – The Role of Media in Development* (pp. 59–80). Springer.

Tamnes, C. K., Herting, M. M., Goddings, A-L., Meuwese, R., Blakemore, S-J., Dahl, R. E., Güroglu, B., Raznahan, A., Sowell, E. R., Crone, E. A., & Mills, K. L. (2017). Development of the cerebral cortex across adolescence: A multisample study of inter-related longitudinal changes in cortical volume, surface area, and thickness. *Journal of Neuroscience, 37*(12), 3402–3412.

Tang, Q., Gu, B., & Whinston, A. (2012). Content contribution for revenue sharing and reputation in social media: A dynamic structural model. *Journal of Management Information Systems, 29,* 41–76.

Tarokh, L., Saletin, J. M., & Carskadon, M. A. (2016). Sleep in adolescence: Physiology, cognition and mental health. *Neuroscience and Biobehavioral Reviews, 70*, 182–188.

Tibber, M., & Silver, E. (2022). A trans-diagnostic cognitive-behavioural conceptualisation of the positive and negative roles of social media use in adolescents' mental health and wellbeing. *The Cognitive Behaviour Therapist, 1,* e7. doi:10.1017/S1754470X22000034

Ullsperger J. M., & Nikolas M. A. (2017). A meta-analytic review of the association between pubertal timing and psychopathology in adolescence: are there sex differences in risk? *Psychological Bulletin. 143*, 903–938.

Valkenburg, P. M. (2022). Social media use and well-being: What we know and what we need to know. *Current Opinion in Psychology, 45*, 101294. https://doi.org/10.1016/j.copsyc.2021.12.006

van Harmelen, A-L., Kievit, R. A., Ioannidis, K., Neufeld, S., Jones, P. B., Bullmore, E., The NSPN Consortium, Fongay, P., & Goodyer, I. M. (2017). Adolescent friendships predict later resilient functioning across psychosocial domains in a healthy community cohort. *Psychological Medicine 47*, 2312–2322.

Vetere, A., & Dowling, E. (Eds.). (2017). *Narrative approaches with children and their families: A practitioner guide to concepts and approaches* (2nd ed.). Routledge.

Waddell, M. (1998). *Inside lives: Psychoanalysis and the growth of personality*. Karnac Books.

Wilmots, E., Midgley, N., Thackeray, L., Reynolds, S., & Loades, M. (2019). *The therapeutic relationship in Cognitive Behaviour Therapy with depressed adolescents: A qualitative study of good-outcome cases*. Psychology and Psychotherapy*: Theory, Research and Practice,* Wiley Online.

Wilson, A., Tuffrey, A., McKenzie, C., & Street, C. (2015). After the flood: Young people's perspectives on transition. *Lancet Psychiatry. 2015*;2, 376–378.

Winstone, L., Mars, B., Haworth, C. M. A., Heron, J., & Kidger, J. (2022). Adolescent social media user types and their mental health and well-being: Results from a longitudinal survey of 13-14-year-olds in the United Kingdom. *JCPP Advances, 102*(2), e12071.

World Health Organization. (2021). Mental health of adolescents. https://www.who.int/news-room/fact-sheets/detail/adolescent-mental-health

World Health Organization. (2022). Adolescent and young adult health. https://www.who.int/news-room/fact-sheets/detail/adolescents-health-risks-and-solutions

Willoughby, T., Heffer, T., Good, M., & Magnacca, C. (2021, September). Is adolescence a time of heightened risk taking? An overview of types of risk-taking behaviors across age groups. *Developmental Review, 61,* 100980.

Winstone, L., Mars, B., Haworth, C. M. A., Heron, J., & Kidger, J. (2022). Adolescent social media user types and their mental health and well-being: Results from a longitudinal survey of 13-14-year-olds in the United Kingdom. *JCPP Advances, 102*(2), e12071.

Yang, C.-C., Holden, S. M., & Ariati, J. (2021). Social media and psychological well-being among youth: the multidimensional model of social media use. *Clinical Child and Family Psychology Review, 24*(3), 631–650.

YMCA. (2020, October). Young and Black: the young Black experiences of institutional racism in the UK. https://www.ymca.org.uk/wp-content/uploads/2020/10/ymca-young-and-black.pdf

11

Sleeping, Feeding and Toileting Difficulties for Young Children

Pinder Kaur and Lauren Bryan

This chapter aims to provide psychological practitioners with guidance around understanding and providing intervention across specific areas of difficulty that commonly present when working with children under the age five. The focus of this chapter is on issues with sleeping, feeding and toileting; these are challenges that can occur, and re-occur, at different points and stages and may also present concurrently (i.e. difficulties with sleeping alongside toileting). Practitioners are encouraged to hold in mind various factors when attending to these specific presenting issues. An awareness of a child's developmental context is necessary, including attendance to their physical, neurological, cognitive, social and emotional growth. Throughout this chapter there is reference to the contexts within which these issues can emerge and an emphasis on clinicians focussing on parent–child dynamics whilst also holding a systemic lens across their assessment, formulation and intervention.

11.1 Sleep

11.1.1 The Under-five Context

There are multiple settings where input from a psychological practitioner might be needed for support with sleep-related challenges for a child under age five. This includes children's centres, pre-school nursery settings and health clinics. Table 11.1 summarises the contact children under 5 years receive under the universal health visiting service and additional professional contact in England and Wales.

11.1.2 What is a Sleep Problem?

Sleep problems in children under the age of five are common. What constitutes a sleep 'problem' varies considerably. In keeping with a practical and clinical focus this section will view sleep problems based on parent self-reported struggles with their child's[1] sleep and

1 In this chapter 'child' refers to a child aged 0–5. In some cases, 'infant' will be used to refer to a child under 12 months.

Child Psychology: Pathways to Good Practice, First Edition.
Edited by Helen Pote, Anna Picciotto and Clare Norris.

Table 11.1 Universal and potential additional healthcare contact for children under age five.

Universal contact with healthcare 0–5 (England)	Professional involved in universal healthcare contact	Additional healthcare/professional contact examples
• Universal health and wellbeing reviews and contacts: o Antenatal health promoting review o New baby review o 6–8 week review o 3-month contact o 6-month contact o 1-year review o 2.5-year review • Immunisations o 8, 12 and 16 weeks o 1 year o 1–5+ – annual flu o 3 years 4 months	• Health visitors • GP nurses	• Post-birth hospital clinic follow ups (e.g. heart murmur clinic) • Nursery workers • Speech and language therapists • Children centre staff, play workers, nursery staff • Paediatric teams for specific medical investigations and treatment. • Occupational therapists • Other specialist medical teams for specific health care needs • Infant mental health team • Early years practitioners • Social care team involvement if under Section 17 (Child in Need) or Section 47 (Child Protection; see Chapter 5).

who are seeking support for this. Developmentally typical sleep challenges in the under-five age range including sleep resistance, negative sleep associations and night wakings will be presented, and the ways in which a psychological practitioner can support families.

11.1.3 Diagnosis and Problem Descriptions

Whilst the ethos of this chapter is to have a broad, family-led description of sleep difficulties, it is important to be aware of the diagnostic context. This awareness can help differentiate between the range of sleep problems, target interventions or know when to refer the family for further support.

The key sources are the fifth edition of *Diagnostic and Statistical Manual of Mental Disorders* (*DSM-5*, American Psychiatric Association, 2013) and the second and third edition of the International Classification of Sleep disorders (ICSD-2, Thorpy, 2012 and ICSD-3, American Academy of Sleep Medicine, 2014; Sateia, 2014). The ICSD-2 uses the clinical diagnostic category of 'Behavioural insomnia of childhood,' further separated into sleep-onset association type, limiting-setting type (typically implicating the parent's role in the sleep problem) or combined. Both the DSM-5 and ICSD-3 merge paediatric insomnia in to one overarching diagnosis: insomnia disorder and chronic insomnia disorder respectively, taking account of developmental issues. Clinically, symptoms must be frequent, present for a length of time and cause significant impairment to the child, parents and family. Milder symptoms should not be labelled as sleep disorders (Meltzer & Mindle, 2014).

The *International Classification of Diseases*, version 10 (ICD-10, World Health Organization, 2016) similarly classifies non-organic and organic sleep disorders and behavioural

Table 11.2 Six categories of 'sleep disorders'.

Category	Description
Sleep-onset association type	When falling asleep in a reasonable time is only possible in association with a specific form of stimulus and/or or setting. For example, on parent's body in the parent's bed or watching TV. These may evolve from being a strategy that initially brings short-term benefits but leads to longer term unhelpful associations.
Limit-setting type	Difficulties in parents setting limits to support a type of culturally acceptable sleep pattern that is desired.
Delayed sleep phase syndrome	Lack of synchrony between schedule and the individual's environment.
Multiple night wakings	It is common to rouse in and out of sleep between cycles; multiple night wakings refers to waking up and not being able to get back to sleep easily, usually in the context of needing the child's sleep-onset associations to be present.
Partial arousal parasomnias	Parasomnias refers to disruptions of sleep. Partial arousal of sleep refers to sleep terrors (night terrors), sleep walking and confusional arousals.
Rhythmic movement disorders	Repetitive movements of large muscles that tend to occur during sleep-wake transitions.
Sleep disordered breathing	A term to describe breathing related problems during sleeps, the most common being obstructive sleep apnoea where breathing stops and starts. The child may not be aware during the night but does not wake up feeling rested.
Restless legs syndrome	The often-uncomfortable urge to move your leg that is relieved by moving your leg, often worse at night.
Periodic limb movement disorder	Repetitive and stereotyped limb movements during sleep.

Source: Adapted from Ogundele and Yemula, 2022.

insomnia of childhood, noting the distinction between them as a primary diagnosis (the main diagnosis describing the assessed problem) and secondary diagnosis (sleep as a symptom secondary to an assessed overall problem that is better accounted for by another primary diagnosis).

Cortese et al. (2013) and Ogundele and Yemula (2022) provide helpful clinically based categories based on diagnostic categories across the main diagnostic manuals and are summarised in Table 11.2.

11.1.4 A Stepped-care Approach to Sleep

Psychological practitioners may be involved in addressing a sleep difficulty as the primary presenting challenge or in the context of another difficulty for the child and family. The next part of this section will summarise a brief understanding of sleep, what to include in a sleep-focused assessment, formulation development and intervention-based research and guidance. A family-centred 'stepped-care' approach can support guiding the level of your input (from psychoeducation only to structured weekly intervention plan) required for a sleep goals-based intervention.

11.1.5 Sleep Background and Sleep Expectations

It is important to have knowledge on how sleep is understood through the lens of western science in the UK context. This one perspective on how sleep is understood will go on to form the basis of psychoeducation-based support for families, which is the first step in supporting a sleep-based goal. The section will also go on to explore the necessity of contextualising sleep problems with a culturally curious and sensitive approach.

11.1.6 Key Concepts in Understanding How Sleep Works

The detailed complexity of sleep is beyond the scope of this chapter, but the concepts of *sleep pressure* and *circadian clocks* appear to be key in regulating sleep and wakefulness. This, along with an understanding of the *sleep cycle* provides an important physiological context for making sense of why children aged under five appear to sleep differently to adults and have challenges in the area of sleep.

Sleep pressure/drive: This is the physiological, homeostatic-based concept that the longer we stay awake the greater our sleep drive (need/urge) to sleep.

Circadian body clock: This refers to the timing of a powerful internal biological clock, sometimes referred to as a 'body clock'. It contributes to feeling tired at night and awake during the day, regardless of when we last slept. Most of these rhythms are controlled within the body but some external cues such as light, temperature and behavioural patterns can impact this. Melatonin is one example of a hormone implicated in the regulation of the circadian body clock. It is sometimes referred to as the 'darkness hormone'. Darkness prompts its production promoting sleep anticipation and light causes it to diminish. Melatonin production increases around three to four months (Kennaway et al., 1992).

Sleep in Stages and the Sleep Cycle: Sleep typically consists of several cycles made up of rapid eye moment (REM) and non-rapid eye moment (NREM) in the night.

REM: This stage of sleep is characterised by eyes moving rapidly whilst closed, increase in brain activity, breathing and heart rate – similar to awake state.

NREM: Non-rapid eye movement appears to have three distinct stages (N1, N2, N3) with each stage progressing to a deeper state of sleep.

Adult sleep cycles are usually 90 minutes; as adults fall asleep, they enter stage NREM1 (or N1 for short) progressing to stage N2 and going into deeper stage N3 sleep before typically going back to stage N2 and then entering the first REM stage of sleep, completing the first cycle of sleep, where they may experience a light waking or arousal before moving back in to the second cycle of the night. Sleep cycles vary and one often has the deepest sleep early on in the night with longer periods of REM in the sleep cycles as the night progresses. Babies up to the age of 3 months will tend to have equal amounts of NREM and REM, from 3 months onwards they will spend progressively less time in REM, slowly shifting towards a balance closer to the adult cycle by the age of five (Patel et al., 2020).

11.1.7 How Much Should Sleep Should Children Under Age 5 Years Have?

Table 11.3 outlines recommended sleep by age in children aged five and under.

Sleep 0–3 Months: There is a considerable amount of individual variation in sleep at this age. Table 11.3 shows how babies can sleep between 8 to 18 hours in a 24-hour cycle. Babies of this age will typically spend more time asleep then awake in a 24-hour cycle, doing so in blocks of short and long periods through the day and night. When a baby does sleep, their sleep cycles are shorter than an adults, at 45 minutes. Babies also have increased REM sleep so will wake more easily. The neurotransmitter systems involved in the 'sleep-pressure' process are under-developed at birth. Newborns only need to be awake for a short time before feeling tired and need to sleep (Iglowstein et al., 2003). Newborns' sleep-and-wake cycles are also not on a 24-hour cycle yet, but by 8 to 12 weeks their rapid brain development supports a closer synchronicity with day and night. This leads to more sleep consolidation at night, whilst they still continue to have multiple naps during the day. The lived experience of parents may well be one of exhaustion if their own, previously more regulated, sleep pattern becomes disrupted with a newborn's fragmented sleep pattern and night wakings, along with the added transition of caring for their newborn.

Table 11.3 Amount of recommended sleep per age in children aged five and under.

Stage	Age	Recommended sleep including naps (hours)	Naps[2]
Newborn	0–3 months	8 up to 16–18	Multiple naps, long and short stretches of sleep. Length of nap may be longer than usual after the first set of immunisations.
Infant	4–12 months	12–16 hours including naps	Multiple naps between longer periods of being awake and a schedule may emerge in context of a regular routine. May experience a 4-month and 8-month sleep regression linked to developmental and environmental changes.
Toddler	1–2 years	11–14 hours including naps	Naps consolidate from usually two (AM and PM) naps to one midday nap depending on context of a regular daily routine. If naps are too close to bedtime this may impact sleep pressure.
Pre-school	3–5 years	10–13 hours including naps	Typically, naps have stopped and vary from none to occasional (e.g. car naps, naps after a particularly exerting day) and earlier bedtimes support the need for sleep in transition to school, which carries more demands on the child's focus, attention and self-regulation capacities.

Source: Adapted from NHS online (2021) and Paruthi et al. (2016)

2 A note on naps – these are dependent on the routine and daily life of the caregiver.

The 0–3 month range is sometimes referred to as the 'fourth trimester' as it's characterised by a huge adjustment from being inside the womb to the outside world. A soothing, rocking, dark place with muffled sounds is a stark contrast to the world outside, so advice related to sleep at this stage may benefit from being underpinned by helping parents go at the pace of their baby as much as possible. Trying to control sleep is likely to add more stress than working with the biological systems that are slowly developing and the time needed for environmental shaping to support sleep to move closer to regulated adult sleep. Therefore, psychological practitioners may wish to target the following areas for practical suggestions:

- Environment: keeping an environment that is regular, calm and quieter for sleep where possible may support this adjustment (this may be harder with siblings and with overcrowded home environments). The parent's body still forms a key part of the baby's environment so regular physical proximity to the sight of the parent, sounds and touch can support this.
- Managing colds and coughs: it is not uncommon for newborns to have minor colds and coughs that can impact how comfortable they are and how they sleep. Addressing these with support from the GP where needed, and making the baby comfortable as possible can help get through these periods.
- Responding to babies' sleep cues and emerging individual sleep cues: at this stage Infant sleep cues might look like rubbing their eyes, yawning, tugging at their ears. These will change and look a little different in each individual baby but responding to cues earlier can help promote sleep.
- Promoting relaxation for the parent and the baby.
- Encouraging parents to keep up with feeding and getting support and connection from others going through a feeding journey. There are usually local infant feeding teams with drop-in sessions or one-to-one sessions available.
- Seeking support from trusted family or friends to specifically help watch the baby so the parent(s) can catch up on sleep. Often, a lack of network of support can be contributing to the parent's struggles. If there are difficulties in asking for help, the psychological practitioner may carefully explore this, and problem solve towards manageable goals in this area.
- Remind parents that most babies start to sleep more at night around 3 months and this typically increases from this point.
- Remind parents that sleep progress is not linear, and regressions or deteriorations are common. If they are concerned about prolonged disruptions to sleep or excessive crying that isn't easily soothed or addressed with usual strategies to seek help from their health visitor and/or GP to explore underlying causes or contributors.
- Validate with compassion that being sleep deprived as a parent is very difficult and that it can be hard to take a longer-term view that things will eventually change when the 'here-and-now' feeling of a disrupted night, or agitated baby feels intense and long.
- Encourage the use of natural daylight to support the development of the internal circadian clock (which typically emerges around 2–3 months) – differentiating between day and night. Use blackout blinds for the night. This might involve encouraging parents to take the baby for walks in the buggy at the start of the day.
- Encourage parents to seek support from others going through similar sleep adjustments to reduce isolation and feelings of struggle through what is an intense but usually

time-limited period.[3] Attending infant groups, 'stay and plays', and local children centres, soft plays, library 'bounce and rhyme songs and stories' sessions. Each council usually has an 'early years' or 'family information' department that gives lists of places that parents can meet other parents with their infants.

Sleep at 3–6 Months: On average, a 3–6-month-old will sleep 8–17 hours in a 24 period. Babies may start to sleep increasingly longer periods at night, however it is still common for babies to wake through the night. Babies' sleep cycles at this stage are closer to 45–60 minutes. Parents may experience their infant's '4-month sleep regression'. This often happens due to the transition point from newborn fragmented sleep throughout the 24-hour cycle to the developing consolidation of sleep at night. The sleep regression can last days to weeks and may be evident through increased fussiness, difficulties in falling asleep, difficulties in staying asleep and reduced sleep. Whilst the process is highly variable between infants, the process of rapidly developing and growing can create instability, experienced as disrupted sleep before regulating once again.

In addition to the 0–3 month advice, psychological practitioners may want to also advise:

- Developing a consistent and predictable bedtime routine: this might help the baby tune in to their natural body clock. It can be helpful to advise against a fixation on the timing of waking and sleeping but that when in the wake or sleep stage that there is clear differentiation and cues are being established. Open the curtains in the morning, use fresh air and natural daylight during the day. Consistent bedtime routines might consist of having a bath, a calming baby massage, reading a familiar story book, dimming the lights and singing a lullaby.
- Teething: when babies start to cut their first teeth it can sometimes be an uncomfortable experience that can disrupt sleep, and promoting coping with this by giving teething toys, comfort and feeding can help get through some of the more challenging parts of it.

Sleep 6–12 Months: At 6–9 months babies are sleeping 14–15 hours with one to three naps in a 24 hour period. At 9–12 months this reduces to 13–14 hours with usually one nap in a 24 hour period. Parents may experience an '8-month sleep regression'. The rapid development of a typical infant means it is difficult to separate what factors contribute to sleep disruptions but at the stage of an 8-month sleep regression, babies are typically more mobile (sitting and attempting/crawling), teething, are developing greater awareness of their surroundings and also more able to differentiate themselves from their parents prompting separation anxiety experiences. Therefore the 8-month sleep regression can be associated with this realisation that their parent is separate to them. In a western, capitalist context, 8 months may be approaching the end of any maternity/shared-care leave arrangements that parents have, and transition to childcare settings.

Sleep 1–2 Years: At this age sleep will vary from 11 to 14 hours in a 24 hour period. At 12 months they may have one or two naps. At around 18 months their naps may reduce, with most children stopping napping between ages 3 and 4 years. Sleep cycles increase in length to 60 minutes. A child's own style of falling asleep might become more noticeable as they begin to verbalise more. Some children might suddenly have important things they need to

3 A note of caution here, however, as some parents can experience being with other parents with babies of the same as age as competitive rather than supportive.

talk about before bedtime with their parent, or they might fidget for a short while before finally falling asleep. Some children might fall asleep quickly, and deeply. Children will wake briefly at the end of each sleep cycle and some children will call out when they wake. On some occasions a child will be able to settle themselves back to sleep without support as they may not have actually woken up fully. On other occasions, when crying is escalating, they may need more support to settle back to sleep, which is common. All children are different with their own personalities; some will sleep longer than others.

Sleep 2–3 Years: Children between the ages of two and three continue to need more sleep than adults, but their need for total sleep time decreases as they get older. Their sleep needs are met through earlier bedtimes, with an additional daytime nap(s). Daytime naps are typically consolidated in to one longer nap in the day, gradually phasing out at pre-school age (3–4 years). Sleep at this age is closely linked to behaviour and the following areas can impact toddler and pre-school aged children:

- Changes in the family life, such as starting nursery, pre-school, toileting learning, transitioning out of a cot to a bed, a new sibling, going on holiday away from the usual sleep environment.
- A toddler's drive for independence and control and an increase in their social, cognitive and motor skills can interfere with sleep.

A psychological practitioner may wish to use guidance and interventions underpinned by social, emotional and behavioural understanding in supporting parents with sleep-related challenges in this age range. These are described later in this section.

Sleep 3–5 Years: Children between the ages of 3 and 5 years sleep between 11–13 hours. Close to the age of five they have usually dropped their nap but parents may find that big days out and new experiences requiring a lot of their energy may lead to one-off naps. Whilst the child's physical sleep is comparable to an adults, there are social, emotional and behavioural differences. Areas that can affect sleep in this age may be starting pre-school and school, night-time wetting and nightmares.

11.1.8 The Impact of Learning Disabilities, Physical Disabilities and Neurodivergence on Sleep

What has been described so far refers to typical sleep development in infants and children where there is no medical condition or disability that would have an additional impact on sleep. However, having a disability and specific disabilities is associated with disrupted sleep and patterns of sleep that do not fit the typical understanding of sleep. One example is cerebral palsy, a group of lifelong conditions that affect movement and co-ordination resulting from physical differences to the brain developed either in the womb or soon after birth. Pain, chronic pain, muscle spasms and breathing complications are associated with cerebral palsy and can disrupt sleep significantly (Dutt et al., 2015).

Similarly, children may have specific sensitivities to their environment, routines, noise and other sensory stimuli. Autistic children have a higher association with sensory sensitivity and may also experience more of an impact on their sleep due to this. In addition transitioning from wake to sleep may be more challenging if sensitive to change (Devnani & Hegde, 2015). An assessment and formulation is needed with an understanding of what sleep goals look like at that particular point in time for the child and their family, with specific guidance sought on the disability and sleep work (e.g. Cortese et al., 2013).

11.1.9 Sleep Assessment

Gathering information on what underpins the presenting sleep difficulties will help make sense of the experience and see where input may be helpful. The assessment guide that follows, whilst not exhaustive, has some areas that are helpful to cover for specific sleep-related difficulties. It should be carried out in addition to the child and family assessment outlined in Chapter 3 of this book.

- **Begin therapeutic alliance building:** sleep tends to impact the parent in more obvious ways than the child, so have empathy and space to listen to and validate their experiences and fears.
- **Sleep problem description, development and impact on child and parents**: what is the problem? How is it making life difficult for the child, parent and family, how long has the problem been going on for?
- **Bedtime and sleep routine and parental involvement at each stage**
  - What happens prior to bed
  - Bedtime routine
  - Night wakings
  - Morning period

  Contextualise this with the rest of the day-time routine (nursery? Do they go for walks with the buggy, scooting in the afternoon? No matter what the weather? Is the day varied or structured?).
- Use a **Sleep diary:** establish a baseline over 1–2 weeks (from the point of your contact with the family) of the sleep difficulty though a diary (see Figure 11.1).
- **Context**: What is happening for the family, environment, levels of deprivation, inequality
- **Sleep history:** find out about the development of the child's sleep. Have they always struggled? Appeared to challenge routines around sleep? Any patterns, disruptions, regularity of sleep to note?
- Establish whether the sleep problem might be **primary** (a sleep problem not caused by an underlying medical condition) or **secondary** (a sleep problem caused by a medical problem). Ask if medical options have been explored or indicated.
- Developmental history
- **Medical history**: any concerns, medical investigations, outcomes of these.
- **Parent information gathering**
  - Parent's experience of their own sleep
  - Parent's self-efficacy in context of problem: How confident do they feel about their role in helping their child with sleep difficulties?
  - Parent expectations around sleep and what informs these.
- **Cross-cultural stories**: on sleep (e.g., is co-sleeping more common, later bedtimes?), on parenting, on how to support children with difficulties.
- Helpful and less helpful aspects of previously tried sleep interventions.

	Monday – Ali aged 13 months Child goal: Sleep earlier and independently.	Monday – Jude aged 4 Child goal: Increase co-operation before bedtime. Reduce bedtime resistance.
Question		
1. How has the day been? • usual day routine • other, please specify	Usual routine but didn't leave the flat, went on to the balcony for air.	Usual. Playgroup in AM, playground play then pick up siblings from school in PM.
2. Did your child nap today? • When did they nap, where and for how long?	1 nap at 3.00 pm for 90 minutes in baby carrier sling.	No
3. What was your bedtime routine an hour before getting in to bed?	Playing with chew toys Bath	Watched x2 Australian-based cartoon about a dog family. Playing wrestling with sisters Bath, brush teeth after repeatedly asking I to Jude listen to me.
4. what time did your child go to bed at night? • Where and how?	9.00 pm In cot bed Holding my hand after partner did story time with Sheep toy playing white noise and infra-red night light as usual.	7.00 pm Refused bed shouting he's not tired, kept running around. Not listening. Eventually go into his racing car bed next to my bed (2 bedroom maisonette, siblings in bunkbed in other room). With softy and audio story by 8.00 pm. Would not let me leave the room said he was scared of monsters.
5. What time did they fall asleep?	9.30 pm!	8.30 pm
6. Did they wake up during the night? If so: • What time did they wake up? • What did they do? • How did you/other people in home respond? • How long did it take for child to resettle?	11.15 Woke up crying for mummy I went and held their hand and baby went back to sleep by 11.20 1.00 am Woke up crying for mummy, I held hand, offered milk bottle, back to sleep by 1.30 4.00 am woke up crying for mummy, I held hand, put baby in my bed, went back to sleep.	10.00 pm – shouted for me said he heard monsters, got into my bed. Stayed asleep. Partner slept on sofabed in living room. I slept with child in main bed.
7. What time did they wake up for the day?	7.00 am	6.00 am
8. How would you rate the quality of their sleep? (0-5)	2	1
9. Total hours slept in 24 hours	10	9 hours
10. Any other comments		

Figure 11.1 Sleep diary example.

- **Questionnaires**
  - Infant: Brief infant sleep questionnaire (0-3; Sadeh, 2004).
  - Younger child: Child sleep habits questionnaire (Goodlin-Jones et al., 2008; Owens et al., 2000).
- **Goals for change through the intervention**: goals for child, goals for parent. Use goal- based measures (Law & Jacob, 2013) from: https://www.corc.uk.net/outcome-experience-measures/goal-based-outcomes-gbo/

11.1.10 Tracking Sleep: Sleep Diaries and Sleep Apps

Technology to Support Sleep Tracking: The role of technology to support the monitoring of sleep for behavioural interventions in children is limited. Sleep apps Sleepio and CBT-i-based apps are available to adults with insomnia. Sleepio is NICE recommended as a digital therapeutic resource to adults who would otherwise be offered sleep hygiene or medication (NICE, 2022). The app has a function to record and track sleep that could be used, and some CBT-i apps have a feature to share sleep diaries with a practitioner. If a parent is seeking a digital way to record their child's sleep another option is editable sleep diaries, which can be found using an up-to-date internet search. One example at the time of writing this chapter is: https://thesleepcharity.org.uk/information-support/children/sleep-diary-for-kids/

11.1.11 Formulation

Five P's Formulation: The 5Ps in Chapter 3 can be used to support an understanding of how sleep problems have developed, how they have been triggered and maintained. This would be consistent with adult theoretical models of insomnia such as Spielman et al. (1987) who use a diathesis-stress '3P' model that explains sleep problems can develop based on the individual's predisposition to sleep. Precipitants may result in sleep problems that are then perpetuated by changes aimed at short term alleviation of the problem, which unintentionally makes things more difficult.

Transactional Model of Sleep-Wake Development Informed Formulation: Goodlin-Jones et al. (2000) and Sadeh and Anders (1993) proposed a useful, more in-depth bi-directional transactional model of sleep–wake development that highlights the role of the parent-and-child interaction in sleep regulation. It is also useful in highlighting the dynamic and multiplicity of factors that contribute to sleep regulation specifically in infants. In Figure 11.2 it has been adapted to include more detail around contextual influences and the parent factors that may influence the sleep-based referred problem.

A Psychoanalytic-informed Formulation and Approach: Formulating sleep challenges from a psychoanalytic position, specifically in the context of sleep, was developed by Dily Daws who used a brief session(s) format. (Daws, 1989 and Daws & Sutton, 2020). A psychoanalytic informed formulation of sleep according to Daws posed that sleep challenges were challenges in the parent-child relationships that were not known to them consciously. Bringing this in to awareness whelp address the underlying relational issue and create shifts in the relationship to the problem and the sleep behaviour itself. Daws encouraged practitioners involved in providing brief sleep focused-sessions to slow down and refrain from jumping in to offer solutions and strategies to parents straightaway.

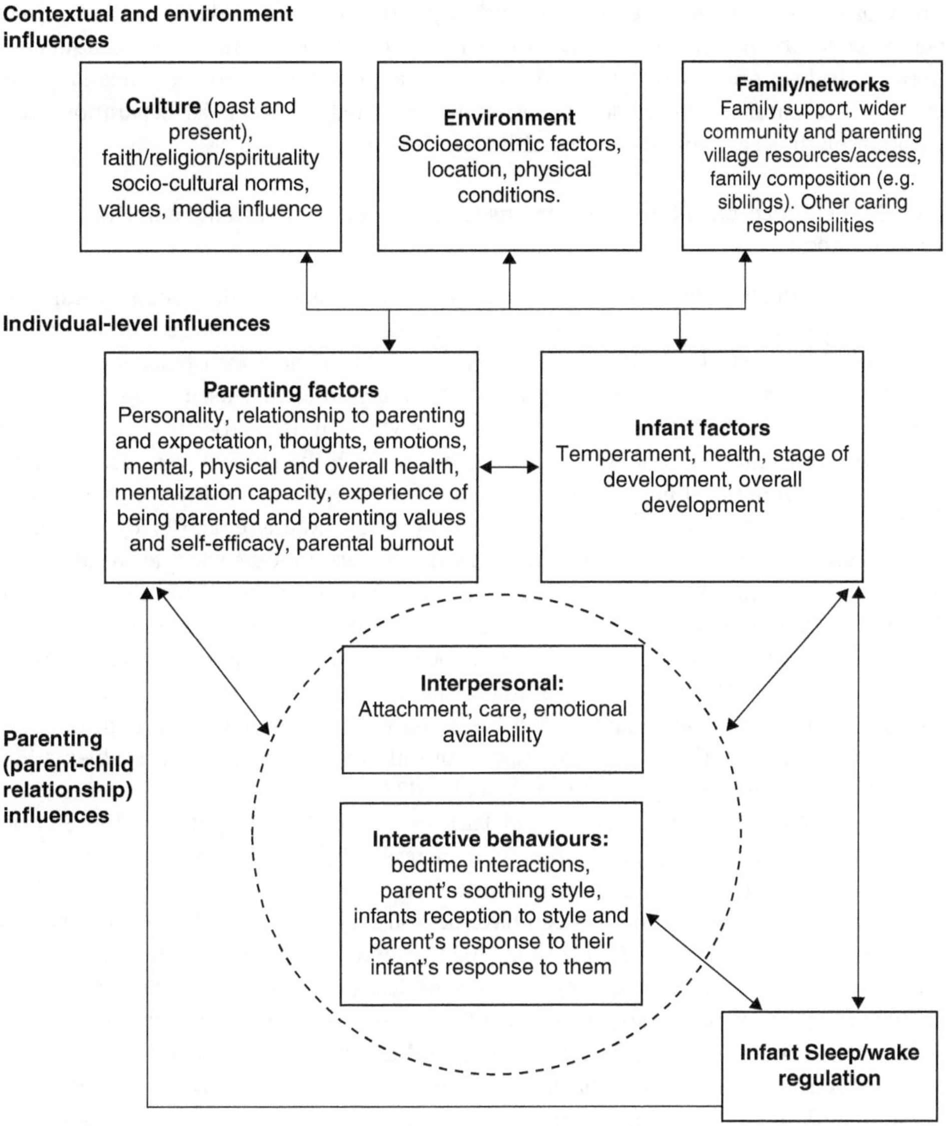

Figure 11.2 0–5 Sleep formulation. *Source:* Adapted from Sadeh et al., 2010.

Instead, Daws used a combination of structured questioning into the baby's timetable and then 'free ranging' open questions into memories of the pregnancy, birth, parent's relationship with each other (where applicable) and the parent's relationship with their own parent (see also see Fraiberg et al., 2003). This observational stance aimed to encourage to discoveries and connections about the baby and themselves as parents. Bringing these connections between emotions and experiences in the parent-child relationship into conscious awareness can creates shifts where things have previously been stuck (Daws & Sutton, 2020). Often this centred around enabling the parents to differentiate themselves and their emotions better from their children.

Some of Daws' influence is embedded within the intervention guidance section below. Notably where the psychological practitioner is encouraged to see the baby's uniqueness to move outside of previously stuck or fixed ways of approaching a problem, meaningfully exploring the parent's experience of sleep, the framing of 'sleep as separation' and individuation thus centring the parent–child relationship.

11.1.12 Evidence-base for Interventions for Sleep-based Challenges in the 0–5 Age Range

In the United Kingdom, the United States and western, industrialised, capitalist countries, behavioural-based interventions are typically used to help families where there are sleep challenges. Reuter et al. (2020) conducted a systematic review into behavioural sleep interventions in the 0–24 month age range, retrieving studies that used sleep education, behavioural interventions and baby massage, reviewing studies across two groupings of 'prevention' and 'intervention'. The countries from which the studies were drawn came predominantly from the United states and Canada for the behavioural-intervention review and New Zealand and Australia for the prevention review. Reuter et al. (2020) concluded from 12 studies that from 6 months onwards there were modest short-term effects of behavioural interventions including extinction methods such as 'cry it out'. 'Cry it out' has a varied definition in research. It typically refers to a parent/carer letting their infant cry and not responding to their cries, and usually occurs in a sleep-based situation at night (Davis & Kramer, 2021). There were limits to the education and mixed results on baby massage. Another systematic review and meta-analysis of 10 randomised control trials showed that behavioural sleep interventions not only reduced child sleep problems but also improved maternal sleep quality (Park et al., 2022).

However, both Reuter et al. (2020) and Park et al. (2022) highlight how there is no one clear definition of sleep difficulties used in research, making evaluating outcomes challenging. Instead, subjective parent reports of total sleep duration, number of night wakings and difficulties settling to sleep have been used as outcomes to indicate success of an intervention. Although Park et al. (2022) highlighted that, despite their review showing reduced sleep problems, there was no significant reduction in night wakings. This challenged what it means for an intervention to be effective and whether extinction-based behavioural methods are meaningfully making a difference. Both reviews are clear that the consequences of extinction behavioural methods are challenging to parents, which is consistent with other studies and commentaries suggesting the overstated and seemingly short-term benefits of extinction methods (e.g. Davis & Kramer, 2021). Reuter et al. (2020) also draw attention to the need to understand how behavioural sleep interventions work across developmental stages, the overlooked area of the role of the other parent/second caregiver in relation to sleep and how to apply cross-cultural sensitivity in sleep research.

There are no specific National Institute of Health and Care Excellence (NICE) guidelines on behavioural management of sleep in the 0–5 age range at the time of writing. Managing sleep as part of a broader difficulty is referred to within in some child-specific NICE guidance (e.g. Autism Spectrum Disorder in under-19s, NICE, 2011 [updated 2017]).

Whilst the research in sleep interventions are growing there is still some way to understand the separate components of intervention (routine, education etc) to see what provides the most effective and sustainable change. In the next section, sleep psychoeducation (commonly used in adult sleep problems) and behavioural sleep-based interventions are described.

11.1.13 Sleep Psychoeducation

Safer Sleep Advice: In this section behavioural-based sleep interventions will be summarised. These are also implicitly underpinned by safer sleep guidance. Typically, parents of newborns are given written safety-based guidance on sleep and how to reduce sudden infant death syndrome (SIDS), how to use slings, swaddle and co-sleep safely. These are reinforced through health visitor appointments. The most up-to-date information can be accessed via the Lullaby Website https://www.lullabytrust.org.uk/. The key pieces of advice you need to hold in mind stem from research supported guidance that aims to reduce the risk of sleep associated SIDS.

- Babies should sleep on their back at the foot of the cot.
- The cot should be kept clear.
- A firm, flat waterproof mattress should be used.
- Keep the environment and baby smoke free.
- Avoid baby overheating.
- Sleep baby in the same room as parents for at least the first six months.

Sleep Hygiene' – Encouraging Sleep Practices that Support more Regulated Sleep: Supporting parents to establish, re-establish and to try to set a foundation of good sleep is an important early step in making changes towards their child-based sleep goals. Often referred to as 'sleep hygiene', the practitioner may wish to use the terms 'positive sleep foundations,' 'setting up for success with sleep', as alternatives. It is important to explain the rationale behind these practices and involve the parent (and child where possible) to shape the guidance to work for their family.

Typical Child Development and Sleep Development: Helping parents understand how sleep typically works in the 0–5 year age range is an important first step. How sleep changes depends on the development of the internal circadian clock and the experience of sleep pressure – both of which are under-developed and will regulate and adjust to their environment over time. Night consolidation of sleep begins at 3 months at the earliest and there are practical strategies to provide external cues to regulate the circadian rhythms. Useful resources include: https://www.nhs.uk/conditions/baby/caring-for-a-newborn/helping-your-baby-to-sleep/ or the sleep foundation: https://www.sleepfoundation.org/baby-sleep/baby-sleep-cycle

Overall Sleep Environment: Our circadian clocks prime us to sleep when it's dark and be active and alert during the day. Parents should be encouraged to keep the bedroom dark, quiet and cool in temperature (approximately 18 °C). If early morning light wakes up the child, then blackout blinds may be needed. Dim night lights are fine if it doesn't disrupt sleep and helps the child feel calm rather than overly alert and active. Research on the role of blue light emitted from smart devices before bedtime has several methodological limitations and strong conclusions and generalisations based on these are cautioned.

Bed–sleep Association: Where possible, it is helpful to try to create an environment that is associated with sleeping. This may not be possible for many reasons. Sometimes changing the bedding, for example, using a 'daytime throw' that is used to cover the bed during the day when it's used for more active things may help differentiate the associations. Involving pre-schoolers in choosing bedding, moving their furniture to create a refreshed environment to start a new bed–sleep association may also help. There may be certain textures that are soothing, pillows that are cosy and cuddly toys specific for the bedtime experience that can build positive associations.

Consistent Bedtime Routine: Regular, consistent bedtime routines offer a strong behavioural cue for sleep. Bedtime routines can include:

- calm activities – colouring, stickers, low frustration toys
- bed-time snack (e.g. banana, yoghurt)
- bath-time
- brush teeth
- story time
- dim lights
- lullaby
- cuddle/kiss/ goodnight

Nap schedules: Keep a consistent age-appropriate nap schedule. Most children being to wean off their daytime nap from age 3 years. Keep daytime nap(s) consistent enough and with enough wakefulness between the nap and the bedtime.

11.1.14 Common sleep challenges in 0–5 years age range

Bedtime Resistance: 'My child refuses to go to bed, they try every trick in the book, it's exhausting. Every night, there's something different but one thing that remains the same is they will do anything, anything to not go to sleep' (Parent of a 5-year-old child).

It is common for children to resist bedtime and understanding what might be going on for the child will support what the practitioner targets. For example, a child might be missing their parent, may be seeking their attention, they may be scared about what happens when they go to sleep. If they cannot verbally articulate what is happening this may make things more difficult. These situations can often result in a power struggle with toddler and pre-schooler and whilst the parent retains their authority and leadership, encouraging a model of shared problem solving rather than parent vs child can support this. It may be important to think about the parent's needs and validate their experiences in order that they might be able to engage with this. Some ideas to support 'bedtime battles' resistance may involve:

- Model a curious approach to what the child might be communicating with their resistance, perhaps it is fear around separation, the dark or too early a bedtime. Help the parent to have space to think about what their feelings are when there is resistance (e.g. feelings about their capacity to parent, fears about pressure on their time). A space for parents to pause to think can sometimes lead to some degree of change because the relationship to the sleep problem has shifted slightly.
- Consider the role of 'special time' or 'connection time' (see Chapter 12) to strengthen the parent–child relationship and increase cooperation. When a child feels connected to their parent they are more likely to be open to changes. Building this 'connection capital' for the referred problem may take a little longer but there is often an 'in-the-moment' impact of a child receiving their parent's attention that is observable and helps keep the special time practice going.
- Developing a consistent routine, considering if there are developmentally adapted ways to include the older toddler, preschooler (e.g. what bedtime story is read together, what soft toy stays in the bed).

- If power struggles are key, help the parent to role play the bedtime routine with their child during daytime play. Parents can support their child to use their favourite soft toy to 'get ready for bedtime'. This can involve pretending to bath it, putting on pretend nightwear, reading a story and getting them all cosy in a pretend bed. Encourage the parents to follow their child's lead and tell them or show them what their teddy likes or doesn't like. This can sometimes be an informative experience for parents. Encourage parents to refrain from asking too many questions and follow play principles.
- Using role play in the day with the older toddler and pre-schooler to walk through the new bedtime plan.
- Create a list of the bedtime routine, magnet boards, white boards or a printed list might be appropriate (free examples can be found from internet searches: https://www.twinkl.co.uk/resource/bedtime-routine-visual-chart-and-cards-us-he-68). This can serve either as a 'now-and-next' step approach. There may be boxes to 'tick' when the stage has been completed.
- If the bedtime resistance is due to an unhelpful association see Section 11.1.15, Breaking Unhelpful Associations.

If parents are articulating their baby is 'resisting' sleep this will require further unpacking. It may be the infant is experiencing 'colic', which is a term used to describe a baby crying without an obvious cause. This can create stress within the parent who may feel they are missing something that could be important for their baby's health. If all else is well medically the parent may need help to gently shift their relationship to the resistance by acknowledging how it is making them feel.

11.1.15 Breaking Unhelpful Associations – Graded or Extinction-based Behavioural Interventions

Unhelpful sleep associations describe links that are developed between sleep and another condition which makes it hard or impossible for the baby or child to sleep without the presence of that condition.

It is important to establish with the parent the context of the unhelpful association and how it developed, for example, whether there are internal and/or external pressures. This may be complicated to establish and it may not be clear cut. There are two types of extinction-based behavioural interventions that have been researched and have shown effectiveness when the outcome has been defined as the infant/child sleeping by themselves and waking less at night.

The Challenge Of Extinction – 'Cry-it-out'-based Methods: Whilst the authors do not advocate for 'cry it out' as a preferred first line approach to sleep challenges, it is important that a psychological practitioner is aware of the method, it's history and guidance. This is a controversial intervention, known as 'controlled crying' that involves a parent putting their child to bed and ignoring their crying for set time intervals in order for their child to learn to 'self-soothe'. As humans we have evolved to respond to cries and, understandably, ignoring crying children has been shown as difficult for parents to accept (Etherton et al., 2016). It challenges attachment-informed responsive parenting, which has established longer-term positive outcomes for the child (e.g. Landry et al., 2006). This is contrasted with controlled crying showing an unclear long-term picture and no clear effects on the immediate reduction of night waking (Park et al., 2022).

The concept of infants being able to self-soothe is also poorly defined; it tends to refer to the infant being able to settle back to bed independently. Although whether this is self-settling or teaching an infant/child that their parent will not support them when they cry in the moment and potentially longer term (the two may co-exist) is not clear. It is an emotive area; the risks of crying it out are poorly understood and may also be overstated and cry it out may unnecessarily villainise parents who are just trying their best. Babies also cry a great deal in contexts where outside of the cry it out the relationship is loving and environment is safe and 'cry it out' needs to be understood in the context of a parent's key task in being able to support their child through difficult feelings and distress. It is important to retain a non-judgemental and curious position as a child psychological practitioner when discussing this strategy.

The cry-it-out method itself has evolved from exclusively ignoring the child's cries at night-time to ignoring their child's cries for a specific set period of time (e.g. a few minutes) sometimes referred to as the 'Ferber method' after Richard Ferber (Ferber, 2006). It typically consists of:

- Putting your child to bed awake in a ready to sleep state.
- Say goodnight and leave the room. Start with checking in after 5 minutes and wait progressively longer periods of time before checking on the child in the night until they fall asleep.
- Increase the initial waiting period before checking each night – usually by 5 minutes increments.
- During each check the advice is to keep it brief, calm and neutral.
- Timings are adjusted based on parent's ability to tolerate crying and the individual child's personality and temperament.
- This is advised from 6 months onwards.
- Parents are advised to be consistent, persistent and follow through.
- Using this method, Ferber (2006) proposes that parents might find their child is able to sleep through, by themselves, within 7–10 days.

Fading/Extinction with Parent's Presence: In this method the parent remains present and gradually 'fades' out of the child's sleeping space over a longer period of time (Mindell & Owens, 2015). This may be more acceptable to parents then 'cry-it-out' and 'controlled-crying' methods. It involves:

- Identifying the specific goal for the parent to do with the child's sleep (e.g. sleeping independently, or not needing to hold my hand to fall asleep).
- Individualise a plan that involves steps to reaching the goal.
  - Establish bedtime routine.
  - Parenting staying with child whilst they fall asleep.
  - Parenting moving further away.
    - Three nights sitting nearby but not next to the bed with accompanying clear script 'Time for bed etc'.
    - Three nights sitting a few more feet away
    - Three nights in the doorway, three nights outside the doorway, in the corridor, on the stairs etc,

Evidence Based Parenting Informed Ideas for Sleep Challenges: There are more ideas to support sleep-based interventions that use social-learning theory and attachment-based principles that underpin evidence-based parenting based work for children with difficult to manage behaviours, encompassing a child-centred, responsive approach. Ideas include:

- For the younger child and infant (0–1 year) see whether parental support and parent self-care can aid their capacity to 'contain' their child's distress associated with sleep. A more rested, more supported parent is likely to feel more self-efficacious in their parenting.
- Help parents develop their own self-soothing or self-supporting statements or regulating actions in the moment, for example, 'this will not last forever, I'm trying my best, my child doesn't need me to solve this but to weather the storm with them' or use visualisations that help bring more calm and regulation.
- Discussing realistic expectations and reminding parents to remember that sleep progress is not linear, although painful! There will be progress and setbacks as with many things, changing like the weather! Expecting sleep quality to remain identical from night to night can cause difficulties.
- Use song and rhyme to communicate safety. 'You are cosy and safe, mummy/daddy/name of parent or carer are close to you/always near and here for you'.
- Explore ways parents can be 'present' in their child's room without being physically present. A transitional object (Winnicot, 1951) that represents the parent might include a photo of them, a cuddly toy that is particularly special because it has been given the parent's 'extra special cuddle' to pass to the child.
- Consider night lights if they are not stimulating or distracting to a child.
- Use stories to help the child manage feelings.
- Try relaxation with the child, baby massage, rocket breaths or hot chocolate breathes that entail short breaths in and 'o' mouth shaped breaths out that are long and slow, as if cooling down a mug of hot drink.
- Roleplay the sleep routine in the day with toys.
- Role play the bedtime routine during the day. Encourage playfulness in this, reverse the roles!
- Encourage the parent to be clear about their necessary boundaries to support good sleep routines for the family and follow through. This means if there is distress, the parent can be present through those feelings and trust the process and their plan.
- It's okay to make mistakes, setbacks are common. It's okay to change the strategy – in a planned way.
- The child might be upset about bedtime separation and going to bed – tolerating their feelings, including their tears with the parent's containing (see Bion's [1962] concept of containment and Winnicott's [1945] concept of 'holding' along with the attachment chapter in this book for more background) presence can help build up the child's own capacity to tolerate distress.

Night Wakings: If night wakings are happening due to sleep-onset associations refer to the earlier section on sleep-association.

Nightmares and Night Terrors: Nightmares are upsetting and distressing dreams that that occur during REM sleep that the individual might wake up from and usually has some memory of.

> *Parent of a 4-year-old child:* 'It's like she was taken over by an intense fear and she stared right through me, flapping and screaming mummy over and over, vocalising sounds I couldn't decipher – she then went immediately back to bed as if nothing had happened, looking peaceful and angelic, and I was left shaken, she was none the wiser the next day.'

This quote describes a night-terror experience from the perspective of a parent. A child is not likely to have any recollection of how much impact their screaming and their lack of responsiveness to their parent's attempts to comfort have had. Night terrors are a type of parasomnia that occurs during NREM sleep, occurring in them the early part of the evening sleep (within the first few hours of sleep). Night terrors are more common in young children but adults can also have them. During night terrors, the person talks and moves about with their eyes open, but they are asleep and usually unable to acknowledge the concerned person in front of them. It is rare to remember having night terrors. They are common between the age of 3 to 8 years and are associated with other sleep conditions such as restless leg and sleep apnoea. Being over-tired or unwell can impact deep sleep and therefore increase the likelihood of night terrors happening. Night terrors are not considered harmful. Some helpful guidance for parents follows.

- Maintain a regular sleep–wake routine to minimise over-tiredness.
- Stay calm when a night terror is happening.
- If the child is moving around, ensure the environment is safe around them. Consider safety gates at the top of stairs and corridor night lights if the child moves around.
- Be present but do not try to 'wake' them as this may prolong the terror or disrupt sleep.
- The night terror will pass, they usually last no longer than a few minutes to 15 minutes and are usually far shorter.
- Guide the child gently back to their bed if they are amenable to do so.
- If they are having night terrors every night at the same time, the parent could try scheduled awakenings 10–15 minutes before the anticipated night terror, which can sometimes disrupt the onset.
- Avoid detailed discussions the next day as the child is unlikely to remember. Discussing the parent's upset and fears about it could lead the development of feelings of shame, avoidance and anxiety in the child.

Other Sleep Supports: Whilst this chapter has focused on behavioural-based interventions, there are other interventions that the psychological practitioner should be aware of and prepared to consider, refer to and recommended. This includes baby massage; a practice widely used outside the west and which commonly forms part of programmes offered in family hubs and children's centres. There may also be music classes, sensory groups, play groups, baby yoga.

A Note on Treatment Delivery Mode and Session Frequency: The Covid-19 pandemic has seen the positive impact of online sessions in increasing accessibility and flexibility to psychological-based interventions, including access to fathers, but this has not been without challenges and it continues to be an evolving landscape. With the need to provide a cost-effective service whilst holding service-user satisfaction and collaboration as key, there are a number of considerations when delivering sleep-based support to families.

Sleep-intervention studies are starting to show that online delivery has been found to be acceptable to parents of children with neurodevelopmental differences (Tan-MacNeill et al., 2023) and low-income families in the United States (e.g. Adams et al., 2023). However, parenting-based literature and NICE guidelines maintain the need to increase effort to reach parents through individualised approaches that may involve community work, home visits and increased weekly contact (NICE, 2013).

Parent Wellbeing: The psychological practitioner's assessment and intervention plan may involve supporting the parent's wellbeing. This may involve supporting referrals to specific parent–child support or adult psychological services such as increasing access to psychological therapies (IAPT) services. It may be that a parent's wellbeing can also be enhanced by helping them to use their own system and network as a source of support. This may also involve connecting with other parents with similar struggles in person through groups or online communities.

Using a Consultation Model: Psychological practitioners may be providing their input to families indirectly, via a another professional involved in the families care. This will involve a consultation process that will draw upon the balance of evidenced-based and formulation-driven work described in this chapter. Whilst a comprehensive overview of consultation models in community settings is beyond the scope of this chapter, one model that may be helpful to psychological practitioners is a 'behavioural consultation' and the 'conjoint behavioural consultation' when working jointly with the system around the child by Bergan and Kratochwill (1990). The model consists of four main stages and involves working with the professional to identify the problem, collaboratively analyse and formulate the problem, plan the intervention and its delivery and subsequent evaluation. It is sometimes referred to as a 'problem-solving consultation' to support the consultee: 1. problem identification; 2. problem analysis; 3. intervention implementation; and 4. treatment evaluation.

Example set of behavioural sleep sessions:

1. Engagement, assessment, baseline measures, goal setting plus sleep diary homework.
2. Review sleep diary plus co-develop formulation and refine goal setting.
3. Psychoeducation around sleep in the 0–5 age group.
4. Behavioural intervention in context, behavioural changes homework.
5. Review, adapt and continue to refine until goal and desired goal rating has been reached.
6. Evaluate, write-up sleep plan blueprint, end of intervention measures, experience of service questionnaire.

See Box 11.1 for a clinical example.

Box 11.1 Clinical example: Ozzy

Tony (he/him) and his partner Nathan (he/him) have been referred for the sleep struggles they are having with their 3-year-old, Ozzy (he/him). They describe Ozzy as an energetic, talkative child who has struggled to sleep by himself since he was a baby. Tony has been the main carer because his work has more flexibility, whilst Nathan works long hours in a hospital, which includes night shifts. Tony reports that he is exhausted and has 'tried everything' to help Ozzy to get to sleep and that 'nothing seems to work'.

(Continued)

Box 11.1 (Continued)

Tony is autistic, and is wandering if Ozzy might also be autistic, this doesn't worry him, but he is wondering whether Ozzy has associated sensory sensitivities that mean Ozzy is unable to fall asleep without having Tony right next to him. Ozzy gets very upset if Tony is not there holding his hand whilst he is falling asleep, and when he wakes up in the night, which usually happens once a night or more if he's had a very busy day. Ozzy has his own room and sleeps in a toddler bed with guard rails. Tony and Nathan have a network of LGBTQ+ multiracial families online but have little practical help outside a daytime nanny three times a week. Ozzy has not been to a nursery yet because Tony worries that 'it will be too much' for Ozzy. There are no medical concerns.

Possible Considerations

Assessment

- Explore the context of the presenting problem and for whom and how it's a problem.
- Ozzy's perspective is not clear, what is the potential to involve him to support him communicating how he feels about his own sleep experience at night? Are their creative ways to do this through child-led play or stuffed toys for example?
- Does Ozzy nap? How different or similar is his sleep during these periods.
- What is the impact of parenting Ozzy on Tony as the 'main' carer and how supported is he, what is the potential for further support?
- Explore the strengths and potential challenges of being a same sex multiracial couple and its relationship to how help around sleep is broached.
- Use a sleep diary to understand what how a week in their life works. Explore Tony's reports of Ozzy's 'sensitivities'.
- Is Ozzy on any waiting list for a neurodevelopmental assessment?
- Does his nanny have a perspective on Ozzy and his sleep, even if she isn't directly involved in this?

Formulation

- Use Sadeh's formulation or the 5Ps.
- It is possible that Ozzy has developed an understandable (because seeking comfort from your caregiver is expected) but unhelpful, sustainable sleep association with only needing to hold Tony's hands to fall asleep and so experiences separation anxiety when Tony let's go? There may also be a sensory need and difficulties with transitions (from wake to sleep and being apart from Tony) that add to the challenge.

Intervention

Depending on Tony and Nathan's goals you might consider the following:

- Reviewing the sleep routine, involving Ozzy, to include familiarity, predictability and perhaps some sensory input alternative to holding Tony's hand the whole time such Toby stroking Ozzy's hand for 5 minutes.
- Fading/extinction with parent's presence. Consider how you would prepare Toby and Nathan to sit with Ozzy's distress when they challenge the sleep association.

Evaluation

- Consider how improvements are evaluated with pre and post measures and session-by session-ratings. Does Ozzy settle to sleep sooner? Does Ozzy need Tony's hand less and less and is coping with this? Has Tony and Nathan's stress reduced and parental self-efficacy improved?
- If Ozzy's sleeping without Tony's presence doesn't improve, reformulate and continue to hold the wider context in mind.

11.1.16 Conclusion

This section has aimed to distil the wide range of sleep differences in the 0–5 year age range by outlining sleep information across this age group and highlighting developmental differences within this age range. A systematic approach has been taken to describe some concepts around sleep, how to assess sleep problems, how the psychological practitioner might formulate sleep challenges, the research on interventions for sleep where there is a behavioural component and a summary of the interventions with plenty of practical guidance.

11.2 Feeding Problems in Children Aged Under 5 Years

11.2.1 Introduction

The focus of this section will be on common, transient, feeding problems that parent/carers often report in this age group, with ideas on how a psychological practitioner might approach these challenges and when to refer a family for further help. More information on eating difficulties for older children can be found in Chapter 15. Other chapters that will be helpful to read alongside this section are Chapter 3, Chapter 12 and Chapter 17.

11.2.2 The Multifactorial Nature of Feeding Problems

The act of feeding is complex. There are a number of influencing factors, occurring in the context of parent–child interactions and it can be an emotional aspect of parenting. A parent wanting to feed their child well is a primitive, basic act, rooted in survival instincts. Therefore, when problems arise, it is understandable that a parent's emotional response (e.g. fear of failing at parenting) forms a part of their conceptualisation of the problem. The causes and contributors to feeding problems include medical, anatomical, developmental, temperamental, social and environmental factors (Goday et al., 2019). Difficulties in these areas can impact nutritional intake, which in turn are associated with reduced growth and reduced weight gain (sometimes described as 'faltering growth' or 'failure to thrive'), developmental impacts, poorer longer-term health outcomes as well as emotional dysregulation

(Tang et al., 2021). Caregiver stress is also associated with feeding problems and societal messaging and financial disparities can contribute to this distress and its impact on child outcomes (e.g. Didehbani et al., 2011).

As a result of these of factors implicated in feeding, professionals including paediatricians, dieticians, occupational therapists and speech and language therapists may become involved in offering feeding-focused assessment, consultation and interventions. Once these medical and mechanical factors in feeding and eating problems have been, or are concurrently being addressed sufficiently, the associated emotional and behavioural influences and challenges can be explored through a psychological practitioner's involvement.

11.2.3 Diagnosis and Problem Description

Children with feeding difficulties may also have a medical diagnosis that is associated with feeding difficulties. For mental health-based diagnoses related to feeding or eating, the fourth edition of the *Diagnostic and Statistical Manual of Mental Disorders* (DSM-IV, American Psychiatric Association, 2000) previously recognised 'Feeding disorders of infancy and early childhood' before replacing this with Avoidant Restrictive Food Intake Disorder (ARFID) in the fifth edition (*DSM-5*, American Psychiatric Association, 2013). ARFID is described as a pattern of eating that avoids certain food groups and/or is restrictive in quantity with a persistent failure to meet nutritional/energy needs associated with weight loss. This is described in more detail in Chapter 15. In this chapter the focus will be on common feeding problems psychological practitioners may come across in the under-five age range.

11.2.4 Feeding Development in the 0–5 Years Age Range

A psychological practitioner should have an understanding of the typical developmental milestones for feeding and use their assessment to understand the differences for each family. Table 11.4 provides a short overview of some of the skills associated with the complex area of feeding and eating and should be read in context with Chapter 3. More detailed descriptions can be helpful and are available on local NHS websites, for example: https://www.justonenorfolk.nhs.uk/child-development-additional-needs/developmental-stages/

11.2.5 Child Development Overview

Typical feeding development begins in utero (mouth opening and swallowing amniotic fluid and the development of the 'non-feeding' suck) and is a dynamic physiological and psychological process. Infants and young children move from sucking to weaning (soft foods to firmer, whole foods) to more mature eating and drinking. This development parallels development in other areas. A brief summary of the early stages of feeding development follows.

Between 3 and 6 months the infant's anatomy evolves from feeding predominately on their back, looking up, to becoming more upright with their increased head control and

Table 11.4 Skills development for eating.

General skills • Facial expressions to show dislike of taste. • Imitating and interacting with others.	
Motor and cognitive • Holding and mouthing • Sitting without support • Pointing at objects • First words e.g. 'no'	**Specific feeding skills** • Sucking and swallowing • Gag reflex • Tongue control and movement • Opening mouth • Biting foods • Chewing foods • Spoon feeding • Self-feeding (e.g. holding food in hand, drinking from closed cups)
Taste, texture and food preferences • Acceptance and rejection • Texture progression (liquid, puree, mashed, lumps) • Eating preferences, smells and tastes	**Appetite regulation** • Signalling hunger • Signalling feeling full up (satiety) and dislike

Source: Adapted from: Infant and toddler forum factsheet: https://infantandtoddlerforum.org/wp-content/uploads/2020/02/ITF206-Factsheet-3.5-Developmental-Stages-Dec19-v1.pdf

sitting balance. Weaning, the early introduction of solid food, typically starts with introducing soft foods at around 6 months of age (NICE, 2015), and with increasing exposure to more solid textures and different temperatures of food, babies develop their sensory and motor skills. Typically, babies initially prefer sweeter textures and tastes. The baby's jaw, tongue and lip movements tend to push food out more than in at first, and with more experience they gain control and range.

Between 6 months and 1 year self-feeding skills such as holding a spoon, accepting harder textures (e.g. crackers, breadsticks, carrot sticks) become common and chewing develops slowly, at this stage consisting of up and down movements. Babies may be drinking from 'sippy' cups or beakers for some drinks, with their milk intake, often due to psychological associations of comfort and habit, remaining with their parent (breast/chest feeding) or bottle. Children are usually teething at this stage, where saliva dribbling, and non-nutritive sucking are common (e.g. dummies, mouthing objects and toys). The combination of different textures of food, saliva and exploration through the mouth means that feeding is messy! Children often want to feel and explore their food with their hands and mouth. This is an important experience that helps them to integrate their sensory system through making links between touch, movement, taste and oral motor functions.

Between 12 and 24 months children are becoming more skilled eaters, chewing and biting with more control. The mouth and throat stages of eating become more distinct which means that children can hold food in their mouth before swallowing, or not swallow and spit it out instead. It is more possible for children to eat mixed textures (sauce, vegetables) but it is common to still require the sorting of food so that they are not mixed, to permit more control for the child. This coincides with 'neophobia', where a child may become suspicious of new food experiences including tastes and textures. Exploration of new food is more possible where the child feels in some control.

From 2 years the fine-tuning process of eating and drinking continues, with biting, chewing and swallowing a range of food. Children are increasingly more mobile, demonstrating their autonomy, asserting their immediate needs. This may mean they are unlikely to sit still for long, can become frustrated easily as their communication, emotional, physical and motor skills develop but may not synchronise to support them with the many tasks that face them (e.g. getting frustrated when they cannot quite verbally communicate an intense negative feeling around food they have been given; they may have wanted their toast cut into squares not triangles and so may throw their food or shout and get upset rapidly). A contributor to what can appear to be fussy eating may be the ongoing development of feeding based self-regulation.

Between 2 and 3 years children continue to refine their feeding skills developed so far. Gradually children learn to express food preferences verbally and tolerate changes and socialise more at family mealtimes. This includes family cultural practices around mealtimes, reflecting how social aspects of mealtimes become part of a child's awareness. Children continue to become more independent in their eating and feeding (and in other areas too). Skills may include being able to use a blunt knife to cut soft foods, using a spoon and fork with less and less spillage over time as their control increases.

11.2.6 'My child does not eat' and Other Parent-reported Feeding Problems

Feeding children provides multiple opportunities, daily, for the parent and child to interact. There are a number of parent-reported eating-related challenges typically seen in the 0–5 year age range. Some of these are problems described by parents are descriptions of their child having 'fussy eating' habits. There is no clear consensus on the definition of fussy or picky eating (Taylor et al., 2015) but some descriptions used by parents include:

- their previously 'good eater' as a baby becoming an erratic eater now that they are a toddler;
- refusing to chew and eat;
- taking a long time to eat;
- refusing to try and eat new foods/suddenly refusing familiar food;
- fussy eating (can often have different interpretations) or selective eating;
- sensory sensitivities/food aversions; and
- other behavioural reported issues at mealtimes (e.g. not sitting still, running back and forth between the table and play, spitting food out, throwing food).

The list provides descriptions of problems so that the psychological practitioner is familiar with some of the ways difficulties may be reported and referred to. These problem descriptions will all require an understanding of their presentation that is connected to the child's broader family and context.

The following sections will summarise an assessment, formulation and intervention model, with brief notes on the contextual factors that might impact how the psychological practitioner understands and supports the referred feeding-based difficulty.

Assessment: Figure 11.3 is an assessment guide to aid psychological practitioners supporting common feeding difficulties. This does not cover a paediatric feeding assessment or an interdisciplinary feeding-based assessment. The assessment is presented in sections, but

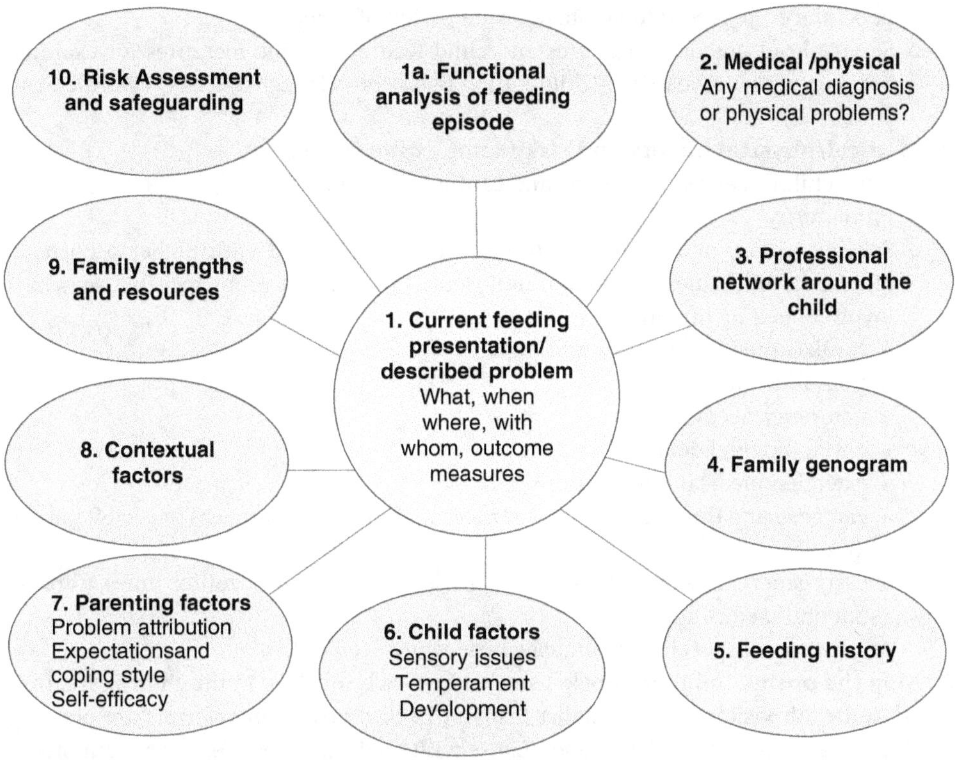

Figure 11.3 Assessment overview.

the process may not always be linear and many of the sections are interconnected. It draws upon a typical child psychological practitioner assessment (see Chapter 3) with specific feeding and eating areas highlighted in Dovey at al., 2008.

1. **Current feeding presentation and parent feeding practices**
   - How are difficulties described? When do the challenges happen: where, with whom, how? What observations from different perspectives are there (e.g. other parent/carers/siblings/nursery/school)?
   - Parent feeding practices (e.g. control and coercive practices).
   - Include a functional analysis (1a), an observational method to record what observable variables impact behaviour in a specific situation of interest. Typically, practitioners use a three column antecedents, behaviour and consequences (ABC chart) to structure observations about what happens before, during and after a problem behaviour. For the purposes of assessing feeding difficulties, the authors recommend starting with this chart and adding notes that occur to the practitioner during an observation in an additional column.
   - Settings, times, child behaviour, parent behaviour and response, quality of interaction, observed distress/emotional response.
   - Emotional climate at mealtimes (e.g. high stress, rushed, family conflict, parent concern).

  - Food diary – to record food intake over a period of time.
  - Service level outcome measures and child feeding specific measures for example, between ages 2–8 years the Child Eating Behaviour Checklist; CEBQ (Wardle et al., 2001).
2. **Medical/physical history and risk factor exploration**
   Explore children at risk of feeding and eating difficulties:
   - Prematurity
   - Specific history or current conditions that are associated with higher occurrence of feeding difficulties due to oral-motor and oral-sensory problems (that may have involved feeding therapy):
     - cardiac and respiratory conditions,
     - gastrointestinal conditions,
     - neurological conditions,
     - developmental delay,
     - extended medical interventions,
     - ear, nose and throat disorders or structural/function differences (e.g. cleft palate), and
     - early experiences of feeding skills, e.g. use of feeding tubes, reflux, tubes, unpleasant oral medications.
   - Any history of speech and language service involvement.
3. **Map the professional network:** Check who else is involved in the child's care, from GP to health visitors and specialist teams. Check if any other referrals are pending. Obtain permission to make contact. Liaise with medical colleagues to confirm predictive growth trajectory for child.
4. **Family genogram:** map the family system and relationships (see Chapter 3). Who is involved in the main feeding role of the referred child? What are their perspectives on the referred problem?
5. **Feeding/eating History**: How has feeding been prior to the presenting difficulty from birth onwards. How was bottle/breast/chest feeding, how was the transition to weaning, any difficulties?
6. **Child factors:** Temperament, style and personality, developmental/neurodevelopmental concerns.
7. **Parenting**
   - Impact of feeding difficulty on family, including parent/carers.
   - Parent expectations and attributions of feeding difficulty.
   - Parent's own experiences of feeding/eating impact on their parenting.
   - Parent beliefs about hunger regulation.
   - Parent awareness of food preference development.
   - Parent feeding practices (see Daniels, 2019 for a summary):
     - coercive, non-responsive to the child, authoritarian, restrictive,
     - emotional feeding – over emphasis on food as response to negative emotions, teaching their child to eat for reasons unrelated to appetite,
     - unstructured, permissive, disorganised feeding environment, and
     - neophobia response that only offers preferred food, forces or pressures to eat food.

- Consider role of Brief Parental Self-efficacy Scale (BPSES; https://www.corc.uk.net/outcome-experience-measures/brief-parental-self-efficacy-scale-bpses/).

8. **Wider context/contextual factors**
   Feeding difficulties in context of wider repetitive or restricted behaviours:
   - culture,
   - societal stories, messaging and norms,
   - family stories, expectations, and
   - faith and spirituality influence on food intake (e.g. fasting, holy days or rules around consumption of food groups).
9. **Family strengths and resources**
   - What has gone well and are there examples of overcoming and getting through difficulties?
   - What support can they harness from within and from their networks?
   - Any observations the practitioner has that they can feedback that might support the work (e.g. the parent's playfulness, creative mind, willingness to try)?
10. **Risk and safeguarding**
    As with all child and family assessments, risk and safeguarding should form part of the assessment and ongoing readiness to assess and respond (see Chapter 3, for more detail). In the context of this chapter, signs of safeguarding flags may relate to harmful parenting practices and the child's faltering growth (see Faltering growth section later in this chapter) and concerns about neglect. The practitioner should seek more information if safe to do so, consult with local safeguarding and Duty social care workers as well as using their own supervision when making assessments of risk and safeguarding, involving the parent if doing so will not increase risk of harm to others.

A clinical example (Box 11.2) illustrates the assessment, formulation, intervention and evaluation process.

Box 11.2 Clinical example: Maya

Maya (she/her) is a 2 year old referred by a health visitor because her mother, Gaby (she/her), reported that she has always been a 'fussy' eater, but things have got 'much worse' recently where she is refusing to eat food she previously ate as well as refusing new foods offered.

Maya is British born Honduran (Central America) living in Kensal Green, an inner-city area of north west London. She was born at 34 weeks and has had a number of successful medical interventions to support her breathing, gastro difficulties and overall growth associated with her premature birth. Her mother reports that since 11 months of age there have been no concerns about her development; she has reached typical milestones. She continues to be monitored by the hospital team.

Gaby is a single parent and has 5-year-old twins who attend the local primary school. Maya's other parent, her father, lives just outside London and she visits him every fortnight with her siblings. Her parents separated a year ago. Maya's mother reports

(Continued)

Box 11.2 (Continued)

that Maya has a small and limited appetite. Her mother says she has stopped eating their cultural food from Honduras, especially 'her favourite' baledas (tortillas that Maya would usually eat with avocado and cheese and a few mashed sweetcorn pieces). When her mother serves her food at mealtimes, Maya refuses. Gaby finds it difficult that Maya rejects food from their culture and worries that Maya and her brothers will not see Honduran practices as relevant to them the older they get. Maya will eat the fruit and cucumber pieces and insists on having cereal when her mother asks her what she wants to eat. Her mother gives her the cereal because she worries all the time that Maya will not get her daily food intake. Maya's mum reports that she throws food, spits it out when she tries to feed her and screams. This can go on for a long time and is disruptive to family meal times. Her father has said she eats better when she with him but 'whenever she feels like it' and describes her as 'grazing' throughout their day and says that this doesn't particularly worry him.

Maya attends nursery 2 days a week and eats the range of food that is served there. Occasionally, Maya will say that she is not feeling hungry at nursery mealtimes and will have a piece of fruit at the next food point (usually snack time).

Formulation

A working, shared hypothesis along with the '5Ps formulation model', referred to in Chapter 3, can be used to support an understanding of the development of feeding and eating difficulties and maintenance factors. An example formulation follows.

Working hypothesis

Maya is potentially presenting with neophobia in the context of typical protesting (adult-boundary resistant) behaviour in a toddler that is communicating the need for control, choice and safety around food and mealtimes. At present, because Gaby is struggling, this is experienced as stressful for them both.

Family

Maya (2 year old, referred child), mother, Lucas and Mateo (5-year-old twin brothers), dad (living 1.5 hours away), dad's partner and newborn daughter, Marissa.

- **Predisposing:** Born prematurely, which is associated with difficulties that can impact feeding. Preference for sweet foods.
- **Precipitating:** Working hypothesis of a developmental stage of neophobia. Impact of parental separation and divorce, plus new baby in dad's family. Transitions might be experienced as unsettling.
- **Presenting/current difficulties:** Food refusal, fear of new foods, unsettled at mealtimes when given new foods and previously 'safe' foods, predominately in main home with mum.
- **Protective/strengths, resources:** Gaby has access to parenting support from families at the hospital who have had shared experiences. Maya has sustained her growth trajectory despite reports of restricted eating by her mother and the food diary that her parents completed showed that she was eating across the range of food groups,

although food in each group was limited when she was with her mum. Nursery team are supportive and keen to share what's worked well for them collaboratively with mum.

- **Perpetuating patterns**
  Maya, in her safe space and relationship with her mum protests loudly about her limited and reduced food preferences. Contributing factors to this behaviour may be the developmentally typical stage of neophobia long along with change that Maya has experienced with her parent's separation and new pattern of being with her parents.

Observation

MUM PRESENTS FOOD TO MAYA: Please eat Maya, you haven't eaten since breakfast
MAYA: No, mama
MUM: You have to eat. (Mum's understandable worry, distress and parenting pressure)
MAYA: No
MUM: You'll grow big and strong like your brothers, eat your dinner, go on, mama spent a long time cooking special food for you, just the way you like (pleading tone)
MAYA: No (repeat x 3) escalates. Coco pops. Screams.
MUM: You've already had coco pops twice today!
MAYA: No. Coco pops now!!!
MUM: Maya...
MAYA: No. I WANT COCO POPS (inhales to take a deep breath) NOWWWW!
MUM: Okay, shh shh shhh, fine, fine, – only tonight, though. We try again after coco pops or tomorrow.
MAYA: Sits quietly and eats coco pops.

In this cycle Gaby's fears of Maya's health and potential poor growth are triggered in the context of her reported feelings of helplessness and sleep deprivation in a stressful single-parenting situation and her fear of her children disconnecting from their heritage. The stress that Gaby experiences with Maya's escalating behaviour results in her giving Maya the food that she would prefer not to give in order to meet some of the needs that Gaby is anxious about and to reduce the unwanted boundary pushing behaviour from Maya, quickly.

Goals
Gaby (parent)-led goals: To be calmer during mealtimes, plan food choices better, to help Maya feel more comfortable around new food experiences and/by increasing her feeling of control. Maya (child)-led goals: Unable to verbalise specific therapy goals due to nature of adult-led intervention but pointed to wanting to try cheese cubes again from food photos in the assessment. Mum's goals for Maya to be more open to trying eat cheese and bean soup again.

11.2.7 Intervention

Behavioural based approaches are generally recommended in University College London's Child and Adolescent Competence frameworks (Douglas, 2002). However, since ARFID is a relatively new, heterogeneous diagnostic category, the evidence base and up to date reviews, especially for the under-five age range, is limited (Archibald & Bryant-Waugh, 2023). This chapter aims to adapt older feeding intervention guides with evidence-based parenting principles (underpinned by social learning theory, behavioural theory and attachment theory, in context) where a more behavioural intervention would be indicated for a family's referred child feeding problem.

Most approaches for this age range advocate for an interdisciplinary assessment/information gathering that leads to a stepwise approach to difficulties (Milano et al., 2019). Following an assessment that has sought to exclude explanations for feeding difficulties that could be accounted for any medical and oral development challenges (often for the psychological practitioner this will involve liaison with the referrer, health visitor team and GP to gather this information), guidelines are offered on limiting aversive feeding practices that have been assessed as contributing to the feeding difficulty.

Psychoeducation Resources: Each NHS Trust is likely to have guidance provided by health visitors and feeding teams. The national website is helpful starting point with clear information in written and video format for parents and carers.

For under 2s, guidance can be found here: https://www.nhs.uk/conditions/baby/weaning-and-feeding/what-to-feed-young-children/

https://www.nhs.uk/conditions/baby/weaning-and-feeding/fussy-eaters/

For over 2s, The Eat Well Guide: the NHS's 'Eat Well Guide' uses a dinner plate image to reflect a type of diet that is considered 'healthy', focusing on five main food groups These are: fruit and vegetables (5 portions a day); starchy foods (1/3 of daily food intake); proteins; milk and dairy alternatives; and oils and spreads. Other fats, salt and refined sugar are outside the Eat Well plate in order to promote the minimal need of these in the diet. https://assets.publishing.service.gov.uk/government/uploads/system/uploads/attachment_data/file/528193/Eatwell_guide_colour.pdf

Whilst the guidelines show the range of food needed for children under age 5 years, the practitioner will need to take a balanced, contextualised approach in setting the above gold standard as the expectation for parents who are struggling with their child. For example, the Children's Future Food Enquiry (2019) showed that only 8% of children over the age of 2 met their fibre recommendations. Current NHS guidance is that in the context of 'fussy eating' parents should focus less on what their child eats in a single day, and more about what they eat across a whole week and ensure there is food eaten across the Eat Well food groups. Provided the referred child is active and gaining weight over time and are generally healthy then it can be assumed that they are getting enough to eat. Food is not only eaten for nutrition.

Behavioural and Parenting-based Interventions: The dominant approach to neophobia, selective eating and fussy eating is graded exposure over time to new foods in the context of a safe parent–child relationship. This is underpinned by evidence-based parenting intervention principles (see Chapter 12, for generalisable principles and parent 'coaching'). Figure 11.4 gives an example treatment outline for Maya with key considerations of the broader context of delivering an intervention.

11.2.8 Working with Parents/carers

Chapter 12, will have a specific focus on how to work collaboratively, using a non-judgemental approach with parents. In general, the practitioner will need to develop a therapeutic alliance with the parents/carers and validate their fears and concerns about their child. Keeping connected with medical colleagues who are supporting aspects of the feeding difficulty and collaborating on the conceptualisation of the social-emotional and behavioural basis of the feeding difficulty will be important.

It may be helpful to consider whether the parent's anxiety is contributing to the development and maintenance of the described feeding difficulty. The psychological practitioner may feel, after speaking with the parents/carers, that the anxiety or distress is broader than

Stage	Steps
1 Assessment and formulation development	• See assessment section
2 Shard Goals	• See assessment section
3 Intervention	• Aim: Repeated, consistent, no pressure, close to neutral, exposure of food to child underpinned by child development knowledge.
Psychoeducation	• How children eat, Maya's developmental stage being consistent with neophobia and asserting her emerging independence.
Joining up the system around Maya	• Although work is directly with Gaby and Maya to include nursery and consistent-enough practices across settings, where feasible.
Increasing Gaby's parental self-efficacy	• Addressing the coco pops: The observation and formulation identifies that Gaby's fears around faltering growth make it hard to say no to Maya and 'contain' and tolerate Maya's distress enough to impose a reasonable boundary. Giving feedback from the food diary and that Maya is thriving aims to reduce Gaby's anxiety. Aim to support Gaby to become aware of triggers in the moment and how they impact food decisions she makes. Gaby does not need to stop giving coco pops, but offer it alongside other preferred or 'safe' foods to work towards her goal of increasing the variety of food Maya eats. Role play can support generalisation of parental skills. Measured, neutral observational or 'descriptive commentary' comments on Maya's efforts may be helpful for example, 'I see how you have tried something new, and it wasn't easy for you, but you gave it go'. Practitioners can help parents prioritise describing the child, their behaviour and their evolving relationship to the food and eating, instead of labelling the food itself 'Yay you ate healthy broccoli!' This form of praise based commentary can be helpful with feeding concerns (e.g., Kohn, 1993; Maimarian & Fishbach, 2014).

Figure 11.4 Example Intervention guide for a therapist working with Maya and her parents.

Graded inclusion of new 'food exposure'	• Choose new, non-preferred food to taste that is close to the range that child already eats. • Present half a centimetre of new food alongside their usual food. Ensure it is served alongside food that Maya typically eats. Have no expectations and give minimal parental fuss over new food presentation and/or if their child decides to eat the new food. • Help parent to adjust to typical child behaviour around exploring food (looking at it with suspicion, smelling, licking and putting it down, poking it). Another recommended behavioural approach is for the child to have to eat the new food before they can continue onwards to their preferred food (Douglas, 2002). However this chapter takes a view that sustainable change is achieved over time, through encouraging intrinsic motivation over time and limiting extrinsic motivation (see Kohn, 1993). • Continue to present non-preferred food regardless of whether they engage with it or not and if child distress is low and remains low and the new food is normalised into the mealtime, consider increasing the size of the food/and or another new food. [Repeat until parent and child goals are reached]. • Consider parent modelling around non-preferred food. It doesn't need to be 'neutral' – they can sit and eat their plate of food alongside their child, model their own curiosity, eat the food and carry on, with no lecture or pressure to child. • Some protocols may indicate use of a reward system such as a sticker chart when new food is eaten. This is not in keeping with the chapter's position on scaffolding a child whose eating is restricted, however the psychological practitioner should consider the use of reward systems on an individual basis, with a view about the likely long-term impact, in supervision, in context. • Meet with Maya's father to explore differences.
4 Review	• Review whether intervention is helping work and meet the goal attainment rating. • This is a process that takes time that may fall outside the number of sessions the practitioner can offer. Use supervision to decide whether more sessions/referral is needed and if not focus on whether the parent has a grasp of the principles and stamina to continue without direct input. Write up an individualised guide for the food, and share it, with permission, with other professionals involved. Consider offering sessions that are more spaced apart and empower parent to monitor their own progress in between.

Figure 11.4 *(Continued)*

the feeding difficulty and supervision will support thinking about the most suited and available service for the family at that point in time, including individual and/or family therapy.

When feeding isn't going well it can highlight ideals of 'good' parenting. The idea that children 'should' eat in a certain way can imply there is a perfect way to parent, which can result in feelings of failure for the parent. Having an understanding of the parenting context and pressures that parents face in a world where parenting can be isolated, and encouraging the positive use of social media, books and aids that help reduce self-blame and increase parental self-efficacy can, in turn, mediate child outcome (Teti et al., 1996).

Information on Children's Eating: Helping parents and caregivers understand that children do not eat like adults can help them to re-evaluate their expectations when this forms part of the formulation of the problem.

- Young children are generally good at knowing when they are hungry and knowing when they are full. This is not always consistent with the structure of meal times that families may have established. Socialising children to this structure takes time and requires a flexible approach, working alongside the child if the parent is experiencing resistance to meal time structure.
- Children's appetites can fluctuate.
- Children need to 'grow', and growth is an important indicator but it is not always linear. There are growth charts that can be referred to in the child's 'red book' (personal child health care record) to show the expected rate of growth.

Some areas relevant to a practitioner's understanding of feeding difficulties with brief notes on how the practitioner might consider these areas with their referred child and family follow.

The Language of 'Good and Bad,' 'Unhealthy and Healthy' and 'It's Not Good For You!':

Food is not inherently 'good' or 'bad' on its own, and the concept of 'healthy' and 'unhealthy' without context can be unhelpful, villainise food, create shame, pressure and contribute to disordered eating in older children and adults. Children, with their more concrete thinking, may internalise eating 'bad' food as being a 'bad' person with morally labelled food. 'Good' food may become confusing too, for example, if 'carrots are good for your eyes' it may create fear that not eating carrots will make you blind. No one food does one thing, particularly in small amounts. Children will also notice that adults do not say similar things about other foods, for example, 'eat ice-cream, it has lots of calcium in it which help you grow big and strong'. Similarly with the use of the word 'healthy'; broccoli might be described as 'healthy' but it might become 'unhealthy' if it's the only thing that is eaten all day for many days. Instead, holding back from labelling foods in general can be more helpful than sending what might seem like positive, but are ultimately reductive messages about food and nutrition.

When parents are asking the practitioner to help their child 'eat healthily', gently exploring what they mean by this and referring to balance, control, choice and trust in their child's agency around food may support a more meaningful shift. It may also reduce future thinking about food that is binary, and could potentially contribute to disordered thinking. In the United Kingdom, childhood obesity often makes the news in alarming ways alongside trends of commentaries on 'processed and ultra -processed food'. Primary schools in England and Wales have an optional (although parents have to opt out not opt in) weighing scheme carried out in Reception (4/5 years) and Year 6 (10/11 years), which gives the child a rating on their weight – contextual factors like this might be understandably impacting on parental behaviour and anxiety.

The Role of Play and Food/eating: Children, and especially children under the age of 5 years, explore their world through play. As part of the assessment, the practitioner should look for instances outside potentially pressurised meal times for the child to 'play' with food. Playing with food can build familiarity and give access to other feelings around food apart from distress. This might involve play food and encouraging the parent to get involved with the play. Perhaps children under five want to plan picnics with their toys and decide what foods can be prepared for this (pretend, play food or even real). Parents over time may feel they can role play showing cautiousness or reluctance around a food item in the picnic (e.g. 'daddy's not sure about this raisin, it feels sticky and looks like a squished fly!') – and watch in wonder at their child's fascination at their parent's reaction, their response, or their complete indifference! If an opportunity presents itself where the child takes the 'bait' – they may give the parent some ideas about strategies to employ (e.g. 'lick it first daddy' or 'try the raisin in a sandwich').

The parent's role in play is associated with greater acceptability of foods by young children (e.g. Coulthard & Sealy, 2017). Involving children in some aspects of food preparation (e.g. spreading butter on toast or naan, scooping houmous on to plate, pulling apart segments of orange, mixing) can also support their exposure to food and take the pressure off food as something given to them that they 'have' to eat. Food isn't always eaten – cornflour, which can be used to thicken liquids, can be added to water to make something referred to as 'Ooblek', which is a bit like slime, acting like a liquid but turning more solid when squeezed. Dried pasta shells can be used as mosaic pieces or necklaces and bananas make great mobile phones. Playing with food may seem frivolous and wasteful and if parents raise these valid concerns it is important to be curious, understand these perspectives and build a shared way forward.

The 'Forbidden Fruit' Effect with Chocolate, Cakes, Sweets: Taking sweets, chocolates and 'treats' off their pedestal reduces their enticing appeal. This can be hard in a western culture that has a tendency to glamorise tasty, usually sweet, treats, that are generally fun and enjoyed by adults too. Restricting food items can be counterproductive. Offering it alongside the main meal can lessen this novelty (e.g. houmous, crudites and a square of chocolate/cake piece/three Smartie sweets). It may involve a huge shift for parents to have to not view it as a type of 'dessert' or reward: the 'eat your main food first, then you have your pudding' approach. The psychological practitioner will need to think carefully about the value of this idea, what informs it and the benefit of sharing this with the family. They should be anchored in the referred problem area and guided by family goals. The general notion here is that children need to experience these foods so that they can learn how to manage them, and restricting or controlling them can limit that from happening.

'Faltering Growth' (previously referred to as failure to thrive) and Obesity: In the United Kingdom there is an NHS focus on childhood obesity. This has not been without criticism and an in-depth discussion is beyond the scope of the chapter. Here, in this context, an individualised, multifactorial approach to supporting a child's feeding difficulty is advised. If there are concerns raised about weight, then specialist support should be sought.

Growth charts are used to 'catch' children who need further support and guidance should be sought on how this is defined locally in order to refer onwards. In children under 5 years, this typically consists of an interruption to expected rate of growth compared to children of a similar age and sex using the World Health Organization (WHO) growth charts (WHO,

2006). This is referred to as 'faltering growth', formally referred to as 'failure to thrive' (NICE, 2017). In the under-fives, weight crossing two centiles on the growth chart, falling below the second centile, weight that is two centiles below the length and height centile and crossing through both weight and length centiles, indicate further input is needed. This may include speaking to the health visiting team and GP to arrange blood tests and a review.

Body Affirming, Body Diversity and Role Modelling: Good advice to parents can be to model eating a variety of foods, normalising the range of individual feelings towards foods, curiosity about new foods, trying previously disliked foods and create opportunities to eat together. Parents can be encouraged to notice their own language about their own body, other people's bodies and their own child's body. They can be encouraged to move their body in ways that feel good (rather than a chore, or to 'make up' for something they ate). Children's books championing body diversity may support the beginnings of these conversations and shifts, for example, *Bodies are cool* (Feder, 2021). Parents may wish to do their own personal work on feelings about their body and its connection to how they view food and body image through their own psychological therapy or reading; *How to Raise an Intuitive Eater* (Brooks & Severson, 2022) and there are resources available on https://www.bodyhappyorg.com/

Cultural Differences in Food Practices: As with all psychological practice, taking a proactive position to explore every referred family's influences, including culture, language, impact of difference of living in the United Kingdom (e.g. experience of racism and discrimination, implicit or otherwise) is essential. The practitioner should consider their own position as a therapist and their proximity to or distance from the family and how this might shape perceptions they have about parenting practices, family life and feeding practices. With respect to food and eating there may be cultural practices that will help the understanding of the family context further. For example, fasting practices in Islam during Ramadan, fasting on specific dates throughout the year for the Hindu community, food during the Shabbat in Judaism and generally specific stories around food and it's function for different cultures and religions. The rejection of cultural food by a child whose parent is trying to nurture their child's identity and preserve their own heritage can add to the picture of emotions around food and the practitioner should explore this meaning when formulating the referred eating-based struggles. Dwivedi and Woodcock's (2011) chapter is an excellent place to start learning more about how to think about culture and feeding. It explores the way Indian, African, Middle Eastern and Caribbean cultures and practices provide a framework in which feeding can be understood. It describes the ways in which feeding practices have developed outside the west, varying influences (e.g. cosmology in the Hindu faith) and the tensions in how minoritized groups navigate adjusting these practices outside their original context.

Learning Disabilities and Neurodivergence: Feeding difficulties are particularly common in autistic children (Mayes & Zickgraf, 2019) and children with a learning disability and can be early indicators of broader, undiagnosed difficulties. An assessment will help explore whether the feeding issues may be related to broader sensory sensitivities and/or other rigidities. Helen Coulthard and Vicky Aldridge (Developmental Psychologist and Clinical Psychologist respectively) have developed and made available online a sensory play toolkit from their studies of the area (Coulthard et al., 2018), which some practitioners may find helpful: https://sensoryplaytoolkit.weebly.com/

When working with a child with a learning disability who has a feeding difficulty it will be important to work in a joined-up way with the team around the child and the various professions involved to do with eating/feeding (see Chapters 18 and 19 for further discussion).

When to Seek Additional Help: In addition to the 'faltering growth' section in this chapter, Milano et al. (2019) outline a number of 'red flags' that would indicate when the psychological practitioner should seek additional help when working with a child with feeding difficulties:

- Pain when feeding: This might be difficult for children who cannot verbalise and will require observations, adapted communication for the developmental state and parent report.
- Persistent vomiting and diarrhoea: Children are often exposed to common bugs whilst their immune system is still developing but persistent vomiting and diarrhoea that cannot be explained should be referred for physical investigations as well.
- Growth failure: see earlier section.
- Force feeding: If this is observed at any point, a careful and child-focused approach must be maintained, an explanation must be sought and safeguarding processes will need to be followed.

11.2.9 Conclusion

In the vast field of eating- and feeding-based difficulties in children, this chapter has focused specifically on common feeding difficulties that a psychological practitioner may come across when working with children aged under 5 years and their parents/carers, and offered an assessment framework, formulation guidance and a broad range of considerations when delivering a predominately evidence-based parenting intervention. Understanding a feeding problem in context is as important as understanding the remits of the psychological practitioner's own role and therefore joined-up working and knowing when to seek additional help outside the specific feeding difficulties context has been emphasised.

Further resources and links: For more information on the paediatric population 'Feeding Problems in Children' by Southampton and Martin (2011), whilst written a while ago, has a helpful range of topics and resources to support assessment and intervention with this group.

Child eating behaviour questionnaire: https://www.ucl.ac.uk/epidemiology-health-care/sites/epidemiology-health-care/files/cebqnoscore.pdf

UCL Child and Adolescent mental health competence frameworks
https://www.ucl.ac.uk/clinical-psychology/competency-maps/camhs-map.html.
https://www.nhs.uk/conditions/baby/weaning-and-feeding/fussy-eaters/

11.3 Toileting Difficulties

The final part of this chapter is focussed on toileting issues commonly experienced during childhood. These difficulties can have a significant impact on various areas, including psychological, social and health domains. This section aims to give a general overview of presenting issues that fall within this area and to support psychological practitioners in building basic competencies in the assessment and management of these.

11.3.1 Development of Continence

It is important to situate any toileting issues or difficulties within the context of typical development and common practices during childhood. Faecal continence is gained ahead of urinary continence, starting with nocturnal faecal continence then day-time faecal continence (Radford & Anderson, 2003). Many infants attain voluntary control of their bowels at around 18 months, however there is variability in the ages that complete bowel control is achieved (Bongers et al., 2007). It is suggested that the conscious awareness of a full bladder typically appears after the age of one (Touchette et al., 2005). Children begin to develop voluntary control of voiding urine around the age of two (Bakker et al. 2001). Day-time bladder control is achieved ahead of night-time control (Radford & Anderson, 2003) and by age four most children will have gained full day time and nocturnal urinary continence (Berk & Friman, 1990).

Toilet training is commonly initiated when a child is aged between 18 months and 3 years (Duong et al., 2013, Greer et al., 2016; Schum et al., 2002). However, commencement of toilet training has also been documented from very early on in infancy, from a few weeks to 6 months old (Berk and Friman, 1990; de Carvalho Mrad et al., 2021; Howell et al., 2010). This variance in timescales is likely due to various societal and cultural factors as well as differences in how toilet training is defined (Berk and Friman, 1990; Howell et al., 2010). Sex differences are widely reported: females have been noted to attain continence and toilet training milestones ahead of males (Howell et al., 2010, Mota et al., 2010; Schum et al., 2002). There are documented differences in initiation of toilet training between countries and between groups (i.e. ethnicities, socioeconomic status) within the same geographical locations (Horn et al. 2006, Horstmanshoff et al. 2003; Koc et al., 2008; Schum et al. 2001). There have also been shifts in trends over time; various studies note that the average age of initiation and completion of toilet training is later now than it was in previous decades (Schum et al., 2002; Tarhan et al., 2015; van Nunen et al., 2015).

There can be distinctions made in approaches to toilet training; those that are more structured, and adult led and those that are more child oriented, however there is no clear consensus on the most effective method to use (de Carvalho Mrad et al., 2021). Toilet training may be determined or influenced by a child showing signs they are beginning to develop bladder and bowel control (Schum et al., 2002; Wolraich, 2016) including showing an awareness of a wet or dirty nappy, going somewhere hidden whilst urinating/defecating or naming when they are urinating or need to do so. Practices are also heavily influenced by the context for example, within some developing countries or within specific cultural groups there may be increased motivation to toilet train children early on if there is limited use or access to disposable nappies or washing machines (Thaman & Eichenfield 2014). Furthermore, the parenting styles and practices of some individuals or populations will also impact how and when a child develops toileting skills. For instance, when there is a high level of physical contact and interaction between a caregiver and infant there may be better attunement and response to signals of elimination, such as body language and bowel and bladder noises (Berk and Friman, 1990; de Carvalho Mrad et al., 2021).

Toileting issues can occur at any age or stage of childhood; they can range from bed-wetting or wetting during the daytime, refusal to use a toilet/potty or to urinate in specific settings, defecating outside the toilet/potty or smearing faeces. This chapter highlights some prevalent concerns and those that psychological practitioners may encounter within their clinical work.

11.3.2 Prevalent Concerns

Incontinence: Urinary or faecal incontinence are common concerns within childhood (Collis et al., 2019). Within the clinical and research literature, there is often reference to elimination disorders. This term usually incorporates two main presentations, involving the developmentally inappropriate elimination of waste: enuresis and encopresis. Enuresis is when there is repeated voiding, involuntarily or intentionally, of urine into clothing or bedding. Encopresis is when there is repeated passing, involuntarily or intentionally, of faeces into clothing, bedding or other inappropriate places (i.e. onto the floor). The terms primary and secondary can be used to distinguish the nature and onset of presentations. Children with primary enuresis or encopresis are those who are soiling/wetting having never achieved bladder or bowel control. Those with secondary enuresis or encopresis are those who have achieved bowel or bladder continence but then begin soiling/wetting at a later point.

Withholding: Withholding of faeces can often occur when a child first begins toilet training but can also happen at other points (e.g. following a change of routine, when in an unfamiliar environment, following constipation or a large/painful bowel movement). A child may use their anal muscles to prevent themselves defecating when they feel the urge. Indications that a child is withholding faeces can include refusal to sit on the potty/toilet, denying the need to use the toilet, unusual body positions or posture or hiding away when they feel the urge to defecate. The withholding of urine is less common; this can also occur during toilet training and can also emerge following the withholding of faeces.

Toilet Avoidance or Phobia: Children may refuse to use a toilet/potty and may insist on continuing to use a nappy. This can occur following the initiation of toilet training but can also be a persistent concern. Avoidance may be associated with unpleasant or uncomfortable experiences (e.g. painful bowel movement, cold toilet seat, dislike of toilet flush).

A child may also develop anxiety or a phobia of using the toilet following a specific experience or incident. They may associate going to the toilet with this incident and therefore avoid going as a way of managing or avoiding feelings of anxiety or unease. There may be other worries associated with the toilet (e.g. dirt and germs, animals/ insects). Some children may also find it difficult to use the toilet when others are around; this is known as paruresis (inability to urinate) and parcopresis (inability to defecate) or may be referred to as 'shy bladder or shy bowel syndrome' (Soifer et al., 2009).

Smearing: Smearing refers to the spreading or wiping of faeces, for instance on the body or on walls. Smearing can be a way of communicating a need (e.g. discomfort); it can be a way of receiving sensory stimulation (i.e. sensation or smell). There may also be a desirable outcome following smearing for instance increased attention or opportunity for a preferred activity (e.g. having a bath or shower).

11.3.3 Defining Concerning Presentations

There can be variation in how issues are defined or understood. Some terms may be used interchangeably (e.g. wetting/bedwetting, urinary incontinence and enuresis or soiling, faecal incontinence and encopresis) and there may be overlap in some conceptualisations or descriptors.

It is important to distinguish between issues that are expected for a particular developmental stage and those that are more persistent in nature or significantly impacting on functioning. For instance, soiling or wetting accidents are not uncommon whilst toilet training is ongoing or if there has been a change in this or other routines. Even when toilet training has been effective, many children will still need reminders and prompts to use the toilet.

Incontinence symptoms are usually only considered problematic if they are occurring after the ages of four or five (in line with usual development of continence) and/or if they are impacting a child's functioning. Enuresis and encopresis are included in the *DSM-5* (American Psychiatric Association, 2013) and the *International Statistical Classification of Diseases and Related Health Problems* (11th edition; ICD-11; World Health Organization, 2019) as elimination disorders. Across both classification systems, an enuresis diagnosis can only be considered when a child is aged five or older and that of encopresis only when a child is aged four and over.

There can be variation in clinical presentation; the nature and severity of toileting issues can differ between genders and across the lifespan and concerns can also spontaneously resolve (Harari, 2013; Sarici et al., 2016). It is also important to acknowledge that our understanding and knowledge of these issues are grounded within certain contexts (e.g. social, cultural, historical). The conceptualisations of developmental milestones or specific concerns presented above are from a westernized/industrialized society lens, therefore there will be limits to how these ideas can be interpreted and applied.

Underlying and Contributory Factors: There are specific health conditions (e.g. urinary tract infection, spina bifida, epilepsy, diabetes mellitus, and sleep apnoea) that can impact urinary and faecal continence. Factors such as bladder storage capacity and hormonal imbalances may also impact the process of waste elimination. Many toileting issues can be due to, or impacted by, constipation including faecal incontinence, withholding, avoidance and faecal smearing.

Ineffective toilet training techniques or delaying toilet training until later than necessary can contribute to issues. It is also important to note that those who have had adverse experiences in their early history (e.g. neglect, developmental trauma, changes in caregivers) may have had limited opportunities to achieve these skills.

Whilst genetic, psychological, emotional or social variables may not always have a causal link to common toileting concerns, it is nevertheless important to acknowledge how these factors impact on the emergence and maintenance of presenting issues. For instance, evidence suggests high heritability of incontinence issues (Breinbjerg et al., 2023) therefore there may also be a family/parental history of some toileting concerns. Children may experience a loss or regression in toileting skills due to a change or disruption to their routines (e.g. moving house or arrival of a sibling) or following traumatic events (Mota & Barros, 2008). Some presentations, such as secondary nocturnal enuresis, can coincide with or emerge following psychological or social stressors including parental separation, bereavement or issues within school (Robson & Leung, 2000). Freudian psychoanalytic theories propose that toilet training is a key experience within the anal stage of psychosexual development. During this stage the source of pleasure shifts from the mouth (oral stage) to the anus, bowel and bladder and a child gains satisfaction from the elimination or retention of waste (S. Freud, 1905, 1908). From a psychoanalytic/psychodynamic lens, toileting difficulties can be seen as a manifestation of an underlying conflict, for instance reflecting themes of loss, separation anxiety, aggression and power struggles between a parent and child (A. Freud, 1965; Howe & Walker, 1992; Pinkerton, 1958; Schoenewolf, 1997).

Associations between neglect and abuse (i.e. physical, sexual) and toileting concerns, such as constipation, faecal incontinence and smearing have been explored with variable findings and prevalence rates (Boon, 1991; Cohn, 2007; Dubowitz et al., 1993; Nieuwhof-Leppink et al., 2019). Sexual abuse can result in damage to a child's genital or anal area and may lead to sexually transmitted or urinary tract infections. This may impact continence, for instance an overactive bladder (Lai et al., 2016). Female genital mutilation (FGM) can also lead to difficulties with continence and urinating (Payne et al., 2019). Neglect and abuse could be precipitating factors for toileting issues, equally, toileting concerns may contribute to experience of abuse, neglect or isolation (e.g. in response to accidents). It is important to consider that changes in toileting behaviour and any health problems (e.g. soreness in the genital/anal area, infections) may be possible indicators of risk or safeguarding concerns.

Low socioeconomic status and exposure to poor living conditions have been highlighted as potential risk factors for some toileting concerns (Abali et al., 2006; Rajindrajith et al., 2010; Van der Wal et al., 2005). Access to adequate toilet facilities (i.e. private, accessible, clean) may impact toileting behaviour and the emergence and maintenance of certain concerns.

Some toileting issues can have a high co-morbidity with other conditions; for instance, children with attention deficit hyperactivity disorder (ADHD) are more likely to experience incontinence issues (Mellon et al., 2013). Children presenting with persistent or significant toileting difficulties may experience increased behavioural or emotional difficulties, such as poor self-esteem, isolation or peer conflict (Nieuwhof-Leppink et al., 2019). Attaining full urinary and faecal continence is a key developmental milestone; it is therefore important to hold in mind that any suspected or confirmed concerns around a developmental delay will impact on continence and toileting behaviour.

The Role and Remit of Psychological Practitioners: Support for toileting issues may be sought from a GP or a health visitor in the first instance. These healthcare professionals will be able to evaluate whether the difficulties fall within the range of 'typical' problems and importantly screen or assess for any organic or medical causes that are contributing to the issues.

Psychological practitioners can also use their core clinical skills to good effect, for those presenting with concerns around toileting, within clinical settings. The level and nature of input provided by practitioners will of course be dependent on their role and context.

Table 11.5 Potential support areas for a psychological practitioner.

Potential task	Details
Providing information in relation to typical developmental and key milestones	• Sharing typical ages/timeframes that certain skills may emerge. • Dispelling any myths or misconceptions around child development.
Supporting effective toilet training	• Advice about environmental adaptations (e.g. ensuring child's feet are supported when using an adult toilet, having toys/books near potty). • Effective rewards and reinforcers of skills.
Providing information about the physiology of waste elimination	• Recognising proprioceptive cues to urinate or defecate. • Body parts involved in urinating and defecating and what happens in the body if there are persistent toileting issues.
Outlining the rationale for certain interventions (including medication/medical investigation)	• Intended role of laxatives/stool softeners for constipation. • Maintenance cycle of anxiety/fear and the benefit of graded exposure.

11.3.4 Psychoeducation

One of the key roles that practitioners may play is that of an educator or information provider. In addition to providing general information to support optimal health and wellbeing, the work of a psychological practitioner may also include areas shown in Table 11.5.

For those working within multidisciplinary settings it may be more appropriate for other colleagues to take the lead in providing information relating to physiological processes or medical aspects of care. However, effective psychoeducation does not necessarily require a practitioner to have 'expert' level knowledge; it can also encompass signposting or redirecting to relevant information or services. There is a wealth of information and resources available online including those developed and published by ERIC, the UK's leading Children's Bowel and Bladder Charity (eric.org.uk). Practitioners should also be mindful of the limits of their knowledge and their positioning; for instance, acknowledging their status as a non-medical professional or being clear what is underpinning the guidance they are giving (i.e. personal/lived experience, commonalities in clinical practice, specific policies).

Psychoeducation will be likely to permeate different stages of clinical input. It may be incorporated into triage or assessment processes and more easily facilitate information gathering (e.g. providing information about typical developmental markers may enable a parent/carer to give richer details about a child's history). Equally, standalone psychoeducation could be a sufficient and effective intervention for a child or family.

11.3.5 Assessment

Drawing on the key assessment skills outlined in previous sections of this book will be fundamental for the psychological practitioner's evaluation and management of these concerns. To support the development of initial hypotheses and establishing the priorities for care, particular attention should be given to:

- ascertaining what advice or input has already been sought (including medical evaluation, medication);
- assessing physical health and other lifestyle factors (e.g. diet, eating habits, daily routines, sleep);
- noting what strategies or targeted interventions have been trialled and to what effect
- gathering a full and comprehensive developmental history;
- mapping out the familial and wider network and their perspectives on the concerns;
- evaluating the child and family's psycho-social needs;
- establishing child/parent goals and motivation for change; and
- assessing any risk concerns.

In addition to this, practitioners should consider a numbers of other areas.

Language/terminology: It is important to establish a shared understanding and vocabulary from the outset. As noted earlier, certain terms or labels may be used interchangeably or may have different meanings within different contexts.

It is useful to note how a child or parent/carer talks about specific difficulties and any factors that affect this (e.g. certain terms used or avoided in the presence of the child). Practitioners should also clarify what they mean when using certain terms, including acknowledgement of how this may align or differ to others' use or understanding.

Given the nature of the difficulties (discussion of urinating, defecating, genitalia etc.), assessment should include establishing what terms are preferred and which are appropriate for the child's age and developmental stage.

Understanding the emergence and context of issues: It is important to establish a clear timeline of concerns (i.e. when they first emerged, occasions when difficulties improve or worsen) alongside other relevant contextual factors (i.e. key transition, stressors, significant life events). This will be essential for understanding if there are specific triggers for the presenting issues, for instance a presentation of secondary enuresis/encopresis following a traumatic incident. These details will inform the plan and priorities for intervention and further support.

Individual and familial values: The assessing clinician should aim to get a good sense of the context in which these issues are emerging and to be mindful of the differences and nuances in toileting practices and behaviours. A comprehensive assessment should include attendance to demographic, cultural, religious factors and also the unique perspectives and values of the child/family. Practitioners should demonstrate a curiosity about how the family connects with certain norms (e.g. age to initiate toilet training), their views on what behaviours are considered atypical and also get a sense of attitudes and expectations within a household (e.g. can the potty can be used anywhere or restricted to the bathroom? Is the child allowed to accompany the parent when they are using the bathroom themselves?).

Toileting readiness, habits and patterns: Practitioners should ensure that they have enquired about experiences of toilet training/learning for the child. Within this, clinicians should also evaluate the child's readiness for mastering these skills; Friman and Freeman (2010) propose that this is done across six specific domains:

(a) Physical readiness (e.g. can pull up and down pants, pick up small objects, sit independently).
(b) Bladder readiness (e.g. dry for several hours).
(c) Language readiness (e.g. have learned 'toileting words').
(d) Instructional readiness (i.e. can follow at least one-step commands).
(e) Proprioceptive readiness (i.e. shows some signs of awareness of need, act or outcome of urinating).
(f) Emotional-social readiness (i.e. attuned relationships with caregivers, increased self-determination, ability to emulate the actions of others).

In the case of incontinence issues, the assessor should consider asking the parent and/or child more specific questions to determine the nature and extent of difficulties. The questions shown in Table 11.6 (adapted from Friman & Freeman, 2010) may be posed.

In relation to soiling it may be useful to describe stool using a scale. The Bristol Stool Form scale (Lewis & Heaton, 1997) is a commonly used tool within clinical settings and is often supplemented with images to aid evaluation. The scale details seven types of stool, which are described in Table 11.7.

Voiding diaries, records of toileting successes and accidents, or ABC charts (details Antecedents, Behaviour and Consequences surrounding events, which may be valuable for understanding underlying needs of behaviours such as smearing) may also be helpful tools to establish frequency of accidents, volume of waste and any patterns. Examples are shown in Tables 11.8, 11.9 and 11.10; practitioners should adapt these to suit their needs.

Parental Response to Issues: Practitioners should also discuss with parents/carers what their usual responses are to incidents of incontinence or other undesirable behaviours. Given the nature of these difficulties and the potential for feelings of shame, guilt and embarrassment, it is crucial that practitioners make efforts to name this and to

Table 11.6 Potential questions for specific incontinence issues (adapted from Friman & Freeman, 2010).

Difficulty	Potential questions
Enuresis	1. Does your child ever dribble in their pants during the day? 2. Does your child need to go more frequently than you think is normal? 3. Can your child delay urination for a period of time after sensing the urge without having an accident? 4. Does your child complain that it doesn't feel like they have completely emptied their bladder when finished? 5. Does your child ever complain of burning when they urinate? Have you ever noticed any irritation around their genitals? 6. Has your child ever had an investigation for a urinary tract infection or any other urinary problem?
Encopresis	1. How often does soiling happen? Does it occur at the same time each day? 2. Describe the consistency of accidents and bowel movements (e.g. hard/pebbles, soft, runny). 3. How often does your child have a bowel movement? How long has this pattern been present? 4. When your child has a bowel movement, does it smell worse than it should? 5. Does your child have a history of painful bowel movements?

Table 11.7 Bristol Stool Form Scale (Lewis & Heaton, 1997).

Types	Indication
Type 1: Separate hard lumps, like nuts (difficult to pass)	May indicate constipation
Type 2: Sausage-shaped, but lumpy	
Type 3: Like a sausage but with cracks on its surface	Ideal stools as they are easier to pass
Type 4: Like a sausage or snake, smooth and soft	
Type 5: Soft blobs with clear cut edges	May indicate diarrhoea and urgency
Type 6: Fluffy pieces with ragged edges, a mushy stool	
Type 7: Watery, no solid pieces, entirely liquid	

Table 11.8 Bladder diary example.

	Bladder Diary		
Time	Fluid intake	Amount of urine	Any wetting accidents?
07:00		110 ml	
08:00	150 ml water		
09:00	200 ml juice		
10:00			Yes
11:00			
12:00			
13:00			

Table 11.9 Bowel diary example.

	Bowel Diary		
Day	Bowels opened	Stool type (Bristol Stool Score)	Any soiling accidents?
1			
2	Yes	1	
3	Yes	1	
4			Yes
5	Yes	3	
6			
7			

Table 11.10 ABC chart.

Date/time/place	Antecedent: context or condition when the behaviour occurs	Behaviour: responses or actions of concern	Consequences: events or outcomes that follow the behaviour
09.06 4.00 pm Living room	Asked Charlie to help tidy up toys and games	Charlie ran and hid in the corner. Discovered smeared poo on the wall and on his hands.	Charlie taken upstairs to shower.

acknowledge the range of responses that may arise. Through assessing parental responses, practitioners have the opportunity to highlight the potential detrimental effects of critical or punitive responses and then to suggest and model more adaptive responses. In addition to gleaning the typical responses of parents/carers, it may also be valuable to gauge those of other key people within the child's network (e.g. nursery staff) to see whether there is consistency in approaches (see Boxes 11.3 and 11.4).

Box 11.3 Clinical example: Eva

Eva is a 4-year-old girl presenting with faecal incontinence. The family have sought input from healthcare professionals following the advice of staff at Eva's school (which she has recently transitioned to from nursery). Eva attends the clinic with her mother, Joanne, and her father, Aryan. At the initial meeting the family confirm that Eva has been having regular 'accidents' (i.e. stool in her underwear or on the floor) for the past 12 months and these have increased in frequency over the last few weeks. There are mixed views within the family about these issues. Aryan shares that his mother, Nazra, is visiting the United Kingdom from Malaysia (where Aryan was born and lived for most of his childhood) and is staying in the family home for a few months. Nazra has been very concerned about Eva's incontinence and this has led to some tensions between her and Aryan. Joanne shared that she had not been too concerned initially, as she felt that the issues would resolve over time; however, she had been agreeable to accessing support from a professional following the school's advice.

Possible points to consider for assessment:

- What medical advice has been sought and how has this been used?
- What is the history and success with toilet training and other developmental milestones? What approaches or strategies have been trialled?
- What are the perspectives and norms within the family and the wider network around toileting behaviours? Are these informed by certain cultural or familial practices? What language or terms are used to talk about toileting behaviours?
- When did the difficulties first emerge? What environmental or contextual factors have affected these issues?
- What are the specific hopes or goals that each family member has?

Box 11.4 Clinical example: Eva

Within the assessment sessions, Eva's family provide background about her development and toileting habits. They share that they have not had any marked concerns about her development. She has not experienced any significant health concerns; however, she has had episodes of constipation. They have tried to manage this by adapting her diet (i.e. more fibre) and through laxatives prescribed by the GP. Eva's parents first introduced toilet training when Eva was 18 months old however, as she was reluctant to use a potty and as there was a period of significant change (family moved home) they had decided to pause toilet training. They then initiated toilet training again when she was 22 months old. Eva has now achieved full urinary continence however the picture with bowel control has been mixed. Nazra, Eva's grandmother, had always been critical of the parent's use of disposable nappies and felt that they should have been encouraging Eva to use the toilet from much earlier on (as Nazra had done with all her children). Nazra and other family members suggest that the parents should enforce some punishment or consequence for accidents. Eva's mother, Joanne, shared that she had her own experience of urinary incontinence when she was a child, which resulted in some isolation and ostracizing from peers; however, her issues spontaneously resolved. Both parents feel that they are struggling to be consistent with their use of certain support strategies and find the demands of attending to accidents very challenging particularly now that the school is also expressing concern. Through the assessment process Eva shared that she often tries to use the toilet but sometimes 'it comes out when she is not ready for it'. Eva expressed a wish for things to be different and felt that it would also mean that others (her parents, grandmother, teacher) would not be sad or angry with her anymore.
Possible points to consider for Formulation:

- Biological factors:
  Experience of constipation and use of laxative medication
  Changes to diet
  Familial history of toileting concerns
- Psychological factors:
  Age/developmental stage and associated tasks or demands (i.e. school transition)
  Feelings of worry, sadness, anger, isolation
  Views about rewards and benefits
- Social factors:
  Familial relationships and communication
  Relationships to others (i.e. school staff, professionals)
  Access to support and advice
- Systemic factors:
  Cultural/societal norms and expectations
  Environment (e.g. home, school, geographical location)
  Varying perspectives and needs (i.e. child, parents, grandparent, school)

11.3.6 Formulation

There are a myriad of ways that toileting issues, including specific presentations, can be understood. Information in previous chapters in relation to psychological formulation, alongside the details above regarding underlying/contributing factors, will support practitioners in developing their initial hypotheses.

A biopsychosocial (Engel, 1977) framework may be particularly useful for supporting a clinician's formulation of these difficulties, with attendance to factors such as:

Biological: Physical health, bladder capacity, recognition of proprioceptive cues, use of medication sleep, diet, family history of toileting issues.

Psychological: Mental health needs, motivation for change, expectations of support, beliefs about difficulties, self-esteem.

Social: Socioeconomic status, peer relationships, family communication, professional input, level of resource.

Bischof and Benson (2004) proposed a biopsychosocial systems approach in relation to childhood enuresis. They emphasise how this goes a step beyond Engel's initial biopsychosocial model to consider interactions across different levels of the system. They also highlight the potential benefits of enhancing a child's sense of personal agency, self-control and self-efficacy (e.g. strategies that can be done by the child and not just to the child). This approach, or elements of it, may also be valuable for supporting other toileting issues aside from enuresis. It also allows for the integration of other relevant theoretical perspectives (i.e. cognitive behavioural theory, attachment theory, narrative ideas) or models relating to specific presentations (e.g. enuresis or encopresis), which can support a practitioner in determining the most appropriate intervention.

11.3.7 Intervention

Medication and Dietary Changes: Medical evaluation and management can be the first line of input for some toileting concerns. When faecal incontinence is due to constipation, enemas, laxatives or stool softeners may be recommended. In the case of urinary incontinence in children age over 7, medication that controls the amount of urine produced by the kidneys (i.e. desmopressin) may be trialled (NICE, 2010). In some cases (i.e. lack of response to treatment), an anticholinergic or tricyclic antidepressants (e.g. imipramine) may also be used; they can play a role in the activity of muscles in the bladder. There may be recommendations that a child has a diet that is high in fibre or that they adapt their fluid intake (e.g. increase fluid for constipation or limit fluids ahead of bedtime).

Whilst psychological practitioners may not have a role in the prescribing and review of medication, their input may involve supporting in sharing the rationale for treatments, the adherence to medication or dietary programmes and evaluation of how they affect the presenting symptoms. Medication and dietary changes are often combined with behavioural interventions to increase effectiveness.

Behavioural Interventions: Many interventions aimed at addressing common toileting issues have a behavioural component (supporting the learning/re-learning and reinforcement of required skills). This may include graded exposure to certain environments or redirecting behaviour, for instance building up tolerance by sitting on the toilet with the lid down or providing an alternative to smearing faeces that will evoke a similar sensory experience. An overview of some specific strategies and targeted intervention used in the management of incontinence issues in children is presented in Table 11.12. Some interventions have multiple components and, therefore, it is not always possible to ascertain which elements are the most effective. In addition, certain aspects of multicomponent interventions may be unacceptable because of their punitive nature (NICE, 2010).

Praise and rewards (e.g. for successful use of the toilet) are a key feature of these interventions and are often used in a graded way (e.g. starting with a reward for just going into the bathroom then a further or increased reward for successful elimination in the toilet) (see Table 11.11). These may range from sticker-charts, treats or special time with a parent/carer where the child chooses the activity. It is important to support children and families in understanding the rationale for praise and rewards; this is also a useful context to reiterate the message of avoiding shame or punitive measures if a toileting accident occurs. Practitioners should support families in working out what is feasible and reasonable for them; for instance, providing treats may not be financially viable or equitable if other siblings/children are in the home.

Narrative Approaches: These therapeutic approaches are grounded in constructivist ideas and posit that problems are produced within social, cultural and political contexts (White & Epston, 1990). Such approaches may be useful in relation to the treatment and management of some toileting concerns. White (1984) coined the allegory 'Sneaky Poo' as a means of externalising experiences of encopresis (talking about the 'problem' as if it is distinct and separate from the child). This notion can be introduced by asking about experiences of 'Sneaky Poo' and the influence it has, for instance: 'How often does the Sneaky Poo have its way with you compared to how often you have your way with the poo?' Externalizing exercises may be advantageous in helping a child or family to gain a better perspective of a 'toileting issue' and can avoid locating the presenting concern(s) within the child. White's (1984) clinical work with those presenting with encopresis also included attending to environmental factors (i.e. location and lighting of toilet, routes and timed trials to get to a toilet), understanding and responding to reflexes/proprioceptive cues. These ideas have been adapted and built upon and there are resources, such as *Beating Sneaky Poo* by Heins et al. (1988), that incorporate narrative elements (e.g. stories about Sneaky

Table 11.11 Record chart

	I sat on my potty	I did a wee in my potty	I did a poo in my potty
Monday	★★	★★	
Tuesday	★	★	★
Wednesday	★★	★	
Thursday	★		
Friday			
Saturday			
Sunday			

Table 11.12 Strategies and interventions for toileting issues.

Strategy	Details
Urine alarm	An alarm system (sound and/or vibration) that is activated when the bed is wet. The child may then complete steps such as completing urination in the toilet or changing clothing before returning to bed. Often an alarm may first alert a parent/carer who will then wake the child. NICE (2010) proposes that an alarm should be offered as first-line treatment if bedwetting has not responded to advice on toileting, fluid intake and appropriate rewards.
Night-waking schedule/ Dry-bed training	This involves waking a child at a specific time during the night and prompting them to use the toilet. The waking time is then adjusted dependent on success with continence. It is proposed that this approach can support the strengthening of the child's inhibitory responses and sphincter muscle. Dry-bed training (Azrin et al., 1974) combines night-waking with other strategies, for instance the child may have some responsibility for undertaking certain steps (e.g. changing bedding) if there has been an accident. NICE (2010) advises against the use of dry-bed training for the management of bedwetting in children; this guidance notes that the waking of children at scheduled or random intervals should only be used as a short-term management strategy.
Voiding/toileting schedule	Creating a schedule for consistent elimination whilst the child is awake and prompting/encouraging the child to use the toilet at these times (e.g. urinating every 2-4 hours, using the toilet shortly after food intake, toilet visit as part of the bedtime routine). These may also include scheduled toilet sits for those who are withholding or those with negative associations with the bathroom.
Retention control training	This training can involve giving the child instructions to delay urination from the time they first sense this urge. The child may also be encouraged to increase their fluid intake. Through this it is suggested that the child can strengthen their inhibitory responses and the sphincter muscle and increase functional bladder capacity (Kimmel & Kimmel, 1970). Retention control training was classified as having 'questionable efficacy' for the treatment of nocturnal enuresis following a review of interventions (Shepard et al., 2017). NICE (2010) guidance advises against the use of strategies that encourage infrequent voiding of urine during the day.
Biofeedback	This aims to support the child in recognising their own muscular movements and to learn how to relax/contract anal muscles. Biofeedback may involve the child engaging in exercises targeting the relevant muscles along with the use of sensory and visual prompts. Biofeedback supports effective defecation and faecal continence (Rajindrajith et al., 2013). Biofeedback was classed as 'probably efficacious' for the treatment of encopresis (Shepard et al., 2017). Whilst biofeedback has not shown significant therapeutic value for those with functional faecal incontinence, improvements in defecation dynamics (i.e. ability to relax anal sphincter) has been noted in those with associated constipation (Rajindrajith et al., 2013).

Table 11.12 (Continued)

Strategy	Details
Enhanced toilet training	The training can include education about the physiology of constipation and incontinence, modelling of effective elimination and teaching strategies (e.g. breathing exercises, relaxation) to support the child in learning how to relax and contract muscles (Borowitz et al., 2002). In a randomized trial of treatments for childhood encopresis, enhanced toilet training had a similar cure rate at 1-year follow-up to intensive medical therapy (i.e. enemas, laxatives) and anal sphincter biofeedback therapy; however enhanced toilet training resulted in a significant decrease in daily frequency of soiling for the greatest number of participants (Borowitz et al., 2002). Shepard et al. (2017) classified enhanced toilet training as being 'probably efficacious' for encopresis treatment.

Poo's actions and preferences), with psychoeducation and behavioural strategies to support continence (see Box 11.5).

Considerations for Intervention: Any intervention offered should be informed by the relevant guidance and policies and current research evidence. NICE (2010) does not recommend treatment for children under 5 years old experiencing bedwetting. There may be instances where other presenting issues (e.g. trauma, anxiety, low mood, familial issues) need to be addressed as a priority before an intervention for any specific toileting concern is considered. This may include the use of other targeted intervention (e.g. trauma-focussed work, cognitive behavioural or systemic therapy). If an intervention is delivered there should be adequate consideration on how this is done; this may also be dictated by service context alongside the specific needs of a child or family (e.g. age, cognitive ability, language skills, availability). Whilst an intervention is targeted at the child, a parent/carer will often play a key role in the delivery of this. Even in circumstances where there may be direct psychoeducation or treatment with a child (e.g. biofeedback, relaxation, exposure work), parental input will be needed to support with practice and generalization of skills. Practitioners may find themselves providing indirect (e.g. group-based support) or consultative input to others in a child's network (e.g. other professionals); there should be consideration of how to promote engagement and ways to monitor and evaluate how the intervention is being received.

Whether working directly or indirectly with children and families, it is valuable for practitioners to model the essential principles of an effective intervention. This may include maintaining optimism and enthusiasm about outcomes and modelling praise and language (e.g. noticing and naming how a parent/carer has responded to or managed a challenge).

11.3.8 Evaluation

Practitioners should be mindful of ways to review and evaluate the input offered and establish an understanding together with the child/family of what change or progress might look like. As part of this process, there should be an acknowledgement of more subtle and gradual signs of success; for instance, an increased delay in the time accidents occur. There should also be discussion of how long techniques or approaches should be implemented, even after a practitioner-delivered intervention has been completed. Often, problems can re-occur simply because supportive strategies have been stopped too soon.

If there are barriers to engagement with an intervention or marked limits to progress, a re-formulation of need or a re-prioritising of goals may be needed. This may be the case if there are co-occurring or emerging issues (social, psychological, behavioural, emotional) that have not been appropriately assessed or managed. There may be a need for managing some issues concurrently, for instance if there is high parental stress or anxiety, support may be offered to address this (e.g. couples-based, systemic intervention) in order to increase parental capacity to engage with an intervention for toileting issues.

Practitioners should also be aware of the wider threats to a child's or parent's health and wellbeing if an issue has not been adequately assessed and managed. There can be potentially serious medical consequences, for instance, with faecal incontinence and chronic constipation as a child's colon can become distended and pose a threat to their health. There can also be a significant impact or impairment in other domains, such as peer relationships and family communication if issues persist even after targeted support. Therefore, practitioners should consider whether the complexity or severity of the presenting need, might warrant more specialised or intensive intervention.

Box 11.5 Clinical example: Eva

The family have been engaging with support from a psychological practitioner for a few weeks. There has been psychoeducation around physiological processes involved in bowel control and continence. They have continued to liaise with the GP who supports with the management of any episodes of constipation. The family and school staff have started to implement a regular voiding schedule for Eva and have supplemented this with small rewards for successes (e.g. stickers, trips to the park). Given Eva's age and the impact of difficulties on her and her family, efforts have been made to incorporate narrative principles of externalising both within and outside of sessions. Eva has been able to draw out her version of the 'Sneaky Poo' and shared that it is more likely to make an appearance when she is busy playing or not long after she has eaten. Her parents also shared that 'Sneaky Poo' can sometimes get in the way of the activities they want to do as a family; however, they reassured Eva that they and other adults (i.e. grandmother, school staff) were all part of her team to help her beat 'Sneaky Poo'.

Possible points to consider for continuing and evaluating Intervention:

- How are strategies and approaches adapted to make them appropriate for the child and supporting adults (e.g. creative/playful approaches, resources to use at home and share with others)?
- How can everyone in the familial and wider network ensure they are encouraging and maintaining progress both during the intervention and beyond (e.g. liaison with the GP and school staff, communicating the formulation and rationale for interventions)?

(Continued)

Box 11.5 (Continued)

- What would be the markers of improvements (e.g. less frequent accidents, increased toilet use)? What would be the indicators of more significant concerns or that more specialised support is needed (e.g. referral to guidance or diagnostic classification systems, decline in physical health or mental wellbeing)?

11.3.9 Summary

- Issues with toileting are common within childhood.
- The development of bladder and bowel continence is a key developmental milestone.
- Difficulties may include urinary or faecal incontinence (enuresis and encopresis), withholding or avoiding elimination of waste or smearing stool.
- Evaluation of any concerns should factor in what may be typical or expected for that developmental stage alongside the severity and persistence of the presenting issues.
- Psychological practitioners, alongside other healthcare professionals, can play a valuable role in the assessment and management of issues relating to toileting.
- Psychoeducation is a key part of supporting children and families.
- Within their assessment, practitioners should be mindful of factors such as language, familial values, toileting readiness/habits and parental response to concerns.
- A biopsychosocial systems approach may be valuable for formulating the presenting needs
- Behavioural interventions are commonly used, alongside other input such as medication and dietary adaptations.

11.3.10 Resources

Sleeping

Lullaby Trust: https://www.lullabytrust.org.uk/
Crysis: Support for parents with crying and sleepless babies:

https://www.cry-sis.org.uk/ Helpline: 0800 448 0737
NHS sleep guide: https://www.nhs.uk/conditions/baby/health/sleep-problems-in-young-children/

Feeding

For more information on the paediatric population *Feeding Problems in Children* by Southampton and Martin (2011), whilst written some time ago, has helpful range of topics and resources to support assessment and intervention with this group.

Child eating behaviour questionnaire: https://www.ucl.ac.uk/epidemiology-health-care/sites/epidemiology-health-care/files/cebqnoscore.pdf
UCL Child and adolescent mental health competence frameworks https://www.ucl.ac.uk/clinical-psychology/competency-maps/camhs-map.html

References

Abali, O., Onur, M., Gurkan, K., Celik, O., & Tuzun, D. U. (2006). Enuresis nocturna among school age children and its evaluation according to sociodemographic data. *Turkish Journal of Child and Adolescent Mental Health, 13*, 49–53.

Adams, E. L., Edgar, A., Mosher, P., Armstrong, B., Burkart, S., Weaver, R. G., Beets, M. W. Siceloff, E. R., & Prinz, R. J. (2023). Barriers to optimal child sleep among families with low income: A mixed-methods study to inform intervention development. *International Journal of Environmental Research and Public Health, 20*(1), 862.

American Academy of Sleep Medicine. (2014). International classification of sleep disorders (3rd ed., ICSD-3). *AASM Resource Library, 281*, 2313.

American Psychiatric Association. (2000). *Diagnostic and statistical manual of mental disorders: DSM-4* (4th ed., text revision). American Psychiatric Publishing.

American Psychiatric Association. (2013). *Diagnostic and statistical manual of mental disorders: DSM-5* (5th ed.). American Psychiatric Publishing.

Archibald, T., & Bryant-Waugh, R. (2023). Current evidence for avoidant restrictive food intake disorder: Implications for clinical practice and future directions. *JCPP Advances*, e12160.

Azrin, N. H., Sneed, T. J., & Foxx, R. M. (1974). Dry-bed training: Rapid elimination of childhood enuresis. *Behaviour Research and Therapy, 12*(3), 147–156.

Bakker, J. van Gool, J.-J., & Wyndaele, E. (2001). Results of a questionnaire evaluating different aspects of personal and familial situation, and the methods of potty-training in two groups of children with a different outcome of bladder control. *Scandinavian Journal of Urology and Nephrology, 35*(5), 370–376.

Bergan, J. R., & Kratochwill, T. R. (1990). *Behavioral consultation and therapy*. Plenum Press.

Berk, L. B., & Friman, P. C. (1990). Epidemiologic aspects of toilet training. *Clinical Pediatrics, 29*(5), 278–282.

Bion, W. R. (1962). The psycho-analytic study of thinking. *International Journal of Psychoanalysis, 43*(4-5), 306–310.

Bischof, G. H., & Benson, B. M. (2004). Childhood enuresis: A biopsychosocial systems approach. *Journal of Family Psychotherapy, 15*(3), 1–17.

Bongers, M. E., Tabbers, M. M., & Benninga, M. A. (2007). Functional nonretentive fecal incontinence in children. *Journal of Pediatric Gastroenterology and Nutrition, 44*(1), 5–13.

Boon, F. (1991). Encopresis and sexual assault. *Journal of the American Academy of Child and Adolescent Psychiatry, 30*(3), 509–510.

Borowitz, S. M., Cox, D. J., Sutphen, J. L., & Kovatchev, B. (2002). Treatment of childhood encopresis: A randomized trial comparing three treatment protocols. *Journal of Pediatric Gastroenterology and Nutrition, 34*(4), 378–384.

Breinbjerg, A., Jørgensen, C. S., Borg, B., Rittig, S., Kamperis, K., & Christensen, J. H. (2023). The genetics of incontinence: A scoping review. *Clinical Genetics, 104*(1), 22–62.

Brooks, S., & Severson, A. (2022). *How to raise an intuitive eater: Raising the next generation with food and body confidence*. St. Martin's Essentials.

Children's Future Food Inquiry. (2019). The Food Foundation. https://foodfoundation.org.uk/sites/default/files/2021-09/Childrens-Future-Food-Inquiry-report.pdf

Cohn, A. (2007). The links between continence and child protection. *Continence UK, 1*(4), 57–60.

Collis, D., Kennedy-Behr, A., & Kearney, L. (2019). The impact of bowel and bladder problems on children's quality of life and their parents: A scoping review. *Child: Care, Health and Development*, *45*(1), 1–14.

Cortese, S., Brown, T. E., Corkum, P., Gruber, R., O'Brien, L. M., Stein, M., Weiss, M., & Owens, J. (2013). Assessment and management of sleep problems in youths with attention-deficit/hyperactivity disorder. *Journal of the American Academy of Child & Adolescent Psychiatry*, *52*(8), 784–796.

Coulthard, H., & Sealy, A. (2017). Play with your food! Sensory play is associated with tasting of fruits and vegetables in preschool children. *Appetite*, *113*, 84–90.

Coulthard, H., Williamson, I., Palfreyman, Z., & Lyttle, S. (2018). Evaluation of a pilot sensory play intervention to increase fruit acceptance in preschool children. *Appetite*, *120*, 609–615.

Daniels, L. A. (2019). Feeding practices and parenting: A pathway to child health and family happiness. *Annals of Nutrition and Metabolism*, *74*(2), 29–42.

Davis, A. M., & Kramer, R. S. (2021). Commentary: Does 'cry it out' really have no adverse effects on attachment? Reflections on Bilgin and Wolke (2020). *Journal of Child Psychology and Psychiatry*, *62*(12), 1488–1490.

Daws, D. (1989). *Through the night: Helping parents with sleepless infants*. Free Association Books.

Daws, D., & Sutton, S. (2020). *Parent infant psychotherapy for sleep problems: Through the night*. Routledge.

de Carvalho Mrad, F. C., da Silva, M. E., Lima, E. M., Bessa, A. L., de Bessa Junior, J., Netto, J. M. B., & de Almeida Vasconcelos, M. M. (2021). Toilet training methods in children with normal neuropsychomotor development: A systematic review. *Journal of Pediatric Urology*, *17*(5), 635–643.

Devnani, P. A., & Hegde, A. U. (2015). Autism and sleep disorders. *Journal of Pediatric Neurosciences*, *10*(4), 304–307.

Didehbani, N., Kelly, K., Austin, L., & Wiechmann, A. (2011). Role of parental stress on pediatric feeding disorders. *Children's Health Care*, *40*(2), 85–100.

Douglas, J. (2002). Psychological treatment of food refusal in young children. *Child and Adolescent Mental Health*, *7*(4), 173–180.

Dovey, T. M., Staples, P. A., Gibson, E. L., & Halford, J. C. G. (2008). 'Food neophobia and "picky/fussy" eating in children: A review.' *Appetite*, *50*(2–3), 181–193.

Dubowitz, H., Black, M., Harrington, D., & Verschoore, A. (1993). A follow-up study of behavior problems associated with child sexual abuse. *Child Abuse & Neglect*, *17*(6), 743–754.

Duong, T. H., Jansson, U. B., Holmdahl, G., Sillén, U., & Hellström, A. L. (2013). Urinary bladder control during the first 3 years of life in healthy children in Vietnam: A comparison study with Swedish children. *Journal of Pediatric Urology*, *9*(6), 700–706.

Dutt, R., Roduta-Roberts, M., & Brown, C. A. (2015). Sleep and children with cerebral palsy: A review of current evidence and environmental non-pharmacological interventions. *Children*, *2*(1), 78–88.

Dwivedi, K. N., & Woodcock, J. (2017). Cultural aspects of feeding: Some illustrations from Indian and other cultures. In *Feeding problems in children* (pp. 111–132). CRC Press.

Engel, G. L. (1977). The need for a new medical model: A challenge for biomedicine. *Science*, *196*(4286), 129–136.

Etherton, H., Blunden, S., & Hauck, Y. (2016). Discussion of extinction-based behavioral sleep interventions for young children and reasons why parents may find them difficult. *Journal of Clinical Sleep Medicine, 12*(11), 1535–1543.

Feder, T. (2021). *Bodies are cool.* Penguin Random House.

Ferber, R. (2006). *Solve your child's sleep problems* (revised ed.). Simon & Schuster.

Fraiberg, S., Adelson, E., & Shapiro, V. (2003). Gespenster im Kinderzimmer: Probleme gestörter Mutter-Säugling-Beziehungen aus psychoanalytischer Sicht [Ghosts in the nursery. Problems of disturbed mother–infant relationships from a psychoanalytical perspective]. *Analytische Kinder- und Jugendlichenpsychotherapie, 34*(120), 465–504.

Freud, A. (1965). *Normality and pathology in children.* International University Press.

Freud, S. (1905). *Three essays on the theory of sexuality.* In *Complete psychological works of Sigmund Freud*, Vol. VII. Hogarth Press.

Freud, S. (1908). *Character and anal-eroticism.* In *Complete psychological works of Sigmund Freud*, Vol. IX. Hogarth Press.

Friman, P. C., & Freeman, K. A. (2010). Enuresis and encopresis. In J. C. Thomas & M. Hersen (Eds.), *Handbook of clinical psychology competencies* (pp. 1371–1402). Springer.

Goday, P. S., Huh, S. Y., Silverman, A., Lukens, C. T., Dodrill, P., Cohen, S. S., Delaney, A. L., Feuling, M. B., Noel, R. J., Gisel, E., Kenzer, A,. Kessler, D. B., Kraus de Camargo, Olaf., Browne, J., & Phalen, J. A. (2019). Pediatric feeding disorder: Consensus definition and conceptual framework. *Journal of Pediatric Gastroenterology and Nutrition, 68*(1), 124–129.

Goodlin-Jones, B. L., Burnham, M. M., & Anders, T. F. (2000). Sleep and sleep disturbances: Regulatory processes in infancy. In A. J. Sameroff, M. Lewis, & S. M. Miller (Eds.), *Handbook of developmental psychopathology* (pp. 309–325). Kluwer Academic Publishers. https://doi.org/10.1007/978-1-4615-4163-9_17

Goodlin-Jones, B. L., Sitnick, S. L., Tang, K., Liu, J., & Anders, T. F. (2008). The Children's Sleep Habits Questionnaire in toddlers and preschool children. *Journal of Developmental & Behavioral Pediatrics, 29*(2), 82–88.

Greer, B. D., Neidert, P. L., & Dozier, C. L. (2016). A component analysis of toilet-training procedures recommended for young children. *Journal of Applied Behavior Analysis, 49*(1), 69–84.

Harari, M. D. (2013). Nocturnal enuresis. *Journal of Paediatrics and Child Health, 49*(4), 264–271.

Heins, T., Ritchie, K., & Pryor, G. (1988). *Beating sneaky poo: Ideas for faecal soiling.* Australian Capital Territory Community & Health Service.

Horn, I. B., Brenner, R., Rao, M., & Cheng, T. L. (2006). Beliefs about the appropriate age for initiating toilet training: Are there racial and socioeconomic differences? *The Journal of Pediatrics, 149*(2), 165–168.

Horstmanshoff, B. E., Regterschot, G. J., Nieuwenhuis, E. E., Benninga, M. A., Verwijs, W., & Waelkens, J. J. (2003). Bladder control in 1–4 year old children in the the Eindhoven and Kempen region (The Netherlands) in 1996 and 1966. *Nederlands Tijdschrift Voor Geneeskunde, 147*(1), 27–31.

Howe, A. C., & Walker, C. E. (1992). Behavioral management of toilet training, enuresis, and encopresis. *Pediatric Clinics of North America, 39*(3), 413–432.

Howell, D. M., Wysocki, K., & Steiner, M. J. (2010). Toilet training. *Pediatrics in Review, 31*(6), 262–263.

Iglowstein, I., Jenni, O. G., Molinari, L., & Largo, R. H. (2003). Sleep duration from infancy to adolescence: Reference values and generational trends. *Pediatrics, 111*(2), 302–307.

Kennaway, D. J., Stamp, G. E., & Goble, F. C. (1992). Development of melatonin production in infants and the impact of prematurity. *The Journal of Clinical Endocrinology & Metabolism, 75*(2), 367–369.

Kimmel, H. D., & Kimmel, E. (1970). An instrumental conditioning method for the treatment of enuresis. *Journal of Behavior Therapy and Experimental Psychiatry, 1*(2), 121–123.

Koc, I., Camurdan, A. D., Beyazova, U., Ilhan, M. N., & Sahin, F. (2008). Toilet training in Turkey: The factors that affect timing and duration in different sociocultural groups. *Child: Care, Health and Development, 34*(4), 475–481.

Kohn, A. (1993). *Punished by rewards: The trouble with gold stars, incentive plans, A's, praise, and other bribes.* Houghton, Mifflin and Company.

Lai, H. H., Morgan, C. D., Vetter, J., & Andriole, G. L. (2016). Impact of childhood and recent traumatic events on the clinical presentation of overactive bladder. *Neurourology and Urodynamics, 35*(8), 1017–1023.

Landry, S. H., Smith, K. E., & Swank, P. R. (2006). Responsive parenting: Establishing early foundations for social, communication, and independent problem-solving skills. *Developmental Psychology, 42*(4), 627–642.

Law, D., & Jacob, J. (2013). *Goals and goal based outcomes (GBOs).* CAMHS Press.

Lewis, S. J., & Heaton, K. W. (1997). Stool form scale as a useful guide to intestinal transit time. *Scandinavian Journal of Gastroenterology, 32*(9), 920–924.

Maimaran, M., & Fishbach, A. (2014). If it's useful and you know it, do you eat? Preschoolers refrain from instrumental food. *Journal of Consumer Research, 41*(3), 642–655.

Mayes, S. D., & Zickgraf, H. (2019). Atypical eating behaviors in children and adolescents with autism, ADHD, other disorders, and typical development. *Research in Autism Spectrum Disorders, 64*, 76–83.

Mellon, M. W., Natchev, B. E., Katusic, S. K., Colligan, R. C., Weaver, A. L., Voigt, R. G., & Barbaresi, W. J. (2013). Incidence of enuresis and encopresis among children with attention-deficit/hyperactivity disorder in a population-based birth cohort. *Academic Pediatrics, 13*(4), 322–327.

Meltzer, L. J., & Mindell, J. A. (2014). Systematic review and meta-analysis of behavioral interventions for pediatric insomnia. *Journal of Pediatric Psychology, 39*(8), 932–948.

Milano, K., Chatoor, I., & Kerzner, B. (2019). A functional approach to feeding difficulties in children. *Current Gastroenterology Reports, 21*, 1–8.

Mindell, J. A., & Owens, J. A. (2015). *A clinical guide to pediatric sleep: Diagnosis and management of sleep problems.* Lippincott Williams & Wilkins.

Mota, D. M., & Barros, A. J. (2008). Toilet training: Methods, parental expectations and associated dysfunctions. *Jornal de Pediatria, 84*, 9–17.

Mota, D. M., Barros, A. J., Matijasevich, A., & Santos, I. S. (2010). Longitudinal study of sphincter control in a cohort of Brazilian children. *Jornal de Pediatria, 86*, 429–434.

National Institute for Health and Care Excellence (NICE). (2010). *Bedwetting in under 19s.* Clinical guideline CG111. NICE. https://www.nice.org.uk/guidance/cg111

National Institute of Health and Care Excellence (NICE). (2011). *Autism spectrum disorder in under 19s: Recognition, referral and diagnosis.* Clinical Guideline (CG128, updated 2017). NICE.

National Institute of Health and Care Excellence (NICE). (2013). *Antisocial behaviour and conduct disorders in children and young people: Recognition and management*. Clinical Guideline (CG158, updated 2017). NICE.

National Institute of Health and Care Excellence (NICE). (2015). *Nutrition: Improving maternal and child malnutrition*. Quality Standard (QS98). NICE.

National Institute for Health and Care Excellence. (2017). *Faltering growth: Recognition and management of faltering growth in children*. NICE Guideline (NG75). NICE. https://www.nice.org.uk/guidance/ng75/resources/faltering-growth-recognition-and-management-of-faltering-growth-in-children-pdf-1837635907525

National Institute of Health and Care Excellence (NICE). (2022). *Sleepio to treat insomnia and insomnia symptoms*. Medical Technologies Guidance (MTG70). NICE.

NHS Online. (2021). *Helping your baby to sleep*. https://www.nhs.uk/conditions/baby/caring-for-a-newborn/helping-your-baby-to-sleep/

Nieuwhof-Leppink, A. J., Schroeder, R. P., van de Putte, E. M., de Jong, T. P., & Schappin, R. (2019). Daytime urinary incontinence in children and adolescents. *The Lancet Child & Adolescent Health*, *3*(7), 492–501.

Ogundele, M. O., & Yemula, C. (2022). Management of sleep disorders among children and adolescents with neurodevelopmental disorders: A practical guide for clinicians. *World Journal of Clinical Pediatrics*, *11*(3), 239–252.

Owens, J. A., Spirito, A., & McGuinn, M. (2000). The Children's Sleep Habits Questionnaire (CSHQ): Psychometric properties of a survey instrument for school-aged children. *Sleep*, *23*(8), 1043–1051.

Park, J., Kim, S. Y., & Lee, K. (2022). Effectiveness of behavioral sleep interventions on children's and mothers' sleep quality and maternal depression: A systematic review and meta-analysis. *Scientific Reports*, *12*(1), 4172.

Paruthi, S., Brooks, L. J., D'Ambrosio, C., Hall, W. A., Kotagal, S., Lloyd, R. M., Malow, B. A., Maski, K., Nicholls, C., Quan, S. F., Rosen, C. L., Troester, M. M., & Wise, M. S. (2016). Recommended amount of sleep for pediatric populations: A consensus statement of the American Academy of Sleep Medicine. *Journal of Clinical Sleep Medicine*, *12*(6), 785–786.

Patel, A. K., Reddy, V., & Araujo, J. F. (2020). *Physiology, sleep stages*. StatPearls. https://www.ncbi.nlm.nih.gov/books/NBK526132/

Payne, C. K., Abdulcadir, J., Ouedraogo, C., Madzou, S., Kabore, F. A., De, E. J., & Ethics Committee if the International Continence Society. (2019). International continence society white paper regarding female genital mutilation/cutting. *Neurourology and Urodynamics*, *38*(2), 857–867.

Pinkerton, P. (1958). Psychogenic megacolon in children: The implications of bowel negativism. *Archives of Disease in Childhood*, *33*, 371–380.

Radford, J. O., & Anderson, M. (2003). Encopresis in children on the autistic spectrum. *Early Child Development and Care*, *173*(4), 375–382.

Rajindrajith, S., Devanarayana, N. M., & Benninga, M. A. (2010). Constipation-associated and nonretentive fecal incontinence in children and adolescents: An epidemiological survey in Sri Lanka. *Journal of Pediatric Gastroenterology and Nutrition*, *51*(4), 472–476.

Rajindrajith, S., Devanarayana, N. M., & Benninga, M. A. (2013). Faecal incontinence in children: Epidemiology, pathophysiology, clinical evaluation and management. *Alimentary Pharmacology & Therapeutics*, *37*(1), 37–48.

Reuter, A., Silfverdal, S. A., Lindblom, K., & Hjern, A. (2020). A systematic review of prevention and treatment of infant behavioural sleep problems. *Acta Paediatrica, 109*(9), 1717–1732.

Robson, W. L. M., & Leung, A. K. (2000). Secondary nocturnal enuresis. *Clinical Pediatrics, 39*(7), 379–385.

Sadeh, A. (2004). A brief screening questionnaire for infant sleep problems: Validation and findings for an Internet sample. *Pediatrics, 113*(6), e570–e577

Sadeh, A., & Anders, T. F. (1993). Infant sleep problems: Origins, assessment, interventions. *Infant Mental Health Journal, 14*(1), 17–34.

Sadeh, A., Tikotzky, L., & Scher, A. (2010). Parenting and infant sleep. *Sleep Medicine Reviews, 14*(2), 89–96.

Sarici, H., Telli, O., Ozgur, B. C., Demirbas, A., Ozgur, S., & Karagoz, M. A. (2016). Prevalence of nocturnal enuresis and its influence on quality of life in school-aged children. *Journal of Pediatric Urology, 12*(3), 159-e1.

Sateia, M. J. (2014). International classification of sleep disorders. *Chest, 146*(5), 1387–1394.

Schoenewolf, G. (1997). Soiling and the anal-narcissistic character. *American Journal of Psychoanalysis, 57*(1), 47–62.

Schum, T. R., Kolb, T. M., McAuliffe, T. L., Simms, M. D., Underhill, R. L., & Lewis, M. (2002). Sequential acquisition of toilet-training skills: A descriptive study of gender and age differences in normal children. *Pediatrics, 109*(3), e48.

Schum, T. R., McAuliffe, T. L., Simms, M. D., Walter, J. A., Lewis, M., & Pupp, R. (2001). Factors associated with toilet training in the 1990s. *Ambulatory Pediatrics, 1*(2), 79–86.

Shepard, J. A., Poler Jr, J. E., & Grabman, J. H. (2017). Evidence-based psychosocial treatments for pediatric elimination disorders. *Journal of Clinical Child & Adolescent Psychology, 46*(6), 767–797.

Soifer, S., Nicaise, G., Chancellor, M., & Gordon, D. (2009). Paruresis or shy bladder syndrome: An unknown urologic malady. *Urologic Nursing, 29*(2), 87–94.

Spielman, A. J., Caruso, L. S., & Glovinsky, P. B. (1987). A behavioral perspective on insomnia treatment. *Psychiatric Clinics of North America, 10*(4), 541–553.

Tan-MacNeill, K. M., Smith, I. M., & Corkum, P. V. (2023). Acceptability of an online intervention for insomnia in children with neurodevelopmental disorders. *Research in Developmental Disabilities, 134*, 104423.

Tang, M. N., Adolphe, S., Rogers, S. R., & Frank, D. A. (2021). Failure to thrive or growth faltering: Medical, developmental/behavioral, nutritional, and social dimensions. *Pediatrics in Review, 42*(11), 590–603.

Tarhan, H., Çakmak, Ö., Akarken, İ., Ekin, R. G., Ün, S., Uzelli, D., Helvacı, M., Aksu, N., Yavaşcan, Ö., Mutlubaş-Özsan, F., Cun, S., Koç, F., Özkarakaş, Ö., İlbey, Y. Ö., & Zorlu, F. (2015). Toilet training age and influencing factors: A multicenter study. *The Turkish Journal of Pediatrics, 57*(2), 172–176.

Taylor, C. M., Wernimont, S. M., Northstone, K., & Emmett, P. M. (2015). Picky/fussy eating in children: Review of definitions, assessment, prevalence and dietary intakes. *Appetite, 95*, 349–359.

Teti, D. M., O'Connell, M. A., & Reiner, C. D. (1996). Parenting sensitivity, parental depression and child health: The mediational role of parental self-efficacy. *Early Development and Parenting: An International Journal of Research and Practice, 5*(4), 237–250.

Thaman, L. A., & Eichenfield, L. F. (2014). Diapering habits: A global perspective. *Pediatric Dermatology, 31*, 15–18.

Thorpy, M. J. (2012). Classification of sleep disorders. *Neurotherapeutics, 9*(4), 687–701.

Touchette, É., Petit, D., Paquet, J., Tremblay, R. E., Boivin, M., & Montplaisir, J. Y. (2005). Bed-wetting and its association with developmental milestones in early childhood. *Archives of Pediatrics & Adolescent Medicine, 159*(12), 1129–1134.

Van der Wal, M. F., Benninga, M. A., & Hirasing, R. A. (2005). The prevalence of encopresis in a multicultural population. *Journal of Pediatric Gastroenterology and Nutrition, 40*(3), 345–348.

van Nunen, K., Kaerts, N., Wyndaele, J. J., Vermandel, A., & Hal, G. V. (2015). Parents' views on toilet training (TT) A quantitative study to identify the beliefs and attitudes of parents concerning TT. *Journal of Child Health Care, 19*(2), 265–274.

Wardle, J., Guthrie, C. A., Sanderson, S., & Rapoport, L. (2001). Development of the Children's Eating Behaviour questionnaire. *The Journal of Child Psychology and Psychiatry and Allied Disciplines, 42*(7), 963–970.

White, M. (1984). Pseudo-encopresis: From avalanche to victory, from vicious to virtuous cycles. *Family Systems Medicine, 2*(2), 150–160.

White, M., & Epston, D. (1990). *Narrative means to therapeutic ends*. W. W. Norton & Company, Inc.

Winnicott, D. W. (1945). Primitive emotional development. *The International Journal of Psychoanalysis, 26*, 137–143.

Winnicott, D. W. (1951). *Transitional objects and transitional phenomena*. Tavistock.

Wolraich, M. (2016). *The American Academy of Pediatrics guide to toilet training: Revised and updated second edition*. Bantam.

World Health Organization. (2006). *WHO child growth standards* WHO. www.who.int/childgrowthstandards

World Health Organization. (2016). *International statistical classification of diseases and related health problems* (10th ed.). WHO.

World Health Organization. (2019). *International statistical classification of diseases and related health problems* (11th ed.). WHO. https://icd.who.int/

12

Behavioural Difficulties and Parenting Interventions

Emma Karwatzki and Kajal Patel

12.1 Introduction to the Topic and its Relevance to Current Practice

This chapter aims to cover the key aspects of parenting interventions, which tend to focus predominantly on externalising behaviours, that is, behaviours that are experienced as challenging, destructive or antisocial. As practitioners it is important to be aware of the wider social and educational contexts within which children in the UK are embedded, this creates a particular set of circumstances that are not necessarily generalisable to other contexts, therefore this chapter will draw on UK evidence and experience wherever possible. The term 'parent/s' is used throughout this chapter for brevity and is defined as all adults responsible for the care and upbringing of a child or young person (CYP). This risks being reductionist, but the authors wish to acknowledge the multitude of families and contexts within which young people are raised. Before reading this chapter practitioners are invited to reflect on their own relationships to parenting and being parented, this is an important first step when engaging with parenting work (see Box 12.1).

Young people presenting with extreme behavioural difficulties that prevent them and their families from being able to engage in community-based interventions thereby requiring residential input will be discussed in Chapters 22 and 26. Whilst there are interventions focusing on the parental role for other presentations such as anxiety and attachment difficulties, these are covered in separate chapters. There is also a specific evidence base for parenting approaches where a CYP presents with neurodevelopmental and/or learning disabilities, which will not be covered in any detail here as they are addressed elsewhere within this book.

Child Psychology: Pathways to Good Practice, First Edition.
Edited by Helen Pote, Anna Picciotto and Clare Norris.

Box 12.1 Practitioner position and reflective exercise

In writing this chapter, we are acutely aware of our multiple identities as parents, as clinical psychologists working with children, young people and families and as trainers. These identities intertwine and the lenses we have used to select and filter the contents of this chapter will undoubtedly be influenced.

We invite you to take a moment to consider your own views of parenting and your experiences of being parented. We would like to encourage reflexive engagement throughout the reading of this chapter to help link your own experiences with your feelings about working with parents in a professional context. Consider these questions individually and consider what information would be helpful for you to share in supervision when undertaking a piece of parent focused clinical work.

How might your own experiences of care and discipline impact on your current views of care and discipline?

How much experience do you have of interacting with children and young people, either your own or those of others?

How do your experiences of witnessing the ways in which others parent their children impact your professional opinions?

How does your social, cultural and worldview impact on your perspectives on parenting?

At the point of writing this chapter (2023), although there have been improvements over recent years, services are provided in a way that can lead young people with behavioural difficulties to fall between the gaps in health and social care services due to commissioning arrangements. This may mean that the remit of work as a psychological practitioner, and the related expected outcomes, will be impacted by the service environment. Practitioners may also be working in a consultative capacity for other professionals delivering parenting interventions. The National Institute for Health and Care Excellence (NICE; 2017) recommends integrated care for young people with behavioural difficulties.

There is sometimes problematic use of language involved in this area of practice, and the risks in separating out behaviour from context. As authors we take a critical and contextual position in this chapter and emphasise that care needs to be taken to ensure that the functional, emotional and relational aspects the behaviour represents are not lost.

In defining behavioural difficulties, the International Classification of Diseases (World Health Organization, 2018) categorises conduct disorder into four subtypes one of which is oppositional defiant disorder. According to the Office of National Statistics (ONS) surveys of 1999 and 2004, conduct disorders have a prevalence of 5% among children and young people aged between 5 and 16 years making it one of the most common emotional and behavioural disorders in children and young people. These figures are cause for serious concern, particularly as the rates of conduct disorder are associated with poverty and are significantly higher in social classes D and E relative to social class A and are nearly at 40% in the most vulnerable subgroups of young people such as 'looked after children', those that have experienced abuse and those on safeguarding plans or registers (NICE, 2017).

Conduct disorder has been found to impact adversely on functioning and quality of life, and is associated with poorer educational outcomes, lack of social support, and amongst older young people, with substance misuse and higher rates of criminality. This link has been found to continue into adulthood with lower levels of educational attainment, poorer occupational outcomes, higher rates of criminality, increased prevalence of mental health problems and a higher likelihood of being diagnosed with a lifelong and stigmatising disorder such as personality disorder (for example see Vizard et al., 2007). Concerns about behavioural issues are one of the most common reasons for referral to mental health, primary care and social care teams, which highlights the demand these difficulties place on all services working with children and young people (NICE, 2017).

12.2 The Tasks of Parenting

In a UK context, parents are expected to meet their children's health and developmental needs, provide consistency and routine, put their children's needs first and engage with support when difficulties arise (NSPCC, 2014). This should include emotional warmth, stimulation, guidance and boundaries, and stability.

Parents often experience judgement of their parenting approaches, and, when this is experienced repeatedly or coupled with other vulnerability factors, parents risk experiencing shame and defensiveness when engaging in services that enquire about parenting. There is therefore an important role for psychological practitioners in taking a non-judgemental and collaborative approach that focuses on family goals and priorities.

Readers of this chapter are encouraged to read further about the concept of the 'good enough mother' (Winnicott, 1953, p. 97) in which 'The good-enough (mother) is one who makes active adaptation to the infant's needs, an active adaptation that gradually lessens, according to the infant's growing ability to account for failure of adaptation and to tolerate the results of frustration.' This is a helpful concept to guide collaborative practice with parents.

12.3 Review of the Evidence Base, NICE Guidelines and Policy

This section organises the available evidence base according to the chronological age of the child, as there are differing approaches to intervention with respect to age. The challenges for evidence-based practice are reviewed in the Section 12.3.4.

12.3.1 Early Years (Under Fives)

The evidence-base and approach to parenting in the early years generally relates to the work of universal services and professionals, with specialist services taking more of a consultative approach.

Public Health England (2016, updated 2021) produce guidance to support public health outcomes for children and young people via the Healthy Child Programme. There is a focus on health visitor and school nurse commissioning and practice. The move towards early intervention on a national level aims to act as an opportunity to engage families before difficulties escalate although there is no statutory duty to provide these interventions. The Family Nurse Partnership (2023) has been set up to deliver the Healthy Child Programme for families particularly at risk with demonstrated outcomes in terms of attachment security, language development and behaviour problems (Early Intervention Foundation, 2017). Sanders et al. (2017) argue for a whole population approach to parenting, highlighting the range of factors that impact on parenting including temperament, cognitive ability, learning history and family history.

The Solihull approach (see Douglas, 2018) is an example of a specific approach offering training for professionals working in universal services such as health visitors, school nurses and nursery nurses, in addition to a 10-week groups for parents. The focus is understanding what may lie behind a child's behaviour including exploration of emotions for children and parents, introducing ideas of containment, reciprocity and behaviour management. A growing evidence base demonstrates reduced parental distress, improved perception of child's behaviour (Milford et al., 2006) as well as reduction in child difficulties (Bateson, 2008). A recent RCT concluded that there were improvements in child prosocial behaviour, conduct problems, parental anxiety and stress and the parent-child relationship (Douglas & Johnson, 2019).

Other attachment-based approaches that are recommended in NICE guidance for supporting children with attachment difficulties (NICE, 2015) such as video interaction guidance (VIG; Kennedy et al., 2010), video-feedback intervention to promote positive parenting (VIPP; Juffer et al., 2008) and Mellow Parenting (Puckering et al., 1994; https://www.mellowparenting.org/) are described elsewhere in this text.

12.3.2 Primary Age (Under 11s)

NICE guidance (2017) for conduct disorder in young people highlights the role for parenting interventions using a social learning theory approach (this approach will be detailed later in this chapter). There is a significant UK evidence base for group parenting programmes in the UK, much of which has come from the Bangor University Centre for Evidence Based Early Intervention and Kings College London's National Academy for Parenting Research.

Leijten et al. (2019) conducted a meta-analyses of parenting interventions across settings (i.e. from preventative through to specialist services), including over 200 trials of parenting programmes. They identified that two of the approaches taken on parenting programmes were particularly associated with stronger effects: positive reinforcement (particularly praise) and natural/logical consequences in both preventative and 'treatment' conditions. Relationship building and parental self-management of their own emotions and behaviour were also key in 'treatment' settings, with a conclusion that 'less is more' in preventative settings.

Mindfulness-based parenting programmes have also demonstrated promising results. Here the focus is on awareness, acceptance and compassion with the aim of impacting parenting skills and parent–child relationships. A recent review by Ahemaitijiang et al. (2021) highlighted that 'mindful parenting' (intentionally paying attention to one's thoughts, emotions, physical sensations, to one's child and to the parent–child relationship) is positively correlated with positive parenting styles and high-quality parent–child relationships and interactions and negatively correlation with negative parenting styles. Positive correlations were also found with respect to child outcomes including both internalising and externalising problems in community and clinical samples. They note that a range of programmes have been developed, with Bogels et al.'s (2008) 8-week course 'The Mindful Parenting Programme' indicating particularly strong results.

There is emerging practice-based evidence for interventions such as the 'whole brain child' (Siegel & Payne-Bryson, 2012) for younger children that use the metaphor of the 'thinking upstairs brain' and 'emotional downstairs brain' to explain the relationship between brain functioning and drivers for behaviour. Although there is extremely limited research on the effectiveness of interventions using this approach the concepts fit with research on other developmental and parenting approaches emphasising the need to manage behaviour relationally in the context of a child's developing ability to self-regulate their emotions. Ryan et al. (2017) reviewed the effectiveness of parenting programmes drawing on attachment theory such as parent infant psychotherapy and VIG and highlights the emerging evidence based for these.

12.3.3 Over 11s

NICE (2013, updated 2017) recommend multimodal interventions (such as multisystemic therapy; MST) for over 11s with behavioural difficulties.

Multisystemic therapy (MST) is an empirically validated, family and community-based intervention for young people presenting with antisocial and offending behaviour, with high acceptability levels for young people (Paradisopoulos et al., 2015).

Additionally, non-violent resistance (NVR; Weinblatt & Omer, 2008) approaches demonstrate effectiveness in a UK population (Newman et al., 2014). NVR aims to serve as an alternative to impulsive responses or resignation in parents with a resistance against problematic behaviours. The use of parental presence and 'sit ins', engaging the community and reconciliation gestures to promote positive aspects of the relationship are key features. In an randomised control trial (RCT) with 41 families, Weinblatt and Omer (2008) found that NVR helps to decrease parental helplessness and escalatory behaviours, with a reduction in parent rated child behavioural difficulties.

In a systematic review addressing the efficacy of systemic therapy for externalising difficulties in young people, including 47 randomised control trials (von Sydow et al., 2013), 42 trials showed effective outcomes with stability across longer-term follow up. The authors report that engagement and retention rates were superior to other therapy approaches, that systemic therapies were significantly more effective than control groups, and equally or more effective than other evidence-based interventions. Trials were included from the broad family of systemic approaches including multisystemic therapy, brief strategic family therapy and functional family therapy.

12.3.4 Critical Reflections on the Current Evidence

One of the main limitations of the current evidence base is that the applicability of the evidence to people from the global majority needs further research, particularly within the UK.

It has been argued that the parenting practices of different ethnic groups need to be better understood before this knowledge is then developed into models of parenting styles or existing parenting measures are adapted (Phoenix & Husain, 2007; Stewart & Bond, 2002). Whiteside-Mansell et al. (2001) argue that differences between cultural or ethnic groups may be due to the fact that the measures used are capturing different constructs. This is in line with view of other researchers in the United States for example, Chao (1994) who challenged the use of certain parenting constructs such as 'authoritative' and 'authoritarian parenting' as 'ethnocentric' and not being a relevant or useful reflection of the parenting practices valued by Chinese American families. Chao argues that parenting concepts need to be understood and formulated within the appropriate cultural context to be useful. She also highlights that many of the broader theoretical frameworks from which parenting concepts are derived such as developmental psychology have a greater focus on 'individualism' and 'independence', which may have limited applicability in some cultural groups.

Although there have been concerns about the impact of parenting interventions for those from disadvantaged backgrounds, Gardner et al. (2019) note that there is no significant evidence for this. For example, across 15 European trials of parenting programmes, they found no differences in outcomes according to ethnicity, poverty, single parent families, teen parents, unemployment or educational attainment. However, La Placa and Corlyon (2015) note that the relationship between poverty, parenting and child outcomes is complex and mediated by a variety of factors, and this therefore needs careful untangling in future intervention trials.

Much of the research is focused on specific populations of young people, sometimes with specific diagnosis as an inclusion criteria. The utility of this approach is questionable. A debate about the usefulness or potential harm of diagnostic labels such as conduct disorder is beyond the scope of this chapter. However, it is important to note that diagnoses in children and young people have an additional power differential attached. This is because access to services or requests for intervention are usually requested by the significant adults in their lives. Therefore, particular care needs to be taken to ensure that wider context and impact is always considered and that hypotheses around the function of the behaviour are not overlooked.

Mazzucchelli and Sanders (2014) highlight the risks in abandoning social learning models for attachment-focused interventions, based not on evidence but due to the notion that they are more emotionally satisfying. However, Scott and Dadds (2009) claim that between a quarter and a third of families do not benefit from evidence-based parenting approaches that draw on social learning theory. They argue that in these cases it is beneficial to draw on a range of other theories such as attachment theory, family systems theory, cognitive attribution theory and shared empowerment/ motivational interviewing to supplement social learning theory.

The long-term impact of parenting interventions is uncertain due to a limited number of longitudinal research designs. There have been follow ups to establish the medium-term effects for parenting programmes (for example, Bywater et al., 2009), but it is unknown how long these effects continue and whether they may last into adulthood (Jeong et al. 2021).

Finally, whilst manualised interventions are often critiqued for lacking real-world applicability, there is no clear evidence indicating that effects are poorer outside research trials (Michelson et al. 2013).

12.3.5 Views and Voices of Children about this Area of Practice

Whilst there is a particular interest in centring young people in the work of mental health professionals, there have been a limited number of studies enquiring about young people's experience of behavioural interventions, with there being more of a focus on experiences of specific parenting styles and discipline (for example, see Nixon & Halpenny, 2010). Indeed, research by Madge and Willmott (2007) highlights that despite the range of parenting programmes available aimed at improving outcomes for young people and their families, there is limited evidence of children and young people having the opportunity to be involved in designing, administering or evaluating these interventions.

Paradisopoulos et al. (2015) conducted a qualitative study that aimed to explore the experiences of young people of multisystemic therapy. Some of the key themes identified as contributing to the maintenance of positive outcomes over time included the therapeutic alliance, increased awareness of self and others and taking responsibility for change, systemic changes such as increased awareness of alternative perspectives and altering communication patterns, emotional regulation strategies, positive peer relationships, celebrating successes and identifying and planning for a preferred future. This research discusses the need to consider changes in behaviour as well as family functioning, in a less linear and more reciprocal and circular way. It also emphasises the impact of peer relationships on positive outcomes.

Ghate and Ramella (2002) conducted a national evaluation of the parenting programme run by the Youth Justice Board. They attempted to access the views of young people whose parents participated in the intervention indirectly using questionnaires sent via their parents. There was a very low response rate and incomplete data but based on the responses received there was some suggestion that young people felt there had been an improvement within the communication and quality of the relationship with their parents.

Parenting interventions tend to be mainly targeted at parents alone and vary in the extent to which they involve young people in the process. This may in part be because often the aim is behavioural change and this is not always embedded within a relational context. In interventions that include young people more directly, such as MST, there is more scope to discuss young people's views, feedback and experiences of the work. However, often in parenting interventions there is a significant gap in how much we know and understand about young people's experiences, which is both an area of concern and a missed opportunity to further develop interventions that are relevant and useful.

12.4 Assessment

12.4.1 Goals

When starting the process of shared decision making (for example, see Abrines-Jaume et al., 2016) at the beginning of the assessment a key area to explore is whose idea it was to access additional support with parenting, past experiences of working with professionals and attitudes towards help. This in turn will help facilitate any conversations about goals the family would like to be working towards and set realistic expectations for the intervention (see Chapters 2 and 8 for more details). The clinical rationale for this is that active participation by families in decision making regarding their own care facilitates better engagement and in turn more positive outcomes. This stance of collaboration is key with families where a parenting intervention is viewed as being mandated for example, as part of a safeguarding plan or in order to access additional sources of support. The process of establishing therapeutic goals should be family led and the reflective exercise (see Box 12.1) may provide a useful aid to reflect on your own expectations, beliefs, cultural and worldviews within this process.

It is often possible to develop some insight into values that might be implicit in the goals set by families (for example, see Harris, 2019). Being mindful of this will inform the theoretical underpinnings you draw upon for both the formulation and intervention plan. For example, for parents that value connection or relationship it may be that there is a greater focus on attachment theory in the intervention plan.

In our clinical experience, many children and young people feel criticised due to the impact of their behavioural difficulties and may therefore be reluctant to access services. It is important therefore to actively listen to their concerns, as well as to elicit their strengths ahead of any attempts to goal set. Offering to meet the young person on their own for a period of time can help to build a relationship and support assessment of needs, particularly if there are relational issues between the parents and young person.

12.4.2 Developmental History

Collecting a detailed developmental history can be a way of identifying factors that may be contributing to or maintaining the behaviours of concern. Alongside information about developmental milestones it is important to include details of difficulties with infertility and past losses, hopes and anxieties about parenting during pregnancy and any concerns that may be indicative of additional learning difficulties/needs and/or neurodevelopmental disorders. Discussing the early attachment relationship and how the child is viewed and perceived by different family members can provide a valuable insight into the meaning of the child to the parent/s and within the family, and help generate hypotheses around why and with whom the challenging behaviours may present, and flag up any potential risk factors (Reder & Duncan, 1999). See Chapter 3 for a detailed discussion of assessment areas.

When taking a developmental approach, the broader cultural context of the family and the way in which concepts of development, milestones and transition are regarded should be considered and acknowledged. As part of this process it is useful to help parents consider what typically developing children may present with, in terms of behaviours (for example, 'tantrums' in 3 year olds are expected). More details on a developmental approach to assessment are outlined in Chapter 3.

Given the high prevalence of attention deficit hyperactivity disorder (ADHD), autism spectrum conditions and learning difficulties as co-occurring presentations (for example, see Leitner, 2014), the use of standardised tools such as the Swanson, Nolan, and Pelham rating scale, fourth edition (SNAP-IV, Swanson, 2013), Conners rating scales (Conners, 1999) and the social communication questionnaire (Rutter et al., 2003) may be helpful here.

12.4.3 Family Context

When assessing the family context, it is important to build an understanding of levels of parental stress, anxiety related to parenting and sense of self-efficacy due to the potential impact this may have on parenting behaviour, the parent–child relationship (Mills-Koonce et al., 2011; Omer et al., 2008; Potharst et al., 2019) and parents' ability to engage in an intervention. This is in line with parenting approaches such as non-violent resistance (Weinblatt & Omer, 2008), MST (Henggeler et al., 1986) and the Solihull approach (Douglas, 2018), which are less child focused and highlight the needs of parents and a more family-centred intervention.

Assessment should include both parental and child history of mental and physical health, substance use difficulties, ability to self-regulate, levels of self-compassion, perceived power within the parent–child relationship and access to a support network. NICE (2017) also recommends assessment of parenting style (with harsh and inconsistent parenting being particular vulnerability factors). Alongside this, information on challenges in the areas of employment, finances/debt, housing, access to resources and transport and the impact of these on parenting will help plan interventions that are individualised and accessible. A cross-generational perspective where parents' own experiences of being parented is explored can be used to identify strengths and support systems. Exploring family scripts (replicative and corrective beliefs and patterns of behaviour) that parents bring from their own experience of being parented can span generations and are particularly helpful in understanding what may be contributing to or maintaining current patterns of parenting behaviour (see Byng-Hall, 1995). Standardised questionnaires such as the SCORE-15 (Stratton et al., 2010), the Parental Stress Scale (Berry & Jones, 1995) and the caregiving helplessness questionnaire (George, 2011) may aid this process.

In families where parents are separated or in blended families it is important to clarify any co-parenting arrangements that may be in place and to identify which significant adults are involved in decision making, discipline and care of the named CYP. Linked to this, considering differing roles within multigenerational households will aid consistency and collaboration between significant adult carers. When developing an understanding of the family context, a key part of this is assessing parental motivation and ability to engage in an assessment or intervention. This is conceptually different to parenting capacity assessments, which are usually conducted in the context of safeguarding concerns and are detailed in Chapter 26. However, some of the guidance on establishing engagement in Chapter 26, which focuses on working in social care, may be useful to draw on when working with families that appear resistant or ambivalent about the process.

12.4.4 Assessment of the Behaviour

The main aim of this assessment process is to identify the function of the behaviour and the contextual and relational factors that may be impacting it. This may be the first opportunity to develop a shared narrative between the practitioner, parent and CYP about these functions. In addition to assessing in detail the current concerns, tracking back to when the parent first became concerned and why allows the opportunity to track changes over time and what has been tried to manage the issue to date. It also enables exploration of the family's understanding of and beliefs around the presenting behaviours and what factors may have contributed to them. The impact of the behaviours on quality of life, educational attainment, peer and family relationships, self-esteem and mood is important.

A diary or record that maps the antecedents, behaviours and consequences (ABC) of the target behaviour for both parent and child, including noting what helps and what makes the situation worse for all involved, introduces the idea that parents need to be reflective about their own triggers and behaviour when responding to their child. As part of this it is useful to explore how different family members respond to the behaviour and if the behaviour varies across settings. To do this the assessment process may need to involve or request feedback from all of the adults responsible for parenting the child and making key decisions about them, for example co-parents, grandparents or other extended family members and older siblings. Consent regarding information sharing needs to be clarified and thought about carefully in families where parents are separated, particular if the child's behaviour varies across the two households. It is very useful to include other health, education and social care professionals with knowledge of the child and family as part of the assessment.

To aid analysis of the function on the behaviour other useful assessment tools may include standardised questionnaires such as behaviour or mood questionnaires or checklists, for example the Child Behaviour Checklist (Achenbach, 1999), the Strengths and Difficulties Questionnaire (SDQ; Goodman, 1997) or relational tools such as timelines, genograms and sculpts. The key focus when identifying the function of the behaviour is to develop an understanding of whether there may be an underlying trauma or mental health issue that requires additional assessment or intervention. It is often useful to use a measure of mental health symptomatology in such cases such as the Revised Child Anxiety and Depression Scale (RCADS), which is a 47-item self-report measure that asks about symptoms of anxiety and depression in young people aged 8 to 18 years (Chorpita et al., 2000).

Although there is no substantial evidence base for the use of narrative approaches with young people who have behavioural difficulties per se, in our clinical experience it has been useful to talk about the behaviours as though they are external to the young person – these externalising approaches (see White & Epston, 1990) can enable the family to take a more curious position and also enable the young person to feel less defensive or ashamed about their behaviours.

In assessing risk, it is important to understand the extent of the behavioural difficulties and the risk of harm to the young person themselves, the parents, siblings, peers and animals. It is also important to enquire about theft and destruction of property. All parenting interventions should assess for potential safeguarding concerns and, where present, local protocols should be followed.

Finally, it is important to embed the behaviour of the CYP within a broader context by assessing how they are functioning, both socially and academically in other environments such as education. Teacher reports will be very helpful and may be gathered verbally at network meetings or school observations, through behavioural monitoring charts or from standardised measures such as the teacher version of the SDQ.

Now that we have introduced key aspects on the assessment of behaviours, please take a few moments to engage with the reflective exercise in Box 12.2. Following on from this, there is an opportunity to apply these aspects to the clinical material provided in Box 12.3.

Box 12.2 Assessment process – reflective exercise

In pairs with a colleague or supervisor from your service discuss:

How your service setting approaches assessments with young people, their families and networks.

How might your service contexts enable needs led assessments that centre the voice of the child?

What benefits and barriers are there to your existing frameworks for assessment?

How does your current assessment process ensure that the sociocultural context of the child's behaviour is explored and used to inform formulations and interventions?

What information and narratives about the function of behaviours might be currently prioritised or subjugated by your current assessments?

How might you use the themes and ideas you have just identified to improve the assessment practices in your service?

Box 12.3 Clinical example: Assessment

In this example of clinical practice we are writing from the position of mental health practitioners working in a service for young people with challenging behaviour. This provides direct intervention to families alongside consultation to professionals.

You have received a referral for Matt who is a 10-year-old boy of white British heritage who has been referred following multiple interventions by public health nursing and a school-based behavioural outreach team. Matt has recently been placed on a Child in Need plan, further to concerns about him being smacked by his parents and him being out of parental control, (for example, by leaving the house after dark). There are also concerns about his vulnerability due to local county lines activity.

The family have been well supported until recent months when the parents separated in the context of increasingly escalating arguments, which has impacted on their levels of support. More recently it has become clear that there was historical domestic abuse in the parental relationship, though this is denied by Alan, Matt's father. Matt appears to have increasingly low self-esteem and recently told his behaviour support team worker that he wanted to die.

At initial assessment at CAMHS, attended by Matt and his mother Miriam, the following is identified:

Goals

Matt – although initially he says he just wants everyone off his case, through the process of the assessment he identifies that he would like there to be fewer arguments and to be allowed to take part in football again.

Miriam – to come off the Child in Need plan and for appropriate housing to be sourced.

Developmental history

It has been hard to get a clear idea of Matt's cognitive and social skills as he can find it hard to settle to work and his peers are wary of him.

Family context

Matt lives with his mother and his younger sisters aged 9 and 7. They have a two-bedroom flat and Miriam sleeps on the sofa. There are concerns about antisocial behaviour in the neighbourhood.

Miriam describes that there have been inconsistencies in their parenting of Matt, and that Alan was often undermining of her attempts to parent Matt. The maternal grandparents are involved but critical of Matt's behaviour. Alan does not consider there to be an issue and was reluctant to pursue the referral, having agreed to it due to the Child in Need plan.

Miriam describes feeling anxious about her husband returning to the family home and her ability to keep both Matt and herself safe. She is concerned about who he may be mixing with when he leaves the family home and whether the safety of the family may be further compromised as a result. Miriam is accessing a domestic abuse support group via social care and there are views that she may need a more targeted mental health intervention due to her anxiety levels.

Assessment of the behaviour

The main concerns relate to Matt's destruction of property as a result of 'lashing out'. He is also described to shout and state that he will harm others, though he hasn't been reported to be physically aggressive.

Matt has damaged his knuckles as a result of punching holes in his bedroom door.

Matt's sisters have started to cower when he raises his voice and the youngest sister's teacher is concerned about her becoming withdrawn.

Miriam has completed an SDQ, which indicates high scores on conduct problems and low scores on prosocial and peer-relationship skills.

The RCADS indicates issues with separation anxiety and low mood.

Miriam completes an ABC chart that identifies that these behaviours are most likely to take place on Matt's return from school and on his return from contact with Alan. Since the introduction of the Child in Need plan, Miriam no longer smacks Matt, but feels at a loss regarding how else to manage his behaviour, and therefore takes the girls into her bedroom and they wait there until Matt calms down.

In one-to-one time with Matt, he shares that he is worried about losing control and harming his family.

12.5 Formulation

The formulations used in several of the evidence-based parenting approaches detailed earlier draw on a range of theories including operant conditioning (Skinner, 1963) social learning theory (Bandura, 1977), attachment theory (Bowlby, 1969) and/or systems theory (von Bertalanffy, 1968). Detailed descriptions of these theories are beyond the scope of this chapter, however a brief outline is given to guide the formulation process. Operant conditioning introduced the idea that the consequences of an action or behaviour determine the probability of it being repeated. Behaviour is likely to be repeated if the consequence is pleasant or rewarding, and behaviour that is followed by less pleasant consequences or punishment will be less likely to reoccur. Social learning theory builds on operant conditioning and emphasises that social behaviour is learned, reinforced and maintained by observing and imitating the behaviour of others. Attachment theory highlights the parent–child relationship and the how a child's behaviour and development is impacted by the sensitivity of parental responses. Kerr and Bowen (1988) introduced the idea that family members are interconnected in a complex social system and influence each other's behaviour, meaning that a family should be viewed as a whole rather than as individuals. These theoretical underpinnings highlight that the formulation should include an understanding of individual, family and contextual factors and not just focus on the child's behaviour.

Johnstone and Dallos (2014) remind us that formulations should enable clients working with psychological practitioners to make coherent sense of how their difficulties develop and are maintained, be linked with theory, and importantly should be collaborative, useful, focused and appropriate to the context.

We would also advise that any formulations take into account the multiple contexts within which people develop (for example, see Bronfenbrenner's work on the ecology of human development; Bronfenbrenner, 1979).

The formulation should embed the difficulties within the current family, cultural and social context and include some clear hypotheses regarding why the behaviours are presenting at this point in time. In addition, there should be shared agreement regarding the triggers for specific behaviours and an understanding of the function of the behaviour. This shared view is key as parents are unlikely to accept an intervention plan where the rationale for the work does not feel meaningful. If the behaviour varies across contexts, it is important to link this to different relationships, expectations and responses received.

Maintaining factors should be considered at an individual, parental and systemic level, for example what needs are being communicated or met, the impact of parental responses and the role of peer relationships.

Finally, it is essential to draw out areas of strength, resilience and attempts that may have been made to improve things by any members of the family. This can be invaluable in situations where there are multiple difficulties and both the family and the professionals working with them feel 'stuck' as it can provide a key area to enhance or develop.

We are mindful that in several contexts there will be limitations in the number of sessions available or that you may be working in a consultative capacity. We would argue that a thorough formulation is key even if the intervention that can be offered is limited as this provides the family and/or network with ideas on ways forward.

Now that you have had an opportunity to consider the key aspects involved in developing a formulation, please consider its application to the clinical material provided in Box 12.4.

Box 12.4 Clinical example: Formulation

Parental beliefs and responses

Miriam feels judged and criticised regarding her parenting, which has impacted on her confidence in managing Matt. The experience of accessing multiple interventions without success has led to her feeling underconfident that she can be helped or that their needs can be met. This compounds her negative self-judgement further to her domestic abuse and she is therefore highly sensitive to any perception of criticism.

Young person's beliefs and responses

Matt is struggling at school socially and academically, which leads him to feel different from his peers. He fears being excluded at school and each day tries his hardest to develop more positive relationships, but this is difficult to sustain as others become frustrated with him. Matt feels more accepted by the young people he spends time with in his neighbourhood. He feels confused about how to communicate his needs as a male approaching adolescence, given his experiences of his father.

On return from contact with his father, Matt struggles with the change in routine as his father treats him as an older peer and he has fewer boundaries. This leads him to feel more tired and irritable and he expresses his frustration that his mother has different expectations for him by being uncooperative and argumentative.

Relational and contextual aspects

Both Miriam and Matt seem to have fears regarding safety and Miriam also experiences anxiety about her relationship with Matt becoming physically aggressive, evoking her traumatic experiences of domestic abuse from her relationship with Alan. This causes her to withdraw further that contributes to Matt feeling excluded within the family and results in her shifting her expectations and not implementing boundaries consistently.

In developing the formulation together with the family, Miriam acknowledges that her emotional responses influence her interactions with and expectations of the children. She also feels the lack of physical space at home means their emotions are intensified. Matt has indicated that he feels this is a more helpful way of understanding the experiences he has found confusing and overwhelming.

Exercise: Developing a formulation

Consider the information from the assessment:

What are the key triggers for the behaviour?

What are the functions of Matt's behaviour?

What sociocultural factors are important in understanding Matt's behaviour?

What theories could be applied to this formulation?

How might you test out this formulation?

How are your own beliefs and expectations about parenting practices influencing your formulation? How might Miriam's beliefs and expectations differ from these?

In what way does this formulation help to identify next steps for Matt and his family?

12.6 Interventions

NICE (2017) advocates that individual needs and preferences should be taken into account when planning care, including the acceptability and tolerability of proposed interventions. They recommend parent training programmes for parents of children aged between 3 and 11 years, social and cognitive problem-solving programmes to children aged 9 to 14 years, and 'multimodal' interventions such as MST to young people aged between 11 and 17 years. Where ADHD has also been diagnosed, pharmacological interventions are also recommended.

12.6.1 Parent Training Programmes

NICE (2017) recommends that parent training programmes should be delivered in groups to both parents where possible, with between 10 and 12 parents in attendance. They should be focused on social learning theory, using modelling, rehearsal and feedback. The group programme should last for between 10 and 16 sessions for around 2 hours a session. It is recommended that programmes are adhered to closely to ensure high fidelity. Where it is not possible for parents to engage in group programmes, individual interventions based on these approaches should be considered.

The Incredible Years (IY) programme (see Webster-Stratton, 2019) is a particularly well-used and researched programme in the UK that uses the image of a 'parenting pyramid' to scaffold approaches to parenting. In the early sessions of the programme, parents are introduced to play-based approaches to help increase empathy and listening skills in parents, which parents are encouraged to apply liberally, there is also a strong focus on praise and positive reinforcement. Towards the second half of the programme, there is more of a focus on limit setting, household rules, distraction/redirection and finally, the application of consequences (with the intention that these are applied selectively and only in the context of the other elements of the programme). A wide range of approaches are used in the group including in-session practice, review of recorded scenarios, home-based tasks, diary records and exploration of the parental beliefs that may impact on the use of each element.

12.6.2 Child-focused Programmes

For young people aged between 9 and 14 years, NICE (2017) recommends that group programmes focusing on social and cognitive problem-solving should be considered. These should be appropriate to the young person's developmental stage and use modelling, rehearsal and feedback to enhance skills. The programme should last for between 10 and 18 sessions for around 2 hours a session.

12.6.3 Multimodal Interventions

These should be offered to young people and their networks for those aged 11 years and over. NICE (2017) recommends that interventions are targeted at an individual, family, school, criminal justice or community level (according to need) with frequent sessions (several per week) over 3 to 5 months. These should be based on social learning theory.

Alongside manualised group interventions there may be a need for individual parenting interventions. The starting point for this is developing a shared formulation with agreement to focusing on the challenging behaviour within a systemic context and including all relevant members of the family. This is to manage parental expectations and clarify that behavioural problems need to viewed within a social context and therefore an individual child-focused therapeutic intervention is not indicated.

After the development of a shared formulation a starting point may be psychoeducation around their child's stage of development, behavioural and attachment theory. This is to help develop an understanding of the need for any intervention to be relationally based whilst also clarifying and managing parents' expectations regarding their child's behaviour.

In the initial stages parents may need support in thinking about ways of developing connection such as how to play, setting up special or talking time, shared hobbies or tasks. When a child presents with behaviour that challenges the impact of this can be that parents tend to withdraw, which in turn can maintain behaviours where the function is to communicate or seek connection.

Parents may need guidance to develop strategies to regulate their own emotions and sometimes to manage their mental health in response to their child's behaviour. This may require referral or liaison with an alternative service provision for example, adult mental services or social care. Alongside this, parents may need help to develop or activate their social or other appropriate support network. This needs to be done sensitively as often parents can experience feelings of shame and fear of judgement about their difficulties. Considering parental stress levels provides an opportunity to support parents in developing a more mindful response towards their child in which they are responding to the need being communicated by the behaviour and not simply reacting (McCurry, 2009).

In interventions drawing from social learning theory parents will need input regarding strategies for rewarding or reinforcing behaviour. These may vary from skills training around the communication of praise to more concrete strategies such as star, token or other reward-based systems. These need to be linked to both the formulation and the developmental stage of the child and care needs to be taken to ensure that the behavioural goals are clear, realistic and achievable.

Strategies that may be viewed as 'punishing' or providing consequences for undesired behaviour need to be considered in the context of how this might impact on the parent–child relationship, parental resources available to enforce the consequence consistently, and how the motivation of the CYP to engage in more prosocial behaviour is likely to be impacted.

CYP may need parental intervention to calm down when they are feeling overwhelmed with emotion, to develop alternative ways to communicate their needs and to implement problem-solving skills.

Now that you have had an opportunity to consider the important aspects of interventions for behaviour difficulties, please take a moment to apply this to the clinical material provided in Box 12.5.

Box 12.5 Clinical example: Intervention

In conversation with Matt and Miriam and incorporating the discussion regarding goals you consider the patterns that trigger and maintain the behaviour both in the immediate setting and the wider context. Particular triggers are returning to the family home (restricted space) and returning from contact with Alan seem important as well as regarding concerns about safety at home and in the community. In addition emotional triggers relating to anxious thoughts and feelings, self-doubt and criticism (for both Matt and his mum) are important. Communication, socially and emotionally (of stress and distress) seem key areas for skills development.

Given Matt's age and developmental stage and the available evidence base, you recognise the importance of engaging him directly in the work rather than working solely with his parents. Miriam has spoken of feeling isolated and lacking confidence and you therefore discuss that a group-based intervention such as NVR might facilitate her in accessing a support network, regaining hope and increasing her confidence when responding to challenging behaviours whilst paying attention to their relationship.

In preparation for the group intervention, you use externalising language to connect the family to the underlying distress and reduce feelings of blame and shame. You also work with school staff to think about supporting Matt in developing his social skills and building peer relationships. You work in collaboration with the family's social worker to consider the impact of the crowded accommodation and support their housing application given his vulnerability and the perceived impact on functioning.

Outcomes

The SDQ, RCADS and goals-based outcomes were repeated following interventions and indicated that there was some improvement in the area of low mood, prosocial behaviour and separation anxiety. However, more peer-related interaction has also led to an increase in Matt's levels of social anxiety (as reported by the RCADS). Together, you formulate that this does not represent an emerging new diagnostic presentation, but rather a recognition that Matt is understandably experiencing some challenges in negotiating new ways of interacting with his peers.

Despite feeling anxious about professional input, Miriam is trying her best to implement the suggestions made and is starting to find the NVR group programme of some use. She reports a greater sense of agency and direction as well as feeling more understood and valued.

The social worker has addressed contact with Alan and been working on the benefits of boundary setting and to establish greater consistency across households.

Exercise

What alternative interventions could have been implemented based on the assessment information and formulation?

Are there any ways in which the assessment, formulation or intervention could have been adapted to make it more culturally appropriate?

How might you widen the intervention to include other professionals in the network?

How might externalising language and concepts be useful with the wider network?

12.7 Evaluation

Evaluation of any intervention must start with consideration of the purpose of the evaluation. For example, does the practitioner wish to demonstrate the effectiveness of treatment outcomes to secure funding, or for the purposes of clinical assessment and intervention planning, or to meet another clinical need? If the aim is two-fold a combination of measures may be required. It is essential to include outcomes that are meaningful to the young person and their parents. In addition to observable behavioural changes as measured by standardised assessment tools and questionnaires, it is important that there is a focus on changes in relational aspects and perceived parental efficacy; for example, improvements in family or peer relationships and engagement with services, increased parental efficacy in managing situations and a general sense of feeling able to cope, and decreased parenting related anxiety and helplessness. Families may view no longer requiring intervention from professionals, or stepping down from a safeguarding or Child in Need plan as a positive outcome. It is important these outcomes are linked to the goals identified by families at the start of the intervention and linked to discussions around sustaining changes.

There are a number of standardised measures that may be useful and which are selected will depend on the purpose of the evaluation and the goals set at the start. For example, there are numerous measures looking at behaviour and symptoms such as child behaviour checklist (CBCL; Achenbach, 1999) and the SDQ (Goodman, 1997). Measures that consider family relationships and perceived parental self-efficacy, levels of parental stress and helplessness may be implemented; for example, the tool to measure parenting self-efficacy (TOPSE; Kendall et al., 2005), parenting stress index (Abidin, 2012) or the SCORE-15 (Stratton et al. 2010). Reviewing goals-based outcomes (Law & Jacob, 2015) that link back to the hopes of the family at the start of the intervention can be both empowering and validating and are an effective way to encourage the voice of the young person to be heard. Alternatively, measures such as the session rating scale (SRS; Duncan et al., 2003) and the outcome rating scale (Miller et al., 2003) that can be used with parents and young people may provide useful insight into levels of engagement and families' general experience of the therapeutic intervention.

12.8 Common Challenges and Addressing Them in the Work

One of the biggest challenges to parenting work is with regard to intervention completion rates. A US-based systematic review of the literature by Chacko et al. (2016) found that a quarter of parents that could potentially benefit fail to sign up for parenting interventions. Of those that do start, a further quarter of parents drop out before completing the intervention. Weisenmuller and Hilton (2021) have conducted another US-based review looking at the barriers to accessing parenting interventions that include systemic factors such as funding and a shortage of appropriately trained practitioners, the impact of cultural and religious beliefs about parenting, parents' own childhood experiences and mental health difficulties, and the role of stigma. Some of these findings may also be applicable to the UK context but further investigation is needed. These reviews highlight the need to support engagement even prior to referral by preparing families for a parenting intervention by thinking through potential practical obstacles alongside hopes and goals.

Parenting work can be demanding for practitioners and there is a risk of burnout and lack of empathy. An area of challenge can be when parents present as highly distressed and in need of support but appear unwilling or resistant to implement ideas discussed. The impact of this is a potential reduction in the practitioner's levels of therapeutic effort and caring behaviour, which they hypothesised might in turn influence the family's level of engagement and lack of action in the therapy process (Patterson & Chamberlain, 1994). Hawes and Dadds (2021) have built on Patterson et al.'s research on parental resistance to propose a reflective practice model for managing such scenarios. It includes encouraging practitioners to reflect on their own responses, welcome alternative views and disagreement, reframe resistance, empower parents and revisit a shared agenda.

Alternatively, another way forward when feeling 'stuck' or overwhelmed within the work would be for practitioners to think about the theoretical models underpinning their formulation and intervention, for example, rewards (social learning theory) and providing consistency (attachment theory), and consider applying it to the therapeutic relationship with parents (Scott & Dadds, 2009). This emphasises the need for a safe supervisory or reflective space where these dynamics can be explored to avoid repeating patterns.

Alongside this, managing positioning and alignment with all members of the system requires care and attention. It can be easy to become aligned with a parent who shares the practitioner's views on parenting, or positioning into the role of an expert but this risks alienating family members and may be experienced as coercive. In these instances the use of motivational interviewing can help rebuild the alliance and offer solutions for a more collaborative way forward (Miller & Rollnick, 2002; Scott & Dadds, 2009).

Parents are aware of the influence that social media plays in both offering support to them, and in increasing a sense of self-judgement. For example, there is a movement towards dispelling the myths that parenting is all-rewarding, and this can connect parents in helpful ways. However, the risks of experiencing 'trolling' online remain high, and there is the potential to experience criticism of parenting approaches taken.

Finally, we recognise that the political system in the UK can result in rapid changes in priorities regarding government health investment. This has resulted in a lack of sustainability of many parenting and family initiatives, and creates concern about the longer-term prognosis for young people with emerging behavioural difficulties, for example, the closure of early intervention and prevention initiatives such as Sure Start programmes and family centres.

Engaging all the key adults responsible for parenting a CYP can be challenging depending on family composition. For example, in families where parents are separated and relationships are acrimonious it is helpful early on to explore and understand factors such as parental responsibility, consent, potential alienation of parent/s and how best to set up sessions with families that struggle to be in the same room to most usefully facilitate conversation. Chapter 5 on legal and professional contexts may provide additional guidance. Working closely with colleagues either in a multidisciplinary team and/or clinical supervision are important ways to remain mindful of not losing the child's voice or forming alliances with one parent where there are high levels of conflict.

Historically, practitioners have reported difficulties in engaging fathers, where present, in parenting interventions and there has been much research and discussion in the literature about how best to address this. Over the past few years, partly stemming from the Covid-19 pandemic, services are being offered more flexibly, such as via online sessions, which may be one way to make sessions more accessible for fathers. See also Chapter 24 for further ideas. In addition, there may be other creative ways to include the voice of fathers such as using genograms or chairwork.

12.9 Future Directions

Children's services in the UK are on the cusp on transforming to a THRIVE model of service delivery (Wolpert et al., 2019), from a long-standing tiered model of service delivery. This is intended to reduce gaps between provider services and enable a more needs-led approach to delivery. The move towards more integrated services is hoped to enable communities to access the right support at the right time. This may lead to greater investment in early intervention and prevention services to support the whole family with managing behaviours that challenge, clearer pathways to accessing help and ways for professionals to highlight at risk families.

The NHS Long Term Plan (NHS, 2019) also prioritises preventative care, in addition to integrated care across providers. The dovetailing of these two priorities is likely to be of benefit for CYP with behavioural difficulties who often experience delays in accessing appropriate intervention. One of the challenges is that many of the initiatives being proposed to reduce gaps between services depend on local commissioning arrangements.

The increasing adoption of MST and NVR across services is likely to lead to the role out of these approaches across the UK. This will have an impact on the training of professionals working with CYP and enable a shared language for the conceptualisation and interventions required for young people.

References

Abidin, R. R. (2012). *Parenting stress index* (4th ed.). Lutz.

Abrines-Jaume, N., Midgley, N., Hopkins, K., Hoffman, J., Martin, K., Law, D., & Wolpert, M. (2016). A qualitative analysis of implementing shared decision making in Child and Adolescent Mental Health Services in the United Kingdom: Stages and facilitators. *Clinical Child Psychology and Psychiatry, 21*(1), 19–31. https://doi.org/10.1177/1359104514547596

Achenbach, T. M. (1999). The Child Behavior Checklist and related instruments. In M. E. Maruish (Ed.), *The use of psychological testing for treatment planning and outcomes assessment* (pp. 429–466). Lawrence Erlbaum Associates Publishers.

Ahemaitijiang, N., Fang, H., Ren, Y., Han, Z. R., & Singh, N. N. (2021, August 27). A review of mindful parenting: Theory, measurement, correlates, and outcomes. *Journal of Pacific Rim Psychology, 15*. https://doi.org/10.1177/18344909211037016

Bandura, A. (1977). Self-efficacy: Toward a unifying theory of behavioral change. *Psychological Review, 84*(2), 191–215. https://doi.org/10.1037/0033-295X.84.2.191

Bateson, K., Delaney, J., & Pybus, R. (2008). Meeting expectations: The pilot evaluation of the Solihull Approach Parenting Group. *Community Practitioner*, *81*, 28–31.

Berry, J., & Jones, W. (1995). The Parental Stress Scale: Initial psychometric evidence. *Journal of Social and Personal Relationships*, *12*, 463–472.

Bogels, S. M., Hoogstad, B., van Dun, L., de Schutter, S., & Restifo, K. (2008). Mindfulness training for adolescents with externalizing disorders and their parents. *Behavioral and Cognitive Psychotherapy*, *36*, 193–209. https://doi.org/10.1017/S1352465808004190

Bowlby, J. (1969). *Attachment and loss, vol. 1: Attachment*. Basic Books.

Bronfenbrenner, U. (1979). *The ecology of human development: Experiments by nature and design*. Harvard University Press.

Byng-Hall, J. (1995). *Rewriting family scripts: Improvisation and systems change*. Guilford Press.

Bywater, T., Hutchings, J., Daley, D., Whitaker, C., Yeo, S., Jones, K., Eames, C., & Edwards, R. (2009). Long-term effectiveness of a parenting intervention in Sure Start services in Wales for children at risk of developing conduct disorder. *British Journal of Psychiatry*, *195*(4), 318–324. https://doi.org/10.1192/bjp.bp.108.05653

Chacko, A., Jensen, S. A., Lowry, L. S., Cornwell, M., Chimklis, A., Chan, E., Lee, D., & Pulgarin, B. (2016). Engagement in behavioral parent training: Review of the literature and implications for practice. *Clinical Child and Family Psychology Review*, *19*, 204–215. https://doi.org/10.1007/s10567-016-0205-2

Chao, R. K. (1994). Beyond parental control and authoritarian parenting style: Understanding Chinese parenting through the cultural notion of training. *Child Development*, *65*(4), 1111–1119. https://doi.org/10.2307/1131308

Chorpita, B. F., Yim, L., Moffitt, C., Umemoto, L. A., & Francis, S. E. (2000). Assessment of symptoms of DSM-IV anxiety and depression in children: A revised child anxiety and depression scale. *Behaviour Research and Therapy*, *38*(8), 835–855.

Conners, C. K. (1999). Conners rating scales – revised. In M. E. Maruish (Ed.), *The use of psychological testing for treatment planning and outcomes assessment* (pp. 467–495). Lawrence Erlbaum Associates.

Douglas, H. (2018). *The Solihull approach in practice*. Solihull Approach.

Douglas, H., & Johnson. R. (2019). The Solihull approach 10-week programme: A randomised controlled trial. *Community Practitioner*, *9*(7), 45–47.

Duncan, B. L., Miller, S. D., Sparks, J., Claud, D., Reynolds, L., Brown, J., & Johnson, L. (2003). The session rating scale: Preliminary psychometric properties of a 'working' alliance measure. *Journal of Brief Therapy*, *3*, 3–12.

Early Intervention Foundation. (2017). Early Intervention Foundation guidebook: Family nurse partnership. https://guidebook.eif.org.uk/programme/family-nurse-partnership

Family Nurse Partnership (2023). fnp.nhs.uk. https://www.fnp.nhs.uk

Gardner, F., Leijten, P., Harris, V., Mann, J., Hutchings, J., Beecham, J., Bonin, E-M., Berry, V., McGilloway, S., Gaspar, M., Seabra-Santos, M. J., Orobio de Castro, B., Menting, A., Williams, M., Axberg, U., Morch, W-T., Scott, S., & Landau, S. (2019). Equity effects of parenting interventions for child conduct problems: A pan-European individual participant data meta-analysis. *The Lancet Psychiatry*, *6*(6), 518–527.

George, C. (2011). Caregiving helplessness: Development of a questionnaire to screen for maternal caregiving disorganisation. In J. Solomon & C. George (Eds.), *Disorganised attachment and Caregiving*. (pp. 133–166). Guilford Press.

Ghate, D., & Ramella, M. (2002). *Positive parenting: The national evaluation of the Youth Justice Board's parenting programme.* Policy Research Bureau for the Youth Justice Board.

Goodman, R. (1997). The strengths and difficulties questionnaire: A research note. *Journal of Child Psychology and Psychiatry, 38*(5), 581–586.

Harris, R. (2019). *ACT made simple: An easy-to-read primer on acceptance and commitment therapy* (2nd ed.). New Harbinger Publications.

Hawes, D., & Dadds, M. R. (2021). Practitioner review: Parenting interventions for child conduct problems: Reconceptualising resistance to change. *Journal of Child Psychology and Psychiatry, 62*(10), 1166–1174. https://doi:10.1111/jcpp.13378

Henggeler, S. W., Rodick, J. D., Borduin, C. M., Hanson, C. L., Watson, S. M., & Urey, J. R. (1986). Multisystemic treatment of juvenile offenders: Effects on adolescent behavior and family interaction. *Developmental Psychology, 22*(1), 132–141. https://doi.org/10.1037/0012-1649.22.1.132

Jeong, J., Pitchik, H., & Fink, G. (2021). Short-term, medium-term and long-term effects of early parenting interventions in low- and middle-income countries: A systematic review. *BMJ Global Health, 6*, e004067.

Johnstone, L., & Dallos, R. (2014). Introduction to formulation. In L. Johnstone & R. Dallos (Eds.), *Formulation in psychology and psychotherapy: Making sense of people's problems.* Routledge.

Juffer, F., Bakermans-Kranenburg, M. J., & van Ijzendoorn, M. H. (Eds.). (2008). *Promoting positive parenting: An attachment-based intervention.* Taylor & Francis Group/ Lawrence Erlbaum Associates.

Kendall S., & Bloomfield, L. (2005). TOPSE: Developing and validating a tool to measure parenting self-efficacy. *Journal of Advanced Nursing, 51*(2), 174–181.

Kennedy, H., Landor, M., & Todd. L. (2010). Video interaction guidance as a method to promote secure attachment. *Educational and Child Psychology, 27*(3). https://doi.org/10.53841/bpsecp.2010.27.3.59

Kerr, M., & Bowen, M. (1988). *Family evaluation: An approach based on Bowen theory.* W. W. Norton & Co.

La Placa, V., & Corlyon, J. (2015). Unpacking the relationship between parenting and poverty: Theory, evidence and policy. *Social Policy and Society, 15*(1), 11–28.

Law, D., & Jacob, J. (2015). *Goals and goal-based outcomes (GBOs): Some useful information.* CAMHS Press.

Leijten, P., Gardner, F., Melendez-Torres, G., van Aar, J., Hutchings, J., Schulz, S., Knerr, W., & Overbeek, G. (2019). Meta-analysis: Key parenting program components for disruptive child behavior. *Journal of the American Academy of Child & Adolescent Psychiatry, 58*(2), 180–190.

Leitner, Y. (2014). The co-occurrence of autism and attention deficit hyperactivity disorder in children – what do we know? *Frontiers in Human Neuroscience, 8*, 268. https://doi.org/10.3389/fnhum.2014.00268

Madge, N., & Willmott, N. (2007). *Children's views and experiences of parenting.* Joseph Rowntree Foundation, National Children's Bureau. https://www.jrf.org.uk/sites/default/files/jrf/migrated/files/childrens-views-parenting.pdf

Mazzucchelli, T., & Sanders, M. (2014). Parenting from the outside-in: A paradigm shift in parent training? *Behaviour Change, 31*(2), 102–109.

McCurry, C. (2009). *Parenting your anxious child with mindfulness and acceptance: A powerful new approach to overcoming fear, panic, and worry using acceptance and commitment therapy.* New Harbinger Publications.

Michelson, D., Davenport, C., Dretzke, J., Barlow, J., & Day, C. (2013). Do evidence-based interventions work when tested in the 'real world?' A systematic review and meta-analysis of parent management training for the treatment of child disruptive behavior. *Clinical Child and Family Psychology Review, 16*, 18–34. https://doi.org/10.1007/s10567-013-0128-0

Milford, R., Kleve, L., Lea, J., & Greenwood, R. (2006). A pilot evaluation study of the Solihull Approach. *Community Practitioner, 79*(11), 358–362.

Miller, S. D., Duncan, B. L., Brown, J., Sparks, J., & Claud, D. (2003). The outcome rating scale: A preliminary study of the reliability, validity, and feasibility of a brief visual analog measure. *Journal of Brief Therapy, 2*, 91–100.

Miller, W. R., & Rollnick, S. (2002). *Motivational interviewing: Preparing people for change* (2nd ed.). The Guilford Press.

Mills-Koonce, W., Appleyard, K., Barnett, M., Deng, M., Putallaz, M., & Cox, M. (2011). Adult attachment style and stress as risk factors for early maternal sensitivity and negativity. *Infant Mental Health Journal, 32*(3), 277–285. https://doi.org/10.1002/imhj.20296

Newman, M., Fagan, C., & Webb, R. (2014). Innovations in practice: The efficacy of nonviolent resistance groups in treating aggressive and controlling children and young people: A preliminary analysis of pilot NVR groups in Kent. *Child and Adolescent Mental Health, 19*(2), 138–141.

NHS. (2019). *The NHS Long Term Plan*. NHS England. www.longtermplan.nhs.uk

NICE. (2015). Children's attachment: attachment in children and young people who are adopted from care, in care or at high risk of going into care. National Institute for Health and Care Excellence: Clinical guideline NG26.

NICE. (2017). *Antisocial behaviour and conduct disorders in children and young people: recognition and management*. National Institute for Health and Care Excellence: Clinical guideline CG158.

Nixon, E., & Halpenny, A. (2010). *Children's perspectives on parenting styles and discipline: A developmental approach.* Office of the Minister for Children and Youth Affairs. https://www.tcd.ie/tricc/assets/pdfs/crc-archive/2010-Nixon-Halpenny-Childrens-perspectives-on-parenting-styles.pdf

NSPCC. (2014). *Assessing parenting capacity: An NSPCC factsheet*. https://www.theministryofparenting.com/wp-content/uploads/2015/08/factsheet-assessing-parenting-capacity8.pdf

Omer, H., Schorr-Sapir, I., & Weinblatt, U. (2008). Non-violent resistance and violence against siblings. *Journal of Family Therapy, 30*(4), 450–464.

Paradisopoulos, D., Pote, H., Fox, S., & Kaur, P. (2015). Developing a model of sustained change following multisystemic therapy: Young people's perspectives. *Journal of Family Therapy, 37*(4), 471–491. https://doi.org/10.1111/1467-6427.12070

Patterson, G., & Chamberlain, P. (1994). A functional analysis of resistance during parent training therapy. *Clinical Psychology: Science and Practice, 1*(1), 53–70.

Phoenix, A., & Husain, F. (2007). *Parenting and ethnicity*. Joseph Rowntree Foundation.

Potharst, E., Boekhorst, M., Cuijlits, I., van Broekhoven, K., Jacobs, A., Spek, V., Nyklicek, I., Bogels, S., & Pop, V. (2019, July 17). A randomized control trial evaluating an online mindful parenting training for mothers with elevated parental stress. *Frontiers of Psychology, 10.* https://doi.org/10.3389/fpsyg.2019.01550

Public Health England. (2021). *Best start in life and beyond: Improving public health outcomes for children, young people and families.* Public Health England.

Puckering, C., Rogers, J., Mills, M., Cox, A. D., & Mattsson-Graff, M. (1994). Process and evaluation of a group intervention for mothers with parenting difficulties. *Child Abuse Review, 3*(4), 299–310. https://www.mellowparenting.org/

Reder, P., & Duncan, S. (1999). *Lost innocents: A follow-up study of fatal child abuse.* Routledge.

Rutter, M., Bailey, A., & Lord, C. (2003). *The social communication questionnaire: Manual.* Western Psychological Services.

Ryan, R., O'Farrelly, C., & Ramchandani, P. (2017). Parenting and child mental health. *London Journal of Primary Care, 9*(6), 86–94.

Sanders, M. R., Burke, K., Prinz, R. J., & Morawska, A. (2017). Achieving population-level change through a system-contextual approach to supporting competent parenting. *Clinical Child and Family Psychology Review, 20*, 36–44. https://doi.org/10.1007/s10567-017-0227-4

Scott, S., & Dadds, M. R. (2009). Practitioner review: When parent training doesn't work: Theory-driven clinical strategies. *Journal of Child Psychology and Psychiatry, 50*(12), 1441–1450. https://doi.org/10.1111/j.1469-7610.2009.02161.x

Siegel, D. J., & Payne Bryson, T. P. (2012). *The whole-brain child.* Random House.

Skinner, B. F. (1963). Operant behavior. *American Psychologist, 18*(8), 503–515. https://doi.org/10.1037/h0045185

Stewart, S. M., & Bond, M. H. (2002). A critical look at parenting research from the mainstream: Problems uncovered while adapting Western research to non-Western cultures. *British Journal of Developmental Psychology, 20*(3), 379–392. https://doi.org/10.1348/026151002320620389

Stratton, P., Bland, J., Janes, E., & Lask, J. (2010). Developing a practicable outcome measure for systemic family therapy: The SCORE. *Journal of Family Therapy, 32*, 232–258.

Swanson, J. (2013). The Snap-IV Teacher and Parent Rating Scale. *Therapist's Guide to Learning and Attention Disorders, 487–500.* https://doi.org/10.1016/B978-012256430-7/50022-3

Vizard, E., Hickey, N., & McCrory, E. (2007). Developmental trajectories associated with juvenile sexually abusive behaviour and emerging severe personality disorder in childhood: 3-year study. *British Journal of Psychiatry, 49*, 27–32.

von Bertalanffy, L. (1968). *General systems theory: Foundation, development, application.* Brazillier.

von Sydow, K., Retzlaff, R., Beher, S., Huan, M., & Schweitzer, J. (2013). The efficacy of systemic therapy for childhood and adolescent externalizing disorders: A systematic review of 47 RCT. *Family Process, 52*(4), 576–618.

Webster-Stratton, C. (2019). *The incredible years: A Trouble-shooting guide for parents of children aged 3–8 years* (3rd ed.). The Incredible Years.

Weinblatt, U., & Omer, H. (2008). Nonviolent resistance: A treatment for parents of children with acute behaviour problems. *Journal of Marital and Family Therapy, 34*(1), 75–92.

Weisenmuller, C., & Hilton, D. (2021). Barriers to access, implementation, and utilization of parenting interventions: Considerations for research and clinical applications. *American Psychologist, 76*(1), 104–115. https://doi.org/10.1037/amp0000613

White, M., & Epston, D. (1990). *Narrative means to therapeutic ends.* W. W. Norton.

Whiteside-Mansell, L., Bradley, R. H., Little, T. D., Corwyn, R. F., & Spiker, D. (2001). An examination of cross-racial comparability of mother–child interaction among African American and Anglo American families. *Journal of Marriage and the Family*, *63*(3), 767–778.

Winnicott, D. (1953). Transitional objects and transitional phenomena. *International Journal of Psychoanalysis*, *34*, 89–97.

Wolpert, M., Harris, R., Hodges, S., Fuggle, P., James, R., Wiener, A., McKenna, C., Law, D., York, A., Jones, M., Fonagy, P., Fleming, I., & Munk, S. (2019). *THRIVE framework for system change*. Anna Freud Centre.

World Health Organization. (2018). *International classification of diseases for mortality and morbidity statistics* (11th rev.). World Health Organization.

13

Emotional Difficulties

Vicki Curry and Maria Loades

13.1 Introduction

'Emotional difficulties' is a broad term that encompasses many of the problems child psychological practitioners will come across in Child and Adolescent Mental Health Service (CAMHS) work. It tends to refer to *internalising* (as opposed to externalising or thought disordered) difficulties (see Kotov et al., 2017), primarily those relating to different types of anxiety and low mood, which are the presenting difficulties focused on in this chapter. Although CAMHS often refer to presenting difficulties according to 'disorders' in the *Diagnostic and Statistical Manual* (DSM; American Psychological Association, 2013) and the *International Classification of Diseases* (ICD; World Health Organization, 2018) psychiatric diagnostic classification systems, many of the children and young people (CYP) seen in CAMHS have a range of complex presenting difficulties, and do not fit neatly into these 'disorder-specific' boxes. Recent research using factor analyses to examine the structure of psychopathology and inter-relationships between symptoms has begun to point to general distress present across a range of disorders, referred to as 'the p-factor', which may be conceptualised as a 'reflection of a single underlying source of vulnerability' (Fonagy & Allison, 2017, p. 986). The p-factor has been found to be the best predictor of long-term mental health difficulties (Caspi et al., 2014), and to be relevant to difficulties in CYP (Wright, 2017). This concept will be returned to later in the chapter in the discussion of the issue of co-morbidity across emotional disorders.

This chapter will cover both anxiety and depression. For clarity, anxiety is covered first: assessment, formulation and treatment, and then the same for depression. Fictitious illustrative clinical examples are used but it is not possible to give a formulation for every disorder-specific model of anxiety and low mood. A clinical example of a younger child is given for anxiety and of an adolescent for low mood. As discussed earlier, in practice, many CYP will have elements of both, and a formulation driven approach based on the difficulties a particular individual has and what makes sense to them and their families is recommended. Hence, the chapter concludes with a discussion of some of the common issues and challenges that may arise when working with CYP with emotional difficulties, with a particular focus on co-morbidity, motivation and engagement, working with the wider system, and equality, diversity and inclusion.

Child Psychology: Pathways to Good Practice, First Edition.
Edited by Helen Pote, Anna Picciotto and Clare Norris.

Note, obsessive compulsive disorder (OCD) which was previously considered to be an 'anxiety disorder' but no longer is (American Psychological Association, 2013) is not included in this chapter. Useful reference texts for practitioners on OCD in CYP are: the textbook by Waite and Williams (2009), a therapist manual by Turner et al. (2019b), which has a related workbook for children and adolescents themselves (Turner et al., 2019a), and a CBT guidebook written for children and families by Derisley et al. (2008). Post-traumatic stress disorder is also not included here; both are covered separately in Chapter 14.

CYP with neurodevelopmental disorders (like autism spectrum disorders) are more vulnerable to developing emotional difficulties and assessment, formulation and treatment needs to be adapted (Attwood & Scarpa, 2013; Walters et al., 2016). Similarly, CYP with chronic physical health conditions are more vulnerable to developing emotional difficulties, and work may also need to be adapted (Moore et al., 2019; Morey & Loades, 2020). Again, it is outside the scope of this chapter to cover these adaptations specifically, but they are addressed in Chapter 16.

13.2 Anxiety Disorders

Anxiety disorders are the most common of all psychological and emotional difficulties experienced by CYP. Polanczyk et al. (2015) conducted a systematic review of studies between 1985 and 2012 in 27 countries across the world, with CYP with different languages, religions, cultures and socioeconomic backgrounds. This review found that 6.5% of CYP at any one time would be diagnosed as having an anxiety problem and that 28.8% of people would experience one at some point during their life. In 50% of cases, the anxiety problem started before the age of 12 years; these estimates were not found to vary as a function of geographical location. Current prevalence in the UK is likely to be even higher than this, given that national surveys in England found a 51% increase in reported anxiety disorders between 2004 and 2017 (Vizard et al., 2018). Importantly, even more CYP experience subthreshold symptoms, which may not reach the level of a 'diagnosis', but still cause functional impairment to their lives (Balázs et al., 2013). With regards to differences in prevalence between sexes, the aforementioned national 2017 survey in England found similar rates in girls and boys in most types of anxiety disorder, apart from panic disorder, which had a higher prevalence in girls (1.7%:0.5%). It is clear that anxiety disorders have a negative impact on CYP's lives in a number of ways, including reduced social and academic functioning and increased risk of developing other psychological difficulties. If untreated they have been shown to continue into adulthood, with resultant reduced life satisfaction for the individual as well as economic burden on society. So – anxiety is a real problem – and is certainly one of the most common presenting difficulties practitioners are likely to come across in CAMHS work.

13.2.1 What is Anxiety?

Clearly, anxiety is a 'normal' emotion – everybody gets anxious sometimes. In the right amounts it can be useful: It's the body's automatic alarm signal, alerting and preparing one to deal with danger, and releasing hormones that in the right amount can help one to focus when necessary.

Anxiety has three characteristics:

Physical sensations in the body: These are associated with stress hormones (adrenaline and cortisol) that are released when danger is sensed which prepares one for action. These physical sensations will be slightly different for everyone, but include things like sweating, heart beating faster, trembling, feeling light-headed and sick. A slightly less well known and very 'normal' physical response is 'depersonalisation' or 'derealisation'. This is where the person feels slightly outside themselves, as if they are experiencing themselves and the world from a distance – maybe a bit floaty, or outside looking in. It's worth mentioning this to a young person because they often would not tell you about this because they don't realise it could be related to anxiety. If they search the Internet for these experiences all kinds of information may come up that might make them feel even more anxious, and make them worry about telling other people.

Anxious thoughts: Research has shown that when people are anxious, they tend to overestimate 'danger' – that something bad will happen and underestimate their ability to cope. Fears and worries are normal, and the content of what CYP worry about has been shown to be similar in 'clinical' and 'non-clinical' populations (school, health, harm to self or others, friendships). Children tend to worry about different things at different ages, linked partly to how developed their brain is and partly to other aspects of their development, like their life stage; the nature of these worries and fears impacts on the types of anxiety disorder that are therefore more prevalent at that age (see Beesdo et al., 2009). For example, when children are very young, they are only really aware of their immediate surroundings and tend to spend a lot of their time with close family, so the focus of their worry tends to be things like separation from primary caregivers. Separation anxiety is the most common anxiety disorders in children under the age of 12 years (Shear et al., 2006). As they get older their brains develop so they are able to contemplate the world in bigger ways. Also, they start being apart more from their families and they go to school, so things like academic performance and the peer group become more important and therefore a potential source of anxiety. This correlates with an increase in disorders like generalised anxiety and social anxiety. The other thing that is very normal in children is worrying about illness and death, especially between the ages of about 4 to 7 years. This coincides with their brains being developed enough for them to be getting a sense of more complex concepts and the world around them, but also often coinciding with a life stage where grandparents might get ill or even die. Parents and carers sometimes find it difficult to know how to answer these kinds of questions from their child, and it can be helpful to point them to useful resources that exist to help. The Anna Freud website has a helpful section on dealing with loss and bereavement, which also highlights additional resources practitioners and parents can make use of (https://www.annafreud.org/on-my-mind/dealing-with-loss-and-bereavement/).

Anxious behaviour: When CYP (and adults) are anxious, they understandably tend to behave in ways that help them look out for possible future danger (hypervigilance) and/or avoid future danger, including situations that make them feel scared or worried. An additional behaviour that is very common is seeking reassurance from others around them. Parents will often talk about children becoming withdrawn and wanting to stay with them. Another response that it is worth asking about is increased irritability and tantrums. Although people may assume that these behaviours are caused by anger, in fact they can be a consequence of stress and anxiety and it is important to keep this in mind in the assessment.

When Does Anxiety Become a 'Problem'?: Given that anxiety is a normal part of life, how does one work out whether to worry about it in a particular child? There are three things that it can be helpful to consider with the CYP/parent/carer:

- *Timing:* When did the symptoms develop? Might they be a 'normal' response to something that is happening in the child's life? A lot of children will get a bit anxious around the time of transition to secondary school for example, or if a close relative is ill, or they have had some friendship issues. If they are supported with the difficult life event, their anxiety difficulties will sometimes resolve, so it's worth doing a bit of 'watchful waiting' to see if signs and symptoms of anxiety persist.
- *Pervasiveness:* How strong is their anxiety? Is it starting to spread and impact more than one area of their life? Is it becoming difficult for them/their family/their school to manage?
- *Functional impairment:* To what extent is the child's anxiety stopping them from doing what they *want* to or *need* to be doing? Is it impacting on their social life, and causing friendship difficulties: Is it impacting on their ability to engage academically? Are they starting to feel fed up and miserable because of the impact of their anxiety on their life?

Importantly, it is not just the impact on the CYP themselves that is important to consider, but also the impact on others around them, such as their family. For example, is the CYP's anxiety stopping parents/carers from doing what *they* want to or need to be doing? Does the parent struggle to get a good night's sleep because the child comes into their bed every night? Does the child get distressed to the extent that they don't want their parent to leave home without them to go to work/the shops/for a night out with friends? If the family's life is disrupted by the anxiety in the child – even if the child themselves does not think there is a problem – this might be a reason for parents/carers to seek help.

13.2.2 What about Anxiety 'Disorders'?

Although all anxiety has common underlying characteristics outlined earlier, the exact nature of anxiety varies, and as a result it has been categorised into subgroups in psychiatric manuals. The major anxiety disorders included in DSM-V (2013) are: separation anxiety disorder, generalised anxiety disorder (GAD), social anxiety disorder, specific phobia, panic disorder, agoraphobia, and selective mutism. DSM-V contains detailed criteria, and Creswell et al. (2020) include a helpful table that summarise recent characteristics and prevalence figures for each. A bit of a flavour of how CYP with anxiety disorders might present in practice is provided here. For all disorders, the criteria require that the anxiety/worry is 'excessive' and 'persistent' and causing significant distress or functional impairment in their lives in order to be given a diagnosis. It is important to highlight that the whole issue of categorising the mental health of children into 'diagnoses' is contentious, and this is discussed in more detail later in this chapter. In addition, as mentioned earlier, there are many CYP who might not quite meet all the criteria for any anxiety 'diagnosis', but whose lives are significantly impacted by the following kinds of difficulties:

- Separation anxiety disorder: This is when a CYP's anxiety focuses on a worry about separating from primary caregiver(s), more than one would expect for their stage of development. The child might not want to be in a different room from their parent/carer at home – even following them to the toilet! They might struggle to sleep in their own room at night. They might get upset when their parent goes out without them or when they leave them at school. They often express worries about something bad happening to their parent/carer – but not all children are able to give specific concerns like this. Some of them just say they 'don't like it'.
- Generalised anxiety disorder (GAD): A CYP with GAD could be described as a 'bit of a worrier'. They tend to worry *a lot* about a *range* of things, in contrast to some of the other types of anxiety where the focus of worry is restricted to one particular area like social situations. CYP with GAD also find it difficult to control their worry – they might get reassured about one worry and then another one will pop up in its place.
- Social anxiety disorder: Here, the focus of the CYP's anxiety is social or performance situations. They tend to worry that they will act in a way that is embarrassing and that they will be negatively judged by others. This might lead to them really struggling to spend time with their peer group, for example, or to ask or answer a question in class; sometimes they withdraw completely. Obviously, a lot of adolescents get self-conscious and a bit socially awkward at times, so it can be helpful to ask the CYP if they think they find social situations more difficult than others in their class/year group.
- Panic disorder: This is where the CYP gets repeated and unexpected panic attacks. A panic attack is an intense and sudden surge of fear, accompanied by strong physical symptoms of anxiety, such as heart palpitations, shaking, chest pain, feeling dizzy, feeling sick. These physical symptoms often make the CYP think they are going to die and/or lose control/go 'crazy'.
- Specific phobia: A phobia is where the anxiety is restricted to fear of a specific object or situation, such as dogs, spiders, needles. Exposure to the feared object will induce intense fear/anxiety.
- Selective mutism: This is where a CYP consistently does not speak in certain social situations, whilst speaking normally in other situations. Often practitioners will meet CYP who do not talk at all outside the family home, for example, whereas their parents may describe them as being complete chatterboxes at home, or report that they do not have a problem communicating at home. Sometimes the children will have found other ways of communicating at school, for example, such as non-verbal communication, or will whisper to one or two people who then talk for them.

13.2.3 Assessing Anxiety Difficulties

Assessment in general is covered in Chapter 3. As with all difficulties in CYP, a good assessment will involve multiple perspectives and informants, including the CYP, family and school; and will include a range of factors such as questionnaires, discussion in sessions, behavioural observations and reports. There are many standardised questionnaires for different ages and informants to help with assessment (e.g. parent/child/teacher) (see Creswell et al., 2020 for a review). It can be useful to start off with a more generic screening questionnaire like the Revised Children's Anxiety and Depression Scale (RCADS; Chorpita et al.,

2000), and then focus in on more anxiety-specific ones like the range of Spence children's anxiety scales (Spence, 1998) and the child anxiety impact scale (Langley et al., 2014) if it becomes clear that anxiety is the main problem. With adolescents, it can also be helpful to use a more disorder-specific questionnaire depending on the nature of the anxiety, such as the Liebowitz social anxiety scale for children and adolescents (Masia-Warner et al., 2003).

For an assessment it is important to bear in mind the points already raised when identifying anxiety in CYP as well as taking into consideration whether or not the anxiety has reached a level where it might be 'a problem'. Another key issue to consider in assessment for anxiety and the kind of treatment that will be most helpful is motivation to change. This is particularly the case for anxiety difficulties because many types of treatment (see later) involve encouraging the child to face their fear rather than avoid it. It is very likely that the CYP will experience some of the aforementioned symptoms of anxiety while they are doing this, which will give them a level of discomfort. Part of a good assessment, therefore, will involve thinking with the CYP and family about what will motivate and encourage them to do this. As this issue is also relevant to depression, this is expanded on in Section 13.4.

13.2.4 Formulation of Anxiety Difficulties

What Contributes to the Development of Anxiety in CYP?: In recent years, there has been a huge quantity of research done into factors that contribute to the development and maintenance of anxiety in children (e.g. Rapee, 2001; Murray et al., 2009). This research has pointed to the interaction between multiple factors, including those within the child, such as biology, genetics and temperament as well as environmental factors such as life events and the behaviour of others around them. Cathy Creswell and Lucy Willets (2019) self-help book for parents, *Helping Your Child With Fears and Worries*, helpfully summarises some of this research in a very digestible way. The book discusses a number of factors that can contribute to the development of anxiety in children:

- Genes/temperament: This is just the way children are born. We know that some children are temperamentally more sensitive to noise and startle more easily and some are just more relaxed in nature than others. Parents with more than one child will report differences between their children in this regard.
- Life events: Sometimes things happen in children's lives that contribute to anxiety, such as illness or bereavement in a family, or moving schools or house.
- Learning by example: From birth, children learn by watching others around them. They are very attuned to facial expressions and behaviour, particularly in their primary caregivers, but will also be influenced by other relatives, friends, cousins and so on. For example, they might be fairly confident around insects for example, until one day another child in their class starts panicking when they see a spider. This leads them to think – 'they are scared of the spider; maybe there is a reason to be scared of the spider; maybe I should be scared of the spider'. In similar ways, children can learn to be *confident* by watching others around them.
- Learning from how others react to their behaviour: Children are very good at picking up on how others respond to what they do and say. They will notice if a parent is sceptical about their ability to cope 'are you sure you'll be ok?', and this can impact on their own self-efficacy about their ability to cope with a situation.

- Coping experiences: Children need to experience a bit of anxiety so they can learn that they can cope with it and also that the 'bad thing' they are worrying about does not actually come to fruition. If we protect children too much, they don't try new situations and therefore don't learn that the bad thing might not happen or that they can cope if it does. Adults have a real desire to protect children, however, and to not put them in situations that cause them distress. So, it is understandable that, particularly if a child has a tendency to anxiety, they will collude with their avoidance of fearful situations – which limits the opportunity for this learning.

13.2.5 What Keeps Anxiety Going in CYP?

There are a range of factors that keep the problem going, some involving things that the child does and some involving things that others around the child do to 'help them out'. These perpetuating factors include:

Things a CYP Might Do: When people are fearful of something, they tend to avoid it. They either don't enter the situation in the first place or they leave the situation as they feel their anxiety rising. This works really well for the CYP in the short term, as avoiding the fearful situation results in the anxiety going away. However, avoiding a situation means that the CYP does not learn that a) the bad thing might not happen and b) even if the bad thing does happen that they can cope/survive. This means that avoidance keeps the fear cycle going (See Figure 13.1).

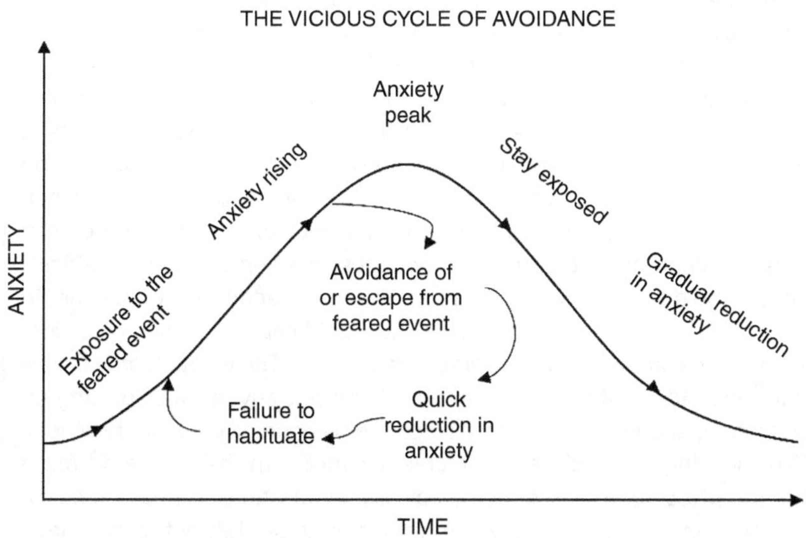

Figure 13.1 The vicious cycle of avoidance.

As discussed earlier, as well as avoiding 'dangerous' situations, CYP will try to protect themselves by being 'hypervigilant' and scanning the environment for signs of possible danger. Additionally they may seek reassurance from others around them that things will be okay to reduce their anxiety.

Things Other People Might Do: Research has shown that adults have a tendance to step in and help children out – particularly those who seem to be vulnerable or have anxious traits. They will step in to solve their problems for them, to try to reduce their distress by not forcing them to do things they seem anxious about doing and to give them lots of reassurance that things will be fine. These are natural things to do, motivated by care and concern and indeed are sometimes part of sensible parenting, especially with younger children. However, as children grow, they have to learn to do things independently without relying on others all the time, which includes solving their own problems and knowing how to get help if they don't know what to do. They also need to learn to cope with difficult emotions like anxiety. Sometimes parental intervention for anxiety can inhibit development of these skills.

The clinical example (Box 13.1) illustrates how these factors might be brought together in a formulation, during a discussion with Emre's mum, Merve.

Box 13.1 Clinical example: Emre

Emre is an 9-year-old boy. He lives with his mother (Merve), father (Asaf), and a 12-year-old sister (Gizem). Asaf is second-generation Turkish British, but Merve moved to the UK from Turkey with her family as a child. Emre's parents referred him to CAMHS because he is extremely shy in social situations. There are days when Merve struggles to get him to school, he refuses to go to family gatherings and won't let his parents go out and leave him with anyone apart from his maternal grandmother. His aunt has asked if he is 'autistic'.

Merve says Emre has always been shy, especially in comparison to his sister. When he was small and his parents went to work, he was looked after at home by his grandmother (whom Emre calls 'Ebe'). She spoke to him in Turkish, although his parents also talked to him in English. When he was little, his speech was a bit delayed and was unclear. At first his family thought it was because he was learning two languages at once, but eventually they took him to the GP who referred him for further investigation at the Ear Nose and Throat Department, and he was diagnosed with Glue Ear. He had grommets fitted when he was 3 years old, and saw a speech and language therapist the following year. When he started primary school, these hearing and speech difficulties meant he had some difficulties with peer relationships. In addition, he was born in August, and Merve was concerned about whether he would cope with starting school so young, particularly in comparison to the others in his class. The whole family is very protective of him. His older sister used to step in if she felt anyone was 'picking on him' in the playground, and Emre misses her since she has gone to secondary school. He does not like speaking out in class, and Merve has met with the teacher to make sure they do not put pressure on him to do this by asking questions. He has friends in school, but there was an issue in Year 1 where he started to get left out by two boys.

He did not tell his mother, and Merve only found out about when she witnessed them doing it on a school trip, which she found very upsetting. Since then, she has made sure she keeps a watchful eye on him when he is with other children and intervenes if she thinks they are being mean to him. Merve says Emre's grandmother has experienced anxiety in the past, and she is also a 'bit of a worrier' herself. She was shy as a child and found it hard moving to the UK and starting school with very little English. She does not want Emre to experience the same anxiety she does.

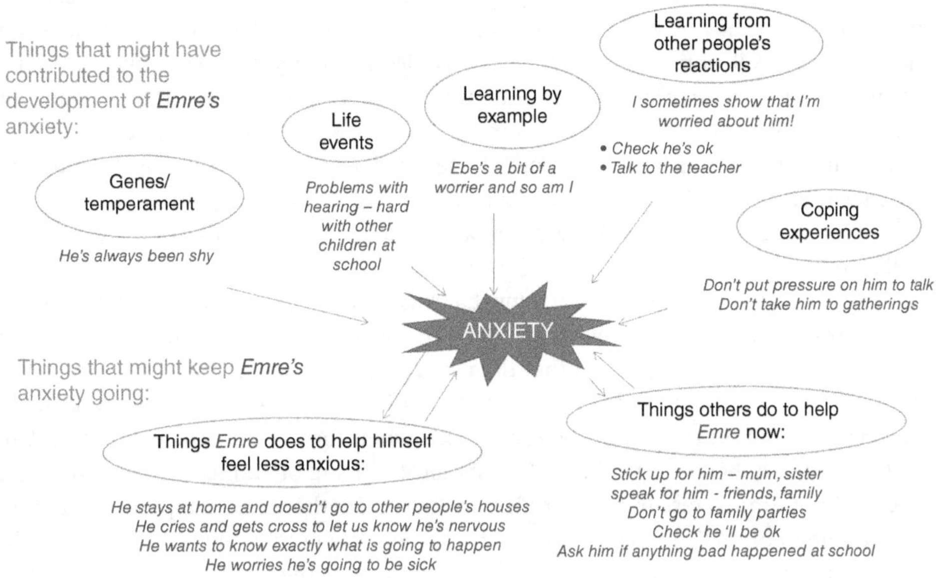

13.2.6 Treating Anxiety: The Evidence Base

It is beyond the scope of this chapter to do a complete review of the evidence base. The National Institute for Health and Social Care guidelines (NICE, 2013) recommend cognitive behavioural therapy (CBT) for social anxiety in CYP and specify four guided self-help digital CBT programmes as initial treatment options for CYP with mild to moderate symptoms (NICE, 2023). Creswell et al. (2020) published a comprehensive and helpful practitioner review of the assessment and treatment of anxiety disorders in CYP, which is recommended for more detailed information. A summary of the conclusions from this review are that CBT shows clear benefits over waiting list controls, with 59.4% of CYP overall no longer having an anxiety diagnosis after treatment. With regards to the long-term impact of CBT, studies have shown mixed results, with some demonstrating positive long-term benefits and others reporting high relapse rates. There are also mixed results regarding individual versus group treatments, both in terms of outcomes and cost effectiveness, and there is emerging evidence for bibliotherapy and computerised and Internet-based treatments. The content of CBT varies between studies, but it tends to include some kind of gradual exposure to the feared situation, with the aim of helping the CYP develop new learning about what *really* happens, as opposed to what they *worry* will happen, when they enter this situation. This is often accompanied by work to address unhelpful thinking patterns, where appropriate, and also skills training such as relaxation or problem solving. In terms of the *evidence* regarding which treatment components are important, however, there is limited research. Creswell et al. (2020) cite a large study in the United States 7 to 17 year olds (Peris et al., 2015) that found exposure and changing self-talk increased the rate of progress, whereas relaxation training had limited effect. This study also highlighted improvements in coping efficacy as being more impactful than improvements in anxious self-talk; similarly other studies point to exposure being more effective than anxiety management strategies. The Wellcome Trust (2021, 2022) is also currently reviewing and publishing more information into which aspects of an intervention contribute to effective outcomes in treatments for anxiety and low mood in CYP. The overall conclusion of Creswell et al. (2020) is that 'treatments might be more efficiently delivered by promoting new learning (particularly about coping) through exposure' (p. 632). 'Learning through doing' is a phrase often used to describe this, and can be used to explain CBT for anxiety to CYP and families well.

It is important to bear in mind problems that exist in the evidence base for treating anxiety problems in CYP (e.g. Creswell et al., 2020; Davis et al., 2011). For example, trials tend to group anxiety diagnoses together rather than studying them individually, so it can be hard to tease out what works for what. There is also an issue of what constitutes 'satisfactory' evidence: how should treatments be catagorised when for example the content of 'CBT' might vary greatly between studies? How should the issue of co-morbidity be managed? There has been limited research undertaken with different therapeutic approaches and very little involving non-CBT-informed approaches commonly used with CYP, such as psychodynamic psychotherapy or systemic psychotherapy. Most of the research, particularly in the UK, has been conducted with white relatively affluent populations (see Section 13.5). It is known that there are sometimes differences in presentations and understandings of mental health and also in help-seeking between different cultural groups and communities, and much of the research informing the theories that many current therapeutic interventions are based on was also conducted with white affluent populations. It is important to do more research with different communities looking at similarities and differences in behaviours that are seen as indicative of an 'anxiety problem' and factors that contribute to these problems. This will inform the co-creation of culturally sensitive ways of working with CYP and families from different communities rather than imposing a Western lens on these understandings and ways of working.

Despite this, there is a fairly clear indication that CBT is an approach worth considering when treating anxiety problems, unless there is a good reason not to. Importantly, CBT with children is very different from CBT with adults, and the context of childhood necessitates the need to consider and often incorporate other theories and models when working with families, and to work with the system around the CYP (see Fuggle et al., 2013). The involvement of parents and carers in treatment for anxiety varies (see Creswell et al., 2020) and decisions about this will be guided by the assessment, formulation and treatment reviews. This is discussed in more detail in Section 13.4.

13.2.7 CBT Treatment for Anxiety

Although there may be a variety of factors that a formulation suggests might have contributed to the development of a CYP's anxiety, CBT treatment tends to focus on the things that are keeping it going (maintenance factors) – at least at first. As highlighted earlier, a key maintenance factor in anxiety is the fear–avoidance cycle, so a key focus of the treatment is breaking this cycle through exposure to fears: encouraging and supporting the CYP in facing the feared object/activity/situation until the anxiety goes away. This is usually done in a gradual way, by working with the CYP to develop a 'step-by-step' plan. There are various mechanisms that are thought to be at play during this 'graded exposure', which are informed by ideas from classical and operant conditioning theory and research. Habituation is a physiological phenomenon in which the amount of anxiety experienced in a fearful situation naturally decreases over time. Extinction is the weakening of previously learned associations between feared thing and bad outcomes. New conditioning sometimes occurs if the originally feared situation becomes associated with something pleasant instead. It leads to the development of self-efficacy, as the CYP learns they can cope with both the feared situation, and with the feeling of fear/anxiety itself. There is also cognitive change in beliefs about the feared object/activity/situation and/or about fear/anxiety itself. The importance of targeting processes that promote inhibitory learning have been shown to be key maximising the benefits of exposure therapy (Craske et al., 2014).

13.2.8 Generic vs Disorder-specific Approaches to Working with Anxiety

Adult CBT for anxiety has tended to organise itself around the different psychiatric diagnostic categories, and there are disorder-specific models and treatments for each one. These models and treatments tend to focus on the factors that keep the anxiety going (maintenance factors) rather than what caused the anxiety to develop in the first place. They share the same underlying ideas about things like avoidance and the importance of 'facing your fear' instead, but each model has some key features that vary according to the anxiety type. For example, the CBT model for GAD (Dugas et al., 1998) suggests that the problem is maintained by the fact that the individual worries, rather than the specific things they are worried about, a difficulty they have in tolerating worry and uncertainty and a low confidence in their ability to problem solve. Therefore, CBT for GAD helps the individual to recognise different types of worry and distinguish between the ones that are worth worrying about and the ones that aren't; learning to tolerate anxiety and uncertainty and learning to let worry wash over them as well as build their confidence in their problem-solving ability. In contrast, the social anxiety model (Clark and Wells, 1995) suggests that the problem is maintained by a focus on the self and other things that people do to keep themselves safe in social situations (safety behaviours) that then backfire and feed into the difficulty. The treatment therefore encourages the person to focus their attention outwards rather than inwards and to identify and drop unhelpful safety behaviours.

There is some emerging evidence for the applicability of both these disorder-specific models and treatment approaches with children and young people (e.g. Leger et al., 2003; Leigh and Clark, 2018), and as practitioners the authors have certainly found them to be helpful especially with some adolescents. However, research is limited to date and it is important for a practitioner to consider the extent to which they might be useful to use with a particular young person on a case-by-case basis. In addition, even if an adult-informed disorder-specific approach *is* taken, it is crucial to ensure systemic and family factors, which are very important in CBT with CYP but are often not part of adult disorder-specific models are considered in the assessment, formulation and intervention. In contrast, many well-established approaches to CBT for anxiety with children, such as the Coping Cat programme (Beidas et al., 2008) take a more 'generic' approach, and this is an equally valid way of working. These generic interventions usually involve the practitioner supporting the CYP in taking a step-by-step approach towards facing their fear, rather than changing what they do according to their specific anxiety diagnosis, as well as engaging in work with the system around the child, such as parents, as appropriate, in order to overcome the child's anxiety. (see Fuggle et al., 2013 for more information about formulating and working with the system in child CBT).

Guided Parent-delivered CBT for Anxiety: Based on the research into the development and maintenance of anxiety in children, in recent years (see Creswell et al., 2020) there has been a real shift in CBT treatment for anxiety especially with primary-school-aged children, away from working one-to-one with the child, to working with parents and carers to promote the kinds of parenting behaviours and choices that help a child manage anxiety and build confidence rather than those which inadvertently feed into the problem. There are lots of reasons why this approach is favoured (see Creswell et al., 2019; Halldorsson et al., 2019), in particular that parents/carers know their child the best and can therefore best support them both between sessions and once the treatment has ended, so it is useful to provide them with strategies they can use at home. Guided parent-delivered CBT for anxiety (Creswell et al., 2019; Halldorsson et al., 2019) involves helping parents put into practice ideas found in Creswell and Willets' book (2019) *Helping your child with fears and worries*. The sessions involve provision of psychoeducation for parents, for example, about the development of anxiety in children and how to overcome it. This includes more and less helpful ways a parent can respond to an anxious child, consideration of possible links between their own responses and their child's anxiety and how to modify these responses if necessary. It also involves thinking with parents how to identify and examine anxious expectations in their child and develop targets for change and graded hierarchies linked to their worries ('learning through doing'), as well as and teaching the child to manage 'real' difficulties and overcome obstacles through problem-solving. Overall, through this approach parents add knowledge about how to help their child build confidence and overcome anxiety to their parenting toolkit. The evidence for this approach to date is very good (Creswell et al., 2017) and it is one of the approaches that is taught as part of many of the NHS England funded CYP-MH Child Wellbeing Practitioner and Education Mental Health Practitioner training programmes.

What Might this Look Like with Emre?: The practitioner would provide Emre's mum, Merve, with psychoeducation about the kinds of factors research suggests might contribute to the development and maintenance of anxiety in CYP and ask her to think whether she thinks any of them might apply to Emre's situation. This would be done in a very collaborative way. For example, as discussed earlier, it is not clear the extent to which the current research into child anxiety fits with children and families from different cultural backgrounds, so it would be important for the practitioner to acknowledge this and ask questions about the extent to which she thinks the theory is relevant to the Turkish-speaking community in the UK, as well as to their particular family situation.

Discussing the anxiety research and developing a shared formulation with parents often involves thinking about things that they and others around the child might have done/be doing that have played a part in their child's difficulties. Given this, it is important for the practitioner to take a stance that reduces the likelihood that parents feel judged and blamed by others, or judge and blame themselves. A good way of doing this is 'normalising' – both the existence of anxiety in children and others around the child, as well as things others around the child tend to do as a result to try to protect them. With Merve, the practitioner talked about how as parents we are designed to worry about our children – it's our job. When they are young, it is important for us to protect them and help them out because they are unable to do it for themselves. They discussed the vulnerabilities in Emre, such as his hearing difficulties, and also certain life events, such as Merve witnessing him being left out by his peers, that contributed to a strong and understandable 'pull' for her and others in his family to protect him. In addition, the practitioner and Merve talked about her memories of arriving in the UK as a child not speaking English, and how she felt quite isolated and anxious when she started school as a result. This had been compounded by the fact that her parents' English had been limited and schools tended not to have access to interpreters when she was young, so it had been difficult for her parents to communicate with her school about how she was feeling. However, the work then included highlighting how it was different for Emre, who spoke good English himself, and also had parents with very good English who had been able to raise their concerns with his teacher and think with her about how to support him in school.

A second part of normalising involved the practitioner talking about how as children get older, they spend more time apart from us, and also become more developed physically and cognitively, so they both need and are able to be more independent from us and learn to do things themselves without us helping them out. Together they thought about how Merve and others around Emre could start helping him to do this. It was important to try to engage Emre in the process of building confidence and facing his fears. However, initially he was reluctant to do this, so Merve and the practitioner started to think about what might motivate him to do this. They talked about things Emre's anxiety was currently stopping him from doing that he wanted to be able to do. Merve told the practitioner about a residential school trip coming up at the end of Year 6, which she knew Emre really wanted to go on, but she knew he was feeling anxious about how he would cope with staying away from his family, which she thought would be a good motivator for him. She began by talking to Emre about this. She explained anxiety to Emre, including why he got the funny feelings in his body and how these would go away eventually if he stayed in a situation rather than leaving it. She also taught him some strategies for managing these physical sensations, such as calm gentle breathing and reminding himself 'it's only anxiety, it will go away', to help him cope. She and Emre talked about his ultimate goal of going on the Year 6 residential trip and worked together to devise a step-by-step plan that would gradually build his confidence so he could achieve this goal. This included doing more social activities in a graded way, starting with safer situations like going to family gatherings, with his parents and sister, where he knew people well. Another step was going to his cousins' house to play. Merve stayed with him to start with, but then gradually started to leave him for increasing lengths of time. Eventually Emre said he wanted to stay overnight, which they thought would be really good practice for his school trip. The first time, Emre had quite strong physical symptoms of anxiety that made him feel quite 'panicky', and in the end his mum had to go to collect him. Following this, Merve reminded Emre about the physical symptoms of anxiety: that although they aren't pleasant, they are normal, and that he had learnt things he could do to that helped the sensations go away (slow breathing and coping thoughts). They thought it would also be a good idea to involve his aunt in this, so that she would be able to normalise his physical symptoms and remind him about his coping strategies if he needed it at the next sleepover. Emre found this helpful, and the second time he went to his cousins' house he was able to stay the whole night. Another thing Merve did to try to help Emre face rather than avoid his fears was talking to his teacher. Rather than asking her not to 'put Emre on the spot' by asking him to talk in class, they came up with a step-by-step plan for building his confidence and involving him more, starting with a learning buddy and then small-group work, and ending with him being able to say his line in the next class assembly. Emre was really into dinosaurs, so Merve bought a tub of toy ones, which he earned for being brave and having a go at each step as he went along. His ultimate reward if he managed to go on the school trip would be a trip to see the dinosaurs at the Natural History Museum in London, where he had always wanted to go. This frequent reward system worked well for Emre as the small rewards were linked to something that was very personally motivating for him. However, the biggest reward was that he managed to go on his Year 6 trip and had a brilliant time!

13.3 Adolescent Depression

Although depression is less common than anxiety disorders in childhood, rates rise steeply during adolescence and girls are more likely to be affected than boys (Lu, 2019). Around 2% of adolescents meet the criteria for a depressive disorder (Shorey et al., 2021) and many more will have subthreshold symptoms. Adolescents with chronic health problems (Ghandour et al., 2019) and those who have experienced adversities like deprivation (Yoon et al., 2021) and racism (Lavner et al., 2021) are more likely to experience depression. Life stressors and adverse events seem to have a cumulative effect on vulnerability (Iob et al., 2021). Depression has an unfavourable impact, even at subthreshold level, both short and longer term; in adolescence, depression is associated with school absenteeism (Finning et al., 2019), poor academic attainment (Wickersham et al., 2021), struggling socially (Schwartz-Mette et al., 2020) and suicidal behaviours (Benarous et al., 2019). Into adulthood, it is linked to mental health problems (Clayborne et al., 2019; Johnson et al., 2018), poor self-rated health (Naicker et al., 2013), and substance abuse, criminality and interpersonal struggles (Copeland et al., 2013).

13.3.1 What is Depression?

Like anxiety, sadness is also a 'normal' emotion. It is often experienced in response to loss. Depression has three core symptoms and is characterised by:

- sadness or 'depressed mood',
- irritability in children and adolescents, and
- loss of interest, enjoyment or pleasure in daily activities.

Common additional symptoms are sleep problems, difficulties concentrating, a lack of motivation and fatigue (Goodyer et al., 2016; Orchard et al., 2016). To meet the DSM-V diagnostic criteria for 'Major Depressive Disorder' (American Psychological Association, 2013), a CYP must have at least one of the core symptoms more than half of the time over the past 2 weeks, and a total of at least five symptoms altogether.

13.3.2 The Experience of Depression

Adolescents with depression describe the experience of misery, despair and tears as well as anger and violence towards themselves and others. Furthermore, they talk about a bleak view of everything, and commonly of isolating themselves from others. They also talk about the impact depression has, particularly on education (Midgley et al., 2015). They tend towards very negative evaluations of themselves, often as worthless (Hards et al., 2019), although they may recognise their positive prosocial behaviours, like viewing themselves as kind to others (Orchard et al., 2019). Struggling with motivation and feeling hopeless are also common features of depression. Adolescents with depression may find it hard to engage and not make use of all the therapy sessions on offer (Goodyer et al., 2016), although this is not necessarily because they haven't found these sessions helpful (O'Keeffe et al., 2019).

13.3.3 When Does Sadness become a 'Problem'?

A key feature to look out for to distinguish between sadness and depression is interference in everyday functioning, as well as symptoms being present and distressing more often than not and lasting for at least 2 weeks. This shouldn't be a lifelong pattern, and it shouldn't be better explained by another factor – for instance, it would be expected that after a bereavement of a loved one, a child or young person may feel sad for a prolonged period, and may also have trouble sleeping, concentrating, may not enjoy things and may be irritable. Although they may fulfil the requirement for having five symptoms of depression, it's likely that a better explanation would be the recent loss, and this would be a normal adjustment response. Box 13.2 gives an illustrative clinical example.

Box 13.2 Clinical example: Depression

Sally, a 15-year-old girl, was referred for help by her GP. Sally had always tended to be a bit of a 'pessimist' as she described it and had experienced some bullying in primary school. She had always done well academically, and this was a source of pride for her. However, Sally really struggled to engage in online learning during the school closures resulting from the Covid-19 pandemic restrictions. This meant that she fell behind academically. Since then, her parents had become increasingly concerned about her ongoing low mood, irritable outbursts and withdrawal from life; she had been less interested than usual in seeing her friends and was also reluctant to go out and about with family members, preferring to stay at home in her bedroom. Her mother had

(Continued)

Box 13.2 (Continued)

noticed that she was much more tearful than usual, and even relatively minor things, like getting a B grade in a test rather than an A, had been very upsetting to her and she had repeatedly told her mother that she didn't think she was good enough, labelling herself as 'rubbish'. Although she was going to school, her grades had slipped, and her teachers were concerned that she was no longer diligent about doing her homework and often seemed not to be able to concentrate in lessons. She opted to give up dancing, which she previously enjoyed, and was taking much less care over her appearance.

Assessing the Nature of the Problem: Central to assessing for depression as part of emotional difficulties is to get a sense of mood. In order to do this the practitioner could ask specific questions for example, asking them to describe in detail a day when they felt low recently. The practitioner could explore what triggers feeling low and ask about good days (or less bad days). It is useful to find out what feeling low encourages the individual to do less of, and to enquire about structure and routine within their day as well as self-care and sleep. A curious enquiry about how mood influences the individual's thinking and whether they have identified any themes in their thinking could be useful, as well as exploring self-confidence and self-esteem, given that self-worth is often impacted in depression. Ask about what they like about themselves, and what they think their strengths are, as well as how they compare themselves to others – using self-esteem measures like the Rosenberg self-esteem scale can help with this (Rosenberg, 1965). It is particularly important to explore current coping strategies both helpful and unhelpful, the latter including self-harm, as well as to thoroughly assess risk, including suicidal ideation, plans and intent. It is worth noting that amongst adolescents (aged 11 to 17) who took part in a CAMHS-based treatment trial for depression one in three reported at least one past suicide attempt, although only 3% were currently engaging in suicidal acts. It may be useful to use guidance to undertake a structured risk assessment (e.g. the University of Oxford's Centre for Suicide Research guide https://www.dpt.nhs.uk/download/2hn1ZTaUXY, and the guide from the Royal College of General Practitioners: https://nspa.org.uk/wp-content/uploads/2022/10/RCGP-Suicide-in-Children-and-Young-People.pdf). Given how common sleep difficulties are, it is a good idea to ask about these too. Often, adolescents who have depression also have some anxieties, particularly social anxiety.

Using questionnaires to supplement the assessment process can be helpful, providing an additional source of information, as well as normalising the symptoms of depression for the individual themselves. One example is the RCADS, which includes 10 depression items and is free to use. There are other examples such as the Mood and Feelings Questionnaire (MFQ; Costello & Angold, 1988) and the Children's Depression Inventory (CDI; Kovacs, 1992). The Patient Health Questionnaire (PHQ-9, Kroenke et al., 2001) can also be used with older teens, and there is an adolescent version (PHQ-A, Johnson et al., 2002). Note that all these existing questionnaire measures may not fully capture the range of experiences described by adolescents with depression (Krause et al., 2020), and in particular, most measures do not separately consider irritability as a symptom of CYP depression, so it may be worth specifically including this in addition to the measure that has been chosen.

13.3.4 Formulation of Depression

What Contributes to the Development of Depression in CYP?: Some adolescents are more likely to develop depression. Risk factors include:

- Demographic and health-related factors that have been found to be associated with increased likelihood of developing depression in adolescence include: gender (females) (Girgus & Yang, 2015; Malooly et al., 2017; Patil et al., 2017; Shore et al., 2017); lower socioeconomic status and minority status with ethnic minority and LGBTQ+ individuals being at greater risk, for example (Mojtabai et al., 2016; Patil et al., 2017; Shore et al., 2017); having an anxiety disorder (Angold & Costello, 1993; Moffitt et al., 2010); obesity in adolescent females (Boutelle et al., 2010); inflammation (Colasanto et al., 2020); dieting (Cairns et al., 2014); and substance use (Cairns et al., 2014; Shore et al., 2017). Protective factors include healthy eating (Cairns et al., 2014) and getting sufficient sleep (Orchard et al., 2020). Certain medications may also increase the risk of developing depression, such as steroids in Inflammatory Bowel Disease (Szigethy et al., 2004).
- Individual factors, including neuroticism and cognitive tendencies like negative thinking style and rumination prospectively predict depression in adolescence (Hankin, 2015; Sfarlea et al., 2019). Other factors, such as higher IQ and cognitive ability, and better problem-solving ability can be protective (Glaser et al., 2011; Spence et al., 2002).
- Family factors including a family history of depression (Murray et al., 2011; Thapar et al., 2012), parenting style including the discouragement of anger expression in childhood (O'Neal et al., 2017), and high perceived parental criticism are associated with an increased risk of adolescent depression (Rapp et al., 2021). Parental somatic illness, parental disability, parental psychiatric problems, parental death and family disruption also increase the risk of depression (Dahl et al., 2017). Likewise, family factors such as family cohesion can also be protective (Askeland et al, 2020).

13.3.5 What Keeps Depression Going in CYP?

At a situation specific level, the interconnected symptoms of depression are reciprocally reinforcing, forming a vicious cycle. This typically includes feelings of sadness, tiredness, lack of motivation and interest, negative thoughts about the self, others and the world, as well as behaviours of withdrawing and isolating the self, doing less. There are different theoretical approaches to understanding (and hence, treating) depression. The behavioural model focuses on the bidirectional link between *behaviours and feelings*, that is, doing less means getting less pleasure, which reinforces the depression (Reynolds & Pass, 2021; Loades & Essau, 2023). The interpersonal psychotherapy model focuses on the link between *relationships and feelings*, whereby, for example, isolating oneself decreases the opportunities for social support and interaction, decreasing pleasure and potentially eroding relationships (Mufson & Sills, 2006; Stuart & Robertson, 2003). The cognitive behavioural model considers *thoughts–feelings–behaviour* interconnections, whereby negative and distorted thoughts, as well as attending selectively to negative information and over-general memory (Smith et al., 2018), further fuels the cycle proposed by the behavioural model (Verduyn et al, 2009). See Figure 13.2 for an example of a situation specific formulation model drawn from these different theoretical approaches using the clinical example, Sally.

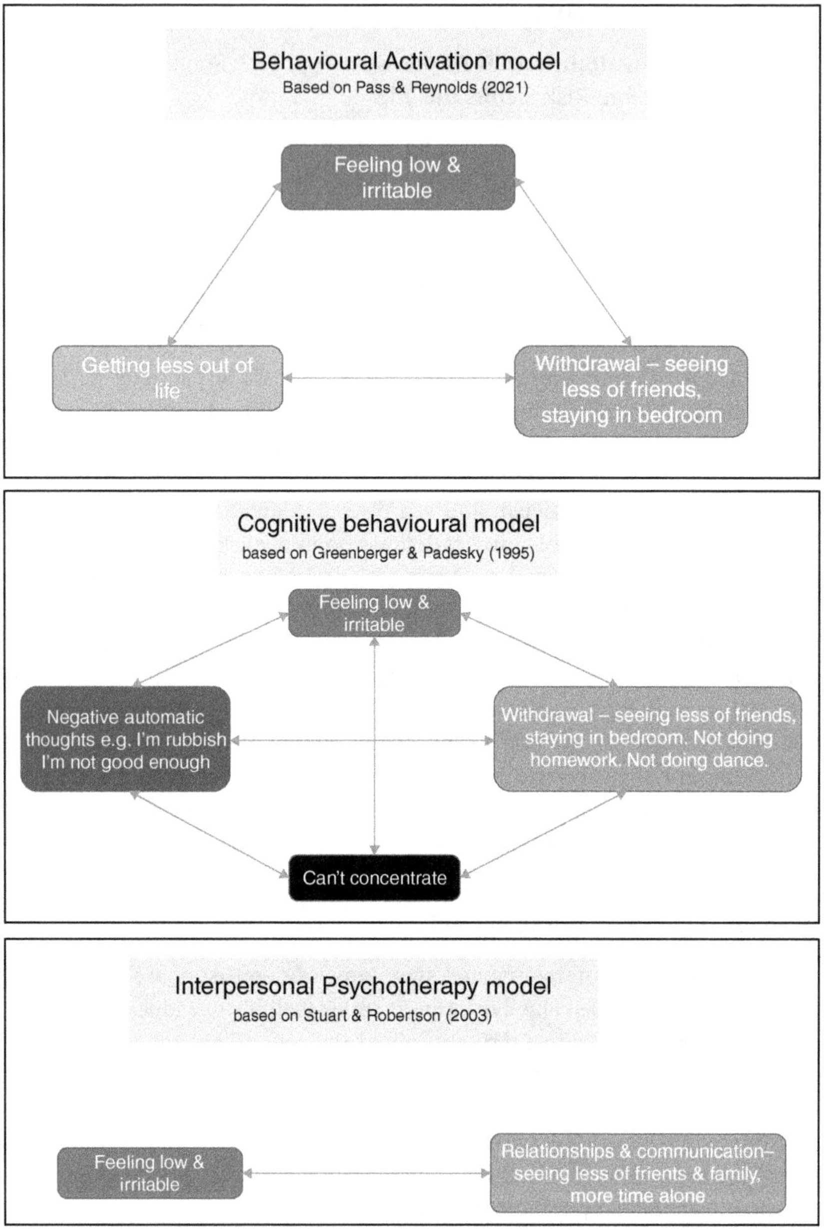

Figure 13.2 Formulating depression using behavioural activation, CBT and IPT models with Sally as a clinical example.

Adolescents with symptoms of both anxiety and depression tend to endorse particularly the negative thinking patterns (a.k.a. cognitive biases) of threat perception, probability estimation, catastrophising and personalisation (Weeks et al., 2017). Overgeneralisation (i.e. taking isolated instances and using them to make sweeping generalisations) and selective abstraction (i.e. a detail is taken out of context and believed whilst everything else in the context is ignored) uniquely predict depression in adolescents (Schwartz & Maric, 2015). Higher cost estimates, mindreading and underestimating the ability to cope uniquely predict anxiety (Schwartz & Maric, 2015; Weeks et al., 2017). Furthermore, it is important to note that as adolescents get older important changes may take place as part of normal development that increase their cognitive biases (particularly threat interpretation, negative attributions and overgeneralising; Slavny et al., 2019).

It is also important to also think about the adolescent developmental context of puberty, brain maturation (which continues until the mid-20s), social development and moral development, as well as to think about how the family, school and peer group contexts might be perpetuating or protective (Blakemore, 2018). It is worth noting that the educational impact of the symptoms of depression in the short term may also feed the negative cycles of depression by providing the young person with extra evidence to feed their negative thoughts and compounding their sense of worthlessness and failure.

13.3.6 Treating Depression: The Evidence Base

When working therapeutically with adolescents with depression, no matter what specific approach is being taken, it is helpful to give them information about depression, the benefits of exercise, physical activity, and advice on sleep hygiene and anxiety management where necessary (NICE, 2005, 2019). The NICE guidelines for child and adolescent depression recommend that those with moderate to severe depression are offered a specific psychological therapy; there are several specific therapies that are at least moderately effective at reducing depression symptoms. The most widely evaluated of these is CBT (Eckshtain et al., 2019). Other effective therapies include interpersonal therapy (IPT) (Eckshtain et al., 2019), short-term psychoanalytic psychotherapy and a brief psychosocial intervention (Goodyer et al., 2016), and there is growing evidence for behaviour activation (which is part of CBT) as a standalone treatment that is also promising (Pass et al., 2015). However, Cuijpers et al. (2023) recently published a meta-analysis of psychological interventions for CYP with depression to examine response, clinically significant change, clinically significant deterioration and recovery as outcomes. They concluded that psychotherapies for depression in CYP are effective compared to control conditions, but more than 60% of youth receiving therapy do not respond. NICE recommends that antidepressant medication is considered for adolescents with severe depression in combination with psychological therapy, or for those who are not able to engage in therapy. Adolescents themselves see medication as a support not a solution and can experience it as a threat to their autonomy if it is against their wishes (Maroun et al., 2018).

Most adolescents with depression see psychological therapy as a process of change through talking, and before starting psychological therapy, they are often anxious and uncertain about what therapy will be like and what they want to achieve (Herring et al., 2022; Midgley et al., 2016; Midgley et al., 2017). Many of those who are seen in CAMHS for depression treatment may have envisaged the therapist as a doctor-like figure who will give advice for them to follow and remove the problem of depression, allowing them to return to their old self. Some see it as a growth process, in which the discussion with the therapist facilitates them to learn new skills and change. Helping CYP to take an active, collaborative approach is important when establishing the therapeutic relationship (see Box 13.3).

Box 13.3 Clinical example: Engaging Sally in treatment

Sally was brought for help by her mother, and was reluctant to engage initially, saying that nothing would help. The therapist focused their efforts in early sessions on getting to know Sally, providing Sally with information about the treatment options and what is known about how effective these are for adolescents with depression, and supporting Sally to think about what she would like to be different, generating goals for therapy. At first, Sally struggled to engage in this, and the therapist had to hold the hope for her that things could be different, and to ensure that initially, they validated how difficult things felt for Sally by curious inquiry, active listening, summarizing Sally's experiences and normalizing hopelessness as part of depression. This enabled Sally to begin to consider change, and starting with very small steps using a behaviour activation approach generated initial momentum. However, Sally's negativity meant that she attributed any changes to external factors, and therefore, the therapist sought supervision and began to incorporate cognitive strategies such as thought catching, checking and changing, into the work. This gradually enabled Sally to recognize her role in generating change, and shifted her hopelessness over time as her mood began to lift and she felt more empowered.

It is beyond the scope of this chapter to thoroughly detail each treatment therefore the authors have focused on behaviour activation as a brief treatment that can be offered by less-skilled therapists and CBT as the best-evaluated treatment both of which are commonly offered in services for CYP.

13.3.7 Behavioural Activation for Depression

Behaviour activation focuses on the links between feeling and doing (see Loades & Essau, 2023) and may be used as a brief, low-intensity support (6–8 sessions; Reynolds & Pass, 2020) or a more intensive therapy (12–15 sessions; McCauley et al., 2016). When people feel low, they get less enjoyment, connectedness and achievement in life and stop doing things that matter to them, all of which interact and reinforce each other in a vicious cycle (Reynolds & Pass, 2020). The aim of behaviour activation is to shift towards a more positive cycle of activity in which the individual does more of what matters *to them*, gets more enjoyment achievement and connectedness in life and feels better. Even within a session, a behavioural experiment approach whereby a preplanned test to see whether a particular thought or assumption is true can be taken to demonstrate how feelings are linked to activities. With a 15-year-old girl, Monica, a behavioural experiment was set up, and for data, rated current mood on a 0 to 10 Likert scale (0 = terrible, 10 = brilliant) before during and after watching a funny video on YouTube together. They then reflected on what we learned about the connections between feelings and doing and how this could inform what Monica could do to help herself to feel better.

Once engaged, adolescents seem to be able to talk readily about what matters to them (Lewis-Smith et al., 2021). The specific areas to ask about can include things that matter like education, things they need to do every day and bigger picture issues like climate change, the people that matter including family friends and intimate relationships, their hobbies and interests, health, and self-care. Creating a list of valued activities can then inform planning for and scheduling doing more activities that matter, whilst monitoring the impact this has on mood (see Reynolds & Pass, 2020).

13.3.8 CBT for Depression

Behavioural activation as described above is a key part of CBT (see Verduyn et al., 2009), typically lasting for 16 to 20 sessions. Alongside this, and driven by the formulation, cognitive aspects of treatment include identifying negative automatic thoughts (i.e. thoughts that pop into one's head automatically), checking these against the evidence and re-evaluating where necessary (cognitive restructuring). When negative thoughts do fit with the evidence and aren't distorted, introducing and working through problem-solving strategies can be helpful. Where recurrent themes in negative, unhelpful thinking are identified, these can inform a longitudinal formulation, including core beliefs and unhelpful rules for living. These may be addressed using techniques like guided discovery, behavioural experiments, surveys and the use of continuum techniques (Clark et al., 2014; Verduyn et al., 2009).

It is important to note that the cognitive components of CBT may be particularly difficult for individuals who are struggling with depression because of the symptoms of depression itself, such as fatigue and lack of energy and poor concentration, as well as potentially being at odds with what feels relevant to the adolescent themselves or what they are able to manage given their developmental level. This does not necessarily matter as evidence suggests that symptom change is predicted by changes in behavioural skills rather than cognitive skills (Webb et al., 2019), and because there are ways in which the practitioner can work on cognitions without explicitly doing cognitive restructuring. One way of doing this is by working on imagery (Pile et al., 2018), another is by introducing positive self-talk (i.e. self-statements or mantras) to say to oneself in difficult situations and a third is using concepts from acceptance and mindfulness within a therapeutic intervention to change the person's relationship to their thoughts rather than to change the thoughts themselves (Loades et al., 2014, Reangsing et al., 2021). Another idea if a young person is finding cognitive work challenging when they are feeling particularly low is to focus on behavioural activation again to try to lift their mood, then returning to the more cognitive work again once they are feeling less low in mood.

13.4 Common Issues Across Emotional Difficulties

13.4.1 Co-morbidity

As discussed earlier, importantly, many CYP have more than one type of emotional disorder. Leyfer et al. (2013) found 63% of a sample of 608 4 to 18 year olds presenting for assessment and treatment for anxiety and related concerns had a co-morbid anxiety or mood disorder. This was similar to previous studies' findings of comorbidity rates in children (Bearman & Weisz, 2015). Similarly at the general population level, many CYP experiencing depression also have elevated anxiety symptoms (Ghandour et al., 2019), and rates of co-morbid depression and anxiety disorders amongst those who present to clinical settings are even higher (Goodyer et al., 2016). There are at least three possible reasons for this:

1) This could be due to an imperfect diagnostic system as symptoms of disorders overlap; for instance, GAD may be more closely related to depression than other anxiety disorders (Cummings et al., 2014), which may explain the particular tendency for these two disorders to co-occur.
2) Co-morbid depression and anxiety may be the result of shared vulnerability factors that increase the likelihood of developing both disorders. The potentially shared vulnerability factors include genetic predisposition, social and cognitive developmental process in adolescence such as heighted self-evaluation, exposure to stressful life events, female gender and low socioeconomic status (Cummings et al., 2014; Dochnal et al., 2019; Terhaag et al., 2021). The concept of the p-factor discussed earlier is also relevant to this point.
3) The consequences of one disorder may increase the chances of developing another. For example, having depression symptoms impacts on functioning (e.g. reduced school attendance or poor academic attainment), which may lead to anxiety and worries about school and schoolwork. Similarly, having anxiety impacts on functioning (e.g. avoidance of enjoyable activities due to worries), which may decrease positive reinforcement and contribute to depression.

One way of addressing this has been the growth of transdiagnostic approaches, which aim to develop single protocols that can treat multiple presenting difficulties. These tend to be divided into *core dysfunction* approaches that target underlying problems common to a range of presenting difficulties, such as the Fairburn (2008) treatment for clinical perfectionism; *common elements* approaches, which combine commonly used components of existing evidence-based treatments, such as the Modular Approach to Therapy for Children with Anxiety, Depression, Trauma and Conduct – MATCH, developed by Chorpita and Weisz (2009); and *principle-guided* approaches, that combine core concepts (rather than core techniques) that contribute to therapeutic change for different presenting difficulties, such as FIRST (Weisz et al., 2017). These approaches have a range of potential benefits and challenges (see Weisz et al., 2017; Fonagy & Allison, 2017 for helpful review papers), and the evidence is emerging, but it will be interesting to see how these develop.

13.4.2 Motivation and Engagement

As discussed earlier, motivation to engage in treatment can be an issue when working with CYP and families with emotional difficulties. Motivation can fluctuate within and between sessions, and this can be impacted by the fact that it is not always the CYP themselves who have sought help. Using ideas and techniques from motivational interviewing (DiClemente & Velasquez, 2002) can be really helpful, such as thinking about the stage of change that an individual is at, and making sure to meet them where they are, using motivational interviewing techniques to help them to move towards change where needed. There are some good chapters on using motivational interviewing ideas in child CBT (see Schmidt, 2005; Stallard, 2005, chapter 2) and also in CBT more generally (Naar and Safren, 2017). Developing collaborative goals and agreeing a plan of work to achieve these goals can help to build therapeutic alliance. One helpful way of doing this is to think with the CYP and family about ways in which the anxiety/depression is impacting the CYP's life. Asking about this in a way that externalises the problem can be helpful: 'What is your anxiety/depression stopping you from doing that you would like to/need to be doing?' Once this has been identified, the practitioner can encourage the CYP to engage by focusing the conversation on things they would really like to be able to do that they can't do now. A CYP is often more likely to be motivated by a goal that involves spending time with a friend or doing an activity that they enjoy like going to play football, than going to school, for example, so this can be talked about a lot about that. It is also worth introducing and offering options for different approaches to change where possible, as this empowers the adolescent to shape their own journey towards their goals. Lowering barriers to action where possible and enlisting social support can be useful, and it is worth identifying any 'quick wins' that could help to build hopefulness, encouraging a try-it-and-see approach; for example, getting a daily routine (re-)established, including some basic self-care activities, like showering, can be a really helpful place to start. In addition, thinking about concrete rewards for 'brave behaviour', or 'doing an activity even if you don't feel like it' can also be helpful in increasing motivation.

13.4.3 Working With the CYP's Support System

Working with the CYP vs Working With the System Around the CYP: As mentioned earlier, working with emotional difficulties most often involves parents/carers and others in the system around the child. It can be helpful (and potentially to involve the CYP themselves in this activity) to identify who the potential sources of support around them are (see Box 13.4). Decisions about who to involve in the work with the CYP will be guided by the assessment and formulation, as well as the wishes of the CYP and family. This will include, for example, the extent to which the formulation suggests that the factors keeping the problem going seem to be associated with things the CYP is doing and the extent to which others around the CYP are playing a role.

Box 13.4 Who is in the system around the child?

- On an A4 sheet, write the client's name in the centre
- Around them position the important people in their lives
  - Near or far?
  - Who is close to who?
  - Who is furthest from whom?
  - Who is helpful and who is unhelpful?
  - Where is the therapist in relation to these people?
  - Who could help to facilitate positive change?

The developmental stage of the CYP is also something to consider: A key developmental task is for an adolescent to individuate from their family of origin. In actuality this tends to mean spending more time with, and placing more importance on, the views of peers, rather than parents. Conflict with parents is, to some extent, a normal part of this process. That said, parents can helpfully be involved in therapy in a number of different potential roles: parents can be a supporter, encouraging change; they can facilitate therapy (enabling the adolescent to attend sessions by driving them to a clinic location, for example); they can be involved as a co-therapist who assists the therapist to enable the adolescent to make adaptive changes, such as engaging in more valued activities; and in some instances, where parental behaviour may be part of problem perpetuation, they may be a co-client (Stallard, 2002, 2005).

How parents are involved will depend on the individual circumstances and formulation, but a general rule of thumb the authors would suggest is that with younger children it is often important to work with parents/carers more with the focus potentially shifting to working more with the young person on a one-to-one basis as they get older. But it is *always* helpful to think with the CYP about educating parents and others in the system who might be appropriate, such as a key person in school, about the treatment approach being used to enable them to support therapy and to promote the transfer of skills from therapy into life more generally, including as part of a relapse prevention plan.

13.5 Equality, Diversity and Inclusion

Inclusivity and addressing issues of power and diversity are covered in detail in Chapter 7 that focuses on this. Relevant to working with children and adolescents with anxiety and/or depression, to ensure fair treatment and opportunity for all CYP, it is important to think about how to meet the needs of the individual from the perspectives of:

- equality of access to help, for example, considering adapting what is offered and how it is offered for a young person who has a chronic illness as well as depression (Morey & Loades, 2020);
- diversity factors of relevance, such as cultural beliefs, language or the experience of being a first-generation immigrant, for example; and
- inclusivity, by making sure that everyone feels welcomed and valued.

Although anxiety and depression exist throughout the world, as with all mental health difficulties, issues arise in relation to understandings of these constructs across different cultures and ethnic groups. Discourse into mental health difficulties has always tended to take a Western perspective, and different understandings of illness and cultural expression can lead to under-diagnosis, misdiagnosis and over-diagnosis of mental health difficulties. In addition, culture and societal values and norms impact how things like anxiety are conceptualised, whether particular 'symptoms' or behaviours are seen as problematic by parents/society, and whether or not they are associated with psychological and emotional difficulties. Borrego et al. (2019), Edge and Lemetyinen (2019) and Rausch (2019) have all published very interesting reviews that discuss these issues, which readers are referred to for further consideration. With regards to anxiety specifically, for example, Borrego et al. (2019)

point to limited research with minority ethnic groups and conclude that research that does exist has found mixed results: some studies have found ethnic differences in the diagnosis of specific anxiety disorders, such as social anxiety, whereas others have not, and there is no consistent pattern. Importantly, most of the research Borrego refers to seems to have been conducted outside the UK, and so the extent to which it is generalisable given societal differences is also called into question. It is therefore important to be cautious with regards to the cross-cultural generalisability of psychological constructs and diagnostic categories, the legitimacy of prevalence figures and also the evidence base with regards to theories of the development, maintenance and treatment of emotional difficulties in in CYP. It is important to consider the potential influence of culture and society with CYP and families on a case by case basis, in order to promote culturally sensitive practice.

References

American Psychiatric Association. (2013). *Diagnostic and statistical manual of mental disorders: DSM-5*. American Psychiatric Association.

Angold, A., & Costello, E. J. (1993). Depressive comorbidity in children and adolescents: Empirical, theoretical, and methodological issues. *American Journal of Psychiatry, 150*(12), 1779–1791. https://doi.org/10.1176/ajp.150.12.1779

Askeland, K. G., Bøe, T., Breivik, K., La Greca, A. M., Sivertsen, B., & Hysing, M. (2020). Life events and adolescent depressive symptoms: Protective factors associated with resilience. *PLoS One, 15*(6), e0234109.

Attwood, T., & Scarpa, A. (2013). Modifications of Cognitive-behavioural therapy for children and adolescents with high-functioning ASD and Their common difficulties. In A. Scarpa, S. W. White, & T. Attwood (Eds.), *CBT for children and adolescents with high-functioning autism spectrum disorders* (pp. 27–44). Guilford Press.

Balázs, J., Miklósi, M., Keresztény, Á., Hoven, C. W., Carli, V., Wasserman, C., Apter, A., Bobes, J., Brunner, R., Cosman, D., & Cotter, P. (2013). Adolescent subthreshold-depression and anxiety: Psychopathology, functional impairment and increased suicide risk. *Journal of Child Psychology and Psychiatry, 54*(6), 670–677.

Bearman, S. K., & Weisz, J. R. (2015). Review: Comprehensive treatments for youth comorbidity – evidence-guided approaches to a complicated problem. *Child and Adolescent Mental Health, 20*(3), 131–141. https://doi.org/10.1111/camh.12092

Beesdo, K., Knappe, S., & Pine, D. S. (2009). Anxiety and anxiety disorders in children and adolescents: Developmental issues and implications for DSM-V. *Psychiatric Clinics, 32*(3), 483–524.

Beidas, R. S., Podell, J., & Kendall, P. C. (2008). Cognitive-behavioral treatment for child and adolescent anxiety: The Coping Cat program. In C. W. LeCroy (Ed.), *Handbook of evidence-based treatment manuals for children and adolescents* (pp. 869–892). Oxford University Press.

Benarous, X., Consoli, A., Cohen, D., Renaud, J., Lahaye, H., & Guilé, J.-M. (2019). Suicidal behaviors and irritability in children and adolescents: A systematic review of the nature and mechanisms of the association. *European Child and Adolescent Psychiatry, 28*(5), 667–683. https://doi.org/10.1007/s00787-018-1234-9

Blakemore, S.-J. (2018). *Inventing ourselves: The secret life of the teenage brain*. PublicAffairs.

Borrego Jr, J., Ortiz-González, E., & Gissandaner, T. D. (2019). Ethnic and cultural considerations. In S. N. Compton, M. A. Villabø, & H. Kristensen (Eds.), *Pediatric anxiety disorders* (pp. 461–497). Academic Press.

Boutelle, K. N., Hannan, P., Fulkerson, J. A., Crow, S. J., & Stice, E. (2010). Obesity as a prospective predictor of depression in adolescent females. *Health Psychology*, *29*(3), 293.

Cairns, K. E., Yap, M. B., Pilkington, P. D., & Jorm, A. F. (2014). Risk and protective factors for depression that adolescents can modify: A systematic review and meta-analysis of longitudinal studies. *Journal of Affective Disorders*, *169*, 61–75. https://doi.org/10.1016/j.jad.2014.08.006

Caspi, A., Houts, R. M., Belsky, D. W., Goldman-Mellor, S.J., Harrington, H., Israel, S., Meier, M.H., Ramrakha, S., Shalev, I., Poulton, R., & Moffitt, T. E. (2014). The p factor: one general psychopathology factor in the structure of psychiatric disorders? *Clinical Psychological Science*, *2*(2), 119–137.

Chorpita, B. F., & Weisz, J. R. (2009). *Modular Approach to Therapy for Children with Anxiety, Depression, Trauma, or Conduct Problems (MATCH-ADTC)*. PracticeWise, LLC.

Chorpita, B.F., Yim, L., Moffitt, C., Umemoto, L.A., & Francis, S.E. (2000). Assessment of symptoms of DSM-IV anxiety and depression in children: A Revised Child Anxiety and Depression Scale. *Behaviour Research and Therapy*, *38*(8), 835–855,

Clark, S., Bowers, G., & Reynolds, S. (2014). Managing negative thoughts, part 1: Cognitive restructuring and behavioral experiments. In E. S. Sburlati, H. J. Lyneham, C. A. Schniering, & R. M. Rapee (Eds.), *Evidence-based CBT for anxiety and depression in children and adolescents: A competencies-based approach* (pp. 157–175). John Wiley.

Clark, D. M., & Wells, A. (1995). A cognitive model of social phobia. In R. G. Heimberg, M. R. Liebowitz, D. A. Hope, & F. R. Schneier (Eds.), *Social phobia: Diagnosis, assessment, and treatment* (pp. 69–93). Guilford Press.

Clayborne, Z. M., Varin, M., & Colman, I. (2019). Systematic review and meta-analysis: Adolescent depression and long-term psychosocial outcomes. *Journal of American Academic Child and Adolescent Psychiatry*, *58*(1), 72–79. https://doi.org/10.1016/j.jaac.2018.07.896

Colasanto, M., Madigan, S., & Korczak, D. J. (2020). Depression and inflammation among children and adolescents: A meta-analysis. *Journal of Affective Disorders*, *277*, 940–948. https://doi.org/10.1016/j.jad.2020.09.025

Copeland, W. E., Angold, A., Costello, E. J., & Egger, H. (2013). Prevalence, comorbidity, and correlates of DSM-5 proposed disruptive mood dysregulation disorder. *American Journal of Psychiatry*, *170*(2), 173–179.

Costello, E. J., & Angold, A. (1988). Scales to assess child and adolescent depression: Checklists, screens, and nets. *Journal of the American Academy of Child & Adolescent Psychiatry*, *27*(6), 726–737. https://doi.org/10.1097/00004583-198811000-00011

Craske, M. G., Treanor, M., Conway, C. C., Zbozinek, T., & Vervliet, B (2014). Maximizing exposure therapy: An inhibitory learning approach. *Behaviour Research and Therapy*, *58*, 10–23.

Creswell, C., Parkinson, M., Thirlwall, K., & Willetts, L. (2019). *Parent-led CBT for child anxiety: Helping parents help their kids*. Guilford Press.

Creswell, C., Violato, M., Fairbanks, H., White, E., Parkinson, M., Abitabile, G., Leidi, A, & Cooper, P. J. (2017). Clinical outcomes and cost-effectiveness of brief guided parent-delivered cognitive behavioural therapy and solution-focused brief therapy for treatment of childhood anxiety disorders: a randomised controlled trial. *The Lancet Psychiatry*, *4*(7), 529–539.

Creswell, C., Waite, P., & Hudson, J. (2020). Practitioner Review: Anxiety disorders in children and young people–assessment and treatment. *Journal of Child Psychology and Psychiatry*, *61*(6), 628–643.

Creswell, C., & Willetts, L. (2019). *Helping your child with fears and worries: A guide self-help guide for parents*. Robinson.

Cuijpers, P., Karyotaki, E., Ciharova, M., Miguel, C., Noma, H., Stikkelbroek, Y., Weisz, J. R., & Furukawa, J. R. (2023). The effects of psychological treatments of depression in children and adolescents on response, reliable change, and deterioration: A systematic review and meta-analysis. *European Child and Adolescent Psychiatry, 32*, 177–192. https://doi.org/10.1007/s00787-021-01884-6

Cummings, C. M., Caporino, N. E., & Kendall, P. C. (2014). Comorbidity of anxiety and depression in children and adolescents: 20 years after. *Psychological Bulletin, 140*(3), 816–845. https://doi.org/10.1037/a0034733

Dahl, S. K., Larsen, J. T., Petersen, L., Ubbesen, M. B., Mortensen, P. B., Munk-Olsen, T., & Musliner, K. L. (2017). Early adversity and risk for moderate to severe unipolar depressive disorder in adolescence and adulthood: A register-based study of 978,647 individuals. *Journal of Affective Disorders, 214*, 122–129. https://doi.org/10.1016/j.jad.2017.03.014

Davis, T. E., May, A., & Whiting, S. E. (2011). Evidence-based treatment of anxiety and phobia in children and adolescents: Current status and effects on the emotional response. *Clinical Psychology Review, 31*, 592–602.

Derisley, J., Heyman, I., Robinson, S., & Turner, C. (2008). *Breaking free from OCD: A CBT guide for young people and their families*. Jessica Kingsley.

DiClemente, C. C., & Velasquez, M. M. (2002). Motivational interviewing and the stages of change. In W. R. Miller & S. Rollnick (Eds.), *Motivational interviewing: Preparing people for change* (pp. 201–216). Guilford Press.

Dochnal, R., Vetro, A., Kiss, E., Baji, I., Lefkovics, E., Bylsma, L. M., Yaroslavsky, I., Rottenberg, J., Kovacs, M., & Kapornai, K. (2019). Emotion regulation among adolescents with pediatric depression as a function of anxiety comorbidity. *Front Psychiatry, 10*, 722. https://doi.org/10.3389/fpsyt.2019.00722

Dugas, M. J., Gagnon, F., Ladouceur, R., & Freeston, M. H. (1998). Generalised anxiety disorder: A preliminary test of a conceptual model. *Behaviour Research and Therapy, 36,* 215–226

Eckshtain, D., Kuppens, S., Ugueto, A., Ng, M. Y., Vaughn-Coaxum, R., Corteselli, K., & Weisz, J. R. (2019). Meta-analysis: 13-year follow-up of psychotherapy effects on youth depression. *Journal of American Academic Child and Adolescent Psychiatry, 59*(1), 45–63. https://doi.org/10.1016/j.jaac.2019.04.002

Edge, D., & Lemetyinen, H. (2019). Psychology across cultures: Challenges and opportunities. *Psychology and Psychotherapy: Theory, Research and Practice, 92*(2), 261–276.

Fairburn, C. G. (2008). *Cognitive Behavior Therapy and Eating Disorders*. Guilford Press.

Finning, K., Ukoumunne, O. C., Ford, T., Danielsson-Waters, E., Shaw, L., De Jager, I. R., Stentiford, L., & Moore, D. A. (2019). The association between child and adolescent depression and poor attendance at school: A systematic review and meta-analysis. *Journal of Affective Disorders, 245*, 928–938.

Fonagy, P., & Allison, E. (2017). Commentary: A refresh for evidence-based psychological therapies: Reflections on Marchette and Weisz. *Journal of Child Psychology and Psychiatry, 58*(9), 985–987.

Fuggle, P., Dunsmuir, S., & Curry, V. (2013). *CBT with children, young people and families*. Sage.

Ghandour, R. M., Sherman, L. J., Vladutiu, C. J., Ali, M. M., Lynch, S. E., Bitsko, R. H., & Blumberg, S. J. (2019). Prevalence and treatment of depression, anxiety, and conduct problems in US children. *Journal of Pediatrics, 206*, 256–267.

Girgus, J. S., & Yang, K. (2015). Gender and depression. *Current Opinion in Psychology, 4*, 53–60. https://doi.org/10.1016/j.copsyc.2015.01.019

Glaser, B., Gunnell, D., Timpson, N., Joinson, C., Zammit, S., Smith, G. D., & Lewis, G. (2011). Age-and puberty-dependent association between IQ score in early childhood and depressive symptoms in adolescence. *Psychological Medicine, 41*(2), 333–343.

Goodyer, I., Reynolds, S., Barrett, B., Byford, S., Dubicka, B., Hill, J., Holland, F., Kelvin, R., Midgley, N., Roberts, C., Senior, R., Target, M., Widmer, B., Wilkinson, P., & Fonagy, P. (2016). Cognitive behavioural therapy and short-term psychoanalytical psychotherapy versus a brief psychosocial intervention in adolescents with unipolar major depressive disorder (IMPACT): A multicentre, pragmatic, observer-blind, randomised controlled superiority trial. *The Lancet Psychiatry, 4*(2), 109–119. https://doi.org/10.1016/s2215-0366(16)30378-9

Greenberger, D., & Padesky, C. A. (1995). *Mind over mood: A cognitive therapy treatment manual for clients*. Guilford Press.

Halldorsson, B., Elliott, L., Chessell, C., Willetts, L., & Creswell, C. (2019). Helping your child with fears and worries: A self-help guide for parents treatment manual for therapists. https://centaur.reading.ac.uk/87041/

Hankin, B. L. (2015). Depression from childhood through adolescence: Risk mechanisms across multiple systems and levels of analysis. *Current Opinions in Psychology, 4*, 13–20. https://doi.org/10.1016/j.copsyc.2015.01.003

Hards, E., Ellis, J., Fisk, J., & Reynolds, S. (2019). Negative view of the self and symptoms of depression in adolescents. *Journal of Affective Disorders, 262*, 143–148. https://doi.org/10.1016/j.jad.2019.11.012

Herring, G. T., Loades, M. E., Higson-Sweeney, N., Hards, E., Reynolds, S., & Midgley, N. (2022). The experience of cognitive behavioural therapy in depressed adolescents who are fatigued. *Psychological Psychotherapy, 95*(1), 234–255. https://doi.org/10.1111/papt.12365

Iob, E., Baldwin, J. R., Plomin, R., & Steptoe, A. (2021). Adverse childhood experiences, daytime salivary cortisol, and depressive symptoms in early adulthood: A longitudinal genetically informed twin study. *Translational Psychiatry, 11*(1), 420. https://doi.org/10.1038/s41398-021-01538-w

Johnson, J. G., Harris, E. S., Spitzer, R. L., & Williams, J. B. (2002). The patient health questionnaire for adolescents: Validation of an instrument for the assessment of mental disorders among adolescent primary care patients. *Journal of Adolescent Health, 30*(3), 196–204.

Johnson, D., Dupuis, G., Piche, J., Clayborne, Z., & Colman, I. (2018). Adult mental health outcomes of adolescent depression: A systematic review. *Depression and Anxiety, 35*(8), 700–716. https://doi.org/10.1002/da.22777

Kotov, R., Krueger, R. F., Watson, D., Achenbach, T. M., Althoff, R. R., Bagby, R. M., Brown, T. A., Carpenter, W. T., Caspi, A., Clark, L. A., & Eaton, N.R. (2017). The Hierarchical

Taxonomy of Psychopathology (HiTOP): A dimensional alternative to traditional nosologies. *Journal of Abnormal Psychology, 126*(4), 454.

Kovacs, M. (1992). *Children's depression inventory*. Multi-health System North Tonawanda.

Krause, K., Midgley, N., Edbrooke-Childs, J., & Wolpert, M. (2020). A comprehensive mapping of outcomes following psychotherapy for adolescent depression: The perspectives of young people, their parents and therapists. *European Child and Adolescent Psychiatry, 30*, 1779–1791. https://doi.org/10.1007/s00787-020-01648-8

Kroenke, K., Spitzer, R. L., & Williams, J. B. (2001). The PHQ-9: validity of a brief depression severity measure. *Journal of General Internal Medicine, 16*(9), 606–613. https://doi.org/10.1046/j.1525-1497.2001.016009606.x

Langley, A. K., Falk, A., Peris, T., Wiley, J. F., Kendall, P. C., Ginsburg, G., Birmaher, B., March, J., Albano, A. M., & Piacentini, J. (2014). The Child Anxiety Impact Scale (CAIS): Examining parent- and child-reported impairment in child anxiety disorders. *Journal of Clinical Child & Adolescent Psychology, 43*(4), 579–591.

Lavner, J. A., Hart, A. R., Carter, S. E., & Beach, S. R. (2021). Longitudinal effects of racial discrimination on depressive symptoms among black youth: Between-and within-person effects. *Journal of the American Academy of Child & Adolescent Psychiatry, 61*(1), 56–65.

Leger, E., Ladouceur, R., Dugas, M. J., & Freeston, M. H. (2003). Cognitive-behavioural treatment of generalised anxiety disorder among adolescents: A case series. *Journal of the American Academy of Child and Adolescent Psychiatry, 42*(3), 327–330.

Leigh, E., & Clark, D. M. (2018). Understanding social anxiety disorder in adolescents and improving treatment outcomes: Applying the cognitive model of Clark and Wells (1995). *Clinical Child and Family Psychology Review, 21*(3), 388–414.

Lewis-Smith, I., Pass, L., & Reynolds, S. (2021). How adolescents understand their values: A qualitative study. *Clinical Child Psychology and Psychiatry, 26*(1), 231–242. https://doi.org/10.1177/1359104520964506

Leyfer, O., Gallo, K.P., Cooper-Vince, C., & Pincus, D.B. (2013). Patterns and predictors of comorbidity of DSM-IV anxiety disorders in a clinical sample of children and adolescents. *Journal of Anxiety Disorders, 27*(3), 306–311.

Loades, M., Clark, S., & Reynolds, S. (2014). Positive imagery, self-talk, thought stopping, and thought acceptance. In E. S. Sburlati, H. J. Lyneham, A. A. Schniering, & R. M. Rapee (Eds.), *Evidence-based CBT for Anxiety and depression in children and adolescents: A competencies-based approach* (pp. 176–193). Wiley.

Loades, M. E., & Essau, C. A. (2023). Behavioral activation. In L. J. Farrell, S. A. Murrihy, & C. A. Essau (Eds.), *Handbook of child and adolescent psychology treatment modules*. (pp. 75–87). Academic Press.

Lu, W. (2019). Adolescent depression: national trends, risk factors, and healthcare disparities. *American Journal of Health Behavior, 43*(1), 181–194.

Malooly, A. M., Flannery, K. M., & Ohannessian, C. M. (2017). Coping mediates the association between gender and depressive symptomatology in adolescence. *International Journal of Behavioral Development, 41*(2), 185–197.

Maroun, R. A., Thackeray, L. A., & Midgley, N. (2018). Meaning and medication: a thematic analysis of depressed adolescents' views and experiences of SSRI antidepressants alongside psychological therapies. *BMC Psychiatry, 18*(1), 374. https://doi.org/10.1186/s12888-018-1961-y

Masia-Warner, C., Storch, E. A., Pincus, D. B., Klein, R. G., Heimberg, R. G., & Liebowitz, M. R. (2003). The Liebowitz social anxiety scale for children and adolescents: An initial psychometric investigation. *Journal of the American Academy of Child & Adolescent Psychiatry, 42*(9), 1076–1084.

McCauley, E., Schloredt, K. A., Gudmundsen, G. R., Martell, C. R., & Dimidjian, S. (2016). *Behavioral activation with adolescents: A clinician's guide*. Guilford Press.

Midgley, N., Holmes, J., Parkinson, S., Stapley, E., Eatough, V., & Target, M. (2016). 'Just like talking to someone about like shit in your life and stuff, and they help you': Hopes and expectations for therapy among depressed adolescents. *Psychotherapy Research, 26*(1), 11–21. https://doi.org/10.1080/10503307.2014.973922

Midgley, N., Parkinson, S., Holmes, J., Stapley, E., Eatough, V., & Target, M. (2015). Beyond a diagnosis: The experience of depression among clinically referred adolescents. *Journal of Adolescence, 44*, 269–279. https://doi.org/10.1016/j.adolescence.2015.08.007

Midgley, N., Parkinson, S., Holmes, J., Stapley, E., Eatough, V., & Target, M. (2017). 'Did I bring it on myself?' An exploratory study of the beliefs that adolescents referred to mental health services have about the causes of their depression. *European Child and Adolescent Psychiatry, 26*(1), 25–34. https://doi.org/10.1007/s00787-016-0868-8

Moffitt, T. E., Caspi, A., Taylor, A., Kokaua, J., Milne, B. J., Polanczyk, G., & Poulton, R. (2010). How common are common mental disorders? Evidence that lifetime prevalence rates are doubled by prospective versus retrospective ascertainment. *Psychological Medicine, 40*(6), 899–909. https://doi.org/10.1017/s0033291709991036

Mojtabai, R., Olfson, M., & Han, B. (2016). National trends in the prevalence and treatment of depression in adolescents and young adults. *Pediatrics, e20161878.*

Moore, D. A., Nunns, M., Shaw, L., Rogers, M., Walker, E., Ford, T., Garside, R., Ukoumunne, O., Titman, P., & Shafran, R. (2019). Interventions to improve the mental health of children and young people with long-term physical conditions: Linked evidence syntheses. *Health Technology Assessment, 23*(22), 1.

Morey, A., & Loades, M. E. (2020). How has cognitive behaviour therapy been adapted for adolescents with comorbid depression and chronic illness? A scoping review. *Child and Adolescent Mental Health, 26*(3), 252–264.

Mufson, L., & Sills, R. (2006). Interpersonal psychotherapy for depressed adolescents (IPT-A): An overview. *Nordic Journal of Psychiatry, 60*(6), 431–437.

Murray, L., Arteche, A., Fearon, P., Halligan, S., Goodyer, I., & Cooper, P. (2011). Maternal postnatal depression and the development of depression in offspring up to 16 years of age. *Journal of the American Academy of Child & Adolescent Psychiatry, 50*(5), 460–470.

Murray, L., Creswell, C., & Cooper, P.J., 2009. The development of anxiety disorders in childhood: An integrative review. *Psychological medicine, 39*(9), 1413–1423.

Naar, S., & Safren, S. (2017) Integrating motivational interviewing and cognitive-behavioral therapy: Rationale approach and evidence. In *Interviewing and CBT: Combining Strategies for Maximum Effectiveness* (pp. 1–10). Guilford Press.

Naicker, K., Galambos, N. L., Zeng, Y., Senthilselvan, A., & Colman, I. (2013). Social, demographic, and health outcomes in the 10 years following adolescent depression. *Journal of Adolescent Health, 52*(5), 533–538. https://doi.org/10.1016/j.jadohealth.2012.12.016

NICE. (2005). Depression in children and young people: Identification and management in primary, community and secondary care. https://www.nice.org.uk/guidance/ng134/evidence/september-2005-full-guideline-pdf-6836038382

NICE. (2013, May 22). Social anxiety disorder: Recognition, assessment and treatment. *Guideline 159*. https://www.nice.org.uk/guidance/cg159

NICE. (2019, June 25). Depression in children and young people: Identification and management. *Guideline 134*. https://www.nice.org.uk/guidance/ng134

NICE. (2023, February 8). Guided self-help digital cognitive behavioural therapy for children and young people with mild to moderate symptoms of anxiety or low mood: Early value assessment. *Evaluation 3*. https://www.nice.org.uk/guidance/hte3

O'Keeffe, S., Martin, P., Target, M., & Midgley, N. (2019, 5 February). 'I just stopped going': A mixed methods investigation into types of therapy dropout in adolescents with depression. *Frontiers in Psychology, 10*, 75. https://doi.org/10.3389/fpsyg.2019.00075

O'Neal, C. R., Weston, L. C., He, X., Huang, K. Y., Pine, D. S., Kamboukos, D., & Brotman, L. M. (2017). Change in depression across adolescence: The role of early anger socialization and child anger. *Journal of Adolescents, 59*(1), 1–7. https://doi.org/10.1016/j.adolescence.2017.05.011

Orchard, F., Gregory, A. M., Gradisar, M., & Reynolds, S. (2020). Self-reported sleep patterns and quality amongst adolescents: Cross-sectional and prospective associations with anxiety and depression. *Journal of Child Psychology and Psychiatry, 61*(10), 1126–1137. https://doi.org/10.1111/jcpp.13288

Orchard, F., Pass, L., Marshall, T., & Reynolds, S. (2016). Clinical characteristics of adolescents referred for treatment of depressive disorders. *Child and Adolescent Mental Health, 22*(2), 61–68. https://doi.org/10.1111/camh.12178

Orchard, F., Pass, L., & Reynolds, S. (2019). 'I am worthless and kind'; The specificity of positive and negative self-evaluation in adolescent depression. *British Journal of Clinical Psychology, 58*(3), 260–273. https://doi.org/10.1111/bjc.12215

Pass, L., Brisco, G., & Reynolds, S. (2015, 18 August). Adapting brief behavioural activation (BA) for adolescent depression: A case example. *The Cognitive Behaviour Therapist, 8*. https://doi.org/10.1017/s1754470x15000446

Patil, P., Porche, M. V., Shippen, N., Dallenbach, N., & Fortuna, L. R. (2017, December). Which girls, which boys? The intersectional risk for depression by race and ethnicity, and gender in the U.S. *Clinical Psychology Review, 66*, 51–68. https://doi.org/10.1016/j.cpr.2017.12.003

Peris, T. S., Compton, S. N., Kendall, P. C., Birmaher, B., Sherrill, J., March, J., Gosch, E., Ginsburg, G., Rynn, M., McCracken, J. T., & Keeton, C. P. (2015). Trajectories of change in youth anxiety during cognitive-behavior therapy. *Journal of Consulting and Clinical Psychology, 83*(2), 239.

Pile, V., Smith, P., Leamy, M., Blackwell, S. E., Meiser-Stedman, R., Stringer, D., Ryan, E. G., Dunn, B. D., Holmes, E. A., & Lau, J. Y. F. (2018, *4* July). A brief early intervention for adolescent depression that targets emotional mental images and memories: Protocol for a feasibility randomised controlled trial (IMAGINE trial). *Pilot Feasibility Study, 4*, 97. https://doi.org/10.1186/s40814-018-0287-3

Polanczyk, G. V., Salum, G. A., Sugaya, L. S., Caye, A., & Rohde, L. A. (2015). Annual research review: A meta-analysis of the worldwide prevalence of mental disorders in children and adolescents. *Journal of Children Psychology and Psychiatry, 56*, 345–365.

Rapee, R. M. (2001). The development of generalized anxiety. In M. W. Vasey & M. R. Dadds (Eds.), *The developmental psychopathology of anxiety* (pp. 481–503). Oxford University Press.

Rapp, A. M., Chavira, D. A., Sugar, C. A., & Asarnow, J. R. (2021, 1 January). Incorporating family factors into treatment planning for adolescent depression: Perceived parental criticism predicts longitudinal symptom trajectory in the Youth Partners in Care trial. *Journal of Affective Disorders, 278*, 46–53. https://doi.org/10.1016/j.jad.2020.09.028

Rausch, R. D. (2019). Narrative matters: The role of culture in the treatment of childhood anxiety. *Child and Adolescent Mental Health, 24*(4), 350–351.

Reangsing, C., Punsuwun, S., & Schneider, J. K. (2021, March). Effects of mindfulness interventions on depressive symptoms in adolescents: A meta-analysis. *International Journal of Nursing Studies, 115*, 103848. https://doi.org/https://doi.org/10.1016/j.ijnurstu.2020.103848

Reynolds, S., & Pass, L. (2020). *Brief behavioural activation for adolescent depression: A clinician's manual and session-by-session guide*. Jessica Kingsley.

Rosenberg, M. (1965). Rosenberg self-esteem scale. *Journal of Religion and Health.*

Schmidt, U. (2005). Engagement and motivational interviewing. In P. Graham (Ed.) *Cognitive-behaviour therapy for children and families* (2nd ed.) (pp. 67–83). Cambridge University Press.

Schwartz, J. S., & Maric, M. (2015). Negative cognitive errors in youth: Specificity to anxious and depressive symptoms and age differences. *Behavioral Cognitive Psychotherapy, 43*(5), 526–537. https://doi.org/10.1017/S1352465814000228

Schwartz-Mette, R. A., Shankman, J., Dueweke, A. R., Borowski, S., & Rose, A. J. (2020). Relations of friendship experiences with depressive symptoms and loneliness in childhood and adolescence: A meta-analytic review. *Psychological Bulletin, 146*(8), 664–700. https://doi.org/10.1037/bul0000239

Sfarlea, A., Lochner, J., Neumuller, J., Asperud Thomsen, L., Starman, K., Salemink, E., Schulte-Korne, G., & Platt, B. (2019). Passing on the half-empty glass: A transgenerational study of interpretation biases in children at risk for depression and their parents with depression. *Journal of Abnormal Psychology, 128*(2), 151–161. https://doi.org/10.1037/abn0000401

Shear, K., Jin, R., Ruscio, A. M., Walters, E. E., & Kessler, R. C. (2006). Prevalence and correlates of estimated DSM-IV child and adult separation anxiety disorder in the National Comorbidity Survey Replication. *American Journal of Psychiatry, 163*(6), 1074–1083.

Shore, L., Toumbourou, J. W., Lewis, A. J., & Kremer, P. (2017). Review: Longitudinal trajectories of child and adolescent depressive symptoms and their predictors – a systematic review and meta-analysis. *Child and Adolescent Mental Health, 23*(2), 107–120. https://doi.org/10.1111/camh.12220

Shorey, S., Ng, E. D., & Wong, C. H. J. (2021). Global prevalence of depression and elevated depressive symptoms among adolescents: A systematic review and meta-analysis. *British Journal of Clinical Psychology, 61*(2), 287–305. https://doi.org/10.1111/bjc.12333

Slavny, R. J., Sebastian, C. L., & Pote, H. (2019, July). Age-related changes in cognitive biases during adolescence. *Journal of Adolescence, 74*, 63–70.

Smith, P., Dalgleish, T., & Meiser-Stedman, R. (2019). Practitioner review: posttraumatic stress disorder and its treatment in children and adolescents. *Journal of Child Psychology and Psychiatry, 60*(5), 500–515.

Smith, E. M., Reynolds, S., Orchard, F., Whalley, H. C., & Chan, S. W. (2018, 1 December). Cognitive biases predict symptoms of depression, anxiety and wellbeing above and beyond neuroticism in adolescence. *Journal of Affective Disorders, 241*, 446–453. https://doi.org/10.1016/j.jad.2018.08.051

Spence, S. H. (1998). A measure of anxiety symptoms among children. *Behavioural Research Therapy, 36*(5), 545–566.

Spence, S. H., Sheffield, J., & Donovan, C. (2002). Problem-solving orientation and attributional style: moderators of the impact of negative life events on the development of depressive symptoms in adolescence? *Journal of Clinical Child and Adolescent Psychology, 31*(2), 219–229.

Stallard, P. (2002). *Think good, feel good : S CBT workbook for young people*. Wiley.

Stallard, P. (2005). *A clinician's guide to think good feel good: the use of CBT with children and young people*. John Wiley.

Stuart, S., & Robertson, M. (2003). *Theory and clinical applications. Interpersonal psychotherapy: A clinician's guide*. Taylor & Francis.

Szigethy, E., Levy-Warren, A., Whitton, S., Bousvaros, A., Gauvreau, K., Leichtner, A. M., & Beardslee, W. R. (2004). Depressive symptoms and inflammatory bowel disease in children and adolescents: A cross-sectional study. *Journal of Pediatric Gastroenterol Nutrition, 39*(4), 395–403.

Terhaag, S., Fitzsimons, E., Daraganova, G., & Patalay, P. (2021). Sex, ethnic and socioeconomic inequalities and trajectories in child and adolescent mental health in Australia and the UK: Findings from national prospective longitudinal studies. *Journal of Child Psychology and Psychiatry, 62*(10), 1244–1267.

Thapar, A., Collishaw, S., Pine, D. S., & Thapar, A. K. (2012). Depression in adolescence. *The Lancet, 379*(9820), 1056–1067. https://doi.org/10.1016/s0140-6736(11)60871-4

Turner, C., Volz, C., & Krebs, G. (2019a). *OCD-tools to help you fight back!: A CBT workbook for young people*. Jessica Kingsley Publishers.

Turner, C., Volz, C., & Krebs, G. (2019b). *OCD-tools to help young people fight back!: A CBT manual for therapists*. Jessica Kingsley Publishers.

Verduyn, C., Rogers, J., & Wood, A. (2009). *Depression: Cognitive behaviour therapy with children and young people*. Taylor & Francis. https://books.google.co.uk/books?id=av9fMczZBh8C

Vizard, T., Pearce, N., Davis, J., Sadler, K., Ford, T., & Goodman, A. (2018). *Mental health of children and young people in England*. NHS Digital.

Waite, P., & Williams, T. (2009). *Obsessive compulsive disorder: Cognitive behaviour therapy with children and young people*. Routledge.

Walters, S., Loades, M., & Russell, A. (2016). A systematic review of effective modifications to cognitive behavioural therapy for young people with autism spectrum disorders. *Review Journal of Autism and Developmental Disorders, 3*(2), 137–153. https://doi.org/10.1007/s40489-016-0072-2

Webb, C. A., Stanton, C. H., Bondy, E., Singleton, P., Pizzagalli, D. A., & Auerbach, R. P. (2019). Cognitive versus behavioral skills in CBT for depressed adolescents: Disaggregating within-patient versus between-patient effects on symptom change. *Journal of Consulting Clinical Psychology, 87*(5), 484–490. https://doi.org/10.1037/ccp0000393

Weeks, M., Coplan, R. J., & Ooi, L. L. (2017, 23 November). Cognitive biases among early adolescents with elevated symptoms of anxiety, depression, and co-occurring symptoms of anxiety-depression. *Infant and Child Development*, *26*(5). https://doi.org/10.1002/icd.2011

Weisz, J., Bearman, S. K., Santucci, L. C. and Jensen-Doss, A. (2017). Initial test of a principle-guided approach to transdiagnostic psychotherapy with children and adolescents. *Journal of Clinical Child & Adolescent Psychology*, *46*(1), 44–58.

Wellcome. (2021). *What science has shown can help young people with anxiety and depression. Identifying and reviewing the 'active ingredients' of effective interventions: Part 1.* Zenodo. https://doi.org/10.5281/zenodo.7327137

Wellcome. (2022). What science has shown can help young people with anxiety and depression. Identifying and reviewing the 'active ingredients' of effective interventions: Part 2. Zenodo. https://doi.org/10.5281/zenodo.7327296

Wickersham, A., Sugg, H. V. R., Epstein, S., Stewart, R., Ford, T., & Downs, J. (2021). Systematic review and meta-analysis: The association between child and adolescent depression and later educational attainment. *Journal of the American Academy of Child & Adolescent Psychiatry*, *60*(1), 105–118. https://doi.org/10.1016/j.jaac.2020.10.008

World Health Organization. (2018). *International classification of diseases for mortality and morbidity statistics (11th Revision).* World Health Organization. https://icd.who.int/browse11/l-m/en

Wright, A. G. C. (2017). The current state and future of factor analysis in personality disorder research. *Personality Disorders: Theory, Research, and Treatment*, *8*, 14–25.

Yoon, Y., Deighton, J., Wickersham, A., Edbrooke-Childs, J., Osborn, D., Viding, E., & Downs, J. (2021, 23 July). The role of mental health symptomology and quality of life in predicting referrals to special child and adolescent mental health services. *BMC Psychiatry*, *21*(1), 366. https://doi.org/10.1186/s12888-021-03364-2

14

Complex Emotional Difficulties

Zoë Maiden

14.1 Introduction

Historically, both obsessive compulsive disorder (OCD) and post-traumatic stress disorder (PTSD) were categorised as anxiety disorders within diagnostic classifications of mental disorders (e.g. Diagnostic Statistical Manual of Mental Disorders [DSM], International Classification of Diseases [ICD]). DSM-5 (American Psychiatric Association [APA], 2013) and ICD-11 (World Health Organization [WHO], 2022) saw the introduction of the obsessive-compulsive and related disorders category, which includes OCD alongside trichotillomania (hair-pulling), hoarding disorder and body dysmorphic disorder (BDD). Similarly, PTSD is now classified under 'Trauma and Stressor Related Disorders' in DSM-5 (APA, 2013) and 'Disorders specifically associated with Stress' in ICD-11 (WHO, 2022).

Despite being distinct disorders, OCD and PTSD share characteristics that render them complex, or often, complicated to treat. Both are debilitating mental health conditions; OCD ranks in the top 10 causes of disability worldwide (Eaton et al., 2008) and the impairment associated with PTSD is comparable to, or greater than that of other severe mental health problems (Kessler, 2000). Both difficulties are associated with high comorbidity rates (e.g. S. J. Lewis et al., 2019; Wewetzer et al., 2001) and complexities with risk assessment and management (e.g. A. Lewis et al., 2020; S. J. Lewis et al., 2019). In addition, despite robust support for evidence-based treatments for both difficulties, research suggests these are under-utilised in routine clinical practice (e.g. Keleher et al., 2020; Smith et al., 2019). Hence it is important for practitioners to understand both difficulties and gain confidence in their assessment, formulation and evidence-based treatments.

14.2 OCD

14.2.1 Presentation

OCD is characterised by the presence of recurrent, unwanted, and distressing intrusive thoughts (obsessions) and/or repetitive acts performed to alleviate anxiety or prevent a feared outcome from occurring (compulsions) (APA, 2013; WHO, 2022). Nevertheless, OCD

Child Psychology: Pathways to Good Practice, First Edition.
Edited by Helen Pote, Anna Picciotto and Clare Norris.

can present very differently for each young person (YP), and previous research suggests there are four common subgroups of symptoms (Abramowitz et al., 2011):

1. Concerns about germs and contamination: often characterised by obsessions about dirt or illness and compulsions relating to washing or cleaning.
2. Responsibility for harm: often characterised by obsessions relating to harm coming to others unless a compulsion is completed.
3. Blasphemous thoughts: involves obsessions relating to 'immoral' or 'taboo' subjects such as violence or sex, accompanied by compulsions (often mental acts) to neutralise or eliminate the thought.
4. Symmetry, completeness, and the need for things to be 'just right': often characterised by sensory-perceptual disturbances regarding the appearance or feeling of internal or external stimuli and repeating, arranging, or counting compulsions to relieve discomfort.

The most common obsessions observed in children and young people (CYP) are worries about dirt, thoughts of something terrible happening and thoughts about illness/death (Williams & Waite, 2009). However, more taboo obsessions, such as intrusions of a paedophilic nature, are also common in CYP with OCD and are likely to be under-reported due to the stigma attached to them (Fernández de la Cruz et al., 2013). The most common compulsions are thought to be washing, checking, repeating tasks, ordering/arranging and counting (Williams & Waite, 2009). The term 'Pure O' is often used to refer to people with OCD who *appear* to experience primarily obsessions. The term is misleading as in reality, the compulsions are present, but they are not readily visible to others (e.g. mental rituals; Williams et al., 2011). Most CYP with OCD endorse multiple obsessions and compulsions at any one time (Geller & March, 2012).

Prevalence rates of OCD for CYP in the United Kingdom are outdated. A study by Heyman et al. (2003) suggests that only 0.25% of 0 to 15 year-olds in the United Kingdom reach diagnostic criteria for OCD at any one time. However, the same study shows that the prevalence is higher in 13- to 15-year-olds (0.6%) than in younger age brackets. Hence the overall figure for adolescents is more likely to be in-line with other research suggesting that 1 to 2% of CYP struggle with OCD (e.g. Douglass et al., 1995; Heyman et al., 2001). Approximately 8 out of 10 people with OCD will have developed symptoms before the age of 18 (Veale & Roberts, 2014). There are some studies indicating OCD is more prevalent in males during childhood but is more common in females during adolescence (Mathes et al., 2019). There is also the suggestion that gender plays a role in the onset, presentation and impact of OCD symptoms (see Mathes et al., 2019 for a review). The typical age of onset is 8 to 11 years with some children as young as 2 years old experiencing symptoms (Swedo et al., 1989). Without intervention, OCD symptoms may increase and decrease over time, but typically follow a chronic course (S. E. Stewart et al., 2004) and is linked to an increased risk for other mental health difficulties in adulthood (e.g. Micali et al., 2010). OCD often has a negative impact across multiple areas of a CYP's life, including school, home and relationships with peers (Piacentini et al., 2003).

Risk Factors

Both nature and nurture are thought to have a role in the aetiology of OCD. Research from twin and family studies suggest a higher heritability of OCD compared to most other anxiety disorders and depression in CYP, with 45 to 65% of the variance explained (Eley et al., 2003;

Taylor, 2011; van Grootheest et al., 2005). This suggests a key role for genetics in the onset of OCD and studies have moved on to investigate which specific genes may be involved (e.g. Mattheisen et al., 2015). Very little is currently known about the contribution of environmental factors to the onset of OCD. In a recent meta-analysis, no factor investigated showed convincing or highly convincing evidence as a risk or protective factor. There was some evidence that early traumatic experiences increased the risk of developing OCD, however the evidence was rated as weak (Fullana et al., 2020).

Family Accommodation

OCD can have a profound effect on members of the CYPs family, with their lives often significantly disrupted (Cooper, 1996). Parent and carers can be affected in multiple domains, including their own psychological wellbeing and social, working and family lives (e.g. Soni et al., 2017). Therefore, family accommodation is common (Lebowitz et al., 2016) and can take many different forms. Generally, the term refers to relatives either supporting a person with their compulsions or even completing them on their behalf. For example, a CYP who experiences intrusions about the security and safety of their house may previously have checked all the windows and doors are locked three times, whereas now the parent or carer completes these checks on their behalf. Accommodation can also occur in the form of providing reassurance. For example, the same CYP being away from the house and experiencing an intrusive thought about the house being unlocked, leading to the parent providing reassurance that it is locked. Parents and carers may also find themselves changing their daily routines. For example, the parent of a CYP who worries about food being contaminated may start washing vegetables multiple times or avoid cooking food that is perceived, by the CYP, to be 'high-risk'. It is also very common for parents or carers to help the CYP avoid situations where their obsessions are likely to be triggered. In the same example, the family avoid getting takeaways or eating out as this causes the CYP's obsessions to occur more intensely.

Cross-cultural Considerations

As with other mental health diagnoses, practitioners should be curious and critical of whether OCD as defined by the DSM and ICD applies across cultures. Much of the OCD research, including that cited in this chapter, is conducted in Europe and the United States. Where cross-cultural differences have been studied, findings are often conflicting. Studies have found that some cultures are more likely to experience particular obsessions, such as religious obsessions in the Middle East (Okasha et al., 1994; Shooka et al., 1998) yet other studies have contradictory findings (Raffin et al., 2009). A recent meta-analysis by Hunt (2020) found that indeed, there are likely to be differences in the content of obsessions experienced across cultures, but that these are more modest than expected as the effect sizes found were very small. Nevertheless, it can be helpful for practitioners to keep these cultural differences in mind to aid with their assessment, engagement, formulation and intervention. Some of the key themes from the meta-analysis were similar to those that had already emerged from the literature. For example, those from Middle Eastern cultures had an increase an religious obsessions, which may be explained by the increased emphasis on religion in the region (Okasha et al., 1994). Contamination and washing compulsions were more common among OCD sufferers from both Asia and the Middle East, which may or may not reflect the importance of purity in Indian culture and Islamic Faith (de

Silva, 2006). Conversely, some findings were new, such as lower proportions of somatic obsessions in those from Asian cultures. Symmetry and ordering obsessions were the only categories that did not significantly differ across cultures. It is important to note that most studies included were conducted with adults and hence require replicating with CYP. In addition, there are many more general criticisms of research currently looking at cross-cultural differences in mental health. For example, the use of overly inclusive cultural groups (e.g. 'Asian') which are arguably reductionist and therefore unlikely to capture the true nuances of different cultures. Practitioners are therefore encouraged to practice, continually, cultural humility in their work with CYP; cultural humility refers to acknowledging that one does not know about and is willing to learn about CYP's cultural experiences, whilst being also being aware of one's own culture (Kirmayer, 2012). See Chapter 7, Inclusivity, Diversity and Power, for further discussion on this.

14.2.2 Assessment

Screening

Practitioners are encouraged to remember that although society typically associates OCD with certain symptoms (for example, excessive hand washing), the disorder is remarkably heterogeneous. The majority of CAMHS services within the United Kingdom now utilise the Revised Children's Anxiety and Depression Scale (RCADS; Chorpita et al., 2000), which includes a subscale for OCD that can be used to screen for the need for further assessment.

Assessment Content

The Child Yale Brown Obsessive Compulsive Scale Second Edition (CY-BOCS-II; Storch et al., 2019) is the gold standard for assessment. It is a semi-structured interview that takes 1 to 2 hours to complete. It involves a comprehensive symptom checklist for both obsessions and compulsions, with additional questions to assess the severity and level of impairment experienced. The questions include calculating the amount of time the CYP spends thinking about obsessions and completing rituals, the level of interference caused by obsessions and compulsions, the level of distress experienced, the amount the CYP tries to resist and their ability to resist when they attempt to. The total score is out of 40, with clinical cut-offs for severity indicated (sub-clinical <10, mild 10–18, moderate 19–29, severe > 29). The CY-BOCS-II can also be used at the end of an intervention to measure symptom change. Notably the adult version of the CY-BOCS-II has been validated for use across several cultures (e.g. Brito et al., 2015; Hiranyatheb et al., 2014; Melli et al., 2015) and hence it is often assumed that the CYP version can be used cross-culturally with confidence.

As well as an assessment tool, the CY-BOCS should be used as an opportunity to engage the client and their caregiver(s). It is a prime opportunity to provide psychoeducation and to normalise the obsessions and compulsions the CYP is experiencing. Practitioners should therefore approach any unusual or potentially embarrassing symptoms (e.g. sexual obsessions) in a gentle but direct manner and ideally without the parent or carer present. In addition, CYP are often relieved to see their obsessions and compulsions listed on a questionnaire as it demonstrates that they are not the only CYP to experience them.

Comorbidity is very common for CYP with OCD, with up to 80% struggling with an additional mental health difficulty (e.g. Heyman et al., 2003; Jans et al., 2007) and anxiety disorders being the most common (Sharma et al., 2021). Therefore, a thorough assessment of their wellbeing and mental health is recommended. Differential diagnosis can often be a challenge in the assessment of OCD, particularly with autism spectrum condition (ASC; discussed later in this chapter), tic disorders and psychosis (Krebs & Heyman, 2015). Regarding tic disorder, whilst this can be a comorbidity, it is important to distinguish the difference between compulsions and tics. Tics are largely involuntary whereas compulsions are performed intentionally to reduce anxiety. In addition, compulsions are often more complex than tics. Obsessions that are seen as 'strange' by society can sometimes be confused with psychotic experiences. For example, obsessions about the fear of being harmed can appear similarly to paranoia. Those with OCD tend to have at least some insight that their obsessions and compulsions are irrational and other symptoms of psychosis (e.g. hallucinations) are absent (Krebs & Hayman, 2015).

Risk Assessment

In addition to standardised risk assessments, it is important to differentiate between primary and secondary risk when working with OCD (Veale et al., 2009). Primary risk refers to the possibility of the CYP acting on an unwanted intrusive thought. This risk is not genuine, rather it is apparent and negligible in the context of experiencing OCD. The content of the obsession is terrifying to the CYP and the compulsions exist because they believe this will prevent the obsession from becoming reality: for example, the fear of pushing someone off the platform at a train station or the fear of stabbing someone. Secondary risk refers to actual risk because of engaging in compulsions and is not intended. For example, not eating enough for fear that food is contaminated.

Thorough assessment and management of these risks whilst completing an intervention is paramount, as practice-based evidence suggests that ineffective management can interfere with treatment in numerous ways (A. Lewis et al., 2020). Both primary and secondary risk can be distracting for practitioners and become the priority, leaving the OCD untreated. Furthermore, where primary risk is present, inexperienced OCD therapists sometimes take measures to reduce the apparent threat. This is problematic as it is not necessary and inadvertently exacerbates symptoms. For example, if a CYP has intrusive thoughts about self-harming with a knife in the context of OCD, implementation of a common safety planning technique of reducing access to knives would reinforce their belief that they will act on the thought. Similarly, therapists may avoid completing the core mechanisms of change in an evidence-based intervention (i.e. Exposure Response-Prevention [ER-P] tasks) due to worries about increasing risk (A. Lewis et al., 2020). In the given example, an appropriate ER-P task would be for the CYP to hold a knife, whilst not completing any compulsions, so that they can learn that they do not harm themselves. As such, the risk assessment described above is paramount. A. Lewis et al. (2020) discuss four case studies of primary and secondary risk in CYP with OCD and provide some guiding principles for assessment and management:

Primary risk:

1. Thoughts are ego dystonic, that is, the CYP finds them distressing and they are unwanted.
2. There is no history of acting on thoughts.

3. Other obsessions are present.
4. Obsessions will be linked to compulsions.

Secondary risk:

1. If the risk will impede CBT, this may need to be managed first (e.g. weight significantly low).

Self-report Outcomes Measures

The RCADS (Chorpita et al., 2000) should be used to get an overall picture of the CYP's emotional difficulties (see Chapter 13 on Emotional Difficulties for further description). Practitioners could choose to use the OCD subscale of the RCADS to measure symptom change. However, for a more in-depth assessment and sensitive measure of change, the Obsessional Compulsive Inventory Revised Self Report (ChOCI-R-S; Uher et al., 2008) can be used. The ChOCI-R-S is a self-report measure validated for use with children and adolescents aged 7 to 17 years. The measure is split into two sections; obsessions and compulsions. There are questions about the presence of common obsessions and compulsions as well as questions regarding severity. A total symptoms and impairment score and/or individual obsession and compulsion symptom and impact scores can therefore be calculated. A parent version (ChOCI-R-P) is also available. Both measures can be used as part of the assessment and track symptom change over time.

Given the importance of family accommodation in the assessment, maintenance and treatment of childhood OCD, having a measure to assess this is recommended. Practitioners have a few options: the Family Accommodation Scale (FAC) is a semi-structured interview, similar to the CY-BOCS-II, that can be conducted by the practitioner. Alternatively, parents and carers can be given the Family Accommodation Scale – Parent Report (FAS-PR), which is a self-report measure (Calvocoressi et al., 1995).

Goal-based Outcomes (GBOs) should also be set collaboratively with the CYP and used as an outcome measure. GBOs are a specific measure of what the CYP wants to achieve by the end of therapy. Setting GBOs allows increased shared decision making about the direction of treatment (Bromley & Westwood, 2013)

NICE Guidelines and Evidence Base

According to the National Institute for Health and Care Excellence (NICE) guidelines (2005), CYP with OCD symptoms resulting in mild functional impairment should be offered guided self-help, in addition to support and information for the family and/or carers. CYP with moderate to severe functional impairment and CYP with mild functional impairment who have not responded/been able to engage with guided self-help, should be offered CBT, including an ER-P component. Furthermore, this should involve the family or carer and should be adapted to the developmental age of the child. Group and individual formats should both be offered, and the treatment commenced should depend on the preferences of the CYP and their family or carers. If psychological treatment is declined by the CYP or they are unable to engage in treatment, medication can be considered; specifically, a selective serotonin reuptake inhibitor (SSRI) that is carefully monitored for adverse events.

The guidelines are based on rigorous randomised controlled trials (RCTs) that have demonstrated CBT and SSRIs to be effective for treatment of OCD in CYP (see J. F. McGuire et al., 2015 for a meta-analytic review). A recent network analysis found that all pharmacological and psychological treatments were more effective than placebo. Combined treatment of medication and CBT was more effective than medication alone (Tao et al., 2022).

There is a proportion of CYP who find some benefit from the outlined treatment but have clinically significant symptoms remaining and there are some CYP with OCD who do not respond to CBT or SSRIs at all. These CYP are often termed 'treatment resistant'. It is recommended that these CYP should trial an alternative SSRI. There is evidence in adults, and emerging research in CYP, that SSRI medication can be augmented with anti-psychotic medication (see Marazziti & Pozza, 2022 for review of current medication options).

Research has attempted to identify predictors of successful treatment. For CYP, there is some evidence that some comorbidities, such as autism, tic disorder and oppositional defiance disorder, predict poorer treatment response (Ginsburg et al., 2008; Russell et al., 2013). A systematic review also found that older age, symptom severity, level of impairment and higher family accommodation predicted poorer outcome to CBT (Turner et al., 2018).

CBT for OCD for CYP – Overview

Mechanisms of Change in CBT for OCD: Cognitive vs Behavioural Techniques: CBT for OCD typically targets changes in both thoughts (obsessions) and behaviours (compulsions). This is usually achieved through a combination of cognitive therapy (CT) and ER-P. The term CBT has been used to describe multiple protocols for working with CYP with OCD, with differing emphasis on the role of CT and ER-P. Despite both techniques deriving from learning theory, they assume distinct mechanisms of change. Cognitive models propose that changing dysfunctional beliefs leads to symptom improvement (e.g. Salkovskis, 1985), whereas behavioural models suggest exposure to feared situations whilst resisting compulsions is the key treatment component (e.g. Arch & Abramowitz, 2015). As such, the amount of cognitive versus behavioural techniques in CBT for OCD manuals can vary immensely, depending on which theoretical approach is taken.

Whilst evidence for the cognitive model of OCD is apparent in the adult literature, the same cannot be said for CYP. Research examining the relationship between dysfunctional beliefs and OCD in CYP is mixed. Some studies found a clear relationship (e.g. Libby et al., 2004; Mather & Cartwright-Hatton, 2004; Matthews et al., 2007) whereas others have not (Barrett & Healy-Farrell, 2003; Verhaak & De Haan, 2007; Wolters et al., 2019). Furthermore, if dysfunctional beliefs were core in the maintenance of childhood OCD, we could expect that modifying these beliefs in treatment would improve outcomes. To date, there is no such evidence and in fact, there is some research demonstrating that changes in OCD symptoms predict changes in dysfunctional beliefs, rather than the other way around (Wolters et al., 2019).

Conversely, there is both expert and research evidence that ER-P is the key component of CBT for childhood OCD. E. Stewart et al. (2016) interviewed childhood anxiety and OCD experts and found that they all endorsed a large use of exposure in treatment. Furthermore, multiple studies have found that adding cognitive strategies to ER-P, have not improved outcomes compared to ER-P alone (e.g. Ale et al., 2015; Peris et al., 2015; Whiteside et al., 2020). Whilst more research in this area would be useful, what is currently known points strongly towards the role of a behavioural approach to CBT for OCD, with ER-P as the main component.

Mechanisms Underlying ER-P: Habituation and Inhibitory Learning: Nevertheless, Craske et al. (2008) have highlighted limitations to the widely accepted and long-standing idea that exposure therapies, including ER-P, works via habituation based on Emotional Processing Theory (EPT; Foa & Kozac, 1986). Habituation is in-essence, the 'getting used to it' effect that is, each time a CYP triggers an obsession and resists completing their compulsions, the distress they feel becomes gradually less and less. For example, a CYP with a fear of contamination touches a door handle without completing any compulsion multiple times and their distress becomes less each time. Craske and colleagues instead propose that inhibitory learning (IL) is key, whereby newly learned, non-threatening connections are encoded and recalled. For example, the same CYP with a fear of contamination completes the same exposure of touching a door handle without any compulsions and learns that they do not become ill from doing so. A thorough explanation of IL is outside the scope of this chapter and readers are encouraged to read Craske and colleagues work to increase their understanding of the theoretical basis. In practical terms, IL suggests that the effectiveness of exposure can be enhanced in several ways, including expectancy violation, combining multiple fear cues, increased variability of stimuli and context, affect labelling and reducing safety-seeking behaviours (see Craske et al., 2014 for details). For example, the CYP with a contamination fear touches multiple door handles and other 'contaminated surfaces' in a variety of places in the community (variability of stimuli and context), is asked by their therapist to label their emotions during the exposure (affect labelling) whilst not using their sleeve to 'protect' their hand (reduction of safety seeking behaviours).

Research on IL and CYP is in its very early stages (see Plaisted et al., 2021 for review) and most of the research in adults has focussed primarily on phobic disorders. Jacoby and Abramowitz (2016) reviewed IL theory and some of the related concepts and applied them specifically to conducting ER-P with sufferers of OCD and concluded that it can be applied to treating OCD. A small case series indicates that IL-based exposure is feasible and acceptable to CYP as well as being superior to exposure based on habituation alone (Kennedy & Hawks, 2021).

Given the current status of the evidence base and the strong evidence for ER-P for OCD based on habituation models, it is important that practitioners understand both habituation and inhibitory learning theories to maximise the effectiveness of ER-P. There is even some early evidence from the adult literature that ER-P set- up with both habituation and inhibitory learning theory in mind maximises the effectiveness (Elsner et al., 2022).

Recommended Manual for CBT for CYP with OCD

The remainder of this chapter therefore focusses on the use of CBT, with a large ER-P component for CYP with OCD. Turner et al. (2018a,b) have written a useful CBT manual for therapists (*OCD: Tools to Help Young People Fight Back!: A CBT Manual for Therapists*) with an accompanying workbook for CYP (*OCD – Tools to Help You Fight Back!: A CBT Workbook for Young People*), which focusses purely on behavioural techniques (i.e. ER-P). This manual has been found to be effective in the treatment of CYP with OCD, even in those who have previously not responded to CBT treatment (Krebs et al., 2015). They recommend a maximum of 14 sessions completed over 8 to 17 weeks, with family members involved throughout. Whilst the manual is very much written in line with habituation theory for simplicity and ease of use, practitioners should also keep inhibitory learning theory in mind in order to optimise the effectiveness of ER-P.

14.2.3 Formulation

Whilst it may still be helpful for practitioners to bear in mind the role of cognitions and dysfunctional beliefs in the maintenance of OCD, in line with the evidence discussed, it is recommended that the formulation shared with the CYP is a simpler, behavioural approach. Turner et al.'s (2018a,b) vicious cycle of OCD starts by identifying the trigger (e.g. touching a door handle). This then leads to obsession(s) (e.g. it's covered in germs and I will get ill), causing an emotion(s) (e.g. distress and anxiety), which in turn leads to a compulsion (e.g. using sleeve of top to cover hand in order to open the door, washing hands three times after touching the door handle). Following completion of the compulsion, a temporary sense of relief is felt, which is reinforcing, meaning that the cycle is more likely to be enacted when the CYP next encounters the trigger. The Turner et al. (2018a,b) model also includes the important role of family accommodation (e.g. parent ensuring all internal doors at home remain open and opening closed doors on behalf of their child), which is seen as a response to the CYP's emotion and contributes to the temporary feeling of relief.

14.2.4 Intervention Components

Early Sessions

Psychoeducation should be woven throughout the intervention but is particularly important during the early stages of therapy. Practitioners should cover what OCD is, provide a definition and examples of both obsessions and compulsions and normalise them. Covering general psychoeducation about anxiety (e.g. fight, flight, freeze) is also recommended. Discussing the potential causes of OCD can be useful to dispel any myths that the young person or family may have. Externalising the OCD as something separate to the CYP is also a key engagement tool (Turner et al., 2018a). Helping both the CYP and their parents/carers see the OCD as a separate entity to the CYP is a powerful part of the intervention. This initially may be achieved by asking the CYP to create a character for their OCD, giving it a name and drawing what it looks like. However, externalising using subtle changes throughout the intervention is equally as important. For example, rather than saying a young person 'obsessively washes their hands', reframing this as 'OCD tells you to wash your hands'. Part of externalising involves setting the stage for therapy as a 'battle against OCD', where the CYP, family and therapist are all working as part of the same team.

Creating a joint understanding of how the CYPs OCD is operating is also important. Practitioners are encouraged to use both a longitudinal formulation (e.g. 5Ps; Macneil et al., 2012) and a cross-sectional formulation. Using the simple cross-sectional formulation described previously (Turner et al., 2018a,b) is encouraged. This should be done collaboratively and utilising examples from the CYP's experiences.

Setting SMART (specific, measurable, achievable, rewarding and time sensitive) goals should also be covered in early sessions. However, practitioners should not become too concerned if the CYP struggles to think of goals as they will naturally emerge in the next part of the work.

ER-P

To engage in ER-P, CYP and their families first need to understand the rationale. Explaining habituation as the 'getting used to it' effect and illustrating this with everyday examples (e.g. living near to an airport and initially noticing when planes fly over, but over time, humans adjust and get used to the sound). The collaborative use of graphs to illustrate how habituation works with anxiety and compulsions is important. For older adolescents, it is also helpful to explain inhibitory learning in a child-friendly manner.

Once they understand the rationale, a hierarchy can be built. Whilst hierarchies for OCD are like hierarchies for anxiety (see Chapter 13, Emotional Difficulties), it is recommended that the generated list focusses on the compulsions that OCD urges the CYP (and other people around them) to do. Practitioners can use the information they gathered from the assessment to help generate the list. CYP should then be asked to rate how anxious they would feel if they had to resist each compulsion and then place them in order. The rating scale used should be adapted to fit the age and developmental level of the CYP. The practitioner may need to help the CYP break down some of the compulsions into smaller steps.

The next stage is to support the CYP to start completing ER-P tasks. Clinical experience suggests that completing ER-P tasks *within sessions* (as well as for between-session tasks outside of the therapy setting) is key for treatment outcomes. Remember that ideally, ER-P tasks should be set up to allow both habituation and inhibitory learning to occur. As such, they should be graded and long enough for habituation to occur, whilst ensuring that the CYP learns something that will be helpful in their battle against OCD. Therefore, prior to the ER-P starting, practitioners should ask the CYP to rate their level of anxiety using an anxiety rating scale (habituation model) and ask them their specific prediction of what will happen (inhibitory learning model). If necessary, the practitioner can model the ER-P task for the young person first.

When completing the ER-P task, therapists should be encouraging and provide praise, whilst being careful not to offer reassurance and/or distract them from the task. They should continue to check-in every few minutes regarding their current anxiety rating. Some CYP will need reminding not to do their rituals during the ER-P task and it can be helpful to ask direct questions about any covert compulsions they may be completing. The habituation model suggests that an ER-P task can end when the CYP's anxiety rating has reduced by at least half. The inhibitory learning model suggests that an ER-P task can end when the CYP has learned enough to progress onto the next step of the hierarchy. Once the task has been completed, there should be a thorough debrief about what the CYP learned during the ER-P task. Clinical experience suggests that sometimes, particularly during early ER-Ps, the CYP needs to learn that their anxiety can habituate (reduce), otherwise they are unlikely to agree to any of the more difficult ER-P tasks.

ER-P tasks should be repeated in sessions each week and for between-session tasks. Each ER-P task should be planned in sufficient detail and continue to consider both habituation and inhibitory learning models. Once the CYP has managed to complete a few ER-P tasks, the practitioner may be able to utilise the hierarchy more flexibly; that is, they may not need to complete every step in order. ER-P tasks that involve overlearning, where the task is pushed beyond the limits of what the CYP would usually experience, can also be introduced later during therapy. For example, if a young person has contamination concerns about food, they could be encouraged to place a piece of food on the floor and leave it there for a few minutes, before eating it. This is not necessarily something they would do in everyday life but is a useful and memorable way to take some of the power back from OCD.

The Role of Cognitive Strategies

In line with the evidence base already discussed, practitioners are actively discouraged from routinely covering general cognitive strategies with CYP with OCD (e.g. thought challenging). However, if practitioners become stuck during ER-P with a clear cognition getting in the way, introducing cognitive strategies can be discussed in supervision. Any cognitive strategies used must be tailored to the CYP's obsessions and developmental level. Some potential cognitive strategies are recognising and relabelling intrusive thoughts as OCD, developing more accurate appraisals of risk/feared consequences and introducing positive self-talk.

Parental Involvement

There are contradictory findings in the literature regarding the benefits of family involvement in CBT for CYP with OCD. For example, Barrett et al. (2004) found that family-based CBT was effective, possibly more so than individual sessions alone. Conversely, Reynolds et al. (2013) found that including a parent in sessions had no effect on treatment. Studies conducted to date are highly heterogenous in their methodologies, perhaps going someway to explain the differences in results. Given the strong evidence for the role of family accommodation in the maintenance OCD for CYP discussed previously in this chapter, it is logical to assume that addressing family accommodation in treatment could improve outcomes. Therefore, future research should be looking at how to maximise the involvement of parents and carers in the treatment of childhood OCD to effectively address accommodation. Some experts also argue that age should be factored into decisions regarding parental involvement in CBT for OCD. Demaria et al. (2021) suggest that primary-school-aged children should have family-based CBT whereas adolescents may respond better to individual CBT with parents attending separate sessions. Addressing family accommodation is a key part of the Turner et al. (2018a,b) manual and is therefore recommended. Please see Box 14.1 for a clinical example.

Box 14.1 Clinical example

Background Information and Referral

Lucas is a 15-year-old cis-gendered male, who identifies as queer. Lucas describes his ethnicity as white, European. Both of his parents are Italian, and they moved to the United Kingdom whilst his mother was pregnant with Lucas. He is an only child and was conceived via IVF. Their extended family remains in Italy and Lucas often spends his summer holidays there. He is bilingual, speaking both Italian and English fluently. The family have a strong Christian Catholic faith and attend church most weeks.

Lucas had been experiencing OCD symptoms for 2 years. After being on a waiting list for 18 months, he received 3 months of CBT from his local CAMHS team. His obsessions focussed on worries of harm coming to others and his compulsions included sending texts to family members to ensure they were okay, checking that doors were locked before bed and avoiding being near sharp objects. The intervention largely consisted of psychoeducation and cognitive interventions, such as relaxation strategies, thought records and thought challenging. The therapists set Lucas some exposure tasks for

(Continued)

Box 14.1 (Continued)

homework, such as not checking the door was locked before bedtime, but he struggled to complete these. Lucas started to become low in mood and was struggling to attend school due to a lack of motivation. He was referred to a specialist OCD clinic for further assessment and intervention.

Assessment

Following problem-free talk, a CY-BOCS was completed with Lucas. During the interview, with direct questioning, Lucas disclosed experiencing sexual thoughts about children. He had not discussed these with anyone before. Lucas also reported intrusive thoughts about causing harm to others that he had previously disclosed. Whilst these were distressing for him, he was very clear that the most distressing thoughts were the sexual thoughts about children. Lucas reported several compulsions related to his obsessions, including calling himself a bad person 10 times in his head, scrubbing his body to remove his sins and praying to God for forgiveness. He also actively avoided places where he was likely to see younger children. This included no longer attending football at the weekends as younger children were often playing nearby. He would also try not to attend church, which caused arguments with his parents. He also struggled to attend school as there was a children's playground opposite. Historically, he had experienced obsessions about contamination and related compulsions of handwashing, but he reported that these were now much less frequent. Lucas's CY-BOCS score was 34, indicating severe OCD.

Lucas also met criteria for a diagnosis of depression. He reported experiencing consistently low mood for the past few months. He was having difficulty getting to sleep and when he woke up he did not feel refreshed. He felt tired constantly and his parents had noticed a reduction in his appetite. Due to no longer attending football, Lucas had stopped seeing his friends outside school. At the assessment, he struggled to identify any activities that lifted his mood. He reported frequent thoughts of self-harm and suicide and attributed these to the obsessions he was experiencing. Lucas often self-harmed in a compulsive manner in response to an obsession (see secondary risk later). He denied any current plans or intention to end his life and cited his faith as preventing him from acting.

Primary risk: The sexual intrusions about children caused Lucas a significant amount of distress and he was making an immense effort to try to stop the thoughts from entering his head, as well as completing compulsions to 'neutralise' having them. He had never acted on these thoughts and was avoiding several situations in order to 'prevent' himself from doing so. As such, he was not considered to be a risk to children.

Secondary risk: Lucas self-harmed a few times a week, cutting using the blade from a razor, as a compulsion to punish himself for having intrusive sexual thoughts about children. When his thoughts were particularly graphic and distressing, he would use bleach to 'wash away his sins' in the shower. Hence there was deemed to be secondary risk, which would be targeted early in the intervention.

Routine outcome measures:
Lucas and his parents completed a set of OCD-specific self-report questionnaires prior to the assessment. Lucas's total symptoms score on the CHOCI-R-S was 22/40 and his total impact score was 40/48. His parents completed the parent version and had a lower symptom score (14/40) and a marginally lower impact score (37/48), reflecting that they were aware of the impact of his symptoms but were not aware of all of the symptoms prior to the assessment taking place. Lucas completed the Family Accommodation Scale and scored 28/76, indicating some levels of parental accommodation.

With the help of his therapist, Lucas set SMART goals, giving them ratings out of 10 (0 = nowhere near achieving the goal, 10 = goal achieved):

1) To be able to go to church on a Sunday and tolerate being near children (2/10).
2) To go back to football training and matches when there are children playing nearby (0/10).
3) To reduce self-harm to once a month (0/10)

Formulation
Presenting Problems: As described earlier, Lucas was experiencing OCD and depression, with the most distressing experiences being obsessions of a paedophilic nature and related compulsions.

Predisposing: Lucas's father also experienced OCD when he was an adolescent. He received medication for this at the time but was not provided with psychological therapy. Lucas's mother described Lucas as always having been a sensitive and thoughtful child, who often worried about other people. Lucas's mother had several health problems including diabetes, which Lucas worried about.

Precipitating: Lucas's initial OCD symptoms (relating to germs and handwashing) were triggered by the COVID-19 pandemic. His mother's diabetes meant she was more at risk of health complications if she contracted COVID-19 and so Lucas did everything he could to reduce the chances of her becoming unwell. Lucas first experienced a paedophilic thought whilst on a family holiday in Italy, approximately 18 months ago, when his younger cousin decided to take their clothes off at the beach. He was really distressed by this thought and tried hard to push it away, but he found himself unable to think about anything else for the rest of the holiday.

Perpetuating: In line with the behavioural theory of OCD, a vicious cycle of OCD was developed. A frequent trigger for Lucas's intrusions was seeing a child under the age of 10, for example, his 6-year-old cousin at a family gathering. This would lead to one or more obsessions, such as "You should touch their genitals" and an image of his cousin naked. This caused Lucas to be incredibly distressed and disgusted at himself. He then completed compulsions in attempt to decrease his distress and 'make up' for having the thoughts. In the moment, this would involve telling himself he was a bad person 10 times and getting as far away from his cousin as possible. When he got home, he would shower himself for at least 60 minutes in a ritualised manner to try

(Continued)

Box 14.1 (Continued)

to '"wash away his sins' and pray before going to bed to ask for forgiveness. These compulsions relieved his distress in the short term but in the long term reinforced the idea that experiencing the intrusive thoughts made him a bad person and he was a risk to children, for which he needed to complete compulsions. Lucas's parents were originally unaware of the content of Lucas's obsessions; however, he frequently asked them for reassurance that he was a good person, which they provided on a regular basis. His parents were concerned about what would happen if people found out about Lucas's intrusive sexual thoughts about children and so they also stopped attending family gatherings and no longer 'pressured' Lucas to go to school.

Lucas's depression was understood in the context of him becoming more isolated from his peers and a reduction in engaging in activities that were important to him, which usually helped to lift his mood. The depression was seen as secondary to that of OCD; i.e. if the OCD was treated, allowing Lucas to engage in more activities outside of his home, then his mood would likely improve. Nevertheless, it was recommended that his depression symptoms be monitored during treatment.

Protective Factors: Other than arguments about attending school and church, Lucas had a good relationship with his parents. He was still in touch with some of his friends and was motivated to engage in treatment. His Christian faith prevented him from acting on his suicidal thoughts.

Treatment

Psychoeducation was adapted to include information regarding the normality of unwanted sexual intrusive thoughts, thoughts about harming others and the role of thought suppression. The therapist contacted the chaplaincy service within their NHS trust and asked the priest to attend a session with Lucas and his parents. The priest also helped to normalise the thoughts that Lucas was having and discussed a Christian approach to OCD. This was helpful for both Lucas and his parents. Lucas and his therapist then devised a hierarchy to tackle previously avoided situations involving children, beginning with photographs of unknown children. The hierarchy also included a gradual reduction of compulsions as Lucas initially struggled to stop them all together. The final step on the hierarchy was to take his cousin swimming and help them learn to swim, which would involve helping them to float in the water, followed by not completing any compulsions. The therapist and Lucas completed ER-P, during his weekly sessions Lucas was set ER-Ps to complete as in-between session tasks. Initially these focussed on reducing self-harm and washing with bleach in order to reduce secondary risk. ER-P tasks were set up so that habitation could occur (i.e. they were long enough for distress to reduce) but also with inhibitory learning theory in mind (e.g. asking Lucas what he expected to happen during the exposure and debriefing afterwards about what actually happened, looking at multiple photographs of different children, Lucas being asked to label his emotions during exposure tasks). As a lot of Lucas's compulsions were 'delayed' until he got home, the therapist recruited his parents to help to remind and support Lucas not to do his compulsions after an ER-P task.

Outcomes

At the end of treatment, Lucas's CY-BOCS score had reduced to 20. His CHOCI-R-S symptom score remained similar at 20/40 but the impact score had reduced to 25/48. He still had symptoms remaining regarding harming others and at times he still struggled to not complete his delayed compulsions. Lucas achieved his goal of going to church on Sundays (10/10). He managed to attend football most weeks (8/10) and had reduced his self-harming to once a fortnight (5/10). The levels of parental accommodation had also reduced (10/76). Lucas and his family were encouraged to continue to make progress after the end of therapy by continuing to complete ER-Ps together and creating their own hierarchy about Lucas's thoughts of harming others.

14.2.5 OCD and ASC

There are high rates of comorbidity of ASC and OCD, with estimates ranging from 17 to 37% (Leyfer et al., 2006; van Steensel et al., 2011) and there is evidence to suggest that CYP with OCD and ASC have significantly distinct clinical symptoms and impairment, compared to CYP who have OCD or ASC only (Griffiths et al., 2017; Lewin et al., 2011; Zandt et al., 2009). Moreover, previous studies have suggested that CBT for co-occurring OCD and ASC are less effective (Griffiths et al., 2017; K. Murray et al., 2015). A recent study in South London by Martin et al. (2020) found that CYP with OCD and ASC were equally likely to receive CBT compared to those with OCD only, but were more likely to be prescribed medication. In addition, they were more likely to use services for longer than either OCD only or ASC only comparison groups. Nevertheless, CYP with OCD and ASC showed significant improvements in functioning after using services but less so than their neurotypical peers. Hence it is important to consider any adaptations specifically for this population.

Research Evidence

A wide range of CBT modifications have been described in the literature in the form of case studies. This includes increasing the number of treatment sessions, increasing the use of visual resources, providing psychoeducation for emotional recognition, incorporating special interests, creating CYP specific anxiety rating scales and increasing parent/carer involvement (e.g. Farrell et al., 2016; Jassi & Krebs, 2020; Krebs et al., 2016).

A treatment manual specifically adapting the Turner et al. (2018a,b) manual for use with CYP with both ASC and OCD was recently created. Similar to the original manual, it consists of a therapist manual titled *Challenging OCD in Young People with ASD. A CBT Manual for Therapists* (Jassi, 2020a) and an accompanying workbook for CYP *Challenge your OCD! A CBT workbook for young people with ASD* (Jassi, 2020b). Early research into the manual has shown very promising results (Jassi et al., 2021). At the end of treatment, 52% of CYP were classified as 'treatment responders' and this increased slightly to 53% at 3-month follow-up. Further research is needed to generalise the results outside the clinic in which the manual was created.

Suggested Adaptations for CBT: Jassi

Firstly, the number of suggested sessions increases from 14 to 20. Sessions may need to be longer or shorter depending on the needs of the CYP. Practitioners are advised to spend longer on psychoeducation (six sessions). Extra sessions could cover the differences and similarities between OCD and ASC and emotion recognition skills training. It is also recommended that a unique anxiety rating scale is developed prior to beginning ER-P. For ER-P itself, Jassi (2020a,b) suggests that tasks will need to be broken down into smaller steps and that visual, mini-hierarchies for each step of the main hierarchy can be helpful in achieving this. Several recommendations are made in order to increase the generalisability of exposure tasks. Firstly, similarities between ERP tasks conducted should be highlighted. Secondly, completing ER-Ps in the community is advised. Thirdly, the importance of training families to lead ER-P tasks to ensure increased practice between sessions and continuation post-treatment is highlighted.

14.2.6 What it's Like to Live with OCD: The Voice of CYP

A short film was co-created by OCD Action, South London and Maudsley NHS Trust and CYP to raise awareness of OCD and the impact if can have on CYP and their families (https://ocdaction.org.uk/resources/ocd-is-not-me/). Therapists can use this resource to aid their own understanding, as well as sharing it as a useful resource with CYP and their families.

Qualitative research on the lived experience of CYP with OCD is limited. Keyes et al. (2018) conducted semi-structured interviews with 10 CYP aged 14 to 17 years old with a diagnosis of OCD in UK CAMHS services. A number of themes were identified. Firstly, CYP stated that formulations should attend to previous difficult life events and that these should be addressed as part of therapy. Whilst this should be captured within a longitudinal formulation (e.g. 5Ps; Macneil et al., 2012), addressing it as part of treatment is arguably lacking in current protocols (e.g. Turner et al., 2018a). This highlights an important area for future research as it would be interesting to discover if addressing previous stressful life events, for example with imagery-based techniques, could further enhance treatment outcomes. Secondly, CYP reported difficulties in responding to their obsessions and compulsions, including struggling to understand their experiences. This reinforces the important role that psychoeducation and normalising OCD symptoms have as part of intervention, but also in society as a whole. All CYP spoke about their battle of living with OCD and the impact this had on their lives. Importantly, the final theme discussed an ambivalent relationship with help. In regard to ER-P specifically, most participants described a conflict between wanting to resist ER-P tasks but an acknowledgment that completing ER-P would probably be helpful in the long term. As such they wanted their therapist and their family to work together to guide them gradually through ER-P. Similarly, there was an acknowledgement from some of the CYP that they wanted their families to accommodate their OCD to reduce their distress in the short term, but that this would probably be unhelpful in the long term. Overall, this suggests that CYP ambivalence should not deter practitioners from implementing evidence-based interventions, that is, ER-P and addressing family accommodation. See Chapter 7, Inclusivity, Diversity and Power, for further discussion on this.

14.2.7 OCD Summary

Whilst a lot of the research on the epidemiology of OCD is outdated and largely based on western, non-diverse samples, OCD remains debilitating for CYP and can impact their lives in many areas. Gold-standard assessment using the CY-BOCS is recommended as is active consideration of primary and secondary risk. Little is known about the risk factors and causes of OCD, which is arguably less important than understanding the maintenance factors and associated treatment techniques. Whilst there is little debate that CBT with an ER-P component is the most effective psychological therapy for CYP, there are differing views on how much cognitive versus behavioural techniques should be included. The limited evidence available suggests that ER-P is the key mechanism of change and hence a largely behavioural approach, focussing on actively completing ER-Ps with CYP is recommended (e.g. manual by Turner et al. 2018a,b). Current evidence indicates that ER-P should be set up and designed with both habituation and inhibitory learning theories in mind, yet further research is needed to determine how ER-P can be fully optimised to improve treatment outcomes. In addition, teaching and training should focus on overcoming barriers to practitioners implementing ER-P. With some adaptations, standardised treatments can also be helpful for CYP with OCD and autism, although further research is needed to improve understanding of the disorder in this population.

14.3 Post-traumatic Stress Disorder

14.3.1 Epidemiology

By the age of 18, approximately 31% of children and young people (CYP) in the United Kingdom will have experienced a traumatic event and 7.8% will meet the diagnostic criteria for PTSD (S. J. Lewis et al., 2019). There is evidence that a proportion of CYP with PTSD will recover naturally, without any intervention, in the 3 months following the trauma (Hiscox et al., 2023). Importantly, a systematic review of the literature found that any PTSD symptoms that remain 6 months post-trauma are unlikely to reduce without therapeutic intervention (Hiller et al., 2016). There is a substantial unmet need for CYP with PTSD in the United Kingdom with only one in three seeing a GP about their symptoms. Furthermore, only one in five will meet with a psychologist, psychotherapist or counsellor and 1 in 10 will meet with a psychiatrist. This leaves approximately 60% without any support related to their PTSD symptoms (S. J. Lewis et al., 2019).

There are several factors that make it more likely a young person will experience PTSD following a trauma exposure, which have been examined in multiple meta-analyses (e.g. Alisic et al., 2014; Cox et al., 2008). The largest was conducted by Trickey et al. (2012), who found that CYP with low social support, high perceived threat to life during the trauma, emotional and physiological distress experienced during or immediately after a traumatic event, social withdrawal, distraction, thought suppression, comorbidity with another mental health difficulty and poor family functioning, led to the largest risk increases for persistent PTSD. Small to medium effects were found for female gender, lower IQ, lower socioeconomic status, life events before and post the trauma, pre-existing mental health difficulties, parental mental health after the trauma, bereavement and trauma severity.

Negligible or small effects were found for younger children and those from ethnic minorities. In addition, there is good evidence that CYP who have experienced multiple traumatic events are more likely to develop PTSD (e.g. Copeland et al., 2007). Similarly, multiple studies have also shown that the nature of the trauma itself is important, with those experiencing a direct interpersonal assault or threat significantly more likely to develop PTSD (Alisic et al., 2014).

14.3.2 Diagnostic Criteria

With both DSM-5 (APA, 2013) and ICD-11 (WHO, 2022) diagnostic manuals being used routinely in the United Kingdom, it is important to note that there are some similarities and differences in their diagnostic criteria. Firstly, the DSM-5 states that CYP must have experienced or witnessed a traumatic event that involved actual or threatened death, serious injury or sexual violence, where the ICD-11 states that the CYP must have experienced an event that was 'extremely horrific'. In recent years, practitioners are becoming more flexible with PTSD diagnoses where the event *does not* strictly meet these criteria, with increasing recognition that a CYP's perceptions of an event being traumatic is more important than sticking rigidly to diagnostic criteria. Both the DSM-5 and ICD-11 also list intrusions or re-experiencing of the event (e.g. nightmares, flashbacks, intrusive memories, repetitive play) avoidance of the event (e.g. talking about it, thinking about it, reminders of what happened) and hyperarousal or sense of current threat (e.g. easily startled, increased irritability, sleep and concentration difficulties) as diagnostic criteria. Symptoms must be present for more than 1 month post trauma, given that the above are also common human reactions to many difficult experiences. The DSM-5 arguably takes a much broader stance to diagnosis and lists more symptoms from each of the diagnostic criteria identified and includes the additional symptom(s) of changes in thoughts and feelings (e.g. distorted thoughts about the causes and/or consequences of the trauma, exaggerated negative believes about themselves, others or the world).

PTSD in younger children often presents differently. As such, there are revised diagnostic criteria for children aged 6 and under (DSM-5, 2013). The criteria for the traumatic event remains the same, however there is an emphasis on assessing for events that have been witnessed. For intrusions and/or re-experiencing symptoms, there is less emphasis on the distress they cause and more focus on their presence. The number of symptoms within the 'avoidance' criteria is reduced to one.

Dissociative Sub-type (DSM-5)

The dissociative sub-type of PTSD is included in the DSM-5. Dissociation is characterised by disruptions in memory, sense of self and perception of the world around us (Briere et al., 2005). The DSM operationalises this with depersonalisation (persistent or recurrent experiences of feeling detached from, and as if one were an outside observer of one's mental processes or body) and and/or derealisation (persistent or recurrent experiences of unreality of surroundings). Dissociation is now understood to be a coping mechanism that can help CYP manage traumatic experiences whilst they are happening, yet for some CYP this experience continues intermittently yet repeatedly once the event is over. There is some evidence that dissociation in CYP is different to that in adults, with adolescents more likely to experience daydreaming, forgetting things and blocking out thoughts. Practitioners should look out for language such as 'feeling foggy' and 'zoning out', which adolescents can use to describe their experience. There is also some evidence that adolescents with the dissociative sub-type of PTSD have experienced more traumatic events and have more severe PTSD symptoms (Choi et al., 2019). Symptoms of dissociation can be frightening to both the CYP and those around them, hence in the past it has been a barrier to them receiving evidence-based interventions. Importantly, there is no evidence that derealisation or depersonalisation moderates outcomes of evidence-based treatments in adults (Hoeboer et al., 2020). Whilst there is little research examining this in CYP, clinical experience suggests that dissociation should not deter practitioners from attempting a psychological intervention.

Complex PTSD

In ICD-11, the WHO introduced a new diagnostic category: Complex PTSD (CPTSD). It is a misconception that those who meet criteria for CPTSD have always experienced multiple traumatic events, perhaps due to the historical and clinical use of the term 'complex trauma', which has long been used to describe those who have experienced prolonged or multiple event traumas. CPTSD can be diagnosed when a single traumatic event has occurred. Similarly, having experienced multiple or prolonged traumatic events, does not mean that the CYP will meet criteria for a diagnosis of CPTSD. Instead, all the following criteria must be met, in addition to the diagnostic criteria for PTSD:

- Severe and pervasive problems in affect regulation (e.g. reckless or self-destructive behaviour, dissociative symptoms, heightened emotional reactivity to small stressors).
- Persistent beliefs about oneself as diminished, defeated or worthless and persistent feeling of shame, guilt or failure in relation to the traumatic event.
- Persistent difficulties in sustaining relationships and feeling close to others (e.g. avoidance of relationships or occasional intense relationships that are not sustained).

As a relatively new diagnosis, CPTSD related research is in its infancy, particularly for CYP. Studies have shown evidence of CPTSD in CYP, as distinct from PTSD, in both community and clinical samples (Haselgruber et al., 2020; Perkonigg et al., 2015; Sachser et al., 2017). Early studies looking at the prevalence of CPTSD suggests that more CYP meet the criteria for CPTSD than for PTSD (e.g. Jensen et al., 2022; Redican et al., 2022).

Clinically, it is important to note that CPTSD and *complexity when treating* PTSD are distinct from each other. A young person who has a diagnosis of PTSD can have symptoms that are complicated or difficult to treat for a multitude of reasons and similarly, those who meet criteria for a diagnosis of CPTSD can be treated by following standardised protocols with minimal adaptation. There is also a common misconception that CPTSD and symptoms of emotionally unstable personality disorder (EUPD) are the same, yet research shows these difficulties as common comorbidities, but distinct (e.g. Ford & Courtois, 2021). Key differences refer to the *pervasiveness* of the symptoms. For example, those with CPTSD have *persistent* negative beliefs about themselves whereas adolescents with emotionally unstable personality disorder traits beliefs about themselves can change drastically from negative to positive in a short space of time.

14.3.3 Cross-cultural Applications

It is important to acknowledge that westernised diagnostic classifications are flawed in multiple ways when considering their applicability across cultures. Patel and Hall (2021) suggest that there are four arguments that reactions to trauma differ across cultures:

- Reactions of PTSD vary across cultures.
- Culturally relevant reactions (i.e. idioms of distress) that are excluded from western diagnostic manuals may be core symptom of PTSD in other cultures.
- Explanations of trauma related distress vary by culture.
- Cultural groups experiencing ongoing adversity may not fit.

In addition, the DSM and ICD do not consider the implications of repeated race-based injustices, systemic racism and white supremacy. This is despite the knowledge that racial trauma and discrimination negatively impacts the mental health of CYP and that adolescents from minoritised ethnic backgrounds often experience higher levels of trauma-related mental health difficulties (e.g. Andrews et al., 2015).

14.3.4 PTSD Assessment

Screening

Actively screening for PTSD is essential. Firstly, CYP will not always spontaneously report traumatic experiences (Bailey et al., 2023). Secondly, the negative impact of experiencing childhood trauma is well documented (e.g. Danese et al., 2009), so early identification and intervention is likely to have many benefits. Despite routine screening being recommended by NICE (2018), mental health practitioners, health authorities and leaders within mental health systems sometimes express concern about harming CYP by asking directly about exposure to trauma (Becker-Blease & Freyd, 2007; Hultmann et al., 2014). Given that distress at reminders of the trauma is one of the key PTSD symptoms it is expected that some level of distress may be elicited by asking CYP about traumatic life events. However, a large study by Skar et al. (2019) found that 68.4% of CYP in a clinical setting reported no or low levels of upset after routine trauma screening, with 27.2% reporting moderate levels of upset and 4.5% reporting high levels.

Routine outcome measures, described later, can be useful in identifying any CYP where a more thorough PTSD assessment would be beneficial. It is important to remember that avoidance is a key symptom of PTSD and therefore it may be possible that even with direct questioning, a CYP will not be forthcoming about their traumatic experiences when first meeting with a professional. Hence involving parents and carers in the assessment, when possible, can be helpful, as they are more likely to be able to disclose any traumatic experiences the CYP has experienced. Practitioners should however remain gentle and cautious when discussing potential traumatic events, as it is not unusual for parents or carers to have experienced the same trauma as the CYP. Nevertheless, it is still important to ask given Skar et al.'s (2019) findings.

Assessment Set Up

For a population that is likely to struggle to trust individuals given their traumatic experiences, several simple steps early on can help the therapeutic relationship. Firstly, being clear about what the assessment will involve (who, what, when, where, why, what happens after?). Similarly, giving the young person as much choice as possible in these factors can be helpful. For example, a choice about the gender of the practitioner if this is feasible for your service. Being aware of their service experiences so far is also valuable; lots of young people will have had multiple assessments by multiple practitioners and repeating their story can be both frustrating and draining. Therefore, collecting as much information from other sources as possible beforehand is recommended.

Assessment Content

A PTSD assessment should contain an exploration of the following topics:

- CYP strengths/interests; the nature of the young person's PTSD symptoms (referring to the diagnostic criteria) including the onset, development and frequency of symptoms.
- A *very* brief account of the trauma (if possible).
- Comorbidity.
- Impact of symptoms.
- How the young person copes with the symptoms.
- Systemic support.
- Risk.
- Protective factors, and
- A brief exploration of what the CYP would like to be different.

At the start of the assessment (or after having screened for PTSD and an indication that further questioning around PTSD would be helpful), the practitioner should quickly inform the CYP that they are not going to ask them to talk about their trauma in a lot of detail. This is a really important point to cover early in the assessment as lots of CYP are understandably anxious about having to talk about their trauma with a stranger. Instead, the practitioner should aim to get a brief description of the event, but only if this is possible. How much the CYP can tell the practitioner about what happened is useful information for your assessment as avoidance of talking about the trauma is a key symptom. If they are not able to tell anything about the trauma, the practitioner can explain that they understand the young person has been through some very difficult things and they are going to ask them some questions about how those things impact on their life currently. If they are able to give some description of what happened, they will likely be watching the practitioner's reactions very closely and so it is important to respond with validation and empathy, whilst not appearing to be too upset; the CYP needs to know that the practitioner can cope with what they are being told. The practitioner should also ask directly about any experiences of discrimination, prejudice, hate crimes and victimisation, which are typically not spontaneously reported by CYP.

Practitioners should remember that CYP who are exposed to traumas generally have high rates of mental health difficulties, including depression (29.2%), conduct disorder (22.9%) and alcohol dependence (15.9%). Comorbidity is also very common (S. J. Lewis et al., 2019). Hence a broad and thorough assessment of the young person's mental health difficulties is imperative.

As with all CYP experiencing mental health difficulties, risk assessment is paramount for those suffering from PTSD. Those who meet diagnosis for PTSD report higher rates of risk to themselves, including self-harm (48.8%) and suicide attempts (20.1%). They are also more likely to have engaged in a violent offence themselves (11.9%) and therefore an assessment of risk to others should also be completed (S. J. Lewis et al., 2019). CYP with PTSD also remain vulnerable to re-victimisation and hence it is imperative to consider any ongoing risks from other people.

It is important to normalise and empathise with young people throughout the assessment process. Some helpful phrases may be 'I'm sorry to hear that happened to you', 'Lots of young people have told me that they experience similar difficulties'. It is also important to instil hope, by letting them know that there are very good treatment options for CYP who have experienced a trauma.

PTSD Outcome Measures

The Children's Revised Impact of Events Scale (CRIES-8; Perrin et al., 2005) is a brief, helpful self-report screening questionnaire for PTSD. Given that CYP are not always forthcoming with traumatic experiences, it is strongly encouraged that the CRIES-8 is completed with all CYP that practitioners work with as standard procedure. The CRIES-8 has been translated into multiple languages, which can be accessed free of charge from the Children and War Foundation (childrenandwar.org) A cut-off above 17 on the CRIES-8 indicates that a more thorough PTSD assessment is warranted. The measure has been validated for use with CYP from ages 8 to 18.

The Child PTSD Symptom Scale (CPSS-V, Foa et al., 2018) is a more in-depth outcome measure that can reliably track change in PTSD symptoms for 8 to 18 year olds. Overall scores are out of 80, with a clinical cut-off of 31. Unfortunately, the CPSS-V has not been translated into many languages and therefore will require the use of an interpreter for CYP whose first language is not English. Similarly, to the CRIES-8, it has been validated for use with CYP aged 8 to 18.

The International Trauma Questionnaire – Child and Adolescent Version (ITQ-CA; Cloitre et al., 2018) is a self-report measure incorporating the core features of PTSD and CPTSD. It has two separate scales for PTSD and CPTSD. It is brief, consisting of 12 questions, with scores ranging from 0 to 48. It is a relatively new measure and has thus far been validated for use with children in foster care (Haselgruber et al., 2020). The ITQ-CA also has a version for parents to complete.

For younger children, the Young Child PTSD Checklist (YCPC; Sheeringa, 2019) is a screening questionnaire that assesses caregiver reported symptoms. It has been validated for CYP aged 1 to 6.

The Parent Trauma Response Questionnaire (PTQR; Williamson et al., 2018) is a measure of how parents have responded to the CYPs trauma and can be a useful tool to begin assessment of parental maintaining factors. The Children's Post Traumatic Cognitions Inventory (CPTCI; Meiser-Stedman et al., 2009) examines a CYP's misappraisals of the trauma, which can be helpful during treatment, as well as being used as an outcome measure.

As previously discussed, a broad and thorough assessment is recommended for any CYP who has been exposed to a trauma and/or has PTSD symptoms. We would therefore encourage the use of other routine outcome measures discussed in previous chapters to assess other emotional difficulties (e.g. RCADS, Chorpita et al., 2000).

14.3.5 PTSD Formulation

The Clark and Ehlers model for PTSD (Ehlers & Clark, 2000) was originally developed for adults and has been successfully applied to the treatment of children and young people. The model proposes that the nature of traumatic memories, negative appraisals of the traumatic event and unhelpful coping strategies maintain PTSD by contributing to an ongoing sense of threat.

Nature of Trauma Memory

Memories of traumatic events are different to memories of 'normal', everyday events (e.g. Brewein et al., 1996; R. McGuire et al., 2021). Memories of everyday events have the following characteristics: stored as words and stories, fluid and updatable, linked to other memories, contextualised in the history of what else was happening at the time, are organised into a coherent narrative and are largely under conscious control. Hence, they feel like they are memories from the past. Memories of traumatic events are very different; perceptual information is contained within little, if any, conceptual framework. Trauma memories are full of vivid sensory information, are static and frozen, isolated from other memories without a historical context, are disorganised, incoherent and fragmented. This leads to them being uncontrollable, easily triggered and feeling like they are happening in the present, rather than in the past.

Negative Appraisals of the Trauma and/or Consequences of the Trauma

The model suggests that CYP will have negative thoughts about themselves (e.g. I am going to die, I am worthless, what happened is my fault) and about others (e.g. everyone blames me for what happened) and the world (e.g. bad things will always happen), as well as misappraisals of PTSD symptoms (e.g. I am going mad, I am damaged) and the consequences of thinking about what happened (e.g. if I talk about it I won't be able to cope). There is evidence to suggest that misappraisals about the traumatic event are the main predictor of a CYP developing PTSD after a traumatic event (Meisier-Stedman et al., 2019).

Unhelpful Coping

The combination of how trauma memories are stored and misappraisals leads to an active sense of current threat, leading to intrusions of the trauma, arousal symptoms and strong emotions. This in turn leads to unhelpful strategies intended to control either the level of threat or the symptoms, which often maintain the CYP's difficulties. This includes thought suppression, rumination, distraction and safety seeking behaviours (Alberici et al., 2018; Meiser-Stedman et al., 2005; Stallard & Smith, 2007). Wider systemic factors should also be considered when thinking about unhelpful coping, although they are arguably not well understood. There is some evidence that parental accommodation, parental emotional over-involvement and the CYP's perception of their parents' expressed emotion are linked to maintaining PTSD (Goddard et al., 2019). It is likely that CYP and their caregivers become locked into cycles of avoidance, each maintaining the other's maladaptive coping strategies, particularly if it is a shared trauma or if the caregiver is suffering from PTSD from having heard about the trauma their child has experienced. However, more research is needed in this area.

Whilst it is essential for practitioners to understand and be able to replicate the Clark and Ehlers model for each CYP with PTSD that they work with, given the complexity of the diagram, it is not recommended that this is shared in this format with CYP. Instead, practitioners can engage the CYP with a thought-suppression exercise to demonstrate that trying not to think about something leads to the thought 'bouncing back' more. For example, asking the CYP to try really hard not to think of a big, pink, fluffy rabbit sat on the practitioner's head.

There are several helpful metaphors that can be used to reinforce the formulation and explain the rationale for the intervention. With CYP, explaining these collaboratively, in a back-and-forth conversation, with some added humour, is often most effective. The most common metaphor used is the wardrobe that was first introduced by Ehlers and Clark (2000), a variation is given here:

> Our memory store is like a well-organised wardrobe; each memory or item of clothing is neatly folded in its own place. So, when you want to find something or think about a certain memory (for example, where were you on New Year's Eve?), you can take it out and think about it. When you're finished, you can slot it back into its usual place and close the wardrobe doors. This is how our memories for every day, non-difficult events work. A trauma memory is like someone throwing a big duvet covered in stinging nettles at you. Most people, understandably, try to get rid of the duvet as quickly as they possibly can, because it is painful to hold. So, they throw the big, stinging-nettle- covered duvet into the wardrobe as quickly as they possibly can. Unfortunately, this means that the wardrobe door won't close properly, and the duvet keeps bursting out when we don't want it to. What we need to do in trauma therapy, is take that stinging-nettle-covered duvet, gently and slowly unravel it, before folding it up and placing it in the wardrobe with the other memories. Sometimes, we might need someone else to help us do this because the stinging nettles are so painful.

Additional CYP-friendly metaphors written by David Trickey, can be found on his website (http://davidtrickey.com/resources). Practitioners can also choose to explain the formulation in a more biological and factual manner, referring to the overactivation of the amygdala and the role of the hippocampus, if developmentally appropriate. For example, the practitioner could ask the young person what they did on New Year's Eve. The practitioner can then explain that when they were asked about that memory, their hippocampus was activated. The hippocampus is like a filing cabinet where our 'normal' memories are stored, which have a number of different characteristics (e.g. those described in 'nature of trauma memories'). When we experience a traumatic event, something 'blocks' the processing and storage of these trauma memories in our filing system with the rest of our memories. Our trauma memories can therefore feel very different to our normal memories, for example, they pop into our head when we do not want them to. These trauma memories are linked very closely with our amygdala, which is another part of our brain that acts like an alarm system. It can be helpful to draw this out visually for the CYP.

14.3.6 Intervention – Evidence Base

For CYP with comorbidity, it is recommended to treat PTSD first when possible. PTSD trials have been representative of CYP with comorbid diagnoses and shown that often comorbidity symptoms reduce as well as PTSD symptoms. PTSD treatment is also very effective for CYP (e.g. Gutermann et al., 2016).

Protocols based on cognitive and behaviour principles currently have the largest evidence base for CYP with PTSD. Hence Trauma-focussed CBTs (TF-CBTs) are recommended in the UK's NICE Guidelines (2018) as the first-line intervention. It is worth noting that several different TF-CBTs exist and have strong evidence bases. Eye movement desensitisation and reprocessing (EMDR) is currently recommended as a second-line treatment for those CYP who do not respond or engage with CBT after 3 months (NICE, 2018). These treatments are described in Sections 14.3.7 and 14.3.8.

It is important to note that the guidelines for adults with PTSD are different; there is evidence that TF-CBTs and EMDR are equivalent in outcome (e.g. Hoppen et al., 2023; C. Lewis et al., 2020) and therefore if available, adults should be offered the choice of TF-CBT or EMDR). For CYP it is not the case that there is research showing that EMDR is less effective that TF-CBTs it is just that there is not *as much* evidence demonstrating its effectiveness. This, combined with the 18 years old cut-off between CAMHS and adult services being arbitrary and increasingly challenged and the NICE guidelines already being half-a-decade old, should all be borne in mind when offering psychological therapy to CYP with PTSD.

It is possible (perhaps likely) that TF-CBT will be more helpful for some CYP with PTSD and EMDR will be more helpful for others. However, research is currently not at a stage to help us predict this. Clinical experience suggests that if a young person can at least start verbalising the narrative of their trauma, TF-CBT should be tried in the first instance. There can be something quite powerful about a CYP being able to share the narrative of their story and this can also be helpful if any safeguarding issues arise during the work that need to be acted upon by the practitioner. If the CYP is not able to talk about their trauma, EMDR may be more appropriate. It may be that EMDR allows CYP with PTSD to access treatment when previously they would have not been able to due to the severity of their avoidance symptoms.

Importantly, there is no evidence for the effectiveness of psychopharmacology and hence medication should not be prescribed for PTSD symptoms. If a CYP has a comorbidity, for example depression, then it may still be appropriate for them to receive medication for this, which should be prescribed by a psychiatrist (NICE, 2018).

14.3.7 Intervention: Trauma-focussed Cognitive Behaviour Therapies

Cognitive behavioural interventions that focus on trauma symptoms are often described as trauma-focussed CBT (TF-CBT). However, this can be confusing given that there are multiple cognitive behavioural interventions for PTSD, which have similarities and differences.

Cognitive therapy for PTSD (CT-PTSD): initially created by Ehlers and Clark (2000) for adults, before being adapted by Smith et al. (2010) for implementation with CYP.

Trauma -focussed CBT (TF-CBT): developed by Cohen et al. (2012) specifically for CYP who had experienced domestic violence and/or sexual abuse, is also based on cognitive-behavioural therapy techniques but has several differences to the CT-PTSD model.

Prolonged exposure (PE): developed by Foa and Rothbaum (1998), which focuses on reducing avoidance by exposure to the traumatic memory.

Narrative exposure therapy (KIDNET): developed by Schauer et al. (2011) for adult asylum seekers and refugees with PTSD, NET for Children and Adolescents (KIDNET; Schauer et al., 2017) can be implemented with those who have faced multiple or complex traumas.

Regardless of which CBT for PTSD protocol is implemented, there is a wealth of evidence for their efficacy. For example, a large meta-analysis of 135 RCTs found that TF-CBT, PE and CT-PTSD were all significantly more effective for PTSD than other psychotherapies (Gutermann et al., 2016). Individual therapy had a larger effect size than group formats, particularly when parents or carers were included. A more recent meta-analyses found that when compared to those on the waiting list, CT-PTSD had the largest effect size, over and above other forms of cognitive behaviour therapies for PTSD (including PE and TF-CBT) and EMDR (Mavranezouli et al., 2020). A recent systematic review found that in research, there are inconsistencies in how TF-CBTs for PTSD are culturally adapted (Ennis et al., 2020). Generally, studies show positive outcomes in reducing PTSD symptoms, however there are many methodological flaws and this is an area that requires further research.

To avoid confusion moving forward, the remainder of this chapter will focus on the CT-PTSD model originally developed by Clark and Ehlers (2000), initially adapted for CYP by Smith et al. (2010) that is currently being adapted and used by National and Specialist CAMHS Trauma, Anxiety and Depression Clinic (N&S TAD) based at the Maudsley hospital within South London and Maudsley NHS Foundation Trust. This model has been chosen because it was designed and developed in the United Kingdom and is therefore frequently taught on psychological therapy courses across the United Kingdom. In addition, the model focusses on modifying the misappraisals of traumatic events, for which there is increasing evidence of its importance (e.g. Meiser-Stedman et al., 2019). There are also freely accessible training videos of some of the aspects of CT-PTSD, which can be found on the UK Trauma Council website (https://uktraumacouncil.org/resources/trauma-and-ptsd-working-with-children-and-young-people). Readers are also encouraged to familiarise themselves with the Cohen TF-CBT model (Cohen et al., 2012), which shares some similarities but also has some key differences.

CT-PTSD focusses on cognitive work interwoven with memory work. The intervention targets the maintaining factors highlighted in the formulation:

1. Reduce disorganisation of trauma memory.
2. Modify misappraisals of the trauma and symptoms.
3. Reduce dysfunctional coping strategies.
4. Modify maladaptive beliefs and behaviours of carers.

The Smith et al. (2010) manual was written for a single-incident trauma and recommends 12 to 14 sessions. For those with multiple traumatic events, CPTSD and/or complicated-to-treat PTSD, the N&S TAD Clinic recommends a minimum of 25 sessions. There is no fixed session-by-session structure and the protocol should be adapted to the needs of each CYP. Core components of the intervention remain relevant for both single-incident and multiple-event traumas, with some additional adaptations for multiple trauma that will be discussed.

CT-PTSD: Early Sessions

The focus of early sessions is building a strong and trusting therapeutic relationship, whilst actively preparing CYP for the memory and cognitive parts of the work. CT-PTSD achieves this with psychoeducation, symptom management and reclaiming life. Stabilisation, which is a term often associated with CBTs for PTSD, was not a part of the original CT-PTSD manual(s) and there is an ongoing debate in the literature regarding the usefulness of this term and an extended early treatment phase. Those in favour argue that a stabilisation phase, which can include a wide range of skills such as distress tolerance and emotional regulation skills, is necessary for CYP to complete memory work safely. However, there is not currently enough research with CYP to make a conclusion about whether stabilisation work is needed or helpful and there is evidence from the adult literature that stabilisation does not improve outcomes (e.g. Oprel et al., 2021). Therefore, whilst the number of sessions spent in this 'early' phase will vary for each CYP, therapists should be aware that spending too long on these topics can be detrimental to treatment outcomes. It is helpful to remember that avoidance is one of the key symptoms of PTSD and hence the CYP may want to delay the memory part of the work. Practitioners with less CT-PTSD experience are also more likely to avoid memory work themselves (Finch et al., 2020).

Psychoeducation: As with all other types of CBT intervention, psychoeducation is an important part of early treatment sessions. Practitioners are encouraged to utilise a variety of psychoeducational resources, including videos. These can be tailored to the age and interests of the CYP. For example, a brief clip from the Marvel movie *Iron Man 2*, can be used to show that even superheroes can suffer from PTSD after a difficult event. As well as psychoeducation about symptoms, CYP should learn about the rationale for treatment, the structure of therapy sessions and also receive information specific to the type of trauma that they experienced: for example, what is domestic violence?

Symptom Management: As a minimum, grounding techniques should be taught and practiced with the CYP to help them to manage their current PTSD symptoms. Practitioners should help the CYP consider different grounding options using each of their five senses and how these may need to be different depending on their environment (e.g. home vs school). Imagery techniques can also be useful to help manage unwanted intrusions and difficult re-experiencing symptoms. For example, watching the images come and go, practicing pausing, playing and manipulating the image in other ways. It may also be helpful to include some sleep hygiene in this session. This is also often when 'calm-place' imagery is first introduced and practiced, which can be utilised as a grounding technique during memory-focussed parts of the intervention.

Reclaiming Life: When experiencing PTSD, CYP often stop doing many of the things that they used to enjoy. This could be because those things remind them of the trauma or because they are feeling low in mood and lack the energy and/or motivation to do them. Reclaiming life is an important early treatment component, where therapists and CYP work together to try to restart as many pre-trauma activities as they can. Therapists may need to use elements of Behavioural Activation (e.g. exploring the CYP's values and using these to increase their activity levels) to help with this, depending on the level of avoidance and the severity of the CYP's low mood. This can be particularly helpful when working cross-culturally. Practitioners should note that pre-trauma activities that are triggers or reminders of the traumatic experience, will be addressed later in trigger work, rather than as part of reclaiming life. Where the trauma experienced has been discrimination or a hate-crime, practitioners are encouraged to think about a safety plan for what the CYP could do in the event of further discrimination (e.g. racism, sexism, ableism). Whilst reclaiming life is often the focus in early sessions, it should continue to be reviewed and monitored throughout the intervention.

CT-PTSD: Memory-focussed Work

There are three stages of memory-focussed work in CT-PTSD:

1. Reliving.
2. Restructuring.
3. Reliving + restructuring = reprocessing.

Step 1: *reliving*, sometimes referred to as imaginal exposure, is a key part of CT-PTSD. It helps to reduce the fragmentation of memory, allows the identification of the worst moments, often referred to as 'hotspots' and identification of meaning misappraisals that require updating, directly counters avoidance and tests out predictions. It is hoped that through habituation, the 'getting used to it' effect, reliving also reduces the frequency and intensity of intrusions.

During reliving, CYP are encouraged to revisit the trauma in their imagination. CYP are usually asked to do this in the present tense, with their eyes closed and in as much detail as possible. It may not always be appropriate to complete reliving in this manner. For example, for younger children or CYP who are prone to dissociation, an alternative method can be used such as drawing, writing or talking with their eyes open. Culturally relevant modes of reliving can also be considered (e.g. song, poem, rap). Regardless of the method, CYP should be encouraged to use their five senses as well as trying to access their thoughts and feelings at the time of the traumatic event.

The post-reliving debrief is equally important. Once they have ensured the CYP is grounded in the here and now, practitioners should prompt the CYP to explain their experience of what just happened. It can be useful to ask for SUDs (subjective units of distress) ratings here, as well as ratings of 'nowness' on a similar 0 to 10 scale. The practitioner should ask about the worst moments of the memory, as well as whether there was anything that surprised them about what came up. It is not unusual for CYP to remember things that they could not previously. When discussing the worst moment, practitioners should be aware of not making their own assumptions and being curious about what was so bad about that moment for the CYP.

Step 2: *restructuring*, the next stage is to modify the appraisals of the hotspots that have been identified during the reliving. Therapists will probably need to use multiple cognitive therapy strategies to do this. It is suggested that you start with an 'updates table' where CYP are gently and socratically (i.e. asked questions to help them re-evaluate a previously held idea) asked what they know now that they could not have possibly known then. For example, if during a mugging the CYP had the thought of 'I'm going to die and never see my family again' a useful update for them to reach through socratic questioning would be 'I did not die and I saw my family again at the hospital and most days since the attack'. Some updates will require more cognitive work than others and therapists are encouraged to employ other cognitive strategies they are familiar with. For example, responsibility pie charts, challenging hindsight bias, conducting surveys and other behavioural experiments. Guilt and shame are often powerful emotions that need to be specifically targeted as part of this work.

Step 3: reliving + restructuring = reprocessing, is the third step. The practitioner helps the CYP to insert the newly acquired knowledge from Step 2 (restructuring) into the original memory described in Step 1 (reliving). In the case of the example here, the CYP would be asked to close their eyes and complete imaginary reliving of the event again, and with the help of the therapist, insert the new information (i.e. I did not die and I saw my family again) at the hotspot where the original cognition emerged. Some CYP may prefer to update each individual hotspot one-by-one in shorter reliving exercises, or to update all hotspots at the same time.

CT-PTSD: Additional Treatment Components

Rescripting: Updating the memory in the way described earlier is sometimes enough to enable meaningful symptom change. For other CYP, rescripting the memory can be used to target any remaining misappraisals that were difficult to shift with updates alone. Whereas reprocessing involves inserting newly learned information into the original memory, rescripting aims to change or alter the image of the memory in some way. In the example above, the misappraisal of 'I am weak' could be targeted by rescripting the memory to the CYP fighting back against their attacker(s). There is no right or wrong way to rescript an image. Rescripting should be designed collaboratively with the CYP and they should be encouraged to use their imagination and creativity.

Working with Triggers: It is recommended that triggers work is commenced after reprocessing has been completed. It can be helpful to start by keeping a trigger or intrusion diary between sessions. The practitioner should then explain to a CYP what a trigger is, why memories get triggered, to identify a trigger and to practice exposure to a trigger whilst using the stimulus discrimination technique (sometimes referred to the 'now vs then' technique). As part of the trigger work, a visit to the site of the original trauma is recommended where this is possible.

Targeting Rumination: When thinking about the traumatic event, it is common for CYP to think repeatedly about why questions. These questions are often unanswerable and maintain symptoms. Practitioners should try to address rumination using rumination-blocking techniques (e.g. switching to a valued activity instead, changing 'why' to 'how' thinking).

Behavioural Experiments: These can be used to address any remaining PTSD symptoms including hypervigilance. For example, a CYP who still walks into a room scanning for the perpetrator of an assault could practice walking into places without scanning to find out the impact of this on their levels of anxiety.

CT-PTSD: Adaptations for Multiple Events

The main adaptation when working with CYP who have experienced multiple traumatic events is to create and use a timeline. This involves talking through the CYP's life experiences so far and plotting them in chronological order. As well as being a good engagement tool, the process can help to start the process of organising the memories and providing contextual information to how they are stored. Talking through some of their traumatic experiences can help with processing them and highlight where more detailed reliving work (described earlier) is needed. There is no set time for how long a timeline will take; for some CYP it will be complete in a session, whereas others will need multiple sessions. This exercise can be very difficult for young people. In addition to empathising and validating the CYP's experiences, it can be helpful to also talk about and include some happier memories on their timeline (where possible). There is no right or wrong way to complete a timeline; practitioners are encouraged to work collaboratively with the young person and be creative.

CT-PTSD Cultural Adaptations

Within the adult literature, there have been some attempts to implement cultural adaptions to TF-CBTs for PTSD. A systematic review found that nine studies had made substantial changes to the interventions, including making adaptations to the conceptualisation of the effects of trauma (e.g. added spiritual approach) and adding techniques in line with the culture of the client (e.g. relaxation strategies). Eight studies described surface-level adaptations including translating materials into the client's first language and changing analogies (Ennis et al., 2020).

There is a lack of research looking at CT-PTSD across cultures for CYP. In clinical practice, therapists are encouraged to practice cultural humility and be curious about the CYP's culture, including how trauma and mental health are perceived. If relevant, some of the above adaptations could be included, as well as those described throughout the chapter.

CT-PTSD: Involving Parents and/or Carers

If the CYP consents, parents and carers should be involved as much as possible in all components of the intervention. Practitioners should pay particular attention to parent's/carer's attitudes to treatment and any avoidance taking place within the family. Parents and carers can be particularly helpful when updating with new information, as they are sometimes able to fill gaps in the CYP's narrative and/or provide useful information to counteract the CYP's misappraisals. It may be necessary to update the parents' own misappraisals of the trauma as part of the intervention, including working with parental guilt. Signposting to adult mental health services for their own support is also encouraged if required.

CT-PTSD: Adaptations for Younger Children

The Scheeringa manual for treating PTSD in pre-schoolers (Scheeringa, 2015) can be used for younger children. Key differences include creating an exposure hierarchy of difficult memories, an increased focus on drawing and parents/carers being present in all memory-focussed sessions if this is appropriate.

CT-PTSD: Overcoming Difficulties with Memory Work

CT-PTSD with CYP is rarely straightforward and hence it is important for practitioners to be supervised by a practitioner with PTSD experience and expertise. Discussing common difficulties is outside the scope of this chapter and further reading is recommended. Murray and El-Leithy (2022) provide a thorough and practical guide to working with complexity within the CT-PTSD model.

14.3.8 Intervention: EMDR

To practice EMDR, practitioners must attend EMDR-specific training, ideally accredited by the European Association for EMDR, which usually consists of three parts. Hence the following is for information and knowledge only; anyone wishing to practice EMDR should receive further specialist training.

EMDR is a talking therapy, first introduced by Shapiro in 1989. It integrates several elements of a range of therapeutic approaches and combines them with bilateral stimulation (BLS) of the brain. The original form of BLS, eye movements, is how the treatment originally received its name, however there are now multiple ways of achieving BLS (Shapiro 1991, 1994, 2007). For example, butterfly hug, buzzers in alternate hands and marching on the spot. This leads to the brain's information processing system being stimulated.

EMDR is an eight-phased treatment approach (Shapiro, 1999):

1. History taking: A detailed history of the CYP's difficulties is conducted to help the therapist ascertain the CYP's readiness for treatment.
2. Preparation: This is similar to the stabilisation phase of TF-CBTs, where the CYP is taught any skills that may be helpful to them in order to complete the memory processing. For example, calm- or relaxed-place imagery. In EMDR, this phase is thought to be helpful for relationship building.
3. Assessment: The therapist and the CYP collaboratively identify the memory to be targeted. CYP are then asked to identify the worst part of the 'event', bringing a picture about it to mind, identifying a positive and negative cognition around it, the feeling and a location in the body where the feeling is experienced. The feeling is rated on a SUDs scale with 0 = no distress and 10 = very distressing. The positive cognition is rated on a scale, called the validity of cognition, 1 = not true at all and 7 = very true.
4. Desensitisation: To reprocess the traumatic event, the CYP is asked to attend to the target image and complete BLS of the brain at the same time. After each set of BLS, the CYP is asked to take a deep breath and asked 'what came up?' during the processing.
5. Installation: The therapist attempts to increase the strength of the positive cognition, until it reaches 7/7 (or a realistic equivalent).
6. Body scan: The CYP is asked to scan their body for any remaining physical sensations. If any are present, they are targeted in further processing.
7. Closure: The techniques practiced and taught in the preparation phase are utilised. Some sessions may skip phases 5 and 6 if the SUD score does not sufficiently reduce in one session.
8. Re-evaluation of treatment effect: A review of the CYPs symptoms is completed and other potential memories to target are identified.

EMDR is guided by the adaptive information processing (AIP) model, which suggests that trauma responses arise when a difficult experience is inadequately processed, leading traumatic memories to be stored in their own neural networks and detached from more adaptive networks (Shapiro, 2007). Central to the theory is the notion that humans have an inherent physiologically system that processes information, which directly impacts the mental health of the person (Shapiro, 2018). The model proposes that a wide range of experiences can interfere with this intrinsic information-processing system, leaving memories in a maladaptive form, isolated from more adaptive memories. EMDR involves accessing the stored trauma memory and stimulating the innate human processing system, allowing the trauma memory to be reintegrated with more adaptive memory networks (Solomon & Shapiro, 2008). There are mixed views in the literature regarding the AIP model, with some stating that it is not relevant or proven (e.g. Perkins & Rouanzoin, 2002), yet the evidence base for EMDR as an effective psychological treatment for CYP continues to grow.

A recent review examined 25 studies looking at EMDR for PTSD in CYP (Matthijssen et al., 2020). This included 11 RCTs for individual EMDR and two RCTs for group EMDR. The remaining were case studies. From the individual RCTs, all but one study found that PTSD symptoms significantly reduced following EMDR, when compared to controls of waiting list, psychoeducation or standard care. Notably session numbers were small (3–9). When compared directly to TF-CBT(s), the interventions were found to be equally effective. There is some early evidence that EMDR can achieve the same results in fewer sessions. However, there are several methodological flaws in the RCTs currently published; most of the samples were small, there was often a lack of a diagnostic interview for PTSD, a lack of checks of model fidelity and missing long-term follow-ups. This has led to a difference between the international guidelines with regards to EMDR for PTSD. The International Society for Traumatic Stress Studies (ISTSS; 2019) and World Health Organization (WHO, 2013) both recommend EMDR therapy for CYP with PTSD, whereas the NICE Guidelines in the United Kingdom, recommend EMDR only if TF-CBT has been unsuccessful (NICE, 2018). To improve the reliability and validity of research for EMDR for CYP, further methodologically rigorous studies are required. There is also notably a lack of evidence for very young children and for those who present with CPTSD.

14.3.9 PTSD and Autism

The clinical features associated with autism mean that adaptations to standard evidence-based psychological treatments are needed (NICE, 2013). In addition, it is likely that PTSD presents differently in this population (see Section 14.3.1, Epidemiology). Hence it is important to consider adaptations specifically for these CYP.

Epidemiology

Research regarding PTSD and autistic CYP is currently limited. What we currently know is that CYP on the autism spectrum show a similar or elevated prevalence of PTSD in comparison to the general population (Rumball, 2020). There are some hypotheses that the sociocognitive features typically associated with autism (e.g. difficulties with theory of mind, executive functioning and cognitive flexibility) may increase their risk of developing PTSD due to the impact these abilities may have on memory processing and appraisals of events (King, 2010; Kerns et al., 2015). There is also emerging evidence that their increased sensory sensitivities could increase the likelihood that an event is experienced as traumatic (Kerns et al., 2015). It is also possible that autistic CYP are more at risk of experiencing traumatic events. There is evidence that they are more likely to experience physical abuse and neglect than their neuro-typical peers (e.g. Dmour et al., 2019; Maiano et al., 2016). Those with co-occurring learning disability are also at a higher risk for experiencing sexual and emotional abuse (McDonnell et al., 2019).

There is an acknowledgement in the literature that autistic CYP are likely to perceive some events as traumatic, where their neurotypical peers would not (Ng-Cordell et al., 2022). There is some adult literature to support this, for example, autistic adults have described events relating to their mental health, changes to routine or excessive sensory input, as traumatic experiences (Kerns et al., 2023; Rumball et al., 2020). Whilst similar studies are needed for CYP, clinical experience suggests that this is also likely to be the case for CYP with autism. Many of the events that they may find traumatic are excluded from standardised screening measures and moreover, these events would typically be excluded from diagnostic criteria for PTSD. In addition, symptoms of autism and PTSD overlap in several ways and hence it could be easy for practitioners to assign a young person's difficulties to an existing autism diagnosis, rather than screening and thoroughly assessing for PTSD. For example, nightmares being masked as sleep difficulties, or social withdrawal being perceived as a lack of interest in peer relationships (Stavropoulos et al., 2018). Similarly, there is evidence that experiencing a traumatic event could lead an autistic CYP to present with an increase in autism features, including repetitive behaviours and emotional outbursts (Brenner et al., 2018; Fuld, 2018).

Assessment

Whilst the literature we have is limited, all of the above suggest that PTSD is common in autistic CYP but is likely to present differently in several ways. Hence it is important for practitioners to be flexible with their screening and assessment processes. Notably, there is evidence that practitioners do not always screen for and treat trauma symptoms in autistic people (Kerns et al., 2020). Clinical experience suggests it can be useful to consider a broader range of events that could be perceived by the CYP as traumatic where evidence of the other criteria is present. In addition, practitioners should be curious about changes in autism features following the traumatic event and consider whether these could be considered under any of the diagnostic criteria. As when working with younger children, assessments may need to be adapted to reduce reliance on verbal communication and the involvement of multiple informants is even more essential. Importantly, validated outcome measures for autistic CYP and PTSD are needed.

Formulation

Clinical experience suggests that the Clark and Ehlers (Ehlers & Clark, 2000) formulation is relevant and helpful for autistic CYP. However, there is currently no known research examining the relevance of the different components previously described.

Intervention

Research into treatment of PTSD for autistic CYP is also urgently needed. The literature is currently limited to case studies and small case series, predominantly with adults. Nevertheless, potential treatment modifications have been suggested for trauma-based CBTs (e.g. Peterson et al., 2019; Stack & Lucyshyn, 2019) and EMDR (Fisher et al., 2022). In addition, clinical experience suggests that NICE recommended treatments can be effective for this population, with some adaptations.

CT-PTSD: The involvement of parents/carers is even more paramount, and all aspects of the intervention should be adapted to the CYP's developmental level and to include their special interests where possible. As with other CBT interventions adapted for autistic CYP, psychoeducation materials may need to be modified to include more visual resources, about both PTSD symptoms and what to expect from therapy. Autistic CYP struggle to generalise skills across different contexts and hence will be likely to need support, from both the practitioner and parents/carers to practice grounding and symptom management techniques in different settings. Additional psychoeducation regarding emotional literacy and recognition may also be needed. Practitioners should however remain mindful that the key mechanism of change is still the memory work and therefore additional skills building should not overly delay the memory part of the intervention. Metaphors can still be used to explain the rationale for reliving, with caution; generally, doing something active in the room to demonstrate (e.g. changing the wardrobe metaphor to a waste-paper bin and acting it out in the therapy room). During reliving, the SUDS may need to be adapted (e.g. reduced/simplified scale, visual representation). Clinical experience suggests that the misappraisals held are often more rigid than those of their neurotypical peers, and hence cognitive updates are likely to take longer and require multiple strategies to target. Therefore, generally, a larger number of sessions are required.

EMDR: Whilst there is no specific research looking at adaptations for autistic CYP, Fisher et al. (2022) completed a survey with over 100 EMDR therapists about the adaptations they make for autistic adults. Over 100 adaptations were identified, with 27 being used often or always by at least 80% of therapists. Notably, the majority of these adaptations would also be considered important for working with CYP more generally (e.g. be flexible and creative, use very clear language, take time to understand the language they use around thoughts and emotions). Others were more EMDR specific, such as trying a range of different bilateral stimulation to see which one they prefer. Clinical experience suggests that some autistic CYP prefer EMDR to CT-PTSD due to the lack of emphasis on verbalising their thoughts, whereas others struggle to tolerate the intense physical sensations that can emerge. Hence at present, practitioners are encouraged to follow the evidence base and try CT-PTSD first.

14.3.10 The Voice of the CYP in PTSD Treatment

The implementation of trauma-focussed therapies may be hindered by practitioners' concerns about how treatment is experienced by CYP. There is evidence that these concerns are unfounded. For example, a systematic review of eight studies examining CYP and caregiver experiences of TF-CBT found that whilst there were concerns from the CYP prior to starting treatment (e.g. that they would not be compatible with their therapist), once treatment had started, they found the experience very validating and safe. Notably, this was enhanced by therapist competence and how confidentiality was managed. The same review found that both CYP and their carers said talking about the trauma was essential for recovery (Neelakantan et al., 2019). Similarly, Eastwood et al. (2021) conducted semi-structured interviews with CYP regarding their experience of TF-CBT. The CYP reported that talking about trauma was difficult, sometimes distressing but imperative for recovery. In addition, the CYP interviewed emphasised the importance of retaining autonomy and control during the intervention. To date, there are no known studies examining the experiences of CYP who complete EMDR.

Although the research into the qualitative experiences of CYP in trauma-focussed therapies is limited, what is available fits with clinical experience that giving as much choice as possible to the CYP during treatment is incredibly important. This can be in the form of small, seemingly minor decisions. For example, in the timeline exercise, would they like to start from the beginning of their life and work forwards, or start from the present and work backwards. It can also be in the form of larger decisions. For example, if a CYP has experienced multiple traumas, the therapist should discuss with them all the different options for how to proceed with memory processing, for example, would they like to start with the least distressing memory, the first memory or the most recent memory? Box 14.2 provides a clinical example of the assessment and treatment of a young person with CPTSD.

Box 14.2 Clinical example: Aaliyah

Background

Aaliyah is a 17-year-old cis-gendered female of Black Caribbean heritage, who lives at home with her mother, father and older sister. Aaliyah was first referred to CAMHS following an attempt to take her own life at age 12. She was admitted to an in-patient ward due to concerns that her parents would not be able to keep her safe at home. Aaliyah had a short stay on the ward and was discharged home. She has since had several more admissions following multiple attempts to end her life and significant self-harm. She was open to social care and placed on a Child in Need plan due to concerns about the family dynamics at home; there were lots of explosive verbal arguments between Aaliyah and her parents, as well as parents struggling to follow safety plans to reduce Aaliyah's risk to herself. During her final admission at age 15, she disclosed historical sexual abuse at the hands of a family friend from the ages of 6 to 9 years. This was reported by the ward to the police. As part of the discharge plan, Aaliyah was referred to a specialist trauma service for young people.

Assessment

Aaliyah attended the assessment alone and refused for her parents to be involved. At assessment, Aaliyah met criteria for a diagnosis of CPTSD. She reported daily flashbacks of the sexual abuse she had experienced, as well as nightmares and intrusive memories. She tried hard to avoid thinking about her traumatic experiences and did her best to stay away from reminders, including a onesie and music by a certain artist. She also tried to avoid being alone with males and romantic relationships. In addition to the core symptoms of PTSD, Aaliyah reported consistent negative beliefs about herself, including that she was "broken", "disgusting" and "unlovable". She also experienced persistent feelings of shame in relation to the abuse. Aaliyah had a long history of difficulties with affect regulation, as evidenced by her self-harm and suicidal behaviour. She also had difficulties in sustaining relationships; she only had one friend, which was from her most recent in-patient admission, which was described by members of staff as 'intense'. Her relationships with her family remained fraught and difficult.

Aaliyah also met criteria for a diagnosis of depression. She reported persistently low mood for several months. She had difficulty sleeping, although she mostly attributed

(Continued)

Box 14.2 (Continued)

this to the nightmares she experienced. She struggled with her self-care and would often not shower or get dressed. She reported a lack of interest in things that she used to enjoy and spent most of the day in her bedroom. She was not engaging in education or employment. As described in more detail later, Aaliyah continued to experience thoughts and urges to self-harm and end her life. Aaliyah reported multiple previous experiences of the same symptoms and hence this was unlikely to be her first episode of depression.

Aaliyah also met criteria for a diagnosis of social anxiety; she reported worrying about what other people thought of her, specifically that they would think she is weird and that when in public, she would do 'something awful' to embarrass herself. This led to Aaliyah avoiding social situations as much as possible and when this was not possible, she engaged in several behaviours to try to prevent others from interacting with her. For example, she avoided eye contact, put her hood up, pretended to be busy on her phone and would not ask questions back during conversations.

In terms of risk to herself, Aaliyah had worked hard during her recent admission to reduce her self-harming behaviour. She still experienced thoughts and urges to self-harm and end her life daily but was currently managing not to act on these by using some skills (e.g. distraction) that she had learned from the in-patient ward.

In terms of risk from others, the family friend was now living abroad and hence the police investigation had not progressed. After attending family therapy sessions on the in-patient ward, Aaliyah's relationship with her parents had somewhat improved, however there were still times when they had arguments and said some hurtful things to Aaliyah. Social care remained involved.

Outcome measures

Aaliyah completed several self-report questionnaires as part of her assessment. For PTSD, she scored 55 on the CPSS-V and 46 on the ITQ-CA. She also completed the RCADS to assess for comorbidities. The RCADS demonstrated that she was also above the clinical cut off for symptoms of social anxiety, depression, and panic.

With the help of her therapist, Aaliyah set the following SMART goals: 1) To reduce the frequency of nightmares to once a week; 2) To reduce the frequency of intrusive memories to once a day.

Formulation

Presenting problems: Aaliyah suffered from CPTSD, depression and social anxiety as described earlier in the assessment.

Predisposing: Aaliyah's mother had an extensive trauma history herself but had struggled to engage with adult mental health services and so had been discharged. Aaliyah's ethnicity meant that, unfortunately, she was more likely to experience racially based discrimination and trauma. Being assigned female at birth also meant she was more likely to experience a sexual trauma. There was a family narrative of not talking about problems or difficulties and that people should just 'get on with it'.

Precipitating: Aaliyah's CPTSD symptoms began following a sex-education class in school, when she realised that what had happened to her was not 'normal' or okay.

Perpetuating: Aaliyah had spent many years becoming expert at trying to avoid thinking about what had happened to her as well as avoiding any potential reminders. She also had multiple negative appraisals of her experience and herself, such as she was to blame for what happened to her and she was now 'broken, disgusting and unlovable'. Her depressive and trauma symptoms were also maintained by a lack of engagement in enjoyable activities. Social anxiety was maintained by an avoidance of social situations and by engaging in multiple safety behaviours when she could not avoid being around people.

Protective: Aaliyah was relieved when she received her CPTSD diagnosis as she felt it explained why her life had been so difficult for so long. As such, she was motivated to engage in treatment. She was also a kind, caring and considerate CYP who had some interest in working with animals in the future.

Intervention

Aaliyah had not yet received an evidence-based intervention for CPTSD. Due to her age, both CT-PTSD and EMDR were then explained as options for treatment, including the evidence bases for each. Aaliyah chose CT-PTSD because even though she thought talking about her trauma experiences would be difficult, she did not like the idea of being 'less in control' in EMDR. CT-PTSD treatment consisted of 25 90-minute sessions. Risk was monitored in every session and a safety plan was in place. It is important to note that Aaliyah did not consent to her parents being involved in treatment. This was frequently revisited by the therapist, but Aaliyah did not change her decision.

Early sessions focussed on relationship building as Aaliyah understandably had difficulties trusting adults. This was achieved through problem-free talk, psychoeducation and creating a timeline of her life so far. Psychoeducation included information about the symptoms of PTSD, plus the role of avoidance and thought suppression in maintaining distress. Psychoeducation about sexual abuse was also included. The wardrobe metaphor was used to explain the rational for treatment and the therapist also explained the role of the hippocampus and amygdala in PTSD. Two sessions were spent on 'reclaiming life'; Aaliyah identified values that were important to her, and some activities were planned each week to try to help her live more in line with these (for example, walking her neighbour's dog was in line with Aaliyah's values of helping others and animal welfare). For the timeline exercise, Aaliyah chose to start from the beginning of her life and work up to the present. Aaliyah struggled to include any positive events and so the therapist balanced encouraging Aaliyah to think about any times in her life that were 'slightly better' whilst being mindful of not invalidating her experiences by insisting positive life events were included. Aaliyah's timeline exercise took multiple sessions due to the significant amount of trauma she had experienced, including the sexual abuse she was originally referred for, emotional abuse at the hands of her parents and difficult experiences during some of her in-patient admissions. A focus of the exercise was to establish which memories were most linked

(Continued)

Box 14.2 (Continued)

to her PTSD symptoms and which memories were the most distressing. With the help of her therapist, Aaliyah identified three memories that were often the content of her flashbacks and nightmares; two of these were linked to the sexual abuse and the third was related to a particularly upsetting argument with her mother.

Aaliyah was given the choice of which memory she would like to start with. Aaliyah chose the least distressing memory, which was related to the sexual abuse. Aaliyah initially struggled to verbalise what happened during reliving and so she created a written narrative first. Eventually, she was able complete reliving in the traditional format, with her eyes closed, speaking in the present tense. Multiple hotspots were identified and restructuring work took place across several sessions. A responsibility pie chart and a survey of other people's thoughts were created to explore if Aaliyah was to blame for what happened. This updated information was then reinserted into the memory.

The memory work was repeated with the other two most distressing memories. Themes were then examined across the three memories and any remaining misappraisals were explored (e.g. I am unlovable). Whilst there was some shift in the belief in these misappraisals, they remained to some extent. Hence the therapist decided to use imagery rescripting techniques to challenge them further. Final sessions covered working with triggers and conducting behavioural experiments around hypervigilance symptoms. A blueprint was created in the final session.

Outcomes

Overall, Aaliyah reported a decrease in her PTSD symptoms. This was reflected in her outcome measures; her CPSS-V score decreased to 25 and her ITQ-CA score decreased to 30. Her depression symptoms had also improved, as evidenced by being below the clinical cut off on the RCADS. Importantly, by the end of treatment, Aaliyah had gained part-time employment at a local animal shelter and enrolled in a college course relating to animal care. She also had not self-harmed and she had met her two goals for treatment. Nevertheless, Aaliyah was still exhibiting symptoms of PTSD, albeit to a lesser extent than at the start of treatment. As such, it was recommended that she have a break from therapy before considering undertaking a second evidence-based intervention, EMDR.

14.3.11 PTSD Summary

A percentage of CYP who experience a trauma will develop PTSD or a related diagnosis. There is very good evidence that TF-CBTs can be helpful for PTSD arising from both single and multiple traumatic events, and emerging evidence that these protocols are also effective for the relatively new diagnosis of CPTSD. As such, TF-CBTs are recommended as first-line treatment for CYP in the United Kingdom. The evidence base and popularity of EMDR for CYP is growing, yet higher quality RCTs are still needed. Research examining which CYP respond better to TF-CBT and which respond better to EMDR is also needed to help practitioners guide their decision making. Research examining the combination of both interventions also has the potential to further boost the success of a outcomes. Whilst there is a lack of research on the voice of CYP in PTSD treatment, the evidence to date supports the notion that talking about their trauma was an imperative part of the intervention. Future research should therefore focus on determining the value of stabilisation early in treatment for CYP with PTSD, as well as continuing to examine the effectiveness of current interventions for the relatively new diagnosis of CPTSD.

References

Abramowitz, J. S., McKay, D., & Taylor, S. (Eds.). (2011). *Obsessive-compulsive disorder: Subtypes and spectrum conditions*. Elsevier.

Alberici, A., Meiser-Stedman, R., Claxton, J., Smith, P., Ehlers, A., Dixon, C., & Mckinnon, A. (2018). The preliminary development and validation of a trauma-related safety-seeking behavior measure for youth: The Child Safety Behavior Scale (CSBS). *Journal of Traumatic Stress*, *31*(5), 643–653.

Ale, C. M., McCarthy, D. M., Rothschild, L. M., & Whiteside, S. P. (2015). Components of cognitive behavioral therapy related to outcome in childhood anxiety disorders. *Clinical Child and Family Psychology Review*, *18*, 240–251.

Alisic, E., Zalta, A. K., Van Wesel, F., Larsen, S. E., Hafstad, G. S., Hassanpour, K., & Smid, G. E. (2014). Rates of post-traumatic stress disorder in trauma-exposed children and adolescents: Meta-analysis. *The British Journal of Psychiatry*, *204*(5), 335–340.

American Psychiatric Association. (2013). *Diagnostic and statistical manual of mental disorders: DSM-5* (5th ed.). American Psychiatric Publishing.

Andrews, A. R., Jobe-Shields, L., López, C. M., Metzger, I. W., De Arellano, M. A., Saunders, B., & Kilpatrick, D. G. (2015). Polyvictimization, income, and ethnic differences in trauma-related mental health during adolescence. *Social Psychiatry and Psychiatric Epidemiology*, *50*, 1223–1234.

Arch, J. J., & Abramowitz, J. S. (2015). Exposure therapy for obsessive-compulsive disorder: An optimizing inhibitory learning approach. *Journal of Obsessive-Compulsive and Related Disorders*, *6*, 174–182.

Bailey, C., Shaw, J., & Harris, A. (2023). Mandatory reporting and adolescent sexual assault. *Trauma, Violence, & Abuse*, *24*(2), 454–467.

Barrett, P., & Healy-Farrell, L. (2003). Perceived responsibility in juvenile obsessive-compulsive disorder: An experimental manipulation. *Journal of Clinical Child and Adolescent Psychology*, *32*(3), 430–441.

Barrett, P., Healy-Farrell, L., & March, J. S. (2004). Cognitive-behavioral family treatment of childhood obsessive-compulsive disorder: a controlled trial. *Journal of the American Academy of Child & Adolescent Psychiatry*, *43*(1), 46-62.

Becker-Blease, K. A., & Freyd, J. J. (2007). The ethics of asking about abuse and the harm of 'don't ask, don't tell'. *American Psychologist*, *62*(4), 330–332.

Brenner, J., Pan, Z., Mazefsky, C., Smith, K. A., & Gabriels, R. (2018). Behavioral Dissociation is characterised by disruptions in memory, sense of self and perception of the world around us inpatient settings. *Journal of Autism and Developmental Disorders*, *48*, 3727–3735.

Brewin, C. R., Dalgleish, T., & Joseph, S. (1996). A dual representation theory of posttraumatic stress disorder. *Psychological Review, 103*(4), 670–686.

Briere, J., Weathers, F. W., & Runtz, M. (2005). Is dissociation a multidimensional construct? Data from the Multiscale Dissociation Inventory. *Journal of Traumatic Stress: Official Publication of the International Society for Traumatic Stress Studies, 18*(3), 221–231.

Brito, M. J. D., Sabino Neto, M., de Oliveira, M. F., Cordás, T. A., Duarte, L. S., Rosella, M. F., Felix, G. A., & Ferreira, L. M. (2015). Yale–Brown obsessive compulsive scale modified for body dysmorphic disorder (BDD-YBOCS): Brazilian Portuguese translation, cultural adaptation and validation. *Brazilian Journal of Psychiatry, 37*, 310–316.

Bromley, C., & Westwood, S. (2013). Young people's participation: Views from young people on using goals. *Clinical and Family Psychology Review, 1*, 41–60.

Calvocoressi, L., Lewis, B., Harris, M., Trufan, S. J., Goodman, W. K., McDougle, C. J., & Price, L. H. (1995). Family accommodation in obsessive-compulsive disorder. *The American Journal of Psychiatry, 152*(3), 441–443.

Choi, K. R., Ford, J. D., Briggs, E. C., Munro-Kramer, M. L., Graham-Bermann, S. A., & Seng, J. S. (2019). Relationships between maltreatment, posttraumatic symptomatology, and the dissociative subtype of PTSD among adolescents. *Journal of Trauma & Dissociation, 20*(2), 212–227.

Chorpita, B. F., Yim, L. M., Moffitt, C., Umemoto L. A., & Francis, S. E. (2000). Assessment of symptoms of DSM-IV anxiety and depression in children: A Revised Child Anxiety and Depression Scale. *Behaviour Research and Therapy, 38*, 835–855.

Cloitre, M., Bisson, J. I., Brewin, C. R., Hyland, P., Karatzias, T., Lueger-Schuster, B., & Shevlin, M. (2018). International trauma questionnaire-child and adolescent version (ITQ-CA). [Unpublished measurement instrument].

Cohen, J., Mannarino, A. P., & Deblinger, E. (2012). *Treating trauma and traumatic grief in children and adolescents.*

Cooper, M. (1996). Obsessive-compulsive disorder: Effects on family members. *American Journal of Orthopsychiatry, 66*(2), 296–304.

Copeland, W. E., Keeler, G., Angold, A., & Costello, E. J. (2007). Traumatic events and posttraumatic stress in childhood. *Archives of General Psychiatry, 64*(5), 577–584.

Cox, C. M., Kenardy, J. A., & Hendrikz, J. K. (2008). A meta-analysis of risk factors that predict psychopathology following accidental trauma. *Journal for Specialists in Pediatric Nursing, 13*(2), 98–110.

Craske, M. G., Kircanski, K., Zelikowsky, M., Mystkowski, J., Chowdhury, N., & Baker, A. (2008). Optimizing inhibitory learning during exposure therapy. *Behaviour Research and Therapy, 46*(1), 5–27.

Craske, M. G., Treanor, M., Conway, C. C., Zbozinek, T., & Vervliet, B. (2014). Maximizing exposure therapy: An inhibitory learning approach. *Behaviour Research and Therapy, 58*, 10–23.

Danese, A., Moffitt, T. E., Harrington, H., Milne, B. J., Polanczyk, G., Pariante, C. M., Poulton, R., & Caspi, A. (2009). Adverse childhood experiences and adult risk factors for age-related disease: Depression, inflammation, and clustering of metabolic risk markers. *Archives of Pediatrics & Adolescent Medicine, 163*(12), 1135–1143.

de Silva, P. (2006). Culture and obsessive-compulsive disorder. *Psychiatry, 5*(11), 402–404.

Demaria, F., Pontillo, M., Tata, M. C., Gargiullo, P., Mancini, F., & Vicari, S. (2021). Psychoeducation focused on family accommodation: A practical intervention for parents of children and adolescents with obsessive-compulsive disorder. *Italian Journal of Pediatrics, 47*(1), 1–7.

Dmour, H. H., Alodwan, M. E., Marashdeh, M. F., Obaisat, M. A., & Hasan, R. S. A. (2019). Abuse of children with autism: Risk of abuse and prevention. *Journal of the Royal Medical Services, 26*(3), 84–91.

Douglass, H. M., Moffitt, T. E., Dar, R., McGee, R. O. B., & Silva, P. (1995). Obsessive-compulsive disorder in a birth cohort of 18-year-olds: Prevalence and predictors. *Journal of the American Academy of Child & Adolescent Psychiatry, 34*(11), 1424–1431.

Eastwood, O., Peters, W., Cohen, J., Murray, L., Rice, S., Alvarez-Jimenez, M., & Bendall, S. (2021). 'Like a huge weight lifted off my shoulders': Exploring young peoples' experiences of treatment in a pilot trial of trauma-focused cognitive behavioral therapy. *Psychotherapy Research, 31*(6), 737–751.

Eaton, W. W., Martins, S. S., Nestadt, G., Bienvenu, O. J., Clarke, D., & Alexandre, P. (2008). The burden of mental disorders. *Epidemiologic Reviews, 30*(1), 1–14.

Ehlers, A., & Clark, D. M. (2000). A cognitive model of posttraumatic stress disorder. *Behaviour Research and Therapy, 38*(4), 319–345.

Eley, T. C., Bolton, D., O'Connor, T. G., Perrin, S., Smith, P., & Plomin, R. (2003). A twin study of anxiety-related behaviours in pre-school children. *Journal of Child Psychology and Psychiatry, 44*(7), 945–960.

Elsner, B., Jacobi, T., Kischkel, E., Schulze, D., & Reuter, B. (2022). Mechanisms of exposure and response prevention in obsessive-compulsive disorder: Effects of habituation and expectancy violation on short-term outcome in cognitive behavioral therapy. *BMC Psychiatry, 22*(1), 1–16.

Ennis, N., Shorer, S., Shoval-Zuckerman, Y., Freedman, S., Monson, C. M., & Dekel, R. (2020). Treating posttraumatic stress disorder across cultures: A systematic review of cultural adaptations of trauma-focused cognitive behavioral therapies. *Journal of Clinical Psychology, 76*(4), 587–611.

Farrell, L. J., James, S. C., Maddox, B. B., Griffiths, D., & White, S. (2016). Treatment of comorbid obsessive-compulsive disorder in youth with ASD: The case of Max. In E.A. Storch & A. B. Lewin (Eds.), *Clinical handbook of obsessive-compulsive and related disorders: A case-based approach to treating pediatric and adult populations* (pp. 337–355). Springer.

Fernández de la Cruz, L., Barrow, F., Bolhuis, K., Krebs, G., Volz, C., Nakatani, E., Heyman, I., & Mataix-Cols, D. (2013). Sexual obsessions in pediatric obsessive-compulsive disorder: Clinical characteristics and treatment outcomes. *Depression and Anxiety, 30*(8), 732–740.

Finch, J., Ford, C., Grainger, L., & Meiser-Stedman, R. (2020). A systematic review of the clinician related barriers and facilitators to the use of evidence-informed interventions for post traumatic stress. *Journal of Affective Disorders, 263*, 175–186.

Fisher, N., Patel, H., van Diest, C., & Spain, D. (2022). Using eye movement desensitisation and reprocessing (EMDR) with autistic individuals: A qualitative interview study with EMDR therapists. *Psychology and Psychotherapy: Theory, Research and Practice, 95*(4), 1071–1089.

Foa, E. B., Asnaani, A., Zang, Y., Capaldi, S., & Yeh, R. (2018). Psychometrics of the Child PTSD Symptom Scale for DSM-5 for trauma-exposed children and adolescents. *Journal of Clinical Child & Adolescent Psychology, 47*(1), 38–46.

Foa, E. B., & Kozak, M. J. (1986). Emotional processing of fear: Exposure to corrective information. *Psychological Bulletin*, *99*(1), 20–35.

Foa, E. B., & Rothbaum, B. O. (1998). *Treating the trauma of rape*. The Guilford Press.

Ford, J. D., & Courtois, C. A. (2021). Complex PTSD and borderline personality disorder. *Borderline Personality Disorder and Emotion Dysregulation*, *8*(1), 16.

Fuld, S. (2018). Autism spectrum disorder: The impact of stressful and traumatic life events and implications for clinical practice. *Clinical Social Work Journal*, *46*(3), 210–219.

Fullana, M. A., Tortella-Feliu, M., De La Cruz, L. F., Chamorro, J., Perez-Vigil, A., Ioannidis, J. P., Sloanes, A., Guardiola, M., Almodovar, C., Miranda-Olivos, R., Ramella-Cravaro, V., Vilar, A., Reichenberg, A., Mataix-Cols, D., Vieta, E., Fusar-Poli, P., Fajto-Vilas, M., & Radua, J. (2020). Risk and protective factors for anxiety and obsessive-compulsive disorders: An umbrella review of systematic reviews and meta-analyses. *Psychological Medicine*, *50*(8), 1300–1315.

Geller, D. A., & March, J. (2012). Practice parameter for the assessment and treatment of children and adolescents with obsessive-compulsive disorder. *Journal of the American Academy of Child & Adolescent Psychiatry*, *51*(1), 98–113.

Ginsburg, G. S., Kingery, J. N., Drake, K. L., & Grados, M. A. (2008). Predictors of treatment response in pediatric obsessive-compulsive disorder. *Journal of the American Academy of Child & Adolescent Psychiatry*, *47*(8), 868–878.

Goddard, E., Onwumere, J., Meiser-Stedman, R., Sutherland, E., & Smith, P. (2019). Relationship between posttraumatic stress symptoms, caregiving response, and parent mental health in youth exposed to single incident trauma. *Journal of Affective Disorders*, *251*, 15–22.

Griffiths, D. L., Farrell, L. J., Waters, A. M., & White, S. W. (2017). Clinical correlates of obsessive compulsive disorder and comorbid autism spectrum disorder in youth. *Journal of Obsessive-Compulsive and Related Disorders*, *14*, 90–98.

Gutermann, J., Schreiber, F., Matulis, S., Schwartzkopff, L., Deppe, J., & Steil, R. (2016). Psychological treatments for symptoms of posttraumatic stress disorder in children, adolescents, and young adults: A meta-analysis. *Clinical Child and Family Psychology Review*, *19*, 77–93.

Haselgruber, A., Sölva, K., & Lueger-Schuster, B. (2020). Validation of ICD-11 PTSD and complex PTSD in foster children using the international trauma questionnaire. *Acta Psychiatrica Scandinavica*, *141*(1), 60–73.

Heyman, I., Fombonne, E., Simmons, H., Ford, T., Meltzer, H., & Goodman, R. (2001). Prevalence of obsessive–compulsive disorder in the British nationwide survey of child mental health. *The British Journal of Psychiatry*, *179*(4), 324–329.

Heyman, I., Fombonne, E., Simmons, H., Ford, T., Meltzer, H., & Goodman, R. (2003). Prevalence of obsessive-compulsive disorder in the British nationwide survey of child mental health. *International Review of Psychiatry*, *15*(1–2), 178–184.

Hiller, R. M., Meiser-Stedman, R., Fearon, P., Lobo, S., McKinnon, A., Fraser, A., & Halligan, S. L. (2016). Research review: Changes in the prevalence and symptom severity of child post-traumatic stress disorder in the year following trauma: A meta-analytic study. *Journal of Child Psychology and Psychiatry*, *57*(8), 884–898.

Hiranyatheb, T., Saipanish, R., & Lotrakul, M. (2014). Reliability and validity of the Thai version of the Yale–Brown obsessive compulsive scale–second edition in clinical samples. *Neuropsychiatric Disease and Treatment, 10*, 471–477.

Hiscox, L. V., Bray, S., Fraser, A., Meiser-Stedman, R., Seedat, S., & Halligan, S. L. (2023). Sex differences in the severity and natural recovery of child PTSD symptoms: A longitudinal analysis of children exposed to acute trauma. *Psychological Medicine, 53*(6), 2682–2688.

Hoeboer, C. M., De Kleine, R. A., Molendijk, M. L., Schoorl, M., Oprel, D. A. C., Mouthaan, J., Van der Does, W., & Van Minnen, A. (2020). Impact of dissociation on the effectiveness of psychotherapy for post-traumatic stress disorder: Meta-analysis. *BJPsych Open, 6*(3), e53.

Hoppen, T. H., Jehn, M., Holling, H., Mutz, J., Kip, A., & Morina, N. (2023). The efficacy and acceptability of psychological interventions for adult PTSD: A network and pairwise meta-analysis of randomized controlled trials. *Journal of Consulting and Clinical Psychology. 91*(8), 445–461.

Hultmann, O., Möller, J., Ormhaug, S. M., & Broberg, A. (2014). Asking routinely about intimate partner violence in a child and adolescent psychiatric clinic: A qualitative study. *Journal of Family Violence, 29*, 67–78.

Hunt, C. (2020). Differences in OCD symptom presentations across age, culture, and gender: A quantitative review of studies using the Y-BOCS symptom checklist. *Journal of Obsessive-Compulsive and Related Disorders, 26*, 100533.

International Society for Traumatic Stress Studies. (2018). New ISTSS prevention and treatment guidelines. https://www.istss.org/treating-trauma/new-istss-prevention-and-treatment-guidelines.aspx

Jacoby, R. J., & Abramowitz, J. S. (2016). Inhibitory learning approaches to exposure therapy: A critical review and translation to obsessive-compulsive disorder. *Clinical Psychology Review, 49*, 28–40.

Jans, T., Wewetzer, C., Klampfl, K., Schulz, E., Herpertz-Dahlmann, B., Remschmidt, H., & Warnke, A. (2007). Phenomenology and co-morbidity of childhood onset obsessive compulsive disorder. *Zeitschrift fur Kinder-und Jugendpsychiatrie und Psychotherapie, 35*(1), 41–50.

Jassi, A. (2020a) *Challenging OCD in young people with ASD: A CBT manual for therapists*. Jessica Kingsley.

Jassi, A. (2020b). *Challenge your OCD!: A CBT workbook for young people with ASD*. Jessica Kingsley.

Jassi, A., Fernández de la Cruz, L., Russell, A., & Krebs, G. (2021). An evaluation of a new autism-adapted cognitive behaviour therapy manual for adolescents with obsessive–compulsive disorder. *Child Psychiatry & Human Development, 52*(5), 916–927.

Jassi, A., & Krebs, G. (2020). Treatment of obsessive-compulsive disorder in a young person with autism spectrum disorder. In E. A. Storch, D. McKay, & J. S. Abramowitz (Eds.), *Advanced casebook of obsessive-compulsive and related disorders* (pp. 137-159). Academic Press.

Jensen, T. K., Braathu, N., Birkeland, M. S., Ormhaug, S. M., & Skar, A. M. S. (2022). Complex PTSD and treatment outcomes in TF-CBT for youth: A naturalistic study. *European Journal of Psychotraumatology, 13*(2), 2114630.

Keleher, J., Jassi, A., & Krebs, G. (2020). Clinician-reported barriers to using exposure with response prevention in the treatment of paediatric obsessive-compulsive disorder. *Journal of Obsessive-Compulsive and Related Disorders, 24*, 100498.

Kennedy, S. M., & Hawks, J. L. (2021). Lessons learned from a randomized controlled pilot trial testing an inhibitory learning approach to exposure in anxious youth. *Cognitive and Behavioral Practice, 28*(2), 241–258.

Kerns, C. M., Berkowitz, S. J., Moskowitz, L. J., Drahota, A., Lerner, M. D., Usual Care for Autism Study (UCAS) Consortium, & Newschaffer, C. J. (2020). Screening and treatment of trauma-related symptoms in youth with autism spectrum disorder among community providers in the United States. *Autism, 24*(2), 515–525.

Kerns, C. M., Newschaffer, C. J., & Berkowitz, S. J. (2015). Traumatic childhood events and autism spectrum disorder. *Journal of Autism and Developmental Disorders, 45*, 3475–3486.

Kerns, C. M., Robins, D. L., Shattuck, P. T., Newschaffer, C. J., & Berkowitz, S. J. (2023). Expert consensus regarding indicators of a traumatic reaction in autistic youth: A Delphi survey. *Journal of Child Psychology and Psychiatry, 64*(1), 50–58.

Kessler, R. C. (2000). Posttraumatic stress disorder: The burden to the individual and to society. *Journal of Clinical Psychiatry, 61*, 4–14.

Keyes, C., Nolte, L., & Williams, T. I. (2018). The battle of living with obsessive compulsive disorder: A qualitative study of young people's experiences. *Child and Adolescent Mental Health, 23*(3), 177–184.

King, R. (2010). Complex post-traumatic stress disorder: Implications for individuals with autism spectrum disorders. *Journal on Developmental Disabilities; Toronto, 16*(3), 91–100.

Kirmayer, L. J. (2012). Rethinking cultural competence. *Transcultural Psychiatry, 49*(2), 149–164.

Krebs, G., & Heyman, I. (2015). Obsessive-compulsive disorder in children and adolescents. *Archives of Disease in Childhood, 100*(5), 495–499.

Krebs, G., Isomura, K., Lang, K., Jassi, A., Heyman, I., Diamond, H., Advani, J., Turner, C., & Mataix-Cols, D. (2015). How resistant is 'treatment-resistant' obsessive-compulsive disorder in youth? *British Journal of Clinical Psychology, 54*(1), 63–75.

Krebs, G., Murray, K., & Jassi, A. (2016). Modified cognitive behavior therapy for severe, treatment-resistant obsessive-compulsive disorder in an adolescent with autism spectrum disorder. *Journal of Clinical Psychology, 72*(11), 1162–1173.

Lebowitz, E. R., Panza, K. E., & Bloch, M. H. (2016). Family accommodation in obsessive-compulsive and anxiety disorders: A five-year update. *Expert Review of Neurotherapeutics, 16*(1), 45–53.

Lewin, A. B., Wood, J. J., Gunderson, S., Murphy, T. K., & Storch, E. A. (2011). Phenomenology of comorbid autism spectrum and obsessive-compulsive disorders among children. *Journal of Developmental and Physical Disabilities, 23*, 543–553.

Lewis, A., Stokes, C., Heyman, I., Turner, C., & Krebs, G. (2020). Conceptualizing and managing risk in pediatric OCD: Case examples. *Bulletin of the Menninger Clinic, 84*(1), 3–20.

Lewis, C., Roberts, N. P., Andrew, M., Starling, E., & Bisson, J. I. (2020). Psychological therapies for post-traumatic stress disorder in adults: Systematic review and meta-analysis. *European Journal of Psychotraumatology, 11*(1), 1729633.

Lewis, S. J., Arseneault, L., Caspi, A., Fisher, H. L., Matthews, T., Moffitt, T. E., Odgers, C. L., Stahl, D., Teng, J. Y., & Danese, A. (2019). The epidemiology of trauma and post-traumatic stress disorder in a representative cohort of young people in England and Wales. *The Lancet Psychiatry*, *6*(3), 247–256.

Leyfer, O. T., Folstein, S. E., Bacalman, S., Davis, N. O., Dinh, E., Morgan, J., Tager-Flusberg, H., & Lainhart, J. E. (2006). Comorbid psychiatric disorders in children with autism: Interview development and rates of disorders. *Journal of Autism and Developmental Disorders*, *36*, 849–861.

Libby, S., Reynolds, S., Derisley, J., & Clark, S. (2004). Cognitive appraisals in young people with obsessive-compulsive disorder. *Journal of Child Psychology and Psychiatry*, *45*(6), 1076–1084.

Macneil, C. A., Hasty, M. K., Conus, P., & Berk, M. (2012). Is diagnosis enough to guide interventions in mental health? Using case formulation in clinical practice. *BMC Medicine*, *10*(111), 1–3.

Maiano, C., Aime, A., Salvas, M. C., Morin, A. J., & Normand, C. L. (2016). Prevalence and correlates of bullying perpetration and victimization among school-aged youth with intellectual disabilities: A systematic review. *Research in Developmental Disabilities*, *49*, 181–195.

Marazziti, D., & Pozza, A. (2022). An overview of the pharmacological options for pediatric obsessive-compulsive disorder. *Expert Opinion on Pharmacotherapy*, *23*(16), 1793–1800.

Martin, A. F., Jassi, A., Cullen, A. E., Broadbent, M., Downs, J., & Krebs, G. (2020). Co-occurring obsessive–compulsive disorder and autism spectrum disorder in young people: Prevalence, clinical characteristics and outcomes. *European Child & Adolescent Psychiatry*, *29*(11), 1603–1611.

Mather, A., & Cartwright-Hatton, S. (2004). Cognitive predictors of obsessive–compulsive symptoms in adolescence: A preliminary investigation. *Journal of Clinical Child and Adolescent Psychology*, *33*(4), 743–749.

Mathes, B. M., Morabito, D. M., & Schmidt, N. B. (2019). Epidemiological and clinical gender differences in OCD. *Current Psychiatry Reports*, *21*, 1–7.

Mattheisen, M., Samuels, J. F., Wang, Y., Greenberg, B. D., Fyer, A. J., McCracken, J. T., Geller, D. A., Murphy, D. L., Knowles, J. A., Grados, M. A., Riddles, M. A., Rasmussen, S. A., McLaughlin, N., C., Nurmi, E., L., Askland, K. D., Qin, H-D., Cullen, B. A., Piacentini, J., Pauls, D. L. … Nestadt, G. (2015). Genome-wide association study in obsessive-compulsive disorder: Results from the OCGAS. *Molecular Psychiatry*, *20*(3), 337–344.

Matthews, L., Reynolds, S., & Derisley, J. (2007). Examining cognitive models of obsessive compulsive disorder in adolescents. *Behavioural and Cognitive Psychotherapy*, *35*(2), 149–163.

Matthijssen, S. J., Lee, C. W., de Roos, C., Barron, I. G., Jarero, I., Shapiro, E., Hurley, E. C., Schubert, S. J., Baptsit, J., Amann, B. L., Moreno-Alcazar, A., Tesarz, J., & de Jongh, A. (2020). The current status of EMDR therapy, specific target areas, and goals for the future. *Journal of EMDR Practice and Research*, *14*(4), 241–284.

Mavranezouli, I., Megnin-Viggars, O., Daly, C., Dias, S., Welton, N. J., Stockton, S., Bhutani, G., Grey, N., Leach, J., Greenberg, N., Katona, C., El-Leithy, S., & Pilling, S. (2020). Psychological treatments for post-traumatic stress disorder in adults: A network meta-analysis. *Psychological Medicine*, *50*(4), 542–555.

McDonnell, C. G., Boan, A. D., Bradley, C. C., Seay, K. D., Charles, J. M., & Carpenter, L. A. (2019). Child maltreatment in autism spectrum disorder and intellectual disability: Results from a population-based sample. *Journal of Child Psychology and Psychiatry*, *60*(5), 576–584.

McGuire, J. F., Piacentini, J., Lewin, A. B., Brennan, E. A., Murphy, T. K., & Storch, E. A. (2015). A meta-analysis of cognitive behavior therapy and medication for child obsessive–compulsive disorder: Moderators of treatment efficacy, response, and remission. *Depression and Anxiety*, *32*(8), 580–593.

McGuire, R., Hiller, R. M., Ehlers, A., Fearon, P., Meiser-Stedman, R., Leuteritz, S., & Halligan, S. L. (2021). A longitudinal investigation of children's trauma memory characteristics and their relationship with posttraumatic stress disorder symptoms. *Research on Child and Adolescent Psychopathology*, *49*, 807–816.

Meiser-Stedman, R., McKinnon, A., Dixon, C., Boyle, A., Smith, P., & Dalgleish, T. (2019). A core role for cognitive processes in the acute onset and maintenance of post-traumatic stress in children and adolescents. *Journal of Child Psychology and Psychiatry*, *60*(8), 875–884.

Meiser-Stedman, R., Smith, P., Bryant, R., Salmon, K., Yule, W., Dalgleish, T., & Nixon, R. D. (2009). Development and validation of the child post-traumatic cognitions inventory (CPTCI). *Journal of Child Psychology and Psychiatry*, *50*(4), 432–440.

Meiser-Stedman, R., Yule, W., Smith, P., Glucksman, E., & Dalgleish, T. (2005). Acute stress disorder and posttraumatic stress disorder in children and adolescents involved in assaults or motor vehicle accidents. *American Journal of Psychiatry*, *162*(7), 1381–1383.

Melli, G., Avallone, E., Moulding, R., Pinto, A., Micheli, E., & Carraresi, C. (2015). Validation of the Italian version of the Yale–Brown Obsessive Compulsive Scale–Second Edition (Y-BOCS-II) in a clinical sample. *Comprehensive Psychiatry*, *60*, 86–92.

Micali, N., Heyman, I., Perez, M., Hilton, K., Nakatani, E., Turner, C., & Mataix-Cols, D. (2010). Long-term outcomes of obsessive–compulsive disorder: Follow-up of 142 children and adolescents. *The British Journal of Psychiatry*, *197*(2), 128–134.

Murray, H., & El-Leithy, S. (2022). *Working with complexity in PTSD: A cognitive therapy approach*. Routledge.

Murray, K., Jassi, A., Mataix-Cols, D., Barrow, F., & Krebs, G. (2015). Outcomes of cognitive behaviour therapy for obsessive–compulsive disorder in young people with and without autism spectrum disorders: A case controlled study. *Psychiatry Research*, *228*(1), 8–13.

Neelakantan, L., Hetrick, S., & Michelson, D. (2019). Users' experiences of trauma-focused cognitive behavioural therapy for children and adolescents: A systematic review and metasynthesis of qualitative research. *European Child & Adolescent Psychiatry*, *28*(7), 877–897.

Ng-Cordell, E., Wardell, V., Stewardson, C., & Kerns, C. M. (2022). Anxiety and trauma-related disorders in children on the autism spectrum. *Current Psychiatry Reports*, *24*(3), 171–180.

National Institute for Clinical Excellence. (2005). *Obsessive-compulsive disorder and body dysmorphic disorder: Treatment. Clinical Guideline* CG31. https://www.nice.org.uk/guidance/cg31

National Institute for Clinical Excellence. (2013). *Autism spectrum disorder in under 19s: support and management*. Clinical Guideline CG170. https://www.nice.org.uk/guidance/cg170

National Institute for Clinical Excellence. (2018). *Post-traumatic stress disorder. Clinical Guideline* NG116. https://www.nice.org.uk/guidance/ng116

Okasha, A., Saad, A., Khalil, A. H., El Dawla, A. S., & Yehia, N. (1994). Phenomenology of obsessive-compulsive disorder: A transcultural study. *Comprehensive Psychiatry, 35*(3), 191–197.

Oprel, D. A., Hoeboer, C. M., Schoorl, M., Kleine, R. A. D., Cloitre, M., Wigard, I. G., van Minnen, A., & van der Does, W. (2021). Effect of prolonged exposure, intensified prolonged exposure and STAIR+ prolonged exposure in patients with PTSD related to childhood abuse: A randomized controlled trial. *European Journal of Psychotraumatology, 12*(1), 1851511.

Patel, A. R., & Hall, B. J. (2021). Beyond the DSM-5 diagnoses: A cross-cultural approach to assessing trauma reactions. *Focus, 19*(2), 197–203.

Peris, T. S., Compton, S. N., Kendall, P. C., Birmaher, B., Sherrill, J., March, J., Gosch, E., Ginsburg, G., Rynn, M., McCracken, J. T., Keeton, C. P., Sakolsky, D, Suveg, C., Aschenbrand, S., Almirall, D., Iyengar, S., Walkup, J. T., Albano, A. M., & Piacentini, J. (2015). Trajectories of change in youth anxiety during cognitive behavior therapy. *Journal of Consulting and Clinical Psychology, 83*(2), 239–252.

Perkins, B. R., & Rouanzoin, C. C. (2002). A critical evaluation of current views regarding eye movement desensitization and reprocessing (EMDR): Clarifying points of confusion. *Journal of Clinical Psychology, 58*(1), 77–97.

Perkonigg, A., Höfler, M., Cloitre, M., Wittchen, H. U., Trautmann, S., & Maercker, A. (2015). Evidence for two different ICD-11 posttraumatic stress disorders in a community sample of adolescents and young adults. *European Archives of Psychiatry and Clinical Neuroscience, 266*, 317–328.

Perrin, S., Meiser-Stedman, R., & Smith, P. (2005). The Children's Revised Impact of Event Scale (CRIES): Validity as a screening instrument for PTSD. *Behavioural and Cognitive Psychotherapy, 33*(4), 487–498.

Peterson, J. L., Earl, R. K., Fox, E. A., Ma, R., Haidar, G., Pepper, M., Berliner, L., Wallace, A., & Bernier, R. A. (2019). Trauma and autism spectrum disorder: Review, proposed treatment adaptations and future directions. *Journal of Child & Adolescent Trauma, 12*, 529–547.

Piacentini, J., Bergman, R. L., Keller, M., & McCracken, J. (2003). Functional impairment in children and adolescents with obsessive-compulsive disorder. *Journal of Child and Adolescent Psychopharmacology, 13*(2, Supplement 1), 61–69.

Plaisted, H., Waite, P., Gordon, K., & Creswell, C. (2021). Optimising exposure for children and adolescents with anxiety, OCD and PTSD: A systematic review. *Clinical Child and Family Psychology Review, 24*, 348–369.

Raffin, A. L., Guimarães Fachel, J. M., Ferrão, Y. A., Pasquoto de Souza, F., & Cordioli, A. V. (2009). Predictors of response to group cognitive-behavioral therapy in the treatment of obsessive-compulsive disorder. *European Psychiatry: The Journal of the Association of European Psychiatrists, 24*(5), 297–306.

Redican, E., Hyland, P., Cloitre, M., McBride, O., Karatzias, T., Murphy, J., Bunting, L., & Shevlin, M. (2022). Prevalence and predictors of ICD-11 posttraumatic stress disorder and complex PTSD in young people. *Acta Psychiatrica Scandinavica, 146*(2), 110–125.

Reynolds, S. A., Clark, S., Smith, H., Langdon, P. E., Payne, R., Bowers, G., Norton, E., & McIlwham, H. (2013). Randomized controlled trial of parent-enhanced CBT compared with individual CBT for obsessive-compulsive disorder in young people. *Journal of Consulting and Clinical Psychology, 81*(6), 1021–1026.

Rumball, F., Happé, F., & Grey, N. (2020). Experience of trauma and PTSD symptoms in autistic adults: Risk of PTSD development following DSM-5 and non-DSM-5 traumatic life events. *Autism Research, 13*(12), 2122–2132.

Russell, A. J., Jassi, A., Fullana, M. A., Mack, H., Johnston, K., Heyman, I., Murphy, D. G., & Mataix-Cols, D. (2013). Cognitive behavior therapy for comorbid obsessive-compulsive disorder in high-functioning autism spectrum disorders: A randomized controlled trial. *Depression and Anxiety, 30*(8), 697–708.

Sachser, C., Keller, F., & Goldbeck, L. (2017). Complex PTSD as proposed for ICD-11: Validation of a new disorder in children and adolescents and their response to trauma-focused cognitive behavioral therapy. *Journal of Child Psychology and Psychiatry, 58*(2), 160–168.

Salkovskis, P. M. (1985). Obsessional-compulsive problems: A cognitive-behavioural analysis. *Behaviour Research and Therapy, 23*(5), 571–583.

Schauer, M., Nuener, F., & Elbert, T. (2011). *Narrative exposure therapy: A short-term treatment for post traumatic stress disorder*. Hogrefe.

Schauer, M., Neuner, F., & Elbert, T. (2017). Narrative exposure therapy for children and adolescents (KIDNET). In M. A. Landolt, M. Cloitre, & U. Schnyder (Eds.), *Evidence-based treatments for trauma related disorders in children and adolescents* (pp. 227–250). Springer.

Scheeringa, M. S. (2015). *Treating PTSD in preschoolers: A clinical guide*. The Guilford Press.

Shapiro, F. (1991). Eye movement desensitization and reprocessing procedure: From EMD to EMDR: A new treatment model for anxiety and related traumata. *Behavior Therapist, 14*(5), 133–135.

Shapiro, F. (1994). Alternative stimuli in the use of EMD(R). *Journal of Behavior Therapy and Experimental Psychiatry, 25*(1), 89.

Shapiro, F. (1999). Eye movement desensitization and reprocessing (EMDR) and the anxiety disorders: Clinical and research implications of an integrated psychotherapy treatment. *Journal of Anxiety Disorders, 13*(1–2), 35–67.

Shapiro, F. (2007). EMDR, adaptive information processing, and case conceptualization. *Journal of EMDR Practice and Research, 1*(2), 68–87.

Shapiro, F. (2018). *Eye movement desensitization and reprocessing (EMDR) therapy. Basic principles, protocols, and procedures* (2nd ed.). Routledge.

Sharma, E., Jacob, P., Dharmendra, A., Reddy, Y. J., Seshadri, S. P., Girimaji, S. C., & Vijaysagar, K. J. (2021). Preschool-onset OCD: A review of literature and clinical experience. *Bulletin of the Menninger Clinic, 85*(3), 298–315.

Shooka, A., Al-Haddad, M. K., & Raees, A. (1998). OCD in Bahrain: A phenomenological profile. *International Journal of Social Psychiatry, 44*(2), 147–154.

Skar, A. M. S., Ormhaug, S. M., & Jensen, T. K. (2019). Reported levels of upset in youth after routine trauma screening at mental health clinics. *JAMA Network Open, 2*(5), e194003–e194003.

Smith, P., Dalgleish, T., & Meiser-Stedman, R. (2019). Practitioner review: Posttraumatic stress disorder and its treatment in children and adolescents. *Journal of Child Psychology and Psychiatry, 60*(5), 500–515.

Smith, P., Perrin, S., Yule, W., & Clark, D. M. (2010). *Post traumatic stress disorder: Cognitive therapy with children and young people*. Routledge.

Solomon, R. M., & Shapiro, F. (2008). EMDR and the adaptive information processing model: Potential mechanisms of change. *Journal of EMDR Practice and Research, 2*(4), 315–325.

Soni, S., Poornima, C., & Ahamed, P. C. A. (2017). Understanding and management of caregivers' stress and burden of person with obsessive compulsive disorder. In B. V. Prasad (Ed.), *Chronic mental illness and the changing scope of intervention strategies, diagnosis, and treatment* (pp. 124–142). IGI Global.

Stack, A., & Lucyshyn, J. (2019). Autism spectrum disorder and the experience of traumatic events: Review of the current literature to inform modifications to a treatment model for children with autism. *Journal of Autism and Developmental Disorders, 49*(4), 1613–1625.

Stallard, P., & Smith, E. (2007). Appraisals and cognitive coping styles associated with chronic post-traumatic symptoms in child road traffic accident survivors. *Journal of Child Psychology and Psychiatry, 48*(2), 194–201.

Stavropoulos, K. K. M., Bolourian, Y., & Blacher, J. (2018). Differential diagnosis of autism spectrum disorder and post traumatic stress disorder: Two clinical cases. *Journal of Clinical Medicine, 7*(4), 71.

Stewart, E., Frank, H., Benito, K., Wellen, B., Herren, J., Skriner, L. C., & Whiteside, S. P. (2016). Exposure therapy practices and mechanism endorsement: A survey of specialty clinicians. *Professional Psychology: Research and Practice, 47*(4), 303–311.

Stewart, S. E., Geller, D. A., Jenike, M., Pauls, D., Shaw, D., Mullin, B., & Faraone, S. V. (2004). Long-term outcome of pediatric obsessive–compulsive disorder: A meta-analysis and qualitative review of the literature. *Acta Psychiatrica Scandinavica, 110*(1), 4–13.

Storch, E. A., McGuire, J. F., Wu, M. S., Hamblin, R., McIngvale, E., Cepeda, S. L., Schneider, S. C., Rufino, K. A., Rasmussen, S. A., Price, L. H., & Goodman, W. K. (2019). Development and psychometric evaluation of the children's Yale–Brown obsessive-compulsive scale second edition. *Journal of the American Academy of Child & Adolescent Psychiatry, 58*(1), 92–98.

Swedo, S. E., Rapoport, J. L., Leonard, H. L., & Lenane, M. (1989). Obsessive compulsive disorder in children and adolescents: Clinical phenomenology of 70 consecutive cases. *Archives of General Psychiatry, 46*, 335–341.

Tao, Y., Li, H., Li, L., Zhang, H., Xu, H., Zhang, H., Zou, S., Deng, F., Huang, L., Wang, Y., Wang, X., Tang, X., Fu, X., & Yin, L. (2022). Comparing the efficacy of pharmacological and psychological treatment, alone and in combination, in children and adolescents with obsessive-compulsive disorder: A network meta-analysis. *Journal of Psychiatric Research, 148*, 95–102.

Taylor, S. (2011). Early versus late onset obsessive–compulsive disorder: Evidence for distinct subtypes. *Clinical Psychology Review, 31*(7), 1083–1100.

Trickey, D., Siddaway, A. P., Meiser-Stedman, R., Serpell, L., & Field, A. P. (2012). A meta-analysis of risk factors for post-traumatic stress disorder in children and adolescents. *Clinical Psychology Review, 32*(2), 122–138.

Turner, C. (2018a). *OCD: Tools to help young people fight back!: A CBT manual for therapists*. Jessica Kingsley Publishers.

Turner, C. (2018b). *OCD: Tools to help you fight back!: A CBT workbook for young people*. Jessica Kingsley Publishers.

Turner, C., O'Gorman, B., Nair, A., & O'Kearney, R. (2018). Moderators and predictors of response to cognitive behaviour therapy for pediatric obsessive-compulsive disorder: A systematic review. *Psychiatry Research, 261*, 50–60.

Uher, R., Heyman, I., Turner, C. M., & Shafran, R. (2008). Self-, parent-report and interview measures of obsessive–compulsive disorder in children and adolescents. *Journal of Anxiety Disorders*, *22*(6), 979–990.

Van Grootheest, D. S., Cath, D. C., Beekman, A. T., & Boomsma, D. I. (2005). Twin studies on obsessive–compulsive disorder: A review. *Twin Research and Human Genetics*, *8*(5), 450–458.

Van Steensel, F. J., Bögels, S. M., & Perrin, S. (2011). Anxiety disorders in children and adolescents with autistic spectrum disorders: A meta-analysis. *Clinical Child and Family Psychology Review*, *14*, 302–317.

Veale, D., Freeston, M., Krebs, G., Heyman, I., & Salkovskis, P. (2009). Risk assessment and management in obsessive–compulsive disorder. *Advances in Psychiatric Treatment*, *15*(5), 332–343.

Veale, D., & Roberts, A. (2014). Obsessive-compulsive disorder. *BMJ*, *348*, g2183.

Verhaak, L. M., & De Haan, E. (2007). Cognitions in children with OCD: A pilot study for age specific relations with severity. *European Child & Adolescent Psychiatry*, *16*, 353–361.

Whiteside, S. P., Sim, L. A., Morrow, A. S., Farah, W. H., Hilliker, D. R., Murad, M. H., & Wang, Z. (2020). A meta-analysis to guide the enhancement of CBT for childhood anxiety: Exposure over anxiety management. *Clinical Child and Family Psychology Review*, *23*, 102–121.

Wewetzer, C., Jans, T., Müller, B., Neudörfl, A., Bücherl, U., Remschmidt, H., & Herpertz-Dahlmann, B. (2001). Long-term outcome and prognosis of obsessive–compulsive disorder with onset in childhood or adolescence. *European Child & Adolescent Psychiatry*, *10*, 37–46.

Williams, M. T., Farris, S. G., Turkheimer, E., Pinto, A., Ozanick, K., Franklin, M. E., Liebowitz, M., Simpson, H. B., & Foa, E. B. (2011). Myth of the pure obsessional type in obsessive–compulsive disorder. *Depression and Anxiety*, *28*(6), 495–500.

Williams, T., & Waite, P. (2009). Introduction to obsessive compulsive disorder. In P. Waite & T. Williams (Eds.), *Obsessive Compulsive Disorder* (pp. 13-30). Routledge.

Williamson, V., Hiller, R. M., Meiser-Stedman, R., Creswell, C., Dalgleish, T., Fearon, P., Goodall, B., McKinnon, A., Smith, P., Wright, I., & Halligan, S. L. (2018). The parent trauma response questionnaire (PTRQ): Development and preliminary validation. *European Journal of Psychotraumatology*, *9*(1), 1478583.

Wolters, L. H., Prins, P. J., Garst, G. J. A., Hogendoorn, S. M., Boer, F., Vervoort, L., & de Haan, E. (2019). Mediating mechanisms in cognitive behavioral therapy for childhood OCD: The role of dysfunctional beliefs. *Child Psychiatry & Human Development*, *50*, 173–185.

World Health Organization. (2013). *Guidelines for the management of conditions specifically related to stress*. WHO.

World Health Organization. (2022). *ICD-11: International classification of diseases* (11th revision). *WHO.* https://icd.who.int/

Zandt, F., Prior, M., & Kyrios, M. (2009). Similarities and differences between children and adolescents with autism spectrum disorder and those with obsessive compulsive disorder: Executive functioning and repetitive behaviour. *Autism*, *13*(1), 43–57.

15

Eating Difficulties and Disorders

Tara Porter

15.1 Introduction

Working with children and young people (CYP) with eating disorders in the UK seems to be a real 'marmite' area of practice: practitioners love it or hate it, with two unique aspects of the work that either attract or repel potential practitioners. The first challenge is that CYP with eating disorders largely don't want to change; it is an ego-syntonic disorder. Patients are metaphorically dragged to clinic by worried parents, family or friends, and a big chunk of the work is around motivation and engagement. Second, it is a mental disorder with a physical component, and these intertwine and exacerbate each other as the CYP spirals into the disorder. Consequently, in treatment it is often difficult to see where the physical aspects end and the mental aspects begin. Potential practitioners may find these two things challenging and fascinating, or off putting.

The CYP's reluctance to change and the physical component also contribute to eating disorders being a potentially extremely serious illness, with long-term consequences for the child, their family and society. For example, the CYP with anorexia can do permanent damage to their body, particularly in relation to their bone health, putting them at risk of osteoporosis in their future life. For the CYP with bulimia, tooth decay, caused by the acid in the stomach, can be a long-term consequence. For both disorders, heart complications can result. In the long term, anorexia has the highest mortality rate of any psychiatric disorder, caused through both the physical damage and the suicide risk. Thus, there exists a high financial cost to society with lengthy inpatient admissions necessary for a substantial minority of CYP and, if untreated, long-term physical consequences into adulthood. This was recognised by NHS England in 2015 as they put CYP with eating disorders as part of the first wave of Transformation Funding (NHS England, 2015). There was evidence that outcomes are better for CYP in specialist teams (Gowers et al., 2010), so where they didn't exist already, specialist teams sitting separately to CAMHS were created in England, and a comprehensive national programme of team training was put in place.

This is an important chapter for all psychological practitioners, because even if it is an area you do not work in, it is important that you have enough information to recognise and refer on if necessary when working within other child mental health contexts.

Child Psychology: Pathways to Good Practice, First Edition.
Edited by Helen Pote, Anna Picciotto and Clare Norris.

15.2 Diagnosis and Formulation

Every edition of the Diagnostic and Statistical Manual (DSM) has increased the number of eating disorders categorised and changed the definition of those eating disorders. In DSM-1, published in 1952, there was only one type of eating disorder, anorexia. Bulimia was added in DSM-3, and at this stage, in the 1980s, eating disorders were a subcategory of disorders of childhood and adolescence. For the fifth edition in 2013 the number of different disorders was expanded to eight different conditions: pica (the eating of non-food items); rumination (repeated regurgitation of food); ARFID (avoidant restrictive food intake disorder); anorexia; bulimia; binge eating disorder (sometimes called BED), and OSFED (other specified feeding and eating disorder – a category that is largely used for anorexia and bulimia conditions that do not reach clinical threshold. This is sometimes also referred to as EDNOS which was used in DSM-IV). Eating disorders are no longer included as a subcategory of conditions of childhood but are a stand-alone category. However, it is worth noting that many eating disorders do have a strong developmental element: ARFID is largely a younger child's difficulty, and anorexia has the peak onset of 14–15 years old. The disorders of bulimia and binge eating tend to have an older onset. This chapter will not be covering pica, rumination disorders or ARFID. This reflects how services are generally divided, with these disorders linked to developmental delay, neurodiversity and parenting, whereas anorexia, bulimia, binge eating and OSFED are linked more by attitudes towards food, eating, weight and shape. Of course, this is not a perfect dichotomy and there is overlap between them which is largely beyond the scope of this chapter.

Eating disorders are prominently female illnesses – approximately 90% of patients in Eating Disorders CAMHS are girls. This in part may link to the tendency for girls to more frequently express distress through internalised channels, and boys by externalised means, and in part to a reluctance for boys to seek help or be recognised as needing help. However, it is also clear that the incidence of body dissatisfaction is linked to cultural attitudes and standards around women's bodies. Becker's seminal research in Fiji linked the exposure to Western standards of female beauty – that is, thinness – to the onset of eating disorders pathology (Becker et al., 2011). Renee Tiggemann's work has tracked this in relation to social media (e.g. Vandenbosch et al., 2022). Through a social constructionist lens, there is some evidence that restrictive eating disorders emerge more in countries that hold a thin ideal, whereas bulimic and binge disorders occur more frequently in countries that hold a curvier body shape as ideal (Hoek, 2016).

The categorisation of separate eating disorders can at best be seen as a work in progress, but at worst an inaccurate attempt to place overlapping problems into categories with arguable validity. It is a moot point whether these diagnoses have clinical significance except to provide a gatekeeper to services. Many anorexics over time, and especially in adulthood, develop bulimic symptoms; nearly all bulimic patients start each day with an anorexic mindset, that they will eat as little as possible for as long as possible, and they won't eat any 'unhealthy' food; many binge-eaters have attempted compensatory behaviours such as vomiting, and some, but for a physical inability to self-induce vomit, would be bulimic. Many binge eaters also spend time on strict, extreme diets. It is frequently the case in CYP eating disorders services (CYPEDS) that CYP who span two or more of the eating disorders, or morph between them at different times, are seen. The less-distinct OSFED category is useful for this reason.

Certainly, the key mentalities for anorexia, bulimia and often binge eating disorder are very similar, centring around a pre-occupation (an obsession if you like) with food, eating, weight and shape. It is this preoccupation that triggers strict dieting. A subproportion of these, because of pre-existing personality characteristics such as rigidity, control, perfectionism and a strong work ethic, go on to develop an anorexic-type disorder. However, for other CYP the body will respond to a strict diet with an overwhelming drive to eat, and binge eating can result. The binge eating, whether it is followed by compensatory behaviours such as vomiting, laxatives or extreme exercise, increases the preoccupation with food, eating, weight and shape, and typically the next day, the extreme diet starts again. A negative cycle is set up, best illustrated by Fairburn's transdiagnostic formulation of eating disorders (Figure 15.1, Fairburn et al., 2023).

Central to our understanding of this are some seminal experiments regarding the impact on a restrictive eating mindset on subsequent overeating. Dubbed the 'what the hell' experiments, Polivy and Herman (2020) showed that dieters tricked into breaking their diet would subsequently eat more than non-dieters or dieters who hadn't overeaten. In

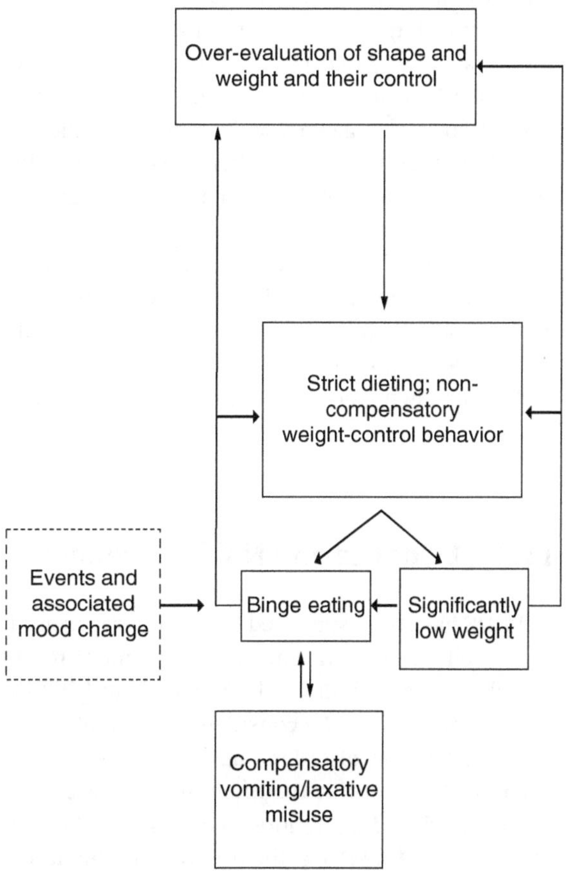

Figure 15.1 Fairburn's transdiagnostic formulation. Source: https://www.cbte.co/site/download/f2-5-transdiagnostic-cbt-e-formulation/?wpdmdl=652&masterkey=5c6fc28dc82bf.

contrast, non-dieters tend to eat more intuitively, tuning into their hunger and satiety cues, thus eating less if they'd eaten more earlier, and eat more if they'd eaten less earlier. This gives an insight to the dieting mindset: dieters are taking cognitive control over what is a biological drive, to eat, and trying to ignore their biological cues. However, if the biological drive overwhelms cognitive control, the dieter tends to think they have 'failed' by breaking the dieting rules, and then think 'what the hell, I've ruined dieting for today, I may as well eat as much as I like', which can lead to overeating and binge eating. The dieting industry exacerbates this through peddling ideas full of inconsistencies and often unproven, such as an arbitrary calorie cut off for a day; or foods being banned or allowed. These warp people's cognitions about food and eating, which contributes to an obesogenic society providing the setting for cognitions for eating disorders.

The triad of anorexia, bulimia and binge eating also share a similarity in that they are often a solution to a problem for a CYP. That is the CYP feels distress (anxiety, depression, loneliness, desperation), and for some the diet or the binge eating temporarily numbs or relieves this distress. Or starting a diet gives a CYP an illusion of control when they are feeling out of control or distracts them from their worries and concerns. For the perfectionists, they have a sense of being successful or the best at something. Binge eating and vomiting can generate a feeling of release from the pressure of life.

The Covid-19 pandemic of 2020–2022 has seen a huge increase of CYP using food, eating, weight and shape to manage their distress. At the time of writing there is not a definitive answer as to why that is, but in the longer term we might hope that it will increase our understanding of the mechanisms of onset. As with all aspects of mental health, it is unlikely to be a single factor. Practitioners believe that CYP have used food and weight as something they can control when the world is feeling out of control. During the lockdowns there was a huge emphasis on maintaining physical exercise, and some young people took on a lockdown project to finally go on a diet or get fit in this context. There also seemed to be a group of young people who, pre-pandemic, were already suffering with anxiety, depression, deliberate self-harm and so forth, whose access to support such as CAMHS, their friends, their social lives or activities was limited, and who developed a food and eating obsession in the absence of their normal coping mechanisms. In addition, in some cases, lockdown exacerbated pre-existing familial conflicts adding an additional source of stress.

15.3 Evidence and NICE Guidelines

CYPEDS have been subjected to two different sets of National Institute for Health and Clinical Excellence (NICE) guidelines, the more recent being in 2017. The NICE guidelines consider anorexia, bulimia, binge eating and OSFED under the same guidelines, with pica, rumination and ARFID considered separately. They focus on CYP in the same document with adult eating disorders, despite the treatment recommendations being significantly different. The first-line treatment for CYP is eating disorder focused family therapy, commonly called FT-ED, or more specifically FT-AN or FT-BN (family therapy with respectively anorexia or bulimia), but the first-line treatment for adults is individual therapy.

Of course, this is a false dichotomy, and this difference emerges from the way research and services are organised. A young adult, who is still at school or university and living with their parents, with a good relationship with them, is likely to benefit more from a family-based approach. Conversely, some child–parent relationships break down in early teens, and some parents have little of the warm authority that is necessary in a FT-ED approach. Similarly, some parents are unable or unwilling to put in the hours of therapy, or support or supervision of meals necessary for FT-ED to be successful. Thus, FT-ED should be offered but individual therapy may be necessary if this is unsuccessful, or in conjunction with the family work.

FT-ED focuses first and foremost on establishing good eating habits, and for those young people with anorexia this also involves weight restoration. Many CYP and their families are surprised that the focus is so much on food and eating, but as practitioners we are all too aware that without regular nutrition in both bulimia and anorexia, and, in addition, being at a healthy weight for our anorexic patients, psychological therapy is rarely successful. When the brain is starving, it is rarely able to take a meta-view or reflective position on the self that individual therapy requires. It finds it difficult to focus on anything but food.

NICE guidelines state that the standard of evidence is low by their medical, scientific standards, with only a few randomised control trials (RCTs) in this area. As with other areas of psychological practice, it is difficult to establish the RCTs necessary not least due to the difficulties highlighted around diagnoses and in terms of treatment establishing a standard treatment protocol whilst allowing for the infinite variation a complex family system presents with.

There are fewer RCTs for bulimia than there are for anorexia, but there is a particular paucity of evidence for binge eating. The NICE guidance is to follow the same treatments as adults, but the author is not aware of any evidence showing the success of these treatments with CYP (see Table 15.1).

Table 15.1 NICE guidelines for eating disorders.

	NICE guidelines
Anorexia	• Consider anorexia-nervosa-focused family therapy for children and young people (FT-AN), delivered as single-family therapy or a combination of single- and multifamily therapy. • If FT-AN is unacceptable, contraindicated or ineffective for children or young people with anorexia nervosa, consider individual CBT-ED or adolescent-focused psychotherapy for anorexia nervosa (AFP-AN).
Bulimia	• Offer bulimia-nervosa-focused family therapy (FT-BN) to CYP with bulimia nervosa • If FT-BN is unacceptable, contraindicated, or ineffective, consider individual eating-disorder-focused cognitive behavioural therapy (CBT-ED) for children and young people with bulimia nervosa.
Binge eating	• For children and young people with binge eating disorder, offer the same treatments recommended for adults with binge eating disorder (guided self-help in the first instance and eating disorder CBT-ED (group and then individual))

Source: NICE (2017, updated 2020)

15.4 Identification of Eating Disorders in Primary Care and Generic CAMHS

It is a tricky skill for a generic mental health practitioner to spot an eating disorder in a young person and to know when to refer on. On the one hand, dieting, inconsistent eating (e.g. skipping lunch but eating lots of biscuits when you get in from school, or doing a late night toast run), and body dissatisfaction are ubiquitous amongst teenage girls. On the other hand, early identification is linked with the best long-term outcome. CYPEDS are also mindful of not bringing those flirting with weight loss into a setting where they could gain 'thinspiration' from the waiting room: weight-loss can be a competitive business amongst the susceptible.

It should also be remembered by the generic practitioner that food and eating changes are linked to many other mental health disorders: many young people stop eating because they are depressed, anxious or in deep trauma. These conditions can cause them to lose their appetite and then find that hunger holds a secondary gain in that it is all-encompassing and numbs emotion. In these cases, it is not clear cut whether they should be treated in generic CAMHS or CYPEDS. One view is that, if possible, they should have the opportunity to make links in their local CAMHS with specialised consultation for the eating component. One needs to ask which came first, the dieting/weight loss or the low mood, as this can give a clue about the best treatment pathway. Having said that, for some CYP their food restriction is so severe, that whatever the pathway into it (i.e. whether via dieting or mood disorder) they are best treated in a specialist team with knowledge about the physical side effects of starvation.

How to distinguish? A young person with a weight-related eating disorder is typically obsessed with food, eating, weight and shape. It takes up about two-thirds of their waking brain space, with the other third often reserved for academic work. They think about these issues instead of all the other normal pre-occupations of adolescent life for example, socialising, sexuality, hobbies and interests. They show severe accommodations to eating normally such as hiding food and lying, and they often think they are too big. Many CYP with the weight-loss associated with other mental health issues will recognise that they have got too thin and be motivated to gain weight. They often cite nausea as the reason not to eat, which is probably secondary both to reduced intake and to anxiety.

Of course, a word of caution: CYP with eating disorders will often lie to protect their illness or worse, simply have no insight, having convinced themselves that this is just how they prefer to eat and they are not hungry. But it is also true that services see some CYP who have serious medical conditions that cause weight loss and who have not been believed about their physical symptoms. Primary health practitioners have to be careful not to just assume that a teenager with weight loss has an eating disorder and then not fully investigate physical causality.

If practitioners are not sure, making a telephone call to local CYPEDS who will probably offer a telephone consultation with duty staff is recommended. They may be able to suggest what extra information should be collected to help identify the correct pathway.

15.5 Triage and Assessment

In the NHS in England since 2017, eating disorders assessments have been subject to referral to treatment 'key performance indicators' (KPIs): a measure of the time between the service receiving the referral and treatment starting. These are for emergency patients to be seen within 24 hours, urgent patients within 7 days and routine patients seen within 28 days. Urgency is determined by the clinical team based on physical health risk, using the MARSIPAN guidance (Management of really sick patients under 18 with anorexia nervosa; College of Psychiatrists, 2014). Many services that were previously achieving this standard are no longer meeting these requirements, as demand has doubled during the Covid-19 pandemic.

Other parts of the UK have not yet set baseline standards. Scotland has recently published their own evidence-based clinical guidelines (Scottish Intercollegiate Guidelines Network, 2022). In Wales, BEAT (the eating disorders charity) conducted research into waiting times and called for the Welsh Government to implement an access-and-waiting-times model back in 2017, and has recently followed up on this call, by publishing a scathing report into the lack of improvements in services (Kelly & Whitfield, 2017). Northern Ireland is working towards trying to see CYP within 3 months for generic CAMHS, and doesn't set any specific standards for eating disorders.

Given the complex physical and mental health components, the interaction between them, and the plethora of differential diagnoses, assessment of a CYP with an eating disorder should be through a multidisciplinary team (MDT). Depression, anxiety and suicidality can all present with loss of appetite, and mental health professionals are perhaps skilled at untangling this. However, serious physical illnesses such as Crohn's disease and Coeliac's disease can be associated with weight loss. Unexplained vomiting can be a side effect of a brain tumour as well as bulimia. It is too easy to assume weight and shape concerns in a teenage girl, where discontentment with body image is normal in society, but ruling out other rare physical explanations of symptoms are crucial. Rather more routinely, it is necessary to check out blood pressure and heart rate, as well as weight and height.

Unfortunately, since the Covid-19 crisis, the enormous increase in referrals has meant that the routine MDT assessment has been scaled back to a single professional. This is likely to lead to misdiagnosis and missed diagnoses.

Assessment will nearly always include a CYP and their parents, as it is often the parents who are more concerned than the CYP about the lack of food intake and weight loss, and it is often here that we start the assessment. CYPEDS practitioners will invite all views about what the problem is, and its onset and course. With an attitude of warmth and curiosity, the practitioner will ask about food intake yesterday, and any nausea, vomiting, exercise and laxative use. As in any mental illness assessment, the practitioner will want to understand the context of the problem, including family dynamics, school and friendship issues.

Crucially, for a diagnosis of an eating disorder to be made cognitions about weight, shape, food and eating need to be assessed. This is perhaps the most skilled part of the assessment as whilst some CYP will willingly share their worries about food, eating, weight and shape, many others don't want to. The reasons for this vary: some CYP have no insight into their own worries and have justified their 'lack of appetite' or 'only liking' certain types of food. Others are reluctant to talk about their thoughts out loud as they are very protective of the eating disorder, and don't want to admit to it for fear it will be taken from them or they don't want to 'lose face'. Young people have often been battling with their parents about whether or not they have an eating disorder, and sometimes the CYP is scared or reluctant to be honest about it. It often involves a practitioner using tact, warmth and empathy to second-guess what maybe going on internally for the young person, and to create an environment where they feel understood or safe to open up. Sometimes this part of the assessment is best done away from parents and can be part of a chat had when physical assessment takes place.

A significant subgroup of anorexic patients have undiagnosed Autistic Spectrum Disorder (ASD), and this should be born in mind. Girls with ASD often 'mask' their symptoms by copying others. As body dissatisfaction and dieting are so normal amongst teenage girls, the CYP with ASD begins copying this in teenage years. This can have a secondary gain of reducing feeling for the CYP, and over time become part of a special interest or obsession. Accurately assessing this is extremely complex as most weight-restricted anorexic patients will also present with a perseverative and obsessive quality. Questions about early history may help distinguish between the two, but sometimes it is only possible once weight restoration has happened.

15.6 Treatment

15.6.1 Engagement in Treatment and Psychoeducation

Given the urgency of the eating disorder, the treatment often starts at the assessment. Many teams will take a break during the assessment, determine their diagnosis and formulation, before meeting again with the family to feedback, and then start the treatment process. The importance of treatment starting is reflected in the structuring of the KPI requirement of NHS England, that is, the waiting time 'clock' only stops on treatment starting. However, this requirement only reflects what is good practice.

The first stage of treatment for anorexia, bulimia and binge eating should involve establishing a regular eating pattern, and with anorexia on establishing weight gain. FT-ED involves engaging the parents in taking an active role in those goals and engaging a CYP in accepting that help. This is sometimes described as parents taking responsibility or control for the food and eating. If a CYP can accept this, it relieves them of the guilt of eating, as the eating becomes someone else's 'fault'. Whilst still often being torturously difficult and painful, it tends to relieve the eating disorder 'voice' in the CYP's head of the blame element of eating.

The anorectic voice is an interesting phenomenon, which places anorexia somewhere in the middle on the old continuum of psychotic or neurotic illness. Not all patients experience it, and many recognise it as a warped, extreme version of their own views. However, many experience as somewhat other, a bullying, coercive 'best friend' in their head.

Having an understanding of and empathy for this, is crucial at this moment of getting the CYP's buy-in to treatment. Being able to connect to their true self and persuade them to join you in the fight against this voice can be a profound moment. For this to happen the CYP needs to be heard, understood and held by the assessing practitioner, and trust in their expertise to help them.

It often involves a large amount of psychoeducation about the psychological impact of starvation: thinking about the impact of giving their family pet half the amount of food can be a helpful analogy. The CYP is able to reflect that their pet would lose their joie de vivre, would stop wagging their tail or chasing squirrels. The CYPED practitioner will often encourage patients to look at Ancell Keyes' seminal Minnesota Studies (Keyes et al., 1950), into the effect of starvation. This is research that was started at the end of World War II where healthy male volunteers had their calorie intake reduced by approximately a half, and their body weight reduced by about a quarter. These studies show that many of the physical and psychological symptoms that co-exist with an eating disorder are actually caused by starvation, such as becoming obsessed with food, as Keyes' participants bought food for strangers in the street and collected cookbooks. They developed strange habits about food for example, with the seasoning of food or the way they ate. They became weak, cold, withdrawn from usual interests and any sort of sexual or romantic relationships.

Referring twenty-first-century, mainly young, women to these grainy photos from two generations ago, can be quite powerful. The penny begins to drop for them and their parents about a causal relationship between their food restriction and some of their other psychological and physical symptoms.

For bulimic patients, co-creating a formulation is crucial; specifically making the link that it is the restrictive eating that drives the binges. It is also crucial for the CYP to feel that the practitioner is joining them with their problem, which is generally the binge eating and not the restriction, and to them help them understand that is only through stopping the restriction that the binge eating will also stop. The bulimic or binge-eating patient is often attracted by the anorectic position, and deeply envious of their capacity to restrict their eating. At heart the bulimic patient often wishes to be a better restrictive eater and through the formulation practitioners help them see this is not an option, and that anorexia often results in binge eating at some point (Eddy et al., 2008).

The triune model of the brain can be helpful in this discussion: a three-layer model, with a core brain at the centre similar to an animal's; a limbic middle centre and a top layer cortical brain involving thinking, planning and language. The practitioner may reflect on how the decision to diet can be made in the top layer, but that the core brain doesn't recognise what is going on and thinks the CYP is in a famine. In these circumstances, the core brain will effectively push very hard to take control, in the same way as it would if their cortical brain decided not to pee or sleep. Eventually animalistic instincts would take control.

15.6.2 Psychoeducation and Support Groups for Parents

Parents are key to the treatment approach, taking a major role in the feeding of their CYP. Parent groups can allow for the maximum amount of information to be offered in a short amount of time. It also allows parents to receive peer support and a sense of camaraderie that they are 'not in this alone'. As in all groups, hearing techniques and experiences from peers (in this case other parents) tends to be more powerful than from seasoned professionals.

There is not a standard protocol for parents' groups but they tend to cover: introduction to eating disorders and the team they are working with; dietetic advice about meal plans and serving sizes; information about supporting and supervising meals, such as length of meals and snacks; the sorts of things CYP find helpful to hear; information about cycles of change and motivational interviewing techniques that they can incorporate into supporting their CYP; and common parental responses to an eating disorder and traps to avoid falling into, which are often referred to as the animal analogies in eating disorder work (Treasure et al., 2016); behavioural and problem-solving principles and self-care for the parents.

15.6.3 FT-ED

Family therapy for eating disorders originated from practitioners working in the Maudsley Hospital in South London led by Christopher Dare, who completed the first RCT into FT-ED (Dare et al., 1990). The work continued at the Maudsley under Ivan Eisler and colleagues (Eisler & Simic, 2012), but a second group split off, James Lock and Daniel LeGrange, and led clinics and published research in California (Lock & Le Grange, 2013). Both groups have completed further RCTs of their treatment approaches and demonstrate the best evidence for a first approach of treatment in anorexia and bulimia, and there have been long-term follow ups in some anorexia studies.

Whilst both these approaches grew out of systemic psychotherapy roots, and share common themes and ideas, over the years differences emerged. The different socioeconomic and cultural differences in the UK and United States have possibly contributed to the way common ideas have developed in practice: in the United States it seems that CYP have fewer rights than their peers in the UK and are more often treated under parental authority. Most treatment in the United States is subject to limits from medical insurance, which is likely to have shaped treatments into a more directive model.

Confusingly, both the UK and US approaches continued to be called the Maudsley approach for many years, although the US approach is now generally referred to as FBT (family-based treatment) and in the UK practitioners tend towards the NICE language of FT-AN and FT-BN. The differences between the two approaches are perhaps less important than the similarities when considering what causes the therapeutic change. Both are staged approaches, with the parental authority over food and eating enhanced in the early stages, which allows weight restoration to occur, and separate subsequent stages where other psychological or systemic difficulties for the CYP and their family are addressed, and where a CYP is encouraged to take over control of their eating and food in a developmentally appropriate way again.

It is also of note that, whilst based on the systemic tradition of treating the family,[1] and borrowing many systemic and narrative techniques, such as externalising the problem, FT-ED also borrows from cognitive and behavioural traditions, as well as neurobiology. The original proponents are largely not systemic psychotherapists, and the techniques are designed to be used by a MDT staff group.

For both FT-AN and FT-BN, typically each session will begin with seeing the parents and patient to hear how eating has gone over the past week. It can be extremely helpful if the family or young person completes a food diary of what has been offered, eaten and significant internal or external events around the food and meals. This is helpful as a practitioner

1 In systemic psychotherapy often the family is seen as a whole with all siblings present, and that continues in FBT. More typically in the UK with FT-ED just the parents and CYP are included.

can quickly scan these and get a lot of relatively accurate information very quickly. Family memory can be warped by recent events or by strong emotions (e.g. successes early in the week forgotten, as more recent days were difficult).

In FT-AN, the goal is to help the family restore the CYP's weight, so an accurate report of how much has been eaten can be crucial in recommending the optimal amount of food. It is worth saying that most families tend to underestimate how much food and how regularly a CYP needs to eat in order to gain weight. This is often warped as a CYP may 'not like' food with a higher calorie density, such as sweet or fatty foods, or even any carbohydrate, and prefer only vegetable-based foods. These are so low in calories that it can feel that the CYP is eating all day and large portions but are unlikely to gain weight on such a diet.

In FT-BN, early sessions involve an emphasis on regular eating. Engagement with a bulimic CYP is made through working on what they see is the problem, which is the binge eating. However, this is unlikely to change if the CYP continues to try to restrict their eating either in time (i.e. trying to go long periods without meals) or in food types (i.e. banning certain food types). Developing the formulation so that they make the connection between restriction and bingeing is key, and then returning to this over and over, as they find it incredibly difficult to give up the dream of dieting, since they are generally as desperate as the anorexic patients to lose weight.

At some point in the session the CYP should be weighed. Whether the CYP should know their weight is a contentious point, and whilst typically they may have been weighing themselves daily or several times a day before the treatment started, they are often reluctant to know their weight as it begins to go up. If the CYP knows, this is exposure to facing the fear that their weight has to go up. In addition, CYP with anorexia and bulimia almost invariably overestimate how much weight they will gain by eating regularly: their fear of weight gain is far worse than the reality. Generally, the only times there is a surprise jump in weight is because a CYP is binge eating. However, engagement with a CYP is so crucial at this time, that sometimes the psychological practitioner has to compromise and accept that the CYP doesn't know their weight. It is best, in any case, not to get drawn into reading too much into any single weight, as this replicates the mindset of the anorexic obsessing about short-term changes in weight when these are rarely significant. In treatment, practitioners are looking for an upwards trajectory, which requires a minimum of three data points.

The stance of the psychological practitioner is to join with the family against the eating disorder, externalising the eating disorder from the CYP. In the US FBT model, this more takes the form of strengthening the parental subsystem to take control over the situation; whereas in the UK, with its higher emphasis on user involvement, this would more involve motivational interviewing approaches to strengthen the CYP's resolve to fight the eating disorder with the support of their parents, or other key adults in the CYP's life.

Whilst discussing the weight trajectory, the written and verbal reports of the eating and any additional information about compensatory behaviours such as vomiting or laxatives, the psychological practitioner will be modelling the techniques of calm curiosity to the family. The aim is to invoke the family's own coping strategies to the eating disorder: what has worked and not worked so well for the family during the previous week; and what the family think the next steps are. In US FBT they use the therapeutic technique of intensifying the seriousness of the problem if parents fail to take up their responsibility, for example, saying 'your parents will want to be able to reassure themselves, if you die from AN, that they have done everything possible to save your life'. It leads one to wonder if this type of extreme statement would work outside the context of a world-renowned expert/clinic. One fears in an NHS clinic it may seem blaming or over-dramatic.

The approach in the UK tends to be rather more pragmatic, and in the UK Maudsley manual, Eisler et al. (2012) 'suggest options and examples of what other families have done'. A MDT might draw on their own discipline expertise in problem solving, which allows multiple therapeutic and clinical approaches to be introduced, for example, applied behavioural analysis to understand the function of the CYP's behaviour and the impact of parent behaviour on it; motivational interviewing to help the CYP see the pros and cons to their own behaviour; psycho- and biological education about the impact of starvation; and circular questions to raise different ideas and points of view within the family. The practitioner will avoid getting drawn into arguments with the eating disorder (e.g. when the CYP tries to negotiate a smaller portion size) and instead may reflect on the process, e.g. 'I can see your eating disorder is really fighting back and trying to take charge.').

A family meal, where the psychological practitioners join the family at their own home, or the family are encouraged to bring a snack or meal into the clinic, is recommended. This can serve as an assessment or treatment intervention for example, to see how the parents manage the eating disorder or to model meal support. It is helpful to clarify the purpose before this is attempted to avoid confusion about who should do what: 'I know it's hard but try to act just as you might at home as I want to understand what is going on' or 'I will lead on this meal and you can just observe me. See if I do anything which helps or doesn't help.'

NICE recommends that family-based approaches last for 1 year comprising 18 to 20 sessions, probably based on RCT results. However, in practice in clinic some CYP have mild eating disorders, which have been caught early, and quickly resolve. Others have more serious conditions that will require a lot more than 20 sessions.

Later in the treatment, once regular eating (BN) or weight restoration (AN) has occurred, the psychological practitioner will turn their attention to the other psychological or systemic concerns. The eating disorder is often a solution to a problem for the CYP. The psychological practitioner often expresses or draws this out as the tip of the iceberg: the bit of the iceberg (problem) that is above the water. Once the tip/eating disorder is removed, other issues rise above the water line. There is no one problem that underlies eating disorders, although there are some more common issues. For example, many anorexic patients suffer with more pervasive perfectionism, which creates and results from high anxiety about performance and being 'good' in all areas of their life. Similarly, many seem to suffer with social anxiety and are obsessed with others' judgments of them. Some CYP find it difficult to negotiate developmental change: puberty, sexual attraction, and separation and individuation from their parents. Sometimes these factors interlink, so a CYP has always been a 'good girl', getting full marks in primary school and never arguing with her parents. As she moves through the middle teenage years, it becomes impossible to sustain 100% achievement academically, and not arguing with your parents prevents normal teenage separation for example, meeting with your friends rather than a family event. The eating disorder can provide a solution to these problems, which now needs to be addressed in the family work or individual therapy. To quote from a recovered patient who took part in the National Training focus group 'you won't be getting your old child back … my mum definitely struggled with how sassy I've become' (Walter, 2017).

For the bulimic patient, once regular eating is established and the dream of dieting has gone, they may find that they still enter the binge–vomit cycle occasionally. The later stages of work tend to look at the events and moods that trigger this, both within the family and in the individual. The work may turn to emotional regulation as the CYP tries to give up their coping mechanism of dysregulated eating and vomiting.

15.6.4 Individual Work

Individual work is cited in NICE guidelines when FT-ED is unacceptable or hasn't worked. It is certainly worth considering the appropriateness of FT approaches for an older and independent teen. When individual work is the only treatment being offered this tends to be either CBT-ED or individual adolescent-focused psychotherapy for anorexia nervosa (AFP-AN). NICE suggests these are longer treatments than FT-ED, running to 40 sessions. The former, CBT-ED, is well established in adult work as a transdiagnostic approach to AN and BN, focusing on: establishing regular eating; addressing dietary restraint; addressing body image concerns (e.g. mirror use; body checking); and how mood and events impact on eating. Recent research has suggested that individual CBT can be as successful as family therapy, but tends to take longer (Le Grange et al., 2020). In AFP-AN, the focus is on how the CYP is using eating to solve interpersonal stress and distress, and to address issues of identity.

Rather than being a stand-alone separate treatment, individual work often follows family work either with the same psychological practitioner (but the parents not attending as regularly or at all) or with a new practitioner, particularly when co-morbidities emerge that seem more suitable for an individual space. Other times there are aspects of the eating disorder that are unresolved and the CYP wishes to discuss them alone rather than in the family situation for example, body image issues.

15.6.5 Day-patient and Inpatient Treatment Models

If a young person is unresponsive to treatment and continues to lose weight or self-induced vomiting is extreme, day-patient or inpatient models of care may be considered. Day-patient models vary, some involving therapeutic groups whilst others focus more on providing FT-AN in a more intensive setting. Initially the former may be intuitively considered better than the latter, but with anorexia being such a competitive disorder, the disadvantages of group work always need to be considered. Recent service evaluation from the author's own unit highlighted the benefits of young people not spending time together but focusing on their eating with their families (Porter et al., 2022).

Inpatient treatment is now used as a last resort and often in conjunction with detention under the Mental Health Act. In the past, when it was used for milder cases, research indicated that specialist outpatient care was the recommended treatment option in terms of treatment adherence and outcome, with a stepped care approach of inpatient care being used when patients are unresponsive to outpatient care (Gowers et al., 2010).

15.7 Views and Voices of CYP

How CYP's voices are heard is a dilemma at the heart of eating disorder treatment because most CYP are at best ambivalent about treatment and at worst not consenting at all. The therapeutic practitioner needs to be constantly reflecting on the CYP's consent in order to provide an ethical treatment. Of course, a CYP's motivation and engagement in treatment will vary, and whilst a skilled psychological practitioner can often establish some mutually agreeable goal-based outcomes in the assessment appointment, when the seriousness of the medical concerns and the diagnosis are first discussed, it is often the case that the CYP's engagement will wane whilst they are sitting down to eat six times a day over the forthcoming weeks.

This ambivalence needs to be addressed in therapy, and the CYP encouraged to verbalise their mixed feelings. These feelings can be acknowledged, empathised with, heard and supported, whilst the team and parents still hold a line that, feelings or no feelings, everyone needs adequate nutrition. Natural and logical consequences result from not eating. For example, if a CYP has physical consequences of not eating it may not be safe for them to attend school or social events. They may need to attend to the clinic more, or receive day patient treatment, naso-gastric feeding tubes, or in the most severe cases, inpatient treatment.

With any of these consequences there is a thin line between, on the one hand, letting CYP know about the consequences of not eating and threatening them or depriving them of their liberty on the other. For example, a CYP has a universal human right to an education, however, a CYP may not be safe to go to school if they are dizzy or fainting, or unable to take adequate nutrition or water, and a school should be informed if a particular CYP is unsafe in school. Does a parent have the right to stop a 16-year-old going out for a walk? Generally, not. Does a parent have a safeguarding responsibility if they know that 16-year-old is physically weak, hasn't eaten and is likely to walk for miles as fast as possible? Probably, yes. These are not clear issues; the word 'leverage' is used in the eating disorder literature to discuss them (Tan et al., 2010).

In these more serious cases, when deprivation of liberty issues arise regularly, the Mental Health Act can be evoked to provide clarity, and this protects the CYP's rights as well as the team's responsibilities. In the recent past, services were more willing to work in 'shades of grey' where leverage was used to persuade a CYP into a particular treatment, or they were treated, if under 16, with parental consent only. For example, if a CYP had been saying no to a particular NG tube feed when the tube was already inserted, but was not actively fighting it, the feed may have gone ahead with a young person's hand being held both for emotional support and to gently prevent them stopping the feed. Nowadays, CAMHS teams would usually look for the protection of the law, through the Mental Health Act, to provide clarity for themselves and a CYP in such a situation.

An MDT has an important role in these issues. Psychiatrists are given enormous power by the law in relation to issues of deprivation of liberty. Good psychiatric practice should involve thorough an MDT discussion to think these issues through, and good MDT working should be able to discuss concerns and, if necessary, challenge that power. The CYP's rights need to be represented in decision making.

However, perhaps most importantly, Tan et al. (2010) highlighted how important the therapeutic relationship is for a young person in accepting treatment – they are less likely to consider a treatment coercive when they recognise the practitioners are making it in their best interests.

In thinking about these issues, feedback given to CAMHS from a service-user group of young adults treated for eating disorders as CYP may be helpful: 'early on in your recovery, you should definitely not be allowed to make decisions on your recovery, because that will just go absolutely terribly so in the early stages when you are too ill to make any decisions, the best thing to do is … we came up with a phrase of transparency … so when the therapist … or anyone are making decisions about your treatment to be able to … listen in and to be able to hear the reasoning behind the decision as because then it combats the anxiety of why people are making these decisions … they know what they are doing' (Walter, 2017). Many of the issues of treatment are illustrated in the clinical example in Box 15.1.

Box 15.1 Clinical example: Chloe

Chloe's referral into the specialist eating disorder service arrived in mid-September from her GP. Her parents reported to be shocked at how much weight she had lost, having seen Chloe in a swimming costume for the first time for ages on their summer holidays. She was 14.

Chloe's Mum received a triage phone call that day and the practitioner heard how they had initially been so pleased when Chloe had been 'eating healthily' and being taking an interest in running during lockdown, but they hadn't realised it had gone so far. They also realised how infrequently in the past few months they'd actually seen her eat. Chloe had always been at a friend's, or eaten later (or earlier), and got up too late for breakfast. When they'd spoken to Chloe about eating more, she said yes of course she would, it wasn't a big deal, but then had often seemed to have an excuse for a meal: a tummy ache, nausea, or that she didn't like things. They were now beside themselves with worry, but if they tried to insist on her eating, it often ended in a row. This wasn't like their Chloe, 'she's always been such as good girl': she was the oldest of three girls, and her parents said she'd always set such a good example to her sisters. Chloe's parents were directed to self-help resources as they waited for a first assessment, and encouraged to hold the expectation that Chloe ate at least three meals and two snacks a day.

In the clinic, a couple of months later, Chloe met the MDT. She had continued to lose weight. Her periods had stopped, she was wearing multiple jumpers and she had light lanugo hair on her body. Her parents had diligently taken the advice from triage and Chloe was now at least eating regularly, however, the number of foods she liked or didn't make her feel sick, had decreased. She was largely vegan, although a year previously she had eaten meat. Sometimes when her Mum got really upset, she would eat some white fish to placate her. She was sugar-free and found carbs 'really hard'. She had persuaded her parents into all sorts of carb substitutes such as cauliflower rice or spiralised vegetables.

(Continued)

Box 15.1 (Continued)

The rows with her parents since triage had moved Chloe to a point where she knew there was a problem. She reassured the team that she was much better now, as she was eating regularly, but when queried about the continued weight loss, she wasn't sure, because she was eating 'all the time'. Her parents too seem flummoxed by the downward trajectory, but it became apparent that Chloe was eating very few calories, with a diet of largely vegetables. It also wasn't clear whether Chloe was eating anything at school: she took a packed lunch but no-one supervised her eating it. The team encouraged Chloe to be open about whether she hid food, exercised excessively or vomited. She was asked about calorie or step counting apps, and thinspiration on social media. Chloe denied vomiting vehemently, and her parents confirmed that she had always hated being sick. Gently exploring a bit more what she did on her phone, it emerged that she was both counting calories and steps. Despite the regular meals and snacks she estimated that she was eating 1200 calories a day, but this was 'too much' and she thought she'd 'get fat'. Her Dad said 'Oh, Chloe.'

After a short break in the assessment for the MDT to confer, the diagnosis of anorexia was fed back to the family, and by that point it was not a surprise to them. It was explained to Chloe that a lot of the changes she was experiencing were probably due to chronic starvation, for example: her body was struggling to keep itself warm and to emotionally regulate. Crucially, it was explained how starvation itself creates an obsession with food and eating, and that obsession was being channelled into dieting. Chloe was encouraged to work with the service, and let her parents take charge of her eating, that they would be supported and wouldn't let her 'get fat', but that she urgently needed to gain weight. Chloe tearfully and silently nodded her head. The practitioner thanked her for being so brave and acknowledged that it wasn't going to be easy.

It was then explained how anorexia could often be a war of attrition, with Chloe having worn her parents down with her food refusal, so that now her parents had normalised providing a smaller range of foods, because they were so scared that she wasn't going to eat anything. A return to 'normal' food was prescribed, as without this it was unlikely that Chloe would gain weight. The family were asked to reintroduce immediately carbs, proteins and normal foods the family would eat. Chloe sat up in shock, and turned to her Mum and Dad appealingly, 'I can't do that' she said. The practitioner then handed her parents a meal plan, and Chloe was reassured 'its ok; we're going to have a think about what you can do'. Over the next 30 minutes her parents were encouraged to claim back some of their expectations, that Chloe would have normal family meals such as fish fingers, pasta with tomato sauce and curry with rice, but they wouldn't insist on chocolate bars and cake. There was also the expectation that she needed to be supported or supervised for lunch and morning snack at school, and the parents went away to talk about how this could be facilitated. Chloe was also asked to stop doing PE at school and all other exercise.

The following months were up and down. Chloe struggled with the new expectations, and often refused to eat completely. There were slammed doors and arguments, and her parents were rightly concerned about the impact on her little sisters. Her family were encouraged to stay calm and supportive but also to keep offering the right food.

In the new regime, some meals continued to be impossible, mac 'n' cheese and pizza, particularly. She'd had to take some time out of school as the school had not been able to facilitate meal supervision, but eventually it was agreed she would eat lunch with a friend in her Head of Year's office. At times, it was discovered that Chloe was hiding food up her sleeves and in her pockets, and also that she falsified her weight by putting weights in her underwear. Chloe was mortified each time these things were discovered, and her ambivalence to recovery was shown. In the calm of the clinic room, she intellectually knew she wanted to get better. She hated what this was doing to her family, to her social life, to her freedom. But the eating disorder drove her to do these things. She was encouraged to talk about it, so the team and her parents could understand her and support her better.

It was the following year on holiday that the penny really dropped for Chloe. She was really dreading the holiday: they always went to the same place, and 'everyone was going to see how big she'd gotten'. She self-harmed with self-loathing before the holiday, and her Mum had wondered about cancelling the whole thing, but her Dad had said through gritted teeth that they were going on bloody holiday. However, whilst sitting at the pool, covered up with a hoodie and towel over her legs, she looked around and realised that nobody cared two hoots about how slim or fat she was. She wanted to play in the pool with her friends. She had a moment where she could see how silly it looked, being by a pool all covered up. She fully committed to recovery in that moment.

It wasn't all plain sailing after that – there were definitely days when her motivation waned. She had some individual sessions where we learnt more about what she was doing that maintained the illness, including hours of mirror use and body checking. She was encouraged to think about the perceptual distortions that happened in the mirror, and how checking did not reflect reality: pinching the stomach 'fat', which was actually skin, muscles, ligaments, veins, arteries and organs. Family therapy facilitated discussion about the big and interesting life that Chloe wanted to have rather than spending hours in her room agonising about her thigh gap, including travelling and about how difficult it was to have that big life if you couldn't be flexible about food for example, eat pizza.

Chloe was discharged from the service 2 years after she started. She had gone from scared little girl to a wonderfully stroppy adolescent in that time. She, much to her Dad's horror, had had a nose ring piercing, and done an under-shave on her long hair. She still got moments when the eating disorder thoughts came back, but she hated them now. She saw them as part of a patriarchal society, and the objectification of women. The CAMHS team thought she was going to be okay.

15.8 Future Directions

There seems to be plenty of scope for further research and therapeutic advancement in the treatment of CYP's eating disorders. FT-ED approaches achieve full remission in RCTs in approximately 40–50% of patients (Jewell et al., 2016). Other directions include the provision of multifamily groups, where several families are seen together using FT-AN principles, which allow for an intensification of the therapeutic approach and achieves similar outcomes (Eisler et al., 2016). Given the differences in practice emerging between the FT-ED streams it is worth noting that 'the theoretical mechanisms proposed for any of these therapies, including FBT itself, are unproven' (Lock & LeGrange, 2013). Establishing what is therapeutic about the FT-ED approach will inevitably improve treatment.

Further work is also required to untangle the relationship between eating disorders and other areas of neurodiversity and mental distress. Practitioners are only beginning to understand the over-representation of girls with ASD in eating disorders services, with dieting seen as a special interest or obsession, providing the secondary gain of numbing or removing CYP with ASD from the bewildering world of teenage friendships. As well as the increase in the incidence of eating disorders discussed here, there has been a well-documented more recent increase in the incidence of gender dysphoria especially amongst girls (Block, 2023). Is there a relationship here? This raises sociological issues about what (mainly) girls are learning about food, eating, weight and shape in this obesogenic society, where they are taught 'healthy' eating from aged four in schools, and have a constant stream of doctored images of bodily perfection surrounding them in the traditional and social media. Professionals and society are only beginning to understand the toxic impact this new media can have on CYP (Porter, 2022; Vandenbosch et al., 2022).

Covid-19 has raised a number of new questions in the eating disorders world, not simply why the huge increase in cases? Hypotheses include the impact of the narratives around exercising each day and about CYP seeking control, as the world spirals out of control. There has also been an increase in what is being called 'disordered eating', CYP who do not reach any of the traditional diagnoses, but whose relationship with food and eating has become a conduit for the expression of distress. The changes in working practice offer many opportunities for understanding 'what is therapeutic' better. For example, how online compares with real life therapy (Stewart et al., 2021).

15.9 In Conclusion

It is important that all psychological practitioners in CAMHS understand how to recognise eating disorders because of the unique and high physical and psychological risks. It is a rewarding area to work in because of the challenges understanding the interaction between physical and mental health, and because it is an ego-syntonic disorder, where young people are rarely motivated to recover. There is an established research base, but still many questions left without clear answers, such as which patients will benefit and which won't from these treatments. Thankfully many CAMHS patients make a full or significant recovery, although a significant minority will pass on to adult services.

References

Becker, A. E., Fay, K. E, Agnew-Blais, J., Nisha Khan, A., Striegal-Moore, R. H., & Gilman, S. E. (2011). Social network media exposure and adolescent eating pathology in Fiji. *British Journal of Psychiatry, 198*, 43–50.

Block, J. (2023). Gender dysphoria in young people is rising – and so is professional disagreement. *British Medical Journal (BMJ), 380*, 382.

College of Psychiatrists. (2014). *MARSIPAN: Management of Really Sick Patients with Anorexia Nervosa* (2nd ed.). Royal College of Psychiatrists.

Dare, C., Eisler, I., Russell, G. F. M., & Szmukler, G. I. (1990). The clinical and theoretical impact of a controlled trial of family therapy in anorexia nervosa. *Journal of Marital and Family Therapy, 16*(1), 39–57.

Eddy, K. T., Dorer, D. J., Franko, D. L., Tahilani, K., Thompson-Brenner, H., & Herzog, D. B. (2008). Diagnostic crossover in anorexia nervosa and bulimia nervosa: Implications for DSM-V. *American Journal of Psychiatry, 165*(2), 245–250.

Eisler, I., & Simic, M. (2012). *Maudsley service model for the management of child and adolescent eating disorders*. South London & Maudsley NHS Foundation Trust. (Unpublished manuscript).

Eisler, I., Simic, M., Hodsoll, J., Asen, E., Berelowitz, M., Connan, F., Ellis, G., Hugo, P., Schmidt, U., Treasure, J., Yi, I., & Landau, S. (2016). A pragmatic randomised multi-centre trial of multifamily and single family therapy for adolescent anorexia nervosa. *BMC Psychiatry, 16*(1), 422.

Fairburn, C., Cooper, Z., & Shafran, R. (2023). Cognitive behaviour therapy for eating disorders: a 'transdiagnostic' theory and treatment. *Behavior, Research and Therapy, 41*(5), 509–528.

Gowers, S. G., Clark, A. F., Roberts, C., Byford, S., Barrett, B., Griffiths, A., Edwards, V., Bryan, C., Smethurst, N., Rowlands, L., & Roots, P. (2010). A randomised controlled multicentre trial of treatments for adolescent anorexia nervosa including assessment of cost-effectiveness and patient acceptability: The TOuCAN trial. *Health Technology Assessment, 14*(15), 1–98.

Hoek, H. W. (2016). Review of the worldwide epidemiology of eating disorders. *Current Opinion in Psychiatry, 29*(6), 336–339.

Jewell, T., Blessitt, E., Stewart, C. S., Simic, M., & Eisler, I. (2016). Family therapy for child and adolescent eating disorders: A critical review. *Family Process, 55*(3), 577–594.

Kelly, J., & Whitfield, J. (2017). *The Welsh eating disorder service review: 3 years on. Beat Eating Disorders.* https://www.beateatingdisorders.org.uk/support-our-work/campaign-for-beat/current/welsh-eating-disorder-service-review-3-years-on/

Keyes, A., Brosek, J., & Henschel, A. (1950). *The biology of human starvation*. North Central Publishing Company.

Le Grange, D., Eckhardt, S., Dalle Grave, R., Crosby, R. D., Peterson, C. B., Keery, H., Lesser, J., & Martell, C. (2020). Enhanced cognitive-behavior therapy and family-based treatment for adolescents with an eating disorder: A non-randomized effectiveness trial. *Psychological Medicine, 52*(13), 1–11.

Lock, J., & Le Grange, D. (2013). *Treatment manual for anorexia nervosa: A family-based approach*. Guilford Press.

National Institute for Health and Care Excellence (NICE). (2017, updated 2020). *Eating disorders: Recognition and treatment (NICE guideline NG69)*. NICE. https://www.nice.org.uk/guidance/ng69

NHS England. (2015). *Local transformation for children and young people's mental health and wellbeing: Guidance and support for local areas. NHS England.* https://www.england.nhs.uk/wp-content/uploads/2015/07/local-transformation-plans-cyp-mh-guidance.pdf

Polivy, J., & Herman, P.C. (2020, March 19). Overeating in restrained and unrestrained eaters. *Frontiers in Nutrition, 7*(30). https://doi.org/10.3389/fnut.2020.00030

Porter, T. (2022). *You don't understand me: The young woman's guide to life*. Bonnier.

Porter, T., Chapman, V., & Snashall, E. (2022). *Better? Or faster? Intensive day patient treatment for CYPED pre and post covid*. Presentation at EDIC conference.

Scottish Intercollegiate Guidelines Network. (2022). *SIGN 164 eating disorders: A national clinical guideline. Healthcare Improvement Scotland.* https://www.sign.ac.uk/our-guidelines/eating-disorders/

Stewart, C., Konstantellou, A., Kassamali, F., McLaughlin, N., Cutinha, D., Bryant-Waugh, R., Simic, M., Eisler, I., & Baudinet, J. (2021). Is this the 'new normal'? A mixed method investigation of young person, parent and clinician experience of online eating disorder treatment during the Covid-19 pandemic. *Journal of Eating Disorders, 9*(78).

Tan, J. O. A., Stewart, A., Fitzpatrick, R., & Hope, T. (2010). Attitudes of patients with anorexia nervosa to compulsory treatment and coercion. *International Journal of Law Psychiatry, 33*(1), 13–19.

Treasure, J., Smith, G., & Crane, A. (2016). *Skills-based caring for a loved one with an eating disorder: The New Maudsley Method*. Routledge.

Vandenbosch, L., Fardouly, J., & Tiggemann, M. (2022). Social media and body image: Recent trends and future directions. *Current Opinion in Psychology, 45*, 101289. doi:https://doi.org/10.1016/j.copsyc.2021.12.002

Walter, L. (2017). *Transcript of service users' feedback*. National Training in Eating Disorders.

16

Paediatrics and Long-term Health Conditions

Sophie Bennett and Kristina Soon

16.1 Introduction

Paediatric psychology has been defined as 'an interdisciplinary field of research and practice that addresses physical, behavioural, and emotional development as it interacts with health and illness in children, adolescents, and families' (APA Dictionary of Psychology, 2023). In this chapter, we specifically consider current practice for psychological practitioners working with children who have long-term physical health conditions, or in paediatric settings. Long-term physical health conditions (sometimes known as LTCs) can be defined as those lasting for at least 3 months, which cause functional impairment, necessitate medical care and where cure is considered unlikely (Mokkink et al., 2008). Common chronic physical illnesses in childhood include asthma, eczema, cancer, epilepsy and diabetes and approximately 28% of children and young people in England have a long-term condition requiring medical follow up (Wijlaars et al., 2016).

In general, practitioners working in paediatrics aim to 'maximize health outcomes, minimize the emotional consequences of living with chronic disease and improve the quality of life for children, young people and their relatives' (Duff & Bryon, 2005).The National Health Service (NHS) is placing greater emphasis on the importance of recognising that our mental and physical health are closely linked and so integrating a psychological perspective when working with children and young people with long-term physical health conditions is extremely important. Children with long-term conditions may be more able to manage the burdens associated with their condition if their psychological needs are considered together with their physical health needs.

The majority of children with long-term physical health conditions do not meet criteria for a range of indices of psychological problems and therefore should not be subjected to unnecessary, deskilling or stigmatising psychological input. We know that psychological interventions have the potential to harm and treatments should not be offered without good reason and full assessment of the child and family's needs (Rozental et al., 2016). However, whilst children may not meet 'cut-off' for mental health diagnoses, many still

Child Psychology: Pathways to Good Practice, First Edition.
Edited by Helen Pote, Anna Picciotto and Clare Norris.

report feeling stressed and burdened by the challenges of living with a medical condition. For example, children with LTCs have lower levels of self-esteem on average compared to their physically healthy peers (Pinquart, 2013) and can have difficulties with academic and social functioning (Pinquart & Teubert, 2012). Such factors may have greater impact on quality of life than the severity of the physical symptoms associated with the medical condition (Fayed et al., 2015). This means many children and young people can benefit from psychological input for adjustment and coping rather than for a mental health diagnosis. For example, some services run groups for children with chronic illnesses to meet each other and learn from others' experiences. The groups can help normalise and validate their own experiences and may improve psychosocial and health outcomes. Sometimes these are for children and young people with specific chronic illnesses so that children and young people feel part of a group with shared understanding of their medical journeys and challenges (Salvo et al., 2022).

Overall, rates of mental health difficulties are elevated in children with a chronic physical illness compared to children who are otherwise healthy (Pinquart & Shen, 2011a,b,c) with prevalence around four times higher than the general population (Hysing et al., 2007). The most common mental health difficulties are the same for healthy children and those with chronic illness: anxiety disorders, low mood and challenging behaviour. Some chronic physical illnesses, particularly neurological conditions, are also associated with increased rates of intellectual and/or neurodevelopmental neurodivergences such as autism spectrum disorder. However, this overall figure masks significant differences between health conditions; in some, such as epilepsy, rates of mental health difficulties are highly elevated, whereas for others, such as diabetes, figures are similar to those in children without a chronic illness (Laurens et al., 2019). Practitioners might therefore treat these common mental health difficulties using standard evidence-based treatments, such as Cognitive Behaviour Therapy for anxiety or depression, or parenting interventions for behavioural difficulties, but making modifications to account for the chronic illness. Modifications might include using examples specific to the chronic illness (e.g. worries about having a seizure for young people with epilepsy), or being more flexible with appointment times, perhaps timing them to happen at the same time as hospital visits if a child has frequent medical appointments. Physical differences might also need to be considered when setting therapy tasks. For example, behavioural activation will need to be carefully planned if the young person has compromised immunity and cannot visit crowded public places or if the young person has limited mobility. Positive reinforcement systems will need to avoid rewards that might exacerbate a child's allergies or contradict medical advice.

Sometimes, children may need input for specific challenges relating to their medical condition, such as procedural anxiety, which is a fear of medical, dental or surgical procedures that might interfere with completing necessary procedures, or a phobia of needles (e.g. Nunns et al., 2018). Parents and siblings of children with long-term conditions may also need support (Barlow & Ellard, 2006). Parents report greater levels of parenting stress particularly associated with physical healthcare, and higher rates of mental health difficulties (Pinquart, 2018, 2019a,b) and whilst many siblings of children with LTCs report positive experiences and that their lives have been enriched by having a sibling with a chronic illness or disability, some also may choose to conceal their emotions about their sibling or other areas of life, perhaps to avoid 'burdening' their families (Haukeland et al., 2015). Siblings and parents may benefit from individual support for worries, or low mood, for example, or psychological practitioners may facilitate groups where family members can meet others in similar circumstances.

Child psychological practitioners may work with children and young people with LTCs and their families in a variety of settings. The majority of paediatric psychologists work in acute medical settings rather than a mental health setting (BPS, n.d.). For example, many psychological practitioners work within paediatric hospitals in outpatient and inpatient settings. Some may be based in mental health services integrated within a physical health setting and vice versa for example, providing liaison psychiatry services, where they may provide mental health assessment and intervention for children and young people with a physical illness. They may also conduct risk assessments in the hospital setting, for example following admissions for self-harm. Some provide community-based services directly linked to physical health settings, for example those working with life-threatening illnesses or in palliative care (holistic care of individuals across all ages with serious health-related suffering due to severe illness and especially of those near the end of life). Finally given the high proportion of children and young people who have a long-term physical health condition, practitioners may work with them in the context of other settings described in this book, such as schools and children and young people's mental health services, in both low-intensity and high-intensity services.

16.2 Review of the Evidence Base, NICE Guidelines and Policy

16.2.1 Therapist Competencies

A framework has now been developed outlining the competencies required to deliver psychological interventions in a paediatric context (Roth & Donnan, 2019). This is based on the existing evidence base and expert advice.

The framework therefore brings together generic therapeutic skills for working with children and young people that are discussed throughout the chapters of this book, together with the specific skills a psychological practitioner may need for working with young people with chronic illness.

The roles of psychological practitioners within paediatric settings are too varied and the research too broad to provide a comprehensive overview, but here we provide further detail about some of the areas described within the competency framework:

16.2.2 Models of Adjustment to Physical Health Conditions

There is a broad ranging literature regarding the psychological impact of having a long-term physical health condition and the relationship between physical and mental health. Historically, this has been published in medical rather than psychology journals and has often been defined by the medical condition rather than the psychological need. Many of the existing studies are descriptive and there is a relative lack of intervention studies.

Box 16.1 Clinical example: Formulation of a young person, Jo, with epilepsy and low mood, Adapted from the Wallander and Varni Risk-Resistance model

DISEASE/DISABILITY

e.g., diagnosis, severity, visibility, brain damage, cognitive function

Poor physical health growing up and a recent diagnosis of aepilepsy which is comparably less 'visible' vs, other physical health conditions until has a seizure, which for Jo are tonic-clonic, involving dropping to the floor and losing consciousness. Finds it difficult to concentrate, and some learning difficulties, particularly in maths.

FUNCTIONAL INDEPENDENCE

e.g., hygiene, ambulation, communication

Struggles to keep up with personal care such as eating healthily, showering or brushing his teeth.

Father helps Jo with many day-to-day tasks

PSYCHOSOCIAL STRESS

e.g., handicap-related problems, daily hassles, major life event

Lots of missed school due to attending many medical appointments making the transition to secondary school and forming/maintaining new friendships even more difficult. School did not allow him to take part in residential trip.

Adjusting to new changes such as worsening epilepsy, undergoing puberty

Being a victim of bullying and feeling isolated

ADJUSTMENT/ADAPTATION

e.g., mental, social, physical

Internalises a negative view of self and ruminates on how he is "unliked"

Socially becomes more withdrawn and spends less time doing activities he enjoys and more and more time in bed.

Constantly feels tired and finds it difficult to keep up with school work or day-to-day demands.

STRESS PROCESSING

e.g., cognitive appraisal, coping strategies

Negative appraisal of events (e.g., feels he is unliked when friends stopped reaching out) and stops reaching out to friends to avoid further disappointment

Copes by avoiding activities and sleeping all day

PERSONAL FACTORS

e.g., temperament, competence, effectance motivation, problem solving ability

Was previously active and friendly with a 'happy go lucky' approach; now Jo is more withdrawn and quieter.

Demotivated and feels like nothing will change

Struggling with problem solving

SOCIAL-ECOLOGICAL FACTORS

e.g., family environment, family member's adjustment, social support

Overprotective but supportive and understanding family

High levels of parental stress and anxiety in helping Jo with his day-to-day tasks

A number of models have been proposed to explain the relationship between mental and physical health in children with long-term physical health conditions. One of the most widely cited is Wallander and Varni's 'Risk-resistance model' (Wallander & Varni, 1998). According to this model 'despite the biomedical uniqueness of each illness, there is considerable commonality in psychosocial ramifications' (p. 29). They describe factors that interact with and influence adjustment in children with a chronic physical illness, where 'good adjustment' is defined as 'behavior that is age-appropriate, normative and healthy and that follows a trajectory toward positive adult functioning'. These contributory factors include:

- variables associated with specific illnesses such as the severity and visibility of the LTC;
- presence of brain damage and associated cognitive functioning;
- level of functional independence (i.e. what daily activities children are able to do for themselves);
- psychosocial stress, for example illness-related stressors such as having to follow a medication regime;
- intrapersonal factors, for example, a child's temperament;
- social-ecological factors such as family functioning;
- and stress processing, meaning the appraisal of circumstances and use of cognitive and behavioural strategies to manage these;

(see Box 16.1 for a clinical example). Psychological practitioners may therefore work with one or more of these areas to promote positive adjustment.

16.2.3 Interventions

According to the Paediatric Psychology Network UK (Young et al., 2018) psychological therapy interventions in this context may be used to:

Improve medical outcomes through increasing adherence: A systematic review of 20 studies found that, compared to control interventions, effective adherence promotion interventions both improved patient quality of life and family-level outcomes, such as caregiver quality of life and family functioning, as well as decreasing overall usage of healthcare in children and young people with chronic medical conditions (McGrady et al., 2015).

Improve psychological functioning: As can be seen in the other chapters of this book, we know that psychological interventions are highly effective for young people with mental health conditions without physical illness (Chorpita et al., 2011) and reviews show that they are also effective in children and young people with mental health difficulties in the context of LTCs (Moore et al., 2019). Qualitative research suggests that the interventions are acceptable to young people and their families and that one of the key factors that may be associated with maintaining engagement over time is the ability of the intervention to adapt flexibly to the physical and mental health needs of the young person. Overall, the research suggests that children and young people value an approach that addresses both their mental and physical health needs. The competence framework suggests that children and young people who have co-existing mental and physical health conditions should therefore receive standard mental health assessments where required, leading to an evidence-based intervention.

Improve overall family functioning: Parent- and family-based psychological therapies such as problem-solving therapy (PST) that includes parents can improve parent outcomes.

PST teaches effective problem-solving skills and coping strategies (D'Zurilla & Goldfried, 1971) and has been found to improve both parent adaptive behaviour and parental mental health (Eccleston et al., 2015; Law et al., 2014). Parent adaptive behaviour includes using labelled praises (Antonini et al., 2014) or demonstrating more constructive problem-solving behaviours, assessed using part of the 'Social problem-solving inventory – revised' (D'Zurilla et al., 2002) with items such as 'Before I try to solve a problem, I set a specific goal so that I know exactly what I want to accomplish.'

Reduce disability and pain: Psychological interventions have a large evidence base in treating chronic pain and have been demonstrated to be effective in reducing pain and increasing physical functioning in children (Fisher et al., 2022).

Reduce procedural anxiety and distress: Children with chronic physical illnesses may have to undergo a range of uncomfortable, painful or otherwise distressing procedures for their physical health, ranging from blood tests and injections, taking medications and scans to surgeries. Psychological interventions such as distraction, hypnosis, cognitive behaviour therapy (CBT) and breathing interventions can effectively reduce the associated pain and distress (e.g. Birnie et al., 2018; Mathias et al., 2022).

Improve communication between families and medical teams: Dovey-Pearce and Flannery (2021) state that 'every healthcare contact provides an opportunity to contribute to relationship building between young people and the healthcare teams' and that psychological practitioners can help teams focus on the relational processes that will make even brief consultations more effective, accessible and satisfactory'. They can also implement approaches with the young person that may support young people's own decision making with medical team, such as shared decision making (Santana & Feeny, 2014) and motivational interviewing (Christie & Channon, 2014). For a fuller discussion of these issues see Chapters 8 and 9.

Mental health and psychological problems in the context of chronic illness are known to be under-recognised and under-treated. There are many reasons for this, but they include diagnostic overshadowing, with the physical health condition being prioritised over mental health problems, or a lack of understanding of the relationship between physical and mental health. Practitioners may assume that a mental health disorder is understandable in the context of the illness or an inherent part of the illness, and therefore not able to be treated. Training and supporting medical staff to identify and respond to psychological needs can ensure better patient-centred care (BPS, 2016).

16.2.4 NICE Guidance and Policy

The National Institute for Health and Care Excellence (NICE) guidance for psychological interventions for children with long-term physical conditions is found within guidance for specific medical conditions in children and young people. Many point to the need to considering psychological and psychosocial aspects and/or make appropriate referrals, for example epilepsy (NICE, 2021a), alopecia areata (NICE, 2018) and asthma (NICE, 2021b).

The NICE guidance for psychological support in children and young people with diabetes is one of the most comprehensive (NICE, 2022) and recommends integrated psychological therapy for children with diabetes, stating that children and young people with Type 1 diabetes 'have a greater risk of emotional and behavioural difficulties' and that they and their families should be offered emotional support after diagnoses, which is tailored to their emotional, social, cultural and age-dependent needs, as well as 'timely and ongoing access to mental health professionals with an understanding of diabetes'. The interventions suggested are dependent on the primary difficulty, for example: counselling or CBT for health-related quality of life; motivational interviewing or multisystemic therapy (MST) for adherence to diabetes treatment; MST for blood glucose management; or behavioural family systems therapy for diabetes-related family conflict. In line with the overarching team role of a psychological practitioner working in a paediatric setting, the guidance also suggests that 'diabetes teams should have access to mental health professionals to support them in psychological assessment and providing psychosocial support'.

Considering mental health disorders, medical condition-specific NICE guidance points to existing NICE guidance for children without long-term conditions. For example, the diabetes guidance suggests treatment for depression, behavioural difficulties and eating disorders according to the standard NICE guidance for these difficulties. In adults, there is overarching guidance for identification and treatment of common mental health difficulties in those with chronic illness (NICE, 2009) but there is no equivalent guidance in children and young people.

16.2.5 Cost-effectiveness

Psychological distress has been found to be associated with more use of healthcare and therefore it follows that psychological intervention may reduce healthcare usage with resultant cost savings. For example, psychological intervention for procedural anxiety may reduce the number of cancelled scans and surgeries, which can be costly. Psychological treatments may result in better self-management of a chronic illness, increased adherence and therefore reduced medical complications. This evidence is strongest in the adult literature, where meta-analyses indicate that psychological interventions are effective in adults with physical and mental ill-health and reduce the use of medical services with an average savings of 20% (Chiles et al., 1999). It is estimated that for each £1 spent on mental health care in the UK, roughly £1 is saved on welfare benefits and another £1 is saved on physical health care (Layard, 2016).

Research suggests that such cost savings also apply to children and young people, for example a study of an interdisciplinary paediatric chronic pain rehabilitation programme found that the programme resulted in significant reductions in a number of areas, including the number of days the children were hospitalised, the number of visits to medical professionals, the use of physical and occupational therapy services, the number of psychotherapy visits and the number of days the parents missed from work (Evans et al., 2016). Similarly, a randomised controlled trial of MST for young people with poorly controlled Type 1 diabetes found that the young people receiving MST had significantly fewer hospital admissions than the control group. Given the high cost of inpatient admissions, this resulted in substantial cost savings (Ellis et al., 2008). Overall, there is an economic argument to increase the provision of psychological therapies for children and young people with chronic physical illnesses. The cost of psychological treatment is more than offset by the resulting savings in physical healthcare costs, such that treatment of the mental health conditions 'costs the NHS nothing' due to the positive impact on physical health services (CEPMHPG, 2012; Layard & Clark, 2015).

16.3 Critical Reflections on the Current Evidence

16.3.1 The State of the Evidence Base

Overall, there are relatively few intervention trials that compare treatments to other treatments or control groups. Some of the interventions that are widely used within paediatric psychology settings do not have a significant evidence base. That is not to say that they are not effective, but that research has not yet been conducted to investigate this. This may be partly due to a lack of 'manualisation' in some areas. In addition, trials may demonstrate efficacy in one group (for example, a certain age group or children with a certain medical condition) but this does not mean that they are efficacious in a different group. The competency framework we described earlier and associated clinical practice in this area is therefore heavily influenced by professional experience rather than evidence from randomised controlled trials.

16.3.2 Over-pathologising Children with Medical Conditions

The literature is clear that healthcare professionals and parents of children with medical conditions show elevated rates of psychological difficulties. As such, concerns located in the child can be a manifestation of problems in other parts of the system. For example, even in children with epilepsy, who are known to have a high rate of mental health difficulties, studies have shown that parents' reporting of their child's behavioural difficulties is highly influenced by the emotional and time impact of epilepsy on themselves (i.e. they may report more difficulties if they are more emotionally impacted by the epilepsy; Eom et al., 2016). It is therefore extremely important to conduct thorough assessments, ideally with separate discussions with different parts of the system, as well as observations if possible. Support should be available for the whole family, as well as professionals.

16.3.3 Use of Standard versus Adapted Interventions

For children who have a specific mental health condition (e.g. an anxiety disorder) in addition to a medical condition, the extent to which interventions need to be adapted for the presence of chronic illness is not clear from current evidence (Cottrell et al., 2015), as no trials directly compare standard evidence-based therapies with those adapted for chronic illness. Whilst modifications to the structure are often necessary (such as timing sessions to coincide with hospital visits or having shorter sessions for young people experiencing fatigue), adaptations to the content of interventions may not always be needed (Bennett et al., 2015; Bennett & Shafran, 2023). There is inherent personalisation of any psychological intervention, for example, using examples from the client's own experience to illustrate a concept such as thought challenging. In the case of chronic illness, this may include challenging thoughts related to the illness (Morey & Loades, 2021). Overall, these are the same principles of flexibility that child practitioners should be developing with all client groups. Gregory and colleagues (2023) suggest that going forward, practitioners and researchers consider whether challenges related to specific illnesses may reduce the efficacy, safety or acceptability of treatments. Where this is the case, then they should develop pilot and trial-modified interventions compared to the best available standardised treatments.

16.4 Inclusive Practice, Including the Views and Voices of Children and Young People about this Area of Practice

16.4.1 Inclusive Practice

It is clear that children and families from minority backgrounds receive poorer care and have poorer health outcomes and so the competence framework for working in this field includes the 'ability to work with difference (cultural competence)' as a key area of required knowledge and skills. Further information around working with difference can be found across this book, and particularly in Chapter 7. However, considering the specific role of psychological practitioners in paediatric settings, the NHS staff is majority white, female, heterosexual, English speaking and physically able and this can be excluding to those who do not share these identities (NHS, 2023). It is therefore important for the practitioner to start by checking their own privileges and biases. Children and families may hold different values, beliefs and expectations regarding physical health, medical care, appearance and disability. Families and children can struggle to relate to a government authority such as the NHS and withdraw from treatment and/or struggle to express their needs, particularly as many children/families from minority backgrounds will recall experiences of feeling marginalised. Psychological practitioners should take responsibility for initiating conversations with children and families about how easy or difficult is has been to relate to the healthcare system and factors and experiences that have obstructed this. Psychological practitioners must then take responsibility for advocating for their patients, 'calling-in' colleagues and organisations to reduce barriers to care and positive health outcomes in minoritised patients/families (Melton, 2018). Whilst interpreters can be useful cultural advisors as well as language translators, they must be trained and supported by the practitioner to interpret in a way that is helpful to family and practitioner.

16.4.2 The Views and Voices of Children and Young People

A child's boundaries with adults can be altered due to medical illness-related experiences, for example removing clothing at the request of an unknown adult, tolerating pain inflicted by strange adults and complying with instructions from strangers without resistance. As such, a psychologist can be important in reinstating adaptive boundaries between the child and adults. This would include explicit collaborative process and centring the child's experiences/wishes/priorities, including explaining clearly what is going to happen so there is no 'hidden agenda' (CWDC, 2009). As described further in this chapter, goal setting with the child's views and wishes is extremely important.

16.5 A Developmental Approach to Assessment, Formulation and Intervention

Child psychological practitioners may support MDTs within medical settings as well as providing individual and group therapy. The goal of the psychologist in a medical MDT is often to ensure that the child remains as close as possible to an adaptive developmental trajectory in order to ensure a successful entry into independent, adult life. Chronic illness and medical treatments can be barriers to this, and the role of the psychologist can be to minimise these obstacles/provide means of overcoming the obstacles as opposed to, or in addition to, treating a mental health condition. They hold safeguarding principles in mind, for example, the Children Act (1989): protecting children from (medical) maltreatment, preventing impairment of children's health or development, ensuring that children are growing up in circumstances consistent with the provision of safe and effective care, undertaking that role so as to enable those children to have optimum life chances and to enter adulthood successfully, and considering issues of competence and consent.

Referral is often initiated by a healthcare professional or parents and the child or young person can also be unclear about the purpose of the referral. Healthcare professionals who may not be knowledgeable about or trained in mental health and psychosocial issues may miss key issues, and so referrals may be misleading or miss key information. Due to elevated levels of psychological difficulties in other parts of the system around the child, it is always important to assess the system to ensure that you are intervening in the right place. Interventions in medical settings often involve parents and family as well as individuals and teams in the healthcare system and other professional systems for example, education professionals. Practitioners should also be mindful of involvement of local health, education and social services, specialist NHS services and third-sector organisations that can all impact on a child's medical condition and development (Dovey-Pearce et al., 2020; Ham et al., 2012). Patients and their parents who are anxious about the child's health can struggle to disagree with medical advice from the referring professional as well as the psychologist. As such, motivation for and feasibility of psychological involvement should be discussed carefully and informed consent sought.

In addition, mental health difficulties can be under-recognised in those with some medical conditions. A key first step in assessment of the mental health problems is therefore to identify them. Instruments used in routine child and adolescent mental health services, such as the strengths and difficulties questionnaire (SDQ) have been shown to be effective in detecting the presence of an emotional or behavioural disorder in those with chronic illness (Glazebrook et al., 2003; Hysing et al., 2007). Measures of quality of life may also be particularly useful in this population for example, the PedsQL (Varni et al., 1999). Guidance for some conditions states that children and young people should be routinely screened for anxiety and depression, for example those with Type 1 diabetes who have persistent difficulty with blood glucose management (NICE, 2004). Providing a self-referral option, as well as actively asking young people/carers in paediatric outpatient clinics if they think they would benefit from support around emotions and/or behaviour, may also increase detection of mental health problems.

The development of children with chronic illnesses can look different to that of children who do not have the added challenge of living with a medical condition. For example, children may demonstrate sophisticated understanding of medical practices and how to interact with adults but struggle with peer interactions. Some conditions can be associated with learning differences. Families will also develop differently, for example, children may remain dependent on their parents for longer due to medical needs or disabilities that require extra support. As such, the child's and the family's development should be carefully observed to ensure a meaningful interaction with the child. The concept of developmental trauma has been applied to children and young people who have experienced aversive medical treatments in their childhood (van der Kolk 2005; see chapter 17 for further discussion of developmental trauma).

Discussion with the team about who is the client is particularly important as healthcare professionals can have different goals to the child and to the family. For example, a medical professional may want to optimise medical treatment, a child may want to have friends and their parents may want them to attend school regularly. As such, a patient-centred discussion about the reason for referral is crucial and negotiation of therapeutic focus is very important. Goals for psychological therapy are frequently unclear to the parent and/or child and should be explicitly discussed and agreed. Goals and outcomes should be set in such a way that take into consideration some of the uncontrollable aspects of medical disease. For example, treatment adherence for eczema should be focused on observable behavioural change, such as frequency of the child using emollients, rather than the state of their eczema/skin, which can be affected by environmental or physiological variables. See Chapter 9.

Children will often be socialised into norms of medical practice and may need clarity about how psychology works. For example, children will often be used to medical doctors speaking mostly to their parent not them – medical consultations are usually with parents and child together so the child may be surprised by and unused to speaking independently with a psychologist. Box 16.2 presents a case example from clinical practice.

Box 16.2 Clinical example: Jo

Referral

Jo is a 13-year-old British boy who lives with his parents and three older brothers. He has epilepsy and was referred to the psychology team by his paediatric consultant as he was struggling with low mood. The referral stated that Jo's mood had deteriorated over the past 6 months after he had a prolonged seizure after being seizure-free for several months prior.

Assessment and formulation

A psychological practitioner met with Jo and his parents for an assessment session to explore his current difficulties and identify goals for treatment. Prior to the assessment, Jo completed the Revised Children's Anxiety and Depression Scale (RCADS; Chorpita et al., 2005) and scored in the borderline clinical range for depression. The assessment and intervention were conducted remotely over video-conferencing, as Jo and his parents were keen to avoid the long journey to hospital, which was tiring for Jo and meant that his father had to take time off from work. The practitioner checked beforehand that there was a private space that Jo could be away from his parents to talk freely, but that his parents were in the house and available when they were needed.

The practitioner followed the assessment template described earlier in this chapter. They initially spent time discussing the plan for the assessment with Jo and his parents, and then spent some time with Jo alone, after checking with him that he was okay to

(Continued)

Box 16.2 (Continued)

do so. Jo initially presented visibly low in mood, keeping his head down and not speaking to the psychological practitioner unless his father prompted him to do so when the family were together. Throughout the session the practitioner's rapport helped to facilitate Jo's disclosure of sensitive information through the use of open questions ('can you tell me a bit more about what's been happening?') as well as, following client's language ('you say you're unliked') and interests and encouraging statements. Jo said that he wanted to get back to the person he used to be – happy-go-lucky and active with a positive outlook on life.

Formulation

Using the '5Ps' as a framework for formulation, we can begin to understand and better conceptualise the development of Jo's difficulties. The 5Ps include: presenting issues (what Jo is struggling with), predisposing (what increases Jo's chance of experiencing these difficulties), precipitating (what may have triggered these difficulties), perpetuating (the factors keeping this problem ongoing) and protective factors (the child or young person's strengths that counteract such difficulties?).

Predisposing factors Jo explained that due to his epilepsy and related treatments including medication and surgery, he already struggled with fatigue more than his peers and missed a lot of school. The adverse experiences associated with his condition and missing out on important time with his peers therefore may have made Jo more vulnerable to developing difficulties with his mood. At the same time, he had moved to a secondary school where he did not know anyone. His school had told him he could not attend the residential trip for new students because of his recent epilepsy surgery, as they were worried he may have a seizure during some of the activities. This knocked his confidence, leading him to feel left out and different from others. He had always struggled with learning, and sometimes had a learning support assistant in the classroom for lessons he found more difficult, such as maths. This increased his thoughts about being different from others.

Jo was diagnosed with epilepsy when he was seven and his parents were protective of him so he very rarely did anything independently. As a result, Jo remained reliant on his parents to help him with daily activities (taking medication, eating at specific times, sticking to a schedule, speaking with professionals, resolving conflicts with peers, etc.), which may have contributed to Jo struggling to find his own identity at a crucial age when his peers were becoming increasingly independent.

Precipitating factors Jo's mood began to deteriorate significantly following a prolonged seizure that made him drop to the floor, which was witnessed by others in his class. He felt embarrassed about the seizure and the young people in his class had made comments about it. He had more trouble with learning around this time and was struggling to keep up with his classmates. He started spending more time in bed, sleeping or ruminating about how unhappy he had become.

Presenting problems Jo's daily thoughts were characterised by pessimism, self-criticism, sadness and hopelessness, corresponding to common themes of depressive thinking (Beck, 1967). He felt hopeless about the future, for example, he thought that he would never go to university or have a good job because he was not clever enough.

He also described feeling fatigued, lacking concentration and motivation and had bouts of sadness and crying spells. He isolated himself from his friends and when not at school, spent most of his time in his room without eating nutritious meals or attending to his personal care. Jo also reported ruminative thoughts centred around being unliked and unable to change, in a world that was not made for him and would not get better – a pattern resembling the cognitive triad of negative thoughts about the self, world and future (Beck, 1979).

Perpetuating factors In addition to the ruminative thinking pattern, at the time of assessment, Jo was struggling to get out of bed, sleeping up to 12–14 hours a day, which made him feel helpless and even more fatigued with little energy. Consequently, he stopped reaching out to or responding to friends and avoided his family, instead ruminating about his perceived failures and sinking deeper into low mood. He would spend breaktimes alone and stopped playing football, which he loved to play in primary school.

His friends also stopped reaching out to him, which he interpreted as a confirmation of his negative beliefs about being unliked and excluded. His absences from school perpetuated his difficulties even further leaving him without a structured routine. This pattern of withdrawing socially as well as from rewarding activities resulted in Jo missing out on potentially positive experiences as well as perpetuating the cycle of being low, disconnected and demotivated with thoughts of excessive self-criticism.

Protective factors

Jo loved sports, particularly football. He was passionate about science and liked to watch science TikTok videos, which gave him motivation even when he was feeling down. Jo also had an excellent relationship with his family. His parents were very supportive of him and offered him encouragement and guidance.

Goals

Jo identified the following goals for psychological treatment:

1. To be able to talk to strangers (professionals and peers) without mum or dad by my side.
2. To have a normal routine to the day (8 hours of sleep, personal hygiene, activities throughout the day) and wake up in time for school.
3. To meet new people and be able to feel comfortable being myself, for example telling people what I really like rather than agreeing with their opinions.

Intervention

Based on the assessment and in line with NICE guidelines for depression (NICE, 2005), Jo was offered an evidence-based treatment for depression; individual sessions CBT, beginning with strategies for low mood. The overall aim of the sessions was to help him understand the cyclical connections between thoughts, feelings and behaviours, and

(Continued)

Box 16.2 (Continued)

work to find more helpful ways of thinking, feeling and/or behaving to work towards the goals he set for himself.

Through formulation, it came to light that many of Jo's attempts to cope with his negative thoughts were worsening his mood with avoidance and disengagement characterising his behaviours. Early sessions focused on psychoeducation for depression to aid Jo's understanding of his symptoms and normalise his difficulties in the context of his experiences. Using the 5Ps formulation described earlier, the psychological practitioner discussed how Jo's apparent solutions contribute to the maintenance of his problems whilst also helping him understand the links between his thoughts, emotions and behaviours. For example, Jo learnt that by stopping the activities he used to enjoy, his mood and his thoughts about things being hopeless worsened. The psychological practitioner began to address inactivity and rumination through behavioural activation (Martell et al., 2001) hoping to break the self-maintaining cycle of Jo's low mood.

Jo's goals all required problem solving. He described hoping to make new friends and feeling more confident in himself – however, he saw these goals as impossible and himself as helpless. The psychological practitioner began to work with Jo to break down his goals to smaller, more manageable steps, which Jo thought were still difficult but more achievable. The steps towards his goals were then rated based on difficulty and the therapist developed a behavioural activation chart to ensure he re-engaged with routine, necessary and pleasurable activities that he was missing out on (Figure 16.1).

Jo progressed well with behavioural activation; by starting to do more, his mood lifted. The practitioner also helped him to look back on what he had learned from doing the activities, supporting him to re-evaluate his beliefs about himself and his abilities. For example, when the practitioner asked Jo what he had learned from doing more activities with his friends, he was able to recognise that he could do activities independently, and that people did respond to his messages when he messaged them, countering his belief that he was unlikeable. Evaluating the changes in his thinking and associated emotions and behaviours following the completion of an activity helped to integrate successes into his new view of himself as capable and likeable.

Whilst implementing the activity scheduling, it was important to consider the potential impact of physical health difficulties and apply the strategies flexibly. Jo often struggled to concentrate for one-hour long sessions. It was difficult to delineate the impact of low mood and his physical health condition on this difficulty and working in collaboration with Jo, the psychological practitioner devised routines around session times and shortened sessions rather than cancel them if he struggled with concentration difficulties. The practitioner also encouraged Jo to make notes during the sessions and provided him with recordings that he could listen to. This supported his engagement with the sessions and built his confidence in being able to do things even on difficult days, allowing him to make use of the treatment rather than dropping out early due to non-attendance. Jo had some worried thoughts that he would have a seizure in front of other people again, which also contributed to his avoiding activities. It was possible, and even likely, that Jo would have a seizure in front of other people in the future and so it was not the practitioner's job to minimise this possibility. Instead, they thought with Jo about the pros and cons of his strategy of avoiding activities (pro – I won't have a seizure in front of other people; con – I won't make friends or meet my goals), and how much his thoughts about himself if he did have a seizure were true (even if I did have a seizure, it doesn't mean people won't like me – there are lots of likeable things about me). Jo's practitioner also arranged a meeting with his school, parents and paediatrician, so that his school could learn about what activities were safe for him to do and how they could support him in being able to join in with all of the school trips and not exclude him.

As Jo began to re-engage with valued activities in his life, his mood started to lift and he reported that he was feeling happier and more confident in himself. Jo rejoined a football club and began to reach out to new people in the group. However, they all lived far away and struggled to make time to meet, which Jo interpreted as the confirmation of his beliefs about being disliked. As these negative thoughts were preventing Jo from engaging in valued activities that would bring him closer to his goals, the practitioner refocused on the restructuring of his particularly difficult thoughts. For example, they discussed how Jo was interpreting apparently neutral stimuli (her friends being busy due to homework and living far away) as negative (his friends not liking him). This is a common information processing bias observed in depression, where people process information in a way that is congruent with their depressive mood (Beck, 1967). Through homework and in-session practice, Jo began to identify his biased thinking patterns and evaluated the evidence for and against his negative thoughts. This resulted in more accurate and balanced re-evaluations of his negative thoughts and supported the development of a more balanced view of himself, the future and the world.

16.6 Evaluation

Ultimately, it is important to ensure that you monitor whether psychological intervention is having a net positive effect on a child and family that is already very vulnerable. As in other areas, this can be evaluated by formal measures of both symptoms and experience, before, during and after interventions, as well as through 'qualitative' feedback from the family and clinical team. Measures of symptoms and experience are detailed in other chapters in this book.

Considering measures of symptoms, the extent to which commonly used measures of mental health, such as the SDQ, are suitable to capture change in this population in unclear, particularly when there is additional complexity such as an intellectual or developmental neurodivergence. Using quality of life measures such as the PedsQL (Varni et al., 2001) and goal-based outcomes (Cooper & Law, 2018) may therefore be important additions to the standardised outcomes measures used for mental health disorders in children who do not have a chronic illness. The PedsQL considers overall quality of life, considering functioning across important areas of a child's life such as school, family and friends in addition to 'health-related quality of life': functional health status, psychological and social well-being, health perceptions, disease-related and treatment-related symptoms, considering the whole child and not only the medical condition (Wallander & Koot, 2016).

Routine	Necessary	Pleasurable
- Good sleeping pattern o 8 hours of sleep and wake up at 8am – go to bed by midnight at latest - Regular showers - Family time - Brushing teeth before bed - Keeping in touch with friends	- Eating - Exercising - Socialising - Medication	- Football - Bike rides with my family - Socialising - Netflix - Watch/make TikToks -
Easy	**Medium**	**Hard**
- Music alarms in the morning - Netflix (wind-down) - Shower alarm with a song - Going for a gentle walk - Messaging friends	- Reading before bed (wind-down) - Wind-down alarm with song (30-60 minutes before bedtime) - Brisk walk - Playing football with family or friends in the garden - Going out with old friends	- Good sleeping pattern – 8 hours and waking up at 9 - Regular showers - Joining a local football club - Making and going out with new friends

Figure 16.1 Behavioural activation routine – necessary and pleasurable activities.

16.6.1 Jo's Measures and Outcomes

Jo's scores on the RCADS (Chorpita et al., 2005) moved from the borderline clinical to the subclinical range, suggesting that low mood was no longer having a significant impact on his life. Furthermore, weekly goal-based outcome measures (Law & Jacob, 2013) were also used to evaluate the effectiveness of the interventions and Jo made significant progress towards all of his therapy goals. By the time of the final session, Jo also had numerous personal achievements, for example he made new friends and had been awarded 'player of the match' in his most recent football match with the club he had joined. Jo was able to share his honest opinions about things with people in his class, and learnt that this did not stop people being his friend; in fact he could make new friends easily when he shared his opinions about things.

16.7 Common Challenges and Addressing them in the Work

16.7.1 The Relationship between Psychological Practitioners and Medical Team Members

It is absolutely crucial to be able to relate effectively to the medical MDT and the priorities and norms of that MDT in order to be able to effectively influence patient care. Therefore, it is important that child psychological practitioners working in this area develop their team-working, consultation and liaison skills in addition to therapy skills.

16.7.2 Flexibly Applying Approaches

Regarding modifications, whilst evidence for adapting content for the context of chronic illness is equivocal, some changes to the format/delivery of interventions have been identified as potentially helpful from the literature (Morey & Loades, 2021) and clinical experience. The most obvious is the need for increased flexibility around appointments, both as cancellations/did-not-attends from illness are more likely in this group, but also as families and young people may already be very time poor due to existing medical appointments and unplanned emergency admissions. Offering families the option of telephone/video delivered therapy, or sessions scheduled around hospital appointments can be helpful.

Evidence-supported treatment can be personalised in the same way as those for children without a chronic illness. For example, using more behavioural than cognitive strategies for treating anxiety in a young person with a mild intellectual disability and having shorter sessions to account for fatigue. There may be more family involvement in order to consider the family's wider narrative about the chronic illness.

As chronic illnesses vary, specific strategies need to be personalised to the individual child and family. For example, a young person with epilepsy may have previously enjoyed swimming with friends but post-diagnosis is understandably worried about returning due to fear of having a seizure. As in Jo's case, the psychological practitioner would need to liaise closely with the young person, their family and the medical team to problem-solve strategies that support graded exposure to feared situations whilst ensuring the young person's safety, for example, ensuring that the young person's friends knew what to do in the event of a seizure. From experience, we have found that it is best to liaise with the medical team and bring these issues of personalisation to supervision. Nursing staff or other health professionals are often able to tell you what would or would not be a safe and appropriate activity given the diagnosis and level of severity. Using goal-based outcomes in addition to standardised measures is key in ensuring that the intervention meets the needs of the family.

16.7.3 Ensuring Families Do Not Fall Through Gaps in Services

As stated in the competencies framework, 'there is a risk that in a paediatric context, mental health problems are seen as the province of Child and Adolescent Mental Health Service (CAMHS), and an equal risk that CAMHS services will be deterred from intervening where there is an evident physical health problem. This can result in the child or young person falling through an "organisational net"'. As described earlier, standard evidence-based treatments should be effective in this group, with personalisation to account for individual differences. Children and young people should always be offered intervention where indicated and the presence of a chronic illness should not be seen as a reason to decline a referral (NICE, 2021b). If a psychological practitioner needs more information about a medical condition they can seek consultation with the child's medical care team.

16.8 Future Directions

Many children and young people with LTCs in the UK may not have any access to psychological therapies. Future work therefore needs to consider new ways of working to ensure that all children and young people have equal access to this support. Psychological interventions are equally effective when delivered in different formats, including via the telephone, which increases accessibility, reduces the stigma associated with attending mental health services and minimises disruption to patients and costs. 'Low-intensity' approaches, such as guided self-help delivered in person or over the telephone/video conferencing are offered in adult pathways for people with LTCs in the NHS. Brief and low-intensity approaches are also effective in children and young people, including those with chronic physical illnesses (Bennett et al., 2019; Catanzano et al., 2020). Further research is needed to understand how these effective interventions can best be integrated into physical healthcare services to optimise care for children and young people with LTCs. An increased focus on prevention studies is also needed (Mattson et al., 2019) to best understand the effects of protective factors like stable relationships or self-esteem (Moore et al., 2019).

Some hospitals and services in England are able to provide truly joined-up working, with psychological practitioners fully embedded within paediatric teams and given the advantages of these models, this is something that should be available to all children with long-term conditions. Overall, this is an exciting area of child psychology to be in. Psychological practitioners can use their unique skills not only to work with children and their families, but also to support the wider team to truly make a difference to the lives of children and young people with long-term physical conditions.

References

Antonini, T. N., Raj, S. P., Oberjohn, K. S., Cassedy, A., Makoroff, K. L., Fouladi, M., & Wade, S. L. (2014). A pilot randomized trial of an online parenting skills program for pediatric traumatic brain injury: Improvements in parenting and child behavior. *Behavior Therapy*, *45*(4), 455–468. https://doi.org/10.1016/j.beth.2014.02.003

APA Dictionary of Psychology. (2023). *Paedatric Psychology*. APA.

Barlow, J. H., & Ellard, D. R. (2006). The psychosocial well-being of children with chronic disease, their parents and siblings: An overview of the research evidence base. *Child: Care, Health and Development, 32*(1), 19–31. https://doi.org/10.1111/j.1365-2214.2006.00591.x

Beck, A. (1967). Depression: Clinical, experimental, and theoretical aspects. *The British Journal of General Practice, 18*(87), 249.

Beck, A. T. (1979). *Cognitive therapy of depression*. Guilford Press.

Bennett, S. D., Cuijpers, P., Ebert, D. D., McKenzie Smith, M., Coughtrey, A. E., Heyman, I., Manzotti, G., & Shafran, R. (2019). Practitioner Review: Unguided and guided self-help interventions for common mental health disorders in children and adolescents: a systematic review and meta-analysis. *Journal of Child Psychology and Psychiatry, 60*(8), 828–847. https://doi.org/10.1111/jcpp.13010

Bennett, S. D., & Shafran, R. (2023). Adaptation, personalization and capacity in mental health treatments: a balancing act? *Current Opinion in Psychiatry, 36*(1), 28–33. https://doi.org/10.1097/YCO.0000000000000834

Bennett, S., Shafran, R., Coughtrey, A., Walker, S., & Heyman, I. (2015). Psychological interventions for mental health disorders in children with chronic physical illness: A systematic review. *Archives of Disease in Childhood, 100*(4), 308–316. https://doi.org/10.1136/archdischild-2014-307474

Birnie, K. A., Noel, M., Chambers, C. T., Uman, L. S., & Parker, J. A. (2018, October 4). Psychological interventions for needle-related procedural pain and distress in children and adolescents. *Cochrane Database of Systematic Reviews*, 2020(10). https://doi.org/10.1002/14651858.CD005179.pub4

BPS. (n.d.). *How are paediatric clinical psychology services organised*. British Psychological Society.

BPS. (2016). *Children and young people with physical health needs*. How psychological services contribute to the care pathway. British Psychological Society.

Catanzano, M., Bennett, S. D., Sanderson, C., Patel, M., Manzotti, G., Kerry, E., Coughtrey, A. E., Liang, H., Heyman, I., & Shafran, R. (2020). Brief psychological interventions for psychiatric disorders in young people with long term physical health conditions: A systematic review and meta-analysis. *Journal of Psychosomatic Research, 136*, 110187. https://doi.org/10.1016/j.jpsychores.2020.110187

CEPMHPG. (2012). *How mental illness loses out in the NHS*. London School of Economics and Political Science.

Chiles, J. A., Lambert, M. J., & Hatch, A. L. (1999). The impact of psychological interventions on medical cost offset: A meta-analytic review. *Clinical Psychology: Science and Practice, 6*(2), 204–220.

Chorpita, B. F., Daleiden, E. L., Ebesutani, C., Young, J., Becker, K. D., Nakamura, B. J., Phillips, L., Ward, A., Lynch, R., Trent, L., Smith, R. L., Okamura, K., & Starace, N. (2011). Evidence-based treatments for children and adolescents: An updated review of indicators of efficacy and effectiveness. *Clinical Psychology: Science and Practice, 18*(2), 154–172. https://doi.org/10.1111/j.1468-2850.2011.01247.x

Chorpita, B. F., Moffitt, C. E., & Gray, J. (2005). Psychometric properties of the Revised Child Anxiety and Depression Scale in a clinical sample. *Behaviour Research and Therapy, 43*(3), 309–322. https://doi.org/10.1016/j.brat.2004.02.004

Christie, D., & Channon, S. (2014). The potential for motivational interviewing to improve outcomes in the management of diabetes and obesity in paediatric and adult populations: A clinical review. *Diabetes, Obesity and Metabolism, 16*(5), 381–387. https://doi.org/10.1111/dom.12195

Cooper, M., & Law, D. (Eds.). (2018). *Working with goals in psychotherapy and counselling*, Vol. *1*. Oxford University Press. https://doi.org/10.1093/med-psych/9780198793687.001.0001

Cottrell, D. (2015). Prevention and treatment of psychiatric disorders in children with chronic physical illness. *Archives of Disease in Childhood, 100*(4), 303–304.

CWDC. (2009). *Early identification, assessment of needs and intervention*. A guide for practitioners*: The common assessment framework*. CWDC.

Dovey-Pearce, G., & Flannery, H. (2021). Integrating psychology into paediatric healthcare: A UK perspective. *Clinical Child Psychology and Psychiatry*, *26*(2), 313–322. https://doi.org/10.1177/13591045211000786

Dovey-Pearce, G., Rapley, T., & McDonagh, J. E. (2020). Delivering developmentally appropriate health care: roles for psychologists as members of the multi-disciplinary health care team. *Clinical Child Psychology and Psychiatry, 25*(3), 579–593.

Duff, A. J. A., & Bryon, M. (2005). Consultation with paediatric teams. *Clinical Child Psychology and Psychiatry*, *10*(1), 102–111. https://doi.org/10.1177/1359104505048795

D'Zurilla, T. J., & Goldfried, M. R. (1971). Problem solving and behavior modification. *Journal of Abnormal Psychology*, *78*(1), 107–126. https://doi.org/10.1037/h0031360

D'Zurilla, T. J., Nezu, A. M., & Maydeu-Olivares, A. (2002). *Social problem-solving inventory – revised*. Multi-Health Systems.

Eccleston, C., Fisher, E., Law, E., Bartlett, J., & Palermo, T. M. (2015). Psychological interventions for parents of children and adolescents with chronic illness. *Cochrane Database of Systematic Reviews*. https://doi.org/10.1002/14651858.CD009660.pub3

Ellis, D., Naar-King, S., Templin, T., Frey, M., Cunningham, P., Sheidow, A., Cakan, N., & Idalski, A. (2008). Multisystemic therapy for adolescents with poorly controlled Type 1 Diabetes. *Diabetes Care*, *31*(9), 1746–1747. https://doi.org/10.2337/dc07-2094

Eom, S., Caplan, R., & Berg, A. T. (2016). Behavioral problems and childhood epilepsy: Parent vs child perspectives. *The Journal of Pediatrics*, *179*, 233–239. e5. https://doi.org/10.1016/j.jpeds.2016.08.096

Evans, J. R., Benore, E., & Banez, G. A. (2016). The Cost-effectiveness of intensive interdisciplinary pediatric chronic pain rehabilitation. *Journal of Pediatric Psychology*, *41*(8), 849–856. https://doi.org/10.1093/jpepsy/jsv100

Fayed, N., Davis, A. M., Streiner, D. L., Rosenbaum, P. L., Cunningham, C. E., Lach, L. M., Boyle, M. H., & Ronen, G. M. (2015). Children's perspective of quality of life in epilepsy. *Neurology*, *84*(18), 1830–1837. https://doi.org/10.1212/WNL.0000000000001536

Fisher, E., Villanueva, G., Henschke, N., Nevitt, S. J., Zempsky, W., Probyn, K., Buckley, B., Cooper, T. E., Sethna, N., & Eccleston, C. (2022). Efficacy and safety of pharmacological, physical, and psychological interventions for the management of chronic pain in children: A WHO systematic review and meta-analysis. *Pain*, *163*(1), e1–e19. https://doi.org/10.1097/j.pain.0000000000002297

Glazebrook, C., Hollis, C., Heussler, H., Goodman, R., & Coates, L. (2003). Detecting emotional and behavioural problems in paediatric clinics. *Child: Care, Health and Development*, *29*(2), 141–149. https://doi.org/10.1046/j.1365-2214.2003.00324.x

Gregory, A. M., Rutter, M. K., Madrid-Valero, J. J., Bennett, S. D., Shafran, R., & Buysse, D. J. (2023). Therapies for mental health difficulties: Finding the sweet spot between standardization and personalization. *Journal of Child Psychology and Psychiatry*, *64*(2), 213–216.

Haukeland, Y. B., Fjermestad, K. W., Mossige, S., & Vatne, T. M. (2015). Emotional Experiences Among Siblings of Children With Rare Disorders. *Journal of Pediatric Psychology*, *40*(7), 712–720. https://doi.org/10.1093/jpepsy/jsv022

Ham, C., Smith, J., Davies, A., Rosen, R., Dixon, J., Goodwin, N., & Dixon, A. (2012). *Integrated care for patients and populations: Improving outcomes by working together*. The King's Fund.

Hysing, M., Elgen, I., Gillberg, C., Lie, S. A., & Lundervold, A. J. (2007). Chronic physical illness and mental health in children. Results from a large-scale population study. *Journal of Child Psychology and Psychiatry*, *48*(8), 785–792. https://doi.org/10.1111/j.1469-7610.2007.01755.x

Laurens, K. R., Green, M. J., Dean, K., Tzoumakis, S., Harris, F., Islam, F., Kariuki, M., Essery, C. M., Schofield, J. M., & Carr, V. J. (2019). Chronic physical health conditions, mental health, and sources of support in a longitudinal Australian child population cohort. *Journal of Pediatric Psychology*, *44*(9), 1083–1096. https://doi.org/10.1093/jpepsy/jsz048

Law, D., & Jacob, J. (2013). *Goals and goal based outcomes (GBOs)*. CAMHS.

Law, E. F., Fisher, E., Fales, J., Noel, M., & Eccleston, C. (2014). Systematic review and meta-analysis of parent and family-based interventions for children and adolescents with chronic medical conditions. *Journal of Pediatric Psychology*, *39*(8), 866–886. https://doi.org/10.1093/jpepsy/jsu032

Layard, R. (2016). The economics of mental health. *IZA World of Labor*. https://doi.org/10.15185/izawol.321

Layard, R., & Clark, D. M. (2015). Why more psychological therapy would cost nothing. *Frontiers in Psychology*, *6*, 1713. https://doi.org/10.3389/fpsyg.2015.01713

Martell, C. R., Addis, M. E., & Jacobson, N. S. (2001). *Depression in context: Strategies for guided action*. W. W. Norton & Company.

Mathias, E. G., Pai, M. S., Guddattu, V., & Bramhagen, A.-C. (2022). Non-pharmacological interventions to reduce anxiety among children undergoing surgery: A systematic review. *Journal of Child Health Care*, *136749352110623*. https://doi.org/10.1177/13674935211062336

Mattson, G., Kuo, D. Z., Yogman, M., Baum, R., Gambon, T. B., Lavin, A., Esparza, R. M., Nasir, A. A., Wissow, L. S., Apkon, S., Brei, T. J., Davidson, L. F., Davis, B. E., Ellerbeck, K. A., Hyman, S. L., Leppert, M. O., Noritz, G. H., Stille, C. J., & Yin, L. (2019). Psychosocial factors in children and youth with special health care needs and their families. *Pediatrics*, *143*(1), e20183171. https://doi.org/10.1542/peds.2018-3171

McGrady, M. E., Ryan, J. L., Gutiérrez-Colina, A. M., Fredericks, E. M., Towner, E. K., & Pai, A. L. H. (2015). The impact of effective paediatric adherence promotion interventions: systematic review and meta-analysis. *Child: Care, Health and Development*, *41*(6), 789–802. https://doi.org/10.1111/cch.12271

Melton, M. L. (2018). Ally, activist, advocate: Addressing role complexities for the multiculturally competent psychologist. *Professional Psychology: Research and Practice*, *49*(1), 83–89. https://doi.org/10.1037/pro0000175

Mokkink, L. B., van der Lee, J. H., Grootenhuis, M. A., Offringa, M., & Heymans, H. S. A. (2008). Defining chronic diseases and health conditions in childhood (0–18 years of age): National consensus in the Netherlands. *European Journal of Pediatrics, 167*(12), 1441–1447. https://doi.org/10.1007/s00431-008-0697-y

Moore, D. A., Nunns, M., Shaw, L., Rogers, M., Walker, E., Ford, T., Garside, R., Ukoumunne, O., Titman, P., Shafran, R., Heyman, I., Anderson, R., Dickens, C., Viner, R., Bennett, S., Logan, S., Lockhart, F., & Thompson Coon, J. (2019). Interventions to improve the mental health of children and young people with long-term physical conditions: linked evidence syntheses. *Health Technology Assessment*, *23*(22), 1–164. https://doi.org/10.3310/hta23220

Morey, A., & Loades, M. E. (2021). Review: How has cognitive behaviour therapy been adapted for adolescents with comorbid depression and chronic illness? A scoping review. *Child and Adolescent Mental Health*, *26*(3), 252–264. https://doi.org/10.1111/camh.12421

NHS. (2023, January). *Health Education England children and young people's mental health workforce census*. https://www.hee.nhs.uk/sites/default/files/documents/Children%20and%20Young%20People%27s%20Mental%20Health%20Workforce%20Census%202022_National%20Report_24.1.23.pdf

NICE. (2004). *Diagnosis and management of Type 1 Diabetes in children, young people and adults*. NICE.

NICE. (2005). *Depression in Children and Young People: Identification and Management in Primary, Community and Secondary Care*. NICE.

NICE. (2009). *Depression in adults with a chronic physical health problem: recognition and management*. NICE.

NICE. (2018). *Scenario: Management of alopecia areata*. NICE.

NICE. (2021a). *Epilepsies in children, young people and adults*. NICE.

NICE. (2021b). *Asthma: diagnosis, monitoring and chronic asthma management*. NICE.

NICE. (2022). *Diabetes (type 1 and type 2) in children and young people: diagnosis and management*. NICE.

Nunns, M., Mayhew, D., Ford, T., Rogers, M., Curle, C., Logan, S., & Moore, D. (2018). Effectiveness of nonpharmacological interventions to reduce procedural anxiety in children and adolescents undergoing treatment for cancer: A systematic review and meta-analysis. *Psycho-Oncology*, *27*(8), 1889–1899. https://doi.org/10.1002/pon.4749

Pinquart, M. (2013). Self-esteem of children and adolescents with chronic illness: a meta-analysis. *Child: Care, Health and Development*, *39*(2), 153–161. https://doi.org/10.1111/j.1365-2214.2012.01397.x

Pinquart, M. (2018). Parenting stress in caregivers of children with chronic physical condition-A meta-analysis. *Stress and Health*, *34*(2), 197–207. https://doi.org/10.1002/smi.2780

Pinquart, M. (2019a). Posttraumatic stress symptoms and disorders in parents of children and adolescents with chronic physical illnesses: A meta-analysis. *Journal of Traumatic Stress*, *32*(1), 88–96. https://doi.org/10.1002/jts.22354

Pinquart, M. (2019b). Featured article: Depressive symptoms in parents of children with chronic health conditions: A meta-analysis. *Journal of Pediatric Psychology*, *44*(2), 139–149. https://doi.org/10.1093/jpepsy/jsy075

Pinquart, M., & Shen, Y. (2011a). Depressive symptoms in children and adolescents with chronic physical illness: An updated meta-analysis. *Journal of Pediatric Psychology, 36*(4), 375–384. https://doi.org/10.1093/jpepsy/jsq104

Pinquart, M., & Shen, Y. (2011b). Anxiety in children and adolescents with chronic physical illnesses: a meta-analysis. *Acta Paediatrica, 100*(8), 1069–1076. https://doi.org/10.1111/j.1651-2227.2011.02223.x

Pinquart, M., & Shen, Y. (2011c). Behavior problems in children and adolescents with chronic physical illness: a meta-analysis. *Journal of Pediatric Psychology, 36*(9), 1003–1016. https://doi.org/10.1093/jpepsy/jsr042

Pinquart, M., & Teubert, D. (2012). Academic, physical, and social functioning of children and adolescents with chronic physical illness: a meta-analysis. *Journal of Pediatric Psychology, 37*(4), 376–389. https://doi.org/10.1093/jpepsy/jsr106

Roth, A. D., & Donnan, J. (2019). Developing a competence framework for psychological interventions in a multidisciplinary paediatric context. *BMJ Paediatrics Open, 3*(1), e000447. https://doi.org/10.1136/bmjpo-2019-000447

Rozental, A., Kottorp, A., Boettcher, J., Andersson, G., & Carlbring, P. (2016). Negative effects of psychological treatments: An exploratory factor analysis of the negative effects questionnaire for monitoring and reporting adverse and unwanted events. *PLOS ONE, 11*(6), e0157503. https://doi.org/10.1371/journal.pone.0157503

Salvo, T., Huckridge, J., Daniilidi, X., Kambakara Gedara, C., & Valentino, C. (2022). Developing groups in a paediatric psychology service: Centring the voices of children and young people. *Clinical Child Psychology and Psychiatry, 28*(1), 24–34. https://doi.org/10.1177/13591045221111215

Santana, M.-J., & Feeny, D. (2014). Framework to assess the effects of using patient-reported outcome measures in chronic care management. *Quality of Life Research, 23*(5), 1505–1513. https://doi.org/10.1007/s11136-013-0596-1

van der Kolk, B. A. (2005). Developmental trauma disorder: Toward a rational diagnosis for children with complex trauma histories. *Psychiatric Annals, 35*(5), 401–408. https://doi.org/10.3928/00485713-20050501-06

Varni, J. W., Seid, M., & Kurtin, P. S. (2001). PedsQL™ 4.0: Reliability and Validity of the Pediatric Quality of Life Inventory™ Version 4.0 generic core scales in healthy and patient populations. *Medical Care, 39*(8), 800–812. https://doi.org/10.1097/00005650-200108000-00006

Varni, J. W., Seid, M., & Rode, C. A. (1999). The PedsQLTM: Measurement model for the pediatric quality of life inventory. *Medical Care, 37*(2), 126–139. http://www.jstor.org/stable/3767218

Wallander, J. L., & Koot, H. M. (2016). Quality of life in children: A critical examination of concepts, approaches, issues, and future directions. *Clinical Psychology Review, 45*, 131–143. https://doi.org/10.1016/j.cpr.2015.11.007

Wallander, J. L., & Varni, J. W. (1998). Effects of pediatric chronic physical disorders on child and family adjustment. *Journal of Child Psychology and Psychiatry, and Allied Disciplines, 39*(1), 29–46.

Wijlaars, L. P. M. M., Gilbert, R., & Hardelid, P. (2016). Chronic conditions in children and young people: learning from administrative data. *Archives of Disease in Childhood, 101*(10), 881–885. https://doi.org/10.1136/archdischild-2016-310716

Young, J., O'Curry, S., Mastroyannopoulou, K., Deiros Collado, M., Gibbins, J., Donnan, J., Gray, V., & Griffiths, H. (2018). Paediatric Psychology Network United Kingdom (PPN-UK): From inception to the current day. *Clinical Practice in Pediatric Psychology*, *6*(4), 331–340. https://doi.org/10.1037/cpp0000257

Further Reading

Roberts, M. C., & Steele, R. G. (Eds.). (2017). *Handbook of pediatric psychology* (5th ed.). Guilford Press.

17

Disrupted Attachments

Clare Norris and Jade Weston

17.1 Introduction

An exciting area of development for child psychological practitioners over the past decade in England has been within children's social care. There are, increasingly, models of practice where practitioners provide consultation, training, assessments and interventions with children and their caring networks who are involved with children's social care. This can be with children on Child Protection (CP) plans, Child in Need (CiN) plans or with children who have been removed from their family of origin and become Children Looked After (CLA), who are placed for adoption or, increasingly, Special Guardianship Orders (SGOs). Chapter 26 focuses on the innovations in psychology providing services to children on CP plans. This chapter will focus on the roles child psychological practitioners have developed with CLA, children placed for adoption or on SGOs and care leavers.

Psychological practitioners may have contact with these children and young people (CYP) in many different clinical contexts such as in generic CAMH services or school-based mental health services, not only within targeted or specialist CLA services. Adults who have a care experienced history will also present to mental health services, including as parents of children referred to CAMHS. This chapter is relevant to all child psychological practitioners and other professionals working in mental health services, across all settings and age ranges.

17.2 The Lens of the Authors

The authors of this chapter have professional and personal experiences in this area that make them passionate about mental health support being accessible for this group of vulnerable CYP. Jade Weston is care experienced and Clare Norris was a 'birth child' of a family that fostered and adopted many children. Both have worked for the majority of their professional careers as psychologists with Children Looked After, adopted children, CYP on SGOs and children involved with Child Protection.

Child Psychology: Pathways to Good Practice, First Edition.
Edited by Helen Pote, Anna Picciotto and Clare Norris.

17.3 Definitions of CLA, Adopted Children and SGOs

In England, the term 'Children Looked After' (CLA) refers to children who are looked after by the local authority under the terms laid out under the Children Act (1989) and the Adoption and Children Act (2002). This includes children who are:

a. Subject to a Care Order (placing them under the care of the local authority on an interim or permanent basis where the local authority has parental responsibility (PR) for the child (shared with the parents).
b. Subject to a Placement Order (which grants the local authority permission to seek adopters for the child).
c. Accommodated by the local authority for a period of 24 hours or more (this includes children accommodated under a voluntary arrangement with the parents where the parent maintains PR, also known as a section 20 of the Children Act 1989).

The legal definition for a care leaver is someone who exits care, who has been in the care of the local authority for a period of 13 weeks or more spanning their 16th birthday (the Children Leaving Care Act, 2000).

Adoption is the legal process where children are placed with adoptive carers and PR transfers from their birth parents or local authority (if CLA) to their new carers. In SGOs the special guardians appointed by the court are usually known to the child's birth family (relatives or friends) and PR is shared with the birth parent/s, although the special guardians can make most decisions without their knowledge or consent. There is usually more contact with the birth family in SGOs than in adoptions, when contact is often prevented or limited. However, open adoptions (where CYP have contact with their birth parents and family) are increasing, particularly in this digital age where many CYP can find their birth parents via social media (Goldberg, 2019).

Usually, children placed for adoption or on SGOs have been CLA prior to being placed permanently via the courts with their new carers. Thus, throughout this chapter CLA will be used to include all children removed from their birth parents (including those that are later adopted or placed in SGOs). Where separate research evidence exists that is different for children adopted or on SGOs compared to CLA then this will be discussed.

17.4 Government Statistics for CLA, Adoption and SGOs

According to Department for Education (DfE) statistics for England for Children Looked After including adoptions (2022a) the number of CLA by local authorities rose to its highest level. As of March 2022, there were 82,170 CLA (up 2% from the previous year). That is 70 CLA per 10,000 children. The total number of children being looked after has increased annually since 2010, with the exception of 2021 where the number dropped due to the Covid-19 pandemic, probably due to the impact on court proceedings being delayed in this time period. Similar patterns have been recorded in Scotland, Northern Ireland and Wales (National Institute for Clinical Excellence, 2021a).

National Institute for Clinical Excellence (NICE) guidance for looked after children and young people (2021a) records that in England, most CLA are cared for in foster placements

Table 17.1 Ethnicity of CLA.

Ethnicity	White British	Mixed or Multiple Ethic Groups	Black African, Caribbean or Black British	Asian or Asian British	Other	Not Known
Percentage of CLA	73	10	7	5	4	1

(72%), with 14% in connected care (with relatives or friends) and 13% in residential care, secure units or semi-independent living accommodation. In addition to these, 7% of CLA are placed with birth parents (such as those returned home but remaining on an order for a short period). Adoptions rose sharply from 2011 to a peak in 2015 but have since been falling. This decrease follows two court rulings in 2013, which stated that adoption orders should be made only when there was no other alternative (such as placing a child with birth relatives). Since then, the number of SGOs have increased. Most SGOs were granted to relatives or friends (87%) the remainder were largely to former foster carers (11%) (Department for Education, 2022a).

The general demographics of CLA in 2022 are similar to previous years (DfE, 2022a). Males account for 56% and females 44%. In terms of age, the majority of CLA are over the age of 10 (64%) and only 5% are under 1 year. Table 17.1 shows the ethnicity of CLA according to government statistics for England (DfE, 2022a).

According to the DfE statistics (2022a) 'abuse or neglect' was recorded as the primary need for becoming CLA for 66% of children, 'family dysfunction' (13%) was the next most common reason followed by 'family in acute stress' (7%). The latter is defined as the family going through a crisis that diminishes parental capacity to meet CYP's needs and there being no parent available to care for the child.

17.5 Attachment Difficulties and Disorders

Children who enter the care system will necessarily have experienced separation from and loss of their primary caregivers. Many will also have experienced abuse and neglect from these caregivers, leading to them being placed in care. Attachment difficulties or disorders are therefore common in children removed from their parents. Attachment theory, developed by John Bowlby in the 1960s (e.g. Bowlby 1969, 1976, 2005), has been the basis of many of the assessments, formulations and interventions for CYP with disrupted attachments.

Attachment theory's origins and developments are described in Chapter 2 so will not be repeated here. It is important to highlight, however, that the concept of *pervasive shame* experienced by CYP (Hughes, 1997, 2006, 2007) who have experienced abusive and neglectful attachment relationships and the failure of primary caregivers to repair disruptions in attachment, is central to many therapies for children removed from their parents (e.g. Dyadic Developmental Psychotherapy (DDP), Hughes 1997, 2006, 2007). These therapies will be described in the interventions section later in this chapter.

In terms of attachment disorders, the main classification of psychiatric disorders, the American Psychiatric Association, Diagnostic and Statistical Manual of Mental Disorders

(DSM-V, 5th edition, 2013) recognises two distinct forms of attachment disorder: Reactive Attachment Disorder and Disinhibited Social Engagement Disorder. The first involves the inability of a child to attach to a referred caregiver, and the second involves indiscriminate sociability and disinhibited attachment behaviours. The alternative classification of disorders, International Classification of Diseases, 11th edition (ICD-11, WHO, 2022a), recognises similar diagnoses of Reactive Attachment Disorder and Disinhibited Attachment Disorder, within the category of Unspecified Behavioural and Emotional Disorders with Onset Usually Occurring in Childhood or Adolescence.

Insecure avoidant and ambivalent attachment styles are not considered 'pathological' and it is estimated that approximately 40% of the general population have an insecure attachment style (Hazan & Shaver, 1994). However, insecure disorganised attachment styles are less prevalent, can have a significant impact on the child or young person's relationships and ability to function in everyday life, and can be a risk factor for mental health difficulties (Hughes, 2006). Disturbed or disordered attachment can lead to chronic difficulties in relating to others, contribute to a poor self-identity and can be a vulnerability to developing emotionally unstable (borderline) personality traits or disorder as an adult (Agrawal et al., 2004).

There is also a body of research demonstrating the impact of early attachment experiences and maltreatment on a child's brain development (e.g. Fonagy et al., 2002; Perry & Pollard, 1997; Schore, 2001; Siegal 2007). Attachment difficulties, neglect and abuse can contribute to neurodevelopmental and cognitive difficulties (Newman et al., 2015; Nishitani et al., 2021; Teicher et al., 2016; Tomoda, Navalta et al., 2009; Tomada, Suzuki et al., 2009; Tomoda et al., 2011, 2012;).

Attachment difficulties and maltreatment in childhood have also been associated with difficulties with emotion processing and regulation across the lifespan (Camras et al., 1983; Cicchetti & Toth, 2015; Jedd et al., 2015; Pollak et al., 2000). Emotion regulation is developed through a child's relationship with their main attachment figures in childhood. It is usually associated with secure attachments, attuned responses to children's emotions and the caregiver demonstrating their ability to regulate their own emotions (Eisenberg et al., 1998, 2010; Morris et al., 2007). Difficulties with social functioning, academic achievement and emotional wellbeing have been associated with deficits in emotion regulation in childhood (Cole et al., 2004; Eisenberg et al., 2010; Graziano et al., 2007; Zeman et al., 2006).

17.6 The Impact of Adverse Childhood Experiences

Almost all CLA and adopted CYP will have experienced trauma in some way. Many experience multiple traumas and adverse childhood experiences (ACEs). As well as physical, psychological, sexual abuse and neglect, trauma can also include exposure to domestic abuse or alcohol, drug misuse and violence. All children are unique and will have their own protective factors and vulnerabilities, and some CLA show remarkable resilience despite their abusive childhood experiences. However, there is a large body of research showing the negative impact of ACEs on a child's development leading to negative outcomes on both their physical and mental health, personality development and ability to form and maintain heathy relationships that often continues into adulthood (Anda et al., 2006; Feeney et al., 2000; Koplan & Chard, 2015). See Chapter 27 for further discussion.

In terms of ACEs for CLA, many will have taken place in their family of origin. The particular and pervasive impact of abuse and neglect within the family on a child's development has been well documented (e.g. Cook & Cook, 2005; Gerhardt, 2004; Perry, 2002, 2006; van der Kolk, 2005). ACEs research and as a concept have, however, not been without criticism (see Chapter 27).

17.7 Developmental Trauma

The term developmental trauma is increasingly used to describe the distress experienced by children who have experienced repeated childhood trauma (van der Kolk, 2014). The impact of this is well documented: numerous studies of chronically traumatised children find problems with aggression and impulse control, attentional and dissociative problems and difficulty negotiating relationships with caregivers, peers, and, later in life, intimate partners. A history of childhood physical and sexual assault is associated with many other psychiatric diagnoses in adolescence and adulthood (van de Kolk, 2014).

The current diagnosis that is usually applied to those having developed mental health symptoms as a result of exposure to an isolated traumatic event is post-traumatic stress disorder (PTSD). Isolated traumatic events can result in conditioned behavioural and biological responses to the trauma, such as symptoms of re-experiencing (e.g. flashbacks/nightmares), avoidance and alterations to cognitions and mood (see Chapter 13).

However, many CLA do not meet the criteria for a diagnosis of PTSD due to having been exposed to repeated trauma throughout childhood rather than an isolated traumatic event, and usually showing a different presentation of symptoms and difficulties. Furthermore, a PTSD diagnosis does not capture the complex emotional, behavioural and neurobiological sequelae of childhood trauma and the recommendations for treatment for PTSD are not always appropriate or effective for repeated childhood trauma. *DSM-V* includes complex PTSD type, for those exposed to numerous traumas, and there are some suggestions of how interventions might be adapted or differ. However, experts in this field assert that this does not go far enough.

Developmental Trauma Disorder was put forward for inclusion in *DSM-V*, with a definition and a set of diagnostic criteria developed by van De Kolk and his colleagues at the National Child Trauma Stress Network (van der Kolk, 2005, 2014). However, the addition was not accepted. The World Health Organization's (WHO) ICD released its 11th edition in 2022 and it included an updated diagnosis of Complex PTSD, separate from PTSD within the category of Disorders Specifically Associated with Stress. Importantly, it was a distinct diagnosis and highlighted that individuals who meet the criteria for PTSD and Complex PTSD are significantly different in terms of their trauma history and the impact on the individual's functioning (see Chapter 27 for a fuller discussion of diagnostic categorisation of trauma and Chapter 14 for an in-depth account of PTSD).

In the absence of an adequate diagnostic framework for children who have experienced multiple childhood traumas, effective interventions cannot be developed. Furthermore, the lack of a diagnosis may act as a barrier to accessing appropriate services. Many children will be misdiagnosed with alternative diagnoses, frequently neurodevelopmental disorders or attachment disorders, or diagnosed with other psychiatric conditions, and non-effective treatments offered in practice. The complexity of assessing CLA and teasing apart if a CYP's difficulties are neurobiological in nature, are due to negative attachment experiences or exposure to neglect and trauma or, indeed, are due to all factors will be further discussed in the assessment section of this chapter.

There is also criticism and controversy surrounding diagnostic frameworks. Alternative frameworks have been developed that focus on describing an individual's difficulties and developing a comprehensive formulation of how they may have developed and be maintained. These are commonly used by psychological practitioners (see Chapters 2 and 3, for more on theory, diagnosis, assessment and formulation).

17.8 Outcomes for CLA and Adopted Children

Unsurprisingly, given the high rates of ACEs in this population, research has consistently shown that the rate of mental health disorders is much higher in the CLA population, at 45% for those in foster care and 72% for those in residential care, than in children in the general population (NICE, 2021a). NHS digital figures from the Mental Health Survey for Children and Young People (MHSCYP; NHS Digital, 2021), which surveyed CYP's mental health from 2017 to 2021, found rates of probable mental disorders in 2021 were one in six (17.4%) in 6 to 19 years old (NHS Digital, 2021).

Despite the known high rate of mental health disorders in CLA, it can be difficult for these CYP and their carers to access appropriate psychological services. In addition to the absence of an appropriate diagnosis, other barriers to access include long waiting lists, stigma, lack of awareness and support for carers, placement instability, poor information, lack of home visiting, off-putting venues and inconvenient appointment times (Blower et al, 2004; Golding, 2010; Street & Davies, 2002; York & Jones, 2017).

Studies have also shown that, compared to children living with their birth families, CLA are likely to have poorer educational outcomes (Meltzer et al., 2003; Tarren-Sweeney, 2010). They are more likely to have special educational needs requiring Education Health and Care Plans (EHCPs), have diagnoses of neurodevelopmental disorders (e.g. Attention Deficit Hyperactivity Disorder (ADHD) and Autistic Spectrum Disorder (ASD)), and are more likely to be excluded from school and to leave school with no qualifications than the general population of children (NICE, 2021a). CLA continue to be over-represented in all areas of the Youth Justice System, police, court and within the prison population (Rose et al., 2006). They are also 88 times more likely to be involved with drug use and 60 times more likely to be homeless than CYP in the general population (Barnardo's et al., 2000). Care leavers as a group also have poorer outcomes on key measures such as housing, health, employment and continuing in education and training post-16 than the general population of CYP (DfE, 2022a; Dixon et al., 2006; NICE, 2021a; Viner & Taylor, 2005).

Delays in a child entering care (prolonging the exposure to abuse and neglect), placement instability and instability of educational settings when in the care system contribute to poorer outcomes for CLA (Hannon et al, 2010; NICE, 2021a, Rubin et al., 2007; Simmonds, 2010; Vostanis, 2007; Ward et al., 2008). On a positive note, studies demonstrate the positive difference that alternative care can make to a child's physical and emotional wellbeing and educational outcomes (Schofield et al, 2012; Van IJzendoorn & Juffer, 2006; Wade et al, 2011). This has led the drive towards placement permanency and adoption of CLA.

The data is also positive for children placed in SGOs in terms of wellbeing, health and education (DfE, 2021; Harwin et al., 2019). Older children (aged four or above), children with emotional and behavioural problems, children who are placed with unrelated carers and those who experienced a greater number of placement moves prior to the SGO are associated with greater risk of disruption (Harwin et al., 2019; McGrath, in press; Selwyn et al., 2014; Wade et al., 2010, 2014).

17.9 Diversity and Inclusion

Many CLA, adopted children and those on SGOs are from groups that are already disadvantaged. NICE (2021a) emphasises that it is crucial that their needs are met and that they do not face further marginalisation. These groups include those from Black, Asian and other minoritised ethnic groups (such as Gypsy, Roma and Traveller communities) and vulnerable groups such as, refugees and unaccompanied asylum-seeking children, disabled children with complex needs, CYP with a learning disability or neurodevelopmental disability, lower socioeconomic groups and people who identify as LGBTQ+.

Research into the impact of transracial fostering and adoption identified a negative impact on children's ethnic identity development that in turn may have an indirect influence on subsequent adjustment (DeBerry et al., 1996; Hollingsworth, 1997; Reynolds & Wing, 2020). Further research showed that white families were minimising the cultural background of their adoptees by infrequent or non-engagement in cultural socialisation practices, not addressing racial discrimination that occurred outside the family and colour-blindness (McRoy & Zurcher, 1983; McRoy et al., 1984; Reinoso et al., 2012).

Services have come a long way in recognising the importance of diversity in fostering and adoption and considering these issues when matching children with carers. There have also been positive changes in who can apply and be approved as foster carers and adoptive parent(s). Where previously this was open only to heterosexual, married couples, nowadays there is greater representation of single carers, same-sex couples, carers from different ethnic groups and from the LGBTQ+ community (Goldberg, 2019). These changes are welcome given the increasing number of children entering care and the national shortage of foster and adopted placements.

17.10 Service Delivery

17.10.1 The Law and Statutory Guidance

In the England and Wales, the health and wellbeing of CLA and care leavers is governed by law and by statutory guidance from the DfE and the Department of Health and Social Care (DoH). NICE (2021b) lists the following: The Children Act (1989), The Children Act (2004), Care Standards Act (2000), Care Planning, Placement and Case Review Regulations (2010), Children and Social Work Act (2017), Fostering Services Regulations (2011), Children and

Adoption Act (2006), the Safeguarding Vulnerable Groups Act (2006), Working Together to Safeguard Children (2018) and Keeping Children Safe in Education (2021).[1] These provide the legal framework for local authorities, providers of fostering services and children's homes. NICE and the social care equivalent, Social Care Institute of Excellence (SCIE) also produce guidelines on best practice for services for CLA.

NICE guidelines (2021a) for child and adolescent mental health services for CLA stipulate:

> To avoid delays in care, provide intermediate therapeutic or specialist support for the care network around looked-after children and young people who are on a waiting list for child and adolescent mental health services (CAMHS), for example a specialist outreach team. This should not be used as a replacement for CAMHS.
> Offer a range of dedicated CAMHS that are tailored to the needs of looked-after children and young people – for example, making them longer term, more trauma informed and relationship based.
> Offer preventive services based on assessed need with timely delivery to prevent serious mental health problems that need tier 3 or 4 specialist services.
> Be aware that children moving placements must not lose their place in the waiting list for CAMHS, as there is a statutory right to not lose a place in a waiting list for a health service.
> Provide specialist, trauma-informed mental health and emotional wellbeing support for unaccompanied asylum-seeking children. Take into account cultural sensitivities (for example, the different perspectives of unaccompanied asylum-seeking children about mental health services) and that symptoms of trauma could come to the surface over the long term.

In the following sections there will be further discussion of current mental health services for CLA and adopted CYP and potential barriers to achieving the aims set out in these guidelines.

17.10.2 The Structure of Mental Health Services for CLA

Traditionally, psychological practitioners working in child health and mental health did not have much involvement in the area of adoption and fostering, viewing it as the remit of social workers. Psychologists, Hobday and Lee (1995) highlighted the lack of training and expertise in the psychological theory or interventions needed to assess, advise and intervene with CLA and adopted children and their families/caring networks and outlined a role for psychologists. Their article outlined some examples of the roles a psychological practitioner could contribute to: the assessment of adoptive parents; placement matching; interventions to prevent placement breakdown; working with foster and adoptive families and birth children; and assessment of children's placement and therapeutic needs. However, the number of psychological practitioners involved in this field remained low with significant postcode variation and the mental health needs of this population remained unaddressed for the many who could not access traditional mental health services such as CAMHS.

1 Scotland and Northern Ireland are covered by different legislation.

The development of specific services to address the physical and mental health needs of CLA flourished following the British government's launching of the Quality Protects programme (Department of Health, 1998), which was a key part of the government's wider strategy for tackling social exclusion. This recognised that CLA needed dedicated physical and mental health services and introduced a set of mandatory national objectives for these services with requirements for multiagency partnership working. A key objective was to ensure that CLA gained maximum life chance benefits from educational opportunities, healthcare and social care.

As part of the programme, there was a requirement for joint commissioning between Health and Social Care. The recommendations for CLA mental health services were the provision of a comprehensive assessment and plan for treatment without a prolonged wait, consultation to social care and primary care, availability of a range of evidence-based treatments and inpatient care in a specialist setting. However, use of the funds attached to Quality Protects was locally determined by health and social care services leading to continued geographical variation in the provision of services across the country.

For some time in the early 2000s, Quality Protects led to increased and improved CLA-specific mental health services. In some areas, there were dedicated services targeted at CLA, leading to an increase in mental health professionals being trained in approaches specific to the mental health of CLA. Teams were offering both indirect work involving consultation and training to social work teams and staff working directly with CLA and their caring networks and direct clinical assessments of and interventions with CLA and parents and carers. Psychological practitioners were amongst these professionals leading to an increase in the development and implementation of specialist therapies for these children and the evaluation of these interventions.

Over time, increases in mental health difficulties in CYP in the general population and a chronic underfunding of mental health services for children (Association of Child Psychiatrists, 2018) have meant that some of these dedicated and well-resourced mental health services for CLA have been cut or severely reduced. The current picture has reverted to many CLA not having access to timely mental health services that meet their needs. However, it is recommended by the DfE and Department of Health Publication (2015, p. 21) that:

> CCGs, local authorities and NHS England should ensure that CAMHS and other services provide targeted and dedicated support to looked-after children according to need. This could include a dedicated team or seconding a CAMHS professional into a looked-after children multi-agency team. Professionals need to work together with the child to assess and meet their mental health needs in a tailored way.

NICE (2021a) and Silver et al. (2015) emphasise the barriers and difficulties this population has accessing traditional mental health services, exacerbated by higher thresholds for accessing services, due to the increase in demand and limited recourses. CAMHS frequently focus on diagnosable mental health difficulties rather than the consequences of ACEs/trauma such as emotional difficulties, which may not meet the criteria for a diagnosis, and therefore CAMHS. Mental health services for CLA require assertive engagement, proactive inclusion work, building relationships and flexible arrangements so that assessments and interventions can take place in less stigmatising settings such as the CLA's home or community venues. The capacity for working with carers and systems and not only individual children is an essential aspect of the work (NICE, 2021a; Silver et al., 2015) and targeted mental health services for CLA need to ensure that these are key features of the services they offer.

National specialist centres, mainly located in London, have been developed and continue to operate with good outcomes, leading on the provision and evaluation of assessments and therapy and resources for these children, their carers and networks. However, these are often highly specialist and costly interventions available for very few, and often the most complex children showing high levels of difficulties.

17.10.3 Mental Health Services for Adopted Children and their Families and CYP on SGOs

In terms of adopted CYP and their families, there has been an increased focus on their needs, with some targeted increase in funding in England (DfE, 2018a. 2021). The strategy's aim is to enable children who have been adopted or who are on an SGO and who have experienced abuse and neglect to get the therapeutic support they need. Additional resources will also go to the Regional Adoption Agency (RAA) to improve recruitment and the adopter approval process.

A large research study carried out by the DfE (2022b) suggests that there has been considerable progress at national and regional levels in implementing the Adoption Support Framework. It found that families feel more confident about asking for help and support is generally more accessible. There is more to be done, however, as it is recommended that funding is sustained and there is an emphasis on building on and consolidating these improvements (DfE, 2022b).

17.10.4 Embedded Models of Mental Health Service Provision

The past 10 years has seen the development of models where psychological practitioners or mental health professionals are co-located, or 'embedded' within social care (e.g. Hackney's Reclaiming Social Work model – Cross, Hubbard, & Munro, 2010; Islington's Motivational Practice Model – Holt et al., 2020; Hertfordshire's Family Safeguarding Model – Forrester et al., 2017; North Yorkshire's Psychologically Informed Partnership Approach – North Yorkshire County Council, 2018). These models all recognise the value of psychological and systemic theory and its application in this area. They recognise the need for early intervention to prevent difficulties escalating and to build children's, their carers' and the system's resilience. They also recognise the need to intervene at multiple levels, directly and indirectly with systems and networks, and that the unique skill set psychological practitioners bring can make a significant impact when they work as *part* of children's social care teams. On a systemic and organisational level, they can present psychological knowledge and practice to forums for strategic leadership and best practice, and their research skills are contributing to the growing knowledge base and literature on CLA and adoption and on therapeutic interventions, which will be described later in this chapter.

17.11 Clinical Practice with CLA and Children placed for Adoption or on SGOs

17.11.1 Critical Reflections on the Current Evidence

The evidence base in this area, particularly around the mental health needs of CLA and adopted children and the evaluation of interventions for this population has lagged in comparison to other areas of child mental health with a lack of methodologically robust studies from which to draw sound conclusions (Bergström et al., 2020; Hambrick et al., 2016).

17.11.2 Systematic Reviews and NICE Guidelines

NICE guidelines for CLA and CYP adopted or on SGOs (2015, 2017, 2021a) have summarised the findings of systematic reviews of interventions for this population (Bergström et al., 2020; Hambrick et al., 2016; Kohloff et al., 2022; Lorenc et al., 2020; Ní Chobhthaigh & Duffy, 2019; Van IJzendoorn & Bakermans-Kranenburg, 2019). All of these reviews have found evidence of interventions that have positive outcomes for CYP that are in care or adopted but they highlight the lack of high-quality evaluative studies and report that it is difficult to draw firm conclusions.

Readers are signposted to the NSPCC's review of the research literature for CLA (Rahilly & Hendry, 2014), which brings together leading academics, practitioners and policy analysts to set out the implications of the latest research and examine the challenges faced by CLA. A summary of the recommended interventions along with those with a growing evidence base will be discussed later in this chapter.

In addition to generic criticisms of the evidence base for psychological therapies (see Chapter 2) there are specific reasons for the lack of an evidence base with CYP and adopted CYP. The ethics of carrying out research with this population is complex: CLA frequently have a lack of trust in professionals that can make it hard to be sure they have given informed consent; many may have additional difficulties (e.g. neurodevelopmental or learning disabilities), which also make gaining informed consent difficult; using control groups in research trials, and thereby depriving children, who often have a high level of need, of an intervention may not meet ethical guidelines standards; and CYP with a history of ACEs may be retraumatised by participating in research that may focus on their past traumatic experiences.

There are also methodological difficulties with defining meaningful outcomes for this population; outcomes being distal to the intervention and standardised measures not fitting well with CYP who are CLA or adopted. This will be discussed further in the outcomes section of this chapter.

In the absence of a sound evidence base for interventions specific for CLA, existing therapies have been offered to these children without adaptation or consideration of the complexity of the client group (Hambrick et al., 2016). Interventions with an established evidence base for treating trauma in the general CYP population, for example, eye movement desensitisation and reprocessing (EMDR, Shapiro & Solomon, 2010) and trauma-focused-cognitive behaviour therapy (TF-CBT, Mannarino et al., 2014) need adapting for CLA and adopted children and need to consider the impact of complex developmental trauma and multiple repeated traumatic experiences. Leenarts et al. (2013) and Bennett et al. (2021), in their systematic reviews of interventions for PTSD in CYP with maltreated children, both conclude that TF-CBT has the strongest evidence base with maltreated children however, there is a paucity of methodologically robust research on other trauma-focused therapeutic models with this population.

It is important that more randomised controlled trails (RCTs) and methodologically robust studies are carried out in this area. However, other research methods are also valuable in being able to understand the experiences of CLA and adopted children, including qualitative methodologies, and these are important in the co-production of mental health and therapeutic services for CLA and adopted CYP. Psychological practitioners, with their research and therapeutic skills, are well placed to continue to develop the evidence base for psychological interventions for CLA and adopted CYP using different methods.

17.12 Clinical Practice

The following sections focus on applying the evidence base in clinical practice with CLA using the structure of assessment, formulation, intervention, outcome and evaluation, illustrated with a clinical example and some ideas for reflection.

17.12.1 Assessment

It is important to clearly define the purpose and remit of a psychological assessment with this client group, as the queries and concerns of the referrer can be broader than a child's mental health and therapeutic needs. For example, referrals may request recommendations about placement needs (including matching with prospective adopters or carers), assessment of whether siblings should be kept together or separated, assessments to inform decisions about contact arrangements or whether a carer has the capacity to meet the child(ren)'s needs.

Consultation with the Referrer and Professional Network: Ideally, a thorough understanding of the referrer's concerns and needs would be gathered through an initial consultation with the referrer and possibly others from the child's professional or caring network. This also helps to identify who needs to be part of the assessment and what sources of information can be drawn upon, in order to limit the impact of the assessment process on the child or family. Consideration needs to be given to how informed consent can be obtained from the CYP and who has parental responsibility to make these decisions.

The initial consultation should include gathering information pertaining to the child's early developmental history, trauma/safeguarding experiences, placement moves and experiences and presenting concerns prior to meeting the child, as these subjects can often be difficult for this cohort of CYP to hear or talk about and may elicit anxiety or shame-based responses. The CYP may not be aware of the details of the situation that led to them becoming looked after or adopted and/or there may be concerns that would be sensitive and potentially detrimental for the CYP to hear from their carers, but which are important to understand (for example, their carer's feelings towards them and possible instability of the placement). Children's services', educational and medical records can also be useful sources of information about the CYP's history and current presentation.

There may be many unknowns in the history for these children who have been removed from their parents' care (such as their in-utero experiences and early infant experiences) and also details about their parents' or extended family characteristics or history (e.g. mental health or neurological difficulties that present in their family). Every effort should be made to find out as much information as possible from multiple sources, but gaps may remain.

Assessment processes for this client group can be lengthy and may often require meetings with different parts of the system around the child, as well as the CYP and their caregivers (both separately and together). It is important to consider the child's behaviour as embedded within their context, holding a framework of mental health and child development, alongside consideration of attachment and trauma. It may also be helpful to meet with the identified child's siblings (including birth, foster and adoptive siblings) and observe the sibling relationship(s), particularly where there are concerns about mental health needs of the sibling(s), which may or may not be related to living with a sibling with a high range of needs. Observations of the CYP in different settings can be valuable (e.g. their education environment). Psychometric assessments and standardised tools and measures can be used to complement clinical interviews (these will be discussed later in assessments of different areas). However, care needs to be taken not to subject traumatised children and young people to batteries of tests or questionnaires as part of the assessment as CLA and adopted CYP may find some of the questions (e.g. about past traumas or experiences) trigger emotional distress.

Difficulties in engagement with CLA and CYP who have been adopted and on SGOs can be common due to mistrust of adults, given their past experiences of abuse and adverse childhood experiences by adult carers. Furthermore, they may have had many different professionals in their lives and may be reluctant to engage with yet another. Time needs to be taken to engage with the CYP and gain their trust.

The assessment should cover:

- The child's in-utero and post-natal experiences: whether they were exposed to alcohol/ substances or domestic violence during pregnancy.
- Developmental history: developmental milestones, any unusual traits or behaviours that have developed.
- Any co-existing neurodevelopmental difficulties or disorders already identified.
- Family factors: who is in the birth family/ carer family and the quality of relationships.
- The child's parenting and attachment experiences, both past and current.
- The child's relationships with birth family/carers, professionals and peers and their interpersonal and social skills.
- The child's placement history: the quality of placements, transitions and losses, contact arrangements.
- Information about the child's past traumas and losses, the child's understanding of these experiences and any sense of blame, shame or trust issues as a result.

- Presenting difficulties and its impact, including on those around them. Areas of concern may include difficulties that may not always be conceptualised by mental health systems as 'mental health difficulties', such as lying, stealing, soiling, hoarding, neglect of personal hygiene, controlling behaviour, disinhibited behaviour and sexually harmful behaviour.
- Education experiences and achievements and any difficulties for example, in cognitive, sensory and executive functioning skills.
- The child's/family's strengths, positive qualities, resources and protective factors.
- Risk and safety factors related to the parents/carers, the child and social risk factors both current and historical.
- Wider contextual and systemic factors: cultural, religious and economic.

Assessments of Attachment and Relationships: Identifying attachment difficulties and disorders is crucial in this population of children, predicting future difficulties in relationships and the need for attachment-based interventions for the CYP, their carers and systems. There are many different methods and tools for assessing attachment relationships and identifying attachment difficulties and disorders, which differ according to the age of the CYP involved. Methods vary, with some focusing on behavioural observations, some examining the CYP's representation of attachment relationships, for example through the CYP completing stories, and some assessing the coherence of the CYP's account of their attachment relationships through interviews. Some of these are described later, but the reader is directed to NICE (2015) for a full systematic review of methods and tools available.

NICE (2015) recommends the assessment tools outlined should be used in conjunction with comprehensive clinical assessment, according to the age of the CYP.

Observational methods such as the Strange Situation (Ainsworth et al., 1978) and modified versions of it (e.g. the preschool assessment of attachment, Crittenden, 1992 or the Attachment Q Sort observational method, Waters & Deane, 1985) are recommended for children aged one to four. The Strange Situation procedure includes observations of the carer–child relationship during times of stressful separation and reunion and can be useful for assessing both the child's reactions and also the caregiver's ability to provide emotional containment on reunion. The Attachment Q Sort method involves observations of the child during a non-stressful situation (e.g. playing with a carer). It is comprised of 90 cards with statements about the child's behaviour, which are sorted into nine piles by the assessor, ranging from 'most descriptive of this child' to 'least descriptive of this child'. It includes items on secure-base behaviours, dependency, affectivity, social interaction, object manipulation and social perceptiveness.

Completing stories to access children's representations of attachment relationships are recommended for children aged four to seven (e.g., the Story Stem Assessment Profile, Hodges et al., 2003). For older children (aged 7 to 15) the Child Attachment Interview (Shmueli-Goetz et al., 2008) and the Attachment Interview for Childhood and Adolescence (Ammaniti et al., 2000) are recommended.

Many of the child–carer therapeutic approaches described in Section 17.12.3 use structured assessment measures of the nature of the attachment relationship and the child–carer interaction to assess where there might be difficulties that need to be addressed (e.g. the use of the Marshak Interaction Method (MIM), commonly used for Theraplay® assessments,

Marshak, 1960). Video Interactive Guidance (VIG, Kennedy and Underdown, 2018) uses videos of parent–child interaction to assess their interaction and relationship and then to show to parents for feedback.

Children's representations of attachments can also be sought more informally and creatively through, for example, the child drawing a picture of their family. Asking children to represent important people in their lives using miniature figures within a sand tray or on a large piece of paper or cloth (sometimes referred to as an eco-map) can also support children to convey non-verbally how they view themselves and important people in their lives. Stone (2021) developed a digital method for conducting these play assessments using a virtual sand tray using the Virtual Sandtray App®©. Treisman (2016) outlines example questions and tools for undertaking attachment and trauma-informed assessments.

As well as assessing the child it is important to consider the carer's attachment experiences and behaviours, such as their sensitivity and attunement towards the child. Caregivers may experience 'blocked care' (Hughes & Baylin, 2012), where they start to lose empathy for and withdraw care from the child as a result of experiencing repeated rejection from the child. The caregiver's own attachment and parenting history might lead them to make unhelpful assumptions about the child's behaviour (Hughes & Baylin, 2012). Measures that can support an assessment of the caregiver's own experiences include the Adult Attachment Interview (George et al., 1985), the Parenting Stress Index (Abidin et al., 2006) and the Parental Reflective Functioning Questionnaire (Luyten et al., 2017).

Assessments of Children's Presenting Difficulties: When assessing presenting difficulties of those in alternative care arrangements, it can be helpful to supplement traditional measures of mental health difficulties such as the Child Behaviour Checklist (CBCL, Achenbach, 1994) with measures that have been specifically designed for this cohort of CYP. The Assessment Checklist for Children (ACC) and the Assessment Checklist for Adolescents (ACA) (Tarren-Sweeney, 2013a, 2013b) are carer-report measures that include empirically derived attachment and trauma-related clinical scales. More general trauma-based measures can also be useful within assessments for this population, such as the Trauma Symptom Checklist for Children (Briere & Spinazzola, 2005), the Children's Impact of Traumatic Events Scale (Wolfe et al., 1991), the Child Dissociative Checklist (Putnam et al., 1993) and the Adolescent Dissociative Experiences Scale (Armstrong et al., 1997). When considering the impact of trauma experiences, it is imperative to consider the full range of trauma experiences and not just those listed within the ACE definitions. These include the impact of racism and being exposed to institutional prejudices, intergenerational trauma such as genocide, being a victim of terrorism, being a victim of bullying, being a child carer, bereavement and family breakdown. Entering care can also in itself be traumatic for some CLA and adopted CYP.

Differential Diagnoses – Attachment and Neurodevelopmental Disorders: CLA and adopted CYP who have experienced developmental trauma and disrupted attachments can present with behaviours and traits consistent with those shown in neurodevelopmental disorders (e.g. autistic spectrum disorder (ASD) and attention deficit hyperactivity disorder (ADHD)). It can be difficult to determine if the behaviours are due to an attachment disorder, a neurodevelopmental disorder or if both are contributing to their presentation. For example, CYP might present as over familiar and friendly towards unfamiliar adults, a behaviour found in children diagnosed with ASD and disinhibited attachment disorders

(DAD) (APA, 2013; WHO, 2022b). Furthermore, one of the diagnostic criteria for ASD is for the CYP to show restrictive and repetitive behaviours, however this is also found in children with reactive attachment disorders (RAD) (Davidson et al., 2015; Sadiq et al., 2012). Attention difficulties, hyperactivity, sensory sensitivities and processing difficulties and conduct issues are associated with neurodevelopmental disorders but can also be present in CYP with a history of trauma and abuse and CYP exposed to harmful substances in utero (Pinto, 2019).

The Coventry ASD vs Attachment Problems Grid (Moran, 2010) and the Coventry Grid Interview (Flackhill et al., 2017) are useful tools for teasing out the subtle differences in the presentation of ASD vs attachment disorder. However, if neurodevelopmental disorders are suspected then a comprehensive assessment for ASD and ADHD should be carried out by specialists within an ASD/ADHD pathway/service to rule this out before considering a diagnosis of attachment disorder. Pinto (2019) warns against diagnosing CYP with adverse childhood experiences with attachment disorders and neglecting to consider any biological or neurological factors in their presentation.

Similarly, children who have experienced neglect and abuse may present with difficulties with their speech, language, social communication, problem solving, sensory processing and executive functioning skills (Bryck & Fisher, 2012). These difficulties may be the result of their early experiences, such as through missing out on consistent education and learning experiences. The CYP may have also been stuck in survival modes of fight/flight/freeze and therefore not being able to attend to or develop new ways of learning and being (Golding, 2008, 2010). It could also be the case that they have additional needs alongside attachment and trauma related difficulties. Developing a good understanding of the nature, onset and duration of difficulties, details about developmental trajectory and the impact of supportive interventions to address difficulties or delays is important and can form the basis of decision making for specialist assessments for neurodevelopmental or learning difficulties.

A significant proportion of children in care are considered to have been exposed to noxious substances, such as drugs and alcohol, pre-natally (Bandstra et al., 2010). Exposure to drugs and alcohol in-utero can lead to a range of difficulties (neurological, cognitive, physical, social, behavioural and emotional) that can have a lifelong impact (e.g. foetal alcohol spectrum disorder (FASD), Vorgias, Bynum, & Bernstein, 2022). Understanding this presentation and referring on for specialist assessment when needed is important to inform a comprehensive understanding of the CYPs presentation and to indicate the most appropriate interventions.

Please take some time to consider the questions in Box 17.1

Box 17.1 Reflective exercise

Consider how your service settings would approach assessments with young people, their families and networks. How might this need to be adapted to meet the needs of CYP who are adopted or looked after?

Box 17.2 provides the assessment phase in the clinical example discussed further in Boxes 17.3 and 17.4.

Box 17.2 Clinical example: David

David is an 11-year-old boy of white British heritage who is referred to a specialist mental health service for looked after and adopted young people following multiple interventions from mainstream CAMHS and private therapy providers.

The initial assessment consists of a detailed referral, a consultation with the referring social worker, a parent interview with the adoptive parents, Lucy and John (together and separately, whilst the other parent was in one of the joint sessions with David), an individual child assessment of David, time with David and John together, Lucy and David together and for the family together. This necessitated a team approach of two psychological practitioners so that sessions could run in parallel.

David was removed from his birth parents at the age of three and placed in foster care following neglect and physical abuse, alongside concerns about him being exposed to 'unsafe adults' with criminal histories, which included sexual offences against children. David experienced several moves whilst in foster care until he was adopted at the age of seven by Lucy and John and subsequently moved to another part of the country. His older siblings remain in foster care and continue to have direct contact with birth family members. David has only had indirect 'letterbox' contact with his birth parents since being placed for adoption. He sees his birth siblings twice a year.

John and Lucy felt worried about David's wellbeing and future, fearing that he may end up like his birth parents despite their love and support of him. They were devoted to helping him heal, but felt unprepared for managing David's difficulties, unsupported, and felt that the social workers had not been honest about the level of difficulties that he had prior to him coming to live with them. The clinical interviews and review of the parents' prospective adopter reports from the adopter assessment process did not highlight any known significant traumas in either of the parent's own histories, and the parents did not report feeling dislike for, or lack of interest in David or feelings of regret about the adoption.

David is described as having difficulties concentrating at school, getting along with others, and can be controlling, angry and defiant in relationships with his parents and peers. He can be easily triggered by changes or if things don't go his way and this can be difficult to predict. He can present at different times as withdrawn and low in mood, anxious and distracted or fidgety. He struggled with the transition to secondary school with teachers raising concerns that he may have ADHD.

The parent–child dynamics were assessed using the Marshak Interaction Method (Marshak, 1960) alongside an observation of the family during a task in which they were to work together to represent their family life and what was important to them. Both parents were observed to be child-led, engaging, curious and nurturing towards David although somewhat hesitant in creating structure and managing boundaries. David presented as self-reliant and rejecting of physical intimacy except through rough-and-tumble play, which his father, John, was particularly receptive to and appeared to enjoy.

(Continued)

Box 17.2 (Continued)

During David's individual assessment session, an eco-map was used alongside a story-stem exercise (Hodges et al., 2003). David's eco-map was notable in that he chose to not only represent his adoptive family but included his ex-foster carer and one sibling. When asked about his birth parents, David chose miniatures for these that were dangerous looking creatures but did not want to place them within the sand tray and instead placed them on the edge of the box. The story-stem brought up a reoccurring theme of catastrophic and violent endings with little evidence of repair or ordinary family representations.

The Child Behaviour Checklist (Achenbach, 1994) and the Assessment Checklist for Children (Tarren-Sweeney, 2013a, 2013b) were completed by parents and school to identify presenting difficulties, as well as a sensory functioning and executive functioning measure. These highlighted significant difficulties in a range of areas for David: emotional, behavioural, interpersonal, executive functioning and attachment seeking strategies.

Questions for reflection

- In what other ways might you assess the quality of the parent–child relationship?
- How else might you gather information about the parents' own histories to inform your formulation about what parents may be bringing into the dynamic, in terms of their own potential unresolved attachment/trauma difficulties and/or their expectations of parenting/children?

17.12.2 Formulation

Models of formulation applied to CYP in other contexts can be applied to this population of CYP. Outlined are particular areas of consideration for CLA, adopted and attachment-disordered CYP.

Bio-psycho-social Formulations: A bio-psycho-social formulation incorporates biological, social and psychological factors to assist in the understanding of a child's presentation. It is recommended for CLA, CYP who are adopted or on SGOs as their presentations are often complex with an interplay of multiple factors contributing (Chaffin et al., 2006; Pinto, 2019). The importance of attachment frameworks to understand CYP difficulties has been outlined earlier in the chapter as well as, theories of the impact of multiple childhood traumas (see Chapter 14 for further details on PTSD formulations). However, frequently, attachment frameworks that mainly focus on the social and psychological factors are used to account for this population of CYP's presentations without considering biological factors, such as neurodevelopmental disorders, intergenerational genetic disorders or traits, the impact of pre-natal harmful experiences, and the impact on the developing brain of early experiences of trauma (Pinto, 2019). If biological factors are not assessed for and included in formulations, it can lead to inappropriate interventions or a lack of access to appropriate services (Barth et al., 2005), for instance if a CYP with undiagnosed ASD is instead diagnosed with attachment disorder, attachment-based interventions would be recommended and the CYP and their carers would not be able to access specialist education, services and interventions for CYP with a diagnosis of ASD.

As outlined earlier in the chapter, van der Kolk (2014) proposed Developmental Trauma Disorder as a framework for understanding the complex impact of childhood abuse, neglect and loss on a child's development, and the range of behavioural and emotional presentations that may develop. As well as exposure to multiple or chronic forms of 'adverse interpersonal trauma', a pattern of dysregulation can be triggered in response to trauma cues. This can include dysregulation in affective, somatic, behavioural, cognitive, relational and self-attributional domains, the presence of persistently altered attributions and expectations (e.g. loss of trust) that impacts negatively on relationships with others and the ability to integrate within society's systems, such as in education.

Beacon House Therapeutic Service and Trauma Team have developed useful resources that expand the concept of developmental trauma and map out the impact on the child's brain from the bottom of the brain to the top (Lyons et al., 2020), drawing on neurodevelopmental theory and research. The brain stem (the 'primitive brain') develops first and manages sensory motor input and survival, the midbrain and limbic areas relate to attachment and emotional development, and the 'cortical brain', which develops later, manages processing, learning, thinking, language and inhibition. Neurodevelopmental theory can be helpful in understanding the development of a range of problems across different domains and the order in which to begin to address the difficulties. For example, it's not uncommon for children in care who have experienced developmental trauma to present with a range of difficulties across the domains, such as poor co-ordination, dislike for touch/being overly tactile, having jumpy and restless behaviour (all linked to sensory systems), day dreaming and having rapid regressions (dissociation linked to the sensory-somatic systems), struggles with transitions, losses and changes (attachment system), prolonged meltdowns, aggression and rule breaking (emotional dysregulation), lying, stealing, hoarding and over or under eating (behavioural dysregulation), black-and-white thinking and difficulties problem solving (cognition), becoming jealous when a caregiver gives others attention and fear of failure (linked to poor self-concept and identity).

Understanding the impact of developmental trauma on the CYP is crucial to developing a comprehensive formulation that can assist the CYP, their carers, families and professional networks to have greater understanding of the CYP's behaviours and difficulties. It can assist in comprehending some of the barriers that the CYP may have in engaging in interventions and how interventions can be adapted to take into account the impact of developmental trauma, for example, the benefit of adaptations to their environment to take into account sensory sensitivities or the need for frequent breaks in therapy to undertake sensory stimulating activities to aid emotional regulation.

Systemic Formulations: Systemic formulations are particularly important in this area as CLA and adopted children are embedded in many different systems, including, for example, professional networks, their family of origin, a foster or adopted family. A formulation should include an understanding of the family in its widest sense to include the foster/adoptive family and extended birth family, and the wider context in which the child is situated, and consider in what way these factors might be contributing to difficulties the child is presenting with (see also Carr et al., 2020; Dallos & Stedman, 2014;

Ochs, Borsca, & Schweitzer, 2020; Rivett & Buchmüller, 2017; Vetere & Dallos, 2018 for further reading on systemic theory and formulations).

When considering factors that may be maintaining the difficulties of the CYP, within a formulation, the role of caregivers and systems around the child are crucial. These can include teachers' responses and school behavioural policies, how informed the system is about the child's early experiences (all too often schools and carers are not given information about the child's history and therefore can struggle to make sense of the child's presentation or how to respond) and how attachment and trauma responsive the system is (see Chapter 27 for further discussion). Caregivers and other adults around the child may unwittingly reinforce the child's survival responses by, for example, becoming dysregulated themselves and losing their temper or through employing behavioural strategies that may be triggering for the CYP, such as 'time out'. Time out can be experienced as particularly anxiety provoking for children who have experienced neglect, multiple losses and disruptions in their lives, as well as potentially giving a message that the caregiver's love and attention is conditional, and that the child needs to manage their emotions and difficulties alone (Hughes, 2009).

The adoptive/foster, special guardian carers may be contributing towards the child's difficulties through responses that can arise, for example, from their own attachment histories, unresolved feelings of loss for the longed-for birth child they could not have, their own mental health difficulties, and/or through vicarious trauma after struggling to parent a child who has experienced trauma for a long time and without adequate support from professionals (Hughes, 2009; Hughes & Baylin, 2012). It is important to consider these factors in the formulation so interventions can address these difficulties and reparative parenting experiences can be fostered for the CYP (Hughes, 2009). However, these formulations need to be sensitively shared with carers and the professional networks so that carers or other professionals surrounding the child do not feel blamed.

Inclusion of Positives and Strengths: The importance of incorporating strengths and protective factors for the child and the systems they are in within the formulation cannot be understated (Treisman, 2016). Children in care are often repeatedly given labels as a result of their care status or due to the challenging behaviour they may present as a result of the hurt and pain that they have experienced. Although labels of 'trauma' and the language of neuroscience may be more helpful and elicit more empathy and understanding than labels such as 'oppositional', 'naughty', 'damaged' and 'attachment disordered', they are still labels that may imply that the child is broken in some way. Such descriptions can further impact the child's developing self-concept and confidence in their ability to overcome difficulties. It is important that the child is viewed as more than their traumas, and that the child and system are asked to fully consider their strengths and ways not only that the child has survived their hardships but their hopes and dreams for the future, their interests and hobbies and what sustains them (Treisman, 2016).

Collaborative Formulations: Children removed from their parents may have many aspects of their history that they cannot recall or have limited information about due to not being with members of their birth families who can pass on these details. They are likely to have many unanswered questions. Developing collaborative formulations with CYP in care, on SGOs or adopted is therefore important for the CYP to understand their own life stories and what may have contributed to some of their strengths and difficulties.

Allowing CYP who may have had little control over their lives to develop a narrative of their life story can be empowering, helping them make sense of their lives and possible routes to recovery (Harper & Moss, 2003). Therapeutic life-story work is covered in more detail later in this chapter. It must be done in a sensitive and strengths-based way to avoid any re-traumatisation or shame from recalling past difficulties. Box 17.3 covers the formulation for the clinical example introduced in Box 17.2.

Box 17.3 Clinical example: David, continued

Presentation: David is presenting with dysregulation in multiple domains that could be considered under the umbrella of developmental trauma: affective (rapidly changing emotional states), somatic (seeking movement, easily startled), behavioural (defiant, intimidatory behaviour), cognitive (struggling with learning), relational (difficulties maintaining friendships) and self-attributions (saying that his parents shouldn't have adopted him because he doesn't deserve it). Loss of trust was displayed towards adults (based on parent and teacher reports and from parent–child observations and story stems) and functional impairment in education (some school avoidance, behind in learning), the family (arguments, family more isolated as David struggles to go out with them or be around others) and with peers.

Predisposing factors: David has experienced a history of neglect, abuse, possible sexual abuse and exposure to parental mental health difficulties in his birth parents' care. He has witnessed domestic violence and alcohol misuse with his birth parents. He has been removed from his primary caregivers and has experienced numerous placement moves.

Precipitating factors: Experiences of failure (e.g. not being able to do homework, losing at a game), limit setting (hearing 'no'), disappointment (when something hasn't gone as hoped/anticipated), perceived rejection (friend doesn't want to join in his game), changes in routine (e.g. change of teacher). David appears to experience chronic shame as a result of these factors, which can lead to defensive responses (anger, lying, minimises actions, blames others) and/or withdrawn and anxious strategies (hiding, running away, regressing, crying). Transition to secondary school and adjusting to new people, more rules/less support/ less-nurturing environment than primary school. Contact with birth sibling can lead to an increase in anxious behaviours in anticipation and defiance, aggression and rejection of adoptive parents after contact.

Perpetuating factors: Parents experience a lack of confidence in boundary setting due to his reactions and feeling overwhelmed/sorry for David and wanting to compensate for his past, as well as not wanting to be like their own parents (strict and quite cold). They can swing into stricter parenting when fearful, such as when David presents with risky or controlling behaviours. Inconsistency in parenting approaches is likely to be experienced as unpredictable and unsafe for David. His school views David's behaviour as attention seeking and oppositional and are enforcing behavioural policies, such as him losing break time for not engaging in learning. This is likely to be compounding

(Continued)

Box 17.3 (Continued)

David's poor self-esteem and reduces his time for engaging in movement and play, which is regulating for him.

Protective factors: Parents are committed to caring for David, advocating for him and engaging in the work. Parents are not displaying blocked care and David is able to receive some of the nurture and support that his parents are providing. David has developed a talent for horse riding, and he is skilled at and enjoys climbing, trampolining and swimming.

Question for reflection

- What theories could be applied to this formulation?
- In what way does this formulation identify the next steps for intervention for David and his family?

17.12.3 Interventions

This section summarises NICE guidance (2015) on interventions for CLA and adopted CYP with attachment disorders or difficulties and therapeutic models that have been developed specifically for children removed from their carers who have attachment difficulties or disorders and traumatic histories, which has a growing research evidence base.

Parenting Interventions: Reparative parenting experiences are key to recovery for CYP removed from their parents due to abuse and neglect (Hughes, 2009, 2012). However, parenting an attachment disordered and traumatised child can be hugely challenging and exhausting (Hughes, 2009, 2012). The lack of confidence in fostering/residential carers/adopters in being able to manage presentations of behaviour that challenges is often a key factor in the disruption of placements (Sinclair et al., 2005). Training, consultation, group work and individual parenting advice that supports the understanding and implementation of therapeutic parenting approaches can increase parenting confidence and a sense of efficacy (Golding, 2014). Dan Hughes has written a number of books on therapeutic parenting approaches for CYP with attachment difficulties. He recommends *Communicating with PACE* (playfulness, acceptance, curiosity and empathy) as a way of being and communicating with the attachment-disordered or traumatised CYP that can be used by caregivers, educators and therapists to increase empathy and attunement and avoid emotional dysregulation. There is also a focus on the need for parents to develop self-care skills to be able to manage the challenges they face (See Hughes (2009) on therapeutic parenting for further techniques and methods of parenting the attachment disordered child).

Ní Chobhthaigh and Duffy's (2019) systematic review of interventions for adopted parents concluded that those that drew on psychological theories, particularly attachment theory, and used video feedback had the most evidence of efficacy. NICE guidelines (2015) recommend a video-feedback parenting programme for pre-school or primary school aged CYP who are in care or adopted who present with attachment difficulties. A minimum of 10 sessions over 3 to 4 months is recommended, delivered by a professional trained in the approach. The aim is to increase parental sensitivity, responsiveness and communication, to give feedback on parenting strengths and weaknesses and acknowledge positive changes in the carer and child's behaviour. Video Interaction Guidance (VIG, Kennedy and Underdown, 2018) is one such approach which has growing evidence base and is increasingly used in the UK.

An alternative to video feedback is a parental sensitivity and behaviour training intervention over 6 months focused on parental attunement, increasing understanding of the child's behaviour, coaching the parents in behaviour management strategies and limit setting. The Incredible Years (Webster-Stratton, 2005) and Attachment and Biobehavioral Catch-Up (ABC, Bernard et al., 2012; Dozier et al., 2009, 2018) parenting programmes have been reported to have the best evidence of efficacy in a systematic review of interventions for foster parents and children (Bergström et al., 2020). Chapter 12 describes parenting programmes in more detail.

In terms of older CYP (late-primary and early-secondary age), an educational group-based intervention for foster carers, alongside a group for the CYP is recommended by NICE (2015). The group for the carers is to support management of behaviours and other issues, such as school transitions or peer-relationship difficulties, and for the CYP the group is a skills teaching, mentoring programme. For all ages, intensive support and training to carers is recommended before the CYP's placement starts, as well as ongoing supervision, weekly support sessions and telephone support offered.

Examples of group programmes for foster carers and adoptive parents include the Fostering Attachments/Nurturing Attachments group programme (Golding, 2007), which provides a psychoeducation component on attachment theory and its applications to therapeutic parenting approaches linked to the needs of the child. Later revisions also incorporate a focus on supporting caregivers' stress levels and increasing the carer's ability to reflect on their own and others' mental states. The AdOpt parenting programme (delivered by the National Implementation Service and adapted from the US based KEEP programme (Harold et al., 2017), is a group programme for adoptive parents of children who are 3 to 8 years of age. The programme is 16 weeks in length and draws on social learning theory and attachment theory models of child development. It is designed as a preventative programme targeting those within the first 2 years of their placement with their adoptive family.

Reflective parenting interventions (Redfern, 2015) to increase mentalisation and attunement towards the child and non-violent resistance (Omer, 2004) for violent and aggressive behaviours are two parenting approaches not developed for this population but which have been applied with adaptations with some success (Byrne, Murphy, & Connon, 2020; Holen et al., 2016). See Chapter 26 for more details of these approaches and their evidence base.

Attachment-based Therapeutic Interventions for Carers and CYP: There are several therapies that have been developed to intervene in the relationships between the CYP and their carer, aiming to promote secure attachments.

Theraplay® (Booth & Jernberg, 2009; Booth & Lindaman, 2000; Booth & Winstead, 2015, 2016; Jernberg & Booth, 2001) draws on common games, songs and nursery rhymes to support the attachment relationship; helping the caregiver to provide engagement, nurture, structure and challenge appropriate to the child's developmental level, and for the child to be able to receive and accept these. There have been some positive studies of Theraplay®'s effectiveness within different contexts with CYP and their carers (Bentzen & Hart, 2015;

Francis, et al., 2017; Hiles Howard et al., 2018; Tucker et al., 2017; Weir et al., 2013; Wettig et al., 2011). Money et al. (2020) present a systematic review of the evidence base.

DDP (Hughes, 1997, 2006, 2007, 2009, 2011; Hughes et al., 2019) was designed specifically for children who had experienced abuse and neglect and separation from birth parents, in the context of traditional therapies not proving effective and children struggling to develop a safe enough therapeutic relationship. DDP helps the child to develop greater levels of emotional security, safety and connection in relation to the therapist and their caregivers through offering new relational experiences modelled on healthy parent–child relationships. Through the attitude of PACE (described earlier), the therapist models to the parent/s a way of relating that can support the child to begin to identify, regulate and express emotion safely. New narratives are created about their experiences as their reflective capacities increase and they're supported to make sense of their experiences, with therapists often making connections between present difficulties and past experiences and supporting parents to respond with empathy. There is a developing evidence base for its efficacy (Hughes et al., 2015, 2019). Although there have been criticisms that the therapy is difficult to evaluate due to its complexity and lack of Manualisation (Mercer, 2014), others have concluded that it is possible to carry out an RCT to evaluate its effectiveness (Turner-Halliday et al., 2014 and the DDP Network are currently undertaking an RCT in England).

Child-based Therapy Approaches: NICE (2017) recommends that skills-based educational and mentoring groups for CYP run alongside groups for foster and adopted carers to assist with peer relationships difficulties, transitions and to teach resilience and encourage community participation facilitated by trained mentors or professionals. Take Charge is a self-determination intervention for improving the transition outcomes of those highly at-risk youth who are in both foster care and special education and has been well-evaluated (Bergström et al., 2020).

Hambrick et al.'s (2016) systematic review of mental health interventions for CLA concluded that many approaches not developed for CLA and adopted children were applied to this cohort of CYP but there was a lack of agreement on how to adapt them or rigorous evaluation of their efficacy, and further research is needed. Traditional individual therapy approaches used to address trauma (e.g. EMDR, narrative therapies, narrative exposure therapy, CBT and/or DBT informed work to manage emotional distress) can be adapted and applied to this population, potentially with the parent present to support the child/young person. A recent systematic review found evidence for the effectiveness of TF-CBT with children with a history of abuse and neglect (Bennett et al., 2021).

Creative therapeutic approaches that are multisensory are often helpful in engaging children and young people and can support with processing experiences on different levels; for example, non-directive therapies, play, drama, dance, movement and/or art-based approaches and the use of sensory integration-based/ informed work and sensory diets; a tailored plan of physical activities and adaptations designed to meet a child's sensory needs such the use of a trampoline, swing or by bouncing on an exercise ball to regulate when talking about big feelings. The aim is to increase the CYP's emotional tolerance and support emotional regulation particularly when children experience hyper- or hypo-arousal (Treisman, 2016).

Therapeutic life-story work is an intervention technique that allows the child to gain ownership of their life story, which can often be fragmented or confusing. It is a child-centred approach that explores a child's life history, utilising a therapeutic approach. In practice this involves the practitioner amalgamating information from interviews and health and social care records and talking with the child and primary carer to ultimately answer any gaps in the child's knowledge and complete the life story (Jones, 2017; Rose, 2004, 2012, 2017a, 2017b; Rose & Phillpot, 2005). Although considered to be a social work task, in reality many social work staff will not have appropriate access to training and supervision to undertake the depth of work needed for children who are looked after or adopted. There is a growing evidence base for this approach (Lucas et al., 2022).

Working with Systems: This could include systemic family therapy with the CYP and their foster or adopted family or working with larger systems surrounding the CYP such as their professional caring networks, residential care settings and school, through consultation, training and facilitating reflective practice groups, ensuring these systems are trauma and attachment informed (see Chapter 27 for further details). Many local authorities have established 'virtual schools' (DfE, 2018b), that include a head teacher and a team of educational professionals with expertise in the difficulties presented by CLA located in children's services that provide an additional resource providing training, consultation and advice to mainstream schools with looked after or adopted pupils.

There has been a growing evidence base for systemic interventions aimed at increasing placement stability for children within foster care and residential care. The NICE guidelines (2021a) review the different models and their effectiveness. A model with a growing evidence bases is Multidimensional Treatment Foster Care, also known as Intensive Fostering (Chamberlain, 2003), which has its foundations in the social learning model. It includes 24-hour intensive support to the foster placement, family and relationship therapy and trauma-informed approaches. It has been shown to be successful in the UK (Eyberg et al., 2008). Fisher and Gilliam (2012) provide a review of the research and advocate its use as an alternative to residential care.

In terms of programmes for residential care there have been many different models based on trauma theory, trauma-informed practices and attachment theory such as the attachment regulation and competency (ARC) programme co-developed by Blaustein and Kinniburgh (2017), which has been used as an organisational framework in residential care homes to support trauma-informed care (see Chapter 27 for more details on ARC). It has a growing evidence base for its effectiveness with CLA and adopted children in a number of settings (Arvidson et al., 2011; Bartlett et al., 2015; Hodgdon at al., 2013, 2016). At a minimum, NICE guidance (2017) for CYP with attachment difficulties or disorders in residential care recommends that professionals with expertise of attachment difficulties consult with the staff about CYP and offer carer sensitivity and behaviour management training, similar to that outlined for foster and adoptive carers.

Multimodal Approaches: Although presented as separate interventions, it can often be crucial for therapists to work in a multimodal way that incorporates a range of direct therapeutic work approaches, work with caregivers and work with the wider system in order to be effective. Complex difficulties often require complex, intensive solutions at a systemic, dyadic and individual level.

An example of a multimodal approach is the neurophysiological psychotherapy (NPP) model developed by Family Futures (a voluntary adoption agency) designed to meet the therapeutic needs of CYP with early maltreatment who have been removed from their parents and who present with complex symptomatology in terms of their somatosensory processing, affect regulation, attachment, cognitive and behavioural systems (Burnell & Vaughan, 2012; Vaughan et al., 2016). NPP integrates interventions for somatosensory difficulties (e.g. Ayres sensory integration, Ayres, 2005), with Theraplay® (Booth & Jernberg, 2009), DDP (Hughes, 1997) and therapeutic life-story work (Burnell & Vaughan, 2008) to intervene with affect regulation and attachment difficulties and to enable the CYP to develop a coherent narrative of their life experiences. Research has shown it to be more effective in improving outcomes for CYP who engage in the whole programme than a control group (McCullough & Mathura, 2019). NPP is however a long, intensive and expensive intervention, which restricts the number of CYP and their families that can access it and benefit, but it could be argued that this is necessary given the complexity of the CYP it is designed to treat. Box 17.4 provides an example of the multimodal approach in operation in our clinical example.

Box 17.4 Clinical example: David, continued

Support to the system

The assessment report and formulation were shared with school to support with their understanding of David's difficulties and more appropriate ways to respond to him which were attachment and trauma informed. Regular meetings with school and social workers were arranged to review progress and provide advice and guidance. An assessment for an EHCP was recommended and contributions made to support with this to enable David to receive greater support at school (initially one-to-one in mainstream setting, and then later for specialist education provision).

Support to caregivers

Psychoeducation regarding developmental trauma was provided to the parents together with individual support and guidance and group-based training on therapeutic parenting approaches. Further information was sought from social care records regarding David's early experiences and shared with parents to support their developing understanding of David's survival strategies, likely triggers and where they had stemmed from. This also allowed space for parents to process their feelings regarding the harm David experienced, so that they could provide greater containment of his emotions, and as preparation for life-story work.

Parents' expectations, family patterns and beliefs and early experiences were explored using genograms, family-script exercises, helping to identify barriers to maintaining structure/boundaries and exploring patterns in relationships. The parents' relationships towards the system and the birth parents were also explored.

Support to child

Initial individual child work focused on regulation, drawing on sensory integration (SI) principles and sensory diets (informed by an SI assessment and input from an occupational therapist qualified in SI) for in- and outside-session work. Movement-based activities and play were used to support regulation and attachment between David and his parents, and trust with the therapists. Theraplay® activities and DDP-informed approaches were utilised to support attachment relationships and in making sense of current experiences/triggers and past experiences. Exploration of thoughts and feelings were supported through creative mediums such as drawing, acting/role play, music, games, as well as the use of tools (e.g. Treisman's cards, Treisman, 2017). Life-story work was incorporated into the latter stages of the therapeutic work, creating a timeline together depicting David's early experiences, transitions and noting experiences of safety, joy and protection, as well as including the more challenging experiences. This was supported by liaison with previous social workers and foster carers who could provide positive memories of David and their experience of him as well as photographs. Somatic processing of information was supported through movement and physical games, as well as therapists and parents modelling anger (high energy and language but without aggression) and sadness in relation to David's early experiences whilst engaging the senses, for example, by throwing clay bombs, punching through paper, making a volcano explode.

The intervention lasted over 2 years, with sessions taking place on a fortnightly basis for half-a-day at a time, alongside informal contact and support to parents and the network.

17.12.4 Evaluation

Routine outcome measures utilised in generic child mental health services (e.g. those recommended by CORC – Clinical Outcome Research Consortium) are also applied to this population. However, many have limitations in being insufficiently sensitive to measure and monitor change with CLA. There are also the difficulties of the ethics of subjecting this population of often traumatised children to lengthy questionnaires or other evaluation tools. There is a need to develop and validate outcome measures specifically for this population.

Due to the complexity of CLA and adopted children's presentations, often with multiple neurodevelopmental, developmental, social, behavioural and emotional difficulties, it can be difficult to track progress. There have been some attempts (e.g. BERRI, Silver, 2005), however it is not widely used. Goal-based outcomes seem to work well for this population, identifying and tracking progress toward goals, not just the young person's, but also the carers' and the system's goals (Law & Jacob, 2015). Measures of family functioning or carer stress, such as the parental stress scale (Berry & Jones, 1995) can measure change in how well a placement is coping with managing the CLA and their needs.

Local authorities often use the Strengths and Difficulties Questionnaire (SDQ, Goodman, 1997) to measure change and will also use other indicators, such as attendance at school or further education, school achievement (exams), placement stability, involvement with the criminal justice system or emergency services. CAMHS and other mental health services for CYP sometimes use the SDQ to determine threshold and access to teams and treatment as a routine outcome measure. However, there has been widespread criticism of the use of it with this population of children (e.g. Lehmann et al., 2014, 2017; Milburn et al., 2008) and evidence suggests that the single-report SDQ should not be relied upon as a sole means of identifying mental health difficulties in a vulnerable and high-risk population but should be complemented with additional measures.

Other measures include self-report measures focusing on internalising difficulties, such as the Revised Children's Anxiety and Depression Scale (RCADS, Chorpita et al., 2000) and the Child Revised Impact of Events Scale (CRIES, Perrin et al., 2005). The Assessment Checklists for Children (ACC, Tarren-Sweeney, 2007) and Adolescents (ACA, Tarren-Sweeney, 2013b), completed by the child's carer, may help to highlight types of internalising difficulties commonly found in children who have experienced maltreatment, such as insecure or anxious/distrustful behaviours or negative self-image.

17.13 Listening to the Voices of CLA and adopted CYP

Going forward it is crucial that the voices of CLA and adopted CYP are represented in the development, design and evaluation of services (SCIE, 2017a). They have usually experienced little control over their lives, with decisions often made for them by professionals. It is important that their experience of services, particularly therapeutic services, is understood and listened to and leads to meaningful change. Service user feedback in a user-friendly form is essential. Many areas have developed groups of CLA and adopted children that they draw upon to co-produce service development and to obtain feedback (see SCIE, 2017b, 2022 for further guidance on co-production with CLA).

Organised service-user groups for CLA and adopted children, such as Voice of the Child and Barnardo's, can be consulted by services to ensure they meet the needs of the children they serve. Services also need to learn from mistakes from the past by reading the stories of CLA, although they are inevitably difficult and emotive reads (e.g. *Hackney Child; A true Story of Surviving Poverty and the Care System*, Daniels & Livingstone, 2011; *My Name is Why*, Sissay, 2019).

The increase in qualitative research in this area also allows the voices of CLA, adopted CYP and care leavers to be heard. Bazalgette's (2014) in-depth life-story interviews with CLA, in collaboration with NSPCC's Young Ambassadors, is particularly illuminating. Although their individual experiences were unique and there were variations in their experiences, many common themes were identified in their stories that services can learn from. This research found that nearly all participants reported positive experiences in care and that their lives had been enhanced in some way through their care experiences. On a negative note, many had experienced disrupted relationships, such as frequent changes of foster carer, residential staff and social workers, having a negative impact on their wellbeing. The young people talked about the challenges and various reasons for going missing from care: many reported discrimination and stigmatisation from the general public as a result of being in care; some reported harmful experiences in care such as emotional neglect and rejection; and others had experienced abuse from their carers or other young people in their placement.

Further research is required to elicit the experiences and views of CLA, care leavers, adopted young people and young people placed in SGOs. Psychologists with their research and clinical practice skills are in a unique position to be able to promote this work.

17.14 Conclusion

This chapter focused on the increasing role child psychological practitioners have with CYP with disrupted attachments both in a clinical and research capacity. CLA, adopted CYP and CYP on SGOs are likely to have experienced many difficulties in their lives (such as neglect, abuse, traumatic experiences and disrupted attachments) that can lead to lasting social, emotional and behavioural issues that can have a profound impact on individuals and their families and, if left unaddressed, also place a financial burden on society (Conti et al., 2021). Developing targeted mental health services for CYP who are in care or adopted and effective psychological interventions is therefore of crucial importance. There is a growing evidence base evaluating the efficacy of different therapeutic approaches for CYP with disrupted attachments, however, further research is much needed.

References

Abidin, R., Flens, J. R., & Austin, W. G. (2006). The parenting stress index. In R. P. Archer (Ed.), *Forensic uses of clinical assessment instruments* (pp. 297–328). Lawrence Erlbaum.

Adoption and Children Act. (2002). Adoption and Children Act, 2002. https://www.legislation.gov.uk/ukpga/2002/38/contents.

Agrawal, H. R., Gunderson, J., Holmes, B. M., & Lyons-Ruth, K. (2004). Attachment studies with borderline patients: A review. *Harvard Review of Psychiatry, 12*(2), 94–104. https://doi.org/10.1080/10673220490447218.

Ainsworth, M. D., Blehar, M., & Waters, E. (1978). *Patterns of attachment: A psychological study of the strange situation*. Lawrence Erlbaum.

American Psychiatric Association (2013). Diagnostic and statistical manual of mental disorders (5th ed.). American Psychiatric Publishing.

Ammaniti, M., Van IJzendoorn, M. H., Speranza, A. M., & Tambelli, R. (2000). Internal working models of attachment during late childhood and early adolescence: An exploration of stability and change. *Attachment & Human Development, 2*(3), 328–346. https://doi.org/10.1080/14616730010001587.

Anda, R. F., Felitti, V. J., Bremner, J. D., Walker, J. D., Whitfield, C., Perry, B. D., Dube, S. R., & Giles, W. H. (2006). The enduring effects of abuse and related adverse experiences in childhood: A convergence of evidence from neurobiology and epidemiology. *European Archives of Psychiatry and Clinical Neuroscience, 256*(3), 174–186. https://doi.org/10.1007/s00406-005-0624-]4.

Armstrong, J. G., Putnam, F. W., Carlson, E. B., Libero, D. Z., & Smith, S. R. (1997). Development and validation of a measure of adolescent dissociation: The Adolescent Dissociative Experiences Scale. *The Journal of Nervous and Mental Disease, 185*(8), 491–497. https://doi.org/10.1097/00005053-199708000-00003.

Arvidson, J., Kinniburgh, K., Howard, K., Spinazzola, J., Strothers, H., Evans, M., Andres, B., Cohen, C, & Blaustein, M. E. (2011). Treatment of complex trauma in young children: Developmental and cultural considerations in application of the ARC intervention model. *Journal of Child & Adolescent Trauma, 4*(1), 34–51.

Association of Child Psychiatrists (ACP) (2018). *Silent catastrophe: Responding to the danger signs of children and young people's mental health services in danger*. ACP.

Ayres, J. (2005). *Sensory integration and the child* (25th anniversary ed.). Western Psychological Services.

Bandstra, E. S., Morrow, C. E., Mansoor, E., & Accornero, V. H. (2010). Prenatal drug exposure: Infant and toddler outcomes. *Journal of Addictive Diseases, 29*(2): 245–258.

Barnardo's, Child Poverty Action Group, Children in Wales, the Children Society, NSPCC, SCF (2000). *Wales' children, our future: A manifesto*. NSPCC Cymru.

Barth, R.P., Crea, T.M., John, K., Thoburn, J., & Quinton, D. (2005). Beyond attachment theory and therapy: Towards sensitive and evidence-based interventions with foster and adoptive families in distress. *Child and Family Social Work, 10*(4), 257–268.

Bartlett, J. D., Barto, B., Griffin, J. L., Fraser, J. G., Hodgdon, H., & Bodian, R. (2015). Trauma-informed care in the Massachusetts child trauma project. *Child Maltreatment, 21*(2), 101–112.

Bazalgette, L. (2014). The views of looked after children and young people on the care system. In T. Rahilly & E. Hendry (Eds.) *Promoting the wellbeing of children in care: Messages from research* (pp. 25–50). NSPCC.

Bennett, R. S., Denne, M., McGuire, R., & Hiller, R. M. (2021). A systematic review of controlled-trials for ptsd in maltreated children and adolescents. *Child Maltreatment, 26*(3), 325–343. https://doi.org/10.1177/1077559520961176.

Bentzen, M., & Hart, S. (2015). The limbic compass and Theraplay. In M. Bentzen & S. Hart (Eds.), *Through the windows of opportunity: A neuroaffective approach to child psychotherapy* (pp. 67–94). Karnac.

Bergström, M., Cederblad, M., Håkansson, K., Jonsson, A. K., Munthe, C., Vinnerljung, B., Wirtberg, I., Östlund, P., & Sundell, K. (2020). Interventions in foster family care: A systematic review. *Research on Social Work Practice, 30*(1), 3–18.

Bernard, K., Dozier, M., Bick, J., Lewis-Morrarty, E., Lindhiem, O., & Carlson, E. (2012). Enhancing attachment organization among maltreated children: Results of a randomized clinical trial. *Child development, 83*(2), 623–636. https://doi.org/10.1111/j.1467-8624.2011.01712.x.

Berry, J. O., & Jones, W. H. (1995). The Parental Stress Scale: Initial psychometric evidence. *Journal of Social and Personal Relationships, 12*(3), 463–472. https://doi.org/10.1177/0265407595123009.

Blaustein, M. & Kinniburgh, K. (2017). *The attachment, regulation, and competency (ARC) treatment model*. In M. Landolt, M. Cloitre, & U. Schnyder (Eds.), *Evidence-based treatments for trauma-related disorders in children and adolescents* (pp. 299–320), Springer International.

Blower, A., Addo, A., Hodgson, J., Lamington, L., & Towlson, K. (2004). Mental health of 'looked after' children: A needs assessment. *Clinical Child Psychology and Psychiatry, 9*, 117–129. https://doi.org/10.1177/1359104504039176.

Booth, P. B., & Jernberg, A. M. (2009). *Theraplay: Helping parents and children build better relationships through attachment-based play*. John Wiley & Sons.

Booth, P. B., & Lindaman, S. (2000). Theraplay for enhancing attachment in adopted children. In H. G. Kaduson & C. E. Schaefer (Eds.), *Short term play therapy for children* (pp. 194–227). Guilford Press.

Booth, P. B., & Winstead, M. L.-R. (2015). Theraplay®: Repairing relationships, helping families heal. In D. A. Crenshaw & A. L. Stewart (Eds.), *Play therapy: A comprehensive guide to theory and practice* (pp. 141–155). Guilford Press.

Booth, P. B., & Winstead, M. L.-R. (2016). Theraplay: Creating secure and joyful attachment relationships. In K. J. O'Connor, C. E. Schaefer, & L. D. Braverman (Eds.), *Handbook of play therapy* (pp. 165–194). John Wiley & Sons.

Bowlby, J. (1969). *Attachment and loss: Vol. 1: Attachment*. Basic Books.

Bowlby, J. (1976). *Attachment and loss: Vol. 2: Separation, anxiety and anger*. Basic Books.

Bowlby, J. (2005). *A secure base. Clinical applications of attachment theory*, Routledge.

Briere, J., & Spinazzola, J. (2005). Phenomenology and psychological assessment of complex posttraumatic states. *Journal of Traumatic Stress, 18*(5), 401–412.

Bryck, R. L., & Fisher, P. A. (2012). Training the brain: Practical applications of neural plasticity from the intersection of cognitive neuroscience, developmental psychology, and prevention science. *American Psychologist, 67*(2), 87–100. https://doi.org/10.1037/a0024657.

Burnell, A., & Vaughan, J. (2008) Remembering never to forget and forgetting never to remember: Re-thinking life story work. In B. Luckock (Ed.), *Direct work with children*. BAAF.

Burnell, A., & Vaughan. J. (2012). *Family futures' neuro-sequential approach to the assessment and treatment of traumatised children: Neuro-physiological psychotherapy (NPP)*. Family Futures.

Byrne, G., Murphy, S., & Connon, G. (2020). Mentalization-based treatments with children and families: A systematic review of the literature. *Clinical Child Psychology and Psychiatry, 25*(4), 1022–1048. https://doi.org/10.1177/1359104520920689.

Camras, L. A., Grow, G., & Ribordy, S. (1983). Recognition of emotional expression by abused children. *Journal of Clinical Child Psychology, 12*(3), 325–328.

Carr. A., Pinquart, M., & Haun, M. W. (2020), Research-informed practice of systemic therapy. In M. Ochs, M. Borcsa, & J. Schweitzer (Eds.) *Systemic research in individual, couple and family therapy and counseling* (pp. 319–348). Springer.

Chaffin, M., Hanson, R., Saunders, B. E., Nichols, T., Barnett, D., Zeanah, C., Berliner, L., Egeland, B., Newman, E., Lyon, T., LeTourneau, E., & Miller-Perrin, C. (2006). Report of the APSAC task force on attachment therapy, reactive attachment disorder, and attachment problems. *Child Maltreatment, 11*(1), 76–89.

Chamberlain, P. (2003). The Oregon multidimensional treatment foster care model: Features, outcomes, and progress in dissemination. *Cognitive and Behavioral Practice, 10*(4), 303–312. https://doi.org/10.1016/S1077-7229(03)80048-2.

Children Act (1989). Children Act (1989). https://www.legislation.gov.uk/ukpga/1989/41/contents.

Children Act (2004). Children Act (2004). http://www.legislation.gov.uk/ukpga/2004/31/contents

Children Leaving Care Act (2000). Children (Leaving Care) Act 2000. https://www.legislation.gov.uk/ukpga/2000/35/contents.

Chorpita, B. F., Yim, L., Moffitt, C., Umemoto, L. A., & Francis, S. E. (2000). Assessment of symptoms of DSM-IV anxiety and depression in children: A revised child anxiety and depression scale. *Behaviour Research and Therapy, 38*(8), 835–855. https://doi.org/10.1016/s0005-7967(99)00130-8.

Cicchetti, D., & Toth, S. L. (2015). Child maltreatment. In M. E. Lamb & R. M. Lerner (Eds.), *Handbook of child psychology and developmental science: Vol. 3. Socioemotional processes* (7th ed.) (pp. 513–563). Hoboken, NJ: Wiley.

Cole, P. M., Martin, S. E., & Dennis, T. A. (2004). Emotion regulation as a scientific construct: Methodological challenges and directions for child development research. *Child Development, 75*, 317–333.

Conti, G., Pizzo, E., Morris, S., & Melnychuk, M. (2021). The economic costs of child maltreatment in UK. *Health Economics, 30*(12), 3087–3105. https://doi.org/10.1002/hec.4409.

Cook, J. L., & Cook, G. (2005). *Child development: Principles and perspectives*. Pearson Education New Zealand.

Crittenden, P. M. (1992). Quality of attachment in the preschool years. *Development and Psychopathology, 4*(2), 209–241. https://doi.org/10.1017/S0954579400000110.

Cross, S., Hubbard, E., & Munro, E. (2010). *Reclaiming social work.* Borough of Hackney Children and Young People's Services, Human Reliability, and London School of Economics and Political Science.

Dallos, R., & Stedmon, J. (2014). Systemic formulation: mapping the family dance. In L. Johnstone & R. Dallos (Eds.), Formulation in psychology and psychotherapy: Making sense of people's problems (pp. 67–95). Routledge.

Dallos, R., Stedmon, J., & Johnstone, L. (2014). Integrative formulation in theory. In L. Johnstone & R. Dallos (Eds.), *Formulation in psychology and psychotherapy: Making sense of people's problems* (pp. 173–190). Routledge.

Daniels, H., & Livingstone, M. (2011). *Hackney child: A true story of surviving poverty and the care system.* Simon & Schuster.

Davidson, C., O'Hare, A., & Mactaggart, F, (2015). Social relationship difficulties in autism and reactive attachment disorder: Improving diagnostic validity through structured assessment. *Research in Developmental Disabilities, 40*: 63–72. https://doi.org/10.1016/j.ridd.2015.01.007.

DeBerry, K. M., Scarr, S., & Weinberg, R. (1996). Family racial socialization and ecological competence: Longitudinal assessments of African-American transracial adoptees. *Child Development, 67*(5), 2375–2399. https://doi.org/10.2307/1131629.

Department for Education (2018a). Adoption support fund (ASF). https://www.gov.uk/guidance/adoption-support-fund-asf.

Department for Education (2018b). Promoting the education of looked after children and previously looked after children. https://www.gov.uk/government/publications/promoting-the-education-of-looked-after-children.

Department for Education (2021). Adoption strategy: Achieving excellence everywhere. https://www.gov.uk/government/publications/adoption-strategy-achieving-excellence-everywhere.

Department for Education. (2022a). Children looked after in England including adoptions. https://explore-education-statistics.service.gov.uk/find-statistics/children-looked-after-in-england-including-adoptions.

Department for Education. (2022b). Evaluation of the adoption support fund 2018 to 2022. https://www.gov.uk/government/publications/evaluation-of-the-adoption-support-fund-2018-to-2022.

Department for Education and Department of Health (2015). Promoting the health and wellbeing of looked after children. https://www.gov.uk/government/publications/promoting-the-health-and-wellbeing-of-looked-after-children--2.

Department of Health (1998). *Quality protects: A framework for action*. The Stationery Office

Dixon, J., Wade, J., Byford, S., Weatherly, H., & Lee, J. (2006). *Young people leaving care: A study of costs and outcomes: Final report to the Department for Education & Skills*. York University, Social Work Research and Development Unit. http://www.york.ac.uk/inst/spru/research/pdf/leaving.pdf.

Dozier, M., Lindhiem, O., Lewis, E., Bick, J., Bernard, K., & Peloso, E. (2009). Effects of a foster parent training program on young children's attachment behaviors: Preliminary evidence from a randomized clinical trial. *Child & Adolescent Social Work Journal : C & A*, *26*(4), 321–332. https://doi.org/10.1007/s10560-009-0165-1.

Dozier, M., Roben, C. K. P., Caron, E., Hoye, J., & Bernard, K. (2018). Attachment and biobehavioral catch-up: An evidence-based intervention for vulnerable infants and their families. *Psychotherapy Research: Journal of the Society for Psychotherapy Research*, *28*(1), 18–29. https://doi.org/10.1080/10503307.2016.1229873.

Eisenberg, N., Cumberland, A., & Spinrad, T. L. (1998). Parental socialization of emotion. *Psychological Inquiry*, *9*, 241–273.

Eisenberg, N., Spinrad, T. L, & Eggum, N. D (2010). Emotion-related self-regulation and its relation to children's maladjustment. *Annual Review of Clinical Psychology*, *6*, 495–525.

Eyberg, S. M., Nelson, M. M., & Boggs, S. R. (2008). Evidence-based psychosocial treatments for children and adolescents with disruptive behavior. *Journal of Clinical Child and Adolescent Psychology, 37*(1), 215–237. https://doi.org/10.1080/15374410701820117.

Feeney, J. A., Noller, P., & Roberts, N. (2000). Attachment and close relationships. In C. Hendrick & S. S. Hendrick (Eds.), *Close relationships: A sourcebook* (pp. 185–201). Sage. https://doi.org/10.4135/9781452220437.n14.

Fisher, P. A., & Gilliam, K. S. (2012). Multidimensional treatment foster care: An alternative to residential treatment for high risk children and adolescents. *Intervencion Psicosocial*, *21*(2), 195–203. https://doi.org/10.5093/in2012a20.

Flackhill, C., James, S., Milton, K., & Soppitt, R. (2017). The coventry grid interview (CGI): Exploring autism & attachment difficulties. *Good Autism Practice*, *18*(1), 62–80.

Fonagy, P., Gergely, G., Jurist, E. L., & Target, M. (2002). *Affect regulation, mentalization, and the development of the self*. Other Press.

Forrester, D., Lynch, A., Bostock, L., Newlands, F., Preston, B., & Cary, A. (2017). *Family safeguarding: Hertfordshire evaluation report*. Department for Education (DFE).

Francis, Y. J., Bennion, K., & Humrich, S. (2017). Evaluating the outcomes of a school based theraplay® project for looked after children. *Educational Psychology in Practice*, *33*(3), 308–322. doi: https://doi.org/10.1080/02667363.2017.1324405.

George, C., Main, M., & Kaplan, N. (1985). *Adult attachment interview (AAI)* [Database record]. APA PsycTests. https://doi.org/10.1037/t02879-000.

Gerhardt, S. (2004). *Why love matters: How affection shapes a baby's brain*. Routledge.

Goldberg, A. E. (2019). *Open adoption and diverse families: Complex relationships in the digital age*. Oxford University Press. https://doi.org/10.1093/oso/9780190692032.001.0001.

Golding, K, (2007) 'Developing group-based parent training for foster and adoptive parents', *Adoption & Fostering* 31: 3, pp 39–48.

Golding K. (2008). *Nurturing attachments: Supporting children who are fostered or adopted.* Jessica Kingsley.

Golding, K.S. (2010). Multi-agency and specialist working to meet the mental health needs of children in care and adopted. *Clinical Child Psychology and Psychiatry, 15*(4), 573–587. doi: https://doi.org/10.1177/1359104510375933.

Golding, K.S. (2014). Meeting the therapeutic and support needs of children in care who have experienced early abuse and neglect. In T. Rahilly & E. Hendry (Eds.) *Promoting the wellbeing of children in care: Messages from research* (pp. 135–170). NSPCC.

Goodman, R. (1997). The strengths and difficulties questionnaire: A research note. *Child Psychology & Psychiatry & Allied Disciplines, 38*(5), 581–586. https://doi.org/10.1111/j.1469-7610.1997.tb01545.x.

Graziano, W. G., Bruce, J., Sheese, B. E., & Tobin, R. M. (2007). Attraction, personality, and prejudice: Liking none of the people most of the time. *Journal of Personality and Social Psychology, 93*(4), 565–582. https://doi.org/10.1037/0022-3514.93.4.565.

Hambrick, E. P., Oppenheim-Weller, S., N'zi, A. M., & Taussig, H. N. (2016). Mental health interventions for children in foster care: A systematic review. *Children and Youth Services Review, 70*, 65–77. doi: https://doi.org/10.1016/j.childyouth.2016.09.002.

Hannon, C., Wood, C., & Bazagette, L. (2010). '*To deliver the best for looked after children the state must be a confident parent*'. *In loco parentis.* Demos.

Harold, G., Hampden-Thompson, G., Rodic, M., & Sellers, R. (2017). *An evaluation of the AdOPt parenting programme.* Department for Education.

Harper, D., & Moss, D. (2003). A different kind of chemistry? Reformulating 'formulation'. *Clinical Psychology, 23*, 6–10.

Harwin, J., Alrouh, B., Golding, L., McQuarrie, T., Broadhurst, K., & Cusworth, L. (2019). *The contribution of supervision orders and special guardianship to children's lives and family justice.* Nuffield Foundation. https://www.cfj-lancaster.org.uk/app/nuffield/filesmodule/local/documents/HARWIN_SO_SGO_FinalReport_V2.1_19Mar2019.pdf.

Hazan, C., & Shaver, P. R. (1994). Attachment as an organizational framework for research on close relationships. *Psychological Inquiry, 5*(1), 1–22. https://doi.org/10.1207/s15327965pli0501_1

Hiles Howard, A. R., Lindaman, S., Copeland, R., & Cross, D. R. (2018). Theraplay impact on parents and children with autism spectrum disorder: Improvements in affect, joint attention, and social cooperation. *International Journal of Play Therapy, 27*(1), 56–68. https://doi.org/10.1037/pla0000056.

Hobday, A., & Lee, K. (1995). Adoption: A specialist area for psychology. *Psychologist, 8*(1), 13–15.

Hodgdon, H. B., Blaustein, M., Kinniburgh, K., Peterson, M. L., & Spinazzola, J. (2016). Application of the ARC model with adopted children: Supporting resiliency and family well being. *Journal of Child & Adolescent Trauma, 9(1)*, 43–53.

Hodgdon, H. B., Kinniburgh, K., Gabowitz, D., Blaustein, M. E., & Spinazzola, J. (2013). Development and implementation of trauma-informed programming in youth residential treatment centers using the ARC framework. *Journal of Family Violence, 28*(7), 679–692.

Hodges, J., Steele, M., Hillman, S., Henderson, K., & Kaniuk, J. (2003). Changes in attachment representations over the first year of adoptive placement: Narratives of maltreated children. *Clinical Child Psychology and Psychiatry, 8*(3): 351–367.

Holen, F. van, Vanderfaeillie, J., Omer, H., & Vanschoonlandt, F. (2016). Training in nonviolent resistance for foster parents: A randomized controlled trial. *Research on Social Work Practice*, *28*(8), 931–942.

Hollingsworth, L. D. (1997). Effect of transracial/transethnic adoption on children's racial and ethnic identity and self-esteem: A meta-analytic review. *Marriage & Family Review, 25*(1–2), 99–130. https://doi.org/10.1300/J002v25n01_07.

Holt, M., Crouch, L., Milward, J., Tankelevitch, L., Vinnitchok, A., & Barnard, M. (2020). *Motivational practice: evaluation report*. Department for Education.

Hughes, D. (1997). *Facilitating developmental attachment*. Jason Aronson.

Hughes, D. (2006). *Building the bonds of attachment* (2nd ed.). Jason Aronson.

Hughes, D. (2007). *Attachment-focused family therapy*. W. W. Norton.

Hughes, D. (2009). *Attachment-focused parenting*. W. W. Norton.

Hughes, D. (2011). *Attachment-focused family therapy workbook*. W. W. Norton.

Hughes. D. (2012). *Parenting a child with emotional and behavioural difficulties (Parenting matters)*. British Association for Adoption and Fostering.

Hughes, D. A., & Baylin, J. (2012). *Brain-based parenting: The neuroscience of caregiving for healthy attachment*. W. W. Norton.

Hughes, D., Golding, K., & Hudson, J. (2015). Dyadic developmental psychotherapy (DDP): The development of the theory, practice and research base. *Adoption & Fostering*, *39*(4). https://doi.org/10.1177/0308575915610943.

Hughes, D. A, Golding, K. S., & Hudson, J. (2019) *Healing relational trauma with attachment-focused interventions: Dyadic developmental psychotherapy with children and families*. Norton and Company.

Jedd, K., Hunt, R. H., Cicchetti, D., Hunt, E., Cowell, R. A., Rogosch, F. A., & Thomas, K. M. (2015). Long-term consequences of childhood maltreatment: Altered amygdala functional connectivity. *Development and Psychopathology*, *27*, 1577–1589.

Jernberg, A. M., & Booth, P. B., (2001). *Theraplay: Helping parents and children build better relationships through attachment-based play*. Jossey Bass.

Jones, A. (2017), Project logic: Providing services and support for the provision of therapeutic life story work. In R. Rose (Ed.), *Innovative therapeutic life story work: Developing trauma informed practice for working with children, adolescents and young adults*. Jessica Kingsley.

Kennedy, H., & Underdown, A. (2018). Video interaction guidance: Promoting secure attachment and optimal development for children, parents and professionals. In P. Leach (Ed.), *Transforming infant wellbeing: Research, policy and practice for the first 1001 critical days* (pp. 224–237). Routledge. https://doi.org/10.4324/9781315452890-23.

Kohlhoff, J., Lieneman, C., Cibralic, S., Traynor, N., & McNeil, C. B. (2022). Attachment-based parenting interventions and evidence of changes in toddler attachment patterns: An overview. *Clinical Child and Family Psychology Review*, *25*(4), 737–753. https://doi.org/10.1007/s10567-022-00405-4.

Koplan, C., & Chard, A. (2015). Adverse early life experiences. In M. T. Compton & R. S. Shim (Eds.), *The social determinants of mental health* (pp. 47–75). American Psychiatric Publishing.

Law, D., & Jacob, J. (2015). *Goals and goals based outcomes (GBOs): Some useful information* (3rd ed.). CAMHS Press.

Leenarts, L. E., Diehle, J., Doreleijers, T. A., Jansma, E. P., & Lindauer, R. J. (2013). Evidence-based treatments for children with trauma-related psychopathology as a result of childhood maltreatment: A systematic review. *European Child & Adolescent Psychiatry, 22*(5), 269–283. https://doi.org/10.1007/s00787-012-0367-5.

Lehmann, S., Bøe, T., & Breivik, K. (2017). The internal structure of foster-parent completed SDQ for school-aged children. *PLoS ONE*, 12(6): e0176625. https://doi.org/10.1371/journal.pone.0176625.

Lehmann, S., Heiervang, E. R., Havik, T., & Havik, O. E. (2014). Screening foster children for mental disorders: Properties of the strengths and difficulties questionnaire. *PLoS ONE, 9*(7), e102134.

Lorenc, T., Lester, S., Sutcliffe, K., Stansfield, C., & Thomas, J. (2020). Interventions to support people exposed to adverse childhood experiences: Systematic review of systematic reviews. *BMC Public Health, 20*, 657. https://doi.org/10.1186/s12889-020-08789-0.

Lucas, J. J., Velik, J., Matthews, L., Brady, K., Breguet, R., & Parson, J. (2022). *Therapeutic life story work Barwon pilot program: Final report*. Geelong. https://www.mackillop.org.au/about-mackillop/publications/therapeutic-life-story-work.

Luyten, P., Mayes, L. C., Nijssens, L., & Fonagy, P. (2017). The parental reflective functioning questionnaire: Development and preliminary validation. *PLoS ONE, 12*(5), e0176218. https://doi.org/10.1371/journal.pone.0176218.

Lyons, S., Whyte, K., Stephens, R., & Townsend, H. (2020). *Developmental trauma: Close up*. Beacon House Therapeutic Services and Trauma Team. https://beaconhouse.org.uk/wp-content/uploads/2020/02/Developmental-Trauma-Close-Up-Revised-Jan-2020.pdf.

Mannarino, A.P., Cohen, J.A., & Deblinger, E. (2014). Trauma-focused cognitive-behavioral therapy. In S. Timmer & A. Urquiza (Eds.). *Evidence-based approaches for the treatment of maltreated children. Vol. 3: Child maltreatment*. Springer. https://doi.org/10.1007/978-94-007-7404-9_10.

Marshak, M. (1960). A method for evaluating child-parent interaction under controlled conditions. *The Journal of Genetic Psychology: Research and Theory on Human Development, 97*, 3–22. https://doi.org/10.1080/00221325.1960.10534309.

Mccullough, E., & Mathura, A. (2019). A comparison between a neuro-physiological psychotherapy (NPP) treatment group and a control group for children adopted from care: Support for a neurodevelopmentally informed approach to therapeutic intervention with maltreated children. *Child Abuse & Neglect.* 97. 104128. https://doi.org/10.1016/j.chiabu.2019.104128.

McGrath, P. (forthcoming). Grandparents experiences of being a special guardian: An interpretative phenomenological analysis. Interim research briefing. 4

McRoy, R. G., & Zurcher, L. A. (1983). *Transracial and inracial adoptees*. Charles Thomas.

McRoy, R. G., Zurcher, L. A., Lauderdale, M. L., & Anderson, R. E. (1984). The identity of transracial adoptees. *Social Casework, 65*(1), 34–39.

Meltzer, H., Gatward, R., Goodman, R., & Ford, T. (2003). Mental health of children and adolescents in Great Britain. *International Review of Psychiatry, 15*(1–2), 185–187. https://doi.org/10.1080/0954026021000046155.

Mercer, J. (2014). Examining dyadic developmental psychotherapy as a treatment for adopted and foster children: A review of research and theory. *Research on Social Work Practice, 24*(6), 715–724. https://doi.org/10.1177/1049731513516514.

Milburn, N. L., Lynch, M., & Jackson, J. (2008). Early identification of mental health needs for children in care: A therapeutic assessment programme for statutory clients of child protection. *Clinical Child Psychology and Psychiatry, 13*(1), 31–47.

Money, R., Wilde, S., & Dawson, D. (2021). Review: The effectiveness of theraplay for children under 12: A systematic literature review. *Child and Adolescent Mental Health, 26*(3), 238–251. https://doi.org/10.1111/camh.12416.

Moran, H. (2010). Clinical observations of the differences between children on the autism spectrum and those with attachment problems. *The Coventry Grid Good Autism Practice Journal, 11*(2), 46–59.

Morris, A. S., Silk, J. S., Steinberg, L., Myers, S. S., Robinson, L. R., & Orleans, N. (2007). The role of the family context in the development of emotion regulation. *Social Development, 16*, 361–388.

Newman, L., Sivaratnam, C., & Komiti, A. (2015). Attachment and early brain development : Neuroprotective interventions in infant–caregiver therapy. *Translational Developmental Psychiatry, 3*, 10.3402/tdp.v3.28647.

NHS Digital. (2021). Mental Health of Children and Young People Surveys. https://digital.nhs.uk/data-and-information/publications/statistical/mental-health-of-children-and-young-people-in-england.

Ní Chobhthaigh, S., & Duffy, F. (2019). The effectiveness of psychological interventions with adoptive parents on adopted children and adolescents' outcomes: A systematic review. *Clinical Child Psychology and Psychiatry, 24*(1), 69–94. https://doi.org/10.1177/1359104518786339.

NICE. (2015). *Children's attachment: Attachment in children and young people who are adopted from care, in care or at high risk of going into care*. NICE.

NICE. (2017). *Child abuse and neglect*. https://www.nice.org.uk/guidance/ng76/chapter/Recommendations#factors-that-increase-vulnerability-to-child-abuse-and-neglect.

NICE. (2021a). Looked after children and young people. https://www.nice.org.uk/guidance/ng73.

NICE. (2021b). NICE support for commissioning for the health and wellbeing of looked-after children and young people.

Nishitani, S., Fujisawa, T., Hiraoka, D., Makita, K., Takiguchi, S., Hamamura, S., Yao, A., Shimada, K., Smith, A., & Tomoda, A. (2021). A multi-modal MRI analysis of brain structure and function in relation to OXT methylation in maltreated children and adolescents. *Translational Psychiatry, 11*. https://doi.org/10.1038/s41398-021-01714-y.

North Yorkshire County Council (2018). Psychological informed partnership approach (PIPA): Annual review. https://cyps.northyorks.gov.uk/sites/default/files/Partnerships/childrens%20trust%20agendas/12.06.19/Enc.%205%20PIPA%20annual%20review%202018.pdf.

Ochs, M., Borcsa, M., & Schweitzer, J. (Eds.). (2020). *Systemic research in individual, couple, and family therapy and counseling* (EFTA Book Series, Vol. 4). Springer International.

Omer, H. (2004). *Nonviolent resistance: A new approach to violent and self-destructive children*. Cambridge University Press.

Perrin, S., Meiser-Stedman, R., & Smith, P. (2005). The children's revised impact of event scale (CRIES): Validity as a screening instrument for PTSD. *Behavioural and Cognitive Psychotherapy, 33*(4), 487–498. https://doi.org/10.1017/S1352465805002419.

Perry, B. D. (2002). Childhood experience and the expression of genetic potential: What childhood neglect tells us about nature and nurture. *Brain & Mind, 3*(1), 79–100. https://doi.org/10.1023/A:1016557824657.

Perry, B. D. (2006). Applying principles of neurodevelopment to clinical work with maltreated and traumatized children: The neurosequential model of therapeutics. In N. B. Webb (Ed.), *Working with traumatized youth in child welfare* (pp. 27–52). The Guilford Press.

Perry, B., & Pollard, M. (1997). *Altered brain development following global neglect in early childhood*. Child Trauma Academy

Pinto, C. (2019). Looked after and adopted children: Applying the latest science to complex biopsychosocial formulations. *Adoption & Fostering, 43*, 294–309. https://doi.org/10.1177/0308575919856173.

Pollak, S. D., Cicchetti, D., Hornung, K., & Reed, A. (2000). Recognizing emotion in faces: Developmental effects of child abuse and neglect. *Developmental Psychology, 36*, 679–688.

Putnam, F. W., Helmers, K., & Trickett, P. K. (1993). Development, reliability, and validity of a child dissociation scale. *Child Abuse & Neglect, 17*(6), 731–741. https://doi.org/10.1016/s0145-2134(08)80004-x.

Rahilly, T., & Hendry, E. (2014). *Promoting the wellbeing of children in care: Messages from research*. NSPCC.

Redfern, S. (2015). *Reflective parenting: A guide to understanding what's going on in your child's mind*. Routledge. 10.4324/9781315764108.

Reinoso, M., Juffer, F., & Tieman, W. (2012). Children's and parents' thoughts and feelings about adoption, birth culture identity and discrimination in families with internationally adopted children. *Child & Family Social Work, 18*, 264–274.

Reynolds, J. D., & Wing, H. M. (2020). Transracial adoption and transracial socialization: clinical implications and recommendations. In E. P. Conngess and M. J. González (Eds,), *Multicultural perspectives in working with families: A handbook for the helping professions* (pp. 39–55). Springer.

Rivett, M., & Buchmüller, J. (2017). *Family therapy skills and techniques in action*. Routledge.

Rose, R. (2004). *The child's own story: Life story work with traumatized children*. Jessica Kingsley.

Rose, R. (2012). *Life story therapy with traumatized children: A model for practice*. Jessica Kingsley.

Rose, R. (2017a). The vital process of recovery. In R. Rose (Ed.), *Innovative therapeutic life story work: Developing trauma-informed practice for working with children, adolescents and young adults* (pp. 30–51). Jessica Kingsley.

Rose, R. (2017b). Communicating with children: Therapeutic life story work techniques. In R. Rose (Ed.), *Innovative therapeutic life story work: Developing trauma-informed practice for working with children, adolescents and young adults* (pp. 52–91). Jessica Kingsley.

Rose, R., & Philpot, T. (2005). *The child's own story life story work with traumatized children*. Jessica Kingsley.

Rose, W., Gray, J., & McAuley, C. (2006). Child welfare in the UK. In C. McAuley, P. J. Pecora, & W. Rose (Eds.), *Enhancing the wellbeing of children and families through effective interventions* (p. 25). Jessica Kingsley.

Rubin, D. M., O'Reilly, A. L., Luan, X., & Localio, A. R. (2007). The impact of placement stability on behavioral well-being for children in foster care. *Pediatrics, 119*(2), 336–344. https://doi.org/10.1542/peds.2006-1995.

Sadiq, F. A., Slator, L., Skuse, D., Law, J., Gillberg, C., & Minnis, H. (2012). Social use of language in children with reactive attachment disorder and autism spectrum disorders. *European Child & Adolescent Psychiatry, 21*(5), 267–276. https://doi.org/10.1007/s00787-012-0259-8.

Schofield, G., Beek, M., & Ward, E. (2012). Part of the family: Planning for permanence in long-term family foster care. *Children and Youth Services Review, 34*, 244–253.

Schore, A. N. (2001). Effects of a secure attachment relationship on right brain development, affect regulation, and infant mental health. *Infant Mental Health Journal, 22*(1–2), 7–66. https://doi.org/10.1002/1097-0355(200101/04)22:1<7::AID-IMHJ2>3.0.CO;2-N.

Selwyn, J., Wijedasa, D., & Meakings, S. (2014). *Beyond the adoption order: Challenges, interventions and adoption disruption*. Department for Education. https://assets.publishing.service.gov.uk/government/uploads/system/uploads/attachment_data/file/301889/Final_Report_-_3rd_April_2014v2.pdf

Shapiro, F., & Solomon, R. M. (2010). EMDR. In I. Weiner and W. E. Craighead (Eds.), *The Corsini encyclopedia of psychology* (4th ed.). Vol. 2, Wiley.

Shmueli-Goetz, Y., Target, M., Fonagy, P., & Datta, A. (2008). The child attachment interview: A psychometric study of reliability and discriminant validity. *Developmental Psychology, 44*(4), 939–956. https://doi.org/10.1037/0012-1649.44.4.939.

Siegel, D. J. (2007). *The mindful brain: Reflection and attunement in the cultivation of well-being*. W. W. Norton.

Simmonds, J. (2010). The making and breaking of relationships: Organizational and clinical questions in providing services for looked after children? *Clinical Child Psychology and Psychiatry, 15*(4), 601–612. doi: https://doi.org/10.1177/1359104510375930.

Silver. M. (2005). About BERRI. https://berri.org.uk/about-berri

Silver, M., Golding, K., & Roberts, C (2015). Delivering psychological service for children, young people and families with complex social care needs. In D. Law, Faulconbridge, J., & Laffan, A. (Eds.), What good looks like in psychological services for children young people and their families. Special edition of the *Child and Family Clinical Psychology Review*.

Sinclair, I., Wilson, K., & Gibbs, I. (2005). *Foster placements: Why they succeed and why they fail*. Jessica Kingsley.

Sissay, L. (2019). *My name is why*. Canongate Books

Social Care Institute for Excellence (SCIE) (2017a). Improving mental health support for our children and young people. Expert Working Group final report. https://www.scie.org.uk/children/care/mental-health/report.

Social Care Institute of Excellence (SCIE) (2017b). *Looked after children and mental wellbeing. The importance of co-production*. SCIE. https://www.scie.org.uk/news/opinions/expert-group-coproduction

Social Care Institute if Excellence (SCIE) (2022). *Co-production, what it is and how to do it*. SCIE. https://www.scie.org.uk/co-production/what-how.

Stone, J. (2021). *Digital play therapy: A clinician's guide to comfort and competence*. Routledge.

Street, E., & Davies, M. (2002). Constructing mental health services for looked after children. *Adoption & Fostering, 26*(4), 65–75. https://doi.org/10.1177/030857590202600409.

Tarren-Sweeney, M. (2007). The assessment checklist for children – ACC: A behavioral rating scale for children in foster, residential and kinship care. *Children and Youth Services Review, 29*, 672–691.

Tarren-Sweeney, M. (2010). It's time to re-think mental health services for children in care, and those adopted from care. *Clinical Child Psychology and Psychiatry*, *15*(4), 613– 626. doi: https://doi.org/10.1177/1359104510377702.

Tarren-Sweeney, M. (2013a). *Assessment checklist for adolescents (ACA)* [Database record]. APA PsycTests.

Tarren-Sweeney, M. (2013b). The assessment checklist for adolescents – ACA: A scale for measuring the mental health of young people in foster, kinship, residential and adoptive care. *Children and Youth Services Review*, *35*(3), 384–393.

Teicher, M. H., Samson, J. A., Anderson, C. M., & Ohashi, K. (2016). The effects of childhood maltreatment on brain structure, function and connectivity. *Nature Reviews Neuroscience*, *17*, 652–666.

Tomoda, A., Navalta, C. P., Polcari, A., Sadato, N., & Teicher, M. H. (2009). Childhood sexual abuse is associated with reduced gray matter volume in visual cortex of young women. *Biological Psychiatry*, *66*, 642–648.

Tomoda, A., Polcari, A., Anderson, C. M., & Teicher, M. H. (2012). Reduced visual cortex gray matter volume and thickness in young adults who witnessed domestic violence during childhood. PLoS ONE, *7*, e52528.

Tomoda, A., Sheu, Y. S., Rabi, K., Suzuki, H., Navalta, C. P., Polcari, A., & Teicher, M. H. (2011). Exposure to parental verbal abuse is associated with increased gray matter volume in superior temporal gyrus. *NeuroImage*, *54*(Supp. 1), S280–S286.

Tomoda, A., Suzuki, H., Rabi, K., Sheu, Y. S., Polcari, A., & Teicher, M. H. (2009). Reduced prefrontal cortical gray matter volume in young adults exposed to harsh corporal punishment. *NeuroImage*, *47*, T66–T71.

Treisman, K. (2016). *Working with relational and developmental trauma in children and adolescents*. Routledge.

Treisman, K. (2017). *A therapeutic treasure deck of feelings and sentence completion cards*. Jessica Kingsley.

Tucker, C., Schieffer, K., Willis, T., Hull, C., & Murphy, Q. (2017). Enhancing social-emotional skills in at-risk preschool students through theraplay based groups: The sunshine circle model. *International Journal of Play Therapy, 26*(4), 185–195. https://doi.org/10.1037/pla0000054.

Turner-Halliday, F., Watson, N., Boyer, N. R., Boyd, K. A., & Minnis, H. (2016). The feasibility of a randomised controlled trial of dyadic developmental psychotherapy. *BMC Psychiatry*, *14*, 347. https://doi.org/10.1186/s12888-014-0347-z.

Van der Kolk, B. A. (2005). Developmental trauma disorder: Toward a rational diagnosis for children with complex trauma histories. *Psychiatric Annals, 35*(5), 401–408. https://doi.org/10.3928/00485713-20050501-06.

Van de Kolk, B. A. (2014). *The body keeps score: Brain, mind and body in the healing of trauma*. Viking Press.

van IJzendoorn, M. H., & Bakermans-Kranenburg, M. J. (2019). Bridges across the intergenerational transmission of attachment gap. *Current Opinion in Psychology*, *25*, 31–36. https://doi.org/10.1016/j.copsyc.2018.02.014.

Vaughan, J., McCullough, E., & Burnell, A. (2016). Neuro-physiological psychotherapy (NPP): The development and application of an integrative, wrap-around service and treatment programme for maltreated children placed in adoptive and foster care placements. *Clinical Child Psychology and Psychiatry, 21*(4), 568–581. https://doi.org/10.1177/1359104516635222.

Vetere, A., & Dallos, R. (2018). *Working systemically with families: Formulation, intervention and evaluation*. Karnac.

Viner, R. M., & Taylor, B. (2005). Adult health and social outcomes of children who have been in public care: Population-based study. *Pediatrics, 115*(4), 894–899. doi: https://doi.org/10.1542/peds.2004-1311.

Vorgias, D., Bynum, F. D., & Bernstein, B. (2023). *Fetal alcohol syndrome*. StatPearls Publishing.

Vostanis, P. (2007). *Mental health interventions and services for vulnerable children and young people*. Jessica Kingsley

Wade, J., Biehal, N., Farrelly, N.,& Sinclair, I. (2011). *Caring for abused and neglected children: Making the right decisions for reunification or long-term care*. Social Policy Research Unit, University of York.

Wade, J., Dixon, J., & Richards, A. (2010). *Special guardianship in practice*. BAAF.

Wade, J., Sinclair, I. A. C., Stuttard, L., & Simmonds, J. (2014). *Investigating special guardianship: Experiences, challenges and outcomes*. Department for Education,

Ward, H., Holmes, L., Soper, J., & Olsen, R. (2008), *Costs and consequences of placing children in care*. Jessica Kingsley.

Waters, E., & Deane, K. E. (1985). Defining and assessing individual differences in attachment relationships: Q-methodology and the organization of behavior in infancy and early childhood. *Monographs of the Society for Research in Child Development, 50*(1–2), 41–65.

Webster-Stratton, C. (2005). The incredible years: A training series for the prevention and treatment of conduct problems in young children. In E. D. Hibbs & P. S. Jensen (Eds.), *Psychosocial treatments for child and adolescent disorders: Empirically based strategies for clinical practice* (pp. 507–555). American Psychological Association.

Weir, K. N., Lee, S., Canosa, P., Rodrigues, N., McWilliams, M., & Parker, L. (2013). Whole family theraplay: Integrating family systems theory and theraplay to treat adoptive families. *Adoption Quarterly, 16* (3–4), 175–200. https://doi.org/10.1080/10926755.2013.844216.

Wettig, H. H. G., Coleman, A. R., & Geider, F. J. (2011). Evaluating the effectiveness of theraplay in treating shy, socially withdrawn children. *International Journal of Play Therapy, 20*(1), 26–37. https://doi.org/10.1037/a0013979.

Wolfe, V. V., Gentile, C., Michienzi, T., & Sas, L. (1991). The children's impact of traumatic events scale: A measure of post-sexual-abuse PTSD symptoms. *Behavioral Assessment, 13*(4), 359–383.

WHO. (2022a). *The ICD-11 classification of mental and behavioural disorders: Clinical descriptions and diagnostic guidelines*.

WHO. (2022b). *ICD-11 mortality and morbidity statistics*. https://icd.who.int/browse11/l-m/en.

York, W., & Jones, J. (2017). Addressing the mental health needs of looked after children in foster care: The experiences of foster carers. *Journal of Psychiatric and Mental Health Nursing, 24*(2–3), 143–153. https://doi.org/10.1111/jpm.12362.

Zeman, J., Cassano, M., Perry-Parrish, C., & Stegall, S. (2006). Emotion regulation in children and adolescents. *Journal of Developmental & Behavioral Pediatrics, 27*(2), 155–168.

18

Young People with Intellectual Disabilities

Nancy Sheppard and Catherine Day

Practitioner psychologists working in the field of neurodevelopment face both challenges and opportunities that allow them the capacity to develop their practice to meet the needs of the children and young people with intellectual disabilities (ID) accessing mental health services. There are a number of factors that can help to develop practitioner confidence in this area and this chapter will aim to impart some of this learning in order to help aspiring and newly qualified practitioners gain some insight into what can be a fascinating and rewarding career.

In comparison to other chapters in this book readers will notice that there is a limited evidence base around working with children with ID. This can leave practitioners feeling particularly unconfident. This chapter will describe the areas where there is strong evidence for effective intervention and illustrate some of the adaptations needed through practice-based evidence in order to offer meaningful support. It will also aim to develop an understanding of the impact of the 'stigma by association' that can occur as stigma is a factor that fundamentally underlies work with this population and explains some of the challenges faced regarding funding, value and recognition in this field. There is a separate chapter on neurodiversity (ND), so this chapter will focus mainly on ID, whilst bearing in mind that 31% of autistic people also have an ID and another 25% have borderline intellectual functioning (IQ = 71–84) (Autism Speaks, 2021).

18.1 Definitions: Who Do We Work With?

It is estimated that 2.5% of the population of children under 17 have an ID; in 2020 this equated to 353,000 children in the UK (ONS, 2020. Precise definitions of ID are confusing as terminology differs across statutory services. Health services define and diagnose young people with ID using *ICD-11* (World Health Organization, 2019) or *DSM-V* (American Psychiatric Association, 2013) definitions that have three criteria:

- deficits in intellectual functioning (i.e. reasoning, problem solving, planning, abstract thinking, judgment, academic and experiential learning, with standardised IQ scores below 70);

Child Psychology: Pathways to Good Practice, First Edition.
Edited by Helen Pote, Anna Picciotto and Clare Norris.

- deficits in adaptive functioning (i.e. social skills, communication, personal independence at home / in the community / school / work functioning); and
- onset in childhood.

Focusing on young people's needs and levels of support over cognitive ability as a means of classification may be more helpful (Carr et al., 2016) and in education services there is a more inclusive definition of learning disability including children with significant learning difficulties or specific learning disorders (i.e. dyslexia, dyscalculia, dyspraxia), which have an impact on a student's capacity to engage in education and learning. Additional health difficulties and co-morbidities and are important for practitioners to consider alongside ID as the health outcomes for young people may be compromised and ID is associated with behaviours that challenge, physical health complications, elevated rates of mental health problems, social inequality and premature death (National Institute for Health and Care Excellence, 2022b; Totsika et al., 2022).

In an effort to bring all of these different aspects together the Education and Health Care Plan (EHCP) system was introduced in 2014 as a means of improving outcomes for children with Special Educational Needs (SEN).

The EHCP aims to:

- establish and record the views of the parents or young person;
- describe the educational needs and any health or social care needs;
- describe the outcomes that, with support, are expected; and
- set out how services will work together to meet these needs.

An EHCP that indicates a significant ID/ND would be a reason to refer to specialist disability Child and Adolescent Mental Health Services (CAMHS). Young people might be referred if they or others close to them see that their mental health is being impacted by their disability in some way, for instance: if they are struggling with anxiety or low mood, related to social skills and friendship difficulties; if they are communicating their feelings by engaging in behaviours of concern; or if family members are struggling with expectations and understanding their needs.

In general, in the UK children with ID, autistic spectrum disorder (ASD) and mental health difficulties will be able to access a specialist CAMHS. Services are organised differently according to area, with some teams integrating specialist provision into generic CAMHS teams and others offering a separate service alongside generic CAMHS.

Similar services exist in other countries outside the UK and have developed according to a number of factors (such as historical and social construction, stigma and understanding of disability, the needs of this population, and the characteristics of health service provision e.g. government health insurance schemes or private health care). Given the disparity of services both across the UK and globally it is important to understand some of the barriers that might be experienced by children with disabilities and their families in accessing mental health support.

18.2 Vulnerability to Mental Health Difficulties and Barriers to Accessing Services

It is well documented that people with ID are vulnerable to experiencing mental health difficulties (e.g. Deb et al., 2001; Zaman et al., 2007). Cooper et al. (2007) report that people with lower intellectual ability are 25% more likely to complain of symptoms of common mental health problems than those with higher abilities. Emerson and Hatton (2007), show that children with ID are 4.5 times more likely to experience mental health difficulties than those without ID. Whilst Austin et al. (2018) note that young people with ID are particularly vulnerable to depression and anxiety at transition to adulthood as they may experience increasing dependence at a time when independence traditionally develops.

Scior (2016) has focused on the area of stigma and ID and explores how this group of people are vulnerable to negative stigmatisation across cultures. Scior also shows how stigmatisation can have negative effects on these individuals, associated with their marginalised group identity, she suggests that:

> It can lead to their exclusion from community life, being denied opportunities and equal rights, and being avoided in social situations (Jahoda & Markova, 2004). Stigma has also been linked to psychological distress (Dagnan & Waring, 2004), decreased self-esteem (Paterson et al., 2012), and increased vulnerability to mental health problems (Mak et al., 2007). (Scior, 2016, p. 7)

Throughout history people with ID have been marginalised in society and denied access to services. Ali et al. (2013) note that discrimination and failure to make reasonable adjustments acted as barriers to accessing care for people with ID and Emerson et al. (2012) also show that people with ID face significant difficulties in accessing health services. The impact of stigma may also have a profound effect; in their review Mitler et al. (2019) show that 'courtesy stigma' (stigma experienced as a result of being close to someone from a stigmatised group) can be internalised by family members and impact on their capacity to cope as social withdrawal and concealment become more likely and asking for help or accessing services for the young people they support becomes more difficult.

A number of government papers and speaking-up campaigns have been published aiming to address the fundamental inequalities and access to safe, effective services. In the UK, Valuing People (Department of Health, 2001) set out to develop a national strategy to support people with intellectual disabilities built on the principles of human rights, developing independence, affording choice and encouraging inclusion. Limited funds resulted in slow progress with these objectives necessitating Valuing People Now (Department of Health, 2009) to revisit the strategy and prompt additional funding.

In the UK in 2012, an undercover journalist filmed footage in a private secure hospital for people with ID that revealed severe levels of systematic abuse.[1] The footage represented an example of extreme devaluation and marginalisation of people with ID in society, and exposed a culture of bullying and abuse rather than care. In response NHS England recommended service models directing the provision of comprehensive community support, and safeguards to prevent hospitalisation for people with ID (NHS England, 2017, 2023).

Mencap has also tried to address the devastating consequences of inequalities in health care for people with ID introducing, *Treat Me Right* (Mencap, 2004), which offered guidance to health professionals around barriers to accessing services. However, 'Closing the Gap' (Disability Rights Commission, 2006) showed that these recommendations had not been implemented and in fact highlighted a number of deaths in people with ID who had been denied access to medical care (see *Death by Indifference*, Mencap, 2007).

1 'Undercover Care; the Abuse Exposed'. BBC Panorama, 2012.

Further efforts to manifest change have been directed by Healthcare for All (Department of Health, 2008) and the Equalities Act (Department of Health, 2010). Despite all of these supports, awareness raising campaigns and policy changes it is clear that inequality in access, particularly in mental health services continues to be a major issue (e.g. Whittle et al., 2019) and as a result there currently remains a need for specialist services.

18.3 Building Confidence in Practitioners

Hronis et al. (2018) suggest that many practitioners working with people with ID and mental health problems have adequate skills but that confidence is needed to use these skills effectively. Hinde and Mason (2020) found that knowledge of issues facing people with ID was key in building confidence and in effective work with this population. It is therefore important to explore factors that may impact gaining relevant knowledge and building practitioner confidence. Bender (1993) suggested that limited access to emotional support for people with ID might be driven by the fact that:

> Psychotherapy involves intensely relating over quite a long period to another person – a certain kind of intimacy. The giving of this intimacy is more difficult, aversive and more energy consuming when the person is seen as unattractive. (Bender, 1993, p. 11)

For most therapists, communication skills and use of words are key in this intense relationship; working with people with limited communication skills requires attunement to non-verbal communications and the emphasis is on the therapist to understand those communications rather than for the client to make themselves understood.

Handley et al. (2019) also note the emotional impact of the work and argue that therapists need 'to engage in advocacy and be in touch with powerful feelings of exclusion and powerlessness' p. 92. Powerlessness and exclusion may therefore become barriers to practitioner confidence and feeling competent in the work. It is well documented that the extreme impact of therapeutic work, particularly trauma related work, can be so powerful as to traumatise the therapist (Corbett 2014). As much of the work undertaken in ID services features underlying chronic, trauma presentations, vicarious trauma may also be a factor affecting confidence. It follows that offering therapeutic support for marginalised, stigmatised individuals is challenging work and may not be as attractive as offering therapy to those where change might come more easily. Shouldering the weight of this kind of history, marginalisation and discrimination needs support.

As described in Chapter 4, supervision for practitioners and reflective spaces to voice the pain and powerlessness present in the work and receive peer support are all vital elements that help provide safe and attuned therapeutic spaces to individuals with ID and their families. Working with colleagues, in multidisciplinary teams, linking with special interest groups and supervision are immensely important in supporting and maintaining energy and curiosity in this work. Developing spaces for reflection and to maintain compassion to navigate the complexities of the work are vital in building confident effective practitioners.

18.4 Evidence Base for Psychological Intervention for Children with ID

The National Institute for Health and Clinical Excellence (NICE) (2016a) recommends that children with ID are offered the full range of psychological interventions with adaptations. The evidence base for psychological interventions with children with ID is, however, limited and as Koslowski et al. (2016) note from their review, the methodologies used in the majority of studies were weak, rendering the existing evidence base fragile. Oshodi and Turk (2017) reviewed the evidence for psychotherapeutic support and Cameron et al. (2021) reviewed the literature relating to children with ID and psychological treatments for depression. Both reviews highlight that despite the paucity of randomised control trials (RCTs), there is evidence from clinical case reports and experimental research that indicates improvements in behaviour for children with ID following psychological interventions. It is, therefore, hoped that a review of the current literature will give practitioners an understanding of the how skills they already have might be helpfully applied to this field.

Carr et al. (2017) have compiled a helpful handbook that details adaptations to assessment and intervention methods to make them accessible for people with ID. Scior (2009) notes that change is likely to be slower in this work and approaches will require significant adaptations to ensure they are person centred and will effect meaningful, positive change. The summary later shows the areas where there is a developing body of evidence to help plan effective interventions.

18.4.1 Parent Support

Hastings and Beck (2004) reviewed interventions that offered parents' support and identified that parental stress had a significant impact on treatment efficacy; they concluded that professional support could reduce parents' stress. Cognitive behavioural therapy (CBT) parenting support models were most frequently studied, but a small number of multicomponent or systemic models also had positive outcomes in terms of reducing parental stress. Hastings and Beck (2004) noted that coordinated support linking different teams and services is a vital element of parent support. Hastings et al. (2012) show the importance of parent-based behavioural support programmes in supporting children with ID. NICE (2013c) recommends parent training for conduct issues and to support the management of ADHD (2019); both areas where there may be adaptations to include support for parents of children with ID. See clinical examples in Box 18.1.

Box 18.1 Clinical example: Jessie

Jessie (10) and her parents were referred by a psychiatrist who had diagnosed mild learning disabilities and ADHD. Jessie's parents wanted to trial medication but agreed for a period of behavioural support as a first line of treatment. Meeting Jessie's parents they were exhausted particularly by the morning routine that frequently ended in Jessie screaming and them both arguing about what had led to the escalation. Jessie's dad felt she was being defiant whilst her mum was trying to see things from a neurodevelopmental perspective, which dad believed let Jessie get away with bad behaviour.

Work started with some psychoeducation looking at how Jessie might be experiencing the world; both parents agreed that they wanted to improve Jessie's experience of life and said it was helpful to mentalise Jessie's experience. The parents were asked to complete some ABC (antecedent–behaviour–consequences) behavioural monitoring charts to gather information about difficult encounters and times when things went well. Looking at the antecedents and consequences of the behaviour with the parents it was clear that the routine needed to start earlier than they expected, that is, sleep was identified as a crucial factor so a good bedtime regime was also as vital as the morning routine.

The intervention then focused on offering a number of behavioural strategies that might support both their evening and morning routine for example, getting things ready the night before, eating dinner together earlier in the evening, getting up a bit earlier, using a visual timetable to help keep Jessie on track and in control, using incentives, for example, making pancakes for breakfast only once all the tasks were done within the timescale and listening to a chapter story in the car on the way to school to motivate Jessie into the car. The practitioner and parents continued to talk through the difficulties Jessie experienced and the impact of these on her self-esteem. Using a goal-based outcome measure (GBOM) the parents rated themselves as understanding Jessie better and also feeling more confident in their parenting task. Although there were still bad mornings they were fewer and as sleep was better for the whole family, Jessie's parent's felt more able to work together and de-escalate difficulties when Jessie became anxious or unfocused.

18.4.2 Behavioural Approaches including Positive Behaviour Support

Sturmey and Hersen (2012) highlight that the majority of studies with children with ID, ASD and Pica (eating of non-foods and substances) favoured behavioural interventions, however this is largely due to the paucity of studies for other interventions rather than evidence that they are ineffective. Grey and Hastings (2005) show that applied behaviour analysis (ABA) interventions have a strong evidence base for children with ID. O'Reilly et al. (2007) give a good overview to the main tenets of ABA, which is underpinned by the behavioural premise that all behaviour is caused and that the cause of the behaviour is external and is triggered by either physical or environmental stimuli. ABA breaks tasks into components and teaches new skills through positive and negative reinforcement (extinguishing behaviour by ignoring it for example). ABA uses functional assessments to understand the causes of difficult behaviour and to identify barriers to accessing opportunities (O'Neill et al., 1990).

Positive behaviour support (PBS) is similarly based on the principle that all behaviour is a communication and close observation can help in understanding its communicative function, however, it has a wider remit than ABA, with emphasis on the network rather than the individual. PBS (e.g. Carr et al., 2002; Hasting, 2013; LaVigna & Willis, 2012) incorporates cognitive, biophysical and environmental psychology with behavioural science as a means of increasing positive behaviours and avoiding the need for a young person to use negative behaviour to communicate their needs. PBS aims to support the family and the network to discover different ways to support needs (Sailor et al., 2009).

In recent years PBS and functional assessments have been expanded to include the impact of trauma (e.g. Paterson et al., 2017) in order to further understand the internal triggers and high arousal that can manifest as behaviours that challenge. There is also a call for PBS to include deeper attention to attachment and relationships in order to holistically understand the individual's needs (BPS, 2017). In practice this has been found to be essential in order to provide effective, holistic interventions for children with ID.

PBS can have significant results; McClean et al. (2007) showed that PBS leads to reduced reliance on medication and improved quality of life, whilst Reid et al. (2013) documented a PBS service approach that included therapeutic short breaks and psychological support and resulted in significant reduction in placement (home or school) breakdown. See the clinical example in Box 18.2.

Box 18.2 Clinical example: Positive behaviour support

A referral was received for Finn, a 15-year-old boy with a diagnosis of ID and visual impairment, who attended the local special school. School had noticed a change in Finn's behaviour and his parents were also struggling to manage at home. There were increasingly frequent angry outbursts accompanied with a new behaviour of banging his head with his hand, which the support network were finding particularly distressing. Following initial assessment, it was agreed that as the family had successfully implemented behavioural strategies in the past, a PBS approach would be most helpful. It was agreed by all that the target behaviour was head banging and a functional analysis, based on interviews with key members of the support network and observations at both home and school, allowed the team to put together a comprehensive PBS formulation (Figure 18.1) to understand what Finn was trying to communicate by this behaviour.

The Head banging behaviour was understood as a means for Finn to communicate a number of different things to the people around him; for instance:

- I don't like this activity and I want it to stop,
- I'm bored,
- this activity is too loud,
- I feel pain
- I am overwhelmed by too many choices

The formulation was presented and agreed by the network and then a number of suggested strategies (Figure 18.2) were introduced to the family, school and the short-breaks support workers. These strategies included offering training to the network to be able to read Finn's communication and feel confident to use the context of the behaviour to work out his particular messages. Over the next few weeks regular network meetings monitored how the introduction of the strategies was going, and parents and carers used the Sheffield Learning Disabilities Outcome Measure (S-LDOM) and the goal-based outcome measure (GBOM) to monitor outcomes; improved scores on both suggested that parental confidence and understanding had increased. There were some adjustments made to the strategies to fit with parent's experience but both home and school reported improved communication as a result of the PBS process.

Under the Transforming Care agenda (NHS England, 2017, 2023), it is important to address the fact that in some services, the restraint of young people with ID remains

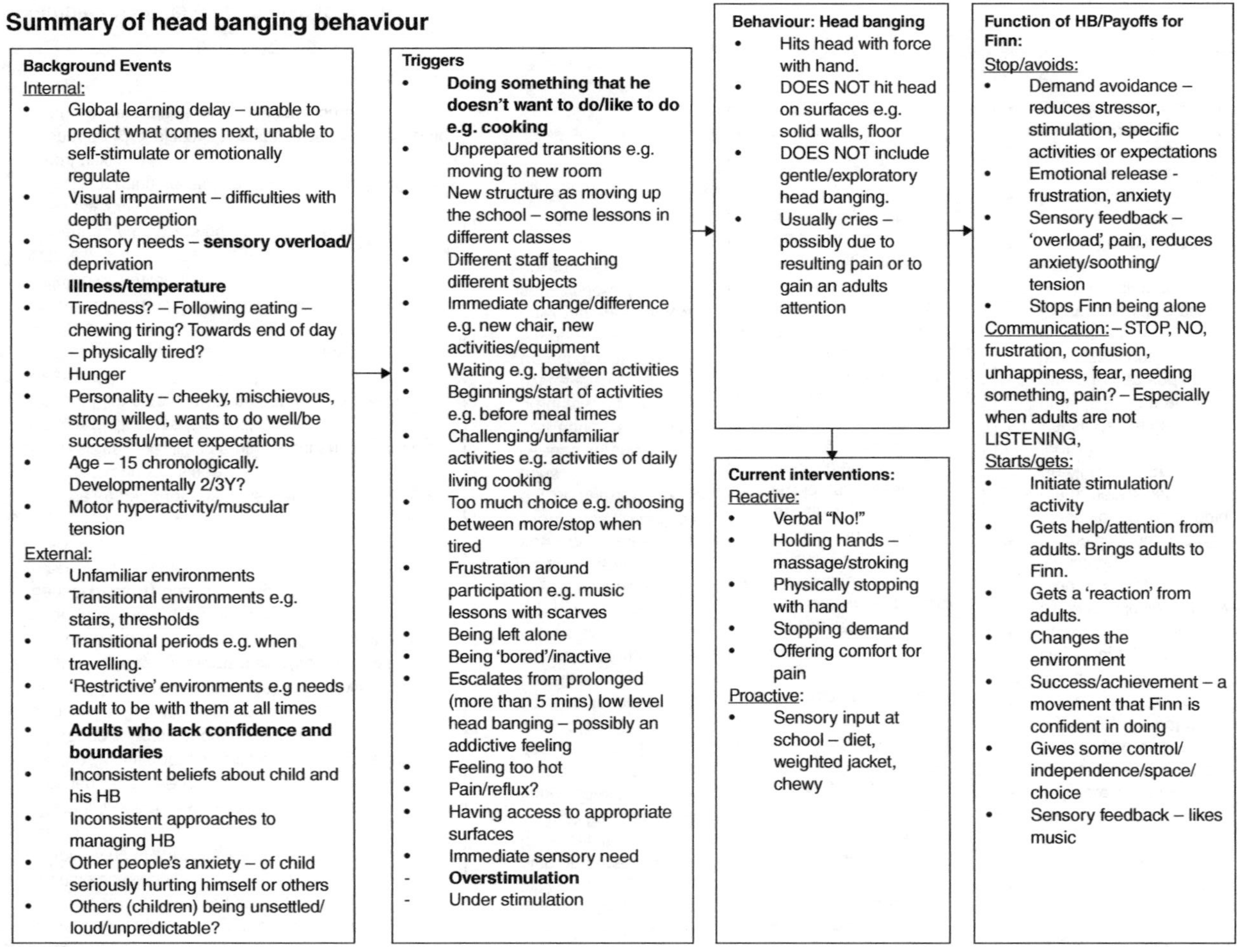

Figure 18.1 Collaborative PBS formulation developed for Finn.

Yellow (background proactive) strategies:

School and home:

- Understand, agree with and be confident and consistent with the PBS plan.
- Training sessions:

1. 'Tolerating my anxiety' training – for family and staff.
2. **'Let's talk about child session – Finn's** capabilities, needs
3. Intensive interaction training / child directed play
4. Feedback from paediatric review

- Sensory/activity visual timetable
- **Provide balance** between rest and activity throughout day – **including rest/down times.**
- Provide alternative sensory stimulation frequently throughout the day (tactile to head and auditory) Sensory/activity brainstorming session headphones to play soft music e.g. Mozart Sonata

Home:

- Provide adapted routine consistently – slightly later timings to support sleep
- Allow some flexibility in routines but ensure child is prepared/offer time to adjust.
- Ensure Finn eats something before activities at weekends
- Provide access to smaller contained environment e.g. bed tent
- Provide opportunities for child to spend time with children of similar age.

School:

- Planned handovers between staff at start of school year.
- Daily morning session to go over the staff/subjects that day
- Sharing PBS plan with all staff who work with child e.g. TAC meetings, new staff induction

Green (trigger proactive) strategies:

- **LISTEN to Finn,** If he communicates 'STOP', 'NO', or 'enough' then stop or pause if demand is necessary.
- Provide frequent social interactions (close physical proximity/low demand e.g. intensive interaction).
- Reduce impact of transitions where possible through routine and preparation – give Finn time!
- Give Finn time to 'settle' or 'readjust' in new environment, even if head banging e.g. no demands for 15 mins
- Graded introduction of new equipment/tasks – gradually increasing use over a term
- Be mindful of temperature of environment – remove shoes/socks if environment is warm.

Orange (when unsettled) strategies:

Unsettled times:

Pre meal/bed times, temperature/illness, transitions, new environments, transitional environments, introducing new activity/task, beginning/start of activities, low level/exploratory head banging

- Standing not sitting for tasks e.g. working, eating
- Reduce/remove choices where possible
- Reduce/remove physical and verbal stimulation where possible
- Avoid unnecessary non-preferred activities where possible.
- Provide breaks in unavoidable non-preferred activities
- Dim lighting and/or reduce noise where possible
- Be patient – don't give up if introducing something new!

Red (after head banging has occurred) strategies:

- Ignore low level head banging (unless continues for more than 5 minutes)
- **Tolerate your own anxieties - take d deep breath and count to 5 – try to appear calm**
- Do NOT say "No" or "Stop"
- **Say "Happy Head"**
- Provide immediate close physical proximity – do NOT hug or 'constrain'
- If Finn continues to HB – use your hand to hold Finn's hands gently – **do NOT hug or 'constrain'**
- Pause demands and provide a short break – return to demand if necessary until completed.
- Provide activity if not occupied/change activity
- Do NOT get stressed/ 'wound up'/shout
- Provide access to alternative head stimulation, music, massage etc
- See stop-think-react plan

Figure 18.2 Example PBS intervention plan for Finn.

common practice. It is preferable to avoid the need for any form of restraint by using functional analysis methods to understand behaviour, however NICE does include guidance on restrictive interventions. Menon et al. (2012) reviewed studies detailing restrictive intervention and concluded that although a variety of techniques are currently used for children with ID including; physical restraint, chemical restraint (medication), mechanical restraint (i.e. protective clothing such as helmets to prevent injury from self-injurious behaviour) and environmental restraints (e.g. padded rooms) there is little evidence to suggest that personal (i.e. seclusion) or chemical restraints are effective. Evidence supporting reduction in medication underlies the STOMP and STAMP[2] campaigns (NHS England 2018) that aim to reduce the use of medication in children with ID. Physical restraint was, in fact, shown by Menon et al. (2012) to be significantly associated with undesirable behavioural consequences and therefore careful ethical consideration is needed before restraint techniques are applied.

18.4.3 Cognitive Behaviour Therapy

Dagnan and Proudlove (1997) and Dagan et al. (2002) have adapted cognitive therapy approaches for people with ID; they advocate that the importance of developing a deep understanding of communication skills and focusing on the therapeutic relationship is central in adapting CBT. They also note the importance of engaging with networks and support systems in order for therapeutic support to be effective and meaningful as so few people with ID are afforded the autonomy to foster real change in their lives.

Harchick et al. (1992) reviewed studies exploring the use of self-management techniques with people with ID and showed that the majority of these studies addressed social skill development. Sams et al. (2006) showed that people (aged 17–60 years) with mild to moderate ID were able to understand the concept of emotion recognition and could distinguish between thoughts, feelings and behaviours and therefore advocated the possibility of offering adapted CBT to young people and adults with ID. See clinical example in Box 18.3.

Box 18.3 Clinical example: Cognitive behaviour therapy

Fatima is 14 and has Downs Syndrome, she was referred by her school to CAMHS as she was regularly crying at school saying she was being bullied. The teachers said when they had investigated her complaints they felt she was misinterpreting things that the other children were saying in response to some quite controlling behaviour from Fatima. In the initial assessment, the therapist heard that Fatima felt that the children didn't like her, that they were talking meanly behind her back and that as she wanted friends, she was telling them to do things she thought friends should do. It was agreed that Fatima would be offered some CBT sessions. In the first session Fatima set a goal of wanting to worry less about friends – it took a couple of sessions to break this

(Continued)

2 STOMP – 'Stop the over medication of people' with autism, learning disabilities STAMP – 'Supporting treatment and appropriate medication in paediatrics'.

Box 18.3 (Continued)

goal downs into a SMART (specific, measurable, achievable, realistic and time limited) goal. Fatima's SMART goals were:

- Fatima will understand what friends do together.
- Fatima will look for evidence (clues) to help her judge if the other young people were being kind or mean.
- Fatima will learn to use tools to help her read the other young people's behaviour.

Fatima and her therapist used 14 sessions of CBT to work out her thoughts and physical feelings when she was worried and developed some strategies to manage her worry in a different way. Through the work together they devised a number of different ways for Fatima to identify her negative, worry thoughts and to learn what feelings accompanied these thoughts. Tools included spotting different words, and facial expressions in other young people, and asking an adult to help her work it out. Fatima's scores on the Revised Child Anxiety and Depression Scale (RCADS) (Chorpita et al., 2000) improved suggesting she felt less anxious and low and this concurred with her verbal report. School and home reported that she was spending less time crying and that she had talked about her strategies to trusted adults.

18.4.4 Other Therapeutic Modalities

There are several third-wave therapeutic modalities that show efficacy for this population including compassion-focused therapy (CFT), acceptance and commitment therapy (ACT), dialectical behaviour therapy (DBT), mindfulness (Patterson et al., 2019) and solution-focused therapy (SFT) (Carrick & Randle-Phillips, 2018). Patterson et al. (2020) describe the adaptations to DBT that make it increasingly accessible for people with ID whilst Cowles et al. (2020) suggest CFT can be adapted to support people with ID who have experienced trauma, attachment difficulties and low self-esteem. Other trauma-focused modalities have also successfully been adapted to be accessible including: eye movement desensitisation and reprocessing (EMDR; Shapiro, 2018) (see Box 18.4), sensori-motor psychotherapy (Fisher & Ogden, 2009) and trauma-focused CBT (Kliethermes et al., 2017). There is a growing body of evidence from RCT's and other studies (e.g. Katatzias et al., 2019, Mevissen et al., 2022) of EMDR with people with ID and from practice that this is an effective modality which does not have to rely on language ability to process trauma. The clinical example in Box 18.4 uses what Marich (2011) refers to as Face 3 of the four faces of EMDR (i.e. the toolbox approach, integrating EMDR techniques into another modality, in this case Disability Psychotherapy).

Box 18.4 Clinical example: Eye movement desensitisation

Ellie, an 18-year-old woman with a mild ID, autism and only scripted or echolalic language was able to use a modified form of eye movement desensitisation (EMD) to reduce her perseverative thinking and anxiety over the health of her mother after she suffered a minor stroke. Ellie was imitating acts of destruction, self-harm and risk taking that she had watched on YouTube. Ellie was a keen artist and she was able to draw her emotions out by copying images from the Internet that she felt represented them. The therapist asked her to choose an emotion card that went with the drawing, and Ellie allowed the therapist to provide bilateral stimulation (BLS) via tapping her hands while she focused on the drawing and the emotion word and what she was feeling in her body.

While Ellie was unable to verbalise this spontaneously, she was able to identify the body sensation and where she felt it. She was also able to rate the intensity of the feeling using a visual subjective units of distress (SUDS) scale. Ellie produced multiple drawings that illustrated her different feelings: sadness, frustration, anger, worry, nervousness, upset, crying, broken, running away, vomiting (see Figure 18.3). Using BLS on each one, her SUDS reduced to zero for all pictures and her behavioural presentation of her anxieties dissipated.

Himmerich (2020) reviewed the literature exploring psychodynamic psychotherapy approaches and showed that psychodynamic support can be helpful (e.g. James & Stacey, 2013; Shepherd & Beail, 2017; Simpson, 2002; Sinason, 2010). However, as most research supporting this approach uses individual case studies or qualitative methodologies, Himmerich concludes that there is not yet enough evidence for psychodynamic psychotherapy to be recommended as a routine clinical intervention but that it should be considered if assessments indicate issues that this model could address. In practice, however, psychodynamic psychotherapy can be extremely helpful in formulating, understanding and supporting people with ID as the case illustration of Alex illustrates (see Box 18.5).

Other attachment-based approaches are also forming a growing body of practice-based evidence. For example, Theraplay® attachment-based play therapy (Booth & Jernberg, 2010; Norris & Lender, 2020), and dyadic developmental psychotherapy (DDP, Hughes et al., 2019). NICE guidelines recommend specific social-communication intervention for the core features of autism but these are also relevant with children and young people with ID. These interventions include play-based strategies with parents, carers and teachers to increase joint attention, engagement and reciprocal communication in the child or young

Crying *Vomiting* *Destroying things*

Figure 18.3 Ellie's drawing and chosen emotion cards used in adapted EMDR.

Table 18.1 Relevant NICE Guidelines and summary of content.

GUIDELINE	SUMMARY
Challenging behaviour and learning disabilities: prevention and interventions for people with learning disabilities whose behaviour challenges	This guideline covers interventions and support for children, young people and adults with a learning disability and behaviour that challenges, and ways of preventing challenging behaviour. It aims to improve quality of life. The guideline also covers support and intervention for family members or carers.
Children's attachment	This quality standard covers the identification, assessment and treatment of attachment difficulties. It focuses on children and young people up to age 18: on the edge of care (those considered to be at high risk of going into care) looked after by local authorities in foster homes (including kinship foster care), in special guardianship, adopted from care, in residential settings and other accommodation
Early years: promoting health and wellbeing in under-fives	This quality standard covers services to support the health, social and emotional wellbeing of children under age five. This includes: home visiting, childcare, early intervention services in children's social care and early education. The standard includes vulnerable children who may need additional support. It does not cover clinical treatment or the role of child protection services
Learning disabilities: behaviour that challenges	This quality standard covers the care of children, young people and adults with a learning disability and behaviour that challenges.
Learning disabilities: identifying and managing mental health problems	This quality standard covers the prevention, assessment and management of mental health problems in people with learning disabilities in all settings (including health, social care, education, and forensic and criminal justice). It also covers family members, carers and care workers.
Mental health problems in people with learning disabilities: prevention, assessment and management	This guideline covers preventing, assessing and managing mental health problems in people with learning disabilities in all settings (including health, social care, education, and forensic and criminal justice). It aims to improve assessment and support for mental health conditions, and help people with learning disabilities and their families and carers to be involved in their care.
Transition from children's to adult's services	This quality standard covers all young people (aged up to 25) using children's health and social care services who are due to make the transition to adult's services. It includes young people with mental health problems with disabilities and with long-term, life-limiting or complex needs in secure settings under the care of local authorities.

Source: NICE Guidelines 2011, 2012a, 2012b, 2013a, 2013b, 2015a, 2015b, 2016a, 2016b, 2018a, 2018b, 2022a, 2022b.

person. Play-based interventions have been found to improve creative and symbolic play, communication and social interactions with peers (Kossyvaki & Papoudi, 2016). Studies of attachment issues of children with autism found they are less likely to demonstrate attachment security than their neurotypical peers and that the more severe the autism, the more impacted their attachment relationships (Kahane & El-Tahir, 2015).

18.4.5 NICE Guidelines

NICE guidance (2022a) has been produced recently to highlight some of the principles in working with children and families with complex difficulties. In essence the guidance states that professionals should ensure that the child is at the centre of any treatment. Timely intervention and planning are key and there is an emphasis on coordination of services and relationship building as central to understanding the child's position and attending to parents' experience as expertise. As described earlier many interventions are adapted to make them accessible for people with ID/ND and therefore all NICE guidelines for working with children are relevant. There are specific guidelines relevant to the field and these are summarised in the Table 18.1.

18.5 Critique of the Evidence Base

The evidence base in this area is largely centred around RCTs, in the same way that there are barriers for the population in accessing services and being afforded a voice in service development, there are also barriers to engaging in research. The majority of studies analysing effectiveness of interventions are based on a medical model of disability focusing on achieving change in the individual to better manage challenges in their environment (e.g. CBT, ABA). Understanding the construction of disability and difference is important in making a distinction between medical models and social or analytical models of disability and how interventions within these models might differ accordingly. Social models of disability propose that change should focus on the environment and the context in order to minimise the impact of the impairment on the individual's opportunities, community participation and choice (e.g. PBS and parents' support). Analytic models focus on understanding and changing the internal experience of the person with a disability (e.g. individual psychotherapy). Another alternative model is a more relational model, which can help the therapist to support individuals in finding ways to engage with society and with the system around them, which supports their best potential to build confidence and self-esteem and to move individuals and their families from a position of powerless to powerful (Wilson 2003). Brown (2019) also acknowledges the particular importance of recognising power imbalance in the therapeutic relationship with marginalised groups and advocates naming the power differences as a means of supporting meaningful attunement.

By adopting a framework of attachment-based thinking and drawing from trauma-informed understanding to build effective therapeutic relationships, practitioners can develop accessible services that highlight the importance of working at different levels within a system, not just focusing on change within the client. Within all of these models of disability, working at many different levels of the system is important. Consultation, advocacy and change in the systems supporting individuals is as valuable as face-to-face individual therapeutic appointments with clients with ID. Using systemic frameworks for understanding difficulties, offering comprehensive assessment of needs within the whole system, and capturing the family's voice are all vital elements of practice-based evidence, demonstrating what is effective work in this field.

18.6 Views and Voices of Children about this Area of Practice

Throughout this chapter a common theme highlighted in the literature, NICE guidance and policy is one of co-creation and inclusion. Traditionally, as in all areas of child mental health, taking account of the child's voice in relation to services was deemed problematic and difficult, so children were simply not asked. Thompson et al. (2020) highlight that children with disabilities are rarely considered as co-producers in the development of services. With new technology and sensitive participation approaches there are better opportunities for inclusion in research (e.g. Schock & Lee, 2016). Despite improvements in mainstream services, in the ID field inclusive research and service development remains a rarity. There are, however, a handful of studies focusing on children's views.

Following recommendations in Valuing People Now (DoH, 2009), Boyden et al. (2013) developed a set of quality standards for engaging children, aged 11–17 with ID, in giving views of services they were receiving; they established a number of areas that their participants had identified as key aspects of meaningful services; the experience of the service, communication with and between professionals, impact of the work carried out, and addressing difficulties encountered. They listened to experiences of families engaging in PBS support and found that participants felt that they experienced more than just strategies to support behaviour change but valued the therapeutic relationship and understanding the difficulties within a family context.

Children and Young People - Improving Access to Psychological Therapies - Autistic Spectrum Conditions and Learning Disabilities models (CYP-IAPT-ASC-LD) (Chinn et al., 2014) advocates services using routine outcome measures to improve participation. In our services we use the Experience of Services Questionnaire (ESQ, Brown et al., 2014) and a Goal Based Measure (Law & Jacob, 2015). Children also use symptom focused session by session rating (e.g. RCADS, Chorpita et al., 2000) to rate their progress in therapeutic support. The clinical examples have illustrated how different outcome measures might be used and how they can enhance work with children and families with intellectual disabilities.

Since the pandemic hit in 2020, the benefits of offering on-line work to some children following an in-person assessment session have supported improved access to services. Many families and young people have expressed their preference for on-line sessions and attendance has improved as a result.

18.7 Frameworks for Practice

Given the limitations and the critiques of evidence-based practice in this field it is also important to incorporate practice-based evidence. In order to enhance practice it can be helpful to draw on two main frameworks for assessment in order to design person-centred, adapted interventions for young people with ID.

18.7.1 Disability as a Form of Complex/developmental Trauma

Disability psychotherapy posits that almost all people with ID have experienced some form of trauma (e.g. Beail et al., 2021; Frankish, 2016). Many authors have written about the ongoing traumatic experiences of people with disabilities from birth, throughout childhood and into adulthood. This type of trauma may differ from conventional forms that are understood in trauma-related services but can be fundamental in understanding a person's presenting difficulties. The impact of stigmatisation, marginalisation and societal attitudes or as Sinason (2010) describes, 'society's death wish' (the unconscious desire to eradicate the existence of certain genetic conditions), all compound the experience of people with ID in their everyday lives and account for increased vulnerability to traumatisation. Delays in meeting developmental milestones can impact relationships with parents, family, teachers and peers. People with ID have a higher vulnerability to adverse experiences (Sullivan & Knutson, 2000) and can be understood to have early and ongoing encounters akin to what is known as complex or developmental trauma (Herman, 2015; *ICD-11*, World Health Organization, 2019).

This vulnerability to trauma is attributed to multiple factors:

- Contextual factors – including social isolation, institutionalised care, minimal access to a trusted person or private space for disclosure, limited understanding and access to adapted personal, social, health and economic education (PSHE), limitations of legal and safeguarding frameworks for individuals with disabilities, lack of participation and choice in decisions.
- Individual factors – increased dependency for personal/intimate care or finances, decreased communication and help seeking skills, vulnerability to bullying, intimidation and abuse, perceived limited capacity to consent to marriage or sexual relationships and a propensity for acquiescence.

In the most recent *DSM*-V and *ICD-11*, definitions of trauma include negative alterations in cognition and mood, and a dissociative subtype, linked to prolonged childhood exposure to interpersonal trauma. This framework can be helpful in understanding presentations such as behaviours that challenge, since many of the common issues that emerge in psychotherapy with individuals with ID can be seen as interpersonal or intrapersonal trauma. Sinason and Hollins (2000) give a deeper understanding of the impact of this type of traumatic experience and suggest that in order to help individuals through therapy a number of themes need to be understood with the individual:

- the existence of the disability itself, including conscious and unconscious fantasies that accompany it;
- loss (of the 'healthy' self);
- sexuality (impacted by the disability);
- dependency (unable to live autonomously);
- fear of annihilation and death (being part of a group that society wishes to eliminate); and
- 'secondary handicap' and 'handicapped smile' (learned helplessness and placating/neutralising others' negativity through false 'cheerfulness').

18.7.2 Attachment Theory

Another helpful framework in understanding the impact of life experience is attachment theory (Ainsworth & Bowlby, 1991; Bowlby, 1988; Main & Solomon, 1986); people with ID can be vulnerable to relational difficulties or mis-attunement from early in life due to differences in communication and social signals, and/or emotional problem solving (such as making relational repairs following a rupture.) The family life cycle is significantly altered compared to families without disability (Goldberg et al., 1995) and this may have an impact on attachment relationships within the parent–child dyad, the parent–parent relationship and sibling bonds. Rhode and Grayson (2021) have explored the initial impact of the disability on the early bonding process and describe a 'cycle of discouragement', which can undermine confidence in parenting and set up a difficult cycle resulting in both parent and child feeling disheartened and 'not good enough'.

Hughes and Baylin (2012) also refer to 'blocked trust' in the child and 'blocked care' in the child–parent dyad; this concept, adapted from DDP, is helpful in understanding how ID might impact the attachment relationships for some children. If a carer experiences early parenting as difficult due to the child being slow or unable to respond to the parents' care and nurture, the parent is at risk of experiencing blocked care. The parent may be able to continue functioning at a practical level but the engagement and enjoyment of natural bonding is impacted: the parent's response is an innate attempt to protect themselves from the emotional pain of managing this experience. For the child, this type of early experience can have devastating neurobiological effects, the child does not develop the trust that adults can attune or consistently attend to their needs. The child can be left with feelings of shame, self-doubt, worthlessness, unlovability, which may lead them to unconsciously fear intersubjective, reciprocal relationships (Hughes & Baylin, 2012) even with loving, nurturing caregivers. Porges' (2017) polyvagal theory further elaborates on this (de)activation of the social engagement system. Fletcher (2004) looked at attachment relationships in parents of children with disabilities and quotes one mum's experience:

> because … when they're younger you always have this hope that when they get older they might grow out of it, or it's going to get better, it's going to get easier and it doesn't get any easier. I'm not sure it's going to get any better, it's just different to be honest … it's much harder when you've got a nine year old girl walking down the road screaming her head off or throwing a wobbly than it is to have a two year old sitting in a pushchair throwing a wobbly … and as you get older you realise that in actual fact you could have this adult of 30 on your arm screaming or throwing a wobbly and that's very difficult to come to terms with Fletcher (2004, p. 40).

Many authors have understood that the birth of a child with disabilities can lead to a need to process the loss of the expected child and this process may have vastly different degrees of emotional impact ranging from adjustment to trauma (Beaumont, 2016; Bicknell, 1983; Ditchfield, 1992; Fletcher, 2016; Hodges, 2003). Goldberg et al. (1995) highlighted that there can be a re-emergence of this initial shock of the diagnosis at each life stage; they described the recapitulated grief that make natural transitions (generally celebrated with neurotypical children) times of extreme anxiety for families. According to the work of Mahler, in neurotypical development, an individual's emotional maturity develops *in relation* to the primary caregivers, that is, within the context of an attachment relationship. Frankish (2016) draws on Mahler's five stages: symbiotic, differentiation, practising, rapprochement and individuation (Mahler et al., 1975/2008) and suggests that individuals with ID/ND often become 'stuck' at one of these stages. This can occur for a number of reasons including difficulty in the primary attachment relationship, traumatic separations and/or medical procedures, having multiple caregivers or being placed into residential care.

Hence, an understanding of the attachment relationships and the emotional stage of development of our clients is essential to understanding how they are currently functioning and where there might be some areas of healing that can be targeted for intervention.

18.8 Assessment

Practitioner psychologists use assessments as a means of exploring the factors that indicate the potential for change in the young person or family system. Hodges (2003) identifies the need for practitioner be aware of their own assumptions when making an assessment, to explore different understandings of presenting difficulties, different beliefs that underlie this understanding and what their individual understanding is of the part each person might play in the difficulties occurring or being maintained. It is also important to assess the relationship to help, what has been their experience of asking for help in the past and what have they made of the help they have received. This will determine the capacity of the young person or their family in taking on and effectively using the support offered. (See Chapter 3 for further discussion).

The importance of a comprehensive trauma- and attachment-informed assessment of strengths and needs cannot be underestimated with young people with ID. This lens can capture the support needs of an individual from a developmentally sensitive perspective and signpost to the social, psychological, educational and interpersonal or relational interventions that will enable the young person to have the best chance of success and growth. This perspective can also lead to better understanding of the systemic nature of the difficulties presented and explore the specific contexts in which the difficulties arise.

18.8.1 Psychological Testing with Young People with ID

As discussed earlier, definitions of intellectual disability generally encompass three core components (NICE, 2022a): lower intellectual ability (usually an IQ of less than 70), significant impairment of social or adaptive functioning and onset in childhood. So, when ID is suspected by the family, health visitor, school or GP a referral for a developmental assessment might be made, often to a multidisciplinary diagnostic assessment service, including paediatricians, clinical psychologists, occupational therapists, speech and language therapists, physiotherapists and sometimes social workers.

As part of this multidisciplinary assessment process CYP may require psychological testing using psychometric assessments across a range of domains (Moss & Moss-Racusin, 2021), including:

- developmental status;

- intelligence and academic achievement;
- speech-language and visual-motor abilities;
- memory, attention/concentration, and executive functioning; and
- behavioural and social-emotional functioning.

Standardised tests of intellectual functioning and adaptive behaviour are available for the psychological practitioner to use such as the Wechsler Intelligence Scale for Children – 5th ed. (*WISC-V-UK*). Only appropriately trained psychological practitioners should be conducting psychometric assessments with young people as the outcomes of psychological assessments have serious consequences for the young person, in relation to receiving diagnostic labels and accessing appropriate education, financial and health resources. Professional practice guidelines on testing should be carefully adhered to (see British Psychological Society: Guidelines on Testing and Test Use, https://www.bps.org.uk/guidelines-testing-and-test-use).

If a diagnosis is given the child or young person will automatically be included in the register of people with an intellectual disability, which is part of the Quality and Outcomes Framework, in order that they can receive appropriate health, educational and social care. Diagnosis of ID, and other developmental difficulties, is only one description of the young person's functioning and it is important to understand their functioning and relationships more broadly in order to develop a psychologically informed formulation.

18.9 Formulations

Once a picture has been established of how the young person's needs interact with their social and relational environment it is possible to formulate how problems may have arisen and are maintained. Creating an intervention plan for young people with ID requires a broad knowledge base of therapeutic modalities that come from many other fields of clinical work alongside psychological interventions (such as occupational therapy, speech and language therapy and art therapy). This is enhanced by experience and by collaboration with multidisciplinary colleagues so that ideas can be shared, problem solved and so that consultation, mentoring and supervision are possible.

Formulations help the practitioner to make an appropriate intervention plan encompassing the immediate and wider context and cultural perspectives, which aims to work at multiple levels.

1. Social/environmental
   - To build up safe connections and attachment relationships in all areas in which the person operates (home, school/vocational).
   - To remove barriers such as misunderstanding of teachers/colleagues through accommodation, adaptation, training, education, advocacy.
   - To provide enrichment opportunities primed through meaningful activities such as joining a club focused on a special or intense interest.
   - Person-centred planning, which puts CYP at the centre of planning and decisions that affect them and their care.

- Positive behaviour support plan and help to implement strategies identified through functional analysis.

2. Individual
   - to address trauma symptoms or reactivations
   - to heal relational / attachment injuries which have led to certain patterns of relating
   - to build specific skills e.g. social skills, independent living skills, Relationship & Sexuality Education (RSE)
3. Relational
   - Systemic family therapy to support family relationships through identifying patterns of behaviour, assumptions and family scripts (Baum & Lyngaard, 2006).
   - Specific attachment work through emotional and behavioural support with a safe caregiver, partner, peers or siblings.
4. Cultural
   - Recommendations are appropriate for and respectful of the:
     - Immediate context (e.g. family, carers)
     - Environmental context (e.g. school, workplace)
     - Community context (e.g. making use of available resources in the local area)
     - Cultural context (e.g. faith beliefs and support networks, cultural traditions)

18.10 Adapting Interventions

Formulation is informed by a range of frameworks and theoretical models, which then lend themselves to the specific evidence-based interventions described earlier many of which may need to be adapted to support the specific needs of children with ID.

Therapies that take a right-brain approach rather than requiring left-brain skills are particularly suited for the first phase of work with those with cognitive impairments or social communication difficulties. As the literature suggests, involvement of parents and caregivers is essential for most effective change and growth. Using a right-brain, 'doing' approach rather than, or in conjunction with, left-brain approaches such as psychoeducation or skills training, can be particularly effective. Perry and Dobson's (2013) neuro-sequential model is helpful as a means of supporting formulations and coordinating support. This is a developmentally and biologically sensitive framework that can be used to organise information gathering and current functioning in order to structure assessment and identify areas of strength and need. From there, the most effective sequence for interventions can be planned to meet those needs. Whilst this model has been developed with traumatised and neglected children in mind, it can be equally valid for guiding work with children and adults with neurodevelopmental conditions. The typical development of the brain is sequential from bottom up: brain stem, limbic system, diencephalon and cortex. This development can be disrupted by trauma and neglect, either by abuse and maltreatment, or by organic impairment, epilepsy, autism, cerebral palsy and so on. Hence this framework can be used to identify strengths and needs regardless of the cause, and to create a care plan for intervention.

Assessment, formulation and intervention plans do not follow an exact pathway. Integrating knowledge and frameworks can be different for each child and family. The clinical example in Box 18.5 aims to illustrate some of the challenges described above and the complexities of the work in this field.

18.11 Measuring Outcomes

Measuring emotional and behavioural outcomes for children and young people with intellectual disabilities is complex for practitioners as individual functioning (such as language abilities), developmental level and sociocultural factors for the child need to be considered in determining if standardised measures are appropriate for use. The British Psychological Society in collaboration with the Child Outcomes Research Consortium have recently developed guidance on appropriate outcome tools for children and young people with intellectual disabilities and these should be consulted for further information (Philips &

Table 18.2 Summary analyses of the 'core' outcome measures used by psychological practitioners working with children and young people with learning disabilities to determine the most appropriate use of each. Data from Phillips, N. & Demjen, E. (2021). *Measuring outcomes and change for children and young people with learning disabilities and their families; A clinical perspective.*

MEASURE (number of respondents in brackets)	LEVEL OF LEARNING DISABILITY[1] (✓ indicates routinely used with this group, X indicates not)				CLINICAL UTILITY[1] (see key at foot of table)				QALITATIVE ANALYSIS[3] Appropriate for use with CYP with learning disabilities?
					Practitioner		Parent/carer		
	Mild	Moderate	Severe	Profound	Useful?	Detects change?	Useful?	Easy?	
GBO (44)	✓	✓	✓	✓	✓✓	✓✓	✓✓	✓✓	✓
CHI-ESQ (24)	✓	✓	✓	✓	✓✓	?	✓	✓✓	✓
BPI-01 (14)	×	✓	✓	×	✓	✓✓	✓	✓	✓
Nisonger (8)	✓	✓	✓	✓	✓	✓✓	?	?	✓
RCADS-P (18)	✓	×	×	×	✓	?	✓	?	CYP with mild learning disabilities only
SLDOM (32)	✓	✓	✓	✓	✓	?	?	✓	✓
DBC (19)	×	✓	✓	×	✓	?	?	?	✓
SDQ Impact (17)	✓	✓	✓	×	?	?	?	✓✓	?
SDQ Parent (32)	✓	✓	✓	×	?	?	?	✓	CYP with mild learning disabilities only
SDQ YP (29)	✓	×	×	×	?	?	××	××	CYP with mild learning disabilities only
CGAS (9)	✓	✓	✓	×	××	?	××	?	×

[1] 'routine use' is defined as where 50% or more of respondents use a measure with each subgroup

[2] clinical utility key – 95% confident that:

✓✓	both highly rated (mean score is >50/100) and better than at least some other measures;
✓	highly rated (mean score is >50/100);
?	no firm conclusions can be drawn;
×	poorly rated (mean score is <50/100); and
××	poorly rated (mean score is <50/100) and poorer than at least some other measures

[3] based on whether overall themes/comments indicated this

Demjen, 2021). They summarise a survey of over 100 psychological practitioners' use of common psychological outcome measures with this population of young people (see Table 18.2).

Box 18.5 Clinical example: Working with Alex

Alex is an 11-year-old Latino boy with mild ID and a diagnosis of ADHD who was supported by creating a neurodevelopmentally sensitive care plan. The work with Alex illustrates intervention at a number of different levels over time in order to fit with what was understood to support his development in emotional and cognitive functioning.

Referral

Alex was referred for urgent CAMHS assessment following a violent altercation with a peer and Alex expressing suicidal ideation. Alex had grown up in a kinship foster care placement with his maternal grandmother, having been removed at birth from his biological mother who used substances throughout the pregnancy.

Assessment

During the assessment Alex reported that he had been bullied for some time by the peer he got into a fight with, and he had been watching pornography and playing violent video games for long hours; it was established in this initial assessment that he had made no attempt to self-harm and had no plan or intent to end his life. A number of self-report and informant measures were used to assess Alex's mental health, such as the RCADS (Chorpita et al., 2000), Beck Youth Inventories (BYI-2, Beck et al., 2005), Behavior Assessment System for Children (BASC3, Reynolds & Kamphaus, 2015) and his adaptive functioning (Vineland Adaptive Behaviour Scales, Sparrow et al., 2016). He had high anxiety and poor adaptive functioning, particularly in socialisation. Alex had begun to experience intrusive thoughts and images about committing sexual offenses and violent acts, and talked about this repeatedly, raising anxiety in the professional network. The network agreed that the exposure to pornography constituted harmful sexual behaviour, damaging to his own sexual development, and potentially increasing risk to others. His grandmother consistently struggled to manage parental controls or supervise Internet use and a child protection process was implemented.

Formulation

Based on the initial information, it appeared that Alex had had little parental supervision and minimal support to manage his anxiety. He was dysregulated and in 'threat response' most of the time and had developed 'strategies' of avoiding going out, excessive gaming and watching pornography to self-soothe. However, the more he watched, the more intrusive thoughts he experienced and the more he fantasised about committing offenses. It was hypothesised that his poor socialisation skills might be compounded by lack of sexual knowledge and that this needed further assessment.

Intervention

Alex was found to have gaps in his sexual knowledge and understanding of issues such as consent. A range of measures were used to assess this such as the Strengths and Difficulties Questionnaire (SDQ), the Adapted Questionnaire on Attitudes Consistent

(Continued)

Box 18.5 (Continued)

with Sex Offending (QASCO) and Assessment of Sexual Knowledge (ASK), along with measures of family functioning such as the SCORE-15.

Taking account of the neuro-sequential model it was considered that Alex could use both a 'bottom-up' approach where his grandmother was supported to provide more co-regulation for Alex (lower- and mid-brain work) and he was provided with a 'top-down', skills-based approach (cortex-level work) to fill the knowledge gaps.

However, grandmother declined support to develop her understanding of Alex's diagnosis and needs. It was therefore, felt that a DDP-informed (Hughes et al., 2019) process might serve to strengthen the parental presence in their relationship. Co-creating narratives with individuals and families about their current difficulties is a therapeutic technique used in many modalities including systemic approaches, DDP and trauma-informed approaches. This model was also applied to support the network; multiagency practice that is delivered using the principles of DDP. The aim is to build relational strength in the network and find the most helpful or effective impact that everyone in the network can have on the child or family. DDP supports developing shared narratives and modelling co-regulation so that the network can support building trust and safety rather than mirroring the blocked care, splitting and blaming. The DDP practitioner uses the principles of PACE (playfulness, acceptance, curiosity and empathy), and affective-reflective dialogue to explore and understand the dynamics.

Alex engaged well with a child-caregiver psycho-education programme based on the Keep Safe© Harmful Sexual Behaviour programme (Malovic et al., 2018). He reintegrated in school and no further concerns were reported. However, Alex's grandmother was in poor health and her attendance at the parent group was sporadic. She was a quiet and proud woman who held tightly to the ideal that her own authoritarian parenting style and strong moral values, which she felt had successfully raised her own children, were what Alex needed. This was understood in the context of the family's culture and wider community where many women were single parenting with support of their female relatives.

Outcome measures

Initial post-intervention measures showed great improvement in sexual knowledge, relationship skills and emotional literacy, a reduction in behavioural problems and increase in pro-social behaviours. However, Alex continued to seek out pornography and needed assistance to clarify the issues of consent. Using the neuro-sequential framework, this outcome fits with the fact that Alex only received a cognitive intervention and other needs were not met, hence he was still using sensori-motor and reward-system activation to self-soothe and manage his emotional responses (functions of the lower-brain areas).

Alex's scores indicated an improvement in family functioning, but his grandmother's scores did not, and she continued to express concerns. With his grandmother not at the stage of readiness to engage in any further work or child–parent dyad work, Alex was discharged and care handed over to the network, following a consultation to school and social worker and recommendations for safeguarding Alex and others, and supporting the family. Ongoing consultation to the network was made available.

Re-referral

Alex was referred again 18 months later, now aged 14 years, having made a disclosure that he had been sexually assaulted by a stranger sometime in the past. His grandmother continued to report behavioural difficulties at home.

Re-assessment

Assessment this time focused on Alex's trauma and attachment history and helping him to tell his own narrative about his life experiences. It was established that around the time of the initial referral he had been sexually assaulted by a male stranger in a public toilet, which he had not told anyone about. During this assessment Alex again expressed suicidal ideation and a sense of hopelessness; he was struggling at his mainstream school and they requested further assessment.

Using a trauma- and attachment-informed neuropsychological approach the assessment included understanding about:

- Alex's cognitive and academic ability;
- mental health and trauma symptomatology using adapted measures;
- level of risk to himself and others including risk of exploitation;
- protective and resilience factors; and
- internal working model and his attachment relationships.

Re-formulation

Alex met the criteria for post-traumatic stress disorder (PTSD); his cognitive profile was typical for children with in-utero alcohol exposure in addition to cocaine. That is, poor social emotional skills, and significantly impaired maths/money skills and independent living skills, though for Alex, verbal skills were in line with chronological age (or slightly advanced), and he had good functional reading ability. This profile gave some insight into the likely assault his developing brain suffered in-utero, as well as his risk and vulnerability factors for the future. Studies show that children exposed to substances in utero are at higher risk of negative outcomes in cognitive, academic, emotional, social and behavioural functioning. They have lower cognitive functioning at an early age and do not 'catch up' over time, even when placed in low-risk stable families in infancy. (BMA, 2007, updated 2016; SAMHSA, 2014).

This additional information served to inform an improved neurodevelopmentally sensitive care plan, and gave some explanation as to why the previous intervention had had limited success.

Attachment insecurity with the grandmother was also indicated, and she reported episodes of escalating violence and aggression. A risk assessment determined that Alex was a low risk to himself and others, but at high risk of exploitation, and due to his level of impulsivity there were safeguarding concerns for his elderly grandmother. She requested that he be removed from her care and be placed in a residential facility.

Intervention

Alex was placed in a residential home, and although this came with many negatives for him, it also allowed him to live in a state of safety and stability, which opened up the

(Continued)

Box 18.5 (Continued)

possibility of additional therapeutic intervention. Once his placement was stabilised, Alex was able to engage in individual therapy: trauma-focused work using a disability psychotherapy model. Liaison and consultation were provided to the care network. Stability was reinforced through the use of phase 1 and 2 of EMDR (resourcing) and a DDP approach with the whole care network, including grandmother and extended family, who, without caring responsibility for Alex were better able to engage and support successful home visits. EMDR processing was not attempted as Alex's cognitive profile, high distractibility and impulsivity led the therapist to judge that he would not cope well with opening up the trauma networks in a safe contained way or be able to shut them down again safely even with an adapted approach. Instead, a DBT-informed approach was used for: psychoeducation about trauma, 'hot/cold/warm/wise mind' and resiliency building. A narrative approach was used to co-create and strengthen positive aspects of his life story from before he was born to present day, including the assault, without going into painful details. With help from his network and social worker, he was gradually introduced to other siblings and half-siblings who had also been placed in care. His therapeutic web was built and reinforced, but it remained difficult for him to engage in extracurricular or social activities. In this way, a combination of cognitive/cortex level interventions (e.g. DBT, narrative work) and lower-brain interventions (e.g. EMDR resourcing, (re)building the family relationships and therapeutic web) was used to form his intervention plan.

Outcome measures

Alex was discharged from therapy when trauma symptoms were no longer in clinical range (as indicated by the Traumatic Stress Checklist for Children and Impact of Events Scale – Intellectual Disability). Continued care coordination and liaison was given to the network, and Alex was involved in all meetings.

Re-referral and ongoing support

At transition age, when he was 17, Alex was re-referred due to high anxiety and concerns about independent living. He returned for some 'booster' therapy sessions, to review the EMDR resourcing and reinforce his ability to regulate and stay in his 'window of tolerance'. Person-centred planning Pearpoint, O'Brien, Forest, M. (1993) was initiated with the therapeutic web. Skills based groups were offered to assist in preparing for community living, specifically the Program for the Evaluation and Enrichment of Relational Skills (PEERS©) group.

Alex is now 20 and has just left the After-Care programme due to his age. He has been successfully living in the community with support from his therapeutic web for 2 years. There are continued concerns about him maintaining employment, and risk of financial or sexual exploitation. He has had some short-term romantic relationships, but remains anxious about sexual relationships. He continues to experience social anxiety but is increasingly involved in community activities such as the Special Olympics, a church group, traditional boat building and vocational training.

Alex may need additional work at crucial life cycle stages, for example if he becomes involved in a long-term relationship or becomes a parent. But for now, he is a stable and functioning member of the community.

18.12 Common Challenges and Addressing Them in the Work

This chapter aimed to address many of the common challenges faced when working with people with ID in addressing equalities, diversity and inclusion (EDI) as these are fundamental issues. In working with children and families from varied cultures, it is important to understand the double discrimination that clients with ID who are from racially or culturally minoritised communities may face. It is therefore particularly important to work with cultural sensitivity and to address the possibility of assumptions being made in the work. Haque (2008) talks about how working with any kind of difference, but particularly referencing cultural differences and disability, raises anxiety in the therapist and client. This anxiety can be stifling and needs acknowledging and exploring.

With Alex, the therapist drew on the strong cultural tradition of oral storytelling to pass down wisdom, customs and folklore. In general, this can be helpful in the engagement process and is a respectful way to include family perspectives without imposing assumptions underlying different therapeutic models. Using the principles of PACE can be helpful in maintaining curiosity and supporting empathy with family feelings and beliefs. However, with Alex's grandmother this posed a difficulty as she was not happy to share her perspective; perhaps due to previous discrimination or perceived differences between herself and the professional network (age, cultural background, racial heritage, faith background and values). Kareem and Littlewood (1999, p. 14) note that: 'The very fact of being from another culture involves both conscious and unconscious assumptions in both the patient and the therapist.'

It is therefore important for practitioners to use a number of means to raise awareness to unconscious assumptions. Individual and peer supervision are vital tools to this end. Using EDI observers in team meetings and asking directly about the experience of racism can also be helpful as a means of highlighting openness to the likelihood of this as an experience and allow the possibility to be explored (see Chapter 7 for a fuller discussion).

Measuring outcomes in this population can also pose a challenge, however they are a means of improving practitioner confidence by measuring change and monitoring progress. Change may be slow, with subtle incremental change or rapid change may occur simply by allowing space for a young person to communicate emotionally in a way they feel understood and for therapists to support 'translating' that understanding to caregivers and networks. Using outcome measures as a matter of routine can also support change.

There are a number of adapted, accessible measures available and a recent CORC project has collated and summarised these (see CORC, n.d.).

18.13 Future Directions

It is appreciated that experience in the field supports the development of confidence to work within a limited evidence base and to adapt and integrate psychological models to enable children using ID services to reach their potential. Becoming comfortable with facing difference and diversity, and to support others to develop this confident stance can take time and experience. The common factors that underlie this confidence are:

- Understanding the impact of living in our society with disability as a form of chronic trauma and attending to the importance of attachment relationships in healing. Therapeutic relationships are inherently attachment relationships and practitioner psychologists act as agents of healing. By using knowledge, skills and 'expertise' to target particular areas of hurt, practitioners can affect great change and growth with service users and in themselves.
- Understanding that fundamentally, underlying all of this is the ability to be with another person who may be different to ourselves, who may look different, communicate differently, act or behave differently, but whose human needs are the same as every human.

Undoubtedly future directions will require more research to be undertaken, giving voice to the young people that ID services support and continuing to support mainstream colleagues to offer their therapeutic work with confidence to people with ID and their families. Addressing the issues of discrimination, stigma and inequality, the ID field is far ahead of other specialities in some areas yet dragging behind in others – a strong evidence base for the practices that are most helpful being one area for growth.

Websites and other useful resources including inspirational practice

American Association of Intellectual and Developmental Disabilities. Available at https://www.aaidd.org/.

Autism Speaks. Available at https://www.autismspeaks.org/.

British Institute of Learning Disabilities. Available at https://www.bild.org.uk/.

Cerebra – Working Wonders for Children with a Brain Condition. Available at https://cerebra.org.uk/.

Challenging Behaviour Foundation. Available at https://www.challengingbehaviour.org.uk/.

Change – Learning Disability Rights Charity. Available at https://www.changepeople.org/.

Chickenshed – Theatre Changing Lives. Available at https://www.chickenshed.org.uk/.

Down's Syndrome Association. Available at https://www.downs-syndrome.org.uk/.

Foundation for People with Learning Disabilities. Available at https://www.learningdisabilities.org.uk/.

Institute of Psychotherapy and Disability. Available at https://instpd.org.uk/.

Mencap – Learning Disability Explained. Available at https://www.mencap.org.uk/learning-disability-explained.

National Association for Down's Syndrome. Available at https://www.nads.org/.

National Autistc Society. Available at https://www.autism.org.uk/.

People First – A Voice for People with Learning Disabilities. Available at https://www.peoplefirstltd.com/.

Respond – From Hurting to Healing. Available at https://respond.org.uk/.

The Association for Child and Adolescent Mental Health (ACAMH). Available at: https://www.acamh.org/.

References

Ainsworth, M. S., & Bowlby, J. (1991). An ethological approach to personality development. *American Psychologist, 46*(4), 333–341. https://doi.org/10.1037/0003-066X.46.4.333.

Ali, A., Scior, K., Ratti, V., Strydom, A., King, M., & Hassiotis, A. (2013). Discrimination and other barriers to accessing health care: Perspectives of patients with mild and moderate intellectual disability and their carers. *PLoS ONE*, 8(8), e70855.

American Psychiatric Association. (2013). *Diagnostic and statistical manual of mental disorders* (5th ed.). American Psychiatric Association.

Austin, K. L, Hunter, M., Gallagher, E., & Campbell L. E. (2018). Depression and anxiety symptoms during transition to early adulthood for people with intellectual disabilities, *Journal of Intellectual Disability Research*, *62*(5), 407–421.

Baum, S., & Lynggaard, H. (Eds.). (2006). Intellectual disabilities: A systemic approach. Routledge. https://doi.org/10.4324/9780429476037.

Beail, N., Frankish, P., & Skelly, A. (Eds.). (2021). *Trauma & intellectual disabilities: Acknowledgement, identification & intervention*. Pavilion.

Beaumont, H. (2016). *Hole in the heart: Bringing up Beth*. Myriad.

Beck, J. S., Beck, A. T., Jolly, J. B., & Steer, R. A. (2005). *Beck youth inventories for children and adolescents: Second edition*. NCS Pearson.

Bender, M., (1993). The unoffered chair: The history of therapeutic disdain towards people with learning disabilities, *Clinical Psychology Forum*, *43*, 2–6.

Bicknell, J. (1983). The psychopathology of handicap. *British Journal of Medical Psychology*, *56*(2), 167–178.

British Medical Association. (2007, updated 2016). *Alcohol and pregnancy: Preventing and managing fetal alcohol spectrum disorders*. BMA. https://www.bma.org.uk/media/2082/fetal-alcohol-spectrum-disorders-report-feb2016.pdf.

Booth, P. B., & Jernberg, A. M. (2010). *Theraplay: Helping Parents and Children Build Better Relationships through Attachment-Based Play*. Third edition.

Bowlby, J. (1988). *A secure base: Clinical applications of attachment theory*. Routledge.

Boyden, P., Munia, M., & Laxton-Kane, M. (2013). Listening to the views of children with learning disabilities: An evaluation of a learning disability CAMHS service. *Journal of Intellectual Disabilities*, *17*(1), 51–63. https://doi.org/10.1177/1744629512469923.

British Psychological Society. (2017). Guidelines on testing and test use. BPS. https://www.bps.org.uk/guidelines-testing-and-test-use.

Brown, A., Ford, T., Deighton, J., & Wolpert, W. (2014), Satisfaction in child and adolescent mental health services. *Administration and Policy in Mental Health and Mental Health Services Research*, *41*(4), 436–446.

Brown, H. (2019). Reciprocal roles in an unequal world. In J. Lloyd, & R. Pollard (Eds.), *Cognitive analytic therapy and the politics of mental health* (pp. 20–37). Routledge.

Cameron, L. A., Phillips, K., Melvin, G. A., Hastings, R. P., & Gray, K. M. (2021). Psychological interventions for depression in children and young people with an intellectual disability and/or autism: Systematic review. *The British Journal of Psychiatry*, *218*(6), 305–314. doi: https://doi.org/10.1192/bjp.2020.226.

Carr, A., Linehan, C., O'Reilly, G., Noonan Walsh, P., & McEvoy, J. (Eds.). (2016). *The handbook of intellectual disability and clinical psychology practice* (2nd ed.). Routledge.

Carr, A., Linehan, C., O'Reilly, G., Noonan Walsh, P., & McEvoy, J. (Eds.). (2017). *The handbook of intellectual disability and clinical psychology practice* (3rd ed.). Routledge.

Carr, E. G., Dunlap, G., Horner, R. H., Koegel, R. L., Turnbull A. P., Sailor, W., Anderson, J. L., Albin, R. W., Koegel, L.K., & Fox, L. (2002). Positive behaviour support: The evolution of an applied science. *Journal of Positive Behavioural Interventions, 4*(1), 4–14.

Carrick, H., & Randle-Phillips, C. (2018). Solution-focused approaches in the context of people with intellectual disabilities: A critical review. *Journal of Mental Health Research in Intellectual Disabilities, 11*(1), 30–53.

Chinn, D., Abraham, E., Burke, C., & Davies, J. (2014). *IAPT and learning disabilities.* King's College and Foundation for People with Learning Disabilities.

Chorpita, B. F., Yim, L. M., Moffitt, C. E., Umemoto L. A., & Francis, S. E. (2000). Assessment of symptoms of DSM-IV anxiety and depression in children: A revised child anxiety and depression scale. *Behaviour Research and Therapy, 38*, 835–855.

Cooper, S. A., Smiley, E., Finlayson, J., Allan, L., Williamson, A., Mantry, D., & Morrison, J. (2007). The prevalence, incidence, and factors predictive of mental ill health in adults with profound intellectual disabilities. *Journal of Applied Research in Intellectual Disabilities, 20*, 493–501.

Corbett, A. (2014). *Disabling Perversions; forensic Psychotherapy with people with intellectual disabilities.* Forensic Psychotherapy Monograph series. Series Editor Brett Kahr. Karnac. London.

CORC. (n.d.). Gathering feedback and measuring outcomes and change with children and young people with learning disabilities (LD). https://www.corc.uk.net/outcome-experience-measures/feedback-and-outcome-measures-for-children-and-young-people-with-learning-disabilities/.

Cowles, M., Randle-Phillips, C., & Medley, A. (2020). Compassion-focused therapy for trauma in people with intellectual disabilities: A conceptual review. *Journal of Intellectual Disabilities, 24*(2), 212–232. https://doi.org/10.1177/1744629518773843.

Dagnan, D., Jahoda, A., & Stenfert Kroese, B., (2002). Cognitive behaviour therapy. In A. Carr, G. O'Reilly, P. Noonan Walsh, & J. McEvoy (Eds.), *The handbook of intellectual disability and clinical psychology practice* (pp. 264–280). Routledge.

Dagnan, D., & Proudlove, J. (1997). Using Makaton drawings to access the ability to recognise facial expressions of emotions in people with learning disabilities. *Clinical Psychology Forum, 195*, 3–5.

Dagnan, D., & Waring, M. (2004). Linking stigma to psychological distress: Testing a social cognitive model of the experience of people with intellectual disabilities. *Clinical Psychology and Psychotherapy, 11*, 247–254.

Deb, S., Thomas, M., & Bright, C. (2001). Mental disorder in adults with intellectual disability. Prevalence of functional psychiatric illness among a community-based population aged between 16 and 64 years. *Journal of Intellectual Disability Research, 45*(6), 495–505.

Department of Health. (2001). *Valuing people: A new strategy for learning disability for the 21st century*. Department of Health.

Department of Health, (2008). *Healthcare for all: Report of the independent inquiry into access to healthcare for people into learning disabilities, Sir Jonathan Michael.* Department of Health. https://webarchive.nationalarchives.gov.uk/ukgwa/20130105064250/http:/www.dh.gov.uk/en/Publicationsandstatistics/Publications/PublicationsPolicyAndGuidance/DH_099255.

Department of Health. (2009). *Valuing people now. A new three-year strategy for people with learning disabilities*. Department of Health.

Department of Health (2010). *Equalities Act*. Department of Health.

Disabilities Rights Commission. (2006). *Equal treatment: Closing the gap*. Disability Rights Commission.

Ditchfield, H. (1992). The birth of a child with a mental handicap: Coping with loss. In A. Waitman and S. Conboy-Hill (Eds.), *Psychotherapy and mental handicap*. (pp. 9–23). Sage.

Emerson, E., Baines, S., Allerton, L., and & Welch, V. (2012). *Health inequalities & people with learning disabilities in the UK: 2012*. Department of Health.

Emerson, E., & Hatton, C. (2007). Mental health of children and adolescents with intellectual disabilities in Britain. *The British Journal of Psychiatry : The Journal of Mental Science, 191*, 493–499. https://doi.org/10.1192/bjp.bp.107.038729.

Fisher, J., & Ogden, P. (2009). Sensorimotor psychotherapy. In C. A. Courtois & J. D. Ford (Eds.), *Treating complex traumatic stress disorders: An evidence-based guide* (pp. 312–328). The Guilford Press.

Fletcher, H., (2004). *The loss of the healthy child: Exploring the relationship between mothers' early attachment relationships and their reaction to their child's learning disability*. Unpublished PhD thesis. University College London.

Fletcher, H. K. (2016). Attachment relationships between parents and their children: The impact of the loss of the healthy child. In H. K. Fletcher, A. Flood, & D. J. Hare (Eds.), *Attachment in intellectual and developmental disability: A clinician's guide to practice and research*. Wiley.

Frankish, P. (2016). *Disability psychotherapy: An innovative approach to trauma-informed care*. Routledge.

Goldberg, D., Magrill, L., Hale, J., Damaskinidou, K., Paul, J., & Tham, S. (1995). Protection and loss: Working with learning-disabled adults and their families. *Journal of Family Therapy, 17*(3), 263–280.

Grey, I. M., & Hastings R.P., (2005). Evidence-based practices in intellectual disabilities and behaviour disorders. *Current Opinion in Psychiatry, 18* (5), 469–475.

Handley, E., Greenhill, B., & Beard, K. (2019). Using CAT to bridge the gap: Attending to the ultimate and the intimate. In J. Lloyd & R. Pollard (Eds.), *Cognitive analytic therapy and the politics of mental health* (pp. 92–111). Routledge.

Haque, S. (2008). Differences, differences, differences: Working with ethnic, cultural and religious diversity. In T. Cottis (Ed.), *Intellectual disability, trauma and psychotherapy* (pp. 130–147). Routledge.

Harchick, A. E., Sherman J. A., & Sheldon, J. B. (1992). The use of self-management procedures by people with developmental disabilities: A brief review. *Research in Developmental Disabilities, 13*, 211–227.

Hastings, R. P., Robertson, J., & Yasamy, M. T. (2012). Interventions for children with pervasive developmental disorders in low- and middle-income countries. *Journal of Applied Research in Intellectual Disability, 25*(2), 119–134.

Herman, J. L. (2015). *Trauma and recovery: The aftermath of violence – from domestic abuse to political terror*. Basic Books.

Himmerich, J. (2020). Psychodynamic psychotherapy in severe and profound intellectual disability. *Advances in Mental Health and Intellectual Disabilities, 14*(3), 45–60.

Hinde, K., & Mason, J. (2020). Health practitioners' knowledge and confidence in diagnosis and treatment of mental health issues in people with intellectual disabilities. *Journal of Intellectual and Developmental Disabilities*, *45*(3), 269–278.

Hodges, S. (2003). *Counselling adults with learning disabilities*. Palgrave Macmillan.

Hronis, A., Robert, L., & Kneebone, I. (2018). Assessing the confidence of Australian mental health practitioners in delivering therapy to people with intellectual disabilities. *Journal of Intellectual and Developmental Disabilities*, *56*(3), 202–211.

Hughes, D. A., & Baylin, J. (2012). *Brain-based parenting: The neuroscience of caregiving for healthy attachment*. W. W. Norton & Company.

Hughes, D. A., Golding, K. S., & Hudson, J. (2019). *Healing relational trauma with attachment-focused interventions: Dyadic developmental psychotherapy with children and families*. W. W. Norton & Company.

Jahoda, A., & Markova, I. (2004). Coping with social stigma: People with intellectual disabilities moving from institutions and family home. *Journal of Intellectual Disability Research*, *48*(8), 719–729.

James, C., & Stacey, J. M. (2013). The effectiveness of psychodynamic interventions for people with learning disabilities: A systematic review. *Tizard Learning Disabilities Review*, *19*(1), 17–24.

Kahane, L., & El-Tahir, M. (2015). Attachment behaviour in children with autistic spectrum disorders. *Advances in Mental Health and Intellectual Disabilities*, *9*, 79–89. http://dx.doi.org/https://doi.org/10.1108/AMHID-06-2014-0026.

Karatzias, T. Brown, M., Taggart. L. Truesdale, M., Sirisena, C, Walley, R., Mason-Roberts, S., Bradley, A., & Paterson, D. (2019). A mixed methods, randomised controlled feasibility trial of eye movement desensitization and reprocessing (EMDR) plus standard Care (SC) versus SC alone for DSM-5 posttraumatic stress disorder (PTSD) in adults with intellectual disabilities, *Journal of Applied Research in Intellectual Disabilities*, *32*(4), 806–818.

Kareem, J., & Littlewood, R. (Eds.). (1999). *Intercultural therapy: Themes interpretations and practice* (2nd ed.). Wiley-Blackwell.

Kliethermes, M. D., Drewry, K., & Wamser-Nanney, R. (2017). Trauma-focused cognitive behavioural therapy. In M. A. Landolt, M. Cloitre, & U. Schnyder (Eds.), *Evidence-based treatments for trauma related disorders in children and adolescents* (pp. 167–186). Springer International Publishing/Springer Nature. https://doi.org/10.1007/978-3-319-46138-0_8.

Koslowski, N., Klein, K., Arnold, K., Kosters, M., Schutzwohl, M., Salize, H. J., & Puschner, B. (2016). Effectiveness of interventions for adults with mild to moderate intellectual disabilities and mental health problems; Systematic review and meta-analysis. *British Journal of Psychiatry*, *209*, 469–474.

Kossyvaki, L., & Papoudi, D. (2016). A review of play interventions for children with autism at school. *International Journal of Disability, Development and Education*, *63*, 45–63. https://doi.org/10.1080/1034912X.2015.1111303.

LaVigna, G. W., & Willis, T. J. (2012). The efficacy of positive behavioural support with the most challenging behaviour: The evidence and its implications. *Journal of Intellectual and Developmental Disability*, *37*(3), 185–195.

Law, D., & Jacob, J. (2015). *Goals and goal based outcomes (GBOs): Some useful information* (3rd ed.). CAMHS Press.

Mahler, M., Pine, F., & Bergman, A. (1975/2008). *The psychological birth of the human infant: Symbiosis and individuation*. Basic Books.

Main, M., & Solomon, J. (1986). Discovery of an insecure-disorganised/disoriented attachment pattern. In T. B. Brazelton & M. W. Yogman (Eds.), *Affective development in infancy* (pp. 95–124). Ablex Publishing.

Mak, W. W. S, Poon, C. Y. M, Pun, L. Y. K., & Cheung, S. F. (2007). Meta-analysis of stigma and mental health, *Social Science & Medicine*, *65*(2), 245–261.

Malovic, A., Rossiter, R., & Murphy, G. H. (2018). Keep safe: The development of a manualised group CBT intervention for adolescents with ID who display harmful sexual behaviours. *Journal of Intellectual Disabilities and Offending Behaviour*, *9*(1), 49–58. ISSN 2050-8824.

Marich, J. (2011). *EMDR Made Simple.* Premier Publishing and Media.

McClean, B., Grey, I. M., & McCracken, M. (2007). An evaluation of positive behaviour support for people with very severe challenging behaviours in community-based settings *Journal of Intellectual Disabilities*, *11*(3), 281–301.

Mencap. (2004). *Treat me right*! Mencap.

Mencap. (2007). *Death by indifference*. Mencap.

Menon, K., Baburaj, R., & Bernard, S. (2012). Use of restraint for the management of challenging behaviour in children with intellectual disabilities. *Advances in Mental Health and Intellectual Disabilities*, *6*(2), 62–75.

Mevissen, L., Didden, R., Korzilius, H., & de Jongh, A. (2017). Eye movement desensitisation and reprocessing therapy for posttraumatic stress disorder in a child and an adolescent with mild to borderline intellectual disability: A multiple baseline across subjects study. *Journal of Applied Research Intellect Disabil.* Dec; 30 Suppl 1:34–41. doi: 10.1111/jar.12335. Epub 2017 Mar 26. PMID: 28345176.

Milter, N., Ali, A., and Scior, K. (2019). Stigmas experienced by families of individuals with intellectual disabilities and autism: A systematic review. *Research in Developmental Disabilities*, *89*, 10–21.

Moss, N. E., & Moss-Racusin, L. (2021). *Practical guide to child and adolescent psychological testing*. Springer.

NHS England. (2017). *Transforming care model service specifications: Supporting implementation of the service model.* NHS England. https://www.england.nhs.uk/wp-content/uploads/2017/02/model-service-spec-2017.pdf.

NHS England. (2018). *Supporting treatment and appropriate medication in paediatrics (STAMP).* NHS England. https://www.england.nhs.uk/learning-disabilities/improving-health/stamp/.

NHS England. (2023). *Dynamic support register and care (education) and treatment review: Policy and guidance*. NHS England. https://www.england.nhs.uk/wp-content/uploads/2023/01/PR1486-Dynamic-support-register-and-Care-Education-and-Treatment-Review-policy-and-guide.pdf.

National Institute for Health and Care Excellence [NICE]. (2011). *Autism: Recognition, referral and diagnosis* (updated 2017). NICE.

National Institute for Health and Care Excellence [NICE]. (2012a). *Social and emotional well-being: Early years*. NICE.

National Institute for Health and Care Excellence [NICE]. (2012b). *Autism diagnosis and management* (updated 2021). NICE.

National Institute for Health and Care Excellence [NICE]. (2013a). *Autism: Support and management* (updated 2021). NICE.

National Institute for Health and Care Excellence [NICE]. (2013b). *Learning disabilities: Challenging behaviour*. NICE.

National Institute for Health and Care Excellence [NICE]. (2013c). *Antisocial behaviour and conduct disorders in children and young people*. NICE guideline [CG158]. https://www.nice.org.uk/guidance/cg158.

National Institute for Health and Care Excellence [NICE]. (2015). *Challenging behaviour and learning disabilities: Prevention and interventions for people with learning disabilities whose behaviour challenge*. NICE.

National Institute for Health and Care Excellence [NICE]. (2015). *Children's attachment*. NICE.

National Institute for Health and Care Excellence [NICE]. (2016a). *Mental health problems in people with learning disabilities: Prevention, assessment and management*. NICE.

National Institute for Health and Care Excellence [NICE]. (2016b), *Transition from children's to adult's services*. NICE.

National Institute for Health and Care Excellence [NICE] . (2018a). *Learning disabilities and behaviour that challenges: Service design and delivery*. NICE.

National Institute for Health and Care Excellence [NICE] . (2018b). *Attention deficit hyperactivity disorder: Diagnosis and management (updated 2019)*. NICE.

National Institute for Health and Care Excellence [NICE]. (2019) *Attention deficit hyperactivity disorder: Diagnosis and management*. NICE guideline [NG87]. https://www.nice.org.uk/guidance/ng87.

National Institute for Health and Care Excellence [NICE] . (2022a). *Disabled children and young people up to 25 with severe complex needs: Integrated service delivery and organisation across health, social care and education*. NICE.

National Institute for Health and Care Excellence [NICE] . (2022b). *Clinical knowledge summaries: Learning disabilities*. NICE. https://cms.bps.org.uk/sites/default/files/2022 07/ptc09_code_of_good_practice_amended.pdf.

Norris, V., & Lender, D. (2020). *Theraplay®: The practitioner's guide*. Jessica Kingsley.

Office for National Statistics (ONS). (2020). *Estimates of the population for the UK, England and Wales, Scotland and Northern Ireland*. ONS.

O'Neill, R. E., Horner, R. H., Albin, R. W., Storey, K., & Sprague, J. R. (1990). *Functional analysis of problem behaviour: A practical assessment guide*. Sycamore Publishing.

O'Reilly, M., Sigafoos, J., Lancioni, G. E., Green, V. A, Olive, M., & Cannella, H. (2007). Applied behaviour analysis. In A. Carr, G. O'Reilly, P. Noonan Walsh and J. McEvoy (Eds.), *The handbook of intellectual disability and clinical psychology practice*. (pp. 253–280). Routledge.

Oshodi, O., & Turk, J. (2017). Efficacy of psychotherapeutic and related interventions for children with intellectual disabilities in non-clinical settings: A review of the literature, *International Journal of Developmental Disabilities*, *63*(2), 61–76.

Paterson, B., Young, J., & Bradley, P. (2017). Recognising and responding to trauma in the implementation of PBS? *BILD, International Journal of Positive Behavioural Support*, *7*(1), 4–14.

Paterson, L., McKenzie, K., & Lindsay, B. (2012). Stigma: Social comparison and self-esteem in adults with an intellectual disability. *Journal of Applied Research in Intellectual Disabilities*, *25*(2), 166–176.

Patterson, C., Williams, J., & Jones R. S. P. (2020). DBT and intellectual disabilities: The relationship between treatment fidelity and therapeutic adaptation. *Advances in Mental Health and Intellectual Disabilities, 14*(3), 61–67.

Patterson, C. W., Williams, J., & Jones, R. (2019). Third-wave therapies and adults with intellectual disabilities: A systematic review. *Journal of Applied Research in Intellectual Disabilities, 32*, 1295–1309.

Pearpoint, J., O'Brien, J., & Forest, M. (1993). *Path: planning alternative tomorrows with hope for schools, organizations, business, families: a workbook for planning positive possible futures.* Toronto: Inclusion Press.

Perry, B. D., & Dobson, C. (2013). The neurosequential model (NMT) in maltreated children. In J. Ford & C. Courtois (Eds.), *Treating complex traumatic stress disorders in children and adolescents* (pp. 249–260). Guilford Press.

Phillips, N., & Demjen, E. (2021). *Measuring outcomes and change for children and young people with learning disabilities and their families: A clinical perspective.* Child Outcomes Research Consortium (CORC). https://www.corc.uk.net/media/2864/full-report-measuring-outcomes-and-change-for-children-and-young-people-with-learning-disabilities-and-their-families-a-clinical-perspective.pdf.

Porges, S.W. (2017). *The pocket guide to the polyvagal theory: The transformative power of feeling safe.* WW Norton.

Reid, C., Sholl, C., & Gore, N. (2013). Seeking to prevent residential care for young people with intellectual disabilities and challenging behaviour: Examples and early outcomes from the Ealing ITSBS. *Tizard Learning Disabilities Review, 18*(4), 171–178.

Reynolds, C. R., & Kamphaus, R. W. (2015). *Behavior assessment system for children* (3rd ed.). NCS Pearson.

Rhode, M., & Grayson, K. (2021). An observationally and psychoanalytically informed parent-toddler intervention for young children at risk of ASD: An audited case series and convergences with organicist approaches. In M. Fitzgerald (Ed.), *Autism spectrum disorder: Heterogeneity, neurobiology and intervention*, Intech Open Books.

Sailor, W., Dunlap, G., Sugai, G., & Horner, R (2009). *Handbook of positive behaviour support.* Springer.

Sams, K., Collins, S., & Reynolds, S. (2006). Cognitive therapy abilities in people with learning disabilities. *Journal of Applied Research in Intellectual Disabilities, 19*(1), 25–33.

Schock, R. E., & Lee, E. A., (2016). Children's voices: Perspectives on using assistive technology. *Exceptionality Education International, 26*(1), 76–94.

Scior, K. (2009). Psychological interventions. In A. Hassiotis, D. A. Barron, & I. Hall (Eds.), *Intellectual disability psychiatry: A practical handbook* (pp. 223–236). Wiley-Blackwell.

Scior, K. (2016). Towards understanding intellectual disability stigma: Introduction. In K. Scior & S. Werner (Eds.), *Stigma and intellectual disability: Stepping out from the margins* (pp. 3–13). Palgrave Macmillan

Shapiro, F. (2018). *Eye movement desensitisation and reprocessing (EMDR) therapy: Basic principles, protocols, and procedures* (3rd ed.). Guilford Press.

Shepherd, P., & Beail, N. (2017). A systematic review of the effectiveness of psychoanalysis, psychoanalytic and psychodynamic psychotherapy with adults with intellectual developmental disabilities: Progress and challenges. *Psychoanalytic Psychotherapy, 31*(1), 94–117.

Simpson, D. (2002). Learning disabilities as a refuge for knowledge. *Psychoanalytic Psychotherapy, 16*(3), 215–226.

Sinason, V. (2010). *Mental handicap & the human conditions: An analytic approach to intellectual disability* (revised ed.). Free Association Books.

Sinason, V., & Hollins, S. (2000). Psychotherapy, learning disabilities and trauma: New perspectives. *British Journal of Psychiatry, 176*, 32–36.

Sparrow, S. S., Cicchetti, D. V., & Saulnier, C. A. (2016). *Vineland adaptive behavior scales: Third edition (Vineland-3)*. NCS Pearson.

Sturmey, P., & Hersen, M. (2012). *Handbook of evidence-based practice in clinical psychology: Vol. 1: Child and adolescent disorders*. Wiley.

Substance Abuse and Mental Health Services Administration (SAMHSA). (2014). *SAMHSA's concept of trauma and guidance for a trauma-informed approach*. HHS Publication No. (SMA) 14-4884. Rockville, MD.

Sullivan P. M., & Knutson J. F. (2000). Maltreatment and disabilities: A population-based epidemiological study. *Child Abuse & Neglect. 24*(10), 1257–1273. https://doi.org/10.1016/S0145-2134(00)00190-3.

Thompson, S., Cannon, M., & Wickenden, M. (2020, August .6). How to ethically involve children with disabilities in research. Institute of Development Studies. https://www.ids.ac.uk/opinions/how-to-ethically-involve-children-with-disabilities-in-research/.

Totsika, V., Liew, A., Absoud, M., Adnams, C., & Emerson, E. (2022). Mental health problems in children with intellectual disability. *The Lancet Child & Adolescent Health, 6*(6), 432–444. https://doi.org/10.1016/S2352-4642(22)00067-0.

Whittle, E. L., Fisher, K. R., Reppermund, S., & Troller, J. (2019). Access to mental health services: The experiences of people with intellectual disabilities. *Journal of Applied Research in Intellectual Disabilities, 32*(2), 368–379.

Wilson, S. (2003). *Disability, counselling and psychotherapy: Challenges and opportunities*. Palgrave Macmillan.

World Health Organization. (2019). *ICD-11: International classification of diseases* (11th rev.). World Health Organization. https://icd.who.int/.

Zaman, S. H., Holt, G., & Bouras, N. (2007). Managing mental health problems in people with intellectual disabilities. In A. Carr, G. O'Reilly, P. Noonan Walsh, & J. McEvoy (Eds.), *The handbook of intellectual disability and clinical psychology practice*. (pp. 787–830). Routledge.

Part III

Growing Areas of Practice

19

Neurodivergence

Imogen Newsom-Davis and Anita Marsden

19.1 Introduction

The term *neurodivergence* describes central neurological or brain function (information processing, cognition, behaviour) that differs from what is considered typical, based on population normative data. It is most commonly used to reference the autism spectrum but also has wider applications across neurodevelopmental differences that affect attention, impulsivity and learning, and its use has only become prominent relatively recently. Research and practice in the field of neurodevelopment has traditionally been structured around classification and diagnosis of disorders. These concepts remain important and are discussed later. However, the past two decades have brought a marked shift in emphasis from categorical to dimensional understanding of neurodevelopment, supported by clinical research highlighting the enormous individual variation within such categories, and high levels of overlap between them. Simultaneously, advocacy groups including the autism rights movement proposed that human cognitive variation should be seen in the wider context of biodiversity, using the term *neurodiversity*. The term was first used by Judy Singer in the 1990s to describe the population-wide spectrum of neurocognitive functioning, later explored in detail in her book (Singer, 2017). The idea that 'neurodevelopmental disorders' are not inherently pathological, and that disability arises out of societal barriers interacting with individual differences, emerged alongside (Silberman, 2015). The concept has gained widespread traction and has started to fundamentally change the way people think about individual differences and inclusion. However, support is not universal or unqualified and opponents argue that there is a risk of downplaying the challenges and suffering associated with some disabilities.

An understanding of both typical and atypical patterns of brain development and the range of factors that underlie this neurodiversity, is central to the work of child and adolescent psychologists. When the broadest definition of neurodivergence is used, these differences are estimated to affect approximately 15% of children in the UK. They are lifelong, although the characteristics and impact vary considerably between individuals and intra-individually across time. Practitioner psychologists specialising in neurodevelopment will develop expertise and play a key role in multidisciplinary assessment and provision of

Child Psychology: Pathways to Good Practice, First Edition.
Edited by Helen Pote, Anna Picciotto and Clare Norris.

support and therapeutic interventions. However, a good understanding of neurodivergence will be relevant to child psychologists working in all areas of paediatric, educational and mental health services. Neurodevelopmental conditions are associated with a higher prevalence of distress and emotion dysregulation, often leading to behavioural challenge and parenting stress. A community child psychologist may be the first contact for a family struggling to understand and manage their child's difficulties and seeking professional help. Having the knowledge and skills to identify possible underlying neurodivergence, and then sensitively guide the family towards an appropriate assessment pathway, is crucial.

A growing body of evidence also supports a link between neurodevelopmental and psychiatric diagnoses (Lai et al., 2019), for example, co-presentation of autism with eating disorders, personality disorders and gender dysphoria. Awareness of neurodivergent profiles, and the ability to appropriately incorporate this into ongoing work with young people and their families, will strongly influence outcome. Finally, neurodevelopmental differences – both diagnosed and undiagnosed – are known to constitute a significant risk factor for mental health difficulties, in particular anxiety and mood disorders, both for children/young people and for their parents or carers.

Whilst psychologists and other clinical scientists have begun to adopt a more dimensional view of neurodevelopment, they continue to recognise the relevance of defining boundaries for typicality and atypicality and of using diagnostic categories. Categorisation or 'classification' systems that group similar phenomena together represent a founding cornerstone of scientific thinking that is not limited to psychology. They facilitate observation, hypothesis-generation and opportunities for testing boundaries that can ultimately advance our understanding. In the context of healthcare, the use of diagnosis is specifically and critically linked to guiding and evaluating treatments. The two largest classification systems used in the evaluation of childhood developmental disorders are the *Diagnostic and Statistical Manual of Mental Disorders* (*DSM-5*) (American Psychiatric Association, 2013) and the Mental Behavioral and Neurodevelopmental Disorders chapter of the *International Classification of Diseases* (*ICD-11*) (World Health Organization, 2022). They represent the culmination of many decades of detailed collation of information and scrutiny of research evidence and still underpin clinical assessment processes worldwide. However, it can be argued that rigidly categorical thinking is reductive and encourages assumptions. The National Institute of Economic and Social Research highlighted this point in a study conducted for the Advisory, Conciliation and Arbitration Service (2018) identifying the 'propensity for neurodivergent individuals to be stereotyped according to the more well-known characteristics of their condition'.

It is interesting that some diagnostic categories for developmental disorder have broadened in scope, most interesting the autism spectrum, and there is widespread acknowledgement that our understanding of these conditions – and consequently the taxonomy we have developed for them – is imperfect. This acknowledgement is a major driver for the deployment of more dimensional approaches alongside diagnosis, to more accurately reflect – and effectively support – the infinite variety of individual presentations and experience. We have chosen to use the term *neurodivergence* as the title for this chapter, to refer to those who have a degree of neurodevelopmental difference, either qualitative or quantitative, that significantly affects one or more aspects of their daily functioning. Some, but not all, children and young people who identify as neurodivergent will meet diagnostic criteria for a neurodevelopmental condition. In the neurodivergent community the term 'neurotype' is sometimes used to represent the 'profile' of individual strengths and difficulties.

The categorisation of neurodevelopmental conditions remains important as a framework for organising our existing knowledge and developing clinical skills and insights. One of our aims as practitioner psychologists should be to incorporate categorical and dimensional approaches into our work, recognising the strengths and limitations of each. For ease of reference, we have structured the subsequent sections of this chapter around established neurodevelopmental diagnostic categories, whilst using the more detailed narrative of the text to emphasise the dimensional range and diversity of profiles that can be found within each one.

Conditions that are considered to be part of the wider spectrum of neurodivergence include:

- social communication differences and autism;
- attention, impulse control and executive function differences (including ADHD and tic disorders);
- intellectual disability;
- speech and/or language disorders or differences;
- motor and sensory processing disorders or differences;
- specific learning difficulties or disorders; and
- acquired neurological injury.

This chapter will focus primarily on the first two areas (social communication/autism and attention deficit/hyperactivity). Intellectual disability is not included here because Chapter 18 is dedicated to this topic alone.

Although differences in language, learning, motor and sensory processing development all reflect neurodivergence, they are not discussed in detail in this chapter because their assessment and associated interventions are not generally provided by practitioner psychologists. However, they are referenced because it is essential that we recognise these elements as part of the neurodivergence family and because we should consider and respond to the child as a whole, reflecting all their areas of strength and challenge, actively communicating with our multidisciplinary team (MDT) colleagues where necessary. Language, motor and sensory differences may occur independently or as part of autism (and other) presentations and may therefore be an important consideration for differential diagnosis and when planning assessments and/or intervention. Specific learning disorders most commonly affect reading/spelling ('dyslexia') or numerical abilities ('dyscalculia') and are known to be a risk factor for both low self-esteem and school-related anxiety. There is also a high comorbidity between specific learning differences and ADHD. It is therefore helpful for practitioner psychologists to be sensitive to possible signs of these difficulties, so that they can be integrated appropriately into formulation where relevant, and to facilitate referral to educational psychology services if appropriate.

It is also important to note the mention of acquired neurological injury. Although it may not always conform to the manualised definition of a developmental condition (evidence prior to 3 years of age), even mild brain injury during childhood brings a high risk of adverse cognitive, social and mental health outcomes. These are unequivocally the result of neurodivergence, even if the mechanisms underlying this deviation are different from those responsible for the differences observed in profiles of those with more conventional 'neurodevelopmental' history involving early biological or environmental factors, or no identifiable causes. Again, as assessment and intervention is not generally provided by practitioner psychologists in primary or secondary care, a detailed consideration of this group of children and young people is beyond the scope of this chapter. For a comprehensive overview of this area see Jacobson and Gerner (2021).

In parallel with the shift in our formalisation of typical and atypical neurodevelopment, there has been a move away from approaches based on *normalisation*, the idea that the over-arching goal for neuro-atypical children (or adults) should be to achieve outcomes as close as possible to neurotypical outcomes. The emphasis has changed to one of embracing neurodiversity, recognising the unique qualities in every individual, and the strengths that such diversity brings to society as a whole. In line with this cultural shift, the focus of support has swung away from interventionist approaches that encourage individuals to change their behaviour, and instead now emphasises strengths-based support and environmental accommodation, alongside targeted skill development, guided wherever possible by the goals and wishes of the young person.

This diverse group of children and young people and their families have a high level of need in relation to physical and mental health, social care and education and their right to receive adequate support is enshrined in the Children and Families Act 2014. Where special educational needs and disability (SEND) are identified, the SEND Code of Practice (Department for Education, 2015) provides the over-arching framework to guide provision of support though an application and statutory assessment process managed through local children's services. The economic cost of meeting these needs is significant and likely to increase as diagnosis of neurodevelopmental conditions continues to grow. The UK Government's *Ten Year Plan* (Alderwick & Dixon, 2019) seeks to address inequalities in access to healthcare for minority and vulnerable groups including those with neurodisability. Condition-specific national policies have also been updated, including *The National Strategy for Autistic Children, Young People and Adults* (Department for Education & Department for Health & Social Care, 2021), highlighting planned improvements such as increased access to education and support of transition to adulthood. Failing to adequately meet the needs of neurodivergent people would be likely to result in even higher costs, both economically and in terms of the health and well-being of the population.[1]

19.2 Evidence

19.2.1 Neurobiology and Brain Development

The healthy adult brain is a uniquely complex organ, highly specialised in both structure and function, and capable of executing a vast range of different tasks, often simultaneously. It is extraordinary to consider that it arises from just a small cluster of proliferating cells,

1 *Authors cautionary note:* It is hoped that the language and themes of this chapter reflect our respectful, neuro-affirmative approach, whilst retaining clinical accuracy and utility, in line with current good clinical practice. Neurodivergence is a rapidly changing field, however, and it is likely that there will be further changes to acceptable terminology in the future.

which begin to form a simple structure known as the neural tube at around weeks three to four of gestation. Prenatal cerebral development continues at an astonishing rate, with some estimates that 250,000 brain cells are formed every minute through rapid cell division. The embryonic brain is morphologically recognisable from around 100 days but continues to mature, both prenatally and after birth throughout childhood. Prenatal development is largely structural and genetically predetermined, involving a series of intricate processes including neurulation, migration, dendritic development and synaptogenesis. These processes are most vulnerable to anomalous genetic changes and intrauterine factors with the potential to cause very significant deviation in development, evident at a macroscopic level and/or in gross differences to cerebral structure, and with associated global phenotypic impact. Post-natal development is dominated by myelination, dendritic arborisation and synaptogenesis, processes that are responsible for the elaboration and 'fine tuning' of neural pathways. These processes are more susceptible to environmental and experiential influences, with the potential to interfere with connectivity and establishment of functional neural networks. See Anderson et al. (2019) for a detailed review.

Technological advances in neuroimaging techniques strengthened support for the connectionist view of brain–behaviour relationships that emerged more than two decades ago (Elman et al., 1996) and is now established. This view recognises that whilst certain regions of the brain may play a particularly important part in mediating a given function, it is the integrity of more widely distributed neural networks – involving communication within and between both cortical and subcortical areas of the brain – that form the neural substrate for complex behavioural and cognitive functions in particular, including attention, executive function and social cognition.

We should perhaps not be surprised to observe such rich neurodiversity across the population, given the many opportunities for this developmental trajectory to be interrupted or diverted, and the vast array of influences that the developing brain is subject to, both intrinsic and extrinsic. Whilst our understanding of the precise mechanisms underlying neurodivergent development is not complete, and is a substantial topic in its own right, it is helpful for the neurodevelopmental psychologist to keep in mind the range of potential factors influencing outcome, and likely stage of impact.

1. *Intrinsic factors*
   a. Single gene disorders, for example, Fragile X Syndrome, Down's Syndrome (trisomy 21), Mucopolysaccharidoses, Neurofibromatosis Type 1 (NFT 1);
   b. Polygenic errors, that is, multiple genes of small effect;
   c. Foetal errors in brain development: neurulation defects, for example, anencephaly, spina bifida; migration defects, for example, microgyria, lissencephaly, agenesis of the corpus callosum.
2. *Extrinsic factors*
   a. Intrauterine environment: maternal stress, malnutrition, alcohol (foetal alcohol syndrome, FAS), drugs and toxins.
   b. Prematurity.
   c. Perinatal factors: birth complications leading to oxygen deprivation (causes hypoxic-ischaemic encephalopathy); infection, for example, Zika, Group B Strep.
   d. Postnatal environment: physical neglect, for example, inadequate nutrition, sleep, care; emotional neglect, for example, lack of warmth, responsiveness, stimulation,

communication; cerebral infection, for example, meningitis; environmental toxins, for example, lead, radiation.

e. Cultural, familial and social: peer influences; educational experience; play; adverse childhood events (ACES); parental mental health.

Prevalent neurobiological models conceptualise neurodivergence as the endpoint of a process that will typically arise from the interaction of one or more relatively non-specific forms of disruption to early brain development, both intrinsic and extrinsic (Bishop & Rutter, 2008). Genetic determinants are commonly involved, but not invariably. Furthermore, substantial vulnerability to a range of neurodevelopmental conditions is thought to be conferred by the presence of combined 'generic' genetic influences, rather than being attributable to specific genetic influences on individual conditions.

It is well-established that all neurodevelopmental conditions occur more frequently in boys than in girls (Kanner, 1943; Nowak & Jacquemont, 2020) although the sex ratio is more marked for some conditions than others. A causal role for genetic factors, sex hormones and sociological factors have all been proposed but despite extensive research, these effects remain poorly understood.

19.2.2 Neurodevelopmental Conditions: Classification, Epidemiology, Aetiology and Management

Social Communication Differences and the Autism Spectrum: Autism was first described by Leo Kanner more than 70 years ago (Kanner, 1943). Although we now recognise a wider diagnostic spectrum, the essential features have remained largely unchanged. The formal diagnostic criteria refer to persistent difficulties with social communication and reciprocal social interaction, together with evidence of rigidity, restricted or intense interests, or repetitive behaviours. The latter sometimes present as stereotypic movements or are associated with sensory disturbances. Full *DSM-5* diagnostic criteria are given in Appendix 19.1. In order to meet diagnostic criteria for autism (*DSM-5* or *ICD-11*) there must be evidence of these characteristics from early in life, together with a significant effect on daily life (a 'functional impairment'). With the move towards more dimensional thinking, practitioners will now sometimes refer to social communication differences or 'traits', when there is evidence of some autistic characteristics that is judged to be relevant as part of the formulation, but that does not meet the threshold for an autism diagnosis for one or more reasons.

A systematic review of the global population prevalence of autism identified a median value of 1% (Zeidan et al., 2022), a median male-to-female ratio of 4.2. Increasing prevalence estimates over the past two decades are thought to reflect changes in diagnostic criteria to encompass the wider autism spectrum, and greater public awareness. The marked higher prevalence of autism in boys than girls has shown stability across ethnic and cultural groups and geographical regions (Fombonne, 2009) but a recent review based on epidemiological rather than clinical sampling suggests a more moderate ratio of 3:1 (Loomes et al., 2017). This suggests some ongoing sex differences in autism detection, possibly as a result of male-biased assessment criteria and masking and diagnostic overshadowing in girls. There has been an important and long-overdue surge in interest in this topic, and in female autism presentations more generally, in recent years. For an excellent discussion of this area, see Carpenter et al. (2019).

A number of theories have suggested different central cognitive abilities that might underpin the autism spectrum phenotype. These include theories focusing on 'theory of mind' (the ability to form cognitive representations of others' thoughts or feelings in order to predict or comprehend their behaviour), over-dominance of systematising ('extreme of the male brain'), central coherence (the drive to make sense of global features rather than focusing on detail), social motivation and executive dysfunction. Simultaneously accounting for the range and diversity of autism presentations and providing a good fit with emerging neurobiological correlates has proved challenging, and many now share the view that a single explanatory model for autism is unlikely to be realistic (Happé et al., 2006). However, these ideas continue to stimulate research and exploration that – it is hoped – will lead to gains in our understanding and ability to support those affected.

There is strong support for a dominant genetic contribution to social communication differences (Havdahl et al., 2021). Research has highlighted a number of potential underlying brain atypicalities, for example, in patterns of brain growth (Courchesne et al., 2011), disrupted mitochondrial function (Goh et al., 2014), serotonin pathways, and reduced activation in the fusiform gyrus and amygdala (involved in face and emotion processing) (Dziobek et al., 2010). However, single factor explanations are unlikely to adequately account for the diversity in presentations that is observed. There is now broad acceptance that varied polygenic susceptibility will interact with environmental risk factors, resulting in a range of phenotypic outcomes: the idea that there is not one but many 'autisms'. Indeed, there is a growing body of evidence to support the suggestion that the 'triad' of social, communicative and rigid/repetitive characteristics may be separable genetically, neurally and cognitively, even within a single individual (Happé & Frith, 2020), a view that also accords with current dimensional conceptualisations of neurodevelopment.

It is important to recognise that empirical investigations of this kind may help to further our understanding of aetiology, but they rest heavily on the view of autism as deviance in development. They fail to take account of autism-centred perspectives arguing that the lack of understanding is reciprocal, that is, neurotypical people fail to 'read' people with autism correctly. This is a relatively new and progressive area of professional thinking that is still developing (Milton, 2012).

This acceptance of high phenotypic and aetiological variability fits with the observation that autism commonly co-occurs across a wide range of medical conditions including chromosomal conditions, inherited metabolic conditions and neurological disorders (most notably epilepsy, with most sources estimating comorbidity at 30% or more), (Al-Beltagi, 2021). There is also a high co-occurrence of autism with other neurodevelopmental diagnoses including intellectual disability (50%), ADHD and developmental-coordination disorder (DCD). Language and cognitive differences in autism can make differential diagnosis more complicated and care must be taken to avoid diagnostic overshadowing.

Anxiety disorders are present in approximately 40% of children with autism (van Steensel et al., 2011) and anxiety may play a key role in the rigidity, obsessional behaviours and preference for predictability that is observed (van Engeland & Buitelaar, 2008). Over the past decade there has been increasing recognition of higher prevalence of autism in young people receiving treatment for eating disorders (ED), recently estimated at 35%

(Maudsley PEACE pathway), and leading to the recommendation that this is routinely considered as part of initial ED presentations. Identification of high rates of autism and gender dysphoria co-presentation have led to similar recommendations for this population.

The social, communicative and behavioural characteristics of autism have the potential to severely impair function and reduce the quality of life for children (and their families) and evidence suggests that the majority are unable to lead fully independent lives as adults. Public awareness is gradually increasing. The early identification of need, together with effective support across settings and a high level of agency, provide the best possible opportunity to reduce this impact.

Attention, Over-activity and Executive Function Differences: There are references in medical literature to children with inattentive and impulsive presentations that go back almost 300 years, but the first formalised descriptions of a behavioural 'syndrome' in UK publications appeared in the early 1900s. Initially reported as a post-encephalitic disorder, it was quickly recognised that most children with the pattern of behaviour had no history of infection or other identifiable brain damage. 'Hyperkinetic disorders' were formally described in the *DSM-II* (American Psychological Association, 1968) and subsequently revised (American Psychological Association, 1980) to include greater emphasis on attention deficit. The *DSM-5* defines ADHD as a pattern of behaviour that is persistent, inconsistent with developmental expectations, and interferes with daily functioning. Diagnosis is made on the basis of clinical history, observation and parent and teacher report, with a requirement that a minimum number of different features are present and observed across more than one setting. To date, no definitive biomarkers for ADHD have been identified. Subtypes of ADHD may be classified according to the predominant features: inattentive, hyperactive-impulsive or combined type. The clinical features are diverse and sometimes informally categorised as 'hot' (considered to reflect high excitation/low inhibition) and 'cold' (considered to reflect low activity of the central executive/supervisory attentional system).

Attention deficit and hyperkinetic disorders are the most common of all neurodevelopmental conditions, with community prevalence estimates that range from 3 to 7% globally (Sayal et al., 2017). Table 19.1 shows the cognitive and behavioural characteristics of ADHD. They are more common in boys than girls, although this diagnostic ratio may shift as differing presentations in girls are increasingly recognised (Hinshaw et al., 2022). ADHD has extremely high levels of co-occurrence, to the extent that it is more often found in the presence of other conditions than alone. The range of co-occurring conditions is wide but particularly features central nervous system involvement, including neurological illnesses (particularly epilepsy), acquired brain injury, intellectual disability, autism, Tourette Syndrome (TS) and specific learning disorders. ADHD is also a strong predictor of internalising and externalising psychiatric disorders including anxiety, depression, conduct disorder and oppositional defiant disorder. See Thapar et al. (2017) for a useful summary.

Given the nature of the symptoms, it is not surprising that ADHD has significant and wide-ranging direct effects in childhood. These include academic under-achievement and withdrawal from education, social difficulties/isolation, physical injury (as a result of risk-taking) and breakdown in parent–child relationships. Secondary impact on self-esteem and mood in adulthood is common, particularly where ADHD is diagnosed late (Torgersen et al., 2006). The strong predictive relationship between ADHD and conduct disorder or

Table 19.1 Cognitive and behavioural characteristics of ADHD.

'Cold' characteristics	'Hot' characteristics
Distractibility, difficulty with goal-directed activity	Lower levels of impulse control (affecting behaviour and emotion regulation)
Difficulty focusing on tasks that are less intrinsically interesting	Excitability
Poor anticipation of consequences and time estimation	Low frustration tolerance
Difficulty with planning, organisation and task initiation	High levels of risk-taking and stimulus-seeking behaviour
	Constantly active and 'on the go'
	Noisy, interrupts

anti-social behaviour in adolescence is well-established (approx. 30%), and more recently a link with anxiety and social functioning (Bishop et al., 2019) and obesity (Cortese, 2019) has been highlighted. Approximately one-third of children with diagnosed ADHD have a good prognosis, involving attenuating symptoms and no identified longer-term impact. Around 40% experience symptoms persisting into adulthood, with some degree of impact on social and vocational function. The remaining 30% are affected more severely, with significant anti-social behaviour problems, substance abuse, mental illness and forensic consequences.

Good physical health, high IQ, positive personality traits and high self-efficacy have all been identified as personal protective factors. Better outcomes are also associated with a range of external factors including secure parent–child attachment, authoritative parenting, familial stability, membership of higher socioeconomic groups, well-informed educational placements and multiprofessional input. Conversely, low resources, parental mental health difficulties and higher levels of stress are risk factors for poor outcomes.

Attempts to explain ADHD with reference to a single core deficit, for example, inattention or hypo-arousal, struggled to convincingly account for the wide range of both 'hot' and 'cold' symptoms observed. More elaborate hypotheses proposing a role for various executive functions have intuitive appeal but are weakened by the findings that not all children with ADHD have differences in executive functions (Sonuga-Barke et al., 2008). There is slightly more clarity relating to the pathophysiology of ADHD. Dysregulation of neurotransmission (dopamine and noradrenaline) in fronto-striatal, subcortical and/or cerebellar circuitry is known to play a key role, supported by evidence from neuroimaging studies and by the effectiveness of stimulant medications such as methylphenidate (a dopamine agonist).

Both genetic and environmental factors are implicated in aetiology and this topic is well reviewed by Thapar and colleagues (Thapar et al., 2012). Twin and adoption studies have demonstrated strong heritability of ADHD, with a number of candidate genes identified, including those involved in the dopamine and serotonin pathways. Interestingly, some of the same chromosomal loci are also implicated in autism. Environmental factors are also relevant, possibly in interaction with genetic risk (epigenetics). Increased prevalence of ADHD is associated with prematurity, foetal exposure to drugs and alcohol, and early or severe neurological injury. Socioeconomic deprivation and parenting difficulties are thought to exert an effect by exacerbating behavioural patterns, rather than causing them. It is most likely that a complex interaction of biological and psychosocial factors underpins the observed symptomatology, the precise nature of which may vary considerably between individuals.

Multimodal intervention programmes are widely recommended, containing some or all of the following key elements: medication, psychoeducation, family- and school-based intervention to support behaviour management and learning, and direct cognitive and social skills intervention. However, the efficacy of non-pharmacological interventions has been difficult to establish, due to poor study design and mixed results. In general parent interventions have the strongest support, with better outcomes than child-focused interventions such as cognitive training programmes, which have consistently failed to show generalisation in effects. The largest effect sizes are consistently found for pharmacotherapy although this is not recommended in children under 4 years of age. A recent meta-analysis of 190 studies (Catalá-López et al., 2017) demonstrated best overall efficacy for behavioural interventions in combination with stimulant medication. For a thorough review of current ADHD management practices see Russell Barkley (2022).

Executive function (EF) requires special consideration here. There is still no universally accepted definition of EFs, but they are generally conceptualised as the 'supervisory' cognitive processes that are involved in directed attention, self-regulation, planning/organisation and coordinating information. Correlational studies suggest that EFs are related to, but distinct from, general intellectual abilities (Friedman et al., 2016) and they are broadly accepted to have a 'frontal' (anterior) locus in the brain. The work of Vicki Anderson and colleagues in this field has been particularly influential and is comprehensively described in Anderson et al. (2010). Their model proposes three distinct but integrated domains underpinning the development of cognitive and behavioural aspects of EF through childhood: attentional control, goal setting and cognitive flexibility. Each is supported by a neural network involving frontal cortical regions and processing stimuli from various subcortical, motor and posterior sources. Anderson has argued that the developmental trajectories for these domains differ, in line with different rates of maturation of the associated brain regions. Indeed, a growing body of evidence from paediatric neuropsychological studies corroborates the suggestion that executive skills have a protracted developmental time course, with 'spurts' [at 0–2 years, 7–9 years and 16–19 years] that are closely tied to increments in attention, memory and processing speed and correspond to peaks in neurobiological markers such as synaptogenesis.

The similarity between these core EF domains and the areas of difficulty reported in ADD/ADHD are striking and one imagines the two things are synonymous. In reality, although there is an association between ADHD and deficits on cognitive measures of attention and EF, the correlation is relatively weak. Furthermore, a growing literature has demonstrated the presence of EF impairments across a wide range of other acquired and developmental conditions including autism, specific learning disorders and tics/TS. Executive dysfunction is therefore neither inevitable in hyperkinetic and attention disorders, nor specific to them. However, the frequency with which it is associated with neurodivergent presentations, and the pervasive impact of EF difficulties on educational, social and behavioural outcomes, means that a good understanding of their cognitive basis and approaches to assessment and intervention is essential for psychologists in this field.

Tic Disorder and Tourette Syndrome: A tic is a sudden, repetitive stereotypic movement or utterance that often mirrors some part of normal behaviour. Movements range from eye blinks and facial grimaces to head jerks and larger or more complex movements of limbs. Examples of utterances include throat clearing, complex vocalisations and coprolalia. The behaviours occur out of context, without a conventional trigger and are thought to be involuntary, reflecting reduced neuronal inhibition.

Provisional tic disorder typically involves motor tics only, presenting in children between 3 and 10 years of age. The tics are generally relatively mild and spontaneously remit within 12 months. TS, originally named Gilles de la Tourette Syndrome, is a more severe and persistent tic disorder, characterised by onset of spasmodic motor tics at around 5 to 7 years. Vocal tics then typically develop alongside, and the tics become more severe and complex through middle childhood, often causing significant distress. UK estimates of TS prevalence in children range from 0.5 to 1% (Robertson, 2015) and tic disorders are more common in boys than girls, with a ratio of approximately 4:1. Pathogenesis remains unclear although twin studies point to genetic influences and there is also an association with adverse perinatal events (Leckman & Fernandez., 2016). It is widely accepted that tics themselves arise from disruption to the frontal-striatal-thalamocortical circuits that mediate self-regulation, and over-sensitivity of dopamine receptors in this network has been proposed, supported by evidence that dopamine antagonists reduce tic severity.

Co-occurrence is the norm for tic disorders and only a minority of affected children do not exhibit other neurodevelopmental and/or psychiatric differences, which may be more disabling than the tics themselves. A relatively recent large cross-sectional study (Hirschtrit et al., 2015) demonstrated that 72% of individuals with TS also had a diagnosis of either ADHD or OCD. The onset of additional psychiatric disorder was most common between 4 and 10 years of age and also included anxiety and mood disorder, each of which affected approximately 30% of the cohort. Co-morbid obsessive compulsive disorder (OCD) with TS has generated a high level of interest as evidence suggests that it has slightly different characteristics to 'pure OCD' and may be less amenable to pharmacotherapy (Szejko & Müller-Vahl, 2021). Tic disorders are also over-represented in autism populations (Baron-Cohen et al., 1999). Neuropsychological profiles of children with TS are consistent with disruption to circuits linking the prefrontal cortex and basal ganglia. Findings typically highlight inhibitory deficits affecting motor pathways, together with visuo-perceptual, visuo-motor and visuo-graphic impairments. Co-occurrence is associated with wider ranging cognitive effects, for example, more prominent executive function, memory and learning differences and are associated with **TS and ADHD** when compared to either condition alone (Burd et al., 2005).

Given the high level of burden described earlier, it is perhaps not surprising to find that children with TS, with or without a co-occurring condition, report lower levels of quality of life than their peers and their parents report higher levels of stress. Quality of life correlates inversely with tic severity (Cutler et al., 2009).

The ability to suppress tics, at least for short periods of time, increases with age for some but may be associated with difficulties with concentration, subjective distress and fatigue. For others, tic suppression is never achieved or is too painful or distressing to sustain.

Relaxation, concentration and physical exercise are all reported to attenuate symptoms (Cohen et al., 2013). In TS, tics tend to attenuate through late adolescence and adults typically report reduced tic severity and frequency with an associated decrease in disability. Tics disappear in adulthood for some, although this is not the majority, and the social and emotional sequelae often persist into adulthood (Bloch et al., 2006). There are relatively few studies that have systematically evaluated the effects of pharmacological or behavioural interventions in TS. There is a general consensus that first-line intervention should focus on psychoeducation, together with careful assessment of possible co-occurring conditions, and some evidence base for habit reversal and Exposure Response Prevention (ERP) is acknowledged (Whittington et al., 2016). As tics generally reduce through adolescence there is a cautious approach to pharmacological treatment in childhood.

19.2.3 Current Debates

Developmental neuroscience and its application to clinical practice has seen rapid growth over the past decade, influenced by continuing advances in neurobiological and neuroimaging techniques and by changes in our understanding of, and attitudes towards, neurodiversity. In some areas these developments have generated more questions than they have answered, leading to both professional and public debate. We have selected two key areas to highlight here, based on their relevance to current practice.

Diagnostic Validity: Briefly touched on in the Introduction to this chapter, the absence of any definitive diagnostic tests for ADHD and autism, and the reliance on guidelines, arbitrary 'cut-offs' and individual judgment, has meant that these diagnoses are still regarded as controversial by some. This applies perhaps most obviously to ADHD, where characteristics or 'symptoms' reflect the extreme end of a spectrum that spans the entire population. The recent shift towards more dimensional thinking around neurodivergence and broadening of diagnostic criteria, together with the observation of widely varying rates of diagnosis and prescribing (of stimulant medication) across different services, has led some to question the validity of any such diagnostic classification. They argue that these categories are artificial constructs based simply on interpretation of behaviour and that there is inherent circularity in the diagnostic process. The question is certainly worthy of further exploration.

In reality, the lack of empirical diagnostic tests applies to all psychiatric and neurodevelopmental conditions, but also to many physical conditions as well, such as hypertension or asthma, and does not necessarily invalidate these diagnoses. Furthermore, the UK evaluation of diagnostic reliability carried out as part of the development of the *DSM-5* yielded particularly high test-retest reliability across sites for both ADHD ($r = 0.61$) and autism ($r = 0.69$), much higher than for conditions such as bipolar disorder ($r = 0.56$) and generalised anxiety disorder ($r = 0.20$). The majority of those within scientific and clinical communities share the view that our current approach, although flawed, has sufficient clinical validity to be justified, based on currently available knowledge. However, it is important that we continue to gather information, interrogate our methods and push the boundaries of our understanding so that alternative interpretations remain a possibility, and that we move gradually closer to a 'true' conceptualisation of neurodivergence and a better ability to understand and support all of those who fall somewhere along these spectra. For a more in-depth discussion of this topic see Sayal et al. (2017).

Pathological or Extreme Demand Avoidance: The term pathological demand avoidance (PDA) was originally coined by Elizabeth Newson (Newson et al., 2003) to describe a subgroup of individuals with autism who presented with a particular cluster of traits. The overriding feature is an extreme need for autonomy or control but there are other characteristics that differ in some respects from a 'classically' autistic profile. In January 2022, the PDA society developed some guidance for identifying and assessing a PDA profile, which is generally described as:

- resists and avoids the ordinary demands of life;
- uses social strategies as part of the avoidance;
- appears sociable on the surface but lacking depth in understanding;
- experiences excessive mood swings and impulsivity;
- 'obsessive' behaviour often focused on other people; and
- appears comfortable in role play and pretence, sometimes to an extreme extent (this feature is not always present).

PDA is not a diagnosis and remains controversial, but the group of behaviours characteristic of this profile is widely recognised by both families and professionals and, in practice, many psychologists see it as having some clinical utility. Proponents of the concept argue that it informs approaches to support and intervention because it highlights the limited efficacy of standard behavioural strategies in this context, the increased potential for difficulties with engagement, and the need to very carefully manage anxiety and emotion dysregulation to avoid extreme distress. Other authors, including autistic academics, have criticised the term PDA for undermining the agency of autistic people and failing to properly consider the role of anxiety (Milton, 2013). The use of the term 'pathological' has quite reasonably been questioned and suggested that it should be replaced with 'extreme'. Further research conducted within appropriate methodological parameters is needed, but in the meantime a compromise position is reasonable. This stops short of recognising a separate neurodevelopmental entity but recognises that a PDA symptom cluster exists and urges approaches that increase our understanding by exploring the associated co-occurring characteristics, sensory and cognitive sensitivities and social factors (Green et al., 2018).

19.3 Inclusive Practice

We all have a responsibility, individually and collectively, to ensure that all children and young people (CYP) and their families have an equal opportunity to access services. In relation to neurodivergence, it is argued that services should not just be accessible, they should be actively neurodiversity affirming, shifting away from the medical model of 'disorder', towards understanding of 'difference' and 'preferences'. In this section we will discuss some of the barriers to inclusive practice that are particularly relevant for neurodivergent individuals pre- and post-diagnosis, make suggestions to improve inclusivity, discuss what neurodiversity affirming practice can look like, drawing on the voices of CYP in the literature and signpost to some relevant resources.

19.3.1 Disability

Many of the neurodivergent conditions we are including in this chapter would come under the protected characteristic of 'disability' in the *Equality Act* (2010) and therefore, reasonable adjustments are a legal requirement to make sure our services are accessible to all. Although, it should be acknowledged that not all neurodivergent individuals would consider themselves 'disabled'. Health inequalities have been shown in the literature for neurodivergent people, at the most extreme end, leading to significant impact on life expectancy (Hirvikoskiet al., 2016). Multiple diagnoses are common and it is important to be aware of the impact of diagnostic overshadowing; one condition biasing healthcare professionals from recognising other conditions. For example, higher rates of co-occurring conditions, or additional 'disabilities' have been found in autistic individuals, including visual and hearing impairments, mental health and physical disabilities (Rydzewska et al., 2018). It is important to keep in mind that not all neurodivergent individuals will have a diagnosis or some might not feel comfortable disclosing a diagnosis.

19.3.2 Sex

There is strong evidence for higher prevalence of neurodivergent conditions in males compared to females. For example, in autism, current consensus suggests a male:female bias of approximately 4:1. However, a recent meta-analysis suggested it is actually 3:1, for those children meeting criteria for autism (Loomes et al., 2017). The paper suggested a diagnostic gender bias, with those girls meeting criteria for autism having a greater risk of not receiving a diagnosis. These gender biases may exist and be maintained by a number of factors including diagnostic tools and criteria being predicated on male presentations, bias from practitioners looking for these more recognised male presentations, and higher levels of internalising or masking in females. There are significant risks and health inequalities for autistic females, including highest risk of early death in autistic females with learning disabilities and autistic females being more likely to die by suicide than non-autistic females, and therefore a serious need to mitigate these. The situation is further complicated by the fact that many autistic people will have trans or non-binary identities (either known or unknown).

Practice recommendations:

- Be aware of this potential gender bias and how neurodivergent conditions might present and be reported differently in females and males.
- Use gender neutral language as standard and review accessibility of facilities and inclusion within your service.
- Access further training about female presentations of neurodivergent conditions (such as the NAS Women and Girls online course).
- Stay up to date with research and training with regards to the tools and criteria we use.

19.3.3 Ethnicity

It is well-established that individuals from minority ethnic groups or backgrounds can face barriers when it comes to accessing healthcare and have poorer health outcomes in general.

A recent population-based study in the UK (Roman-Urrestarazu et al., 2021) found varied prevalence rates of autism in different minority ethnic groups. In particular, Roma/Irish Traveller individuals were 60% less likely to be given an autism diagnosis than white pupils, whilst Chinese and black pupils were more likely to receive a diagnosis than white pupils (38% and 26% respectively). The study also found that autism was less likely to be diagnosed in those pupils who spoke English as a second language, more likely in socially disadvantaged pupils (receiving free school meals) and that social disadvantage was found to mediate the increased prevalence in non-white groups. There is an urgent need to review diagnostic assessment processes and decision making to ensure that these are free from cultural and racial bias (whether conscious or unconscious).

The National Autistic Society have conducted various surveys for autistic individuals, including a 'diverse perspective' report in 2014 (Slade, 2014). Focus groups for families from minority ethnic communities with autistic children were used to explore the wide-ranging barriers they face accessing services, and the reported culminated in recommendations at a national and local level.

Practice recommendations:

- Inform yourself and discuss with colleagues, bringing greater awareness.
- Identify possible barriers in your service (the NAS 2014 'diverse perspective' report is a great place to start).
- Regular whole service anti-racism training.
- Engage people with minority ethnic backgrounds in co-production.
- Always consider using interpreters as individuals might want or need to speak in their preferred language.
- Identify if there are different language versions of tools you might use such as the Strengths and Difficulties Questionnaire (https://www.sdqinfo.org/py/sdqinfo/b0.py).

19.3.4 Adaptation for Families

Some of the practice recommendations mentioned earlier are relevant across psychological services and are discussed in other chapters, but they may have a particular salience when considered for neurodivergent populations. It is important to consider that children referred to these services are also more likely than average to have a parent with a neurodevelopmental or learning difference. Further adaptations to consider are:

- Thee journey each family or individual makes through your service:
  - How do they know what your service does?
  - How do they request a referral and find out what will happen next?
  - How are appointments communicated?
  - Where and when do appointments take place? What travel options are there and how manageable with siblings and/or or children and how will they travel?
  - How much agency or choice is offered in relation to the assessment or intervention?
- Methods for sharing information: Can it be adapted or extended for those with additional needs, for example, using pictures or photos of physical environment and staff?
- The physical spaces of your service – not just for those with physical disabilities but also sensory and behavioural needs; consider noise and lighting, space for moving around, security around access points.

- Opportunities for participation and co-production by service users so that these 'experts by experience' can contribute to service development.
- Recommended reading with lots of practical suggestions: *NAS Good Practice Guide for Mental Health Professionals.*

19.3.5 Neurodiversity Affirming Practice

The neurodiversity movement and neurodivergent community are calling for services, schools and wider society to become more neuro-affirmative. This involves moving away from stereotypes and deficit-focused models, which may encourage masking and suppression of a person's true identity, thereby increasing risks to poor mental health. Being neuro-affirmative requires not just an awareness, but acceptance and appreciation of neurodiversity, and working to empower and advocate for neurodivergent individuals (autism level up). This includes adapting services, schools and society for all neurotypes.

There are various practical steps we can take as practitioner psychologists to become more neuro-affirmative:

- Change the language used, both in clinical discussion and written documentation. Remove or reduce references to disorder, disability, impairment, treatment. Talk about differences, characteristics, strengths, accommodations and support. See Appendix 19.2.
- Consider the journey through your service for neurodivergent individuals, looking at how your service is promoted/communicated (online/printed resources), the language that is used, and each step from pre-referral to discharge.
- Consider accommodations you and your service make for neurodivergent individuals in order to increase access (please see Sections 19.3.1, 19.3.2 and 19.3.3 for practice recommendations).
- Consider cascading neuro-affirmative language, messages, resources and signposting to those you work with. This may be in the form of simply sharing resources or could involve facilitating a staff discussion group or even a training or teaching session.
- Co-production: Wherever possible invite neurodivergent children and their families to help you with this process to ensure you are not making assumptions and that your service is shaped by authentic first-person experiences, opinions and knowledge.
- If you are involved in diagnostic assessments, consider moving away from our traditional medical model and diagnostic language, which tends towards 'are they failing as a neurotypical person' towards the question of whether their experiences align with the autistic / ADHD / neurodivergent experience.

Further sources of support for exploring neurodiversity affirming practice include:

- Listening to neurodivergent individuals is one way of becoming more neuro-affirmative (please see Appendix 19.2 for ways to do this).
- *The Nine Degrees of Autism* by Philip Wylie, Wenn Lawson and Luke Beardon, autistic and non-autistic writers and researchers presents a developmental model of neurodivergent conditions (focusing on autism but the model is applicable more widely) to support improved mental health and wellbeing. This is a great book for parents and an alternative to the often given negative prognosis.
- *Neurotribes* by Steve Silberman explores the idea that neurological differences such as autism, dyslexia and ADHD are not 'disorders' or errors of nature but the result of natural

variations in the human genome, reshaping our understanding and implications of neurodiversity.

- The Adult Autism Practice has produced four webinars on neuro-affirmative practice, including one specifically for CYP diagnostic assessments and one for developing CAMHS services to be neurodiversity affirmative (https://www.youtube.com/channel/UCZ7fcjBtaTiVuVBd1yv6WBg). An example of a neuro-affirmative report inspired by one of these webinars in is Appendix 19.3.
- Sandhya Menon is an Australian Psychologist, 'AutADHDer' as she puts it, who is a neurodiversity affirming advocate. At the time of writing her website, onwardsandupwardspsychology.com.au has a blog post with a hugely comprehensive list of neurodiversity affirming resources (https://www.onwardsandupwardspsychology.com.au/post/neurodiversity-affirming-resources).

19.3.6 Neurodivergence in Education

There is increasing acknowledgment of the experience of neurodivergent individuals within educational settings and potential effects on their mental health and wellbeing. Government figures show autistic individuals are twice as likely to be excluded than non-autistic peers (National Autistic Society, 2021) and the PDA society's 'Our Being Misunderstood' report shows that 70% of autistic children with a PDA profile are not in school or regularly struggle to attend. An anonymous blog by an autistic mother of six neurodivergent children (theplightofthesendparent.co.uk) talks about how the school environment is harder for neurodivergent CYP and suggests that separation anxiety represents a child communicating their distress at having their 'auxiliary aid' (the person that understands them the most and accommodates for them) taken away, likening it to removing a child's glasses or hearing aid at the school door.

A paper has been written in 2022 by a group of neurodivergent young people entitled 'How can schools better support neurodivergent children and young people' (Gasselling et al., 2022). It suggests one of the reasons neurodivergent CYP struggle is because schools prioritise grades over wellbeing and uses the NHS five ways to wellbeing as a way of presenting a strong argument for what is foundational to learning. It talks beautifully about the importance of meaningful friendships, self-understanding as well as peer acceptance as a step further than just anti-bullying. It speaks to the importance of staff understanding, voicing a range of quotes from peers about how they have been misunderstood by teachers, including their experience of restraint and exclusion and trauma that has resulted from this. Finally, it makes lots of useful suggestions for improving practice, including prioritising listening to the voices of neurodivergent individuals and their perspective, including this in staff training. It has some great info-graphics about reframing behaviour, seeing behaviour as 'can't' rather than 'won't' and the double empathy problem (Damian Milton), working collaboratively to create neuro-harmony within our schools and wider society.

19.3.7 Listening to the Views of CYP and Families

All of the earlier sections on inclusive practice would not have been possible without listening to the voices of CYP, their families and adults who are neurodivergent. Seeking the views of neurodivergent individuals will enhance our services and practice and ultimately meet their needs better. There are various ways that we can seek to do this:

- Prioritise participation and co-production in every aspect of the work we do for example, run workshops, teaching and groups with parent carers or CYP as co-facilitators.
- Link up with local parent-carer forums and invite members regularly to meetings that pertain to the running or development of services.
- Request feedback from CYP and parents we work with whether that is following their assessment journey or a piece of therapeutic work, constantly seek to hear their views and be willing to listen and adapt our practice.

It is also our responsibility to search out the lived experience of neurodivergent individuals. A summary of some more sources of the voices of neurodivergent individuals, focusing on CYP and their families follows.

- The Autistic Self Advocacy Network (ASAN) is an American non-profit organisation run by autistic people. They have a YouTube Channel with lots of great videos and have written a book.
- *The Spectrum Girls Survival Guide*, written by Siena Castellon, an autistic, dyslexic, dyspraxic, ADHD young neurodiversity advocate.
- *The Reason I Jump*, by Naoki Higashida, a non-speaking autistic advocate who wrote this book at the age of 13 to share insights into his experiences of autism and challenge core assumptions about autism.
- *The Secret Life of Rose; Inside an Autistic Head* by Rose Smitten, a book (and accompanying YouTube channel) by 11-year-old Rose and her mother, explaining her experiences of being autistic, covering topics such as stimming, masking, sensory experiences and emotions.
- *A Different Sort of Normal*, by Abigail Balfe about her experience of growing up autistic.
- *The Brain Forest*, a book for children about neurodiversity, written by Sandhya Menon, an autistic ADHD psychologist.
- The Curly Hair Project is an organisation founded by an autistic author, Alis Rowe intended to support autistic CYP and their families with lots of videos and downloadable resources and option for subscription. There are also regular online webinars often run by parents of autistic young people.
- Kristy Forbes is a neurodivergent parent of four neurodivergent children and runs an organisation called In Tune Pathways.
- The ADHD Foundation is a user-led organisation aiming to offer advocacy and support for multiple neurodivergent conditions (www.adhdfoundation.org.uk).
- Neurodiversity Network aims to provide support to neurodivergent job seekers, students, employers and universities and has a range of great resources (https://www.neurodiversitynetwork.net/).
- The PDA society website (https://www.pdasociety.org.uk/) has a range of case studies, books, as well as blogs and vlogs by autistic and PDA CYP and their families, giving their perspectives on living life as 'PDAers'. Two books include *I'm Not Upside Down I'm Downside Up* by Harry Thompson (also author of the *PDA Paradox*) and Danielle Jata-Hall and *The Family Experience of PDA* by Eliza Fricker.

YouTube channels:

- Amazing Things Project (especially this video: https://www.youtube.com/watch?v=VAogdfYPstU)
- Purple Ella
- Different Not Less; Chloe Hayden
- Yo Samdy Sam
- How to ADHD
- Dyslexia Box

Podcasts:

- Two Sides of the Same Spectrum
- The Neurodivergent Woman

Lis Angoff, an educational psychologist, has compiled a spreadsheet of resources, including videos and books to explain assessment results and neurodivergence to CYP (https://docs.google.com/spreadsheets/d/1rPpqxlufrQlv8Orq7aL8D5TyOD6EooVOGM52wJvVUXI/edit#gid=1073884638).

19.4 Common Challenges and Addressing Them in the Work

In addition to the more generic challenges of applied practice in child psychology, working with neurodivergent populations brings some particular issues of its own.

19.4.1 Complexity and Co-occurring Conditions

There is both a high chance of having more than one neurodevelopmental condition. There is also a wide range of presentations within diagnostic categories and overlap between them. For example, executive function and emotion regulation difficulties are common characteristics of both autism and ADHD. In addition, there are higher rates of other psychiatric problems in the context of neurodivergence, for example, anxiety, tics and OCD. This has a number of implications for the practitioner psychologist: they must hold in mind and weigh up a large number of possible explanatory mechanisms for a given aspect of a presentation; include additional areas of assessment and ensure that sufficient information is collected to allow differential diagnosis; and finally the various elements and their inter-relationships must be considered together and combined in a formulation that should be accurate, empirically sound and clinically plausible.

19.4.2 The (Neuro)developmental Perspective

The dynamic nature of brain development means that even when differences are 'hard-wired' and present from very early in life, neurodivergent patterns of difficulty may emerge at different points through development, or change over time. The timing of your assessment of a CYP must therefore always be considered when evaluating the information gathered. It is likely that an individual's neurodivergent profile or 'neurotype' will become clearer over time and early intervention, alongside watchful waiting, might also be an alternative to drawing premature diagnostic conclusions.

19.4.3 Multiagency and Multidisciplinary Working

Whilst multidisciplinary approaches are widely used and valued across healthcare, and particularly in relation to care of children, they are perhaps particularly salient in the field of neurodevelopment. As discussed, neurodevelopmental diagnostic decisions are typically made by teams composed of professionals from varied medical, psychology and allied health backgrounds, and this multidisciplinary approach forms part of the NICE guidance. An ability to work collaboratively is therefore essential, requiring confidence to express and evidence your professional opinion, as well as to consider other views and to explore differences and seek consensus. Similarly, psychotherapeutic interventions are often offered alongside other forms of treatment including pharmacotherapy, speech and language therapy and occupational therapy (OT) (the importance of the latter, particularly for young people with proprioceptive and sensory challenges associated with autism, should not be under-estimated). The ability to liaise and plan shared care with colleagues is essential, together with an understanding of how best to configure support so that efficacy of individual components is maximised and can be accurately attributed.

19.4.4 Evidence-based Practice

Evidence-based practice is the gold standard for practitioner psychologists in all fields. It is equally important for neurodevelopmental practice but interventions in particular represent a relatively new and rapidly evolving field and randomised controlled trial (RCT) or Cochrane quality evidence for intervention in many areas is still lacking. In practice it may be necessary to rely on smaller-scale pieces of evidence, combined with clinical experience and case discussion with colleagues or in supervision, to devise a plausible intervention plan. Measuring the impact of our individualised interventions case by case is critical in these situations. This is also known as 'practice-based evidence'.

19.4.5 Assessment in the Context of Neglect or Abuse

A significant minority of autistic or ADHD children have a history of neglect, abuse or developmental trauma, or are currently experiencing it. Although rare when the neurodiverse population is considered as a whole, severe adverse social or familial experiences are known to be a causal factor contributing to neurodivergent outcomes for a very small number of the most severely deprived or traumatised children (Rutter et al., 1999). In other cases, children may have pre-existing neurodevelopmental differences that interact with subsequent experiences of neglect, abuse or trauma, creating a mixed aetiological pathway. In these circumstances the process of assessment, formulation and follow-up clearly requires highly specialist expertise and is often referred to specialist teams. Please see Chapter 26 for further discussion.

19.4.6 Future Directions

Rapid ongoing development in neuroscience together with a growing interest in the interface between mental health and neurodevelopment has created a vast range of possibilities for future directions. It is beyond the scope of this chapter to discuss them all, but some key areas most relevant for psychological practice are briefly considered later.

19.4.7 Inclusion

In recent years there has been a welcome and significant shift in practitioner approaches to neurodevelopmental difference, with a move away from 'normalisation' and towards celebration of difference and inclusion. Over the next decade we can expect to see further growth in this direction, with increasing emphasis on relationship-based and multiagency models for supporting children and their families, rather than behavioural modification, and a focus on increasing accessibility and reducing stigma. Inclusion is no longer just about including children with additional needs in mainstream classrooms, it is about ensuring that neurodivergence is understood, identified and appropriately supported across all ethnic, cultural and demographic groups.

19.4.8 Gender Identity and Autism

The recent finding from the University of Cambridge Autism Research Centre that transgender and gender-diverse adults report higher rates of autism diagnosis than cisgender individuals (5% to 24% prevalence respectively, Warrier et al., 2020) has fed speculation about the nature of the relationship between neurodivergence and development of gender identity through childhood and adolescence. Further research is now underway to explore the significance of this finding. Whatever emerges from these studies, we know that both these groups of individuals are classed as vulnerable and more likely to experience health and social inequalities. The need to safeguard rights and to celebrate and support people with differences remains of paramount importance.

19.4.9 Neural and Cognitive Basis for Commonalities and Discrepancies

The relatively new, broader concept of neurodiversity has focused attention on the degree of overlap between conditions. In particular, emotion regulation and executive function difficulties are characteristic across diagnostic categories, as well as being commonly identified in people who are subthreshold for any diagnosis. It is hoped that clinical research seeking to improve the definition and understanding of the underlying cognitive constructs for some of these core functions, and the neural circuits that underpin them, will ultimately lead to a better understanding of the commonalities and discrepancies across neurodivergent presentations in children and adults. There are some related practice developments, focused on 'profiling', that could be transformative. The development of a new standardised profiling tool, originally co-produced by professionals and parents in Portsmouth, UK, aims to support practitioners (originally those in schools and education) to identify a child's profile of neurodevelopmental needs across nine developmental domains; speech, language, energy levels, attention skills, emotion regulation, sensory levels, flexibility, adaptability and empathy. The tool creates a holistic view of the child in order to try to accommodate and support their needs across settings.

19.4.10 Service Organisation

Service provision in neurodevelopmental practice is starting to change. Historically, an age-based division in the referral pathway was adopted. Developmental concerns about younger (pre-school or younger school-aged) children led to assessment within community paediatric teams, whilst older school-aged or secondary school-aged children were referred to their local CAMHS for neurodevelopmental assessments, with some gradually establishing their own clinics or teams specialising in diagnosis of autism and ADHD. However, problems with this dichotomous approach have emerged, highlighted by the shift in our understanding of neurodiversity. Assessment clinics that focused on binary and category-specific diagnostic decisions fail to take adequate account of the dimensional and co-occurring nature of neurodivergence, with children sometimes undergoing multiple assessments with a variety of professionals/teams to separately identify different aspects of their profile. Intervention services were also hindered, with many CAMHS teams initially lacking full collaboration with appropriate therapeutic services, education and other agencies. In another example of division, whilst CAMHS were set up to assess and treat children's mental health problems, in some cases the referral criteria meant that CYP with autism were excluded because they had a 'neurodisability' and must be referred to learning-disability teams. In others, the learning-disability teams excluded autistic CYPs at referral if they did not technically meet criteria for cognitive impairment, leaving them with nowhere to go for support.

The inefficiency and inequity of this approach became apparent and, together with increasing waiting times, formed the basis for a range of initiatives to pilot alternative service models. Embracing Complexity is a coalition of more than 60 different organisations working together to encourage a shift towards an understanding that co-occurring conditions are the norm rather than the exception. It is encouraging to report that in most areas there is now an intention to move towards development of integrated services to identify and support CYP who have neurodevelopmental differences. This has been driven by recognition of the difficulties highlighted and also by the huge increase in demand for these services over the past 5 years. There is no single approach to integrated assessment, and NICE does not make explicit recommendations, other than giving support to multidisciplinary and inter-agency working. Some regions have piloted joint CAMHS/Paediatric assessment teams, whilst others are aiming to create over-arching neurodevelopmental services that include professionals from within paediatrics, CAMHS, speech and language therapy (SaLT), occupational therapy and education. In other regions there are specialist teams that support children with mental health difficulties in the context of autism and/or learning disability. This paradigm shift in our approach will have clear benefits for our services users and very wide support within the clinical community, but it requires a high level of cooperation and coordination between mental health and community paediatric services, both practically and financially, which may delay its implementation on a larger scale.

19.5 Assessment of Neurodevelopment

The UK's National Institute for Health and Care Excellence (NICE) does not currently offer guidelines or evidence relating to neurodevelopmental assessment as a whole, but instead has category-specific guidelines for autism, ADHD and the neurological assessment of children (National Institute for Health and Care Excellence, 2011). Recommended approaches can also be identified from systematic reviews and clinical research, particularly those that meet Cochrane Review standards (this term is explained in Cipriani et al. 2011, and a summary of the key elements for good clinical practice that emerges from this analysis is given later). Before we consider those guidelines, however, it is worth considering current UK service models and how these affect our ability to support neurodivergence in children and young people.

19.5.1 Good Clinical Practice Guidelines for Assessment

Based on the evidence from sources mentioned earlier, the consensus that emerges for key elements of best clinical practice in relation to neurodevelopmental assessments across all conditions are:

- Multidisciplinary involvement, with the composition of the team reflecting the nature of the referral concern and other characteristics, for example, an occupational therapist if sensory features are dominant, or a speech and language therapist where language disorder is suspected.
- Process may be stepped, that is, initial 'intake' consultation with one team member allows the other elements of assessment for that CYP to be determined.
- Clinical interview to gather information including:
  - description of the current concern or presentation and its history;
  - detailed developmental, medical and educational history;
  - evaluation of family environment and resources;
  - child's strengths and interests; protective factors and resources; and
  - previous assessments or input from other professionals.
- Standardised questionnaires measuring behaviour and/or adaptive function; parent report, teacher report and self-report (may be used for screening or as supporting evidence during assessment, but NOT as a substitute for detailed history and observation).
- Formal direct assessment of cognitive and/or other developmental abilities is indicated in some situations but not essential in all and may include (depending on the question):
  - cognitive ability, academic attainments, executive functions, attention and memory;
  - receptive and expressive language;
  - fine and gross motor skills and sensory processing;
  - social communication abilities, for example the *Autism Diagnostic Observation Schedule*, 2nd ed. (*ADOS-2*, Lord et al., 2012); and
  - adaptive behaviour and emotion regulation.

Inclusion of a psychologist in the MDT is recommended for assessment of most neurodevelopmental conditions, including for autism, ADHD, brain injury and a range of syndromes such as foetal alcohol spectrum disorder (FASD). Their role will vary, depending on the psychologist's skills and experience, the MDT composition and the nature of the presenting concerns. However, it will typically include participation in clinical interview with the CYP and/or their family, administration and interpretation of standardised indirect measures, and direct assessment of one or more aspects of development.

In common with other child psychological assessments, it is vital to create opportunities for the child/young person to voice their own view or questions (if they are able to), bearing in mind that they may feel more able to do so at a later point in the process when a rapport has been developed. If possible, appreciative enquiry can be used to balance what are often 'problem'-focused assessments and through these discussions with the CYP and parent/carer key question(s) or goals can be collaboratively elicited. These questions should then guide the assessment process and be referred to throughout, and particularly at feedback and in the written report or letter.

Considering the mental health of the CYP presenting for neurodevelopmental assessment is essential, even when this is not raised as a presenting concern. Co-morbid anxiety disorders are extremely common in the context of neurodivergence, as discussed earlier in this chapter, and care must be taken to ensure they are not missed as a result of diagnostic overshadowing. Studies have shown that these difficulties represent a major barrier in daily life, particularly affecting school.

Although the neurodevelopmental assessment process has parallels with other types of psychologist practitioner assessment, as described earlier, there are some ways in which it differs.

First, there is a greater emphasis on the developmental, medical and educational history, because they are particularly salient to assessment of neurodevelopment. The medical history must be detailed, including antenatal and perinatal history. The family history asks explicitly about developmental delay or disorder in the wider family, in addition to psychiatric illness, and the medical history should include questions about head injuries, neurological illnesses, any loss of consciousness or seizures.

Second, the importance of gathering information from more than one source, which will typically include the child's educational setting and may involve direct observation rather than indirect report. This represents a key element when evaluating neurodevelopment, for a number of reasons: (a) evidence of the pervasive nature of behaviour patterns is critical to some diagnoses; (b) neurodevelopmental difficulties may be more apparent in some settings (where demands are higher) than in others; and (c) to fully understand the functional impact of difficulties.

Third, the nature of risk assessment may be somewhat different. There is a need to screen for the more obvious potential risks associated with, for example, physically aggressive behaviour or self-harm. An awareness of how risks can be obscured in this population is important: young people with communication differences may be less likely to identify or describe internal states or their own experiences, and behavioural change may more often be attributed to their neurodevelopmental condition, rather than being picked up as an index of distress. In addition there are risks that may be difficult to detect, such as patterns of non-attendance at health appointments. Some children with neurodiverse needs are under the care of more than one service, particularly if they have an associated physical health condition or syndrome. A pattern of missed appointments can indicate that a family is struggling to manage, with implications for the child's health and wellbeing in the immediate and longer term. Whatever the external signs, assessment should include evaluation of parent/carer stress and coping capacity. Parents of children with neurodisabilities report higher levels of mental health difficulty and marital breakdown and often experience social isolation and greater financial hardship. Furthermore, it is not uncommon for there to be more than one child with neurodevelopmental differences within the same family (because of heritability), and for one child to be affected by more than one condition (because of the commonality of co-occurrence), increasing the total burden.

Finally, neurodevelopmental assessments differ in the inclusion of physical and/or neurological examination as a standard part of the assessment process for some neurodivergent presentations including autism, cerebral palsy (CP) and acquired brain injury (ABI). Obviously these examinations are not within the remit of psychology. They are usually carried out by the paediatrician or other medical professional in the team but it is necessary to understand and incorporate any findings when interpreting other assessment results and formulating.

An audiological assessment may also be required prior to assessments for suspected autism and language difficulties, to identify whether hearing impairment has contributed to any observed delay or difference in language.

19.5.2 Autism and ADHD Assessment: Special Considerations

Where specific diagnoses are under consideration for autism or ADHD, the protocol is more prescriptive and it is essential that a structure is followed to ensure that all relevant areas are covered. Evaluation is made by reviewing all the information collected from interview, observation and standardised measures, from all sources, and comparing it to criteria as set out in either *ICD-11* or *DSM-5*, to determine whether the threshold is met.

A key issue in the assessment of ADHD is understanding the rather weak relationship between ADHD diagnosis and measures of cognitive inattention, that is, scores on tests of sustained attention. It is important that poor scores on tests of attention are not used as evidence of ADHD in the absence of other signs and, conversely, that lack of impairment on tests of attention is not used as an argument for not diagnosing ADHD when other evidence to support the diagnosis exists. Although there are group differences in neuropsychological test results for children with ADHD and those without, the majority of young people with ADHD do not demonstrate consistent patterns of impairment on cognitive tests of attention and executive functioning (Arnett et al., 2022).

19.5.3 Standardised Assessment

The use of standardised tools in neurodevelopmental assessment is supported in the NICE guidelines but at the discretion of the assessing/treating team. In most cases, if there is evidence of delay in one or more areas of a child's development, then a formal assessment to establish an ability profile is a helpful starting point, although in reality there are often insufficient resources to achieve this consistently.

For younger children this is likely to include assessment of language and/or motor development alongside cognition. A cognitive assessment battery exploring verbal and non-verbal reasoning as well as cognitive proficiency is typically administered to school-aged children. If a developmental delay or learning disability is suspected, a measure of adaptive function is also required, usually a parent or teacher-rated questionnaire (for a detailed discussion see Chapter 18). There is one very important reason to support this approach. Once the child's general ability or developmental level is clarified, whatever the outcome, the presenting behaviours or difficulties can then be more accurately interpreted with reference to this context. For example, a 5-year-old boy who is slow to develop language and is struggling to establish relationships or join in play with his peers, may initially be suspected of having social communication difficulties or autism. However, standardised developmental assessment then shows that he has a delay affecting all aspects of his abilities, which are currently at a 3-year age-equivalent level. His social interactions and language are therefore consistent with his general developmental level, and in fact it is observed that he can interact well with pre-school children. This assessment of underlying ability has therefore averted the need for an autism diagnostic assessment, and has identified developmental needs that can now be supported appropriately.

When diagnostic questions are unclear at an early stage in assessment, screening measures for social communication and other aspects of behaviour are often administered. They are relatively quick and economical to use, with good reliability and validity. They can both shape the direction of the rest of the assessment process and make an important contribution to the formulation and recommendations for support. The tools most commonly used in this context by practitioner psychologists are tabulated in Appendix 19.4.

In the autism diagnostic assessment, many practitioners now also use standardised social communication history tools that are electronically mediated, in place of a traditional 'free-flowing' clinical history interview. For example, the Autism Diagnostic Interview – Revised (ADI-R; Lord et al., 1994) prompts the practitioner to deliver set questions to the parent/carer; their responses are then evaluated by the practitioner and scores entered. At the end of the interview the program algorithm generates a final/summary score, indicating whether the threshold for autism is met in different areas. These instruments help to ensure that the content of interviews is comprehensive and thoroughly explores the social communication history, but it is still acceptable to use a traditional clinical interview instead, provided that the quantity and quality of information is sufficient. Some practitioners feel that the computerised processes are too rigid and 'binary', inhibiting more creative or intuitive clinical evaluation that may be beneficial in some cases.

ADOS-2 is the most established direct standardised measure of a child or young person's social communication. It is a semi-structured, interactive assessment consisting of a number of set activities and 'presses' that provide opportunities to elicit social interaction and communication, to explore understanding of social relationships and emotions and to observe behavioural flexibility/creativity together with sensory characteristics. These are then scored by the practitioner (and often independently by a second observer too) and an algorithm generates a total score that can be compared to a 'cut-off' threshold for autism. The use of the *ADOS-2* is recommended in the NICE guidelines for autism assessment, but is not required. It takes approximately 60 minutes to administer and parsimony must be considered here, particularly with the challenges in meeting the increasing demand for community autism assessments. Many practitioners argue that for children with clear and pervasive social communication differences and repetitive and stereotyped behaviours, sufficient evidence can be provided without the need for formal direct assessment. For the large number of children and young people who present with more subtle or mixed presentations, however, a systematic and standardised method for eliciting evidence of social communication strengths and weaknesses, provided by the *ADOS-2*, has significant benefits.

There is a note of caution that applies to the use of standardised diagnostic instruments like the *ADOS-2* and ADI-R, which practitioners must hold in mind, and is also set out in the NICE guidelines. Although valuable, these tools should never be used in isolation and a score above or below threshold does not necessarily mean a diagnosis is indicated, or ruled out. Standardised assessment results represent one data source and, for a number of reasons, they sometimes yield a false positive or negative. Such results should therefore always be carefully interpreted alongside a number of other sources of information in reaching a final decision, and the application of clinical judgment is vital.

19.5.4 Camouflaging

Camouflaging has been defined as 'acting as behaviourally neurotypical in order to cope in social situations' (Lai et al., 2019) and has been identified as being particularly characteristic of (but not exclusive to) cognitively able autistic females. Although first mentioned as early as 1981 by Lorna Wing, the concept has received much more attention over the past 10 to 15 years, in parallel with increasing interest in presentations of autism in girls. Camouflaging may include both 'masking' components, such as suppressing/controlling repetitive behaviours and mimicking neurotypical social behaviours including eye contact and facial expression, and compensatory techniques such as learning rules/scripts for social chat (see Cook et al., 2021 for a detailed discussion of this important topic). The relevance to neurodevelopmental assessment is clear: it is possible that features of autism will be hidden by the young people we assess (both female and male) and it is important that we do everything possible to ensure that this does not invalidate our findings and interpretation. It can be very difficult to accurately identify social behaviours as genuine rather than performed, but often parent and school reports will provide valuable information to corroborate observations, as well as discussion with the CYP if appropriate. There is also now a standardised questionnaire available that asks young people about their behaviour in social situations, the Camouflaging Autistic Traits Questionnaire or CAT-Q (Hull et al., 2019, which is being increasingly used in these situations.

Whilst the essential components have not changed, as set out earlier, the approach to assessment of autism and ADHD in children has evolved over the past two decades. This reflects our growing understanding of the diversity and complexity of developmental trajectories, our changing attitudes to difference and the importance of looking at the system(s) around the child. Some key ideas that have gained greater attention recently, and are helpful for psychologists to consider as part of their neurodevelopmental process:

- Establish the hopes of the parent/carer and CYP: What is their understanding of the assessment purpose? Have they thought about potential diagnoses? How might they react? How would it be discussed or disclosed to the child or young person?
- Structure the assessment so that it considers dimensional evaluation, rather than simply categorical:
  - screening and stepped assessment format; and
  - do what is necessary, in incremental stages, and explain at every stage.
- Evaluate behaviours in the context of developmental level (this is why it is important to have a measure of development or cognitive ability).

- Consider early attachment experiences and home environment: disordered attachment may mimic social communication difficulties (but be mindful also that children with autism spectrum conditions may not relate to their parents in a typical manner and this does not necessarily reflect a primary attachment difficulty).
- Take into account cultural and language differences when interpreting assessment results.
- Special circumstances may require clinical judgment, for example, where full details of early history is not available due to care history.
- Ecological validity of assessment (use observation in non-clinic settings if possible).
- Differential diagnosis and co-occurring conditions – ensure you collect sufficient information to evaluate more broadly – some comprehensive screening questionnaires include this, for example, the Conners series (Conners, 2008, 2022).
- Atypical profiles of autism and ADHD are common, particularly at the top and bottom of the age range, in girls, and where there are co-occurring conditions.
- Severe or persistent patterns of early neglect or emotional abuse can lead to presentations that replicate some of the characteristics of neurodevelopmental conditions, particularly social communication difficulties.
- Consider developmental stage in determining time spent with parent and CYP on their own and together.
- Adaptations for other disabilities, sensory needs and so forth.
- Pacing and flexibility: need more than one session for assessment; use previous written information to support assessment and/or 'information gathering form'.

19.5.5 Formulation and Interpretation in Neurodevelopmental Assessment

As in any area of psychological practice, a key priority for your formulation and interpretation should be to answer the right questions. This is likely to include one (or more) questions posed by the referrer, which are often diagnostic. Equally important is the need to answer the questions brought by the CYP and parents, which should have been elicited and discussed at an early stage in the assessment process (see Section 19.5.1). The psychologist may also then develop their own questions, which emerge as they move through the assessment process and information gathering. Finally, there will be occasions when you cannot answer a question and it is important to be able to admit this, although difficult, especially for younger practitioners. Usually this message can be given constructively, with an explanation for why the answer isn't clear and suggestions for other avenues to follow, or that a review after a period of time might be helpful.

Whatever the questions posed, a good neurodevelopmental assessment should give as much weight to clear formulation as it does to accuracy of diagnostic conclusions. This is particularly important when working with neurodivergence because of the very wide variability in individual profiles and the likelihood that the presentation is the product of the interaction of characteristics of more than one condition. Even when some features are subthreshold for diagnosis, they may be having a significant functional impact, and it is common to be considering whether any given presentation is the product of the interaction of different neurodivergent characteristics, rather than a reflection of any single condition.

The formulation process will typically involve multidisciplinary discussion and the synthesis of information from multiple sources and the psychologist may play a key role. They are well-placed to do so because the study of psychology, and subsequently the applied training for practice, both have a strong emphasis on integration of information from a range of contexts. This approach has been enshrined in the biopsychosocial model. Widely used by psychologists working in neurodivergent contexts, this model is particularly useful as a framework for understanding how neurobiological or inborn factors drive the development of underlying cognitive and behavioural differences, which in turn are influenced by environmental, social and familial factors.

One key aspect of interpretation and formulation that applies particularly to assessment of neurodivergence is an *understanding of statistical and clinical significance*:

- Neurodevelopmental assessments generally utilise a larger number of standardised instruments than other forms of psychological evaluation. A grasp of basic statistics is essential when handling quantities of clinical data in this way, so that interpretation can be informed by an understanding of concepts such as reliability and measurement error.
- Statistical significance is only part of the story and must be considered alongside evaluation of clinical significance. This is likely to include reference to population base rates and clinical observations that help us to decide whether a child's performance on a task was an accurate reflection of their 'true' ability or influenced by other factors on the day. Attention and motivation have a very significant impact on test performance and are of course often affected by neurodevelopmental conditions. Collateral information is helpful in these situations, to determine whether the pattern of test results is consistent with expectations based on parental report, information from school and any established diagnoses.
- The validity of standardised scores may also be influenced in other ways. The majority of cognitive and neuropsychological assessment batteries and questionnaires are standardised on 'normative' populations that exclude children with neurodevelopmental diagnoses or disabilities. This must be carefully weighed up when interpreting results obtained by a CYP who is neurodivergent.

Requirements for *feeding back and following up* might also differ in neurodevelopmental practice. The nature of some presentations results in lengthy and multi-faceted assessments, involving evaluation of mental health difficulty alongside neurodevelopmental profile and leading to complex formulations that seek to explain the various findings and the relationship between them. Giving a diagnosis of a neurodevelopmental condition, when indicated, will require particular care because of the significant and long-term implications. Where possible the outline of the feedback should have been discussed and planned by the MDT in advance, taking into account a number of factors including:

- Making the process collaborative to try to ensure the family has a sense of agency.
- Discussing with parents, prior to feedback, whether the CYP should be present for feedback – if not then consider how the family is supported to share the findings with them and when.
- Providing guidance about how to discuss the assessment findings, the use of neuro-affirmative language non-verbal signals.

- The hopes and expectations of the parents and CYP – are your findings something they are expecting/wanting, or not? Are there cultural factors that might affect the response to this information?
- The level of language comprehension and ability to process information (parent and CYP). Provide opportunities for re-cap and questions accordingly as there is a higher frequency of neurodivergence amongst parents of young people with neurodevelopmental differences. You may want to consider visual ways of sharing information for those who process information better this way.
- Planning how you will shift between the communication of the 'bigger picture' to the more detailed results and how much detail will be helpful (but be prepared to change this at the time if necessary). Consider whether 'headline' diagnoses should be given first, followed by evidence, or the other way round. It is usually helpful to offer choice.
- Offering feedback as soon as possible after the assessment is completed, and written reports as soon as possible after feedback; it is particularly difficult for families to be 'in limbo' waiting for results that have such significance.
- The possibility of providing a short written summary of key points that the family can take away with them from feedback; the emotional salience of the information and its complexity makes it much more difficult for parents to retain.
- Ensure that the full written report is clear and meaningful. It should focus on describing the CYP both through observation and findings, and relating the conclusions and formulation to the questions/concerns raised. Avoid lengthy test descriptions and repeated reference to statistical findings.
- Considering providing a shorter/simpler version of the report for the child or young person themselves, usually this will outline strengths, needs and recommendations.
- Review: neurodevelopment is dynamic, as is a CYP's social and family environment. It will often be clear that a review could be beneficial, particularly around school transitions or Key Stages changes, although many services are reluctant to make this recommendation due to capacity and waiting list pressures.

19.6 Interventions and Support for Difficulties Associated with Neurodivergence

The neurodiversity movement and a change in attitudes to difference has led to much greater emphasis on adaptations to the environment and/or supporting the system around the individual, to reduce the secondary impact of neurodivergence, rather than interventions that focus on helping the individual to change. The social model of disability, developed out of the disability rights movement in the 1970s, presents the idea that disability arises not directly from the individual's impairment, but from the barriers created by societal responses – both practical and in terms of acceptance. It argues that the concept of 'fixing' or 'treating' a disability is intrinsically discriminatory. Instead we should seek to change societies 'constructs' of disability and the systems around the individual as a way to support them to reach their full potential. This is not only a more inclusive and ethically acceptable approach, but is also supported by some evidence, although more systematic studies are needed in this area.

In this section we will explore: existing guidelines for interventions; different levels of intervention and support provided by psychologists; some of the main reasons for referral and examples of intervention for these.

19.6.1 Clinical Guidelines

NICE has developed a range of individual guidelines pertaining to different neurodevelopmental conditions, including autism diagnosis and follow-up (NICE, 2011) as well as some broader prevention/intervention guidelines, for example, challenging behaviour and learning disabilities (NICE, 2015). There is also a national strategy for autistic children, young people and adults (Department for Education, 2021), identifying how the UK government will work towards improving outcomes for autistic individuals. The NICE guidance for diagnosis and management of ADHD (NICE, 2018) mentions first-line interventions such as parent management training (PMT) especially for under-fives and those with associated behavioural difficulties, although efficacy of behavioural interventions remains unclear (see further discussion later). *Future in Mind* (National Health Service, 2015) identified severe ADHD as one of the most common reasons for referral to mental health services and recommended greater focus on preventative strategies as well as improving access to services, especially for those who are most vulnerable. Indeed, there is overwhelming evidence both from research and clinical experience that early identification of these neurodevelopmental conditions, with appropriate support, is key to preventing a cycle of negative experiences and low self-esteem leading to anxiety and secondary mental health difficulties. At the time of writing, waiting times nationally for ADHD and autism assessment are exceptionally long, in part as a result of backlogs caused by the Covid-19 pandemic but also thought to represent the growing awareness and recognition of neurodivergence. This has become a priority for the NHS with strategic and financial resources now being channelled.

Guidelines are limited for supporting individuals with language disorder, sensory and motor disorders, and specific learning difficulties. Although these interventions and support are generally provided by the relevant therapeutic services (SaLT, OT, physiotherapy and educational psychology), it is important we remain aware of them. Both the potential secondary impact of such difficulties on a child's wellbeing and mental health, and the fact that these differences may be part of a wider behavioural profile or 'neurotype', make the involvement of a practitioner psychologist alongside other agencies quite likely. As a practitioner psychologist within neurodevelopmental services one important part of your role is likely to be consultation with your MDT colleagues, sharing or facilitating formulation and ensuring that a full picture of the child's strengths and needs and wider context are taken into account to support planning. This can be done in case discussion groups and for a wider group of CYP not officially on your caseload. Sharing a psychological perspective, a wider view of neurodiversity and bringing a neuro-affirmative approach are all ways we can intervene indirectly.

The Royal College of Psychiatrists has recently developed a guide for parents of CYP with specific learning difficulties, highlighting the increased vulnerability to effects on wellbeing and behaviour (Royal College of Psychiatrists, 2015), and it is encouraging to note that, at the time of writing, the National Institute for Clinical and Health Excellence [NICE] is due to release a publication relating to rehabilitation of chronic neurological disorders, including acquired brain injury. However, there remains a need to develop more robust guidelines for provision of support to CYP with the full range of neurodiverse profiles.

19.6.2 Levels of Assessment

As a starting point, it is helpful to have a broad view of what constitutes an intervention or therapeutic goal, particularly given that some neurodevelopmental psychology roles are entirely assessment focused. There is also evidence to support this position. When planned and executed well, assessments that include careful feedback of results, formulation and opportunity for discussion and questions result in higher parent satisfaction (McCrimmon & Gray, 2021). Disseminating and discussing this information with other agencies, most often schools (with parental consent), so that a shared understanding of the CYP can be reached, is likely to have further benefits.

In their ground-breaking book, *Feedback that Sticks*, Karen Postal and Kira Armstrong talk about feedback as a systemic intervention, sharing information and recommendations with the individual, family and school/workplace (Postal & Armstrong, 2013). Improved understanding can also help individuals and families become better advocates in their own care. Postal and Armstrong also present that feedback, and the potential therapeutic benefit of this, begins at initial interview (or even at referral/initial contact) and therefore, the relationship we form at this point (trust, respect, safety) has the potential to impact the information we are able to gather, the validity of the formulation we generate and associated diagnoses, and also the potential intervention and outcomes for the CYP. This is aligned with the neuro-affirmative approach. The Family Partnership Model (Davis & Day, 2010), is a great example of an evidence-based (ecological systemic) model, which places the relationship at the heart of the process of helping, explicitly acknowledging the impact relationship has on outcome. This is consistent with meta-analyses that show a moderate but reliable association between therapeutic alliance on outcomes across conditions and ages (Horvath et al., 2011). Whatever the psychologist's role in a child's neurodevelopmental pathway, being aware of the potential to support and facilitate through interactions with clients and colleagues, direct or indirect, written or verbal, is an important starting point.

Beyond the generic psychotherapeutic role in the assessment process there are different 'levels' of more formal intervention, as there are in other areas of psychological practice. These are usually categorised as:

Direct: Work directly with a child or young person, for a particular presenting problem (see below for most common referral reasons).

Indirect:

- Parents/family – this is often the level we work at with emotional dysregulation and behaviour, with parental adjustment to diagnosis and where our formulation identifies systemic factors that may be maintaining the presenting problem for example, parental responses to demand avoidance (O'Nions et al., 2021).
- Multiagency – coming alongside other agencies involved with the CYP, such as school to identify factors impacting their wellbeing or causing some level of functional impairment and working together to ameliorate these.

- Consultation/supervision – this may involve offering support to other members of your team, to discuss cases, consider aspects of your formulation (without involving the CYP or family) and making a plan for ways to move the case along.

19.6.3 General Considerations

Practitioner psychologists working therapeutically with neurodivergent CYPs will most likely be addressing either (a) a primary mental health difficulty but in the context of neurodivergence for example, addressing OCD in the context of autism or (b) mental health or other difficulties that represent the secondary impact of their neurodivergence, for example, high levels of anxiety or low mood as a result of misunderstanding and lack of accommodation in their home or education setting. Interventions will frequently be cross-diagnostic, because of the high levels of co-occurrence of neurodevelopmental 'conditions' and the overlap of characteristics. Some of the most common interventions are described in more detail later, but it is helpful to begin by reviewing a number of factors that should be considered when setting out to work therapeutically with neurodevelopmental difference:

Interventions should address the CYP/family's wishes, not just the referral question; goal-setting and reviewing goals is vital.

- Interventions must be accessible and developmentally appropriate; establish the CYP's level of understanding and communication, and any other barriers.
- It is more often necessary to work with the parents and school primarily or as well as the individual:
  - factor this in from the outset and gain permission;
  - be aware of the possibility for creating conflicting loyalties and consider involving different members of the team to work with different parts of the system if necessary and feasible; and
  - ensure that everyone understands what/when information will be shared and with whom.
- Be careful not to pathologise the individual (locating the problem in them) when there may be systemic changes that need to be made first or alongside therapeutic intervention.
- Promote self-efficacy and using resources; help children and families to engage with voluntary organisations locally and nationally.
- Work collaboratively with professionals from other disciplines and deliver psychological interventions alongside other support including medication.
- Communication: Be aware that receptive language may be weaker than expressive and do not assume a level of understanding; be ready to support communication in other ways:
  - visual presentation of information;
  - use pen and paper to draw out genogram/ important people/timeline etc,;
  - allow more time for reponse;
  - repetition and recap;
  - use special interests as ways to engage and share concepts;
  - building the therapeutic alliance may take longer; tips and strategies;
  - the generalisation of skills/strategies from sessions to daily life may be more difficult and require smaller steps;

- the ability to identify and describe internal states is typically more difficult for CYPs with social communication differences, sometimes known as alexithymia; this needs careful management in the context of planning and delivering interventions relating to mood or emotion regulation (see later); and
- sessions may need to be shorter or longer depending on the processing style and attention/concentration capabilities of the individual.

19.6.4 Intervention for Anxiety

Anxiety is significantly more prevalent in neurodivergent individuals than in the general population (Kent & Simonoff, 2017), it has been identified as a major cause of school refusal. School non-attendance in the UK is at its highest ever level with a UK Government Department of Education figure of 23.4% for 'persistent absence' in 5 to 15 year olds in February 2023. The impact of lockdowns during the Covid-19 pandemic is thought to have had a further significant impact. A 2018 survey of parents of children refusing school found that 90% had suspected or diagnosed special educational needs (Square Peg, 2018). Adapted interventions for anxiety conditions have been shown to be effective in neurodivergent CYP (Sharma et al., 2021) but significant barriers to accessing mental health support remain (Crane et al., 2019).

The essential structure of interventions for anxiety includes many of the same elements described in Chapter 13 for the general child population, but with some adaptations to ensure that it is tailored to the needs of CYPs with neurodivergent profiles:

- Emphasis on assessing the systemic and environmental factors affecting anxiety and how these can be addressed (working with family, school and so forth), with caution not to pathologise the CYP if the anxiety is appropriate to the context.
- Psychoeducation:
  - usually include CYPs and parents and sometimes school;
  - first explore the level of understanding about their neurodivergence, followed by psychoeducation about anxiety and how they are related;
  - may need to include initial work on understanding and identifying emotions.
- Good practice guidelines for practical adaptations for autistic individuals (Cooper et al., 2018) include:
  - more behavioural strategies;
  - concrete and structured approaches;
  - psychoeducation about emotions;
  - visual and written information;
  - discussion of hobbies and interests; and
  - family members in sessions.
- Be cautious about use of exposure – this should always be done with the consent of the CYP and their parent if appropriate.
- Make sure you have a clear formulation about the factors maintaining the anxiety and a measure of the severity of the anxiety.
- Unpick if the anxiety is adaptive or appropriate (e.g. an unsafe school environment, being bullied) or out of proportion or 'inappropriate' (such as fear of worms, spiders).

Anxiety-driven behaviours that are secondary to neurodivergence (e.g. caused by sensory or socially overwhelming elements of the environment) have a significant self-regulating function; exposure that isn't very carefully controlled and prepared may cause severe anxiety spikes that are not only distressing but also serve to embed the anxiety. For example, for anxiety related to attending school, it is critical that the school refusal is considered as 'appropriate' anxiety, indicating a need to change the school environment and consider adaptations including making the environment safe before considering gradual reintroduction to school, this will need to be done in collaboration with the CYP, family and school.

For anxiety disorders (OCD/phobias) in the context of neurodivergence, an adapted exposure and response prevention (ERP) model may be appropriate.

Some great resources for working with anxiety in neurodivergent individuals include:

- *Exploring Feelings*; CBT to manage anxiety, Dr Tony Attwood (Atwood, 2001)
- *Avoiding Anxiety in Autistic Children*, Dr Luke Beardon (Beardon, 2020)
- *The Neurodivergent Friendly Workbook of DBT Skills*, Sonny Jane Wise (@livedexperienceeducator) (Wise, 2022)
- *Helping Autistic Teens to Manage their Anxiety*; Strategies and worksheets using CBT, DBT and ACT skills, Dr Theresa Kidd (Kidd, 2022)

19.6.5 Intervention for ADHD-related Difficulties

Attention and executive function related difficulties are core features of ADHD but are also characteristic of other neurodivergent conditions. These difficulties have been shown to have an impact on individual and systemic functioning and quality of life (Peasgood et al., 2016), and in ADHD, associated with increased negative life outcomes, at the most extreme level related to increased contact with the criminal justice system (Young & Thome, 2011). There is a clear need to offer support as early as possible for these difficulties to mitigate secondary impact and, once again, adaptations of the system around the child or young person are likely to be critical. Unless the identified difficulty poses a risk to others, consideration should also be given as to whether the individual wants to change. For older children and teens, motivational interviewing could be used where there is a discrepancy between the individuals view of their needs and the systems view.

The brief literature overview at the beginning of this chapter outlines the evidence base for psychological and other approaches to supporting ADHD. In this section we aim to set out how these key findings might translate into practice for psychologists working with CYP affected by ADHD and associated neurotypes.

- Psychoeducation: for the parents, the child, school and other agencies. Explaining your formulation, as clearly as possible, and achieving a shared understanding of the child's 'neurotype' and the factors influencing behaviour (many of which are external not internal) provides the best possible springboard for what comes next in the support plan.
- Children with ADHD are often labelled – lazy, inattentive, rude, defiant, naughty – leading to negative self-image, increased anxiety and ultimately increasing the risk of mood disorder. Changing the narrative is a priority. If you have successfully worked through some psychoeducation this stage should follow quite naturally.

- Adapting the environment: focus on changing the system (home and school) both in terms of practical support and expectations. It is sometimes said that ADHD 'sets children up to fail' within conventional environments. They struggle with being ready on time, finishing class work, following instructions, organising themselves ... the list could go on. By adjusting the environment and goals so that they are attainable that is, so that the child is set up to succeed, the cycle can be broken. Common recommendations for education include sitting at the front of the class, movement breaks, fidget toys/wobble cushions, breaking work down into smaller chunks, using checklists, providing written or pictorial instructions to supplement verbal direction, and encouraging physical exercise. However, strategies should always be based on individual need and developed collaboratively for maximum impact.
- Family support: family resources and resilience are important determinants of outcome. Parents will not be able to make changes if they are struggling personally or financially, and many parents of neurodivergent children are neurodivergent themselves. Consider what support is needed and how to help them access this before moving forwards.
- Co-morbidity: Always consider co-occurring conditions (for ADHD this is the norm, not the exception) and adjust your approach or seek support from other agencies as necessary. Time and effort directed towards one area of need may be wasted if you have failed to take account of others or understand their role.
- Integration: Working collaboratively with the family, school, medical and allied health professionals is likely to facilitate better outcomes. It is particularly relevant for a neurodevelopmental condition that has such wide-ranging effects on function, that may be misunderstood by others, and that responds to varied interventions. For example, OT provision of sensory toys or activities that provide proprioceptive feedback can make a significant difference to behavioural and cognitive regulation, whilst evidence for efficacy of stimulant medication in reducing impulsivity and increasing sustained attention remains stronger than for any other single intervention.

19.6.6 Emotional Dysregulation and Behaviours that Challenge

The most widely accepted approach to managing behaviours that challenge is positive behaviour support (PBS) and there is a strong evidence base for its application in the context of neurodivergence (https://www.challengingbehaviour.org.uk/information-and-guidance/positive-behaviour-support/). Please refer to Chapters 12 and 18, which contain more detailed background information about this approach. When developing an intervention plan in any situation, the starting point is to understand that the behaviour is likely to be the expression of emotional dysregulation and distress and may be due to unmet needs. Some important considerations for behavioural interventions in the context of neurodevelopmental conditions are:

- *Behaviour as communication* – this idea is at the centre of PBS approaches but is particularly applicable to CYPs with neurodiverse conditions that affect language and/or social communication. For example, a behaviour may signal an emotional response (most often distress or agitation) or a desire to stop an activity.
- *What function is the behaviour serving?* – functional analysis (FA) identifies patterns in behaviour that tell us about the factors that precipitate or trigger the behaviour, and those

that maintain it. In the context of some neurodiverse conditions, such as autism, there is a higher likelihood of sensory factors (sensation seeking or hypersensitivity) and functions relating to regulation of internal states. Understanding the function of a behaviour for an individual allows exploration of whether there are alternative ways for the same need to be met.

- *Observable behaviour as the 'tip of the iceberg'* – this is critical to successful behaviour support in the context of neurodiversity. A 'pure' FA only considers observable factors but the neurodevelopmental profile, and wider context, play a strong part in driving behaviour and must be factored into this process. This includes a child's skills and abilities, history, temperament and relationships.
- *Brain-based approaches* – relatively recent and informed by a body of neuroscientific and somatic research such as polyvagal theory (Porges, 2009) these approaches conceptualise some behaviours as a 'pre-verbal/cognitive' response of the nervous system to perceived threat, initiating an activation of the nervous system into 'survival mode' of fight or flight or at times 'freeze'. Further evidence is needed but the theory is gaining influence in explaining interpersonal factors in emotional dysregulation and behaviour. See Daniel Siegel (*Whole Brain Child, No Drama Discipline, Yes Brain Child, The Power of Showing Up*) and Mona Delahooke (*Beyond Behaviours and Brain Body Parenting*) for a full discussion of this area.
- *Parental factors* – caring for a child or young person with additional needs places additional stress on parents, which can in turn negatively affect parenting behaviours and ultimately the outcomes for the CYP. Evaluating and reducing parental stress is therefore a useful target for intervention and studies have shown a positive impact on child behaviour. For example, a recent systematic review of mindfulness interventions for parents (predominantly of neurodivergent children) demonstrated improved family outcomes, including in externalising behaviours of children (Burgdorf et al., 2019). *Mindful Parenting: A Guide for Mental Health Practitioners* by Susan Bogels and Kathleen Restifo is a great place to start and discusses neurodivergence as a key referral criteria for this intervention.

Successful interventions require a careful balance between the application of informed, evidence-based strategies and the need to properly hear and engage with the CYP and/or their family, to acknowledge the lived experience and real-life implications. As for practitioner psychologists in other areas of practice, establishing a good therapeutic relationship is key. We can then make sure we are using the evidence base to inform our individualised interventions and working within 'practice-based evidence' to measure the impact and outcome of these interventions.

19.6.7 Evaluation of Outcome in Neurodevelopmental Conditions

Good clinical practice in relation to evaluation of outcome in psychology, as set out in Chapter 8, applies in much the same way to the work of practitioner psychologists working with neurodivergence. There are perhaps two particular issues that need special consideration in this field, however.

First, is the idea that the understanding of a neurodevelopmental presentation in itself can and should be regarded as a potential measure of 'outcome' for CYP and their families. This does not mean that other support and interventions are not necessary or recommended. But it does mean that we could expect to see some measurable benefit when diagnostic decision(s) and formulation, together with communication of this information in feedback and in a written report are well-executed. In our clinical experience there is much evidence to support this idea, both anecdotally and from service audit, but as yet there has been no substantive published research in this area.

Second, is the need to be aware of limitations in the use of established standardised instruments for measuring clinical outcomes. Many such instruments lack suitability for neurodivergent populations, either because they have been standardised only on typically developing populations, or because the content and/or mode of presentation is unsuitable for people with neurodisability. Goal-based outcomes remain a very commonly used measure of outcome, and don't suffer from the issues identified, but they are limited because of their subjective nature and can of course only be used to evaluate intra-individual outcomes.

Box 19.1 describes a clinical example from the point of referral, through assessment, formulation and diagnosis to intervention and outcomes.

19.7 Concluding Remarks

Variation in all aspects of brain function exists across the whole population. This has always been the case, but its application to the field of neurodevelopment – in particular the idea of dimensionality – is fairly new. The term neurodivergence is typically used to refer to significant difference(s) in one or more dimension of neurodevelopment, and the co-occurrence of neurodivergent characteristics is very common. The degree of impact is affected both by the nature and extent of the features, and by the way in which the child and family are supported. Diagnoses of autism, ADHD and other neurodevelopmental conditions associated with specific patterns of neurodivergence have clinical and pragmatic utility but there is a move away from the use of terms such as disorder. The addition of a dimensional approach is thought to offer a more balanced and accurate way to account for the experiences of neurodivergent people and their families. It represents a fundamental element of neuro-affirmative practice, alongside a corresponding shift in provision of support, with a focus on environmental/systemic adaptation and accommodation. This progressive change in attitudes is beginning to have real effects for children and their families, but a more pervasive evolution of health and social care services and education is required, and this will require time and financial resources. Careful planning, including co-production and outcome evaluation, will be critical to optimise development of services.

The need for practitioner psychologists to have an understanding of neurodivergence has never been greater. Current estimates suggest that approximately 15% of the population are neurodivergent, and children with these characteristics are more likely to also have a parent who shares some of the same traits. Furthermore, such differences are associated with an increased risk for a range of social, familial and mental health difficulties. It is difficult to think of another area of psychological practice that is growing and changing so rapidly and in so many ways – in terms of neuroscience, psychological formulation and sociopolitical context, to name a few. There are extraordinary opportunities ahead, to make real changes for this diverse group of children and families, but also many challenges. Psychologists have an important role to play, and we hope you will be one of them.

Box 19.1 Clinical example: Grace

Referral

Grace, 9 years of age, lived at home with her mother, father and younger brother. She was in Year 4 at a mainstream primary school with some additional support in place for her reading and writing that was thought to be about 1 year behind age-related expectations. Her parents had sought referral from their GP as they were finding her behaviour at home increasingly difficult to manage, despite attending parenting courses. Grace was not fully continent at night and had long-standing sleeping difficulties. She was described as 'oppositional', resisting parents' requests for example, to get dressed, brush her teeth and they were having 'battles' to get her to the dinner table, even for her favourite meals. Parents reported lots of challenges in the morning with Grace saying she did not want to go to school. However, school were reporting that Grace appeared to enjoy school once she was there, was very chatty, had great ideas although could be fidgety and distractible. Grace was said to be quite confident at school, seeking out teachers and peers, often 'leading' games or activities.

Further information collected

Developmental, family and educational history

The pregnancy and birth were unremarkable, Grace was said to be a smiley alert baby but difficult to settle, often napping for very short periods of time. She met her motor milestones and had some single words by 12 months but language development was then slow. Nursery raised concerns about speech and language at about 3 years of age, referring to local SaLT but Grace was discharged after a course of therapy. Parents reported some difficulties with loud noises, preference for certain clothes and a limited diet.

With regards to family history, there was a maternal aunt with a late diagnosis of autism and a paternal uncle with suspected autism. There was also a family history of hypermobility and dementia.

There had been some separation anxiety at nursery and at the start of school, although school reported Grace was 'fine' when in school and they did not have major concerns. Parents said Grace often reported playing on her own at break times or seeking out older or younger children and had been increasingly saying she was 'different' to her peers. At home the parents reported 'impulsive meltdowns', often when Grace was asked to do day-to-day activities such as brushing teeth; she would shout, throw things, run away and could be physically aggressive towards parents and her brother.

Grace had strengths in role play, she would often lead her brother through elaborate make-believe games. She often pretended to be a cat or dog and loved talking about animals. She also had strengths in her physical skills, learning to ride a bike at age four and tending to take physical risks, climbing high.

Direct assessment

In the Autism Diagnostic Observation Schedule (ADOS) Grace scored just at the cut off for suspecting autism, she was noted to be socially motivated, initiating interaction

(Continued)

Box 19.1 (Continued)

frequently, offering lots of information about herself. Her preference for eye contact was noted to be variable, often looking intensely at the examiner or talking without looking at all. Grace directed smiles at the examiner throughout, even when talking about things that made her feel sad, like her pet dying. She was observed to be a bit compulsive, insisting on finishing her story about her holiday and did not want to tidy up after a break until she had finished her drawing.

In the QbTest Grace was found to be significantly more fidgety than females of her own age, although these were noted to be 'micro' movements that might not be noticeable in class. She was also found to be significantly more impulsive and inattentive than her peers.

Grace herself reported that she was beginning to feel different from her friends, finding they did not always want to talk about what she wanted to talk about. Grace said she found school hard and boring, especially having to sit still so much. Grace said at home she can get very angry and feels there is a monster inside her that bursts out even when she doesn't want it to.

Feedback of formulation, diagnosis and recommendations

Grace had early language difficulties, long-standing separation anxiety, sensory sensitivities and need for sameness alongside emerging challenges with friendships. On observation she presented with a need for completing activities, sharing information often and in detail and was noted to have differences in her non-verbal communication. The combination of parent and school report plus observation and discussion with Grace aligned with the experience of autistic individuals and she fulfilled the *DSM-V* criteria for autism. Grace also demonstrated high levels of impulsivity and inattention on formal testing, alongside a high level of small movements. It is possible that she is suppressing her need for movement at school, is reported to be very talkative, which may be her way of being hyperactive. Taking into account her whole neurodevelopmental profile Grace also met criteria for ADHD. Grace's emotional dysregulation and resistance around the ordinary demands of everyday life, along with social strategies to avoid these requests and her comfort in role play appear to fit with high levels of demand avoidance and a PDA profile of autism was suspected.

Intervention

Grace's parents requested further support, identifying their goals as: to understand Grace better and to help support her emotional regulation and reduce the 'meltdowns' at home. Grace's parents reported that they had been trying to use rewards and consequences as these were recommended but felt Grace pushed back against them. Her parents were initially supported to monitor Grace's behaviour at home looking at contextual factors and began to see a pattern of behaviour associated primarily with explicit instructions and transitions away from preferred activities. They developed a formulation based around Grace's need for agency and high levels of anxiety associated with a sense of loss of control. Parents engaged in some psychoeducation around Grace's emotional dysregulation at home, understanding that Grace's brain can see a loss of agency as a 'threat' and often has a survival response (fight or flight). They learnt that this can also impact them, possibly triggering them into survival mode, sometimes leading to co-escalation as they tend to get stricter (e.g. 'you can't talk to me like that'). They also hypothesised that during the school day Grace's 'window of tolerance' gets narrower and narrower and when she returns home, to her safe place people and small things can dysregulate her. This led to the idea that initially they needed to help her have some 'downtime' after school to prevent melt-downs but also when she does 'flip her lid', they need to support her to re-regulate, probably by using 'co-regulation', signalling safety to her. They also spent time discussing ways of helping Grace feel in control more throughout her day, using the PANDA acronym from the PDA society; Pick your battles, Anxiety Management, Negotiate and collaborate, Disguise and manage demands, Adaptation and shared ideas with school. They initiated a weekly 'family chat' to collaboratively work alongside Grace and her brother to think about what was important to them and how they could each support each other to live in line with these values.

Outcome

Grace's parents reported a reduction in the frequency, duration and severity of the behaviours, an increase in their understanding of Grace's experience and improved relationships in the family and with Grace's school. The Revised Child Anxiety and Depression Scale (RCADS) parent report showed reduced anxiety across the board and Grace's self-report of generalised anxiety and separation anxiety had reduced marginally. Grace said she had felt good about being given special roles at school and school had also commented that Grace appeared to be more motivated to come into school.

Appendix 19.1 Diagnostic criteria for autism spectrum disorder (*DSM-V*)

Must meet criteria A, B, C, and D:

Criterion A: Are there persistent deficits in social communication and social interaction across multiple contexts, not accounted for by general developmental delays, and manifest by ALL THREE of the following:

§ Deficits in social-emotional reciprocity, ranging, for example, from abnormal social approach and failure of normal back-and-forth conversation; to reduced sharing of interests, emotions, or affect; to failure to initiate or respond to social interactions?

§ Deficits in non-verbal communicative behaviors used for social interaction, ranging, for example, from poorly integrated verbal and non-verbal communication; to abnormalities in eye contact and body-language or deficits in understanding and use of gestures; to a total lack of facial expression and non-verbal communication?

§ Deficits in developing, maintaining and understanding relationships, ranging, for example, from difficulties adjusting behaviour to suit various social contexts; to difficulties in sharing imaginative play or in making friends; to absence of interest in peers?

Criterion B: Are there restricted, repetitive patterns of behavior, interests or activities, as manifested by AT LEAST TWO of the following:

§ Stereotyped or repetitive motor movements, use of objects, or speech (such as, simple motor stereotypies, lining up toys or flipping objects, echolalia, idiosyncratic phrases)?

§ Insistence on sameness, inflexible adherence to routines, or ritualised patterns of verbal or non-verbal behavior (such as, extreme distress at small changes, difficulties with transitions, rigid thinking patterns, greeting rituals, need to take same route or eat same food every day)?

§ Highly restricted, fixated interests that are abnormal in intensity or focus (such as, strong attachment to or preoccupation with unusual objects, excessively circumscribed or perseverative interests)?

§ Hyper- or hypo-reactivity to sensory input or unusual interest in sensory aspects of the environment (such as, apparent indifference to pain/temperature, adverse response to specific sounds or textures, excessive smelling or touching of objects, visual fascination with lights or movement)?

Criterion C: Have the symptoms been present since early childhood? (NOTE: Symptoms may not become fully manifested until social demands exceed limited capacities, or may be masked by learned strategies in later life)?

Criterion D: Do the symptoms cause clinically significant impairment in social, occupational, or other important areas of current functioning?

Appendix 19.2 Neuro-affirmative language

Try not to use...	Consider using...
Person first language e.g. Person WITH autism/disability	Identity first language e.g. autistic person, disabled person, neurodivergent person
Suffers with … e.g. ADHD	Has …
Autism spectrum disorder	Autism/autistic
EF (or abbreviations)	Executive Function (use full words)
Disorder, disease, illness, abnormal, delay, deficit, symptoms, inappropriate, appropriate, poor, limited, odd, unusual, peculiar, absence of, does not…	Difference(s), characteristics, difficulties, challenges, tricky, does…, (describe what you see without judgment)
High/low functioning Mild/severe	Talk about an individual's profile of strengths and needs
Co-morbidities/co-morbid disorders	Co-occurring conditions
Symptoms/impairments	Characteristics/differences
Self-stimulatory behaviour/repetitive movements	Stimming, stims, self-expression body language
Treat/treatment	Support, accommodations, adaptations
Special interests, restricted interests, obsessions	Strong interests, areas of expertise, strengths
Lack of central coherence	Attention to detail
Rigid/lacks imagination	Thrives with predictability and structure
Restless/hyperactive	Energetic
Talks too much	Talkative
School refusal	Not attending school due to (anxiety)

Appendix 19.3 Profile of strengths and needs

Jane was noted to have the following strengths:

Is gentle and caring with a strong sense of social justice.

Is a really interesting person to engage with .

Pays great attention to detail.

Has a love of learning and actively seeks out information on topics of interest.

Can focus for a long time on topics of interest.

Is a creative person with lots of unique ideas.

Is determined and resilien.t

The following needs were identified as priorities for Jane:

Jane would benefit from further understanding the autistic experience and how this might relate to their own experience and identity.

Jane's family, teachers and future college would benefit from learning about the autistic experience in neuro-affirmative ways and adapting their expectations, communication styles and making reasonable adjustments to support Jane.

Jane would benefit from further support from an occupational therapist to understand their sensory profile and how to meet their needs and accommodate for this in everyday life.

Jane would benefit from accessing support for her mental health and ideally a neuro-affirmative therapeutic approach adapting evidence-based interventions to meet their autistic experience.

Diagnostic conclusion and summary

Jane is an especially likable 15-year-old person with caring parents committed to supporting them to reach their full potential. Jane presents with many strengths, including their attention to detail, ability to learn deeply about their interests, being gentle and caring with a strong sense of social justice. Priorities at the time of referral centered around Jane's challenges with peer interactions, feelings of difference and associated difficulties with their mental health and wellbeing. The assessment involved a multielement approach to help identify Jane's profile of strengths and needs, which included a parent interview, detailed interview with Jane about their experiences of the world, which is in line with best practice guidelines.

Jane has preferences and differences in her social communication and interaction with others. She has passions and interests that she likes to engage with intensely and experiences sensory elements of the world differently. In collaboration with Jane and her parents, the assessment therefore indicates that Jane's strengths, the challenges that have arisen and her overall experience aligns with the experience of autistic individuals and she therefore fulfills the *DSM-5* criteria for Autism.

Appendix 19.4 Standardised screening tools for neurodiversity

Social Communication	Social Responsiveness Scale, Second Edition (SRS-2), Constantino, 2012
	The Social Communication Questionnaire (SCQ), Rutter et al., 2003
	The Children's Communication Checklist, version 2 (CCC-2), Bishop, 2003
Sensory Profile	The Sensory Profile 2, Dunn, 2014
Attention and Hyperactivity	Conners Fourth Edition, Conners, 2022

(Continued)

Behaviour and Developmental Screening	Strengths and Difficulties Questionnaire (SDQ), Goodman, 1997
	Strengths and Difficulties Questionnaire (SDQ), Conners, 2008
Adaptive Behaviour	Adaptive Behaviour Assessment System Third Edition (ABAS-3), Harrison & Oakland, 2015
	Vineland Adaptive Behavior Scales, Sparrow et al., 2015

References

Advisory, Conciliation and Arbitration Service. (2018). *ACAS annual report and accounts 2018 to 2018*. https://www.gov.uk/government/publications/acas-annual-report-and-accounts-2017-to-2018.

Al-Beltagi, M. (2021). Autism medical comorbidities. *World Journal of Clinical Pediatrics, 10*(3), 15–28. doi.org/10.5409/wjcp.v10.i3.15.

Alderwick, H., & Dixon, J. (2019). The NHS long term plan. *British Medical Journal (Clinical Research ed.), 364*, l84. doi.org/10.1136/bmj.l84.

American Psychiatric Association. (1968). *Diagnostic and statistical manual of mental disorders* (2nd ed.). American Psychiatric Association.

American Psychiatric Association. (1980). *Diagnostic and statistical manual of mental disorders* (3rd ed.). American Psychiatric Association.

American Psychiatric Association. (2013). *Diagnostic and statistical manual of mental disorders* (5th ed.). American Psychiatric Association. doi.org/10.5409/wjcp.v10.i3.15.

Anderson, V., Jacobs, R., & Anderson, P. J. (2010). *Executive functions and the frontal lobes: A lifespan perspective*. Psychology Press.

Anderson, V., Northam, E., & Wrennall, J. (2019). The developing brain. In V. Anderson, E. Northam, & J. Wrennall (Eds.), *Developmental neuropsychology: A clinical approach*. (2nd ed., pp. 27–45). Routledge.

Arnett, A. B., McGrath, L. M., Flaherty, B. P., Pennington, B. F., & Willcutt, E. G. (2022). Heritability and clinical characteristics of neuropsychological profiles in youth with and without elevated ADHD symptoms. *Journal of Attention Disorders, 26*(11), 1422–1436. doi.org/10.1177/10870547221075842.

Attwood, T. (2001). *Exploring feelings: Cognitive behavioural therapy to manage anxiety*. Future Horisons.

Barkley, R. A. (2022). *Treating ADHD in children and adolescents*. Guilford Publications.

Baron-Cohen, S., Mortimore, C., Moriarty, J., Izaguirre, J., & Robertson, M. (1999). The prevalence of Gilles de la Tourette's syndrome in children and adolescents with autism. *The Journal of Child Psychology and Psychiatry and Allied Disciplines, 40*(2), 213–218. doi.org/10.1111/1469-7610.00434.

Beardon, L. (2020). *Avoiding anxiety in autistic children: A guide for autistic wellbeing*. Sheldon Press.

Bishop, C., Mulraney, M., Rinehart, N., & Sciberras, E. (2019). An examination of the association between anxiety and social functioning in youth with ADHD: A systematic review. *Psychiatry Research, 273*, 402–421. doi.org/10.1016/j.psychres.2019.01.039.

Bishop, D., & Rutter, M. (2008). Neurodevelopmental disorders: conceptual Issues. In M. J. Rutter, D. Bishop, D. Pine, S. Scott, J. Stevenson, E. Taylor, & A. Thapar (Eds.), *Rutter's child and adolescent psychiatry* (5th ed., pp. 32–41). Wiley-Blackwell. doi.org/10.1186/1471-2431-5-34.

Bishop, D. V. M. (2003). *The children's communication checklist, version 2 (CCC-2).* Pearson.

Bloch, M. H., Peterson, B. S., Scahill, L., Otka, J., Katsovich, L., Zhang, H., & Leckman, J. F. (2006). Adulthood outcome of tic and obsessive-compulsive symptom severity in children with Tourette syndrome. *Archives of Pediatrics & Adolescent Medicine, 160*(1), 65–69. doi.org/10.1001/archpedi.160.1.65.

Burd, L., Freeman, R. D., Klug, M. G., & Kerbeshian, J. (2005). Tourette syndrome and learning disabilities. *BMC Pediatrics, 5*(1), 1-6. doi.org/10.1186/1471-2431-5-34.

Burgdorf, V., Szabó, M., & Abbott, M. J. (2019). The effect of mindfulness interventions for parents on parenting stress and youth psychological outcomes: A systematic review and meta-analysis. *Frontiers in Psychology, 10,* 1336. doi.org/10.3389/fpsyg.2019.01336.

Carpenter, B., Happé, F., & Egerton, J. (2019). *Girls and autism: Educational, family and personal perspectives.* Routledge.

Catalá-López, F., Hutton, B., Núñez-Beltrán, A., Page, M. J., Ridao, M., Macías Saint-Gerons, D., Catalá, M. A., Tabarés-Siesdedos, R., & Moher, D. (2017). The pharmacological and non-pharmacological treatment of attention deficit hyperactivity disorder in children and adolescents: A systematic review with network meta-analyses of randomised trials. *PLoS ONE, 12*(7), e0180355. doi.org/10.1371/journal.pone.0180355.

Children and Families Act. (2014). *Children and families act* 2014. www.legislation.gov.uk/ukpga/2014/6/contents/enacted.

Cipriani, A., Furukawa, T. A., & Barbui, C. (2011). What is a Cochrane review? *Epidemiology and Psychiatric Sciences, 20*(3), 231–233. doi.org/10.1017/S2045796011000436.

Cohen, S. C., Leckman, J. F., & Bloch, M. H. (2013). Clinical assessment of Tourette syndrome and tic disorders. *Neuroscience & Biobehavioral Reviews, 37*(6), 997–1007. doi.org/10.1016/j.neubiorev.2012.11.013.

Conners, C. K. (2008). *Conners early childhood* (3rd ed.). Multi-Health System.

Conners, C. K. (2022). *Conners early childhood* (4th ed.). Multi-Health Systems.

Constantino, J. (2012). *Social responsiveness scale, second edition (SRS-2).* Western Psychological Services.

Cook, J., Hull, L., Crane, L., & Mandy, W. (2021). Camouflaging in autism: A systematic review. *Clinical Psychology Review, 89,* 102080. doi.org/10.1016/j.cpr.2021.102080.

Cooper, K., Loades, M. E., & Russell, A. (2018). Adapting psychological therapies for autism. *Research in Autism Spectrum Disorders, 45,* 43–50. doi.org/10.1016/j.rasd.2017.11.002.

Cortese, S. (2019). The association between ADHD and obesity: Intriguing, progressively more investigated, but still puzzling. *Brain Sciences, 9*(10), 256. doi.org/10.3390/brainsci9100256.

Courchesne, E., Mouton, P. R., Calhoun, M. E., Semendeferi, K., Ahrens-Barbeau, C., Hallet, M. J., Barnes, C. C., & Pierce, K. (2011). Neuron number and size in prefrontal cortex of children with autism. *Journal of the American Medical Association (JAMA), 306*(18), 2001–2010. doi.org/10.1001/jama.2011.1638.

Crane, L., Adams, F., Harper, G., Welch, J., & Pellicano, E. (2019). 'Something needs to change': Mental health experiences of young autistic adults in England. *Autism, 23*(2), 477–493. doi.org/10.1177/13623613187570.

Cutler, D., Murphy, T., Gilmour, J., & Heyman, I. (2009). The quality of life of young people with Tourette syndrome. *Child: Care, Health and Development*, *35*(4), 496–504. doi.org/10.1111/j.1365-2214.2009.00983.x.

Davis, H., & Day, C. (2010). *Working in partnership: The family partnership model.* Pearson.

Department for Education. (2015). *Special educational needs and disability code of practice: 0 to 25 Years.* Department for Education. https://assets.publishing.service.gov.uk/government/uploads/system/uploads/attachment_data/file/398815/.

Department for Education & Department for Health & Social Care. (2021). *The national strategy for autistic children, young people and adults: 2021 to 2026.* Department for Education. https://www.gov.uk/government/publications/national-strategy-for-autistic-children-young-people-and-adults-2021-to-2026/the-national-strategy-for-autistic-children-young-people-and-adults-2021-to-2026.

Dunn, W. (2014). *The sensory profile 2.* Pearson Education Ltd.

Dziobek, I., Bahnemann, M., Convit, A., & Heekeren, H. R. (2010). The role of the fusiform-amygdala system in the pathophysiology of autism. *Archives of General Psychiatry*, *67*(4), 397–405. doi.org/10.1001/archgenpsychiatry.2010.31.

Elman, J. L., Bates, E. A., Johnson, M. H., Karmiloff-Smith, A., Parisi, D., & Plunkett, K. (1996). *Rethinking innateness: A connectionist perspective on development.* MIT Press.

Equality Act. (2010). Equality Act 2010. www.legislation.gov.uk/ukpga/2010/15.

Fombonne, E. (2009). Epidemiology of pervasive developmental disorders. *Pediatric Research*, *65*, 591–598. doi.org/10.1203/pdr.0b013e31819e7203.

Friedman, N. P., Miyake, A., Altamirano, L. J., Corley, R. P., Young, S. E., Rhea, S. A., & Hewitt, J. K. (2016). Stability and change in executive function abilities from late adolescence to early adulthood: A longitudinal twin study. *Developmental Psychology*, *52*(2), 326. doi.org/10.1037/dev0000075.

Gasselling, T., Morris, B., Smith, A., & Hughes, J. (2022). *How can schools better support neurodivergent young people?* Greater Manchester Youth Combined Authority. https://drive.google.com/file/d/1DMbqNV3M8xEFXiCbpSHPEd1PRA5Hdfc-/view?fbclid=IwAR2ugaZTKoOZTCJmswTk3ZufDI7IK7osSbE0DDF-I5Ezkc_j1F5ttRQmNOc.

Goh, S., Dong, Z., Zhang, Y., DiMauro, S., & Peterson, B. S. (2014). Mitochondrial dysfunction as a neurobiological subtype of autism spectrum disorder: evidence from brain imaging. *Journal of the American Medical Association (JAMA) Psychiatry*, *71*(6), 665–671. doi.org/10.1001/jamapsychiatry.2014.179.

Goodman, R. (1997). *Strengths and difficulties questionnaire (SDQ).* APA PsycTests.

Green, J., Absoud, M., Grahame, V., Malik, O., Simonoff, E., Le Couteur, A., & Baird, G. (2018). Pathological demand avoidance: Symptoms but not a syndrome. *The Lancet Child & Adolescent Health*, *2*(6), 455–464. doi.org/10.1016/S2352-4642(18)30044-0.

Happé, F., & Frith, U. (2020). Annual research review: Looking back to look forward: Changes in the concept of autism and implications for future research. *Journal of Child Psychology and Psychiatry*, *61*(3), 218–232. doi.org/10.1111/jcpp.13176.

Happé, F., Ronald, A., & Plomin, R. (2006). Time to give up on a single explanation for autism. *Nature Neuroscience*, *9*, 1218–1220. doi.org/10.1038/nn1770.

Harrison, P., & Oakland, T. (2015). *Adaptive behaviour assessment system.* (3rd ed.). Western Psychological Services.

Havdahl, A., Niarchou, M., Starnawska, A., Uddin, M., van der Merwe, C., & Warrier, V. (2021). Genetic contributions to autism spectrum disorder. *Psychological Medicine, 51*(13), 2260–2273. doi.org/10.1017/S0033291721000192.

Hinshaw, S. P., Nguyen, P. T., O'Grady, S. M., & Rosenthal, E. A. (2022). Annual research review: Attention-deficit/hyperactivity disorder in girls and women: Underrepresentation, longitudinal processes, and key directions. *Journal of Child Psychology and Psychiatry, 63*(4), 484–496. doi.org/10.1111/jcpp.13574.

Hirschtritt, M. E., Lee, P. C., Pauls, D. L., Dion, Y., Grados, M. A., Illmann, C., King, R. A., Sandor, P., McMahon, W. M., Lyon, G. J., Cath, D. C., Kurlan, R., Robertson, M. M., Osiecki, L., Scharf, J. M., & Matthews, C. A. (2015). Lifetime prevalence, age of risk, and genetic relationships of comorbid psychiatric disorders in Tourette syndrome. *Journal of the American Medical Association (JAMA) Psychiatry, 72*(4), 325–333. doi.org/10.1001/jamapsychiatry.2014.2650.

Hirvikoski, T., Mittendorfer-Rutz, E., Boman, M., Larsson, H., Lichtenstein, P., & Bölte, S. (2016). Premature mortality in autism spectrum disorder. *The British Journal of Psychiatry, 208*(3), 232–238. doi.org/10.1192/bjp.bp.114.160192.

Horvath, A. O., Re, A. C. D., Flückiger, C., & Symonds, D. (2011). Alliance in individual psychotherapy. In J. C. Norcross (Ed.), *Psychotherapy relationships that work: Evidence-based responsiveness* (2nd ed., pp. 25–69). Oxford University Press. doi.org/10.1093/acprof:oso/9780199737208.003.0002.

Hull, L., Mandy, W., Lai, M. C., Baron-Cohen, S., Allison, C., Smith, P., & Petrides, K. V. (2019). Development and validation of the camouflaging autistic traits questionnaire (CAT-Q). *Journal of Autism and Developmental Disorders, 49*, 819–833. doi.org/10.1177/1362361319864804.

Jacobson, L., & Gerner, G. (2021). Acquired brain injury: A developmental perspective. In L. M. Glidden, L. L. McIntyre, & M. J. Tasse, *APA handbook of intellectual and developmental disabilities: Foundations*. (pp. 239–260). American Psychiatric Association.

Kanner, L. (1943). Autistic disturbances of affective contact. *The Nervous Child, 2*, 217–250.

Kent, R., & Simonoff, E. (2017). Prevalence of anxiety in autism spectrum disorders. In M. C. Kerns, P. Renno, E. A. Storch, P. C. Kendall, & J. J. Wood (Eds.). *Anxiety in children and adolescents with autism spectrum disorder: Evidence-based assessment and treatment* (pp. 5–32). Elsevier. doi.org/10.1016/B978-0-12-805122-1.00002-8.

Kidd, T. (2022). *Helping autistic teens to manage their anxiety: Strategies and worksheets using CBT*, DBT and ACT skills. Jessica Kingsley Publishers.

Lai, M. C., Kassee, C., Besney, R., Bonato, S., Hull, L., Mandy, W., Szatmari, P., & Ameis, S. H. (2019). Prevalence of co-occurring mental health diagnoses in the autism population: A systematic review and meta-analysis. *The Lancet Psychiatry, 6*(10), 819–829. doi.org/10.1016/S2215-0366(19)30289-5.

Leckman, J. F., & Fernandez, T. V. (2016). The origins of Tourette syndrome: Prenatal risk factors and the promise of birth cohort studies. *Journal of the American Academy of Child & Adolescent Psychiatry, 55*(9), 751–753. https://doi.org/10.1016/j.jaac.2016.06.009.

Loomes, R., Hull, L., & Mandy, W. (2017). What is the male-to-female ratio in autism spectrum disorder? A systematic review and meta-analysis. *Journal of the American Academy of Child & Adolescent Psychiatry, 56*(6), 466–474.

Lord, C., Rutter, M., DiLavore, P., Risi, S., Gotham, K., & Bishop, S. (2012). *Autism diagnostic observation schedule: ADOS-2*. Western Psychological Services.

Lord, C., Rutter, M., & Le Couteur, A. (1994). Autism diagnostic interview-revised: A revised version of a diagnostic interview for caregivers of individuals with possible pervasive developmental disorders. *Journal of Autism and Developmental Disorders, 24*(5), 659–685. doi.org/10.1007/BF02172145.

McCrimmon, A. W., & Gray, S. M. (2021). A systematic review of factors relating to parental satisfaction with the diagnostic process for autism spectrum disorder. *Review Journal of Autism and Developmental Disorders, 8*, 334–349. doi.org/10.1007/s40489-020-00224-9.

Milton, D. (2013). 'Nature's answer to over-conformity': Deconstructing pathological demand avoidance. *Autism Experts Online article.* https://kar.kent.ac.uk/id/eprint/62694.

Milton, D. E. (2012). On the ontological status of autism: The 'double empathy problem'. *Disability & Society, 27*(6), 883–887. doi.org/10.1080/09687599.2012.710008.

National Autistic Society. (2021). *Good practice guide.* National Autistic Society. https://s2.chorus-mk.thirdlight.com/file/24/asDKIN9as.klK7easFDsalAzTC/NAS-Good-Practice-Guide-A4.pdf.

National Health Service. (2015). *Future in mind: Promoting, protecting and improving our children and young people's mental health and wellbeing*. National Health Service. https://assets.publishing.service.gov.uk/government/uploads/system/uploads/attachment_data/file/414024/Childrens_Mental_Health.pdf.

National Institute for Health and Care Excellence. (2011). *Autism spectrum disorder in under 19s: Recognition, referral and diagnosis.* (NICE Guideline CG128). NICE. https://www.nice.org.uk/Guidance/CG128.

National Institute for Health and Care Excellence. (2015). *Challenging behaviour and learning disabilities: Prevention and interventions for people with learning disabilities whose behaviour challenges.* (NICE Guideline NG11). NICE. https://www.nice.org.uk/guidance/ng11.

National Institute for Health and Care Excellence. (2018). *Attention deficit hyperactivity disorder: Diagnosis and management.* (NICE Guideline NG87). NICE. https://www.nice.org.uk/guidance/ng87.

Newson, E. L. M. K., Le Marechal, K., & David, C. (2003). Pathological demand avoidance syndrome: A necessary distinction within the pervasive developmental disorders. *Archives of Disease in Childhood, 88*(7), 595–600. doi.org/10.1136/adc.88.7.595.

Nowak, S., & Jacquemont, S. (2020). The effects of sex on prevalence and mechanisms underlying neurodevelopmental disorders. In A. Gallagher, C. Bulteau, D. Cohen, & J. L. Michaud (Eds.). *Handbook of clinical neurology, Vol. 173* (pp. 327–339). Elsevier.

O'Nions, E., Happé, F., Viding, E., & Noens, I. (2021). Extreme demand avoidance in children with autism spectrum disorder: Refinement of a caregiver-report measure. *Advances in Neurodevelopmental Disorders, 5*(3), 269–281. doi.org/10.1007/s41252-021-00203-z.

Peasgood, T., Bhardwaj, A., Biggs, K., Brazier, J. E., Coghill, D., Cooper, C. L., Daley, D., De Silva, C., Harpin, V., Hodgkins, P., Nadkarni, A., Setyawan, J., & Sonuga-Barke, E. J. (2016). The impact of ADHD on the health and well-being of ADHD children and their siblings. *European Child & Adolescent Psychiatry, 25*, 1217–1231. doi.org/10.1007/s00787-016-0841-6.

Porges, S. W. (2009). The polyvagal theory: New insights into adaptive reactions of the autonomic nervous system. *Cleveland Clinic Journal of Medicine, 76*(Suppl 2), S86. doi.org/10.3949/ccjm.76.s2.17.

Postal, K. S., & Armstrong, K. (2013). *Feedback that sticks: The art of effectively communicating neuropsychological assessment results.* Oxford University Press.

Robertson, M. M. (2015). A personal 35 year perspective on Gilles de la Tourette syndrome: prevalence, phenomenology, comorbidities, and coexistent psychopathologies. *The Lancet Psychiatry, 2*(1), 68–87. doi.org/10.1016/S2215-0366(14)00132-1.

Roman-Urrestarazu, A., van Kessel, R., Allison, C., Matthews, F. E., Brayne, C., & Baron-Cohen, S. (2021). Association of race/ethnicity and social disadvantage with autism prevalence in 7 million school children in England. *Journal of the American Medical Association (JAMA) Pediatrics, 175*(6), e210054. doi.org/10.1001/jamapediatrics.2021.0054.

Royal College of Psychiatrists. (July, 2015). *Specific learning disabilities for parents and carers.* Royal College of Psychiatrists. https://www.rcpsych.ac.uk/mental-health/parents-and-young-people/information-for-parents-and-carers/specific-learning-disabilities-for-parents

Rutter, M., Anderson-Wood, L., Beckett, C., Bredenkamp, D., Castle, J., Groothues, C., Kreppner, J., Keaveney, L., Lord, C., & O'Connor, T. (1999). Quasi-autistic patterns following severe early global privation. *The Journal of Child Psychology and Psychiatry and Allied Disciplines. 40*(4), 537–549. doi.org/10.1111/1469-7610.0047.

Rutter, M., Bailey, A., & Lord, C. (2003). *The social communication questionnaire.* Western Psychological Services.

Rydzewska, E., Hughes-McCormack, L. A., Gillberg, C., Henderson, A., MacIntyre, C., Rintoul, J., & Cooper, S, A. (2018). Prevalence of long-term health conditions in adults with autism: observational study of a whole country population. *British Medical Journal Open 8*(8), e023945. doi.org/10.1136/bmjopen-2018-023945.

Sayal, K., Prasad, V., Daley, D., Ford, T., & Coghill, D. (2018). ADHD in children and young people: Prevalence, care pathways, and service provision. *The Lancet Psychiatry, 5*(2), 175–186. doi.org/10.1016/S2215-0366(17)30167-0.

Sharma, S., Hucker, A., Matthews, T., Grohmann, D., & Laws, K. R. (2021). Cognitive behavioural therapy for anxiety in children and young people on the autism spectrum: A systematic review and meta-analysis. *BMC Psychology, 9*(1), 1–16. doi.org/10.1186/s40359-021-00658-8.

Silberman, S. (2015). *NeuroTribes: The legacy of autism and how to think smarter about people who think differently.* Allen & Unwin.

Singer, J. (2017). *Neurodiversity: The birth of an idea.* [Kindle Edition]. Amazon Digital Services, Judy Singer.

Slade, G. (2014). *Diverse perspectives.* The National Autistic Society. https://positiveaboutautism.co.uk/uploads/9/7/4/5/97454370/nas-diverse-perspectives-report-1.pdf.

Sonuga-Barke, E. J., Sergeant, J. A., Nigg, J., & Willcutt, E. (2008). Executive dysfunction and delay aversion in attention deficit hyperactivity disorder: Nosologic and diagnostic implications. *Child and Adolescent Psychiatric Clinics of North America, 17*(2), 367–384. doi.org/10.1016/j.chc.2007.11.008.

Sparrow, S. S., Cicchetti, D. V., & Saulnier, C. A. (2016). *Vineland adaptive behavior scales.* (3rd ed.). Pearson.

Square Peg. (2018). *School attendance difficulties: Parent survey results.* https://img1.wsimg.com/blobby/go/a41082e1-5561-438b-a6a2-16176f7570e9/NFIS%20Parent%20Survey%20Results%20May%202018.pdf.

Szejko, N., & Müller-Vahl, K. R. (2021). Challenges in the diagnosis and assessment in patients with Tourette syndrome and comorbid obsessive-compulsive disorder. *Neuropsychiatric Disease and Treatment, 17*, 1253–1266. doi.org/10.2147/NDT.S251499.

Thapar, A., Cooper, M., Jefferies, R., & Stergiakouli, E. (2012). What causes attention deficit hyperactivity disorder? *Archives of Disease in Childhood, 97*(3), 260–265. doi.org/10.1136/archdischild-2011-300482.

Thapar, A., Cooper, M., & Rutter, M. (2017). Neurodevelopmental disorders. *The Lancet Psychiatry, 4*(4), 339–346. doi.org/10.1016/S2215-0366(16)30376-5.

Torgersen, T., Gjervan, B., & Rasmussen, K. (2006). ADHD in adults: A study of clinical characteristics, impairment and comorbidity. *Nordic Journal of Psychiatry, 60*(1), 38–43. doi.org/10.1080/08039480500520665.

van Engeland, H., & Buitelaar, J. K. (2008). Autism spectrum disorders. In M. J. Rutter, D. Bishop, D. Pine, S. Scott, J. Stevenson, E. Taylor, & A. Thapar (Eds.), *Rutter's child and adolescent psychiatry* (5th ed., pp. 759–781). Wiley. doi.org/10.1002/9781444300895.ch46.

van Steensel, F. J., Bögels, S. M., & Perrin, S. (2011). Anxiety disorders in children and adolescents with autistic spectrum disorders: A meta-analysis. *Clinical Child and Family Psychology Review, 14*, 302–317. doi.org/10.1007/s10567-011-0097-0.

Warrier, V., Greenberg, D. M., Weir, E., Buckingham, C., Smith, P., Lai, M. C., Allison, C., & Baron-Cohen, S. (2020). Elevated rates of autism, other neurodevelopmental and psychiatric diagnoses, and autistic traits in transgender and gender-diverse individuals. *Nature Communications, 11*(1), 3959. doi.org/10.1038/s41467-020-17794-1.

Whittington, C., Pennant, M., Kendall, T., Glazebrook, C., Trayner, P., Groom, M., Hedderly, T., Heyman, I., Jackson, G., Jackson, S., Murphy, T., Rickards, H., Robertson, M., Stern, J., & Hollis, C. (2016). Practitioner review: Treatments for Tourette syndrome in children and young people: A systematic review. *Journal of Child Psychology and Psychiatry, 57*(9), 988–1004. doi.org/10.1111/jcpp.12556.

Wise, S. J. (2022). The neurodivergent friendly workbook of DBT Skills. Independently published.

World Health Organization. (2022). Mental behavioral and neurodevelopmental disorders. In *International Classification of Diseases, 11th Edition*. World Health Organization. https://icd.who.int/.

Young, S., & Thome, J. (2011). ADHD and offenders. *The World Journal of Biological Psychiatry, 12*(supl), 124–128. doi.org/10.3109/15622975.2011.600319.

Zeidan, J., Fombonne, E., Scorah, J., Ibrahim, A., Durkin, M. S., Saxena, S., Yusuf, A., Shih, A., & Elsabbagh, M. (2022). Global prevalence of autism: A systematic review update. *Autism Research, 15*(5), 778–790. doi.org/10.1002/aur.2696.

20

Working in Schools

Anna Picciotto, Joe Hickey and Sian Barnett

20.1 Introduction

After home and family, schools are often the environment in which children and young people (CYP) spend most of their time. They are an immersive social experience as well as centres of learning, and can support the development of good social, emotional and mental health. Schools have the potential to offer a nurturing and protective environment for CYP in the most adverse circumstances. School staff are in loco parentis and can be role models and attachment figures. They often know their CYP and families well, sometimes holding a great deal of information about family history, strengths and risk factors. They are ideally placed to notice early signs of distress. Schools can therefore provide access to timely interventions and support to CYP and their caregivers in a familiar setting.

Any psychological practitioners working with CYP might need to interact with schools during their work, whether for assessment purposes, sharing a formulation or extending an intervention into school time. Increasingly, psychological practitioners are located within schools themselves, working directly with school staff as well as CYP and families. Practitioners may go into a school in an ad hoc way, be employed by the school as part of the pastoral care team or they may be part of an in-reach service to schools provided by CYPs mental health services. They may be part of a team, or they may be a lone mental health professional. Educational psychologists, who have always worked in education settings, continue to perform a vital role in helping schools meet their pupils' learning and emotional needs through assessment (including for statutory purposes), advice, consultation and some direct work with pupils. What is changing is that a wider range of psychological practitioners are now working in schools or considering doing so.

In the first section of this chapter, a rationale for working in schools is introduced, exploring how schools shape CYP's development and mental health, and summarising the policy and legislative context in which this work takes place. The second section covers how to set up in a school, including how they are organised, the roles of key staff and some good ways to get started in a new school. The third section describes the types of intervention available to

Child Psychology: Pathways to Good Practice, First Edition.
Edited by Helen Pote, Anna Picciotto and Clare Norris.

psychological practitioners, assesses the evidence that CYP, families and schools can benefit from such work, and considers how practitioners can measure the impact of what they do. Throughout the chapter, practical pointers towards becoming an established school practitioner are offered, including finding a shared language with staff and building a support network.

Psychological practitioners in schools are often working simultaneously in the health system and the education system. There are great benefits to be found in this overlap, for clients, organisations and practitioners, but it can be a complex matter. Practitioners 'joining' a school, but employed elsewhere, soon find that the core task of any school – learning and development – may not always align with the mental health and wellbeing focus of an applied psychology training. At points in this chapter, therefore, practitioners are encouraged to reflect on their experience of being in school, the impact of this personally, and how this shapes the work.

20.2 What is a School?

Most people reading this chapter will have attended school, so asking this question may sound strange, but it is posed here for two reasons. First, an aim of this chapter is to show that psychological concepts and theory can give many different, useful answers to this apparently simple question. The second reason is to highlight the importance of practitioners examining their most familiar ideas about schools and schooling.

Practitioners' education experiences – whether in a mainstream school, a more specialist setting, or being home educated, in the UK or in a different country – will shape their views about what schools can and should do. Box 20.1 is an invitation to practitioners to begin this chapter by reflecting on their own education.

Box 20.1 Schooling and you

Your education experiences can shape your ideas about schools and your work as a practitioner: how you define your role; your expectations of the environment; your responses to staff and pupils; and how it feels to go 'back to school'. It is recommended that you reflect on these experiences before you start the work, in order to increase awareness of your potential biases and to anticipate how the work might affect you. There are some suggested questions and prompts included. Your answers could be discussed with a supervisor, mentor or colleague. This is part of being a *reflective* practitioner, which is an essential competence for school-based psychological work.

1. What type of school did you attend?	• State or private? • Single sex or co-educational? • A religious school? • Did you board? • Urban or rural? • Large or small? • How many times did you change school?

2. How much did you enjoy learning?	• Were you considered to be 'academic'? • Did you experience teachers in a positive way? • Did you have special educational needs and, if so, were they diagnosed or supported? • Did you feel that you excelled in something and was that valued?
3. How much did you enjoy the social side of school?	• Did you have friends? • Were you part of a social group? • Were you picked on or bullied? • Did your friendships change and if so, how did you manage that? • Were most of your close friendships formed in school or other social settings?
4. How connected did you feel to the school as a community?	• Did you feel that you fitted in? • Were your parents/carers involved with your school? • Did you join in extra-curricular activities (sport/music/drama)? • Did you experience racism or other forms of discrimination?
5. What do you remember about the school's provision for social, emotional and mental health needs?	• Was there formal provision? • Were issues talked about in classes or assemblies? • How did your school respond to bullying?

20.2.1 Schools as Ecosystems

Being an effective psychological practitioner in a school has a lot to do with how the practitioner connects and collaborates with its pupils or students, as individuals or in small groups. But as discussed later, this work can also place practitioners in a helping role towards the school more broadly, as an organisation. They become part of a wider system; influencing it and being influenced in turn. Thinking about schools as systems is therefore an essential foundation for practice.

A useful framework for this is the *ecological model* of child development developed by Uri Bronfenbrenner (Bronfenbrenner & Morris, 2007), which identifies how pupils are influenced by different aspects of a school environment. Bronfenbrenner proposed that development can be understood as a series of systems that interact with each other over time. For example, a CYP and their teacher form a *microsystem*, as does the CYP with their school class and the CYP with their immediate family. These systems can themselves interact and influence each other. This may happen in visible ways, such as a parent or carer attending a school trip. A less direct example might be the influence of a parental separation: a child seeming more dependent on their teacher, and more withdrawn from their peer group, shows how these microsystems are connected. Bronfenbrenner used the term *mesosystem* for these webs of interconnected microsystems.

In this way, the whole network of people and influences around a CYP in school can be modelled. The *exosystem* is the system of connected social structures that influence pupil development without direct contact, such as a caregiver's workplace. Wider aspects of the culture and society where the child and school are located, such as the family's socioeconomic status, or government policy towards exams and assessment, are termed the *macrosystem* in Bronfenbrenner's model. Finally, as this collection of interacting systems around the child moves through time, it is the *chronosystem* that captures the level of environmental changes such as role transitions, and historical shifts such as changing attitudes to corporal punishment.

Four key messages can be drawn from the example provided. Different levels of a school organisation are connected. These connections are often two-way or *bidirectional*. Some risk and protective factors for CYP's wellbeing are unique to schools. Finally, it will be apparent that effective practitioners can intervene at different levels in the school system. It is this flexibility that brings some of the appeal and variety of school-based working.

20.3 Why Work in Schools?

20.3.1 Schools' Influences on Child Development

The ecosystemic model described earlier (Bronfenbrenner & Morris, 2007) is an overall framework for understanding the wide range of influences schools can have on their pupils' development. Next, some of the specific factors are considered in more detail.

Schools can be a positive influence on pupils' emotional development and mental health. They provide an alternative social experience to home, broadening exposure to peer group and other social influences in a wider, but still contained, community environment. Attachment bonds with staff can support pupils' resilience and emotional wellbeing (Verschueren & Koomen, 2012). Schools can teach executive functioning skills such as problem solving, communication and emotion regulation skills within a social context and can provide opportunities for achievement and success outside academia, for example through sport and arts programmes (Department for Education, 2021). Within the school curriculum, pupils will have access to universal psychoeducation on a range of topics including positive social, emotional and mental health. Trained counsellors and psychological practitioners can provide targeted psychological support within the school environment.

Child development reflects the interplay of risk and protective factors (Rutter, 1987), and many aspects of school life can influence wellbeing positively or negatively. For example, academic attainment can have a positive or negative impact on self-esteem and self-worth; exam and workload pressure can negatively impact on anxiety levels; peer groups can provide positive and/or risky influences including sexual harassment and drug and alcohol use; the school can provide a positive social environment but can also be a trigger for social anxiety. The predictable structure and routine of the school environment can help pupils feel safe and learn. For some pupils, however, especially those with neurodevelopmental differences, a relatively inflexible environment with high sensory stimulation (like a busy classroom) requires adaptation to meet their needs.

Sociological, psychological and public health research has examined the 'climate' and 'culture' of schools, but neither term is very precisely nor consistently defined, and they are sometimes used interchangeably. 'Climate' is generally used to refer to a collection of features that shape the pupil and teacher experience (safety, environment, teaching, relationships) whilst 'culture' refers to shared beliefs, norms and values within the school. The latter is more widely used in the UK research literature (Jessiman et al., 2022) and will be used in this chapter.

Individual school cultures vary enormously, but some common elements support pupils' wellbeing and mental health (Barker et al., 2023; Jessiman et al., 2022; Sellström & Bremberg, 2006). For example, qualitative research has linked higher-performing schools with strong leadership, higher teacher expectations for pupil attainment, successful parent engagement and lower job frustration levels for teachers (Baars et al., 2018). An emphasis on reparation and restorative justice by schools may reduce aggressive and violent behaviour in pupils (Bonell et al., 2015). School culture can also influence or mediate the impact of other interventions (Singla et al., 2021).

Some risks for poor child health and educational outcomes do not originate in schools, but schools can buffer or exacerbate their effects. Socioeconomic deprivation is one such factor, widely reported to be associated with worse physical and mental health outcomes (Reiss, 2013). In the UK, for example, schools provide free meals and other benefits to lower-income families through means-tested funding systems. However, there can be stigma attached to these benefits, and in some areas, schools cannot provide curriculum enhancements such as school trips without donations from parents/carers and charities. The Covid-19 pandemic highlighted this dichotomy. When UK schools closed, students from lower-income households – with less access to IT, learning space and parental support at home – experienced greater barriers to their learning and progress, and more social adversity due to more limited access to outdoor space (Blundell et al., 2022).

Schools also present unique risk factors to CYP's mental health. For example, the experience of being bullied or victimised in school is widely recognised to be associated with poor long-term outcomes in mental health, physical health, involvement in the criminal justice system and socioeconomic status (Arseneault, 2017; Bowes et al., 2015; Lereya et al., 2015). Schools in the UK have been required to have an antibullying policy since the 1990s.

Schools can perpetrate and maintain social inequalities, racism and other forms of discrimination. Black Caribbean students are three times more likely to be excluded (both temporarily and permanently) from school than their white peers (Gillborn et al., 2016), and the highest rates of permanent exclusion are seen among White Gypsy, Roma, Irish Traveller, Black Caribbean and Mixed White/Black Caribbean pupils (Barnardo's, 2020; Department for Education, 2023). Systemic racism in the school system has been suggested as an explanation for this difference and for the underachievement of pupils from non-white backgrounds. Examples of this include school discipline policies that inadvertently disadvantage minority ethnic groups, and the increased likelihood of school staff to interpret behaviour that challenges from black students as 'bad' or dangerous rather than as an indication of distress (Swiszczowski, 2022; YMCA, 2020). The disproportionate number of teachers and leaders from BAME backgrounds in UK schools, and the lack of a relevant, inclusive school curriculum, have been cited as further evidence of systemic racism (Demie & Huat See, 2023).

Sexuality and gender identity remain common causes of bullying in schools and are frequently reported to be mishandled by school staff (Menesini & Salmivalli, 2017; O'Donoghue & Guerin, 2017). Of pupils identifying as LGBT, 45% are reported to experience bullying due to their sexuality (Stonewall, 2017). Since 2020, it has been mandatory for English and Welsh schools to teach relationships education in primary schools and relationships and sex education in secondary schools. Schools have some flexibility in designing this curriculum: government advice is for teaching to be tailored to the school's local health priorities and to be politically impartial.

20.3.2 Mental Health Needs in Schools

Having briefly considered some developmental influences on mental health in schools, the outcomes of most relevance for psychological practitioners will now be covered: poorer mental health and impaired functioning, and how these can manifest in school settings.

Rates of probable mental disorders in CYP have increased since 2017 from one in nine (11.6%) to one in six (17.4%) in 6 to 16 year olds, and from 1 in 10 (10.1%) to one in six (17.4%) in 17 to 19 year olds. Rates in both age groups remained similar between 2020 and 2021 (NHS Digital, 2022a). In a school context, this equates to five pupils in every standard state school classroom (Young Minds, 2022). The rates of CYP with a diagnosed neurodevelopmental condition have also increased, with the incidence of attention deficit hyperactivity disorder (ADHD) in childhood now 5% (Sayal et al., 2018) and 1% for autism (NHS, 2022b). Rates of autism are expected to continue to rise, as referrals for specialist assessment continue to increase (NHS Digital, 2022b). Currently, over 70% of CYP with a diagnosis of autism are educated in mainstream schools (National Autistic Society, 2021).

Some symptoms or patterns of behaviour indicating mental health difficulties can become noticeable first in school, such as separation anxiety at drop-off time or difficulties with transitions between classes or into a new school. Conditions such as emotionally based school avoidance (EBSA) refer to behaviours or impairments (non-attendance, in this case) that are specific to school settings. Accordingly, there are school-specific risk factors for EBSA (bullying, transitions, difficult relationships with staff) as well as home/family factors (parental mental health issues, family stress or loss) and individual factors (other mental health difficulties, special educational needs or disability, trauma).

The wellbeing and mental health of school staff is also an important consideration. Prior to the Covid-19 pandemic, it was widely reported that teachers felt poorly skilled in recognising and managing CYP's mental health needs and overwhelmed by the pressure of their work responsibilities. Levels of teacher stress have since increased, with 59% of teachers and education staff considering leaving the profession in 2021/22 due to pressures on their own mental health and wellbeing (Savill-Smith & Scanlan, 2022).

20.3.3 Mental Health and Learning

As described earlier, the links between mental health and learning are bidirectional. This means that mental health problems affect educational access, engagement and attainment, while learning problems, including intellectual disability and adversity in education settings, can lead to a significant mental health burden for CYP.

Associations between mental health and school attendance are a good starting point for understanding this connection. Pupils with poorer mental health and/or neurodevelopmental conditions such as autism and ADHD are more likely to be persistently absent from school than their peers, and persistent absenteeism is an indicator of current or future poor mental health (John et al., 2022). In 2021–2022, 22% of CYP in England were persistently absent, missing 10% or more of their lessons, and 1.5% of CYP attended less than half their lessons (Children's Commissioner for England, 2022). Risk factors for absenteeism include having an Education Health and Care Plan (EHCP; the statutory framework for assessing and funding additional support for pupils with higher needs), being referred to children's social care, previous periods of absence and/or fixed term or permanent exclusions, and missing time in the first week of the school year (John et al., 2022).

The negative impact of poor mental health on CYP's learning trajectories and educational outcomes has been well-documented through international research (e.g. Brannlund et al., 2017; Dalsgaard et al., 2020) and recently more robustly evidenced in the UK. Lereya et al. (2019) found that behavioural difficulties, hyperactivity and inattention difficulties and difficulties with peer relationships were associated with poor attainment, while emotional difficulties and hyperactivity/inattention were associated with absenteeism, which impacts on attainment. In their longitudinal study, Smith et al. (2021) demonstrated that mental health difficulties between the ages of 11 and 14 were linked to poorer educational success at age 16, independent of other factors such as socioeconomic status and parental health. Chapter 27 describes the impact of trauma and developmental trauma on CYP's ability to access education, and the importance of schools adopting a trauma-informed approach to ameliorate that impact and avoiding further traumatisation.

Difficulties with learning, including specific learning difficulties such as dyslexia, can impact negatively on pupils' mental health in multiple ways. CYP with these additional needs can experience low self-esteem, frustration and isolation in school settings; this increases the risk of mental health disorders including anxiety and depression (e.g. Alesi et al., 2014). Special educational needs and disability (SEND) status is associated with increased prevalence of a range of mental health problems (Deighton et al., 2019).

20.3.4 Public Policy and School Mental Health

School provision for mental health is now part of UK government policy, funding conditions and inspection standards. Schools are advised to be aware of and respond to pupils' mental health and emotional wellbeing needs (Department for Education, 2022a) as well as SEND and safeguarding. EHCPs include mental health as a type of need meriting specialist in-school provision in some circumstances. Combining whole-school approaches to mental health (described in more detail later) with individual support is advocated in government advice (Department for Education, 2018). In England, joint inspections are carried out by the education regulatory body, Ofsted, and the health regulatory body, the Care Quality Commission, into localities' SEND provision.

The UK government green paper *Transforming Children and Young People's Mental Health* (Department of Health and Social Care and Department for Education, 2017) introduced a significant expansion of school-based mental health provision in England through the creation of Mental Health Support Teams (MHSTs). In these teams, Education Mental Health Practitioners (EMHPs) carry out school-based mental health prevention work and psychological interventions for common conditions (such as anxiety and depression) at mild to moderate levels of need and complexity. The green paper also outlined a new school leadership role, now called the Senior Mental Health Lead (SMHL). This is a senior member of staff who oversees the promotion of positive mental health in their school, including training and supporting the staff team, and links with local voluntary and NHS providers. MHSTs are tasked with supporting the work of the SMHL, as well as delivering interventions and providing advice and consultation to school staff on a range of mental health topics.

In Scotland, a 'named person' system was introduced under the 'Getting it right for every child' (GIRFEC) policies developed since 2012 (Children and Families Directorate, 2022). The named person is an identified professional within universal services, to provide advice and support from birth to 18, enable access and referrals, and sometimes be the lead professional in a multiagency group for CYP with higher levels of need. For the majority of CYP of school age the named professional is their guidance teacher or another school staff member, giving schools a vital role for CYP needing additional support.

While these policy developments have been welcomed by many in the mental health and education fields, some caution is needed. The MHST programme – including EMHPs and SMHLs – reached about a quarter of England's schools by 2022/2023 (NHS Digital, n.d.) and is not due to achieve 100% coverage until 2027/2028 (Garratt et al., 2022), so is not yet available to most pupils. Some ambiguities remain over roles and responsibilities for school staff, school senior leadership teams and governing bodies in this area. In England, supporting CYP's mental health and wellbeing is not covered in detail in Ofsted inspections or the teacher training curriculum (Department for Education, 2019).

There have been concerns about the 'therapeutic turn' in education settings (Foulkes & Stringaris, 2023). As well as highlighting the burden on educators, critiques of these developments point to the limited evidence for school-based psychological interventions, and have proposed that outcomes, including harms arising from interventions, should be more rigorously recorded. Like any psychological interventions, the potential benefits to CYP must be observed and measured, not assumed. Some of these issues are explored further in later Section 20.5.5 'Considering the Evidence' and Section 20.5.6 'Measuring Change'.

20.3.5 Current Support in Schools

Increasingly, many schools in the UK do have some specialist mental health support in place for students and staff. Sharpe et al. (2016) carried out a sample survey of schools in England and reported that two-thirds had specialist support in place, from a mixture of government funded, NHS, charity or third-sector providers. Mental health provision offered within a school setting is often focused on whole school, universal and preventative levels and on interventions for CYP with mild to social, emotional and mental health difficulties. Despite the mental health support available in many schools, Sharpe et al. (2016) found gaps in the links between schools and specialist CAMH services as well as in the availability of specialist mental health resources. This indicates that local provision can be disjointed, with school-based practitioners frequently working in isolation and no clear pathways between services.

Recent initiatives in school-based provision must therefore be considered in connection with the overall picture of funding and capacity for CYP's mental health. This is because there is an expectation that clinical interventions for CYP with moderate to severe mental health difficulties will be provided by specialist CAMHS. In 2004, it was estimated that fewer than 35% of CYP in the UK with a diagnosable mental health condition access specialist mental health services (Green et al., 2005). Targets to close this 'treatment gap' have been proposed (Mental Health Taskforce, 2015) but levels of need have since increased (Department for Education, 2022b; Garratt et al., 2022), exacerbated by the Covid-19 pandemic (Mansfield et al., 2022). This has been echoed by preliminary findings of the new joint inspections carried out by the education regulatory body in England, Ofsted, and the health regulatory body, the Care Quality Commission into SEND (which includes SEMH) in local areas. In many areas, schools still face difficulties accessing specialist support for CYP with SEMH needs (Care Quality Commission, 2022).

It is certainly true that mental health and emotional wellbeing is now widely talked about in schools, and that this is normalising, to a certain extent. However, receiving support within a school setting can be stigmatising and even shameful for some pupils. Having the choice to access support in alternative, less public settings is essential.

20.4 Setting Up in a School

20.4.1 Where to Start

This section covers some of the key questions when setting up to do psychological work in a school. Depending on the situation, responsibility for these steps might lie with the psychological practitioner, or a manager or supervisor. If senior supervisory relationships are not already in place to offer support, this must be resolved before proceeding.

The psychological practitioner may be working as part of an established service, with financing and allocated time already negotiated. Or they may be an independent practitioner, commissioned directly by a school for the first time. Whatever the setting, both the practical and psychological aspects of setting up will require attention.

20.4.2 Learning About the System

It is crucial to spend some time initially getting to know the school's staff, pupils and parents/carers. Just as practitioners understand the importance of the therapeutic relationship between themselves and their client to positive outcomes in treatment, the alliance between the practitioner and the school they are working in is also key to successful outcomes. Many psychological practitioners working in schools find it helpful to see the school as a 'client' and engaging them through building a positive relationship is key.

The school's aims and ethos, and its experience of working with other agencies that support the school to attend to the social, emotional and mental health needs of its population, will need to be understood. How the school responds to difference, to discrimination and to being challenged should be considered alongside practitioners' personal reflections. All of these will be key factors in building a successful working relationship and to the wellbeing of the practitioner working in the school. The key areas for developing a 'profile' of a school are now summarised.

Types of school

In the UK schools can be broadly categorised on three dimensions: how they are funded, the age of their pupils and the type of pupil need they cater to. Practitioners should also aim to find out the size and demographics of the school, including ethnicity, religion and sexuality, the number of pupils with English as a second language, its catchment area, the number of

Table 20.1 School types by age.

School Stage	Age of pupil	School Year (England and Wales)	School Year (Scotland)	School Year (Northern Ireland)	Key Stage (England)	Key Stage (Northern Ireland)	Curriculum Level (Scotland)	Progression Step (Wales)
Primary	4–5	Reception	P1	1	Foundation	Foundation	Early	1
	5–6	1	P2	2	1	Foundation	1st	1
	6–7	2	P3	3	1	1	1st	
	7–8	3	P4	4	2	1	1st	2
Middle/ Primary	8–9	4	P5	5	2	2	2nd	2
	9–10	5	P6	6	2	2	2nd	
	10–11	6	P7	7	2	2	2nd	3
Secondary	11–12	7	S1	8	3	3	3rd/4th	3
	12–13	8	S2	9	3	3	3rd/4th	
	13–14	9	S3	10	3	3	3rd/4th	4
	14–15	10	S4	11	4	4	Senior	4
	15–16	11	S5	12	4	4	Senior	5
Sixth Form/ Further Education	16–17	12	S6	13	-	-	Senior	5
	17–18	13	–	14	-	-	-	-

CYP on its SEND register and how many are eligible for free school meals. Each UK nation has a different system of stepped levels that mark expected learning and development for a given age range [1] (see Table 20.1). In Wales, Key Stages were replaced in 2022 with a more flexible system (Education Wales, n.d.).

Terms and timetable

The school year runs from September to the third week of July in England and Wales and mid-August to June in Scotland. School terms are arranged into three terms of 10–13 weeks, each with a week's holiday in the middle. In Northern Ireland, children get a longer summer break, with long weekends mid-term, rather than a whole week's break. The school day itself lasts around 6.5 hours, including up to an hour for assembly, breaks and lunch. A school may offer supportive or 'enrichment' activities that wrap around the core timetable such as a breakfast club or homework club. These sometimes incur a cost but may be means tested and subsidised.

School staff

Schools have a leadership hierarchy. The head teacher usually leads a senior leadership team (SLT) of deputies or assistant heads, although the exact terminology varies between schools and UK nations. Some schools may also have an Executive Head Teacher who holds some strategic responsibility for more than one school. Staff outside the SLT may also have important roles overseeing specific areas of the curriculum.

Several different staff might hold the responsibility for a school's provision around psychological wellbeing and mental health. Many schools separate out responsibility for

1 It is possible to defer starting school beyond these ages.

behaviour from pastoral care and it will be important to link with both. All schools have a Designated Safeguarding Lead (DSL) who is responsible for all safeguarding and child protection concerns, and all staff should have basic safeguarding training at least. Special Educational Needs and Disability Coordinators (SENDCOs) hold responsibility for coordinating provision for CYP with SEND, which includes social, emotional and mental health. Class teachers, form tutors and heads of year often hold knowledge of and some responsibility for the pastoral care needs of individual pupils. Teaching assistants in primary schools may support individual CYP, groups or whole classes with additional learning needs.

The school staff member linking with the psychological practitioner will be a key person for the success of the input to the school, so finding out about their role is important. How do they link to other staff involved in social, emotional and mental health and well-being and safeguarding? What is the pastoral care support in the school more generally? Box 20.2 illustrates one way that services can prioritise the working relationship between a school-based practitioner and their link member of staff.

Box 20.2 The 'reviewing' system in one school-based NHS CAMHS

In this service, the school CAMHS team is well-established. One of the key practices for oversight and support is a system of 'reviewers' – senior practitioners with experience of school-based work – to help new practitioners get set up and to provide ongoing support. Reviewers organise and chair a set-up meeting for a new school CAMHS practitioner. This is also attended by the practitioner and the member of school staff who will be the link. The meeting's agenda reflects the setting-up checklist (Box 20.3), and agreements made will form a contract for the forthcoming work.

Since the practitioners already have a supervisor and manager, the reviewer's specific responsibility is the relationship between the school and the practitioner. They hold a formal review meeting at least annually but are involved ad hoc should difficulties arise. Reviewers' allocations to specific schools change much less often than practitioners', where some turnover is inevitable. In this way, the reviewer 'holds' the relationship between the school and CAMHS and knows the history of that collaboration.

The team around the school

A wide range of external professionals can play a part in supporting the school's pupils and staff, directly or indirectly. The services available to a school vary considerably depending on location but are sometimes collectively known as the 'team around the school' or TAS. Psychological professionals working in a school are part of this TAS. Making connections with other TAS members can be key to supporting the work in a school, particularly where there is a lone psychological practitioner. Since the Future in Mind report (Children and Young People's Mental Health Taskforce, 2015), the UK government has recommended that every school has a dedicated named contact point in targeted or specialist mental health services. Table 20.2 outlines some of the professionals or agencies that might be available to a school, but these will vary depending on local resources as will the support they can provide.

Topics and Curriculum

What schools teach is determined by the curriculum they follow. Local-authority-maintained schools must adhere to the National Curriculum (NC) in England, or the local

Table 20.2 The team around the school.

Agency or profession	Role
Educational Psychologists	Core functions: consultation and advice; assessment; intervention; professional development and training; research and strategic development. Statutory responsibility to provide advice for CYP with SEND and to contribute to EHCPs.
Speech and Language Therapists	SLTs work directly with CYP, their families, and other education professionals to develop personalised strategies to support CYP's individual needs. They also provide training to education professionals so they can identify the signs of speech, language and communication needs and support them appropriately.
School outreach teams	Can include outreach support from specialist neurodevelopmental and behaviour support teams.
CAMHS	Linked CAMHS practitioner discusses and provides timely advice on the management and/or referral of CYP, including consultation, co-working or liaison. This may include targeted or specialist mental health staff who work directly in schools/GP practices/voluntary sector providers with CYP and families/carers.
Charities and independent organisations	Can include mentoring and third sector counselling services.
Children's Social Care/Social Work	Some local authorities provide a link social worker and/or early help worker to schools, linking with the school's DSL.

equivalent in Scotland (Curriculum for Excellence), Wales (Curriculum for Wales) and Northern Ireland (Northern Ireland Curriculum). In England, faith schools may diverge in religious studies, and academies and independent schools do not have to follow the NC. Pay particular attention to what the school already does within the curriculum to promote psychological wellbeing, in subjects such as Personal, Health and Social Education (PHSE). Many elements of PHSE can be considered as universally applied interventions for mental health promotion and psychoeducation.

Assessment and inspection

Assessment is an important part of school life, reflecting the core task of teaching and learning and the strong emphasis on standardised assessment in UK education policy and practice. Baseline testing in Key Stage 1 and 2 (or equivalent) varies between UK countries. GCSEs are the most common courses and public assessments at ages 14–16 in England and Wales. At sixth-form level in England and Wales, most students follow 2-year A-level courses in three or four subjects. In Scotland, students complete National Qualifications in S4–S6, Highers at 16 to 17 years and Advanced Highers at 17 to 18 years. It is important to know what assessments a school uses, and how they support pupils around exam time, especially those with additional needs. Exam stress has been a growing problem and some interventions in this area are discussed later.

It is important to know that schools themselves are assessed too. All UK countries have a system of formal inspection, comprising visits, a written inspection report and an overall grading for the school. In England, Ofsted is the government organisation that inspects all state schools and some independent schools about once every 4 years. Other independent schools are inspected by the Independent Schools Inspectorate. In Scotland, schools are inspected by Education Scotland using a sampling model rather than an inspection cycle for each school. Inspections can exert a strong influence on a school community. Well-rated schools will generally find it easier to attract staff and keep pupil numbers at target levels. A school deemed to be 'inadequate' risks having its leadership team replaced, must act quickly to address inspectors' concerns and is likely to be a more stressed organisation.

Box 20.3 Setting-up checklist

- Review the type of school, its pupils, catchment, history, recent inspection reports
- Read school policies for SEND, bullying, mental health, trauma-informed practice, behaviour management
- Get a copy of the school timetable and a staff list
- Identify a key member of staff to link with
- Identify a room and working space that provides an acceptable environment for confidential therapeutic work
- Identify a suitable time and day for regular visits
- Ask what psychological support the school has had before, and what the barriers and facilitators were
- Define the interventions you will offer
- Agree how referrals will be made to you
- Draw up a contract or agreement between you and the link staff member
- Publicise your offer to the wider staff group, and parents/carers and pupils as appropriate
- Contact members of the TAS and attend a TAS meeting
- Spend time observing in a range of classes, breaks and transition times

Consent, confidentiality and safeguarding

This is an essential area for practitioners to clarify when work is contracted, recognising that they are working within a school system with its own information governance framework and safeguarding policy. When offering direct clinical work to CYP and families in a school setting, parameters of confidentiality and consent will necessarily be slightly different. As the referrer, some members of the school staff team will know that the child is being seen. Others will become aware because they know a practitioner's role in the school and the child will leave class to see them. Although this can be normalising, the potential for the child to feel self-conscious or stigmatised should be considered on an individual basis.

When working in schools, the clinical governance arrangements of the psychological practitioner's employer should be made clear. This includes CYP decision making, consent and information sharing. Do not assume that school staff are familiar with the key health concepts and legislation, such as Gillick competence and mental capacity. Some secondary schools stipulate that parental consent must be obtained for CYP to be seen by their school practitioner in school regardless of Gillick competence. It is important to agree with the school and with the individual CYP, parent or carer how much information will be fed back to the school/referrer and how that information will be shared.

The practitioners' role in offering indirect support and consultation to school staff regarding individual or groups of CYP should also be clarified. Some schools introduce their TAS in information to parents/carers and inform them that the school may consult that team if they are concerned about emotional health or wellbeing of any pupil. How those consultations are recorded will depend on the practitioner's organisation and setting but should be agreed in advance with the school. If offering reflective practice consultations to individual or groups of staff, the boundaries and parameters of the work must be included in the contracting (Mattison & Fredman, 2018).

Responsibility for the safeguarding of all pupils in a school (promoting their welfare and protecting from harm) lies with the school's DSL, as described earlier. They will need to be informed about any safeguarding concerns that arise for CYP when working directly or indirectly. If referrals need to be made to children's social care, the practitioner will need to agree who is leading on this (which may depend on who is holding the highest level of concern) and to what extent it can be done jointly. Managing differences in levels of safeguarding concern in a school is complicated and psychological practitioners should find out where to get safeguarding advice from their employer, and key contacts in children's social care for reporting concerns. It is also important to know which safeguarding or child protection meetings need to be attended.

20.4.3 Using Supervision

Supervision has been mentioned several times already (see Chapter 4 for a more detailed discussion). It is important to emphasise one other key task for supervision, which is to support the practitioner in working with the *combination* of issues, systems and relationships they will encounter. Left unexplored, this combination, and the experience of being (in some cases) the sole representative of the employing organisation, has the potential for increased practitioner stress. In addition to supervision, school-based services should consider providing reflective practice and other supportive arrangements such as those described in Box 20.2 . Box 20.4 provides an example of how a practitioner might use supervision.

Box 20.4 Example of using supervision for school issues

A practitioner working in two primary schools and one secondary school meets their supervisor for routine fortnightly supervision. They agreed the following items for discussion.

Agenda

- Brief caseload review and case presentation following assessment of a primary pupil.
- Issue with availability of link staff member in primary school.
- Frequent interruptions of sessions in secondary school.

Discussion

- Caseload and individual client questions were discussed first, prioritising questions relating to risk or safeguarding.
- At the primary school, the practitioner explained, their link staff member (the deputy head) had been cutting short meetings, and last week cancelled it altogether. The supervisor asked questions to review the general engagement level of the school with the practitioner. Staff feedback, referral rates and rapport with the staff link all seemed favourable. It also emerged that the staff link had recently been covering teaching duties for a colleague on sickness absence. Agreed plans were to raise the matter with the staff link, consider changing their meeting times and clarify an alternative staff member in the SEND team that the practitioner could approach when the staff link was unavoidably called away.
- The practitioner described several recent examples of school staff trying to enter their allocated room during 1:1 sessions with pupils. Some staff wanted access to the cupboards in the room, and on another occasion a staff member wanted urgent safeguarding advice. The supervisor agreed with the practitioner that this needed addressing for sessions in school to continue. The supervisor suggested that, as well as raising the issue with their staff link there (the SENDCO), the practitioner consider the staff team's overall understanding of the nature and requirements of their work. The practitioner decided to ask to join a staff meeting to introduce themselves to new staff, describe their work including the importance of a confidential space and answer questions. They agreed that the team manager might also need to liaise with the school if the interruptions continued.

The example in Box 20.4 shows the need for the school to be considered as a 'client' on the supervision agenda at times, without forgoing adequate supervision of specific CYP interventions. It is these interventions, and the wide range of approaches available to school-based practitioners, that are considered next.

20.5 School-based Interventions

Psychological interventions in schools can be grouped along several dimensions. *Prevention* seeks to avert or ameliorate psychological problems before they reach an impairing level, versus *treatment* for pupils already showing significant mental health need. Prevention work is said to be: *universal* if offered to all pupils regardless of need; *targeted* if pupils are selected based on the presence of additional risk factors; and *indicated* if offered based on elevated need. Interventions may involve *direct* pupil contact, or *indirect* work with staff or other adults. The intervention may be *school-specific* in aims and design, or a school-based delivery of a more *general* therapy or group developed in another setting.

20.5.1 Whole-school Approaches

A whole-school approach (WSA) to mental health means developing and implementing a set of policies and practices that aim to promote the mental health and psychological wellbeing of pupils, parents/carers and staff. This is a strand of schools' wider responsibility for health promotion. The World Health Organization's Health Promoting Schools model (Langford et al., 2014, 2017) proposes that schools can effect change through three basic areas, which are directly linked to school culture, as described earlier:

- the formal health curriculum;
- school ethos and environment; and
- engaging with families and communities.

By their nature, WSAs are multifaceted interventions with variable components. There is significant policy support for the use of WSAs and an accumulation of evidence in favour of their impact (Weare & Nind, 2011). Key principles of WSAs have been set out by Public Health England (2015) and Weare (2015a), and these are closely followed by more recent national guidance to schools. For example, in Scotland, schools are advised to consider the following for their WSA (Mental Health in Schools Working Group, 2021).

1. Leadership and management that supports mental health and wellbeing across the school.
2. An ethos and environment that promotes positive and respectful relationships and values diversity.
3. Effective curriculum and learning and teaching to promote resilience and support mental, emotional, social and physical wellbeing and learning.
4. Enabling CYP's voices and participation to influence decisions.
5. Supporting staff professional learning and development to ensure their own and others' wellbeing.
6. Identifying need and monitoring impact of interventions.
7. Working with parents, carers and the wider community.
8. Targeted support and appropriate pathways to the right support.

National Institute for Health and Care Excellence (NICE) guidance in England and Wales (NICE, 2022) recommends that schools in England and Wales should account for neurodiversity and communication needs in their WSA and should employ a stepped-care approach to providing targeted interventions.

Psychological practitioners can be involved in many parts of the WSA, and finding out about it is an essential part of getting to know a school. Schools vary considerably in how far their WSA is codified and explicit, however; some may have a single document but in others, key information may exist across several school policies. Involving CYP in the development of the WSA is recommended and feasible with the right process (Forshaw & Woods, 2022).

Adoption of a WSA is rarely uniform in practice across school staff, especially at first. Implementation of a WSA is usually a staged process that takes place over terms or years, which is why leadership and integration with the curriculum are particularly important for the WSA to be fully delivered and maintained.

Trauma-informed practice is the deliberate creation of school environments that are sensitive to the neurobiological, psychological and relational impacts of adverse childhood events (ACEs) and developmental trauma on pupils (Chafouleas & Overstreet, 2016). Trauma-informed approaches have four core aims (Substance Abuse and Mental Health Services Administration, 2014):

- Realisation of the pervasive effects of trauma;
- recognising the signs of trauma in pupils, staff and parents/carers;
- respond by integrating knowledge about trauma into policies, procedures and practices; and
- resist re-traumatising CYP.

Trauma-informed practice can be one part of a wider WSA, and NICE recommends schools 'take into account the value of trauma-informed approaches' (NICE, 2022). Programmes are multifaceted (Phifer & Hull, 2016), potentially involving changes to staff training, behaviour management approaches, curriculum, assessment, timetable and policies, as well as targeted and indicated trauma-focused interventions for some pupils (Fondren et al., 2020). Successful implementation of a trauma-informed approach is therefore a significant endeavour requiring clear leadership and ongoing maintenance (see Chapter 27 for more information.)

20.5.2 Formulation

A formulation is an explanatory account of a client's needs, difficulties or symptoms based on one or more psychological theories or models (Johnstone & Dallos, 2013). Formulating is the process – typically collaborative and iterative – of constructing a formulation, covered in more detail in Chapter 3.

As discussed, the 'client' may to some extent be the school itself. In this sense, tailoring a WSA model to a specific school's needs is a form of organisational formulation. Formulation has direct and indirect aspects as an intervention. Some parts of the process take place with the client but others happen in supervision or professional discussion.

Two distinctive aspects of school-based formulation for individual CYP are also worth considering. First, the *content* of a formulation will usually include more information about school-specific factors, such as a teacher–pupil relationship, exam stress, school engagement or peer networks. This follows from the additional assessment information it is possible to gather in school. To accommodate this, practitioners may need to amend formulation templates or resources aimed at clinic settings (under supervision as needed). Second, *sharing* a formulation works differently in schools, due to the organisational setting and the nature of indirect working and consultation. The issues discussed in the section 'Consent, confidentiality and safeguarding' apply here. Key ideas from a formulation may need to be understood by several staff members, especially in secondary schools or larger primaries (see Box 20.5 for an example).

Box 20.5 Sharing a formulation in school

A 11-year-old White British boy was referred by the Head of Year in their school (a large urban secondary) to their allocated practitioner from a third-sector child mental health provider. The practitioner was female, in her late 20s and of White European ethnicity. The main concerns were that the boy seemed easily distractible in lessons, could only focus with effort and seemed restless and fidgety. He was attaining several years below

(Continued)

Box 20.5 (Continued)

age expectations and his attendance rate was about 55%. The Head of Year wondered if the boy needed assessing for ADHD.

In the practitioner's initial assessment session, the boy was able to explain that he had been repeatedly bullied by peers in the previous academic year. Most of his lessons now were attended by one or more of these peers, and he felt strong anxiety whenever he was near them. Careful history-taking indicated that the level of distractibility, hyperactivity and lower attainment had appeared in the past year. The boy did not want further action against the bullies, saying it had stopped now, but the practitioner obtained consent to share information with key staff about its aftermath.

In supervision the practitioner developed a provisional formulation of anxiety-driven difficulties, informed by cognitive-behavioural psychological models. The links between bullying, isolation, anxiety and concentration were pivotal in the formulation (Christina et al., 2021), rather than primarily a neurodevelopmental or learning problem. Fear of negative peer evaluation and social avoidance were among the hypothesised maintaining factors (Kingery et al., 2010). The practitioner planned some screening questions for post-traumatic stress disorder (PTSD) to the bullying, as well as discussing the provisional formulation with the boy, in a follow-up session.

After validating the formulation, the practitioner offered the Head of Year and SENDCO a feedback meeting to share it with them. Staff had been aware of some bullying but thought it had been 'dealt with' at the time. The Head of Year suggested some changes to seating and small-group arrangements that could be made without drawing attention to the reason, as well as increasing opportunities for positive social interaction. The practitioner shared some psychoeducation about the impact of bullying on mental health, and how high anxiety can present in the classroom and obstruct learning. The school's antibullying policy was due for review and the SENDCO asked the practitioner to contribute some advice to this process.

20.5.3 Indirect Interventions

Indirect interventions are those that do not include the CYP or family participating in meetings or sessions. These are a natural fit for school-based mental health, as many more pupils are reached than could be seen individually per practitioner.

Consultation is one of the most important forms of indirect intervention. The term refers to discussion between a consultant and consultee, usually with a specific CYP or school issue in mind. In its original sense, the consultee seeks the expertise of a consultant who possesses knowledge they do not. Nowadays, often influenced by systemic or psychoanalytic practices, school consultation is a more collaborative engagement in which there is meaning in each participant's knowledge of the material under discussion (Fredman et al., 2018). For school-based practitioners, staff are the most likely group to take part in consultation. Like any other intervention, practitioners offering consultation should be trained in a relevant model or practices and have adequate supervision and support.

Facilitating *reflective practice* can be an important indirect intervention for psychological practitioners. Reflective practice refers generally to reviewing and reflecting on actions, decisions and experiences and is deemed essential for many practitioner roles (Health and Care Professions Council, 2021; Lilienfeld & Basterfield, 2020). In schools, psychological practitioners often contribute to reflective practice by facilitating groups, adding mutual support and shared learning to the reflective process. In some circumstances, practitioners may also join reflective practice groups as a participant. Unlike consultation, which often takes a single meeting, there are usually multiple sessions or an ongoing commitment to reflective practice.

As well as being intended to influence future staff practice, especially with pupils who might be the focus of group discussion, reflective practice can contribute to the staff wellbeing aspects of a WSA by providing a safe space for staff to consider the emotional impact of their work. Reflective practice is not supervision, and the psychological practitioner does not generally hold any direct management or governance responsibility for the practice under discussion (while retaining their professional safeguarding responsibilities and duty of care). Reflective practice spaces therefore need careful distinguishing from more directive input at the setting-up stage.

Training for school staff is often a valued way for practitioners to support pupils' wellbeing and contribute to the school community. Delivering training with school staff or other agencies has the added benefits of collaborative working, with joint training an established marker of integration between organisations (Cooper at al., 2016). Substantial trainings like the Solihull Approach (Douglas, 2004) can themselves be critical parts of a WSA. Psychological practitioners may also be called on to deliver training on specific topics such as responding to self-harm or anxiety.

Attendance at *professionals' meetings* gives opportunities for psychological practitioners to be involved in the planning and delivery of interventions. Meetings focused on a single CYP or family are held under different names, including Team Around the Child (TAC) meetings or Child's/Young Person's Plan Meeting (CYPPM) in Scotland. TAC meetings are often convened by the school, but any professional can do this; in Scotland the CYPPM is convened by the named person, typically their guidance teacher or similar. Some meetings may be called by social workers under their statutory duties, such as child protection investigations or review meetings for CYP looked after under a care order. In these, the chairing and agenda will be held by the social worker and the practitioner is there to contribute their psychological understanding of the CYP's needs. In all such meetings about a named CYP, psychological practitioners should be ready to talk in simple terms about their work with the CYP; their team's view of the needs, strengths and risks; their formulation of these; and plans for intervention (if any). In doing so, practitioners must respect confidentiality, and its limits, and should seek supervisory or management support as needed in advance of a meeting.

Professional or multiagency meetings with a wider agenda and standing membership are known as TAS meetings. These are attended by school staff with key pastoral responsibilities, plus external professionals connected to the school, reflecting the school's position in a network of services and agencies. The agenda and format can vary considerably but they can consider the needs of specific pupils where inter-agency working is a particular factor, as well as wider issues and incidents in the school community.

Practitioners can also attend to and support the functioning of the professional group itself in settings like TAC or TAS meetings. Models of group process (Yalom & Leszcz,

2005) or team-based mentalising approaches (Bevington et al., 2017) can be useful guides in this area. For example, naming dilemmas and difficulties in the work, perspective-taking, reflecting on one's own experience of a group or meeting, all have the potential to assist the professional group, and in the process contribute to the delivery of the WSA.

Observations involve the practitioner spending time in school watching one or more CYP over time. They may be carried out to support a direct piece of work, such as observing the behaviour of a CYP who is reported to be isolated. Observations can also be focused on a group or whole class, to explore issues such as peer relationships, help-seeking or anxiety. The follow-up to an observation may be informal feedback, a more organised staff consultation, liaison with clinical colleagues or other steps. Remember that observations typically yield valuable information about staff–CYP and staff–staff relationships. If these were not the focus of the request, the practitioners should consider what is appropriate to feed back about these parts of the observation, and how best to do so.

Signposting and referral to other services is a specific form of advice giving in which practitioners recommend services for schools to consider using for a CYP. This can take place in many of the meetings and spaces previously described, and practitioners may also signpost for CYP they see directly. When signposting relates to safeguarding concerns, it is essential to reach clear agreement between professionals about who will make an enquiry or referral, and document this in clinical records.

Since the CYP is not present, it is essential that indirect interventions reflect their needs and wishes. So-called 'Pupil Voice' spaces, focus groups, school councils, feedback from parents or carers, are all viable ways to achieve this.

20.5.4 Direct Interventions

Much universal direct work takes place at the *curriculum* level and is delivered by teaching or pastoral staff or assistants. For example, social and emotional learning (SEL) programmes are designed to promote wellbeing and emotional development, using a combination of games, group tasks, role play and whole-school activities (Weare & Nind, 2011). To avoid repetition or gaps, psychological practitioners should find out what interventions of this kind the school has already delivered for a pupil before starting a piece of direct work.

Large-format *group activities* like assemblies and class workshops allow practitioners to deliver psychoeducation content directly to pupils. Commonly requested topics are exam stress, sleep, anxiety reduction and peer problems. Whether delivered to the whole school, year group or key stage cohorts, or individual classes, practitioners should bear the following general principles in mind when planning assemblies or workshops.

- Make time to discuss the request or 'commission' with the requesting person in school, in order to understand their aims for the session.
- Ask about the group, to learn about what engages them and how best to communicate the material.
- Make sure the content is accurate by using reputable sources (with credit) such as textbooks or journal articles, local or national government documents, university teaching materials or websites of established charities.
- Re-purpose, adapt and tailor existing content from the employing service wherever possible to save time.

- Involve CYP in the development and/or delivery of the session where possible and appropriate.
- Consider how to evaluate the success of your session, through informal feedback, surveying, follow-up curriculum work and so on.

At a more targeted level, several *prevention programmes* for anxiety and depression based on cognitive behaviour therapy (CBT) have been evaluated. For example, FRIENDS groups (Barrett & Turner, 2001) can be delivered on a targeted or indicated basis. In these, pupils learn cognitive, behavioural and physiological strategies to identify anxiety, challenge anxious thoughts and problem-solve. The CUES-Ed programme is a CBT-based whole school approach for primary age children that has been shown to target stigmatising appraisals of emotional expression and cognitive biases (Underwood et al., 2023. There have been calls for school-based prevention programmes to include family members (Gondek & Lereya, 2018), since conflicts with parents are a key risk factor for lower reported wellbeing and mental health problems (Patalay & Fitzsimons, 2016) and parent-led CBT has shown promising results (Creswell et al., 2022).

Assessments and screening may be carried out either as a stand-alone task, or to inform the selection process for further interventions. Assessment (gathering information about a CYP and their mental health, level of functioning and their wishes) is a core activity for most psychological practitioners in any setting. A comprehensive description of CYP mental health assessment practices can be found in Chapter 3, but some school-specific elements may be noted here. Practitioners usually have easier access to school-specific information, including: staff impressions; school engagement; the nature of key staff relationships; learning and attainment; upcoming tests or exams; and transition plans. Standardised questionnaires should be used to augment clinical observations and self-report by CYP. Some common measures are given in Section 20.5.6 'Measuring change'. Cohort screenings, in which all pupils in a class, year group or key stage complete a standardised mental health questionnaire, can be useful when identifying pupils in need proves difficult, but require significant time from schools and practitioners. For example, screenings should only be carried out with appropriate clinical support in place to follow up promptly any CYP expressing suicidality. With all assessment and screening activities, practitioners should consider the extent to which they share membership of the school system with the CYP, and how they are positioned from the CYP's point of view. This is different from a traditional clinic setting, in which an assessing practitioner would never be a part of the CYP's other key systems such as their household. For example, does a practitioner seem more like a staff member or a visitor? Reflection of this kind may give ideas about how best to engage CYP in assessments and screenings.

Counselling interventions – meaning those delivered directly to pupils primarily using non-directive, humanistic or person-centred therapeutic approach – are a mainstay of indicated prevention and early intervention in many schools. It is one of the most frequently delivered mental health approaches for CYP in the UK (Garratt et al., 2022), with 'therapeutic individual counselling' named by most schools as part of their offer (Cooper, 2009). Common presenting issues are family problems, anger and academic problems; CYP often reported helpful aspects of counselling being 'getting things off one's chest', problem solving, guidance and insight (Cooper, 2009). Counselling is sometimes carried out with little or no involvement from the adults around the CYP. When systemic family or school factors seem to be maintaining a CYP's difficulties, links with this network need careful consideration. Department for Education guidance on commissioning and implementing school counselling is in place in England (Department for Education, 2016), and local authorities are legally required to provide school counselling in Wales (Welsh Government/Llywodraeth Cymru, 2013).

Low-intensity psychological interventions derive from more established therapies but are briefer and involve little or no direct input from a practitioner. They have become increasingly common in recent years (Roach et al., 2023). Guided self-help (GSH) is a type of low-intensity intervention used for CYP at the targeted prevention and mild/moderate treatment levels. A GSH protocol is designed to provide a simplified, accessible version of an established evidence-based psychological therapy. They are among the most common interventions delivered under the MHST programme (Ellins et al., 2023). Examples include GSH for anxiety, based on CBT and self-help principles and strategies, or programmes based on Incredible Years (Webster-Stratton, 1992) and social learning theory (Bandura, 1973). Specific considerations for GSH are the ability of the CYP or other client swiftly to form a collaborative working relationship, motivation to work between contacts and lower level of symptoms and risk consistent with brief, manualised help.

Individual *psychological therapies* delivered in schools are higher-intensity interventions for CYP already showing significant or diagnosable mental health needs or conditions. It is possible to use some of the preventative protocols mentioned above in this way. For example, CBT-based approaches such as FRIENDS (Barrett & Turner, 2001) can be delivered effectively in a one-to-one format (Stallard et al., 2005; Stallard et al., 2014). School-specific interventions seem to be effective at reducing depression and anxiety, but it is unclear if these gains are maintained (Gee et al., 2020; Stallard, 2013). Standard evidence-based therapies for common difficulties such as generalised anxiety, depression, OCD and panic can be adapted to the school setting. For example, in CBT the greater accessibility of peer interactions may alter the focus of behaviour experiments; in a range of interventions, key school staff may receive psychoeducation as part of the intervention in addition to parents (with appropriate consent).

Groups are the final main type of direct intervention used by psychological practitioners. They may also be school-specific by design or adapted for school settings. Interpersonal Psychotherapy–Adolescent Skills Training (IPT–AST) is an example of a group programme successfully delivered in schools (Young et al., 2006). IPT-AST is delivered at an indicated level over 12 weeks, with adolescents typically identified by high scores on a depression screening tool. Content includes psychoeducation about depression, exploring links between interactions and feelings, role play and rehearsal of new communication skills, and strategies to reduce conflict and build support in relationship networks. It links emerging symptoms of depression to interpersonal problems such as conflict in important relationships, disruptive transitions, unresolved grief or long-term isolation.

20.5.5 Considering the Evidence

A growing amount of research evidence is available to the school-based practitioner. Best practice decision making arises from combining the available evidence, client preferences and practitioner judgement to make intervention plans that are agreed with supervisors and MDT colleagues (Shafran et al., 2014). When seeking evidence on a specific topic or intervention practitioners should make sure of a range of sources, including: asking colleagues and supervisors; textbooks and manuals; NICE guidance, quick literature searches using Google Scholar or similar; and systematic searches using databases such as PubMed or EBSCO. Systematic reviews that synthesise and evaluate research in a particular area for practitioners may be particularly helpful. The remainder of this section summarises key evidence relating to the main interventions carried out by school-based practitioners.

Before considering specific programmes, it is useful to understand the evidence relating to implementation. This means the decisions and conditions that determine how an intervention is carried out in a particular setting. In research, these factors may also be called moderators and mediators of a programme's effects. For example, most of NICE's recommendations for targeted support (NICE, 2022) are about implementation and apply to any intervention: clear ways of identifying need; involving parents/carers and CYP; links with other agencies; and so forth. Work by Durlak et al. (2011) analysing the wide range of outcomes for SEL programmes defined four elements of the more successful ones. These have wider relevance for many universal and psychoeducation interventions.

- Skills development follows a logical sequence.
- Active learning approaches are used.
- Staff and pupils have time to focus on the programme.
- Programme components explicitly address the desired skills.

Implementation also concerns the barriers and facilitators to successful mental health work in schools. A thematic synthesis of this evidence by Gee et al. (2021) yielded 11 factors relating to interventions, organisation, provider and the wider community (see Figure 20.1).

Gee et al.'s (2021) synthesis could be considered a real-world application of the ecosystemic approach discussed at the start of this chapter. The themes may be used as a template for practitioners planning the introduction of a new intervention, reviewing a completed piece of work, or seeking to troubleshoot implementation challenges. With the importance of implementation in mind, the evidence for different intervention types is now considered.

Whole-school programmes are heterogenous and evolve over time. This means it is challenging to demonstrate real-world efficacy, and standardised ways of measuring their impact are lacking. Nonetheless, some research indicates that common WSA elements, such as teaching, pastoral care and interagency practices, show measurable benefits for pupil wellbeing when delivered together (Weare, 2015b; Weare & Nind, 2011). In this context, it is unsurprising that many elements of effective WSAs are represented in Gee et al.'s (2021) implementation themes described earlier. Despite the systemic aims of most WSAs, Wignall et al. (2022), reviewing WSA evaluations between 2003 and 2017, found that most measured pupil-level effects (e.g. behaviour, attainment or internalising symptoms), rather than wider factors such as school culture and ethos.

Trauma-informed approaches show promise but need more study of their impact. A recent systematic review by Avery et al. (2021) identified just four studies of multi-faceted, school-wide programmes and concluded that this evidence of their efficacy was of low strength. Improving this picture is a priority, given the adoption and currency already achieved by trauma-informed practice. There is more evidence for individual components

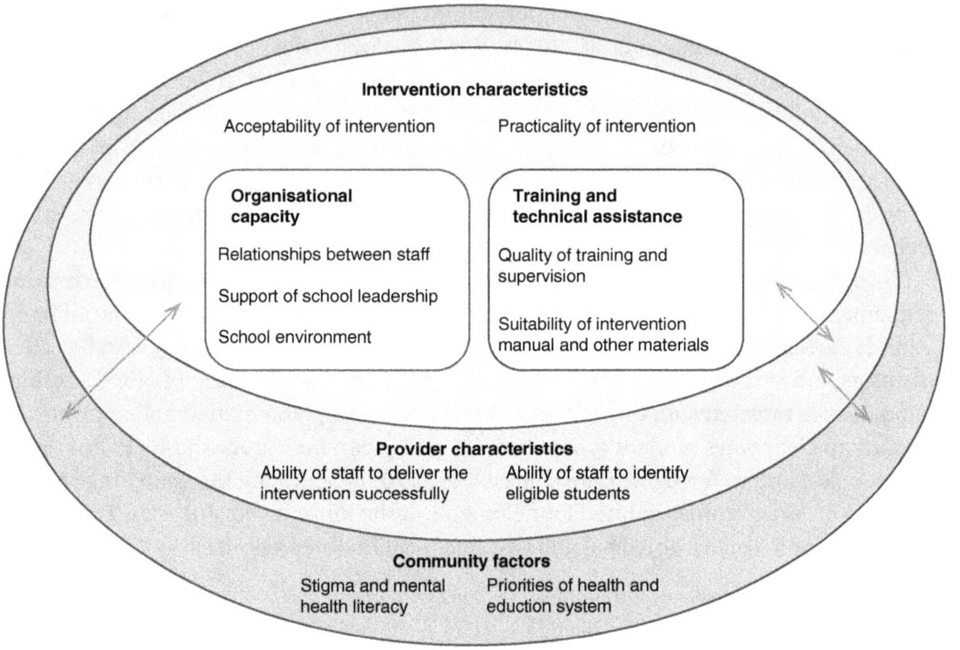

Figure 20.1 Success factors for school-based mental health interventions. Gee et al. (2021) / John Wiley & Sons / CC BY 4.0.

of a trauma-informed approach, for example, some whole-class or individual interventions show small beneficial effects on posttraumatic symptoms in 5 to 11 year olds (Bagneris et al., 2021), and trauma-informed training can successfully influence staff attitudes and reduce burnout (MacLochlainn et al., 2022).

Universal prevention, including classroom sessions, teacher training and parent-focused sessions for internalising or externalising problems (Paulus et al., 2016), can show positive outcomes for staff and pupil behaviour change (Durlak et al., 2011; Public Health Guidelines Team, 2022) and may reduce suicide attempts in adolescents (World Health Organization, 2017). SEL programmes can lead to small to moderate improvements in social and emotional skills, positive social behaviours, academic performance and conduct problems over at least 1 year (Taylor et al., 2017). Across this research, it is still the case that academic outcomes are not routinely included in study designs (Werner-Seidler et al., 2017) and when measured, the impact on attainment tends to be small (Weare & Nind, 2011).

Studies of preventative mental health interventions commonly find larger effects when CYP experiencing more difficulties are recruited (e.g. Stice et al., 2009). This might be expected, since measuring symptom change is best suited to identifying treatment effects. Werner-Seidler et al. (2017) found that, for depression, indicated and targeted programmes outperformed universal interventions, but this difference was not apparent for anxiety. As an example of targeted prevention, depression and anxiety programmes appear to be effective for children of depressed or anxious parents (Havinga et al., 2021). In a more recent analysis, indicated anxiety prevention has been shown to have small positive effects maintained for up to 1 year (Hugh-Jones et al., 2021).

NICE guidance to schools recommends adopting a WSA and using trauma-informed practices (NICE, 2022). In terms of direct prevention, NICE suggests schools choose interventions that focus on strengths, align with the school's WSA, and are 'informed by mindfulness or cognitive behavioural approaches' where suitable training allows (NICE, 2022). Since NICE's review, however, further research found adverse outcomes for some CYP, prompting widespread re-assessment of the suitability of universal mindfulness-based interventions for CYP (Montero-Marin et al., 2022). It should also be noted that the review process for NICE (NICE, 2022) excluded interventions delivered at school but outside teaching hours, somewhat limiting the scope of these recommendations.

School-based counselling using a humanistic model was evaluated in a recent large-scale trial in 18 London secondary schools (Cooper et al., 2021). Small improvements in pupils' distress were found after 12 counselling sessions and persisted at 3-month follow up, relative to a control group receiving pastoral care as usual. This counselling intervention did not demonstrate cost-effectiveness, although this is also unverified for many of the interventions discussed here. In other research, CYP attending counselling report benefits to their capacity to learn and study (Rupani et al., 2014).

Guided and non-guided self-help interventions in schools have received less attention to date, but this is changing as their use in England significantly increases under the MHST programme. A meta-analysis by Bennett et al. (2019) found moderate reductions in anxiety, depression and behavioural symptoms. According to these findings, self-help and GSH overall seem to be more effective than no intervention, but slightly less effective than many face-to-face interventions. Bennett et al. (2019) note that more robust research is needed in this area, and the implementation of GSH in MHSTs specifically remains to be evaluated at scale.

Although there is much still to discover, the evidence for school-based interventions is already sufficient to guide psychological practitioners in selecting and implementing the best available approaches for their clients. It is vital that practitioners include in their 'offer' to schools only those interventions in which they are competent and will receive supervision and support (including managing risk and safeguarding issues). Beyond this, a clear understanding of the interventions already available from school staff and the TAS will help identify what a new practitioner can add.

20.5.6 Measuring Change

For the school-based practitioner, evaluating the efficacy and impact of interventions often takes place in two contexts at once: their employing organisation and the school itself. As seen above, in a mental health paradigm the typical outcomes are a reduction in symptoms, or signs of distress and disorder. A huge range of questionnaires and observation schedules is available to measure change. The choice of measure will be determined by the practitioner's service policy and resources, as well as the needs and intervention type (see Chapter 8). For direct interventions, Measures that include teacher-completed items, such as the Strengths and Difficulties Questionnaire (Goodman et al., 2003) and Connors rating scales (Conners, 2008) are particularly useful.

School staff may be more interested in a pupil's attendance, behaviour and attainment than their symptoms. These can be important markers of wellbeing and functioning, and pupils themselves may have goals for change in these areas. This does not mean psychological practitioners should routinely measure their impact in such ways, however, even though (as discussed earlier) they are closely linked to mental health. Other specialists like educational psychologists are better able to intervene in many aspects of learning and attainment. Rather, it is crucial to discuss hopes for change with key staff when considering a school-based intervention and addressing any misaligned expectations at an early stage.

The impact of indirect interventions can be more difficult to measure, but there are several options available. Feedback scales like the Consultation Partnership Scale and Consultation Outcome Scale (Worwood & Fredman, 2018) can yield rich information, especially when used as the basis for further discussion and reflection. Validated measures are available for some domains that have seen long-standing research interest, such as staff stress and burnout (Kyriacou, 2011). Practitioners can also gather qualitative information about change in school. Observations, teacher report and some of the other assessment approaches discussed earlier can be repeated periodically, and at the end of interventions.

20.6 Conclusion

School-based mental health intervention is a fascinating, cross-disciplinary area of applied psychology. The authors hope that in this chapter they have conveyed their enthusiasm for this work as well as some encouragement for psychological practitioners setting foot in school again after some time. Learning is an essential process in psychological therapies, as well as in education. This fundamental connection should guide practitioners' own learning and development towards skilled and confident practice in schools.

References

Alesi, M., Rappo, G., & Pepi, A. (2014). Depression, anxiety at school and self-esteem in children with learning disabilities. *Journal of Psychological Abnormalities*, *3*(3), 1–8.

Arseneault, L. (2017). The long-term impact of bullying victimization on mental health. *World Psychiatry*, *16*(1), 27–28.

Avery, J. C., Morris, H., Galvin, E., Misso, M., Savaglio, M., & Skouteris, H. (2021). Systematic review of school-wide trauma-informed approaches. *Journal of Child & Adolescent Trauma*, *14*(3), 381–397.

Baars, S., Shaw, B., Mulcahy, E., & Menzies, L. (2018). *School cultures and practices: supporting the attainment of disadvantaged pupils*. LKMCo, Department for Education. https://potentialplusuk.org/wp-content/uploads/2022/02/London_Effect_Qual_Research_-_Research_Report_FINAL_v2.pdf

Bagneris, J. R., Noel, L. T., Harris, R., & Bennett IV,, E. (2021). School-based interventions for posttraumatic stress among children (ages 5–11): Systematic review and meta-analysis. *School Mental Health*, *13*(4), 832–844.

Bandura, A. (1973). *Social learning theory*. Prentice-Hall.

Barker, R., Hartwell, G., Egan, M., & Lock, K. (2023). *The importance of school culture in supporting student mental health in secondary schools*. Insights from a qualitative study.

British Educational Research Journal. Advance online publication. https://doi.org/10.1037/com0000253

Barnardo's. (2020, July 21). *How systemic racism affects young people in the U.K.* https://www.barnardos.org.uk/blog/how-systemic-racism-affects-young-people-uk

Barrett, P., & Turner, C. (2001). Prevention of anxiety symptoms in primary school children: Preliminary results from a universal school-based trial. *British Journal of Clinical Psychology, 40*(4), 399–410.

Bennett, S. D., Cuijpers, P., Ebert, D. D., McKenzie Smith, M., Coughtrey, A. E., Heyman, I., Manzotti, G., & Shafran, R. (2019). Practitioner review: Unguided and guided self-help interventions for common mental health disorders in children and adolescents: A systematic review and meta-analysis. *Journal of Child Psychology and Psychiatry, 60*(8), 828–847.

Bevington, D., Fuggle, P., Cracknell, L., & Fonagy, P. (2017). *Adaptive mentalization-based integrative treatment: A guide for teams to develop systems of care.* Oxford University Press.

Blundell, R., Costa Dias, M., Cribb, J., Joyce, R., Waters, T., Wernham, T., & Xu, X. (2022). Inequality and the Covid-19 Crisis in the United Kingdom. *Annual Review of Economics, 14*, 607–636.

Bonell, C., Fletcher, A., Fitzgerald-Yau, N., Hale, D., Allen, E., Elbourne, D., Jones, R., Bond, L., Wiggins, M., Miners, A., Legood, R., Scott, S., Christie, D., & Viner, R. (2015). Initiating change locally in bullying and aggression through the school environment (INCLUSIVE): Pilot randomised controlled trial. *Health Technology Assessment, 19*(53), 1–109.

Bowes, L., Joinson, C., Wolke, D., & Lewis, G. (2015). Peer victimisation during adolescence and its impact on depression in early adulthood: prospective cohort study in the United Kingdom. *British Medical Journal, 350*, h2469.

Brannlund, A., Strandh, M., & Nilsson, K. (2017). Mental-health and educational achievement: The link between poor mental-health and upper secondary school completion and grades. *Journal of Mental Health, 26*(4), 318–325.

Bronfenbrenner, U., & Morris, P. A. (2007). The bioecological model of human development. In W. Damon, R. M. Lerner, & R. M. Lerner (Eds.), *Handbook of child psychology.* (6th ed., pp. 793-828). Wiley.

Care Quality Commission. (2022, 12 May). *Provider collaboration review: Mental health care of children and young people during the COVID-19 pandemic.* https://www.cqc.org.uk/publications/themes-care/provider-collaboration-review-mental-health-care-children-young-people

Chafouleas, S. M., & Overstreet, S. (2016). Trauma-informed schools: Introduction to the special issue. *School Mental Health, 8*(1), 1–6.

Children and Families Directorate. (2022, September). *Getting it right for every child (GIRFEC): Practice guidance 2 – role of the named person.* Scottish Government. https://www.gov.scot/publications/getting-right-child-girfec-practice-guidance-2-role-named-person/

Children and Young People's Mental Health Taskforce. (2015). *Future in mind: Promoting, protecting and improving our children and young people's mental health and wellbeing.* Department of Health and Social Care. https://www.gov.uk/government/publications/improving-mental-health-services-for-young-people

Children's Commissioner for England. (2022, March). *Where are England's children? Interim findings from the Children's Commissioner's attendance audit.* https://assets

.childrenscommissioner.gov.uk/wpuploads/2022/03/cco-where-are-englands-children-interim-findings-mar-2022.pdf

Christina, S., Magson, N. R., Kakar, V., & Rapee, R. M. (2021). The bidirectional relationships between peer victimization and internalizing problems in school-aged children: An updated systematic review and meta-analysis. *Clinical Psychology Review*, *85*, 101979.

Conners, C. K. (2008). *Conners manual* (3rd ed.). Multi-Health Systems.

Cooper, M. (2009). Counselling in UK secondary schools: A comprehensive review of audit and evaluation data. *Counselling and Psychotherapy Research*, *9*(3), 137–150.

Cooper, M., Evans, Y., & Pybis, J. (2016). Interagency collaboration in children and young people's mental health: A systematic review of outcomes, facilitating factors and inhibiting factors. *Child: Care, Health and Development*, *42*(3), 325–342.

Cooper, M., Stafford, M. R., Saxon, D., Beecham, J., Bonin, E. M., Barkham, M., Bower, P., Cromarty, K., Duncan, C., Pearce, P, Rameswari, T., & Ryan, G. (2021). Humanistic counselling plus pastoral care as usual versus pastoral care as usual for the treatment of psychological distress in adolescents in UK state schools (ETHOS): A randomised controlled trial. *The Lancet Child & Adolescent Health*, *5*(3), 178–189.

Creswell, C., Chessell, C., & Halliday, G. (2022). Parent-led cognitive behaviour therapy for child anxiety problems: Overcoming challenges to increase access to effective treatment. *Behavioural and Cognitive Psychotherapy*. Advance online publication. https://doi.org/10.1017/S1352465822000546

Dalsgaard, S., McGrath, J., Østergaard, S. D., Wray, N. R., Pedersen, C. B., Mortensen, P. B., & Petersen, L. (2020). Association of mental disorder in childhood and adolescence with subsequent educational achievement. *JAMA Psychiatry*, *77*(8), 797–805. https://doi:10.1001/jamapsychiatry.2020.0217

Deighton, J., Lereya, S., Casey, P., Patalay, P., Humphrey, N., & Wolpert, M. (2019). Prevalence of mental health problems in schools: Poverty and other risk factors among 28000 adolescents in England. *The British Journal of Psychiatry*, *215*(3), 565–567.

Demie, F., & Huat See, B. (2023). Ethnic disproportionality in the school teaching workforce in England. *Equity in Education & Society*, *2*(1), 3–27.

Department for Education. (2016). Counselling in schools: A blueprint for the future. https://assets.publishing.service.gov.uk/government/uploads/system/uploads/attachment_data/file/497825/Counselling_in_schools.pdf

Department for Education. (2018). Mental health and behaviour in schools. https://www.gov.uk/government/publications/mental-health-and-behaviour-in-schools--2

Department for Education. (2019). ITT Core content framework. https://assets.publishing.service.gov.uk/government/uploads/system/uploads/attachment_data/file/974307/ITT_core_content_framework_.pdf

Department for Education. (2021). Research and analysis: Education, schooling and health summary. https://www.gov.uk/government/publications/education-schooling-and-health/education-schooling-and-health-summary

Department for Education. (2022a). Promoting and supporting mental health and wellbeing in schools and colleges. https://www.gov.uk/guidance/mental-health-and-wellbeing-support-in-schools-and-colleges

Department for Education. (2022b). State of the nation 2021: Children and young people's Wellbeing. https://assets.publishing.service.gov.uk/government/uploads/system/uploads/attachment_data/file/1053302/State_of_the_Nation_CYP_Wellbeing_2022.pdf

Department for Education. (2023). Permanent exclusions and suspensions in England. https://explore-education-statistics.service.gov.uk/find-statistics/permanent-and-fixed-period-exclusions-in-england/2021-22-spring-term

Department of Health and Social Care & Department for Education. (2017). *Transforming children and young people's mental health provision: A green paper*. https://assets.publishing.service.gov.uk/government/uploads/system/uploads/attachment_data/file/664855/Transforming_children_and_young_people_s_mental_health_provision.pdf

Douglas, H. (2004). *The Solihull Approach resource pack: The school years*. Jill Rogers Associates.

Durlak, J. A., Weissberg, R. P., Dymnicki, A. B., & Taylor, R. D. (2011). The impact of enhancing students' social and emotional learning: A meta-analysis of school-based universal interventions. *Child Development*, *82*(1), 405–432.

Education Wales. (n.d). Education is changing. Welsh Government. https://www.gov.wales/education-changing

Ellins, J., Hocking, L., Al-Haboubi, M., Newbould, J., Fenton, S-J., Daniel, K., Stockwell, S., Leach, B., Sidhu. M., Bousfield, J., McKenna, G., Saunders, K., O'Neill, S., & Mays, N. (2023). *Early evaluation of the Children and Young People's Mental Health Trailblazer programme: a rapid mixed-methods study*. National Institute for Health and Care Research. https://doi.org/10.3310/hsdr-tr-130818

Fondren, K., Lawson, M., Speidel, R., McDonnell, C. G., & Valentino, K. (2020). Buffering the effects of childhood trauma within the school setting: A systematic review of trauma-informed and trauma-responsive interventions among trauma-affected youth. *Children and Youth Services Review*, *109*, 104691.

Forshaw, E., & Woods, K. (2022). Student participation in the development of whole-school wellbeing strategies: A systematic review of the literature. *Pastoral Care in Education. Advance online publication.* https://doi.org/https://doi.org/10.1080/02643944.2022.2148175

Foulkes, L., & Stringaris, A. (2023). *Do no harm: Can school mental health interventions cause iatrogenic harm?* BJPsych Bulletin. Advance online publication. https://doi.org/10.1192/bjb.2023.9

Fredman, G., Papadopoulou, A., & Worwood, E. (Eds.). (2018). *Collaborative consultation in mental health: Guidelines for the new consultant*. Routledge.

Garratt, K., Laing, J., & Long, R. (2022). *Support for children and young people's mental health (England)*. House of Commons Library. https://researchbriefings.files.parliament.uk/documents/CBP-7196/CBP-7196.pdf

Gee, B., Reynolds, S., Carroll, B., Orchard, F., Clarke, T., Martin, D., Wilson, J. & Pass, L. (2020). Practitioner review: Effectiveness of indicated school-based interventions for adolescent depression and anxiety: A meta-analytic review. *Journal of Child Psychology and Psychiatry*, *61*(7), 739–756.

Gee, B., Wilson, J., Clarke, T., Farthing, S., Carroll, B., Jackson, C., King, K., Murdoch, J., Fonagy, P. & Notley, C. (2021). Delivering mental health support within schools and colleges: A thematic synthesis of barriers and facilitators to implementation of indicated psychological interventions for adolescents. *Child and Adolescent Mental Health*, *26*(1), 34–46.

Gillborn, D., Rollok, N., Warmington, P., & Demack, S. (2016). *Race, racism and education: Inequality, resilience and reform in policy & practice*. Society for Educational Studies. https://soc-for-ed-studies.org.uk/wp-content/uploads/2019/02/GillbornD-et-al_Race-Racism-and-Education.pdf

Gondek, D., & Lereya, T. (2018). What are the challenges involved in the prevention of depression in schools? *Contemporary School Psychology*, *22*(4), 395–400.

Goodman, R., Meltzer, H., & Bailey, V. (2003). The Strengths and Difficulties Questionnaire: A pilot study on the validity of the self-report version. *International Review of Psychiatry*, *15*(1–2), 173–177.

Green H., McGinnity A., Meltzer H., Ford T., & Goodman R. (2005). *Mental health of children and young people in Great Britain, 2004*. Office for National Statistics, Department of Health, Scottish Executive. Palgrave Macmillan. https://sp.ukdataservice.ac.uk/doc/5269/mrdoc/pdf/5269technicalreport.pdf

Havinga, P. J., Maciejewski, D. F., Hartman, C. A., Hillegers, M. H., Schoevers, R. A., & Penninx, B. W. (2021). Prevention programmes for children of parents with a mood/anxiety disorder: Systematic review of existing programmes and meta-analysis of their efficacy. *British Journal of Clinical Psychology*, *60*(2), 212–251.

Health and Care Professions Council. (2021, April 8). *What is reflection?* https://www.hcpc-uk.org/standards/meeting-our-standards/reflective-practice/

Hugh-Jones, S., Beckett, S., Tumelty, E., & Mallikarjun, P. (2021). Indicated prevention interventions for anxiety in children and adolescents: A review and meta-analysis of school-based programs. *European Child & Adolescent Psychiatry*, *30*(6), 849–860.

Jessiman, P., Kidger, J., Spencer, L., Geijer-Simpson, E., Kaluzeviciute, G., Burn, A. M., Leonard, N., & Limmer, M. (2022). School culture and student mental health: A qualitative study in UK secondary schools. *BMC Public Health*, *22(*1), 619.

John, A., Friedmann, Y., DelPozo-Banos, M., Frizzati, A., Ford, T., & Thapar, A. (2022). Association of school absence and exclusion with recorded neurodevelopmental disorders, mental disorders, or self-harm: A nationwide, retrospective, electronic cohort study of children and young people in Wales, *UK. The Lancet Psychiatry*, *9*(1), 23–34.

Johnstone, L., & Dallos, R. (2013). *Formulation in psychology and psychotherapy*. Routledge.

Kingery, J. N., Erdley, C. A., Marshall, K. C., Whitaker, K. G., & Reuter, T. R. (2010). Peer experiences of anxious and socially withdrawn youth: An integrative review of the developmental and clinical literature. *Clinical Child and Family Psychology Review*, *13*, 91–128.

Kyriacou, C. (2011). Teacher stress: From prevalence to resilience. In J. Langan-Fox & C. Cooper (Eds.), *Handbook of stress in the occupations* (pp. 161–173). Edward Elgar Publishing.

Langford, R., Bonell, C. P., Jones, H. E., Pouliou, T., Murphy, S. M., Waters, E., Komro, K. A., Gibbs, L. F., Magnus, D., & Campbell, R. (2014). The WHO Health Promoting School framework for improving the health and well-being of students and their academic achievement. *Cochrane Database of Systematic Reviews*, *4*, CD008958, 1-247.

Langford, R., Bonell, C. P., Komro, K., Murphy, S. M., Magnus, D., Waters, E., Gibbs, L., & Campbell, R. (2017). The health promoting schools framework: Known unknowns and an agenda for future research. *Health Education and Behavior*, *44*(3), 463–475.

Lereya, S. T., Copeland, W. E., Costello, E. J., & Wolke, D. (2015). Adult mental health consequences of peer bullying and maltreatment in childhood: Two cohorts in two countries. *The Lancet Psychiatry*, *2*(6), 524–531.

Lereya, S. T., Patel, M., Dos Santos, J. P. G. A., & Deighton, J. (2019). Mental health difficulties, attainment and attendance: A cross-sectional study. *European Child & Adolescent Psychiatry*, *28*(8), 1147–1152.

Lilienfeld, S. O., & Basterfield, C. (2020). Reflective practice in clinical psychology: Reflections from basic psychological science. *Clinical Psychology: Science and Practice*, *27*(4), e12352.

MacLochlainn, J., Kirby, K., McFadden, P., & Mallett, J. (2022). An evaluation of whole-school trauma-informed training intervention among post-primary school personnel: A mixed methods study. *Journal of Child & Adolescent Trauma*, *15*(3), 925–941.

Mansfield, R., Santos, J., Deighton, J., Hayes, D., Velikonja, T., Böhnke, J., & Patalay, P. (2022). The impact of the Covid-19 pandemic on adolescent mental health: A natural experiment. *Royal Society Open Science*, *9*(4), 211114. doi:https://doi.org/10.1098/rsos.211114

Mattison, V., & Fredman, G. (2018). Principles and practices for getting started with consultation in mental health. In G. Fredman, A. Papadopoulou, & E. Worwood (Eds.). *Collaborative Consultation in Mental Health: Guidelines for the new consultant* (pp. 21–39). Routledge.

Menesini, E., & Salmivalli, C. (2017). Bullying in schools: The state of knowledge and effective interventions. *Psychology, Health & Medicine*, *22*(sup1), 240–253.

Mental Health in Schools Working Group. (2021). A whole school approach framework for schools to support children and young people's mental health and wellbeing. Scottish Government, Learning Directorate. https://www.gov.scot/publications/whole-school-approach-mental-health-wellbeing/documents/

Mental Health Taskforce. (2016). *The five year forward view for mental health*. NHS England. https://www.england.nhs.uk/wp-content/uploads/2016/02/Mental-Health-Taskforce-FYFV-final.pdf

Montero-Marin, J., Allwood, M., Ball, S., Crane, C., De Wilde, K., Hinze, V., Jones, B., Lord, L., Nuthall, E., Raja, A., Taylor, L., Tudor, K., MYRIAD Team, Blakemore, S-J., Byford, S., Dalgleish, T., Ford, T., Greenberg, M. T., Ukomunne, O. C., … Kuyken, W. (2022). School-based mindfulness training in early adolescence: What works, for whom and how in the MYRIAD trial?*BMJ Mental Health*, *25*(3), 117–124.

National Autistic Society. (2021). *School Report 2021*. https://www.autism.org.uk/what-we-do/news/school-report-2021

National Institute for Health and Care Excellence. (2022). *Social, emotional and mental wellbeing in primary and secondary education*. NICE Guideline No. 223. https://www.nice.org.uk/guidance/ng223

NHS Digital. (2022a). *Mental health of children and young people in England 2022*. Health and Social Care Information Centre. https://digital.nhs.uk/data-and-information/publications/statistical/mental-health-of-children-and-young-people-in-england/2022-follow-up-to-the-2017-survey#:~:text=Key%20findings,between%202020%2C%202021%20and%202022

NHS Digital. (2022b). *Autism statistics, April 2021 to March 2022*. Health and Social Care Information Centre. https://digital.nhs.uk/data-and-information/publications/statistical/autism-statistics/april-2021-to-march-2022

NHS Digital. (n.d.). Mental health support in schools and colleges. https://www.england.nhs.uk/mental-health/cyp/trailblazers/

O'Donoghue, K., & Guerin, S. (2017). Homophobic and transphobic bullying: Barriers and supports to school intervention. *Sex Education*, *17*(2), 220–234.

Patalay, P., & Fitzsimons, E. (2016). Correlates of mental illness and wellbeing in children: Are they the same? Results from the UK millennium cohort study. *Journal of the American Academy of Child & Adolescent Psychiatry*, *55*(9), 771–783.

Paulus, F. W., Ohmann, S., & Popow, C. (2016). Practitioner review: School-based interventions in child mental health. *Journal of Child Psychology and Psychiatry*, *57*(12), 1337–1359.

Phifer, L. W., & Hull, R. (2016). Helping students heal: Observations of trauma-informed practices in the schools. *School Mental Health*, *8*(1), 201–205.

Public Health Guidelines Team. (2022). Social, emotional, and mental wellbeing in primary and secondary education: [B] Evidence review for universal curriculum approaches. National Institute for Health and Care Excellence. https://www.nice.org.uk/guidance/ng223/evidence/b-universal-curriculum-approaches-pdf-11132505183

Public Health England. (2015). Promoting children and young people's mental health and wellbeing. Public Health England & Department for Education. https://www.gov.uk/government/publications/promoting-children-and-young-peoples-emotional-health-and-wellbeing

Reiss, F. (2013). Socioeconomic inequalities and mental health problems in children and adolescents: A systematic review. *Social Science & Medicine*, *90*, 24–31.

Roach, A., Cullinan, S., Shafran, R., Heyman, I., & Bennett, S. (2023). Implementing brief and low-intensity psychological interventions for children and young people with internalizing disorders: A rapid realist review. *British Medical Bulletin*, *145*(1), 120–131.

Rupani, P., Cooper, M., McArthur, K., Pybis, J., Cromarty, K., Hill, A., Levesley, R., Murdoch, J., & Turner, N. (2014). The goals of young people in school-based counselling and their achievement of these goals. *Counselling and Psychotherapy Research*, *14*(4), 306–314.

Rutter, M. (1987). Psychosocial resilience and protective mechanisms. *American Journal of Orthopsychiatry*, *57*(3), 316–331.

Savill-Smith, C., & Scanlan, D. (2022). *Teacher wellbeing index 2022*. Education Support. https://www.educationsupport.org.uk/media/zoga2r13/teacher-wellbeing-index-2022.pdf

Sayal, K., Prasad, V., Daley, D., Ford, T., & Coghill, D. (2018). ADHD in children and young people: Prevalence, care pathways, and service provision. *The Lancet Psychiatry*, *5*(2), 175–186.

Sellström, E., & Bremberg, S. (2006). Is there a 'school effect' on pupil outcomes? A review of multilevel studies. *Journal of Epidemiology and Community Health*, *60*(2), 149–155.

Shafran, R., Fonagy, P., Pugh, K., & Myles, P. (2014). Transformation of mental health services for children and young people in England. In R. S. Beidas & P. C. Kendall (Eds.), *Dissemination and implementation of evidence-based practices in child and adolescent mental health* (pp. 158–178). Oxford University Press.

Sharpe, H., Ford, T., Lereya, S. T., Owen, C., Viner, R. M., & Wolpert, M. (2016). Survey of schools' work with child and adolescent mental health across England: A system in need of support. *Child and Adolescent Mental Health*, *21*(3), 148–153.

Singla, D. R., Shinde, S., Patton, G., & Patel, V. (2021). The mediating effect of school climate on adolescent mental health: Findings from a randomized controlled trial of a school-wide intervention. *Journal of Adolescent Health*, *69*(1), 90–99.

Smith, N. R., Marshall, L., Albakri, M., Smuk, M., Hagell, A., & Stansfeld, S. (2021). Adolescent mental health difficulties and educational attainment: findings from the U.K. household longitudinal study. *BMJ Open*, *11*(7), e046792.

Stallard, P. (2013). School-based interventions for depression and anxiety in children and adolescents. *Evidence-based Mental Health*, *16*(3), 60–61.

Stallard, P., Simpson, N., Anderson, S., Carter, T., Osborn, C., & Bush, S. (2005). An evaluation of the FRIENDS programme: A cognitive behaviour therapy intervention to promote emotional resilience. *Archives of Disease in Childhood*, *90*(10), 1016–1019.

Stallard, P., Skryabina, E., Taylor, G., Phillips, R., Daniels, H., Anderson, R., & Simpson, N. (2014). Classroom-based cognitive behaviour therapy (FRIENDS): A cluster randomised controlled trial to prevent anxiety in children through education in schools (PACES). *The Lancet Psychiatry*, *1*(3), 185–192.

Stice, E., Shaw, H., Bohon, C., Marti, C. N., & Rohde, P. (2009). A meta-analytic review of depression prevention programs for children and adolescents: Factors that predict magnitude of intervention effects. *Journal of Consulting and Clinical Psychology*, *77*(3), 486–503.

Stonewall. (2017). *The school report: The experiences of lesbian, gay, bi and trans pupils in Britain's schools*. https://www.stonewall.org.uk/school-report-2017

Substance Abuse and Mental Health Services Administration. (2014). *SAMHSA's concept of trauma and guidance for a trauma-informed approach*. U.S. Department of Health and Human Services.

Swiszczowski, L. (2022). *We need to talk about racism in the UK education system*. Teach First. https://www.teachfirst.org.uk/blog/racism-uk-schools

Taylor, R. D., Oberle, E., Durlak, J. A., & Weissberg, R. P. (2017). Promoting positive youth development through school-based social and emotional learning interventions: A meta-analysis of follow-up effects. *Child Development*, *88*(4), 1156–1171.

Underwood, R., Redfern, A., Plant, D., Bracegirdle, K., Browning, S., & Jolley, S. (2023). Identifying and changing cognitive vulnerability in the classroom: Preliminary evaluation of CUES-Ed, a school-based universal cognitive behavioural early intervention service for 7–10 year olds. *Child and Adolescent Mental Health*, *28*: 221–229.

Verschueren, K., & Koomen, H. M. Y. (2012). Teacher–child relationships from an attachment perspective. *Attachment and Human Development*, *14*(3), 205–211.

Weare, K. (2015a). *What works in promoting social and emotional well-being and responding to mental health problems in schools?* National Children's Bureau. https://www.ncb.org.uk/sites/default/files/uploads/files/ncb_framework_for_promoting_well-being_and_responding_to_mental_health_in_schools_0.pdf

Weare, K. (2015b). Editorial: Child and adolescent mental health in schools. *Child and Adolescent Mental Health*, *20*, e6–e8.

Weare, K., & Nind, M. (2011). Mental health promotion and problem prevention in schools: what does the evidence say? *Health Promotion International*, *26*(Sup1), i29–69.

Webster-Stratton, C. (1992). *The Incredible Years. A trouble-shooting guide for parents of children aged 3–8*. Umbrella Press.

Welsh Government/Llywodraeth Cymru. (2013). *Statutory guidance to Welsh local authorities on the provision of independent counselling services.* https://www.gov.wales/sites/default/files/publications/2018-03/statutory-guidance-to-welsh-local-authorities-on-the-provision-of-independent-counselling-services.pdf

Werner-Seidler, A., Perry, Y., Calear, A. L., Newby, J. M., & Christensen, H. (2017). School-based depression and anxiety prevention programs for young people: A systematic review and meta-analysis. *Clinical Psychology Review, 51*, 30–47.

Wignall, A., Kelly, C., & Grace, P. (2022). How are whole-school mental health programmes evaluated? A systematic literature review. *Pastoral Care in Education, 40*(2), 217–237.

World Health Organization. (2017, August 1). *WHO recommendations on adolescent health: Guidelines approved by the WHO guidelines review committee.* World Health Organization. https://www.who.int/publications/i/item/WHO-MCA-17.09

Worwood, E., & Fredman, G. (2018). Evaluating collaborative consultation. In G. Fredman, A. Papadopoulou, & E. Worwood (Eds.). *Collaborative consultation in mental health: Guidelines for the new consultant* (pp. 93–111). Routledge.

Yalom, I., & Leszcz, M. (2005). *The theory and practice of group psychotherapy* (5th ed.). Basic Books.

YMCA. (2020). *Young and Black: The young black experience of institutional racism in the UK.* https://www.ymca.org.uk/wp-content/uploads/2020/10/ymca-young-and-black.pdf

Young, J. F., Mufson, L., & Davies, M. (2006). Efficacy of interpersonal psychotherapy-adolescent skills training: An indicated preventive intervention for depression. *Journal of Child Psychology and Psychiatry, 47*(12), 1254–1262.

Young Minds. (2022). Mental health statistics. https://www.youngminds.org.uk/about-us/media-centre/mental-health-statistics/

21

Perinatal and Infant Mental Health

Jane Iles, Zoe Darwin and Florence Bristow

21.1 The Significance of the Very Beginnings of Childhood

When considering clinical contact with children and young people, it's impossible – and perhaps negligent – to ignore the ways in which infants and children start their lives, and the impact these early beginnings have on their subsequent development and mental health, throughout infancy and across the lifespan. Although the focus in early childhood is often placed on an infant's parents' or caregivers' wellbeing, the circumstances in which a baby is conceived, their in-utero environment, and the environment that they are born into play a significant role in the infant's life story and outcomes. Infant mental health must be acknowledged and considered. The first 1,001 days, from conception into the first years of a child's life, are critical in shaping longer-term development (Department of Health and Social Care, 2021) through laying the foundations for a child's emotional, social and physical health and wellbeing. This period needs to be understood as offering vital opportunity for support and intervention.

> The period from pregnancy to age 3 is when children are most susceptible to environmental influences. Investing in this period is one of the most efficient and effective ways to help eliminate extreme poverty and inequality, boost shared prosperity, and create the human capital needed for economies to diversify and grow (UNICEF et al., 2018).

The perinatal period is a term used to typically define the period spanning pregnancy and the first year of an infant's life (National Institute for Health and Care Excellence, 2014) where mothers (and indeed any birthing or non-birthing parents) face increased risk of experiencing mental ill health. This may be a relapse of a previously experienced mental health difficulty, exacerbation of any existing symptoms or the onset of a first episode (O' Hara & Wisner, 2014). In this chapter, we predominantly refer to women and mothers when considering the experiences of the gestational (or 'birthing') parent during the perinatal period. However, we recognise that this terminology does not fully represent the wide range of people who give birth and have or look after children; specifically, not all

Child Psychology: Pathways to Good Practice, First Edition.
Edited by Helen Pote, Anna Picciotto and Clare Norris.

people who birth are women, and not all women who are parents have given birth. Approximately one-in-five mothers are affected by perinatal mental health difficulties; rates in trans and non-binary birthing people are unknown (Greenfield & Darwin, 2021). When considering the birth rate in England and Wales (Office for National Statistics, 2021), this translates to approximately 123,000 infants potentially impacted annually; numbers that increase further when also considering paternal and partner mental health. If left untreated, perinatal mental health difficulties can lead to profound detrimental effects on parents and children (Kendig et al., 2017). Approximately one-in-five mothers are affected by perinatal mental health difficulties. When considering the birth rate in England and Wales (Office for National Statistics, 2021), this translates to approximately 123,000 infants potentially impacted annually; numbers that increase further when also considering paternal and partner mental health. If left untreated, perinatal mental health difficulties can lead to profound detrimental effects on parents and children (Kendig et al., 2017).

However, the adverse effects of parental perinatal mental health difficulties on children are not inevitable (Howard et al., 2014). Understanding early perinatal and childhood experiences and providing appropriate intervention and support to the family in this time can play a key role in supporting children and young people to reach their optimal outcomes across their lives. Economic analyses estimate that in the UK maternal perinatal mental health difficulties carry long-term societal costs of around £8.1 billion every annual birth cohort, with approximately £6.1 billion associated with perinatal anxiety and depression. The majority (72%) of the costs associated with each birth relate to the adverse impacts on the child, including their mental health and academic attainment (Bauer et al., 2016). We must remember that impacts can also be felt for older children in the family, explored later in this chapter. Whilst specific costs may vary internationally, the messages are the same: perinatal mental health difficulties carry costs to individuals, families and society; the costs of improving services is likely considerably less than the long-term costs of not making such investment. The potential impact of parental mental health means that prompt action is needed (National Institute for Health and Care Excellence, 2014).

This chapter considers the importance of understanding the experiences families face in the perinatal period, but also the significance of being aware of the impact this period has across the lifespan for multiple family members, particularly infants and older children.

21.2 Re-defining the Perinatal Period

The perinatal period is considered the time period that spans conception up until the end of the first year of an infant's life. However, the journey to becoming a parent, for the first time or subsequently, is often far from straightforward and the significance of this period may begin many years beforehand. Individuals and couples may face challenges including fertility, assisted conception and perinatal loss (pregnancy and baby loss). These challenges and any health difficulties that impact (or threaten) the health of the unborn baby can understandably place enormous emotional demands on parents, potentially increasing vulnerability to mental health difficulties – both in the short term and in subsequent pregnancies (Hunter et al., 2017). Pregnancies vary in the extent to which they are (un)intended, (mis)timed, (un)planned and (un)wanted (Klerman, 2000). Whilst these factors can be linked to the likelihood of a baby entering the world in a range of difficult emotional or practical circumstances, *any* parent can experience perinatal mental health difficulties.

21.3 Working Inclusively: Considering Language and the 'Family' System

In addition to considering the infant's experiences and inner-world (see Box 21.1), when working with infants and families during the perinatal period it is essential to consider *who* may be important within the family and who we are referring to when we consider and work with an infant's caregivers. The National Health Service's (NHS) good practice guide on involving and supporting families in the context of perinatal mental health (Darwin et al., 2021) proposed a series of ideas to support this practice, including 'mapping the family'. Family formations can be enormously varied, with diverse experiences – including a single-parent, separated parents, same-sex or same-gender parents, more than two parents being identified by the family, siblings with different parents, children who are care-experienced, multigenerational households and many other formations.

Language is incredibly powerful when working with families; interactions and communication needs to be inclusive, non-stigmatising and culturally sensitive, demonstrating understanding towards different lived experiences and the range of hopes and expectations held towards family life and caring for an infant. As practitioners, we may hold unconscious biases or assumptions about what 'family' means or looks like. Taking a curious, exploratory stance is essential, asking questions to understand *who* is important in the infant's life, who may need to form part of an intervention or support network or who may need support in their own right (Darwin et al., 2021). Practitioners, therefore, need to consider within the psychological services where they work, where a family member is identified as experiencing a mental health difficulty or other psychosocial difficulties (such as financial, housing, or substance misuse) whether there are pathways to support their access to services.

The process of mapping the family needs to be sensitive to difficult family relationships and experiences; mothers/birthing people or children may feel conflicted about who to include. Involving partners and family members in a mother's care must be respectful of the mother's wishes and considerate of the family's culture. When working with families during the perinatal period, hold in mind that domestic violence is known to increase or intensify during this time, likely due to a multitude of changes to physical, emotional, social and economic circumstances and needs (Mojahed et al., 2021). It is estimated that one-in-four mothers in contact with mental health services may be experiencing violence, abuse or coercive control (LARA-VP, 2022). It is always necessary to seek consent about who can be informed and involved, and to prioritise safeguarding – for the mother, but also any children in the family or others who may be at risk of harm.

Specialist perinatal mental health services are predominantly commissioned to work with the gestational parent (usually a mother) as the individual referred to the service. Groups that may be less visible in services, policy and research include gestational (or birthing) parents who are trans men or non-binary people, and other caregivers, including: (non-gestational) fathers; other co-parents and partners; adoptive parents; wider family members or others with parental responsibility on a temporary or long-term basis. This chapter largely discusses *maternal* perinatal mental health, but all individuals in a family can be affected by mental health difficulties.

Box 21.1 Reflective questions for child psychological practitioners in perinatal services

In clinical work, it is important for you to stay curious, to explore the families' own words, to understand their experiences and use language that is acceptable and relevant to them, ensuring that your care is personalised and inclusive. This approach is also important for addressing inequalities; minority groups face increased vulnerability to perinatal mental health disorders and barriers to accessing services (Darwin et al., 2021).

As you read this chapter, we ask you to hold the infant's perspective in mind:

- What are these experiences like for an infant or a child?
- How might they be experiencing the world?
- What impact may these experiences have on them?
- What might they need to mitigate against any difficult or distressing experiences?
- Consider, also, what impact may this have for an older child in the family?

21.4 Mental Health in the Perinatal Period: A time of Increased Risk to Mental Health

Pregnancy and the postnatal period can undoubtedly be times of joy and excitement, as parents and families plan for and welcome a new baby into their lives. However, this is also a time of significant change, and the transition to parenthood is not without challenge. During adaptations to pregnancy or becoming a new parent (whether for the first time or subsequently), there can be many changes to daily life. Becoming a parent may impact on friendships and relationships with significant others, employment, finances, housing, health and fitness, amongst others. Considerable adjustments may be needed, including adapting to interrupted patterns of sleep and routines needed to care for an infant.

Beyond practical challenges, there are a host of emotional and psychological adjustments that can increase vulnerability to mental health difficulties. There may be uncertainties about a baby being wanted and conception may or may not have been planned. Parents may not feel the rush of love and affection portrayed in many societies as a given when having a child. They may be struggling with a physically complicated pregnancy, recovering from birth, and/or establishing infant feeding. Experiencing any difficulties that do not fit with societal narratives can contribute to parents feeling alone, ashamed and a failure, maintaining distress (Cree, 2015).

The psychological adjustment to parenthood can also involve reflecting on one's own experience of being parented and templates for relating to others. Becoming a parent can stir up difficult experiences from childhood, consciously or unconsciously. Psychoanalysts refer to the metaphor of 'ghosts in the nursery' (Fraiberg et al., 1975) to describe a parent's own early experiences and how they can reappear in the task of parenting, impacting on parent–infant relationships. The psychological adjustment to parenthood can be even more challenging for parents who have a history of childhood adversity and trauma, such as parents who experience difficulties consistent with complex post-traumatic stress - sometimes referred to as 'personality disorder'.

Numerous studies have attempted to understand *why* some parents may be at increased vulnerability during this time. These have largely focused on risk for postnatal experiences but are increasingly examining vulnerability to mental health difficulties during pregnancy. Systematic reviews and meta-analyses over the past 20 to 30 years have drawn similar conclusions concerning depression and anxiety both postnatally and antenatally: perceived availability of and satisfaction with social support, satisfaction or conflict within the partner relationship, previous experience of mental health difficulties (including during pregnancy), social deprivation and negative childbirth experiences consistently emerge as significant risk factors (e.g. O'Hara & McCabe, 2013; Robertson et al., 2004). Of note, these risk factors are largely similar across literature looking at both maternal and paternal experiences. For fathers, it also seems that their partner's mental health, inter-parent conflict and parenting stress are significant factors, particularly for paternal postnatal depression (Chhabra et al., 2020). With severe mental illness such as postpartum psychosis (which has rarely been the subject of fathers' and other co-parents' research), other risk factors are indicated including own previous mental health and familial history.

The aetiology of perinatal mental health, whether antenatal or postnatal, is likely due to a complex interplay of risk and protective factors. Although these studies can guide us to pay more attention to parents' life circumstances, which may place them at increased risk, it is important to remember that individuals experience numerous life events and experiences. Some of these may increase risk, yet others will act protectively, mitigating against possible risk factors. It is important to be aware of this when working with parents and families; studies highlight potential vulnerability factors, yet poorer outcomes are not inevitable. Be careful with language; it is important that parents are supported to recognise their own needs and have access to appropriate effective support, without increasing fear of stigma, shame or guilt about consequences for the family, all of which can create barriers to seeking and accepting support.

Less is known about the risks relating to mental illness for fathers, other co-parents and partners. However, with growing recognition of the significance of this period for mothers' wellbeing, focus is slowly shifting to consider the mental health needs of other significant people in the family. Fathers, other co-parents and partners can themselves face challenges in adapting to the changes that pregnancy and the postnatal period bring, including changes in roles and the additional demands that may come with balancing numerous responsibilities. Evidence indicates that 5–10% of fathers experience perinatal depression (Cameron et al., 2016) and 5–15% experience perinatal anxiety (Leach et al., 2016). Initial evidence suggests that vulnerability to perinatal mental health may be higher in marginalised parents, including stepfathers and non-gestational co-mothers (Malmquist et al., 2019; Ross et al., 2007; Wee et al., 2011).

There is evidence to suggest that signs of mental health difficulties may present differently across different groups of parents and barriers to help-seeking may vary. For example, some have argued that behavioural symptoms may be more apparent in fathers, and they may question the legitimacy of their own distress, given that they are not themselves seen to be users of maternity or other perinatal services (Darwin et al., 2017). Research with non-gestational co-mothers indicates similar challenges concerning legitimacy and potential discrimination in healthcare, together with fears that their parenting may be more judged more harshly as LGBTQ+ parents (Howat et al., 2023).

It could be argued that parents today have never been under more scrutiny or vulnerable to mental health difficulties given the presence of social media, societal pressures, absence of social support and increased knowledge of the importance of sensitive caregiving. However, in the UK there is also growing awareness of perinatal mental health difficulties, changing societal narratives and more opportunities for support.

21.4.1 Service Provision for Perinatal Mental Health: Policy Context

Health professionals across services have an important role to play in preventing, identifying and managing perinatal mental health, and alleviating the wider impact this can have on the family. The National Institute for Clinical Excellence (NICE) guidelines on antenatal and postnatal care (NICE, 2017) provide guidance on how professionals in England can recognise, assess and treat mental health difficulties in women who are planning to have a baby, are pregnant or those who have had a baby or have been pregnant in the past year. The themes from this policy context may be relevant to a range of other nations. The importance of early detection is highlighted, with GPs, health visitors and midwives being expected to screen for depression and anxiety in the perinatal period. Recommendations are included for provision and management of good care, importantly highlighting that this should be integrated across all involved services, such as primary care, midwifery services and mental health teams. Referrals should be made to secondary mental health services for all pregnant women who are identified to have a current or previous severe mental health difficulty, and those identified as being at risk of postpartum psychosis following birth. The guidance also includes areas professionals need to cover when completing assessments and care plans during this period.

When a mother/birthing person experiences a perinatal mental health difficulty, psychological therapies are largely recommended as the first-line intervention (NICE, 2017). These are often preferred by mothers due to concerns regarding the *possible* effects of psychotropic medication on the foetus and breastfeeding infant. However, medication may be considered either alongside or instead of psychological therapy. Any decisions relating to stopping or starting any treatment in the perinatal period (medication and psychological therapy) need to carefully consider the risks and benefits of treating and not treating for both the mother and infant.

Changes to clinical guidance for maternity services (National Collaborating Centre for Women's and Children's Health, 2007, 2008) led to the introduction of routine assessment of mental health of mothers in pregnancy, which had previously only been the role of health visitors (also known as child health nurses) and limited to the postnatal period. It took campaigning over many years to make the case for increased investment in specialist perinatal services to meet the needs increasingly being identified within universal services. Alongside support offered through maternity, health visiting and primary care (such as family practitioners), and more generic adult mental health services, dedicated specialist perinatal mental health services are commissioned across England to provide specialist support to mothers experiencing (or at risk of) moderate to severe perinatal mental difficulties. A joint work stream between the Maternity Transformation Programme and the Mental Health Programme has sought to improve access to perinatal mental health services by ensuring access to a specialist community perinatal mental health service in every area of the country and increasing the number of mother and baby units (MBUs) offering inpatient support for mothers experiencing more severe, urgent or complex mental health needs. Unlike other adult inpatient mental health units, MBUs offer space for babies to stay alongside their mothers, enabling mothers and infants to remain together in these crucial early days of an infant's life.

Specialist perinatal mental health teams have a multidisciplinary workforce of practitioners. Although staffing structures may vary, this is typically made up of psychiatrists, psychologists, specialist nurses, nursery nurses, occupational therapy, social workers, administrators, peer support workers and pharmacists. There may also be health visitors, specialist mental health midwives and obstetricians within or linked to the team. The psychology workforce may be made up of clinical psychologists, counselling psychologists, cognitive behavioural therapists, systemic family therapists, adult psychotherapists and parent–infant psychotherapists, and may be supported by assistant psychologists and clinical associate psychologists. Further details of these roles can be found in the 2016 British Psychological Society Briefing Paper (British Psychological Society, 2019) and Royal College of Psychiatry CR232 Report (Royal College of Psychiatrists, 2021).

Alongside the expansion of specialist perinatal mental health services, the NHS long-term plan has outlined the aim that these services should expand their reach beyond the birthing mother to offer psychological therapies for families. This ambition will see the inclusion of parent–infant, couple, co-parenting and family interventions within these services. The plan includes the ambition to offer 'mental health checks' (a mental health assessment) and signposting to professional support, for partners of people who are accessing these services. While the 'index patient' referred into the service will (currently) remain the mother (gestational parent), this proposal indicates the value of working systemically to improve outcomes for the mother and her family system. In the good practice guide on involving and supporting partners and other family members, Darwin et al. (2021) offer underpinning principles, key ideas, practice tips and practice examples for how staff and services may consider meeting these needs.

The expansion of perinatal services has also been supported by the development of maternal mental health services (in partnership with the Maternity Transformation Programme), originally referred to in the NHS long-term plan as maternity outreach clinics. These services are being piloted in a range of formats and with different emphases but share a purpose of offering psychological support for those experiencing mental health difficulties arising from, or related to, their maternity experience, including trauma and loss.

In addition to these specialist services, other mental health provisions are adapting existing services to meet the needs of mothers and families in the perinatal period. For example, within NHS talking therapies services, pregnant women and new mothers are given priority for timely provision. In some locations, this prioritisation extends to fathers and other co-parents. A perinatal competency framework has recently been published for this work within Talking Therapies Services (previously known as Improving Access to Psychological Therapies) (O'Mahen & Healy, 2021).

However, there is growing evidence of inequalities in identifying and managing perinatal mental health difficulties, which needs to be addressed (Prady et al., 2021) both within universal and specialist services.

21.4.2 Considering Perinatal Mental Health across a range of Clinical Contexts

There are many clinical contexts in which contact may occur with infants and children of mothers facing perinatal mental health difficulties, not limited to the specialist services outlined earlier. It is imperative that perinatal mental health is considered across a much wider range of clinical settings. Perinatal mental health, and the unintended consequences of these difficulties, can be relevant across the lifespan, and contact with families facing these difficulties (either currently or a historically) may fall within the context of a wide range of service provision. This may include healthcare providers (e.g. paediatric settings, community general practice), social care settings or community mental health teams. In addition, consideration of perinatal mental health may be highly relevant in services designed specifically for infants and children, such as children's centres, under-fives mental health teams, parent–infant psychotherapeutic settings (PIP) or child and adolescent mental health teams (CAMHS).

The nature and remit of many services and the expertise within them, will likely mean that the focus lies on the index patient referred to the service, rather than considering these more systemic familial experiences. For example, within adult health or mental health settings, the infant or any children in the family are unlikely to be at the forefront of the service provision. Infants and children may not actually be visible to or seen in the service at all. Therefore, although practitioners may be aware of caregiver perinatal or mental health difficulties, the potential consequences, including the impact on the family, may go unseen.

When working across a variety of settings it is therefore imperative that services embody a 'Think Family' approach and that practitioners hold any infants or children in mind, considering their needs and whether they need to be seen, assessed and offered support. Within services designed for infants and children, although children and caregivers are likely to be seen, the referred difficulties may fail to take perinatal mental health into account, therefore potentially missing an important area for intervention. To be a competent practitioner working with children and young people, perinatal mental health and the potential impact of these difficulties need to be taken into account across all settings.

21.4.3 Common Mental Health Difficulties in the Perinatal Period and How These May Impact Children

This section briefly outlines some of the more commonly experienced mental health difficulties. Alongside a brief description of these disorders, we consider what may be *different* about the symptoms or presentation in the context of the perinatal period and what the impact might be on infants and children, and consider the specific elements to hold in mind in assessments of parental mental health during the perinatal period. Babies require consistent, sensitive, responsive caregivers. Where a parent's ability to meet their baby's needs is impaired by poor mental health, the baby's psychosocial and emotional development may warrant specific consideration and assessment. However, it is important to hold in mind, that despite associations between perinatal mental health and poorer outcomes for the child, the majority of children who have been exposed to maternal perinatal mental health difficulties will not experience negative outcomes. When perinatal mental health disorders occur in the absence of social adversity and are of short duration, the risks to the child are generally low (Stein et al., 2014).

Whilst considering the parent's experience of these symptoms, hold in mind the following:

- The infant/child's perspective:
  - What would it be like for an infant to experience this? What might they say if they could?
  - How may life be impacted for any older children in the family?
  - How may the impact vary or manifest as a child gets older, or as a parent recovers or experiences any relapse?
- Admitting difficulties and seeking help:
  - If a parent is unwell, will they feel able to seek or accept support and help?
  - Might there be stigma around mental health and what it means to be a 'good parent' that may prevent disclosure?
  - Are there fears around disclosure regarding the mother or birthing person's perceived ability to care for the baby, or whether the baby will be removed and placed in care?

21.4.4 Perinatal Depression

Depression has been the most frequently explored perinatal mental health difficulty, yet prevalence varies between studies. Antenatal depression is thought to affect 12–20% of mothers (Leigh & Milgrom, 2008). Notably, rates tend to be higher in low- and middle-income countries (Howard & Khalifeh, 2020). The symptoms of antenatal depression may be misinterpreted as 'side-effects' of pregnancy, such as increased fatigue, loss of energy and changes to appetite and sleep. Depression during pregnancy may therefore be missed and go undiagnosed. Depression's symptoms can detrimentally impact on women's ability to care for themselves, including poorer nutrition, reduced attendance at health appointments, and unhelpful coping behaviours (e.g. smoking and increased use of drugs and alcohol). This may therefore have unintended consequences for foetal growth and development during pregnancy, and potentially a longer-lasting impact on infant health at birth and beyond.

Postnatally, around 10–15% of mothers experience depression in westernised countries, and likely considerably higher globally (Gavin et al., 2005). It is important to distinguish between depression and the 'baby blues', a term used to describe the brief experience of feeling tearful, emotional and irritable, typically in the first 3 to 10 days following childbirth. Baby blues is very common, affecting at least half of new mothers, and thought to be accounted for by changes in hormone levels after birth, alongside a period of psychological adjustment to caring for a newborn baby. In contrast to transient baby blues, postnatal depression is more severe, with symptoms persisting more than a few days. The onset can be very gradual or can seem very sudden, with severity varying from relatively mild to very severe. Symptoms of perinatal depression remain in-line with diagnostic features of depression more broadly, such as low mood, fatigue, suicidality, a loss of interest or enjoyment in activities, and withdrawal from others.

Depression is often characterised by persistent and intrusive feelings of worthlessness. In the context of the perinatal period this may manifest in specific beliefs about not being a 'good enough' mother (Law et al., 2021). The transition to motherhood can already be characterised with fears of judgement from others, and pressures to be the 'perfect' parent, causing high levels of stress and guilt (Meeuseen & Van Laar, 2018). Combined with the presence of depression and resulting beliefs about being an inadequate or 'good-enough' mother, new parents can be left debilitated with negative and distressing thoughts and feelings about their role as a parent.

Evidence consistently indicates the significant protective role that social support plays during postnatal depression. However, depression can lead to withdrawal from others and previously enjoyed activities, thereby reducing an important protective factor. Absence of social contact may reduce opportunities for positive affirmations and feedback on parenting, thus perpetuating the cycle of negative self-beliefs regarding parenting ability. Assessment of postnatal depression needs to explore these negative beliefs, including those focused on parenting abilities and judgement from others. The social support network needs to be explored, to understand both the quantity and quality of emotional and practical support available during this transition.

These negative beliefs about parenting combined with a sense of worthlessness, hold the potential to detrimentally impact the parent–infant relationship. As one example, postnatal depression has been linked with a reduced capacity to accurately interpret a baby's cues and behavioural signals, and to mentalise the baby's experiences and needs (Murray et al., 1996), often referred to as parental sensitivity (Ainsworth, 1978). A parent experiencing postnatal depression may be distracted by or overwhelmed with their own emotional state, reducing their ability to interpret infant signals and cues, or respond to them in-line with the baby's needs. For example, infant crying may be inaccurately interpreted as an indication that the baby does not like or need their parent. In response to beliefs about their failings as a parent, they may try to *over*-compensate, focusing on provision of care that strives to prove they are capable. Whilst this is likely to be driven by good intentions, it may have the consequence of being insensitive to the baby's cues and signals (for example, through being intrusive), thereby leading to mis-attunement between the infant and the parent. In other cases, the parent may withdraw from the infant, avoiding emotional or physical contact due to beliefs that they cannot provide what the baby needs, or that the baby is better off without them. This may leave the baby with unmet physical or emotional needs or may impact on the infant's developing parent attachment relationship.

Aspects of caregiving may also be detrimentally impacted if a mother experiences postpartum depression. Studies have shown associations with lower rates of breastfeeding, difficulties establishing safe sleeping routines, reduced attendance at routine child healthcare appointments but higher frequency of visits to emergency healthcare providers, and more difficulties implementing safety practices such as using an infant car seat (Field, 2010).

21.4.5 Perinatal Anxiety

Whilst some degree of anxiety may be expected at a time of such transition and increased responsibility, perinatal anxiety disorders are characterised by the presence of persistent symptoms that cause significant distress, interfere with functioning, social activities and relationships. They include obsessive compulsive disorder (OCD), social anxiety, generalised anxiety (GAD), post-traumatic stress disorder (PTSD), phobias, tokophobia, health anxiety and panic disorder.

Research suggests 15% of women will meet criteria for a clinical diagnosis of anxiety at some point during the perinatal period (Dennis et al., 2017; Howard et al., 2018). Whilst anxiety disorders are potentially more prevalent than depression (e.g. Fairbrother et al., 2016), they remain under recognised and therefore, under treated (Woolhouse et al., 2009). With less public discourse, women are less likely to seek help or have their difficulties recognised by professionals. Women experiencing high levels of anxiety may appear to be very active, masking distress.

Anxiety disorder can begin in the perinatal period, or be exacerbated. It is common for anxiety to focus on perinatal concerns (e.g. pregnancy, birth, parenting and the infant, baby's health and wellbeing). It is not uncommon to meet diagnostic criteria for more than one anxiety disorder and co-morbidity with depression is high. Symptoms can become all-consuming, overtaking and interfering with day-to-day life, and potentially increasing the likelihood of developing unhelpful coping strategies that inadvertently prolong or worsen symptoms, such as avoidance, self-medication with substances or elevated reassurance-seeking. This may include excessive use of health services, or conversely, avoidance of services who may be well-placed to provide support. Antenatal anxiety has been found to be associated with a range of adverse outcomes, including preterm birth, preference for caesarean section (with associated increased costs to the NHS), higher rates of maternal eating disorder and increased risk of suicide (Biaggi et al., 2016). However, results are confounded by co-morbidity between anxiety, depression and other factors, such as deprivation and life stressors (Ding et al., 2014; Grigoriadis et al., 2018). There is no evidence to suggest that high levels of anxiety during pregnancy can cause miscarriage, despite being a common misconception (Stirrat, 1990). Evidence indicates an association between maternal stress and anxiety in pregnancy and alterations to the development of the infant's stress system in utero, known as 'foetal programming', the impact of the in-utero environment on the infant's developing nervous system (e.g. Glover et al., 2015).

The offspring of parents who have anxiety disorders face increased vulnerability to developing mental health problems in childhood (Lawrence et al., 2019). Parents with anxiety disorders may display caregiving behaviours that can limit the child's independence, autonomy and resilience (Wood et al., 2003). Postnatally, anxiety can lead mothers to feel less confident in their parenting, which may reduce maternal sensitivity to infant cues, reduce engagement, and alter emotional tone and warmth during interactions with the infant (Nicol-Harper et al., 2007; Reck et al., 2012). When a child has been exposed to anxiety in utero, sensitive caregiving postnatally has been found to mitigate negative outcomes for the child (Schechter et al., 2017). Whilst there are mixed findings on the impact of maternal anxiety on the quality of the mother–infant relationship, identifying and treating anxiety disorders in the perinatal period is an opportunity to buffer and break the intergenerational transmission of psychological risk.

21.4.6 Perinatal Obsessive-Compulsive Disorder

Unwanted, intrusive thoughts, images, impulses or urges related to a baby are an unpleasant but normal phenomenon of parenting (Fairbrother & Woody, 2008). Intrusive thoughts are likely to occur on a spectrum – more fleeting, less distressing and easier to dismiss at one end, and increasingly persistent, distressing and impacting on functioning at the other. Obsessive-Compulsive Disorder (OCD) is characterised by the unwanted and intrusive presence of obsessions (recurrent and persistent thoughts, urges or images) and/or compulsions (repetitive behaviours or mental acts that are performed in response to an obsession). Approximately 3% of mothers experience OCD during pregnancy, rising to around 7% postnatally (Dennis et al., 2017; Fairbrother et al., 2021). Initial estimates suggest 3.4% of fathers experience OCD during pregnancy, dropping to 1.8% after birth (Coelho et al., 2014). However, further research is needed.

Perinatally, maternal obsessions commonly include thoughts or images about harm coming to the baby, such as distress concerning fear of germs or contamination, or acts of deliberate harm to the baby (Zambaldi et al., 2009). This may result from an increased sense of responsibility that new parents feel towards the care of their infant. These intrusive thoughts or images can be highly distressing, causing anxiety, guilt, disgust and low mood. The resulting compulsions may include a range of rituals or behaviours to reduce the distressing thoughts or prevent the fears from happening, such repeated hand-washing or sanitising, cleaning the infant and the house (e.g. clothes, toys, sterilising equipment), frequent checking, (e.g. checking the baby repeatedly through the night) and reassurance seeking. Avoidance of feared situations or activities is also common, including caregiving of the infant and not trusting others to care for the infant. There may also be attempts to neutralise thoughts through mental rituals, which require directly assessing due to their less overt presence.

There is often a fear of disclosing obsessional thoughts, especially when they are related to harm, due to beliefs that the thoughts mean that they are a bad mother or could result in social care involvement. A parent may worry that their thoughts or images are actually *true,* implicating them as a bad person and parent, fearing that they will subsequently act on the thoughts. This leads to additional fears that others will judge them as being compromised in their parenting capacity.

> *"I see myself throwing my baby down the stairs.*
> *I'm not fit to be a mother"*

Although a thorough risk assessment should always be completed, there is unlikely to be a high level of risk directly related to any obsessions or intrusions (Fairbrother et al., 2022). These are ego-dystonic, meaning that the intrusive thoughts or images are unwanted, inconsistent with a person's values and feelings, and result in distress, anxiety and shame. These fears may reduce disclosure or divulging the extent of symptoms.

Harm-related intrusive thoughts in the context of OCD are very different from thoughts experienced by parents who may impulsively *want* to harm their child when they feel overwhelmed, angry or emotionally dysregulated, or those who have delusions about the baby as a result of postpartum psychosis and have a psychotic belief that the baby *should* be harmed. For more information, Veale et al. (2009) provide a helpful guide on assessing risk alongside OCD.

There may be secondary risks associated with the intrusive thoughts or images, or the resulting coping behaviours. It is imperative to remain sensitive to the distress this is likely to cause and the hypervigilance the mother may be experiencing to any signs she is being judged or seen as a threat to her child. These fears may reduce disclosure or divulging the extent of symptoms.

21.4.7 Birth Trauma and Post-traumatic Stress Disorder

Over the past two decades, there has been a surge in research and understanding relating to parents' experiences of traumatic labour and childbirth. Approximately one-third of women experience childbirth as traumatic (Alcorn et al., 2010), and some may go on to experience post-traumatic stress symptoms resulting from perceived threat to their own life or that of their infant (American Psychiatric Association, 2013). What appears to be important is the subjective view of the experience; trauma symptoms can occur following what is perceived by health professionals to be a 'normal' birth, that is, trauma is 'in the eye of the beholder' (Beck, 2004). Approximately 4% of women develop 'diagnosable' levels of post-traumatic stress, increasing significantly to over 18% in high-risk samples, such as mothers with a history of interpersonal abuse, those who experienced severe pregnancy complications or whose babies' health statuses were compromised or where the infant was born preterm (Yildiz et al., 2017). Some studies find higher rates following obstetric interventions, including emergency caesarean section. An additional proportion also experience subclinical levels of symptoms (Grekin & O'Hara, 2014).

Less is known about fathers' experiences, but a growing body of work highlights that many fathers feel helpless and out of control during their partner's labour and birth, often watching difficult medical situations but unable to help. Prevalence of childbirth-related post-traumatic stress in fathers is inconsistent between studies (0–8%; Ayers et al., 2007; Bradley et al., 2008), but qualitative literature demonstrates the distressing consequences of paternal birth trauma (Daniels et al., 2020).

Post-traumatic stress symptoms during the perinatal period appear to be similar to those experienced following other events, yet there may be specific perinatal factors influencing how these symptoms are experienced and overcome (Iles & Pote, 2015). Postnatal trauma can impact on feeding decisions (Beck & Watson, 2008), as well as perceptions of the bond with the infant (Parfitt & Ayers, 2009). Mothers report feeling disconnected to their infant, lacking confidence in their parenting role and not being a 'good-enough' mother (Molloy et al., 2021). Physical recovery from the birth may impact on parenting behaviours, compounding a sense of guilt and shame already felt alongside trauma symptoms. Avoidance is one of the key features of PTSD, frequently manifested as an attempt to curtail distressing intrusions and flashbacks. Often this avoidance relates to key reminders of the traumatic event itself. With birth trauma these reminders may be the infant themself or healthcare providers, with implications for accessing services. The parent–infant relationship or well-being of the dyad may therefore, unwillingly, be compromised.

It is important to recognise pre-existing PTSD and the impact that a traumatic birth, or other factors in the transition to parenthood, may have in re-triggering trauma symptoms.

21.4.8 Fear of Childbirth (Tokophobia)

Tokophobia refers to a severe fear of childbirth (Hofberg & Ward, 2003) and is at one end of a spectrum of anxiety that women may experience to some degree relating to birth. Tokophobia is not yet well understood and defined. It occurs in approximately 6% of pregnant women, where fears become so extreme that they becomes disabling, interfering with day-to-day functioning and may result in decisions to avoid or terminate a pregnancy, avoid antenatal care or request a caesarean section (Jomeen et al., 2021). Tokophobia in nulliparous women (those who have not previously birthed) is referred to as 'primary', whereas parous women (usually those who have experienced a prior traumatic birth) are referred to as experiencing secondary tokophobia. The nature of the fears can be varied, such as fear of being abandoned during the labour, being unable to manage pain and serious harm coming to the mother or infant (Slade et al., 2019). The new expansion of specialist maternal mental health services within the UK may support women both pre-conception and during pregnancy, working closely with maternity staff to understand and support women's experiences and choices. The services also may offer support post-birth, in the context of traumatic birth experiences.

The increased degree of fear about birth throughout pregnancy may prevent women from enjoying pregnancy, planning for baby, feeling connected to baby and thinking beyond childbirth to parenthood. Subsequently mothers may sense an impairment in their relationship with their infant, although this appears to be mothers' perceptions rather than being a detriment observed by others (Challacombe et al., 2021).

21.4.9 Postpartum (Puerperal or Perinatal) Psychosis

Whilst any perinatal mental health difficulty can become severe in terms of the nature of symptoms, risks, the impact on a person's functioning and on parenting, it is important to consider severe mental illnesses such as bipolar disorder and psychosis. The presence of a pre-existing severe mood disorder, such as bipolar disorder, increases the risk of women experiencing a severe postnatal mental illness (e.g. psychosis, mania) and requiring inpatient psychiatric care (Howard & Khalifeh, 2020).

The onset of psychosis in the postnatal period is rare, affecting 0.2–1% of (birthing) mothers. Postpartum psychosis has an acute and rapid onset, often occurring within 2 weeks of birth, although most mothers date the onset of symptoms to the first 3 days postpartum (American Psychiatric Association, 2013). Following onset, there is a rapid deterioration in a mother's mental health. The symptoms include agitated anxiety and restlessness, delusions (thoughts or beliefs that are unlikely to be true), hallucinations, manic mood (talking/ thinking too quickly, feeling 'high'), low mood (signs of depression, being withdrawn or tearful, lacking energy, loss of appetite or trouble sleeping), loss of inhibitions, feeling suspicious/fearful, behaving out of character and feeling very confused. The delusions or suspicions often involve the partner or family members, which can be very distressing for those involved.

In the immediate acute phase of psychosis there may be concerns about the mother's ability to look after the infant. There are very few studies looking at the potential impact on maternal caregiving during this time, or the impact on the mother–infant relationship. The small body of evidence that exists suggests that these mothers may feel elevated levels of anxiety and reduced confidence in their caregiving, perceiving a detriment to the mother–infant bond (Forde et al., 2020). However, studies also suggest mothers are still able to maintain a level of care and sensitivity towards their infant, and that their interactions may be less impaired than those mothers with severe postnatal depression requiring inpatient admission (Noorlander et al., 2008). This may be dependent on the nature of the delusions experienced, one study found that mothers experiencing infant-related persecutory delusions (beliefs that deliberate harm would come to their infant) were able to show affection towards their baby, demonstrating competence in caring for their baby's needs. These mothers became distressed if separated from their baby. However, mothers with negative beliefs about their baby (i.e. believing the baby was 'evil' or belonged to someone else) were at a greater risk of harm to the infant (Chandra et al., 2006). This highlights the importance of exploring and understanding the nature of postpartum psychotic delusions in order to maintain infant safety as well as preserving the mother–infant relationship.

Onset of postpartum psychosis is viewed as a medical emergency due to increased likelihood of risk to self, others or the infant (predominantly as a result of the delusions), and usually requires a period of inpatient treatment. With the correct intervention, postpartum psychosis usually resolves fairly quickly with mothers making a full recovery. However, there is a high risk of relapse in subsequent pregnancies (up to 75% in some studies; Boyce & Barriball, 2010). It seems that the baby may be central to the mother's recovery; being able to care for the infant may increase sense of parenting self-efficacy. However, this is not always the case as some mothers may feel heighted distress at the pressures of caring for their infant, and feel emotionally detached (Plunkett et al., 2017). Protected sleep is often crucial in recovery from postpartum psychosis, which can be hard to achieve when caring for a newborn with needs throughout all hours. Medication may add to tiredness during this time, increasing difficulties in sense of efficacy in caregiving.

21.4.10 Assessing and Understanding a Perinatal Mental Health Difficulty

It is important to remain sensitive to the fears and difficulties that women may have about disclosing mental health concerns and how this might impact on engagement with services. Any assessment of perinatal mental health difficulties should be done with a 'perinatal frame of mind'; considering the needs of the mother/birthing person the infant, the parent-infant relationship and how this fits with wider family factors (Health Education England, 2018).

This section suggests some areas to guide assessment, which should always be done with appropriate supervision, alongside local policies for managing risk and safeguarding, and in consultation with specialist perinatal services where indicated. For all areas of assessment, consider aspects of diversity and difference as part of understanding the difficulties and experiences in the perinatal period. This may include, ethnicity, culture, language, gender, sexuality and disability.

High levels of co-morbidity and overlap in symptomology must also be taken into account. Hold in mind the possible consequences of this, for example, co-morbid anxiety and depression are more likely to manifest into more severe symptoms with poorer acute and long-term outcomes, harder to treat than each disorder alone, also increasing the risk of suicide (Adams et al., 2016).

Alongside clinical interviews, there are a number of assessment tools that may support understanding and detecting perinatal mental health difficulties (see NICE 2014; Royal College of Psychiatrists, 2018, CR216).

Areas to guide assessment:

- Presenting difficulties, including symptoms, onset, history, frequency.
- Thoughts and beliefs about pregnancy/the baby, childbirth and parenthood.
- Presence of psychosocial stressors and availability/quality of social support (including living conditions, social isolation, immigration difficulties, financial stressors, any inequalities).
- Past psychiatric history (including in the perinatal period) and family mental health history.
- Developmental history (including childhood experiences, experience of being parented).
- Previous mental health support and response to treatment.
- Presence of domestic violence and abuse.
- Circumstances of the pregnancy ((un)intended, (un)planned, (un)wanted).
- Obstetric history (including conception, fertility difficulties, losses, terminations).
- Pregnancy complications, birth details, obstetric interventions.
- Relationship with the baby – including how the baby is perceived by the parent, described, responded to, impacted on by the mental health symptoms and impact of these on caregiving.
- Infant temperament, feeding, sleeping.
- Responsibilities to care for others, including children and adults.
- Understanding the family system – who is in the support network, what is the quality of these relationships, what are their attitudes towards the mother/birthing person and infant, perception of difficulties, what support is available?
- Physical wellbeing (including recovery from birth, wider health, use of substances).

21.5 Maternal Risk and Mortality: Incorporating Risk Management into Perinatal Assessment and Intervention

Risk needs to be held at the forefront of all perinatal work. The 2022 confidential enquiry into maternal deaths in the UK (MBRRACE, 2022) found that during pregnancy, up to 6 weeks after childbirth or the end of pregnancy, 10.9 women per 100,000 died (between 2018 and 2020), a figure rising from previous years. Mental health is one of the leading causes of maternal death during this time, with maternal suicide and drug and alcohol use being the foremost direct causes of death over the first year after pregnancy. Maternal death by suicide was three times more likely in the 2019–2020 period compared to the previous report in 2021. These figures may be lower than the reality as maternal death resulting secondary to self-harm is often not accurately recorded (Mangla et al., 2019). It is also notable that paternal deaths are not yet recorded, despite an increased risk of suicide perinatally (Quevedo et al., 2011).

The MBRRACE report (2022) highlights the importance of immediate and thorough risk management for mothers during the perinatal period. Practitioners need to be aware of the potential for rapid deterioration in women's mental state, particularly postnatally. Recent reporting finds that pregnant teenagers, mothers who have experienced domestic violence and those facing multiple adversities were at notably increased risk. Women residing in the most deprived areas of the UK were two-and-a-half times more likely to die than those in the most affluent areas (MBRRACE, 2022). For 20% of women who died, social care services were involved in their lives this rises to 43% and 85% of those dying due to suicide or substance use respectively.

> There is a need for recognition that women can be placed at additional risk by clinician behaviours which focus on concerns over a woman's pregnancy rather than concerns over a woman herself (MBRRACE, 2021).

There remains a huge disparity in maternal deaths for mothers from minoritised ethnic backgrounds. Mothers and birthing people from black and Asian ethnic groups face a significantly higher risk of dying during the perinatal period compared to white women (MBRRACE, 2022). The reasons behind these inequalities are not yet fully understood but are being increasingly questioned and confronted, although systemic racism may be implicated. As practitioners, it is our role to continue to challenge and change this practice. It is likely that inequities partly stem from socioeconomic factors affecting access to and quality of care, but also stresses of racism and their long-term physiological implications (Omeish & Kiernan, 2020).

Importantly, the MBRRACE reports continue to bring into focus the significant inequalities and adversities that many families face during this period, and the associated increased risks. The nuances in increased risk, and what constitutes elevated risk, need to be thoroughly assessed and managed.

21.5.1 Risk Assessment

Assessing perinatal risk is essential, yet an emotive area for practitioners and clients. Every risk assessment should be made on an individual basis, holding in mind risk of harm to the mother, risks in the mother–infant relationship, and risk of harm to the baby and any older children in the family. Risk must also be considered in the context in which it is occurring – the family environment and wider system – and with consideration of protective factors. Risk in the perinatal period is dynamic and can escalate throughout pregnancy into the postpartum. It is crucial to understand the meaning of a woman's experience, not just the symptoms that exist.

Risk should be a shared responsibility within and across services, with close inter-agency working and information sharing. Always use supervision to discuss and formulate risk.

In addition to a generic assessment of historical and current thoughts of self-harm, suicide and intent, also consider:

- Has there been recent self-harm or a psychiatric admission?
- Is there a sense of hopelessness, thoughts of (violent) suicide, and/or a postpartum onset?
- What is the potential impact of the mother or birthing person's health on the developing foetus or infant, including direct risks such as neglect or abuse?

- Be curious about any thoughts of harm to the unborn/infant – normalise the presence of intrusive thoughts. Establish meaning of these thoughts. Are they present in the context of OCD (e.g. ego-dystonic) or psychosis (e.g. part of delusions)?
- Are there any bonding difficulties (reported or observed)?
- Was this an unwanted pregnancy, or are there any signs of denial of pregnancy?
- Has there been any antenatal neglect (e.g. substance misuse, lack of engagement in antenatal care)?
- Is termination of pregnancy relevant?
- Are there any delusional or persecutory beliefs about the infant?
- Are there any risks involved with medication (non)compliance?
- How is baby experienced by the mother? What is baby's temperament like? (e.g. prolonged crying/unsettled babies can increase the level of stress on a family).
- Is there any risky sexual behaviour, homelessness, lack of engagement with antenatal care?
- How does the mother/birthing person regulate emotions? Is there impulsiveness, irritability, violence?
- Are there risks posed by others (e.g. mental health of others in the family, domestic violence, safeguarding concerns)?
- Are there any secondary risks to the infant (which may need prioritising for treatment)? (e.g. avoidance, excessive washing or restrictions due to other safety strategies, difficulty meeting needs due to other preoccupations, withdrawal, over-compensating or intrusiveness in interactions).

Box 21.2 illustrates an example of a postnatal mother seen by a community perinatal mental health team.

Box 21.2 Clinical example: Celeste

Celeste is a Black African woman in her mid-thirties who was referred to a perinatal service 6 weeks following the birth of her first baby, Tia. Tia was a much longed for baby following over a year of trying for a baby. The labour was long and complicated, resulting in an emergency caesarean section, which left Celeste feeling like she had failed to birth her baby as she had expected. She described feeling anxious, low in mood, withdrawn, lacking in energy and tearful. She found it difficult to soothe Tia when she was crying or distressed. She described feeling overwhelmed when this happened, becoming very upset and believing that she was unfit as a mother because she couldn't comfort Tia. She had started to withdraw from caring for Tia – instead asking Tia's father or other family members to look after her, because she felt they cared for her better than she did.

When Celeste was asked about the thoughts she was experiencing when Tia was crying, she reported that she was having thoughts and images about deliberately harming her. She imagined scenarios in which she was shaking her excessively to stop her crying, or throwing her on the floor in exasperation, after desperately trying to soothe and calm her.

Celeste was caught up in thinking over and over about the thoughts and images she was having, and that this must mean that she was not cut out to be a mother.

At times, she thought that Tia would be better off without her. She spoke about feeling so ashamed that she was having these thoughts. She felt guilty that this was not how she anticipated motherhood would be, and was left wondering if she was doing something wrong and was a bad person.

Celeste was clear that she did not want to harm Tia or act on her thoughts. She was distressed by the presence of the thoughts themselves because she believed that having the thought meant that she would act on it. She sought lots of reassurance from the health team about whether they thought she was a danger to her baby.

Through psychological therapy, Celeste was able to understand that withdrawing from Tia was an attempt to alleviate her distress and reduce what she perceived as her risk to her baby. She recognised that asking others to comfort and meet her needs had an unintended consequence of increasing her perception of being 'not good enough' as a mother and reducing her confidence in being able to care for Tia. Spending time alone gave Celeste time to ruminate and took her away from tasks and activities that she valued and enjoyed. Celeste's difficulties were formulated as perinatal OCD with secondary depressive symptoms.

Celeste and her psychologist worked on her intrusive thoughts and challenged the meaning of these using behavioural experiments (cognitive-behavioural therapy). They worked on building up her emotional capacity to manage Tia's communication through emotions. They used video-interaction guidance (VIG) to support Celeste to see the strengths in the attachment relationship she was developing with Tia and build evidence that she was a good-enough mother and indeed effectively responding to Tia's needs.

Celeste made significant progress in therapy, with the support of the wider perinatal team, to manage these anxious and depressive symptoms. As part of supporting her to maintain progress, treatment considered the significant milestones that might leave her vulnerable to a relapse later in the perinatal period (e.g. comparing developmental milestones with other babies, weaning, Tia becoming more autonomous and expressing her wants and needs in different ways).

Reflections

- What might you have been holding in mind when assessing Celeste?
- What would you need to know and how would you obtain this information to inform your risk assessment?
- Might there be important aspects of ethnicity, culture and identity that could be explored with Celeste? How might you go about sensitively exploring these areas with Celeste?
- What factors may have made Celeste vulnerable to perinatal mental health difficulties, and how would you consider these in understanding her difficulties?
- How might you consider the needs of Celeste's partner and what this experience might be like for him?
- How do you think Tia would have been experiencing her mother?

21.6 Psychological Therapies for Perinatal Mental Health Difficulties

Studies have demonstrated the effectiveness of psychological and psychosocial interventions for a range of presentations during the perinatal period, and found that the evidence base mirrors interventions found to be effective for mental health difficulties outside the perinatal period (Howard & Khalifeh, 2020). Psychological therapies for perinatal mental health difficulties should be guided by NICE recommendations (e.g. NICE, 2014) and the latest evidence base (NHS England et al., 2018). Reviews of perinatal services in low- and middle-income countries suggest the effectiveness of integrating perinatal services into broader maternal services (Prom et al., 2022).

In brief, cognitive behavioural therapy (CBT) is the predominant recommended intervention across perinatal mental health disorders. There are also recommendations for the use of behavioural couples therapy (BCT) and interpersonal therapy (IPT), particularly for depression. Eye movement desensitisation and reprocessing (EMDR) is recommended for PTSD (including post-birth). Family interventions are recommended for the treatment of psychosis. There is growing interest in the applicability and effectiveness of third-wave cognitive and behavioural interventions (e.g. acceptance and commitment therapy (ACT) and compassion-focused therapy (CFT)). There are a range of interventions that draw on an attachment framework (e.g. mentalisation-based therapy (MBT) and schema-informed CBT), which may be particularly relevant in the perinatal period.

Studies have examined the impact of transdiagnostic interventions for the intergenerational cycles of trauma often associated with the perinatal period (Erickson et al., 2019). Many specialist perinatal services in England will provide interventions such as, circle of security parenting (COS-P, Cooper et al., 2005), VIG (e.g. Kennedy & Underdown, 2018), video intervention to promote positive parenting (VIPP, Juffer et al., 2008) and parent–infant psychotherapy (PIP, e.g. Barlow et al., 2015) to support parents to feel more confident in their parenting role or the parent-infant relationship.

21.7 Perinatal Mental Health and Outcomes for the Wider Family

If a mother experiences a perinatal mental health difficulty, the whole family may be affected. Although not always the case, the home environment is likely to be altered: emotions may be high, fluctuating rapidly and unexpectedly. Previous routines may be disrupted and the family may become isolated from their support network due to fears of stigma or judgement or due to the daily challenges associated with managing a mental health difficulty. Partners and other family members have to manage their own worries about the mother, cope with changes to relationships, simultaneously managing other people's concerns and questions (Darwin et al., 2021).

The potential familial consequences of perinatal mental health are increasingly being recognised and national policies are driving change within healthcare services.

If working with a mother/birthing person in the perinatal period, always consider the following:

- Is there anyone else in their family or support network who may need support?
- Has anyone seen or spoken to these family members?
- How are they coping?
- What can you do to ensure all family members are taken into account and offered appropriate care and support?
- If your service is not able to offer direct support, are there any local or national services who you can signpost to?

Other children in the family may be less visible to services, because of the focus on the mother. These children may or may not be biologically related to the mother, or any other parental figures in the house. Older children may find it hard to understand what is happening, feel worried for their parent, feel alone and afraid. They may have been exposed to heightened emotions, witnessed distressing events or been separated from a parent, particularly if a mother is severely unwell and admitted to an inpatient unit. The child may have to take on additional tasks within the home, and their education may be disrupted. If the family has become distanced from support, older children may feel isolated and alone. Furthermore, if the mother and infant are away from the family home in an MBU (or other inpatient setting), this may affect the relationship that older children develop with the baby. Children may need to take on caring responsibilities for other children in the family or for their parent/s. Although they may take pride in this, caring for a parent with a mental health difficulty can bring many pressures (Cooklin, 2009).

Evidence suggests that children living in a home with a parent with a mental health difficulty are at increased risk of emotional, behavioural and developmental difficulties, as well as adverse health outcomes (e.g. Pierce et al., 2020; van Santvoort et al., 2015). The children's needs and safeguarding must be considered and appropriately assessed.

21.8 Challenges and Future Directions for Perinatal Mental Health Provision

A significant challenge faced by professionals as well as families during the perinatal period is the stigma around mental health, and the level of fear, shame and guilt that parents and families face in sharing their experiences and seeking help. Despite societal shifts in acceptability of discussing mental health, there remain pressures and taboos about 'failing' as a parent. Perceived expectations and judgements from others can weigh heavily. Fears of being deemed an unfit parent and the infant or older children being removed from the home may feel overwhelming, leading to withdrawal from others, isolation and a reluctance to seek support. Sadly, many families may therefore suffer on their own during this time. For children in the family, this may mean they go unseen for longer, increasing severity and duration of any distress and difficulties experienced. Family members can feel a sense of betrayal in sharing difficulties experienced in the family, which may be further amplified for those from marginalised backgrounds.

Ongoing challenges for service managers and practitioners include service remits and commissioning constraints. Although there has been a surge in recognising the familial and transgenerational impact of perinatal mental health, and a programme of service development to begin to support this in England, further change is needed. The current emphasis is on service provision for the mother or other birthing parent. Some services are also able to work with the infant. However, we still need to improve visibility of and support for, other family members, including children in the family: fathers, co-parents and partners.

- Other family members, including children in the family and other caregivers.
  - How will services find ways to make families and their needs visible?
- Children impacted by another caregiver's perinatal mental health difficulties.
  - How can services be aware of these needs when fathers, other co-parents and partners are not routinely assessed?
- Older children whose longer-term outcomes may be impacted by perinatal mental health: for some children affected, difficulties may not manifest or be visible for many years.
  - How can services working with older children continue to understand and consider the impact and role of perinatal mental health across the lifespan?

If future developments see services able to offer increased support and interventions for infants and children affected by perinatal mental health, then the workforce within these services need consideration. Many staff working in perinatal services have trained in adult mental health and may not have the required competencies in working with infants or children. Additional training may be required, including assessment and intervention for the mother–infant relationship or systemic approaches.

The significance of perinatal mental health for families across the life course needs to be widely understood. There is an important role for health professionals working in all services to hold in mind perinatal mental health difficulties and their impact.

References

Adams, G. C., Balbuena, L., Meng, X., & Asmundson, G.J. (2016). When social anxiety and depression go together: A population study of comorbidity and associated consequences. *Journal of Affective Disorders*, *206*, 48–54. https://doi.org/10.1016/j.jad.2016.07.031

Ainsworth, M. S., Blehar, M. C., Waters, E., & Wall, S. (1978). *Patterns of attachment: A psychological study of the strange situation*. Lawrence Erlbaum.

Alcorn, K. L., O'Donovan, A., Patrick, J. C., Creedy, D., & Devilly, G. J. (2010). A prospective longitudinal study of the prevalence of post-traumatic stress disorder resulting from childbirth events. *Psychological Medicine*, *40*, 1849–1859.

American Psychiatric Association. (2013). *Diagnostic and statistical manual of mental disorders* (5th ed.). American Psychiatric Association.

Ayers, S., Wright, D. B., & Wells, N. (2007). Symptoms of post-traumatic stress disorder in couples after birth: Association with the couple's relationship and parent–baby bond. *Journal of Reproductive and Infant Psychology*, *25*, 40–50.

Barlow, J., Bennett, C., Midgley, N., Larkin, S. K., & Wei, Y. (2015). Parent-infant psychotherapy for improving parental and infant mental health. *Cochrane Database of Systematic Reviews*, *1*. https://doi.org/10.1002/14651858.CD010534.pub2

Bauer, J., Knapp, M., & Parsonage, M. (2016). Lifetime costs of perinatal anxiety and depression. *Journal of Affective Disorders, 192*, 83–90. https://doi.org/10.1016/j.jad.2015.12.005

Beck, C. T. (2004). Birth trauma: In the eye of the beholder. *Nursing Research, 53* (1), 28–35. https://doi.org/10.1097/00006199-200401000-00005

Beck, C. T., & Watson, S. (2008). Impact of birth trauma on breast-feeding. *Nursing Research, 57* (4), 228–236. https://doi.org/10.1097/01.NNR.0000313494.87282.90

Biaggi, A., Conroy, S., Pawlby, S., & Pariante, C. M. (2016). Identifying the women at risk of antenatal anxiety and depression: A systematic review. *Journal of Affective Disorders, 191*, 62–77. https://doi.org/10.1016/j.jad.2015.11.014

Boyce, P., & Barriball, E. (2010). Puerperal psychosis. *Archive of Womens' Mental Health, 13*, 45–47. https://doi.org/10.1007/s00737-009-0117-y

Bradley, R., Slade, P., & Leviston, A. (2008). Low rates of PTSD in men attending childbirth: A preliminary study. *British Journal of Clinical Psychology, 47*, 295–302.

British Psychological Society. (2019). *Position paper. Perinatal psychology provision in specialist perinatal community mental health services*. https://www.bps.org.uk/guideline/perinatal-psychology-provision-specialist-perinatal-community-mental-health-services

Cameron, E. E., Sedov, I. D., & Tomfohr-Madsen, L. M. (2016). Prevalence of paternal depression in pregnancy and the postpartum: An updated meta-analysis. *Journal of Affective Disorders, 206*, 189–203.

Challacombe, F. L., Nath, S., Trevillion, K., Pawlby, S., & Howard, L. (2021). Fear of childbirth during pregnancy: Associations with observed mother–infant interactions and perceived bonding. *Archives of Women's Mental Health, 24*, 483–492. https://doi.org/10.1007/s00737-020-01098-w

Chandra, P., Bhargavaraman, R., Raghunandan, V. M., & Shaligram, D. (2006). Delusions related to infant and their association with mother–infant interactions in postpartum psychotic disorders. *Archives of Women's Mental Health, 9*, 285–288. https://doi.org/10.1007/s00737-006-0147-7

Chhabra, J., McDermott, B., & Li, W. (2020). Risk factors for paternal perinatal depression and anxiety: A systematic review and meta-analysis. *Psychology of Men & Masculinities, 21*(4), 593–611. https://doi.org/10.1037/men0000259

Coelho, F. M., Silva, R. A. D., Quevedo, L. D. Á., Souza, L. D., Pinheiro, K. A., & Pinheiro, R. T. (2014). Obsessive-compulsive disorder in fathers during pregnancy and postpartum. *Brazilian Journal of Psychiatry, 36*(3), 272–272.

Cooklin, A. (2009). Children as carers of parents with mental illness. *Psychiatry, 8*(1), 17–20.

Cooper, G., Hoffman, K. T., Powell, B., & Marvin, R. S. (2005). The circle of security intervention: differential diagnosis and differential treatment. In: L. J. Berlin, Y. Ziv, L. M. Amaya-Jackson, and M. T. Greenberg (Eds.), *Enhancing early attachments: theory, research, intervention, and policy* (pp. 127–151). Guilford Press.

Cree, M. (2015). *The compassionate mind approach to postnatal depression: Using compassion focused therapy to enhance mood, confidence and bonding*. Robinson.

Daniels, E., Arden-Close, E., & Mayers, A. (2020). Be quiet and man up: A qualitative questionnaire study into fathers who witnessed their partner's birth trauma. *BMC pregnancy and childbirth, 20*(1), 1–12.

Darwin, Z., Domoney, J., Iles, J., Bristow, F., McLeish, J., & Sethna, V. (2021). *Involving and supporting partners and other family members in specialist perinatal mental health services*.

Good practice guidance. https://www.england.nhs.uk/wp-content/uploads/2021/03/Good-practice-guide-March-2021.pdf

Darwin, Z., Galdas, P., Hinchliff, S., Littlewood, E., McMillan, D., McGowan, L., & Gilbody, S. (2017). Fathers' views and experiences of their own mental health during pregnancy and the first postnatal year: A qualitative interview study of men participating in the UK Born and Bred in Yorkshire (BaBY) cohort. *BMC Pregnancy Childbirth*, *17*, 45. https://doi.org/10.1186/s12884-017-1229-4

Dennis, C. L., Falah-Hassani, K., & Shiri, R. (2017). Prevalence of antenatal and postnatal anxiety: Systematic review and meta-analysis. *British Journal of Psychiatry*, *210*(5), 315–323. https://doi.org/10.1192/bjp.bp.116.187179.

Department of Health and Social Care. (2021). The best start for life. A vision for the 1001 critical days. The Early Years Healthy Development Review Report. https://www.gov.uk/government/publications/the-best-start-for-life-a-vision-for-the-1001-critical-days

Ding, X. X., Wu, Y. L., Xu, S. J., Zhu, R. P., Jia, X. M., Zhang, S. F., Huang, K., Zhu, P., Hao J-H., & Tao, F. B. (2014). Maternal anxiety during pregnancy and adverse birth outcomes: A systematic review and meta-analysis of prospective cohort studies. *Journal of Affective Disorders*, *159*, 103–110.

Erickson, N., Julian, M., & Muzik, M. (2019). Perinatal depression, PTSD, and trauma: Impact on mother-infant attachment and interventions to mitigate the transmission of risk. *International Review of Psychiatry*, *31*(3), 245–263. https://doi.org/10.1080/09540261.2018.1563529

Fairbrother, N., Collardeau, F., Albert, A. Y. K., Challacombe, F. L., Thordarson, D. S., Woody, S. R., & Janssen, P. A. (2021). High prevalence and incidence of obsessive-compulsive disorder among women across pregnancy and the postpartum. *The Journal of Clinical Psychiatry*, *82*(2), 20m13398. https://doi.org/10.4088/JCP.20m13398

Fairbrother, N., Collardeau, F., Woody, S. R., Wolfe, D.A., & Fawcett, J. M. (2022). Postpartum thoughts of infant-related harm and obsessive-compulsive disorder: Relation to maternal physical aggression toward the infant. *Journal of Clinical Psychiatry*, *83*(2). https://doi.org/10.4088/JCP.21m14006.

Fairbrother, N., & Woody, S. R. (2008). New mothers' thoughts of harm related to the newborn. *Archives of Women's Mental Health*, *11*(3), 221–229. https://doi.org/10.1007/s00737-008-0016-7

Field T. (2010). Postpartum depression effects on early interactions, parenting, and safety practices: a review. *Infant behavior & development*, *33*(1), 1–6. https://doi.org/10.1016/j.infbeh.2009.10.005

Forde, R., Peters, S., & Wittkowski, A. (2020). Recovery from postpartum psychosis: A systematic review and metasynthesis of women's and families' experiences. *Archives of Women's Mental Health*, *23*, 597–612. https://doi.org/10.1007/s00737-020-01025-z

Fraiberg, S., Adelson, E., & Shapiro, V. (1975). Ghosts in the nursery: A psychoanalytic approach to the problems of impaired infant–mother relationships. *Journal of American Academy of Child Psychiatry*, *14*(3), 387–421.

Gavin, N. I., Gaynes, B. N., Lohr, K. N., Meltzer-Brody, S., Gartlehner, G., & Swinson, T. (2005). Perinatal depression: A systematic review of prevalence and incidence. *Obstetrics and Gynaecology*, *5* (1), 1071–1083. https://doi.org/10.1097/01.AOG.0000183597.31630.db

Glover, V. (2015). Prenatal stress and its effects on the fetus and the child: Possible underlying biological mechanisms. *Advances in Neurobiology, 10*, 269–283.

Greenfield, M., & Darwin, Z. (2021). Trans and non-binary pregnancy, traumatic birth, and perinatal mental health: A scoping review. *International Journal of Transgender Health, 22*(1–2); https://doi.org/10.1080/26895269.2020.1841057.

Grekin, R., & O'Hara, M.W. (2014). Prevalence and risk factors of postpartum post-traumatic stress disorder: A meta-analysis. *Clinical Psychology Review, 34*(5), 389–401. https://doi.org/10.1016/j.cpr.2014.05.003

Grigoriadis, S., Graves, L., Peer, M., Mamisashvili, L., Tomlinson, G., Vigod, S. N., Dennis, C. L., Steiner, M., Brown, C., Cheung, A., dawson, H., Rector, N. A., Guenette, M., & Richter, M. (2018). Maternal anxiety during pregnancy and the association with adverse perinatal outcomes: Systematic review and meta-analysis. *The Journal of Clinical Psychiatry, 79*(5), 17r12011.

Health Education England. (2018). *The competency framework for professionals working with women who have mental health problems in the perinatal period.* https://www.hee.nhs.uk/our-work/mental-health/perinatal-mental-health/competency-framework-perinatal-mental-health

Hofberg, K., & Ward, M. R. (2003). Fear of pregnancy and childbirth. *Postgraduate Medical Journal, 79*, 505–510. https://doi.org/10.1136/pmj.79.935.505

Howard, L. M., & Khalifeh, H. (2020). Perinatal mental health: A review of progress and challenges. *World Psychiatry, 19*, 313–327. https://doi.org/10.1002/wps.20769

Howard, L. M., Piot, P., & Stein, A. (2014). No health without perinatal mental health. *The Lancet, 384*(9956), 1723–1724. https://doi.org/10.1016/S0140-6736(14)62040-7

Howard, L., Ryan, E., Trevillion, K., Anderson, F., Bick, D., Bye, A., Byford, S., O'Connor, S., Sands, P., Demilew, J., Milgrom, J., & Pickles, A. (2018). Accuracy of the Whooley questions and the Edinburgh Postnatal Depression Scale in identifying depression and other mental disorders in early pregnancy. *The British Journal of Psychiatry, 212*(1), 50–56. doi: https://doi.org/10.1192/bjp.2017.9

Howat, A., Masterson, C., & Darwin, Z. (2023). Non-birthing mothers' experiences of perinatal anxiety and depression: understanding the perspectives of the non-birthing mothers in female same-sex parented families. *Midwifery, 120*, 103650. https://doi.org/10.1016/j.midw.2023.103650

Hunter, A., Tussis, L., & MacBeth, A. (2017). The presence of anxiety, depression and stress in women and their partners during pregnancies following perinatal loss: A meta-analysis. *Journal of Affective Disorders, 1*, 153–164.

Iles, J., & Pote, H. (2015). Postnatal post-traumatic stress: A grounded theory model of first-time mothers' experiences. *Journal of Reproductive and Infant Psychology, 33*(3), 238–255. https://doi.org/10.1080/02646838.2015.1030732

Jomeen, J., Martin, C.R., Jones, C., Marshall, C., Ayers, S., Burt, K., Frodsham, L., Horsch, A., Midwinter, D., O'Connell, M., Shakespeare, J., Sheen, K., & Thomson, G. (2021). Tokophobia and fear of birth: A workshop consensus statement on current issues and recommendations for future research. *Journal of Reproductive and Infant Psychology, 39*(1), 2–15. https://doi.org/10.1080/02646838.2020.1843908

Juffer, F., Bakermans-Kranenburg, M. J., & van IJzendoorn, M. H. (Eds.). (2008). *Promoting positive parenting: An attachment-based intervention.* Taylor & Francis Group/Lawrence Erlbaum Associates.

Kendig, S., Keats, J. P., Hoffman, M. C., Kay, L. B., Miller, E. S., Moore Simas, T. A., Frieder, A., Hackley, B., Indman, P., Raines, C., Semenuk, K., Wisner, K. L., & Lemieux. L. A. (2017). Consensus bundle on maternal mental health: Perinatal depression and anxiety. *Obstetrics & Gynecololgy, 129*(3), 422–430. https://doi.org/10.1097/AOG.0000000000001902

Kennedy, H., & Underdown, A. (2018). Video interaction guidance: Promoting secure attachment and optimal development for children, parents and professionals. In P. Leach (Ed.), *Transforming infant wellbeing: Research, policy and practice for the first 1001 critical days* (pp. 224–237). Routledge/Taylor & Francis.

Klerman, L.V. (2000). The intendedness of pregnancy: A concept in transition. *Maternal Child Health Journal, 4*, 155–162. https://doi.org/10.1023/A:1009534612388

LARA-VP. (Linking Abuse and Recovery through Advocacy for Victims and Perpetrators). (2022). *A resource to help mental health professionals identify and respond to Domestic Violence and Abuse (DVA).* lara-vp-online-resource.pdf (kcl.ac.uk)

Law, S., Ormel, I., Babinski, S., Plett, D., Dionne, E., Schwartz, H., & Rozmovits, L. (2021). Dread and solace: Talking about perinatal mental health. *International Journal of Mental Health Nursing, 30(S1)*, 1376–1385. https://doi.org/10.1111/inm.12884

Lawrence, P. J., Murayama, K., & Creswell, C. (2019). Systematic review and meta-analysis: Anxiety and depressive disorders in offspring of parents with anxiety disorders. *Journal of the American Academy of Child and Adolescent Psychiatry, 58*(1), 46–60. https://doi.org/10.1016/j.jaac.2018.07.898

Leach, L. S., Poyser, C., Cooklin, A. R., & Giallo, R. (2016). Prevalence and course of anxiety disorders (and symptom levels) in men across the perinatal period: A systematic review. *Journal of Affective Disorders, 190*, 675–686. https://doi.org/10.1016/j.jad.2015.09.063

Leigh, B., & Milgrom, J. (2008). Risk factors for antenatal depression, postnatal depression and parenting stress. *BMC Psychiatry, 8*, 24. https://doi.org/10.1186/1471-244X-8-24

Malmquist, A., Jonsson, L., Wikström, J., & Nieminen, K. (2019). Minority stress adds an additional layer to fear of childbirth in lesbian and bisexual women, transgender people. *Midwifery, 79*, 102551. https://doi.org/10.1016/j.midw.2019.102551

Mangla, K., Hoffman, M.C., Trumpff, C., O'Grady, S., & Monk, C. (2019). Maternal self-harm deaths: An unrecognized and preventable outcome. *American Journal of Obstetrics and Gynecology, 221*(4), 295–303. https://doi.org/10.1016/j.ajog.2019.02.056

MBRRACE. (2021). *Saving lives, improving mothers' care lessons learned to inform maternity care from the UK and Ireland confidential enquiries into maternal deaths and morbidity 2017–19*. https://www.npeu.ox.ac.uk/mbrrace-uk/reports

MBRRACE report (2022). *Saving lives, improving mothers' care lessons learned to inform maternity care from the UK and Ireland confidential enquiries into maternal deaths and morbidity 2018–20*. https://www.npeu.ox.ac.uk/mbrrace-uk

Meeussen, L., & Van Laar, C. (2018). Feeling pressure to be a perfect mother relates to parental burnout and career ambitions. *Frontiers in Psychology, 9*, 2113. https://doi.org/10.3389/fpsyg.2018.02113

Mojahed, A., Alaidarous, N., Kopp, M., Pogarell, A., Thiel, F., & Garthus-Niegel, S. (2021). Prevalence of intimate partner violence among intimate partners during the perinatal period: A narrative literature review. *Frontiers in Psychiatry, 12*. https://doi.org/10.3389/fpsyt.2021.601236

Molloy, E., Biggerstaff, D. L., & Sidebotham, P. (2021). A phenomenological exploration of parenting after birth trauma: Mothers' perceptions of the first year. *Women and Birth*, *34*(3), 278–287. https://doi.org/10.1016/j.wombi.2020.03.004

Murray, L., Fiori-Cowley, A., Hooper, R., & Cooper, P. (1996). The impact of postnatal depression and associated adversity on early mother–infant interactions and later infant outcome. *Child Development*, *67*, 2512–2526.

National Collaborating Centre for Mental Health. (2007). *Antenatal and postnatal mental health: The NICE guideline on clinical management and service guidance*. The British Psychological Society and The Royal College of Psychiatrists.

National Collaborating Centre for Women's and Children's Health. (2008). *Antenatal care: Routine care for the healthy pregnant woman*. RCOG Press.

National Institute for Health and Care Excellence (NICE). (2014). *Antenatal and postnatal mental health: Clinical management and service guidance*. National Institute for Health and Care Excellence.

NHS England, NHS Improvement, & National Collaborating Centre for Mental Health. (2018). Perinatal mental health care pathways. https://www.england.nhs.uk/wp-content/uploads/2018/05/perinatal-mental-health-care-pathway.pdf

Nicol-Harper, R., Harvey, A. G., & Stein, A. (2007). Interactions between mothers and infants: Impact of maternal anxiety. *Infant Behavior & Development*, *30*(1), 161–167. https://doi.org/10.1016/j.infbeh.2006.08.005

Noorlander, Y., Bergink, V., & van den Berg, M. (2008). Perceived and observed mother–child interaction at time of hospitalization and release in postpartum depression and psychosis. *Archives of Women's Mental Health*, *11*, 49–56. https://doi.org/10.1007/s00737-008-0217-0

Office for National Statistics. (2021). *Births in England and Wales* 2020. https://www.ons.gov.uk/peoplepopulationandcommunity/birthsdeathsandmarriages/livebirths/bulletins/birthsummarytablesenglandandwales/2020

O'Hara, M. W., & McCabe, J. E. (2013). Postpartum depression: Current status and future directions. *Annual Review of Clinical Psychology*, *9*, 379–407. https://doi.org/10.1146/annurev-clinpsy-050212-185612

O'Hara, M. W., & Wisner, K. L. (2014). Perinatal mental illness: Definition, description and aetiology. *Best Practice Research Clinical Obstetrics and Gynaecology*, *1*, 3–12. https://doi.org/10.1016/j.bpobgyn.2013.09.002

O'Mahen, H., & Healy, S. (2021). *IAPT perinatal competency framework*. https://www.ucl.ac.uk/pals/sites/pals/files/iapt_perinatal_competancy_framework_final_version_sept_2021-1.pdf

Omeish, Y., & Kiernan, S. (2020). Targeting bias to improve maternal care and outcomes for Black women in the USA. *eClinical Medicine*, *3*(27), 100568. https://doi.org/10.1016/j.eclinm.2020.100568.

Parfitt, Y. M., & Ayers, S. (2009). The effect of postnatal symptoms of post-traumatic stress and depression on the couple's relationship and the parent-baby bond. *Journal of Reproductive and Infant Psychology*, *27* (2), 127–142. https://doi.org/10.1080/02646830802350831

Pierce, M., Hope, H., Kolade, A., Gellatly, J., Osam, C., Perchard, R., Kosidou, K., Dalman, C., Morgan, V., Di Prinzio, P., & Abel, K. (2020). Effects of parental mental illness on children's physical health: Systematic review and meta-analysis. *The British Journal of Psychiatry*, *217*(1), 354–363. https://doi.org/10.1192/bjp.2019.216

Plunkett, C., Peters, S., Wieck, A., & Wittkowski, A. (2017). A qualitative investigation in the role of the baby in recovery from postpartum psychosis. *Clinical Psychology & Psychotherapy, 24*(5), 1099–1108. https://doi.org/10.1002/cpp.2074

Prady, S. L., Endacott, C., Dickerson, J., Bywater, T. J., & Blower, S. L. (2021). Inequalities in the identification and management of common mental disorders in the perinatal period: An equity focused re-analysis of a systematic review. *PloS One, 16*(3), e0248631. https://doi.org/10.1371/journal.pone.0248631

Prom, M. C., Denduluri, A., Philpotts, L. L., Rondon, M. B., Borba, C. P. C., Gelaye, B., & Byatt, N. (2022). A systematic review of interventions that integrate perinatal mental health care into routine maternal care in low- and middle-income countries. *Frontiers in Psychiatry, 13*, 859341. https://doi.org/10.3389/fpsyt.2022.859341

Quevedo, L., da Silva, R. A., Coelho, F., Pinheiro, K. A., Horta, B. K., & Kapczinski, F. (2011). Risk of suicide and mixed episode in men in the postpartum period. *Journal of Affective Disorder, 132*, 243–246. https://doi.org/10.1016/j.jad.2011.01.004

Reck, C., Noe, D., Gerstenlauer, J., & Stehle, E. (2012). Effects of postpartum anxiety disorders and depression on maternal self-confidence. *Infant Behaviour and Development, 35*(2), 264–272. https://doi.org/10.1016/j.infbeh.2011.12.005

Robertson, E., Grace, S., Wallington, T., & Stewart, D.E. (2004). Antenatal risk factors for postpartum depression: A synthesis of recent literature. *General Hospital Psychiatry, 26*(4), 289–295. https://doi.org/10.1016/j.genhosppsych.2004.02.006

Ross, L. E., Steele, L., Goldfinger, C., & Strike, C. (2007). Perinatal depressive symptomatology among lesbian and bisexual women. *Archives of Women's Mental Health, 10*, 53–59. https://doi.org/10.1007/s00737-007-0168-x

Royal College of Psychiatrists. (2018). *Framework for routine outcome measures in perinatal psychiatry CR216*. https://www.rcpsych.ac.uk/improving-care/campaigning-for-better-mental-health-policy/college-reports/2018-college-reports/cr216

Royal College of Psychiatrists (2021). *Perinatal mental health services: Recommendations for the provision of services for childbearing women CR232*. https://www.rcpsych.ac.uk/improving-care/campaigning-for-better-mental-health-policy/college-reports/2021-college-reports/perinatal-mental-health-services-CR232.

Schechter, J. C., Brennan, P. A., Smith, A. K., Stowe, Z. N., Newport, D. J., & Johnson, K. C. (2017). Maternal prenatal psychological distress and preschool cognitive functioning: The protective role of positive parental engagement. *Journal of Abnormal Child Psychology, 45*(2), 249–260. https://doi.org/10.1007/s10802-016-0161-9

Slade, P., Balling, K., Sheen, K., & Houghton, G (2019). Establishing a valid construct of fear of childbirth: Findings from in-depth interviews with women and midwives. *BMC Pregnancy Childbirth, 19*(96). https://doi.org/10.1186/s12884-019-2241-7

Stein, A., Pearson, R. M., Goodman, S. H., Rapa, E., Rahman, A., McCallum, M., Howard, L. M., & Pariante, C. M. (2014). Effects of perinatal mental disorders on the fetus and child. *Lancet, 384*(9956), 1800–1819. https://doi.org/10.1016/S0140-6736(14)61277-0

Stirrat, G. M. (1990). Recurrent miscarriage. *The Lancet, 15*, 673–675. https://doi.org/10.1016/0140-6736(90)92159-f

UNICEF, World Bank, & World Health Organization. (2018). *Nurturing care for early childhood development: A framework for helping children survive and thrive to transform health and human potential.* https://apps.who.int/iris/bitstream/handle/10665/272603/9789241514064-eng.pdf

van Santvoort, F., Hosman, C. M. H., & Janssens, J. M. (2015). The impact of various parental mental disorders on children's diagnoses: A systematic review. *Clinical Child and Family Psychology Review, 18*, 281–299. https://doi.org/10.1007/s10567-015-0191-9

Veale, D., Freeston, M., Krebs, G., Heyman, I., & Salkovskis, P. (2009). Risk assessment and management in obsessive-compulsive disorder. *Advances in Psychiatric Treatment, 15*(5), 332–343.Wee, K. Y., Skouteris, H., Pier, C., Richardson, B., & Milgrom, J. (2011). Correlates of ante and postnatal depression in fathers: A systematic review. *Journal of Affective Disorders, 130*, 358–377. https://doi.org/10.1016/j.jad.2010.06.019

Wood, J. J., McLeod, B. D., Sigman, M., Hwang, W. C., & Chu, B. C. (2003). Parenting and childhood anxiety: Theory, empirical findings, and future directions. *Journal of Child Psychology and Psychiatry, and Allied Disciplines, 44*(1), 134–151. https://doi.org/10.1111/1469-7610.00106

Woolhouse, H., Brown, S., Krastev, A., Perlen, S., & Gunn, J. (2009). Seeking help for anxiety and depression after childbirth: Results of the maternal health study. *Archive of Women's Mental Health, 2*, 75–83. https://doi.org/10.1007/s00737-009-0049-6

Yildiz, P. D., Ayers, S., & Phillips, L. (2017). The prevalence of post-traumatic stress disorder in pregnancy and after birth: A systematic review and meta-analysis. *Journal of Affective Disorders, 208*, 634–645. https://doi.org/10.1016/j.jad.2016.10.009

Zambaldi, C. F., Cantilino, A., Montenegro, A. C., Paes, J. A., de Albuquerque, T. L., & Sougey, E. B. (2009). Postpartum obsessive-compulsive disorder: Prevalence and clinical characteristics. *Comprehensive Psychiatry, 50* (6), 503–509. https://doi.org/10.1016/j.comppsych.2008.11.014

22

Mental Health Crisis and Inpatient Care for Children and Young People

Aspa Paspali

This chapter is divided into two sections: 1) mental health crisis and 2) psychiatric inpatient care for children and young people (CYP). The majority of the chapter will focus on assessment and treatment in the United Kingdom.

Section 1 discusses what constitutes a mental health crisis in CYP, and the various crisis presentations that a psychological practitioner may encounter. It focusses on self-harm and suicide attempts and will also describe other possible mental health crisis presentations. It discusses the key elements of a comprehensive risk assessment, and interventions to manage acute risk and underlying presentations. This information can be used in acute settings, such as hospital Accident and Emergency (A&E) departments, but also in other settings such as community Child and Adolescent Mental Health Services (CAMHS) or schools. It discusses the challenges associated with the current provision of crisis care for CYP and opportunities for future developments.

Section 2 discusses what happens during a psychiatric admission, the different types of CYP inpatient settings, and the legal frameworks around admission and deprivation of liberty that psychological practitioners need to be aware of. It discusses when a psychiatric admission may be necessary, the benefits and the risks associated with inpatient admissions, and finally, future directions in inpatient care for CYP.

In this chapter, the term 'psychological practitioner' is used to describe clinicians from various professional backgrounds and disciplines who may be assessing and/ or treating CYP who present in mental health crisis or are admitted as psychiatric inpatients. It includes not only psychologists, but also mental health nurses, psychiatrists, psychotherapists, clinical social workers, and other therapists.

22.1 Mental Health Crisis

22.1.1 Introduction

Half of all mental illnesses begin before the age of 14, and three-quarters before the age of 18. Mental health services for CYP are significantly underfunded (Dubicka & Bullock, 2017). Between 1 in 8 and 1 in 10 CYP are currently thought to have a diagnosable mental

Child Psychology: Pathways to Good Practice, First Edition.
Edited by Helen Pote, Anna Picciotto and Clare Norris.

disorder, and between 1 in 12 and 1 in 15 will self-harm (Healthy London Partnership 2016; Sadler et al., 2018). A national UK survey found that in 2022, 18% of children aged 7 to 16 years and 22% of CYP aged 17 to 24 years had a probable mental disorder. These figures had increased between 2017 and 2020 in both groups and have remained stable since then (NHS Digital, 2022).

A 2017 UK analysis (Morgan et al., 2017) showed that girls exhibit a higher annual incidence of self-harm (37.4 per 10,000) than boys (12.3 per 10,000), with a significant increase of 68% in girls aged 13 and 16 between 2011 to 2014. Young adults in the United Kingdom are seeking support for mental health problems, such as anxiety, depression or self-harm in greater proportions that any other generation on record (NSPCC, 2016).

A mental health crisis refers to a situation in which an individual's mental health has deteriorated to the point where they require immediate intervention and support, and the support already available (at home, at school and/or from community services) is no longer sufficient to contain it. Presentations can be varied, for example, a significant deterioration in the individual's mental health condition such as a depressive or anxiety disorder, a severe panic attack, or the emergence of a psychotic illness, which are often accompanied by a weakening of the system of care around the individual, such as a relationship breakup, difficulties with friendships, exam stress, parental separation, a house move, experiencing physical, sexual or emotional abuse and others (Healthy London Partnership, 2016).

Failure to prevent and address mental health crises in CYP presents a missed opportunity for the CYP and their future trajectory (Healthy London Partnership, 2016). A mental health crisis can present in many ways and may lead to a CYP's first presentation to mental health services, or to a hospital A&E department (Healthy London Partnership, 2016).

Mental health crises in CYP differ to those in adults, as CYP are much more embedded in their families, schools, friendship groups and other social systems. Because a crisis episode in a CYP may not be always due to a mental health problem alone, relying solely on healthcare when addressing it is unlikely to lead to an effective solution. A holistic approach involving coordination and communication between all agencies involved in the care of the child is essential, so that factors that contributed to the crisis can be adequately understood and addressed.

Involving a CYP's parents and/or carers in the assessment and management of the crisis episode can help the effective management of the crisis, and possibly avoid the use of more restrictive options, such as a psychiatric admission. Parents and carers can be key in ensuring the safe discharge of a CYP in crisis back into their community. At the same time, understanding and addressing possible underlying safeguarding concerns at home that may contribute to the crisis episode, for example, a chronically critical or invalidating style of interaction in the family, or, in more severe cases, physical, sexual or emotional abuse, is of paramount importance.

Mental health professionals can be in a good position to advise the wider professional network and make recommendations to support the CYP through the crisis. For example, they may recommend adjustments to the timetable at school, or extra time for exams. They may make a safeguarding referral or ask the GP to refer the parent or carer for further support for themselves.

An appropriate crisis intervention aims to reduce the immediate risks and ensure the safety of the CYP. The assessing psychological practitioner may recommend a hospital admission (a psychiatric hospital admission needs to be endorsed by a Consultant Psychiatrist), or intensive community management, for example via crisis services or home treatment teams. In addition to immediate management and support, effective ongoing interventions for the CYP, family, school and professional network should be initiated or recommended.

22.1.2 Mental Health Crisis Presentations

Table 22.1 shows the range of presentations in a CYP in mental health crisis.

A crisis episode can occur at home or in other community settings, for example at school, in a youth hub, during a CAMHS appointment and elsewhere. Teachers, other professionals or parents/carers will be required to respond according to the level of severity and risk. When there is an imminent threat to life and the CYP requires medical attention, they will need to be taken to their local A&E department.

However, not all CYP in mental health crisis present in hospitals or require treatment in hospital. If the CYP does not require immediate medical attention, but there are concerns about their safety (for example, if they have disclosed suicidal thoughts to their parents or teachers but have not yet acted upon these thoughts), the crisis could potentially be managed in the community, with the implementation of a safety plan.

If the CYP is known to CAMHS, their allocated worker can be contacted for advice, or otherwise a duty CAMHS practitioner should be available to provide advice and support. In many areas in the United Kingdom there are now telephone crisis lines, specifically set up for CYP in a mental health crisis, that can be accessed 24 hours a day, 7 days a week, can provide support for CYP, their carers, teachers or other professionals who may be involved,

Table 22.1 CYP in-crisis presentations.

A suicide attempt	An act of self-harm with the intent to take one's own life. This can take the form of an overdose of medication, ingestion of substances such as cleansing fluids, acetone or other chemicals, an attempt at self-asphyxiation or other violent methods such as jumping from height.
An act of (non- suicidal) self-harm of various levels of severity	For example, cutting one's forearms, legs or abdomen, burning skin, headbanging, picking skin, pulling our hair, biting skin or other forms of self-induced injury.
An acute deterioration in mental state	The emergence of an acute psychotic illness that places the CYP or others at risk, for example when the CYP presents with aggressive behaviour in the context of paranoid delusions or perceptual abnormalities; a manic episode; a severe panic attack.
An acute deterioration in physical state	For example, rapid weight loss or dehydration in the context of anorexia nervosa, or a manic, depressive or psychotic episode.
Behaviours that challenge (e.g. self-injury or aggressive behaviour) in the context of a neurodevelopmental disorder (e.g. learning disability or /and autism)	These can pose particular challenges, for example when the CYP is non-verbal and unable to explain their thoughts, feelings and experiences. Moreover, CYP with severe neurodevelopmental difficulties may respond differently to usual interventions; for example, they are more likely to experience side effects from psychotropic medication, which poses significant challenges in the management of such presentations.

and signpost CYP to the appropriate services and resources. This provision is currently a UK national priority (Mental Health Crisis Concordat, H. M. Government, 2014) with the aim of reducing unnecessary presentations to A&E departments. Depending on the presentation, the CYP may be advised to attend A&E, an outpatient CAMHS appointment, or follow their existing safety plan (see Appendix).

In most areas there are intensive outreach CYP community teams or crisis services. These services offer higher frequency of contacts than a generic CAMHS team and can see the CYP in various contexts (at home, at school or elsewhere in the community). Management of a crisis episode in the community requires a robust support system around the CYP. Their family or carers need to demonstrate the ability to support the CYP through the crisis, supervise them more closely if needed and alert emergency services if risks continue to increase.

When a CYP is brought to hospital, this usually signifies that the system around them is no longer able to contain the crisis, and therefore the intervention must also provide support to the system.

22.1.3 How Children are Different to Adults when Presenting in Mental Health Crisis

- Children may present differently depending on their developmental stage, biologically and psychologically. An effective assessment is developmentally sensitive, taking account of the child's chronological age and developmental stage.
- CYP are more vulnerable than adults (for example, in the context of safeguarding concerns in the family home, concerns around grooming, sexual or other exploitation, or in the case of children who are looked after by local authorities).
- There are different legal considerations and obligations of the state depending on their age and maturity. The assessing practitioner is required to have a good knowledge of relevant legal frameworks to inform decisions about sharing information, the use of restrictive practices and the role of parental consent (see Chapter 5).
- CYP are usually in full-time education and living with parents or carers. Parents/carers and education services are key in the further management of the crisis episode.
- CYP mental health crisis presentations are rarely the result of a mental health problem alone but are often due to a complex psychosocial situation. Therefore, holistic approaches are needed to address the crisis.
- CYP are often skilled in digital communication, which can open new opportunities for effective interventions. At the same time, continuous connectivity may contribute to a deterioration in mental state and wellbeing. Social media may encourage unrealistic expectations or provide fertile ground for cyber bullying, may contribute to 'contagion' (copying self-harm or suicidal behaviours) and may increase risks to self via accessing websites that promote suicide. An effective risk assessment includes an assessment of the CYP's online activity (see Chapter 10 and Chapter 24).

22.1.4 Self-harm and Suicide

Suicide is the second leading cause of death in CYP globally (Asarnow & Ougrin, 2019; Wasserman et al., 2015), making it a public health priority in many countries. There are differences in suicide rates internationally, but suicide rates in CYP are increasing in the western world (Naghavi, 2019). Some, but not all deaths by suicide could be prevented (Asarnow & Ougrin, 2019).

The aim of the assessment of a CYP who presents in crisis following self-harm or a suicide attempt is to determine whether the individual is at high risk of attempting suicide again. This assessment will identify immediate next steps: a decision about whether the CYP can be safely discharged into the community with appropriate follow up or whether an inpatient admission should be sought. The ultimate goal of suicide prevention relies on refining the ability to anticipate and identify individuals who are at the greatest risk of self-harm and further suicide attempts (Rodway et al., 2016).

As self-harm is one of the strongest predictors of suicide (Morgan et al., 2017), it is an important focus for suicide prevention strategies globally.

The definition of self-harm is important in clinical practice and research but is contested between countries, and also sometimes within countries (Wilson & Ougrin, 2021). The National Institute for Health and Care Excellence (NICE) in the United Kingdom defines self-harm as 'any act of self-poisoning or self-injury carried out by an individual irrespective of motivation' (NICE, 2022). Motivation can vary from an attempt to manage overwhelming emotional states, to an attempt to take their own life.

The term 'deliberate self-harm' is still used widely, despite the term 'deliberate' having been removed from clinical guidance in the late 2000s due to the stigmatising and blaming connotation of the term. Kapur et al. (2013) and the Royal College of Psychiatrists (2020) argue that the word 'deliberate' implies a calculated act rather than the result of a highly distressed or impulsive state, adding to confusion around the nomenclature of self-harm.

In the United States, non-suicidal self-injury (NSSI) is distinguished from suicide attempts (SA) based on the presence or absence of suicidal intent at the time of self-harm (American Psychiatric Association, 2013; Crosby et al., 2011). However, in clinical practice, differentiating suicidal from non-suicidal self-harm can be challenging, as suicidal intent may change, particularly at times of distress. Individuals in distress may not be able to provide an accurate retrospective account of their thoughts and feelings at the time of the self-harm act. Whilst not differentiating suicidal from non-suicidal self-harm may at times lead to inappropriate treatment and management, the broad use of the term 'self-harm', which encompasses all degrees of intentionality of suicide, may be justified for cases where intention and motivation are uncertain (Wilson & Ougrin, 2021; Zetterqvist, 2015).

Self-harm; epidemiology: Self-harm can present in the form of cutting, scratching or excessive skin picking, hair pulling, overdosing on medication or ingesting harmful substances (e.g. chemicals), headbanging, running into traffic, or engaging in other risky behaviours (for example, substance misuse, unprotected sex) as an indirect form of self-harm.

According to a 2017 Public Health report looking at self-harm amongst school age children in the United Kingdom, the prevalence of self-harm is estimated at 22% amongst 15-year olds in England, with girls reporting three times more self-harm than boys (Public Health England, 2017). However, these figures are likely to be an underestimation as many cases of self-harm are not reported or documented. Less than one-quarter of children and adolescents who self-harm present to mental health services (Ystgaard et al., 2009).

Self-harm happens more often than suicide, but there has been inadequate research on the differences in rates between the two. Hawton & Harriss (2008) examined the rates of self-harm in comparison to suicide rates by gender and method of self-harm, using 10 years of data from a local system. Findings showed that self-harm occurred at a rate 36 times higher than suicide, with an average ratio of 87:9 (self-harm:suicide) in females and 18:7 in males. The ratio of self-harm to completed suicides varied across age, it was higher in adolescents (200:1) than in those over the age of 60 (10:1).

In England, as reported by NHS Digital (2018), one-quarter of 11–16 year olds, and nearly half of 17–19 year olds (46.8%), with a mental disorder reported that they had self-harmed or attempted suicide at some point in their lives. For 11–16 year olds, this represents a greater than eight-fold risk compared to those without a mental health problem (25.5% compared to 3%).

Rates of self-harm have been increasing in recent years. The causes of this increase are complex, and likely to be related to multiple factors, such as socioeconomic deprivation and inequalities, individualism and social isolation, the influence of social media, increasing academic demands, the increasing risk of mental health disorders, such as depression, in CYP and the normalisation of self-harm in the popular culture.

Why do children /young people self-harm? Every CYP (child or young person) who engages in an act of self-harm will do this for different reasons, and a comprehensive assessment is crucial. Every act of self-harm needs to be taken seriously, as it indicates high levels of distress in the CYP, and because it significantly increases the risk of completed suicide.

Self-harm can be associated with a range of mental health difficulties and can also occur without the presence of mental illness. A CYP may engage in self-harm: to distract or find relief from overwhelming emotional pain; to express intense feelings of anger that they feel cannot be expressed in other forms; to escape from an intolerable state of mind or situation; to punish themselves in the context of thoughts of guilt or self-loathing; as part of a ritualistic behaviour; or as a failed attempt to take their own life.

Self-harm is often hidden and may not come to the attention of parents/carers until much later. Signs that could indicate self-harm include: the presence of unexplained cuts, burns or scars; inappropriate dress for the weather, for example, wearing long sleeves or trousers in the summer; unwillingness to participate in activities that require less clothing, such as swimming; withdrawal from friends or family; a change in behaviour, for example withdrawal from social activities; and deteriorating academic performance.

Although many individuals who self-harm have no plans or intention to take their life, it is important for practitioners not to be reassured into a false sense of security. A recent prospective multicentre study (Hawton, Bale et al., 2020) showed that self-harm, especially if repeated, significantly increases the risk of completed suicide (30 times more suicides than expected in the general population). The increase is more pronounced in males and older adolescents.

For some individuals, regular self-harm can be an important coping mechanism and an attempt to alter negative emotional states. They may use it as a release or a distraction from emotional pain. The treating practitioner or team cannot expect that self-harm will just stop, as the individual will not yet have developed alternative coping strategies, and this needs to be explained to families, parents or carers. The practitioner should never encourage self-harm, but should recognise its function for the young person (YP), especially if it has been occurring over a long period of time. In these cases, a safety plan based on gradually trying alternative strategies, and, in the longer term, reducing and eventually stopping self-harm is advisable (see for example, NSPCC [2016] 'Keeping children safe').

Suicide, Epidemiology: Completed suicide is very rare in children of primary school age and becomes gradually more common after the age of 12. Younger children are less likely to attempt suicide, but suicide rates rise sharply in late teens (NCISH, 2022).

Suicide used to be a criminal offence, hence the use of the term 'commit suicide', and was de-criminalised in 1961 in the Suicide Act in the United Kingdom. Suicide remains a crime in 20 countries.

The National Confidential Inquiry into Suicide and Safety in Mental Health (NCISH, 2022) used real-time surveillance data of patients and the general population in the United Kingdom between 2009 and 2019, and reported an average of 6090 deaths by suicide per year, across all ages. The rate of suicide increased by 8% in 2018–2019 compared to 2017, and the increase was seen in both males and females. Historically, suicides by violent methods have been more common in males, but recently there has been a rise in suicides by hanging especially in females and those under the age of 25.

The majority of people who die by suicide are not under the care of mental health services at the time of suicide. NCISH (2022) reports that only 27% of suicides occurred in people who had had contact with mental health services within the previous 12 months.

The inquiry reports that, despite the recent increase in suicide rates, there was no further documented increase in suicides specifically during the Covid- 19 pandemic, in adults or adolescents. It is, however, possible that experiences of the pandemic, for example anxiety, isolation, disruption to care, may have contributed to some suicides in mental health patients.

Increase in suicides in recent years was also found in the adolescent population. There were 1093 suicides in the general population by people aged under 18 in the United Kingdom in 2009–2019, an average of 99 deaths per year. The number increased over the reporting period, mainly due to an increase in girls aged 16 and boys aged 17, and to a rise in deaths by hanging/strangulation in the under 18s. Only 19% of those CYP were under the care of mental health services at the time of death.

Assessment of risk should include enquiry about online experience, as 25% of CYP who died by suicide were known to have had suicide-related online experience, more than other age groups. The potential harms associated with internet and social media use for YP include cybervictimization, cyberbullying, suicidal ideation and self-harm (Sedgwick et al., 2019). Both victims and perpetrators of cyberbullying are at greater risk of self-harm, suicidal ideation and suicidal behaviour (John et al., 2018). Exposure to social media has the potential to suggest and reinforce negative thoughts and behaviours, such as self-loathing, loneliness and feeling unloved.

Risk factors for Suicide: There is no foolproof way to predict suicide risk accurately. CYP's suicidal intent may vary over time, or they may die by misadventure, not recognising the lethality of their chosen method. The method and severity of the self-harm act is important to clarify, but should not be a decisive factor in determining whether the child or CYP is at risk of fatal self-harm.

The risk factors most associated with completed suicide are listed in Table 22.2 and should be explored in the risk assessment.

Table 22.2 Risk factors most commonly associated with completed suicide in CYP.

History of self-harm and/or suicide attempts	A previous history of self-harm is the most significant predictor of suicide (Mars et al., 2019). A person who has made a serious suicide attempt in the past can be thought of as having crossed the 'body barrier' – its strength is then weakened, making it easier to transgress it again (Campbell & Hale, 1991). CYP may learn that self-harm can attract higher levels of care and attention by their families and carers, which may further reinforce self-harming behaviour, to continue to elicit care. In addition, they may develop a sense of invincibility from having repeatedly survived, which may encourage them to repeat self-harm and/ or increase its severity/ frequency. Unfortunately, it is not uncommon for psychological practitioners or services to respond with reducing concern, or minimise the patient's difficulties, as the intensity and/or frequency of self-harm in a patient increases over time, as they may become desensitised or even see it as 'attention-seeking' behaviour. This stance can increase the risk of suicide as services may not respond appropriately due to desensitization to risk. Past suicidal ideation and suicide attempts have also been identified as significant risk factors for suicide (Barzilay et al., 2019).
Social isolation	Social connectedness is an important protective factor that is often overlooked in clinical risk assessment (King et al., 2018). Higher levels of social connection are associated with lower levels of suicidal behaviours in adolescent groups. Interventions to improve social connections may have an important role in suicide prevention (King, Arango et al., 2019).
History of alcohol and substance misuse	A state of intoxication can increase the risk of accidental suicide. Use of cannabis and other illicit substances was found to increase the risk of suicide attempts in YP with suicidal thoughts or history of non-suicidal self-harm (Mars et al., 2019).
Autism spectrum condition	YP with autism who present in mental health crisis are more likely to have entrenched suicidal ideation, which can be more challenging to change in the context of rigidity in their thinking and behaviour. It is not uncommon for YP with undiagnosed autism to experience their first contact with services when in mental health crisis, which can often occur as the result of cumulative stress due to chronic difficulties with school, peer relationships and social isolation. CYP with autism are more likely to present with suicidal thoughts and acts, depression, behavioural problems and bullying than neurotypical CYP, which are all associated with increased risk of suicide (Dickerson Mayes et al., 2013). Assessing practitioners should be aware of indications of possible underlying social communication difficulties to inform the formulation and management.
Affective disorders	Mood disorders such as depression and bipolar disorders significantly increase the risk of suicidal attempts in both genders and all age groups (Bridge et al., 2006), especially when combined with substance misuse. Early identification and treatment of mood disorders is key in suicide prevention.
Recent discharge from hospital	The National Confidential Enquiry in Suicide and Mental Health (2022) found that in adult populations, post-discharge suicides were more frequent in the 1–2 weeks after discharge from hospital. The highest number occurred on day three after leaving hospital. In the United Kingdom it is now recommended that all patients are followed up by mental health teams within 72 hours of discharge from inpatient care.
Male gender	Males have traditionally been more likely to use violent methods of suicide, which are more likely to be successful. Adolescent males are less likely to access mental health services increasing their vulnerability (King, Grupp-Phelan et al., 2019).

(Continued)

Table 22.2 (Continued)

Emotional regulation difficulties and impulsivity	Considering the role of ADHD in self-harming behaviours is important but often overlooked. Difficulties with impulse control, emotional regulation and difficulties in goal-directed activity can often lead to self-harm and increase suicide risk (Wolff et al., 2019). Pharmacological treatment may improve emotional dysregulation in individuals with ADHD and lead to a reduction in self-harming behaviours. Screening for ADHD in individuals who engage in self-harming behaviours is recommended.
Eating disorders	Suicide is one of the predominant causes of death in individuals with bulimia or anorexia nervosa (Pompilli et al., 2006). Those with symptoms of bulimia are at higher risk of suicide attempts than those with restrictive anorexia (Mayes et al., 2014).
Suicide related online experience	Visiting websites that encourage suicide or discuss suicidal intent online, searching for information on suicide methods or posting messages with suicidal content have been found to be linked to completed suicide (The National Confidential Enquiry into Suicide and Mental Health, 2022). The dark web, an under-researched entity, has potentially significant implications for suicidal CYP because of the anonymity conferred by not being indexed by conventional search engines (Sedgwick et al., 2019). Instant and widespread communication within communities about suicidal acts and completed suicides via social media, and exposure to an outpouring of love and affection towards the deceased YP in the comments sections may encourage CYP towards suicidal behaviour. Enquiry about online activity should be a key part of the risk assessment.
A history of maltreatment	Physical, emotional, sexual abuse or neglect are strong predictors of self-harm (Russell et al., 2019; Zelazny, 2019), which increases the risk of suicide. Children Looked After, especially those leaving care, are at increased risk of suicide (NCISH, 2017).
LGBTQ	LGBTQ CYP, especially those with a history of being bullied, are at increased risk of suicide (NCISH, 2017).
Family history of suicide and severe mental illness	A family history of completed suicide and psychiatric illness were found to significantly and independently increase the risk of suicide. These effects were not influenced by the socioeconomic status or psychiatric history of the individuals who died by suicide (Qin et al., 2002). Family history of suicide and severe mental illness should always be explored in the risk assessment.
Recent loss/endings/ life events/ bereavement	Relationship break-ups, loss of friendships, parental separation or divorce and bereavement can increase a sense of abandonment, particularly in CYP with insecure attachment patterns and can contribute to a higher suicide risk.
Exposure to suicide in the family, school, social network or through the media ('contagion')	There is significant association between exposure to the suicide of an adolescent peer and a subsequent suicide attempt. Suicide clusters, also known as contagion or copycat suicides, refer to a phenomenon where a series of suicides occur within a specific time period and geographical area, often among individuals who are connected or share certain characteristics. These clusters can potentially contribute to an increase in suicide rates in CYP. The impact of suicide clusters on communities and institutions can be profound (Hawton, Hill et al., 2020). Ease of communication (Robertson et al., 2012 and the 'glamorisation' of suicide in CYP via social media may contribute to an increase in suicide risk in CYP. Following a suicide, it is preferable to limit information, and avoid publicising details such as method used. Proactive engagement with the media, bereavement support and support for the most vulnerable groups is crucial in responding to suicide clusters.

(Continued)

Table 22.2 (Continued)

Access to lethal means	Restriction of access to specific means can reduce the likelihood of suicide using the specific method, even though it is not possible to completely eliminate the risk of suicide. At a population level, these strategies have been effective (for example, the repackaging of paracetamol in the United Kingdom or restriction to pesticides in Asian countries). The likelihood of people trying to take their own lives may be reduced, at least temporarily, when they are prevented from using their chosen method, as suicide attempts tend to be closely tied to specific methods. Furthermore, if a particularly lethal method is not accessible, individuals may resort to using more easily available, often less-harmful methods, avoiding fatality. At an individual level, the critical moments during a suicidal crisis, especially when the suicidal act is impulsive, may have a short duration, and there may be ambiguity and fluctuation in suicidal intent. Individuals tend to utilize the method that is most easily within their reach. When certain lethal means are not immediately accessible when the impulse arises, there could be a postponement in suicide attempts, which could allow the intense suicidal feelings to subside without resulting in a fatal outcome in some instances (Yip et al., 2012). Access to hazards such as medication or sharps should always be evaluated during assessment.

22.1.5 The Assessment of a Crisis Presentation

Presentation at an A&E Department

Triaging: When a CYP in mental health crisis presents to a hospital site, usually brought by their family/carers or an ambulance, a triage nurse will usually be the first point of contact and will collect details of the CYP and parent/carer, and information on the reason for presentation and risks.

Physical examination and treatment: Typically, the CYP will receive an evaluation from a member of the paediatric team, who will conduct a thorough examination by gathering information from both the CYP and their parent or caregiver, and perform a physical examination. If there is a need for medical intervention due to a severe self-harm or overdose, or if the child is medically unstable due to dehydration or malnourishment, they will be admitted to a hospital, usually to a paediatric ward, to receive the necessary treatment.

Comprehensive psychosocial assessment: The psychosocial assessment is led by a trained mental health professional, such as a mental health nurse, a child and adolescent psychiatrist, a clinical psychologist, psychotherapist or a social worker, who may be part of a paediatric liaison team or a specialist child and adolescent mental health service available at some hospitals. In hospitals where a paediatric liaison team is not available, a psychological practitioner from the community CAMHS teams will be assigned to evaluate the CYP at the hospital.

The assessment usually involves interviews with the CYP and the parent/carer, separately and together. If possible, the practitioner will also obtain a collaborative history from other agencies that are involved with the CYP (e.g. from school and/or children's social care), which can often help understand the events that led to the crisis. The assessment will usually cover the 10 areas outlined in Table 22.3.

Table 22.3 Psychosocial assessment.

1. Circumstances	The circumstances preceding the crisis event and precipitating factors.
2. Details	Details of the crisis event, including the extent of the self-harm/suicide attempt, means used, how they were obtained, whether the event was planned or impulsive, the degree of suicidal intent, whether the YP had taken steps to avoid being found, whether they had left a suicide note.
3. Family circumstances and history	Who lives at home, relationships and patterns of communication within the family, conflict and how this is managed, family history of mental illness/suicide/neurodevelopmental conditions, history of emotional, physical, sexual abuse or neglect. Not all of this information can always be obtained in a crisis setting, and sometimes it is not appropriate to press the CYP/parent or carer who may be in a state of distress and therefore unable to discuss past history, especially relating to traumatic events. The assessing practitioner will need to prioritise engaging the CYP and establishing a positive rapport and trust. Gaps in history can be filled in later after the immediate crisis has been resolved.
4. Psychosocial history	School functioning – academic and social, friendships, romantic relationships, sexual activity, gender identity/dysphoria, early social development.
5. Medical history	Any chronic conditions (epilepsy, asthma, diabetes), history of head injury, allergies, menarche/onset of puberty.
6. Substance use/anti-social behaviour	Use of drugs or alcohol, criminal activity.
7. Mental state examination	To determine possible underlying mental health difficulties that may have contributed to the crisis event such as depressive illness, anxiety disorder, acute stress reaction, affective disorder or psychotic illness, eating disorder.
8. Risk assessment	The practitioner will need to assess whether the CYP is future orientated (e.g. thinking about exams and future studies, discussing a future event that they have planned, such as a holiday) or whether they present with a sense of hopelessness and worthlessness. The practitioner will enquire whether they have regretted their act of self-harm or suicide attempt, or whether they have ongoing plans to take their own life, and assesses whether the crisis has triggered a change in how they view themselves and the world.
9. Evaluation of the system around the CYP	A key part of the risk assessment is an evaluation of how the system around the CYP (parents/carers) is coping and whether they are able to manage the crisis and implement a safety plan, and their attitude to professional help. If parents/carers feel able to follow recommended advice, and provide the increased levels of supervision that may be necessary in the aftermath of the crisis event, then discharging the CYP into their care can be considered. If they appear exhausted and overstressed, if they have their own health needs that compromise their capacity to ensure the child's safety at home, if there is ongoing conflict at home, then a discharge home may not be indicated at this point. The team may decide to keep the child in hospital for a bit longer to consider additional support that the family may benefit from, or a psychiatric hospital admission may be sought.

(Continued)

Table 22.3 (Continued)

10. The CYP's competence or capacity to make decisions about information sharing or treatment	This assessment is relevant if, for example, they do not want to share information about risk with their parents/carers, or when they do not agree with the suggested treatment plan, for example to remain in hospital for further assessment or treatment. A CYP over the age of 16 is expected to have capacity to make decisions, assuming that they are able to understand the information relevant to the decision, are able to retain and weigh up that information as part of the process of making the decision and they do not have an impairment of their brain or mind that makes them unable to make the decision (Mental Capacity Act, 2005; Chapter 4). Children under the age of 16 can consent to treatment if they are believed to have enough maturity and intelligence to be able to understand what is involved in their treatment (they are Gillick competent). The assessing practitioner may be required to breach confidentiality if, for example, the safety of the CYP is compromised, and informing their carers is crucial for maintaining their safety or safety of others (see Chapter 5, for more information). The practitioner should not hesitate to ask for advice from their peers, supervisor or manager when they are not sure about the next steps.

Formulation: A formulation of the CYP's difficulties looks at predisposing, triggering and maintaining factors that contribute to the presentation. It considers biological, psychological and social factors, to allow the psychological practitioner to make recommendations for appropriate treatment or interventions. Examples of factors that contribute to the crisis may include:

- Predisposing factors: family history of suicide or severe mental illness, early trauma/ abuse, history of bullying, underlying neurodiversity or learning needs, underlying genetic or other disorders.
- Triggering factors: loss, relationship break up, exam stress, house move, parental separation, physical illness or pain, intoxication, a traumatic event.
- Maintaining factors: parental health needs that may compromise their ability to be emotionally present and supportive, continuing abuse or neglect/ ongoing safeguarding concerns and/or continuous invalidating home environment, ongoing bullying, unsuitable school environment, avoidance behaviours (e.g. school avoidance), ongoing use of alcohol or substances.

Risk Assessment: The risk assessment provides information about the likelihood of further self-harm, or a self-harm act that is likely to lead to suicide.

CYP often report a negative experience when seeking care and treatment for their self-harm. They report feeling judged or blamed by A&E staff, being given the message that they do not deserve treatment because their injuries are self-inflicted. The first contact with services is often a window of opportunity to intervene. A negative experience is likely to impact on further engagement and their trajectory. A successful early intervention can help the CYP cope differently with their distress and can prevent escalation of self-harm.

Risk assessment tools should not be solely relied upon for clinical decision making, for example, when deciding whether a CYP is safe to be discharged from hospital, or used as a checklist to assess the level of risk. Risk is dynamic and ongoing clinical assessment is necessary (NCISH, 2022). Decisions about positive risk management (for example, deciding to discharge a YP with a safety plan in place, rather than recommending a psychiatric admission) should involve the CYP, parents/ carers, and the whole network around them.

The most important factor in determining the provision of safe care is how well the professional network works together, and the degree of engagement with the CYP and the family. A positive therapeutic relationship can give the message that the CYP is thought about and supported and instil hope that things can get better. Ongoing communication between psychological practitioners, teams and agencies will ensure that information about risk is not lost and will improve safe decision making. A comprehensive risk assessment should include the elements outlined in Table 22.4.

Key Considerations for the Psychological Practitioner: The risk assessment and management of CYP, especially when they are not previously known to the psychological practitioner can trigger significant anxiety, both in the practitioner and the patient. The practitioner should be aware of and follow their local organisational/Trust risk-assessment procedures and policies, make use of their team and supervisor and clearly document all discussions and clinical decisions in patient records.

Direct questioning about suicidal thoughts and plans, when there is history of previous risk events, is particularly important and may bring relief to the suicidal CYP as it can validate their distress and create a space for further exploration (Leicester Partnership NHS Trust, 2013). The assessing practitioner should not hesitate to enquire directly about these. Direct exploration of suicidal thoughts and plans does not increase the risk of self-harm or suicide.

The key factor for an effective risk assessment is the practitioner's capacity to attentively listen to the individual's perspective and their interpretation of events, without interrupting or trying to alter their thoughts or emotions. A sense of not being heard may be experienced as neglectful by a distressed CYP resulting in a sense of alienation and disengagement. The practitioner should not tell the patient how they feel (for example 'I can see you are angry') as this may come across as dismissive and insensitive, further exacerbating feelings of detachment. Additionally, avoiding discussing the CYP's thoughts around suicide or self-harm, or attempting to argue against their suicidal thoughts, can be perceived as unhelpful and invalidating to the CYP's experiences, leading to a sense of helplessness and impacting engagement.

Attributes such as age, race, class, gender, culture, religion are likely to impact on the CYP's and the family's, ability to engage with the assessment and talk openly about deeply personal thoughts and feelings. Establishing a rapport and trust as quickly as possible will positively impact the effectiveness of the first assessment. This can be achieved by actively recognising social and cultural difference and being curious about the CYP's and the family's experience of mental illness, care and adversity.

The psychological practitioner must be aware of their own biases and assumptions and maintain an open mind and curiosity. It is recommended that practitioners are trained in the use of the cultural genogram and are aware of social GGRRAAACCEEESSS (Burnham, 2013) (see also Chapters 4 and 7). The concept of 'social graces' encompasses multiple factors that contribute to power dynamics and diverse perspectives. These factors,

Table 22.4 Comprehensive risk assessment.

Risk to self	1) Current suicidal intent: suicidal intent in CYP may, however, vary over time, and therefore does not accurately predict suicide risk. 2) Details in the sequence of events suggesting serious suicidal intent: whether steps had been taken by the CYP to avoid being found, whether preparations were made in anticipation of the event, whether suicide notes had been left, the extent of planning, failure to alert others following the event. 3) Method used: the lethality of the method used can give an indication of the degree of suicidal intent, and needs to be explored, but it is not always a reliable indicator of the suicide risk. A CYP may misjudge the lethal potential of a certain method, for example, they may take an objectively small (non-lethal) overdose, but they may have believed that the overdose could have killed them and maintain suicidal intent, or they may have a sense of 'invincibility' having engaged in similar degrees of self-harm in the past and survived. 4) Factors that may increase risks: impulsivity, use of drugs or alcohol, environmental factors such as abuse, bullying, school stress, relationship difficulties, a relationship breakup. 5) Past history of self-harm or suicide attempts.
Risk to others[a)]	1) History of aggressive behaviour towards others. 2) History of criminal activity. 3) Current mental state that may increase risk of aggressive behaviour, such as untreated psychotic illness or a manic episode. 4) A neurodevelopmental condition such as autism or learning disability that results in difficulties for the CYP in communicating their needs to others, leading to frustration and higher risk of 'lashing out'.
Self-neglect	1) Amount and pace of weight loss – rapid weight loss is more likely to lead to medical instability and affect mental state. 2) Current mental state that affects sleep and appetite and may increase risk of self-neglect, such as a psychotic illness, severe depressive illness, anorexia nervosa.
Risk from others	1) History of emotional, physical, sexual abuse or neglect. 2) Previous or current safeguarding concerns. 3) Parents'/carers' understanding of current situation and ability to make changes. 4) Indications of social vulnerability, for example risk of sexual exploitation, trafficking, difficulties in social communication and interaction, bullying.
Risk of further deterioration in physical or mental state	1) Social isolation. 2) Lack of daily structure and routine (for example, not attending school). 3) Lack of an adequate support system around the YP (family, friends, teachers, professionals). 4) Safeguarding concerns. 5) Untreated severe mental illness for prolonged periods (which makes resistance to treatment more likely). 6) History of criminal activity. 7) Non-adherence to treatment (e.g. refusing to take prescribed medication or engage in therapeutic interventions). 8) Substance misuse.

a) It is important to note that a known diagnosis of a severe mental illness or a neurodevelopmental condition does not automatically increase the risk to others. A detailed assessment of the individual's current and past behaviour, circumstances, and other relevant factors will determine any impact of these diagnoses on the risk of aggression.

both apparent and hidden, expressed and unexpressed, give rise to distinct experience. Currently, the notion of 'social graces' includes gender, geographic location, race, religion, age, abilities, physical appearance, socioeconomic status, cultural background, ethnicity, educational attainment, employment status, sexual orientation and spirituality.

The psychological practitioner is likely to experience intense emotional responses when assessing an individual presenting with suicidal risk. Recognising these emotions can provide insight into the CYP's emotional state. For example, an angry emotional response within the psychological practitioner, when faced with a suicidal patient, may suggest the same angry feelings within the patient that cannot be expressed safely. Similarly, an anxious emotional response within the practitioner may indicate that the CYP does not feel safe, which can be an indication of heightened risk of suicide.

Emotional disconnection on the part of the psychological practitioner – when they have no emotional response to a CYP when discussing their difficulties, or when they minimise the CYP's difficulties – should be a 'red flag' indicating possible heightened risk. Discussion with the multidisciplinary team or in supervision is necessary to help the psychological practitioner recognise and make sense of their own emotional responses and ensure they are supported. The practitioner's response to the suicidal CYP is crucial, as it affects future engagement and, therefore, future risks. A thoughtful, reflective and well-considered response can solidify the CYP's engagement and instil a sense of hope. On the other hand, an over-anxious, or dismissive response, driven by the psychological practitioner's own emotional responses, can ultimately lead to negative outcomes including declining engagement or escalating self-harm.

The term 'malignant regression' (Balint, 1968) refers to a state of increasing dependency of the patient on the psychological practitioner. The practitioner is likely to experience escalating levels of anxiety and feel compelled to offer more interventions, but these will never be experienced as enough, and the patient will continue to deteriorate. In this situation it is important for the psychological practitioner to acknowledge, collaboratively with the patient, that they have reached the limits of what they are able to offer. Box 22.1 describes a clinical example of a CYP's increasing mental health risk.

Box 22.1 Clinical example

Saira is a 16 year old girl of Pakistani heritage, who had been under the care of an adolescent outreach mental health team for approximately 9 months. She self-harmed regularly, via cutting, burning her skin and ingesting small quantities of acetone or bleach. Saira's parents were supportive but struggled to understand her difficulties, partly due to cultural differences, which increased Saira's sense of not being understood. English was not her parents' first language, and the language barrier and use of an interpreter in family sessions made parental engagement and the family work more challenging for the practitioners. The seriousness of Saira's self-harm appeared to gradually increase. She had a plan to end her life on a specific date and stated to her workers that nothing could make her change her mind. The team responded by increasing the frequency of clinical contacts, and recommended constant close supervision by her parents, 24/7. Despite the team efforts, Saira's presentation seemed to deteriorate. Some practitioners in the team experienced high levels of anxiety, while others reported an increasing sense of apathy, and saw Saira's increasing self-harm and suicidal threats as 'attention seeking' and attempts at manipulation. Saira took an overdose a few days after her discharge from an inpatient adolescent unit. She received treatment on a paediatric ward for a few days and, upon discharge home, she jumped out of the fifth floor window. She sustained a spinal fracture and returned to inpatient care.

It is important for a psychological practitioner and a team to be able to recognise when their interventions are no longer helpful and when it would be more beneficial to the CYP and their family for another service to be involved, which is better equipped to continue providing care.

The quality of the therapeutic connection plays a vital role in effectively evaluating and addressing risks faced by young people who may exhibit persistent suicidal ideation, self-harm or suicide attempts. The assessment and management process should be carried out in a collaborative manner to ensure that the needs and wishes of both the CYP and their family are taken into consideration. Even when it becomes necessary to conduct a Mental Health Act (MHA) assessment (the MHA will be explained later in the chapter), which entails involuntary hospitalization to ensure safety, efforts should be made to consult and involve the CYP and their family as much as possible. In cases where the wishes of the CYP or their family are over-ridden, it is important to treat them with respect and for psychological practitioners to provide clear explanations regarding the decision-making process.

Dealing with a high and continuous risk in isolation is challenging for psychological practitioners who work with CYP with chronic suicidality and recurrent self-harm. Risk assessment and management is complicated, and the psychological practitioner's ability to think clearly when faced with a high-risk situation can be compromised.

The clinical team is the best resource that the psychological practitioner has available. Discussions in multi-disciplinary team meetings and clinical supervision are crucial for effective risk assessment and management, but also provide invaluable support to the psychological practitioner.

It is important to encourage a supportive culture of openness within teams and organisations. Organisations are expected to develop a culture of learning, not blame, for serious incidents when they occur, to encourage honesty and transparency about practice, reflection and thoughtful positive risk taking.

Psychological practitioners must also recognize that there are instances where suicide may be inevitable. A suicide does not necessarily mean inadequate clinical care. Risk assessment and management rely on clinical judgment, and absolute certainty regarding the outcome is never attainable. Psychological practitioners are expected to demonstrate that their clinical decisions were made thoroughly, thoughtfully and collaboratively at all times, regardless of the eventual outcome, including cases involving suicide.

Myths and Facts about Self-harm

Myths about self-harm

- Self-harm is attention seeking.
- Self-harm is for pleasure.
- All people who self-harm want to take their own life.
- It's only a teenage thing and one will grow out of it.
- People who self-harm could stop if they wanted to.
- All people who self-harm have been abused.
- Self-harm is only when you cut yourself.
- If the wound is not bad, the problem cannot be bad.
- Self-harm is cool.
- Self-harm is normal – everyone does it.

Facts about self-harm

- Self-harm is never okay.
- It always indicates a significant amount of emotional distress.
- It can indicate mental illness, or abuse, but not always.
- Factors that lead to self-harm are often complex.
- People can be prejudiced and judgmental against those who self-harm.
- Risk assessment is not static, and risks can change overtime and under different circumstances.
- The harmful effects of an overdose can be delayed, sometimes for several hours or even days and may not be visible.
- A paracetamol overdose can cause serious liver damage and can be fatal.
- Asking about self-harm or suicide thoughts does not increase the risk of self-harm or suicide. The more people talk about a 'taboo' issue, the less alienating and frightening it becomes.

Box 22.2 describes a clinical example of a CYP engaging in self-harm, and her risk assessment.

Box 22.2 Clinical example: Monica

Monica, a 14-year-old girl of Polish parents, was noticed to be missing from her class. She was later located hiding in the school toilets, in a distressed and tearful state, having cut both her arms significantly. One of Monica's teachers and the school safeguarding lead contacted Monica's parents and emergency services. Monica was taken to her local A&E department for her wounds to be treated. She was subsequently assessed by the CAMHS crisis team. Monica was seen alone and with her parents, and the clinician also spoke to the school staff. Even though Monica's parents or teachers had not noticed any recent changes in her behaviour, it emerged that Monica had been excluded by her friendship group after a boy posted nude photos on social media that he claimed were of Monica, two months previously. Monica had not shared these events with her parents or teachers, as she felt deeply ashamed, but was significantly distressed. She gradually isolated herself and started cutting her arms to manage her overwhelming anxiety and thoughts of self-blame. Monica presented with thoughts of hopelessness and worthlessness, had thoughts of wanting to die and had researched methods of suicide online. The CAMHS clinician referred Monica to social care and her local Home Treatment team for follow up. A safety plan was made with Monica, her parents and the school to ensure her safety post discharge. School liaised with the police to investigate the sharing of nude photos and reviewed their safeguarding policy to prevent similar incidents from happening again.

22.1.6 Other Mental Health Crisis Presentations/Acute Deteriorations in Mental State

Acute Psychotic Episode

Mental Health Crisis Presentations can be due to an Acute Psychotic Episode: Psychotic disorders are serious mental health conditions that affect individuals' perception of reality, leading to a range of symptoms such as delusions, hallucinations, disorganized thinking and unusual behaviour. These disorders can affect people of all ages, including CYP. Psychotic disorders in CYP can be particularly challenging, as they can interfere with normal developmental processes, affect academic and social functioning, and have long-lasting consequences. Early identification and treatment are critical to managing the symptoms and improving outcomes for CYP with psychotic disorders. In this context, understanding the causes, symptoms and treatment options for psychotic disorders in CYP is essential.

Epidemiology: Schizophrenia with onset in middle or late adolescence is common, with 1% prevalence. Childhood onset psychosis is very rare, with a prevalence of 0.2-–0.4/10,000 (Courvoisie et al., 2001).

Symptoms: Psychotic symptoms include:

- Positive symptoms:
- Disorganisation of
  - o thought form (formal thought disorder)
  - o thought content (delusions)
  - o or perception (hallucinations)

Delusions are rare in younger children or adolescents presenting with psychosis, and are more likely to appear, or become more systematised, with increasing developmental age.

- Negative symptoms
  - o extreme negativism
  - o flat affect
  - o paucity of thought and speech (thought block)
  - o passivity, avolition
  - o social withdrawal

Hallucinations and delusions are usually required to establish a diagnosis of psychosis. However, these symptoms can occur frequently in CYP and are not always due to a psychotic illness. They may occur in other medical or neurological conditions (such as epilepsy) and are also commonly observed in children with autism. Normally developing children with active fantasy lives can often misinterpret their thoughts or dreams as actual events and describe them as hallucinations.

Non-specific symptoms such as anxiety, irritability, withdrawal and distractibility may precede a psychotic episode (known as a prodromal syndrome). Diagnosis of a psychotic illness can be difficult when a CYP presents for the first time, as symptoms may not always be clear. Often, a period of 'watchful waiting' is required to ascertain the nature and origin of symptoms, as the clinical picture may become clearer with the full emergence of symptoms.

Psychotic disorders are extensively researched in the adult literature. Symptoms and phenomenology, and the evidence base for treatment, are well established. When the criteria are applied in older adolescents, when a first episode of psychosis occurs, the diagnosis is often reliable and the evidence base for treatment that is available from the adult literature can be used successfully. However, in younger children or adolescents, diagnostic accuracy may be affected by issues related to their cognitive or language development (Courvoisie et al., 2001).

Psychotic symptoms in children need to be differentiated from similar non-psychotic symptoms such as obsessions relating to OCD, anxious ruminations relating to anxiety disorders, depressive ruminations, fixated cognitions related to autism spectrum condition, emotional regulation difficulties and affect illusions in the context of PTSD or complex PTSD (e.g. in the context of history of abuse or developmental trauma), or emerging emotionally unstable personality disorder traits and overvalued ideas. Language deficits in children with learning disability or language disorders may also resemble psychotic symptoms. Psychosis should always be considered as a differential diagnosis by the clinical team when a CYP presents in crisis with the symptoms described above but its diagnosis in CYP is complex and can take time.

Assessment: A CYP may present to services in a state of distress, complaining of hearing voices, seeing distressing images or visions, feeling scared or frightened and not being able to trust their family. At other times, a parent or carer may be concerned that their child has gradually become withdrawn, is not leaving their bedroom and is not eating or sleeping. The family or network may or may not be querying a possible diagnosis of a psychotic illness.

The assessing psychological practitioner needs to consider the following:

- a CYP presenting with unusual symptoms or experiences will require a full physical examination and investigations to rule out neurological and other organic conditions that may result in such symptoms (e.g. encephalitis, thyrotoxicosis, Wilson's disease, head injury).
- Substance misuse, for example cannabis, amphetamines, cocaine, can trigger psychotic symptoms. There is evidence that regular use of cannabis predicts risk of reported psychotic symptoms and schizophrenia, particularly in genetically susceptible individuals (for example, those with a family history of psychotic disorders) (Hall & Degenhardt, 2008). It is possible that psychotic symptoms may improve when the CYP is no longer under the influence of the substance. Ongoing substance misuse may maintain psychotic symptoms or interfere with treatment.

- A family history of psychosis, or affective disorders, in the immediate or extended family indicates genetic vulnerability to the development of psychosis and needs to be established.
- CYP with autism and/or learning disability may present with symptoms resembling psychosis. They are also more likely to develop psychosis (Zheng et al 2018).
- Mental state: it is important to assess the CYP's experiences in depth in order to differentiate between psychosis or other difficulties. Perceptual abnormalities, such as hearing voices or seeing visions, may be due to a range of difficulties, such as PTSD, emotional dysregulation, autism, substance misuse. Auditory hallucinations associated with psychosis are usually experienced as being as real as other voices (i.e. they are heard outside the CYP's head, not inside) and are 'third person' (the CYP can hear them talking about them), in addition to hearing them talking to them. Often the CYP is surprised that others cannot hear the voices they hear. When these characteristics are observed, the voices are more likely due to psychotic illness. Visual or other (e.g. tactile or olfactory) hallucinations, when occurring without auditory hallucinations, are more likely due to other difficulties (e.g. emotional dysregulation, substance misuse) rather than psychosis.
- Delusional beliefs should be examined in detail to ascertain whether they constitute paranoid ideation or are anxious/ obsessional thoughts or ruminations. Assessing how fixed these beliefs are, or whether the CYP can accept different perspectives, is helpful in differentiating between the two. Some beliefs may be culturally appropriate (for example, it is normal to believe in ghosts or spirits/'gins' in some cultures). The practitioner will need to ascertain whether the CYP's belief system is culturally appropriate by obtaining history from the family/carers.
- Thought disorder: a CYP may 'not make sense' during conversation, due to making bizarre associations between words, phrases or topics, or using combinations of words that do not make sense ('word salad').
- It is not easy to diagnose a psychotic presentation. Consultation with the clinical supervisor/team psychiatrist is essential.

Behaviours that challenge in neurodiverse CYP: 70–95% of children and adolescents with autism/ learning needs have at least one co-occurring psychiatric disorder, which has implications in terms of diagnosis and appropriate treatment and support (Simonoff et al., 2008; Gjevik et al., 2011). Co- occurring mental health difficulties may delay a diagnosis of autism. Modified interventions are required to treat mental health problems in individuals with autism.

Autism may be identified later in girls as they can 'mask' their difficulties (see Chapter 19, Neurodiversity). They may gradually deteriorate, leading to a mental health crisis, sometimes referred to as 'autistic burnout'. At this point, their difficulties are likely to be already entrenched and of high severity, leading to significant impairment and the need for more resources to be able to support these young people effectively.

Medical instability due to starvation in the context of an eating disorder: a CYP with an eating disorder who severely restricts their dietary intake may be at risk of medical instability. They will require admission to a paediatric ward for medical stabilisation. It is good practice for CAMHS Eating Disorder services to work jointly with the paediatric team to stabilise the CYP and address all risk factors. Many areas have intensive eating disorder services to enable management of acute deterioration of eating disorders at home, once physical health risks are addressed, and avoid long term admissions in eating disorder units (see Chapter 15).

22.1.7 Mental Health Crisis Interventions

Crisis care for young people involves a coordinated response from mental health professionals, medical providers and other support services. The first step in crisis care is often to ensure the safety of the CYP, which may include hospitalisation or referral to an emergency department, or, alternatively and when safe to do so, the involvement of Home Treatment teams or crisis services. Once the immediate danger has been addressed, mental health professionals can work with the adolescent to develop a care plan that meets their individual needs.

Following the initial assessment by a psychological practitioner with experience in the assessment and treatment of CYP, the following outcomes may occur:

- Discharge back to the care of parents/ carers with a safety plan, and a referral to community CAMHS with the request to provide follow up. This is usually referred to as '7-day follow up' (expected to take place within 7 days) but most recent guidance recommends follow up within 72 hours (NCISH, 2022). Many hospitals make a referral to social care as part of their usual crisis management process.
- If a safety plan cannot be made and the CYP is not deemed safe to be discharged, or they need further medical treatment (e.g. after an overdose), a decision may be made for the CYP to be admitted to a paediatric ward (or, in some hospitals, an adult ward if the CYP is over 16 years old). Further investigations or treatment will be offered. Nursing staff will monitor the CYP, which will inform the assessment and formulation. They are likely to be placed under one-to-one observation until their level of risk is assessed to have reduced. The team may invite all agencies involved (school, social care, parents/carers) to share information and discuss next steps. A discharge can then become possible. Alternatively, the CYP may require an inpatient hospital admission.
- A 'safety and coping plan' for all CYP known to mental health services who have a history of mental health crisis presentations is recommended (Healthy London Partnership, 2016). This plan should be drawn up with the contribution of the CYP and their family, be realistic, and be shared with all professionals involved (see example safety plan listed in the Appendix). A safety plan should include:
  - the name and contact details of the CYP's allocated CAMHS worker;
  - all other professionals involved;
  - when and where their next appointment is;
  - how to recognise the early signs of a mental health crisis;
  - clear information on who to contact in the event of a crisis, both during office hours and out of hours;
  - details of other support services that the CYP can access (such as Childline [Rantzen & Cameron, 2016], the Samaritans);
  - a list of strategies to help manage distress, anxiety or other overwhelming mental states. These will need to be agreed with the CYP and their parents/carers.

  - o clear advice for parents/ carers with regards to the level of supervision that is required, and specific advice on reducing access to hazards (e.g. parents/carers may be advised to lock away all medication or sharps temporarily); and
  - o information on what to do in the event of an immediate medical emergency; for example, after an overdose. This will usually involve advice to contact 999 or attend the local A&E department.
- In some cases, a psychiatric hospital admission may be necessary; for example, when a CYP presents with an acute psychotic episode and is not willing to accept treatment in the community, or when a CYP presents at high risk of suicide and their family or carers are no longer able to keep them safe. The CYP may be admitted voluntarily or may need to be detained under the Mental Health Act. It is important to involve parents or caregivers in the care plan to provide ongoing support and guidance for their child. Liaison with school, social care and other agencies as appropriate is crucial.

  Longer term interventions, once the crisis is resolved, depend on the presenting problem and will usually be offered by community CAMHS or inpatient services, in conjunction with other agencies such as social care (to address any possible safeguarding concerns) or education.

For young people presenting with self-harm or a suicide attempt, the underlying condition will need to be addressed. Mental health difficulties such as depressive or anxiety disorders, PTSD, OCD will need to be treated, and difficulties such as substance misuse, behaviours in the context of neurodevelopmental difficulties, will need to be addressed appropriately. This usually involves psychological treatments (CBT, family therapy, IPT-A, psychodynamic psychotherapy) and medication (for example, anti-depressants).

NICE guidelines recommend dialectical behavioural therapy (DBT) for adolescents who self-harm (NICE, 2022). DBT is a mindfulness and acceptance-based cognitive-behavioural therapy adapted for treating people with severe, complex, hard-to-treat multidiagnostic conditions, in particular borderline personality disorder (BPD). It was developed by Marsha Linehan, to target the specific symptoms associated with BPD (Linehan, 1993): emotional instability; interpersonal difficulties; regular suicidal thoughts or self-harm; and impulsive acts. DBT is also helpful for other disorders that involve emotional dysregulation (e.g. substance use disorders, binge eating), and was recently modified for the treatment of recurrent self-harm in adolescents. DBT has emerged from CBT, but encompasses additional elements, such as the dialectical philosophy (that there may be more than one truth at the same time), the focus on the biosocial model and the role of emotions, and mindfulness-based approaches (Chapman 2006).

A psychotic disorder will require long-term treatment with anti-psychotic medication, in conjunction with individual therapy (CBT for psychosis), family intervention and support to return to education.

22.1.8 Risk Assessment and Management – Key Principles for Psychological Practitioners

- Become familiar with common risk factors in people who die by suicide.

  Do not use risk-assessment tools alone to assess the level of mental health risk.

- Be aware of cultural, and other factors that may be a barrier for the CYP from openly discussing their feelings.
- Formulate an understanding of the unique profile, circumstances and constellation of difficulties for each CYP and family, and the unique factors and triggers that may contribute to risk of suicide at this specific time.
- Treat CYP and families with respect, explain your decisions and actions, and take into account their wishes.
- Monitor feelings, particularly anxiety levels.
- Use the team and clinical supervision, do not try to manage high risk situations alone.
- Don't try to cheer the patient up as this will make them feel unheard and misunderstood.
- Be aware of changes or losses in the CYP's life, particularly in the interpersonal domain, as these may increase risks.
- Work together as a team. Ask for help.
- Ensure clinical records are comprehensive and up to date.

22.1.9 Reflections on the Provision of Current Crisis Care, Challenges and How to Address them

Access to and Consistency of Crisis Care: The provision of 24/7 crisis care for CYP in crisis is not consistently available currently in the United Kingdom. Given the relatively small number of CYP presenting in mental health crisis compared to adults, service provision may need to be designed in such a way to cover a bigger geographical area. While a short-term or overnight admission on a paediatric ward can be helpful for some CYP, as it provides an opportunity to 'cool off', reflect and can help resolve a crisis, prolonged paediatric admissions for CYP presenting with mental health difficulties, for example when a psychiatric bed is required but is not available, or when the CYP's placement has broken down, can be problematic. This can be a stressful experience for the CYP, due to the busy ward environment, and at the same time increases the demand on acute paediatric beds.

Despite higher incidences of self-harm in socially deprived areas, referrals within a year of the initial self-harm episode were 23% less likely for young patients registered with GP practices in such areas. This reflects the geographical inconsistencies in the provision of crisis care (Morgan et al., 2017).

Crisis Escalation in the Context of Chronic Underfunding of CAMHS and Social Care: Long waiting times for CAMHS assessments and interventions, particularly for neurodevelopmental assessments, and interventions for common psychiatric conditions (for example, depression and anxiety), may contribute to the deterioration, over time, in the mental health presentation of CYP, and escalation to the point of the mental health crisis. Under-funded services may not be able to provide adequate support for those in crisis. This can lead to increased mental health difficulties and may result in individuals requiring more intensive and costly interventions (e.g. inpatient care). Accessing care at the point of crisis sadly often means that the CYP has endured a great deal of distress and suffering until they become able to access the care that they needed (Children's Commissioner, 2021).

Transitions: transition to adult services can be a difficult and confusing time for CYP in mental health crisis, and can contribute to a feeling of 'falling between the cracks' when there are gaps in service provision, different thresholds for accessing mental health support and long waiting times. It is not uncommon for a vulnerable CYP to present in a mental health crisis as they approach their 18th birthday. Young people may find themselves with no or very little support as they are leaving CAMHS, which can increase mental health risks. It is good practice to consider involving adult crisis services in the case of a CYP at transition age who presents in mental health crisis, and joint management of the crisis between children and adult services may be required. Some areas have established 'transition panels' where CAMHS and adult mental health teams, as well as social care and other services, discuss young people who are anticipated to require support from adult mental health services to ensure a prompt referral to the appropriate team and minimise disruption of care.

22.2 Inpatient Care

22.2.1 Introduction and Relevance to Clinical Practice

Adolescent inpatient psychiatric care is a part of Child and Adolescent Mental Health Services (CAMHS) in the United Kingdom, often referred to as a 'tier 4' service along with specialist outpatient care. The tiered model of mental health care comprises universal and increasingly targeted and specialized community-based care through tiers 1 to 3. This model is currently being phased out, with emphasis being placed on the CYP's needs, which will determine the support they will receive (see Chapter 6).

As described at the start of this chapter, there has been a significant increase in the demand for CAMH services, with a 35% increase in referrals for help in 2019/2020 compared to the previous year and an almost 60% increase compared to 2 years previously (Children's Commissioner, 2020b, 2021). Despite this, there has not been a proportional increase in CAMHS resources, resulting in increased pressure on all services that encounter CYP with mental health problems. However, over the past 20 years, there has been an increase in the provision of adolescent inpatient services, with the number of CAMHS beds in England rising from 844 in 1999 to 1368 beds across 115 wards in October 2020 (Hayes, D. et al 2022). Almost half of these beds are provided by the private sector (NHS England, 2014). The model of care has also shifted towards offering emergency admissions 24/7 for both informal and detained patients, moving away from elective and often lengthy admissions based on therapeutic community principles (Corrigall & Mitchell, 2002). This increase in adolescent inpatient capacity contrasts with the reduction in adult mental health inpatient beds over the same period and a greater emphasis on alternatives to hospital admission for adults that CAMHS have only more recently begun to adopt (Ougrin, 2018).

Although inpatient care can be necessary and beneficial for some CYP, it can also have adverse effects that need to be carefully managed. Lengthy inpatient admissions for young people with self-harm, although sometimes needed, have been linked with a subsequent increase in self-harm (Ougrin et al., 2014, 2018; Reavey et al., 2017) although no link has been identified with the risk of future A&E presentations following self-harm (Ougrin et al., 2020). Given that the inpatient environment contains high levels of emotional dysregulation and risk amongst young people, staff are constantly required to balance safety and freedom, to avoid excessive or unnecessary restrictive practice. Without adequate support and supervision, there is risk that the care provided can become unsafe, or overly restrictive, with a detrimental impact on the CYP their experience of care and recovery (Clark & MacLennan, 2023). Additionally, inadequate or under-resourced community care may lead to inpatient admissions for presentations that could be better managed in the community if the appropriate resources were available. Lack of appropriate community care may lead to prolonged inpatient stay and/or relapse or deterioration post discharge. It is essential to ensure that inpatient interventions are integrated into a broader treatment plan and are used effectively and efficiently. Collaborative working between inpatient units, community teams, other involved services such as social care and education, young people, and their families is critical to achieving optimal outcomes and promoting engagement and independence.

There was a significant increase in the number of adolescent psychiatric inpatient admissions in England between 2008 and 2018 which then plateaued and started to decrease in 2019 (NHS Digital, 2019). There could be multiple reasons for this recent reduction, but the recent and rapid expansion of intensive community care services is likely to be a significant factor.

22.2.2 When is a Hospital Admission Necessary?

Future in Mind (Department of Health, 2015) emphasises the importance of enhancing care for CYP experiencing crises. The objective is to ensure that they receive appropriate treatment in the most suitable location, preferably close to their homes. To achieve this, it is crucial to establish evidence-based pathways for community-based care, including the implementation of intensive home treatment whenever applicable, to minimize unnecessary hospital admissions. However, it is acknowledged that some CYP will still require more intensive and specialised inpatient care. To effectively commission the right type of care in the appropriate locations, a comprehensive whole-system commissioning perspective is recommended. This approach should encompass pre-crisis, crisis and 'step-down' services, in addition to inpatient provisions.

There is no specific mental health problem that automatically requires a CYP to be treated as an inpatient in a mental health hospital, but some conditions may increase the likelihood of requiring inpatient treatment. Patients with specific diagnoses are treated in inpatient settings: the group of patients diagnosed with eating disorders is the largest (20%), followed by those with neurotic, stress-related and somatoform disorders (10%), mood disorders (8%), behavioural and emotional disorders (8%), schizophrenia and related disorders (4%), disorders of psychological development (4%), 'other' disorders (4%), and personality disorders (3%). The largest group (38%) doesn't have a specific diagnosis assigned, and some other groups have poorly defined and heterogeneous diagnoses (Children's Commissioner, 2021).

In January 2021, NHS England commissioned 1350 CAMHS inpatient beds from NHS and private providers (NIHR 2021). This included 56 beds (4%) for those with a learning disability and 210 beds (15%) for those with eating disorders. The total number of psychiatric beds in 2019/20 in England was just over 18,000 (National Institute of Health and Care Research [NIHR](2021) illustrating the limited investment in mental health beds for CYP, despite the recent expansion.

22.2.3 Types of CYP Inpatient Psychiatric Provision

General adolescent units (GAU): Young people admitted to GAUs have access to individual and group therapies, medication management, education, community activities. Young people can be admitted voluntarily or can be detained under the Mental Health Act (MHA, UK Legislation, 1983). The multidisciplinary care team includes mental health nurses, healthcare assistants, psychiatrists, psychologists, family therapists, psychotherapists, occupational therapists, art therapists, dieticians and teaching staff. There is significant heterogeneity amongst GAUs, with differences in staffing levels, the make-up of the multi-disciplinary team and length of stay of patients reflecting the individual differences between units. Nationally in the United Kingdom, the average length of stay in an inpatient unit has been reducing (from 114 days in 2014 to 85 days in 2019/20). But the range is significant, with 32% of patients spending over 90 days as inpatients, and 2% over 1 year (Hayes et al., 2022).

Eating disorder units: The current evidence base supports the treatment of CYP with eating disorder out of hospital, with the provision of community and intensive eating disorder services. However, some CYP will require treatment in an inpatient setting until their weight stabilises and they can continue care and treatment in the community.

Children's units (for under 13 year olds): the multidisciplinary team works closely with the child's family/carers to understand their difficulties. Usually children spend weekends at home, to minimise the time spent away from their families. The treatment programme focuses on therapeutic support and education.

Units for deaf children and adolescents: multidisciplinary teams include deaf clinicians in various roles and sign language interpreters, to ensure the provision or comprehensive care for deaf children with acute mental health needs, often including those with visual impairments.

Psychiatric intensive care units (PICU): These units offer 6–8-week-long admissions under higher security conditions for young people who present as acutely unwell, with high risk to self and/or others, who cannot be managed safely in GAUs. All young people in PICUs are detained under the 1983 MHA. Once stabilised, young people are expected to step down to GAUs, or be discharged to the community.

Low secure units (LSU): these are similar to PICUs but offer longer admissions.

Medium secure units (MSU): these are higher security units that support young people with severe mental health difficulties who have been in contact with the criminal justice system.

Learning disability units (general, LSU and MSU): These units provide specialised care for CYP with severe or profound learning disability who present with behaviours that challenge and a co-morbid severe mental disorder and can no longer be managed safely in the community.

22.2.4 What Happens during an Admission to a CYP Inpatient Psychiatric Unit?

Whilst an inpatient, a CYP will undergo a period of assessment and observation, with the aim of clarifying their current diagnosis and arriving at a comprehensive formulation that takes account of psychological, biological, systemic and social factors. The opportunity to observe a CYP 24/7 allows for a speedier and more in-depth assessment than can be carried out in the community, where practitioners rely on information given by parents or other professionals. Every CYP has a care plan, which is created jointly by the team and the CYP and shared with the CYP and their carer(s), reflecting their needs and wishes as much as possible and is reviewed and updated regularly (usually a minimum of weekly) , according to clinical need and risk (Department of Health, 2018).

The CYP will have access to a therapeutic programme, which may include individual and family therapy, group therapy, community activities, occupational therapy and art therapy, depending on the staff composition of the unit. Usually, a consultant psychiatrist, a matron (a senior nurse) and a ward manager lead the unit. Inpatient care is punctuated by regular multiagency and multidisciplinary reviews attended by the inpatient and community teams, social care, education, the CYP and their parents or carers. These reviews provide a framework to ensure that the care provided addresses all mental and physical health, education, housing, spiritual and cultural needs, as well as considering support for carers, and addressing issues relating to alcohol/substance misuse and offending behaviour. During these meetings, the network is updated on the CYP's progress, any barriers to discharge are identified, and steps are taken to ensure that the CYP will have the appropriate support for a safe discharge in the community. Community teams are expected to continue to visit the CYP during their inpatient stay to maintain the therapeutic relationship and to be kept updated on progress. Where available, home treatment teams or outreach services may offer a 'step-down service', which is an intensive support package to allow for an earlier discharge.

Many units have 'high-dependency' areas (also referred to as 'seclusion'), where young people who present with acute and severe difficulties and pose significant risk to themselves or others are nursed for brief periods, separately from peers, until their mental state is stabilised sufficiently to allow them to return to the ward safely (Department of Health, 2018). Seclusion or segregation is to be used only as a last resort and for brief periods (RCPsych, 2021) as this may result in the deprivation of liberty. Young people nursed in high-dependency areas are usually detained under the 1983 MHA, unless they are able and willing to give consent. Consideration should be given to transferring young people to other more appropriate settings (PICU, LSU) if they require prolonged periods in high-dependency units.

Sometimes, high-risk care decisions may need to be made for example, the team may decide that despite the patient's ongoing difficulties, discharge or transfer is now appropriate, despite ongoing clinical risk. Such decisions should be taken jointly by the treating practitioners and senior members of the team: consultant psychiatrists, clinical lead or clinical director. Other agencies involved with the patient, for example social care and education are also invited to participate in the decision-making process, and discuss their views and concerns.

Multiagency discharge planning meetings take place when the CYP is nearing discharge and will review and plan all aspects of care after they leave the hospital, including a safety plan. The CYP will usually have trial periods of home leave as they are approaching discharge.

Discharge from hospital can be a difficult time for the CYP, especially after a prolonged admission. They and their family may experience the discharge as an acute withdrawal of support, and they may experience feelings of anxiety. Risk of suicide in the initial period following discharge is high, and the active participation of all agencies to ensure appropriate support is in place as part of the discharge planning is of the utmost importance (Hayes et al., 2022).

Planned and marked endings of an admission to an inpatient unit, especially if an admission was long, are important. They can allow CYP the opportunity to say goodbye to staff and peers, see that they can be different to other endings of relationships that they may have experienced and may be therapeutic in themselves.

A clinical case is illustrated in Box 22.3

Box 22.3 Clinical example: Melissa

Melissa, a 15-year-old dual-heritage (White British and Black African), non-binary CYP, was admitted to a GAU as an emergency. In the weeks prior to her admission, Melissa had been referred to and seen by the community outreach service, following an episode of significant self-harm through cutting. Melissa was selectively mute and was not able to engage with the community team. Melissa refused the offer of medication or therapy in the community as they were unable to engage due to their levels of distress. The team was concerned that Melissa may have undiagnosed autistic features that may have contributed to the crisis. They were also concerned that they were unable to support Melissa given the acuity of the presentation, and Melissa's inability to engage with the community team due to high levels of distress. A hospital admission to a general adolescent unit was being considered. Melissa subsequently took a significant overdose (50 paracetamol tablets) and was admitted as an emergency. During admission, Melissa received a diagnosis of autism, and it became clear that the school environment was particularly stressful resulting in 'masking' of difficulties for a significant period. Melissa continued to refuse medication, and struggled to engage in therapy, but benefited from occupational therapy input and discovered an interest in illustration and comics, giving hope and a sense of purpose. Melissa had the opportunity to form relationships with other young people and to participate in many unit activities. Additional Funding was requested for Melissa's education, and an alternative provision was identified for Melissa to attend post discharge. Melissa sat GCSE exams in the unit, which alleviated a significant amount of stress. It was difficult for Melissa and their mother to contemplate Melissa returning home, due to high levels of anxiety about managing without the support of the inpatient unit. Melissa started to spend increasing amounts of time on leave from the unit, until eventually there was a successful discharge, with support from the community team.

22.2.5 The Legal Framework

Consent to Admission and Treatment

The provision of inpatient care is expected to occur collaboratively between the services, CYP and their families. Children and adolescents can be admitted to hospital voluntarily ('informally'), as long as they are able and willing to give informed consent about their admission. It is good practice to involve parents/carers in decisions about the CYP's treatment, but this is not required. There may be times when there is a good reason not to seek parental consent, for example, in the case of ongoing safeguarding concerns in the family home, and/or when there is concern that a parent or carer may not act in the child's best interests.

In order to provide informed consent, the CYP must:

1. Have all the necessary information and support to make the decision.
2. Have made the decision without any undue pressure placed on them.
3. Have the mental capacity (if aged 16 or 17 years old) or be 'Gillick competent' (if aged under 16) to make this decision (see Chapter 5).

A compulsory admission should be considered when it is likely that the person will change their mind either before or soon after their admission, and they pose a risk to themselves or others (MHA Code of Practice, Department of Health, 2017a).

Consent should be obtained for every aspect of care during the admission and should be continuously assessed. A person who passively cooperates with the admission and treatment should not be automatically deemed to be consenting.

When recommending a hospital admission, and in order to obtain informed consent, CYP and parents/carers require information about why a hospital admission is necessary, what medical treatment they will receive, the likelihood of success of the treatment and what alternative treatments may be available, where the hospital is and whether an estimation can be made about the length of their admission. They will need to be given information about the visiting hours, what type of restrictions are likely to be placed upon them (for example, whether they will need to ask permission if they want to leave the ward), the rules of the unit (e.g. electronic devices policy) and be told that they can change their mind even if they initially consent to treatment, and that this may lead to them being assessed under the MHA. Many young people and their families/carers have preconceptions about inpatient care due to wider stigma and negative media reporting, which can trigger understandable anxiety about the recommended admission. It is important to allow time to answer any questions they may have and signpost them to the hospital website.

Deprivation of Liberty: Article 5 of the European Convention of Human Rights (ECHR) requires the implementation of sufficient safeguards and protections in any situation where individuals may be deprived of liberty (European Convention of Human Rights, 1998, article 5.4, Council of Europe 1998).

Deprivation of liberty happens when:

- *An individual is confined (is not free to leave a specific restricted place) for a non-negligible length of time.* This includes situations where the individual is under continuous supervision and control and not free to leave. Consideration needs to be given whether this restriction is developmentally appropriate; for example, a toddler is expected to be subject to different restrictions to an adolescent, as part of a parent's responsibility to protect the welfare of a child. However, deciding the level of restriction that is developmentally appropriate is largely subjective and this, understandably, leads to lack of clarity when needing to decide if an adolescent is confined (deprived of their liberty), for example, in the case of an inpatient admission.
- *The individual has not given valid consent for the confinement. There is no deprivation of liberty if consent is given.* When, however, a YP is not able to consent, for example, if they

lack capacity or are deemed not competent to make this decision, consideration needs to be given to whether the person who holds parental responsibility can consent on their behalf. Parents/carers of 16 and 17 year olds cannot consent on the CYP's behalf. For CYP Looked After under a care order, neither the parent nor the local authority can consent to their confinement whatever their age.
- *Responsibility for the confinement is attributed to the state.* This could be the NHS, in the case of an inpatient psychiatric admission; the local authority, for example, in the case of a looked after child; or another public body (Parker, 2020).

Each of these three elements need to be considered when deciding whether to apply the safeguards under ECHR Article 5.

It is not possible to admit or treat a CYP informally if the admission amounts to deprivation of liberty. The appropriate legal framework will need to be used.

Parental Consent and the Scope of Parental Responsibility (PR)

If a CYP is not able to decide on their treatment, because of their age, or because they have lost their ability to make decisions due to their illness, it may be possible, under certain circumstances, to be admitted under parental consent.

There are limits to the decisions that a parent can make in relation to a CYP's admission to a psychiatric unit (MHA Code of Practice, Department of Health, 2017a) even when they have PR. If the decision is not one that a parent would be routinely expected to make, or there are concerns about the validity of the consent by the parent/carer, then it would not be appropriate to rely on their consent to authorise an inpatient admission. A psychiatric admission, sometimes involving highly restrictive interventions, is unlikely to fall under the scope of PR. When a parent's capacity to give consent may fluctuate, a parent is not deemed to act according to the child's best interests, or there are disagreements between two people with PR, parental consent cannot be relied upon. The CYP's perspective/point of view should always be considered, and their growing independence is expected to gradually reduce reliance on the parent's decision-making capacity.

Where informal admission is not possible, formal procedures need to be followed. These include:

- the Mental Health Act;
- a court authorisation; and
- the Deprivation of Liberty safeguards for 16 and 17 year olds.

The Mental Health Act 1983: The MHA (1983, amended 2007) is a UK law that sets out procedures for the assessment, treatment and detention of people with mental disorders. Mental disorder is defined as 'any disorder or disability of the mind' and can include conditions like schizophrenia, bipolar disorder and depression. This does not include alcohol or substance dependence, when this is the only presentation. A learning disability and autism are considered a disability of the mind, and can be considered as mental disorders when associated with severely aggressive or risky behaviour. People with learning disability and/or autism can only be detained for treatment if they present with such behaviours.

During a MHA assessment, two medical practitioners, one of whom would preferably have had previous knowledge of the patient and/or experience in the assessment of CYP, and an approved mental health professional (AMHP) meet with the YP to assess their mental health, risk to themselves or others and determine their need for treatment. The AMHP carries out a social assessment of the individual, including their family and social background. If the criteria for detention under the MHA are met, the medical professionals provide written recommendations for detention, and the person may be detained in a hospital or mental health unit for treatment. If the criteria are not met, the individual is discharged with advice and a care plan.

Admission for Assessment (Section 2): An application for detention under Section 2 of the MHA (1983) can be made on the following grounds: (a) the individual is experiencing a mental disorder that requires their detention in a hospital for assessment, either for a limited period or for assessment followed by medical treatment, and (b) detention is necessary for the individual's health or safety, or for the safety of others. Once admitted for assessment, the patient can be detained for a maximum of 28 days. After this period, they may either be discharged into the community, remain in the hospital as a voluntary patient, or undergo assessment for detention under section 3 of the MHA (1983).

Admission for Treatment (Section 3): An application for detention under Section 3 of the MHA (1983) can be made on the following grounds: (a) the individual is experiencing a mental disorder that requires medical treatment in a hospital; (b) it is necessary for the individual's health, safety, or the protection of others that they receive such treatment, and it can only be provided if they are detained under this section; and (c) appropriate medical treatment is available, tailored to the patient's age, such as a bed in a children's mental health unit for a child. A patient can be detained under Section 3 of the MHA for a maximum of 6 months, and the section can be renewed for an additional 6 months if necessary. If the patient's mental health improves to the point where they no longer require detention under the MHA, they can be discharged from the section and either remain in the hospital as an informal patient or be discharged completely.

CYP who are detained under the Mental Health Act have certain rights, including being informed of their detention, accessing support from an advocate and appealing against their section. An appeal is reviewed by a Mental Health Tribunal, an independent panel consisting of a judge, a mental health professional and a layperson, who consider evidence from the patient, the inpatient team and the community team, along with relevant reports. The tribunal decides whether the patient needs to continue to be detained in the hospital or should be discharged from their section (MHA Code of Practice, Department of Health, 2017a).

Holding Powers (Section 5(2) and 5(4)): If a voluntary patient (including patients who are treated for physical health problems) wishes to leave hospital but the treating team are concerned about their safety or safety of others, they can hold them in hospital until a MHA assessment takes place. Section 5(2) can be applied by a medical professional and lasts for up to 72 hours. Section 5(4) can be applied by a nurse and lasts up to 6 hours.

Section 136: This applies when a police officer becomes concerned that a person in a public place is suffering from a mental disorder and needs immediate care in a place of safety. The police officer can detain the individual and take them to a place of safety, which can be an A&E department, or in some cases a dedicated '136 suite' on a hospital site. Section

136 lasts up to 24 hours (it can be extended up to 36 hours in some circumstances) during which a comprehensive assessment by a mental health professional needs to take place to decide whether the patient can be discharged, should remain in hospital as a voluntary patient or undergo a MHA assessment.

People with mental disorders should be treated with the least restrictive form of intervention possible, and their human rights should be respected at all times (MHA Code of Practice, Department of Health, 2017a).

Community Treatment Order: A Community Treatment Order (CTO) is a legal provision that allows individuals with a mental disorder to receive compulsory treatment while living in the community rather than being hospitalised. CTOs are typically used when individuals have been discharged from a psychiatric hospital but still require ongoing treatment and support. The order grants mental health professionals the authority to supervise and enforce treatment compliance. If the individual does not comply with the conditions of the CTO, they can be recalled and detained in hospital. This can include medication, therapy, or other forms of treatment. CTOs aim to strike a balance between ensuring individuals receive necessary treatment while preserving their autonomy and enabling them to live in the community. The specific conditions and duration of a CTO can vary depending on local mental health legislation (MHA Code of Practice, Department of Health, 2017a).

The Mental Capacity Act: The MCA is a legislation established in the United Kingdom to provide support for individuals who may lack the capacity to make their own decisions or may be at risk due to their decision-making abilities. This law applies to individuals aged 16 and above, who, following a capacity assessment, have been determined to have an impairment or disturbance in their mind or brain that hinders their decision-making capacity. This can include a learning disability, an impairment of the mind secondary to head injury or other causes.

When acting on behalf of someone lacking capacity, any decisions or actions taken must be in their best interests, while considering their wishes, feelings, beliefs and values as much as possible.

Safeguards are included in the legislation to protect individuals without capacity, such as the involvement of independent mental capacity advocates (IMCAs), the Court of Protection and the Deprivation of Liberty Safeguards (DoLS).

The DoLS is a legal framework that safeguards individuals lacking capacity from being deprived of their liberty. It requires a comprehensive assessment of their circumstances and the utilization of the least restrictive options for managing their care. In 2022, the DoLS were replaced by the Liberty Protection Safeguards (LPS, Department of Health and Social Care, 2020), which offer a more streamlined process and extends to 16 and 17 year olds. The purpose of LPS is to ensure the legality and justification of any deprivation of liberty, with provisions for legal representation and independent review of care arrangements. An example of LPS usage for young people is when they are placed in a residential setting, and concerns arise regarding their safety, such as vulnerability to exploitation due to autism or attachment disorders. LPS can be implemented to prevent the YP from leaving the unit without staff agreement, and their situation will be reviewed by a judge as their needs evolve.

CYP with Autism/learning Disability and Complex Mental Health Needs: Children with a learning disability and/or autism, particularly those with severe difficulties and a higher level of need, are more likely to display 'behaviours that challenge'. Behaviours that challenge arise from intricate interactions between an individual and their surroundings, often indicating unmet needs or a diminished quality of life, whether temporarily or chronically. These behaviours can manifest as aggression, self-injury, stereotypical actions, withdrawal, or disruptive and destructive conduct. Whilst such behaviours can pose challenges for service providers, family members or caregivers, they may serve significant purposes for the individual, such as generating sensory stimulation, seeking social attention, avoiding demands or communicating with others.

These behaviours result from complex interplays between biological, developmental and environmental factors. However, certain key factors contributing to the development and persistence of challenging behaviours can be modified. Through addressing these factors, there can be a notable reduction in the risk of harm, the need for restrictive and aversive interventions, social exclusion and an overall improvement in the quality of life for both individuals and their families. Understanding the factors that may lead to the individual displaying behaviours that challenge can allow systems and services to work together to provide proactive support and prevent an escalation in crisis.

These behaviours, when posing risks to the individuals or others around them, may result in a request for a hospital admission under the MHA. Not all individuals exhibiting behaviours that challenge will require intensive support, but for some CYP, support in the community may no longer be sufficient and inpatient admission may be required (NHS England, 2017).

The *NHS Long Term Plan* (2019) pledged to transform mental health services for CYP with autism and/or learning disability with a focus on improving community services, reducing the over reliance on inpatient care and promoting the effective integration and collaboration between mental health services, schools and councils.

Most CYP with autism who require inpatient admission, will be treated in GAUs or PICUs. A small minority of CYP with severe or profound learning disability require admission in specialist learning disability units.

The inpatient environment can be challenging for CYP with neurodiversity. It can be an unpredictable, noisy environment, with alarms sounding at different times during day or night, staff changing constantly, other YP presenting as highly distressed or engaging in high-risk behaviours. Being away from their family, home, school environment and familiar routines can be particularly challenging. These factors can contribute to further deterioration in the CYP's presentation and risks.

Every effort should be made for these CYP to be able to access treatment and support in their communities. When an inpatient admission is necessary, because of the high levels of risk or because appropriate treatments are not available in the community, admissions should be as short as possible. In recent years, steps have been made to enhance the community support available to these CYP, but significant gaps in the provision of care remain. Inpatient units are encouraged to modify the environment (e.g. with the creation of low stimulus sensory rooms), train staff in understanding the challenges in behaviour associated with neurodiversity, and learn behavioural strategies to manage these appropriately, in an effort to reduce inappropriate restrictive practice.

The MHA and Young People from Black and Minoritized Ethnic Communities: Research consistently demonstrates that black individuals face a higher likelihood of being involuntarily detained under the MHA (UK Legislation, 1983) compared to individuals from other ethnic groups (Race Disparity Audit, Department of Health and Social Care, 2017). The rates of detention among individuals classified as 'any other black background' including black Europeans or black Americans, are more than 10 times higher than those among the white population (NHS Digital, 2017). Moreover, the Race Disparity Audit indicates that approximately 3% of black men experienced a psychotic disorder in the previous year, which is over 10 times the rate observed in white men. This disparity is replicated in CYP groups (e.g. NCEL CAMHS Provider Collaborative Strategic Health Needs Assessment, 2021).

This raises an important question for commissioners and healthcare providers: why are black individuals more prone to detention and diagnosis of mental health conditions? Black ethnicity is linked to social disadvantage across many areas of public life, such as health, education, the criminal justice system and employment. There is a limited cultural awareness within mental health staff and the provision of care is often not culturally appropriate. There are concerns about stigma, racism, stereotyping, overmedication and overdiagnosis, fear and professionals' perceptions of risk, as well as lack of trust in the mental health system by black and minoritized ethic groups (Bevan Brittan, 2018).

Health and social inequalities have a direct impact on health and wellbeing. Tackling mental health inequalities requires a focus on prevention and early intervention, and a whole-system approach to address inequalities at population level.

22.2.6 Review of the Evidence Base and Critical Reflections

Benefits of an Inpatient Admission A psychiatric hospital admission involves various degrees of restrictive practice, and as such, is usually considered as the last resort, in cases where there are high clinical risks that cannot be managed safely in the community. When a CYP is admitted, care should be taken for the admission to be of the shortest duration possible, while appropriate support is being put in place in the community (NIHR 2021).

Inpatient admissions for young people with mental disorders are effective and can have several benefits (Hanssen-Bauer et al., 2011), including a thorough assessment of their condition, which sometimes is not possible in the community, effective monitoring and containment of potential risks, initiation of new treatment options, especially when there are difficulties with adherence to treatment in the community, evaluation of treatment response and side effects, and positive influence from peers and staff (the 'therapeutic milieu'). The impact of positive relationships with staff and peers can be significant in a CYP's recovery journey and experience of care.

Short-term admissions can break the cycle of risk and offer support to families, even if the underlying issues persist. By offering a break from stressful environments (such as family or school), there are opportunities for implementation of additional support and improvement of difficulties, even when the psychopathology persists (Green et al., 2007).

The goal of inpatient care may be symptom and risk management rather than complete resolution of the difficulties, with the minimum effective change to enable a transition to less-restrictive community care, where treatment can be completed.

A minority of CYP present with highly complex difficulties and will require longer hospital admissions and an intensive therapeutic programme before they are able to safely re-integrate into the community.

It is important to note that there is limited research into CAMHS inpatient care, including in obtaining feedback on patient experience, as outcome and service evaluation measures used in community CAMHS are not applicable or always relevant (Clark & MacLennan, 2023). YP's experiences of the ward atmosphere, therapeutic relationships, agency in the care, the experience of parents/carers and the application of evidence-based therapies in these settings are all important considerations for future research.

Risks Associated with a Psychiatric Admission: The potential benefits of inpatient admissions for young people with mental health issues must be considered alongside the risks and drawbacks. Removing a CYP from their usual environment and support structures can be challenging and may expose them to new stressors, especially if they are admitted a long way from home. Restrictions and interventions may impact their autonomy and self-esteem, and some young people may find the experience negative and associated with stigma and alienation (Polvere, 2011). Some young people may find the restrictions associated with an inpatient admission uncomfortable, especially if they were previously used to managing their emotional state via maladaptive strategies (e.g. self-harm), which they no longer have access to. This may lead to escalation in their behaviour, leading to increasing restrictive practice such as the use of restraint or intramuscular medication (Furre et al., 2017).

Use of coercion can negatively affect future engagement and therapeutic alliance (Nyttingnes et al., 2018) and restrictions during inpatient admission may undermine an individual's sense of agency and control (Gill et al., 2016). Continuous monitoring may be experienced as intrusive.

Inpatient environments may also expose young people to potentially harmful behaviours or influence from others with additional risk factors, for example substance misuse, severe self-harm, aggressive behaviour. Noisy and unpredictable hospital environments can be experienced as particularly stressful by CYP with neurodiversity who may present with sensory processing difficulties, potentially leading to higher levels of distress and escalating behaviours that challenge. Inpatient units are expected to provide areas with low stimulation, and staff should be trained in managing behaviours that challenge in this group of patients.

Parents and carers can often feel disempowered and excluded from the CYP's care, which can lead to high levels of anxiety when discharge is suggested. Regular contact with and involvement of parents/ carers throughout the admission is crucial.

The decision to use inpatient services should, therefore, be carefully considered by medical professionals and families, taking into account the profile and individual vulnerabilities of the CYP. Inpatient units are expected to work collaboratively with community services to ensure the CYP does not remain on the unit for longer than necessary, and that transitions to and from the community are as seamless as possible. This assumes the availability of intensive community services, which are not universally available, as there are significant geographical disparities in the provision of mental health care.

CYP's views and experience of inpatient care: Most research on inpatient experience has been focused on adult wards (Wood & Alsawy, 2016). The degree to which an individual felt involved in decisions made about their care during the admission, how well services worked together (for example, adequate discharge planning), relationships with staff and peers, including staff shortages and feeling unheard and dismissed, experience of patient-centred care and the quality of the therapeutic environment emerged as the most important factors that shaped patient experience of inpatient care.

Research in CYP experience from inpatient care is lacking, and is admittedly more complex to obtain reliably (Clark & MacLennan, 2023). The Children's Commissioner briefing (2020a) explored CYP's experience of inpatient care depending on whether they were detained under the MHA or treated informally. Children frequently describe their experience of being detained under the MHA as difficult (Children's Commissioner, 2020a) especially when admitted at a distance from home and unable to see their families frequently. Even though many CYP recognise the good intentions of the treatment team, they may feel that they are 'told how to live their life', many do not understand what a 'section' is and feel confused about their rights (NIHR, 2021).

Many detained CYP struggle with the lack of autonomy and not being able to leave. CYP who were admitted informally raised concerns about the validity of their consent, describing feeling that they had been 'threatened' with a section if they did not agree to the admission. This suggests that they may be deprived of their liberty unlawfully, as informal patients do not have access to the safeguards and protections detained patients have (for example, to appeal against their section).

CYP described feeling that it is very important to have a say in their treatment, to be given clarity about their care plans, their discharge plans, their diagnosis and rationale for treatment. Children experience being restrained, or witnessing others being restrained, as traumatic, and this can often trigger memories of previous traumatic experiences in them. However, when restraint is used effectively, for the shortest amount of time possible and while providing adequate explanation and support, it was experienced as helpful.

CYP with autism and/or learning disability find peer relationships, clinical outcomes, the use of restrictive practices and the normality of experience as important factors in shaping their inpatient experience (NIHR, 2021).

There are, however, no universally agreed measures to accurately capture CYP's experience from inpatient care in a meaningful way, in order to inform future provision of care in inpatient settings, commissioning decisions and service improvement. Findings from adult literature may not always be applicable given the developmental differences in CYP and the ongoing role of peer relationships, parent involvement, social media and education (Clark & MacLennan, 2023). Future research is needed to determine an accurate measure of the CYP's and parents'/carers' experience , as this will help improve the quality of inpatient care and overall outcomes.

22.3 Conclusions and Future Directions in Crisis and Inpatient Care

A mental health emergency can be as devastating as a physical health emergency. However, the provision of urgent mental health care for CYP in crisis is often delayed, fragmented, can add to feelings of stigma or fail to address their needs (Healthy London Partnership, 2016).

The most recent research in the field of crisis care highlights the importance of understanding individualised risk and protective factors, and the various pathways that may lead to suicide. There is a need for improving risk assessment methods, moving away from a limited focus on suicide ideation and suicidal behaviour (Ougrin, 2021).

Currently, DBT has the best evidence base for the treatment of young people who present with recurrent self-harm. The comprehensive DBT programme is offered in the community. DBT is not yet consistently available across the United Kingdom and not all CYP in need will be able to access it. Computerised interventions may hold promise for addressing risks of self-harm and suicide on a broader level (Adrian et al., 2019).

As most CYP who die by suicide present with high risk of self-harm but are not in touch with mental health services, public health measures to reach them are important for suicide prevention on a large scale. One promising strategy involves integrating universal suicide prevention measures that enhance protective factors across the entire population, alongside targeted interventions for young individuals identified as having a risk of suicide or self-harm. Additionally, health and social policies should be implemented to improve access to care (Ougrin et al., 2018) whilst also reducing access to potentially lethal self-harm methods and environmental factors associated with an increased risk of suicide or self-harm such as the contagion effects of social media exposure.

Overall, aims for the future direction of services and treatment places significant emphases on prevention, early intervention and integrated care, before a CYP reaches a mental health crisis and/or requires an inpatient psychiatric admission. At the same time, it is recognised that CYP present with increasing mental health needs. Crisis services are expanding to 24/7 availability, and the number of inpatient psychiatric beds in the United Kingdom has increased.

The *Transforming Children and Young People's Mental Health Provision Green Paper* (Department of Health, 2017b) is a UK government policy document outlining proposals for improving mental health services for CYP. It proposes a new model of care, which involves increasing access to mental health services in schools, expanding community-based services and improving support for those with complex needs.

The Children's Commissioner (2020a) has called for improved access to community and crisis services, so that fewer CYP are admitted to inpatient wards. Priority is also placed on reducing the length of admission to inpatient units, having CYP's rights protected, and improving the quality of care they receive. There is variation in practice in inpatient care, with restrictive practices used to different degrees and different levels of sensitivity to the trauma that it can cause.

Mental health crisis care for CYP is a complex and evolving field. As the understanding of mental health and its impact on YP continues to evolve, there are several future directions:

a) Early intervention: By identifying and addressing mental health issues early, crises can be prevented from developing or becoming more severe, to minimise the need for inpatient care. This may involve the use of screening tools, early assessment and intervention, expansion of community services (including the provision of DBT services), to improve access during early stages of difficulties and ongoing monitoring and support.
b) Intensive alternatives to inpatient care, such as home treatment, outreach teams and day treatment programmes, can provide effective treatment whilst allowing the CYP to maintain their daily routines and relationships within their own community. Research has shown that these alternatives can be effective in managing mental health crises and

reducing the need for inpatient care (Chang et al., 2017; Esposito-Smythers et al., 2011; Khanna et al., 2018).

c) Trauma-informed care: Trauma-informed approaches require a fundamental shift in ideology and service provision, transforming survivors' experiences and therapeutic relationships. This shift is captured by asking 'What happened to you?' instead of 'What's wrong with you?' Practitioners can introduce trauma-informed principles by: acknowledging the prevalence of trauma in its broader sense, to include social trauma such as poverty, racism and abuse; by recognising that behaviours such as self-harm, aggression or avoidance may function as coping strategies to early trauma; by asking sensitively about abuse, ensuring cultural and gender competence; by adopting strengths-based models, acknowledging underlying pain and addressing power imbalances that hinder collaboration and choice. Trauma-informed, authentic patient-centred care in the management of acute crisis and in inpatient psychiatric care, can improve patient engagement, clinical outcomes and staff wellbeing through mutual understanding, respect and trust between clinicians and patients (Sweeney et al., 2018). By providing a safe and supportive environment that emphasizes empowerment and collaboration, trauma-informed care can help CYP feel more engaged in their treatment (see also Chapter 27).
d) Particular attention needs to be paid to the secondary trauma experienced by staff. Staff working in crisis care and inpatient psychiatric settings may experience high levels of burnout and job dissatisfaction (Gilbody et al., 2006), often in the context of the complex demand of caring for CYP with significant levels of emotional dysregulation, the risk of assault, managing clinical presentations of high complexity, and also in the context of staff shortages and under-resourced services, which may lead to a lack of compassionate care. Poor wellbeing and emotional distress diminish the capacity to hold someone else in mind (Fonagy & Bateman, 2008), something that CAMHS staff are required to do daily. Therefore, staff wellbeing within CAMHS crisis and inpatient services is crucial for the provision of safe and effective care. Appropriate supervision, staff support, an open organisational culture and trauma-informed practice are crucial.
e) Digital health and telemedicine: These technologies are likely to play an increasingly important role in mental health crisis care for CYP. They can help to improve access to care, particularly in rural or remote areas, and can provide more flexible and convenient options for young people and their families (see also Chapter 24). In inpatient care, mobile apps that allow for real-time tracking of mood, sleep and medication adherence can help adolescents manage their mental health more effectively (Kaufman et al., 2019).
f) Culturally responsive care: This recognizes the importance of cultural factors in mental health and seeks to provide care that is sensitive to the needs of diverse populations. This may involve the use of culturally tailored interventions and the integration of culturally responsive practices into all aspects of care.
g) Integrated and collaborative care: Mental health crisis and inpatient care will need to become more joined up, involving a range of healthcare professionals, social workers and other support services rather than the responsibility of mental health services. This will ensure that CYP receive comprehensive care that addresses their mental health needs, as well as any other factors that may be contributing to their crisis. Good-quality

care depends on true integration between all partners, so that CYP can move seamlessly between services depending on their level of need at the time.

At present, care is often fragmented, as community and inpatient services, social care, education and primary care are provided by different organisations. This poses a significant challenge, leading to delayed discharges and consequential high risk of institutionalisation. Services are often organised by risk, responding to risk events without considering the whole person as part of a system. A culture of defensive practice may lead to CYP being passed on between services, or getting 'stuck' in inpatient care, often resulting in escalation of risk and 'iatrogenic harm'.

A whole-system culture shift that includes a reconceptualization of risk, and 'ownership' of risk by all agencies involved in the care of a CYP (not only health services), will pave the way for true integration of care and the provision of better-quality care, underpinned by understanding the CYP as a whole.

Appendix 22.1 Example of a coping and safety plan

SAFETY PLAN

PATIENT DETAILS

Name:
DoB:
Date of plan:
Clinician:
Contacts
Young person:
Parent/carer:
CAMHS:
Social Worker:
CAMHS crisis team:

PLEASE KEEP THIS PLAN SOMEWHERE EASILY ACCESSIBLE AND SAFE

HELPING MYSELF TO STAY SAFE

What might my triggers to distress be?

– Hostility from others, people making unkind remarks, shouting or aggressive towards you.

– Feeling stuck.

– Not feeling heard.

How do I reduce distress?
Focus on a task that helps me reduce my distress

– Listening to music.

– Speaking to a good friend.

– Going for a walk and having some fresh air, having some space.

If my emotions feel too much and I feel I might harm myself, I will use TIPP skills to reduce my distress rapidly:
- ***T**emperature – splash my face with some very cold water: 'ice diving' Tip the Temperature: TIP DBT Skill - YouTube*
- ***I**ntense Exercise – 10-15 minutes TIP Skills: Intensive Exercise - YouTube*
- ***P**aced Breathing – I will try to slow my breathing down to 5–7 breaths per minute for one minute TIP Skills: Paced Breathing - YouTube*
- ***P**aired Muscle Relaxation – I will tense each group of muscles in my body one by one for 5 seconds, and then relax (think turning from a robot into a rag doll) TIP Skill: Paired Muscle Relaxation - YouTube*

Remember to PLEASE look after your body and mind:
- ***P**hysica**L** – Treat physical illness, see a doctor, and take medication as prescribed*
- ***E**ating – Eat a balanced diet, not too much or too little*
- ***A**void – Avoid any mood altering drugs*
- ***S**leep – Get enough sleep to feel rested*
- ***E**xercise – Get regular exercise*

If above is not working and I still feel unsafe and out of control, I can:
- Call the Crisis lines as outlined below, for support. Crisis line **XXXXXX** (24/7 availability)
- Attend any Emergency Department at any time of day, seven days a week. My local Emergency Department is **The XXX Hospital**. To access the Emergency Department I can self-present and also call 999 for ambulance if I feel unable to get there safely.

WHAT OTHERS CAN DO TO HELP ME

Current Plans:

- Social Worker
- CAMHS
- The Paediatric Team

CAMHS are going to:

We have referred you to xxxx CAMHS for further emotional and mental health support. They will make contact to arrange a time to meet with you.

My mother/ father/ carer is going to:

– Stick to the written agreement made.

– This includes ensuring that you both have space for 1 hour if argument ensue.

– There will be no physical or verbal altercations between the both of you.

– If there is an altercation the Emergency Duty Team xxxxxxxxx will be contacted for further support.

– If there are concerns around your mental health needs, that Mental Health Crisis Line should be contacted for support.

– Mother can also assist in you coming to the Emergency Department for support.

WHO TO CONTACT IN AN EMERGENCY

Monday to Friday 9.00 am to 5.00 pm: who to call

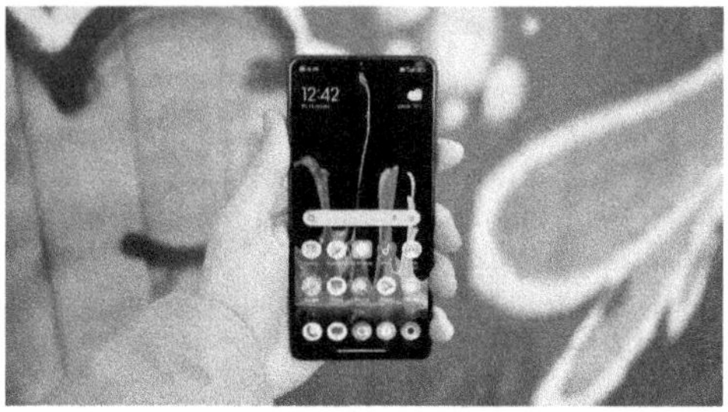

- crisis line xxxxxxxxxx (24/7 availability)
- Go to my local emergency department (name of hospital)
- Telephone 999

Other times
(Anytime between 5.00 pm and 9.00 am during the week and from 5.00 pm on Friday to 9.00 am on Monday over the weekend and on bank holidays).

Other helpful app resources Jmcanally / Shutterstock.com

Other helpful websites. Rock 1997 / Wikimedia Commons / CC BY-SA 4.0

References

Adrian, M., McCauley, E., Berk, M. S., Asarnow, J. R., Korslund, K., Avina, C., Gallop, R., & Linehan, M. M. (2019). Predictors and moderators of recurring self-harm in adolescents participating in a comparative treatment trial of psychological interventions. *Journal of Child Psychology and Psychiatry, 60*(10), 1123–1132. https://doi.org/10.1111/jcpp.13099

American Psychiatric Association (2013). DSM–5 Fact Sheets: Section III. https://www.psychiatry.org/psychiatrists/practice/dsm/educational-resources/dsm-5-fact-sheets

Asarnow, J. R., & Ougrin, D. (2019). Suicide and self-harm: Advancing from science to preventing deaths. *Journal of Child Psychology and Psychiatry, 60*, 1043–1045. https://doi.org/10.1111/jcpp.13131

Balint, M. (1968). *The Basic fault*. Therapeutic aspects of regression. Tavistock Publications.

Barzilay, S., Apter, A., & King, R. A. (2019). Suicidal behavior and health risk behaviors over time among a school-based sample of Israeli adolescents. *Journal of Abnormal Child Psychology, 47*(10), 1725–1736.

Bevan Brittan (2018). Why black men are more likely to be detained: Consideration of significant racial disparity in mental healthcare. https://www.bevanbrittan.com/insights/articles/2018/why-black-men-are-more-likely-to-be-detained-consideration-of-significant-racial-disparity-in-mental-healthcare/

Bridge, J. A., Goldstein, T. R., & Brent, D. A. (2006). Adolescent suicide and suicidal behavior. *Journal of Child Psychology and Psychiatry, 47*(3–4), 372–394. https://doi.org/10.1111/j.1469-7610.2006.01615.x

Burnham, J. (2013). Developments in Social GGRRAAACCEEESSS: Visible-invisible, voiced-unvoiced. In I.-B. Krause (ed.), *Cultural reflexivity in systemic psychotherapy: Mutual perspectives*. Karnac.

Campbell, D., & Hale, R. (1991). Suicidal acts. In J. Holmes (ed.), *Textbook of psychotherapy in psychiatric practice* (pp. 287–306). Churchill Livingstone.

Chang, J. C., Huynh, L., Brettmann, J., & Sapiro, R. (2017). Outcomes of an intensive outpatient program for adolescents with eating disorders. *Journal of Adolescent Health, 60*(4), 11–12.

Chapman, A. L. (2006). Dialectical behavior therapy: Current indications and unique elements. *Psychiatry, 3*(9), 62-68.

Children's Commissioner. (2020a). *Children's experiences in mental health wards*. https://www.childrenscommissioner.gov.uk/resource/childrens-experiences-in-mental-health-wards/

Children's Commissioner. (2020b). *Who are they? Where are they?* https://www.childrenscommissioner.gov.uk/wp-content/uploads/2020/11/cco-who-are-theywhere-are-they-2020.pdf

Children's Commissioner. (2021). *The state of children's mental health services* 2020/21. https://www.childrenscommissioner.gov.uk/resource/29751/

Clark, J., & MacLennan, E. (2023). Measuring experience of inpatient child and adolescent mental health services (CAMHS). *International Journal of Environmental Research in Public Health, 20*(11), 5940. https://doi.org/10.3390/ijerph20115940

Corrigall, R., & Mitchell, B. (2002). Service innovations: Rethinking inpatient provision for adolescents. *Psychiatric Bulletin, 26*, 388–392.

Council of Europe. (1998). European convention of human rights. https://www.echr.coe.int/documents/d/echr/convention_ENG

Courvoisie, H., Labellarte, M. J., & Riddle, M. A. (2001). Psychosis in children: Diagnosis and treatment. *Dialogues in Clinical Neuroscience, 3*(2), 79–92. https://doi.org/10.31887%2FDCNS.2001.3.2%2Fhcourvoisie

Crosby, A., Ortega, L., & Melanson, C. (2011). *Self-directed violence surveillance, uniform definitions and recommended data elements*, version 1.0. https://www.cdc.gov/suicide/pdf/self-directed-violence-a.pdf

Department of Constitutional Affairs. (2007). *Mental Capacity Act (2005) Code of Practice*. London: HMSO.

Department of Health. (2015). Future in mind: Promoting, protecting and improving our children and young people's mental health and wellbeing. https://assets.publishing.service.gov.uk/government/uploads/system/uploads/attachment_data/file/414024/Childrens_Mental_Health.pdf

Department of Health. (2017a). Code of practice: *Mental Health Act 1983*. https://assets.publishing.service.gov.uk/government/uploads/system/uploads/attachment_data/file/435512/MHA_Code_of_Practice.PDF

Department of Health. (2017b). Transforming children and young people's mental health provision: A green paper. https://assets.publishing.service.gov.uk/government/uploads/system/uploads/attachment_data/file/664855/Transforming_children_and_young_people_s_mental_health_provision.pdf

Department of Health. (2018). Child and adolescent mental health services tier 4(CAMHS T4): General adolescent services including specialist eating disorder services. https://www.england.nhs.uk/wp-content/uploads/2018/02/tier-4-camhs-general-adolescent-service-specification-v3.pdf

Department of Health and Social Care. (2017). Race disparity audit. https://assets.publishing.service.gov.uk/government/uploads/system/uploads/attachment_data/file/686071/Revised_RDA_report_March_2018.pdf

Department of Health and Social Care. (2020). Mental Capacity (Amendment) Act 2019: Liberty protection safeguards (LPS). https://www.gov.uk/government/collections/mental-capacity-amendment-act-2019-liberty-protection-safeguards-lps

Dickerson Mayes, S., Gorman, A., Hillwig-Garcia, J., & Syedet, E. (2013). Suicide ideation and attempts in children with autism. *Research in Autism Spectrum Disorders, 7*(1), 109–119.

Dubicka, B., & Bullock, T. (2017). Mental health services for children fail to meet soaring demand. *BMJ, 358*: j4254. https://doi.org/10.1136/bmj.j4254

Esposito-Smythers, C., Spirito, A., Kahler, C. W., Hunt, J., & Monti, P. (2011). Treatment of co-occurring substance abuse and suicidality among adolescents: A randomized trial. *Journal of Consulting and Clinical Psychology, 79*(6), 728–739.

Fonagy, P., & Bateman, A. (2008). The development of borderline personality disorder: A mentalizing model. *Journal of Personality Disorders, 22*(1), 4–21.

Furre, A., Falk, R. S., Sandvik, L., Friis, S., Knutzen, M., & Hanssen-Bauer, K. (2017). Characteristics of adolescents frequently restrained in acute psychiatric units in Norway: A nationwide study. *Child and Adolescent Psychiatry and Mental Health, 11*(3). https://doi.org/10.1186/s13034-016-0136-1

Gilbody, S., Cahill, J., Barkham, M., Richards, D., Bee, P., & Glanville, J. (2006). Can we improve the morale of staff working in psychiatric units? A systematic review. *Journal of Mental Health, 15*(1), 7–17.

Gill, F., Butler, S., & Pistrang, N. (2016). The experience of adolescent inpatient care and the anticipated transition to the community: Young people's perspectives. *Journal of Adolescence, 46*, 57–65. https://doi.org/10.1016/j.adolescence.2015.10.025

Gjevik, E., Eldevik, S., Fjaeran-Granum, T., & Sponheim, E. (2011). Kiddie-SADS reveals high rates of DSM-IV disorders in children and adolescents with autism spectrum disorders. *Journal of Autism and Developmental Disorders, 41*(6), 761–769. https://doi.org/10.1007/s10803-010-1095-7

Green, J., Jacobs, B., Beecham, J., Dunn, G., Kroll, L., Tobias, C., & Briskman, J. (2007). Inpatient treatment in child and adolescent psychiatry: A prospective study of health gain and costs. *Journal of Child Psychology and Psychiatry, 48*(12), 1259–1267. https://doi.org/10.1111/j.1469-7610.2007.01802.x

Hall, W., & Degenhardt, L. (2008) Cannabis use and the risk of developing a psychotic disorder. *World Psychiatry*, *7*(2), 68–71. https://doi.org/10.1002/j.2051-5545.2008.tb00158.x

Hanssen-Bauer, K., Heyerdahl, S., Hatling T., Jensen, G., Olstad, P. M., Stangeland, T., & Tinderholt, T. (2011). Admissions to acute adolescent psychiatric units: A prospective study of clinical severity and outcome. *International Journal of Mental Health Systems, 5*(1). https://doi.org/10.1186/1752-4458-5-1

Hawton, K., Bale, L., Brand, F., Townsend, E., Ness, J., Waters, K., Clements, C., Kapur, N., & Geulayov, G. (2020). Mortality in children and adolescents following presentation to hospital after non-fatal self-harm in the Multicentre Study of Self-harm: A prospective observational cohort study. *The Lancet: Child & Adolescent Health, 4*(2), 111–120. https://doi.org/10.1016/S2352-4642(19)30373-6

Hawton, K., & Harriss, L. (2008). How often does deliberate self-harm occur relative to each suicide? A study of variations by gender and age. *Suicide and Life-Threatening Behavior, 38*, 650–660. https://doi.org/10.1521/suli.2008.38.6.650

Hawton, K., Hill, N. T. M., Gould, M., John, A., Lascelles, K., & Robinson, J. (2020). Clustering of suicides in children and adolescents. *The Lancet: Child & Adolescent Health*, *4*(1), 58–67. https://doi.org/10.1016/S2352-4642(19)30335-9

Hayes, D., Thievendran, J., & Kyriakopoulos, M. (2022). Adolescent inpatient mental health services in the UK. *Archive of Disease in Childhood, 107*, 427–430. https://doi.org/10.1136/archdischild-2020-321442

Healthy London Partnership. (2016). Improving care for children and young people with mental health crisis in London. https://www.transformationpartnersinhealthandcare.nhs.uk/wp-content/uploads/2017/11/Improving-care-for-children-and-young-people-with-mental-health-crisis-in-London.pdf

H. M. Government. (2014). Mental Health Crisis Care Concordat: Improving outcomes for people experiencing mental health crisis. https://assets.publishing.service.gov.uk/government/uploads/system/uploads/attachment_data/file/281242/36353_Mental_Health_Crisis_accessible.pdf

John, A., Glendenning, A. C., Marchant, A., Montomery, P., Stewart, A., Wood, S., Lloyd, K., & Hawton, K. (2018). Self-harm, suicidal behaviours, and cyberbullying in children and young people: Systematic review. *Journal of Medical Internet Research, 20*, e129. https://doi.org/10.2196/jmir.9044

Kapur, N., Cooper, J., O'Connor, R. C., & Hawton, K. (2013). Non-suicidal self-injury v. attempted suicide: New diagnosis or false dichotomy? *British Journal of Psychiatry, 202*, 326–328.

Kaufman, N. J., Broth, M. R., Smith, C. O., & Collins, M. H. (2019). Family-based interventions in inpatient child and adolescent psychiatric settings. *Journal of Child and Adolescent Psychiatric Nursing, 32*(4), 202–208. https://doi.org/10.1111/j.1752-0606.2011.00257.x

Khanna, R., Madhavan, S. S., & Smith, M. J. (2018). Mobile crisis teams and crisis stabilization units: An updated systematic review. *Administration and Policy in Mental Health and Mental Health Services Research, 45*(1), 133–149.

King, C. A., Arango, A., Kramer, A., Busby, D. R., Czyz, E. C., Ewell Foster, C. J., & Gillespie, B. W. (2019). Association of the youth-nominated support team intervention for suicidal adolescents with 11- to 14-year mortality outcomes. Secondary analysis of a randomized clinical trial. *JAMA Psychiatry, 76*, 492–498.

King, C. A., Gipson, P. Y., Arango, A., Lernihan, D., Clark, M., Foster, C. E., Caldwell, C., Ghaziuddin, N., & Stone, D. (2018). LET's CONNECT community mentorship program for youths at risk of suicide: A randomized controlled trial. *Journal of the American Academy of Child & Adolescent Psychiatry, 58*(7), 104–110. https://doi.org/10.1002%2Fjcop.21979

King, C. A., Grupp-Phelan, J., Brent, D., Dean, J. M., Webb, M., Bridge, J. A., Spirito, A., Chernick, L. S., Mahabee-Gittens, E. M., Mistry, R. D., Rea, M., Keller, A., Rogers, A., Shenoi, R., Cwik, M., Busby, D. R., & Caspar, T. C. (2019). Predicting 3-month risk for adolescent suicide attempts among pediatric emergency department patients. *Journal of Child Psychology and Psychiatry 60*(10), 1055–1064. https://doi.org/10.1111/jcpp.13087

Leicester Partnership NHS Trust. (2013). *Guidelines for the psychological management of suicide risk*.

Linehan, M. M. (1993) *Cognitive-behavioral treatment of borderline personality disorder*. Guilford Press.

Mars, B., Heron, J., Klonsky, E. D., Moran, P., O'Connor, R. C., Tilling, K., Wilkinson, P., & Gunnell, D. (2019). Predictors of future suicide attempt among adolescents with suicidal thoughts or non-suicidal self-harm: A population-based birth cohort study. *Lancet Psychiatry, 6*(4), 327–337. https://doi.org/10.1016/s2215-0366(19)30030-6

Mayes, S. D., Fernandez-Mendoza, J., Baweja, R., Calhoun, S., Mahr, F., Aggarwal, R., & Arnold, M. (2014). Correlates of suicide ideation and attempts in children and adolescents with eating disorders. *Eating Disorders, 22*(4), 352–366. https://doi.org/10.1080/10640266.2014.915694

Morgan, C., Webb, R. T., Carr, M. J., Kontopantelis, E., Green, J., Chew-Graham, C. A., Kapur, N., & Ashcroft, D. M. (2017). Incidence, clinical management, and mortality risk following self-harm among children and adolescents: Cohort study in primary care. *BMJ, 359*, j4351. https://doi.org/10.1136/bmj.j4351

Morgan, H. G. (1979). *Death wishes: The understanding and management of deliberate self-harm*. Wiley.

Naghavi, M. (2019). Global, regional, and national burden of suicide mortality 1990 to 2016: Systematic analysis for the Global Burden of Disease Study 2016. *BMJ, 364*, j194. https://doi.org/10.1136/bmj.l94

National Confidential Inquiry into Suicide and Safety in Mental Health. (2022). *Annual report 2022: UK patient and general population data, 2009–2019, and real time surveillance dat*a. University of Manchester. https://sites.manchester.ac.uk/ncish/reports/annual-report-2022/#:~:text=During%202009%2D2019%2C%20over%20a,half%20were%20on%20agreed%20leave

National Institute for Health and Care Excellence [NICE]. (2022). *Self-harm: Assessment, management and preventing recurrence*. https://www.nice.org.uk/guidance/ng225

National Institute of Health and Care Research [NIHR]. (2021). *Experience of children and young people cared for in mental health, learning disability and autism inpatient settings*. https://evidence.nihr.ac.uk/themedreview/children-young-people-mental-health-learning-disability-autism-inpatient-settings/

NCEL CAMHS Provider Collaborative Strategic Health Needs Assessment. (2021). Executive summary. https://www.northeastlondonhcp.nhs.uk/wp-content/uploads/2023/05/CAMHS-HNA-summary.pdf

NCISH. (2017). *National confidential inquiry into suicide and homicide by people with mental illness. Suicide in children and young people*. University of Manchester.

NHS. (2019). *Long term plan*. https://www.longtermplan.nhs.uk/wp-content/uploads/2019/08/nhs-long-term-plan-version-1.2.pdf

NHS Digital. (2017). Mental health act statistics, annual figures: 2016-17, experimental statistics. https://digital.nhs.uk/data-and-information/publications/statistical/mental-health-act-statistics-annual-figures/mental-health-act-statistics-annual-figures-2016-17-experimental-statistics

NHS Digital. (2018). *Mental health of children and young people in England,* 2017. https://digital.nhs.uk/data-and-information/publications/statistical/mental-health-of-children-and-young-people-in-england/2017/2017#key-facts

NHS Digital. (2022). Mental health of children and young people in England 2022: Wave 3 follow up to the 2017 survey: Data tables. https://digital.nhs.uk/data-and-information/publications/statistical/mental-health-of-children-and-young-people-in-england/2022-follow-up-to-the-2017-survey/data-sets

NHS England. (2014). Child and adolescent mental health services (CAMHS) tier 4 report, 2014. https://www.england.nhs.uk/wp-content/uploads/2014/07/camhs-tier-4-rep.pdf

NHS England. (2017). *Transforming care model specifications* 2017. https://www.england.nhs.uk/wp-content/uploads/2017/02/model-service-spec-2017.pdf

NSPCC. (2016). *Keeping children safe*. https://www.nspcc.org.uk/keeping-children-safe/childrens-mental-health/self-harm/

Nyttingnes, O., Ruud, T., Norvoll, R., Rugkasa, J., & Hanssen-Bauer, K. (2018). A cross-sectional study of experienced coercion in adolescent mental health inpatients. *BMC Health Services Research, 18*(389). https://bmchealthservres.biomedcentral.com/articles/10.1186/s12913-018-3208-5

Ougrin, D. (2020). Debate: Emergency mental health presentations of young people during the COVID-19 lockdown. *Child and Adolescent Mental Health, 25*(3), 171–172. https://doi.org/10.1111%2Fcamh.12411

Ougrin, D., Corrigall, R., Stahl, D., Poole, J., Zundel, T., Wait, M., Slater, V., Reavey, P., Byford, S., Ivens, J., Crommelin, M., Hayes, D., Middleton, K., Young, P., & Taylor, E. (2018). Comparison of effectiveness and cost-effectiveness of an intensive community supported discharge service versus treatment as usual for adolescents with psychiatric emergencies: A randomised controlled trial. *The Lancet Psychiatry, 5*(6), 477–485. https://doi.org/10.1016/s2215-0366(18)30129-9

Ougrin, D., Corrigall, R., Stahl, D., Poole, J., Zundel, T., Wait, M., Slater, V., Reavey, P., Byford, S., Ivens, J., Crommelin, M., Hayes, D., Middleton, K., Young, P., & Taylor, E. (2020). Supported discharge service versus inpatient care evaluation (SITE): A randomised controlled trial comparing effectiveness of an intensive community care service versus inpatient treatment as usual for adolescents with severe psychiatric disorders: Self-harm, functional impairment, and educational and clinical outcomes. *European Journal of Child and Adolescent Psychiatry, 30*(9), 1427–1436. https://doi.org/10.1007/s00787-020-01617-1

Ougrin, D., Zundel, T., Corrigall, R., Padmore, J., & Loh, C. (2014). Innovations in practice: Pilot evaluation of the supported discharge service (SDS): Clinical outcomes and service use. *Child and Adolescent Mental Health, 19*(4), 265–269. https://doi.org/10.1111/camh.12038

Parker, C. (2020). *Adolescent mental health care and the law*. Legal Action Group.

Polvere, L. (2011). Youth perspectives on restrictive mental health placement: Unearthing a counter narrative. *Journal of Adolescent Research, 26*, 318–343.

Pompilli, M., Girardi, P., Tatarelli, G., Ruberto, A., & Tatarelli, R. (2006) Suicide and attempted suicide in eating disorders, obesity and weight-image concern. *Eating Behaviour, 7*(4), 384–394.

Public Health England. (2017). *Intentional self-harm in adolescence: An analysis of data from the health behaviour in school-aged children (HBSC) survey for England, 2014*. https://assets.publishing.service.gov.uk/government/uploads/system/uploads/attachment_data/file/621068/Health_behaviour_in_school_age_children_self-harm.pdf

Qin, P., Agerbo, E., & Mortensen, P. B. (2002). Suicide risk in relation to family history of completed suicide and psychiatric disorders: A nested case-control study based on longitudinal registers. *The Lancet, 360*, 1126–1130. https://doi.org/10.1016/S0140-6736(02)11197-4

Rantzen, E., & Cameron, J. (2016). *Childline: 30 years of listening to children*. NSPCC.

Reavey, P., Poole, J., Corrigall, R., Zundel, T., Byford, S., Sarhane, M., Taylor, E., Ivens, J., & Ougrin, D. (2017). The ward as emotional ecology: Adolescent experiences of managing mental health and distress in psychiatric inpatient settings. *Health & Place, 46*, 210–218. https://doi.org/10.1016/j.healthplace.2017.05.008

Rodway, C., Tham, S. G., Ibrahim, S., Turnbull, P., Windfuhr, K., Shaw, J., Kapur, N., & Appleby, L. (2016). Suicide in children and young people in England: A consecutive case series. *The Lancet Psychiatry, 3*(8), 751–759. https://doi.org/10.1016/s2215-0366(16)30094-3

Royal College of Psychiatrists. (2020). Self-harm. https://www.rcpsych.ac.uk/mental-health/mental-illnesses-and-mental-health-problems/self-harm

Royal College of Psychiatrists. (2021). *CAMHS quality network for inpatient care CCQI standards for services* (11th ed.). https://www.rcpsych.ac.uk/docs/default-source/improving-care/ccqi/quality-networks/child-and-adolescent-inpatient-services-(cahms)/qnic-standards-11th-ed477e94a4a56143b8928b84877532c9c6.pdf?sfvrsn=661fd7da_2

Russell, B. S., Hickie, I. B., & Mykletun, A. (2019). Evidence-based prevention and treatment interventions for youth suicide. *Australian & New Zealand Journal of Psychiatry, 53*(3), 189–190.

Sadler, K., Vizard, T., Ford, T., Goodman, A., Goodman, R., & McManus, S. (2018). *Mental health of children and young people in England, 2017: Trends and characteristics*. NHS Digital.

Sedgwick, R., Epstein, S., Dutta, R., & Ougrin, D. (2019). Social media, internet use and suicide attempts in adolescents. *Current Opinions in Psychiatry, 32*(6), 534–541. https://doi.org/10.1097/YCO.0000000000000547

Simonoff, E., Pickles, A., Charman, T., Chandler, S., Loucas, T., & Baird, G. (2008). Psychiatric disorders in children with autism spectrum disorders: Prevalence, comorbidity, and associated factors in a population-derived sample. *Journal of American Academic Child and Adolescent Psychiatry, 47*(8), 921–929. https://doi.org/10.1097/chi.0b013e318179964f

Sweeney, A., Filson, B., Kennedy, A., Collinson, L., & Gillard, S. (2018) A paradigm shift: Relationships in trauma-informed mental health services. *British Journal of Psychiatry, 24*(5), 319–333. https://doi.org/10.1192%2Fbja.2018.29

UK Legislation. (1983). Mental health act 1983 c. 20. https://www.legislation.gov.uk/ukpga/1983/20/contents

Wasserman, D., Hoven, C. W., Wasserman, C., Wall, M., Eisenberg, R., Hadlaczky, G., Kelleher, G., Sarchiapone, M., Apter, A., Balazs, J., Bobes, J., Brunner, R., Corcoran, P., Cosman, D., Guillemin, F., Haring, C., Iosue, M., Kaess, M., Kahn, J-P., ... Carli, V. (2015). School-based suicide prevention programmes: The SEYLE cluster-randomised, controlled trial. *The Lancet, 385*, 1536–1544.

Wilson, E., & Ougrin, D. (2021), Defining self-harm: How inconsistencies in language persist: A commentary/ reflection on Ward and Curran (2021). *Child and Adolescent Mental Health, 26*(4), 372–374. https://doi.org/10.1111/camh.12502

Wolff, J. C., Thompson, E., Thomas, S. A., Nesi, J., Bettis, A. H., Ransford, B., Scopelliti, K., Frazier, E. A., & Liu, R. T. (2019). Emotion dysregulation and non-suicidal self-injury: A systematic review and metaanalysis. *European Psychiatry, 59*, 25–36. https://doi.org/10.1016/j.eurpsy.2019.03.004

Wood, L., & Alsawy, S. (2016). Patient experiences of psychiatric inpatient care: A systematic review of qualitative evidence. *Journal of Psychiatric Intensive Care, 12*, 35–43. https://doi.org/10.20299/jpi.2016.001

Yip, P. S. F., Caine, E., Yousuf, S., Chang, S., Wu, K. C., & Chen, Y. (2012). Suicide 3: Means restriction for suicide prevention. *The Lancet, 379*(9834), 2393–2399. https://www.proquest.com/scholarly-journals/suicide-3-means-restriction-prevention/docview/1022967728/se-2

Ystgaard, M., Arensman, E., Hawton, K., Madge, N., van Heeringen, K., Hewitt, A., de Wilde, E. J., De Leo, D., & Fekete, S. (2009). Deliberate self-harm in adolescents: Comparison between those who receive help following self-harm and those who do not. *Journal of Adolescence, 32* (4), 875–891. https://doi.org/10.1016/j.adolescence.2008.10.010

Zelazny, J., Melhem, N., Porta, G., Biernesser, C., Keilp, J. G., Mann, J. J., Oquendo, M. A., Stanley, B., & Brent, D. A. (2019). Childhood maltreatment, neuropsychological function and suicidal behavior. *Journal of Child Psychology and Psychiatry, 60* (10), 1085–1093. https://doi.org/10.1111/jcpp.13096

Zetterqvist, M. (2015). The DSM-5 diagnosis of nonsuicidal self-injury disorder: A review of the empirical literature. *Child and Adolescent Psychiatry and Mental Health, 9*, 31. https://doi.org/10.1186/s13034-015-0062-7

Zheng, Z., Zheng, P., & Zou, X. (2018). Association between schizophrenia and autism spectrum disorder: A systematic review and meta-analysis. *Autism Research, 11*(8), 1110–1119. https://doi.org/10.1002/aur.1977

23

Youth Offending and Forensic Interventions

Simone Fox and Vicky Thakordas-Desai

23.1 Introduction

Young people who come into contact with the Criminal Justice System (CJS) present many challenges to and dilemmas for society. In the eighteenth and nineteenth centuries young people were not distinguished from adults and were placed in adult prisons. Approaches to managing young people have gradually moved away from punitive to preventative; recognising early intervention and diversion and rehabilitation as critical to their adjustment in society. Identifying and understanding the needs of young people who are already in, or at risk of entering, the CJS is essential from developmental, societal and political perspectives.

In England and Wales (E&W) and Northern Ireland, the minimum age of criminal responsibility (MACR) is 10 years and in the Republic of Ireland (ROI) and Scotland it is 12. In other countries it ranges widely, from 7 to 10 in the United States to 18 in Belgium. Children under the age of criminal responsibility are deemed to lack capacity to commit crime, as they may be insufficiently capable of moral reasoning. The low age of 10 has been the source of contention for many years, with the European Commissioner on Human Rights recommending that the UK adopt an age of criminal responsibility in line with the European norm, on the grounds that children under 12 years cannot have sufficient consciousness of the nature and consequences of their actions to be held criminally responsible. The MACR also results in inconsistencies within UK law, where children of the same age are understood differently in different legal contexts. Few children under the age of 14 commit crimes and their offences are largely minor (Youth Justice Board (YJB), 2021).

Over the past 15 years or so, there has been a significant reduction in the number of children and young people involved in youth justice proceedings (YJB, 2021). In 2019–2020, the number of young people under 18 in custody in E&W was 780 (YJB, 2021). This is a fall of 68% compared with 10 years previously (YJB, 2021). There continue to be reductions in the number of first-time entrants to the Youth Justice System (YJS) and in the number of young people receiving a youth caution or court sentence. However, the average custodial sentence length has increased by over 7 months over a 10-year period (from 11.3 to 18.6 months) (YJB, 2021). The YJB data for 2020–2021 support these trends but are further complicated by the impact of the Covid-19 pandemic (YJB, 2022).

Child Psychology: Pathways to Good Practice, First Edition.
Edited by Helen Pote, Anna Picciotto and Clare Norris.

The reduced rates of offending, re-offending and custody within the YJS do not translate to youth from minority ethnic backgrounds. These young people are disproportionately represented across many stages of the YJS. The proportion of young people from minority ethnic backgrounds in the YJS has steadily increased over the past 10 years, with the percentage of black children given a caution or sentence doubling and the proportion of black children in remand or custody increasing by over a third (YJB, 2021). Institutional racism was highlighted in the Macpherson report in 1999 (Macpherson, 1999) at all stages of the CJS including from stop-and-search to arrests, conviction, imprisonment and deaths in custody. The Lammy review (2017) further explored the over-representation of minority ethnic groups within the YJS.

The health, education, social and emotional needs of children and young people in forensic settings are high (Chitsabesan et al., 2006; Lader et al., 2000). Studies consistently suggest significant levels of mental health needs (e.g. Lennox & Khan, 2013; Teplin et al., 2002) and neurodevelopmental disorders amongst young offenders (see Hughes et al., 2012 for summary). Compared to young people in the general population where prevalence rates for various mental health disorders such as anxiety, depression and post-traumatic stress disorder range from 0.4 to 3.3%, reported prevalence rates for young offenders can range from 8 to 29% (Chitsabesan & Hughes, 2016). A review of research and government data drawn from a variety of national contexts also suggests a disproportionately high rate of neurodevelopmental disorders amongst young people in forensic settings. This includes those with a learning/intellectual disability, communication disorders, Attention Deficit Hyperactivity Disorder (ADHD) and autistic spectrum disorders (Hughes, 2015). The higher prevalence rates in young people within the CJS may be a consequence of shared risk factors in the development of both antisocial behaviour and mental health disorders. Young people in forensic settings have had high levels of exposure to traumatic and stressful life events (Lader et al., 2000).

There is considerable research into the causes and correlates of adolescent offending, which include several longitudinal studies following children well into adulthood (e.g. Farrington et al., 2021; Koops & Orobio de Castro, 2004). Risk factors for offending and violence support a socioecological view (Bronfenbrenner, 1979) and relate to: the individual (e.g. as low verbal skills, antisocial attitudes and beliefs, cognitive bias to attribute hostile intentions to others, substance misuse); the family (e.g. lack of monitoring and supervision, ineffective discipline, low warmth, high conflict, parental difficulties such as substance abuse, criminality and psychiatric conditions); peers (e.g. rejection, peer delinquency, low association with pro-social peers); school (e.g. poor attendance/attainment); and the community (e.g. high mobility, criminal subculture, low community support). Research has also supported a range of protective factors across the different systems that will reduce the risk of engagement in violence or antisocial behaviour, these include: individual factors (e.g. intelligence, good problem-solving skills, 'easy' temperament); family (e.g. attachment to parents, supportive family environment); peer (e.g. bonding with pro-social peers); school (e.g. academic achievement, motivation, positive relationships and class/school climate); and community (e.g. a strong indigenous support network). Early intervention and prevention is based on the assumption that life course trajectories can be changed by actively reducing the risk factors associated with antisocial behaviour and increasing the strengths or protective factors that support desistance.

It can be difficult to define what constitutes a forensic setting. This could encompass both community and secure environments that would include anything from Forensic Child and Adolescent Mental Health services (FCAMHs) to Young Offenders' Institutions (YOIs). Rather than have a distinction between forensic and non-forensic contexts, this chapter will focus on services and settings where psychological practitioners may come into contact with young people who present with high-risk forensic behaviours (either to self and/or others).

23.2 Psychological Therapists within the Context of the Criminal Justice System

Recent developments and innovation within public sector services have provided opportunities for aspiring and qualified psychological practitioners to gain a range of skills in order to develop breadth and depth of psychological practice and experience across a variety of settings and populations. Whereas in previous years these roles have been limited to a set few psychological specialities, recent advances have recognised the valid contributions individuals with a background in psychology and advanced psychological training can bring to multiagency and professional teams. Within the CJS, psychological therapists are employed in both secure and community settings across the country. Their contribution is not limited to CJS settings. Psychological therapists are increasingly employed in a variety of capacities within public and private sector organisations such as local authority teams, mental health, education, police and residential healthcare settings. Whilst they may not always be employed specifically in the capacity of a 'psychological practitioner', their psychological knowledge base and skills versatility mean that they can be recruited into a variety of roles where psychologically informed practice is utilised.

More commonly, psychological practitioners have played an important role in supporting children and young people in secure settings such as secure training centres (STCs), in YOIs, secure mental health hospitals and within children's secure welfare services. Young people will often transition between these settings as a result of the legal framework they are subjected to. In the community, psychological practitioners are engaged within: the YJS (see Box 23.1 for an example); harmful sexual behaviour teams; in local authorities within specialist family intervention teams (such as multisystemic therapy (MST), family functional therapy (FFT) and edge of care teams); FCAMHS; mental health liaison and diversion teams; within specialist residential and educational settings; and in more bespoke and specialist roles within the police (such as the violence reduction unit – see later in the chapter) and specialist mental health teams. They may work alongside children and young people's Liaison and Diversion nurses, which are specific posts funded through National Health Service Education (NHSE) Youth Justice specialist commissioning and whose role is to screen and assess the mental health needs of all children and young people in police custody.

Whether within secure or community settings, the role of the psychological practitioner can vary considerably on the basis of their area of specialty, qualification, registration and experience. The psychological practitioner role has expanded to include not only specialist/registered roles, but also psychologically trained and experienced practitioners who are employed in a number of specialist mental health, therapist and support worker roles that do not require formal registration but are often found working under the supervision and oversight of a qualified practitioner. Such teams and roles within this range of settings are largely influenced by the commissioning and funding of forward-thinking and innovative services and leaders who appreciate the value of embedding psychological practice within their services.

More recently, there have been local and national drives for public sector services and organisations to adopt psychologically and trauma informed ways of working. The publication of high-profile reports such as *Punishing Abuse* (Chard, 2021) and *Secure Children's Homes: Placing Welfare and Justice Children Together* (Hart & La Valle, 2021) highlight the complexities and significant levels of vulnerabilities of children who come into contact with the CJS. The *Punishing Abuse* report draws upon research that indicates how multiple childhood adversities including abuse, neglect, trauma, loss and disrupted attachments lead to poor outcomes in later life (Chard, 2021). It reports a close correlation between adversity in childhood and involvement in subsequent offending behaviour. On the basis of their skills and training, psychological practitioners are key professionals leading and driving forward initiatives relating to evidence-based and psychologically informed practice as a response to the growing evidence of the impact of early childhood trauma and adversity in the lives of children and young people who enter the CJS. This includes a range of direct and indirect methods aimed at engaging colleagues from a wide range of agencies to offer consultation and formulation-based support to training and supervision.

Box 23.1 Professional example: Faith, forensic psychologist

Faith is a forensic psychologist based within a Youth Justice Team. She is working alongside case managers to support colleagues to understand, manage and consider appropriate interventions for children and young people who present with complex forensic histories. Her work includes undertaking risk assessments to aid legal decision making and sentencing, undertaking training with colleagues in relation to areas linked to forensic risk and mental health, providing supervision and reflective practice groups to her colleagues to negate the impact of vicarious trauma and supporting the development and implementation of appropriate interventions with children/young people. Faith also undertakes one-to-one work with the child/young person where appropriate, but often engages the child's family and caregiver system to enable them to manage their young person's risks and needs. In order to do this, she uses trauma-informed practices and systemic approaches to ensure that all of the people around the child can work together in the same way to meet their needs. She is seen as a valuable and knowledgeable resource to her colleagues and the wider service.

Within the context of a CJS setting, the psychological practitioner has the opportunity to become involved in a range of tasks and assessments. The nature and complexity of these will often be experience and speciality dependent and will require appropriate oversight and supervision from a suitably qualified psychological practitioner. Typically, the psychological practitioner can expect to become involved in the following core areas of practice:

- Undertaking specialist assessments and formulations to understand risk, needs and strengths relating to the young person, communicating this understanding to colleagues and aid decision-making within legal settings.

- Delivery of structured interventions aimed at an individual, a group, family-focused or systemic.
- Provision of consultation to other psychological and non-psychological colleagues in relation to the psychological evidence base and recognising and understanding levels of risk, needs, vulnerabilities and safety factors.
- Offering supervision and training to psychological and non-psychological colleagues within CJS settings.
- Involvement in service and clinical evaluation and research to support the development of new and innovative approaches.

The core areas highlight a number of benefits associated with having a psychological practitioner sitting alongside youth justice teams to aid evidence-based decision making.

23.3 Assessment

In order to support a child or young person's journey within the CJS and to ensure that their needs are targeted effectively, it is critical that comprehensive assessments are undertaken in order to understand their offending behaviour and the context within which this behaviour is occurring. Psychological practitioners undertaking assessments of children and young people should aim to ensure that their approach, method and technique takes into account a multidimensional and holistic approach to the concerns and is grounded in evidence-based practice. Psychological assessments and formulations undertaken within the context of a forensic setting will in most instances require an opinion in relation to future risk of harm towards others as well as themselves. Therefore, it is essential that the assessment process is undertaken in a logical and structured way with appropriate oversight and supervision by a senior practitioner.

Assessment in forensic settings involves 'the systematic collection of relevant information in order to detect clinically relevant phenomena or problems in functioning, in order to provide clear treatment targets and risk management strategies' (Vess & Ward, 2011, p. 175). The aim of a forensic assessment of a child or young person is so that a formulation can be understood and offered regarding their presenting risks, needs and vulnerabilities so that targeted support and interventions can be provided, and further risk scenarios can be mitigated against by utilising protective factors across the child or young person's system. Furthermore, aside from their individual needs, the assessment should also take into account and understand the complexities and interactions of the systems around them. Hence, assessments of children and young people should employ multiple methods of assessment, should be multilayered in order to consider the dynamics of the systems around them and should draw on the relevant evidence base relating to offending behaviour and mental health. It is also prudent for ethical considerations to be taken into account from the outset bearing in mind professional and organisational requirements. Ethical considerations can range from the nature and type of contact with the child/young person and people around them, ensuring appropriate informed consent is gained in relation to information governance, recording and storage. It is advisable that these challenges are reflected upon and addressed with a senior practitioner prior to commencing the assessment process.

The process of assessment can be divided into the following generic steps which will be discussed in further detail:

- methods of assessment;
- types of assessment; and
- formulation.

23.3.1 Methods of Assessment

When undertaking forensic assessments of children and young people, it is critical that the psychological practitioner gathers data from multiple sources and systems in order to gain a comprehensive understanding of the child/young person's developmental history and life experiences. Active engagement and dialogue with relevant services and agencies that have been involved with the child/young person is critical in being able to gather historical reports as well as more recent dynamic assessments undertaken by professionals. Developmental history details cannot always be gleaned from the child/young person themselves bearing in mind their level of development, maturity and reliability. Accuracy in relation to historical and clinical factors is vital to inform the correct treatment needs and pathways in order to reduce risk of future offending and thus improve the child/young person's life outcomes. Obtaining a clear developmental history can be difficult due to family factors as previously outlined. The psychological practitioner should consider a variety of creative methods and opportunities in order to gather the relevant information to undertake the assessment in question. These methods typically include:

- Review of collateral reports in order to generate an integrated chronology and understanding of significant events in the child or young person's life.
- Consultations and discussions with relevant professionals who have been involved in the child or young person's care.
- Interviews with parents/carers, school/college staff and significant others within the community which may include the completion of observation schedules or behavioural monitoring tools.
- Clinical interview with the child (where required/possible) which may also include the administration of necessary psychometric measures or neuro-cognitive assessments.

23.3.2 Types of Assessments

Prior to assessment, it is important to consider the reason for the referral, the referrer's concerns and their specific instructions/questions that require investigation. Referrals for assessments may be requested to support legal decision making in relation to sentencing, understanding risk and dangerousness, understanding mental health or trauma and the interventions associated with these needs. Topics of assessments can vary but typically relate to cognitive assessments, personality assessments, mental health and attitudes towards and risk of offending behaviour. These assessments require a comprehensive developmental and psychosocial history that takes into account the child/young person's early life experiences from the point of pregnancy to the present-day covering areas such as early development, family and parental experiences, exposure to early trauma or adversity, educational and school-related experiences, social interactions and relationships, mental health, substance misuse and forensic history. In doing so, the psychological practitioner can develop a formulation of the onset, development and maintenance of the child/young person's presenting needs and vulnerabilities. In addition, for specific and serious offending behaviour, the assessment may require a specialist protocol that is aimed at determining future risk. It is important to recognise that practitioners need to be familiar with professional networks, types of reports and assessment undertaken that are held by different agencies so that a reliable developmental history is compiled. If a comprehensive clinical history is unavailable, it is critical that the psychologist seeks support from senior colleagues to source data and other resources. Depending on their level of qualification and experience, psychological practitioners may be involved at various points of these assessments in the capacity of assessor and/or contributor supporting the process of collateral data review and formulation.

Over the past two decades, there have been significant advances in our understanding and assessment of children and young people at risk of committing serious offending, but there continues to be an ongoing debate about these approaches and their application to children and young people within the context of providing risk judgements in relation to violent or sexual offending. It is accepted that there is no single aetiology for juvenile delinquent behaviour and the extant literature places a much stronger emphasis on the inclusion of protective factors when considering risk in children and young people (Fox & Latham, 2014). Furthermore, risk factors associated with youth offending may not be generalisable, highlighting the need for a robust risk formulation that takes into account the degree of presence and impact of risk and protective factors within the core domains: child/young person, family, school, peer group and community. In addition, it is crucial to recognise that children and young people who engage in serious offending behaviour are themselves vulnerable and marginalised often presenting with complex presentations consisting of multiple and co-morbid developmental and mental health underpinned by significant trauma and adversity during their formative years (Johnstone & Gregory, 2015). As a result, it is vital that psychological practitioners recognise the challenges that lie in reliably conceptualising the complex and potentially inter-related risks and needs and how these precipitate and perpetuate offending behaviour.

There is a wealth of information available in relation to the use of risk assessment tools and their methodologies, the pros and cons of which have been extensively deliberated (Cooke & Michie, 2013; Logan & Hart, 2011; Logan & Johnstone, 2013). These discussions will not be replicated here, but a short summary of contemporary approaches to risk assessment is offered in Table 23.1.

Structured professional judgement tools represent the 'gold standard' when it comes to risk assessment for violent and sexual offending. This is due to the integration of empirically validated risk and protective factors along with scenario planning and risk management.

Examples of structured professional judgement tools include:

- Structured Assessment of Violence Risk in Youth (SAVRY) (Borum et al., 2002), which was developed in order to assist practitioners in the evaluation of violence risk in male and female adolescents aged 12 to 18 years.
- Short-term Assessment of Risk and Treatability: Adolescent Version (START: AV) (Nicholls et al., 2010), which is designed to capture a range of dynamic risk items,

Table 23.1 Summary of contemporary approaches to risk assessment.

Risk assessment approach	Description	Advantages	Disadvantages
Unstructured clinical judgement	• Based on subjective risk factor selection from one practitioner • Drawn from individual clinical experiences • No use of standardised protocols, decision of risk at the discretion of one person/group of people	• Flexible and adaptable • Takes into account dynamic risk factors amenable to change	• Vulnerable to decisional bias • Unclear explicit decision-making structure • Low reliability and validity • Methodology differs across practitioners
Actuarial risk assessment	• Application of algorithms to risk factors in order to reach a predictive decision • Predictions about likelihood of an individual reoffending on the basis of data for a specific offending cohort	• Improved accuracy and consistency of predictions of recidivism rates compared to unstructured clinical judgement • Risk factors are empirically associated with offending type	• Focus on static risk factors and does not take into account dynamic risk that is amenable to change • Group data is applied to individual cases and may overestimate risk
Structured Professional Judgement	• Combines professional judgement alongside empirically validated risk factors with clear coding rules for assessors. • Relevance of risk is considered and evaluated along a spectrum of risk • Risk factors are linked to plausible scenario planning and risk management strategies to assess the likelihood, frequency, severity and prevention of future offending	• Methodical: standardises approaches to increase reliability and validity across practitioners • Ability to create tailored intervention and target risk management • Takes into account static, dynamic and protective factors, and can be utilised alongside an actuarial risk assessment	• Expertise of assessor is critical in understanding and applying risk judgements and therefore these can vary • Process is time and resource intensive and requires access to a variety of collateral data including a clinical interview with the client

strengths and vulnerabilities in youth displaying harmful behaviour to themselves and others.
- Estimate of Risk of Adolescent Sexual Offence Recidivism V2 (ERASOR) (Worling & Curwen, 2001) designed to assess the risk of sexual recidivism in adolescents aged 12 to 18 years who have previously committed a sexual offence.
- Sexually Harmful Adolescent Risk Protocol (SHARP) (Richardson, 2009) that assesses 50 factors across 12 domains that may be relevant in understanding sexually harmful behaviour of children.

Generic services and organisations who do not employ appropriately qualified psychological practitioners may choose to utilise non-validated screening or decision-making tools that are locally derived and lack the requisite criteria to be considered a structured professional judgement tool. These checklists or decision-making tools aim to capture and/or monitor risks in order to support local risk-assessment processes and are derived from the work of one or a group of individuals. Psychological practitioners may be required to undertake or contribute towards these assessments depending upon the remit of their roles. Examples of commonly used decision-making tools within youth justice settings across England and Wales include:

- AssetPlus (YJB, 2014), which is a revised version of the 'Onset' and 'Asset' assessments and has been designed to provide holistic end-to-end assessment and intervention planning that prompts practitioners to take into account a wide range of risk and protective factors derived from the core record. This record is intended to follow the child or young person throughout their time in the YJS. The AssetPlus assessment is intended to be dynamic and iterative, reflecting the complexity of the young person's personal circumstances rather than a 'one-size-fits-all' approach (AssetPlus Model document, YJB, 2014). The assessment allows for key ratings to take place in order to provide a score and an indicator of risk using the Youth Offender Group Reconviction Score (YOGRS) for likelihood of offending and risk of serious harm. An overall safety and well-being judgement is also made by the practitioner.
- Assessment, Intervention and Moving-on (AIM) (Henniker et al., 2002) assesses children and young people aged 10 to 17 years of age who display harmful sexualised behaviour. It contains factors pertaining to both risks and strengths and relies on inter-agency and multidisciplinary liaison and communication to develop a shared language and approach.

23.4 Formulation

The psychological formulation process aims to 'develop an aetiological understanding of the person's difficulties and to ascertain which individual and systemic factors continue to maintain a person's problem' (Harvey, 2014, p. 24). Essential features of all formulations regardless of the modality include: a summary of the core problems; using psychological theories and models to understand how the difficulties relate to one another, drawing on theory to understand the reasons for maintenance of the problem behaviour; and initiating a plan of intervention on the basis of psychological processes and principles identified and revise and reformulate (Johnstone & Dallos, 2006). Whilst there may be differences in training according to specialism and modalities, formulation is a core skill for psychological practitioners to develop and become involved with (see Chapter 3 for more details on generic assessment and formulation).

Formulation within the context of forensic risk assessment is a critical component of the overall process (Cooke & Michie, 2013; Logan & Johnstone, 2013). It targets those factors that are most relevant to understanding why and how offending behaviour has occurred in the past and what might increase the risk of offending in the future. The formulation process provides a framework by which the practitioner can structure, organise and 'make-sense' of complex and multifaceted information, synthesising and considering across a broad range of literature base associated with criminogenic factors (dynamic risk factors that are linked to criminal behaviour) and biopsychosocial theoretical models. Structured professional judgement tools are incomplete without a comprehensive formulation that provides theoretical and multilevel insight into the behaviours of concern. The 5Ps framework (Weerasekera, 1996) is an appropriate framework to organise data pertaining to risk. This framework includes an assessment of all the 'presenting' issues, 'predisposing' influences that link to genetic vulnerabilities and relevant contextual risk markers, 'precipitating' factors that marked the onset of the problem behaviour, 'perpetuating' aspects that exacerbate and maintain the problem issues and 'protective' factors that prevent further deterioration and can help to reduce risk. Johnstone and Gregory (2015) recommend that when formulating in relation to risk-related behaviours for children and young people that the following should also be kept in mind to allow for a more balanced view of risk:

- Developmentally informed – takes into account developmental versus chronological functioning on a number of different domains such as cognitive, emotional, social, physical and moral development.
- Systems informed – acknowledging that the child or young person is embedded in family, school and community systems that also has an impact on their behaviour; they cannot be understood in a vacuum. Therefore, it is critical to adopt a whole systems approach to risk assessment.
- Trauma informed – accepting that exposure to multiple childhood adversity is linked to poor outcomes in life including antisocial behaviour. A trauma-informed conceptualisation will allow for the behaviour to be understood within the context of the trauma experienced. In addition, vicarious trauma should also be considered and addressed, taking into account the experience of 'traumatised' systems.
- Vulnerability informed – recognises that children and young people who offend are a vulnerable group of individuals who have multiple difficulties that have complex interactions.

Due to the changeable nature and experience of children and young people's behaviour, it is vital that the formulation process is:

- dynamic,
- highlights strengths and positive progress,
- developed in a multidisciplinary way that is shared and agreed upon,
- linked into the development of interventions, and
- actively revisited, reformulated and revised in order to support assertive risk management.

23.5 Interventions and Risk Management

The subject of early interventions for children and young people who present with antisocial behaviour is often a source of contention among practitioners and researchers alike. There are those who argue that the behaviour should not be pathologised, as defiant, disruptive and aggressive behaviours are often thought of as developmentally normative in the pre-school period. In contrast, others argue that conduct disorder and oppositional defiant disorder are the two most prevalent mental health disorders diagnosed in childhood (e.g. Baker, 2012) and these children present significant concerns both to their family and to the wider society.

A young person's antisocial behaviour may occur in one setting (for example, in the home, at school or with peers in the community), or it may be pervasive across different contexts. The types of antisocial behaviour may also range from aggression towards family members, peers or professionals, to substance misuse or criminal behaviour (e.g. shoplifting, robbery or drug dealing). Multiple agencies and providers may be involved in the care and treatment of these children and young people. Multiagency involvement can present a challenge to effective co-ordination or care, which will be discussed later in this chapter.

Psychological practitioners have been widely utilised in the facilitation and delivery of various individual and group-based interventions within both secure and community settings. Treatment programmes can vary in terms of their content and approaches across different settings, but meta-analytic studies show that those that conform to risk, needs and responsivity principles (Bonta & Andrews, 2007) demonstrate more superior effects to those that do not. Within secure settings, accredited offending behaviour programmes are designed to develop cognitive, interpersonal, emotional and adaptive skills. These interventions help young people build skills in problem-solving, emotional regulation, interpersonal communication and social skills. Group-based programmes like Juvenile Enhanced Thinking Skills (JETS; Nichols & Mitchell, 2004) were developed to focus on cognitive skills deficits, are goals-based and skills oriented and are manualised standardised approaches. Interventions in the community can vary including individualised (traditional) approaches depending on the need, group-based interventions as well as family-focused interventions that are based upon the ecological systems theory (Bronfenbrenner, 1979) such as multisystemic therapy (MST; Henggeler et al., 2009), functional family therapy (FFT; Alexander et al., 2013) or treatment foster care Oregon (TFCO; Chamberlain & Smith, 2003).

23.6 Consultation, Supervision/Training, Reflective-practice Research and Service Evaluations

Alongside the clinical elements of their work, psychological practitioners may be involved in other areas of service delivery as their competence and skills set increase. This could include training, advice, guidance and consultation, clinical supervision and the provision of reflective spaces for other staff. FCAMHs are a good example of where a psychological practitioner may provide advice and consultation to wider systems including courts, general children and adolescent mental health services (CAMHS) and other professionals who are working directly with young people and their families. FCAMHs are based on a consultation-and-liaison model where young people within the CJS may present with concerns around mental health. Within the secure estate, the Framework for Integrated Care (SECURE STAIRS), takes a trauma-informed approach to addressing the needs of young people. Psychological practitioners may take a lead role in the training, supervision, support and provision of a reflective practice space for prison officers. In addition to this, psychological practitioners may be actively involved in research and audit to support service development and the improvement of intervention delivery.

Working in this way and taking a whole systems approach allows for a much more holistic and systemic lens to be applied to the issues facing practitioners in forensic settings. Young people in these settings do not often fall neatly into traditional diagnostic models – so taking a formulation-driven and trauma-informed approach allows for more flexibility that 'makes sense' given the setting. It also allows for improved relationships and a collaborative approach in 'coming alongside' the staff in the shared task of understanding the young people in custody, rather than being 'split' into 'punitive' and 'caretaking' roles. For example, providing training on trauma-informed practice, vicarious trauma and re-traumatisation in a secure setting allows for health and discipline staff to come together and discuss their experiences and can lead to improved perspective-taking amongst colleagues (see Chapter 27 for a detailed description of this).

Some of the challenges of this work are that practitioners are sometimes faced with ethical dilemmas of trying to provide support to staff within a system that may, by its nature, be working in opposition with some core beliefs or moral values. The idea of 'moral injury' is relevant here – and space needs to be given to the potential for these personal conflicts in supervision. There are also challenges in balancing the 'professional-expert' position with a collaborative stance, so as to work effectively with frontline staff from different disciplines.

23.7 Review of the Evidence Base, NICE Guidelines and Policy

The evidence around what works for young people in or at risk of involvement in the CJS comes from systematic reviews and meta-analyses of international research evidence and from UK practice. These reviews cover a range of approaches including individual interventions with the young person, parenting interventions and school approaches. Some of the practices are well evidenced, whereas other approaches may be lacking any evidence at all and may even be harmful. The Early Intervention Foundation completed a rapid review of interventions in the UK and abroad to understand what works to prevent gang involvement, youth violence and crime (O'Connor & Waddell, 2015). The findings from this report were largely consistent with those from key systematic reviews. The most reviewed psychosocial approaches included cognitive and behavioural interventions, systemic family therapy and mentoring, as well as police-led diversion, curfews, drug treatment courts, restorative justice and pharmacological treatments.

In general, programmes that are delivered in court settings have been found to be less effective than those delivered in community or home settings (de Vries, 2015). Furthermore, exposure to prison facilities such as Scared Straight (a programme involving exposing young people to custodial facilities), processing through the YJS and custodial sentences have all been found to increase the likelihood of future offending (Petrosino et al., 2013; Villettaz et al., 2015).

There is a large and established evidence base for parenting programmes when used with parents of very young children with behavioural difficulties (Waddell et al., 2018). These include behavioural modelling, parent skills training and behavioural contracting. The National Institute for Health and Clinical Excellence (NICE) and the Social Care Institute of Excellence (SCIE) have developed guidelines in the UK for recognition, intervention and management of the difficulties associated with antisocial behaviour. Parent training programmes are recommended for parents of children and young people between 3 to 11 years (NICE, 2013). However, whilst the evidence for parent training programmes is well established for children aged 11 years or younger, there is limited evidence for these programmes in older children despite the recognition that parenting difficulties continue to impact on the development and maintenance of conduct disorders (NICE, 2013). NICE (2017) recommends child-focused programmes should include group social and cognitive problem-solving programmes for 9 to 14 year olds that use modelling, rehearsal and feedback to improve skills whilst adhering to a developer's manual in order to ensure consistency of implementation. Multimodal interventions, such as MST, are recommended for children and young people aged between 11 and 17 years for the treatment of conduct disorder. NICE (2016) guidance on harmful sexual behaviour amongst children includes several recommendations for specific therapies including MST, CBT, family interventions and multiagency work.

There are no NICE guidelines specifically for the Youth Offending Service (YOS). Standards for Children in the Youth Justice Service (YJB, 2019), specifies that for court and out-of-court disposals, all children need to have a comprehensive assessment. In current practice, Youth Offending Teams (YOTs) claim to use an individualised approach to each young person, taking into consideration their specific contexts. However, despite the use of decision-making tools such as AssetPlus, there is much variation across teams, subjectivity in decision making and lack of consideration of the evidence base to target appropriate interventions based on risk, need and responsivity.

In terms of individual intervention, Riise and colleagues (2021) completed a review of CBT for externalising disorders. They found 38% and 48% remission rates for ADHD and conduct disorder respectively. Mentoring has also been found to have positive impact on aggression, substance misuse and antisocial behaviour (Tolan et al., 2013). However, the studies reviewed varied considerably in terms of their approach to mentoring and their research methods.

There are various criminal justice approaches to addressing antisocial behaviour in young people. There is some evidence that police-led diversion schemes, using cautions, restorative actions and referrals to other services to avoid arrest, reduce re-offending rates by about 20% relative to usual practice (Wilson et al., 2018). However, caution needs to be applied as contact with the CJS has been shown to increase re-offending rates and care must be applied when using police-led approaches not to increase negative contacts with the police and contact with offending communities. Youth curfews, where a young person is not allowed in public areas during certain times, have not been found to be effective in reducing criminal behaviour (Wilson et al., 2018).

23.8 Public Health Approach to Addressing Youth Violence

Although there are different ways to reduce violent behaviour, a public health approach (PHA) is being increasingly discussed. This uses evidence-led methodology to reduce and prevent violence in communities (Local Government Association, 2019). This approach moves away from addressing violence through a criminal justice lens and treats violence like an infectious disease. It suggests that policy makers should search for the 'cure' by using scientific evidence to identify the causes and find interventions that prevent it from spreading. The UK Government has slowly adopted the terminology 'public health approach' to describe its policy on tackling violent crime.

In March 2019, the Home Office announced £35m of funding targeted to support multiagency approaches to tackling and preventing serious violence at a local level. This funding was awarded to 18 Police and Crime Commissioners in areas worst affected by violent crime to establish Violence Reduction Units (VRUs). A further £35m was provided for 2020/2021. The aim of the units was to bring together different organisations including the police, local government, health, education, community leaders and other key partners to understand the root causes of serious violence and provide a coordinated strategic response to reduce violence. The approach is based on the work of the Scottish Violence Reduction Unit (SVRU), also referred to as the Glasgow model, which adopts the World Health Organization's (WHO) definition of a PHA (Craston et al., 2020).

A 2-year evaluation of the VRUs concluded that they have made progress in implementing and delivering on the aims of the whole systems approach to violence reduction (Home Office, 2022). There were early indications of VRUs impacting violence reduction. The biggest impact was found to be around multiagency working and data sharing. At a strategic level, VRUs were found to strengthen partnerships, streamline approaches and identify and facilitate collaboration. Multiagency working was believed to be more developed at a strategic level as opposed to an operational level. Various challenges were identified due to the Covid-19 pandemic, which affected progress with elements of delivery.

23.9 Recent Developments

In 2021, further services were commissioned by the Home Office, the Youth Endowment Fund and NHS England (Health and Justice Mental Health Programme) across England to deliver a multisystems, trauma-informed approach to tackling youth violence. These services are very much based on a PHA to address offending. The Framework for Integrated Care (Community) has recently been developed to support improved outcomes and a reduction of health inequalities for this specific group of young people (NHS England & NHS Improvement, 2022). The framework is evidence based and has evolved through learning from previous projects that were part of Children and Young People's Mental Health Transformation within NHS England and NHS Improvement, including the roll-out of FCAMHS, the introduction of the Framework of Integrated Care (SECURE STAIRS) in the secure estate and the development of collaborative commissioning networks.

The Vanguard model uses the Framework of Integrated Care. It is currently being rolled out over 12 areas across England. There are three Vanguards in London that bring together

Table 23.2 Your Choice and London Vanguard

Area	Your Choice CBT	London Vanguard: Community Multi Systems Violence Reduction Model
Target cohort	11–18 year olds most at risk of extra-familial harm	0–25 years who are affected by violence directly or indirectly
Referral pathway	32 x Multi Agency Child Exploitation Panels (MACE) or pre-MACE or equivalent to assess eligibility	Multi sources of referral - referral pathway may vary depending on how the ICSs propose to implement the London Vanguard.
Geographical coverage	32 London boroughs	13 London boroughs across North Central, North East and South East London ICSs. Coverage of all components of the London Vanguard model varies from borough to borough, and is based on evidenced need
Programme timescale	3 years (October 2021 – March 2024)	4 year pilot up to end of September 2025
Funding agency	Home Office, Youth Endowment Fund and London Violence Reduction Unit	NHS England (Health and Social Justice and Mental Health Programme)
Accountable body for funding	London Violence Reduction Unit (Mayor's Office)	NHS England (Health and Justice and London Violence Reduction Programme)
Delivery organisations	32 London boroughs	3 ICS pilots (joint delivery between health services, LAs and voluntary and community sector organisations)
Delivery model	Embedded within local authority existing service environment and based on Child First principles, working towards personal goals and building a pro-social identity. The programme offers key additionalities: trained practitioners (Your Choice Coaches) are provided with regular specialist Clinical Supervision and are part of a Your Choice Network; the Coaches work with children (3 contacts a week) using CBT-informed tools and techniques including those from third-wave CBT. The intervention lasts 12–18 weeks. At the end of the programme, the young person is linked into their communities where they can continue their journey of personal development.	The model aims to implement the framework for integrated care, using local organisations and partnerships. Case workers act as key advocate for the YP building trust, providing advocacy, coordinating services, pathway navigation, working with the network, managing risks and attending relevant meetings alongside individuals if necessary. The case worker is ideally fully embedded in the community, and has access to appropriate clinical supervision. The clinical case management is delivered by clinicians.
Delivery location	Where the child is – e.g. youth centre	Will vary depending on what components of the model are being delivered. Key ethos is that services are embedded within local communities

(Continued)

Table 23.2 (Continued)

Area	Your Choice CBT	London Vanguard: Community Multi Systems Violence Reduction Model
Recruitment requirement	Additional qualified youth practitioners to provide extra capacity and/or mental health practitioner-supervisor, according to local need	Case workers and wider staff psychologist, OT, Family therapist, SLT, access to specialist resource within Children' or Adult's Mental Health Service, Local Authorities or Social Care
Training/supervisory requirement	Existing youth practitioners trained and supervised to deliver CBT-informed practice within interventions. Requirement of 3 contacts per week	Training and supervision will vary across the team. Trauma informed approaches, AMBIT, NVR, attachment based models, working with health, social and race inequalities, promotion of positive practice models which support thriving and diverse workplaces, CBT informed practice, CBT, counselling skills, case management skills, goal setting and care planning, strength based approaches, risk management, boundaries, safeguarding, training to support the delivery of low intensity interventions.
Training organisation	NHS/LIIA	Mix between NHS/VCSE/Local Authority
Intervention	CBT-informed practice embedded within interventions delivered by LA adolescent services	Prevention, intervention (including CBT) and case management
Evaluator/s	Anna Freud Centre and IFS (Evaluation Lead). YEF projects require random controlled trials - details to be agreed	Anna Freud National Centre for Children and Families

Source: London Violence Reduction Programme

the London Integrated Care Systems the London boroughs, NHS Trusts and voluntary sector organisations. The aim for the Vanguards is to be co-produced and co-delivered with young people and carers with lived-experience. In London, a second initiative, Your Choice, is also being implemented. Table 23.2 shows some of the key features of each approach.

23.10 Inclusive Practice

Collaboration and co-production between children and young people and relevant systems involved in their care is highly recommended and encouraged where possible. Engaging the child and young person in decision making, and understanding about their presentation, strengths and needs allows practitioners to guide, enhance and manage the therapeutic relationship as well as demonstrate transparent and collaborative goal setting and planning. Listening to and understanding the child/young person's voice, journey, views and lived experiences provides a rich and constructive dialogue that can significantly impact longer-term outcomes particularly in relation to mental health needs and risk.

Increasingly (and rightly), practitioners in forensic settings are adopting a trauma-informed approach where a child or young person's presentation and behaviour is understood in the context of their early adversity and experience of developmental trauma. It is recognised that strengths-based and compassion-focused approaches are crucial in supporting children and young people navigate their journey within the CJS given the challenges and complexities involved. Therefore, it is critical for practitioners and psychologists working with children and young people in the CJS to balance an understanding of their early life experiences and challenges as well as a need to identify and manage areas of risk. This can be a highly complicated and difficult task for practitioners to undertake and therefore requires input from both direct and indirect data sources.

Direct sources of data include listening to and recording the voice of the child or young person in relation to their journey. Depending on their training and experience psychological practitioners and CJS practitioners will utilise a range of strategies in order to build rapport and motivation to engage children and young people in the process of contributing towards their care.

The following examples have been provided by a social worker embedded within the YOS describing their approach to promoting the voices of children/young people:

> As many of the children and young people that we work with have suffered from trauma, I use the trauma-informed model to engage with them, i.e. recognising that before I can try to build a positive rapport, they first need to have their basic needs met (food, safety, home, etc.); once this has been secured, I look to build an open, trusting relationship with them by clearly defining the rules and boundaries of our engagement (which includes a behaviour agreement, which both I and the young person sign to say that we have agreed to, which includes things like being on time, respecting each other's views, confidentiality) and a very informal, relaxed approach in the early stages of engagement, focusing on getting to know them and demonstrating my commitment to them. I find that very small gestures such as giving them a lift home, or getting them a snack, really can promote the relationship, as can showing that you have listened to them (e.g. remembering something they have said in a previous session and referring to it later on).
>
> Every intervention plan is made in conjunction with the child/young person; depending on their level of need/understanding, for example, for some I use a whiteboard and marker to mind-map changes they want to make, which I then type up into a more formal intervention plan. For others, I might use the Signs of Safety and Wellbeing / Three Houses model, to identify their worries, strengths and the actions to address these. The child/young person's voice is integral to the plan, as otherwise it is likely to be ineffective. Every plan that is created with the child/young person is then also agreed to by the parent, and I send a copy to them in the post, so they can monitor their own progress (I encourage them to tick things off as they go), and it is reviewed every three months.

Whilst a collaborative journey with the child and young person is preferred, this may not always be possible. For instance, the child/young person may not be willing or ready to engage in such a process or there may be barriers that prevent the practitioner from working with the child/young person directly in a productive or meaningful way. Therefore, inclusive practices should also bear in mind the value and relevance of taking a systems-based approach to understanding the child/young person as a whole and not in isolation. In line with the evidence base for this cohort, some practitioners within CJS settings are shifting their practice by moving the focus away from the child/young person, to engaging the perspectives of relevant systems within which the child/young person is placed. To this end, where traditional intervention is not indicated or possible, indirect methods of data collation through systems such as family members, teachers and professionals can provide valuable information and aid with supporting formulations and psychologically informed practice. As previously discussed, children/young people in the CJS present with complex emotional, social, health and educational needs. There are often multiple professionals involved both with the young person and the wider family. Shared team formulations that incorporate factors relevant to both the system and the child/young person allow for a wider, richer and holistic understanding of current and historical strengths, needs and experiences. This shared narrative and conceptualisation enables a collaborative and logical approach to risk assessment and management. Therefore, it is essential that systems communicate, share information and work well together. Some strengths and challenges of working in this way are described in Table 23.3.

The clinical example in Box 23.2 demonstrates how multiagency collaboration can enable and support a young person in contact with the CJS.

Table 23.3 Strengths and challenges of joint working.

Strengths of systemic and joint working	Challenges of systemic and joint working
• Shared understanding of risk and formulation • Regular and ongoing lines of communication • Shared understanding of roles and responsibilities • Single point of contact for the professional network • Professionals holding accountability and responsibility for their role • Joint/shared problem-solving and decision-making vs in isolation • Professionals presenting as one voice to client • Recognising and naming challenges associated with interagency working • Supporting information sharing and joint working in order to manage risk and ensure safety • Collaborative working principles and practices	• Differences of views and opinions • Individual preferences and perspectives get in the way of joint working • Difficulties in consistent communication and information sharing • Different professional agencies with differing priorities and ways of working • The child's journey not being held in mind • Systems experiencing wider organisational barriers to change

Box 23.2 Clinical example: Callum

At time of referral to the MST team Callum was sentenced to a 12-month Youth Referral Order (YRO), for a robbery with a knife. The MST therapist and social worker did a lot of joint visits as Callum and his mum struggled to engage with professionals. Callum had a missing episode and was found in a property known to police as a county-lines property. During this missing episode, the MST therapist shared with the YOS worker the safety plans that had been completed with mum around de-escalation, weapon safety (key for his YRO) and his vulnerability in the community. The YOS worker in turn supported with building a bigger picture that included peer and location mapping. Where YOS struggled to engage with the family, they found it helpful collaborating with the MST therapist in order to understand the difficulties for Callum and his mum in building trusting relationships with professionals. The professional network was also able to leverage the strengths regarding Callum's and mum's positive relationship with his mentor to build a stronger working relationship and agree on intervention plans together.

23.11 Critical Reflections and Future Directions

As discussed within this chapter, children and young people at risk of entering/or within the criminal justice system present with a range of complex needs and vulnerabilities. As a result of their presentation they are likely to come into contact with a wide variety of professionals, from a range of backgrounds. Services across multiple sectors collectively struggle to meet the needs of these young people. Furthermore, young people often find it hard to access, respond and maintain progress with the support and interventions offered.

Outcomes for this cohort may be impacted by a whole host of factors ranging from the individual, organisational to the systemic. At an individual level race, gender and socioeconomic status may affect their pathway with the huge, well-documented, inequality in provision leading to a 'postcode lottery' determining access to appropriate intervention. Existing services may not meet the specific needs of the individual young person and may lack expertise to respond and intervene, having their own inclusion criteria that will exclude certain groups, such as those with neurodevelopmental disabilities or those already in care.

At an organisational level, there is evidence of siloed working with a lack of partnership or collaboration between statutory and voluntary organisations. The involvement of multiple professionals may lead to an inconsistency in approach and a lack of continuity of care. This may happen on the ground and at a higher level. New services that develop may duplicate those already in place. Interventions are often a single modality (such as CBT or medication) and involve the young person individually without adequate consideration of the wider systemic context. In addition, there appears to be a lack of psychological leadership of new provisions/services as well as a lack of psychological practitioner presence within many local authority and youth justice teams. This is disappointing given the significant value psychologically trained colleagues and psychologically informed thinking can bring to strategic, operational and clinical development of services. Examples that include the input of psychological staff and psychological practice across the country are limited.

At a systemic level, there is a lack of clarity and continuity of care; different regions and areas have their own specific needs and consequent service provision may be inequitable and inconsistent with other areas. Services may develop due to local need that are not necessarily evidenced based and do not have rigour. Sometimes the interventions offered are diluted, cheaper versions of evidenced-based approaches that are adopted in order to cut costs but fail to demonstrate efficacy.

Funding streams further dictate the type of service that is being developed and a lack of collaboration between organisations tackling the same issues leads to discrepancies and duplication of work. Each source of funding has its own agenda and outcomes, despite the young people being the same; funding from NHS streams tends to have more of a mental health focus, Home Office funding looks at crime reduction, and social care may have more of an emphasis on keeping young people out of care. The challenge has been on creating joined-up pathways with shared goals.

A further concern is the fragility of funding with a lack of longevity and difficulties in embedding programmes. Funding is often provided for a 2-to-3-year period to support and develop new initiatives. It takes time for services to get off the ground and demonstrate their impact. These new initiatives are often linked to research, but research takes time and many services are not sustained after their initial funding has run out. These issues are embedded in a wider context where links between research, policy makers, funders and practitioners are unclear thus leading to a lack of streamlined pathways of care of children and young people.

Whilst the described difficulties are real and present, the commitment from clinicians and practitioners to achieve positive outcomes for children and young people cannot be questioned. Their skill and determination to find solutions, overcome barriers and enable and empower understanding of the child/young person continues to grow. Despite the challenges, creative initiatives are being established across the country that allow for the development of exciting services for psychological therapists and practitioners to be a part of.

Future directions for change require the integration of research embedded within policies to allow funders and practitioners (commissioners and providers) to work together to evaluate and understand the problems that are present so that investments can be directed more meaningfully over a longer period of time. Psychological practitioners have the opportunity to contribute towards such learning and advancement through their practice, but more importantly, their desire to make a difference.

Acknowledgements

We would like to thank the MST team in Birmingham, Niamh Doherty-Ingram from Birmingham YOS for providing some examples of good practice and Rhiannon Lewis, Consultant Clinical Psychologist, for providing reflections on SECURE STAIRS. Pseudonyms have been used to protect anonymity. Thank you also to Georgia Merchant for reading drafts and finding references.

References

Alexander, J., Waldron, H. B., Robbins, M. S., & Neeb. A. A. (2013). *Functional family therapy for adolescent behaviour problems*. American Psychological Association.

Baker, K. (2012). Conduct disorders in children and adolescents. *Paediatrics and Child Health, 23*(1), 24–29.

Bonta, J., & Andrews, D.A. (2007). Risk-need-responsivity model for offender assessment and rehabilitation: User report 2007–06; Public Safety. Canada, 2007.

Borum, R., Bartel, P., & Forth, A. E. (2002). *Manual for the Structured Assessment of Violent Risk in Youth (SAVRY)*. University of South Florida.

Bronfenbrenner, U. (1979). *The ecology of human development*. Harvard University Press.

Chamberlain, P., Smith, P. (2003). Antisocial behaviour in children and adolescents: The Oregon multidimensional treatment foster care model. In A. E. Kazdin & J. R. Weisz (Eds.), *Evidence-based psychotherapies for children and adolescents* (pp. 282–300). Guildford Press.

Chard, A. (2021). *Punishing abuse: Children in the West Midlands criminal justice system*. West Midlands Combined Authority and West Midlands Police and Crime Commissioner. YCTCS Ltd.

Chitsabesan, P., & Hughes, N. (2016). Mental health needs and neurodevelopmental disorders amongst young offenders: Implications for policy and practice. In J. Winstone (Ed.), *Mental Health, Crime and Criminal Justice* (pp. 109–130). Palgrave Macmillan.

Chitsabesan, P., Kroll, L., Bailey, S., Kenning, C., Sneider, S., MacDonald, W., & Theodosiou, L. (2006). Mental health needs of young offenders in custody and in the community. *British Journal of Psychiatry, 188*, 534–540.

Cooke, D.J., & Michie, C. (2013). Violence risk assessment: From Prediction to understanding–or from what? to why? In C. Logan and L. Johnstone (Eds.), *Managing clinical risk: A Guide to effective practice* (pp. 3–25). Routledge.

Craston, M., Balfour, R., Henley, M., Baxendale J., & Fullick. (2020). *Process evaluation of the Violence Reduction Units*. Research Report 116. Home Office.

de Vries, S. L., Hoeve, M., Assink, M., Stams, G.J., & Asscher, J. J. (2015). Practitioner review: Effective ingredients of prevention programs for youth at risk of persistent juvenile delinquency – recommendations for clinical practice. *Journal of Child Psychology and Psychiatry, 56*(2):108–121. https://dxdoi.org/10.1111/jcpp.12320

Farrington, D., Jolliffe, D., & Coid, J. (2021). Cohort profile: The Cambridge study in delinquent development. *Journal of Development and Life-course Criminology, 7*, 278–291.

Fox, S., & Latham, R. (2014). Managing risk in community settings. In Z. Ashmore & R. Shuker (Eds.), *Forensic practice in the community* (pp. 173–193). Routledge.

Hart, D., & La Valle, I. (2021). *Secure children's homes: Placing welfare and justice children together research report*. Department for Education.

Harvey, J. (2014). Assessment in community settings. In Z. Ashmore & R. Shuker (Eds.), *Forensic practice in the community* (pp. 22–39). Routledge.

Henggeler, S. W., Schoenwald, S. K., Borduin, C. M., Rowland, M. D., & Cunningham, P. B. (2009). *Multisystemic therapy for children and adolescents* (2nd ed.). Guildford Press.

Henniker, J., Print, B., & Morrison, T. (2002). An inter-agency assessment framework for young people who sexually abuse: Principles, processes and practicalities. *Child Care in Practice, 8*, 114–126.

Home Office. (2022). Violence reduction unit year ending March 2021 evaluation report. https://www.gov.uk/government/publications/violence-reduction-unit-year-ending-march-2021-evaluation-report/violence-reduction-unit-year-ending-march-2021-evaluation-report

Hughes, N. (2015). Neurodisability in the youth justice system: recognising and responding to the criminalisation of neurodevelopmental impairment. Working Paper. Howard league for Penal Reform.

Hughes, N., Williams, P., Chitsabesan, P., Davies, R., & Mounce, L. (2012). *Nobody made the connection; the prevalence of neurodisability in young people who offend*. Office of the Children's Commissioner.

Johnstone, L., & Dallos, R. (Eds.). (2006). *Formulation in psychology and psychotherapy: Making sense of people's problems*. Routledge.

Johnstone, L., & Gregory, L. (2015). Youth violence risk assessment: A framework for practice. In A. Rogers, J. Harvey, & H. Law (Eds.), Young people in forensic mental health settings. Palgrave Macmillan.

Koops, W., & Orobio de Castro, B. (2004). The development of aggression and its linkages with violence and youth delinquency. *European Journal of Developmental Psychology, 1*, 241–269.

Lader, D., Singleton, N., and Meltzer, H. (2000). *Psychiatric morbidity among young offenders in England and Wales*. London: Office for National Statistics.

Lammy, D. (2017). *The Lammy review: an independent review into the treatment of, and outcomes for, Black, Asian and minority ethnic individuals in the criminal justice system*. HM Government.

Lennox, C., & Khan, L. (2013). Youth justice. In *Our Children Deserve Better: Prevention Pays. Annual Report of the Chief Medical Officer*. Department of Health. https://www.gov.uk/government/publications/chief-medical-officers-annual-report-2012-our-children-deserve-better-prevention-pays

Local Government Association (2019). Public health approaches to reducing violence. https://www.local.gov.uk/sites/default/files/documents/15.32%20‐%20Reducing%20family%20violence_03.pdf

Logan, C., & Hart, S. (2011). Forensic case formulation. In P. Sturmey & M. McMurran (Eds.), *Forensic case formulation* (pp. 81–106). Wiley-Blackwell.

Logan, C., & Johnstone, L. (2013). *Managing clinical risk: A guide to effective practice*. Routledge.

Macpherson, W. (1999). *The Stephen Lawrence Inquiry: Report of an inquiry by Sir William Macpherson of Cluny*. HMSO.

NICE. (2013). Antisocial behaviour and conduct disorders in children and young people: recognition, intervention and management. Clinical guideline *158*. http://guidance.nice.org.uk/CG158

NICE. (2016). *Harmful sexual behaviour among children and young people*. NICE.

NICE. (2017). *Antisocial behaviour and conduct disorders in children and young people: Recognition, intervention and management*. Clinical guidelines 158. NICE.

NHS England & NHS Improvement. (2022). Framework for integrated care (Community).

Nichols, C. E., & Mitchell, J. (2004). *The JETS living skills programme: An integrated cognitive behavioural programme for juvenile offenders. Theory manual*. HMPS Offending Behaviour Programmes Unit, Home Office.

Nicholls, T., & Viljoen, J., & Cruise, K., & Desmarais, S., & Webster, C. (2010). *Abbreviated manual for the Short-Term Assessment of Risk and Treatability (START): Adolescent version*.

Forensic Psychiatric Services Commission and BC Mental Health and Addiction Services, Port Coquitlam BC and Simon Fraser University, Burnaby BC.

O'Connor, R., & Waddell, S. (2015). *What works to prevent gang involvement, youth violence and crime: A rapid review of the interventions delivered in the UK and abroad*. Early Intervention Foundation.

Petrosino, A., Turpin-Petrosino, C., Hollis-Peel, M. E., & Lavenberg, J. G. (2013). Scared straight and other juvenile awareness programs for preventing juvenile delinquency: A systematic review. *Campbell Systematic Reviews*. The Campbell Collaboration.

Richardson, G. (2009). Sharp practice: The sexually harmful adolescent risk protocol. In M. C. Calder (Ed.), *Sexual abuse assessments: Using and developing frameworks for practice* (pp. 108–147). Russell House Publishing.

Riise, E. N., Wergeland, G.J. H., Njardvik, U., & Öst, L-G. (2021). Cognitive behavior therapy for externalizing disorders in children and adolescents in routine clinical care: A systematic review and meta-analysis. *Clinical Psychology Review, 83*, 101954. doi: 10.1016/j.cpr.2020.101954

Teplin, L. A., Abram, K. M., McClelland, G. M., Dulcan, M., & Mericle, A. (2002). Psychiatric disorders in youth in detention. *Archives of General Psychiatry, 59*, 1133–1143

Tolan, P., Henry, D., Schoeny, M., Bass, A., Lovegrove, P., & Nichols, E. (2013). *Mentoring interventions to affect juvenile delinquency and associated problems: A systematic review. Campbell Systematic Reviews, 9*(1), 1–158.

Vess, J., & Ward, T. (2011). Sexual offences against children. In P. Sturmey & M. McMurran (Eds.), *Forensic case formulation* (pp. 175–194). Wiley.

Villettaz, P., Gillieron, G., Killias, M. (2015). The effects on re-offending of custodial vs. non-custodial sanctions: An updated systematic review of the state of knowledge. *Campbell Systematic Reviews, 11*(1), 1–92. https://doi.org/10.4073/csr.2015.1

Waddell, C., Schwartz, C., Andres, C., Barican, J. L., & Yung, D. (2018). Fifty years of preventing and treating childhood behaviour disorders: A systematic review to inform policy and practice. *Evidence Based Mental Health, 21*(2), 45–52.

Weerasekera, P. (1996). *Multiperspective case formulation: A step towards treatment integration*. Krieger Publishing Company.

Wilson, D. B., Brennan, I., & Olaghere, A. (2018). Police-initiated diversion for youth to prevent future delinquent behaviour: A systematic review. *Campbell Systematic Reviews, 14*(1), 1–88. HTTPS://doi.org/10.4073/csr.2018.1

Worling, J., & Curwen, T. (2001). Estimate of Risk Of Adolescent Sexual Offense Recidivism (Version 2.0: The 'ERASOR'). In M. C. Calder, *Juveniles and children who sexually abuse: Frameworks for assessment* (pp. 372–397). Russell House.

YJB. (2014). *AssetPlus: Assessment and planning in the youth justice system*. Youth Justice Board.

YJB. (2019). Standards for children in the youth justice service. https://yjresourcehub.uk/legislation-and-guidance-documents/item/636-standards-for-children-in-the-youth-justice-system-youth-justice-board-2019.html#:~:text=The%20standards%20for%20children%20in%20the%20youth%20justice%20system%2C%20(2019),in%20the%20youth%20justice%20system.

YJB. (2021). *Youth Justice Statistics: England and Wales: 2019–2020*. Youth Justice Board.

YJB. (2022). *Youth Justice Statistics: England and Wales: 2020–2021*. Youth Justice Board.

24

Digital Practice

Helen Pote

24.1 Introduction

Digital technology is part of young people's everyday communication, social interaction, work and recreation (Bakker et al., 2016). Young people are often referred to as 'digital natives' with 90% of children owning their own mobile phone by age 11 and 70% of 3–17 year olds using mobile phones and tablets for online access in the UK (Ofcom, 2022). In this context, digital mental health technologies such as apps, mobile text messaging, video conferencing, wearables (e.g. smart watches), websites and Internet interventions, games and extended reality (virtual and augmented) have all been used to support young people to manage their mental and physical health (Liverpool et al., 2020). The use of technology might help young people's services achieve greater reach to clients and offer other presumed service efficiencies such as saving time, money and reliance on expensive professionals to deliver routine interventions such as psycho-education. In addition, digital interventions offer young people greater autonomy, flexibility and anonymity. This chapter will detail the current digital health policy context, review some of the research and practice evidence for digital child mental health and consider the ways in which psychological services and individual psychological practitioners might adapt their practice to this emerging digital health reality (Domhardt et al., 2021).

24.2 Why Consider Digital Interventions for Young People

24.2.1 Policy Context

In the past 10 years most health policy in the UK has had a strong digital focus. The NHS Long Term Plan (NHS, 2019b) has a clear digital future in mind across physical and mental health services with expansion of online delivery and more effective use of data to improve clinical decision making – this policy context has important implications for child psychological practitioners. The broader international policy context also sees the future of mental health services as embracing digital practice and the World Innovation Summit for Health (WISH) details the ways digital mental health technologies will be used by the public and

Child Psychology: Pathways to Good Practice, First Edition.
Edited by Helen Pote, Anna Picciotto and Clare Norris.

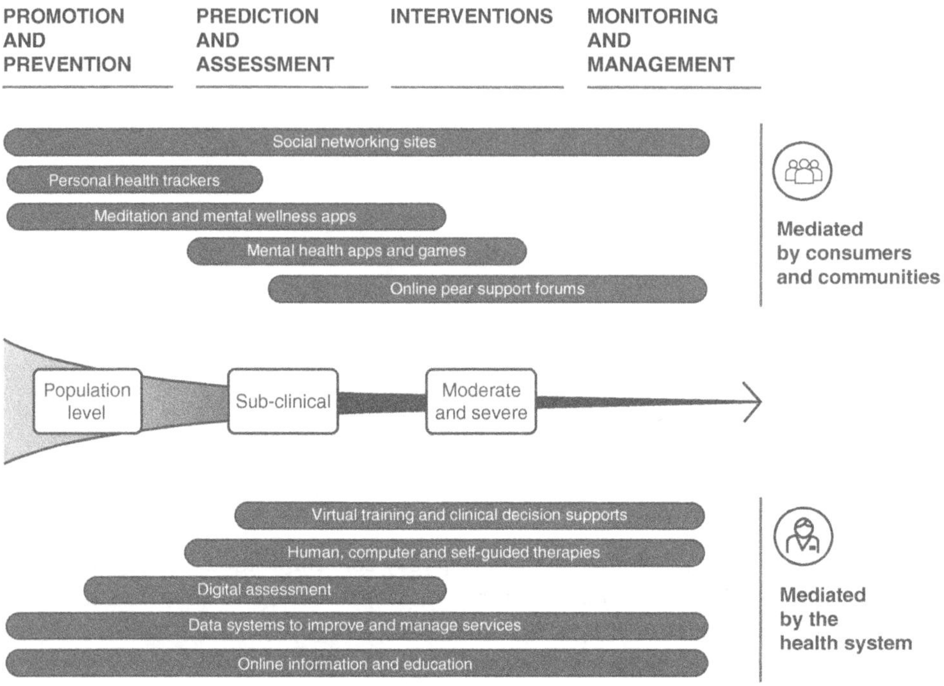

Figure 24.1 Pieces of the Puzzle: A framework for understanding digital technologies in mental health. Taken from WISH Report: The Digital Mental Health Revolution (Roland et al., 2020, p. 5/Qatar Foundation).

professionals across mental health services, ranging from population level health promotion, through to individual prevention, assessment, and interventions, with follow up health maintenance (Roland et al., 2020). This is depicted in Figure 24.1.

Implementation of digital psychological interventions is not a simple process. The recent Topol report in the UK emphasised the need to support and develop the current health workforce in digital skills if the digital transformation of health services was to be realised (Topol, 2019). For psychological practitioners this policy context presents obvious workforce and digital training needs that are often not addressed in pre-registration training (Pote et al., 2021). Child practitioners need to develop skills in engaging children online and negotiate the complexities of consent, confidentiality, equality of participation and managing risk when working with whole families using digital formats (Burbach & Pote, 2021).

24.2.2 Advantages of Digital Interventions for Youth

Digital interventions might improve the reach of psychological services for young people. There are many effective traditional, in-person psychological interventions for young people with mental health concerns but limited resources, difficulties with access to services and problems engaging young people persist (Gee et al., 2021). As reflected in previous chapters, this can result in the majority of young people with mental health problems not having access to evidenced-based psychological interventions that might help to alleviate their psychological distress. Digital solutions may address this resource gap. In one national government survey of the young people in the UK with mental health concerns, 44% reported using online or telephone support to address their difficulties and 35% of their parents were also accessing digital mental health support (NHS Digital, 2021). For young people, more reported accessing digital support than were accessing traditional in-person health services (37%, NHS Digital, 2021).

Increasing engagement with psychological interventions is a key advantage of digital delivery. What teenager really wants to sit with a well-meaning adult as the only choice of delivery method for psychological therapies? Liverpool et al. (2020), explored young people's engagement in digital health interventions in a systematic review of 83 studies. They found that young people preferred digital health interventions, which included videos, the ability to personalise and to connect with others, as well as options to receive text message reminders. Text-heavy digital resources were not favoured, with young people enjoying more active engagement. In the research reviewed there was a high average retention rate of 79% across various digital interventions though many of these studies were not in naturalistic settings and those that were showed reduced retention with the digital intervention. In their model of youth engagement in digital mental health interventions they highlighted the importance of the social context and social connectedness as an influence on youth engagement.

Co-production with young people is critical to the success of digital mental health interventions for young people (Bevan Jones et al., 2020; Hill et al., 2017). The World Health Organization (2020) offers a framework for planning, developing and implementing digital health interventions with and for young people, which highlights the utility of digital interventions for improving physical and mental health outcomes for young people if design is approached with the users in mind. The key messages of the framework are:

- Young people should be involved at every stage of the digital development process.
- Digital is not always the best solution and solutions should follow a clear needs assessment.
- It is better to reuse digital interventions than reinvent them.
- Digital should integrate with existing health interventions, not function as stand-alone solutions.

A final positive of the digital developments in youth mental health has been online access to digital forms of outcomes measures and feedback methods to inform individual self-monitoring and increase feedback for services. Digital measurement of outcomes for young people can provide an engaging format for gathering brief, sensitive and meaningful data in an accessible and cost-effective manner. Young people consider the use of technology in routine outcome data collection positively and may prefer electronic measures over paper-based versions when offered the choice (Bushnell et al., 2003; Hall et al., 2014). Some digital apps have been co-designed with practitioners and young people to record young people's routine mental health outcome data and these have been established as valid, reliable and sensitive to change when compared to paper-based measures (e.g. MyLifeTracker, a digital routine monitoring measure integrated into the Headspace app for young people aged 12–25 years; Kwan & Rickwood, 2021; Kwan et al., 2018). The Child Outcomes Research Consortium (CORC) offers a range of free psychological outcome and service evaluation measures that are suitable for use online (see https://www.corc.uk.net/outcome-experience-measures). Their guidance on working remotely with outcome measures is helpful (CORC, 2022); it reminds psychological practitioners to consider carefully the psychometric validity and reliability of measures adapted for use online so that the measure can be meaningfully used with the young person and compared across contexts and over time. Simply uploading in-person measures into online formats is not advisable, as formats can affect how young people respond (perhaps due to online disinhibition), and change already established normative data for the measure, altering scoring criteria and clinical cut-offs (e.g. Patalay et al., 2016).

24.2.3 Disadvantages of Digital Interventions for Youth

Digital mental interventions for children and young people have several potential limitations, which psychological practitioners must consider before offering them in clinical practice.

Firstly, most practitioners and young people are concerned that digital delivery will negatively impact on the therapeutic alliance and human factors that are important in successful therapy outcomes. Whilst this is a valid concern and choice about the mode of delivery (digital vs in-person) should always be a priority, the adult therapeutic alliance literature suggests that digital therapeutic alliance is at least as strong as in-person alliance, but the processes may be somewhat different (Simpson & Reid, 2014; Simpson et al., 2021). Clients report satisfaction with the alliance through video -conferencing, but therapists may be more concerned about alliance quality (Cataldo et al., 2021). The research with children and young people is not so advanced regarding therapeutic alliance in online therapy, but qualitative research has illustrated positive accounts of therapeutic alliance from young people's perspectives (Hanley, 2012). In child practice, Fonagy and colleagues (2020) have highlighted the need for therapists to exaggerate or combine ostensive cues such as subtleties in tone of voice or facial expression, which will be disrupted in remote communications, in order to address issues of therapeutic mistrust (Fisher et al., 2020). The digital therapeutic alliance processes may vary across client groups, therapeutic modalities and digital methods (Tremain et al., 2020) and so careful adaptations and a position of curiosity (seeking feedback) is required by the therapist to ensure that alliance is maintained. Cataldo et al. (2021), have developed a new model of digital therapeutic alliance from adult research that includes the computer as the invisible third party and this may be a useful framework for research into youth digital therapeutic alliance.

Secondly, practitioners are concerned about the safety of digital mental health forums and psychological interventions and whether appropriate risk assessments and risk management can be achieved. Of particular concern is whether psychological practitioners can pick up on the usual signs of self-harm and suicidal risk when delivering online and blended interventions. Research with young people on this issue is lacking. Practitioners will need to be explicit in sensitively asking young people questions about risk to self and risk from others regularly when working online, in the absence of physical signs (e.g. bruises or scars from self-harming) practitioners need to include risk screens as a regular part of their session by session outcome monitoring.

The concept of digital self-harm; 'the anonymous online posting, sending or otherwise sharing of hurtful content about oneself' has been documented in large-scale studies of US adolescents, and found to be associated with a five-to-seven-fold increase in the reporting of suicidal thoughts and a 9-to-15-fold increase in the likelihood of a suicide attempt (Patchin et al., 2023). The activities that young people are undertaking online are important for their mental health outcomes, and those at risk of digital self-harm require support. Practitioners and developers need to take risk assessment within digital forums and interventions seriously.

An additional safety risk is that of privacy and data concerns, young people may not have access to a safe private space to speak at home and may fear how and with whom their data (e.g. from online symptom management tools) will be shared, or lack awareness and skills to deal with cybersecurity concerns (Department for Digital, Culture, Media & Sport, 2022). Ensuring a safe and consistent physical space will be important for young people to make good use of online interventions and connect well with their psychological practitioners in the same way as it is for in-person interventions. This is particularly important for young people who have experienced violence and abuse or are currently at risk of abuse. In addition, ensuring data security and developing creative ways to ensure informed consent to data storage is essential in any digital youth interventions.

To address the limitations discussed, psychological practitioners need to be trained in digital competences to know how to carefully set up online therapeutic work with clients. Free eLearning to develop digital mental health competences has been developed for psychological practitioners by the Division of Clinical Psychology, Digital Healthcare Committee (this can be accessed at www.digitalhealthskills.com).

Finally, the economic burden of digital youth interventions should not be underestimated. Although many digital interventions are offered without cost, access is reliant on device and data access and poverty will impede young people's access to digital mental health interventions. The importance of promoting digital inclusivity is critical.

For a fuller discussion of the strengths and limitations of youth digital mental health interventions practitioners are referred to *Child and Adolescent Mental Health*, special issue Technology and mental health for children and adolescents: pros and cons, 2023, vol. 28.

24.2.4 Choice and Digital Inclusion

Young people themselves indicate a desire for choice in the delivery methods of their psychological interventions. Co-production, client choice and digital inclusion and exclusion are important considerations for individual practitioners and services as they need to offer digital health interventions that are both inclusive and accessible (Aisbitt et al., 2023 NHS, 2019a; World Health Organization, 2020). The importance of informed consent and choice in deciding whether to undertake digital or in-person psychological interventions should not be underestimated and practitioners and health commissioners need to work together to ensure a range of interventions and modalities are available for young people (NHS Confederation, 2020). Digital delivery of psychological interventions should not be the only option.

Digital divides do exist internationally, which 'mirror broader socioeconomic divides – between rich and poor, men and women, cities and rural areas, and those with education and those without' (World Health Organization, 2020, p. 2). The NHS Confederation (2020), note that 9 million people in the UK (16% of the population) cannot access the Internet independently, probably as a result of poverty, lack of interest, confidence or skills. In the UK, one in four children are living in poverty and one-third of working-class households do not have access to the Internet at home (Francis-Devine, 2020; Joseph Rowntree Foundation, 2023). The intersectionality of digital exclusion is important as poverty, as well as experiences of mental health problems vary by ethnicity; digital services may unintentionally exclude young people coming from particular ethnic groups or with particular mental health problems, compounding the impacts of poverty and racism, by making mental health interventions inaccessible for some (for a more detailed and nuanced discussion see Aisbitt et al., 2023).

Piers et al. (2023), systematically reviewed the features, acceptability and efficacy of seven digital mental health interventions for socioeconomically and digitally marginalised youth, which were reported across 10 quantitative and qualitative research studies. They concluded that there is moderate, but limited evidence, that digital interventions designed for marginalised populations, improve youth mental health. Further research is needed before the digital divide in youth mental health can be addressed.

Digital divides are not just about physical access to technology and economic issues but connect to educational, cognitive and emotional factors. The NHS Confederation (2020) recommends four principles for digitally inclusive mental health services in order to address concerns about health inequalities and to address a digital divide in access to future mental health services:

1. Understand the needs of people who use services – know who can and cannot access the digital services, co-produce and co-design digital services to overcome any access difficulties.
2. Prioritise flexibility and adaptability – plan in advance about how to address problems when digital access goes wrong.
3. Ensure ongoing communication and feedback – recognise the novelty for many clients in using digital services and allow time and opportunity for them to feedback on their experiences.
4. Provide a personalised approach – support informed choice about service uptake and understand barriers to access from an individual perspective, offering solutions which can be tailored to a diverse range of need.

24.3 Evidence for Digital Interventions with Young People

As well as issues of reach and engagement it is important to consider if digital mental health and wellbeing interventions are effective for young people. In answering this question, one must take a developmental approach; digital approaches might be more effective for adolescents than younger children for example, or those with strong reading abilities compared to those with developmental difficulties (Domhardt, 2020; Hollis et al., 2017).

The evidence base for adult digital mental health interventions is fairly well established but the effectiveness research with young people is less well developed and research designs are sometimes not robust, with interventions not well described, a reliance on self-report and non-standardised measures, and studies sometimes using small samples with pre- and -post data analysis but no controlled comparison. Researchers have questioned the appropriateness of traditional outcome research designs, such as randomised controlled trials, for digital interventions, which are quickly adapted by rapidly changing technology.

Iterative, adaptive designs may better capture the utility of digital interventions and users' experience (Wilson et al., 2018). This is clearly a rapidly growing field, and the evidence base is building to suggest that young people with mental health problems may benefit from digital interventions.

24.3.1 Computerised CBT and Digital Wellbeing Apps

Digital psychological interventions for youth anxiety and depression have been the most studied, and initial systematic reviews have shown them to be efficacious for these common mental health problems, long-term physical health problems, chronic pain and insomnia, with small- to medium-effect sizes (Calear & Christensen, 2010; Ebert et al., 2015; Pennant et al., 2015; Podina et al., 2015; Thabrew et al., 2018; Vigerland et al., 2016). For example, Hollis and colleagues (2017) conducted a meta-review of youth digital mental health interventions overall. Across 21 existing reviews they found some clinical benefit for digital youth mental health interventions particularly computerised cognitive behavioural therapy (cCBT), for depression and anxiety in adolescents and young adults. Given the quality and quantity of evidence it was difficult for this meta-review to draw any firm conclusions about the cost effectiveness of digital interventions, and they could not offer support for other disorders where digital interventions are available for young people, namely: ADHD, autism, psychosis and eating disorders (Hollis et al., 2017). More recent reviews of digital mental health interventions have replicated these early findings (Christ et al., 2020; Domhardt et al., 2020; Wickersham et al., 2022). See example in Box 24.1.

Box 24.1 Digital intervention example I: cCBT – MoodGYM

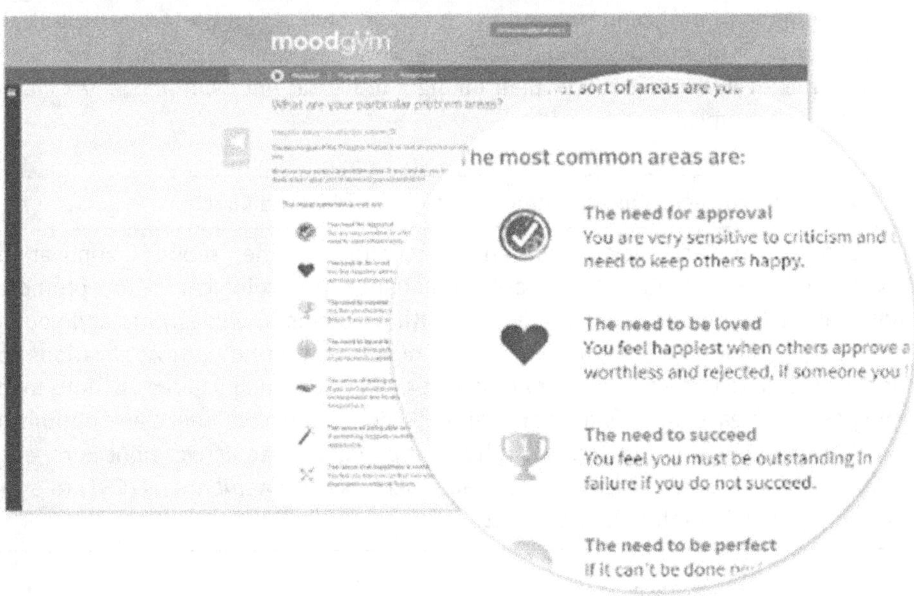

Source: Image taken from https://moodgym.com.au/

(Continued)

Box 24.1 (Continued)

MoodGYM, for anxiety and depression, is a widely implemented low-cost digital intervention for adults and young people developed by psychologists and medical researchers. It is an online, self-directed cognitive-behavioural therapy programme, developed in Australia, which has been implemented for over 1 million users internationally. With five skills-based modules it covers psychoeducation about feelings, thoughts and their connection; thought challenging; destressing techniques; and managing relationships. Quizzes, exercises and diaries offer interaction for the user.

In robust research with adolescents in Australia, the intervention initially showed significant but small effects for reduced anxiety post-treatment and at 6-month follow up when compared to a wait-list control (Calear et al., 2009). These effects were not replicated for depression and the later large-scale REEACT trials with adults showed no significant improvement in depression symptoms for those using MoodGYM compared to an alternative paid for cCBT programme (Beating the Blues) or GP care as usual (Gilbody et al., 2015) though small to medium effects were found when MoodGYM was supplemented with telephone support (Brabyn et al., 2016). As the evidence is mixed for many cCBT interventions for adults and children, psychological practitioners should be cautious about assuming self-directed digital interventions will be helpful to young people with mental health problems and examine the evidence for new interventions carefully.

Mobile applications have also been used to promote emotional wellbeing and prevent mental health problems in children and young people (CYP). Research findings suggest that (in keeping with in-person preventative interventions) digital prevention and health promotion tools for mental health and wellbeing work best when targeting young people who are at risk of difficulties rather than taking a universal interventions approach. See Box 24.2 for an example.

Box 24.2 Digital intervention example II: EcoWeB – MyMood Coach

The ECoWeB project developed and disseminated the mobile application MyMoodCoach – a personalised tool to enhance psychological skills, promote emotional wellbeing and prevent mental health problems in adolescents and young adults (16 to 22 years). The app offers daily mood monitoring with notifications to help young people understand what influences their mood, and includes CBT informed strategies to increase emotional understanding, motivation, confidence and optimism as well as reduce worry. The app was rolled out and evaluated across eight European nations and delivered empirically supported psychological interventions (CBT) to over 3,800 young people in the research trials.

Source: Image taken from https://www.mymoodcoach.com/find-out-more. Credit Marcos / Adobe Stock. Ian Stauffer / UnSplash. Ian Dan Nelson / UnSplash.

The PROMOTE randomised controlled trial of the app, where a low-intensity CBT intervention was offered universally to a well-functioning group of young people did not reduce depression or improve wellbeing. However, the PREVENT randomised trial, which was targeted at young people who were at a higher risk of mental health problems showed increases in low mood were prevented and quality of life was improved. The researchers conclude that mental health apps need to be tailored to individual needs and are more likely to be effective when tailored to higher risk groups of young people (Watkins, 2022). Results are awaiting peer-reviewed publication.

Digital online interventions that use models other than CBT and focus on counselling and peer-support approaches have been well received by young people and integrated into mainstream NHS and Social Care services and into US healthcare providers. The most successful of these has been Kooth (see Box 24.3).

Box 24.3 Digital intervention example III: Kooth

Kooth is an online synchronous and asynchronous, co-produced, digital intervention that provides psychoeducation and free, safe and anonymous online text-based support and counselling to young people from trained counsellors. The intervention aims to develop an online support community and help children and young people 'feel safe and confident in exploring their concerns and seeking professional support'. It includes features such as discussion boards for social connection and peer support, personalised goal setting and journaling features to track mood and identify triggers for negative and positive mood. These enable the young person to gain agency over their mental health concerns. Importantly, Kooth has integrated a risk-profiling system across all parts of the platform that allows the intervention to prioritise and reach out to young people at risk. The intervention has been evaluated in the UK, with positive practice-based evidence supporting its use (e.g. Prescott et al., 2019).

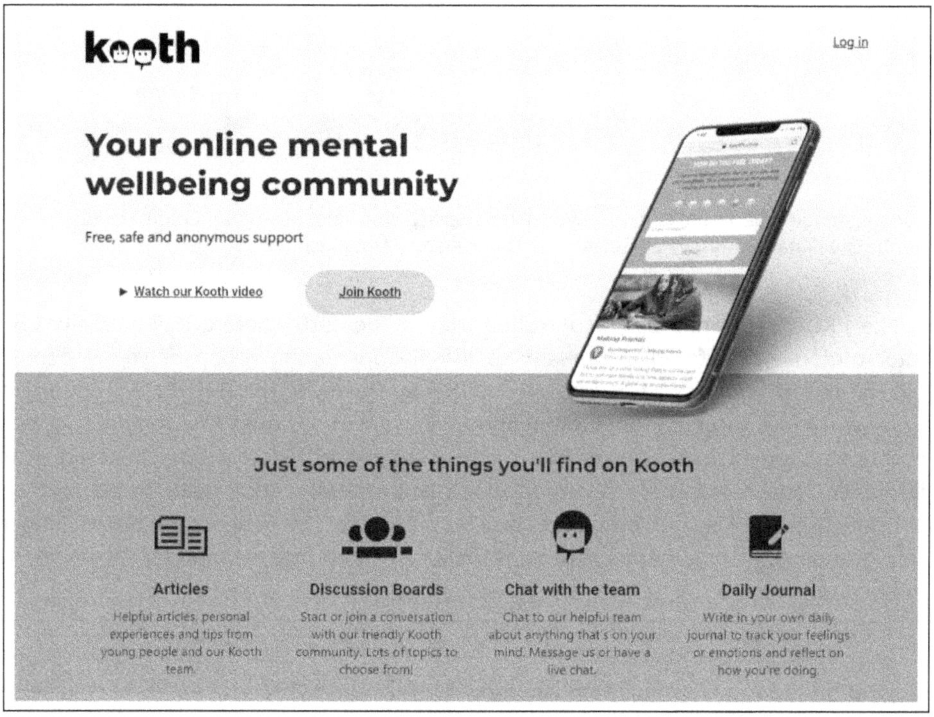

School-community-focused digital interventions to improve young people's knowledge and skills regarding mental health knowledge, stigma and access to help (Mental Health Literacy, Jorm, 2012) have also been popular internationally, particularly in the UK, Australia, Canada, the United States and Hong Kong. A systematic review of digital mental health literacy interventions with young people (10 to 24 years – including videos, health ecards, websites, online modules and online games) found these were useful in enhancing mental health literacy (MHL) for anxiety disorders and anorexia, but not depression (Tay et al., 2018). Digital MHL interventions for young people were as effective as those delivered in-person, with the biggest improvements seen for mental health knowledge (see Box 24.4) (Bemrose & Pote, 2022).

Box 24.4 Digital intervention example IV: MindAid Youth, digital mental health literacy

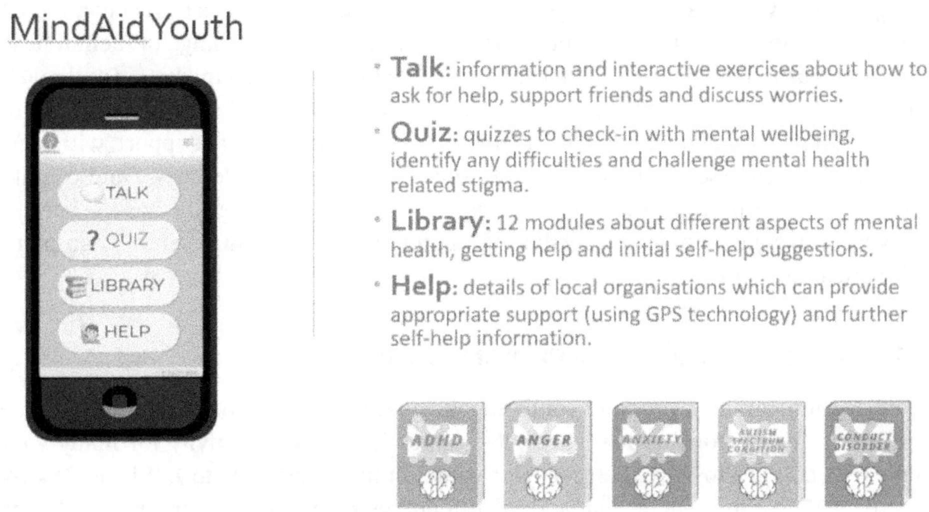

Source: Image taken from https://mindaid.org/youth/

MindAid Youth is a freely available interactive MHL web-based app for young people that has been co-designed by psychologists, teachers and young people. It acts as a teaching tool and aims to improve young people's MHL knowledge of mental health difficulties, accessing mental health support and addressing mental health stigma.

Interactive contents include information on mental health difficulties, available support (external and self-help), exercises to challenge stigmatising attitudes, and tools to explore current mental health. MindAid Youth has an accompanying teacher's version, which helps them to communicate with pupils about mental health, recognise mental health difficulties and support pupils to seek appropriate help.

In two recent cluster-controlled trials, MindAid Youth was evaluated in UK schools with 686 young people and found high youth engagement with improvements in adolescents' mental-health-related knowledge compared to control groups completing personal and social health education as usual (Bemrose et al., 2022). Results are awaiting peer reviewed publication.

Research is still in its infancy, so the efficacy of digital psychological interventions for youth mental health problems and those to support broader wellbeing is not yet fully established, though the results of CBT-informed and targeted digital interventions are looking promising. Research trials are indicating that mental health apps and online platforms need to be tailored to individual needs and are more likely to be effective when offered to higher risk groups of young people compared to whole community populations.

Psychological practitioners are starting to understand what might engage young people in digital interventions from co-production and qualitative accounts but quantitative research into the active ingredients of digital interventions is only just emerging. This will be an important next step in using artificial intelligence to develop personalised digital psychological interventions for young people. Domhardt and colleagues (2021) conducted a systematic review of 25 studies of digital interventions for a broad range of mental health problems (mostly Internet based, CBT informed) that had explored mediators and mechanisms of change with young people. The review could not make definitive conclusions due to study variability and quality, but 21 mediators had some empirical support, with significant affective processes (emotional factors such as fear and hopelessness) and cognitive processes (such as perceived control and post-event processing) identified as the variables that were actively changing and mediating the impact of digital interventions on mental health outcomes for young people.

24.3.2 Computer Games for Youth Mental Health

Recently gamification to promote youth engagement with traditional psychological interventions has been growing. Playing digital games is a popular activity for many young people with 60% of 3 to 17 year olds playing games online, increasing to 75% in adolescence (Ofcom, 2022). Serious games that address difficulties such as mental and physical health problems have been employed in health settings to support adults and young people. These interventions require minimal staff resources to implement and are intrinsically rewarding to play so can lead to high levels of intervention fidelity (Francis et al., 2021).

Conclusive evidence for the effectiveness of these games is yet to be established, though there is some evidence that they are helpful for common mental health problems (Lau et al., 2017; Townsend et al., 2022). SPARX, a CBT computer game designed for adolescent depression, is the world leader in this field having been designed and implemented since 2010. In robust research trials SPARX has been shown to be effective in reducing adolescents' symptoms of depression when compared to treatment as usual, with improvements maintained at 3-month follow up (Merry et al., 2012). Perhaps most impressively this game has had broad impact; it has been adapted for a culturally diverse user group and implemented nationally across New Zealand, where it was developed, as well as being offered to young people in countries internationally. See Box 24.5 for further information about SPARX.

Shepherd et al. (2018) qualitatively explored adolescent perceptions of using the SPARX serious game for low mood and focused particularly on cultural narratives and images in the games design. Personalisation of the game enhanced user engagement that, in turn, assisted participants with learning relaxation and cognitive restructuring skills through the gameplay.

Box 24.5 Digital intervention example V: SPARX – CBT computer game for youth depression

Source: Image taken from https://landing.sparx.org.nz/

SPARX stands for Smart, Positive, Active, Realistic, X-Factor Thoughts. It is a CBT-focused computer game for mild to moderate depression experienced by adolescents. It incorporates fantasy role playing and traditional Maori design elements in a video game environment over seven modules.

CBT techniques include: relaxation skills, problem solving, challenging and replacing negative thoughts and social skills development. For each module the 'Guide' presents mood and safety assessments, coaches young people on coping with depression, reviews CBT skills and assigns homework. Users create an avatar and use CBT skills to defeat GNATs (Gloomy Negative Automatic Thoughts).

Modified versions of SPARX have been created for gender diverse adolescents and for addressing general mental health. It's a freely available and there is 24-hour clinical back-up support provided in partnership with charities offering telephone contact from professional counsellors and additional resources are also available online. Initial trials in Australia (Merry et al., 2012), and subsequently internationally, show positive effects of the intervention on mood symptoms, immediately after use and at follow up (as reported in Section 24.3.2).

Determining whether the mechanisms of change for serious games and online cCBT interventions for young people's mental health are working is difficult. The factors that are changing when young people are engaging in these digital interventions and showing improvements in their mental health is still uncertain but research into the mechanisms of change or 'active ingredients' in digital psychological games is emerging (Wellcome, 2022).

24.3.3 Immersive Technologies: Virtual and Augmented Reality

Immersive technologies are growing in popularity to address youth mental health and wellbeing, but it is too early to determine the evidence base for extended reality (XR) interventions in this field. A recent systematic review by Halldorsson et al. (2021), found evidence of success for XR interventions aimed at youth anxiety and depression, as well as improving pain management and social skills for young people. However, as in previous digital outcome evaluations, effect sizes were small when controlled comparisons were used. In general, the quality of quantitative study designs was poor, including low use of controlled comparisons and a limited range of outcome measure that focus on the specific features of the digital intervention. In addition, qualitative research offering the perspectives of young people in using these immersive mental health and wellbeing interventions are only just emerging.

Extended reality (XR) interventions have also been developed for youth wellbeing and evaluation of community samples has shown mixed results, depending on the intervention used and research design. It is difficult to make comparisons between studies as the depth of immersion for the young person varies greatly from watching videos in virtual reality to augmented reality games (see Box 24.6). Some outcome research does report significant improvements in youth mental health and wellbeing after XR interventions that use immersive videos (for example, Liu et al., 2020; Rupp et al., 2019).

Box 24.6 Digital intervention example VI: Dragons of Afterlands, augmented reality board game to support youth wellbeing

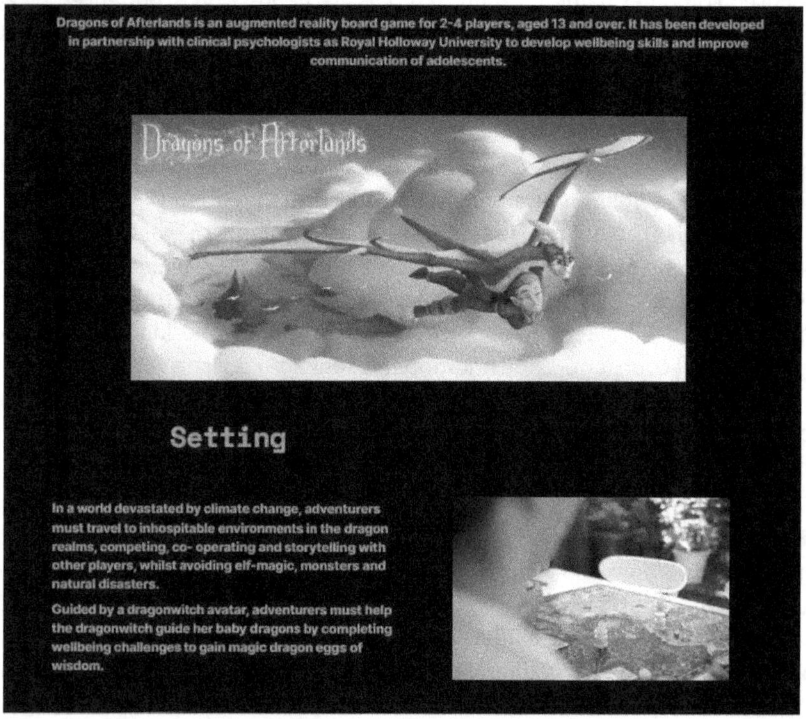

Source: Image taken from https://playwellforlife.com/dragons-of-afterlands

Dragons of Afterlands is an immersive board game for adolescents, using augmented reality (AR) and game-based learning to develop adolescent mental health and social skills through collaborative storytelling in a school setting. It has been co-designed by psychologists, teachers and adolescents (Campbell et al., 2022).

Players must win magical dragon eggs by completing social challenges across four wellbeing realms: physical, social, cognitive and emotional. Gameplay facilitates social interaction storytelling for building wellbeing skills, utilising a blended online and offline experience.

Piloting of Dragons of Afterlands in UK schools with adolescents (N = 100) has shown positive outcomes for young people playing the game when compared to those completing usual personal/social lessons but it needs to determine if this is sustained at follow-up.

24.4 Conclusion

Digital mental health interventions for young people are gaining in popularity due to their potential for engaging 'digital natives' in addressing common mental health difficulties such as anxiety and depression and more broadly improving their psychological wellbeing and mental health knowledge. Early evidence of success is available from research trials and practice-based evidence with young people. Co-production of digital mental health tools with children and young people is strongly endorsed: from planning and design to implementation and evaluation in order to make these applications relevant, engaging, personalised and effective.

References

Aisbitt, G. M., Nolte, T., & Fonagy, P. (2023). Editorial perspective: The digital divide – inequalities in remote therapy for children and adolescents. *Child and Adolescent Mental Health, 28*(1), 105–107.

Bakker, D., Kazantzis, N., Rickwood, D., & Rickard, N. (2016). Mental health smartphone apps: Review and evidence-based recommendations for future developments. *JMIR Mental Health, 3*(1), e4984.

Bemrose, H., & Pote, H. (2022). *A systematic review of the modalities of mental health literacy interventions for young people: Are digital interventions helpful?* {Poster session]. International Society for Research on Internet Interventions. 11th Scientific Meeting, Pittsburgh, United States, 19–21 September.

Bemrose, H., Pote, H., & Good, H. (2022). *A cluster-controlled trial of a digital mental health literacy intervention in UK Schools: MindAid youth.* [Paper presentation]. International Society for Research on Internet Interventions. 11th Scientific Meeting, Pittsburgh, United States, 19–21 September.

Bevan Jones, R., Stallard, P., Agha, S. S., Rice, S., Werner-Seidler, A., Stasiak, K., Kahn, J., Simpson, S. A., Alvarez-Jimenez, M., Rice, F., Evans, R., & Merry S. (2020). Practitioner review: Co-design of digital mental health technologies with children and young people. *Journal of Child Psychology and Psychiatry, 61*(8), 928–940. https://doi.org/10.1111/jcpp.13258.

Brabyn, S., Araya, R., Barkham, M., Bower, P., Cooper, C., Duarte, A., Kessler, D., Knowles, S., Lovell, K., Littlewood, E., Mattock, R., Palmer, S., Pervin, J., Richards, D., Tallon, D., White, D., Walker, S., Worthy, G., & Gilbody, S. (2016). The second Randomised Evaluation of the Effectiveness, cost-effectiveness and Acceptability of Computerised Therapy (REEACT-2) trial: Does the provision of telephone support enhance the effectiveness of computer-delivered cognitive behaviour therapy? A randomised controlled trial. *Health Technology Assessment, 20*(89), 1–64. https://doi.org/10.3310/hta20890.

Burbach, F. R., & Pote, H. (2021). Digital approaches – a paradigm shift? *Journal of Family Therapy, 43*, 169–184.

Bushnell, D. M., Martin, M. L., & Parasuraman, B. (2003). Electronic versus paper questionnaires: A further comparison in persons with asthma. *Journal of Allergy, 40*(1) 1–11.

Calear, A. L., & Christensen, H. (2010). Review of internet-based prevention and treatment programs for anxiety and depression in children and adolescents. *The Medical Journal of Australia, 192*(S11), S12–14. https://doi.org/10.5694/j.1326-5377.2010.tb03686.x

Calear, A. L., Christensen, H., Mackinnon, A., Griffiths, K. M., & O'Kearney, R. (2009). The YouthMood project: A cluster randomized controlled trial of an online cognitive behavioral program with adolescents. *Journal of Consulting Clinical Psychology, 77*(6), 1021–1032. https://doi.org/10.1037/a0017391

Campbell, S., Pote, H., & Stock, M. (2022). *Dragons of Afterlands: Co-designing and piloting an augmented reality board game to enhance youth wellbeing*. [Poster presentation]. International Society for Research on Internet Interventions. 11th Scientific Meeting, Pittsburgh, United States, 19–21 September.

Cataldo, F., Chang, S., Mendoza, A., & Buchanan, G. (2021) A perspective on client-psychologist relationships in videoconferencing psychotherapy: Literature review. *JMIR Ment Health, 8*(2), e19004. https://doi.org/10.2196/19004

Child Outcomes Research Consortium (CORC). (2022). *Advice and guidance on working remotely with outcome measurement and feedback questionnaires*. CORC. https://www.corc.uk.net/media/2561/summary-guidance-working-with-measures-remotely-v01-final.pdf

Christ, C., Schouten, M. J., Blankers, M., van Schaik, D. J., Beekman, A. T., Wisman, M. A., Stikkelbroek, Y. A., & Dekker, J. J. (2020) Internet and computer-based cognitive behavioral therapy for anxiety and depression in adolescents and young adults: Systematic review and meta-analysis. *Journal of Medical Internet Research, 22*(9), e17831. https://doi.org/10.2196/17831

Department for Digital, Culture, Media & Sport, (2022). *mapping informal cyber security initiatives for young people aged 5–19*. https://www.gov.uk/government/publications/mapping-informal-cyber-security-initiatives-for-young-people-aged-5-19/mapping-informal-cyber-security-initiatives-for-young-people-aged-5-19

Domhardt, M., Engler, S., Nowak, H., Lutsch, A., Baumel, A., & Baumeister, H. (2021). Mechanisms of change in digital health interventions for mental disorders in youth: Systematic review. *Journal of Medical Internet Research, 23*(11), e29742. https://doi.org/10.2196/29742

Domhardt, M., Steubl, L., & Baumeister, H. (2020). Internet- and mobile-based interventions for mental and somatic conditions in children and adolescents. *Zeitschrift der Kinder- und Jugendpsychiatrie und Psychotherapie, 48(*1), 33–46.

Ebert, D. D., Zarski, A., Christensen, H., Stikkelbroek, Y., Cuijpers, P., Berking, M., & Riper, H. (2015). Internet and computer-based cognitive behavioral therapy for anxiety and depression in youth: A meta-analysis of randomized controlled outcome trials. *PLoS One, 10*(3), e0119895.

Fisher, S., Guralnik, T., Fonagy, P., & Zilcha-Mano, S. (2020). Let's face it: Video conferencing psychotherapy requires the extensive use of ostensive cues. *Counselling Psychology Quarterly, 34*, 508–524.

Fleming, T., Dixon, R., Frampton, C., & Merry S. (2012). A pragmatic randomized controlled trial of computerized CBT (SPARX) for symptoms of depression among adolescents excluded from mainstream education. *Behavioral and Cognitive Psychotherapy, 40*(5), 529–541. https://doi.org/10.1017/S1352465811000695

Fonagy, P., Campbell, C., Truscott, A., & Fuggle, P. (2020). Debate: Mentalising remotely – The AFNCCF's adaptations to the coronavirus crisis. *Child and Adolescent Mental Health, 25*, 178–179.

Francis, J., Vella-Brodrick, D., & Chyuan-Chin, T. (2021). Effectiveness of online, school-based positive psychology interventions to improve mental health and wellbeing: A systematic review. *International Journal of Wellbeing, 11*(4), 1228–1254.

Francis-Devine, B. (2020). Poverty in the UK: Statistics.(House of Commons Library Briefing Paper No. 7096. https://researchbriefings.files.parliament.uk/documents/S

Gee, B., Wilson, J., Clarke, T., Farthing, S., Carroll, B., Jackson, C., King, K., Murdoch, J., Fonagy, P., & Notley, C. (2021). Review: Delivering mental health support within schools and colleges – a thematic synthesis of barriers and facilitators to implementation of indicated psychological interventions for adolescents. *Child and Adolescent Mental Health, 26*(1), 34–46.

Gilbody, S., Littlewood, E., Hewitt, C., Brierley, G., Tharmanathan, P., Araya, R., Barkham, M., Bower, P., Cooper, C., Gask, L., Kessler, D., Lester, H., Lovell, K., Parry, G., Richards, D. A., Andersen, P., Brabyn, S., Knowles, S., Shepherd, C., Tallon, D., White, D., & REEACT Team. (2015). Computerised cognitive behaviour therapy (cCBT) as treatment for depression in primary care (REEACT trial): Large scale pragmatic randomised controlled trial. *British Medical Journal, 35*, 5627 https://doi.org/10.1136/bmj.h5627

Granic, I., Lobel, A., & Engels, R. C. (2014). The benefits of playing video games. *American Psychologist, 69*(1), 66.

Hall, C. L., Moldavsky, M., Taylor, J., Sayal, K., Marriott, M., Batty, M. J., Pass, S., & Hollis, C. (2014). Implementation of routine outcome measurement in child and adolescent mental health services in the United Kingdom: A critical perspective. *European Child & Adolescent Psychiatry, 23*(4), 239–242. https://doi.org/10.1007/s00787-013-0454-2

Halldorsson, B., Hill, C., Waite, P., Partridge, K., Freeman, D., & Creswell, C. (2021). Immersive virtual reality and digital applied gaming interventions for the treatment of mental health problems in children and young people: The need for rigorous treatment development and clinical evaluation. *Journal of Child Psychology and Psychiatry, 62*(5), 584–605.

Hanley, T. (2012). Understanding the online therapeutic alliance through the eyes of adolescent service users. *Counselling and Psychotherapy Research, 12*(1), 35–43.

Hill, C., Martin, J., Thomson, S., Scott-Ram, N., Penfold, H., & Creswell, C. (2017). Navigating the challenges of digital health innovation: Considerations and solutions in developing online and smartphone-application-based interventions for mental health disorders. *The British Journal of Psychiatry, 211*(2), 65–69. https://doi.org/10.1192/bjp.bp.115.180372

Hollis, C., Falconer, C. J., Martin, J. L., Whittington, C., Stockton, S., Glazebrook, C., & Davies E. B. (2017) Annual research review: Digital health interventions for children and young people with mental health problems – a systematic and meta-review. *Journal of Child Psychology & Psychiatry, 58*(4), 474–503. https://doi.org/10.1111/jcpp.12663.

Jorm, A. F. (2012). Mental health literacy: Empowering the community to take action for better mental health. *American Psychologist, 67*(3), 231–243. https://doi.org/10.1037/a0025957

Joseph Rountree Foundation. (2023). UK Poverty: The Essential Guide to Understanding Poverty in the UK. Joseph Rowntree Foundation. https://www.jrf.org.uk/sites/default/files/jrf/uk_poverty_2023_-_the_essential_guide_to_understanding_poverty_in_the_uk_0_0.pdf

Kuosmanen, T., Clarke, A. M., & Barry, M. M. (2019). Promoting adolescents' mental health and wellbeing: Evidence synthesis. *Journal of Public Mental Health, 18*(1), 73–83. https://doi.org/10.1108/JPMH-07-2018-0036

Kwan, B., & Rickwood, D. J. (2021). A routine outcome measure for youth mental health: Clinically interpreting MyLifeTracker. *Early Intervention in Psychiatry, 15*(4), 807–817. https://doi.org/10.1111/eip.13016

Kwan, B., Rickwood, D. J., & Telford. N. R. (2018). Development and validation of MyLifeTracker: a routine outcome measure for youth mental health. *Psychology Research and Behaviour Management, 11*, 67–77. https://doi.org/10.2147/PRBM.S152342

Lau, H. M., Smit, J. H., Fleming, T. M., & Riper, H. (2017). Serious games for mental health: are they accessible, feasible, and effective? A systematic review and meta-analysis. *Frontiers in Psychiatry, 7*, 209.

Liu, Q., Wang, Y., Yao, M. Z., Tang, Q., & Yang, Y. (2020). The effects of viewing an uplifting 360-degree video on emotional well-being among elderly adults and college students under immersive virtual reality and smartphone conditions. *Cyberpsychology, Behavior, and Social Networking, 23*(3), 157–164.

Liverpool, S., Mota, C. P., Sales, C. M. D, Čuš, A., Carletto, S., Hancheva, C., Sousa, S., Cerón, S. C., Moreno-Peral, P., Pietrabissa, G., Moltrecht, B., Ulberg, R., Ferreira, N., & Edbrooke-Childs, J. (2020). Engaging children and young people in digital mental health interventions: Systematic review of modes of delivery, facilitators, and barriers. *Journal of Medical Internet Research, 22*(6), e16317. https://doi.org/10.2196/16317.

Mandryk, R. L., & Birk, M. V. (2017). Toward game-based digital mental health interventions: player habits and preferences. *Journal of Medical Internet Research, 19*(4), e6906.

Merry, S. N., Stasiak, K., Shepherd, M., Frampton, C., Fleming, T., & Lucassen, M. F. G., (2012, April 19). The effectiveness of SPARX, a computerised self-help intervention for adolescents seeking help for depression: Randomised controlled non-inferiority trial. *British Medical Journal, 344*. https://doi.org/10.1136/bmj.e2598

NHS. (2019a, July). Digital inclusion guide of health and social care. https://digital.nhs.uk/about-nhs-digital/corporate-information-and-documents/digital-inclusion#chapter-index

NHS. (2019b). Long Term Plan Report. https://www.longtermplan.nhs.uk/

NHS Confederation. (2020). Digital inclusion in mental health: A guide to help increase choice and improve access to digital mental health services. https://www.nhsconfed.org/publications/digital-inclusion-mental-health

NHS Digital. (2021). *Mental health of children and young people in England, 2021: Wave 2 follow up to the 2017 survey*. NHS. https://files.digital.nhs.uk/97/B09EF8/mhcyp_2021_rep.pdf

Ofcom. (2022). Children and parents: Media use and attitudes report 2022. Ofcom '22 childrens-media-use-and-attitudes-report-2022.pdf

Patalay, P., Hayes, D., Deighton, J., & Wolpert, M. (2016). A comparison of paper and computer administered strengths and difficulties questionnaire. *Journal of Psychopathology and Behavioral Assessment, 38*(2), 242–250.

Patchin, J. W., Hinduja, S., & Meldrum, R. C., (2023). Digital self-harm and suicidality among adolescents. *Child and Adolescent Mental Health, 28*(1), 52–59.

Pennant, M. E., Loucas, C. E., Whittington, C., Creswell, C., Fonagy, P., & Fuggle, P. (2015). Computerised therapies for anxiety and depression in children and young people: A systematic review and meta-analysis. *Behavioral Research Therapy, 67*, 1–18.

Pham, Q., Wiljer, D., & Cafazzo, J. A. (2016). Beyond the randomized controlled trial: A review of alternatives in mhealth clinical trial methods. *JMIR Mhealth and Uhealth, 4*(3), e107. https://doi.org/10.2196/mhealth.5720.

Piers, R., Williams, J. M., & Sharpe, H. (2023). Review: Can digital mental health interventions bridge the 'digital divide' for socioeconomically and digitally marginalised youth? A systematic review. *Child and Adolescent Mental Health, 28*(1), 90–104 https://doi.org/10.1111/camh.12620

Podina, I. R., Mogoase, C., David, D., Szentagotai, A., & Dobrean, A. (2015). A meta-analysis on the efficacy of technology mediated CBT for anxious children and adolescents. *Journal of Rational-Emotive & Cognitive Behavior Therapy, 34*(1), 31–50.

Pote, H., Rees, A., Holloway-Biddle, C., & Griffith, E. (2021, February 11). Workforce challenges in digital health implementation: How are clinical psychology training programmes developing digital competences? *Digital Health, 7*. https://doi.org/10.1177/2055207620985396

Prescott, J., Hanley, T., & Ujhelyi Gomez, K. (2019). Why do young people use online forums for mental health and emotional support? Benefits and challenges. *British Journal of Guidance & Counselling, 47*(3), 317–327. https://doi.org/10.1080/03069885.2019.1619169

Roland, J., Lawrance, E., Insel, T., & Christensen, H. (2020, November). *The digital mental health revolution: Transforming care through innovation and scale-up.* World Innovation Summit for Health & Qatar Foundation Report. https://2020.wish.org.qa/app/uploads/2020/09/IMPJ7849-03-Digital-Mental-Health-WISH2020-201103-WEB.pdf

Rupp, M. A., Odette, K. L., Kozachuk, J., Michaelis, J. R., Smither, J. A., & McConnell, D. S. (2019). Investigating learning outcomes and subjective experiences in 360-degree videos. *Computers & Education, 128*, 256–268.

Shepherd, M., Merry, S., Lambie, I., & Thompson, A. (2018). Indigenous adolescents' perception of an emental health program (SPARX): Exploratory qualitative assessment. *JMIR Serious Games, 6*(3), e13. https://doi.org/.2196/games.8752

Simpson, S. G., & Reid, C. L. (2014). Therapeutic alliance in videoconferencing psychotherapy: A review. *Australian Journal of Rural Health, 22*(6), 280–299.

Simpson, S., Richardson, L., Pietrabissa, G., Castelnuovo, G., & Reid, C. (2021). Videotherapy and therapeutic alliance in the age of Covid-19. *Clinical Psychology & Psychotherapy, 28*(2), 409–421.

Tay, J. L., Tay, Y. F., & Klainin-Yobas, P. (2018). Effectiveness of information and communication technologies interventions to increase mental health literacy: A systematic review. *Early Intervention in Psychiatry, 12*(6), 1024–1037. https://doi.org/10.1111/eip.12695

Thabrew, H., Stasiak, K., Hetrick, S. E., Wong, S., Huss, J. H., & Merry, S. N. (2018, August 15). E-health interventions for anxiety and depression in children and adolescents with long-term physical conditions. *Cochrane Database of Systematic Reviews, 8*(8), CD012489. https://doi.org/10.1002/14651858.CD012489.pub2

Topol, E. (2019). The Topol review: Preparing the healthcare workforce to deliver the digital future. NHS and Health Education England. https://topol.hee.nhs.uk/the-topol-review

Townsend, C., Humpston, C., Rogers, J., Goodyear, V., Lavis, A., & Michail, M. (2022). The effectiveness of gaming interventions for depression and anxiety in young people: systematic review and meta-analysis. *British Journal of Psychology Open, 8*(1), e25.

Tremain, H., McEnery, C., Fletcher, K., & Murray, G. (2020). The therapeutic alliance in digital mental health interventions for serious mental illnesses: Narrative review. *JMIR Mental Health, 7*(8), e17204. https://doi.org/10.2196/17204

Vigerland, S., Lenhard, F., Bonnert, M., Lalouni, M., Hedman, E., Ahlen, J., Olen, O., Serlachius, E., & Ljotsson, B. (2016). Internet-delivered cognitive behavior therapy for children and adolescents: a systematic review and meta-analysis. *Clinical Psychology Review, 50*, 1–10.

Watkins, E., (2022). *ECoWeB: Large-scale controlled trials of a digital app to promote wellbeing and prevent poor mental health in young people across Europe.* [Presentation]. NIHR MindTech MIC National Symposium, London, UK, 24 November.

Wellcome. (2022, November 22). What science has shown us can help young people with anxiety and depression. https://wellcome.org/reports/what-science-has-shown-can-help-young-people-anxiety-and-depression

Wickersham, A., Barack, T., Cross, L., & Downs, J. (2022). Computerized cognitive behavioral therapy for treatment of depression and anxiety in adolescents: Systematic review and meta-analysis. *Journal of Medical Internet Research, 24*(4), e29842. https://doi.org/10.2196/29842.

Wilson, K., Bell, C., Wilson, L., & Witteman, H. (2018). Agile research to complement agile development: A proposal for an mHealth research lifecycle. *Digital Medicine, 1*, 46. https://doi.org/10.1038/s41746-018-0053-1

World Health Organization. (2020). *Youth-centred digital health interventions: A framework for planning, developing and implementing solutions with and for young people.* World Health Organization. https://www.who.int/publications/i/item/9789240011717

25

Youth Community Practice

Collaboration and Co-production in Action (MAC-UK)

Katerina Alexandraki, Laura Casale, Jessica Davies, Rupert Goodman, Tasir Joseph, Jake Lake, Rachel McKail and Jon Oliver

25.1 Introduction

This chapter illustrates the frameworks for co-production and collaboration introduced in Section 1 using the example of MAC-UK.

MAC-UK is a mental health charity, founded in 2008 in recognition of the fact that marginalised young people needed a different kind of mental health support to that which was being offered by mainstream services. MAC-UK has over 15 years of experience working in communities that are marginalised, institutionally under-resourced and experience high levels of social exclusion. As an organisation, the vision is for a society where excluded young people inspire and lead the solutions to inequality and the impact of this on mental health, with the resources, capabilities and investment to do so. Central to the work is co-production, which strives to have young people and other stakeholders as equal partners in the design, delivery and evaluation of the work, and promotes shared decision making along the way.

MAC-UK has a track-record of being able to support young people in numerous ways, and work at multiple levels simultaneously. MAC-UK's INTEGRATE model (see Section 25.3.3) works to support young people and services where they are at, building relationships and offering support through those relationships in order to improve the wellbeing of young people. To create long-lasting change, MAC-UK seeks to also impact services and systems. Alongside the expertise of young people, communities and services, the work draws on ideas from youth work, psychology and public health to inform practice.

Experience has shown that there is a fundamental need for this work to continue at a number of levels, including community practice, examples of which will be shared within this chapter. This chapter will first give a brief introduction to MAC-UK's history, the INTEGRATE model and ways of working, a critical review of the evidence base relevant to community-based approaches, along with challenges of working in this way and ideas about evaluation.

Child Psychology: Pathways to Good Practice, First Edition.
Edited by Helen Pote, Anna Picciotto and Clare Norris.

25.1.1 Approaching the Chapter

When invited to write this chapter, MAC-UK staff came together to think about what youth and community practice means to them and to identify the key messages to share with people training to work with children and young people. Hoping to ensure voices and diversity of experience within the team were accurately represented, each section has a different author, which means a different tone and lens has been brought. Even though perhaps a little unfamiliar, this is representative of the way of working and of the message MAC-UK hopes to bring about collaboration and space for difference. Conversations as a team were recorded, and the quotations used to structure this chapter.

25.2 The Need for Alternative Mental Health Provision for Marginalised Young People

Increasing evidence supports the significant links between social inequality, lower socioeconomic status and racism, and poor mental health and social outcomes (Deighton et al., 2019; Marmot et al., 2010, 2020; Nagata et al., 2019; Nazroo et al., 2020; Vargas et al., 2020); in the United Kingdom, diagnosed mental health 'disorders' increase as one moves further down the income scale (e.g., see Public Health England, 2019; World Health Organization and Calouste Gulbenkian Foundation, 2014). Despite tremendous resilience and creativity, communities facing structural disadvantage can experience chronic exposure to environmental stressors, resulting in various forms of psychological distress (Miller & Townsend, 2005). Young people from racially minoritised[1] groups in particular, are disproportionately exposed to mental health risk factors (Ayo et al., 2020). However, for the members of these communities most in need of mental health support, accessible and appropriate services are often entirely out of reach.

Inequalities across mental health services in the United Kingdom are well documented. Access to and experience of mental health services varies across racial group education level and gender, with those at multiple intersections likely to be most disadvantaged (Department of Health and Social Care, 1999, 2018; Hussain et al., 2022). In recent years, there have been ongoing recommendations for Child and Adolescent Mental Health Services to develop more flexible services for marginalised children and young people (Ayodeji et al., 2021; Wintermeyer, 2020). However, disparities remain. A range of explanations have been offered, but much of the research tends to locate the problem within marginalised communities in the form of differing social/cultural understandings of mental health, and a historic lack of trust in services. Other research has acknowledged the role that services play (Byrne et al., 2017; Keating and Robertson, 2004; Robards et al., 2018; Street et al., 2005), with young people of varying racial groups, genders identities and socioeconomic positions reporting negative experiences of clinical settings. For example, 27% of the videos on TikTok using the #CAMHS hashtag shared negative perceptions and experiences (Chadee & Evans, 2021).

1 The author recognises the problematic nature of the term 'racially minoritised' in that, similarly to 'BAME', it fails to recognise the unique cultural identities and experiences within the acronym (Aspinall, 2020). 'Racially minoritised' is used, in the place of 'ethnic minority', to acknowledge that groups have been actively 'minoritised' by people and systems, as opposed to naturally existing as a minority, as other terms can imply (Gunaratnam, 2003).

Barriers to access are said to include: previous negative interactions with professionals (Plaistow et al., 2014), believing support would not be appropriate to their needs (Ayo et al., 2020) or that they would not be taken seriously (Plaistow et al., 2014). Similarly, young people who MAC-UK have worked alongside have reported that, within mainstream clinical settings, they felt positioned as the 'problem', and the practitioner the 'expert'. If being 'the problem' is a label that some young people are used to repeatedly receiving, from both services and wider society, this approach is unlikely to prove conducive to healing.

25.2.1 Changing the Dynamic

It is increasingly understood across the youth mental health sector that interventions can exist beyond the therapy room, that effective therapeutic work need not rely on 1:1 interactions within a clinical setting (Birch et al., 2020; Zlotowitz et al., 2016), making room for a broader definition of therapeutic work and engaging young people in more creative ways. Despite this, the value of academic knowledge and traditional clinical 'expertise' continue to be emphasised within mental health professional training and clinical settings. The necessity of thorough training to practise to a professional standard is not disputed. Rather, thinking encouraged about how the 'expert' position, a label often ascribed within the field of mental health, can, at times, reinforce unhelpful power dynamics. This is particularly relevant to young people, where the value of their knowledge is often underestimated.

The 'expert' label exists in direct opposition to positions advocated for in the approach taken by MAC-UK in working alongside young people and other professionals, communities and services, where a position of 'not knowing' and curiosity are adopted as intentional stances, rather than positioning oneself as the expert. When it comes to 'trauma-informed' youth community practice, MAC-UK maintains the importance of trying to level the playing field, with practitioners sharing the power that they have been granted by virtue of their occupations, whilst considering wider conceptualisations of trauma, including community and systemic trauma inflicted by the state and systems around young people. It is important for practitioners to acknowledge that not everything can be learned through academic study and placements in 'traditional' mental health settings; valuing the expertise of young people is vital in developing practice. Fundamentally: '[It's about] listening to young people, finding out what they want. Almost throwing your approaches and your theory out, to just actually hear young people.' (MAC-UK staff member)

25.2.2 Changing the Narrative

> I was thinking about some of the teaching that we [MAC-UK] did recently, and talking to some trainees about gangs … and they were saying, 'oh, well I don't really know much about gangs, just aside from what I've seen on TV'. And I thought, like, these are … they're obviously the people that are going to become … are gonna be delivering the therapy.
>
> (MAC-UK staff member)

Within statutory mental health services, views of marginalised young people are often one-dimensional, based upon dominant societal narratives (Turnbull, 2016). Such views can, inadvertently, further marginalise, pathologising individual responses to structural forces such as poverty and racial inequality (Turnbull & Spence, 2011). In addition, beyond mental health services, many of the narratives perpetuated around marginalised young people are created and upheld by those with little direct contact. Therefore, to create a ripple effect across policy and service provision, services and practitioners are in a position to use the power they hold to challenge discriminatory narratives and 'thicken' alternative, subjugated stories about young people (White, 2003), both inside and outside the workplace.

Practitioners also have a responsibility to interrogate not only the preconceived ideas others may hold, but their own prejudices. For example, it is understood that the media can be powerful in shaping conceptions, particularly if they are the sole forms of exposure (Ford, 1997). Since people from marginalised groups are frequently portrayed in the media as largely one-dimensional, devoid of visible family lives, or problematic in other ways, they are, to some extent, denied full humanity (Entman & Rojecki, 2000; Tucker, 2009). Similarly, the disproportionate representation of Black men on the news has been said to reinforce negative stereotypes, positioning them as violent, untrustworthy and threats to society (Aubrun et al., 2005; Entman & Rojecki, 2000). The absence of contextual explanations, including any underlying or structural reason for the circumstances of some young people, can promote these discriminatory views further (Entman & Gross, 2008), providing real-life repercussions including in mental health provision.

As well as being upheld by wider society, these narratives can also be internalised by young people, particularly during adolescence where identity and critical-thinking skills are still developing (Marin & Halpern, 2011). A strengths-focussed approach and ongoing involvement of youth voice is therefore vital, as is the need for systemic change. Without denying young people's agency MAC-UK advocates the use of a systemic, intersectional lens, aware of the ways race, class, gender can intersect to exclude young people from services, whilst simultaneously exacerbating their trauma (Sweeney et al., 2018; Woodall et al., 2010). Therefore an alternative, preventative approach to mental health support is fundamental.

25.3 MAC-UK

Across the years that MAC-UK has existed, it has evolved and developed practice in response to the needs of the young people, communities and services that it works alongside, moving from initial co-produced partnership projects with young people to disseminating work alongside existing voluntary and statutory organisations. Core across all of MAC-UK's work has been co-production with socially excluded young people that recognises that they hold the solutions to the challenges that services face. We will provide a short introduction to the earlier projects, and how MAC-UK currently operates.

25.3.1 A Brief History

MAC-UK was born out of a recognition that traditional approaches to mental health care were not serving marginalised young people, and therefore the need to go to where people were physically, rather than providing individual therapy in clinic spaces. MAC-UK's original project, Music and Change (later shortened to MAC-UK) was set up in the borough of Camden alongside young people. Later projects each had their own name; named by the young people who were employed as part of the project, or were attending early on in a project's development. Within each of these, young people identified activities that would support them and their peers to progress, and to make changes to their community. They were then supported to co-produce these activities, including working on logistics, costings, risk assessment, risk management, facilitation and evaluation, and dissemination where possible.

The topic of mental health was present throughout the projects, seen as part of what enables us all to progress, and in exploring barriers to general wellbeing. Those who attended the projects learnt about mental health as a contextual idea, impacted by wider circumstances and woven into the way we are viewed and treated in society. Individual mental health was discussed if it was raised, from informal conversations whilst planning activities to more formal sessions where this was a preference. Of the four initial projects, two projects ran in Camden, one in Peckham, and one in Haringey. From these four projects, other projects developed and received funding, led by the needs identified through the work and often led by young people who were employed or attending the project.

Projects ran increasingly in partnership with local authorities and NHS Trusts as well as the Police and other local organisations. While staff may have been employed in the project by different organisations, they were seen as one team, along with young people. Leads from the organisations sat on operational and steering groups, met regularly and co-developed governance, risk management and HR processes that would reflect the project's approach, which in turn impacted on their own organisations.

25.3.2 MAC-UK Today

In line with MAC-UK's approach of being flexible and responsive to the ongoing needs of young people, communities and services, in response to the changing sociopolitical and economic landscape and the learning from previous projects, the work and focus of MAC-UK continues to evolve. Since the earlier days of developing co-produced partnership projects offering direct interventions with young people in their communities, MAC-UK's practice and positioning has changed to where it is today, with current core components being dissemination, public health and prevention, and youth employment. The vision is to continue to see a society where marginalised young people inspire and lead the solutions to inequality and it is understood that improving mental health is best achieved outside a clinic, and at the core are values of co-production, relationships, lived experience and equality. The MAC-UK team is made up of people with expertise across youth work, public health, psychotherapy and psychology and vitally many have lived experience of the areas worked across (e.g. mental health issues, discrimination, youth violence, accessing statutory and community services). A short summary of MAC-UK's current work follows.

Dissemination: Often, third-sector organisations receive short-term funding, build good relationships with young people and communities and do really important work. However due to the instability of the funding streams, these projects may need to close and can potentially cause harm by replicating the pattern of services engaging then terminating relationships with young people. Moreover, there are many incredible organisations, services and practitioners rooted in communities who are working with young people, who already hold strong relationships. The work has therefore evolved to disseminate and embed learning within other organisations through meaningful partnerships (e.g. with local authorities, NHS, universities and third-sector organisations), teaching and training opportunities, training placements for people training to work in mental health and offering consultation to other organisations. MAC-UK's approach to dissemination is in line with the INTEGRATE model – a collaborative approach that was developed through direct co-produced projects alongside young people, and guides inclusive practice for those who are so called 'hard to reach' (see later for a full description of the model). Broadly, the approach involves making sure time is spent getting to know the organisation/service/community and building meaningful relationships in order to understand the challenges, gaps and ways in which MAC-UK's learning might support these organisations. From there, embedded in other teams, MAC-UK collaborates on the aims of the work together, to implement and share the INTEGRATE model to embed co-production, psychologically informed environments and youth employment.

Youth Employment: MAC-UK continues to employ young people within the organisation, many of whom are introduced to MAC-UK through partner organisations. Employing young people makes a difference to their material reality, as well as supporting people to participate in creating real social change that has a meaningful and lasting impact. MAC-UK offers wrap-around support, project management skills and work with young people to amplify their voices in places from which they are usually excluded.

Public Health and Prevention (PHP): PHP was developed to support MAC-UK articulate its strategic aims and objectives regarding influencing policy and addressing the underlying social, systemic and legislative issues that impact the young people and the systems worked with. PHP aims to work with young people to support them to articulate the challenges they face, and advocate for them in the decision-making processes that they are often excluded from, as well as working in more conventional policy-influencing ways, such as engaging with stakeholders through forums (e.g. The Alliance for Youth Justice), speaking at conferences and teaching students about public health approaches to mental health.

MAC-UK's work in a legislative setting includes attending policy influencing spaces, responding to calls for evidence and contributing to white papers, as well as collaborating with other organisations and the young people they work with to articulate a collective position on a particular government agenda or decision (e.g. over-policing or media representation of young people).

25.3.3 MAC-UK's INTEGRATE Model

The INTEGRATE model developed through learning what worked for young people when working alongside them in the four delivery projects, whilst also drawing on psychological and youth work knowledge of staff members (Zlotowitz et al., 2016). This approach consists of principles that the young people believed were essential for meaningful work. The model continues to evolve alongside the work of the organisation. INTEGRATE is an approach that guides the delivery of interventions that create change at multiple levels of our social environments. It outlines ways to co-produce services with those who have lived experience of the issues that are trying to be addressed, as well as offering guidance to those offering direct support to young people.

This section outlines the process of an INTEGRATE project or piece of work (Figure 25.1) and demonstrates how the INTEGRATE principles are part of this process (Figure 25.2).

In each project the stages shown in Figure 25.1 were followed, though rather than following in order, multiple stages could occur at different times, or simultaneously. A little more detail of each stage is given, with examples shared by staff, including those who were formerly young people attending one of the projects.

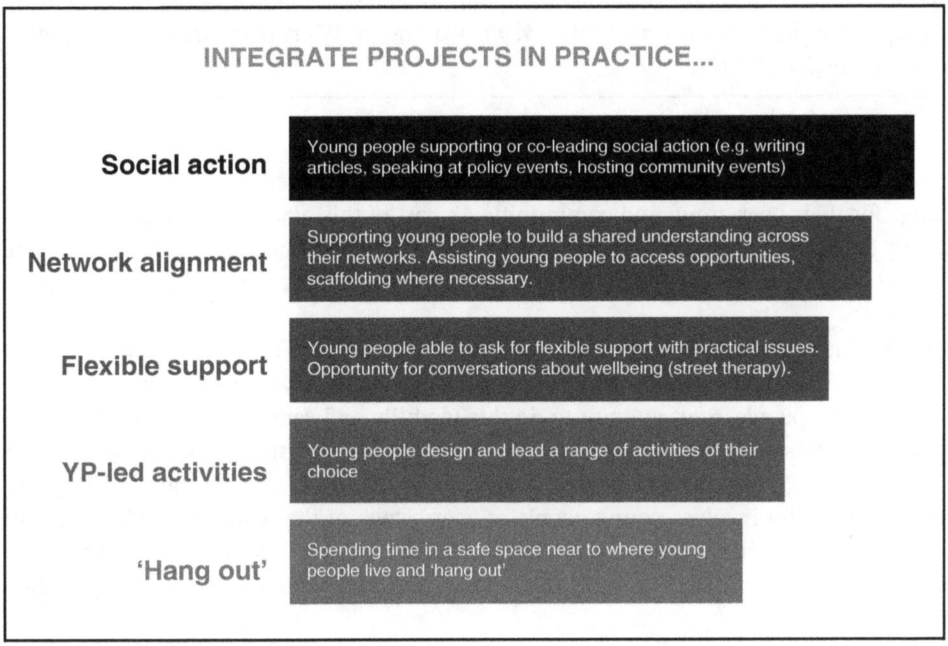

Figure 25.1 INTEGRATE project process.

INTEGRATE PRINCIPLES
(AN ASSET-BASED APPROACH)

SERVICE LEVEL	PRACTICE LEVEL
1. Harness experts by experience	1. Everything is an opportunity
2. Take services to young people	2. Ask for young people's help
3. Create flexible and responsive services	3. Do 'with' young people, and not 'for'
4. Co-produce services with excluded and 'vulnerable' young people and partners	4. Be empathic, non-judgmental and share dilemmas
5. Address people in context	5. Adopt a 'not-knowing' and curious position
6. Build meaningful partnerships	6. We are a team and we work as one
7. Work at multiple levels of the system	7. We deliver what we promise and don't promise what we can't deliver
8. Build psychologically informed systems	8. From the eyes of the young person
9. Focus on and build resources and resiliencies	9. 'I could lose my job' - boundaried stance
10. Evidence-based working and evaluation	10. What needs changing around us?

Figure 25.2 INTEGRATE principles.

'Hang Out': To reach those who are most excluded, the MAC-UK approach is to go out to where young people are and offer a flexible, responsive and holistic service that goes beyond just providing one-to-one therapy. This means working out in communities, or other settings that are not clinics.

> How did you first come across MAC-UK?
> *OK. Two clinical psychologists who walked around the area, wanting to get to know the youth. At first, there were suspicions from a lot of young people who assumed that they were police officers. Wondering what....Yeah, two, I guess. White man, white woman, plain clothes – definitely CID.*

Young Person-led Activities: Young people are then asked for their help to make change for their peer group and community. As part of this, young people alongside staff identify opportunities for change, and young people then co-produce (design, develop and lead) all or part of these activities. Further examples of this are given in the 'Principles' section.

Whether it be through informal conversation, paid feedback sessions or more formally embedded co-production frameworks, there are a myriad of ways of gathering the perspectives of young people. Staff attempt to do this tactfully and sensitively, not attempting to claim full understanding of a community they are not a part of, nor to take the suggestions of young people from them and apply them simply as they see fit. Rather, where possible, co-production involves young people at every stage of the work, throughout service development and delivery, welcoming their voices at every level. Rewarding young people for their input is another important way to share power, placing 'equal' value upon their contributions.

> What happened next?
> *I recall daily and for weeks on end, they ventured into the more dangerous parts of the area behind the estate etc., but not being afraid to be vulnerable. They were consistent on their side, to say the least. Forever inquiring (but not getting much reception) and trying to figure out what it was missing for young people, how they could be supportive; on the flip how they needed young people's help in creating something – an opportunity to make a difference within our area and support our community.*
>
> How did it progress from there?
> *Eventually, one or two young people decided to hear them out. Gave them a shot to really see what they had to say. Early interactions were happening in a local cafe, KFC or on the street. Anywhere a young person felt comfortable and flexible.*

Flexible Support: Whilst working on young person-led activities, conversations are varied, ranging from practical support with housing, employment and education to mental health and wellbeing, to heated debates about sport, music and food. These conversations are all welcomed, and take place in spaces that have been identified as comfortable for the young people. Mental health is seen as impacted by wider factors (such as economic stability, social status or experiences of discrimination) and is considered to be one aspect of the whole person, rather than the sole focus.

What was it like being in the project?

Our backgrounds being predominantly Afro Caribbean and Irish, growing up with 'tough love' and a lot of stigma around mental health and opening up about yourself, not being allowed to be vulnerable and how that was a sign of weakness being a theme for the majority of young people who participated... but something about having the space to do that, without judgement, encouraged others to do so. A real sense of trust and a rapport was built through/off the back of that. For us to share a little bit about our stories and who we were and learn obviously about who they are, conversations around mental health and wellbeing was new and a breath of fresh air for so many of us coming from where we were from.

Network Alignment: Staff assist young people to access opportunities, scaffolding this where needed. Young people work with staff to build a shared understanding across their network, reducing duplication, unnecessary referrals, and potentially diverting costly crisis management resources to the voluntary and community sector, focusing on prevention rather than reaction.

If a young person was involved in more than one service or organisation, staff would coordinate shared meetings where, in whatever way the young person was comfortable, a plan would develop for future support. For example, probation requirements could be met through holding meetings at the project where they could work together on something that the young person had shared an interest in, rather than having to juggle a lot of different appointments in different places.

Social Action: Staff then look for opportunities for young people where they can experience that they have the knowledge, the skills, the power and the support to engage in social action and create social change. This occurs in part through the structure of the project, including through collaboratively developing activities, being peer researchers, paid members of the staff team or being invited to consultation sessions. It also occurs through the change young people make to local and national policies and services, through creating different stories of young people in their community, setting up community events and connecting with local leaders (such as council leaders or MPs) to further the aims of the project.

Young people shared how they were often viewed negatively within their community, while also being viewed similarly negatively as a whole community by those in neighbouring areas and beyond. Through discussion, their passion for bringing the community together was shared. Young people worked together to create community days. They used their passion, contacts and skills to create days where young people and the wider community could express themselves, eat together and enjoy themselves. Young people took the opportunity to lead on different aspects such as leading street dance workshops with children, selling t-shirts that had been designed by young people as part of a connected local social enterprise, cooking and MCing, with young people showcasing their skills, while also developing new skills and gaining experiences. Local statutory partners were invited to attend, and experience a different version of the community and of the young people. These community days continue now. Others made films, facilitated local council events, co-delivered training sessions to statutory bodies, took council leaders on tours of their neighbourhoods or set up their own projects working with younger people in their communities.

This process attempts to transform traditional statutory mental health services for excluded and 'vulnerable' young people through disrupting systems leadership, delivering differently and disseminating ideas. Activities challenge harmful cultural and societal norms which perpetuate inequality and exclusion.

The INTEGRATE approach, as shown in Figure 25.2, consists of service- and practice-level principles that serve as a guide to develop services to deliver flexible and responsive provision, and also guide direct approaches with young people. These principles inform how a young person, service or community is approached and leave room for the work to be co-produced in collaboration with others to influence change at multiple levels. In response to the focus of this book, the focus below is on practice-level principles.

25.3.4 INTEGRATE Practice-level principles

Everything is an Opportunity: Every interaction is seen as an opportunity to engage in the work; by building a respectful and trusting relationship. When practitioners see *everything* as an *opportunity*, they open themselves up to the possibility of learning from challenging situations, for creating a lens through which they look for what is possible within the current context. For example, in situations when a young person is opposed to a policy or a rule, one can use the opportunity to think about why the rule is there, think about the impact of the rule on the system, and consider with the young person if the rule needs to be thought about more, adapted and/or explained differently.

If a young person disengages, this is an opportunity to actively seek feedback and improve skills in offering services that are relevant and meet their needs, or respond to the reasons that have been discovered. MAC-UK practitioners find that often, even with the most negative feedback and in situations where 'things didn't work', there are very important lessons to be learnt that can help the team in their work for the future. Practising this principle with young people can help them and practitioners re-evaluate their situations, without denying the challenges, supporting their ability to continue growing despite adversities.

Ask for Young People's Help: Asking for young people's help has been one of the most engaging ways to initiate and build meaningful and authentic connections with young people; they are the experts in their lives and have good ideas about what they need. Their ideas are always worth exploring first. Practitioners need to refrain from putting on the expert 'hat' and explaining their own experience. Acknowledging that the young person is the expert gives respect, ownership and empowerment. It is one of the ways to actively show that their views and experiences are valued. By turning help seeking on its head, young people can be supported to participate in the service more: they can make decisions about how the service is run, as well as be involved with youth-led activities. It also provides the opportunity for workers to show that they don't have all of the answers, and also need to ask for help at times, hopefully encouraging confidence for young people to, in turn, be more likely to ask for help.

Often, young people report that professionals and other adults in positions of power have told them what is best for them. By asking young people for their help, they developing more trust in their own autonomy and ability to make decisions. This also allows them to direct their lives in meaningful ways, whilst being validated by adults. For example, a young person previously affected by youth violence helped MAC-UK by co-designing and co-delivering training on 'gangs' for local services, leading to a very collaborative and meaningful piece of work.

Engaging young people meaningfully in responding to a challenge or opportunity requires time to plan, discuss and decide together. Although this approach can be slower, service delivery is more attuned to what young people need and therefore outcomes are generally significant. This also shifts the wider narrative around who is the 'problem', allowing young people to provide support, and not only be seen as 'requiring support'.

Do '*With*' Young People and Not 'For': We are taught that 'helping professions' step in and help out young people, often by taking action *for* them. At MAC-UK staff work to step back and take action *together*. This can be practised with the smallest steps, like making a phone call to a professional, school or work opportunity. Depending on their starting point, supporting a young person to make the telephone call and not doing it for them can be part of scaffolding their skills and autonomy.

Doing 'with' is often a new experience, which young people have shared feels empowering as it acknowledges they have something to offer. Alongside young people, staff can figure out what the problem is and collaborate to achieve a better outcome. For example, in a school settings when pupils have reported there are issues with teachers, staff do not talk directly to the teachers without the young person. Instead they think with the young person about how they could respond, with support. This may lead to arranging with the young person a space to meet together with the teachers. This way, young people have the opportunity express how they are feeling and how it is affecting them, without feeling that only adults can get heard. Young people are supported to participate in a way that they want to. This can include them co-hosting their own meetings, setting the agenda together, deciding on who should be invited or writing something to be read out. This can give the young person a boost in self-esteem, and gives further experience in utilising problem-solving skills. In the future young people are likely to feel more confident, knowing they have the skills to resolve other problems themselves or know who to ask.

Be Empathic, Non-judgemental and Share Dilemmas: Working alongside young people is about opening up conversations and demonstrating empathy for the person. Marginalised young people so often experience little empathy, with root causes of their circumstances not being considered and rather their 'behaviour' being judged; this different approach can be a first-time experience from professionals. Also, professionals often work together with other professionals when they have dilemmas working with young people. In this way of working it is good practice to share the dilemma directly with the person so they are actively aware and involved in moving forward. This builds confidence to help others, helps with sharing power in the relationship and promotes trust.

In every interaction with young people, active listening can open up conversations and promote a culture of empathy, understanding and transparency, building trust. If a young person presents something that the practitioner disagrees with, the practitioner aims to remain non-judgemental about their position. For example, if they are concerned about an interaction a young person had with their new relationship, they can invite them to think about it together. They can put it back to them: 'How is this working for you?' acknowledging they might have a different experience, different opinions and feelings about it. They can have a discussion about their concerns and ask their views on them. These are steps to open up dialogue, encouraging a meaningful discussion within a trusted relationship.

This stance can have more positive outcomes, rather than telling the young people what they should do, or pretending that there are straight answers to complex human experiences and relationships. This can model a process of talking through dilemmas, appreciating different perspectives and understanding others, which are valuable relational skills for young people and their networks. Young people say that this process makes them feel genuinely listened to and supported.

Adopt a Not Knowing and Curious Position: The team at MAC-UK are often positioned as experts, however staff are reminded to hold the position of 'not knowing' with others; being confident to share that they genuinely do not know. It is good practice to remember we do not ever fully know what is going on for a young person.

Taking an intentional position of 'not knowing' and curiosity also supports the notion that the young person is the expert in their lives and is likely to have some solutions to problems. This contributes to more authentic, genuine relationship building and opens up new conversations, where power is more shared.

MAC-UK usually gets the feedback that this helps young people warm to them more, and that being honest is very appreciated. This stance does not mean not having confidence in their professional competencies, practitioners do hold certain knowledges, they are experts in their expertise, but young people are the experts in their experiences and worlds: together, as a team, they are exploring the world, to change it meaningfully.

We are a Team and We Work as One: Practitioners and young people are a team. It is more helpful to move away from divisions of them and us, 'professionals and patients' and focus on the common values and goals. In MAC-UK, young people and staff are part of the team and so they make decisions based on what is good for the whole team. MAC-UK staff and young people think together about how to address the challenges the young people face. Emphasis is put on the fact that help is sought and provided by the whole team. The success or not of any intervention, piece of work and effort is a reflection of everyone's contributions and reflections.

Choosing not to turn the young people into 'others' within services can be a new experience, and of course means a change in organisational ethos and language. It is important to acknowledge that there can be challenges in getting professionals from different contexts and different viewpoints to work together 'as a team' with young people. Sometimes because of systemic pressures there can be unhelpful exchanges, when the role is to work together to advocate and support young people. Practitioners bridging young people in to work as a team should consider what support the 'system' or professionals need to be ready for this approach.

We Deliver What We Promise and Don't Promise What We Can't Deliver: When working with young people who have often been let down by society at large, and professionals they have encountered, it is crucial to only promise what is possible – it is important to not commit to something that cannot be guaranteed to be delivered.

This helps to build trust and consistency within relationships and prevents the repetitive experience of being let down by professionals or those in positions of power. It shows respect for the person. It can be challenging to say no when you want to help and are enthusiastic about supporting positive outcomes; it can lead to professionals not feeling like they're doing a good-enough job. In the moment, it can lead to disappointment for who you are working with, however, it gives a different experience of being offered something that doesn't get followed through. Talking about what can be put in place can help develop a trusting relationship. Following through with any agreed action improves the working relationship and demonstrates that the practitioner is reliable.

From the Eyes of the Young Person: This relates to always thinking and asking how a young person might interpret what has been said or why they might be behaving in a certain way. MAC-UK emphasises implementing this principle at every level of a system; consistently trying to think from a young person's perspective, their ideas and view of the world.

This includes bringing the perspective of young people to professional settings if they are absent from the room, for example, if they are being spoken negatively about, 'What would x say if they were here?' 'What else is going on which means x can't get here on time?' Thinking from a young person's perspective can help people you are working with to think about other people's perspectives. This can help shift 'stuckness' in moving forward. It can build skills in mentalising others (being curious about someone else's perspective and actions).

I could lose my job – Boundaried Stance: It is important to support young people to understand the reason why practitioners work with boundaries, and the impact of respecting them for everyone involved in the work. Being clear about professional boundaries and sticking to them, and ensuring young people understand why those boundaries are in place, is the cornerstone of forming respectful working relationships. Often young people are informed about boundaries, but not the reasons for them, both professional and personal.

Being open and engaging in dialogue about rules and boundaries removes this from a personal realm and judgement, and fosters an understanding of consequences. This can help young people make informed decisions and have a different relationship to boundaries. For example, if you are working with a young person and they ask your views on whether drugs should be legal, or why they can't meet up with you in a bar on a Saturday night, you can invite reflection on such issues, considering why the boundary/law is in place, what consequences it would have on your life or your role if they are not adhered to, and what society at large might say about the issues being discussed.

What Needs Changing Around Us?: When there are issues faced by young people, families and services, often the solutions are only focused on how young people should change – it is imperative to shift the focus to find what can change around the young people. For young people to be agents of change and feel empowered to make changes for themselves, practitioners need to consider how to encourage them into looking for changes around them.

Young people often bring issues affecting them in their lives, and are used to a relationship with adults and professionals where they take over and solve the problem, or be resolved that no change is possible, believing '*it is what it is*'. For example, if a young person is expressing a problem with a service they have received, how can you work with them to identify what change might be possible? Young people can be very helpful in assessing issues and problems in the way services are run, and they can be very helpful to problem solve, suggest innovative ideas and solutions that meet their needs.

It can be easier to find what needs changing, but finding what steps young people need to take in order to make those changes can require a longer route. For example, if they find discriminatory ideas being shared by a teacher, MAC-UK would work together with young people to consider what can be done about it, who would take which action and how they would evaluate the outcome. It is empowering to young people to do something about it themselves and realise they are their own agents of change.

Box 25.1 provides a description of some work at one of the projects, where several aspects of both the process and the principles are demonstrated.

Box 25.1 INTEGRATE example

One area of interest identified by a young person involved in the project was fitness, health and the gym. This interest was coupled with a lack of opportunity in the area for young people to access gyms and gym memberships, which was having an impact on their wellbeing. An idea from the young person was to co-create a space that could fill this gap. In particular, a gym space was seen as beneficial as it would give an opportunity for young people to build their strength and knowledge about physical appearance and health, as well as building confidence and self-esteem. This idea was shared with professionals and young people involved in the project and there was broad agreement that there was an issue in the local area.

From this, the project team and young people began co-designing a project that could be a gym space for young people. A mapping phase with all members included considering the budget, contacting the Sports Centres, understanding gym memberships options, getting a sense internally about who would be interested in using the space and using memberships, gym training days/time slots, workout regime/structures and how to rotate gym passes so other young people were included. A local space was found and a relationship established with an understanding of the purpose of the project. The project began rolling out and young people were engaging and interested from the start. The space ran about three times a week and involved sessions being facilitated by the young people (e.g. focusing on particular muscle groups). Practitioners would also take part in sessions with young people, where conversations about mental health and what it personally meant to each young person were started. Crucially, the space reinforced the idea that therapy could be taken out of a clinic and a safe place to offload stressful 'life stuff'. A key part of the space was the flexibility to support young people about whatever was coming up in their life. For example, housing issues, criminal justice system issues and education issues. Young people felt safe to bring those issues into the space, which built trust between the young people and the professionals. It provided a place to be transparent and open about their experiences and helped break down the stigma around talking about mental health.

For the young people involved in the gym project, this was a new chance to do something positive and meaningful and to co-produce something from the ground up, based on their passions and interests. Being involved in all phases gave a sense of ownership over the project, which was a different experience for many of the young people and their interactions with services. Specifically, it provided an opportunity to create, develop, project manage and improve communication skills, time keeping as well as build confidence. The project ran for over the course of about 6 months, which taught dedication and consistency for those involved, as well as being involved in something where they were accountable and could see outcomes (e.g. meeting at said location at set time or space would be taken up).

The project adopted a peer-referral model, which meant that young people could bridge their network or friends into the project without formal paperwork and forms but based on word of mouth and personal contact. Having peers involved gave an established connection for people to motivate one another, especially people with perhaps less experience, to reach their goals and spark their interest. It also allowed people not to immediately dive in, but maybe dip their toe in gradually. This flexible project was a new asset in the area that gave a different place and space for young people to go and to get off the streets.

The impact of the project was that young people began to feel more confident with their appearance and fitness. They became more conscious and aware of both their physical and mental wellbeing and both professionals and young people developed ways of communicating about their mental health and experiences and new relationships. As well as this, the gym sparked a passion for some young people to pursue training as a hobby post-project or look into a career as a Fitness Instructor or Personal Trainer.

At the project a whole variety of other activities took place. They all harnessed or developed young people's skills, including street art talents. For example, after collectively naming the project, looking through numerous sketched logo ideas drafted by a street artist, then cohesively deciding on the final product, there was a paid opportunity to design/spray paint the logo inside the space. Young people had learnt about typography in school but not realised there was a potential career that could come out of it. Instead of being forced to 'vandalise street properties', this small project sparked the desire to take their ideas to local small businesses and actually build a brand.

25.4 Examining the Evidence Base

It is important to look at the evidence base for supporting practitioners and services to implement alternative ways of working, and to guide safe and effective services for children and young people. Therefore, this section is a critical exploration[2] and appraisal of how research, and health and social care publications connect with youth community practice along with evidence from MAC-UK's own research evaluations.

25.4.1 Examining Traditional Guidelines

Traditionally, mental health care for children and young people has been commissioned on a 1:1 or family basis, either in community or in-patient settings, and guidelines for support are provided to 'treat' individual problems (e.g. depression, anxiety). Guidelines, such as those provided by the National Institute of Health and Care Excellence (NICE) are drawn upon to inform service delivery, and though are intended only as guidance to be used alongside client choice and practitioner expertise, they are often the only guidance used to inform what services deliver. Historically, and currently, this is traditionally individual psychological therapies such as cognitive behavioural therapy, and/or medication, and change is measured by a reduction in 'symptoms' or behaviour the person is experiencing or exhibiting. Moreover, the evidence that such interventions draw on are not representative of all children and young people or the realities of complex lives, networks and societies; change is measured by statistical rather than clinical or personal significance and interventions may be considered as superior to alternative, non-westernised, community-based approaches. Though such interventions and evidence has its place, this model is largely deficit based, placing both the problem and solutions within individuals and ignoring the powerful role that context and societal factors play in influencing mental health.

What do NICE Guidelines and International Practice-Based Evidence say about Youth and Community-Based Practice?: NICE guidelines (NICE, 2016, 2021) provide guidance for engaging communities, and working with excluded young people, for example children in care. On an individual level, a core part of the guidance about working with young people advises practitioners to focus more on being part of positive relationships, and less on traditional therapeutic interventions that prioritise reducing symptoms (NICE, 2021). Although relationship-based approaches require more resources in the short term (e.g. flexible practitioners who are able to offer informal support at times when it is most useful to young people), they promote engagement and help prevent increased distress in the long term (NICE, 2021). Central principles of NICE's (2021) relationship-based guidance include listening in a non-judgemental way, consistently trying to understand the context of young people's behaviour and communicating fair boundaries. These principles are underpinned by a focus on promoting young people's agency through shared decision making, and showing genuine care (NICE, 2021).

So, how can practitioners apply these relationship-based principles? NICE guidance (2021) advises helping young people to build their identity, skills and relationships by

2 MAC-UK encourages critical engagement with all 'evidence' to question who the research informing this is based on and who it is for, as well as which groups may not have been included in research.

supporting them to pursue their interests and says that this will not require significant resources from services as there are existing projects that young people can be signposted to. This perspective could be seen as having flaws; ignoring how existing projects may have been designed without meaningful input from a diverse range of young people, making them less accessible, particularly to marginalised groups. For practitioners in areas without accessible existing projects, practitioners could make it part of their therapeutic work to help groups of young people to realise their ideas about the kinds of activities they want to engage in.

Another aspect of the NICE (2021) relationship-centred guidance is supporting young people to form and maintain positive relationships with others. The value of friendships and mentoring relationships is highlighted, particularly with peers who have had similar life experiences. Whilst this appreciates the strengths that exist within communities, there appears to be an assumption that mentoring relationships will inevitably be voluntary and informal (and therefore come at no extra cost to services). Although it is important to consider communities' existing resources (see asset-based approaches: Foot & Hopkins, 2010; Rippon & Hopkins, 2015) and challenge the 'expert' position often assumed within mental health services, in the context of the significant spending cuts implemented by successive UK governments from 2010, it is crucial that services take opportunities to re-distribute their funding and support communities to build upon their own resources. As excluded young people face particular barriers to accessing employment (Durcan et al., 2017), services that attempt to work alongside communities by offering paid mentoring opportunities could be especially useful.

At an organisational level, NICE guidance (2016) advises that services should invest resources in building trusting relationships with community members, enabling their involvement in designing and delivering interventions. The guidance acknowledges the need to continually ensure that collaborative work is accessible to all groups within the local population, particularly groups that do not currently access services (e.g. by working in an accessible location, or by using multiple methods of communication). Despite efforts towards inclusivity, NICE (2016) suggests that community members should work with services in a 'non-professional capacity'. In a similar way to their assumption that mentoring relationships will inevitably be voluntary, this raises questions about a commitment to equal partnerships between services and communities.

On a societal level, NICE guidance (2016, 2021) notes the specific need to involve under-served communities in designing wellbeing interventions. The content states that many young people come from groups that experience additional disadvantages, advising practitioners about the importance of meeting the needs of those from marginalised groups, in order to avoid further exclusion. Although this connects with the respect for diversity that is central to MAC-UK, NICE (2021) undermines this connection by arguing that the attention and expertise required to prevent further marginalisation will not incur significant additional cost. This overestimates the inclusivity of existing mental health services and under-estimates the systemic changes that are needed to move towards equitable access. Without institutions making the argument for systemic change, there is even more onus upon individual practitioners to seek out their own learning about how to practise in a way that minimises further exclusion for people from marginalised groups.

25.4.2 Health and Social Care Policies

Discussions about involving excluded communities in service design and delivery have been present in health and social care policies and legislation over the past 10 years (NHS England, 2014, 2017; Social Care Institute for Excellence, 2015). Recently, the *NHS Long Term Plan* (NHS, 2019) advocates innovation within psychological services, and the need for stronger action on prevention and health inequalities across the NHS. Autonomy has long been seen by researchers as an important component of wellbeing (see self-determination theory: Ryan and Deci, 2000), with wellbeing associated with the level of power or control that people have over their lives (National Collaborating Centre for Mental Health [NCCMH], 2019). Therefore, by sharing power with those accessing mental health services, and with excluded community members for whom services are inaccessible, co-production is a potential intervention that could play a role in both addressing health inequalities and preventing/reducing distress.

Although discussion about involving communities is present within policies and legislation, the extent to which they advocate for genuine co-production is questionable. For example, The Care Act (UK Government, 2014) uses the term co-production, but talks about communities influencing services, rather than working in equal partnerships, perhaps associated with the more tokenistic forms of 'involvement' or 'consulting' (Arnstein, 1969; also see 'Ladder of Engagement', University Hospitals of Leicester [UHL] NHS Trust, 2019). This finding is reflected in reviews of patient and public involvement across various NHS Trusts in Scotland in which the most commonly reported form of involvement was patient satisfaction questionnaires, with practitioners considering this a form of co-production (Forbat et al., 2009, cited in NCCMH, 2019). This form of 'tokenism' or 'consulting' (Arnstein, 1969; also see "Ladder of Engagement", UHL NHS Trust, 2019) is different from co-production as professionals retain power by seeking feedback about things that they have already designed, and excludes people who are not engaging with services, significantly limiting the extent to which services can become more accessible and challenge health inequalities.

Though there is an increasing emphasis on co-production, understandably, trainees or recently qualified practitioners may feel a lack of ability or limited power to influence their service when it comes to co-production, particularly if the institution itself has limited focus on this approach. However, one should be encouraged and supported by the notion that NHS England's (2017) patient and public participation policy encourages all staff to have a 'role to play in strengthening patient and public participation in our work, both individually and collectively. All staff are responsible for considering the need for patient and public participation in their work and undertaking this as appropriate' (p. 7).

Whilst managers have a responsibility to shape team cultures that embed meaningful forms of community participation, all practitioners have the potential to include communities in their work (see Chapter 9 for further examples of this in practice) (NHS England & NHS ICPC, 2020).

25.4.3 Impact of Co-production Approaches

While it is important to acknowledge that true co-production is not always the easiest route, research has found evidence of wide-ranging positive effects on practitioner wellbeing, including confidence for developing new peer relationships, increased employability, higher levels of practitioner empathy and reduced rates of depression (New Economics Foundation, 2013; What Works Wellbeing, 2017; for further discussion of the evidence base, see Chapter 9).

At a service level, although co-production can be seen as a risk because it requires an initial investment of planning and resources, it has been linked to services being more cost-effective, and having better satisfaction and health outcomes in the long term due to being better aligned with the needs of communities (Barker, 2010; Charles et al., 2018). Co-produced mental health services (e.g. Croydon Service User Network) have been found to help people develop the skills necessary to reduce their use of acute services, and to work with community leaders (e.g. in churches or mosques) to help communities reduce stigma around mental health (New Economics Foundation, 2013).

Despite these promising findings, the research literature about the impact of co-production is small (New Economics Foundation, 2013). Funding for more high-quality research is needed to improve understanding of the links with individual wellbeing, and to investigate further the impact on wellbeing at a community level (NCCMH, 2019). To be most effective, co-production needs to be clearly understood throughout a team, so practitioners talking about the impact that it can have can play an important role in helping further this kind of work (NCCMH, 2019).

25.4.4 MAC-UK's Contribution to the Evidence Base

MAC-UK has contributed to the growing evidence base of co-produced, community-based mental health work with young people and has been cited as best practice in several government and policy reports (see https://mac-uk.org/publications-and-evidence/). Four of the initial projects that MAC-UK co-produced with young people were independently evaluated by the Centre for Mental Health. Findings indicated that young people's wellbeing improved across their time engaging with the projects (e.g. see Durcan et al., 2017; Stubbs & Durcan, 2017) and included a more positive view of self, an ability to be more open and to see issues from different perspectives, and the development of skills such as emotional regulation, communication and teamwork (Durcan et al., 2017; Stubbs & Durcan, 2017). Young people also reported that being engaged in positive activities led them to feel safer, and therefore less in need of taking measures to protect themselves (e.g. carrying a knife) (Durcan et al., 2017; Stubbs & Durcan, 2017). Young people, the Police and other community stakeholders all perceived a reduction in offending behaviour (Durcan et al., 2017; Stubbs & Durcan, 2017).

Important indicators of young people becoming more open and developing skills included them going on to access other services (e.g. health, housing, benefits), as well as opportunities in education, employment or training (Durcan et al., 2017; Stubbs & Durcan, 2017). Moreover, by bridging young people into other services and professionals, there was more likelihood of forming useful relationships with other professionals and on the other side of this 'bridge' other professionals trusted young people more because their engagement in the project helped humanise the participants, seeing them as less 'dangerous' (Durcan et al., 2017; Stubbs & Durcan, 2017). The impact that one project had upon wider professional systems was further evidenced by the rollout of co-production and service-user involvement within the local authority and NHS trusts (Stubbs & Durcan, 2017). Other projects supported young people to influence national policy, engaging with the Home Office to successfully advocate for an increased focus on mental health within plans to address youth violence (Durcan et al., 2017).

25.5 Addressing Challenges of Working in Community-based Approaches

Working with young people in a turbulent sociopolitical and economic climate, in a way that sits outside a mainstream individual therapeutic approach can be challenging to navigate.

This is an essential area to explore and MAC-UK takes opportunities to learn and adapt through challenges, these will always be present and need constant attention from any professional working alongside communities. Below are some of the common challenges that come along with the work, alongside ideas of how these can be navigated and explored.

25.5.1 Engagement – Working Outside Your Comfort Zone

> I always think about how the context of maybe supporting young people, has changed dramatically, even from say, when, when I was a young person. I feel as though sometimes a challenge could be having a knowledge of the intersectional experiences of adolescents in today's world where technology is a big thing, and there are other big themes that can probably be quite hard to go on a course and learn about...
>
> (MAC-UK staff member)

MAC-UK's work has historically been alongside young people and communities that have been marginalised by society and institutions, and who rightly have, at times, been hesitant to trust or engage with services and professionals and who have generously brought our attention to the inherent challenges of professionals attempting to work alongside them. Therefore, working with young people in any capacity as a member of the systems that young people interact with, requires an understanding and acceptance that young people might be suspicious of people representing these systems, as it is so often these systems that have harmed them in the first place. Working to address this will mean being outside your comfort zone some of the time. Young people will challenge those around them, they will question decisions, and encourage those working with them to think differently.

There is no one singular way to describe, accurately, how to work with young people. In this group there are endlessly different personalities, experiences, attitudes and talents, as well as an immeasurable amount of potential to change society for the better. Working flexibly requires taking time to ask questions, to try to understand their perspective, and to support them with articulating what they need.

Working with Difference: Professionals in UK mental health systems are not often from a similar demographic to the young people that services try to interact with; of course young people are not a monolith and neither are those that work with them. However there tends to be a broad difference between those mental health professionals and the communities that often require greater levels of mental health support (whether they access them or not). This means that if professionals enter a community from a background or social identity that is different to those with which they work, it is essential that they are willing to leave some of their sensibilities behind. This isn't to say that middle-class, white professionals shouldn't hold the values they might have, or work within different communities (in fact it is important that they do), but that they should be prepared to learn from the people they are working with. If a practitioner is not from a community that has experienced significant disadvantages, then they shouldn't pretend. Don't feel sorry for people, though continue to empathise and try to understand.

> That idea of not being part of communities and being curious and not knowing and all of that, but also just **knowing when you're just not the right person to do the work**, you know, for whatever reason that might be, maybe not just assuming it is you, because young people might have connections to other people that you could support in your, you know, using your skills whatever they might be. **And not taking that personally**, as well as, like, doing your own learning about the community, if you're not a part of it, and listening when it's your place to listen. Also just not being, not carrying that sense of difference with you the whole time, and being paralyzed with it, and knowing that there will be similarities as well as differences.
>
> (MAC-UK staff member)

The fact that community and youth practitioners are more likely to work with communities that require a greater level of mental health support by virtue of their class position, requires an understanding of inequality (Wilkinson & Pickett, 2010). This requires practitioners to be able to focus on the broad foundations of society and infrastructure of how society developed. It is essential to understand how and why the services that are in place are there, and the role they play in the ways in which society has been formed over the past few hundred years.

> Working in groups with young people takes guts, and those guts have got to be okay with being clueless most of the time. In a world that moves so fast, with the discourse pacing along, it is impossible to keep up, and you would be foolish to try. But ask questions, be curious, have jokes, bring joy into your work.
>
> (MAC-UK staff member)

Working in a truly young-person led way means ensuring their interests, language, ideas and ways of engaging are central to the work, which can leave practitioners feeling out of their depth, and not being able to keep up with youth culture. This can be different to how mental health professionals are traditionally trained, to be the 'experts' with the answers, and who will be continued to be positioned as such. This approach can take some 'unlearning', which can be challenging, but poses opportunities for new learning. Young people can be helpful in supporting this process of new learning. MAC-UK emphasises that it is a real strength to own 'not knowing', as outlined in the INTEGRATE approach, but recognise that this can feel uncomfortable for practitioners after training for so long, and being asked to know so much!

Position in the System: A further challenge is how practitioners position themselves, in between the young person and the services that might be trying to work with them. For example, a young person might not want social services' involvement in their lives, but safeguarding concerns means that there is no choice for them. This puts the practitioner in a position where, in the best interests of the young person, they have to act as both an advocate for the young person, articulating to the services involved what the young person needs, but also as a professional who is potentially going against the young person's wishes by working with social services. This is a difficult position to be in and requires delicacy to maintain an effective working relationship with both parties, and ensuring that they have a working relationship with each other. In this instance it is essential to truly listen to what the young person wants, not to force them into anything, but to try to understand where they are coming from and why they might be distrustful of the services involved in their lives.

There can be a disconnect between traditional ways that mental health services work (operating out of a therapy room, not being truly involved in the lives of the young people accessing support) and community work (being embedded in the lives of young people, being available to them and offering a place to go that doesn't necessarily look or feel like a mental health service). As an example, if the work is embedded in the community, then practitioners are committed to spending time within the environment that young people are faced with growing up; the service becomes a part of their lives, rather than a person behind a desk. If this is done well then young people come to trust the space that has been created, which in turn means they will reach out when things have got too much for them or when they are facing particular challenges in their lives. This is to say that the relationship is valued in a way that other relationships they may have with services aren't, which means they may be more forthcoming about what is going on with them. It is in these circumstances that some of the things they disclose can be challenging. The important thing is to remain as a trusted person in their lives, but to ensure that they are as safe as possible. This might mean that the practitioner might have to do things the young person doesn't want to be done, but if the thinking is done together and the process is one that values the relationship, then there is more chance the young person will come on the journey alongside the practitioner, rather than push them away. This is another challenge, what happens if the young person pushes the practitioner away? How can a relationship be repaired that might have been damaged because of a disclosure that had to be dealt with? It comes down to the consistency of, and respect within, the relationship. It doesn't always work, and dealing with rejection is something that, as a professional, it is important to come to terms with and explicitly get support with, as practitioners are people too! Young people might not always like the practitioner, especially if they can sense judgement rather than respect.

Working Inside 'the System': It is important to remember, even if there are challenges faced when working with individual young people, that there are wider systemic issues at play in everyone's lives (Bronfenbrenner, 1979). Therefore, some of the biggest challenges come from tackling issues at a structural level, rather than the issues that young people present with.

The systems with which young people are interacting: school, police, mental health, children's services and central government legislation, all exert pressure on them, sometimes forcing them to exist and operate outside the parameters of what we define as acceptable. Rarely do these systems operate in ways that attempt to understand the context in which young people exist and treat those who do operate outside these systems with compassion. These systems often fail to understand the realities of young people's lives, and instead operate as rigid, punitive forces. As a practitioner the job is often going to be bringing the young people, or at least their voices, into the room and trying to persuade the systems, and those that represent them, to work differently. It requires building relationships within these systems and convincing them of the efficacy of trying something new, potentially adjusting their position on risk for example, and more often than not to allow for time and care to be taken over supporting someone who is maybe making what are perceived as mistakes. Of course, the other challenge across the board is the resourcing of services, and the resourcing of services that are doing things differently, which can be done by forming meaningful relationships with commissioners, but also trying to help them to operate slightly away from the conventional 'key performance indicators' model of working.

Balancing Reflection and Action: MAC-UK understands the value of spending time to reflect, think together and ensure decisions are made with intention, and not simply reacting to a situation without proper consideration. However, this can be a huge challenge for a number of reasons; firstly because of the sometimes immediate nature of the situations young people are faced with, either by the systems around them (housing insecurity, for example) or by their individual personal circumstance (threat of violence, for example). To try to balance the need for time to be taken to think with the young person and to try to support them to learn the skills of reflection and consideration, with the sometimes non-negotiable need for action, can be extremely difficult. Additionally, too much time thinking can be a sign to young people that things aren't changing and that as practitioners we're not taking enough action to support changes to their environment. It is a balance to strike between reflection and action (Freire, 1972).

> A challenge that I've come upon, it's like, I guess it's the liberation psychology idea that, like of 'praxis', that balance between reflection and action. And I think it's a hard balance in terms of time, of how much time do you spend reflecting, how much time do you do action, and if there's lots of pressures maybe you're pulled towards action more and haven't done enough, like, thinking, or if you're doing too much thinking and not doing enough action, that's a problem as well.
>
> (MAC-UK staff member)

25.6 Evaluation

> When you work in different settings, you need, you need support and evidence to prove that this way of working, you know if you believe in it you might need to convince other people in your team or your manager, for example even just to go out of your office.
>
> (MAC-UK staff member)

To provide high-quality, effective and safe services for young people and sustain provision, evaluation is essential. Evaluation can be a further challenge of working in less- traditional ways. There are often multiple stakeholders who may be informed by different evaluation frameworks, targets and work demands, as well as ideas about what is perceived as a good 'outcome'.

Therefore, a similar flexible and responsive approach is required for evaluation that is bespoke for the intervention, project or service that has been offered. Mainstream 'evidence base' and intervention guidance documents for young people tend to draw on evaluations that favour manualised and prescriptive interventions. Often, research has been undertaken in controlled settings with unrepresentative and non-complex populations, and use outcome measures where change is represented by statistical significance, rather than a detailed understanding of how the interventions have improved someone's life or in areas that are meaningful for them (Guy et al., 2012; Hunsley, 2007; Kazdin, 2008; Mollon, 2009). Though these approaches have benefits, they are not sufficient at measuring flexible, co-produced and responsive service delivery that meet where people are at.

When evaluating community-based approaches that incorporate complex social issues and experiences of young people and communities, evaluation must acknowledge the multiple 'realities' that may exist within the work, and develop a framework that can capture an in-depth representation of such realities (Williams & Zlotowitz, 2013).

Given the complexities described, it is challenging to provide a one-size-fits-all approach to evaluation. Following are some ideas from MAC-UK's experience about evaluation principles.

> A common challenge of the work is what's the measure of success? That's going to be dissemination projects or working with a young person, yeah, what either party, or even us as a team or organisation, what we measure success as, and what's seen as meaningful work ... exploring being curious about what the meaningful outcome is, and what is the sustained, sustained intervention that we wanna co-create, yeah, and that takes, obviously we all know it takes time, and a lot of conversations.
>
> (MAC-UK staff member)

Start at the Beginning: Whether evaluating a small, individual/group piece of work or a larger-scale project that involves multiple services and young people, a core principle is to *start at the very beginning*. Though a meaningful approach, it is important to bear in mind that co-production with others can take a longer time for evaluation. Starting with the end in mind, factoring time and resources (including a budget) into the planning can support the development of evaluation. Thinking about evaluation at the start can also set the scene for ensuring that everyone is on the same page for the work and has a shared goal in the overall objectives. This can become a core feature of co-production and collaboration, as it is often the place where misunderstandings can be thought through.

Mapping out the stakeholders: However big or small, it can be useful to map out the stakeholders involved in evaluation to understand the needs of each. In this stage, you can find out what parameters can and can't be moved. For example, if a service has an existing evaluation measure that is required to be used for all work, this is crucial to know at the beginning, to understand how to include it or question its use. Crucially, within this process is the consideration of what young people hope to achieve from the work, in order to ensure this is built into the infrastructure of any evaluation – it is at this stage helpful conversations can occur about what is possible and what is not; make sure you don't promise what can't be delivered. Moreover, here agreements can be made not only about the evaluation, but the goals for the work, the needs of each person/group involved (including competing service demands if present), timeline, what is meaningful work and what measures of success people value, what the roles and responsibilities of each person involved are, what skills and resources people have to offer to evaluation, and what the gaps are.

Mutual benefits: As with any form of co-production, consideration of how the work can be mutually beneficial is imperative: What is it that young people can gain/develop from being a part of the work? It is important to continually consider power and equity within this process-, a balance of people's ideas and hopes and ensuring that where possible equity of access and benefit is underpinning the decisions. For example, where staff are being paid in the project or the work is part of their ongoing professional development, what consideration has been given to young people for payment/development? Many clinical research funding bodies outline standard pay rates for involvement of 'experts by experience' and these should be considered in project development, as a minimum benchmark.

Developing a Framework: A key part of a successful evaluation is a collaborative and robust framework. Here a decision can be made about what the key questions are and how they will be answered and measured. The main aims of evaluating interventions are to ensure that the impact of the work is understood, to implement service improvement, and to establish quality, safe and meaningful support for young people. Keeping these in mind, the framework will need to include consideration of how to evidence the outcome/impact of the work and how this will be measured: using qualitative information or quantitative data, or a combination? Collecting baseline information from which to compare future data points?

Co-Production: Co-production with young people and stakeholders/communities is at the core of evaluation; the work is most successful when people continue to work together and are included at each step of the way. It is important to acknowledge that this way of working can be challenging, slow, even frustrating at times. At times, a person may step out of co-production and be tempted to stride on and do their own thing. This is to be expected, but it's important to keep a check on who is leading/driving the work, whose decisions are being prioritised, whose demands are being centred and who is being left behind. Evaluations that are co-produced doesn't mean that everyone has to do the same amount or the same task; each person's contribution can look different and play to their strengths. Co-production brings creativity and enables the sharing of strengths and resources; you never know what could come of the process so embrace the journey.

Zooming In and Out: After embarking on the evaluation journey, it is helpful to have a balance of 'zooming in' on the details, making sure a person is checking in with the process, timeline and learning throughout the work, and 'zooming out', to keep connected to the wider aims and objectives of the work/evaluation to see if these are being achieved.

Sharing the Learning: An exciting part of evaluation is considering how learning can be shared. Co-production continues at this stage, and the more creative the better. The conversations at the beginning of the work included consideration of what each organisation/stakeholder might need, and these should inform dissemination of learning. This may take a more formal route such as a report evidencing the impact of your work. Even so, this can be done creatively drawing on the strengths and skills of the group working together. Remember that, although the work might feel small, others working in this area or other young people considering working alongside professionals may love to hear about it and it may encourage further progress in others' work. Consider the ways in which dissemination will have most impact: Which spaces and places do these people access? Do they read, listen to podcasts, access art/poetry? This can guide some creative ways to share the learning and messages that come from your collaborative and community-based working and projects; think outside the box.

25.7 Conclusion

In this chapter, MAC-UK has shared some context of their work across the past decade, working alongside young people and communities, with a critical review of the evidence base, to support the value of community-based approaches and co-production. Taking into consideration the economic, social and political contexts that continue to disproportionately affect marginalised communities and the impact on wellbeing and mental health, an alternative to individual, clinic-based mental health support is needed. MAC-UK's approach advocates locating the problems outside young people and in systems, and providing multi-levelled interventions that support people and communities, and contribute to systemic change.

Ultimately, there is no 'right' or perfect way to work with young people; the approach taken by MAC-UK advocates delivering flexible and responsive support, meeting people where they are at both emotionally and physically – taking support outside clinic spaces. The INTEGRATE approach encourages the co-production of services that young people access. This includes co-production with both young people who have the lived experience of the issues that services are trying to address, and professionals working within services; through collaboration, such change is possible.

Appreciating the ever increasing demands on public-sector workers, and those working to support young people struggling with their mental health, it is hoped that practitioners can take these ideas and integrate them into what they are already doing well and feel supported to propose changes to the way things are done; at the core is developing trusted relationships and working collaboratively to effect change.

The evidence base for community-based and co-produced ways of working is small, but growing, and MAC-UK encourages those trialling innovative and alternative ways of working with young people and their systems to consider evaluation and sharing this learning to influence the ongoing practice of others, contributing to a community of practice.

Adjusting to new ways of working, or suggesting changes within already stretched systems can feel a daunting task. MAC-UK appreciates that change is slow and requires commitment and faith in the process. Though challenging, the smallest of changes can have a big impact, such as co-producing individual or group interventions, sharing power in meetings, creating small social-action initiatives with colleagues and people who access support, and/or collaborative policies and evaluations. It is hoped that this chapter is a stepping stone to reading and learning more about co-produced and youth-led community approaches, with encouragement for people at all stages of their career to lean in and try out the ideas!

References

Arnstein, S. (1969). A ladder of citizen participation. *Journal of the American Institute of Planners*, *35*(4), 216–224.

Aspinall, P. J. (2020). Ethnic/racial terminology as a form of representation: A critical review of the lexicon of collective and specific terms in use in Britain. *Genealogy*, *4*(3), 87.

Aubrun, A., Emanatian, M., & Grady, J. (2005). *Six harmful patterns in newspaper presentations of race*. Frameworks Institute.

Ayo, Y., Morley, D., & Steven, W. (2020). Delivering culturally competent services. In L. Theodosiou, S. Bailey, P. Knightsmith, and P. Lavis (Eds.), *Children and young people's mental health: Early intervention, ongoing support and flexible evidence-based care* (2nd ed., pp. 57–67). Pavilion Publishing and Media.

Ayodeji, E., Dubicka, B., Abuah, O., Odebiyi, B., Sultana, R., & Ani, C. (2021). Editorial perspective: Mental health needs of children and young people of Black ethnicity: Is it time to reconceptualise racism as a traumatic experience? *Child and Adolescent Mental Health*, *26*(3), 265–266.

Barker A. (2010). *Co-production: A series of commissioned reports*. Local Authorities & Research Councils' Initiative. https://www.govint.org/fileadmin/user_upload/publications/LARCI_CoproductionPapers_2010.pdf

Birch, J., Rishbeth, C., & Payne, S. R. (2020). Nature doesn't judge you: How urban nature supports young people's mental health and wellbeing in a diverse UK city. *Health & Place*, *62*, 102296.

Bronfenbrenner, U. (1979). *The ecology of human development: Experiments by nature and design*. Harvard University Press.

Byrne, A., Mustafa, S., & Miah, I. Q. (2017). Working together to break the 'circles of fear' between Muslim communities and mental health services. *Psychoanalytic Psychotherapy*, *31*(4), 393–400.

Chadee, P., & Evans, S. (2021). Representation of # CAMHS on social media platform TikTok. *BJPsych open*, *7*(S1), S241–S242.

Charles, A., Ham, C., Baird, B., Alderwick, H., & Bennett, L. (2018). *Reimagining community services: Making the most of our assets*. The King's Fund. https://www.kingsfund.org.uk/publications/community-services-assets

Deighton, J., Lereya, S. T., Casey, P., Patalay, P., Humphrey, N., & Wolpert, M. (2019). Prevalence of mental health problems in schools: Poverty and other risk factors among 28,000 adolescents in England. *The British Journal of Psychiatry*, *215*(3), 565–567.

Department of Health and Social Care. (1999). *National service framework for mental health. Modern standards and service models*. HM Government. https://www.gov.uk/government/publications/quality-standards-for-mental-health-services

Department of Health and Social Care. (2018). *Modernising the Mental Health Act: Increasing choice, reducing compulsion*. HM Government. https://assets.publishing.service.gov.uk/

media/5c6596a7ed915d045f37798c/Modernising_the_Mental_Health_Act_-_increasing_choice__reducing_compulsion.pdf

Durcan, G., Zlotowitz, S., & Stubbs, J. (2017). *Meeting us where we're at. Learning from INTEGRATE's work with excluded young people.* Centre for Mental Health, MAC-UK

Entman, R. M., & Gross, K. A. (2008). Race to judgment: Stereotyping media and criminal defendants. *Law and Contemporary Problems, 71*(4), 93–133.

Entman, R. M., & Rojecki, A. (2000). The black image in the white mind: Media and race in America (book review). *Journalism and Mass Communication Quarterly, 77*(4), 921.

Foot, J., & Hopkins, T. (2010) *A glass half full: How an asset approach can improve community health and wellbeing.* Improvement and Development Agency.

Forbat, L., Hubbard, G., & Kearney, N. (2009). Patient and public involvement: Models and muddles. *Journal of Clinical Nursing, 18*(25), 47–54.

Ford, T. E. (1997). Effects of stereotypical television portrayals of African-Americans on person perception. *Social Psychology Quarterly, 60* (3) 266–275.

Freire, P. (1972). *Pedagogy of the oppressed.* Penguin.

Gunaratnam, Y. (2003). *Researching 'race' and ethnicity: Methods, knowledge and power.* Sage.

Guy, A., Loewenthal, D., Thomas, R., & Stephenson, S. (2012). Scrutinising NICE: The impact of the National Institute for Health and Clinical Excellence Guidelines on the provision of counselling and psychotherapy in primary care in the UK. *Psychodynamic Practice, 18*(1), 25–50. https://doi.org:10.1080/14753634.2012.640153

Hunsley, J. (2007). Addressing key challenges in evidence-based practice in psychology. *Professional Psychology: Research and Practice, 38*(2), 113–121. https://doi.org:10.1037/0735-7028.38.2.113.

Hussain, B., Hui, A., Timmons, S., & Nkhoma, K. (2022). Ethnic mental health inequalities and mental health policies in England 1999–2020. *Journal of Public Mental Health, 21*(2), 162–173

Kazdin, A. E. (2008). Evidence-based treatments and practice. New opportunities to bridge clinical research and practice, enhance the knowledge base and improve patient care. *American Psychologist, 63*(3), 146–159. https://doi.org:10.1037/0003-066X.63.3.146

Keating, F., & Robertson, D. (2004). Fear, black people and mental illness: A vicious circle? *Health & Social Care in the Community, 12*(5), 439–447.

Marin, L. M., & Halpern, D. F. (2011). Pedagogy for developing critical thinking in adolescents: Explicit instruction produces greatest gains. *Thinking Skills and Creativity, 6*(1), 1–13.

Marmot, M., Allen, J., Boyce, T., Goldblatt, P., & Morrison, J. (2020). *Health equity in England: The Marmot Review 10 years on.* Institute of Health Equity.

Marmot, M., Allen, J., Goldblatt, P., Boyce, T., McNeish, D., Grady, M., & Geddes, I. (2010). *Fair society, healthy lives. The Marmot review, strategic review of health inequalities in England post-2010.* The Marmot Review.

Miller, D. B., & Townsend, A. (2005). Urban hassles as chronic stressors and adolescent mental health: The urban hassles index. *Brief Treatment & Crisis Intervention, 5*(1), 85–94.

Mollon, P. (2009) The NICE guidelines are misleading, unscientific and potentially impede good psychological care and help. *Psychodynamic Practice, 15*(1), 9–24. https://doi.org:10.1080/14753630802614457

Nagata, J. M., Palar, K., Gooding, H. C., Garber, A. K., Whittle, H. J., Bibbins-Domingo, K., & Weiser, S. D. (2019). Food insecurity is associated with poorer mental health and sleep outcomes in young adults. *Journal of Adolescent Health, 65*(6), 805–811.

National Collaborating Centre for Mental Health [NCCMH]. (2019). *Working well together: Evidence and tools to enable co-production in mental health commissioning*. NCCMH. https://www.rcpsych.ac.uk/improving-care/nccmh/service-design-and-development/working-well-together

National Institute for Health and Care Excellence [NICE]. (2016). *Community engagement: improving health and wellbeing and reducing health inequalities*. NICE guideline NG44. https://www.nice.org.uk/guidance/ng44

National Institute for Health and Care Excellence [NICE]. (2021). Looked-after children and young people. NICE guideline NG205. https://www.nice.org.uk/guidance/ng205

Nazroo, J. Y., Bhui, K. S., & Rhodes, J. (2020). Where next for understanding race/ethnic inequalities in severe mental illness? Structural, interpersonal and institutional racism. *Sociology of Health & Illness, 42*(2), 262–276.

New Economics Foundation. (2013). *Co-production in mental health A literature review*. Mind. https://neweconomics.org/uploads/files/ca0975b7cd88125c3e_ywm6bp3l1.pdf

NHS. (2019). *The NHS long term plan*. NHS. https://www.longtermplan.nhs.uk/publication/nhs-long-term-plan/

NHS England. (2014). *Five year forward view*. NHS England. https://www.england.nhs.uk/wp-content/uploads/2014/10/5yfv-web.pdf

NHS England. (2017). *Patient and public participation policy*. NHS England. https://www.england.nhs.uk/publication/patient-and-public-participation-policy/

NHS England and NHS Improvement and Coalition for Personalised Care. (2020). *A co-production model*. NHS and C4PC. https://coalitionforpersonalisedcare.org.uk/resources/a-co-production-model/

Plaistow, J., Masson, K., Koch, D., Wilson, J., Stark, R. M., Jones, P. B., & Lennox, B. R. (2014). Young people's views of UK mental health services. *Early Intervention in Psychiatry*, *8*(1), 12–23.

Public Health England. (2019). *Mental health: Environmental factors*. Public Health England. https://www.gov.uk/government/publications/better-mental-health-jsna-toolkit/2-understanding-place#fn:6

Robards, F., Kang, M., Usherwood, T., & Sanci, L. (2018). How marginalized young people access, engage with, and navigate health-care systems in the digital age: Systematic review. *Journal of Adolescent Health*, *62*(4), 365–381.

Ryan, R. M., & Deci, E. L. (2000). Self-determination theory and the facilitation of intrinsic motivation, social development, and well-being, *American Psychologist*, *55*, 68–78.

Rippon, S., & Hopkins, T. (2015). Head, hands and heart: Asset-based approaches in health care. The Health Foundation.

Social Care Institute for Excellence. (2015, October). *Co-production in social care: what it is and how to do it – At a glance*. https://www.scie.org.uk/publications/guides/guide51/at-a-glance/

Street, C., Stapelkamp, C., Taylor, E., Malek, M., & Kurtz, Z. (2005). *Minority voices. Research into the access and acceptability of services for the mental health of young people from black and minority ethnic groups*. Young Minds Research https://www.yumpu.com/en/document/view/50350364/minority-voices-research-into-the-access-and-acceptability-of-mmc

Stubbs, J., & Durcan, G. (2017). *Unlocking a different future. An independent evaluation of project future*. Centre for Mental Health.

Sweeney, A., Filson, B., Kennedy, A., Collinson, L., & Gillard, S. (2018). A paradigm shift: Relationships in trauma-informed mental health services. *BJPsych Advances, 24*(5), 319–333.

Tucker, L. G. (2009). *Lockstep and dance: Images of Black men in popular culture*. University Press of Mississippi.

Turnbull, G. (2016). The price of youth: Commodification of young people through malleable risk practices. *Journal of Youth Studies, 19*(8), 1007–1021.

Turnbull, G., & Spence, J. (2011). What's at risk? The proliferation of risk across child and youth policy in England. *Journal of Youth Studies, 14*(8), 939–959.

United Kingdom Government. (2014). Care Act 2014, c. 23. https://www.legislation.gov.uk/ukpga/2014/23/contents/enacted

University Hospitals of Leicester NHS Trust. (2019). *Patient and public involvement (PPI) strategy*. UHL NHS Trust. https://www.leicestershospitals.nhs.uk/EasysiteWeb/getresource.axd?AssetID=45536&type=full&servicetype=Attachment

Vargas, S. M., Huey, S. J. Jr., & Miranda, J. (2020). A critical review of current evidence on multiple types of discrimination and mental health. *American Journal of Orthopsychiatry, 90*(3), 374–390. https://doi.org/10.1037/ort0000441

What Works Wellbeing. (2017). *Scoping review of review-level evidence on co-production in local decision-making and its relationship to community wellbeing*. https://whatworkswellbeing.org/wp-content/uploads/2020/02/Co-production-scoping-review-July-2017.pdf

White, M. (2003). Narrative practice and community assignments. *International Journal of Narrative Therapy & Community Work, 2003*(2), 17–55.

Wilkinson, R., & Pickett, K. (2010). *The spirit level: Why greater equality makes societies stronger*. Bloomsbury Press.

Williams, G. A., and Zlotowitz, S. (2013). Using a community psychology approach in your research. *PsyPAG Quarterly*, (*86*), 21–25.

Wintermeyer, C. E. (2020). *Exploring the experiences of young people from an ethnic minority background in accessing and engaging with CAMHS*. [Doctoral dissertation, University of Leeds].

Woodall, A., Morgan, C., Sloan, C., & Howard, L. (2010). Barriers to participation in mental health research: Are there specific gender, ethnicity and age related barriers? *BMC Psychiatry, 10*, 1–10.

World Health Organization and Calouste Gulbenkian Foundation. (2014). *Social determinants of mental health*. World Health Organization.

Zlotowitz, S., Barker, C., Moloney, O., & Howard, C. (2016). Service users as the key to service change? The development of an innovative intervention for excluded young people. *Child and Adolescent Mental Health, 21*(2), 102–108.

26

Working within Children's Social Care

Clare Norris and Omar Timberlake

26.1 Introduction

This chapter will focus on the developing roles of psychological practitioners within Children's Social Care (CSC) (also referred to as Children's Services) and accompanies Chapter 17, which focuses on children removed from their biological parents (e.g. Children looked after, adopted children, children in kinship care or subject to special guardianship orders (SGOs)). It will focus on children involved with CSC (e.g. those on Child in Need (CiN) or Child Protection (CP) Plans). The chapter has relevance to all psychological practitioners working in different settings and contexts with children and families who are currently involved or have had contact with Children's Services including those on CP plans.

The aim of the chapter is to introduce some of the definitions, legislation (see also Chapter 5), terminology, the latest epidemiology, the development of the role of the psychological practitioner in this area and the rise of embedded service models. Furthermore, the chapter reflects critically on the evidence base and details the practice of psychological assessment, formulation, intervention and evaluation, illustrated with a clinical example.

26.2 Context

Safeguarding children in society is everyone's responsibility. Professionals working with children have a particular duty to ensure those children are not at risk of harm. That said, in the UK, referrals to Child Protection Services are at an all-time high, increasing year on year putting strain on the system. At the time of writing this chapter, the Department for Education (DfE) recorded 3.3% (404,310 children) of all children as being categorised as CiN (children assessed as needing help and protection because of risks to their health or development) in England. This is the highest number since 2018, up 4.1% in the last year. Of those categorised as CiN 12% (50,920 children) are on CP plans with the local authority (a statutory plan outlining the need for significant support and close monitoring to safeguard the child from risk of harm) (DfE, 2022). This has led some researchers (e.g. Bilson,

Child Psychology: Pathways to Good Practice, First Edition.
Edited by Helen Pote, Anna Picciotto and Clare Norris.

2022; Bilson & Macleod, 2023; Bilson & Martin, 2016) to highlight that there has been an 'investigative turn' in society (a growing trend in the UK to refer to children's services and investigate families). Often these children and families are from the most deprived communities (Bywaters et al., 2016), families living in poverty with limited resources that probably contributes to their difficulties meeting their children's needs.

The CP system within the UK is considered to be one of the best in terms of implementing good practice in comparison to other similar nations (Spratt & Nett, 2013). The system has strived to develop and improve in response to child fatalities, following recommendations of serious case reviews, government enquiries and independent reviews (e.g. Laming, 2003; Munro, 2011), leading to a reformation of safeguarding acts for local authority (LA) and other agencies (e.g. health, education) around safeguarding children (see Chapter 5 for further information on acts and legislation). However, there are still lessons to be learned and improvements that need to be made. The government recently commissioned an independent review on Children's Social Care. The report concluded that the current Children's Social Care system needed radical reformation as it was geared towards crisis intervention with poor outcomes and high costs (MacAlister, 2022).

Children's Social Care, particularly Children's Safeguarding or Protection Services in the UK, has experienced a huge amount of transformation and innovation in the past decade. The DfE have evaluated many of these innovations contributing further to the evidence base. The Social Care Institute of Excellence (SCIE) and other institutions (e.g. Research in Practice) have been established to disseminate research, publicise the evidence base and to offer training in evidence-based approaches. The evidence base is in its infancy compared to other areas of practice and there is still much that needs to be evaluated and researched.

There has long been recognition that services (e.g. health, education, voluntary, housing, police and social care) need to work together to safeguard children (DfE, 2018). The failure of services to work together effectively to protect children from harm was identified as a key area for improvement in many serious case reviews and independent review of children's social care (e.g. Laming, 2003; Munro, 2011). Overcoming barriers to this joint working across agencies has been the main focus of a number of the innovations in services that are showing signs of being effective in practice. There has been an increase in the numbers of mental health professionals and psychological practitioners being embedded in children's services due to recognition of the impact Safeguarding concerns can have on the mental health and emotional needs of the children and carers, and identification of the barriers for these vulnerable children and adults in accessing traditional mental health services. The success of these psychology-led services has led to an increased demand for psychological practitioners as these innovations are scaled up throughout the United Kingdom. This is an exciting new area for psychological practitioners to make a real difference to the most vulnerable and risky families in the UK and beyond (see DfE, 2021a for further information).

26.3 The Safeguarding Process

There are many acts, guidance, legislation and policy in this area that detail the safeguarding process. These use acronyms extensively, that can at first baffle a psychological practitioner new to the area. It is therefore crucial when working in this field to refer to publications such as the Children Act (1989 and 2004), Adoption and Children Act (2002), The Adoption Support Agencies Regulations (2010), Children and Social Work Act (2017) and Working Together to Safeguard Children (2018). Collectively, these set out the specific duties of the LA and partner organisations (health, education, voluntary sector and the police) to work together to safeguard children in their area. Safeguarding and promoting the welfare of children is defined as 'protecting children from maltreatment; preventing impairment of children's mental and physical health or development; ensuring that children grow up in circumstances consistent with the provision of safe and effective care; taking action to enable all children to have the best outcomes' (DfE, 2018, pp. 6–7). The guidance puts the child at the centre of the process and emphasises that safeguarding children is everyone's responsibility.

The general processes, terminology and structure of safeguarding services is outlined later, but the reader is encouraged to refer to the original documents for further detail. Referral processes and the structure of Children's Social Care in different areas of the country have similarities but LAs can also work differently. The UK's four nations also have different CP systems and laws to protect children from neglect and abuse. Psychological practitioners are required to read and adhere to the national and local safeguarding policy and guidance where they are working.

The statutory CP process starts with a referral to Children Services. Anyone concerned about a child's welfare can make a referral. The referral will then be screened by Children's Services in terms of the needs and risks to the child and a decision will be made as to whether to investigate the referral further. In many services this screening is carried out by a multidisciplinary team based in Children's Services. The possible outcomes are as follows:

1. No additional need – the child's health and development needs can be met by universal services (e.g. health or education).
2. Early help – where children/families have additional needs and are showing early signs of abuse and neglect. Children receive an assessment and are directed to either universal services or receive support from targeted services (but do not meet the threshold for an assessment by Children Services under Section 17 – CiN).
3. Children with complex multiple needs – this is the threshold for children to be referred to and assessed by Children's Services under Section 17 (voluntary). These children require specialist services in order to achieve or maintain a satisfactory level of health or development or to prevent significant impairment of their health and development and /or who are disabled (CiN).
4. Children in acute need – these children have more complex needs and meet the criteria for an investigation (Section 47) as there is reasonable cause to suspect that a child is suffering or likely to suffer significant harm.

Only referrals considered to be at points 3 and 4 in the above list will proceed to a statutory assessment by Children's Safeguarding Services. If it is considered that the child is suffering or likely to suffer significant harm a strategy discussion will take place (a multiagency meeting involving the Police, health and other agency professionals involved in the child/ren's life) and it will be decided if a Section 47 (safeguarding) investigation is needed. (The investigation could be joint, which means Police and Children Services, or single agency, which is only Children Services). However, information from all agencies, parents/carers and CYP is requested in completing this investigation in line with the working-together process.

If the outcome of the investigation is that the child is suffering or likely to suffer significant harm then a CP case conference is held to bring together the family and multidisciplinary team (MDT) to develop a CP plan, to promote the child's health and development and to support the family in doing this and to reduce risk of harm to children and young people (CYP). The MDT and parents form a core group and meet at regular intervals to check on the progress and review the plan.

If the assessment concludes the child is a CiN, then a CiN plan is put place (a plan detailing the services and support needed to meet the identified needs and reduce the level of assessed risk). The MDT and the parents meet together regularly for meetings to assess and review progress towards the plan.

Ongoing assessments, interventions and support continue throughout the period where CYP are subject to a CP/CIN plan.

If Children's Services consider that the child is suffering significant harm then they will apply to the court for a Care Order. This process is called care proceedings. The court then make a decision as to what should happen to the child. Outcomes could be:

1. No order – the child remains with their parents, and they maintain parental responsibility (PR).
2. Interim care order or full care order (at conclusion of court proceedings). The LA shares PR with the parents and a child becomes a 'child looked after' (CLA).
3. Supervision order – this is an order obliging the LA to advise, befriend or assist the subject child or children. It gives the LA legal power to monitor the child's needs and progress whilst the child remains at home or living elsewhere. The parents maintain PR.
4. A placement/adoption order – a child is removed from their parents and placed with foster carers, in a residential care, or with adoptive parents (this is the only occasion where parents lose parental responsibility for their child)
5. A special guardianship order (SGO) is when a carer (usually known to the child) applies to be the child's special guardian via the courts. The court can grant an SGO, giving that carer PR (shared with birth parent) to care for the child and make decisions about the child until they are 18. Birth parents cannot apply for an SGO. Contact with birth parents can continue if agreed with the special guardian.

The Public Law Outline (PLO) process takes place when the LA is considering care proceedings. The PLO is the last opportunity the parents have to make improvements to their parenting before care proceedings are issued. The PLO process sets out the duties that the LA has when it is considering taking a case to court for a care or supervision order. The PLO process is about getting social workers and parents together along with legal representation (for both the parents and the LA) to discuss the concerns they have and make a plan for improvement. The process usually lasts around 3 months, but this can vary depending on the circumstances.

As mentioned earlier there can be significant variation between LAs as to the organisation of children's services. The structure of one LA is outlined in Table 26.1.

Table 26.1 Organisation of Children's Services in one LA.

Level	Target
1. Early help service	Prevention/Family support 0–18 years (25 if child has a learning need or disability)
2. Family Safeguarding	CiN/Child protection/PLO/Care Proceedings 0–18 years
3. Children with Disabilities Service	0–25 years, Children with learning needs and disabilities
4. Specialist Service for Adolescence	11–17, Edge of care, homeless, child exploitation, youth justice,
5. Children Looked After and Care Leavers	0–18, Children subject to a care order or 16–25 leaving care when they have been in care for 13 weeks or care spanning their 16th birthday

This chapter will focus predominantly on number 2: Family Safeguarding/Child Protection/Children in Need.

26.4 Demographics of Children and Families Involved with Child Protection

There can be huge variation in the demographics of children referred to Children's Services and on CP plans. Psychological practitioners embedded in Children's Services should familiarise themselves with their local demographics and ensure that there is equal access to their services and caseloads are representative of the families involved with CP services in their area. Being involved with Children's Services can be stigmatising for all families but it has particular impact on certain minoritised groups within society. Developing an understanding of the different minority communities in the area and the impact on the families of being involved with Children's Services is important in order to form empathic therapeutic relationships.

Ahmed et al.'s (2022) report on ethnicity and social care revealed that there is huge regional variation of children categorised as CiN. For example, 73% of children categorised as CiN are from minoritised communities in London but the figure is only 11% in the North East of England. Nationally, children of mixed white and black Caribbean ethnicity were around 30% more likely than white British children to have a CP plan following a referral. There are also higher percentages of children from white Irish Traveller, Roma and Gypsy ethnic groups involved with CP services (around four times the general population of CYP). However, there are fewer CYP from Asian ethnic groups (Indian, Bangladeshi and Pakistani) with CP plans (with the exception of those that identify as other Asian ethnic groups). The research on ethnic disparities in social care is small and it is a complex area and beyond the remit of this chapter. Psychological practitioners are encouraged to read the full report for further discussion for the reason in disparities.

26.4.1 Characteristics of Parents/Children/Families Involved in Child Protection

Chapter 5 outlines some of the factors (societal, systemic, parental and child) that increase the likelihood of children in a family being abused, along with the different types of abuse.

In terms of parental factors, much currency has been given to the concept of the 'toxic trio' within government and social work policy and practice. Analysis of serious case reviews commissioned by the DfE led to the development of this concept (Brandon et al., 2009), now renamed 'trio of risk' due to the derogatory language of the original term. The analysis found that the parental risk factors most associated with abuse and neglect of children were (i) domestic violence and abuse, (ii) parental mental health issues and/or learning disability and (iii) parental alcohol and/or drug misuse. This concept has much influence on the family justice system, CP assessment processes, social work policy, the training of social workers and national data collection. There has, however, been criticism of the concept and its evidence base as it neglects to focus on other important social and economic factors that have serious negative consequences for children and their families. These include the impact of poverty, poor-quality housing or homelessness, precarious employment or unemployment, as well as identity and demographic factors, such as ethnicity or the parents' age (Skinner et al., 2020).

Government statistics show, similar to CLA, that children involved with CP are more likely to be diagnosed with neurodevelopmental disorders, have Special Educational Needs (SEN), have developmental delay, to experience health concerns and social emotional and behavioural difficulties, to have higher absence rates from school and poorer educational achievements than the general population (DfE, 2022).

Child risk factors, parental risk factors and economic and social disadvantage combine to increase the risk of neglect and abuse and all need to be the focus of assessments and interventions aimed at supporting families. Neglect remained the most common initial category of abuse recorded for children on CP plans in 2021, accounting for almost half of children. The next most common category (one-third of children) was emotional abuse (DfE, 2022).

26.4.2 Prevalence of Mental Health Disorders

The mental health of children on a CP and CiN plan is not routinely monitored (as it is with CLA). There is, however, a large body of research detailing the negative impact of abuse, neglect and adverse childhood experiences (ACEs) on a child's development, physical health, neurological and cognitive abilities and mental health (see Chapter 17). The prevalence rates of mental health difficulties in CLA is much higher than the general population due to their experiences of maltreatment, abuse and neglect prior to entering care (NICE, 2021: 45% for those in foster care and 72% for those in residential care; Ford et al., 2007; Tarren-Sweeney, 2010; Teggart & Menary, 2005). As the majority of CLA were previously on CP and CiN plans it can be assumed that mental health difficulties of these children will also be higher, and that is the experience of those that work in this area. Further research is needed to confirm the level of need.

Children and their families involved with CP will have similar barriers to CLA in gaining access to mental health services and may be more disadvantaged as (unlike CLA) the majority remain in their family where abuse and neglect has occurred or is continuing to occur, and are likely have parents who are struggling to access health, and mental health services for themselves and their children. There may be many other barriers, such as instability in their family, chaotic lifestyles of the parents, economic barriers, parents' difficulties engaging due to substance abuse or their own mental health issues and the stigma of attending mental health services. Mental health services will often not accept referrals for children who remain living in unsafe situations, holding the view that the children will be unable to benefit from psychological or other therapeutic interventions whilst they continue to be exposed to neglect and abuse. Very vulnerable children are therefore denied access to evidence-based psychological interventions to improve their mental health and wellbeing.

26.5 Development of Psychologists' Roles in Safeguarding Services

Children involved in CSC and on safeguarding plans were previously referred to traditional Child and Adolescent Mental Health Services (CAMHS) and there were very few targeted services or mental health workers embedded in Children's Social Care. Over the past decade, as with CLA, this situation has started to change, as the recognition of the need of these children in terms of their mental health and emotional wellbeing due to their traumatic and abusive childhood experiences has increased. There has also been an increase in awareness of the barriers these children and their families face in accessing traditional mental health and psychological services.

Over the past 10 years more targeted services have developed for children involved with social care, which have included embedding mental health workers (including psychological practitioners) in CSC. In East London, Hackney's 'Reclaiming Social Work' model, introduced in 2007 (Cross et al., 2010) was one of the first practice models that integrated evidence-based approaches (social learning theory and systemic theory) and mental health practitioners to create MDTs within social care. It was positively evaluated and other LAs adopted the approach (Bostock et al., 2017). However, this was not consistent practice across the UK and in many areas the barriers to these children and families receiving timely services for their children's mental health or neurodevelopmental difficulties remained.

Prior to recent innovations, one of the main roles for psychologists within this area was conducting psychological assessments of children and parents and acting as expert witnesses in care proceedings. Although there were some reputable services providing these assessments the majority were from independent experts, acting alone or forming private businesses, and the assessments and reports varied in quality, often making recommendations for interventions and services that were not available. The focus was also on gathering evidence once the case had escalated to care proceedings rather than using psychological knowledge and skills preventatively to support these children and their families to make positive changes to keep families together. These issues remain problematic in current services.

The DfE's Children's Social Care Innovation Programme was set up in 2014 to encourage the development of new approaches to deliver significant and sustained improvement. Wave 1 of the programme saw £110 million invested in 57 projects, many of which highlighted multiagency working, integrating psychologists, mental health professional and other disciplines (such as recovery workers and domestic abuse workers) and embedding them into MDTs within CSC.

The evaluation of the programme, which was undertaken for 42 of the innovations between 2014 and 2016 (DfE, 2017), found that the most successful practice models were those that were:

- Using a systemic, family-focused, strengths-based approach that supported families and young people to take more responsibility for their own lives.
- Using multiprofessional working that involved a wide range of services including specialist workers in substance abuse, domestic violence, mental health, childhood sexual exploitation (CSE), female genital mutilation (FGM) and offending to make a distinctive but synthesised contribution to case reviews and decision making.
- Providing consistent support to parents, young people and foster carers through one consistent 'key worker'.
- Maximising direct contact with families and young people that is flexible and reflective.
- Providing high-quality social work supervision by practitioners or consultant social workers.

The DFE provided Wave 2 funding for the most successful programmes in the longer term (3 to 4 years). They identified the seven practice measures and seven outcomes shown in Table 26.2 that they want to examine further with more robust evaluation.

It is beyond the scope of this chapter to outline all of the different practice models that have been implemented in the UK, and readers are directed to Isokuortti et al. (2020) for a systematic review of the evidence base.

Models that have had positive evaluations of their impact that contain most of the elements outlined in Table 26.2 are Hertfordshire's Family Safeguarding Service, Leeds' Family Valued and North Yorkshire's No Wrong Door (DfE, 2021a). These approaches also embed psychological practitioners and other multidisciplinary team members in CSC.

Strengthening Families, Protecting Children (SFPC) is the current 5-year programme set up by the DfE to support local authorities to improve their work with families, with the aim of more children staying at home in stable family environments and fewer children needing to be taken into care. A total of 18 LAs are being supported to embed one of three whole-system change projects, developed by Leeds, Hertfordshire and North Yorkshire (DFE, 2021a).

Table 26.2 Practice measures and outcomes.

Practice measures	Outcomes
Strengths-based practice frameworks	Create greater stability for children
Systemic theoretical models	Reduce risk for children
Multidisciplinary skills sets	Increase wellbeing and resilience for children and families
High intensity/consistency of practitioner	Reduce days spent in state care
Family focus	Increase staff wellbeing
Skilled direct work	Reduce staff turnover and agency rates
Group case discussion	Generate better value for money

26.5.1 Evaluations of Psychologists' Specific Contributions

Although there has been much evaluation of new practice models and the positive contribution that multidisciplinary teams make when embedded in CSC, there have been very few published studies evaluating the specific contributions that psychologists have made. One exception is a study on the Psychologically Informed Partnership Approach (PIPA) in North Yorkshire (Snodgrass & Selman, 2019).

PIPA provides access to a psychological service for vulnerable and marginalised children and young people across the 0 to 25 age range. The service model is primarily of embedded psychologists in LA children and young people's teams, many of which have statutory duties, from Early Help Teams, through to Safeguarding and Looked After Children's teams, Children's Residential Units and Leaving Care Services. Service evaluation and inspections of PIPA has evaluated the model as having an overwhelmingly positive impact on the children and young people's emotional wellbeing and also on the confidence and psychological understanding of social care staff resulting in reduced anxiety of workers (e.g. Lushey et al., 2017; Snodgrass & Selman, 2019).

Practice models and interventions in CSC are being widely adopted in the UK and other countries. Although the conduct of outcome evaluations in CSC involves multiple challenges, the results of Isokuorrti et al.'s (2020) systematic review suggest that more high-quality studies are urgently needed to evaluate which, if any, of these practice models improve outcomes for child-protection-involved families. There has been intense debate over whether randomised controlled trials (RCTS) are applicable for evaluating social care models due to the complexities of the situations being studied (De Jong et al., 2015) and the lack of generalisability of findings. However, others have argue that RCTs are still the best choice in terms of being able to make causal inferences (Deaton & Cartwright, 2018).

Despite these challenges in evaluating the effectiveness of practice models, there have been recent attempts at evaluations using rigorous mixed-method studies such as realist randomised trial designs or other kinds of high-quality study designs, measuring child and family-level outcomes, including multiple data sources and informants (such as data gathered directly from children and young people). Effective study designs require sufficient time and funding (Baginsky et al., 2019). The evidence base for psychological interventions for children on CP plans will be presented in Section 26.10.

The recent innovations in strength-based practice models and evidence of their successful impact have challenged the long-held view that children and families with high levels of safeguarding needs cannot benefit from psychological therapy. They have shown that targeted strengths-based interventions and multidisciplinary interventions can produce positive change, reducing the risk of potential harm in families and keeping families together. Much more research is needed into what specific psychological interventions benefit these children and their families and the specific contribution psychologists embedded in children's social care make.

26.6 Voice of CYP and their Families Involved with Child Protection Services

Collaboration and co-production with CYP involved with social care and their families is key given their mistrust of professionals and services and lack of power within the child protection system (see Chapter 8 for further discussion of this area).

Although the recent evaluations of models of social work have included family views (mainly parents and carers) not focusing on the views of CYP who have CP plans has been an important omission. A summary of serious case reviews highlighted the need to include the views of CYP and noted that listening to their voices may have prevented serious harm occurring (Ofsted, 2011).

Social workers within these new innovative practice models are given more time to carry out direct interventions with children and young people and their wishes and feelings are frequently sought and included as part of the plan. Psychologists and practitioners working in this area also utilise service-user feedback on their service that includes the views of CYP. However, there is a lack of published research allowing these children's voices to be heard. In addition, the collective action and organised groups of service users found in CLA contexts are absent. Supporting CYP with self-advocacy and to gain a voice within social care contexts is an area for future development and is something psychological practitioners would be well placed to carry out.

26.7 Clinical Practice: Issues to Consider in Clinical Practice with Children on a Child Protection Plan with Children's Social Care

When carrying out psychological assessments and interventions in this area psychological practitioners need to be aware of many factors, sometimes unique to this cohort of children, that can impact on the success of clinical practice.

26.7.1 Consent and Engagement

Referrals to psychological practitioners working in CSC usually come from social workers involved with the families. It might be the case that the referral is part of the CP or CiN plan. The assessment/intervention forms part of the parenting assessment or parenting/family interventions with the aim of improving family functioning and keeping the family together. In either case, the families do not have a choice to be on a CP plan and they therefore may feel they have no choice to engage with what is on the plan or referrals made by the social worker. CiN plans are more voluntary so this is less of an issue but there is still a power differential between the professional and the family with regard to the plan that can be difficult to negotiate. These systemic structures can create issues around consent to psychological assessments and interventions for both the parents and children as they have not themselves initiated the referral and may feel ambivalent or opposed to engaging in the work. Although good practice in social work is to discuss and seek the adult or children's consent, the power differential and fear of children being removed can lead to parents and children agreeing to referrals that they have not given informed consent to, or feel they neither want or need. This poses very difficult ethical and professional dilemmas for the psychological practitioner.

These issues need to be addressed by the psychological practitioner before any assessment or interventions take place otherwise they are likely to affect the parent or child's engagement. Eliciting their views on the referral and understanding their level of consent is the first step. When a social worker has made the referral, the practitioner may find that their goals are different to the parent or child's goals and again this also needs to be resolved. Joint meetings with the referrer and the parent or child can be a productive way forward.

26.7.2 Mistrust of Professionals

Children and parents involved in Children's Services are more likely to have a mistrust of professionals or other people in general (Cooper et al., 2003). They will often have had many professionals in their lives, and this is unlikely to have been their choice. Many parents of children on a CP plan are care experienced or will have been on CP plans themselves. They may have had negative experiences or not found professionals supportive. Both parents and children are likely to have experienced ACEs, trauma and abuse at the hands of adults or even professionals leading to issues with trust. In some circumstances, the children in the family may be 'coached' by the parents not to talk to professionals or share information for fear of the consequences from professionals (such as being removed from their family) or fear of the reaction by the parent (particularly if the parent is abusive). Again, these issues need to be addressed and it may take longer to establish trusting therapeutic relationships with these families.

Psychological services in childrens social care often implement assertive engagement and strength-based approaches, such as motivational interviewing (Miller & Rollnick, 2013) to promote engagement. It can take a long time to engage parents and children using many different methods, for example, visiting in non-stigmatising venues or where the client feels comfortable. Taking interventions to the CYP and their families in their home removes barriers such as an inability to attend venues due to financial issues, mental health, disorganisation or chaotic lives and substance misuse. However, if this venue is where abuse has taken place, it may be counter therapeutic. Children centres or schools can be alternative venues, although some children do not want practitioners to visit schools due to stigmatisation and not wanting to appear different from their peers (see Chapter 20) and choice is particularly important for this cohort.

26.7.3 Confidentiality

There are more limits to confidentiality in psychological practice in social care due to the aim of safeguarding children. Information is shared within the professional network surrounding the family and there are regular professional meetings where everyone involved with the child on a plan comes together to discuss the plan (such as CP case conferences and core and CiN group meetings) and at which sensitive information is often shared. It is important that this is made explicit by the psychological practitioner when they first meet with the parent or child even though it may create barriers and impact what the parent or child is willing to share. The area of confidentiality can often raise dilemmas for the psychological practitioner who wants to develop and maintain a trusting therapeutic relationship with the child or parent but has a professional duty to report on safeguarding issues. Making decisions about what information needs to be shared can be challenging and confusing for novice practitioners and it takes some time to develop confidence making clinical decisions in this area. Parents or children may disclose information and ask for it not to be shared, leaving the psychologist practitioner in a dilemma about what is relevant to disclose (e.g. if parents relapsed on drugs or alcohol or a young person started self-harming). Supervision is therefore of critical importance to seek support regarding these issues and develop skills in determining the boundaries of confidentiality in safeguarding settings.

26.7.4 Stigma of being involved with Children's Social Care

There is usually a huge amount of shame and stigma attached to having a CP plan with Children's Social Care. Many parents feel criticised and judged and report feeling under constant scrutiny. The impact of being involved with Children's Services can result in anxiety for parents and children, and often leads to a worsening of mental health issues. This is heightened further when in care proceedings or PLO (the step before care proceedings). It can, therefore, be a difficult time to try to engage parents/children in psychological assessments and interventions. Careful consideration is needed of what they may be able to engage in at that time and services should ensure there is a 'no-blame approach' if they struggle to engage. Although the aim of CSC is to provide intensive support and interventions as part of the plan to enable the family to stay together and improve parenting, in care proceedings these interventions can often be directed by judges following advice from expert psychological assessments. Parents and children may therefore feel they have little choice to engage, fearing the consequences if they don't, and this can impact on engagement and the success of the intervention.

26.7.5 The Professional System Surrounding the Child and Family

Issues in the professional network surrounding the child and family can contribute to problems and impact on families' ability to engage in interventions. There may be heightened anxiety in part of the network, polarisation between different professionals, the network (or parts of it) may mirror some of the difficulties presented in the family and biases may occur (Featherston et al., 2019). This can be particularly the case with separated parents where there is high conflict between the parents, cases where contact or living arrangements are contested or cases where parents attempt to get professionals to take sides. This is a particular complication when working with families on CP plans due to the large number of professionals and agencies involved. Assessments, formulations and interventions need to include the professional network. Psychological practitioners' roles may be to offer reflective spaces to the network to develop insight and address these issues rather than direct work with the families themselves.

26.7.6 The Impact on Professionals

Psychological practitioners involved with children and parents that have had multiple traumas in their lives (past and present) and have possibly witnessed or overheard abuse are likely to be impacted themselves. The concept of professionals experiencing vicarious traumatisation (a negative impact on their emotional wellbeing) from being exposed to these traumatic experiences applies to this area of clinical practice (Tsirimokou et al., 2022). Self-care and self-reflexivity are critical in enabling practitioners to notice when the work may be having a negative impact and to take steps to ameliorate it. Forums that aid this process are supervision, practitioners having their own personal therapy and accessing peer support. There is commonly much anxiety surrounding safeguarding cases from public and professional networks that can have an impact on the professional network surrounding the child. It is crucial to be able to step back and reflect on these issues as a psychological professional in order to offer containing and effective work to families and other professionals.

26.7.7 Children Remain in Unsafe Situations

Children on child protection plans remain in situations where safeguarding concerns are ongoing. There needs to be a careful consideration and a comprehensive assessment to ascertain if the child can engage in a therapeutic intervention or if an intervention will have any impact given these concerns or if changes need to take place first to ensure the child is safe. Interventions may first need to take place with the parents to improve their parenting, or ensure their situation made safer (e.g. an unsafe or abusive adult may need to be removed from the home). Psychological practitioners can often experience a pressure from other professionals to provide an intervention directly to the child when it is clear they are suffering emotional distress due to their circumstances. The professional network may need to be educated about the challenges of providing interventions to children in these circumstances and what such an offer might communicate to the child (i.e. that they are the ones that need to change, leading to sense of blame for the situation). Ensuring that professionals are part of the decision-making process about the most useful level to offer an intervention can help to avoid frustration between professionals and agencies.

26.7.8 Need to Formulate and Apply Multisystemic Interventions

As mentioned earlier in the chapter the role of a psychological practitioner working within CSC is varied. Practitioners will need to have specialist skills in assessing, formulating and intervening with both adults (regarding their own mental health and their parenting) and CYP's mental health. Furthermore, the psychological practitioner needs skills in working with relationships between children and carers and systemically with children, their carers, their family and larger systems such as schools and the caring networks surrounding the child. Multidisciplinary team working is central along with skills in being able to disseminate psychological ideas, formulations and techniques via consultation, supervision and training to social work teams and other professionals. Usually, psychological practitioners working in this area are a limited resource and will not have capacity to assess and intervene directly with all referred CYP with mental health concerns. Thus, a large part of the work is consultation with the social work teams and MDTs as well as identifying other services that might be able to work directly with the child and the family if needed and supporting them to engage. Consultations with the network surrounding the child and the referrer following a referral is common, enabling the identification of cases to prioritise for psychological assessment and intervention by the psychological practitioners embedded in the service.

26.7.9 Model of Service Delivery

Psychological practitioners embedded in children's services are usually a unidisciplinary service with no direct access to psychiatry, although they may be part of a MDT within childrens social care (with social workers, drug and alcohol workers and other mental health professionals). Thus, in terms of the Thrive framework (Wolpert et al., 2014, 2019) for child mental health services they will usually offer interventions within the 'getting advice' and 'getting help' needs-based groupings (see Chapter 6 for a full account of the Thrive framework). If the adult or child presents with severe and enduring mental health difficulties with risks (such as self-harm) then it is more appropriate to refer to secondary mental health services that have access to high-risk pathways and psychiatry (e.g. Children's mental health team and CAMHS). Embedded psychological practitioners will generally offer brief interventions so that they do not develop long waiting lists. If longer, more intense interventions are indicated then the CYP/family may need to be referred to other mental health services.

26.7.10 Family Courts

Psychological practitioners working in this area may be required to submit reports and provide evidence to the family courts when a case they have been involved with is in care proceedings. Developing skills in this area in an important competency. Further post-qualification training may be beneficial such as having the opportunity to practice delivering evidence and being cross-examined in mock courts.

26.8 Clinical Practice

The next section focuses on applying the evidence base in clinical practice with children and families involved with CSC using the structure of consultation, assessment, formulation, intervention, outcome and evaluation. This is illustrated with an anonymised clinical example which highlights the contribution psychological practitioners may make at each stage.

26.8.1 Referrals and Consultation

One advantage of having psychological practitioners embedded in Children's Services is the ease with which informal consultations can take place. For example, a social worker or another member of the MDT might seek out the psychological practitioner informally (over coffee or in an open plan office) to get an alternative professional view or to consider if a formal referral is appropriate. In this way, inappropriate referrals may be prevented, and the practitioner is able to offer informal mental health advice and support to other professionals.

Professionals often seek out more formal consultation with psychological practitioners to support psychological thinking, applying models to their work with clients and developing their own skills. This can also include seeking out a space to reflect on troubling issues that are impacting them professionally or personally. Those seeking consultation are not always clear themselves about what they want or need and co-contracting to clarify what the work will involve at the start is helpful (Fredman et al., 2018).

Formal case consultations with the MDT or professional network surrounding the child usually occur after a referral to the service. They may have several aims.

1. *Seeking a referral for an assessment or intervention:* The consultation is used to determine: The appropriateness of the referral, Can the service meet the needs and goals of the CYP and their family? Has consent has been obtained from the CYP and family? What are the goals of the referrer? Where should the assessment or intervention should take place and who should be involved? The family may be involved at this stage in the consultation, or it may just involve professionals. The benefit to having all stakeholders present means that any issues regarding consent, motivation to engage and practical issues can be addressed in the consult. If it is felt that the service is not the most appropriate to meet the child or family's needs, then the psychological practitioner can use their knowledge of child and family services in the area to signpost and assist with referrals to these services (e.g. if the case requires CAMHS due to risk and complexity).
2. *When professionals feel stuck with a case or to discuss barriers to engagement:* Professionals may seek out a consultation when they are feeling 'stuck' with a case, having exhausted all other ideas and feel that they are not progressing. This offers an opportunity to take a step back and reflect on what might be done to make a difference in working with the child and family, to consider barriers to engagement and ways to increase engagement by using strengths-based, motivational methods (e.g. motivational interviewing).
3. *To understand the client's mental health difficulties more thoroughly, develop psychological and trauma-focused formulations and to develop ways of working with CYP and their families:* This includes when clients present with complex mental health difficulties or if learning disabilities are suspected. Consultations can often involve supporting fellow professionals to understand aspects of their work using psychological theories and models (e.g. attachment, cognitive and social learning theory) and systemic approaches (theories of the functioning of systems and families). These consultations focus upon deepening understanding, utilising formulation, helping professionals to think about their client's cultural and other differences, early life history, familial relationships, environment, experience of parenting, and how trauma has contributed to their difficulties and the safeguarding issues. It can be helpful to support professionals in seeking out the strengths of clients and any exceptions to the problem. Consultation here is aimed at developing and enhancing reflective practice within a creative and collaborative space.

26.8.2 Assessment

This section aims to act as a guide for carrying out psychological assessments with parents/caregivers and children within the context of children's services. There may be many different requests for different types of assessments by the social work teams and other professionals with differing aims and this issue needs to be explored prior to starting the assessment, usually in the consultation. The different types of assessment are outlined together with factors to consider when carrying out an assessment in social care settings. It will give an overview of useful tests and questionnaires that psychological practitioners may use and the different sources of information that are useful to consider when carrying out assessments with children and adults.

26.8.3 Types of Assessments

1. Psychological or mental health assessments of the parents/carers. This includes assessing the impact of their difficulties on their capacity to parent and recommendations for support/interventions.
2. Assessments of parents with a suspected learning disability.
3. Assessments of the nature and quality of the relationship between the parent/carer and children.
4. Psychological or mental health assessments of the CYP (can sometimes include neurodevelopmental and cognitive assessments).
5. Sibling relationship assessments.
6. Family system assessments.

Assessments of the parent/carer: This is usually a broad mental health/psychological assessment including general mental health and functioning, relationship difficulties, personality difficulties, substance misuse, risk to adult and child and any other factors that may be impacting on parental capacity. It includes the parent's childhood experiences, any ACEs or trauma in their background, their experiences of being parented, family relationships and relationships with peers, their experiences and achievements in education and occupational history and any forensic history. It should also include a detailed history of the development of any difficulties and any support or interventions they may have engaged in, as well as the client's understanding of the concerns of professionals, insight into their difficulties, motivation to change or engage in support and, strengths and positive factors. Consideration of the parent's background, current context (impact of poverty, if appropriate) and support network and impact of any of the Social Graces (Burnham, 1992) is also important. It will include a psychological formulation of their difficulties followed by recommendations for further support and guidance for professionals working with the family (usually compiled and circulated to the MDT in a report).

Assessments of parents and carers usually involve interviews with the parent(s), reviewing and summarising Children's Services' and other services' records (e.g. medical records if available) and interviews with the social worker or other professionals involved with the family. Psychometric assessments and self-report questionnaires may aid the process e.g. self-report symptom checklists for depression (BDI, Beck et al., 1961), anxiety (BAI, Beck et al., 1988) and personality disorders questionnaires/measures (e.g. revised Minnesota Multiphasic Personality Inventory (MMPI-2, Graham, 2006)).

The main aim of this assessment is to assess the parent's mental health and give an opinion on the impact these difficulties may have on their ability to safely parent the child and consistently meet their needs. Although the parent is being assessed, the child remains at the centre of the assessment.

Assessment of parents with suspected learning disability: Cognitive assessments (such as the *Weschler Assessment of Intelligence Scale* 4th Edition (*WAIS-IV*, Drozdick et al., 2012) are sometimes carried out if it is suspected that the parent has an undiagnosed learning disability that may be impacting on their parenting, their ability to function in everyday life and their ability to engage with Children's Services or with other professionals' assessments and interventions. Children's Services have a duty to adapt their way of working to take these difficulties into account. This information will inform the parenting assessments and how the parents can best be supported in terms of disseminating information to them so it can be retained and understood. Parents may require referral to other services for adults with learning disabilities for support or to advocacy services. The ethics of carrying out cognitive assessments on parents that are involved with Children's Services needs to be considered, given it is likely to be a time of heightened stress. It should therefore only be considered if there is significant evidence that the parent may have a learning disability (see Working Together with Parents Network (WTPN), 2021 and BPS, 2011 for more information).

Assessments of the nature and quality of the relationship between the parent/carer and children: These assessments are common, particularly when abuse or neglect has occurred. Their function is to assess the security of the attachment relationship and whether the parent is attuned to the child and able to meet the child's emotional needs. The main aim is to assess if any attachment-based interventions are needed to repair or build relationships. Observations of the child and parent/carer are key to these assessments.

An assessment of the child's relationship with the non-resident parent (in parental separation cases) is often carried out to inform Children's Service's contact plans (i.e. frequency, duration of contact and where it should take place and if it should be supervised or unsupervised) (see Chapter 17 for further information on attachment assessments and measures).

Child assessments: Psychological assessments of children are often likely to run parallel to assessments of parents and caregivers. Their aim is to assess if the child has any social, emotional, behavioural, neurodevelopmental or learning difficulties that need further assessment, support and intervention. There may be additional requests for other types of assessments to assist with the Children's Service's assessments and care planning (such as assessments of sibling relationship, relationship between parent/carer and child and family functioning).

Central to these assessments is the need to consult multiple sources of information (e.g. Children's Service's records and documents, health records, education records and reports) and to carry out interviews with the child, parents, immediate and extended family and the professional network surrounding the child (e.g. social workers, teachers, special needs coordinators). Observations of the child in different settings can be invaluable to the assessment (see Chapter 3 for further details on child assessments and Chapter 18 for information on psychometric assessments that aid this process).

26.8.4 Engagement

As mentioned previously, children involved with social care can be mistrusting of professionals: they may fear the consequences of reporting difficulties to professionals, or they may have been coached by their parents to not be honest and open. Thus, time needs to be taken to build up a rapport with CYP and to gain their trust. Meeting the CYP on their own, with different trusted adults (such as teachers) and in different contexts can help them to be more open.

Games and other activities such as drawing tasks can act as ice breakers, develop trust and increase engagement. This can also involve the parents or other members of the family and presents an opportunity to see children with their parents, or siblings, engaging in a fun task, which can add to assessments of parent–child, or family, relationships. Genograms are useful to undertake with the entire family to get all members talking about a subject on which they are the experts, and it offers valuable information about the family and intergenerational factors. Mapping the other professionals involved can also be useful in this context where a large number of professionals and services can be working with CYP and their families (see Chapter 3).

26.8.5 Experiences In utero and Developmental History

Gaining a comprehensive developmental history can help inform an understanding of any earlier experiences of trauma or developmental issues (e.g. developmental delays) that may contribute to the child's presenting difficulties. Key areas of childhood development will include their motor skills, cognitive, language, social, emotional and development of attachment relationships (see Chapter 3). The in utero experience of the child and mother's experiences during pregnancy are particularly important in this area as the child may have been exposed to stressful or harmful experiences when in utero (such as alcohol and illicit substances and/or domestic violence and abuse; Huestis & Choo, 2002) and research has shown that this can impact negatively on a child's development (e.g. Davis et al., 2011).

Gathering information on the adverse life experiences the CYP and how they may contribute to the current presentation is essential. There are questionnaires that can assist (e.g. Impact of Life Events Scale; Weiss & Marmar, 1997), however completing these questionnaires can be triggering as they can remind CYP of past trauma. This information can also be gleaned from other sources, such as social care records or interviews with professionals and the family. Creating a timeline with CYP can be a more positive, strengths-based method of eliciting both the difficult and enjoyable times in their lives, as described in Narrative Exposure Therapy for Children (KIDNET; Neuner et al., 2008).

Neurodevelopmental screening is a frequent request from social workers, parents and schools. However, caution has to be exercised as many behaviours and traits associated with neurodevelopmental conditions (such as autistic spectrum disorder (ASD) and attention deficit hyperactivity disorder (ADHD)) can be presented by children who have been subject to childhood trauma and abuse due to their experiences (e.g. poor concentration, hyperactivity, hypervigilance, difficulties with social communication and peer relationships). Screening for these diagnoses may be warranted but children should be referred to specialist services that can make differential diagnoses in these complex circumstances. Professionals are reluctant to make diagnoses of neurodevelopmental disorders if the child remains in a neglectful or abusive environment, which is often the case with children on CP plans (see Chapters 18 and 19 for more information on neurodevelopmental and learning disability assessments in children. See Chapter 17 for further discussion of these assessments in children who have been abuse or neglected).

26.8.6 Other Assessments

Psychological practitioners might also receive requests to assist Children Service's social workers in assessing the relationship between siblings (for instance, if abuse between siblings is suspected or with a view to them being placed together or separately if they are removed from the parents' care). Assessments of the parents' relationships or of family functioning are also sometimes needed to inform the children's services' care plans (e.g. is the parent's relationship or the way the family functions having a negative emotional impact on the child). Separated and divorced families where there is high parental conflict can have a huge emotional impact on children who are caught the middle. Assessments of the nature of the relationship difficulties, the impact on the children and whether the parents are able to mentalise (the ability to understand the mental state of another person, their children or themselves) with the child and understand the negative impact can be useful in these circumstances. Social workers frequently have to conduct 'viability' assessments of friends or family members to assess if they can safely care for the children either temporarily or permanently to avoid CYP going into care. They may seek the input of psychological practitioners to assist with these assessments or to consult with them regarding their findings (see Chapter 17 for more details on carrying out these assessments and measures and tools that may be applied).

26.9 Formulation

Formulation in this context is similar in many ways to that in the practice of child psychology in other contexts. There are many psychological models and approaches that practitioners can call upon, including psychodynamic, attachment, cognitive behavioural, systemic, integrative and social constructionist. (See Chapters 2 and 3 for further information). Key theoretical models for this cohort follow.

- *Attachment theory* (e.g. Bowlby, 1969, 1976, 2005) is especially relevant for this cohort of CYP and families given the likelihood of difficulties in attachment relationships due to abuse, loss and neglect.
- *Systemic theory* (e.g. Bateson, 1972; Bronfenbrenner, 2000; Palazzoli et al., 1978) As the children involved with social care are part of many systems, more than is typical with children in the population in general, systemic theory has value to support the understanding of the interaction of the different systems.
- *Trauma-informed formulations* (e.g. Johnstone, 2017, Johnstone & Boyle, 2018) Trauma and adverse experiences are high in this population, and trauma-informed formulations that are free from blame and highlight what has happened to the child or parent that might contribute to their difficulties or behaviours are also useful (see Chapter 27).
- *Cognitive and behavioural theories* (e.g. Ehlers, 2013; Monson & Shnaider, 2014) of the development and maintenance of post-traumatic stress disorder (PTSD) can help in the understanding both for parents and CYP presenting with PTSD.

- *Narrative theory* (e.g. White & Epsom, 1990) is also valuable in this area, as it explores the discourses that have shaped these parents and children's lives.
- *Strength-based, solution-focused theories* (e.g. De Shazer et al., 1986) highlight the positive strengths and resilience the parents and CYP involved with social care, and their systems that can be harnessed to overcome difficulties.
- *The 5Ps framework of formulation* (Padesky, 2020), explained in detail in Chapters 2 and 3, is a popular way of structuring formulations and is also useful for sharing formulations with the MDT. One of the main roles of the psychologist practitioner in this area is to disseminate psychological understanding of parents, children and their systems in a trauma-informed way that may change the way other professionals view them and improve their ability to work collaboratively with these families. It is important to include bio-psycho-social factors in these formulations (see Chapter 17) as well as factors associated with the individual/personal and the system/context for each of the five areas (see Carr, 2006). An example of a formulation using the framework of the 5Ps is presented in the clinical example in Box 26.1.

Box 26.1 Clinical example

Background

Sophia is a single parent and mother to Christine (8 years old) and Jonathon (4 years old). Sophia was in a relationship with Mark, Christine and Jonathon's father, for 10 years. Sophia and Mark are both white British. The family are living in an area with high social deprivation in a tower block in the heart of a busy city. Sophia lives close to her former foster carers, Jane and Timothy, but described that her relationship with them had been strained since difficulties arose in her relationship with Mark. Sophia reported having a limited social network around her but had developed a friendship with a fellow neighbour who was also a single mother of a child close to Christine's age. Sophia was unemployed. She said she wanted to look for employment and aimed to do this once Jonathon began primary school but was lacking confidence and found the practicalities of managing the needs of the children were challenging.

Sophia was herself removed from the care of her parents at the age of 4 years due to domestic abuse and neglect and had been placed in foster care with Jane and Timothy until she was 6 years old. She was then returned to the care of her birth parents. However, similar safeguarding concerns continued, and this led to her being removed from her parents again and placed back with Jane and Timothy at the age of 8 years. Sophia had her last contact with her birth parents when she was 10 years old, as they stopped attending arranged contacts. She spent the remainder of her childhood living with Jane and Timothy.

Sophia reported previously having had a positive relationship with her foster carers and that her experience in childhood in the placement was positive. She highlighted difficulties in education, noting that she frequently struggled with her behaviour at school. Sophia met Mark shortly after finishing college, through a mutual friend. This relationship was characterised by domestic abuse from Mark towards Sophia, including physical and verbal abuse. Towards the end of the relationship, Sophia and Mark began misusing cocaine and cannabis regularly. The relationship came to an end following the involvement of Children's Services. Sophia attended the freedom programme regarding domestic abuse support and reported ceasing using cocaine but noted that she continued using cannabis. Following the end of the relationship, Sophia ceased being involved in the care of the children, often going for long periods of time not seeing them.

Referral

The referral noted that Children's Services became involved with the family due to safeguarding concerns for the children regarding domestic abuse and substance misuse in the home when Sophia and Mark were in a relationship and living together. This referral came through the Police, following a callout to the family home as a result of an altercation between Sophia and Mark. The police had described concerns regarding the conditions of the family home and reported that both parents were likely to be under the influence of recreational drugs. Christine had also disclosed witnessing violence between her parents at home to a member of staff at her school and a referral was also made to Children's Services by the school.

Following professional involvement, Sophia was described as working with professionals, ending her relationship with Mark and completing domestic abuse and substance misuse support. However, professionals had observed that Christine had been presenting at school with emotional difficulties, including appearing withdrawn, highly anxious, disengaged from her learning and having difficulties separating from her mother at the school gates in the morning. Whilst working with a teaching assistant, Christine had reported that she had nightmares and was anxious about something 'bad' happening to her mother. The team requested a psychological assessment of Christine's needs.

Consultation

A consultation was held with the social worker, domestic abuse worker, team manager, school staff and children's practitioner. It was identified that the team were experiencing a sense of feeling 'stuck' with supporting Sophia to make changes in the family home. Her parenting style was noted as not being sensitive to the children's experiences. It was reported that Sophia had been struggling with acknowledging the impact on the children of witnessing domestic abuse, parents being under the influence of drugs, poor home conditions and the absence of the children's father from their lives.

The domestic abuse worker shared that Sophia had engaged well with the support that was offered to her and she was described as resilient and strong willed. However, concerns were raised regarding Sophia's wellbeing and sense of social isolation and how this might be impacting on her parenting.

Positively, there had recently been significant improvement in the conditions of the family home and the children's attendance at school was greatly improving.

(Continued)

Box 26.1 (Continued)

The children's practitioner highlighted concerns for Sophia's relationship with Christine, but felt that Jonathon had a better relationship with his mother and was coping well. The social worker raised the request of wanting support in how to engage with Sophia to make further improvements to her parenting and to explore therapeutic support for Christine.

Christine: 5Ps formulation

Presenting factors:

Christine was identified as presenting with several difficulties, including being anxious, having upsetting thoughts regarding her sense of safety, struggling to stop worrying, and having difficulties sleeping at night. She disclosed thoughts of feeling rejected and disliked by others around her if they got to know her fully and was described as having low self-esteem and self-worth. Christine reported having thoughts of not feeling worthy of love from others and not deserving happiness and perceived the difficulties that had taken place in the family home as her own fault. She described feeling responsible for supporting her mother Sophia and that she worried about her mother's safety and wellbeing when she is not with her.

Predisposing factors

Christine has experienced instability, neglect, parental substance misuse and witnessed domestic abuse in her life with her parents. There had been identified difficulties in Christine's attachment with her mother, and her mother's ability to mentalise. It was hypothesised that that Sophia's attachment difficulties to her own birth parents and experience of trauma and abuse in her relationship with Christine's father prior to, during and following the birth of Christine might be impacting on her attachment with Christine and her ability to be attuned and mentalise with her children.

Precipitating factors

Christine reported observing her mother being upset and emotional and she highlighted that this would leave her worried that something bad would happen or that she and her brother Jonathon would be taken into care. Leaving her mother to go to school was particularly difficult for Christine as she would worry about how her mother was doing and feel that she might be lonely, and that she should be at home with her. Christine also identified that being reminded of her father Mark would bring about difficult emotions due to having not seen him in a long time.

Perpetuating factors

Christine was experiencing difficulties in her peer relationships and feeling isolated at school. She felt reluctant to seek support from others as she worried she would be a burden. Her withdrawal had meant that she had lost opportunities to develop peer relationships in the school environment and falling behind in her learning further added to her feelings of low self-esteem and low confidence. Alongside this, despite the improvements in the family home, there were concerns around the ongoing impact of home life and the absence of Christine's father in her life.

Protective factors

It was identified in a family group conference that Christine had good relationships with her mother's foster carers Jane and Timothy, and they had expressed commitment to the children and providing support by offering childcare to the family. Alongside this, there had been an improvement in warmth between Sophia and Christine identified by the professionals working with the family.

Christine had developed a good relationship working with the family children's practitioner and reported having a good relationship with members of staff at the school. The family's home conditions had improved as had the children's school attendance.

Intervention

Support to the system

The assessment report and formulation were shared with Sophia and Christine alongside the wider professional network to aid them in developing a greater understanding of Christine's difficulties. This helped to support staff in understanding the factors that might be impacting upon Christine's wellbeing. The assessment highlighted the role for professionals in utilising a strengths-based approach towards the family and Sophia, such as motivational interviewing. Further to this, it included supporting staff to consider the trauma across the family lifespan that Sophia and the children had experienced and the impact this was having on their current situation, helping the professionals to hold in consideration other ideas to understand the challenges that they were facing.

Support for Sophia and Christine

Psychoeducation regarding developmental trauma was recommended for Sophia in supporting her understanding of the experiences of Christine and Jonathon, along with individual support and guidance and group-based training on therapeutic parenting approaches. A family group conference was held to support Sophia in strengthening her relationship with her wider family and in developing a specific plan of how they could further support her. Alongside this, a therapeutic intervention was recommended for Sophia to access whilst the children were at school. This consisted of cognitive behavioural therapy for anxiety and depressive symptoms, along with her ongoing engagement with domestic abuse support. The social worker worked with Sophia to identify opportunities both in future employment, and in the community on her own and with the children, to develop new friendships and a support network for herself. Additionally, it was advised that Sophia continue to work with the substance misuse team to support her in addressing her use of cannabis.

Alongside this, it was felt that Sophia and Christine would benefit from accessing Video Interactive Guidance (VIG) to improve communication, strengthen their relationship and build on attuned moments in their relationship. It was also felt that Christine would benefit from support at school with CBT for anxiety alongside therapeutic life story work. The psychological practitioner offered the CBT for anxiety and supervised the children's practitioner to implement therapeutic life story work (an approach she had recently been trained in).

(Continued)

Box 26.1 (Continued)

The social work team had further consultations with the psychologist practitioner to discuss ways of engaging Mark to evaluate whether he could be a positive recourse in the children's lives.

Outcome measures

CORC recommended outcomes measures were administered pre- and post-intervention that included:

Child

SDQ – parent, child (Christine) and teacher rated

Revised Children's Anxiety and Depression Scale (RCADS) – parent and child

Parent

PHQ-9 Patient Health Questionnaire (PHQ-9) and Generalised Anxiety Disorder (GAD)

Parent stress scale

Reflective parenting measures

Goal-based outcomes for parent, child and referrer

Patient feedback questionnaire

Outcomes

Symptoms report measures showed a decrease in Christine's anxiety and an improvement in her peer relationships. Christine presented as less withdrawn at school and her teachers were less concerned about her. She reported understanding her life story better following the therapeutic life story work.

Similarly, Sophia reported a reduction in her anxiety and depressive symptoms post-therapy in self-rated measures. Sophia had engaged well with the parenting interventions and was more attuned to her children and able to mentalise. She reported a reduction in parental stress. She had engaged well with the domestic abuse work but had started a relationship with a new partner who had a history of domestic abuse, so this remained an ongoing concern. She had engaged with drug recovery services and had reduced cannabis intake but was not abstinent. The social worker, mother and Christine reported being closer to their goals post-therapy. They indicated satisfaction on patient feedback questionnaires, but Sophia had wanted therapy to continue beyond the commissioned 20 sessions.

The improvements in the home conditions and school attendance were maintained, and Mark had started to engage with the social worker. There were plans for him to gradually be re-introduced to the children and to have more regular contact. His life was more stable than it had been as he was living with a new partner and the relationship was assessed by Children's Services as being healthy and stable. They had a 6-month-old daughter together and, as his life was more stable, he was considered to be in a better position to form positive relationships with his older children, despite some concerns about how Christine and Jonathan would feel about the new baby.

26.10 Intervention

Therapeutic interventions applied to children, parents and families involved with CP are similar to those for children with a history of developmental trauma, abuse and neglect, attachment difficulties or disorders and overlap considerably with those for children in care, adopted children or those on SGOs. Children on a CP or CiN plan present challenges to traditional child mental health services that only offer services based on diagnosable mental health difficulties CYP involved with CP services may present with many symptoms of emotional distress that do not fall neatly into diagnostic categories.

There is a lack of evidence for the efficacy of mental health interventions for children involved with CP and their caring networks (Kohlhoff et al., 2022). Approaches that have been applied and evaluated in the general population of children (e.g. cognitive behaviour therapy) or specific populations of children with similar characteristics (e.g. CLA or adopted children) are often adapted and utilised with these vulnerable children with limited evaluation of their effectiveness. Approaches developed for CLA and/or adopted children, who have complex developmental trauma and disorganised attachments, that have a growing evidence base (e.g. dyadic developmental psychotherapy; Hughes, 1997, 2006); Theraplay® (Booth & Jernberg, 2009), therapeutic life story work (Rose, 2012), developmental trauma creative approaches (Triesman, 2016) and non-verbal creative therapies (e.g. art, drama, music therapy), are often applied by practitioners working in CP due to the similarities of their cohort in terms of their experiences of childhood abuse, adverse childhood experiences and poor parenting/attachment relationships (see Chapter 17).

However, an important difference between CLA and those involved in CP is that the latter usually remain with their family of origin where these difficulties have taken place, with often vulnerable parents or carers (and siblings) who may continue to have their own difficulties that need addressing. In contrast, for CLA, foster carers, SGOs and adopted parents can usually offer a more stable parenting environment. Practitioners embedded in social care therefore need to be able to intervene with the family of origin, and support parents/carers' mental health difficulties, the child's difficulties and broader systemic and family difficulties to be able to enable change.

26.10.1 National Institute of Health and Clinical Excellence Guidelines

National Institute of Health and Clinical Excellence (NICE) guidelines of child abuse and neglect (NICE, 2017) and child maltreatment (NICE, 2009) are essential guides for psychological practitioners working in this area. Several other NICE guidance have relevance, including those for CLA (NICE, 2021), Children's Attachment (NICE, 2015) and Domestic Violence and Abuse (NICE, 2016). However, there is a lack of RCTs in this area and most of the evidence comes from a single research study with less robust methodology (see Kohlhoff et al., 2022).

It is beyond the scope of this chapter to outline all the guidance. However, included is a summary of conclusions for therapeutic interventions with neglected, abused and maltreated children from the NICE guidance for child abuse and neglect (NICE, 2017) as this is based on the most recent reviews of the evidence base. The guidance considers the different approaches needed based on the types of abuse and the age of the child.

26.10.2 Attachment-based Parenting Interventions for Younger Children who have Experienced Neglect and Abuse

In terms of physical, emotional abuse and neglect in the 0 to 5 years age range, attachment-based interventions (minimum 10 sessions) with the parent or child/parent psychotherapy (of minimum 1 year duration) is the recommended treatment (based on the Cicchetti and Toth model: Cicchetti & Toth, 1991). This model is based on Pre-School Parent Psychotherapy (PPP) developed by Fraiberg et al. (1975) and then further evolved by Leiberman (1991). The model is also referred to as toddler/ parent psychotherapy or infant/parent psychotherapy depending on the age of the child. The model emphasises the importance of the child–parent relationship in developing more positive attachments and reducing parental maltreatment. Therapy is carried out with the child–parent dyad, as a way to link the parent's past with their current representations of the child. Its effectiveness has been researched by Cicchetti et al. (1999) particularly on depressed mothers (see also systematic review of attachment-based interventions by Kohlhoff et al., 2022).

For children under 12 years, the guidance recommends a comprehensive parenting intervention for 6 months and parent–child interaction therapy. Group sessions for parents are combined with individual child–parent sessions focusing on developing child-centred interaction and effective discipline skills (see Chapter 12 for more details on parenting interventions). Safecare is one such parenting intervention. It is an 18-session, home-based intervention that has its foundations in behavioural theory, teaching positive parent–child interactions, skills in keeping the home environment safe and meeting the child's health needs (see Whitaker et al., 2020 for a recent RCT evaluating its effectiveness).

26.10.3 Multisystemic Therapy for Adolescents that have Experienced Neglect and Abuse

For adolescents (17 and under) multisystemic therapy for child abuse and neglect (MST-CAN) for 4 to 6 months is recommended. MST-CAN (Swenson et al., 2010) is an adaptation of the Standard Multisystemic Therapy (Henggeler et al., 2009) for CYP and their families aged 6 to 17 years who have been exposed to abuse and/or neglect. The intervention provides CYP and their families with focused individual and family support (usually in their homes) to target specific risk factors that contribute to child abuse and neglect. Strategies include CBT for managing anger and addressing the impact of trauma, safety planning and interventions for adult substance misuse and family therapy focused on communication and problem solving. It emphasises the need to involve the whole family in order to address the multiple factors contributing to the problem. It includes a 24-hour on-call service to support families to manage crises (see Schaeffer et al., 2021 and Bauch et al., 2022 for evidence of the programme's effectiveness with CYP who have experience neglect and abuse and their families.

26.10.4 Evidence-based Interventions for CYP who have experienced Sexual Abuse

The NICE guidance for CYP and their families who have experienced sexual abuse (NICE, 2017), recommends group or individual trauma-focused cognitive behavioural therapy (a minimum of 12 to 16 sessions) for CYP who have been sexually abused and show symptoms of anxiety, sexualised behaviour and/or post-traumatic stress disorder. Separate trauma-focused cognitive behavioural therapy sessions should also be provided for the non-abusing parent or carer. For CYP aged 8 to 17 who have been sexually abused, the intervention should:

- Emphasise the importance of the therapeutic relationship between the CYP and therapist.
- Offer support tailored to the CYP's needs, drawing on a range of approaches including counselling, socio-educative and creative (such as drama or art).
- Include individual work with the child or young person (up to 20 sessions, extending to 30 as needed).
- Offer parallel work with non-abusing parents or carers (up to eight sessions).

An example of such a treatment is the Letting the Future In (LFTI) intervention developed by the NSPCC that was positively evaluated by Carpenter et al. (2016).

NICE (2017) recommends that girls aged 6 to 14 who have been sexually abused and who are showing symptoms of emotional or behavioural disturbance, should be assessed carefully, and treatment from the following options should be considered: individual focused psychoanalytic therapy (up to 30 sessions) *or* group psychotherapeutic and psychoeducational sessions (up to 18 sessions). Again, separate supportive sessions for the non-abusing parent or carer is recommended, helping them to support the child's attendance at therapy, as well as addressing issues within the family (see Macdonald et al., 2012 and Parker & Turner, 2013 for systematic reviews of interventions for CYP who have experienced sexual abuse).

26.10.5 Video-based Feedback Interventions on Parenting

Video-based feedback parenting interventions are highlighted as an evidence-based approach in the NICE guidelines for children's attachment (2015). Video-interaction guidance (VIG, Kennedy & Underdown, 2018) is one such model. It is a brief intervention for parents that highlights and builds on attuned moments in parent–child interactions. This is done through guided reflection on video clips of interactions between the parent and their child. It is based on theories of attachment, intersubjectivity, mentalisation and positive psychology. It has also been included in systematic reviews (e.g. O'Hara et al., 2019). However further research is needed on its application to parents and children who are involved in CP.

26.10.6 Other Approaches Implemented with Growing Evidence Bases

Non-violent resistance: Child to parent violence or oppositional behaviour is common in this area of practice and approaches such as non-violent resistance (NVR; Omer, 2004) have been implemented (See Chapter 17 for further details). NVR has a growing evidence base and has been found to be effective in reducing problematic behaviour in CYP and reducing stress in their parents (Weinblatt & Omer, 2008). More recently an RCT has also found it to be effective with foster carers (Holen et al., 2016). Further research is needed into this approach for children who have experienced abuse and neglect.

Mentalising-based interventions: Parents with particular mental health diagnoses (e.g. emotionally unstable personality disorder (EUPD)) and substance misuse can struggle with attachment and mentalising (Fonagy & Bateman, 2016). Parenting interventions that focus on managing the children's behaviour, promoting attachments and the parent's ability to mentalise can therefore be beneficial in either a group or individual format (e.g. reflective parenting interventions, Redfern, 2015). Parental self-mentalising has been found to have a greater effect on parent–child interactions than on the parent's mentalising of the child (Suchman et al., 2010) and should therefore be a focus for interventions. (See Byrne et al.'s 2020 systematic review of MBT with children.)

26.11 Child-based Therapy Approaches

26.11.1 Interventions for Complex Trauma

There has been a great deal of debate about whether trauma-focused interventions for PTSD (e.g. Trauma-focused CBT, eye movement rapid desensitisation (EMDR)) can be effective for CYP who have complex trauma as a result of childhood abuse and neglect. Bennett et al. (2020) carried out a systematic review of the evidence base of psychological treatments for PTSD for CYP who have experienced maltreatment. They included 15 RCT and five non-RCTS with interventions ranging from trauma-focused CBT to creative-based therapies. They concluded that trauma-focused CBT was the most effective intervention, with symptom reduction being maintained at follow-up 1 year later. However, the evidence base for the other interventions was limited, and more methodologically robust research needs to be carried out on CYP with complex trauma (see Bennett et al, 2020 for further details). The reader should see Chapter 14, for further discussion on treatment for trauma.

Narrative exposure therapy for children (KIDNET, Neuner et al., 2008) has a growing evidence base and can be considered as an alternative to CBT and EMDR. Research studies have demonstrated the effectiveness of NET/KIDNET for reducing PTSD symptoms in children who have experienced single or multiple traumas, including children with autism spectrum disorders and those with intellectual impairments (Fazel et al., 2020; Karam et al., 2019).

26.11.2 Individual Interventions for Parents

Parents will present with a range of adult mental health issues prevalent in the adult population in general, so consulting NICE guidelines as to the most effective evidence base for those presentations is important. The psychological practitioner should also consider the limitations of the evidence, the parent's preferences in terms of intervention and what they are motivated or able to engage in given their circumstances. There has been limited research carried out examining what mental health difficulties are most prevalent in parents that abuse and neglect their children (Friedman & McEwan, 2018) but unpublished service audits of the child and parental mental health service within Hertfordshire's Family Safeguarding service show complex PTSD, depression, anxiety and EUPD traits or disorders are the most common presentations. CBT and dialectical behaviour therapy (DBT) are interventions often implemented, in groups or individually (see Chapter 2 for further details of these approaches). Parents may find it difficult to engage in trauma-focused interventions when they may remain in an unsafe situation and the trauma is continuing, or they may feel their life is too chaotic and unstable to engage in an intensive intervention. However, the stabilisation phase of CBT for PTSD and helping the parent develop healthy ways of coping and emotion regulation can be beneficial.

26.11.3 Interventions Focused on Parents' Relationships

Relational issues can typically arise for couples in this area. These can include difficulties regarding intimacy, issues regarding power dynamics in the relationship, sexual problems, infidelity, domestic abuse, substance misuse and eventual relationship breakdown. Intimate partner violence is prevalent in parents of CYP on CP plans and is a contributory factor to child abuse and neglect. Behavioural (Fals-Stewart et al., 2009), cognitive behavioural (Baucom et al., 2015) and solution-focused (Stith et al., 2011) couple therapy programmes for intimate partner violence have a promising evidence base (see Carr, 2019 for a systematic review of the evidence base of couple therapy, family therapy and systemic therapy for couples with relationship difficulties).

26.12 Working with Systems

Systemic approaches with the CYP and their family or working with larger systems surrounding the CYP (e.g. professional caring networks, residential care settings and schools) through consultation, supervision, training and facilitating reflective practice groups is a common role for psychological practitioners in this area of practice. Ensuring these systems are trauma and attachment informed (see Chapter 27 for further details). Many LAs have established 'virtual schools', an additional resource of a head teacher and a team of educational professionals who provide training, consultation and advice to mainstream schools. The pilot and roll out was originally for CLA but has recently been extended to include all children with a social worker (DfE, 2022). The virtual schools may also seek the advice of the psychological practitioners based within CSC regarding children on their case load.

26.13 Outcome Measures

The Strength and Difficulties Questionnaire (SDQ) (Goodman, 1997) is routinely used by CSC to measure social, emotional and behavioural difficulties in children. It may also be used as a threshold criterion for children and families to access more mental health support via CAMHS or mental health services. This is despite the SDQ being widely criticised as a measure for children with abusive and traumatic backgrounds (Lehmann et al., 2014; Milburn et al., 2008. See Chapter 17 for further details). There are no routine outcome measures (ROMs) specifically developed for children involved with social care (as with CLA and adoption). Thus, psychological practitioners tend to utilise those developed on the population as a whole and that are recommended by research bodies (e.g. the Child Outcomes Research Consortium (CORC)) for child symptoms and behaviours, and the Parental Stress Scale (Berry & Jones, 1995) for measuring parental stress.

Goal-based outcomes (GBO, Law & Jacob, 2015) often make the most sense to the families and children and practitioners in these services where the aim is collaboration with clients to meet their goals (see Chapter 8 for a detailed discussion of ROMs). It can also elicit the goals of the network in relation to the parents and children.

Key performance indicators (KPIs) are collected by CSC as indicators of the success of social care models (assessments and interventions). These may include the length of time a CYP is on CP plan, the numbers of CYP stepped up or down in terms of CP plans, the number of care proceedings initiated, attendance at school, attendance at A & E or by emergency services, involvement with mental health crisis teams and in-patient admissions (for parents and children) (see Forrester et al., 2017 for an evaluation that included KPIs).

Feedback from CYP and families is crucial in services where the clients (children and parents) are often in a powerless position, struggling to get their voices heard. Patient feedback questionnaires (CORC) for children and adults can be used for this purpose. As a large quantity of the work involves consultation with the network, getting feedback from social workers and the larger MDT is also beneficial for monitoring and improving services. Feedback from other stakeholders such as social workers is also valuable for evaluating the impact and quality of the psychological professionals' assessments, interventions, training events and consultations (see Worwood and Fredman, 2018 for tools to use to evaluate collaborative consultations).

26.14 Summary and Conclusions

This is a new, exciting and fast-growing area for psychological practitioners that provides the opportunity to make a real difference to often the most disadvantaged vulnerable families within society. Recommendations of many government reviews and reports emphasise partnership working and the value of MDTs embedded within children's services. Further reform of children's services is clearly needed given the findings from the recent independent review of children's services (MacAlister, 2022). There is optimism, however, given the growth in evidence based, of strengths-based approaches being applied in this field with promising outcomes. However, the evidence base is still in its infancy and much more research is needed; is research that is focused on: the specific contribution of embedding psychological practitioners in CSC; improving outcome measures; developing evidence-based interventions for CYP who are involved with social care and have experienced neglect and abuse; and long-term outcomes for children and their families. Psychological practitioners are well placed to contribute to the future evidence base in this important area for CYP their families and caring networks.

References

Adoption and Children Act. (2002). https://www.legislation.gov.uk/ukpga/2002/38/contents.

Adoption Support Agencies Regulations. (2010). https://www.legislation.gov.uk/uksi/2010/465/made.

Ahmed, N., James, D., Tayabali, A., & Watson, M. (2022). Ethnicity and children's social care. https://www.gov.uk/government/publications/ethnicity-and-childrens-social-care.

Baginsky, M., Moriarty, J., & Manthorpe, J. (2019). Signs of safety: Lessons learnt from evaluations. *Journal of Children's Services, 14*(2), 107–123. doi:https://doi.org/10.1108/JCS-11-2018-0028.

Bateson, G. (1972). *Steps to an ecology of mind: Collected essays in anthropology, psychiatry, evolution, and epistemology*. Jason Aronson.

Bauch, J., Hefti, S., Oeltjen, L., Pérez, T., Swenson, C. C., Fürstenau, U., Rhiner, B., & Schmid, M. (2022). Multisystemic therapy for child abuse and neglect: Parental stress and parental mental health as predictors of change in child neglect. *Child Abuse & Neglect*, *126*, 105489. https://doi.org/10.1016/j.chiabu.2022.105489.

Baucom, D. H., Epstein, N. B., Kirby, J. S., & LaTaillade, J. J. (2015). Cognitive-behavioral couple therapy. In A. S. Gurman, J. L. Lebow, & D. K. Snyder (Eds.), *Clinical handbook of couple therapy* (pp. 23–60). Guilford Press.

Beck, A. T., Epstein, N., Brown, G., & Steer, R. A. (1988). An inventory for measuring clinical anxiety: Psychometric properties. *Journal of Consulting and Clinical Psychology*, *56*(6), 893–897. https://doi.org/10.1037//0022-006x.56.6.893.

Beck, A. T., Ward, C. H., Mendelson, M., Mock, J., & Erbauch, J. (1961). *Beck depression inventory (BDI)* [Database record]. APA PsycTests. https://doi.org/10.1037/t00741-000.

Bennett, R. S., Denne, M., McGuire, R., & Hiller, R. M. (2020). A systematic review of controlled-trials for PTSD in maltreated children and adolescents. *Child Maltreatment*, *26*(3), 325–343. doi: https://doi.org/10.1177/1077559520961176.

Berry, J. O., & Jones, W. H. (1995). The parental stress scale: Initial psychometric evidence. *Journal of Social and Personal Relationships*, *12*(3), 463–472. https://doi.org/10.1177/0265407595123009.

Bilson A. (2022, 10 June). Why the evidence does not support multi-agency child protection units. *Community Care*. https://www.communitycare.co.uk/2022/06/10/why-the-evidence-does-not-support-multi-agency-child-protection-units/.

Bilson, A., & Macleod, M. (2023). Social work interventions with children under 5 in Scotland: Over a quarter referred and one in seventeen investigated with wide variations between local authorities. *The British Journal of Social Work*, *53*(4), 2217–2236. https://doi.org/10.1093/bjsw/bcad079.

Bilson, A., & Martin, K. E. (2016). Referrals and child protection in England: One in five children referred to Children's Services and one in nineteen investigated before the age of five. *British Journal of Social Work*, *47*(3), 793–811.

Booth, P. B., & Jernberg, A. M. (2009). *Theraplay: Helping parents and children build better relationships through attachment-based play*. John Wiley & Sons.

Bostock, L., Forrester, D., Patrizo, L., Godfrey, T., Zonouzi, M., Antonopoulou, V., Bird, H., & Tinarwo, M. (2017). *Scaling and deepening the Reclaiming Social Work model. Children's social care innovation programme evaluation report 45*. Tilda Goldberg Centre for Social

Work and Social Care, University of Bedfordshire & CASCADE: Children's Social Research and Development Centre, University of Cardiff. https://www.gov.uk/government/publications/scaling-and-deepening-the-reclaiming-social-work-model.

Bowlby, J. (1969). *Attachment and loss*, Vol.1: *Attachment*. Basic Books.

Bowlby, J. (1976). *Separation, anxiety and anger*. Basic Books.

Bowlby, J. (2005). *A secure base. Clinical applications of attachment theory*. Routledge.

Brandon, M., Bailey, S., Belderson, P., Gardner, R., Sidebottom, P., Dodsworth, J., Warren, C., and Black, J. (2009). Understanding serious case reviews and their impact: A biennial analysis of serious case reviews 2005–2007. Department for Children, Schools and Families.

British Psychological Society [BPS]. (2011). *Good practice guidance for clinical psychologists when assessing parents with learning disabilities*. BPS.

Bronfenbrenner, U. (2000). Ecological systems theory. In A. E. Kazdin (Ed.), *Encyclopedia of psychology* (Vol. 3, pp. 129–133). Oxford University Press.

Burnham, J. (1992). Approach-method-technique: Making distinctions and creating connections. *Human Systems*, *3*(1), 3–26.

Byrne, G., Murphy, S., & Connon, G. (2020). Mentalization-based treatments with children and families: A systematic review of the literature. *Clinical Child Psychology and Psychiatry*, *25*(4), 1022–1048. doi: https://doi.org/10.1177/1359104520920689.

Bywaters, P., Brady, G., Sparks, T., & Bos, E. (2016). Inequalities in child welfare intervention rates: The intersection of deprivation and identity. *Child & Family Social Work*, *21*(4), 452–463. https://doi.org/10.1111/cfs.12161.

Carpenter, J., Jessiman, P., Patsios, D., Hackett, S., & Phillips, J. (2016). *Letting the future in: A therapeutic intervention for children affected by sexual abuse and their carers: An evaluation of impact and implementation*. Project Report. National Society for the Prevention of Cruelty to Children (NSPCC).

Carr, A. (2006). *The handbook of child and adolescent clinical psychology: A contextual approach* (2nd ed.). Routledge/Taylor & Francis Group.

Carr, A. (2019). Couple therapy, family therapy and systemic interventions for adult-focused problems: The current evidence base. *Journal of Family Therapy*, *41*(4), 492–536. https://doi.org/10.1111/1467-6427.12225.

Children Act. (1989). https://www.legislation.gov.uk/ukpga/1989/41/contents.

Children Act. (2004). http://www.legislation.gov.uk/ukpga/2004/31/contents.

Children and Social Work Act. (2017). http://www.legislation.gov.uk/ukpga/2017/16/contents/enacted.

Cicchetti, D., & Toth, S. L (Eds.). (1991). *Rochester symposium on developmental psychopathology*, vol. 3. *Models and integrations*. University of Rochester Press.

Cicchetti, D., Toth, S. L., & Rogosch, F. A. (1999). The efficacy of toddler-parent psychotherapy to increase attachment security in offspring of depressed mothers. *Attachment & Human Development*, *1*(1), 34–66. https://doi.org/10.1080/14616739900134021.

Cooper, A., Hetherington, R., & Katz, I. (2003). *The risk factor: Making the child protection system work for children*. Demos.

Cross, S., Hubbard, E., & Munro, E. (2010). *Reclaiming social work: London Borough of Hackney children and young people's services*. Human Reliability and London School of Economics and Political Science.

Davis, E. P, Glynn, L. M., Waffarn, F., & Sandman, C. A. (2011). Prenatal maternal stress regulation. *Journal of Child Psychology and Psychiatry and Allied Disciplines*, *52*(2), 119–129.

De Jong, G., Schout, G., Meijer, E., Mulder, C., Abma, T. (2015). Enabling social support and resilience: Outcomes of family group conferencing in public mental health care. *European Journal of Social Work*, *19*, 1–18. https://doi.org/10.1080/13691457.2015.1081585.

De Shazer, S., Berg, I. K., Lipchik, E., Nunnally, E., Molnar, A., Gingerich, W., & Weiner-Davis, M. (1986). Brief therapy: Focused solution development. *Family Process*, *25*(2), 207–221. https://doi.org/10.1111/j.1545-5300.1986.00207.x.

Deaton, A., & Cartwright, N. (2018). Understanding and misunderstanding randomized controlled trials. *Social Science & Medicine* (*1982*), 210, 2–21. https://doi.org/10.1016/j.socscimed.2017.12.005.

Department for Education. (2017). *Children's social care innovation programme final evaluation report*, DfE. https://www.gov.uk/government/publications/childrens-social-care-innovation-programme-final-evaluation-report.

Department for Education. (2018). *Working together to safeguard children. Statutory guidance on inter-agency working to safeguard and promote the welfare of children*. DfE. https://www.gov.uk/government/publications/working-together-to-safeguard-children--2.

Department for Education. (2021a). Guidance: Strengthening families protecting children (SFPC) programme. DfE. https://www.gov.uk/guidance/strengthening-families-protecting-children-sfpc-programme#sfpc-projects.

Department for Education. (2021b). Promoting the education of children with a social worker: Virtual school head role extension. DfE. Virtual school head role extension to children with a social worker - GOV.UK (www.gov.uk)

Department for Education. (2022). Characteristics of children in need: 2021 to 2022. DfE. https://www.gov.uk/government/statistics/characteristics-of-children-in-need-2021-to-2022.

Drozdick, L. W., Wahlstrom, D., Zhu, J., & Weiss, L. G. (2012). The Wechsler adult intelligence scale – fourth edition and the Wechsler memory scale – fourth edition. In D. P. Flanagan & P. L. Harrison (Eds.), *Contemporary intellectual assessment: Theories, tests, and issues* (pp. 197–223). Guilford Press.

Ehlers, A. (2013). Trauma-focused cognitive behavior therapy for posttraumatic stress disorder and acute stress disorder. In G. Simos & S. G. Hofmann, (Eds.), *CBT for anxiety disorders: A practitioner book* (pp. 161–190). John Wiley & Sons.

Fals-Stewart, W., Lam, W. K., & Kelley, M. L. (2009). Learning sobriety together: Behavioural couples therapy for alcoholism and drug abuse. *Journal of Family Therapy*, *31*, 115–125.

Fazel, M., Stratford, H. J., Rowsell, E., Chan, C., Griffiths, H., & Robjant, K. (2020). Five applications of narrative exposure therapy for children and adolescents presenting with post-traumatic stress disorders. *Frontiers in Psychiatry, 11, Article 19*. https://doi.org/103389/fpsyt.2020.00019.

Featherston, R. J., Shlonsky, A., Lewis, C., Luong, M.-L., Downie, L. E., Vogel, A. P., Granger, C., Hamilton, B., & Galvin, K. (2019). Interventions to mitigate bias in social work decision-making: A systematic review. *Research on Social Work Practice*, *29*(7), 741–752. https://doi.org/10.1177/1049731518819160.

Fonagy, P., & Bateman, A. W. (2016). Adversity, attachment, and mentalizing. *Comprehensive Psychiatry*, *64*, 59–66. https://doi.org/10.1016/j.comppsych.2015.11.006.

Ford, T., Vostanis, P., Meltzer, H., & Goodman, R. (2007). Psychiatric disorder among British children looked after by local authorities: Comparison with children living in private households. *The British Journal of Psychiatry, 190*(4), 319–325.

Forrester, D., Westlake, D., Glynn, G., Barnes, J., & Pavlou, T. (2017). *Family safeguarding Hertfordshire evaluation report*. Department for Education.

Fraiberg, S., Adelson, E., & Shapiro, V. (1975). Ghosts in the nursery. A psychoanalytic approach to the problems of impaired infant-mother relationships. *Journal of the American Academy of Child Psychiatry, 14*(3), 387–421. https://doi.org/10.1016/s0002-7138(09)61442-4.

Fredman, G., Papadopoulou, A., & Worwood, E. (2018). Introduction: Collaborative consultation in mental health. In G. Fredman, A. Papadopoulou, & E. Worwood (Eds.), *Collaborative consultation in mental health: Guidelines for the new consultant* (pp. 1–18). Routledge. https://doi.org/10.4324/9781315696652-1.

Friedman, S. H., & McEwan, M. V. (2018). Treated mental illness and the risk of child abuse perpetration. *Psychiatric Services (Washington, DC), 69*(2), 211–216. https://doi.org/10.1176/appi.ps.201700120.

Goodman, R. (1997). The strengths and difficulties questionnaire: A research note. *Child Psychology & Psychiatry & Allied Disciplines, 38*(5), 581–586. https://doi.org/10.1111/j.1469-7610.1997.tb01545.x.

Graham, J. R. (2006). *MMPI-2: Assessing personality and psychopathology* (4th ed.). Oxford University Press.

Henggeler, S. W., Schoenwald, S. K., Borduin, C. M., Rowland, M. D., & Cunningham, P. B. (2009). *Multisystemic therapy for antisocial behavior in children and adolescents* (2nd ed.). Guilford Press.

Holen, F. van., Vanderfaeillie, J., Omer, H., & Vanschoonlandt, F. (2016). Training in nonviolent resistance for foster parents: A randomized controlled trial. *Research on Social Work Practice, 28*(8), 931–942. https://doi.org/10.1177/1049731516662915.

Huestis, M., & Choo, R. (2002). Drug abuse's smallest victims: In utero drug exposure. *Forensic Science International, 128*, 20–30.

Hughes, D. (1997). *Facilitating developmental attachment*. Jason Aronson.

Hughes, D. (2006). *Building the bonds of attachment* (2nd ed.). Jason Aronson.

Isokuortti, N., Aaltio, E., Laajasalo, T., & Barlow, J. (2020). Effectiveness of child protection practice models: A systematic review. *Child Abuse & Neglect, 108*, 104632. https://doi.org/10.1016/j.chiabu.2020.104632.

Johnstone, L. (2017). Psychological formulation as an alternative to psychiatric diagnosis. *Journal of Humanistic Psychology. 58*(1). https://doi.org/10.1177/0022167817722230.

Johnstone, L., & Boyle, M. (2018). The power threat meaning framework: An alternative nondiagnostic conceptual system. *Journal of Humanistic Psychology*. https://doi.org/10.1177/0022167818793289.

Karam, E. G., Fayyad, J. A., Farhat, C., Pluess, M., Haddad, Y. C., Tabet, C. C., Farah, L., & Kessler, R. C. (2019). Role of childhood adversities and environmental sensitivity in the development of post-traumatic stress disorder in war-exposed Syrian refugee children and adolescents. *The British Journal of Psychiatry, 214*(6), 354–360. https://doi.org/10.1192/bjp.2018.272.

Kennedy, H., & Underdown, A. (2018). Video interaction guidance: Promoting secure attachment and optimal development for children, parents and professionals. In P. Leach

(Ed.), *Transforming infant wellbeing: Research, policy and practice for the first 1001 critical days* (pp. 224–237). Routledge. https://doi.org/10.4324/9781315452890-23.

Kohlhoff, J., Lieneman, C., Cibralic, S., Traynor, N., & McNeil, C. B. (2022). Attachment-based parenting interventions and evidence of changes in toddler attachment patterns: An overview. *Clinical Child and Family Psychology Review, 25*(4), 737–753. https://doi.org/10.1007/s10567-022-00405-4.

Laming, W. H. (2003). The Victoria Climbie inquiry: Report of an inquiry by Lord Laming (Cm. 5730). The Stationery Office. https://assets.publishing.service.gov.uk/government/uploads/system/uploads/attachment_data/file/273183/5730.pdf.

Law, D., & Jacob, J. (2015). *Goals and goals based outcomes (GBOs): Some useful information* (3rd ed.). CAMHS Press.

Lehmann, S., Heiervang, E., Havik, T., & Havik, O. (2014). Screening foster children for mental disorders: Properties of the Strengths and Difficulties Questionnaire. *PLoS ONE, 9*(7), e102134. https://doi.org/10.1371/journal.pone.0102134.

Lieberman, A. F. (1991). Attachment theory and infant-parent psychotherapy: Some conceptual, clinical and research considerations. In D. Cicchetti & S. L. Toth (Eds.), *Rochester symposium on developmental psychopathology,* vol. 3. *Models and integrations* (pp. 261–287). University of Rochester Press.

Lushey, C., Hyde-Dryden, G., Holmes, L., Blackmore, J., & Department for Education (DfE) Loughborough University. (2017). *Evaluation of the no wrong door innovation programme. children's social care innovation programme evaluation report*. DfE.

MacAlister, J. (2022). *The independent review of children's social care: Final report*. DfE

Macdonald, G., Higgins, J. P. T., Ramchandani, P., Valentine, J. C., Bronger, L. P., Klein, P., O'Daniel, R., Pickering, M., Rademaker, B., Richardson, G., & Taylor, M. (2012). Cognitive-behavioural interventions for children who have been sexually abused. *Cochrane Database of Systematic Reviews*, (5), CD001930. https://doi.org/10.1002/14651858.CD001930.pub3.

Milburn, N. L., Lynch, M., & Jackson, J. (2008). Early identification of mental health needs for children in care: A therapeutic assessment programme for statutory clients of child protection. *Clinical Child Psychology and Psychiatry, 13*(1), 31–47. https://doi.org/10.1177/1359104507086339.

Miller, W. R., & Rollnick, S. (2013). *Motivational interviewing: Helping people change* (3rd ed.). Guilford Press.

Monson, C. M., & Shnaider, P. (2014). *Treating PTSD with cognitive-behavioral therapies: Interventions that work*. American Psychological Association.

Munro, E. (2011). *The Munro review of child protection. Final report. A child centred system*. DfE.

National Institute for Health and Care Excellence [NICE]. (2009). *Child maltreatment: When to suspect maltreatment in the under 18s*. NICE. https://www.nice.org.uk/guidance/cg89/chapter/1-Guidance.

National Institute for Health and Care Excellence [NICE]. (2015). *Children's attachment: Attachment in children and young people who are adopted from care, in care or at high risk of going into care*. NICE.

National Institute for Health and Care Excellence [NICE]. (2016). *Domestic violence and abuse*. NICE. https://www.nice.org.uk/guidance/ng76.

National Institute for Health and Care Excellence [NICE]. (2017, October). *Child abuse and neglect*. NICE. https://www.nice.org.uk/guidance/ng76/chapter/Recommendations#factors-that-increase-vulnerability-to-child-abuse-and-neglect.

National Institute for Health and Care Excellence [NICE]. (2021). *Looked after children and young people*. NICE. https://www.nice.org.uk/guidance/ng73.

Neuner, F., Catani, C., Ruf, M., Schauer, E., Schauer, M., & Telber, T. (2008). Narrative exposure therapy for the treatment of traumatized children and adolescents (KidNET): From neurocognitive theory to field intervention. *Child and Adolescent Psychiatric Clinics of North America*, *17*(3), 641–664.

O'Hara, L., Smith, E. R., Barlow, J., Livingstone, N., Herath, N. I., Wei, Y., Spreckelsen, T. F., & Macdonald, G. (2019). Video feedback for parental sensitivity and attachment security in children under five years. *The Cochrane database of systematic reviews*, *11*(11), CD012348. https://doi.org/10.1002/14651858.CD012348.pub2.

Ofsted. (2011, April). The voice of the child: Learning lessons from serious case reviews. Ofsted. https://assets.publishing.service.gov.uk/government/uploads/system/uploads/attachment_data/file/526981/The_voice_of_the_child.pdf.

Omer, H. (2004). *Nonviolent resistance: A new approach to violent and self-destructive children* (trans, S. London-Sapir). Cambridge University Press.

Padesky, C. A. (2020). Collaborative case conceptualization: Client knows best. *Cognitive and Behavioral Practice*, *27*(4), 292–404. https://doi.org/10.1016/j.cbpra.2020.06.003.

Parker, B., & Turner, W. (2013). Psychoanalytic/psychodynamic psychotherapy for children and adolescents who have been sexually abused. *Cochrane Database of Systematic Reviews*, (7), CD008162. doi: https://doi.org/10.1002/14651858.CD008162.pub2.

Redfern, S. (2015). *Reflective parenting: A guide to understanding what's going on in your child's mind*. Routledge. https://doi.org/10.4324/9781315764108.

Rose, R. (2012). *Life story therapy with traumatized children: A model for practice*. Jessica Kingsley.

Schaeffer, C. M., Swenson, C. C., & Powell, J. S. (2021). Multisystemic therapy - building stronger families (MST-BSF): Substance misuse, child neglect, and parenting outcomes from an 18-month randomized effectiveness trial. *Child Abuse & Neglect*, *122*, 105379. doi: https://doi.org/10.1016/j.chiabu.2021.105379.

Selvini-Palazzoli, M. (1978). *Self-starvation: From individual to family therapy in the treatment of anorexia nervosa*. Jason Aronson.

Snodgrass, C., & Selman, M. (2019). The psychologically informed partnership approach: Innovation in working with vulnerable and marginalised children, young people and families. *Clinical Psychology Forum*, *321*, 12–18.

Skinner, G. C., Bywaters, P. W., Bilson, A., Duschinsky, R., Clements, K., & Hutchinson, D. (2020). The 'toxic trio' (domestic violence, substance misuse and mental ill-health): How good is the evidence base? *Children and Youth Services Review*, 105678.

Spratt, T., & Nett, J. (2013). *Child protection systems: An international comparison of good practice examples of five countries (Australia, Germany, Finland, Sweden, United Kingdom) with recommendations for Switzerland*. 10.13140/RG.2.1.3737.2249

Stith, S. M., McCollum, E. E., & Rosen, K. H. (2011). Domestic violence–focused couples therapy within a solution-focused framework. In S. M. Stith, E. E. McCollum, & K. H. Rosen,

Couples therapy for domestic violence: Finding safe solutions (pp. 31–42). American Psychological Association. https://doi.org/10.1037/12329-003.

Suchman, N., Decoste, C., Leigh, D., & Borelli, J. (2010). Reflective functioning in mothers with drug use disorders: Implications for dyadic interactions with infants and toddlers. *Attachment & Human Development*, *12*, 567–585. https://doi.org/10.1080/14616734.2010.501988.

Swenson, C. C., Schaeffer, C. M., Henggeler, S. W., Faldowski, R., & Mayhew, A. M. (2010). Multisystemic therapy for child abuse and neglect: A randomized effectiveness trial. *Journal of Family Psychology, 24*(4), 497–507. https://doi.org/10.1037/a0020324.

Tarren-Sweeney, M. (2010). It's time to re-think mental health services for children in care, and those adopted from care. Clinical Child Psychology and Psychiatry, *15*(4), 613–626. doi: https://doi.org/10.1177/1359104510377702.

Teggart, T., & Menary, J. (2005). An investigation of the mental health needs of children looked after by Craigavon and Banbridge health and social services trust. *Child Care in Practice*, *11*, 39–49.

Treisman, K. (2016). *Working with relational and developmental trauma in children and adolescents*. Routledge.

Tsirimokou, A., Kloess, J. A., & Dhinse, S. K. (2022). Vicarious post-traumatic growth in professionals exposed to traumatogenic material: A systematic literature review. *Trauma, Violence, & Abuse*, *24*(3). https://doi.org/10.1177/15248380221082079.

Weinblatt, U., & Omer, H. (2008). Nonviolent resistance: A treatment for parents of children with acute behavior problems. *Journal of Marital and Family Therapy*, *34*(1), 75–92. https://doi.org/10.1111/j.1752-0606.2008.00054.x.

Weiss, D. S., & Marmar, C. R. (1997). The impact of event scale – revised. In J. P. Wilson & T. M. Keane (Eds.), *Assessing psychological trauma and PTSD* (pp. 399–411). Guilford Press.

Whitaker, D. J., Self-Brown, S., Hayat, M. J., Osborne, M. C., Weeks, E. A., Reidy, D. E., & Lyons, M. (2020). Effect of the SafeCare© intervention on parenting outcomes among parents in child welfare systems: A cluster randomized trial. *Preventive Medicine*, *138*, 106167. doi: https://doi.org/10.1016/j.ypmed.2020.106167.

White, M., & Epston, D. (1990). *Narrative means to therapeutic ends*. W.W. Norton.

Wolpert, M., Harris, R., Hodges, S., Fuggle, P., James, R., Wiener, A., McKenna, C., Law, D., York, A., Jones, M., Fonagy, P., Fleming, I., & Munk, S. (2019). *THRIVE framework for system change*. CAMHS Press. https://www.annafreud.org/media/9254/thrive-framework-for-system-change-2019.pdf.

Wolpert, M., Harris, R., Jones, M., Hodges, S., Fuggle, P., James, R., Wiener, A., Mckenna, C., Law, D., & Fonagy, P. (2014). *THRIVE: The AFC-Tavistock model for CAMHS*. CAMHS Press. https://repository.tavistockandportman.ac.uk/941/1/Thrive%20model%20for%20CAMHS.pdf.

Working Together with Parents Network [WTPN] (2021). Good practice guidance on working with parents with learning disabilities. WTPN.

Worwood, E., & Fredman, G. (2018). Evaluating collaborative consultation. In G. Fredman, A. Papadopoulou, & E. Worwood (Eds.), *Collaborative consultation in mental health: Guidelines for the new consultant* (pp. 93–111). Routledge. https://doi.org/10.4324/9781315696652-6.

27

Trauma-informed Practice

Sian Barnett

This chapter will focus on the impact of complex developmental trauma on children and the value of trauma-informed practice as a whole system approach. The chapter will start by defining trauma, complex developmental trauma and trauma-informed practice, reviewing the theory and research underpinning this area of work. It will go on to outline the value of trauma-informed practice in organisations and discuss the benefits and challenges for staff and practitioners using trauma-informed practice, the evidence base and areas for development. Trauma-informed practice in school settings will be described to illustrate the implementation of trauma-informed practice within a system.

27.1 Introduction

There is a growing awareness of how widespread trauma is and an increasing understanding of the significant impact of complex developmental trauma on mental health across the lifespan (Alexander et al., 2023). Trauma-informed practice has guided developments in psychological practice in clinical and community settings for many years. The ideas and psychological theories associated with trauma-informed practice are therefore not new. They are however, increasingly grounded in well-tested psychological theory, knowledge about child development, evolving research developments in neuroscience, practice-based and evidence-based practice, in an increasing number of health, public service, and community settings. For these reasons, and because of concerns about increasing levels of adversity for children and young people, as a result of global events (Covid-19 pandemic, war, racial inequalities and the current cost of living crisis), trauma-informed practice has become part of the zeitgeist.

27.2 Defining Trauma

Everyone experiences some adversity in life and managing and overcoming adversity is an important part of human development that can build resilience. In understanding

Child Psychology: Pathways to Good Practice, First Edition.
Edited by Helen Pote, Anna Picciotto and Clare Norris.

trauma and its impact, it is important to acknowledge that different people have different temperaments, capacities to cope and different resources to draw upon to support them. How a person reacts to trauma will vary depending on multiple factors, including the nature of the traumatic event, support networks, age, developmental stage, family, cultural background, race, religion and community. An essential aspect of understanding and working with trauma therefore involves consideration of context and aspects of people's identity, culture, and experience, or Social Graces (Burnham, 2012; Burnham & Roper-Hall, 2017)). See Chapter 7 for further details on Social Graces.

Dictionary definitions describe trauma as an injury (or wound) caused by an extrinsic agent, or an emotional/ behavioural state resulting from severe, mental, emotional stress or physical injury. The *Diagnostic and statistical manual of mental disorders* 5th ed. (APA, 2013) (*DSM-5*) defines trauma as actual or threatened death, serious injury or sexual violence, including stressful events not involving immediate threat to life or physical injury.

There is a consensus in the literature that trauma is an adverse event or series of events experienced as potentially threatening to one's safety, life, or sense of self. This threat may overwhelm a person's capacity to cope, either temporarily or in the longer term. In addition to the actual level of threat, an individual's perception of the event, how they respond at the time and in the aftermath, may determine how traumatic an event is for an individual. The trauma experience and perception of that experience has the potential to negatively impact an individual's ability to function and their wellbeing. It is notable that definitions of trauma are largely focused on the individual, and an individual's response to traumatic events, despite the significant interpersonal, political and community context of many traumatic incidents, or in the case of racial trauma, incremental incidents or lived experience. Perhaps it is time to embrace a wider definition of trauma that takes account of the interpersonal impact of trauma on families and communities. As well as the importance of relationships, communities and systems in influencing recovery from trauma and even the opportunities for growth, development and change following trauma.

The research literature on the prevalence of trauma indicates that trauma is relatively common, with estimates that one-half to two-thirds of children experience some form of traumatic event (Fondren et al., 2020; Treisman, 2021). Many adults and children will recover from trauma by processing what happened, through play, or talking with friends or family, coming to terms with the event over time. Following a traumatic event, approximately one in eight people experience symptoms diagnosable in *DSM-5* as post-traumatic stress disorder (PTSD) (NICE, 2018). This means that they are likely to be hypervigilant (on high alert for danger and easily startled) and to be reliving the experience (having nightmares and symptoms such as flashbacks, where the event feels like it is happening in the present). They may also avoid cognitive, sensory and situational reminders of what happened. PTSD in young children has been shown to present slightly differently, with more changes in behaviour, events replicated in play and less obvious avoidance. This has been reflected in changes to the *DSM-5* diagnostic criteria, which now includes a subtype for pre-school children.

Some children and adults will need additional support to recover from traumatic experiences and for young children the literature supports a systemic rather than individual approach for the provision of PTSD interventions (Bartlett et al., 2017; Holmes et al., 2014). Many children will not have the words to describe their experience. This is significant for children, who experience trauma pre-verbally or with language difficulties, who may struggle to develop a verbal narrative to help them process or make sense of the trauma (Shonkoff et al., 2012).

27.3 The Impact of Complex Developmental Trauma on Children

Single event trauma such as an assault, accident, car crash or robbery may be experienced differently from complex trauma. Complex trauma can impact individuals at any age and includes multiple occurrences of interpersonal, community threat or natural disasters over what may be a prolonged period.

Complex developmental trauma specifically describes the cumulative experience, and impact of a child experiencing abuse (physical, sexual, emotional), or neglect, physical illness, losses or ongoing racial, cultural or community traumas, witnessing domestic violence or significant parental mental health problems. Complex developmental trauma effects children and young people at a critical developmental time and stage in life, whilst their brains and bodies are still growing, and whilst they are learning about the world, themselves and other people. It often happens within the context of close relationships and sometimes over the duration of many years. For lots of children, these traumatic experiences will occur within the parental attachment relationships (Bowlby, 1951), designed to keep them safe and help them to develop and grow. This may impact their developmental trajectory, cognitively, socially, emotionally, psychologically, neurologically and biologically. In summary, there is a potential impact of complex developmental trauma on all areas of child development.

27.3.1 Adverse Childhood Events and Complex Developmental Trauma

Researchers Felitti and Anda (Felitti et al., 1998) identified 10 adverse childhood experiences (ACES) within the family context. They asked 17,000 adults to rate whether they had experienced these ACES. The key findings of their study were that ACES were common, and that there was a correlation between ACES and long-term serious physical and mental health issues.

There have been criticisms of the retrospective nature of ACES research, the fact that Felitti and Anda identified a relatively small number of ACES, and the lack of differentiation between the potential impact of adverse experiences such as divorce, as compared to childhood sexual abuse. Since the original study, research into ACES has developed to include the experiences of racism, bullying and community violence. In recognition of the range of ACES, it is not advisable to simply count ACES to determine a clinical intervention, or to assume that each ACE is likely to have the same impact. However, ACES can be a useful aid to prompt consideration of whether a child or adult may have experienced trauma, and how this contributes to a formulation or intervention to support them. Since the original ACES study, research studies have continued to demonstrate that children who have experienced complex developmental trauma are more at risk of future incidents of assault, abuse, interpersonal violence, relationship difficulties and intergenerational trauma (Labella et al., 2018). This provides a compelling argument for the allocation of public health and government funding of early intervention and prevention projects and services (Stubley, 2020).

27.4 The Neuroscience of Trauma

Researchers in the field of neuroscience have explored the impact of complex developmental trauma on brain development. This contributes to the understanding of why children who have experienced trauma may develop PTSD, anxiety, depression or emotion regulation difficulties, or demonstrate withdrawn behaviour, and difficulties making or maintaining relationships.

Traumatic experiences are processed by the limbic system in the brain. To ensure survival, humans have developed an alarm system that provides us with a rapid response to threat. The amygdala, which effectively sounds the threat alarm, sits within the limbic system and is the area of the brain responsible for processing emotions. The thalamus interprets information from the external world, via our senses. With the help of the hippocampus, which stores memories of previous experiences, the thalamus decides quickly whether the amygdala or the cortex (the thinking part of the brain) is best placed to respond to a situation. If there is danger, the amygdala triggers the endocrine system to flood the body with cortisol and adrenalin so that we can fight the danger, flee, freeze or flop (play dead) to survive. If there is no danger or the danger subsides, the cortex takes over.

Cicchetti (2010) reported that complex developmental trauma can lead to differences in cortisol levels, executive functioning, information processing, reward and motivation, mood and managing emotions, sleep, appetite, activity levels and survival responses. McCrory et al. (2011) found that shockingly, but perhaps unsurprisingly, children exposed to physical abuse and domestic violence show hypervigilance to danger and similar activation in their amygdala as that observed in soldiers before and after involvement in combat situations.

The threat system of a child who has experienced complex developmental trauma has been compared to a smoke alarm reacting to the smoke from burnt toast rather than a fire: because they have become sensitised to threat. Children in survival mode have less capacity to access the cortex, which is still growing and developing into a person's 20s. The cortex is responsible for the executive functioning skills required to think things through, problem solve and plan; essential skills in positive decision making and learning. Children who have experienced complex developmental trauma may therefore miss out on learning and develop a skills lag, socially, academically and emotionally (Perlman et al., 2008). The need to support children to calm down, to feel safe enough to be able to think and learn has significant implications for parents, carers and professionals working with children. The good news is that the plasticity of the human brain means that children and adults can continue to learn and develop new skills with support and time.

27.5 Attachment Theory

Alongside the neuroscience, attachment theory (Bowlby, 1951) is a helpful way of explaining why safe adult relationships are so important for child development, but may be challenging for children who have experienced complex developmental trauma. Bowlby described how in terms of evolution, attachment relationships are necessary for survival, protecting helpless babies and young children from danger. Babies and children get their basic needs: safety, food, sleep and comfort met, and come to make sense of the external world around them, as well as their internal, emotional and cognitive world, through these relationships. They learn about themselves and whether or not they are worth thinking about and loveable. If adults provide containment (Bion, 1959) – demonstrating care and attention, trying to help make sense of, name and respond to their emotions and experiences, and give them back to the child in a processed more manageable form, they will continue to communicate, and learn. A behaviour like crying is recognised as an expression of a child's need, that requires meeting, and the adult tries to read the child's cues, in order to do this, for example, 'I think you may be hungry, let's give you a feed/a snack, I think you are feeling sad, I will give you a cuddle.' Over time, with good enough parenting (Winnicott, 1973), when caregivers try to meet a child's needs, children learn to identify their own needs and start to name and manage their emotions for themselves. They also learn to seek help from others when they have difficult feelings and experiences (co-regulation). Available, caring attachment figures provide a safe base from which a child can explore the world. Attachment relationships with adults also provide a child with internal working models, or templates for how they expect to be treated by others in their future relationships.

Research into child development has looked in detail at reciprocity, or intersubjective attunement, in adult–child relationships (Tronick, 1989). Reciprocity describes the two-way interaction between children and adults, where they respond to each other. Good enough parenting acknowledges that reciprocity is a dance, and that caring adults and children will get out of step with each other, having ordinary ruptures or misunderstandings in their relationships. Adults do not have to get things right all the time. If relationship ruptures are acknowledged, repaired and balanced with positive interactions, then children tolerate these missteps in relationships, continue to learn, develop, grow and are more likely to go on to explore healthy relationships. In fact, with the experience of rupture and repair comes resilience. Without repair, however, children may be left to deal with difficult or traumatic experiences, without the resources to cope. This can be detrimental to child development (Tronick, 1989). When children experience, abuse or neglect, within relationships that are meant to keep them safe, they may struggle to feel safe, trust others, understand or process their experiences, and their own, or other's emotions (Baylin, 2017).

The ability of children and adults to form different attachment relationships with different people is significant and hopeful for practitioners working with individuals impacted by trauma.

27.6 Trauma-informed Systems

In understanding the impact of trauma on children and young people, we need to consider how to develop trauma-informed services to ameliorate these experiences. This also involves supporting the staff working within these systems. Understanding the impact of trauma is highly relevant to adults and staff working in child services, as we know that dysregulated or traumatised adults will struggle to support children or other adults to regulate. Many adults working in child-focused services may have experienced childhood trauma, or be experiencing current adversity in their lives. Large systems like the NHS, (out-patient services, CAMHS and inpatient wards), Children's Social Care, Youth Justice, Education; including early years and schools, as well services in the private and voluntary sector) are designed to support and meet the health, social, and learning needs of children and their families. These services risk inadvertently re-traumatising children and families and their staff, without a comprehensive understanding of the impact of trauma, reflective management, and positive planning.

Staff who work in Youth services, health, the Police/Safer Schools officers, fire fighters and ambulance crews, social care and education are in direct contact with young people and communities experiencing high levels of trauma. They may be working with individuals and communities with a history of trauma directly associated with previous interactions with their services. Community members may be fearful of the organisation, avoidant or triggered into survival mode, despite the best intentions of the individual professional they are working with. Skilled, well-supported trauma-informed community-based practitioners have the opportunity to become the 'friendly-face' of a service and to provide a community with an alternative, positive experience. However, staff in these organisations also risk exposure to trauma in their work and in the helping professions there is a risk of vicarious trauma, PTSD or burnout (Figley, 1998; Sprang et al., 2011). Staff may lose sight of why they took on the role in the first place expressing thoughts of failure, low mood, anxiety and low self-esteem (Treisman, 2017). Staff therefore require training and support to recognise and understand trauma reactions in themselves and others.

Alongside training in trauma-informed practice, work with trauma-informed practitioners, is important to help staff in a system understand trauma and consider how trauma-informed ideas fit with the dominant culture of their organisation. Curiosity and empathy from trauma-informed practitioners is key in meeting a system where it is at, supporting a system through change and introducing new ideas in a way that they can be taken forward and owned within an organisation. To do this well requires a clear understanding of the process of organisational change (Lawson & Price, 2003) and methods of evaluating change. Staff need to understand the approach, be able to ask questions, see how trauma-informed practice is relevant and helpful to themselves and their peer group and worth the time and effort to implement; they need to be part of the process of change, providing a helpful feedback loop. The individual strengths and skills of team members can be utilised in a working group, that represents the service and supports the transition to trauma-informed practice, whilst hearing and responding to voices of disagreement. This creates an organisation in which connection and access to opportunities are prioritised, with open, honest communication to develop services.

Trauma-informed practice as a whole system approach is valuable. Therapy is not the only helpful intervention for traumatised children, families or staff, and will not be desirable to or needed by everyone. Trauma-informed practice can allow practitioners to have a bigger reach and impact through intervening in the whole system, with every interaction having the potential for positive impact.

For these reasons, a gold-standard service delivery is underpinned by a trauma-informed approach and a cascading model of containment (Douglas, 1997). Leaders should try to model and champion trauma-informed practice, taking collective care of each other, and the staff working for them. In this way they can provide a secure base and sense of belonging to staff, so that they have the emotional and cognitive capacity to continue to take care of children and families. The trauma-informed approach is ideally then owned and implemented at all levels of the organisation. It can also be helpful to appoint a champion and working party for staff wellbeing and self-care.

Trauma-informed systems need to be open and curious to allow for continual learning. They recognise their strengths and limitations and work to be responsive to feedback, to diversity of culture, experiences, training and opinion. They actively demonstrate an appreciation and respect for difference. This includes being culturally aware and sensitive and being able to identify and be committed to addressing systemic racism, structural inequality and all forms of discrimination. Treisman (2021) describes this as cultural humility, on the basis that we can never truly be competent in someone else's cultural experience. Minority staff need to be represented across all levels of an organisation and be part of recruitment and interviewing, decision making and raising issues, as well as proposing solutions. It is essential to enable staff and service users to have a voice that is actively listened to, facilitating an experience of safety, dignity, confidentiality and choice in service provision.

Organisations need dedicated time and spaces for supervision, line management, service user groups, working parties and reflective practice groups. These spaces are vital to enable thinking and reflection; the executive functioning capacities that risk being shut down in the face of trauma and stress. Reflective spaces where staff come together can help counteract or provide something of an antidote to the way in which trauma is absorbed within systems.

A trauma-informed organisation should be welcoming, attending carefully to physical and felt safety. In this way it tries to provide an environment that staff and service users want to come to, and meets the needs of and represents the community it serves. Whilst taking account of and acknowledging practical limitations, learning walks and user feedback or focus groups are excellent ways to consider the physical environment of a service, from the point of information giving, to accessibility for different members of the community. Leaflets, letters and information should be available through different media, including online, and in different languages and adapted for people of different ages and abilities. Signs should be worded positively with visual images informing people where to go or what to do, rather than what not to do for example, 'This is a calm, quiet area, please use a quiet voice', rather than 'No talking.' Reception areas and décor should be inviting, with toys that are cared for and developmentally appropriate and the environment should be sensitive to neurodiversity. Staff should be welcoming, friendly, and calm in their words, body language and facial expressions, sensitive to the anxiety or even trauma that someone might feel entering the building or accessing their service. Some examples are:

- A CAMHS service had a bright, child-friendly mural painted by a local charity, at the entrance, and pictures drawn by children decorating the reception walls.
- A youth and community centre displayed inspirational quotes along the corridor that the young people had identified as personally important to them.
- A school's senior leaders greeted pupils each morning with a friendly smile, 'good morning' and a tray of bagels. This supported a smooth transition into school. Breakfast helped with children's concentration and regulation during the day, and parents and pupils felt held in mind and cared for.

Trauma-informed systems should celebrate good ideas, and 'shining moments' in meetings, newsletters, displays or emails. In line with the attention rule in social learning theory, (Bandura, 1977), when positive practice is attended to and shaped through specific praise and encouragement, it increases. Trauma-informed practice takes a strengths-based rather than a problem saturated approach, which can too easily become the dominant narrative, both in traumatised systems, and formulations around traumatised children. Individuals feel appreciated through the recognition of birthdays, life events and celebrations as well as transitions, the losses of staff leaving and difficult individual and community events. This helps create a safe environment in which teams can learn together, acknowledging and learning from mistakes and managing change.

Team meetings and team away days help to ensure a supportive environment and shared understanding and approach. See Box 27.1 for an example of using the Tree of Life (Ncube, 2006) as a team building activity in an away day.

Box 27.1 The Tree of Life

The Tree of Life (Ncube, 2006) is a narrative strengths-based community approach developed to support children in Zimbabwe affected by the trauma of HIV/AIDS. A trauma-informed team used The Tree of Life at their away day as a creative way to support staff to explore their relationship to their work. They developed a collage of a tree with roots representing their background, culture and experiences. The ground represented their hobbies and everyday tasks. The trunk represented their skills and strengths. The branches depicted their hopes and goals and the leaves depicted significant people in their work lives. The fruits were the gifts or pleasure they received in their work. The team could also have created a forest of trees representing individual staff. The team tree was then used to support a conversation about the storms they faced and how they might weather them together. This enabled them to continue the work they were doing and to consider how to further develop the service offer.

Like all high-quality services, trauma-informed systems should provide clear roles, responsibilities and expectations for staff and service delivery, with Specific, Measurable, Achievable, Realistic and Time-bound (SMART) goals. The service ethos and philosophy should be outlined in policy and mission statements, with a focus on early intervention and prevention. Staff should be trained in trauma-informed practice and able to access information about the emerging evidence base.

Appraisals and line management are an important way of identifying an individual's professional strengths as well as any needs and areas for development. Staff can be supported to develop skills and knowledge, and access continuing professional development (CPD) and mentoring. Challenging behaviour in an organisation or system can be addressed thoughtfully when behaviour is seen as the tip of an iceberg and a communication of need. This enables management to remain curious about what is behind (or beneath the surface of) the communication and the purpose it serves the individual, or the system, in order to understand how to respond to it.

Caseloads and responsibilities should be titrated according to individual abilities, needs and any triggers or hotspots, and the physical work environment considered and adapted for staff who identify as neurodiverse or with social, learning, emotional or physical needs. See Box 27.2 for examples of trauma-informed adaptations in clinical services.

Box 27.2 Adapting practice: Tany and Roberto

Tany worked in a trauma-informed clinical service. She reflected in supervision on the impact of her experiences of trauma. She agreed with her supervisor that she would not work with cases where similar aspects of trauma were explicit in the referral, whilst she explored her own experiences in therapy. Her caseload was carefully managed and adjusted. This was regularly reviewed, and additional supervisory support provided when similar trauma experiences were disclosed by families she was already working with.

Roberto has autism and ADHD. He is easily distracted and overstimulated by noise. He experiences pressure to talk when others are in an office with him. His workplace have set up a quiet room where a maximum of two staff can work at any one time.

27.7 Defining Trauma-informed Practice in Organisations

Despite an increase in interest in this approach, until recently, there was no working definition of trauma-informed practice and it was seen as an amorphous concept (Hanson & Lang, 2014). The Department of Health and Social Care (2022) sought to rectify this by adopting principles based on those developed by the US Substance Abuse and Mental Health Services Administration, (SAMHSA, 2014). Within this definition, trauma-informed practice: **realises** that trauma can affect individuals, groups and communities and that the impact can be wide ranging; aims to support those in a system to **recognise** the signs and symptoms of trauma, and the negative impact on the ability of individuals and communities to feel safe or to develop trusting relationships. It also seeks to improve accessibility and quality by creating culturally sensitive, safe environments that people trust, **responding** by integrating knowledge into policies, procedures and practices. It prepares staff to work in collaboration and partnership with people and empowers them to make choices about their health and wellbeing. Trauma-informed practice acknowledges the need to see beyond an individual's presenting behaviours, and to ask, 'What does this person need?' rather than 'What is wrong with them?' and to avoid **re-traumatisation**. It **recognises** that those working within the system may also have experienced trauma. There are six principles of trauma-informed practice: safety, trust, choice, collaboration, empowerment and cultural consideration.

Looking at these principles and reading this chapter, many psychological practitioners may argue that what is described is simply good clinical practice applied to supporting the development of compassionate systems. Although there is some truth in this, in addition to taking a caring approach that sees behaviour as the tip of the iceberg, trauma-informed practice provides a clear and specialist focus for understanding the evidence base and impact of complex developmental trauma on children, adults, families, communities, and systems, as well as staff working in those systems.

It feels important and necessary to clarify that being a trauma-informed practitioner or system does not mean believing that all emotional or mental health difficulties are the result of trauma. A trauma-informed approach recognises the value of diagnosing mental health difficulties, neurodevelopmental difficulties and learning difficulties. These approaches can coexist in a complementary way.

27.7.1 Challenges for Trauma-informed Systems

Alongside the huge benefits of trauma-informed systems, there are challenges inherent in introducing change and adopting trauma-informed practice. Organisational transformations are reportedly three times more likely to be effective if potential barriers are identified and addressed (Keller et al., 2010) so it is important to consider potential challenges in advance and solve unforeseen challenges as they arise.

Senior leaders and staff in an organisation need to know which trainings, models and methods of evaluation to choose as the options continue to increase with the popularity of trauma-informed practice. Some financial and personnel resources are needed to commit to trauma-informed practice. Internal pressures like staff illness, workload, budget cuts, increasing waiting times, alongside external pressures like Ofsted/CQC inspections and the Covid-19 pandemic can reduce capacity for trauma-informed practice. Staff under stress may be more resistant to, or less able to manage, the uncertainty of change despite the project being a potential resource to support with their challenges. Systemic and psychoanalytic theories are helpful in recognising that staff in traumatised or stressed systems can function like unwieldly extended families in which the dynamics risk splitting (Treisman, 2021), with some people being idealised as holding all the organisational knowledge and success and skills, and others being denigrated. The same can happen with initiatives, and trauma-informed ideas may be seen by some people as irrelevant or a passing trend, which has the potential to undermine practice.

One of the challenges in embedding trauma-informed practice over the longer term is sustainability. Organisations need to work with trauma-informed practitioners, to develop sufficient ownership of the ideas and integrate practice with any other organisational approaches and initiatives. Changes of leadership and staff turnover can make it challenging to keep ideas alive in an organisation, so it is important for senior leadership to be committed to embedding the ideas and seeing the work as an ongoing process, rather than something to be achieved in order to move on to the next initiative. Descriptions that show the striving or working to become trauma informed include: interview questions, ways of welcoming and inducting new staff, mentoring systems, working groups, network meetings, communities of practice, that can come together to explore challenges and access to training for new staff.

27.7.2 Outcome Measures for Trauma-informed Systems

Ways of measuring the impact of trauma-informed practice on systems and on clients will vary depending on the service or system that practitioners are working in and can be selected and adapted according to need. Self-assessment tool kits have been developed for services wanting to evaluate their trauma-informed practice, including the Welsh and Scottish ACES Toolkits (ACE Hub Wales, 2021; Scotland Children and Families Directorate, 2021; Welsh Government, 2021). These toolkits have been developed based on staff and trauma-impacted service-user views of what trauma-informed practice means in organisations.

Staff belief questionnaires can be used to evaluate the understanding and impact of trauma-informed practice, along with staff wellbeing questionnaires and surveys. Staff recruitment and retention rates, child attendance and exclusion rates and user-satisfaction or feedback questionnaires contribute to outcome data. However, it is important to recognise that there are multiple extraneous variables affecting this data.

There is a comprehensive list of questionnaires in Treisman (2017, p. 140) *Working with relational and developmental trauma in children and adolescents*. Examples include:

- The Professional Quality of Life Scale (Stamm, 2009–2012), which measures the positive and negative effects of those who help others experiencing trauma.
- The Areas of Work Life Scale, which measures person-job match in six areas of work life (Leiter & Maslach, 2000).
- Coping Strategies Inventory (Bober et al., 2006) measures beliefs and behaviours about coping amongst trauma counsellors.

Information can also be gathered from the NHS staff survey and the CHI-ESQ patient feedback questionnaire (Brown et al., 2014). These can be used alongside standard clinical assessment and routine outcome measures of change in child services.

27.7.3 Summary of the Evidence Base for Trauma-informed Systems

The current evidence base suggests that trauma-informed practice in services leads to improved outcomes for service users, including a reduction in symptoms, increased feelings of safety and empowerment and improved functioning. This has been demonstrated in a variety of settings including: the criminal justice system (Greenwald et al., 2012), inpatient settings (Azeem et al., 2011), and social services and healthcare (Gatz et al., 2007), where there is evidence of increasing engagement with 'hard-to-reach' populations. Trauma-informed practice has also been linked to increased staff wellbeing and reduced burnout. Supporting staff to look out for each other results in improvements in staff wellbeing (Bailey and West, 2020). ACES' guidance for the Education Sector (Association of Directors of Public Health and the WAVE Trust, 2021), reviewed trauma-informed practice across education, health, housing and policing, reporting that outcomes and interviews indicate that trauma-informed approaches could have a profound impact on society when applied as part of a whole-system effort to tackle ACES.

A review by the National Institute for Health and Care Excellence (NICE, 2015) found substantial evidence for the efficacy of trauma-informed approaches in supporting young people in school and recommended further development of training for teachers. There is mounting evidence that professionals believe that trauma-informed interventions in school have a positive impact on young people's wellbeing and educational engagement. Qualitative feedback indicates that the trauma-informed approach is very well regarded by headteachers, who feel that it brings about important changes within school that are instrumental in improving experiences for young people. Feedback from senior leadership, staff across the school community and pupils, gathered in focus groups and questionnaires, reflects similar themes. Staff in trauma-informed schools report being better equipped to support children who may be dealing with underlying trauma. They can define trauma, understand its impact, understand the ARC framework and are better able to self-regulate and respond to the needs of vulnerable children. They know how to seek support and work well with partner agencies and make referrals (Harrison 2022).

There is emerging evidence that trauma-informed approaches work best when they are appropriately financed and resourced, and established using a borough-wide, interagency approach (Trivedi & Harrison, 2022). Interestingly despite the initial need for some financial investment in becoming trauma informed, Domino et al. (2005) reported that as well as improving outcomes, integrated, trauma-informed services were cost effective, costing no more than standard services.

27.7.4 Areas for Further Research

A systematic review of the research into trauma-informed practice in schools indicates the need for the establishment of clear models of trauma-informed practice, research into approaches for working directly with children, and randomised control trials (Fondren et al., 2020). A systematic review of trauma-informed organisational settings by Purtle (2020) suggested similarly, that despite promising research, the strength of evidence for trauma-informed practice has been limited due to inconsistent use of assessment measurements, methods of analysis and short follow-up periods. Purtle also recommended that further research is needed to improve understanding of user perceptions of care and mechanisms for change in trauma-informed practice.

27.8 The Importance of Trauma-informed Practice in Schools

This section will focus on the research behind and implementation of trauma-informed practice in school settings to further illustrate the approach.

As is described in Chapter 20, most children spend a significant amount of their lives in the school environment; therefore schools can be an important place of safety and learning. However, we know that they can also be a place of adversity and even trauma (Blitz & Lee, 2015) for children who experience bullying, difficulties with adult or peer relationships, or struggle to feel safe in the school environment, due to learning needs, neurodiversity, race, language, culture, gender or complex developmental trauma (Dorado et al., 2016; Teicher & Samson, 2016).

Children who experience complex developmental trauma are reportedly three times more likely to drop out of school than their peers. Studies have consistently demonstrated a link between more frequent and more traumatic experiences and difficulties in school (Delaney-Black et al., 2002; Shonk & Cicchetti, 2001) and a risk of poor school attendance. Children in need and children looked after are also five times more likely than peers to receive fixed-term exclusions from school (Department for Education, 2019). Blodgett and Lanigan (2018) reported that children with complex developmental trauma histories had higher rates of fixed-term and permanent exclusions overall, and higher rates of challenging behaviour, lower grades, difficulties with attention and concentration, delays in expressive and receptive language, developmental delay and special educational needs (SEN), lower reading ability, and difficulties with memory, organisation and emotion regulation.

These potential areas of challenge for children who have experienced complex developmental trauma can make it more difficult to have a positive experience of school, and there is a real risk that traumatised children may expect to fail, which can damage their confidence and self-esteem. They may not have the executive functioning skills, attention or concentration skills, needed for academic work. They may have a skills lag, from their focus on keeping safe, or an unidentified learning need. They may be able to do their schoolwork sometimes and not at other times, which can be frustrating and confusing for teachers.

Children experiencing repeated criticism, disappointment and frustration, and little repair or positive feedback, may become avoidant of work or give up on activities. They might argue, refuse to follow instructions, destroy work, become angry and aggressive towards their peers or teacher, or avoid the classroom. They may find it difficult to manage relationships, or social interactions, because they become emotional, experience sensory overload or struggle with rules and limits.

For these reasons, support for children in the school environment seems increasingly important and perhaps even more so in the current context. According to the Department of Education, the number of children in care and with an Education Health and Care Plan (EHCP) has increased and the mental health needs of vulnerable children have been exacerbated by the Covid-19 pandemic (Skripkauskaite et al., 2021).

27.8.1 The Impact of Working with Complex Developmental Trauma on Teaching Staff

Teachers can understandably experience traumatised children as challenging to teach. Trauma-impacted children may be easily triggered by sounds, smells, physical sensations, memories or facial expressions. They may have big emotional reactions or become withdrawn or distressed by seemingly innocuous events or interactions. Their responses to situations may be difficult to predict or understand, leaving staff feeling confused, angry or upset themselves. Adults may find that they struggle to maintain empathy in the face of perceived challenging behaviour. This might be because their own stress response system is triggered, or their sense of what is appropriate behaviour is undermined, and they feel worn down by continued efforts to support a child. If teaching staff have themselves experienced complex developmental trauma or difficulties in their attachment relationships are concurrently experiencing trauma or stress in their own lives, then the work may feel particularly challenging, increasing the risk of vicarious trauma or burnout.

As children spend so much time in school, and accessing an education is so important in terms of future life chances, there is a clear need for understanding complex developmental trauma and interventions that support vulnerable children to engage with education, as well as supporting the teaching staff who work with them.

27.8.2 Developing Trauma-informed Practice in Schools

The theory and evidence base described in this chapter illustrates why school systems should help traumatised children to feel safe and secure through building positive relationships, providing a calm learning environment, supporting education staff and teaching them to provide trauma-informed care (Bartlett et al., 2017). Trivedi and Harrison (2022) reported that as a result, schools are increasingly working with other services to access training for staff and support for their vulnerable pupils.

Becoming a trauma-informed school is an ongoing process that means supporting vulnerable children to have improved life chances and better educational outcomes, whilst trying to avoid creating further adversity for, or further traumatising of, children and adults. The good news is that what is helpful for traumatised children is also likely to be helpful for all children in a school environment, including children with neurodiversity or additional learning needs. There is a recognised benefit for all pupils in a safe, supportive school community that nurtures its pupils' social-emotional development and learning in a way that is sensitive to their individual needs. Trauma-informed practice in a school therefore starts with recognising the importance of safe environments and caring relationships for children, families and teaching staff, in order to bring about positive change for children and young people (Cook et al., 2017).

Over the past 15 years, programmes have been developed to support schools to become 'attachment-aware' or 'trauma-informed', by implementing whole-school changes in ethos, policy and practices (Colley & Cooper, 2017; Harlow, 2021; Parker & Levinson 2018). Between 2009 and 2014, Dorado and colleagues piloted a whole-school approach in San Francisco called the HEARTS programme. This approach utilised the Attachment, Regulation and Competency (ARC) framework developed by Blaustein and Kinniburgh (2018). The ARC framework provides an effective structure for understanding and working with children in schools who have experienced complex developmental trauma. It also provides a shared language and a rationale for staff self-care in the context of what is often highly challenging work. The programme showed promising outcomes and contributed to the evidence that trauma-informed practices in schools can increase attendance and reduce exclusions (Durlak & Weissberg, 2011). The approach has since been adapted and developed for UK schools. See the ARC website (https://arcframework.org/) for further details and research on the ARC model.

27.9 Trauma-informed Practice in Schools: An Example of Whole-system Trauma-informed Practice

This section explores how this approach has been piloted in an inner-city borough, with a diverse community.

27.9.1 Local Context

Referrals to children's social care and to CAMHS reflect the level of need and complex developmental trauma experiences of many children in the borough. Since a pilot with five schools in 2017, 38 schools have been or are working with a trauma-informed practitioner, over a two year period, to embed trauma-informed practice in their school.

The aim of introducing trauma-informed practice to schools in the borough was to recognise and ameliorate the negative impact of complex developmental trauma on children, by creating responsive, inclusive and happier learning environments in which all children can have a sense of physical and felt safety, can thrive and can reach their potential. It was also part of a long-term project to reduce violent youth crime.

Trauma-informed training in the borough builds on a history of using the Solihull Approach (Douglas, 1997) to develop a shared language, understand child development in the context of caring adult relationships and to support work with children and families. The offer sits alongside a school wellbeing service offering preventative and early intervention work in schools, and the community CAMHS in Schools service, which works clinically with children and families in the school alongside staff consultation and training.

It has been shown to be helpful when agencies work in partnership with schools to support vulnerable children, Barnes (2017), and trauma-informed practice was introduced as a shared innovation across education, health, the local authority and public health. Most local authorities using trauma-informed approaches in schools are led and delivered by Educational Psychology Services or CAMHS. In this service, a clinical psychologist in CAMHS manages a team of educational psychologists and CAMHS clinicians who deliver the service and the team's work is supported by a multiagency working party. Following its initial success, the project has been extended to include early years settings (children's centres and nurseries) and voluntary and independent youth settings in the community.

27.9.2 Contracting and Setting Up

In order to be part of the project, schools have to commit resources, time and make a financial contribution (although schools can access help with the investment). Introducing trauma-informed practice is not a quick fix and planning service delivery means developing an offer to support schools with trauma-informed practice longer term, adopting a focus on sustainability.

Tah et al. (2021) identified common elements across schools implementing a trauma-informed approach, including training for teaching and non-teaching staff, a commitment to building trusted and respectful relationships between children and staff, emotion coaching techniques that validate children's feelings and support them to regulate their responses, the use of calming down spaces and strategies, restorative approaches and a reduced reliance on sanctions, alongside the use of nurture groups or links to therapeutic support.

Trauma-informed practitioners use the ARC framework to develop a bespoke whole-school approach. Within each school a link person, who is part of the school's senior leadership team (SLT), is identified to work with the practitioner. This relationship is key because it helps to develop the work and enables the practitioner to get to know the school history, culture and ethos (see Chapter 20). The school link person meets with the school's trauma-informed practitioner when they visit the school.

Most trauma-informed approaches involve the delivery of whole staff training. Trauma-informed practice in this borough provides the equivalent of 2 days of training for the whole school staff team, to promote the development of a shared ethos across the school and to start to support the understanding of the principles and practice, to identify any concerns and answer questions. Schools start with the introduction to complex developmental trauma training, providing psychoeducation about the impact of trauma on children and families and the staff working with them. The rest of the ARC training is delivered flexibly over inset days or half days, either at the start of the project or across the 2 years.

> 'Whole school training during inset days works really well. It's a chance for discussion together as a staff team.' (Headteacher)

> 'It was helpful that the admin team were also a part of the training, allowing for a universal approach.' (Staff member)

School staff have the opportunity to consider what the school is already doing well that is trauma informed and start to identify areas for development.

The trauma-informed practitioner helps the school link to establish a working group, The working group should have six to eight members with a mix of skills and interests and the willingness to take on projects. The group should be comprised of teaching and non-teaching staff across year groups, with staff of different genders at different ages and stages in their career, who as far as possible represent the culture, race, religions and backgrounds of the school community. The working group will meet regularly to identify the strengths and needs of the school and to take forward change; problem solving challenges and dilemmas. The working group will continue to lead trauma-informed practice in the school once their trauma-informed practitioner's time in the school comes to an end.

27.9.3 Developing Action Plans

In order to support their work, the working group can complete an audit or quick needs assessment, using a mental health and resilience framework, and develop an action plan for work in the school (three to five areas that the school plans to work on (less is more) and a named lead in the school to be responsible for the area. Action plans require SMART goals and identified timescales for change). The working group can then review progress. This encourages the school to share ownership of trauma-informed practice in the school from the start.

A common area identified as a focus for trauma-informed work in a school is a review of the physical school environment, including the playground. The practitioner can offer a 'learning walk' and focus groups with staff and pupils to help consider how the school looks, feels and sounds to visitors, parents, staff and pupils. They can help or advise about displays, projects and changes to the school layout, and the setting up and introduction of calming spaces in classrooms and communal areas for pupils.

Many schools choose to review their school policies and procedures. This might include a review or rewriting of the school behaviour policy, to include language that demonstrates the school is trauma informed. A trauma-informed behaviour policy should explain that the response to behaviour will be differentiated in the same way a school differentiates responses to learning. This means responding to behaviour in line with a child's developmental stage, age and needs, and with a focus on praise, encouragement and restorative approaches rather than punishment.

There may be work around transitions into and out of the school for reception and year 6 children and for all year groups before and after school holidays, at the beginning and end of the school day, as well as during the school day between lessons and break times. Practitioners can also support with the development of school and class rules and routines and communication with parents.

> In order to sensitively support children at the beginning of the year, a teacher sent a postcard to their students telling them how much they were looking forward to having them in their class. Parents reported how much they appreciated this gesture and how significant it felt for their child to receive the postcard. The postcard contributed to children feeling enthusiastic about starting their new class. The children experienced being thought about, wanted and welcomed, which helped the settling in process.

Trauma-informed practice can support the embedding of whole-school approaches around understanding and managing emotions, and which recognise the importance of co-regulation for children with adults such as the Zones of Regulation (Kuypers, 2011). Schools use assemblies and Personal Social Health Education (PSHE) time to introduce visuals and language around identifying and managing emotions. The work is also complemented and supported by links with the school CAMHS clinician and the School Well-Being practitioner who can offer individual sessions and groups to staff and pupils alongside work with parents or carers.

Classroom observations help teaching staff considering how to support a group of children in the classroom, impacted by trauma, who might be struggling, or who the teacher might be finding challenging. Scripts for managing incidents and for restorative conversations help staff learn to model talking about and managing their own feelings first, to acknowledge and name what the child might be feeling for example, 'I think that you might be feeling angry/sad/frustrated/worried/confused right now' and to ask or suggest ways that they might be able to support them to manage the feeling (co-regulation).

Staff find it helpful to learn about the impact of their proximity to a distressed child and can learn when it helps a child to calm down by being close or maintaining a small distance between them and the child, to avoid escalating a situation (proximity management/ distance regulation).

For many teaching staff it has been an important learning point that you can't talk through an event with a dysregulated child, and that you can't help a child as a dysregulated adult. It is therefore important to wait until everyone is calm before restorative conversations take place and for any learning from a situation to happen. Staff have reported finding it very helpful to know that there will be times when they feel that they cannot manage a situation well, and that they can ask someone else to take over, to support them.

> 'Watching other staff members in a challenging situation helped me to learn effective strategies. Reflecting together afterwards helped me to learn about what worked in a situation and what didn't work for a particular child and why.'

27.9.4 Consultation and Reflective Practice

Staff support and staff wellbeing is a key aspect of trauma-informed practice. Many schools becoming trauma informed focus on staff wellbeing and support through the introduction of staff wellbeing days, breakfasts or coffee and cake afternoons, as well as knowing where to signpost staff to for additional support.

Through consultation and reflective practice, the trauma-informed practitioner provides the role of 'container', in a cascading model of containment (Alexander et al., 2023; Bion, 1959; Douglas, 1997). The practitioner is contained by their team, and consultation and reflective practice spaces in school provide an opportunity for staff to reflect on and make sense of the complexity of their work and the impact that it has on them. This enables them to process their experience and maintain empathy towards themselves and the children and the families that they work with. Models of reflective practice can be flexible depending on the training of the practitioner. Some practitioners use a work discussion group (Jackson, 2008), others a systemic reflecting team model. This team uses a collaborative consultation approach (Fredman et al., 2018) for setting up, contracting, establishing who wants the reflective space and agreeing the limits of confidentiality and safeguarding, as well as considering systemic issues of power and Social Graces. The practitioner brings the ARC framework and clinical knowledge, and school staff bring their educational knowledge and day-to-day expertise working with children in a school, to develop a shared understanding.

There is scope for staff to talk about their own feelings and wellbeing, as well as support to discuss children that they may be struggling to connect with or to know how to help. It is not uncommon for a member of teaching staff to find a particular child or group of children is affecting them more than others. It might be difficult to make sense of a child's behaviour, because it connects to their own experience of trauma or relationships, because they are finding the child's history distressing, or because the child's behaviour transgresses their rules or beliefs about how children should behave. As narratives around some children can be problem saturated, it can be very helpful to bring together a group of staff with a shared challenge or knowledge about a child, or group of children, to co-create a trauma-informed understanding. This understanding takes account of a child's strengths, their history and their needs and considers what works to support them. Feedback shows that reflective practice and consultation provide an increase in opportunities to discuss, and problem solve around individual children and their experience and behaviour.

> 'Consultation helped me to understand the children more and develop some ideas for supporting them in a different way. I feel less anxious and more confident now in the classroom.' (Teacher)

Please see example in Box 27.3 of a child supported through teacher consultation.

Box 27.3 Clinical example: A child supported through consultation

Samir seemed to have unpredictable outbursts or to become very withdrawn and disengaged in class. Talking through specific situations in consultation, the teacher and trauma-informed practitioner were able to make sense of these outbursts in relation to Samir's trauma history. Samir had experienced significant changes and losses in their life. It was hypothesised that school was a place of relative safety and predictability and at times when there were changes to Samir's routine in school, this unpredictability, felt alarming and frightening. Simple changes to classroom plans or having to wait for something longer than usual, triggered their fight response.

(Continued)

Box 27.3 (Continued)

Being clear with the class about when and why a change might happen, using social stories around small changes to routines, naming the feelings this elicited and potential ways of managing them, helped to prepare Samir. It also helped to give Samir choices to increase their sense of agency in situations. The teacher described some real successes in building their relationship with Samir and praising steps Samir made towards using the calming down space in the classroom. Samir started to use words to describe feelings and to fight less. The teacher reflected that consultation had helped them to look after themselves and retain a sense of empathy for Samir. Learning from and together with the teaching assistants in the class about what worked, also built supportive staff relationships. Team Around the Child meetings enabled a wider professional network to come together and think with the family about their wishes. This facilitated the provision of an integrated and comprehensive package of support across services and improved communication between home and school.

See Box 27.4 for examples of qualitative feedback from staff on pupils on the impact of trauma-informed practice.

Box 27.4 Feedback from staff and pupils on the impact of trauma-informed practice

Staff feedback

The environment

'I am definitely noticing, from walking around the school, that more pupils are taking a minute outside the class to self-regulate, and then returning to learning. The trauma-informed approach has enabled us to set up a calm learning environment for the children.'

Self-care and emotions

- 'Trauma-informed practice has helped us (staff team) recognise the importance of self-care in order to help others.'
- 'I have seen a language change with the majority of staff beginning to name emotions.'
  Head Teacher
- 'As a whole, the staff have slowed down. For example, there is no rush to get back to learning if a child is distressed. They know they need to help a child to calm down before they can learn.' SLT

Pupils feedback

The children and young people in trauma-informed schools report seeing their school as a more sensitive and caring environment and one in which there is an adult who they feel comfortable talking to.

- Pupils said they have learnt about emotions in assemblies, which helps them to use a shared language to communicate their feelings.

- Pupils shared different ways they self or co regulate. Some pupils go to the playground and kick a ball, others go and talk to a member of support staff and play games.
- A teacher described how after an incident in the playground a child said 'I've come to talk to you because I'm really angry about what happened. I wanted to run away, but I didn't.' They have a language to talk about feelings rather than just acting on them.

Schools have reported that they have seen a reduction in time out of lessons from exclusions or internal isolation for the pupils, meaning they remain in school when they might otherwise have been excluded or moved to alternative provision.

Qualitative feedback from pupils and staff in the borough's schools was also supported by changes on a staff belief questionnaire over 2 years. Staff reported improvements in managing challenging behaviour, understanding the impact of trauma on pupil behaviour and an increase in confidence in knowing how to respond to vulnerable children in their care. Exclusion rates and the number of days pupils were excluded for, reduced, as did permanent exclusions (Aspland et al., 2020). Since then, evaluating attendance data has been complicated by the impact of Covid-19, but fixed-term and permanent exclusions have continued to decrease in trauma-informed schools.

27.10 Challenges for Trauma-informed Practice in Schools

Covid-19 proved a significant challenge globally and in this inner-city borough. For staff trying to embed trauma-informed practice, there were long periods of remote teaching and learning, illness and losses, children in school being taught in 'bubbles' and the transition back to school to manage for children educated remotely.

The war in Ukraine meant that schools in the borough provided essential educational placements to families fleeing from the trauma of war, facing upheaval to their lives and trying to integrate into a new country, language and system. The teaching and wider community have risen to the challenge of thinking about how to support a transient population of children and families experiencing this trauma, and practically and emotionally support them with the challenges and the complex transitions that they faced.

An ongoing challenge discussed by school staff is how the trauma-informed approach fits with implementing behaviour management strategies. This has been the focus of much discussion in training sessions, consultation and SLT support sessions. Teaching staff have concerns about how you support one child who might be demonstrating traumatised or challenging behaviour, when it impacts negatively on other children in the class. There may be other children who have experienced trauma or are affected by this challenging behaviour and children simply wanting to focus and learn. These are genuine dilemmas and questions that need hearing and validating. Whilst behaviour policies that differentiate behaviour are important, and the need to support vulnerable children to try to keep them in school is at the heart of the approach, trauma-informed practice does not reject limits and boundaries around behaviour. Limits and boundaries are an important part of how children learn about rules in society and they keep children safe. Trauma-informed practice takes the approach of positive discipline through building relationships, improving communication and routines. It is within these relationships that clear agreements, rules and responsibilities are established. Trauma-informed practice assumes that children are doing the best they can with the skills and experience that they have, and that adults need to attune to them and meet their needs. Adults need to teach children new skills, when they are calm and have the capacity to learn, if they want to see a different or new behaviour. Repeating ineffective consequences will not lead to a different outcome, only to further stress, and sometimes shame and misery for a child. There is therefore a restorative approach to difficulties in trauma-informed practice.

27.10.1 The Way Forward

During and after the 2 years of trauma-informed practice, schools are invited to join a termly network meeting to share their ideas and experiences remaining part of the community of practice and supporting new schools joining the programme. The hope is that trauma-informed practice will be embedded in a school and supported by practice across the borough. New staff joining the school can access a centralised trauma-informed training so that they understand the approach and ARC framework.

27.11 Conclusion and Summary

In summary, trauma-informed practice in systems and organisations is a promising emerging area of psychological practice, with a bright future despite some ongoing challenges and room for further development. There is now broad agreement about what trauma-informed practice in a system looks like. Further research is needed into models of trauma-informed practice and methods of evaluation. Randomised control trials of trauma-informed practice would be helpful, and there is also work to be done around ensuring the sustainability of trauma-informed practice in systems. Longitudinal studies could demonstrate whether changes are sustained in services over time. Greater understanding of the impact of racial trauma and ensuring that cultural humility is an integrated part of any trauma-informed training and practice offer is also an area for future development.

There is a clear agreement amongst clinicians, trauma-informed practitioners, research, the evidence-base and amongst policy makers that trauma-informed practice is grounded in good psychological theory and practice. It looks as though trauma-informed practice has an important role to play in supporting services to promote positive, inclusive outcomes for children and young people, impacted by trauma, as well as staff in organisations working with young people.

References

ACE Hub Wales. (2021). *ACE Hub Wales TrACE toolkit*. ACE Hub Wales. https://aceawarewales.com/traceorgtoolkit/.

Alexander, L., Barnett, S., & Wilkinson, V. (2023). Working with trauma: Finding new ports of entry. *Journal of Child Psychotherapy*, *49*(1), 39–59. https://doi.org/10.1080/0075417X.2023.2167103.

American Psychiatric Association. (2013). *Diagnostic and statistical manual of mental disorders* (5th ed.). American Psychiatric Association.

Aspland, H., Cameron, H., Strelitz, J., Clarke, S. E., Fahy, L., Mansour, H., & Shelemy, L. (2020). *Developing trauma-informed practices in inner London schools – the iTIPS Pilot*. The Dartington Hall Trust. www.rip.org.uk.

Association of Directors of Public Health and the WAVE Trust. (2021). *Guidance for the education sector*. ADPH. https://www.adph.org.uk/wp-content/uploads/2021/12/ACES-Guidance-for-the-education-Sector.pdf.

Azeem, M., Aujla, A., Rammerth, M., Binsfeld, G., & Jones, R. (2011). Effectiveness of six core strategies based on trauma-informed care in reducing seclusions and restraints at a child and adolescent psychiatric hospital. *Journal of Child & Adolescent Psychiatric Nursing*, *24*(1), 11–15.

Bailey, S., & West, M. (2020). *Covid-19: Why compassionate leadership matters in a crisis*. King's Fund. www.kingsfund.org.uk/blog/2020/03/covid-19-crisis-compassionate-leadership.

Bandura, A. (1977). *Social learning theory*. Prentice-Hall.

Barnes, D. (2017). *Re-affirming the role of the Local Authority in education*. Association of Directors Children's Services. https://adcs.org.uk/blog/article/re-affirming-the-role-ofthe-local-authority-in-education.

Bartlett, J. D., Smith, S., & Bringewatt, W. (2017). *Helping young children who have experienced trauma: Policies and strategies for early care and education*. Columbia University: National Center for Children in Poverty. https://academiccommons.columbia.edu/doi/10.7916/d8-f1gn-7n98.

Baylin, J. (2017). Social buffering and compassionate stories: The neuroscience of trust building with children in care. *Australian and New Zealand Journal of Family Therapy*, *38*(4), 606–612. https://doi.org/10.1002/anzf.1272.

Bion, W. R. (1959). Attacks on linking. In *Second thoughts* (pp. 93–109). Karnac.

Blaustein, M. E., & Kinniburgh, K. M. (2018). *Treating traumatic stress in children and adolescents: How to foster resilience through attachment, self-regulation and competency* (2nd ed.). Guildford Press.

Blitz, L., & Lee, Y. (2015). Trauma-informed methods to enhance school-based bullying prevention initiatives: An emerging model. *Journal of Aggression, Maltreatment & Trauma*, *24*(1), 20–40. https://doi.org/10.1080/10926771.2015.982238.

Blodgett, C., & Lanigan, J. D. (2018). The association between adverse childhood experience (ACE) and school success in elementary school children. *School Psychology Quarterly*, *33*(1), 137–146.

Bober, T., Regehr, C., & Zhou, Y. R. (2006). Development of the coping strategies inventory for trauma counsellor. *Journal of Trauma and Loss*, *11*(1), 71–83.

Bowlby, J. (1951). *Maternal care and mental health*. World Health Organization.

Brown, A., Ford, T., Deighton, J., & Wolpert, W. (2014). Satisfaction in child and adolescent mental health services. *Administration and Policy in Mental Health and Mental Health Services Research*, *41*(4), 436–446.

Burnham, J. (2012). Developments in social GRRRAACCEEESSS: Visible-invisible and voice unvoiced. In I. B. Krause (ed.), *Culture and reflexivity in systemic psychotherapy: Mutual perspectives* (pp. 139–160). Routledge.

Burnham, J & Roper-Hall, A. (2017). *Commentaries on this issue*. Context, *151*, 47–50.
Cicchetti, D. (2010). Resilience under conditions of extreme stress: A multilevel perspective. *World Psychiatry*, *9*(3), 145–154. https://doi.org/10.1002/j.2051-5545.2010.tb00297.
Colley, D., & Cooper, P. (2017). *Attachment and emotional development in the classroom: Theory and practice*. Jessica Kingsley Publishers.
Cook, A., Spinazzola, J., Ford, J., Lanktree, C., Blaustein, M., Cloitre, M., DeRosa, R., Hubbard, R., Liautaud, J., Olafsen, E., Kagan, R., Mallah, K., & van der Kolk, B. (2017). Complex trauma in children and adolescents. *Psychiatric Annals*, *35*(5), 390–398.
Delaney-Black, V, Covington, C., Ondersma, S. J., Nordstrom-Klee, B., Templin, T., Ager, J., Janisse, J., & Sokol, R. J. (2002). Violence exposure, trauma, and IQ and/ or reading deficits among urban children. *Archive of Pediatric and Adolescent Medicine, 156*(3), 280–285. https://doi.org/10.1001/archpedi.156.3.280.
Department for Education. (2019). *Timpson review of school exclusion*. Department for Education.
Department of Health and Social Care, Office of Health Improvement and Disparities. (2022). *Guidance: Working definition of trauma-informed practice*. Department of Health and Social Care.
Domino, M. E., Morrissey, J. P., Chung, S., Huntington, N., Larson, M. J., & Russell, L. A. (2005). Service use and costs for women with co-occurring mental and substance use disorders and a history of violence. *Psychiatric Services*, *56*, 1223–1232.
Dorado, J. S., Martinez, M., McArthur, L. E., & Leibowitz, T. (2016). Healthy environments and response to trauma in schools (HEARTS): A whole-school, multi-level, prevention and intervention program for creating trauma-informed, safe and supportive schools. *School Mental Health*, *8*(1), 163–176.
Douglas, H. (1997). *Containment and reciprocity: Integrating psychoanalytic theory and child development research for work with children*. Routledge.
Durlak, J., & Weissberg, R. (2011). Promoting social and emotional development is an essential part of students' education. *Human Development*, *54*(1), 1–3.
Felitti, V. J., Anda, R. F., Nordenberg, D., Williamson, D. F., Spitz, A. M., Edwards, V., Koss, M. P., & Marks, J. S. (1998). Relationship of childhood abuse and household dysfunction to many of the leading causes of death in adults: The adverse childhood experiences (ACE) study. *American Journal of Preventive Medicine*, *14*(4), 245–258.
Figley, C. R. (1998). *Burnout in families: The systemic costs of caring*. CRC Press.
Fondren, K., Lawson, M., Speidel, R., McDonnell, C. G., & Valentino, K. (2020). Buffering the effects of childhood trauma within the school setting: A systematic review of trauma-informed and trauma-responsive interventions among trauma affected youth. *Children and Youth Services Review*, *109*, 1046.
Fredman, G., Papadopoulou, A., & Worwood, E. (2018). *Collaborative consultation mental health guidelines for the new consultant*. Routledge.
Gatz, M., Brown, V., Hennigan, K., Rechberger, E., O'Keefe, M., Rose, T., & Bjelajac, P. (2007). Effectiveness of an integrated, trauma-informed approach to treating women with co-occurring disorders and histories of trauma: The Los Angeles site experience. *Journal of Community Psychology*, *35*(7), 863–878.
Greenwald, R., Siradas, L., Schmitt, T., Reslan, S., Fierle, J., & Sande, B. (2012). Implementing trauma-informed treatment for youth in a residential facility: First-year outcomes. *Residential Treatment for Children and Youth*, *29*(2), 141–153.

Hanson, R. F., & Lang, J. (2014). Special focus section: A critical look at trauma informed care (TIC) among agencies and systems serving maltreated youth and their families. *Child Maltreatment*, *19*(3–4), 275. https://doi.org/10.1177/1077559514557018.

Harlow, E. (2021). Attachment theory: Developments, debates and recent applications in social work, social care and education. *Journal of Social Work Practice*, *35*(1), 79–91. https://doi.org/10.1080/02650533.2019.1700493.

Harrison, N. (2022). *Attachment and trauma awareness training: Headteachers' perspectives on the impact on vulnerable children, staff and the school.* Rees Centre.

Holmes, C., Levey, M., Smith, A., Pinne, S., & Neese, P. (2014). A model for creating a supportive trauma-informed culture for children in preschool settings. *Journal of Child and Family Studies*, *24*, 1650–1659.

Jackson, E. (2008). The development of work discussion groups in educational settings. *Journal of Child Psychotherapy*, *34*(1), 62–82.

Keller, S., Meany, M., & Pung, C. (2010). What successful transformations share, *McKinsey Quarterly*.

Kuypers, L. (2011). *The zones of regulation*. Social Thinking Publishing.

Labella, M. H., Johnson, W. F., Martin, J., Ruiz, S. K., Shankman, J. L., Englund, M. M., Collins, W. A., Roisman, G. I., & Simpson, J. A. (2018). Multiple dimensions of childhood abuse and neglect prospectively predict poorer adult romantic functioning. *Personality and Social Psychology Bulletin*, *44*(2), 238–251. https://doi.org/10.1177/0146167217736049.

Lawson, E., & Price, C. (2003). The psychology of change management. McKinsey Quarterly.

Leiter, M., & Maslach, C. (2000). The areas of work life scale which measures person-job match in six areas of work life. In P. L. Perrewe & D. C. Ganster (Eds.), *Research in occupational stress and well-being* (pp. 91–134). Elsevier.

McCrory, E. J., De Brito, S. A., Sebastian, C. L., Mechelli, A., Bird, G., Kelly, P. A., & Viding, E. (2011). Heightened neural reactivity to threat in child victims of family violence. *Current Biology*, *21*(23), R947–R948.

National Institute for Health and Care Excellence. (2015). *Children's attachment: Attachment in children and young people who are adopted from care, in care or at high risk of going into care.* NICE.

National Institute for Health and Care Excellence. (2018). *NICE Guidelines post-traumatic stress disorder: Treatment for children and young people.* NICE.

Ncube, N. (2006). The tree of life project: Using narrative ideas in work with vulnerable children in Southern Africa. *The International Journal of Narrative Therapy and Community Work*, *1*, 3–16.

Parker, R., & Levinson, M. P. (2018). Student behaviour, motivation and the potential of attachment aware schools to redefine the landscape. *British Educational Research Journal*, *44*(5), 875–896. https://doi.org/10.1002/berj.3473.

Perlman, S. B., Kalish, C. W., & Pollack, S. D. (2008). The role of maltreatment in children's understanding of the antecedents of emotion. *Cognition and Emotion*, *22*, 651–670.

Purtle, J. (2020). Systematic review of evaluations of trauma-informed organizational interventions that include staff training. *Trauma Violence Abuse*, *21*(4), 725–740. https://doi.org/10.1177/1524838018791304.

Scottish Government, Children and Families Directorate. (2021). *Trauma-informed practice: toolkit*. Scottish Government. ISBN: 9781800045606. https://www.gov.scot/publications/trauma-informed-practice-toolkit-scotland/pages/11/.

Shonk, S. M., & Cicchetti, D. (2001). Maltreatment, competency deficits, and risk for academic and behavioral maladjustment. *Developmental Psychology, 37*(1), 3–17. https://doi.org/10.1037/0012-1649.37.1.3.

Shonkoff, J. P., Garner, A.S., Committee on Psychosocial Aspects of Child and Family Health, Committee on Early Childhood, Adoption, and Dependent Care, Section on Developmental and Behavioral Pediatrics, Siegel, B. S., Dobbins, M. I., Earls, M. F., McGuinn, L., Pascoe, J., & Wood, D. L. (2012). The lifelong effects of early childhood adversity and toxic stress. *Pediatrics, 129*(1), e232–e246. https://doi.org/10.1542/peds.2011-2663.

Skripkauskaite, S., Shum, A., Pearcey, S., McCall, A., Waite, P., & Creswell, C. (2021). *Changes in children's mental health symptoms from March 2020 to June 2021 (Report 11).* Co-SPACE study. http://cospaceoxford.org/findings/changesinchildrens-mental-health-symptomsfrommarch-2020-to-june2021/.

Sprang, G., Craig, C., & Clark, J. (2011). Secondary traumatic stress and burnout in child welfare workers: A comparative analysis of occupational distress across professional groups. *Child Welfare, 90*(6), 149–168.

Stamm, B. H. (2009-2012). *Professional quality of life: Compassion satisfaction and fatigue Version 5.* ProQOL. www.proqol.org.

Stubley, J. (2020). The early response to Covid 19: A psychoanalytic and trauma perspective. NHS England.

Substance Abuse and Mental Health Services Administration. (2014). *SAMHSA's concept of trauma and guidance for a trauma-informed approach.* HHS Publication No. (SMA) 14-4884. Substance Abuse and Mental Health Services Administration.

Tah, P., Trivedi, H., Brown, A., Sebba, J., & Harrison, N. (2021). *Attachment and trauma awareness training: Analysis of pre-Covid staff interviews and pupil focus groups in five case study schools.* Rees Centre.

Teicher, M. H., & Samson, J. A. (2016). Annual research review: Enduring neurobiological effects of childhood abuse and neglect. *Journal of Child Psychology and Psychiatry, 57*(3), 241–266.

Treisman, K. (2017). *Working with relational and developmental trauma in children and adolescents.* Routledge.

Treisman, K. (2021). *A treasure box for creating trauma-informed organizations* (vols. 1 and 2). Jessica Kingsley Publishers.

Trivedi, H., & Harrison, N. (2022). *Attachment aware and trauma-informed schools programmes. Positive practice examples from local authorities.* Rees Centre.

Tronick, E. Z. (1989). Emotions and emotional communication in infants. *American Psychologist, 44*, 112–126.

Welsh Government. 2021. *Review of Adverse Childhood Experiences (ACE) policy: Report: How the ACE policy has performed and how it can be developed in the future.* Welsh Government. https://www.gov.wales/review-adverse-childhood-experiences-ace-policy-report-html.

Winnicott, D. W. (1973). *The child, the family and the outside world.* Penguin.

Index

a

abuse 28–31, 48, 50, 53, 93, 110, 112–120, 122, 125, 154, 193, 197, 219, 278, 299, 308, 311, 388, 391–394, 453, 455, 460, 463, 466, 467, 469, 490, 494, 507, 511, 548, 556, 594, 615, 625, 628, 643, 650, 653, 655, 660, 679, 691, 693, 717, 765–791, 802, 804
  coercion 153–154, 676
  domestic abuse and violence 48, 50, 118, 226, 308, 311, 381, 463, 471, 615, 628, 629, 768, 780, 782–786, 791, 802, 803
  emotional 119, 124, 388, 393, 556, 768, 788
  maltreatment 116–121, 454, 457, 478, 650, 765, 768, 788
    indicators of 119–120
  neglect 110, 113, 116, 118, 120, 219, 278, 388, 453, 455, 460, 466, 467, 469, 470, 474, 533, 548, 556, 650, 655, 693, 768, 769, 782–788, 791, 804
  physical 50, 119, 388, 467, 803
  sexual 28–31, 119, 278, 391–394, 454, 789, 802
  sexual assault 455, 515–516
  victimisation 377, 378, 605
  violence 50, 54, 170, 213, 226, 337, 358, 374, 454, 463, 471, 515, 615, 628, 629, 691, 692, 696, 701, 703, 705, 717, 737, 743, 752, 770, 780, 783, 801, 802
    child to parent 789
    sexual 374, 801
    violence reduction 703, 705
    youth 701, 703, 737, 743
  vulnerability 117–120, 212, 323, 336, 344, 494, 507, 534, 559, 614, 616, 617, 623, 649, 655, 661, 673, 699
activity(ies) 21, 83, 183, 220, 225, 276, 286, 341, 342, 345, 385, 440, 498, 536, 537, 650, 724
  criminal activity 652, 655
  enrichment opportunities 510
  exercise 341
  fitness 200, 616, 746–747
  inactivity 440
  online activity 220, 650, 724
  physical activity 341
  scheduling 440
  sexual activity 105, 219, 652
  stimulus-seeking behaviour 537
adolescence 11, 26, 58, 114, 211–231, 336–343, 455, 537, 540, 659, 736
puberty 58, 212, 213, 215, 216, 217, 219, 341, 418, 430, 652
adult mental health services 4, 144, 229, 230, 235, 386, 392, 618, 665
anxiety 6, 8, 18, 28, 57, 60, 65, 70, 84, 87, 110, 131, 146, 156, 168, 191, 193–196, 213, 214, 218, 221, 227, 229, 269, 276, 307, 309, 314, 323–336, 338, 339, 341, 344, 346, 347, 357, 361, 363, 366, 391–394, 412, 413, 418, 428, 432, 443, 493, 499, 500, 513–517, 535, 537, 540, 541, 552, 562–563, 567–569, 582,

Child Psychology: Pathways to Good Practice, First Edition.
Edited by Helen Pote, Anna Picciotto and Clare Norris.

anxiety (*contd.*)
595–596, 599, 600, 602, 617, 622–623, 626, 643, 664, 719, 720
emotional-based school avoidance 584
fear 8, 42, 57, 157, 246, 252, 256, 325, 327, 328, 333, 334, 361, 499, 624–626, 773
parental anxiety 301
procedural anxiety 428, 432, 433
school-based anxiety 18
separation anxiety 57, 70, 244, 278, 309, 314, 325, 326
social anxiety 226, 326–328, 331, 333, 391–394, 513–516, 582
assessment tools
Applied Behaviour Analysis 497
Attachment Q Sort method 464
Autism Diagnostic Interview 554
Autism Diagnostic Observation Schedule 551, 567
Camouflaging Autistic Traits Questionnaire 565
Child Outcome Rating Scale 182
Child PTSD Symptom Scale 378
Children's Revised Impact of Events Scale 29
Child Yale Brown Obsessive Compulsive Scale 360
Cognitive Behaviour Therapy Scale for Children and Young People 81
Coventry ASD vs Attachment Problems Grid 466
Diagnostic and Statistical Manual of Mental Disorders (DSM-5) 17, 32, 239, 260, 530, 801
Family Accommodation Scale 362
feedback scales 604
Gillick Competence Test 105, 111
ideographic patient-rated outcomes 179
International Classification of Diseases (ICD, 11) 19, 299, 454, 530
International Trauma Questionnaire-Child and Adolescent Version 378
observational tools 81
Obsessional Compulsive Inventory Revised Self Report 362
outcome tools 144, 178–185
Parent Trauma Response Questionnaire 378
Revised Children's Anxiety and Depression Scale 29
risk assessment tools 653–654, 696
self-esteem measures 338
Session Rating Scale 82, 115, 182, 315
Story Stem Assessment 464
Strange Situation 464
Strengths and Difficulties Questionnaire 29, 791
symptom-focused tools 180, 181
visual subjective units of distress scale 503
Wechsler Intelligence Scale for Children 510
Welsh and Scottish ACES Toolkits 810
Young Child PTSD Checklist 378
attachment
difficulties 301, 453–454, 464, 472, 475, 476, 504, 784
style 23, 24
theory 23–24, 29, 70, 215, 302, 303, 305, 310, 453, 472, 473, 475, 508–509, 803–804

b

behaviour
activation 341, 342
behavioural consultation 257
behavioural difficulties 11, 24, 48, 157, 298–317, 428, 432–434, 585, 702
bias
gender 542
sampling 60
unconscious 21, 92, 615
bullying 80, 92, 113, 119, 222, 337, 401, 414, 430, 465, 494, 507, 545, 581, 583, 584, 591, 596, 604, 605, 609, 610, 645, 649, 653, 655, 802, 811

burnout 9, 80, 90, 91, 96, 98, 249, 316, 602, 604, 638, 661, 679, 805, 810, 812, 822

C

caregiver stress 260
carer support groups 198
leaver 452
child protection 42, 45, 49, 50, 100, 113, 117, 122, 124, 125, 127, 128, 239, 291, 451, 487, 504, 513, 589, 592, 597, 763, 766, 767, 771, 772, 775, 793
clinical practice
aptitude 7
career 9, 10, 89, 221, 815
clinical
competence 5, 75, 83, 98
confidence 5–10, 75
decisions 22, 88, 654, 657, 773
governance 591
outcome 28, 145
utility 512, 541
contracting 42–45, 592, 702, 777, 814–816
cost-effectiveness 17–18, 433, 603
expert label 735
collaborative 22
systemic 66, 95
imposter syndrome 8, 87, 91
perfectionism 410, 418, 424
powerlessness 152, 191, 495
unstructured clinical judgement 697
cognition
appraisal 378, 379, 382, 384, 390, 393, 430, 431, 599, 807
automatic thoughts 340, 343, 725
cognitions 25, 343, 365, 410, 413, 455, 660
cognitive
development 40, 215, 227
flexibility 288, 538
inattention 553
identification 130, 197, 257, 353, 384, 536, 559, 649, 659, 764, 775
judgements 15, 88, 135, 199, 214, 633, 696, 697
labelling 138, 157, 269, 271, 364, 367
memory 374, 379–391, 394, 417, 510, 538, 539
focused work 380–391
metaphors 155, 164, 380, 390, 393, 616
myth 40, 142, 143, 279, 316, 365, 658
reappraisal 215
rescripting 385, 394
scripts 55, 306, 511, 816
unconscious 21–23, 63, 79, 89, 92, 508, 517, 615, 616
communication
non-verbal communication 327, 569
open communication 78, 182
community
accommodation 20, 314, 359, 362, 363, 365, 367, 453, 504, 532
approach 807
community-based practitioners 805
violence 802
confidentiality 43, 45, 50, 67, 78, 103, 115, 116, 122, 151, 197, 390, 591, 595, 597, 653, 706, 714, 773–774, 806, 817
limits of 78, 817
consent
informed 42, 436, 461, 462, 669, 670, 717, 772
Gillick Competence Test 105, 111
withdrawing 110
coping
efficacy 332
strategies 28, 30, 336, 338, 370, 382, 417, 430, 623, 647, 679, 810
unhelpful coping 379, 621, 623
co-production 11, 136–138, 140, 183, 188–208, 214, 432, 462, 478, 543, 544, 546, 566, 705, 715, 717, 724, 727, 733, 736–738, 740, 750, 751, 756, 757, 759, 771
crisis
care 642, 662, 664–665, 677–679
intervention 643, 764
mental health crisis 49, 229, 643–665, 670, 678
critical thinking 7, 760

d

death 41, 51, 106, 114, 213, 251, 339, 374, 493, 494, 542, 628, 629, 645, 650, 682, 691, 801
  bereavement 9, 141, 145, 278, 328, 373, 465, 650
  early death 542
  grief 508, 600
  loss 29, 47, 51, 141, 228, 325, 336, 337, 469, 507, 508, 614, 619, 628, 650, 693
  palliative care 429
deprivation 111, 170, 234, 246, 267, 336, 420, 499, 533, 538, 617, 623, 642, 647, 668, 670, 671
development(al)
  delay 69, 264, 278, 408, 466, 499, 507, 552, 553, 768, 780, 812
  factors 17, 18
  faltering growth 259, 265, 269, 272, 273
  history 47, 55, 246, 280, 305, 462, 628, 695, 696, 780
  perspective 9, 104, 211, 547
diagnosis 17, 19, 25, 239, 240, 260, 263, 277, 303, 324, 326, 331, 346, 374, 389, 394, 408–410, 413, 414, 428, 430, 443, 448, 455, 466, 510, 529, 530, 532, 535, 536, 539–543, 549, 554–557, 560, 566, 584, 623, 659, 661, 666, 667, 669, 675
  atypical profiles 529, 532, 556
    diagnostic frameworks 13, 20, 48, 62, 456
    overshadowing 432, 534, 535, 542, 552
  misdiagnosis 346, 413, 455
digital
  apps 53, 200, 248, 422, 679, 713–715, 719, 721, 724
  augmented and virtual reality 83, 97, 713, 726
  computer games 724–725
  cyberbullying 113, 648
  exclusion and inclusion 717, 718
  health policy 713
  online support 51, 221, 715, 722
  phone 119, 122, 199, 412, 422, 433, 444, 473, 664, 713, 715, 720
  social media 53, 106, 122, 201, 214, 220–222, 227, 271, 316, 408, 422, 452, 645, 647, 648, 650, 658, 678
  technology 147, 184, 200, 221, 248, 506, 713, 715, 718
  therapeutic alliance 716
  video feedback 472, 473
discrimination
  anti-discriminatory practice 93
  class position 753
  disparity 213, 629, 675, 683
  exclusion 152, 157, 213, 217, 459, 494, 495, 545, 583, 674, 718, 733, 749
  homophobia 152, 166, 167
  inequality 130, 135, 136, 147, 151, 152, 158, 159, 161–163, 166, 170, 171, 246, 493, 495, 708, 733, 734, 736, 742, 753, 806
    health 135–137, 150, 542, 675, 703, 718, 750
    racial 736, 800
    social 154, 161, 171, 493, 549, 583, 675, 734
  intersectionality 166–171, 718
  marginalisation 152, 162, 457, 494, 495, 507, 749
  prejudice 90, 135–138, 163, 377, 465, 658, 736
  racism 52, 92, 93, 136, 137, 162, 163, 166, 167, 170, 172, 174, 214, 229, 237, 273, 336, 376, 384, 465, 517, 543, 581, 583, 629, 679, 718, 734, 759, 761, 791, 802, 806
    institutional 163, 691
  representation 159, 161, 457, 736
    under-representation 17, 171
    over-representation 424, 691
  sexism 136, 166, 167
  white privilege 162, 163
diversity 17, 37, 72, 96, 120, 151–171, 198, 199, 346, 457, 535, 555, 627, 749, 806

cultural
  competence 158–161, 435
  humility 159–161, 360, 386, 806, 820
  identity 160, 213, 224
  reflexivity 92, 683
demographic factors 17, 190, 280, 339, 767, 768
ethnic
  differences 347
  identity development 457
Eurocentricity 152, 162, 168, 169
high-income countries 17
low-and middle-income countries 15, 621, 632
minority groups 135, 136, 153, 154, 157, 158, 161, 162, 168, 347, 435, 532, 542, 543, 583, 616, 691, 734, 767, 806
multigenerational households 306, 615
poverty 17, 118, 137, 154, 155, 299, 303, 679, 717, 718, 736, 764, 768, 778
religion 47, 52, 53, 118, 122, 152, 163, 164, 167, 249, 273, 359, 587, 654, 656, 801, 815
Roma 457, 543, 583, 767
Western perspective 346
working-class 162, 718

e

early life
  early
    childhood 58, 114, 194, 260, 570, 613, 693
    life events 65
    years 112, 216, 239, 244, 300–301, 504, 814
  infancy 55, 57, 184, 260, 275, 515
  infant mental health 239, 613–634
  post-natal experiences 463, 621
  primary age 59, 301–302, 599
  toddlerhood 57, 242, 245, 252, 253, 261, 266, 670, 788
  under-five 55, 238, 239, 260, 268, 273, 504, 559
early help 124, 590, 767, 771
education
  academic attainment 336, 344, 582, 614
  classroom 50, 146, 549, 582, 584, 596, 602, 812, 815, 816, 817–818
  dyscalculia 493, 531
  dyslexia 91, 493, 531, 544, 547, 585
  educational outcomes 300, 456, 457, 583, 585, 813
  exam stress 590, 595, 598, 643, 653
  personal social health education 816
  secondary school 213, 219, 326, 430, 592
  school
    based mental health provision 585
    culture 583, 594, 601
    non-attendance 562, 584, 603
    policies 470, 591
  teacher stress 584
  team around the school 589, 590
  virtual schools 475, 791
  whole-school approach 593–595
emotions
  emotional
    instability 214, 663
    state 196, 622, 656, 676
    support 197–199, 420, 432, 495
    volatility 118
  processing 454, 535
  rumination 339, 379, 385, 408, 410, 440, 660, 661
  sadness 191, 284, 336, 337, 339, 438, 439, 477
  temperament 55, 56, 118, 249, 254, 259, 263, 264, 301, 328, 331, 430, 565, 628, 630, 691
  uncertainty 88, 189, 214, 333, 809
empathy 6, 7, 16, 57, 80, 91, 92, 136, 246, 312, 316, 377, 414, 465, 470, 472, 474, 514, 517, 549, 744, 751, 805, 812, 817
engagement 189, 220, 695, 715
environment
  chronosystem 155, 582
  clinical environment 9
  environmental adaptation 279, 510, 566
  environmental stressors 54, 676

environment (*contd.*)
  intrauterine environment 533
  lockdown 410, 421, 562
  macrosystem 155, 582
  mesosystem 155, 581
  microsystem 155, 581
  school environment 545, 562, 563, 581, 582, 602, 653, 811–813
ethics 77, 114, 461, 477, 779
  ethical standards 76
  ethical practice 7, 77

f

family
  based treatment 416
  composition 40, 249, 306, 316
  divorce 9, 43, 52, 109, 266, 650, 781, 802
  functioning 304, 373, 431, 453, 477, 514, 772, 779, 781
  generational differences 228
  history 47, 51–55, 68, 89, 285, 301, 339, 552, 579, 650, 652, 661
  mapping 280, 615, 708, 780
  meal 262, 263, 266, 271, 418
  safeguarding 767, 770, 791
  scripts 306, 511
  siblings 46, 47, 49, 54, 56, 59, 70, 119, 243, 249, 307, 428, 445, 463, 511, 543, 576, 780, 781, 787
  systems theory 26
flexibility 46, 86, 125, 142, 194, 230, 256, 257, 388, 443, 500, 554, 556, 582, 584, 701, 718, 747
food intake
  diabetes 134, 277, 427, 428, 433, 436, 446
  diet 268, 409, 410, 412, 414, 417, 419, 424, 474, 499, 661, 681
  dieting mindset 409, 410
  fasting 265, 273
  feeding 259–274, 415, 557, 616, 618, 625, 628, 661
  food diary 264, 266, 269, 416
  fussy eating 262, 268, 292
  obesity 271, 272, 339, 446, 537
  weight restoration 411, 416, 418
forensics
  assessment 694–698
  confinement 670, 671
  court 109, 452, 701, 702, 776
  Criminal Justice System 136, 137, 148, 156, 157, 184, 477, 583, 667, 675, 692–693, 708, 810
  custodial sentence 690, 701
  custody 690–692, 701
  deprivation of liberty 111, 429, 642, 668, 670–671, 673
  offending behaviour 302, 668, 693–696, 700
  punishment 310, 582, 815
  prison 456, 690, 691, 701
formulation 19, 20, 22, 23, 29, 39, 62–71, 108, 109, 119, 188, 248, 257, 258, 266, 269, 285, 309–311, 328, 339, 365, 372, 379, 408–410, 415, 430, 438, 468–472, 498, 510–511, 547, 556–558, 595–596, 653, 698–699, 781–786
fostering
  adoption 451, 453, 457, 458, 460, 461, 766
  foster placement 28, 475
  looked after children 108, 184, 229, 299, 452, 771
functioning
  adaptive functioning 493, 509
  autonomy 58, 83, 84, 202, 215, 227, 262, 341, 390, 541, 623, 676, 713, 743, 750
  capabilities 94, 95, 214, 500, 562, 733
  core skills 6–8, 143
  functional impairment 323, 347, 362, 427, 471, 534, 560
  independence 58, 212, 231, 245, 269, 303, 430, 431, 493, 494, 499, 666, 671
  intellectual functioning 61, 492, 510
funding 134, 135, 147, 315, 459, 460, 494, 586, 664, 669, 703, 704, 749, 751, 757, 771, 802

g

gender
  differences 216, 236, 401
  disparity 213
  dysphoria 213, 424, 425, 530, 536
  identity 51, 58, 216, 232, 549, 583, 652
  transgender 51
genetic(s)
  genes 328, 331, 359, 537
  genogram 29, 51–53, 72, 93, 263, 264, 561, 654
  influences 534, 539
  risk 537
goal setting 140, 143, 179, 257, 435, 538, 705, 722
guided self-help 331, 362, 411, 444, 600, 603
guidelines
  AssetPlus 698, 702
  Child Outcomes Research Consortium 512, 792
  codes of conduct 95
  Deprivation of Liberty Safeguards 111, 671, 673
  Eat Well Guide 268
  Education Health and Care Plan 585, 812
  Framework for Integrated Care (Community) 703
  Framework for Integrated Care (SECURE STAIRS) 701
  Fraser Guidelines 42, 101, 105
  Getting it right for every child policies 586
  guided self-help 331, 362, 411, 444, 600, 603
  MARSIPAN guidance 413
  Maudsley approach 416
  National Confidential Inquiry into Suicide and Safety in Mental Health 648
  NHS Long-Term Plan 230, 619
  Psychologically Informed Partnership Approach 460, 771
  public health and prevention 737, 738
  SEND Code of Practice 532
  SMART goals 369, 392, 502, 815
  Supervision: Adherence and Guidance Evaluation 82
  Think-family approach 620
  United Nations Convention on the Rights of the Child 101
  Video Interactive Guidance 24, 465

i

identity 41, 51, 58, 75, 117, 120, 159, 160–167, 213–218, 220, 224, 228, 454, 457, 494, 544, 549, 583, 736, 768
  gender 51, 216, 549, 583
  group 120, 161, 494
  identity development 214–216, 228, 457
information
  contextual factors 64, 66, 85, 86, 152, 156, 262, 263, 265, 271, 280, 283, 310, 507
  dissemination 159, 737, 738, 756, 758
  sensitive 438, 773
  sharing 29, 79, 307, 591, 629, 653, 707
  signposting 279, 386, 544, 598, 619
intervention plan 20, 105, 241, 257, 305, 310, 500, 510, 516, 548, 564, 698, 706
in-patient settings
  admission 111, 407, 429, 433, 443, 627, 629, 642–678, 792
    in-patient 111, 391, 627, 646, 670, 671, 674–676
    psychiatric hospital 644, 652, 663, 675
    short-term 664, 674, 675
  discharge 544, 643, 646, 649, 652, 653–654, 657, 659, 662, 666, 667, 669, 672, 673, 676, 677, 680
  in-patient care 111, 419, 632–682
  physical restraint 498, 501, 545, 676, 677
intersectionality 166–171, 718

j

job planning 141–143

k

key performance indicators 413, 755, 792

l

learning
 continual 806
 difficulties 184, 305, 430, 466, 493, 531, 559, 585, 779, 809
 by example 328, 331
 through doing 332, 334
legal acts and orders
 Children Act 101, 102, 108, 112, 113, 123, 436, 452, 479, 764
 Children and Social Work Act 112, 113, 457, 765
 Community Treatment Order 673
 Human Rights Act 101
 Interim Care Order 108
 Mental Capacity Act 101, 102, 112, 653, 673
 Prohibited Steps Order 108
 Special Guardianship Orders 451, 763
 Youth Referral Order 708

m

medical
 asthma 427, 432, 540, 652
 biofeedback 287, 288
 cancer 134, 427
 cerebral palsy 245, 511, 553
 colds 243
 comorbidity rates 344, 357, 360, 371, 377
 eczema 427, 437
 epilepsy 277, 427, 428, 430, 432, 434, 437, 438, 443, 511, 535, 536, 652, 659
 long-term health conditions 427–44
 magnetic resonance imaging 217, 218
 medical condition 245, 246, 428, 429, 433, 434, 436, 441, 444
 medical instability 655, 661–662
 pain 197, 217, 245, 274, 327, 432, 433, 435, 470, 498, 499, 509, 626, 647–648, 679, 719, 726
mental health disorders
 acute psychotic episode 659, 663
 anorexia nervosa 215, 407, 409–411, 413–415, 417, 419, 422, 644, 650, 655, 723
 attachment disorders 453, 455, 465, 466, 472, 673
 attention deficit hyperactivity disorder 61, 71, 157, 278, 305, 312, 319, 456, 465–467, 535–540, 544, 546, 548, 551, 553, 555, 556, 563–564, 566, 568, 584, 702, 719, 780
 autism spectrum disorder 61, 146, 305, 324, 361, 388, 428, 529–531, 534, 535, 556, 569, 570, 790
 avoidant restrictive food intake disorder 260, 408
 binge eating disorder 408, 409, 411
 body dysmorphic disorder 357
 borderline personality disorder 25, 454, 663
 bulimia nervosa 146, 409–411, 413, 414, 416, 417, 497, 650
 conduct disorder 157, 213, 299–301, 377, 536, 700, 702
 developmental-coordination disorder 535
 developmental trauma disorder 455, 469
 disinhibited attachment disorder 454, 464, 465
 elimination disorder 276
 generalised anxiety disorder 326, 327
 hoarding disorder 357
 hyperkinetic disorders 536
 learning disorder 493, 531, 536, 538
 major depressive disorder 337
 neurodevelopmental disorder 305, 324, 444, 455, 456, 465, 466, 768
 obsessive compulsive disorder 27, 180, 324, 357, 539, 623
 oppositional defiant disorder 299, 536, 700
 panic disorder 25, 324, 326, 327, 623
 postnatal depression 617, 621, 622, 627
 post-traumatic stress disorder 25, 324, 357, 373–395, 455, 616, 623, 625, 691, 781, 789, 801

reactive attachment disorder 454
separation anxiety disorder 326, 327
sleep disorders 239, 240
social engagement disorder 454
Tourette syndrome 539
tic disorder 361, 363, 539
insomnia 239, 240, 248, 719
phobia 24, 276, 563, 623
neophobia 261, 264–267, 269
tokophobia 623, 626
pica 408, 410, 497
selective mutism 326, 327
trichotillomania 357
meta-analysis 15, 250, 341, 359, 382, 538, 542, 603
mindfulness 25, 26, 35, 343, 502, 565, 603, 663
models
adaptive information model 387, 551
affective-appraisal approach 196, 207
attachment, regulation and competency framework 813
behavioural activation model 340
bio-psycho-social formulation 468
Bronfenbrenner, Uri 39, 40, 155, 581
cascading model of containment 805, 817
cognitive behavioural model 339, 340
cognitive behavioural supervision model 85
competence models 84
Choice and Partnership Approach (CAPA) 140–143, 144, 146, 147
circle of security 24, 37, 632, 635
developmental models 84
ecological model 581
family life cycle model 40, 41
Foucault, Michael 27, 153–154
Freud, Anna 138
humanistic model 603
integrated models 83, 733, 738
lean theory 140
life-span wisdom model 218
medical model of disability 505
mentalising theory 116
of mind 388, 535
model of containment 805, 817
model of service delivery 317, 776
neuro-sequential model 511, 514
operant conditioning 24, 87, 309, 310, 333
PACE (playfulness, acceptance, curiosity, and empathy) 472, 514
peer-referral model 747
Piaget, Jean 215
5Ps model 29, 63–66, 69, 71, 248, 266, 365, 438, 440, 699, 782
reclaiming social work model 460, 769
reflecting team models 85
relational model 505
risk-resistance model 430, 431
Rogers, Carl 6
seven-eyed supervision model 84
social graces model 92, 163–166, 654, 817
social learning theory 24, 40, 268, 301, 303, 309, 310, 312, 313, 316, 473, 600, 604, 769, 777, 807
social model of disability 558
stepped care approach 419
stress-vulnerability model 64
THRIVE model 317
triune model of the brain 415
Vanguard model 703, 704

n

National Institute for Health and Care Excellence 11, 14, 118, 362, 493, 550, 551, 576, 594, 609, 613, 614, 639, 646, 686
neuro-affirmative 544, 566, 570
neurodevelopmental screening 780
neurodivergence 61, 71, 245, 273–274, 441, 529–571
neurodiversity 54, 184, 408, 424, 492, 529, 532, 533, 541, 544–546, 549, 550, 558, 559, 565, 571, 653, 661, 674, 676, 806, 808, 811, 813
neurology
acquired neurological injury 531
amygdala 380, 393, 535, 803
bilateral stimulation 387, 390, 503
brain

neurology (*contd.*)
atypical 535
based approaches 565
damage 430, 431, 536
function 529, 566
cortex 218, 236, 511, 514, 516, 803
cortisol 325, 803
dopamine 537, 539
dysregulation of neurotransmission 537
executive function 58, 388, 406, 464, 466, 468, 510, 553, 582, 803, 806, 812
foetal brain development 553
hippocampus 380, 393, 803
hormones 216, 324, 325
limbic system 511, 803
neuronal change 217
reward system 270, 336
right-brain approach 511
social brain 217
synapses 217
thalamus 803
normalising 47, 273, 335, 338, 372, 587, 591
not knowing position 6, 735, 739, 744

o

outcome monitoring 82, 144, 177, 187, 716
client feedback 82, 185

p

parent(s)
adaptive behaviour 432
co-habitting 109
divorced 781
estranged 108
father 109, 214, 430, 681
groups 415
intersubjective attunement 804
mother 617, 631
parental
attunement 473
authority 111, 416
consent 43, 111, 420, 560, 592, 645, 670, 671
criticism 339
responsibility 29, 42, 43, 100, 101, 104, 108, 109, 316, 452, 462, 615, 671, 766
self-management 301
sensitivity 472, 473, 622
stress 32, 118, 289, 306, 313, 315, 430, 477, 496, 565, 792
parent-child interaction 125, 259, 465, 472, 473, 622, 788–790
parent-infant psychotherapeutic settings 302, 620, 632, 788
parenting
authoritarian 264, 318
mindful 301, 302, 565
negative beliefs about parenting 622
parenting capacity assessment 306, 778
parenting style 228, 275, 302, 306, 318, 339, 783
positive parental monitoring 229
responsive 215, 253
support 496
unresponsive 215
parenting interventions 24, 35, 298–317, 428, 472, 701, 788–790
parenting programmes
ACHIEVE 5, 7
ADHD Foundation 546
Child in Need plan 766, 768, 772, 787
Closing the Gap 494
Curly Hair Project 546
Dragon of Afterlands 727
MAC-UK 136, 137, 140, 733–752, 755, 758
MindAid youth 723, 727
Minding the Gap 230
MoodGYM 719, 720
MyMoodCoach 720
prevention programmes 599
Quality Protects 459
Solihull approach 301, 306, 597, 814
SPARX 724, 725
Strengthening Families, Protecting Children 770
Tree of Life 807
Valuing People Now 494, 506
Video Interactive Guidance 24, 465
Your Choice 704, 705
Parent Management Training 312, 559, 702
AdOpt 472
Incredible years 24, 473, 600

Mindfulness - based parenting 301
Power Up for Parents 198–9, 201
participation 17, 29, 75, 82, 129, 131, 140, 144, 147, 183, 189, 304, 474, 505–507, 544, 546, 551, 594, 669, 714, 750, 761
perinatal
anxiety 614, 617, 622
depression 617, 621, 635
mental health 613–634
obsessive-compulsive disorder 623
play 23, 56–60, 67, 272, 312, 465, 474, 500, 505
practitioner confidence 492, 495, 517
pregnancy
antenatal anxiety 623
birth 452, 453, 474, 766
foetus 618, 629
in-utero/pre-natal experiences 466
infertility 305
maternal perinatal mental health 613–634
perinatal period 613–634
postnatal depression 617, 621, 622, 627
pregnancy 47, 52, 54–56, 101, 248, 305, 463, 513, 613–634, 695, 780
prematurity 264, 538, 553
prevalence 19, 132–134, 158, 188, 208, 278, 296, 297, 299, 300, 305, 324, 326, 347, 358, 375, 388, 520, 530, 534–537, 539, 542, 543, 549, 572, 585, 625, 646, 659, 691, 768, 801
problem of the referring person 42, 48
professional bodies
British Psychological Society 11, 20, 76, 78, 101, 114, 126, 152, 161, 510, 512, 619
Health and Care Professions Council 9, 78, 152, 597
protective factors 3, 29, 63, 64, 71, 339, 347, 377, 444, 454, 464, 470, 472, 537, 551, 617, 677, 678, 691, 694, 696–698
psychoeducation 18, 25, 30, 188, 195, 221, 222, 241, 250, 268, 269, 279, 288–290, 313, 334, 360, 365, 367, 370, 371, 373, 383, 388, 390, 393, 397, 414, 415, 476, 497, 511, 516, 538, 540, 562, 563, 568, 582, 590, 596, 598, 600, 601, 720, 722, 785, 814

q

quality of life 194, 205, 292, 296, 300, 427, 431, 433, 436, 441, 446, 449, 498, 504, 536, 539, 563, 574, 674, 721, 810

r

relationships
friendships 53, 212, 216, 221, 223, 325, 424, 430, 545, 581, 616, 643, 650, 652, 749, 785
peers
peer-group discussion 141, 143
support 8, 221, 234, 415, 495, 619, 722, 775
reciprocity 160, 301, 569, 757, 804, 822
relationship-based approaches 748
reflection
reflective spaces 495, 700, 774, 806
reflexivity 21–22, 62, 90, 92, 99, 165, 171, 774
reinforcement 301, 312, 344, 428, 497
positive reinforcement 301, 312, 344, 428
research methods
audit 6, 20, 21, 193, 199, 500, 566, 675, 684, 701, 791, 815
Cochrane quality evidence 548
generalisability 16, 17, 347, 372
hypotheses 116, 227, 266, 530
longitudinal 303
meta-analysis 15, 250, 341, 359, 382, 538, 542, 603
naturalistic observations 56, 59, 60
observational data 16
outcome monitoring 82, 144, 177, 187, 716
client feedback 82, 185
practice-based evidence 20, 21, 184, 302, 361, 492, 503, 506, 548, 565, 722, 727, 748
qualitative 21, 46, 372, 431, 478, 583, 718, 726
qualitative feedback 810, 819

research methods (*contd.*)
  quality improvement 21, 144
  randomised controlled trials 15, 27, 362, 434, 718, 771
  reliability 19, 81, 320, 388, 399, 449, 482, 488, 489, 540, 554, 557, 695, 697, 716
  routine outcome measures 60, 61, 178, 369, 376, 378, 477, 506, 810
  sampling methods 60
  screening 61, 71, 132, 193, 296, 327, 360, 376, 378, 389, 551, 554–556, 571–572, 596, 599, 600, 650, 678, 698, 765, 780, 797
  self-report 16, 81, 85, 307, 362, 369, 478, 551, 569, 599, 718, 778
  statistical significance 323, 344, 557, 756
  validity
    diagnostic 482, 540
    ecological 556
    external 17
    internal 17, 81
restriction
  restrictive intervention 501
  seclusion 501, 668
risk
  factors 49, 63, 278, 305, 339, 358, 373, 535, 537, 579, 584, 585, 593, 617, 648, 662, 663, 676, 691, 696, 697, 699, 734, 759, 768, 788
  management 5, 80, 146, 229, 628–631, 654, 675, 694, 696, 697, 699, 700, 705, 716, 737
  support 145–147, 176
  taking 58, 217, 218, 220, 222, 228, 232, 235–237, 657

S

safeguarding
  boundaries 41, 59, 70, 71, 95, 108, 115, 127, 161, 194, 213, 224, 225, 228, 255, 300, 311, 435, 467, 476, 499, 530, 540, 592, 705, 706, 739, 745, 748, 774, 820
  child protection 42, 45, 49, 50, 100, 113, 117, 122, 124, 125, 127, 128, 239, 291, 451, 487, 504, 513, 589, 592, 597, 763, 766, 767, 771, 772, 775, 793
  disclosure 80, 121–123, 126, 193, 224, 507, 624, 625, 754
scientist-practitioner 13, 14, 20, 31, 35, 38, 86
self
  self-awareness 78, 83, 160
  self-care 22, 80, 255, 338, 343, 345, 392, 416, 472, 655, 774, 806, 813, 818
  self-compassion 10, 306
  self-esteem 58, 65, 92, 219, 278, 285, 307, 308, 338, 354, 428, 444, 448, 472, 485, 494, 497, 502, 531, 536, 559, 582, 585, 604, 676, 743, 746, 784, 805, 812
  self-evaluation 7, 87, 159, 344, 353
  self-reflective approach 9
  self-regulation 218, 236, 242, 262, 538, 539
self-harm 25, 28–30, 49, 50, 213, 227, 338, 368–370, 378, 392, 410, 429, 552, 597, 608, 628, 629, 638, 642, 643, 645, 647, 648, 650, 654, 655, 657, 658, 663, 665, 669, 676, 679, 682, 716, 717
  non-suicidal self-injury 644, 646
services
service user
  feedback 46, 772
  participation 183
sexuality
  harmful sexual behaviour 513, 702
  LGBTQIA+ 109, 135, 258, 339, 457, 617, 650
sex
  sexual knowledge 513, 514
  sexual offending 969
shame 45, 191, 256, 271, 281, 286, 300, 313, 314, 375, 385, 391, 453, 462, 463, 471, 508, 617, 624, 625, 633, 774
shared decision making 42, 48, 147, 179, 189–192, 196–199, 304, 317, 362, 432, 733, 748
sleep
  apps 248
  assessment 245, 248
  bedtime

resistance 247, 252, 253
routine 244, 246, 247, 252–255, 287
cycle 241, 245
diary 246, 247, 257, 258
disturbance 28, 30, 220
Ferber method 254
hygiene 248, 250, 251, 341, 383
naps 242, 244, 245
nightmares 28–30, 68, 70, 245, 255, 374, 389, 391, 392, 394, 455, 783, 801
night wakings 239, 240, 243, 246, 250
pressure 241, 242, 251
problems 238, 239
regression 242, 244
social
action 172, 739, 741
antisocial behaviour 691, 699, 700, 702
class 153, 299
communication differences 531, 534, 535, 551, 554, 562
comparison 234, 524
and emotional learning 598
identity 163, 166, 704, 753
inequality 493, 734
interaction 60, 464, 534, 554, 596, 713, 727
isolation 217, 507, 552, 628, 648, 649, 655, 783
motivation 535
psychosocial stress 430, 431
sensitivity 217
social-emotional reciprocity 569
socioemotional change 216
support 118, 154, 300, 339, 345, 373, 430, 617, 618, 622, 628
social media 53, 106, 122, 201, 214, 220–222, 227, 271, 316, 408, 422, 424, 452, 618, 645, 647, 648, 650, 658, 677, 678
socioeconomic status 53, 70, 152, 155, 167, 275, 278, 285, 339, 373, 582, 583, 585, 650, 656, 708
special needs
inclusive practice 11, 435–444, 541–547, 705–708, 738
inclusivity 9, 21, 151–172, 198, 346, 541, 655, 717, 749
intellectual disability 61, 402, 443, 509, 510, 516, 519, 531, 535, 546, 585, 691
intelligence quotient 339, 350, 373, 492, 509, 537
secondary handicap 507
Special Educational Needs 42, 456, 493, 532, 562, 581, 584, 585, 589, 768, 812
Special Educational Needs and Disability Coordinators 589
staff
support 90, 602, 679, 816
wellbeing 679, 770, 806, 810, 816, 817
stigma 19, 80, 133, 137, 144, 157, 191, 213, 358, 444, 456, 492, 493, 494, 518, 549, 617, 621, 632, 633, 677, 722, 723, 741, 747, 751, 768, 774
substance misuse 118, 300, 615, 630, 646, 649, 655, 661, 663, 676, 691, 696, 700, 702, 773, 778, 783, 785, 788, 790, 791
substances
alcohol 54, 228, 377, 454, 463, 466, 538, 551, 582, 621, 628, 649, 653, 668, 768, 774, 776, 780
drugs 170, 227, 228, 466, 533, 538, 621, 652, 655, 745, 774, 783
suicide
attempt 338, 644, 649, 650, 652, 663, 686, 717
prevention 646, 649, 678, 689
suicidal ideation 338, 513, 648, 649, 657
suicidal risk 656, 716
suicidal thoughts 49, 50, 177, 194, 644, 649, 654, 663, 686, 717
supervision 77, 80, 82, 766
cognitive behavioural 85
seven-eyed supervision model 84
supervisory alliance 81, 82, 84–86, 88, 90, 95, 117
systemic supervision 85, 93
symptom/s
avoidance 29, 31, 65, 189, 256, 276, 277, 329, 333, 344, 374, 376, 377, 381, 383, 384, 386, 393, 440, 455, 471, 499, 541, 560, 576, 584, 596, 623–625, 630, 653, 679, 801

symptom/s (*contd.*)
compulsions 357–373, 624
delusions 624, 626, 627, 630, 635, 644, 659
demand avoidance 132–134, 139, 142, 143, 300, 413, 459, 499, 500, 541, 550, 560, 568, 576, 664, 665, 679, 764
derealisation 325, 374, 375
deterioration 341, 349, 626, 629, 643–645, 655, 662, 664, 666, 674, 699
dissociation 374, 375, 384, 395, 396, 399, 469
distractibility 516, 537, 596, 660
executive dysfunction 535, 538, 577
fight/flight/freeze reaction 365, 466, 565
hallucinations 193, 361, 626, 659–661
harmful behaviour 464, 698
hyper-/hypo-reactivity 570
hypervigilance 325, 385, 394, 625, 780, 803
impulsivity 218, 515, 516, 529, 541, 564, 568, 650, 655
instability 214, 244, 456, 463, 655, 661–662, 663, 737, 784
internalising symptoms 216, 601
intrusive thoughts 357, 361, 367, 368, 370, 513, 623–625
irritability 189, 325, 336, 338, 347, 374, 630, 660
loss of interest 336, 621
low mood 65, 102, 146, 180, 191, 194, 195, 214, 223, 288, 309, 314, 323, 332, 337, 368, 383, 391, 412, 428, 430, 437, 439, 440, 442, 493, 561, 621, 624, 626, 721, 724, 805
malignant regression 656
mistrust 17, 157, 463, 716, 771, 773
negative
appraisals 379, 393
self-image 478
thinking patterns 341
neuroticism 339
over-activity 536
relapse 331, 346, 613, 621, 627, 631, 666
selective abstraction 341
subthreshold symptoms 324, 336
threats 289, 657, 736
withdrawal 110, 112, 119, 337, 340, 373, 389, 494, 536, 621, 622, 630, 633, 647, 659, 660, 668–669, 674, 784

t

team work
collaborative formulation 22
co-regulation 514, 569, 804
experience-based co-design 197, 203
flexible support 739, 741
group case discussion 770
multiagency 63, 117, 124, 147, 459, 514, 548–553, 560, 586, 597, 668, 692, 700, 702, 703, 707, 765, 769, 814
multiagency meetings 117, 124, 597
multidisciplinary working 551, 708, 770, 773
network alignment 739, 741
organisational change 21, 805
stakeholders 189, 194, 199, 201, 733, 738, 751, 756, 757, 777, 792
therapeutic interventions
adolescent mentalisation-based integrative therapy 120
attachment-focused therapy 303, 788
Behavioural Interventions 24, 248, 250, 252, 253, 285, 290, 304, 497, 538, 540, 559, 564, 632, 701
cognitive therapy
Cognitive Behaviour Therapy 16, 27, 73, 81, 411, 428, 432, 448, 461, 501, 599, 787, 789,
couple therapy 791
Dialectical Behavioural Therapy 663, 791
digital therapy 200, 713–727
disability psychotherapy 502, 507
Dyadic Developmental Psychotherapy 24, 453, 485, 522, 787
Dynamic Interpersonal Therapy 23, 27, 227, 339, 340
Exposure Response Prevention tasks 361

exposure therapy 30, 31, 250, 333, 381, 382, 474, 780, 790
graded exposure 8, 146, 268, 279, 285, 333, 443
narrative exposure therapy 31, 474, 780, 790
for children 780, 790
Eye Movement Densitation Reprocessing 31, 381, 382, 387–390, 393, 394, 397, 401, 403, 503, 516, 632
indirect Intervention 596–598, 604
life-story work 471, 474, 476
mentalisation-based therapy 24, 632, 790
motivational interviewing 303, 316, 344, 345, 416–418, 433, 446, 563, 773, 777, 785
multimodal 302, 312–315, 702
narrative therapy 27, 32, 129, 169
non-pharmacological 538
non-violent resistance 302, 306, 473, 789
play therapy 23, 503
positive behaviour support 24, 497, 498, 511, 520, 523, 564
psychoanalytic therapy 22, 23, 789
school-based 593–604
specialist family intervention teams 692
systemic therapy 26, 27, 85, 288, 302, 410, 411, 700, 791
therapeutic
alliance 84, 179, 180, 182, 183, 246, 269, 304, 345, 560, 616, 676
alliance-focused tools 182–183
relationship 23, 30, 31, 43, 84, 90, 104, 115, 117, 123, 180, 182, 224, 225, 316, 342, 376, 383, 474, 505, 506, 654, 668, 705, 773, 789
therapist adherence 16
Theraplay 24, 464, 473, 476, 477, 503
toileting
bowel control 275, 276, 284, 289
continence 275–278, 284, 287–290
encopresis 276, 277, 280, 281, 285–288, 290
enuresis 276–278, 280, 281, 285, 287, 290
readiness 280, 290
smearing of faeces 276, 286
toilet avoidance 276
toilet training 56, 58, 275–280, 288
withholding of faeces 276
trauma
adverse childhood experiences 454, 463, 466, 768, 787
adverse events 336, 362
complex developmental trauma 462, 787, 800, 802, 803, 809, 811–814
complex PTSD 29, 375, 455, 660, 791
developmental trauma 146, 277, 437, 455–456, 462, 465, 469, 471, 507, 548, 585, 594, 706, 785, 787, 800, 802, 803, 809–814
re-traumatisation 471, 701, 808
trauma-informed
approach 585, 595, 602, 701, 703, 706, 781, 805, 806, 809, 810, 811, 815, 818, 819
practice 591, 594, 595, 601, 679, 701, 800–820
schools 811, 813, 818, 820
training 602, 814, 820
traumatic event 373–395, 455, 635, 653, 801
treatment
adherence 15, 16, 82, 128, 285, 419, 431, 433, 437, 447, 570, 655, 675, 679
ambivalence 110, 138, 372, 420
confidentiality 43, 45, 50, 67, 78, 103, 115, 116, 122, 151, 197, 390, 591, 595, 597, 653, 706, 714, 773–774, 806, 817
limits of 78, 817
disclosure 80, 121–123, 126, 193, 224, 507, 624, 625, 754
drop-out rate 157, 183
sustainability 809, 814, 820
tolerance 286, 383, 474, 516, 537, 569
triggers 30, 45, 64, 216, 269, 280, 307, 310, 311, 314, 338, 364, 383, 385, 394, 409, 476, 477, 498, 499, 664, 680, 722, 803, 808

u

unconditional positive regard 6, 7

w

wellbeing 154, 220, 454, 456, 458, 503, 583, 585, 587, 720, 760, 771, 774

y

youth 154, 220, 454, 456, 458, 503, 583, 585, 587, 720, 760, 771, 774
 employment 737, 738
 offending 690–709
 youth-led activities 743

www.ingramcontent.com/pod-product-compliance
Lightning Source LLC
LaVergne TN
LVHW081958200926
848481LV00010B/2762